ARAKI

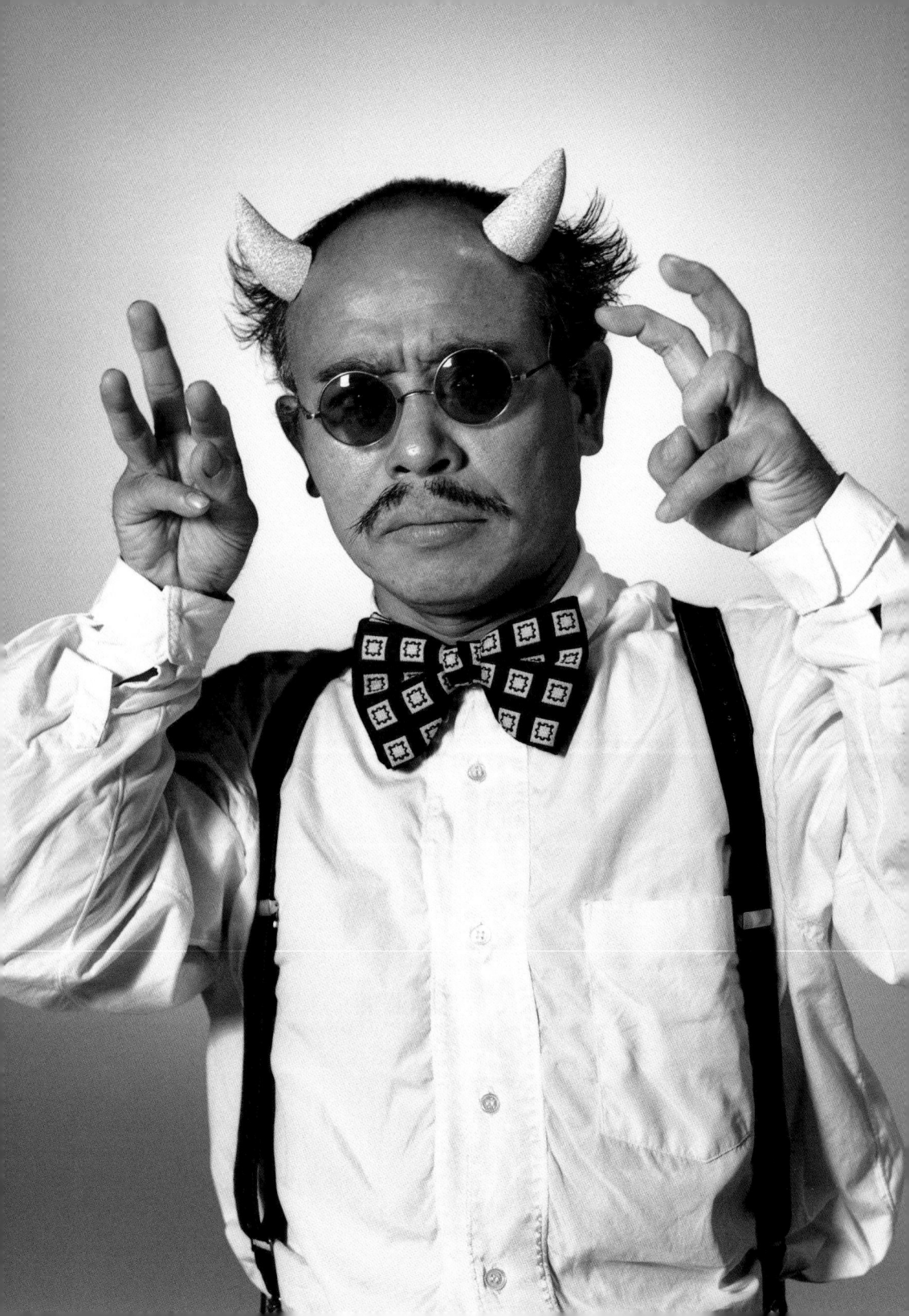

ARAKI

TASCHEN

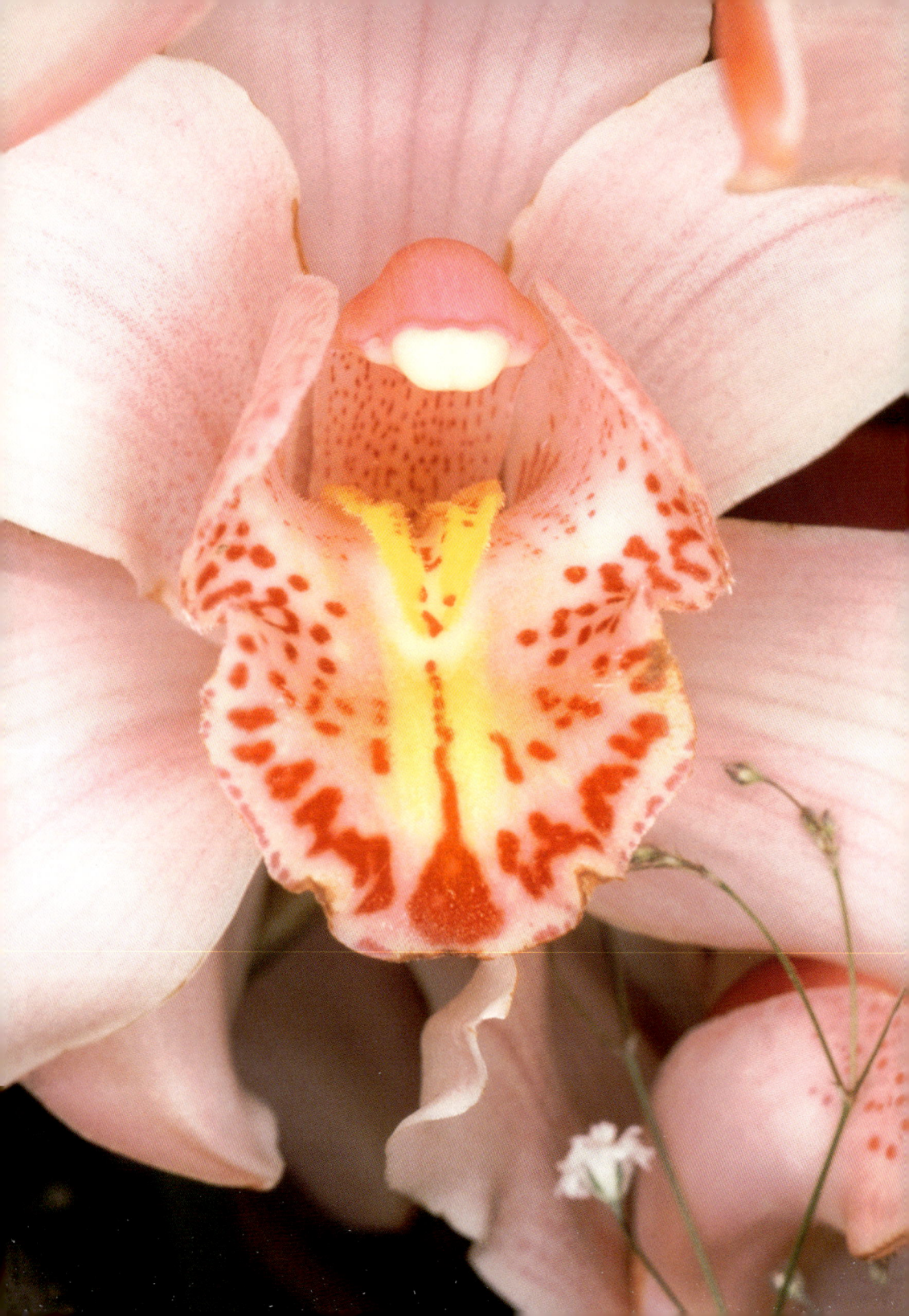

6

NOBUYOSHI ARAKI

interviewed
by Jérôme Sans

32
Colorscapes

42
Tokyo Story

66
Love in Winter

90
Flower Rondo

106
Private
Photography

184
Kyoto White
Sentiment

188
Chiro

190
Novel
Photography

198
Tokyo Comedy

246
Angel's Festival

260
Tokyo Love

264
Naked
Faces

268
In Ruins

298
Sensual
Flowers

304
Erotos

344
Sexual Desire

354
A's Paradise

364
Tokyo
Nostalgia

382
The Banquet

388
Shino

396
A's Lovers

402
Photo-Maniac
Big Diary

412
Color Rays

420
Private Diary

426
Tokyo Nude

474
Tokyo
Autumn

502
Appendix

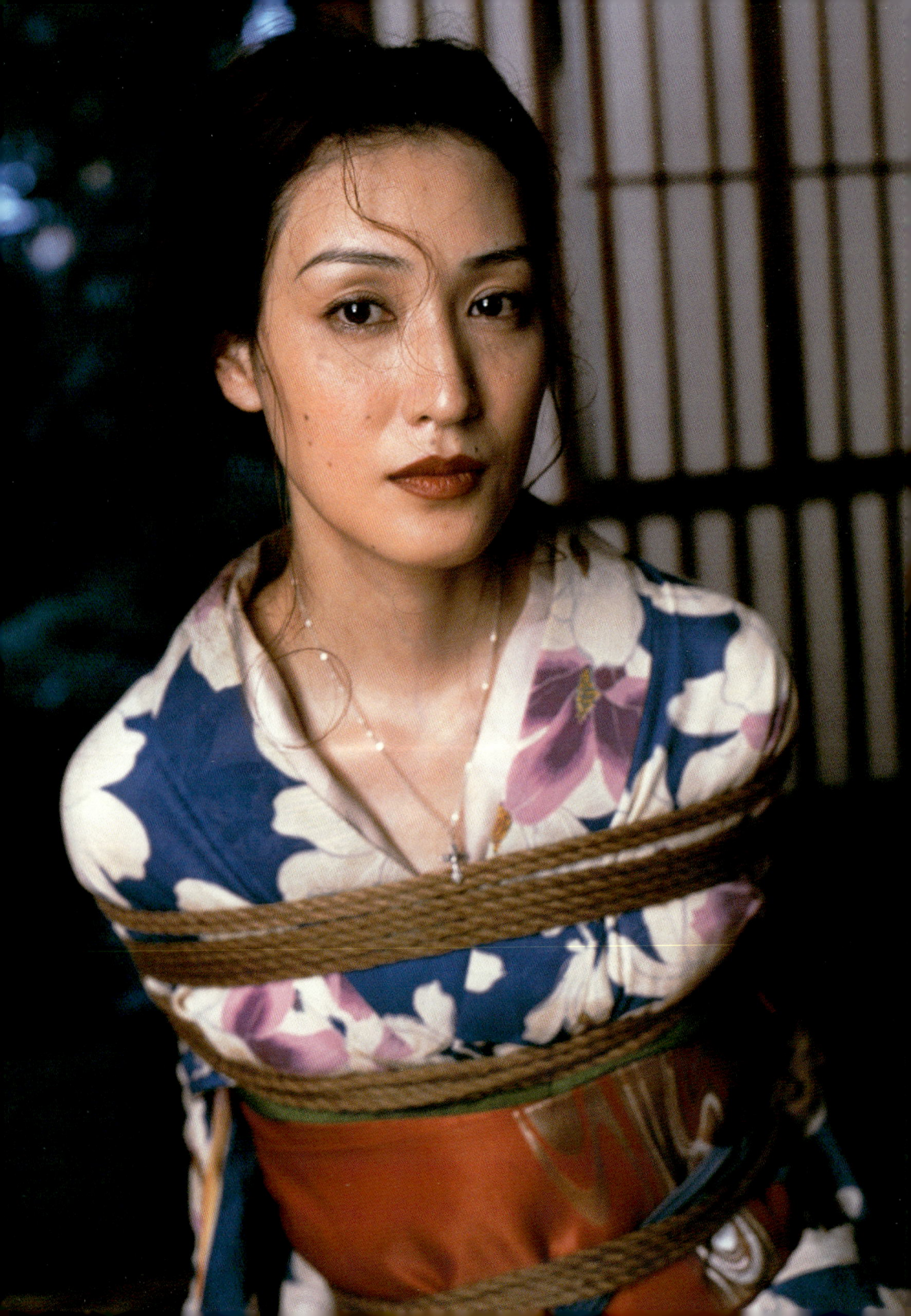

Nobuyoshi Araki

interviewed by Jérôme Sans

Jérôme Sans: Why call your book *Araki by Araki* when you have edited most of your own books yourself? Was there something special about this one? Nobuyoshi Araki: I turned 60 at the end of the 20th century. In Japan, the 60th birthday is called *Kanreki*; it's a special celebration. One cycle of life finishes and another begins. It's a passage, a fresh start. For this occasion, I decided to bring all my work together. I've kept the best for the end, like "Picasso's Picassos." My first thought was to publish everything myself, here in Japan. But finally it seemed more interesting to do it through someone else's vision, more especially through someone unknown to me. For me, other people are always the unknown, and this time the stranger is a foreigner, which is even better. In the final analysis, this book is not *Araki by Araki*, but *Araki by TASCHEN*, and no less interesting for that. When a foreigner chooses my works, unknown aspects of me emerge. I've had lots of exhibitions abroad (in Austria at the Wiener Secession, in Italy at the Centro per l'Arte Contemporanea Luigi Pecci, Prato …) and it's always turned out that way. Things I don't find very significant finish up interesting other people.

People tend to think that the ideas or thoughts get into photos through editing and juxtaposition. Well, not for me. My photos have plenty of strength and energy of their own. I can afford just to hand them over to an editor

because I'm confident of the quality and power of my photos. Normally what you get is the editor's vision. But I have confidence in my photographs. They never change.

How does this book differ from the other books? The distinctive thing is that I can show everything about me—my women, my wife, and my city … It shows the ramifications of feelings—it records something of the organic development of my work. The individual elements are the leaves of a big tree, as it were. I hope that the tree will start to blossom. *Araki by Araki* is an epitaph for my first 60 years. I've been taking photographs since the moment I was born. I was no sooner out of my mother's womb than I turned around and photographed her sex! After reincarnation, in my new life, photography will still be the first word I utter. It's been a 60-year contract, near enough. Photography is love and death—that'll be my epitaph.

How do you define love? Love is hard to define. When you love a woman, she survives in photos and in your memory. And feelings survive, too. For example, I loved my wife, and traces of this remain in my feelings and my body, traces that survive in the photos. (I say this only about my wife—otherwise I'll get into trouble!) That is what it means to say you have loved someone.

At the moment I love Chiro, my cat, and flowers. The cat is flesh and the flowers are genital. They prompt the feelings felt for those one loves. When I am at home, my feelings for Chiro well up when she comes up to me. Or when I wake up and see flowers, I photograph them; it's this feeling of proximity. These instant feelings come to me quite naturally. (I always have a lot of flowers in my home.) It's instant feelings I love, though my feeling for photography is absolute.

For me love is about proximity, familiarity, things one can touch. That's why there is no such thing as love on the Internet. Love implies intimacy of smells, sensations, surroundings.

So I photograph my friends, people I'm close to, the things around me. That's photography, for me. For example, I'm taking a photograph of you now because we've met today.

You've taken pictures in many Asian cities, but Tokyo is at the centre of your universe. Your work conveys a strong sense of belonging to your immediate environment. Do you think there is a correlation between it and those old traditional Japanese houses where there's a sense of shared intimacy? When I say Tokyo, I'm not interested in the city as a whole, only in the places I'm familiar with, where I go every day. I don't take photos just anywhere, just in Shinjuku and the neighborhoods I know really well. Photography means the things that relate to me. I don't go places simply to take photographs. If I might use the word "introduce" about my work, I'd say I "introduce" the women, places, and moments I love.

Everything is determined by the place you were brought up. I was born in a humble part of Tokyo called Minowa, in a traditional little house divided into two homes, and everything in these two homes was on top of everything else. You could go from one house through to the next. There was always a neighbor bringing something to the back door. They would bring you food, saying it was leftovers when in fact it had been cooked specially. Everyone cooked

for everyone else. It was a very humane place. I was brought up there, so that's how I am. Minowa's on the outskirts of the Taito-Ku district in the north-eastern part of Tokyo. If you go further north to where Takeshi Kitano was born, people are more tyrannical, the way he is *(laughs)*.

I lived near Yoshiwara, the *filles de joie* district. Close by was a temple called Jokanji, where courtesans with no family were buried. That's where I played as a child. In that temple, there were graves (death) and there were prostitutes. That place has left its mark on my life. The mud of that humble district is still on me. Life and death were at large there. It was like that from my earliest days—I acquired a feeling for life and death automatically.

My favorite color is red. Red expresses the complexity of life and death. That's why I asked the landlord of this bar we are sitting in to do the whole place over in red. The place is even called the ROUGE. When the incendiaries from the American B-29s dyed Japanese skies red, I found it very beautiful. I was five years old at the time. My interest in red comes from that. All my photographic work derives from childhood. For me, Minowa is like the womb. I don't live there any more, but my roots are there. Because I grew up in a traditional wooden house, I am warm-hearted and sentimental through and through. There were morning glories flowering in the little street: that was the milieu I was brought up in. My whole life was determined by this. Paris also has its very ordinary districts, but all in stone, and very dry. In today's Japan, there's stone everywhere. Robots are replacing the human voice. The things there were to photograph are disappearing. If the world takes a turn for the worse, photography follows. Nothing holds the eye any more. That's my epitaph, at 60, for the end of the world.

Your work is all about women. I took my very first photograph just after I had left my mother's uterus. For me, woman is photography. The next photo I took was of a girl I was secretly in love with in primary school. As I grew up, a woman immediately meant her vulva. I often took close-ups of vaginas and in 1970 described this position in my exhibition "Sur-sentimentalist Manifesto," a photographic manifesto dating from the time when I started taking shots of women. I thought then I was going to be an anarchist. So I called myself "Ararky." That was the beginning.

At the time, I was working for Dentsu, a Japanese advertising agency. There I met Yoko, who became my wife. Till then I'd taken women by shooting their vaginas, as sex-objects. As soon as I photographed Yoko, I began to grasp the relationship between me and the woman before me as a mutual, two-way thing. For the first time I was photoing a woman the way she was, not as an object.

Growing out of that relationship, there are many branches (women) to my tree. Although I've always said that I was faithful to my wife and that she was the center of my work, even then I was already photographing lots of other women. This book reveals these things for the first time and, indeed, everything about me. I'm revealing more and more about myself. There's a statute of limitations: I'm 60 now. After my wife's death, I went on taking more and more photos of women. So, lots of ramifications, lots of leaves (women) have unfolded around me, and it's been paradise! *(laughs)*

Can your passion for sex be considered a contemporary version of the *Shunga*, the erotic prints from the Edo period [c. 1600–1868]? I'd like it if my photos were like *Shunga*, but I haven't got there yet. There is a degree of reserve in *Shunga*. The genitals are visible, but the rest is hidden by the kimono. The colored woodcuts do not show everything. They express the mystery of love. *Shunga* don't just reveal sex, they reveal the secret of love between two people, between a man and a woman.

I often appear in my photographs in which scenes of bondage or having sex are shown. But I don't have the starring role. I'm like a minor character in a *Shunga* print, a secondary or spectator's role. I prefer photography to sex. These days

I won't even go out with a girl. Because they all expect sex. Just having dinner isn't enough for them. I won't do that any more, I prefer taking photographs.

In sex, I rank second or third. I just take advantage of sex to take good photos. I'm hard on sex the way I am on the woman I'm making love to.

I am putting all this in the book because it'll be published abroad and the Japanese won't see it. For me, photography's the essential thing.

What do you express in your photos? I don't have anything to say. There's no special message in my photos. The messages come from my subjects, men or women. I wait for my subjects to give of themselves, offer themselves up. I have things to photograph, so I've nothing to express. Right now, I'm showing the joy of life rather than the sadness of death. Some people I know think life is sad. But these days I think the opposite. Death is sadder.

Why are you obsessed with women in your photographic work? Women have all the charms of life itself. They have all the essential attributes: beauty, ugliness, obscenity, purity … much more so than nature. In woman, there is sea and sky. (This may sound affected.) In woman, there is the bud and the flower …

A photographer who doesn't take photos of women is no photographer, or only a third-rate one. Women teach you much more about the world than reading Balzac's *Human Comedy*. Whether it's your wife, a one-night stand or a prostitute, women teach you how the world goes round. Besides, I stopped reading when I left primary school. I've built my life on meeting women.

You are a cult figure in Japan for your iconography. How do you react to the paradox of censorship in this country, which behind its façade and official manner offers a whole other world of "forbidden pleasures," and in particular "love hotels" for adulterous rendezvous? I don't take photos to shove everything in everyone's face. In fact, I'm quite content to show my photos to my friends if I think they're good. As regards censorship, I'm not socially or artistically committed. I have no special ideology, no ideas about art, no thoughts or philosophy. It's as though I'm just a little rogue getting up to mischief.

I think this attitude reflects a paradox of Japan, which has laws against pornography. Yes, and that's been so since the Edo period. It may seem ambiguous, or paradoxical. There may be a strict law on censorship, but you can still find anything and everything in Japan. Chaos is the rule. Rigid strictness co-exists with the glamour of deviant opportunities. And these contrasting things often get mixed up. In Japan, no one's going to condemn a photographer to death for tying up a girl and taking photos of her. It's astonishingly relaxed. Christian countries are much more severe in that respect. Europe remains tolerant. The Vatican does not approve of that kind of thing, but it accepted my work nonetheless. The United States is particularly strict and draconian. I can't risk showing little girls nude or women in bondage over there. Compared to the Edo period, I think our period is an impoverished one as regards sex, but there's still a confused atmosphere about sex that I like.

Why is bondage a recurrent theme in your work? *Kinbaku* [making knots with ropes] is different from bondage. I tie women's bodies up because I know their souls can't be tied. Only the physical self can be tied. Putting a rope round a woman is like putting an arm round her.

What are the little plastic dinosaurs doing in your universe? What exactly do they represent? Does each one have a specific identity? I'm the kind of person who needs company all the time. I really need friends around me because I'm often lonely. These monsters are my alter ego. They signify my desire to be in my photos, as though they were parts of my body. I love these dinosaurs,

and I just want to be with them all the time and to collect them. That is a sexual desire. I want to take photos of the things I love and spend all my time with them.

My balcony's empty right now because the dinosaurs aren't back from my Paris show. They're still stuck in Japanese customs, and I miss them terribly. So now my cat Chiro is also feeling lonesome and sulking a little bit. She's lying on top of Waneen (a large crocodile-object), but she misses them too.

Each dinosaur has its own specific meaning. But it's more important for me that they all stay together. I often feel lonely and want my house to feel inhabited. Of course, each one has its own charm. In fact, I give each of them a name. But basically the reason I'm interested in them is because I'm often lonely and prefer being with them just for the company. I have lots of flowers for the same reasons. Sentimentally lonely! I love warmth. The warmth of the womb. I'm a baby and a child. I can't forget the warmth of the womb. I like hot springs too, they're a sort of womb for me.

Sometimes you paint colors on your black and white photos. Why? Black and white photos represent death. To take a photo is to kill the subject. Another way I have of showing black and white photos is the "Arakinema" performances. Photos presented in motion with sound.

Monochrome photos represent death, so I want to resuscitate them. I want to add erotic feelings, passion, the warmth of the body. All this gives me an unconscious desire to paint them. It's not that I want to turn these black and white photos into paintings. I just want to make them more like the ideal photos I have in my head.

I'm not trying to do painting on a photographic basis, just trying to believe in the photos and reveal them by painting. I often choose colors like red and green, and I entitle these pictures "red-green sentimental colors."

The black and white photos I just showed you are from my book *Photographs from the End of the*

Century. The next book to come out will be all in color, and its title will be *Photographs from the New Century*. These two books complete a cycle.

In your series of women in black and white, why do you systematically paint over the vaginas? First and foremost, this is censorship by retouching, so that the genitals can't be seen. It works like that because there are lots of strict rules in Japan. But it's better for me that there are some rules. And it's also an indication of my desire to mess around, as if I were touching them or putting my sex into them.

It's as though I'm swimming in the river, swimming to and fro between the color bank, the bank of our world, and the bank of the next world, the world of black and white. Depending on how I feel, I decide if I should go to monochrome Paradise, stay in this color world, or take the same subject and treat it simultaneously in monochrome and color.

When I'm tired I float on my back and photograph the sky. Paris has the Seine, while Tokyo has two rivers, the Sumidagawa and the Arakawa. But Japan also has a river called the Sanzu no Kawa [river of the dead]. It's the river the dead must cross to reach Nirvana.

Time is never specified in your photos. What is your relationship to time? A photograph takes place only at a certain instant. And this instant is unidentifiable. The instant is the eternal and eternity an instant. This, more than any other element, is the notion photography carries within it.

When I release the shutter, that's the eternal. Down comes the shutter and makes eternity. The effect is extremely direct. It's more an action than an art. Consequently, I claim the right to mix photos without attention to the dates when they were taken. On the other hand, I also take photographs that have the date printed on the print, and these I can show in chronological order. The flow of daily life constitutes a narrative. Like a diary. The passage of time is extremely dramatic. So I use several temporal meanings. But if I *have*

to choose, I go with chronological order, which I find ultimately more interesting. This is why I take photos as a diary, and often decide to leave them as they are without any editorial work.

Then the editorial work is done automatically by life, by the times we live in. Which means, the moment I sort the photos into the order they were taken in, god or someone – in my case Shashin, the god of photography—does the editorial work for me. The most dramatic order would be the unconscious one. That's how most of my photography books work. It's not worth thinking about order. For example, if I want a photo of Chiro, I don't need to think. This image appears spontaneously.

Why do you sometimes put dates on photos? It's meant as parody, as a way of saying that perfection was neither achieved nor sought. If there's a date printed on a photo, it can't be a masterpiece, can it? It means these photos are just what happened on a certain day. That's photography! Photography just says this day, this instant was wonderful. That's life! Nothing's better than a journal. Even in literature, the journal's head and shoulders above the novel. The journal is life, and the date's photography. Or else it's up to the photographer to erase the date. Photo, *c'est la vie*!

Is that why you've never stopped taking pictures? You have to go on photographing the moments of life; you have to go on living. For me, taking photos is life itself.

Which artists, writers or film directors who used the journal format do you feel close to? I probably feel closest to the Japanese writer Kafu Nagai [1879–1959], who wrote a novel in 1917 called *Danchotei Nichijo* [Danchotei's Diary]. If the events of any given day were fascinating, he knew it would be even more wonderful to place fiction within it. Before him, journals were supposed to describe daily reality. He was the first to break the rule and mix in a few lies, which makes a journal more enticing. In *Danchotei Nichijo*, everything is lies. It's much more interesting that way. I also feel close to the Lithuanian film director Jonas Mekas, although he doesn't include dates in his work. He has an access to the sublime that I lack. But we're quite alike. For me, Minowa is the womb, for Mekas it is probably Lithuania, his homeland. For him, nature and family in Lithuania are the main thing. My Minowa has lost its attractions and is in ruins, and his Lithuania is in ruins but was once really a paradise. This is what we have in common. We're both fascinated by the city or quarter where we were born. This place and time or another, that's what a diary is about. This day, that, and another. But I don't think about that, I just keep taking photos every day. Punctuating these movements would be like putting the date in.

Like the English artists Gilbert & George you aim for accessibility, the widest possible distribution of your work, and favor art for everyone. Does this stem from your past in advertising? When I was working for Dentsu, I made ads for other people. But I wanted to make ads for myself. You could call that art. I thought it would be good to show my photos to friends. On the other hand, I've always wanted to be known by loads of people, as many as possible. I want to know that the iguanas in the Galapagos want to see my work. I'd like them to cross the ocean to Japan and let me take their photos. Then I would take them to Yoshiwara.

How many books have you published so far? More than 250, I guess. Right at the beginning, I got tired of the countless unproductive meetings with Japanese publishers, so I began by publishing my first books in photocopy form. My first book, *Xeroxed Photo Albums*, was done that way. Then, when I did *Sentimental Journey*, no publisher would print my honeymoon. Later on, many publishing houses published my books, like TASCHEN now. Sometimes I take photos and I want to make a book of them immediately, like a premature ejaculation. Sometimes I just can't bear to wait three months to get a book out after the shoot. I want the book out in a month, right after doing the last picture. That's why I did *Photographs from the End of the Century* myself, to satisfy my desire for haste. It's a "live" photo book in which the speed and heat of the shot can still be felt. With some other books, it seems to me that the publisher brought some enthusiasm to them, too.

Photocopying has come on in leaps and bounds since the 1970s. Do you still make photocopybooks? Today, copying's much too good, it's no longer of any interest. A photocopy in the 1970s was not just mechanical, it was rough, rugged, and approximate. It fitted in with my ideas and those of the time, which was a very crude decade. They were copies of my unbridled feelings of the time. I gave up on the word "copy" and turned to "reproduction." Photography reproduces feelings during the shoot, or those I shared with someone I met then, or those of my relationships of the time. It's not expression. And it's not an attempt to express the feelings of the subject I am photographing. Through the subject, I make a copy of myself. Thanks to these subjects, I make "reproductions." Without them, I couldn't. That goes for life too. I need subjects. It can be flowers, the sky or of course women. I live through women. I shall always photograph women. If women were to disappear from the planet one day, I should hope to be long dead.

Have you any projects that haven't materialized and that you wish to undertake in future? I haven't any unrealized projects. My surroundings will dictate what I do next. May god/dess Woman guide me.

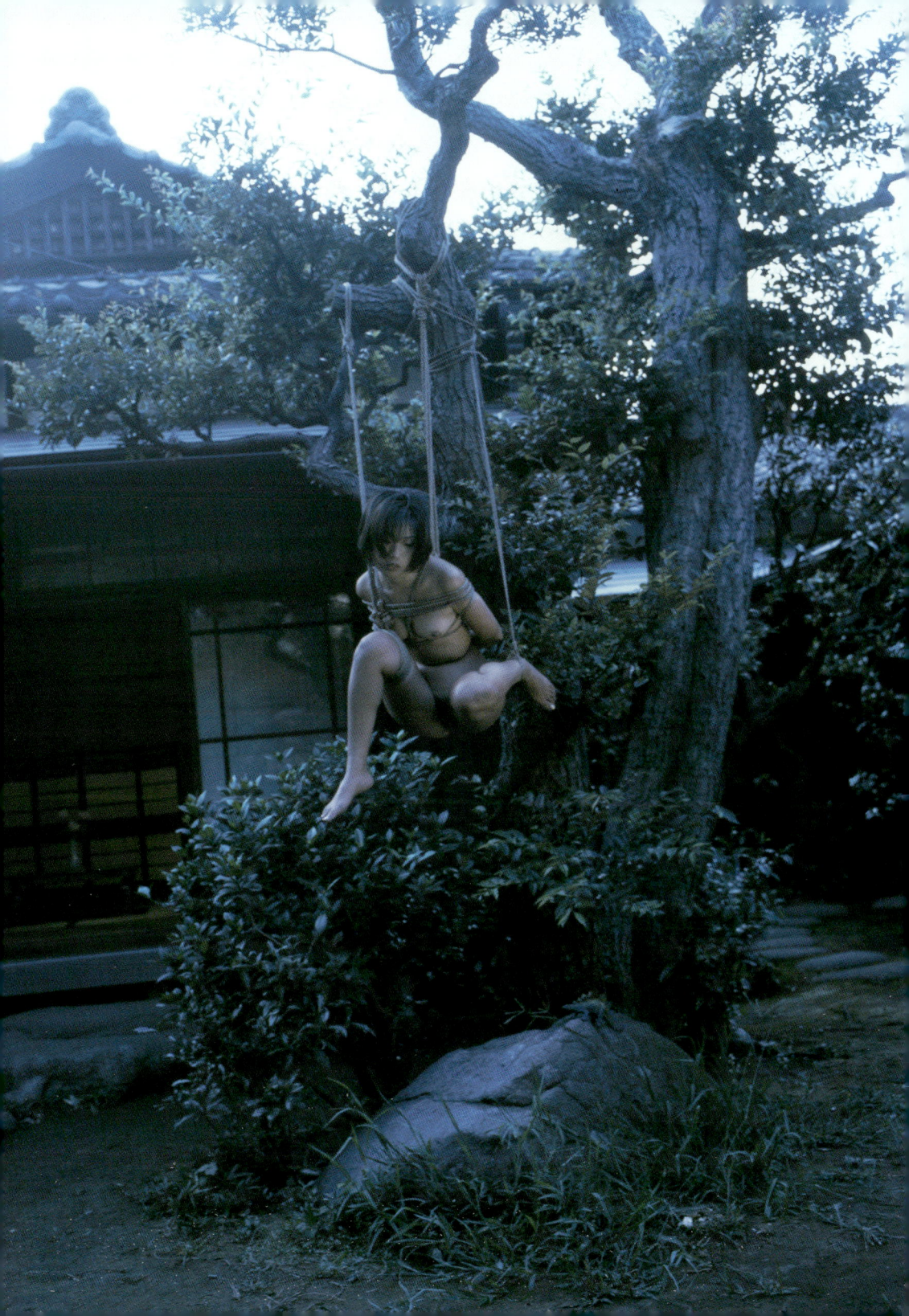

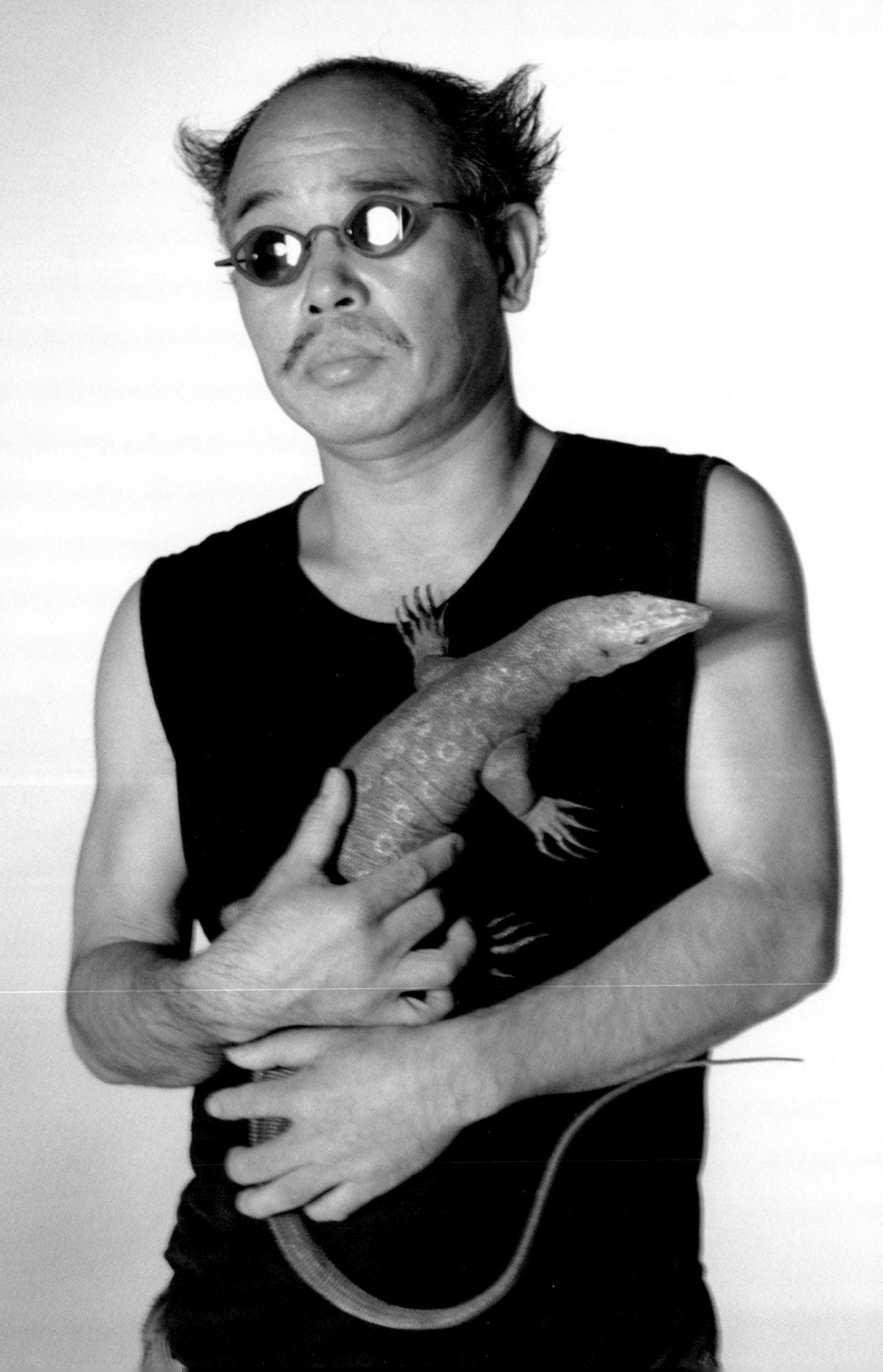

Nobuyoshi Araki

im Interview mit Jérôme Sans

Jérôme Sans: Sie haben das vorliegende Buch *Araki by Araki* genannt. Warum das, wo Sie doch die meisten Ihrer Bücher selbst herausgeben? Verbinden Sie damit eine besondere Aussage? Nobuyoshi Araki: Als das 20. Jahrhundert zu Ende ging, bin ich 60 geworden. In Japan heißt der 60. Geburtstag „Kanreki" und ist ein ganz besonderes Fest, mit dem ein Lebenszyklus endet und ein neuer beginnt. Es ist ein Übergang und ein neuer Ausgangspunkt. Bei dieser Gelegenheit kam ich auf den Gedanken, alle meine Arbeiten zu kompilieren. Vergleichbar mit „Picasso's Picassos" habe ich die besten bis zum Schluss aufgehoben. Zunächst hatte ich vor, das Buch hier in Japan selbst herauszubringen. Interessanter erschien mir jedoch letztlich der Blickwinkel eines anderen, eines Fremden zumal. Für mich ist ein anderer immer ein Fremder. Und diesmal handelt es sich um einen wirklich Fremden, was dem Vorhaben etwas Frisches gibt. Letztlich ist dieses Buch kein *Araki by Araki*, sondern ein *Araki by TASCHEN*. Ich denke, es ist deshalb nicht minder spannend.

Wenn jemand Fremdes die Auswahl der Arbeiten vornimmt, erkenne ich möglicherweise unbekannte Seiten meiner selbst. Bei meinen zahlreichen Ausstellungen außerhalb Japans (in Österreich bei der Wiener Secession, in Italien im Centro per l'Arte Contemporanea Luigi Pecci, Prato …) habe ich immer wieder diese Erfahrung gemacht. Auch ist es schon vorgekommen, dass Dinge, die ich nicht besonders wichtig finde, von anderen für ausgesprochen interessant gehalten werden.

Im Allgemeinen glaubt man, die Fotografie durch die Zusammenstellung oder das Layout mit Ideen oder Gedanken aufzuladen. Das funktioniert bei mir nicht. Meine Fotos besitzen sehr viel Kraft und Energie aus sich selbst heraus. Ich kann es mir erlauben, sie in die Hände eines Herausgebers zu legen, weil ich mir der Qualität und der Kraft meiner Fotografien sicher bin. In der Regel macht sich der Blick dessen bemerkbar, der sie zusammenstellt. Aber ich vertraue meinen Fotos. Sie verändern sich nie.

In welchen Punkten unterscheidet sich dieses Buch von den anderen Büchern? Der Punkt ist, dass ich alles von mir zeigen kann – die Frauen, meine Frau, die Stadt … Das Buch zeigt Empfindungen in ihren Verästelungen und Verzweigungen, es bietet so etwas wie eine organische Entfaltung meiner Arbeit. Die einzelnen Elemente sind gleichsam die Blätter eines großen Baumes. Ich hoffe, dass dieser Baum anfängt zu blühen. *Araki by Araki* ist ein Epitaph zu meinem 60. Geburtstag. Ich mache Fotos seit meiner Geburt. Nachdem ich aus dem Bauch meiner Mutter gekommen war, habe ich mich umgedreht und ihre Vulva fotografiert! Das erste Wort, das ich nun nach meiner Reinkarnation, in meinem neuen Leben, in den Mund nehme, ist noch immer Fotografie. Das ist eben ein Kontrakt, der seit nunmehr fast 60 Jahren besteht. Mein Epitaph: Fotografie ist Liebe und Tod.

Wie definieren Sie Liebe? Liebe ist schwer zu definieren. Wenn man eine Frau liebt, so bleibt sie auf dem Foto oder auch im Gedächtnis erhalten. Und ebenso bleiben die Gefühle bestehen. So zum Beispiel habe ich meine Frau geliebt und davon sind in meinen Empfindungen, in meinem Körper Spuren zurückgeblieben, Spuren, die auch aus einer Fotografie nicht verschwinden. (Ich nenne hier nur meine Frau, sonst gäbe es Probleme!) Das ist es, wenn man sagt, man hat jemanden geliebt.

Zurzeit liebe ich meine Katze Chiro und Blumen. Die Katze steht für den Leib, die Blumen für die Genitalien. An ihnen entzünden sich Gefühle, wie ich sie für geliebte Menschen habe.

Wenn ich zu Hause bin und Chiro sich zu mir gesellt, spüre ich, wie meine Gefühle für sie wachsen. Wenn ich aufwache und Blumen sehe, nehme ich sie mit der Kamera auf, und zwar immer aus einem Verhältnis der Nähe, aus einem natürlichen Gefühl heraus (zu Hause habe ich immer viele Blumen). Solche Augenblicksempfindungen sind es, die ich mag – dennoch ist es die Fotografie, für die ich absolute Gefühle hege.

Liebe ist für mich etwas Vertrautes, das man berühren kann. Deshalb gibt es im Internet keine Liebe. Liebe bedarf einer Nähe der Gerüche, der sinnlichen Wahrnehmungen, einer gemeinsamen Umgebung.

Aus diesem Grund fotografiere ich meine Freunde, die Menschen, die mir nahe sind, meine Umgebung. Das eben ist Fotografie. Mit anderen Worten, ich nehme Sie jetzt mit der Kamera auf, weil ich Ihnen heute begegnet bin.

Im Mittelpunkt Ihrer Welt steht Tokio, auch wenn Sie in anderen Städten Asiens fotografiert haben. Ihre Arbeit spricht von der Nähe zu Ihrer unmittelbaren Umgebung. Sehen Sie **da einen Zusammenhang zur Nähe in den alten, traditionellen japanischen Häusern, die ja den Eindruck geteilter Intimität erwecken?** Wenn ich von Tokio spreche, dann interessiere ich mich nicht für die Stadt in ihrer Gesamtheit, sondern nur für die Orte, mit denen ich vertraut bin und an denen ich mich jeden Tag bewege. Ich fotografiere nicht irgendwo, sondern ausschließlich in Shinjuku oder in der Nachbarschaft, die ich gut kenne. Fotografie ist gleichbedeutend mit dem, was zu mir in Beziehung steht. Nie nehme ich mir vor, irgendwohin zu gehen, um dort zu fotografieren. Falls ich meine Arbeit als „Vergegenwärtigung" bezeichnen darf, dann wäre sie eine „Vergegenwärtigung" von Frauen, Orten oder intensiven Momenten, die ich liebe.

Alles wird durch die Umgebung bestimmt, in der man aufgewachsen ist. Ich bin in Tokios Kleine-Leute-Viertel Minowa zur Welt gekommen, in einem kleinen traditionellen Haus, das aus zwei aneinander grenzenden Wohnungen bestand, sodass sich das Leben in engster Nähe abspielte. Man konnte von einem Teil des Hauses zum anderen hinübergehen. Immer war da ein Nachbar, der einem durch die Hintertür etwas brachte. Die Nachbarn kamen mit Essen und sagten, es sei von ihrer Mahlzeit übrig geblieben, aber in Wirklichkeit hatten sie es auch für uns zubereitet. Man kochte nicht für sich allein, sondern für die anderen mit. Es war ein Viertel, in dem große Menschlichkeit herrschte. Und weil ich dort geboren bin, bin ich auch so. Minowa liegt an der Grenze des Stadtbezirks Taito-ku im Nordosten von Tokio. Bewegt man sich noch weiter Richtung Norden, dorthin, wo Takeshi Kitano zur Welt kam, so sind die Menschen dort ein wenig tyrannischer, so wie er. *(lacht)*

Ich lebte nahe Yoshiwara, dem Freudenviertel. Ein paar Schritte von meiner Haustür entfernt stand ein Tempel namens Jokanji, in dem Kurtisanen, die keine Angehörigen hatten, bestattet wurden. Als Kind war dieser Tempel mein Spielplatz. In ihm fand sich zweierlei vereint, Gräber (der Tod) und Prostituierte. Mein ganzes Leben war von diesem Ort geprägt. Der Schmutz dieses volkstümlichen Viertels wird mir stets gegenwärtig bleiben. Leben und Tod gingen dort ein und aus. So hat sich mir schon im frühesten Kindesalter die Erfahrung von Leben und Tod eingeprägt.

Meine Lieblingsfarbe ist Rot. Diese Farbe spricht von der Komplexität von Leben und Tod. Deswegen habe ich den Inhaber der Bar, in der wir gerade sitzen, gebeten, seine ganze Einrichtung in Rot zu halten – „ROUGE" ist übrigens auch ihr Name. Als die Brandbomben der amerikanischen B 29-Bomber den Himmel über Japan rot färbten, fand ich das sehr schön. Ich war damals fünf Jahre alt. Mein Interesse an der Farbe Rot geht auf dieses Erlebnis zurück. Meine gesamte fotografische Arbeit leitet sich aus dieser Kindheit her. Minowa ist für mich wie eine Gebärmutter. Zwar lebe ich nicht mehr in dem Viertel, aber meine Wurzeln sind dort.

Da ich in einem traditionellen Haus aus Holz aufwuchs, bin ich von Warmherzigkeit und Sentimentalität durchdrungen. Ich bin in einer Umgebung aufgewachsen, wo in der kleinen Straße Morgenwinden blühten. Diese Umgebung hat mein Leben geprägt. Paris hat ebenfalls seine einfachen Viertel, aber sie sind ganz aus Stein und sehr trocken. Heute besteht auch Japan nur aus Steinen. Roboter ersetzen die menschliche Stimme. Was zu fotografieren wäre, ist im Verschwinden begriffen. Wenn die Welt schlecht wird, nehmen die Fotos denselben Weg. Alles wird uninteressant. Das wäre also, mit 60 Jahren, mein Epitaph zum Ende der Welt.

Ihre Arbeit ist den Frauen gewidmet. Meine allererste Fotografie machte ich, nachdem ich den Uterus meiner Mutter verlassen habe – für mich ist die Frau Fotografie. Als nächstes habe ich ein Mädchen aufgenommen, in das ich in der Grundschule heimlich verliebt war. Mit dem Erwachsenwerden war für mich der Anblick einer Frau unmittelbar mit der Vorstellung ihrer Vulva verbunden. Ich habe oft Großaufnahmen davon gemacht und diese Position 1970 mit meiner Ausstellung „Sur-sentimentalist Manifesto" vertreten, einem fotografischen Manifest aus der Zeit, als ich mit dem Fotografieren von Frauen begann. Zu jener Zeit glaubte ich, dass ich Anarchist werden müsse. Deshalb hatte ich mir den Namen „Ararky" zugelegt.

Ich arbeitete damals bei Dentsu, einer japanischen Werbeagentur. Dort lernte ich meine spätere Ehefrau Yoko kennen. Bis dahin hatte ich Frauen über ihren Sexus aufgenommen, als „Objekte". Als ich Yoko fotografierte, begann ich die Beziehung als ein Verhältnis der Gegenseitigkeit zu sehen, das sich zwischen der Frau, mit der ich mich auseinander setzte, und mir selbst abspielte. Damals habe ich eine Frau zum ersten Mal so genommen, wie sie ist, und nicht als Objekt.

In dieser Beziehung wurzelnd hat mein Baum viele Zweige (Frauen) entwickelt. Wenngleich ich immer gesagt habe, dass ich meiner Frau treu war und meine damalige Arbeit sich ausschließlich um sie drehte, habe ich auch damals schon viele andere Frauen fotografiert. Diese und andere Tatsachen, die mich betreffen, werden in diesem Buch erstmals enthüllt. Ich offenbare mich immer mehr. Mit 60 Jahren darf ich Verjährung in Anspruch nehmen. Nach dem Tod meiner Frau habe ich dann noch viele Frauen aufgenommen. So sind am Ende um mich herum viele Verzweigungen, viele Blätter (Frauen) entstanden, und es wurde das Paradies! *(lacht)*

Kann man Ihre Leidenschaft für den Sexus als eine zeitgenössische Version der Shunga betrachten, jener erotischen Farbholzschnitte der Edo-Zeit [um 1600–1868]? Ich würde meine Fotografien gerne wie Shunga gestalten, doch ist mir das bisher noch nicht geglückt. In den Shunga gibt es eine verborgene Seite. Die Geschlechtsorgane sind sichtbar, aber der Rest wird von den Kimonos verdeckt. Diese Farbholzschnitte geben also nicht alles preis. In ihnen kommt das Mysterium der Liebe zum Tragen. Die Shunga stellen nicht bloß den Sexus dar, sondern ein Liebesgeheimnis zwischen zwei Menschen, zwischen Mann und Frau. Oftmals erscheine ich auf meinen Fotos, auf denen verschnürte Frauen oder ein Geschlechtsakt zu sehen sind. Aber ich spiele nicht die Hauptrolle. Ich bin wie eine kleine Figur in einem Shunga, spiele einen Neben- oder Zuschauerpart. Ich ziehe das Fotografieren dem Sex vor. Heute lehne ich sogar jedes Angebot, mit Mädchen auszugehen, ab. Sie erwarten, dass man mit ihnen ein sexuelles Verhältnis unterhält; zusammen Abendessen zu gehen genügt nicht. Aber das könnte ich nicht mehr ertragen, denn ich ziehe das Fotografieren vor.

Beim Geschlechtsakt bin ich zweit- oder gar drittklassig. Ich benutze Sex nur, um gute Fotos aufzunehmen. Ich bin streng mit dem Sex wie mit der Frau, mit der ich schlafe.

Ich setze dies alles in dieses Buch, weil es sich um eine Publikation im Ausland handelt, die die Japaner nicht zu Gesicht bekommen werden. Für mich ist die Fotografie das Wesentliche.

Was wollen Sie durch Ihre Fotos mitteilen oder zum Ausdruck bringen? Ich habe in meinen Fotografien nichts mitzuteilen, keine besondere Aussage zu machen. Die Aussagen kommen von den Sujets der Darstellung, seien es Männer oder Frauen. Ich warte, bis diese Sujets sich ergeben, sich hergeben. Ich habe etwas zu fotografieren, aber nichts auszudrücken. Derzeit zeige ich eher die Freuden des Lebens als die Tristesse des Todes. Ich kenne einige Menschen, die das Leben für traurig halten. Ich sehe das heute anders. Der Tod ist trauriger.

Woher rührt eigentlich diese Obsession für Frauen in Ihrer fotografischen Arbeit? Die Frau vereint alle Reize des Lebens, alle seine Wesenszüge: Schönheit, Hässlichkeit, Obszönität, Reinheit … weit mehr, als man in der Natur findet. In der Frau ist der Himmel und das Meer. (Auch wenn das irgendwie affektiert klingt.) In der Frau ist die Blume und die Knospe …

Ein Fotograf, der keine Frauen fotografiert, ist kein Fotograf oder doch nur ein drittklassiger. In der Begegnung mit Frauen lernen wir weit mehr über die Welt als durch die Lektüre der *Menschlichen Komödie* von Balzac. Ob die eigene Frau, eine Zufallsbekanntschaft oder eine Prostituierte, sie erschließen uns die Welt. Übrigens lese ich nicht mehr, seit ich die Grundschule verlassen habe. Ich gestalte mein Leben durch das Zusammentreffen mit Frauen.

In Japan sind Sie mit Ihrer Ikonografie zur Kultfigur geworden. Wie reagieren Sie auf die widersinnige Zensur in einem Land, in dem hinter der Fassade ganz offiziell eine zweite Welt existiert, die Welt der „verbotenen" Lüste, besonders die der Love Hotels für außereheliche Begegnungen? Ich fotografiere nicht, um aller Welt alles offen zu legen. Eigentlich bin ich damit zufrieden, meine Fotos, wenn es denn gute Fotos sind, in meinem Freundeskreis zu zeigen. Was die Zensur betrifft, so geht mich diese weder gesellschaftlich noch künstlerisch etwas an. Ich habe keine besondere Weltanschauung und auch keine besondere Ansicht von der Kunst, vom Denken oder der Philosophie. Man könnte sagen, ich bin ein kleiner Schlingel, der verbotenen Unfug treibt.

Ich glaube, diese Haltung weist auf eine Paradoxie hin, die in Japan bezüglich des Gesetzes gegen die Pornografie herrscht. Ja, und das ist seit der Edo-Zeit so. Es mag zwiespältig und widersinnig erscheinen. Auch wenn in Japan ein strenges Zensurgesetz erlassen worden ist, geht dort alles Mögliche munter weiter. Es herrscht eben ein gewisses Drunter und Drüber. Äußerste Strenge steht neben dem Glamour abweichender Möglichkeiten. Häufig kommt es sogar vor, dass diese Gegensätze sich vermischen.

Wenn man in Japan ein Mädchen verschnürt und fotografiert, so wird dies dem Urheber der Fotos niemals die Todesstrafe einbringen. Da ist man unerwartet großzügig. Christliche Länder sind in dieser Hinsicht viel strenger, aber Europa ist nach wie vor tolerant. Selbst wenn der Vatikan diese Art von Praktiken nicht gutheißt, nimmt er doch meine Arbeit hin. In den USA hingegen herrschen außerordentlich strenge und rigorose Sitten. Ich würde nicht das Risiko eingehen, dort nackte Mädchen oder gefesselte Frauen zu zeigen.

Meiner Ansicht nach leben wir heute, verglichen mit der Edo-Zeit, in einer sexuell ärmeren Epoche, aber es gibt noch Sphären einer vielgestaltigen Sexualität, die ich sehr mag.

Weshalb thematisieren Sie in Ihren Fotografien immer wieder die Praxis des Bondage? Der Kinbaku [Verknotung mit Seilen] ist etwas anderes als Bondage. Ich umschnüre den Körper der Frauen, weil ich weiß, dass ich ihre Seele nicht zu fesseln vermag. Binden lässt sich nur ihre Physis. Die Frauen zu umschnüren läuft in einem gewissen Sinne darauf hinaus, sie zu umarmen, zu liebkosen.

Warum bauen Sie kleine Dinosaurier aus Kunststoff in Ihre Welt ein? Wofür genau stehen sie? Haben sie jeweils eine eigene Identität? Ich bin jemand, der ständig Gesellschaft braucht. Ich habe das Bedürfnis, Kameraden oder Freunde um mich zu haben, denn ich fühle mich häufig einsam. Diese Monstren sind mein Alter Ego. Sie sind Zeichen meines Wunsches, in meinen Fotos anwesend zu sein, so als wären sie Teile meines Körpers. Ich mag diese Dinosaurier sehr und ich habe einfach das Verlangen, ständig mit ihnen zusammen zu sein und sie zu sammeln. Dieses Verlangen ist sexueller Art. Ich will die Wesen, die ich liebe, fotografieren, und ich möchte immer mit ihnen zusammenleben.

Augenblicklich ist mein Balkon leer, weil die Dinosaurier noch nicht von meiner Ausstellung in Paris zurückgekommen sind. Sie stecken zurzeit beim japanischen Zoll fest und fehlen mir schrecklich. Chiro, meine Katze, fühlt sich ebenfalls einsam und schmollt ein bisschen. Sie liegt auf dem Rücken von Waneen (einem großen Krokodil-Objekt), aber auch ihr fehlen die Saurier.

Jeder Dinosaurier hat eine eigene Bedeutung. Wichtiger ist mir jedoch, dass sie alle zusammenbleiben. Ich fühle mich häufig allein, deshalb wünsche ich mir immer, mein Haus zu beleben. Selbstverständlich hat jeder Saurier seinen eigenen Charme. Ich habe ihnen sogar Namen gegeben. Doch der Hauptgrund für mein Interesse

an diesen Wesen ist, dass ich mich oft ganz allein fühle und es schön finde, wenn sie da sind und mir Gesellschaft leisten. Und deshalb umgebe ich mich auch mit Blumen. Sentimentally lonely! Ich liebe die Wärme, die Wärme der Gebärmutter. Ich bin ein Baby und ein Kind. Ich kann die Wärme des Uterus nicht vergessen. Auch mag ich Thermen, die für mich eine Art Uterus sind.

Sie übermalen Ihre Schwarzweiß-Fotografien gelegentlich mit Farben. Was möchten Sie damit zum Ausdruck bringen? Die Schwarzweiß-Fotografien stellen den Tod dar. Ein Foto zu machen heißt, dessen Sujet zu töten. Eine weitere Möglichkeit, Schwarzweiß-Fotos in lebendiger Form zu zeigen, sind für mich die „Arakinema", in denen ich die Fotos in Bewegung und mit Ton vorführe.

Die Schwarzweiß-Fotografien stellen den Tod dar, und ich möchte sie wieder zum Leben erwecken. Ich will ihnen erotische Gefühle, Leidenschaften oder die Wärme eines Körpers geben. Daher kommt auch der unbewusste Wunsch, sie zu bemalen. Es geht mir jedoch nicht darum, diese Schwarzweiß-Fotos in Malerei zu verwandeln. Ich versuche nur, sie so weit wie möglich den idealen Fotografien anzunähern, die ich im Kopf habe.

Mein Ziel ist es nicht, Malerei auf fotografischer Grundlage zu betreiben, sondern an Fotos zu glauben und durch Bemalung darzustellen, was sie bedeuten. Ich entscheide mich oft für die Farben Rot oder Grün, und ich nenne die entstandenen Bilder „rotgrün sentimentale Farben".

Die Schwarzweiß-Fotos, die ich Ihnen gerade gezeigt habe, entstammen dem Buch *Photographs from the End of the Century*. Das nächste wird ausschließlich Farbfotos enthalten und den Titel *Photographs from the New Century* tragen. Diese beiden Bücher ergänzen sich zu einem Zyklus.

Warum übermalen Sie in den entsprechenden Serien durchgängig das Geschlecht der schwarzweiß dargestellten Frauen? Das ist zunächst eine zensurbedingte Retusche, die die

Genitalien verbergen soll. Und zwar deshalb, weil es in Japan strenge Regeln gibt. Vielleicht ist es aber besser für mich, dass ein paar Regeln herrschen. Gleichzeitig ist diese Übermalung jedoch auch ein Zeichen meines Verlangens, Unfug zu treiben, sie anzufassen oder mein Glied hineinzustecken.

Es ist, als ob ich in einem Fluss hin- und herschwimme zwischen dem farbigen Ufer – der heutigen Welt – und dem monochromen Ufer – dem Jenseits. Meinen momentanen Gefühlen folgend entscheide ich, ob ich ins Paradies des Schwarzweiß gehe, in der hiesigen Welt der Farbe bleibe oder dasselbe Sujet sowohl in Farbe als auch in Schwarzweiß behandele.

Wenn ich müde bin und mich auf dem Rücken treiben lasse, fotografiere ich den Himmel. Paris hat die Seine, Tokio die beiden Flüsse Sumidagawa und Arakawa. Japan hat aber auch einen Fluss namens Sanzu no Kawa [Totenfluss]. Diesen Fluss müssen die Toten durchqueren, um das Nirwana zu erreichen.

Ihre Fotografien sind zeitlich völlig unbestimmt. Welches Verhältnis haben Sie zur Zeit? Eine Fotografie kann nur den Augenblick der Aufnahme beschreiben. Und dieser Augenblick bleibt unidentifizierbar. Ein Augenblick ist eine Ewigkeit und die Ewigkeit ein Augenblick. Mehr als alle anderen Aspekte ist es dieser Gedanke, den die Fotografie in sich birgt. Wenn ich auf den Auslöser drücke, ist dieser Moment ewig. Die Ewigkeit wird somit erzeugt durch die Freigabe des Verschlusses. Das ist eine ungemein direkte Handlung. Es ist mehr Tat als Kunst.

Folglich behaupte ich, dass ich meine Fotos miteinander vermischen kann, ohne das Aufnahmedatum berücksichtigen zu müssen. Andererseits mache ich auch Fotografien, bei denen das Aufnahmedatum auf dem Abzug steht, so dass ich sie in chronologischer Reihenfolge zeigen kann. Wie in einem Tagebuch formt die alltägliche Kontinuität eine Geschichte. Der Fluss der vergehenden Zeit ist höchst dramatisch und spannend. Ich arbeite also mit mehreren Zeitbegriffen. Wenn ich aber unter den beiden wählen darf, halte ich mich lieber an die chronologische Reihenfolge, die ich im Endeffekt interessanter finde.

Deshalb mache ich Fotografien nach Art eines Tagebuchs und beschließe häufig, sie zu lassen, wie sie sind, ohne zu versuchen, sie zu bearbeiten.

Dieses Bearbeiten ergibt sich nachher von selbst, durch das Leben oder die Zeit, in der wir leben. Das bedeutet, wenn ich die Fotos in chronologischer Reihenfolge ordne, wird sich Gott oder irgendwer anders – bei mir Shashin, der Gott der Fotografie – an meiner Stelle darum kümmern. Die dramatischere Wirkung entsteht aus einer unbewussten Zusammenstellung. Die meisten meiner Fotobücher funktionieren so. Es lohnt sich nicht, über eine bestimmte Ordnung nachzudenken. Wenn ich zum Beispiel ein Foto von meiner Katze Chiro machen will, brauche ich mir darüber keine Gedanken zu machen. Dieses Bild entsteht auf ganz natürliche Weise.

Weshalb versehen Sie dann manche Fotos mit einem Datum? Das ist eine Parodie, ein Hinweis darauf, dass hier Vollkommenheit weder erreicht noch angestrebt wird. Wenn auf einem Foto ein Datum gedruckt steht, wird es niemals ein Meisterwerk sein können. Das datierte Foto ist nicht mehr als ein schlichtes Zeugnis eines Tages. Aber gerade das ist ja wiederum Fotografie!

Das Foto besagt einfach, dass dieser Tag, dieser besondere Augenblick wunderbar war. So ist das Leben. Nichts geht über das Tagebuch. Selbst in der Literatur ist das Tagebuch dem Roman überlegen.

Das Tagebuch ist das Leben, und das Datum ist das Foto. Oder aber es liegt am Fotografen, das Datum zu löschen. Photo, c'est la vie!

Ist das der Grund, warum Sie unaufhörlich fotografieren? Man muss die Augenblicke des Lebens fortwährend fotografieren. So wie man weiterleben muss – für mich heißt fotografieren soviel wie leben.

Welchen Künstlern, Schriftstellern oder Cineasten, die Tagebücher führen, fühlen Sie sich nahe? Am stärksten fühle ich mich vielleicht dem japanischen Schriftsteller Kafu Nagai [1879–1959] verbunden, der 1917 den Roman *Danchotei Nichijo* [Danchoteis Tagebuch] verfasst hat. Nagai wusste, dass die Ereignisse des jeweiligen Tages zwar sehr interessant sind, es aber noch wundervoller wäre, in das alltägliche Leben Fiktionen einzubauen. Vor ihm galt es als abgemacht, dass ein Tagebuch die Realität des Tages schildern sollte. Er hat als Erster diese Regel durchbrochen, indem er sein Tagebuch mit ein wenig Lüge versetzte, so dass es einen zusätzlichen Reiz bekam. An seinem *Danchotei Nichijo* ist alles falsch, aber dadurch wird der Text spannender.

Nahe fühle ich mich auch dem litauischen Filmemacher Jonas Mekas, auch wenn er in sein Werk keine Daten einfügt. Er hat einen Zugang zum Erhabenen, den ich nicht besitze, aber es gibt viele Berührungspunkte zwischen uns. Für mich ist Minowa die Gebärmutter, für Jonas Mekas ist dies wahrscheinlich Litauen, sein Heimatland. Am meisten liegt ihm an den charakteristischen Formen der Natur und an seiner Familie in Litauen. Mein Minowa hat schon etwas an Schwung verloren und liegt in Trümmern, und sein Litauen, das ebenfalls ein Trümmerhaufen ist, war einmal ein Paradies. Das sind unsere Gemeinsamkeiten. Wir interessieren uns beide für die Städte und für die Viertel, in denen wir geboren sind. Wechsel von Orten, von Zeiten. Das ist ein Tagebuch: Wechsel der Tage. Ohne viel über diesen Gedanken nachzusinnen, mache ich nach wie vor jeden Tag Fotos. Sich weiterbewegen heißt lebendig bleiben. Und diese Bewegungen mit einer Interpunktion zu versehen, bedeutet, ein Datum zu setzen.

Wie die englischen Künstler Gilbert & George verfolgen Sie das Ziel der Zugänglichkeit, der weitestmöglichen Verbreitung Ihrer Arbeit. Sie sind Anhänger einer Kunst für alle. Gründet dieser Ansatz in Ihrer Vergangenheit in einer Werbeagentur? Als ich bei Dentsu arbeitete, machte ich Werbung für andere. Aber ich wollte Werbung für mich selbst machen. Man könnte es als Kunst bezeichnen. Ich dachte, es wäre schon etwas erreicht, wenn ich meine Fotografien meinen Freunden zeigen könnte. Auf der anderen Seite aber hatte ich seit jeher den Wunsch, von möglichst vielen Menschen gekannt zu werden. Beispielsweise würde es mich freuen zu erfahren, dass die Leguane von den Galapagos-Inseln sich meine Arbeiten anschauen. Außerdem fände ich es schön, wenn sie über den Ozean nach Japan kämen, um sich von mir fotografieren zu lassen. Ich würde sie dann nach Yoshiwara mitnehmen.

Wie viele Bücher haben Sie bis heute veröffentlicht? Ich glaube, mehr als 250. Da ich die unzähligen fruchtlosen Besprechungen mit japanischen Verlegern satt hatte, gab ich meine Bücher zunächst selbst heraus, und zwar in fotokopierter Form. Mein erstes Buch, *Xeroxed Photo Albums*, kam so zustande. Zu der Zeit, als ich *Sentimental Journey* in Arbeit hatte, wollte kein Verlag ein Buch über meine Flitterwochen publizieren. Später haben viele Verlage meine Bücher veröffentlicht, wie TASCHEN heute. Manchmal mache ich Fotos und habe Lust, auf der Stelle ein Buch herauszubringen, wie bei einer Ejaculatio praecox. So bin ich mitunter nicht imstande, nach den Aufnahmen drei Monate auf das Erscheinen des Buches zu warten. Am liebsten wäre es mir, das Buch entstünde binnen eines Monats, gleich nach den Aufnahmen. Das Buch *Photographs from the End of the Century* habe ich selbst produziert, um diesem Bedürfnis nach Schnelligkeit nachzukommen. Es handelt sich um ein „Live"-Fotobuch, das die Geschwindigkeit und die Hitze der Aufnahmesituation bewahrt. Bei anderen Büchern scheinen auch die Herausgeber einen bestimmten Enthusiasmus entwickelt zu haben.

Die Technik der Fotokopiermaschinen hat sich seit den 70er Jahren sehr stark weiterentwickelt. Machen Sie immer noch Fotokopien-Bücher? Heute habe ich kein Interesse mehr daran, Bücher mit der Kopiermaschine zu machen, gerade weil die Qualität sich so stark verbessert hat. In den 70er Jahren waren Fotokopien roh, ungenau, körnig. Dies entsprach meinen Vorstellungen und überhaupt denen jenes Jahrzehnts, das ein sehr rohes war. Es waren Fotokopien meiner wilden Gefühle jener Zeit.

Nachdem ich mit dem Begriff der „Kopie" gearbeitet hatte, wandte ich mich dem Begriff der „Reproduktion" zu. Denn ein Foto ist die Reproduktion der Empfindungen zum Zeitpunkt der Aufnahme oder die Reproduktion der Empfindungen von Menschen, denen ich zu einem bestimmten Zeitpunkt begegnet bin, oder auch die Reproduktion von Beziehungen, die ich hatte. Gleichwohl sind meine Fotos kein Ausdruck der Gefühle der Sujets, die ich ablichte, noch wollen sie diese zur Darstellung oder zur Erscheinung bringen. Insofern kopiere ich mich selber und schulde dies der Existenz meiner Sujets. Dank ihrer kann ich „Reproduktionen" machen. Ohne sie könnte ich es nicht. Das gilt nicht nur für die Fotos, sondern auch für das Leben. Ich brauche Sujets. Das können Blumen sein, der Himmel oder selbstverständlich die Frauen. Ich lebe durch die Frauen. Ich werde sie weiterhin fotografieren. Sollten eines Tages die Frauen vom Erdball verschwinden, würde ich lieber rechtzeitig vorher sterben.

Haben Sie unrealisierte Projekte oder Vorhaben, die Sie in Zukunft angehen wollen? Ich habe kein Projekt, das nicht umgesetzt worden wäre. Über das, was ich in Zukunft tun werde, wird meine Umgebung entscheiden. Auf jeden Fall wird die Gottheit – die Göttin – „Frau" mich leiten.

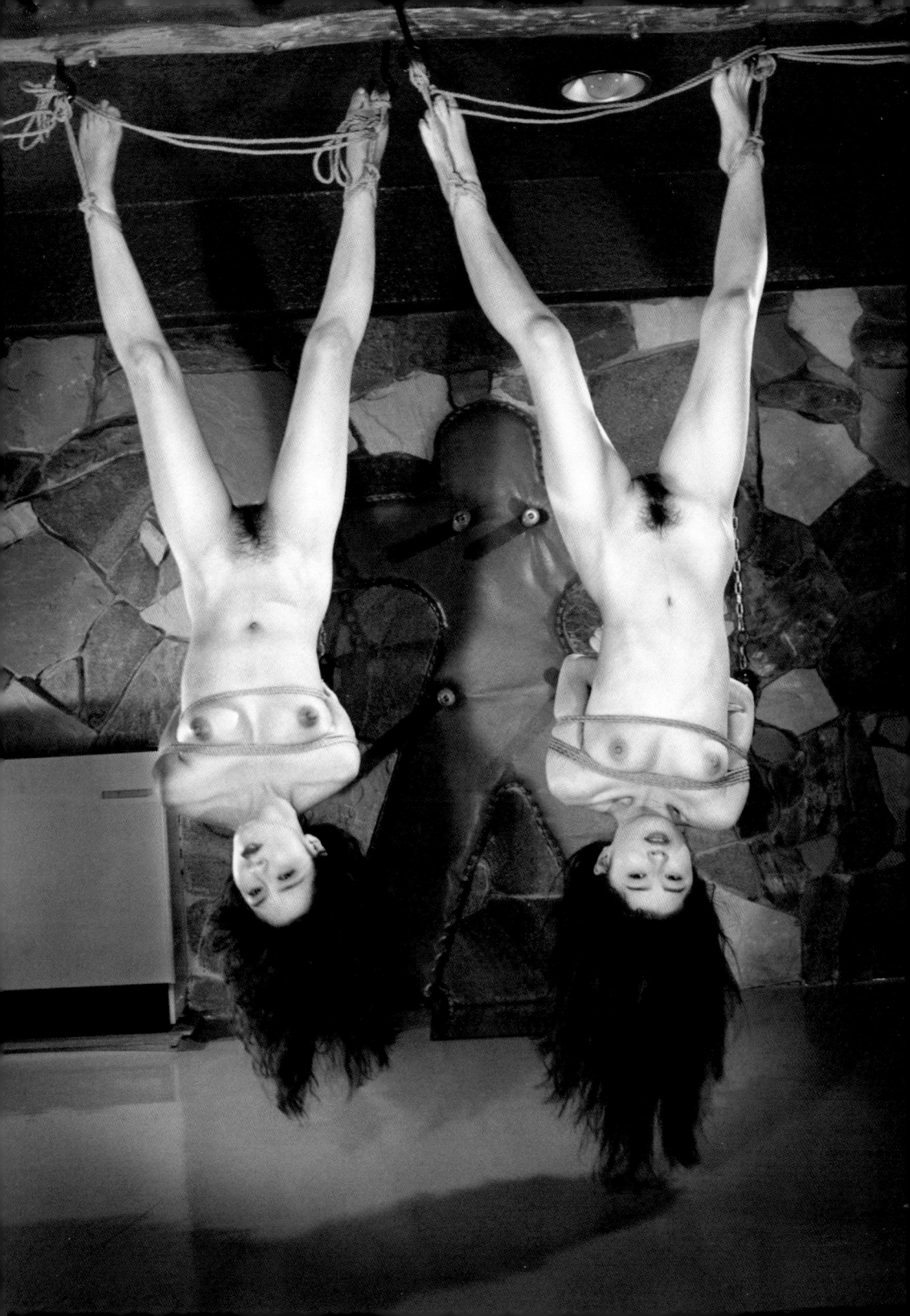

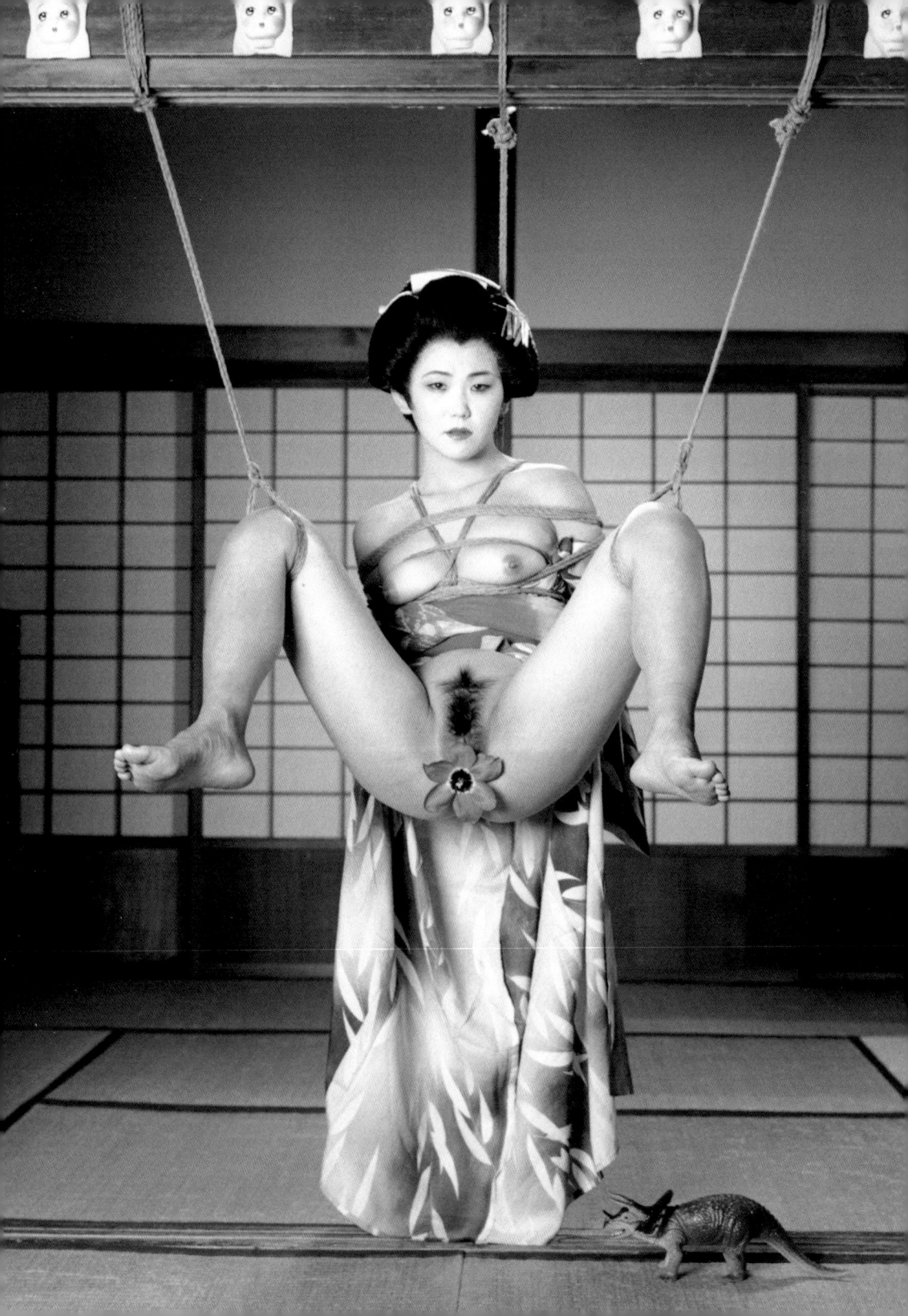

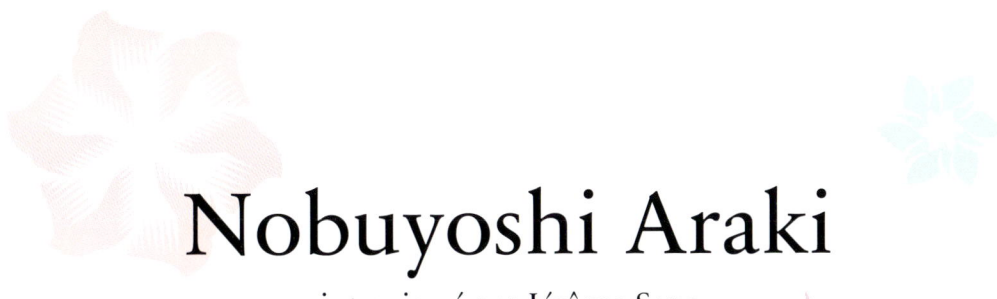

Nobuyoshi Araki

interviewé par Jérôme Sans

Jérôme Sans : Pourquoi avez-vous intitulé ce livre *Araki by Araki* alors que vous avez vous-même réalisé la plupart de vos livres ? S'agirait-il d'une démarche particulière ? Nobuyoshi Araki : J'ai eu 60 ans à la fin du XXᵉ siècle. Au Japon, le 60ᵉ anniversaire, appelé *Kanreki*, est une fête particulière, celle d'un cycle de vie qui s'achève pour un autre. C'est un passage et un nouveau départ. À cette occasion, j'ai pensé rassembler tous mes travaux. J'avais gardé les meilleures choses pour la fin de ma vie comme « Picasso's Picassos ». D'abord, j'avais pensé tout éditer moi-même au Japon. Mais finalement il m'a semblé plus intéressant de le faire à travers la perspective du regard d'une autre personne, et surtout de celle d'un étranger. Pour moi, l'autre est toujours un étranger. Et cette fois il s'agit vraiment d'un étranger, ce qui est très rafraîchissant. Finalement, ce livre n'est pas *Araki by Araki* mais *Araki by TASCHEN*. Je pense qu'il reste tout aussi intéressant. Quand une personne étrangère fait le choix de mes travaux, cela peut me faire concevoir des aspects inconnus chez moi. J'ai eu beaucoup d'expositions dans de nombreux pays (en Autriche à la Wiener Secession, en Italie au Centro per l'Arte Contemporanea Luigi Pecci, Prato…) et, à chaque fois, j'ai eu cette expérience. Il m'est déjà arrivé que des choses que je ne trouve pas particulièrement importantes semblent très intéressantes à d'autres. Généralement on croit donner à la photographie des idées ou des pensées par l'édition ou le montage. Cela ne fonctionne pas pour moi. Mes photos ont en elles-mêmes beaucoup de force ou d'énergie. Je peux me permettre de les mettre dans les mains d'un éditeur, car je suis sûr de la qualité et de la force de mes photographies. Normalement cela devient le regard de celui qui les édite. Mais j'ai confiance en mes photos. Elles ne changent jamais.

Quels sont les points différents de ce livre par rapport aux autres livres ? Le point qui diffère est que je peux tout montrer de moi – les femmes, ma femme, la ville… le livre montre les émotions et leurs ramifications, il offre au lecteur une sorte de déploiement organique de mon travail. Les éléments particuliers sont en quelque sorte les feuilles d'un grand arbre. J'espère que cet arbre se mettra à fleurir. *Araki by Araki* est une épitaphe pour mes 60 ans. Je prends des photos depuis que je suis né. Après être sorti du ventre de ma mère, je me suis retourné et ai photographié le sexe de ma mère ! La photographie est toujours le premier mot que j'emploie après ma réincarnation dans ma nouvelle vie. C'est un contrat de presque 60 ans maintenant. Mon épitaphe : la photo est amour et mort.

Comment définissez-vous l'amour ? L'amour est difficile à définir. Quand vous aimez une femme, elle reste en photo et aussi en mémoire. De même, les sentiments demeurent. Par exemple, après avoir aimé ma femme, il reste des traces dans mes sentiments, dans mon corps, traces qui ne disparaissent pas d'une photographie. (Je ne cite ici que le nom de ma femme sinon cela poserait problème !) C'est ainsi quand on dit qu'on a aimé quelqu'un.

Actuellement, j'aime Chiro, ma chatte, et les fleurs. Le chat représente la chair tandis que les fleurs sont les parties génitales. Le sentiment de personnes aimées.

Quand je suis chez moi, je sens mes sentiments grandir pour Chiro lorsqu'elle vient vers moi. Quand je me réveille et que je vois des fleurs, je les prends en photo toujours dans un rapport de proximité. Des sentiments instantanés me viennent tout naturellement (j'ai toujours beaucoup de fleurs à la maison). Ces sentiments instantanés sont ce que j'aime, même si j'ai pour la photographie des sentiments absolus.

L'amour pour moi c'est une histoire de proximité, de familier, que l'on peut toucher. C'est la raison pour laquelle il n'y a pas d'amour sur Internet. L'amour implique une proximité d'odeurs, de sensations, d'environnement. C'est pour cette raison que je photographie mes amis, mes proches, ce qui m'entoure. C'est cela la photo. En d'autres termes, je vous prends en photographie maintenant parce que je vous ai rencontré aujourd'hui.

Tokyo est au centre de votre univers, même si vous avez réalisé des photographies d'autres villes asiatiques. Votre travail parle de cette proximité à votre environnement direct. Y voyez-vous un rapport avec celle des vieilles maisons traditionnelles japonaises où il y a cette sensation d'intimité partagée ? Quand je parle de Tokyo, je ne m'intéresse pas à la ville dans sa globalité, mais simplement aux endroits qui me sont familiers et que je fréquente quotidiennement. Je ne photographie pas n'importe où mais uniquement Shinjuku ou le voisinage que je connais bien. La photographie est synonyme de ce qui est en relation avec moi. Je ne vais

pas quelque part intentionnellement pour faire des photos. Si je pouvais utiliser le mot « présentation » pour parler de mon travail, ce serait une « présentation » de femmes, de lieux ou de temps forts que j'aime.

Tout est déterminé par l'environnement dans lequel vous avez été élevé. Je suis né dans le quartier populaire de Tokyo qui s'appelle Minowa, dans une petite maison traditionnelle qui était constituée de deux foyers contigus où chacun de ces foyers évoluait dans une grande proximité. On pouvait passer d'une maison à l'autre. Il y avait toujours un voisin qui vous amenait quelque chose par la porte de derrière. Il vous apportait de la nourriture, disant qu'il s'agissait de restes de leur repas, alors qu'il l'avait fait spécialement pour vous. On y faisait des plats pour tous. C'est un quartier où il y avait beaucoup d'humanité. Puisque je suis né là, je suis comme cela.

Minowa est à l'extrémité de l'arrondissement Taito-ku au nord-est de Tokyo. Si vous allez encore plus au nord, où Takeshi Kitano est né, les gens sont un peu plus tyranniques, comme lui. (Il rit.)

J'habitais près de Yoshiwara, le quartier des filles de joie. Juste à côté de chez moi se tenait un temple nommé Jokanji où les courtisanes sans famille étaient enterrées. Enfant, ce temple était mon terrain de jeux. Se trouvaient conjointement dans ce temple des tombes (la mort) et des prostituées. Toute ma vie a été marquée par ce lieu. Il me restera toujours les traces mouillées de boue de ce quartier populaire. Il y avait là toujours la vie et la mort errante. C'est comme cela que dès le plus jeune âge, j'ai automatiquement appris ou senti la vie et la mort.

Ma couleur préférée est le rouge. Cette couleur parle de la complexité de la vie et de la mort. C'est pourquoi j'ai demandé au patron du bar où nous nous trouvons de faire tout son décor en rouge. D'ailleurs, il se nomme bar « ROUGE ». Quand les bombes incendiaires des chasseurs américains B 29 ont teinté le ciel japonais de rouge, j'ai trouvé cela très beau. J'avais alors cinq ans. Mon intérêt pour la couleur rouge vient de cette expérience. De cette enfance, j'ai développé tout mon travail photographique. Pour moi Minowa est comme un utérus. Même si je ne vis plus dans ce quartier, mes racines sont là. Ayant grandi dans une maison traditionnelle en bois, je suis imprégné de sentiments humains ou romanesques. J'ai vécu dans un environnement où les volubilis fleurissaient dans la petite rue. Cet environnement a déterminé ma vie. Paris a aussi ses quartiers populaires, mais tout en pierres, ils sont très secs. Aujourd'hui, le Japon lui aussi n'est plus que pierres. Les robots remplacent les voix de la chair. Les éléments à photographier sont en train de disparaître. Quand le monde devient mauvais, les photos prennent le même chemin. Tout devient inintéressant. Voici donc mon épitaphe, à l'âge de 60 ans, pour la fin du monde.

Votre travail est dédié aux femmes. La toute première photographie que j'ai réalisée, c'était après la sortie de l'utérus de ma mère. Pour moi, la femme incarne la photographie. Ensuite, j'ai pris celle d'une fille dont j'étais amoureux en cachette à l'école primaire. Quand je suis devenu adulte, une femme, pour moi, cela signifiait tout de suite son sexe. Je les ai souvent pris en gros plans et ai décrit cette position en 1970 dans mon exposition « Sur-sentimentalist Manifesto », un manifeste photographique du temps où j'ai commencé à prendre les femmes en photo. À cette période, je croyais que je devais devenir anarchiste. Aussi me suis-je surnommé « Ararky ». C'était le début.

Je travaillais alors chez Dentsu, une agence de publicité japonaise. J'y ai rencontré Yoko qui est devenue ma femme. Jusque-là je prenais des photos de femmes à travers leurs sexes comme des « objets ». Dès que j'ai photographié Yoko, j'ai commencé à prendre notre relation à deux, la femme à laquelle je me confrontais et moi-même. C'était la première fois que je prenais vraiment une femme comme elle est et non comme un objet.

À partir de cette relation, mon arbre a plein de branches (des femmes). Bien que j'aie toujours dit que j'étais fidèle à ma femme et que mon travail d'alors n'était axé que sur elle, je prenais déjà en photographie à cette époque beaucoup d'autres femmes. Ce livre révèle pour la première fois ces faits et tout ce qui me concerne. Je me révèle de plus en plus. À 60 ans, il y a prescription. Après la mort de ma femme, j'ai continué à prendre constamment des photos des femmes. Finalement beaucoup de ramifications, de feuilles (des femmes) sont apparues autour de moi et c'est devenu le paradis ! (Il rit.)

Est-ce que votre passion pour le sexe peut être envisagée comme une version contemporaine des *Shunga*, ces gravures sur bois érotiques de l'époque Edo [env. 1600–1868] ? Je voudrais faire mes photos comme des *Shunga*, mais je n'y suis pas encore arrivé. Il y a un côté réservé dans les *Shunga*. Le sexe est visible, mais le reste est caché par les kimonos. Ces gravures sur bois ne révèlent pas tout. Les *Shunga* comportent le secret amoureux. Ils ne révèlent pas uniquement le sexe mais un secret amoureux entre deux personnes, entre l'homme et la femme.

J'apparais souvent sur mes photos qui représentent des femmes ligotées ou faisant l'amour. Mais je ne joue pas le rôle principal. Je suis comme un petit personnage dans un *Shunga*. Un rôle secondaire ou de spectateur. Je préfère la photo au sexe. Maintenant, je refuse même toute proposition de sortir avec une fille. Elles attendent d'avoir une relation sexuelle. Dîner ensemble ne suffit pas. Je ne pourrais plus car je préfère la photo. Dans l'acte sexuel, je suis de deuxième ou troisième classe même. Je ne fais que profiter du sexe pour prendre de bonnes photos. Je suis dur avec le sexe comme avec la femme avec qui je fais l'amour. Je mets tout cela dans le livre car c'est une publication étrangère que les Japonais ne verront pas. Pour moi, l'essentiel c'est la photo.

Qu'est-ce que vous voulez dire ou exprimer dans vos photos ? Je n'ai rien à dire, aucun message particulier dans mes photographies. Les messages proviennent de mes sujets, hommes ou femmes. J'attends que les sujets se donnent, s'offrent. J'ai des choses à photographier alors que je n'ai rien à exprimer. Actuellement, je montre la joie de vivre plus que la tristesse de la mort. Certaines personnes que je connais trouvent que la vie est triste. Je pense aujourd'hui l'inverse. La mort est plus triste.

Mais pourquoi cette obsession de la femme dans votre travail photographique ? La femme a tous les charmes de la vie. Elle en a tous les éléments essentiels : la beauté, la laideur, l'obscénité, la pureté… bien plus que la nature n'en comprend. Dans la femme, il y a le ciel et la mer. (Dans un sens, cela peut paraître affecté.) Dans la femme, il y a la fleur et le bourgeon…

Un photographe qui ne photographie pas les femmes n'est pas un photographe, ou seulement un photographe de troisième classe. Les femmes vous apprennent beaucoup plus de choses sur le monde que la lecture de *La Comédie humaine* de Balzac. Qu'il s'agisse de votre femme, d'une rencontre ou d'une prostituée, elles vous apprendront le monde. D'ailleurs je ne lis plus depuis que je suis sorti de l'école primaire. Je crée ma vie en rencontrant des femmes.

Figure culte au Japon pour votre iconographie, comment réagissez-vous à la censure paradoxale de ce pays où réside derrière la façade et de manière officielle un deuxième monde, celui des plaisirs « interdits » avec notamment les « love hotels » pour les rencontres adultères ? Je ne fais pas de photos pour tout révéler à tout le monde. Je suis content en effet de montrer mes photos à mon cercle d'amis quand ce sont de bonnes photos. Pour ce qui est de la censure, je ne suis engagé ni socialement ni artistiquement. Je n'ai aucune idéologie particulière, ni d'idée sur l'art, sur la pensée ou sur la philosophie. C'est comme si j'étais un sale gosse faisant des bêtises interdites.

Je pense que cette attitude montre un paradoxe au Japon avec la loi contre la pornographie. Oui, et cela continue depuis l'époque Edo.

Cela peut paraître ambigu, paradoxal. Même si une loi stricte sur la censure a été établie, tout et n'importe quoi subsistent malgré tout au Japon. C'est toujours un peu le bordel. L'extrême rigueur côtoie malgré tout le glamour de la différence de possibilité. Et il arrive souvent que ces choses paradoxales se mélangent.

Au Japon, ficeler une jeune fille et la photographier n'entraînera jamais une condamnation à la peine de mort pour l'auteur de ces photos. C'est étonnamment bienfaisant. Les pays chrétiens sont bien plus sévères par rapport à cela. L'Europe reste tolérante. Même si le Vatican n'approuve pas ce type de pratique, il a quand même accepté mon travail. Les États-Unis sont particulièrement stricts et sévères. Je ne risque pas d'y montrer des jeunes filles nues ou des femmes ligotées.

Par rapport à l'époque Edo, je trouve que nous sommes aujourd'hui dans une époque plus pauvre en ce qui concerne le sexe, mais il demeure encore des atmosphères confuses de sexe que j'aime.

Pourquoi cette récurrence de la pratique du bondage dans vos photographies ? Le *Kinbaku* [nœuds de cordes] est différent du bondage. Je ligote le corps des femmes parce que je sais que je ne peux attacher leur âme. Seul leur physique peut être noué. Lacer les femmes revient en quelque sorte à les embrasser.

Pourquoi intégrez-vous des petits dinosaures en plastique dans votre univers ? Que représentent-ils exactement ? Ont-ils chacun une identité spécifique ? Je suis une personne qui a continuellement besoin de compagnie. J'ai besoin d'avoir des camarades ou des amis autour de moi car je me sens souvent solitaire. Ces monstres sont mon alter ego. Ils signifient mon désir d'être dans mes photos, comme s'ils étaient des parties de mon corps. J'aime ces dinosaures et j'ai le désir simple d'être avec eux tout le temps et de les collectionner. Ce désir est d'ordre sexuel. Je veux prendre en photo ceux que j'aime et je veux être toujours avec eux.

Mon balcon est actuellement vide car ces dinosaures ne sont pas encore rentrés de Paris après mon exposition. Ils sont encore bloqués en ce moment à la douane japonaise et ils me manquent terriblement. Chiro, ma chatte, se sent également seule et boude un peu. Elle est couchée sur le dos de Waneen (un grand objet crocodile) mais ils lui manquent à elle aussi.

Chaque dinosaure a une signification particulière. Mais il est plus important pour moi qu'ils restent tous ensemble. Je me sens souvent seul donc je voudrais toujours que ma maison soit animée. Bien sûr, chaque dinosaure a son propre charme. Je leur donne même à chacun un nom. Mais la raison de base de cet intérêt pour eux est que je me sens souvent tout seul et préfère être avec eux pour avoir de la compagnie. J'ai également des fleurs pour les mêmes raisons. *Sentimentally lonely!* J'aime la chaleur. Celle de l'utérus. Je suis un bébé et un enfant. Je ne peux pas oublier cette chaleur de l'utérus. J'aime également les thermes qui sont pour moi une sorte d'utérus.

Vous peignez quelquefois les photos noir et blanc de couleurs, qu'est-ce que vous voulez dire par là ? Les photographies noir et blanc représentent la mort. Prendre une photo revient à tuer son sujet. Une autre manière pour moi de montrer des photos noir et blanc en tant que performance, ce sont les « Arakinema ». Des photographies que je présente en mouvement et avec du son.

Les photos noir et blanc représentent la mort, je souhaite les ressusciter. Je veux leur ajouter des sentiments érotiques, des passions ou la chaleur d'un corps. Cela me donne aussi envie de les peindre inconsciemment. Je ne souhaite pas pour autant transformer ces photos noir et blanc en peinture. Je voudrais simplement qu'elles se rapprochent le plus possible des photographies idéales que j'ai dans ma tête.

Je ne prétends pas faire de la peinture avec des bases photographiques. Mais en les peignant en couleur, croire en ces photos et les révéler une nouvelle fois.

Je choisis souvent des couleurs comme le rouge et le vert et j'intitule ces photos : « Couleurs sentimentales rouge-vert ». Les photos noir et blanc que je viens de vous montrer sont tirées de mon livre *Photographs from the End of the Century*. Le prochain à paraître qui sera tout en couleur s'intitulera : *Photographs from the New Century*. Ces deux livres complètent un cycle.

Pourquoi dans vos séries picturales peignez-vous systématiquement sur les sexes des femmes représentées en noir et blanc ? D'abord, c'est une retouche par la censure afin que leurs parties génitales ne soient pas montrées. C'est comme ça parce qu'il y a des règles strictes au Japon. Mais finalement il est mieux pour moi qu'il y ait quelques règles. Mais c'est aussi un signe de mon désir de vouloir faire des bêtises, comme si je les touchais ou y mettais mon sexe.

C'est comme si je nageais dans la rivière en traversant entre la rive couleur, celle du monde actuel, et la rive monochrome, celle de l'au-delà. Suivant mes sentiments du moment, je décide si je vais au Paradis du noir et blanc, si je reste dans ce monde de couleur, ou si je prends le même sujet en le traitant simultanément en couleur et en noir et blanc.

Je photographie le ciel lorsque je suis fatigué et me laisse flotter sur le dos. Paris a la Seine alors que Tokyo a deux rivières, la Sumidagawa et l'Arakawa. Mais le Japon a aussi une rivière nommée Sanzu no Kawa [la rivière des morts]. C'est une rivière que les défunts doivent traverser pour atteindre le Nirvana.

D'ailleurs vos photographies ne spécifient aucune temporalité. Quel rapport entretenez-vous avec le temps ? Une photographie ne peut décrire que l'instant de la prise de vue. Et cet instant reste non identifiable. Un instant est une éternité et l'éternité un instant. La photographie porte en soi cette notion plus que tout autre élément. Quand je déclenche l'obturateur, ce moment est éternel. L'éternité est alors produite par le déclenchement de l'obturateur. C'est une action extrêmement directe. Il s'agit plus d'une action que d'art.

En conséquence, j'affirme pouvoir mélanger les photos sans regarder leur date de prise de vue. D'un autre côté je prends également des photographies qui ont la date de prise de vue imprimée sur le tirage et là je peux les montrer dans leur ordre chronologique. À l'instar d'un journal intime, la continuité journalière est une histoire. Le flot du temps qui passe est extrêmement dramatique et intéressant. J'utilise donc plusieurs sens temporels. Mais si je me permets de choisir entre les deux, je préfère conserver l'ordre chronologique. Je trouve en effet qu'il est plus intéressant.

C'est pourquoi je prends des photos comme un journal intime et je dis souvent de les laisser telles quelles sans essayer de les éditer.

L'édition se fait ensuite automatiquement par la vie ou le temps dans lequel nous vivons. Ce qui signifie que dès que je classe les photos dans leur ordre chronologique, Dieu ou quelqu'un d'autre, dans mon cas Shashin, le dieu de la photographie, s'en chargera pour moi. Ce serait plus dramatique si elles étaient placées dans un ordre inconscient. La plupart de mes albums photo fonctionnent de cette manière. Ce n'est pas la peine de penser à l'ordre. Par exemple, si je veux une photo de ma chatte Chiro, je n'ai pas besoin d'y penser. Cette image apparaît tout naturellement.

Pourquoi mettez-vous parfois des dates sur les photos? C'est une parodie du fait de ne pas avoir atteint ni visé la perfection. Si une date est imprimée sur une photographie, elle ne pourra jamais être un chef-d'œuvre. La photo datée n'est rien de plus qu'un simple témoin d'un jour. Mais c'est ça la photo!

La photo dit simplement que ce jour, cet instant particulier était merveilleux. C'est la vie. Rien n'est supérieur au journal intime. Même dans la littérature, il est supérieur au roman. Le journal intime c'est la vie, et la date c'est la photo. Ou bien c'est au photographe d'effacer la date. La photographie c'est la vie!

Est-ce pour cette raison que vous n'arrêtez pas de photographier? Il faut continuellement photographier les instants de la vie. Comme il faut continuer à vivre, pour moi, prendre des photographies revient à vivre.

Quels sont les artistes, écrivains ou cinéastes qui pratiquent le journal intime, dont vous vous sentez proche? Je me sens peut-être encore plus proche de l'écrivain japonais Kafu Nagai [1879–1959] qui a notamment écrit en 1917 le roman appelé *Danchotei Nichijo* [Le journal de Danchotei]. Il savait que si les événements de la journée étaient très intéressants, il serait encore plus merveilleux d'insérer de la fiction dans la vie quotidienne. Avant lui, il était convenu qu'un journal intime devait décrire la réalité du jour. C'est le premier à avoir cassé cette règle en y incorporant un peu de mensonge, ce qui donne plus de charme au journal intime. Dans son *Danchotei Nichijo*, tout est faux. Mais il est plus intéressant comme cela.

Je me sens proche aussi du cinéaste lituanien Jonas Mekas bien qu'il n'insère pas de date à son travail. Il a un accès au sublime que je ne possède pas. Mais nous partageons beaucoup de points communs. Mon Minowa c'est l'utérus, chez Jonas Mekas c'est vraisemblablement sa Lituanie, son pays natal. Le plus important pour lui sont les caractéristiques naturelles et sa famille en Lituanie. Mon Minowa a déjà perdu ses bons vents et est en ruine alors que sa Lituanie qui est aussi une ruine était bien un paradis. Ce sont nos points communs. Nous avons tous les deux un intérêt quant aux villes ou aux quartiers natals. Des transferts de lieux, de temps. C'est cela un journal: des transferts de jours. Sans réfléchir à cette idée, je continue à prendre des photos tous les jours. Se déplacer, c'est rester vivant. Mettre une ponctuation à ces déplacements revient à mettre une date.

Comme les artistes anglais Gilbert & George, vous visez l'accessibilité, la diffusion la plus large et êtes partisan d'un art pour tous? Cette disposition vient-elle du fait de votre passé en agence publicitaire ? Quand je travaillais chez Dentsu, je faisais de la publicité pour les autres. Mais je voulais en faire pour moi-même. Cela pourrait être appelé de l'art. Je pensais que cela serait déjà bien de montrer mes photographies à mes amis. Mais d'un autre côté, j'ai toujours eu le désir d'être connu par le plus de monde possible. J'aimerais entendre, par exemple, que les iguanes des îles Galápagos aimeraient voir mon travail. En plus, j'aimerais qu'ils viennent au Japon en traversant les océans pour se faire photographier par moi. Alors, je les emmènerais à Yoshiwara.

Combien de livres avez-vous publiés à ce jour ? Je crois plus de 250. Au début, fatigué des innombrables rendez-vous infructueux avec des éditeurs japonais, j'ai d'abord édité moi-même mes livres photocopiés. Mon premier livre *Xeroxed Photo Albums* a été fait comme ça. Quand j'ai fait *Sentimental Journey*, aucune maison d'édition à l'époque, ne voulait publier une lune de miel personnelle. Ensuite, beaucoup de maisons d'édition ont publié mes livres, comme TASCHEN aujourd'hui. Parfois, je prends des photographies et ai envie de sortir un livre immédiatement, comme une éjaculation précoce. Il m'arrive de ne pas pouvoir attendre trois mois pour sortir un livre après la prise de vue. Je voudrais que le livre soit fait en un mois, juste derrière la prise. Le livre *Photographs from the End of the Century* a été fait par moi-même pour exaucer ce désir de rapidité. Il s'agit d'un livre photo « live » qui conserve la vitesse ou la chaleur de la prise de vue. Pour d'autres livres, je pense que les éditeurs apportent également un certain enthousiasme.

La technologie des photocopieurs a beaucoup évolué depuis les années 70, faites-vous toujours des livres en photocopies ? Aujourd'hui, je n'ai plus intérêt à faire des livres avec un photocopieur car la qualité s'est beaucoup améliorée. Les photocopies des années 70 n'étaient pas seulement mécaniques, leur rendu était brut, approximatif, rugueux. Ce qui correspondait à mes sentiments, comme à ceux de cette décennie qui était très brute. C'étaient des photocopies de mes sentiments fougueux d'alors.

Après avoir utilisé le terme « copie », je me suis tourné vers celui de « reproduction ». Car la photo est la reproduction des sentiments des moments de prises de vue, ou la reproduction des sentiments de personnes que j'ai rencontrées à un moment donné, ou encore la reproduction de relations que j'ai eues. Ce n'est pas pour autant une expression, ni la volonté de représenter, d'exprimer les sentiments des sujets que je photographie. C'est pourquoi je me copie moi-même en dette à l'existence de mes sujets. Grâce à ces sujets, je peux faire des « reproductions ». Sans eux, je ne pourrais pas. C'est aussi le cas dans la vie, pas seulement pour les photos. J'ai besoin de sujets. Cela peut être des fleurs, le ciel et bien sûr les femmes. Je vis par les femmes. Je continuerai à les photographier. Si un jour les femmes venaient à disparaître de la planète, je préférerais mourir bien avant.

Avez-vous des projets non réalisés ou des projets que vous voulez faire dans le futur ? Je n'ai pas de projet qui n'ait été matérialisé. Ce que je ferai dans le futur est ce que mon environnement décidera. De toute façon, dieu (déesse) « femme » me guide.

Colorscapes

色景

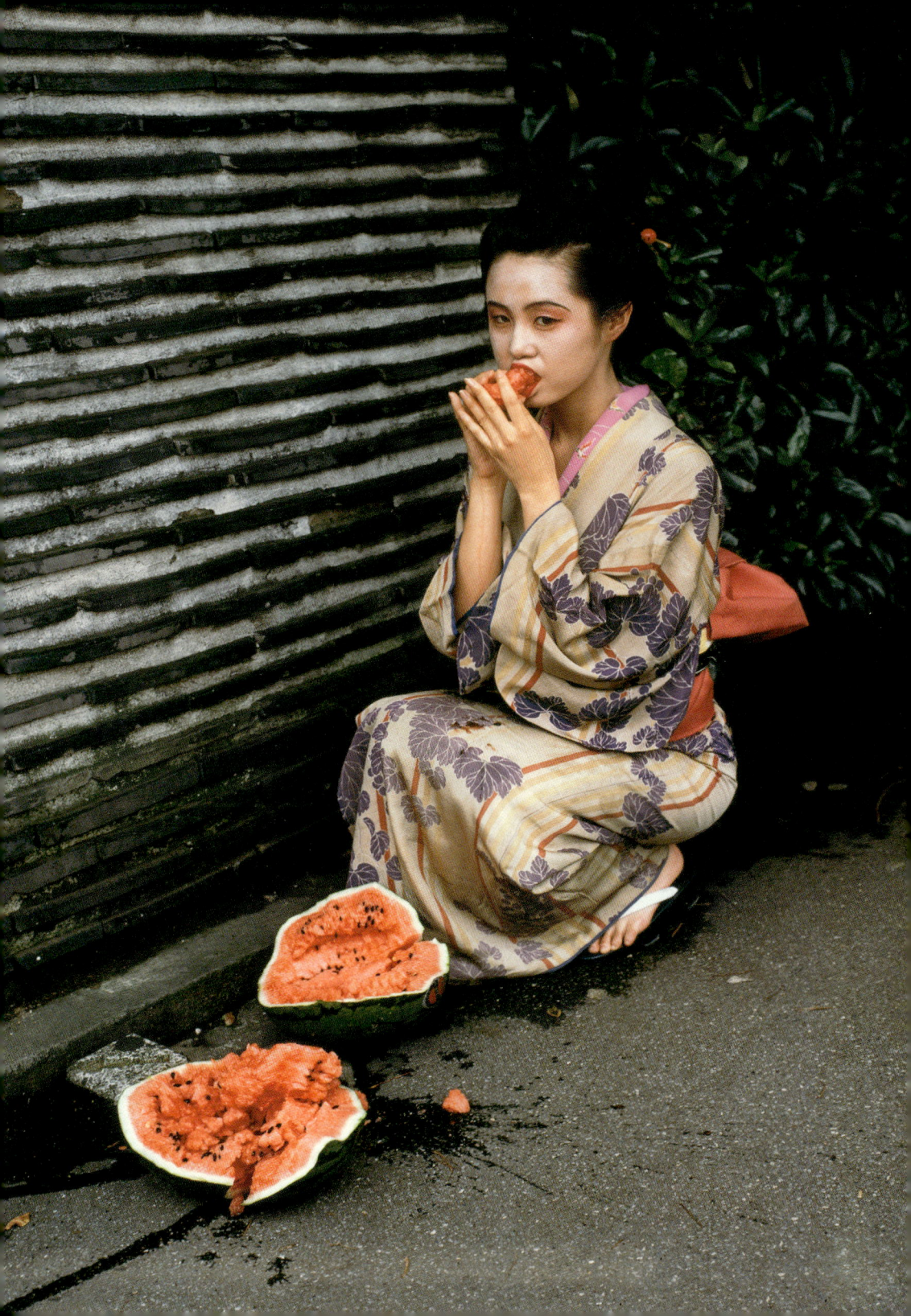

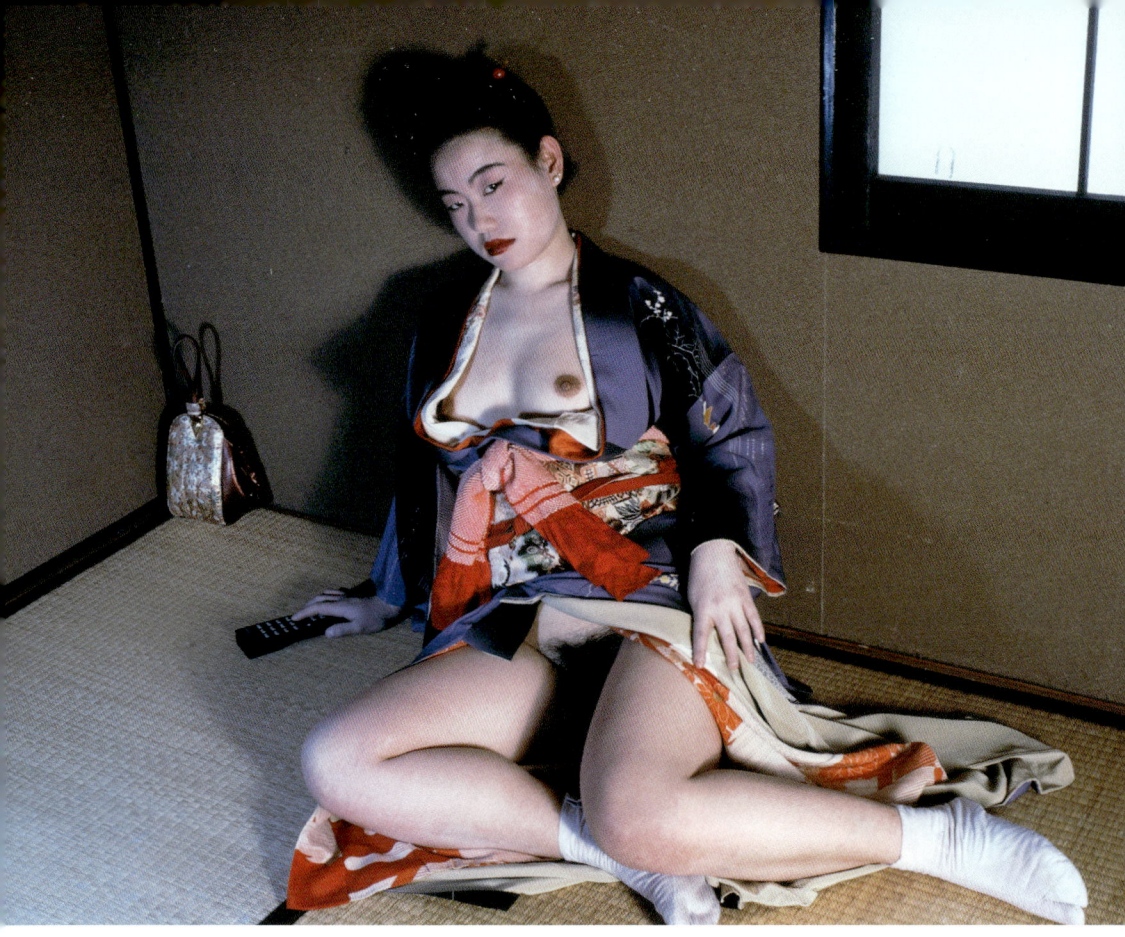

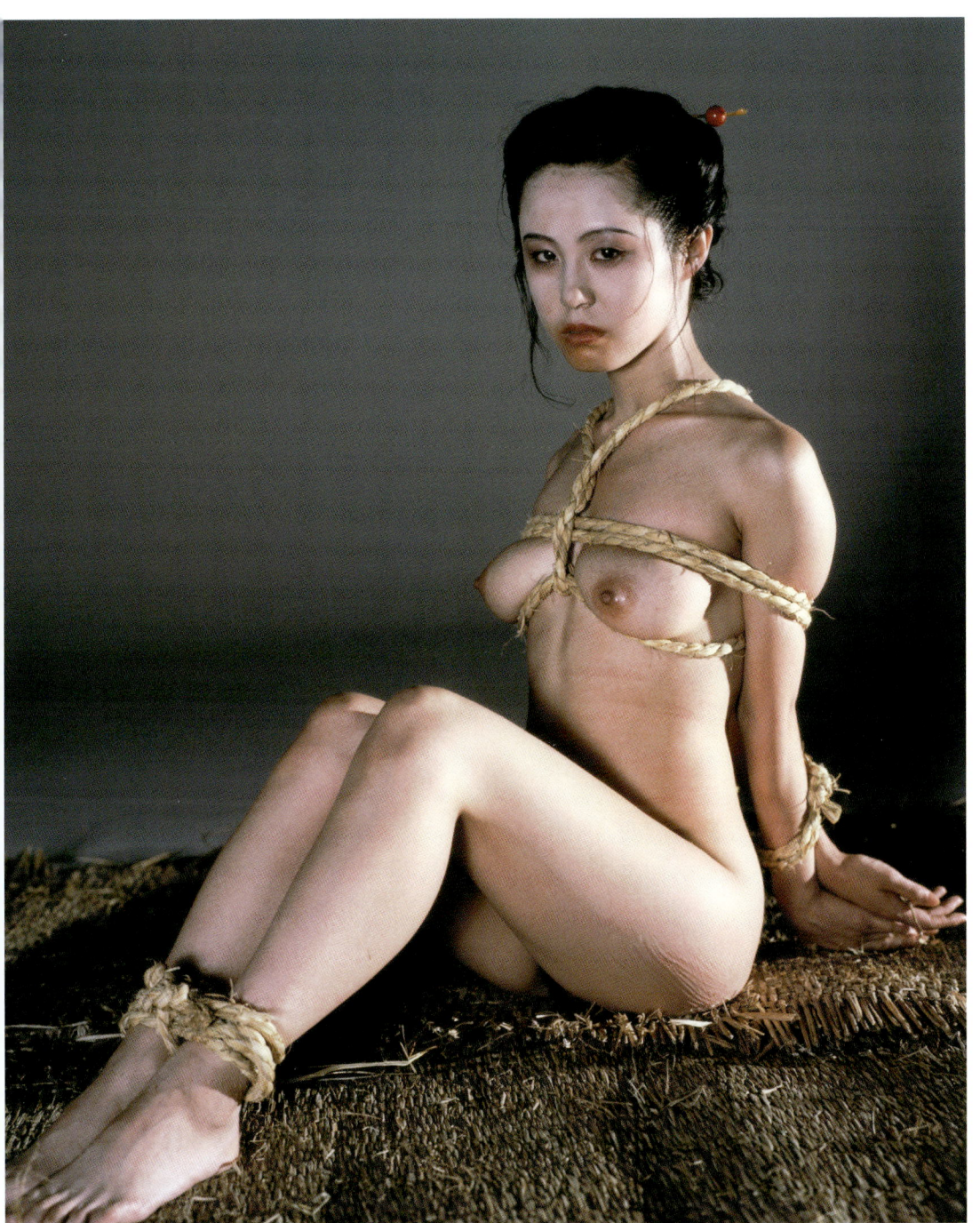

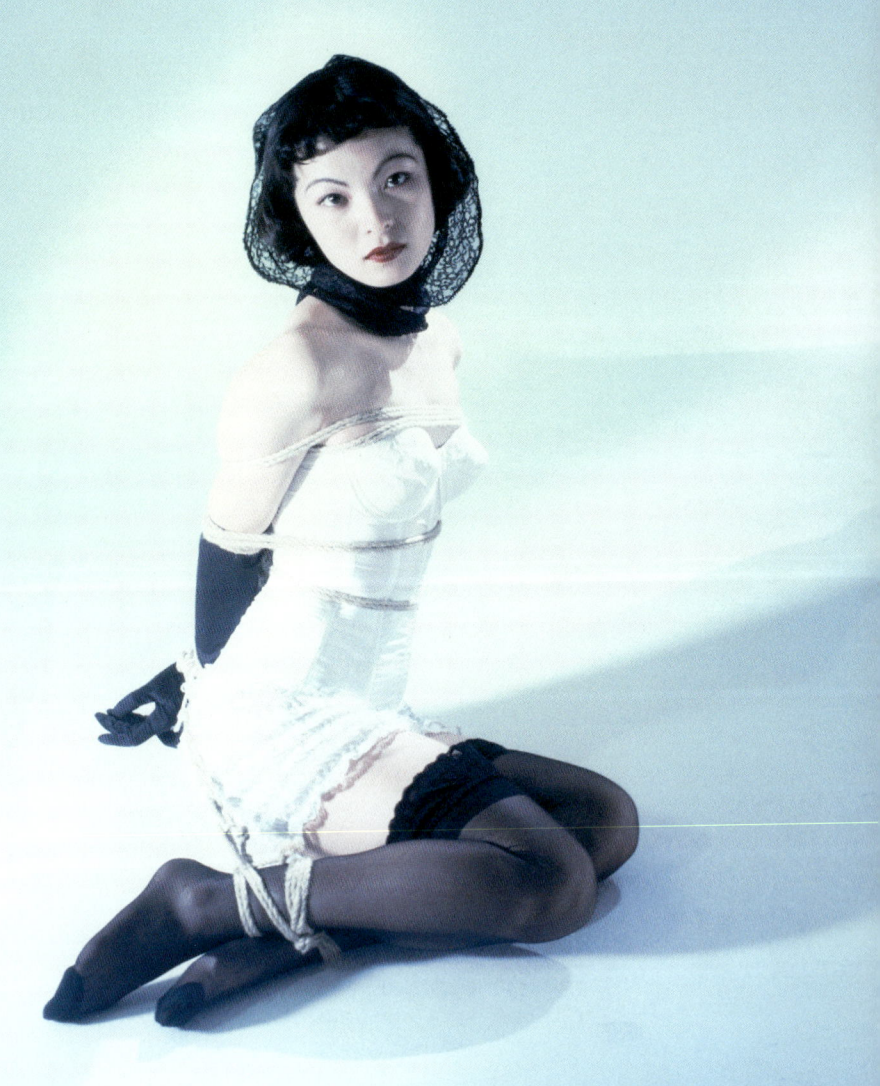

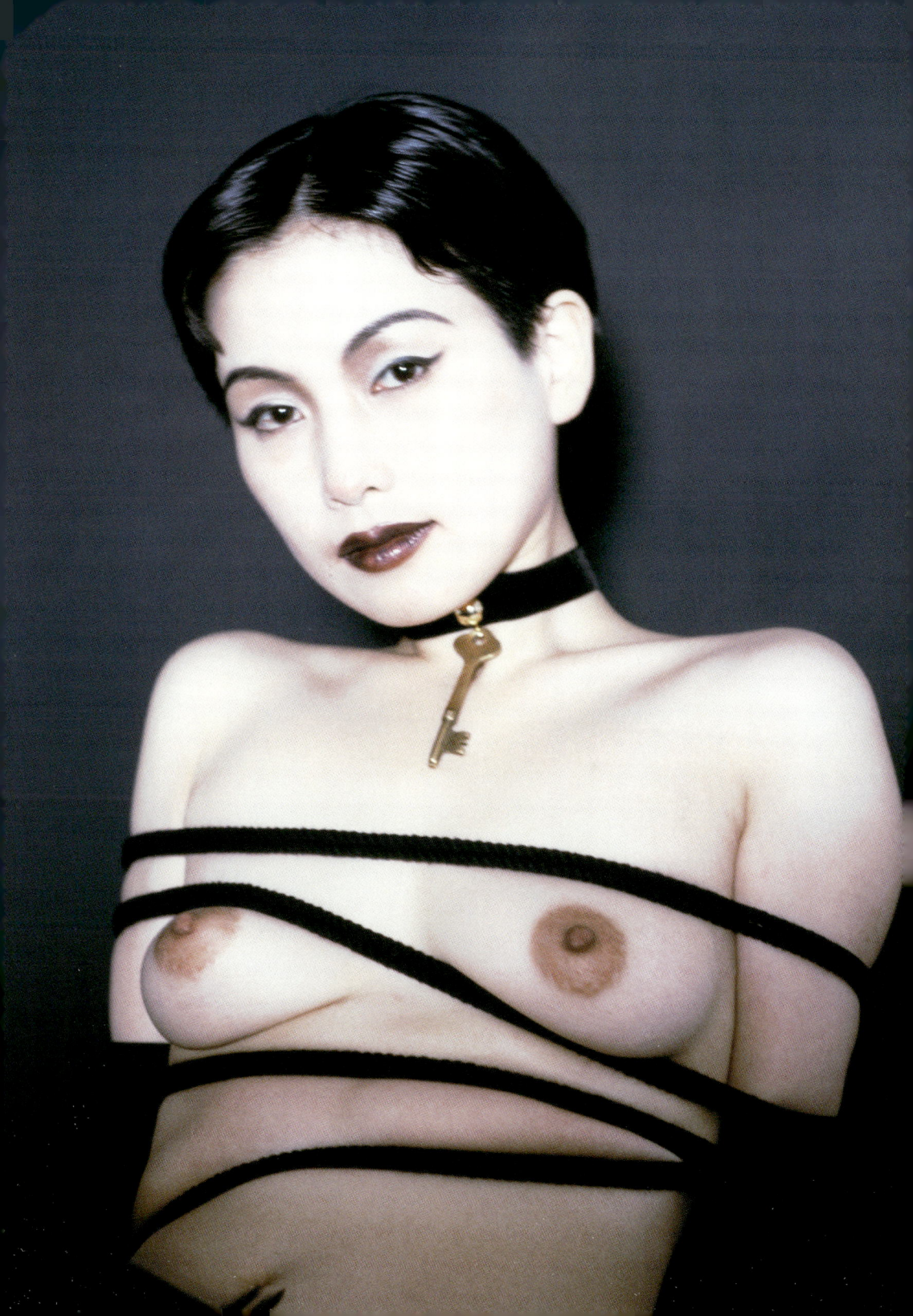

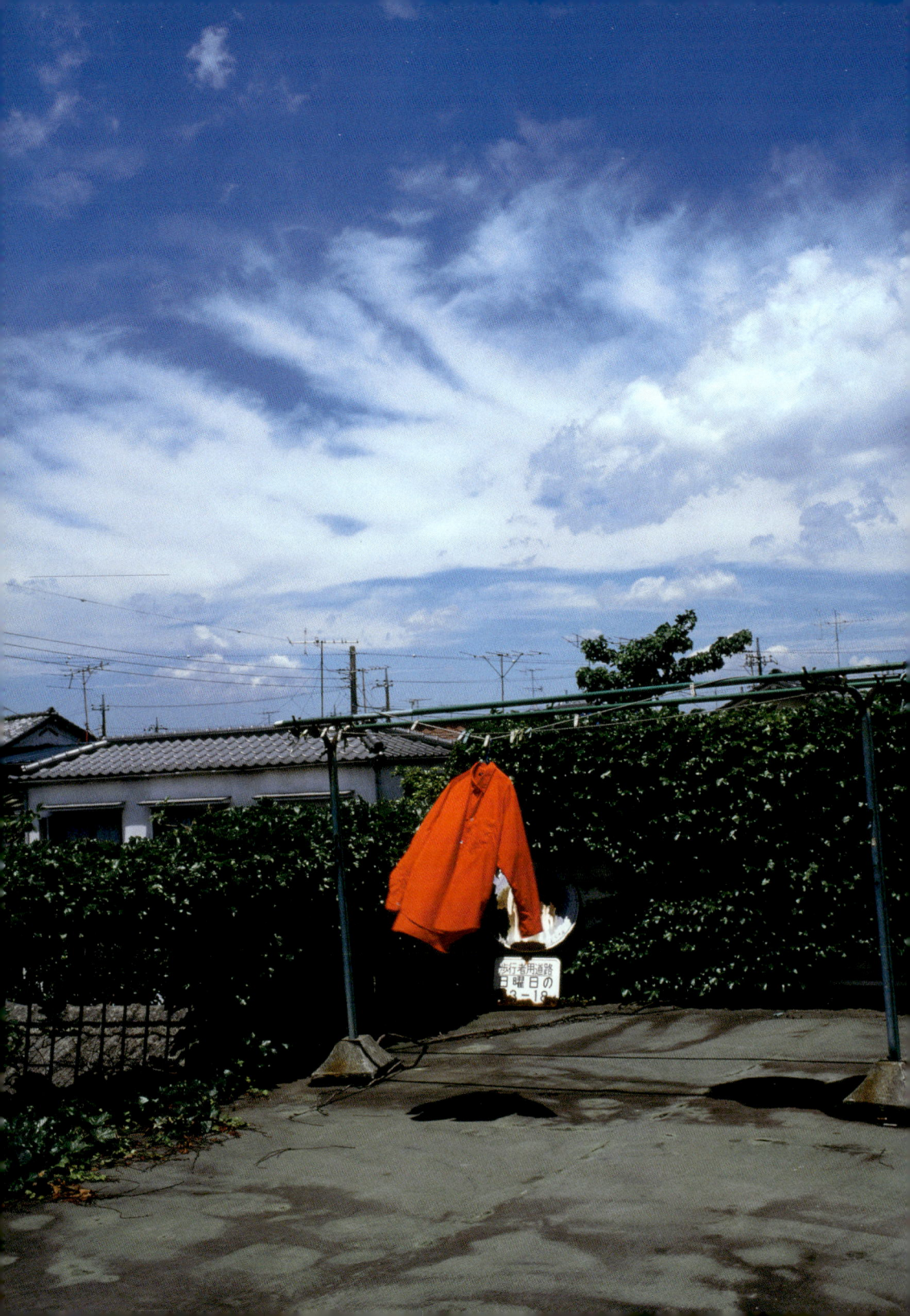

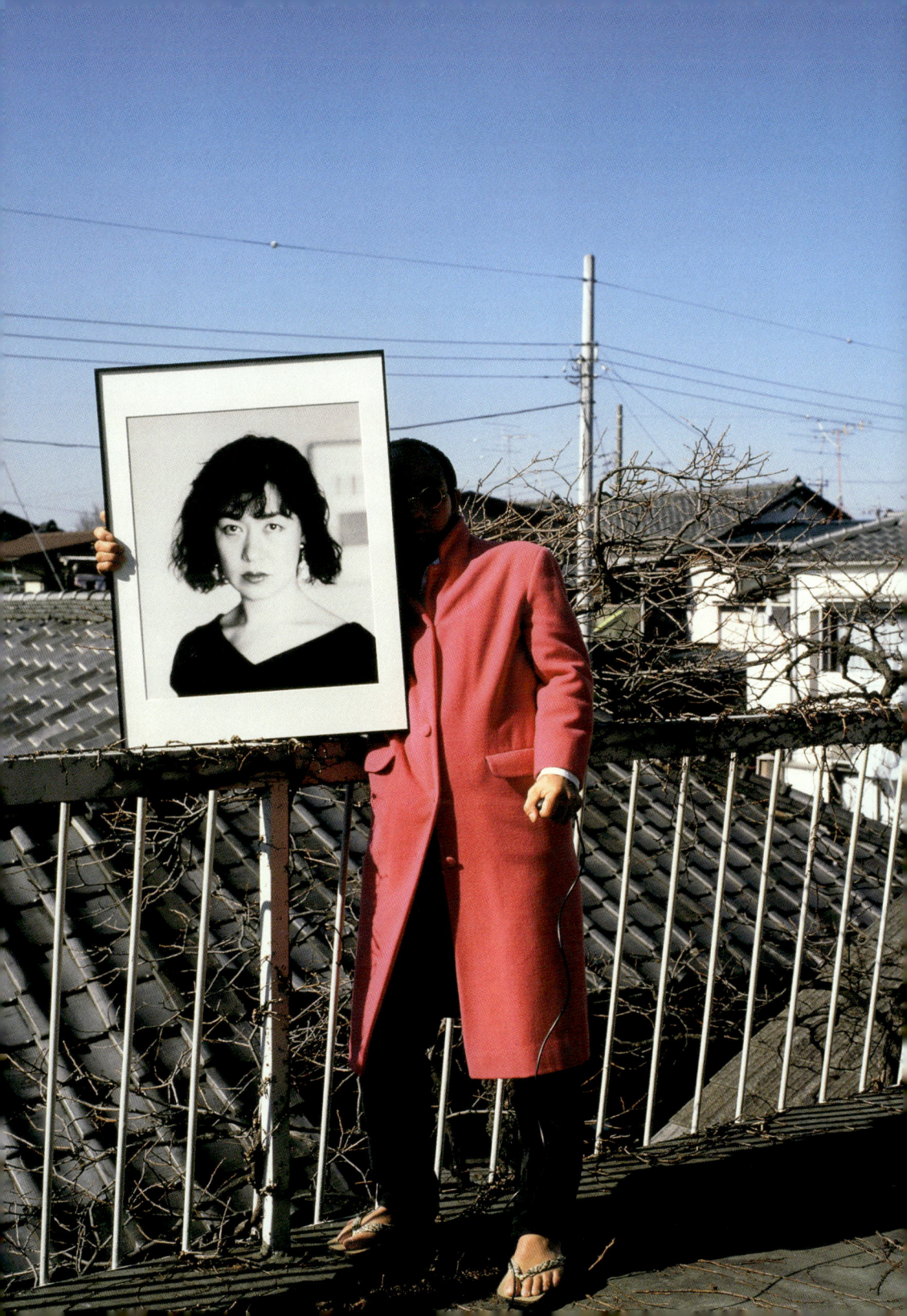

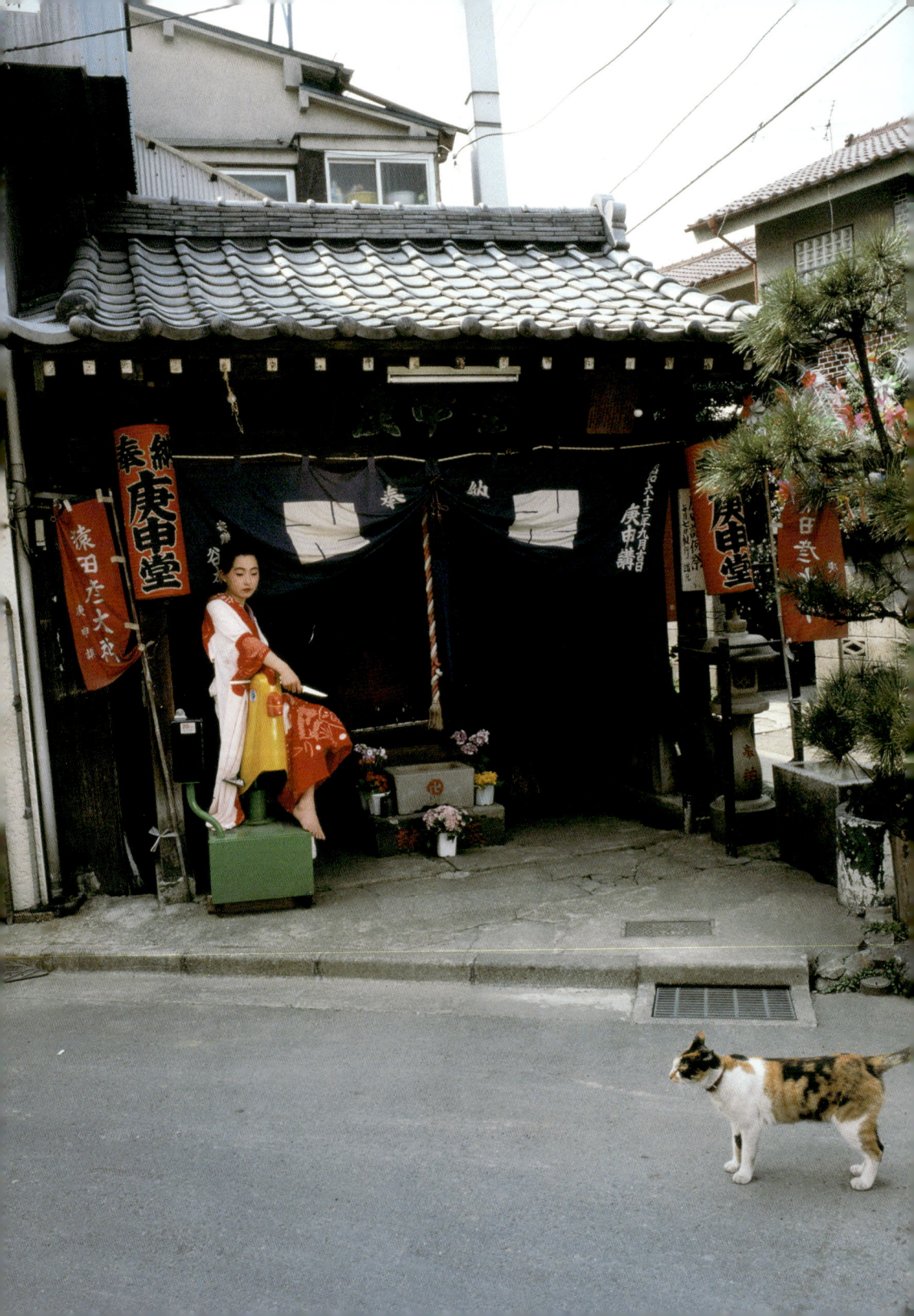

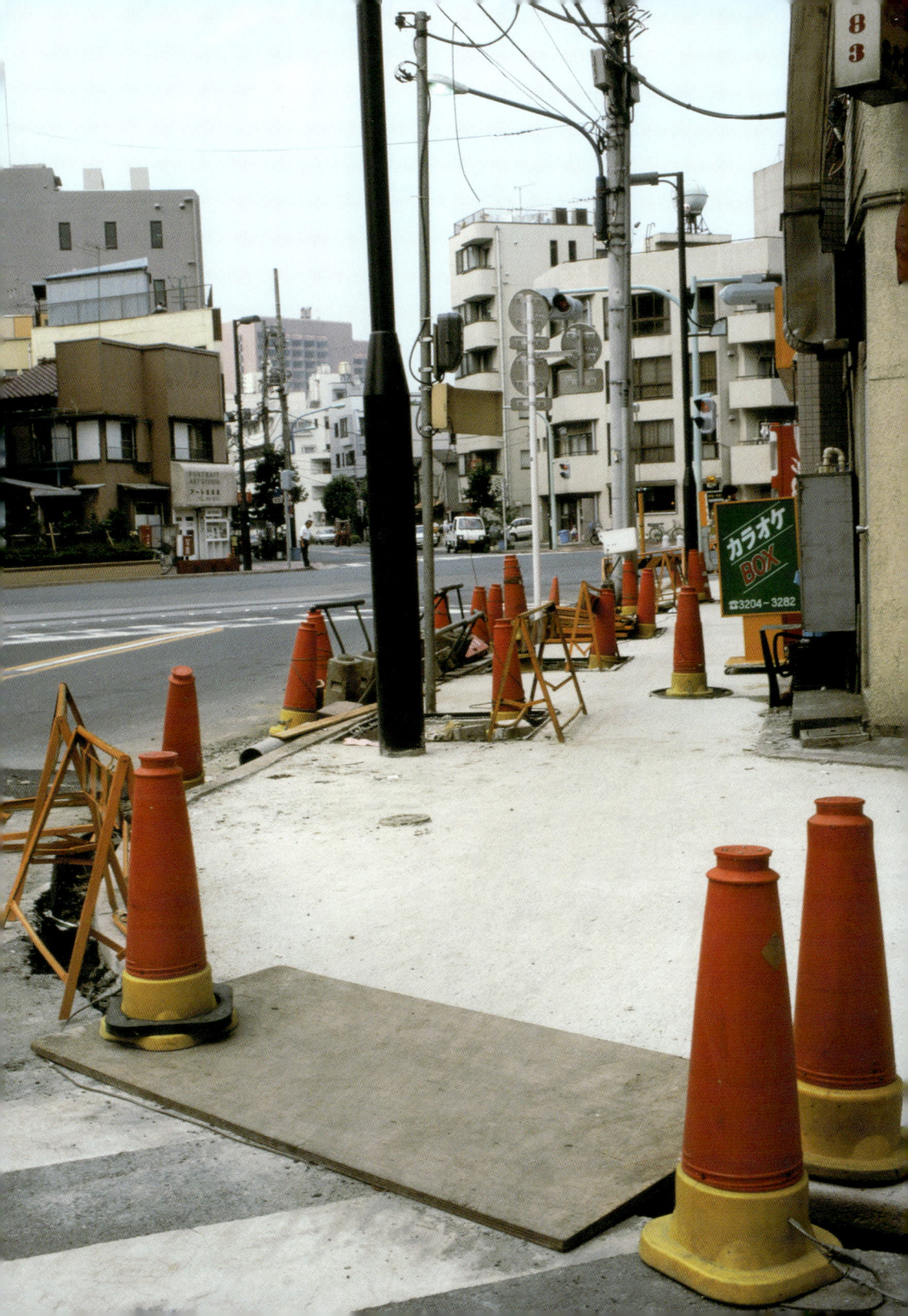

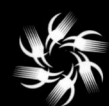

Tokyo Story

東京物語

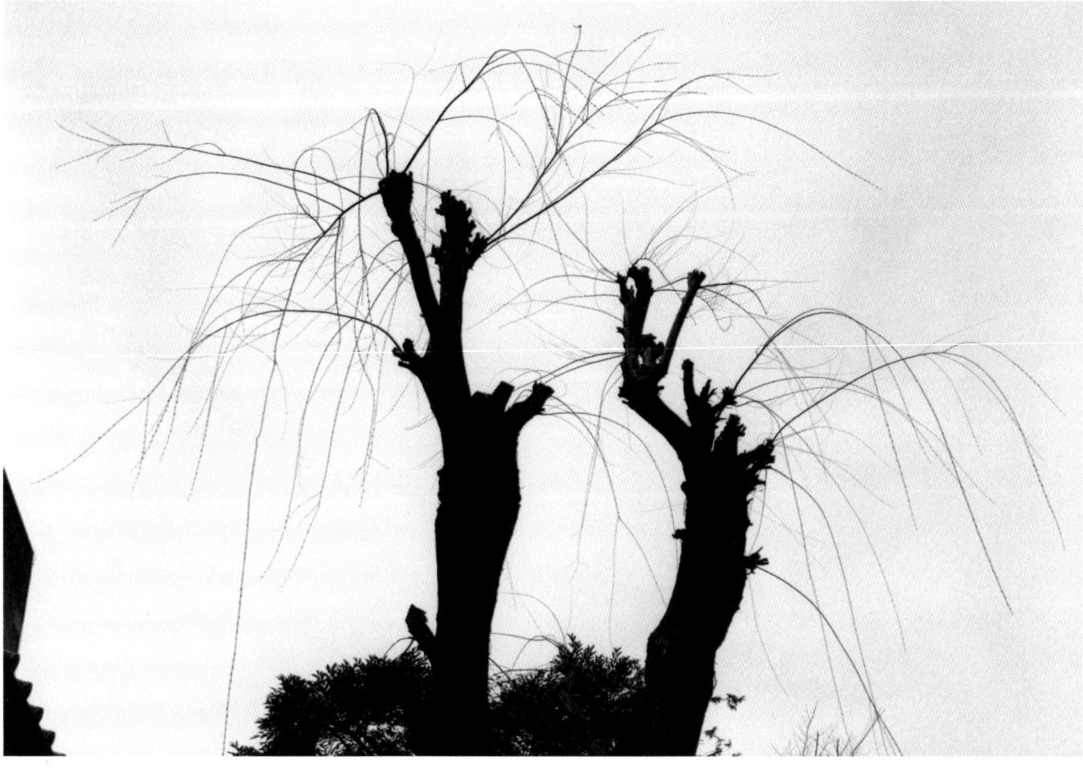

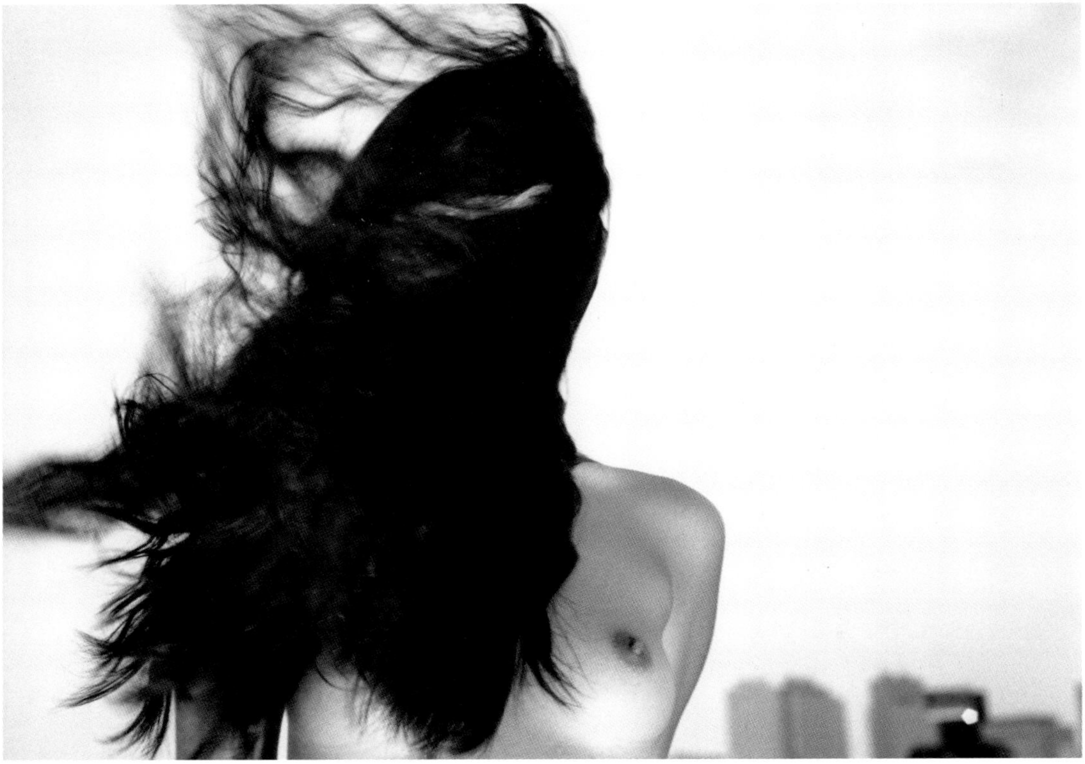

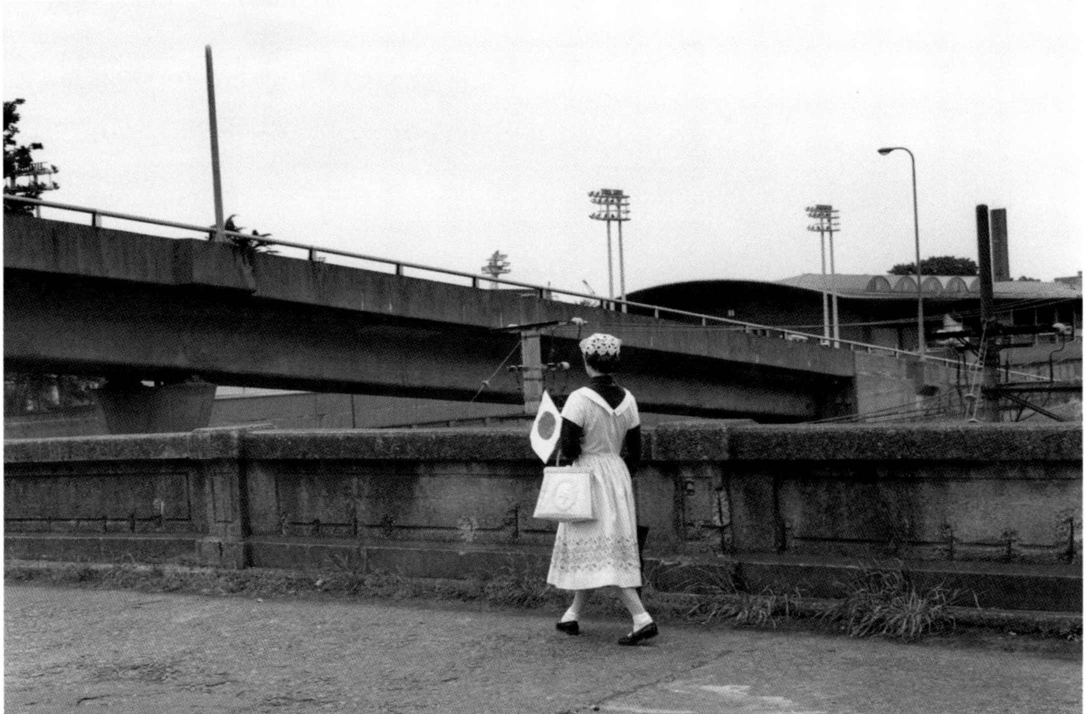

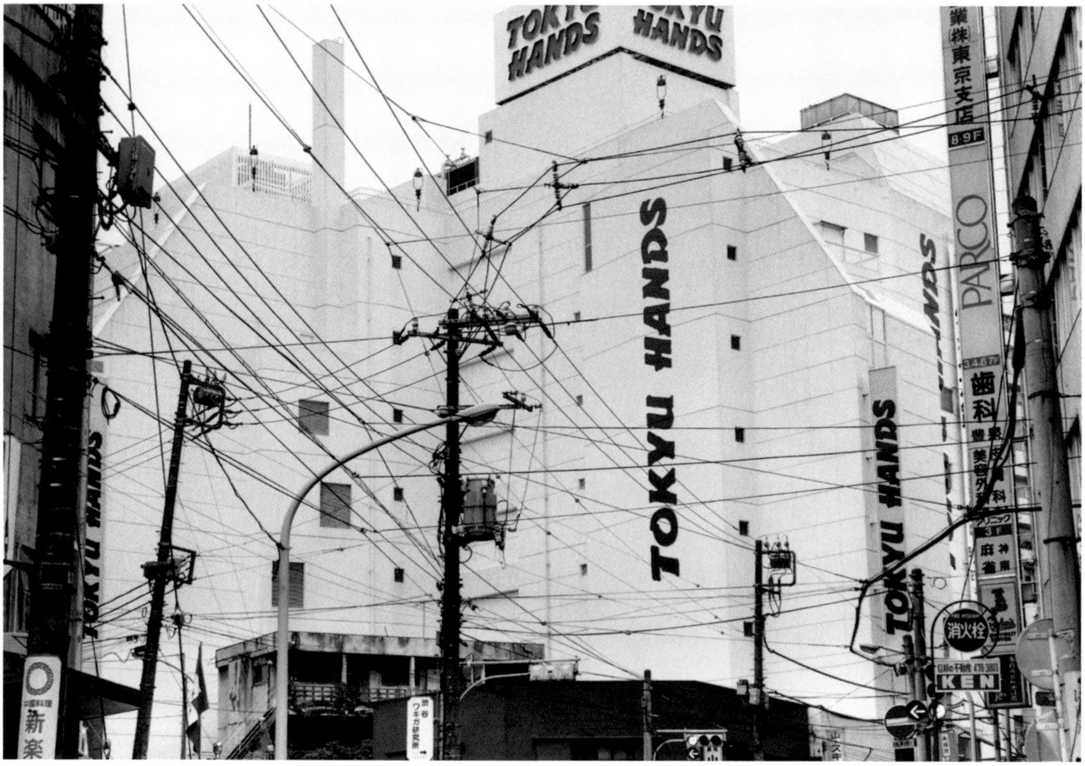
TOKYU HANDS
TOKYU HANDS
TOKYU HANDS
TOKYU HANDS
TOKYU HANDS
東京支店
8·9F
PARCO
歯科
消火栓
KEN
新楽

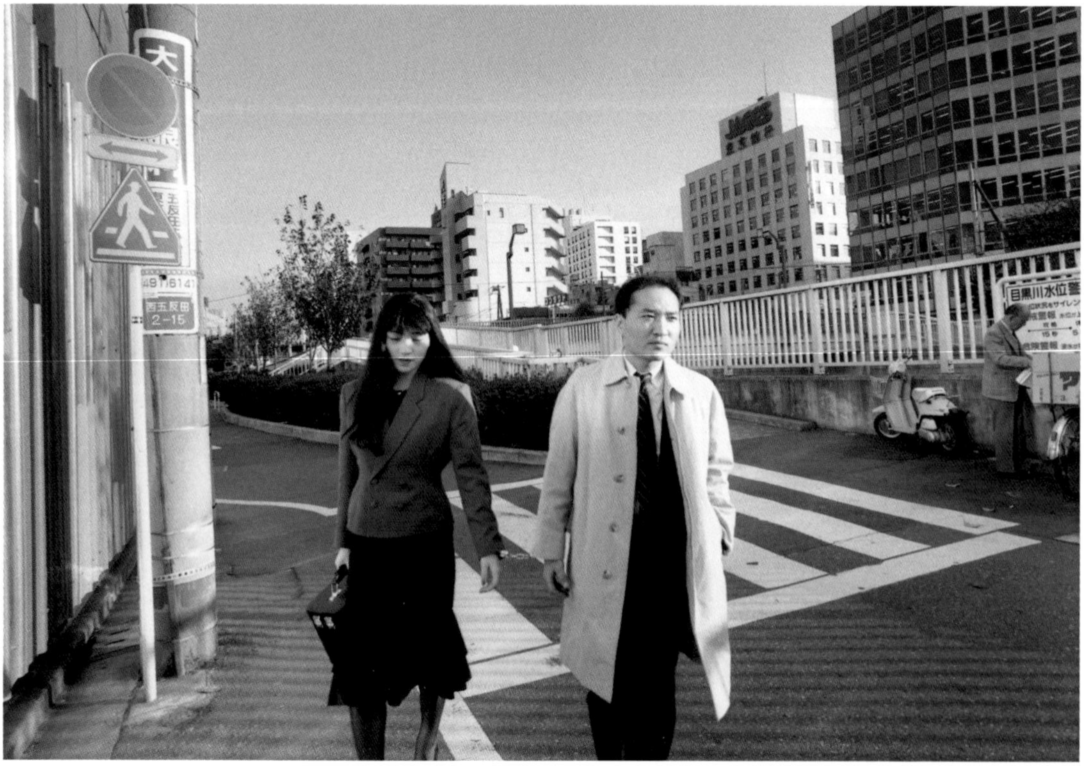
西五反田
2-15
目黒川水位

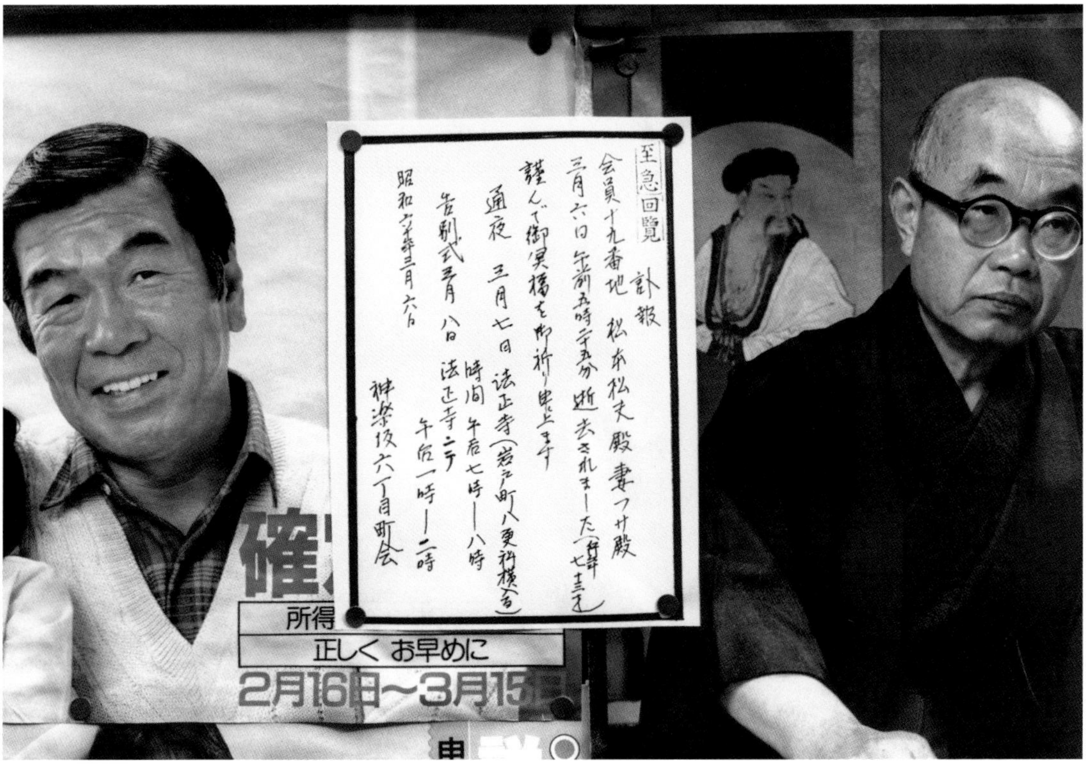

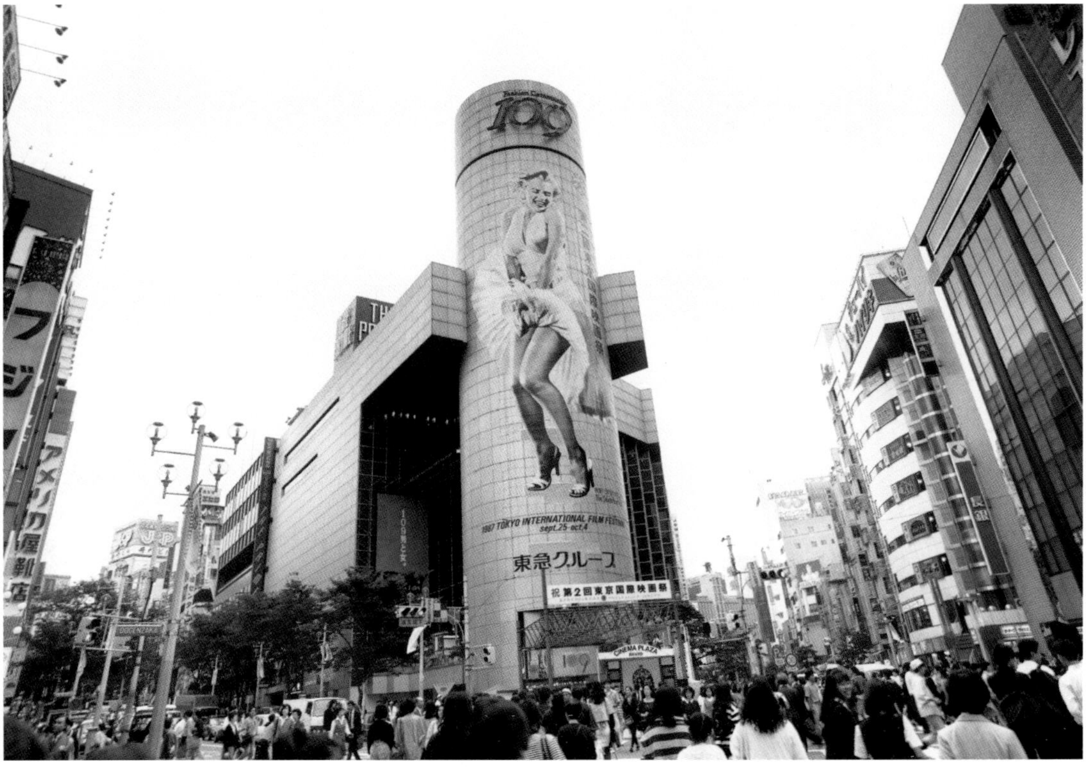

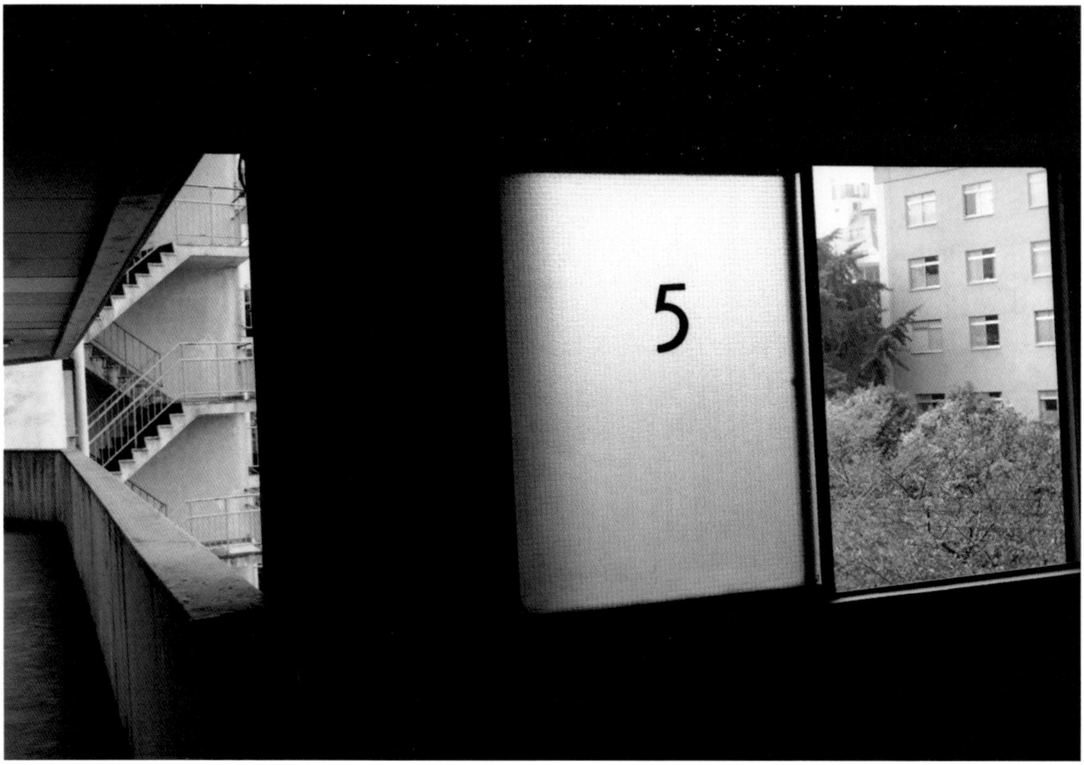
5

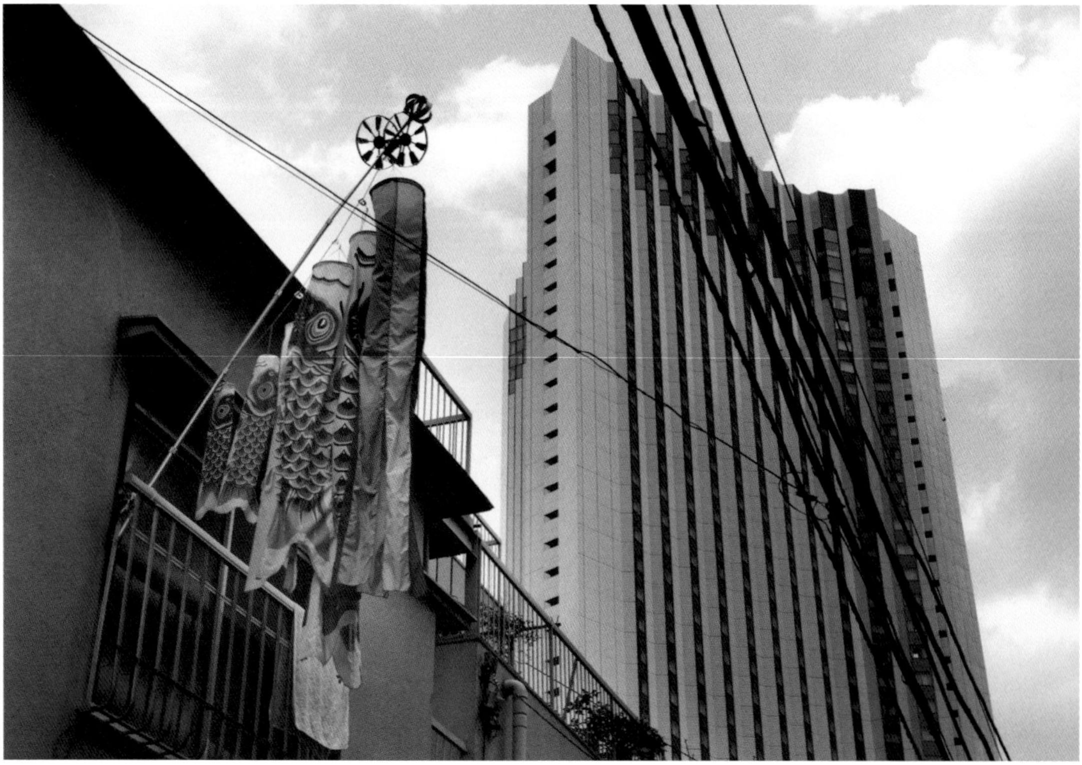

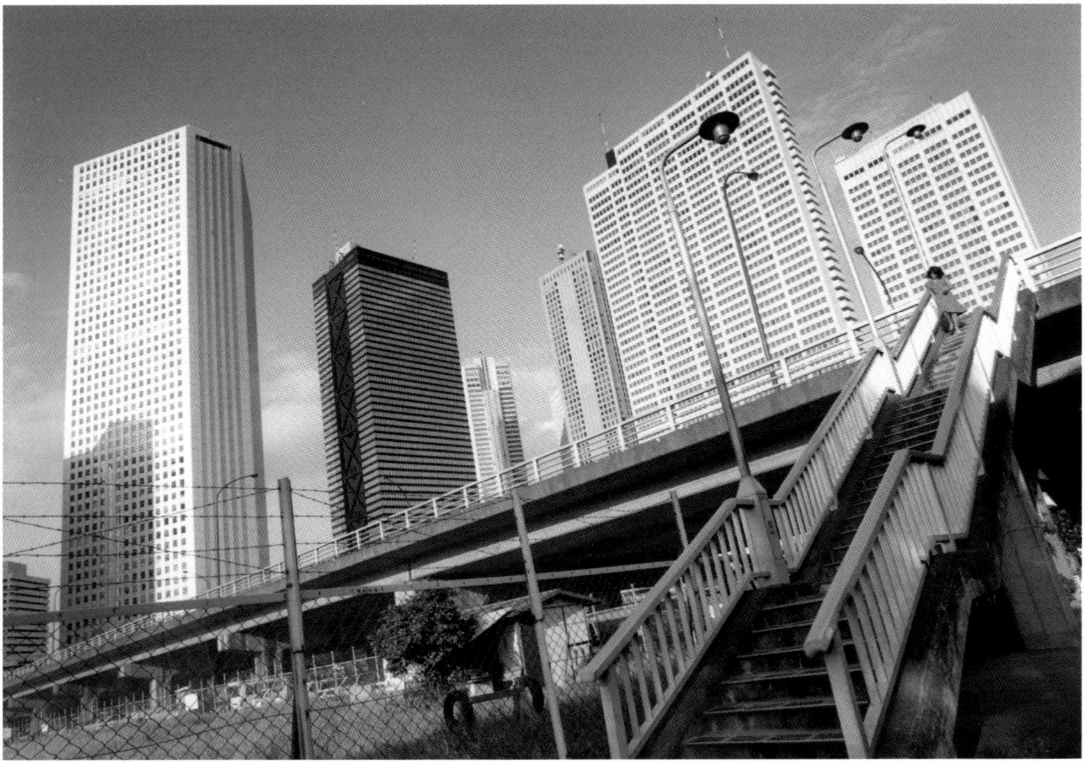

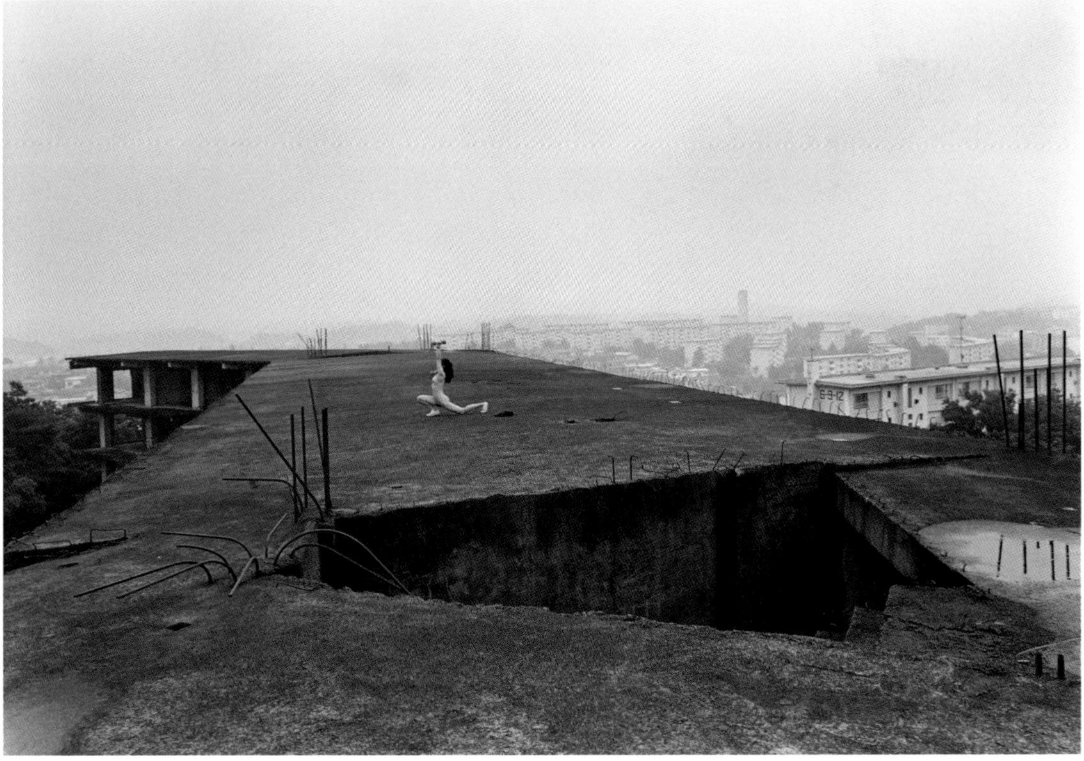

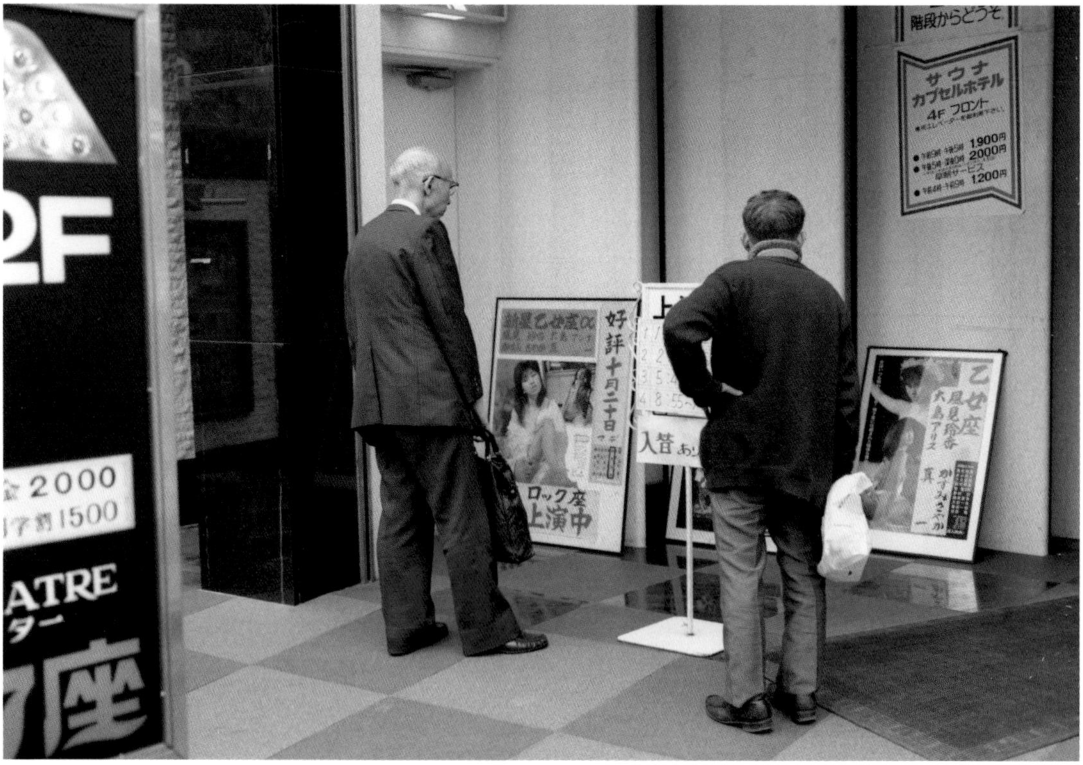

2F
階段からどうぞ
サウナ
カプセルホテル
4F フロント
1.900円
2000円
サービス
1.200円
好評十月二十日
ロック座
上演中
乙女座
風見玲香
大島アリス

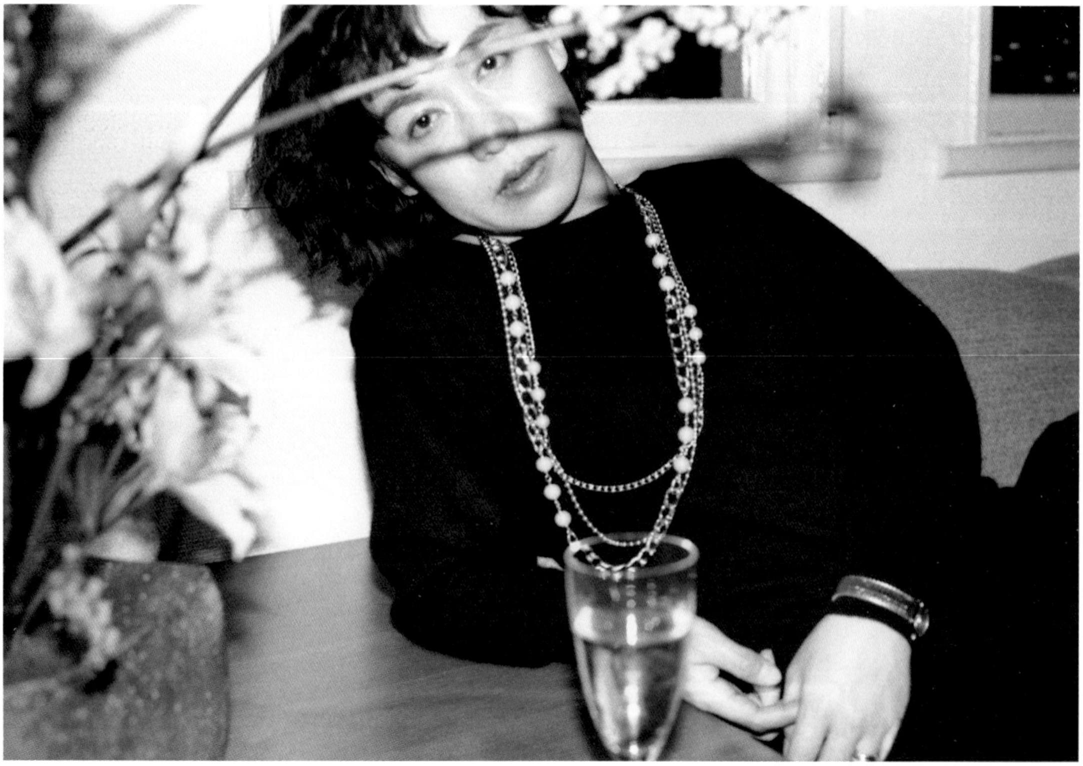

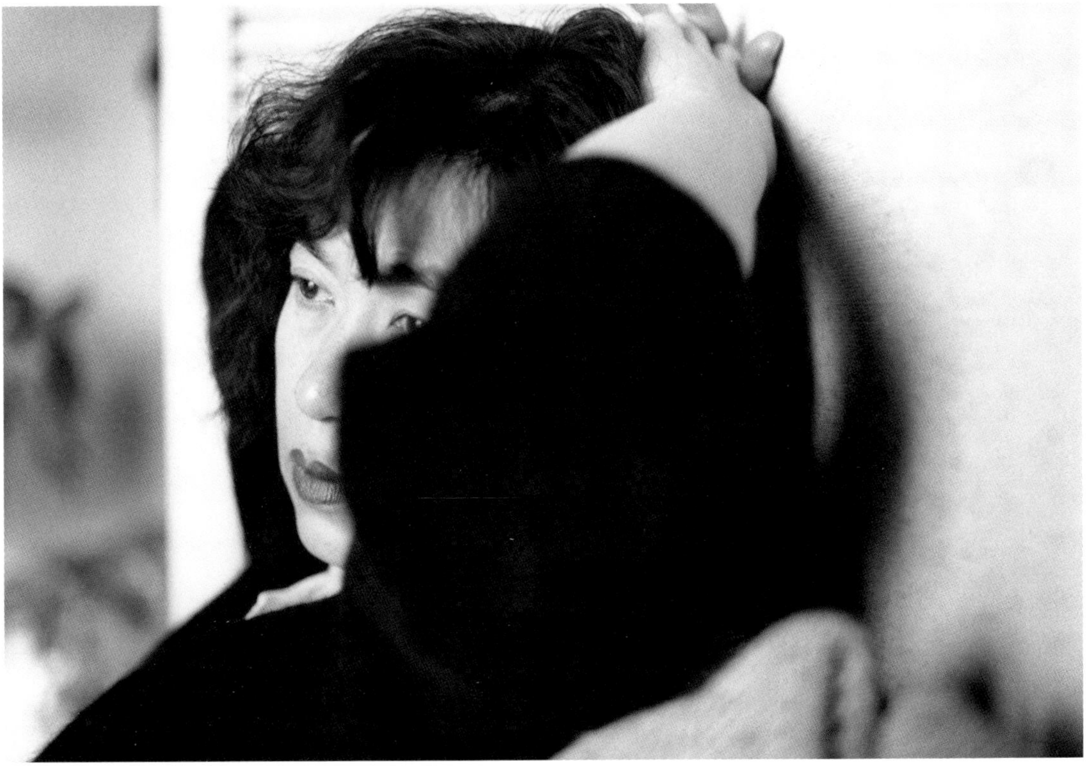

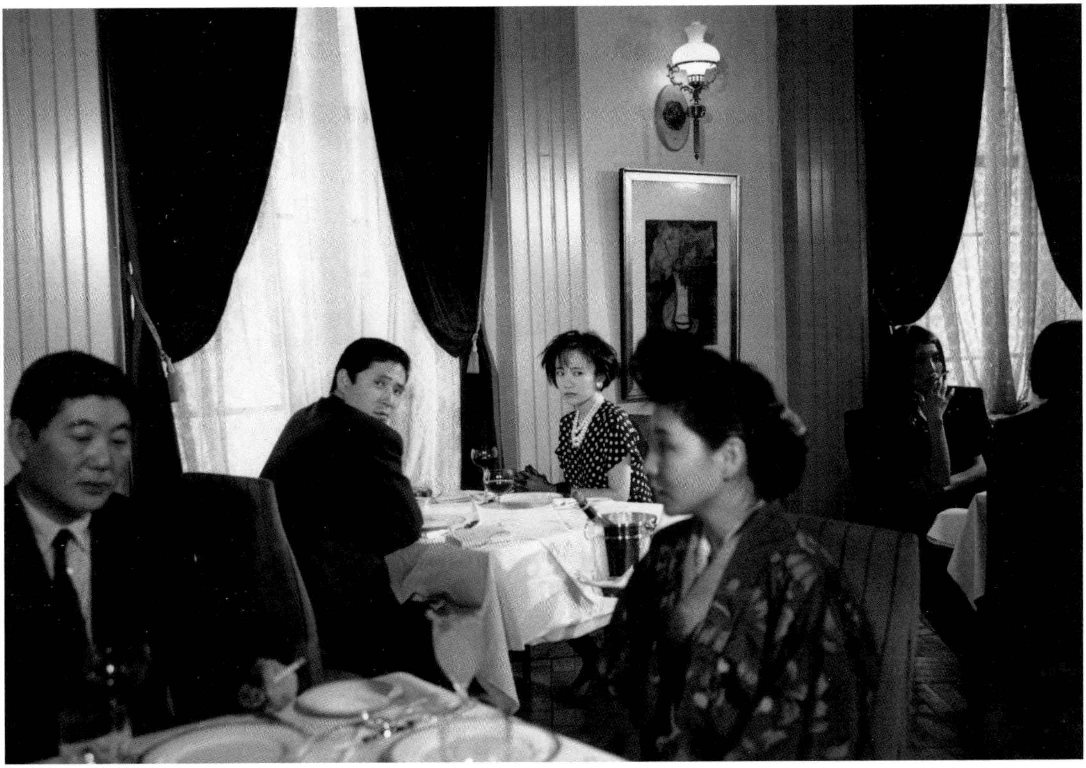

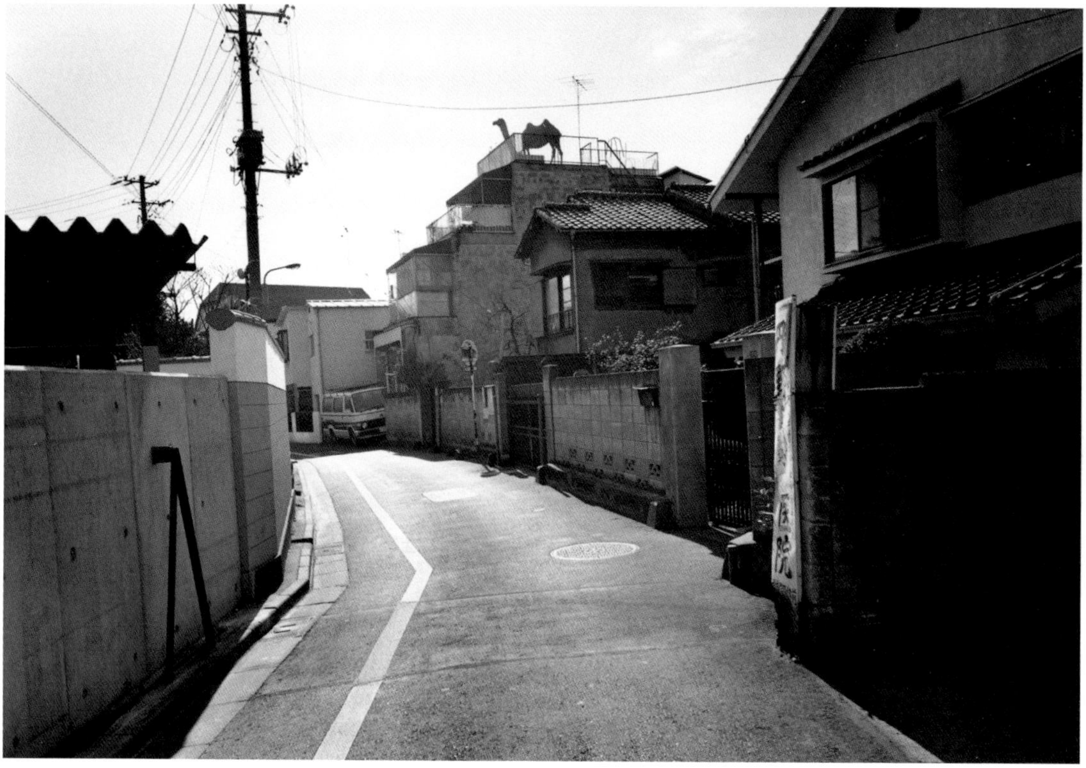

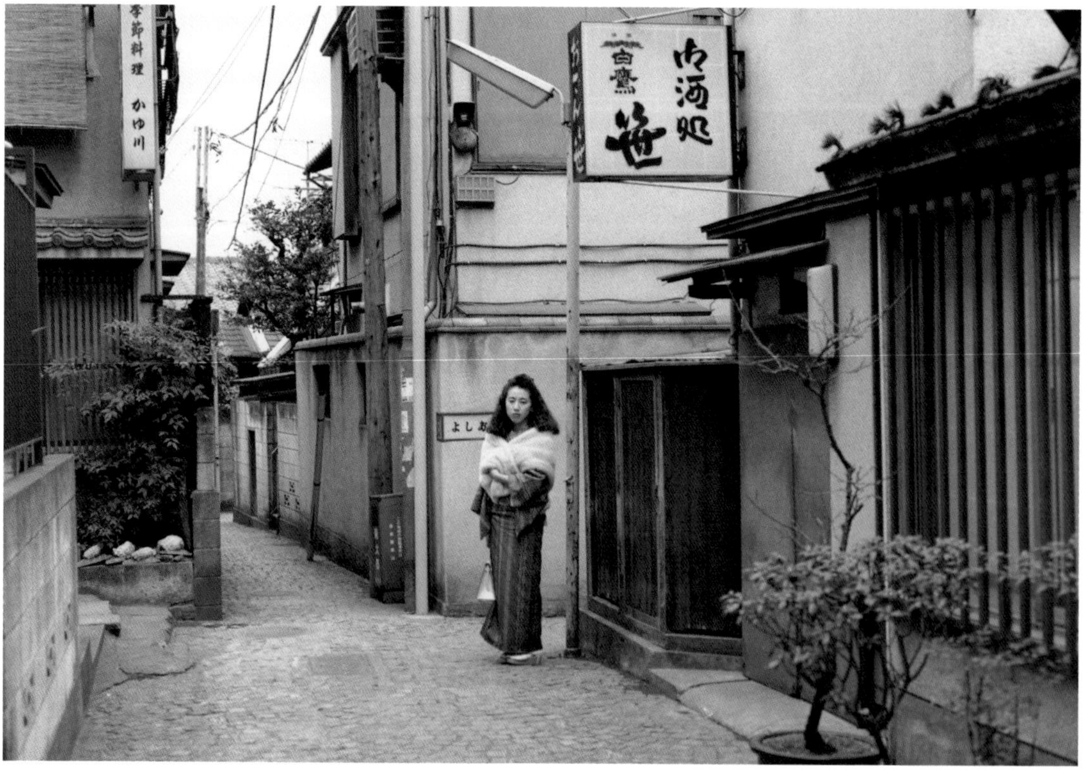
季節料理
かゆ川
白鷹
お酒処
笹

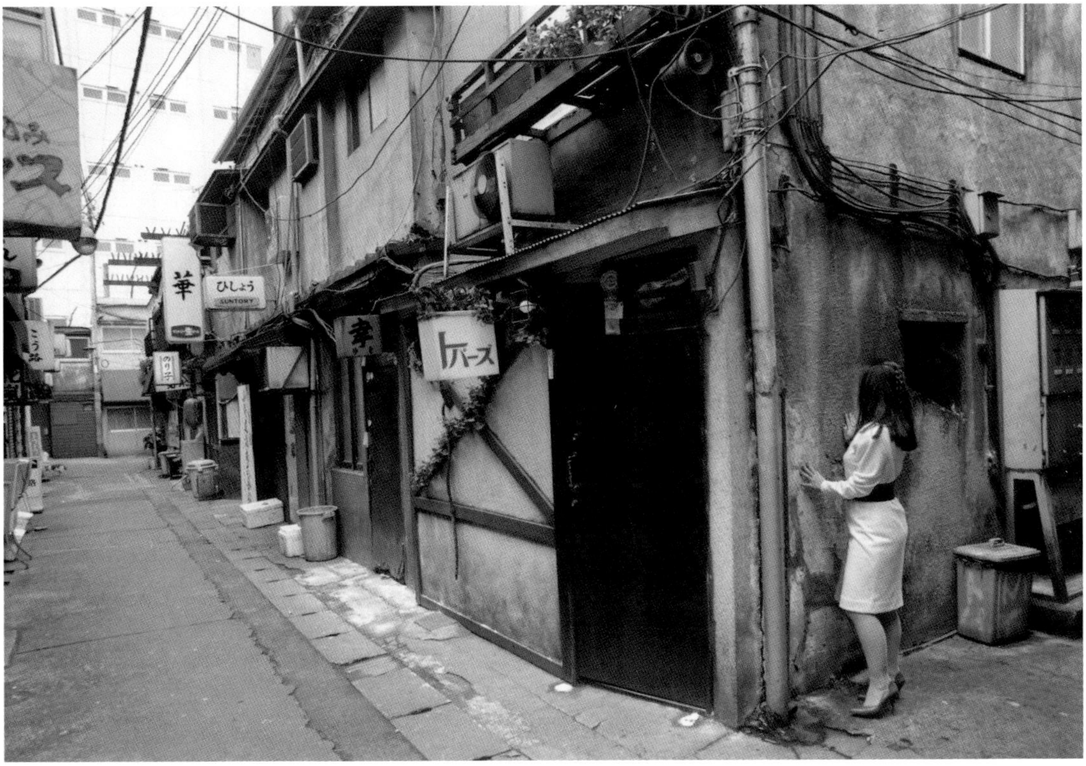
華
ひしょう
SUNTORY
トパーズ

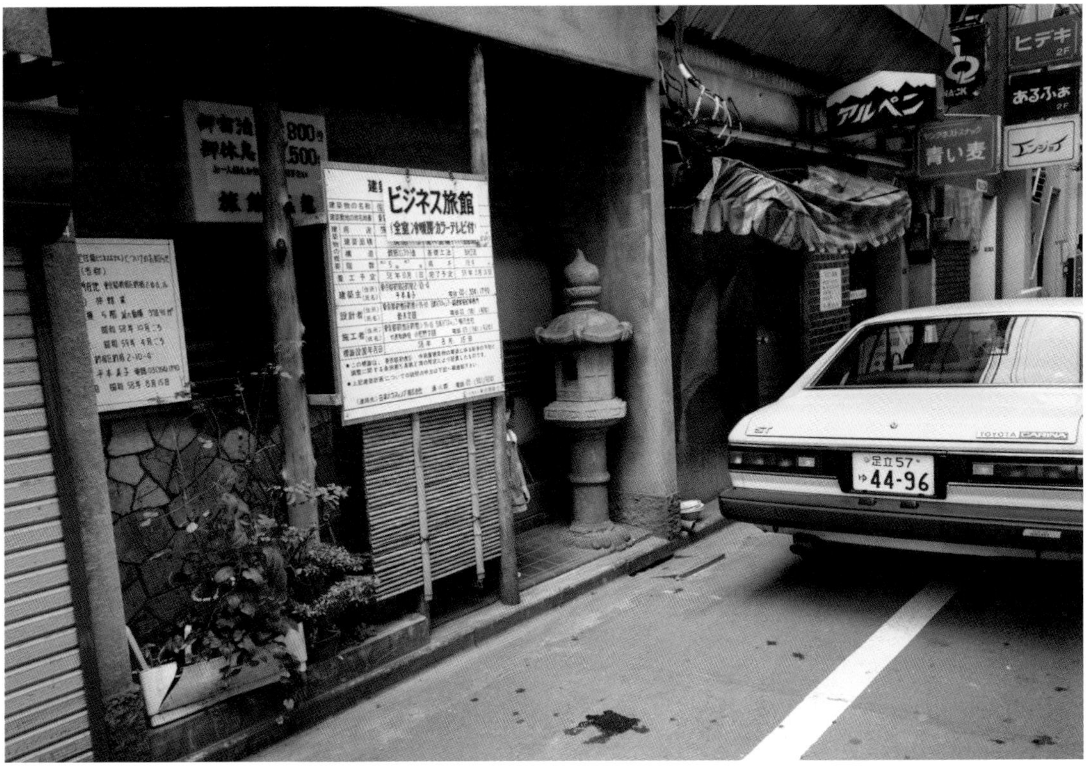
ビジネス旅館
(全室)冷暖房·カラーテレビ付
アルペン
ヒデキ
2F
あるふぁ
2F
青い麦
エンジョイ
TOYOTA CARINA
足立57
ゆ 44-96

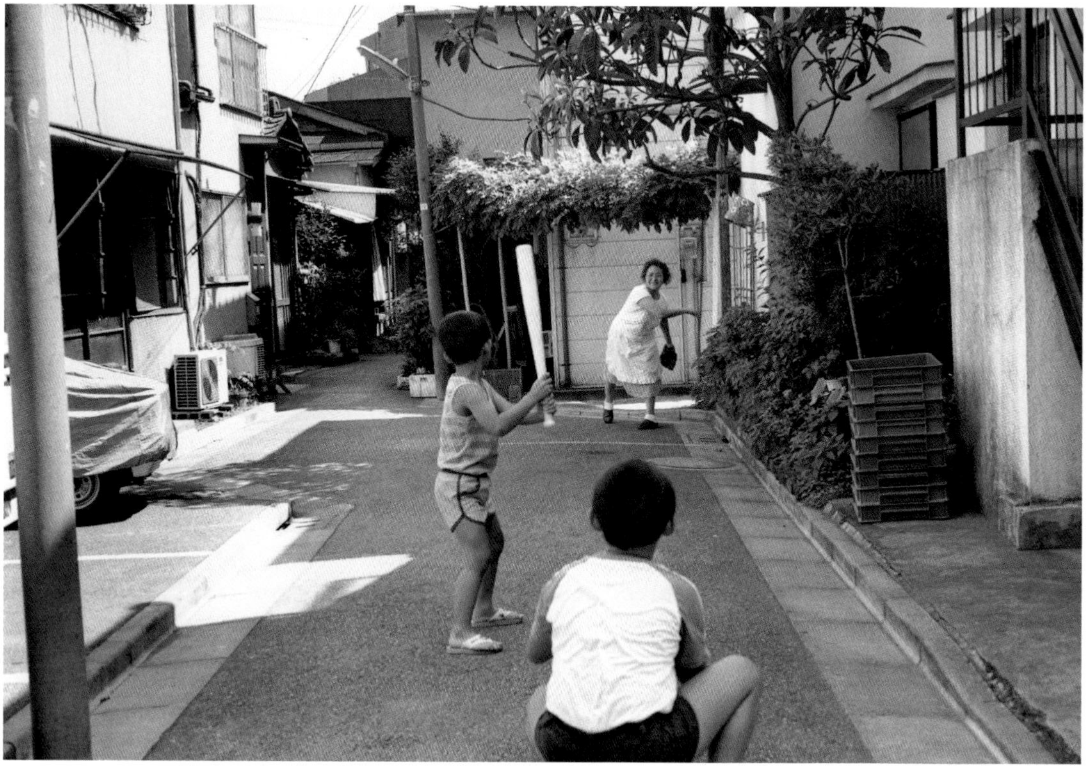

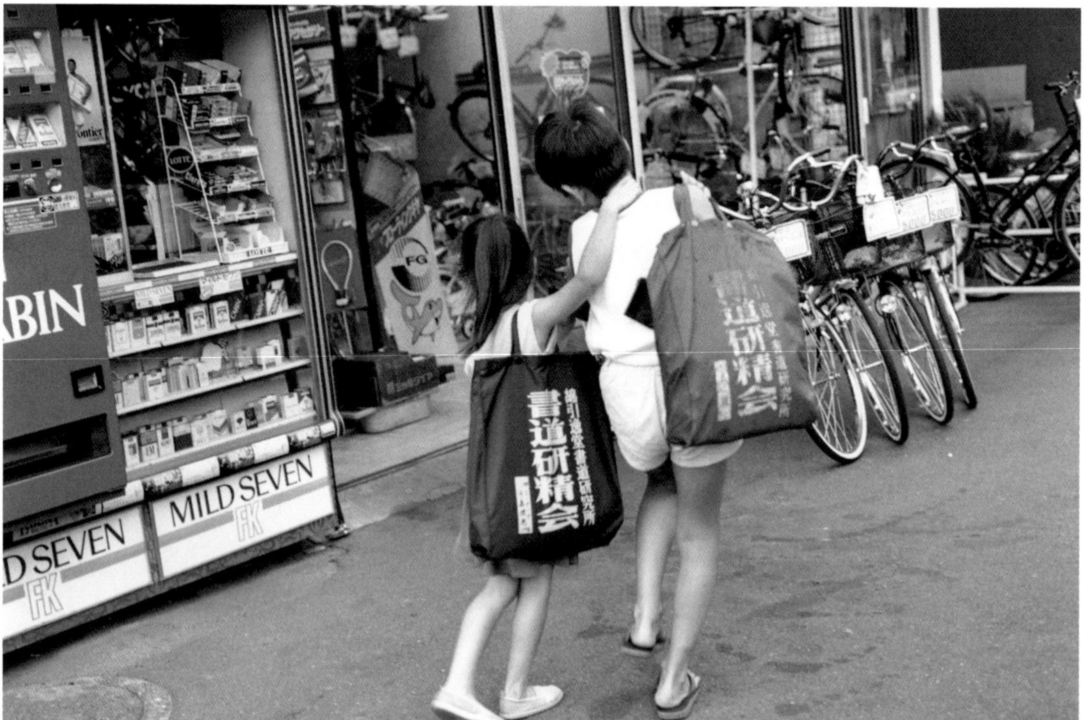

BIN
LOTTE
MILD SEVEN
FK
D SEVEN
FK
書道研精会
書道研精会

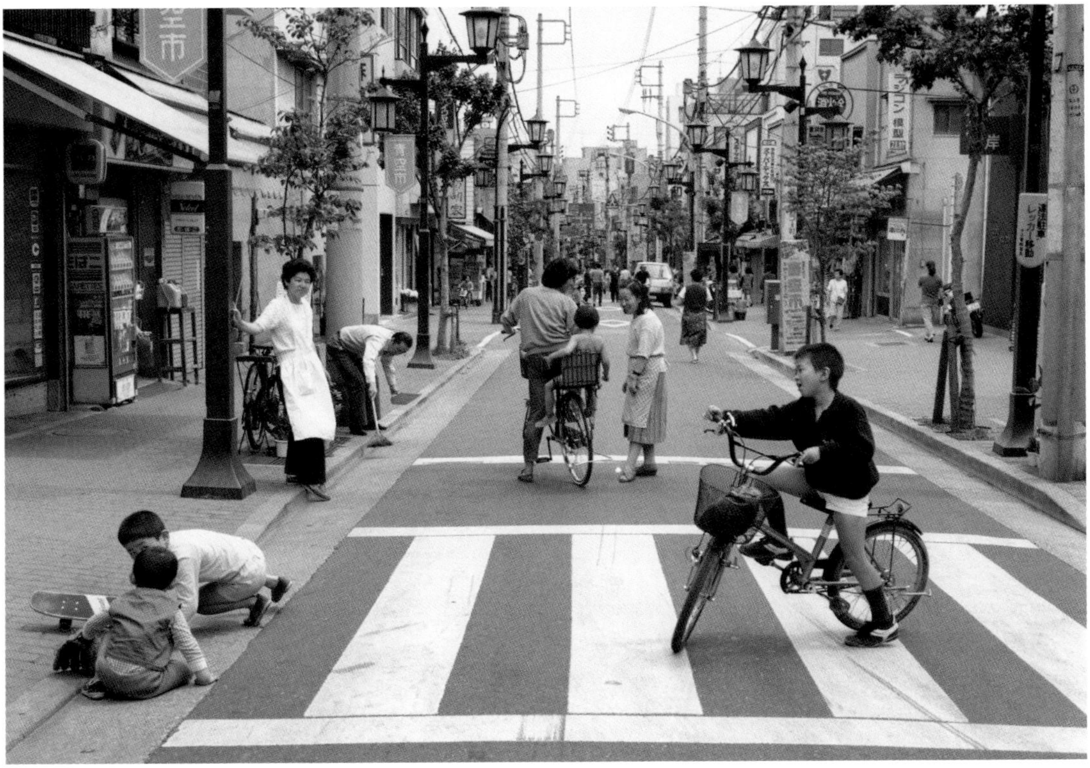

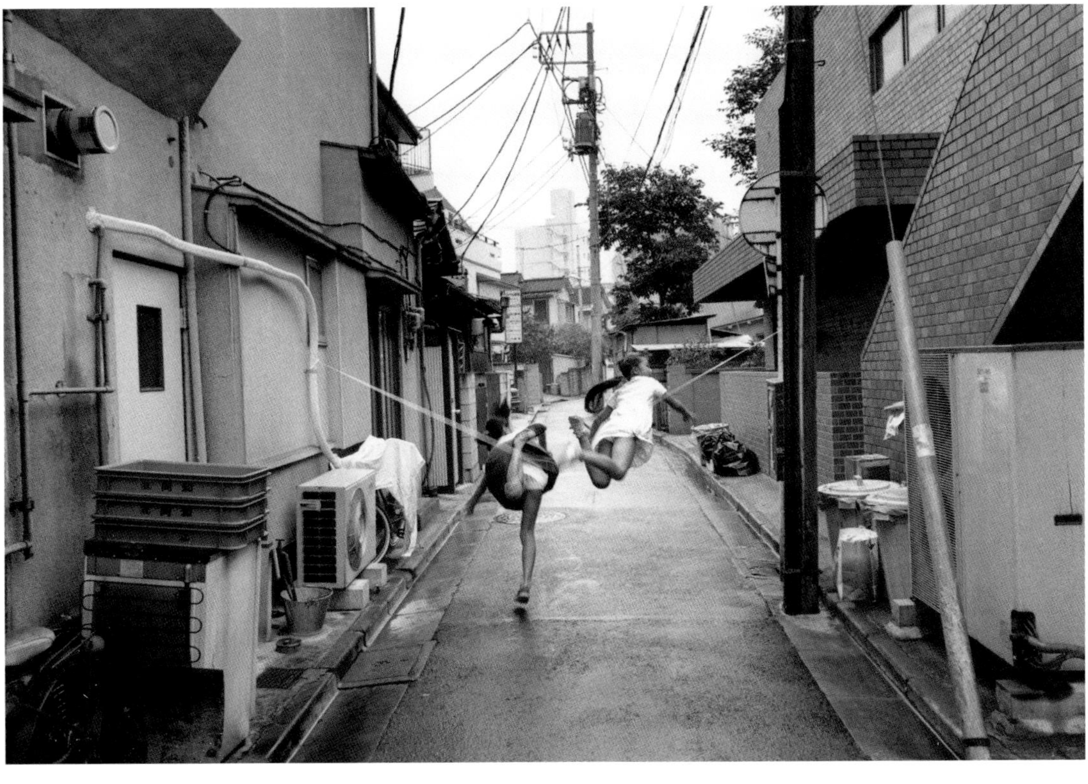

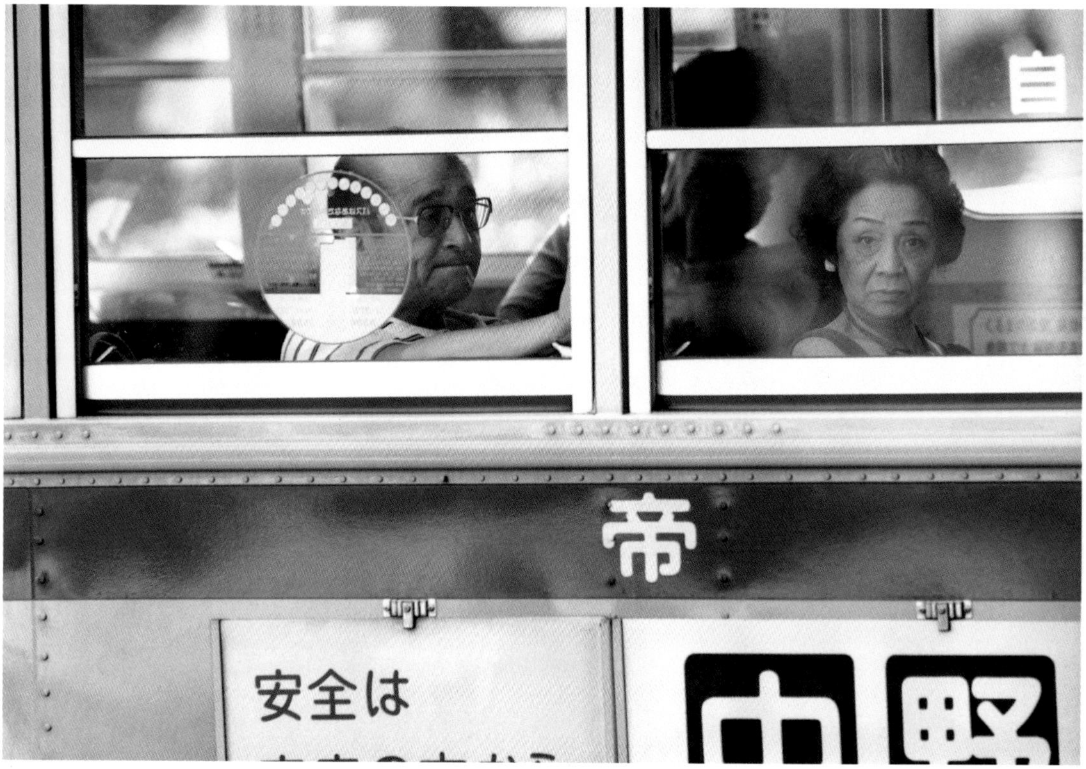
帝
安全は

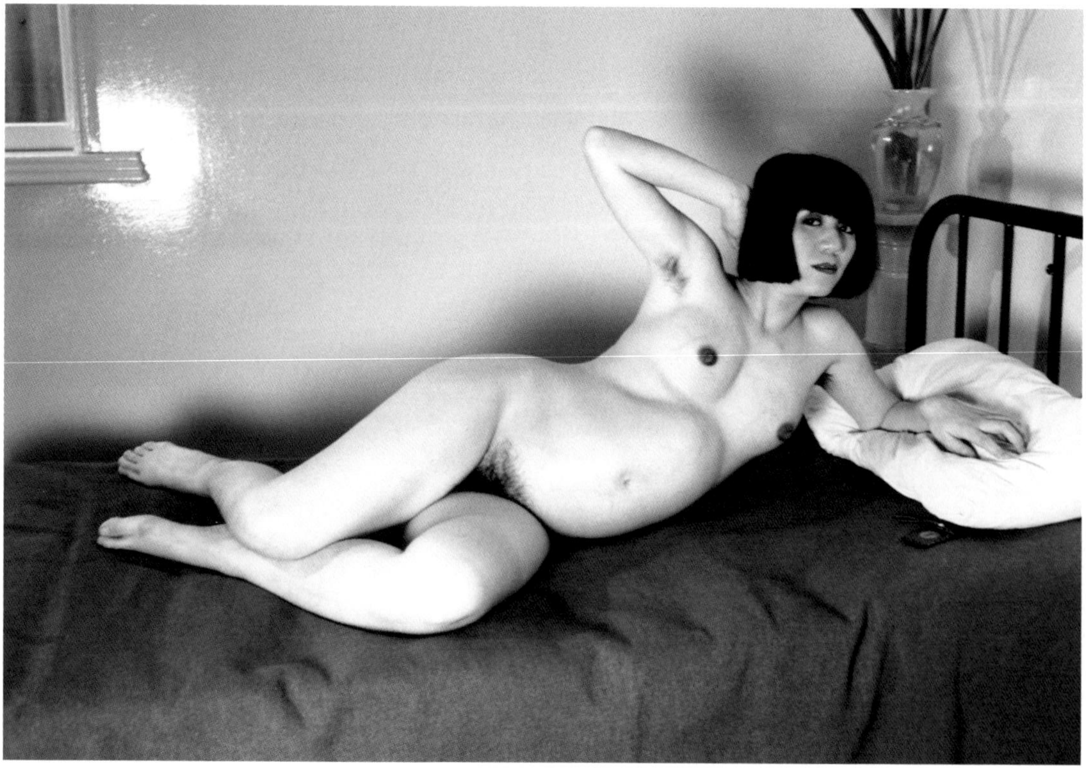

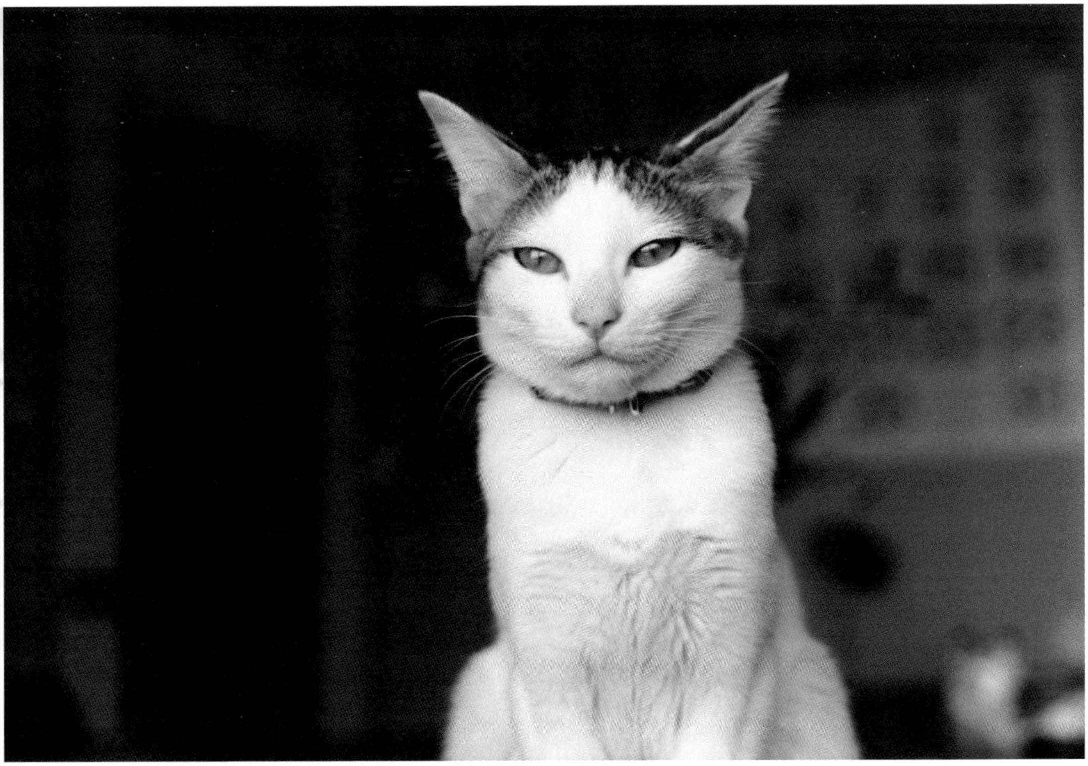

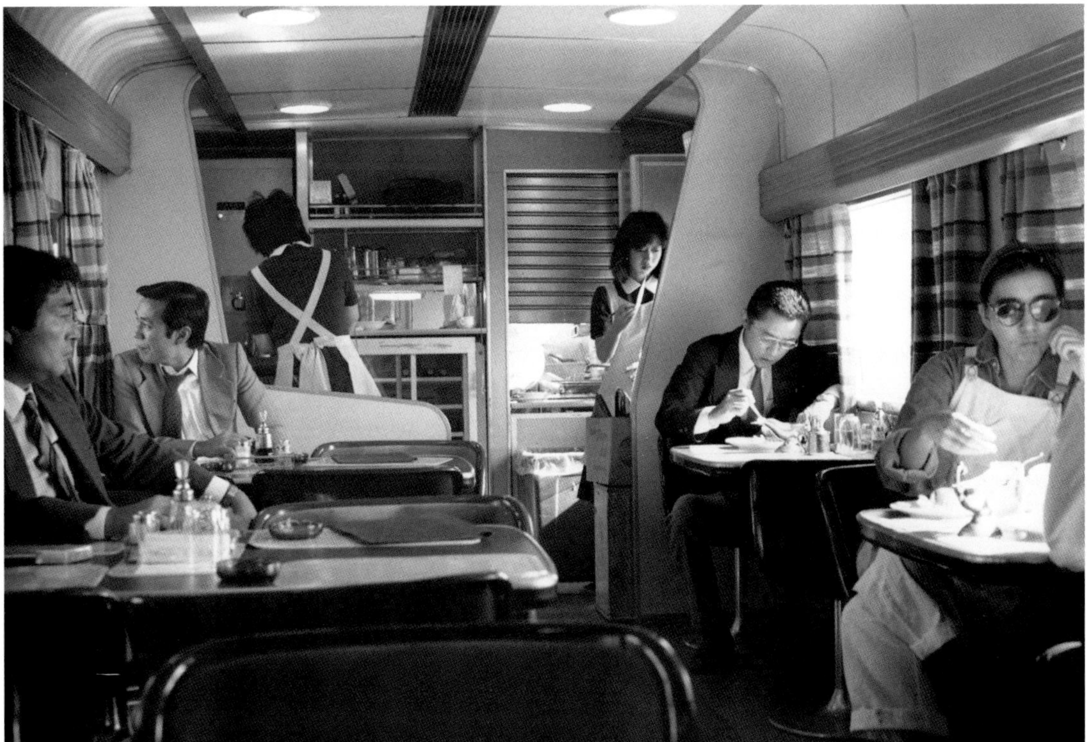

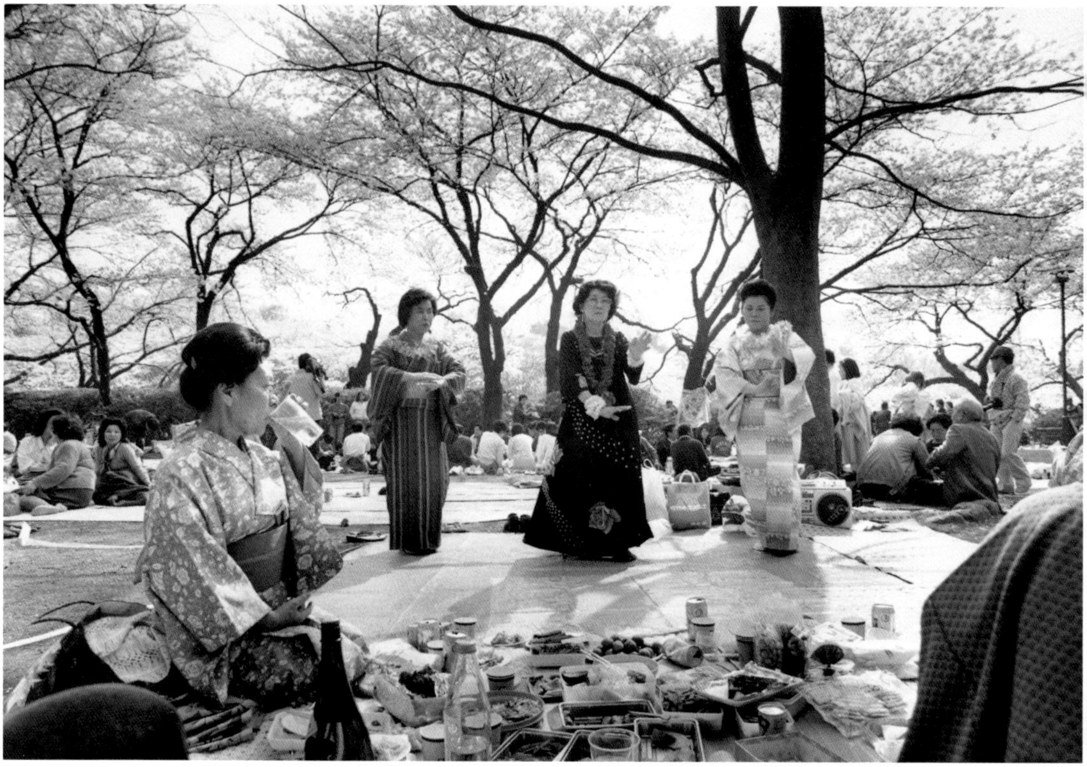
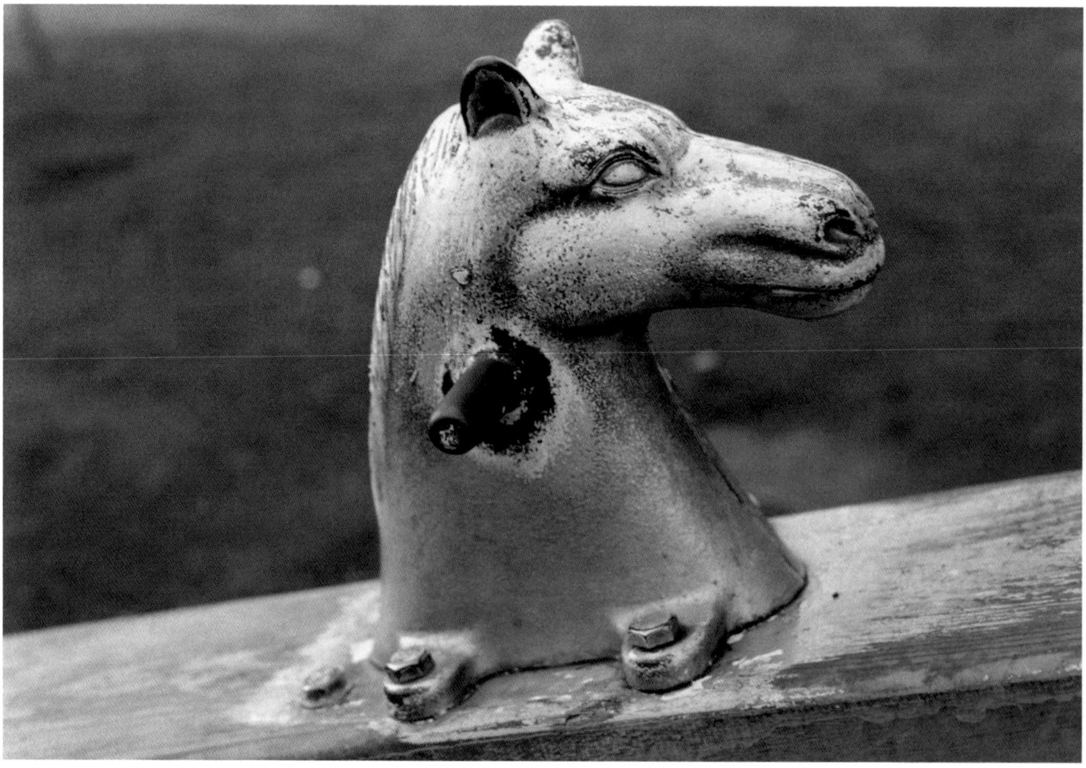

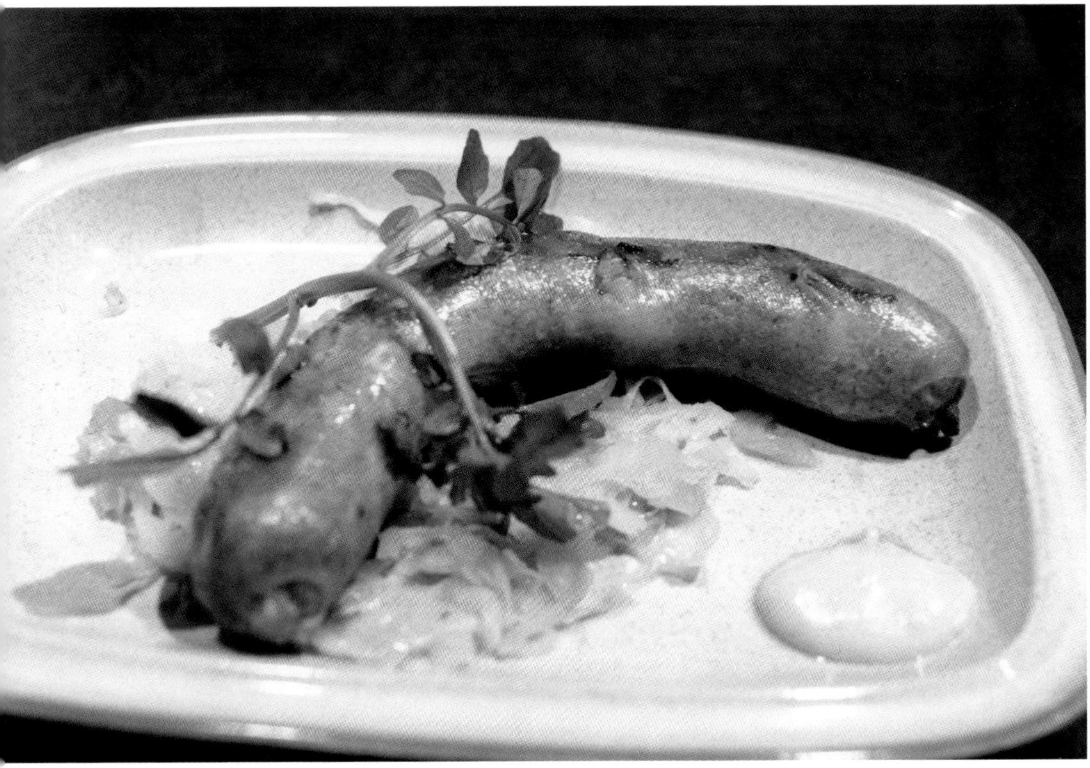

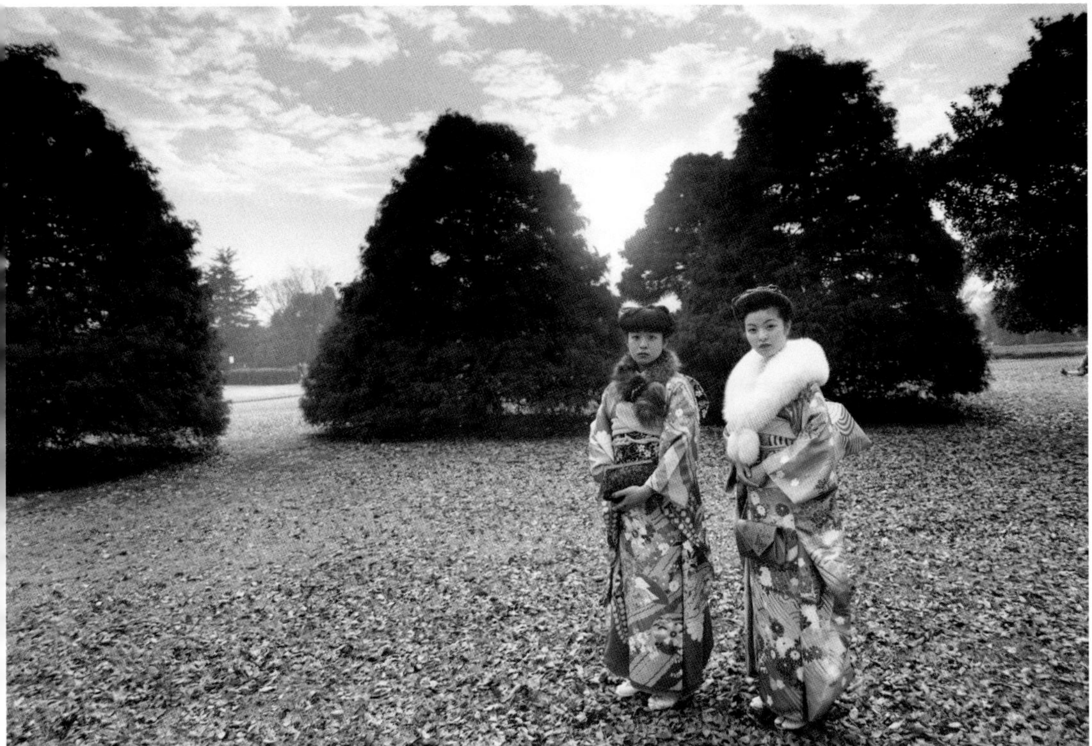

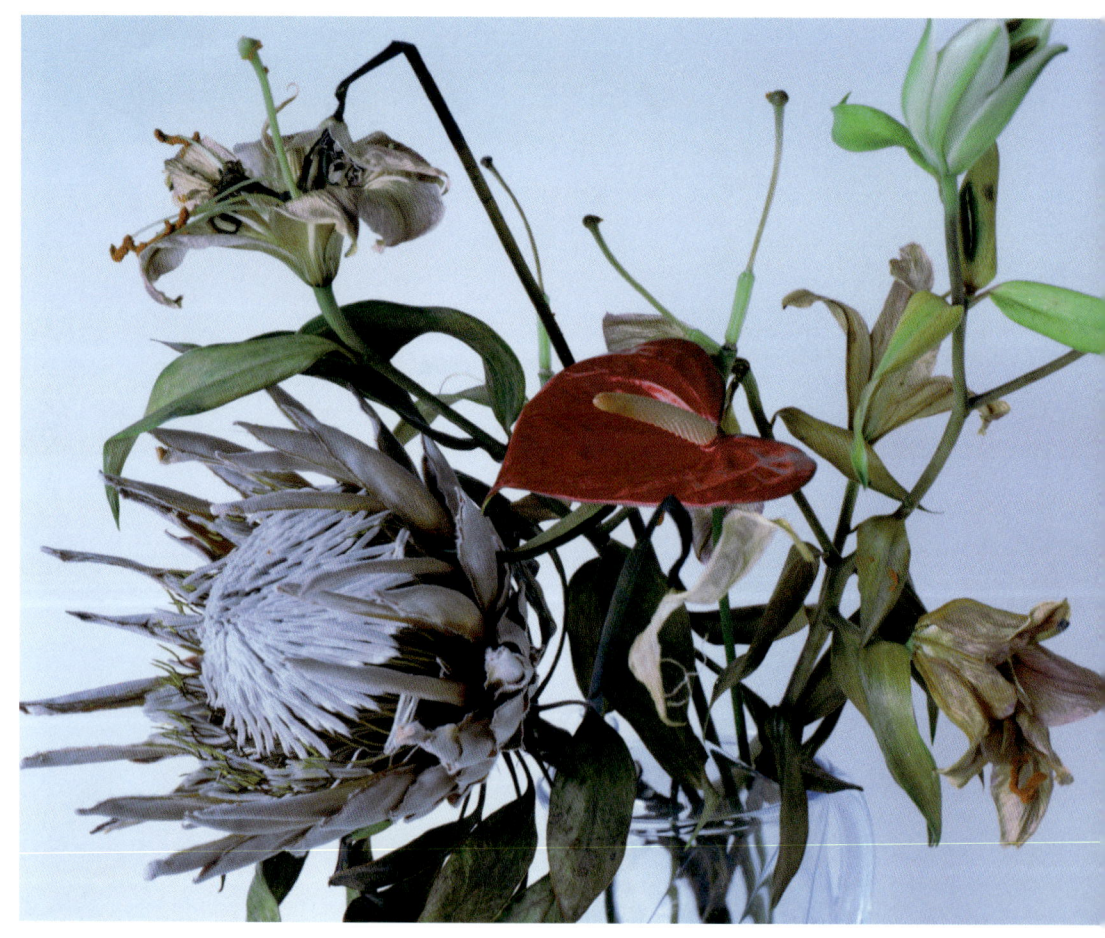

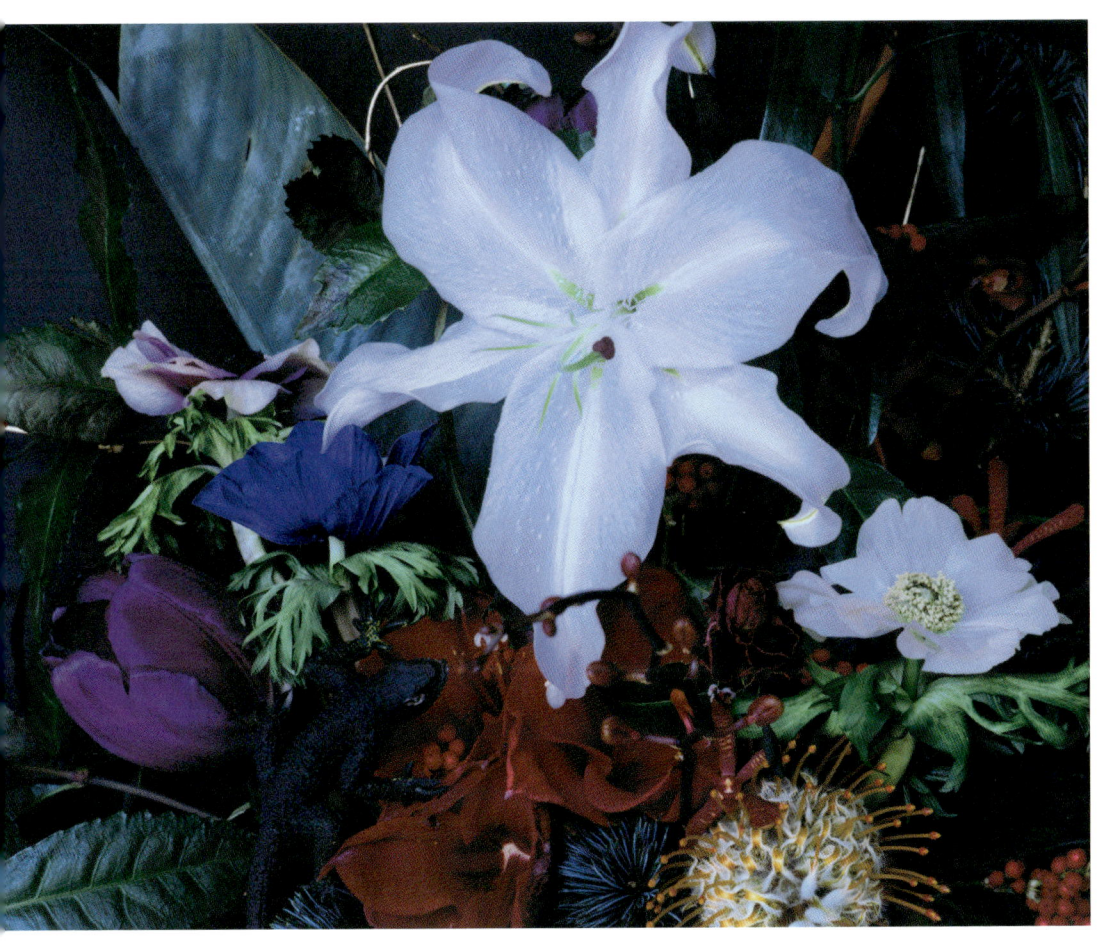

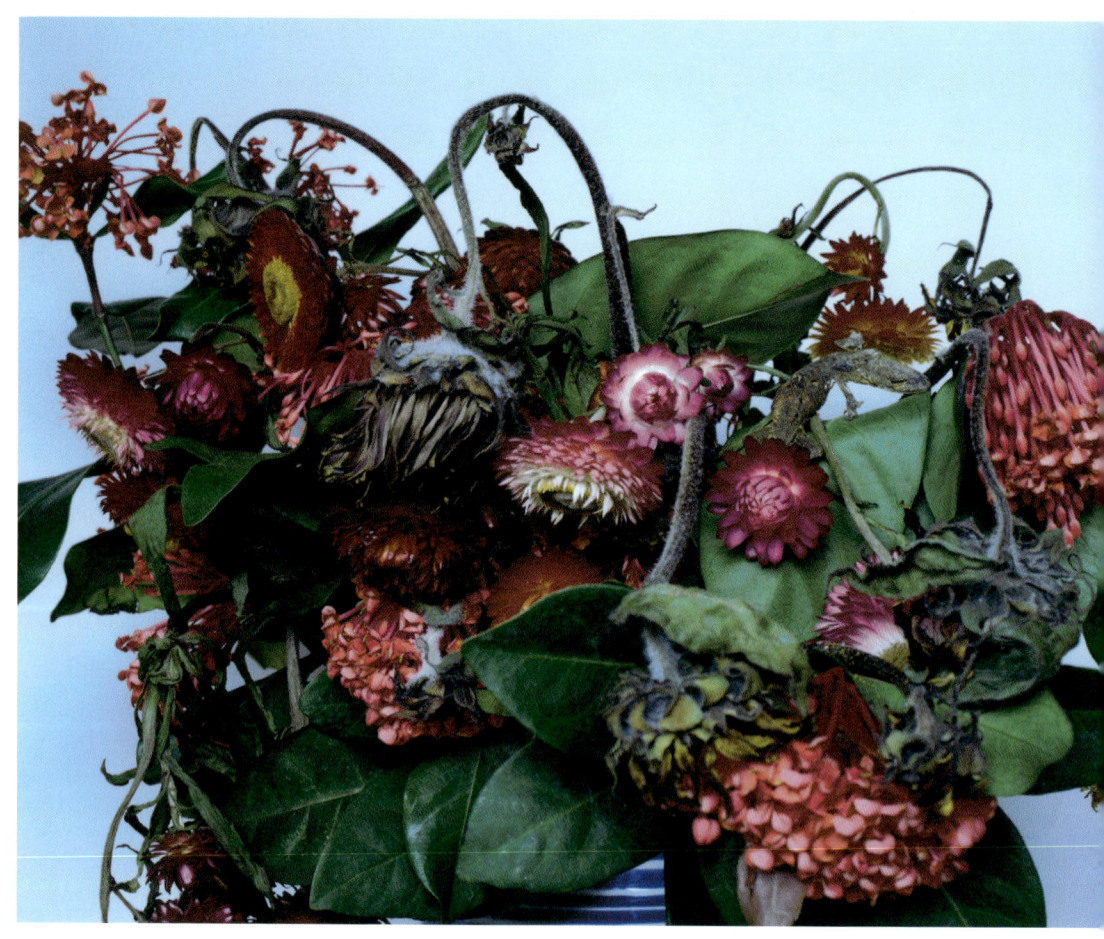

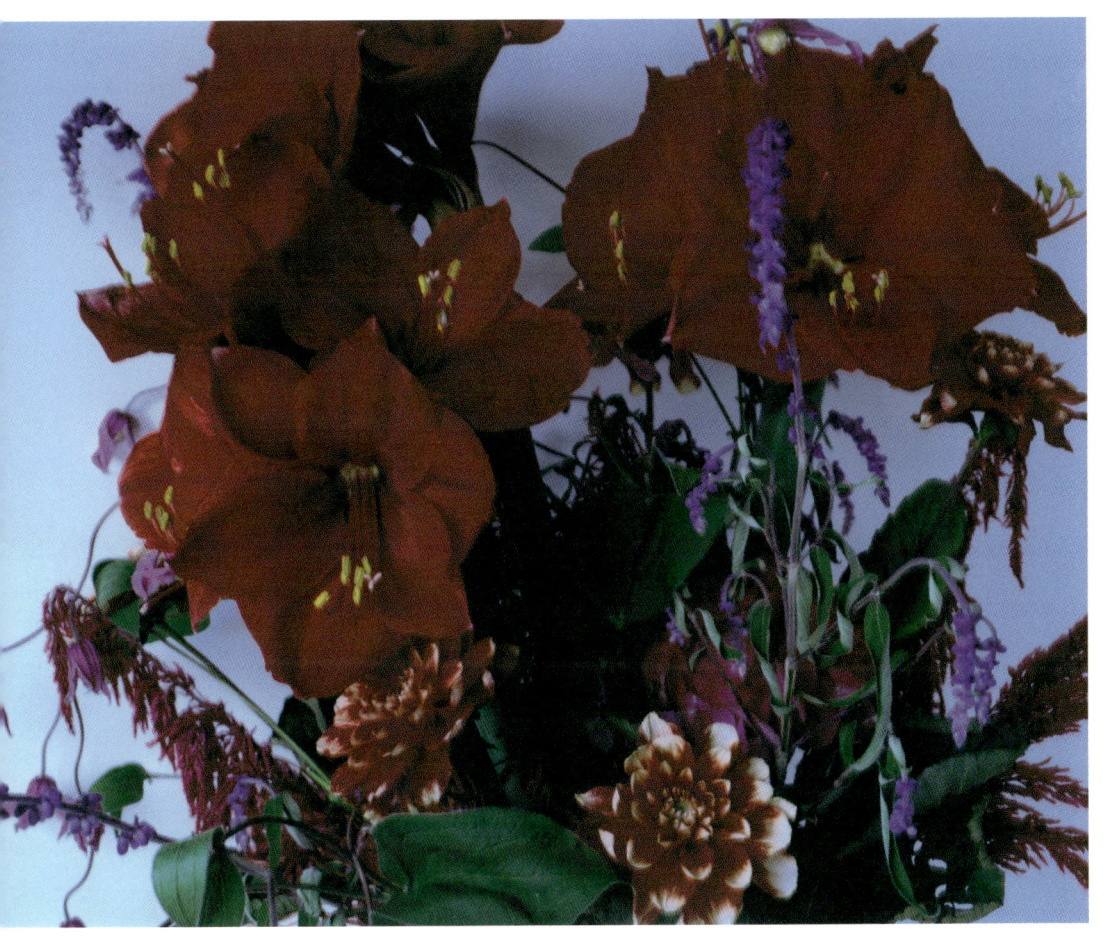

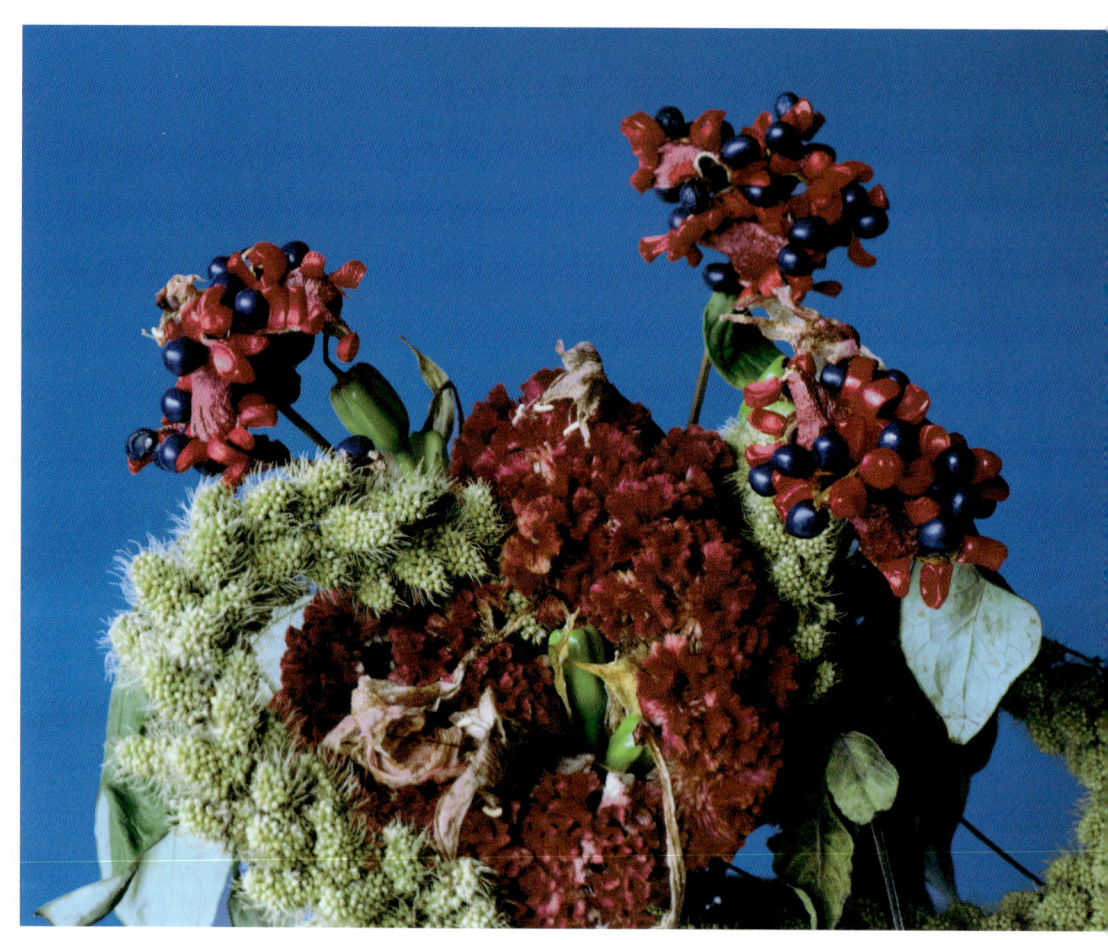

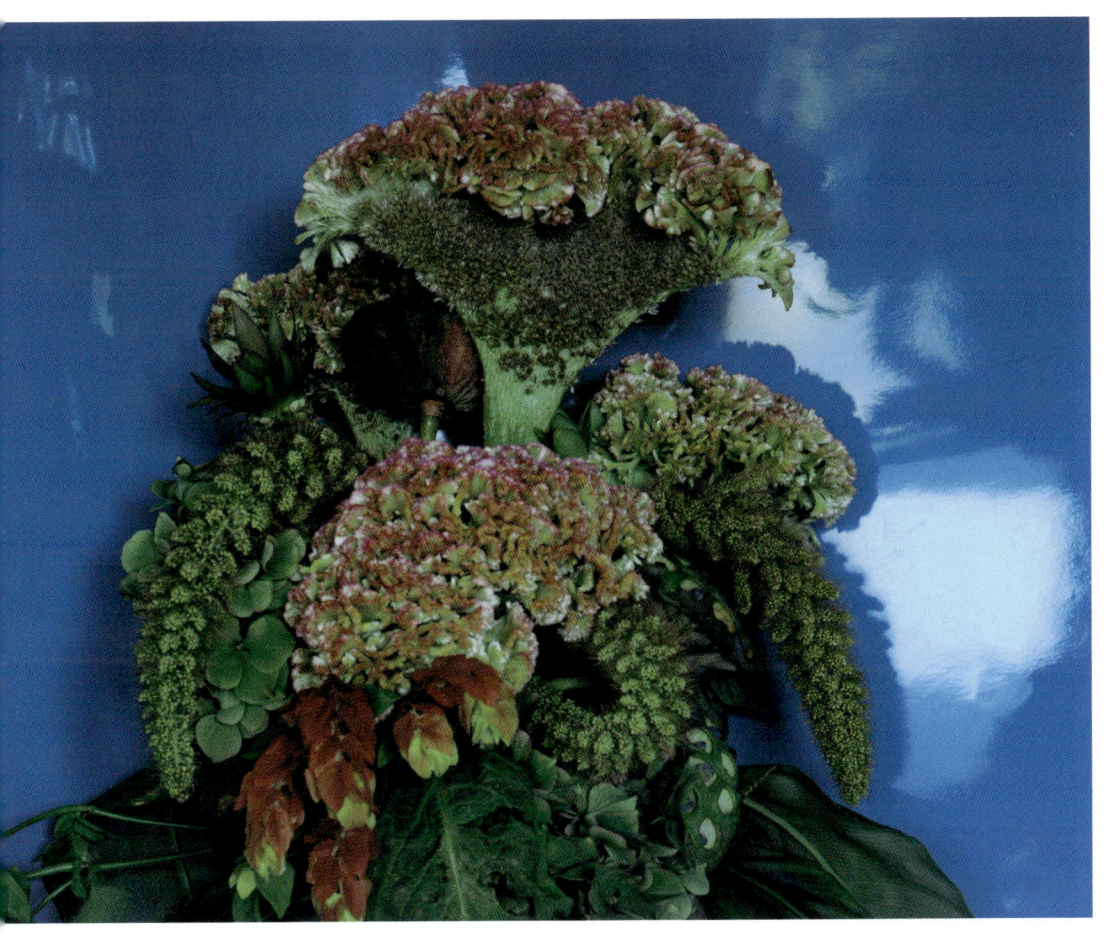

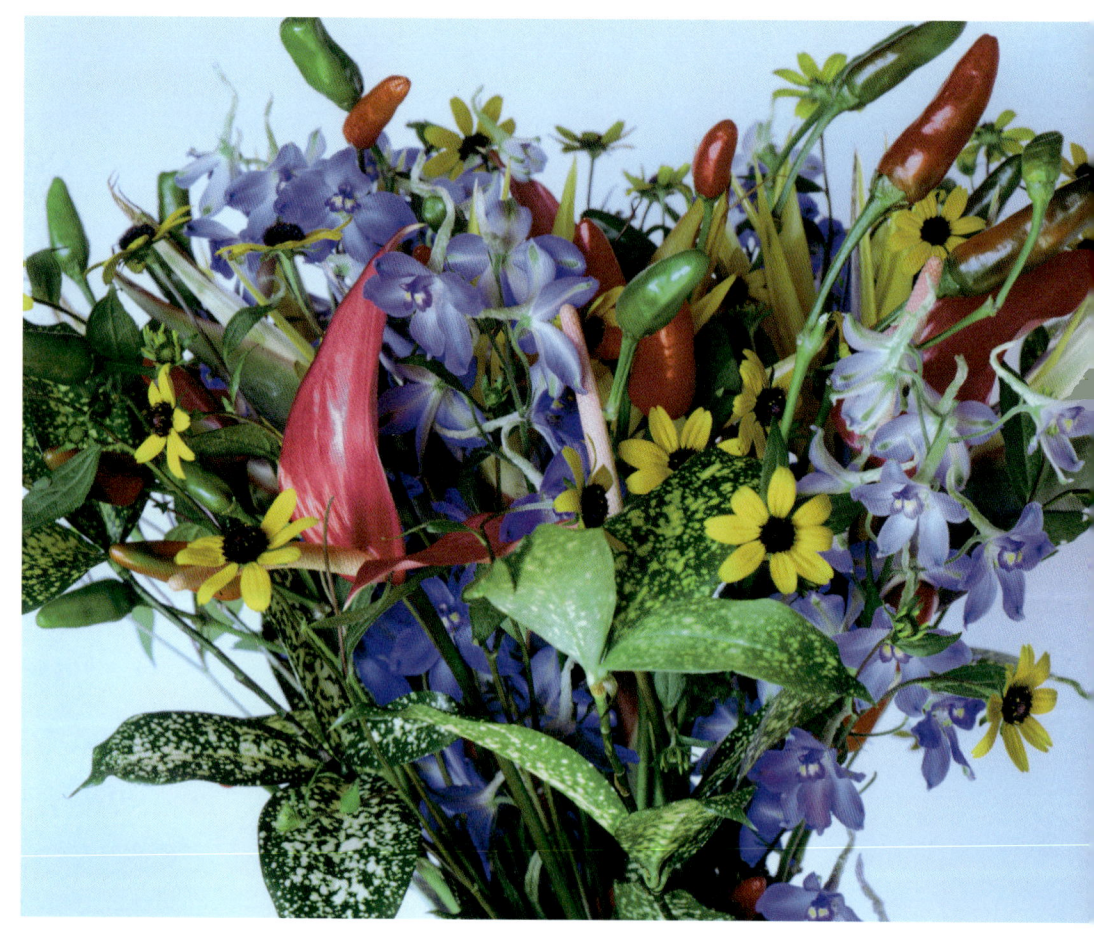

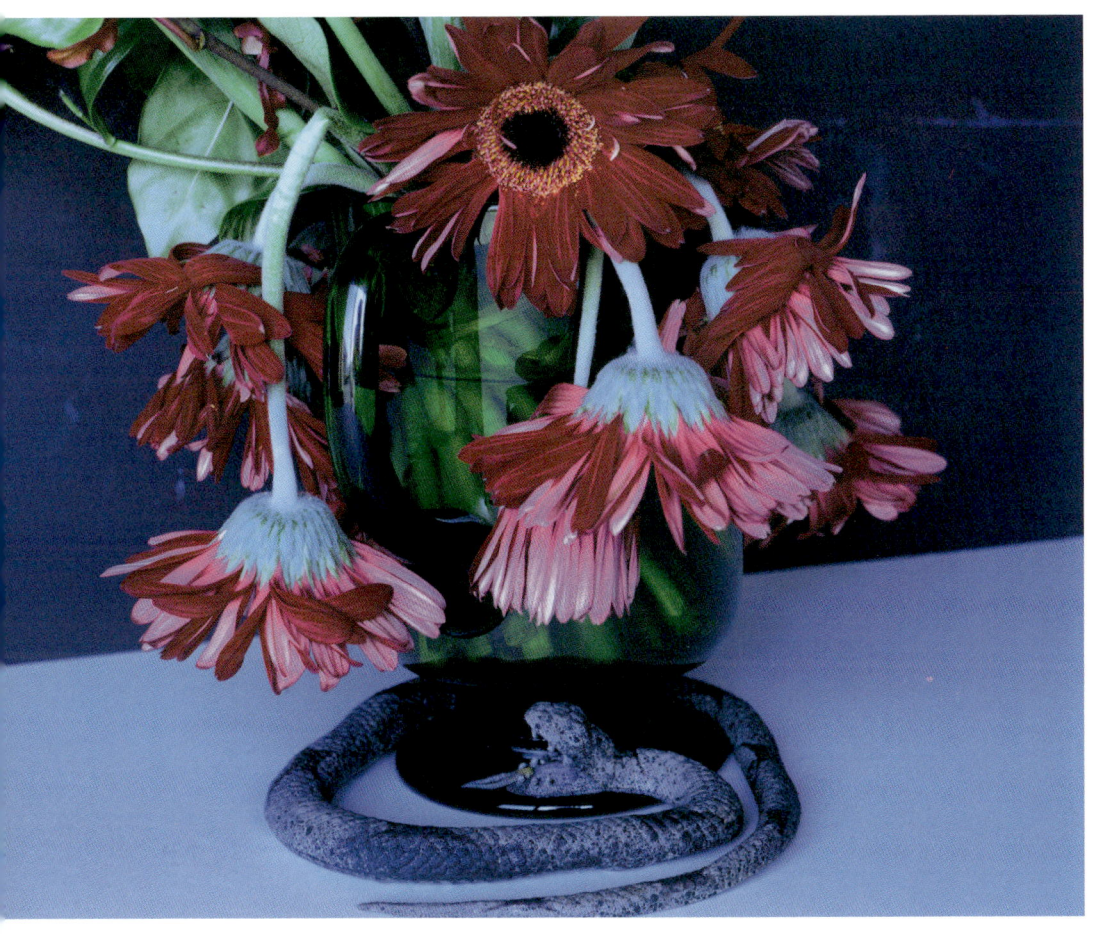

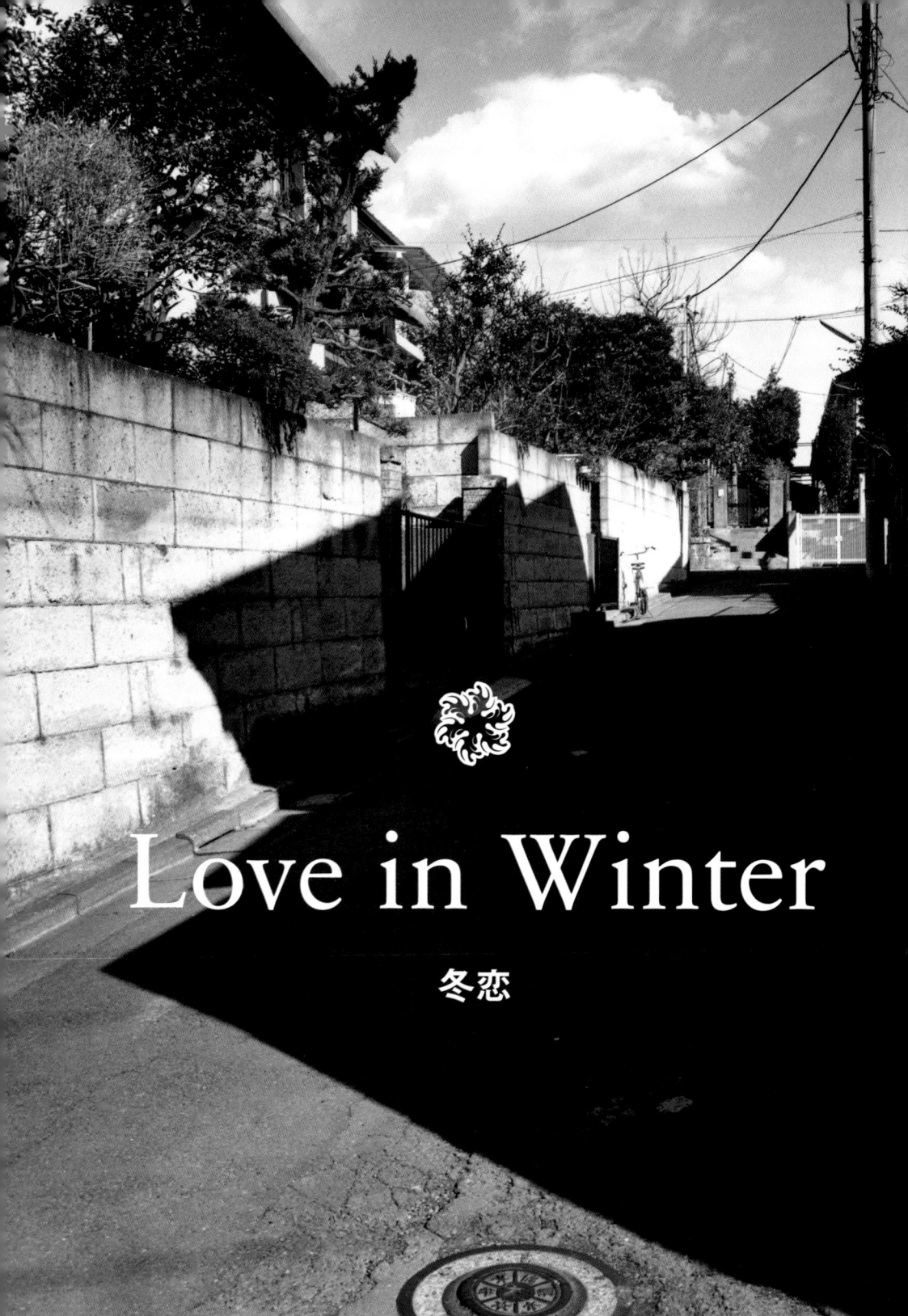

Love in Winter

冬恋

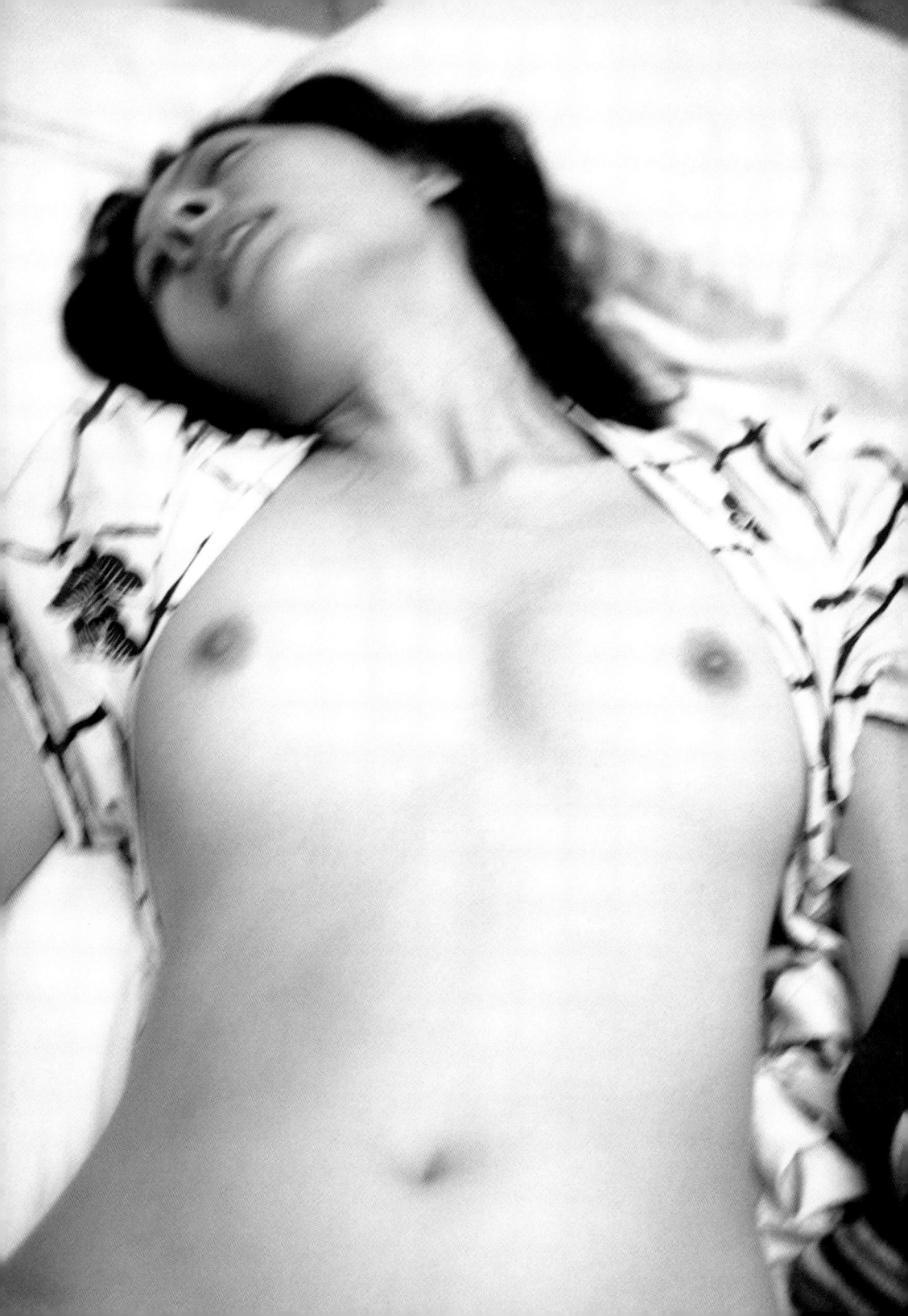

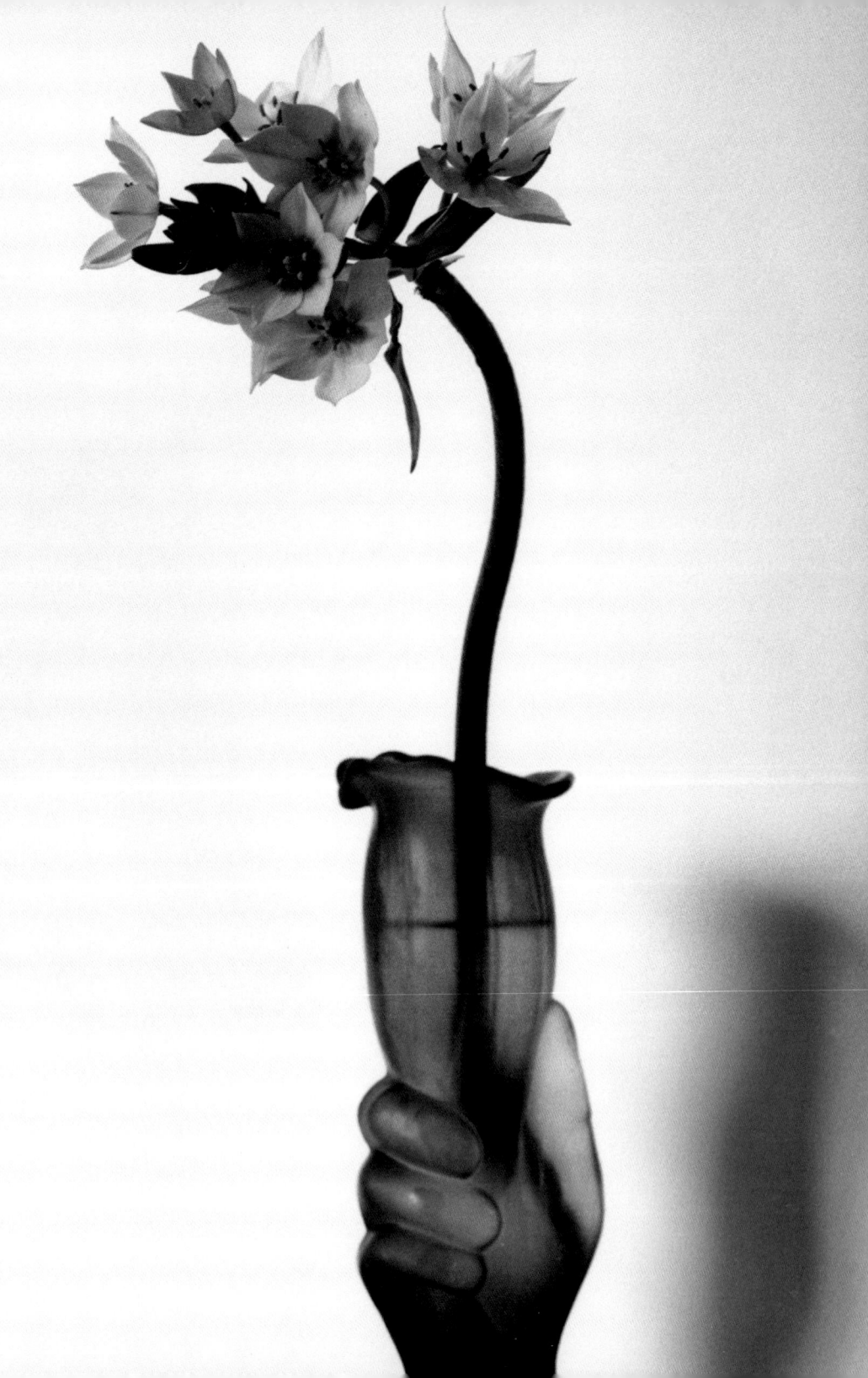

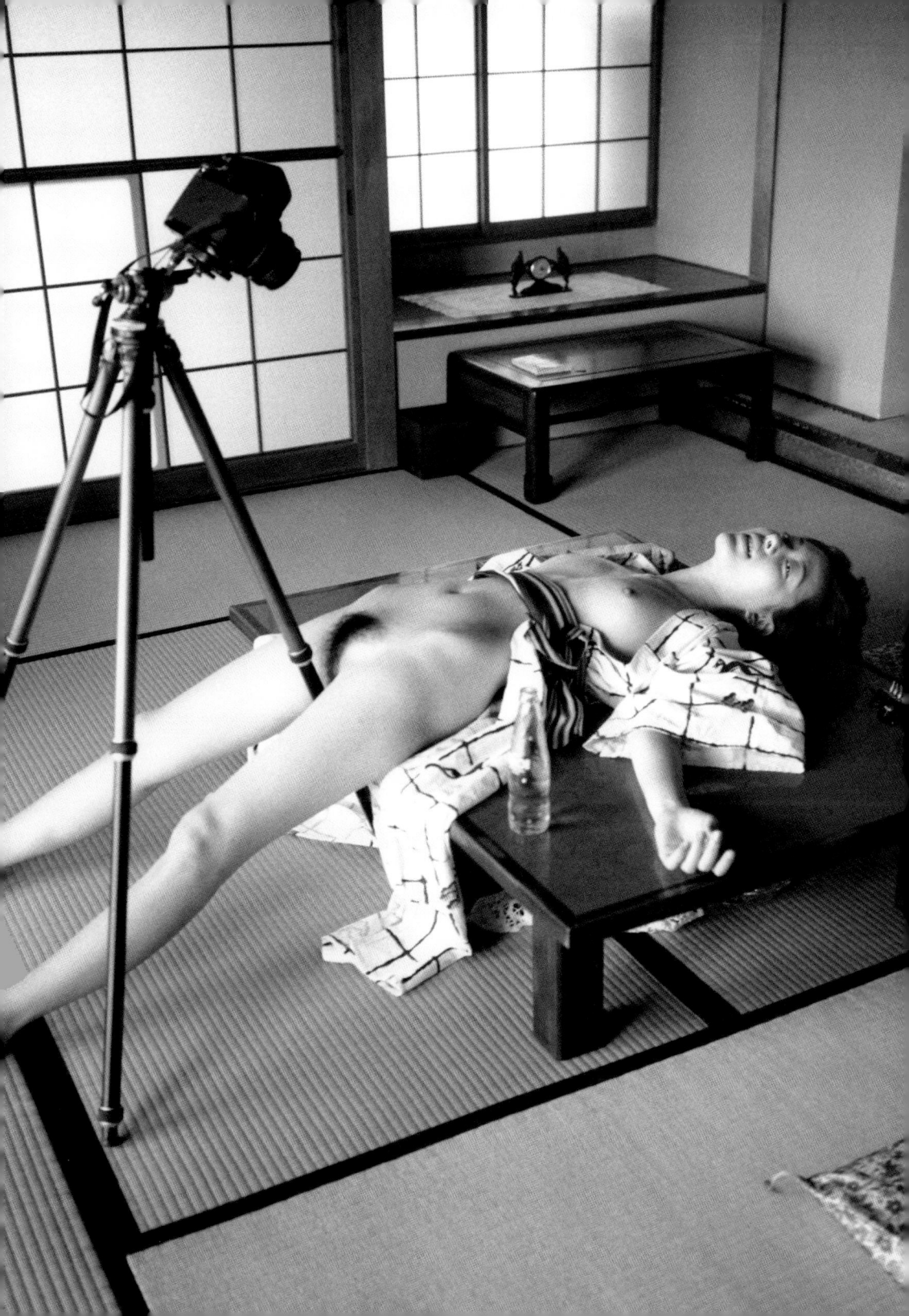

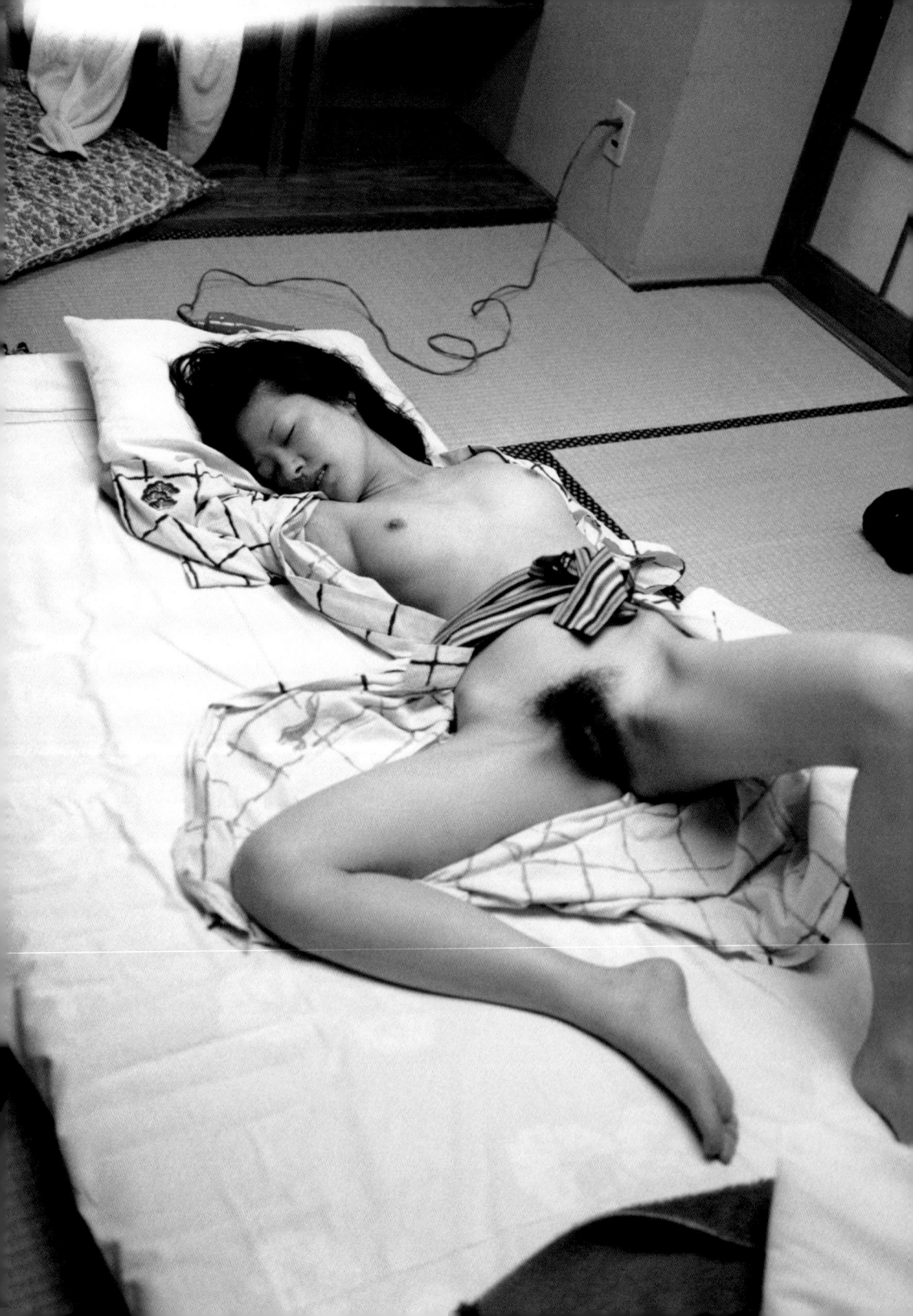

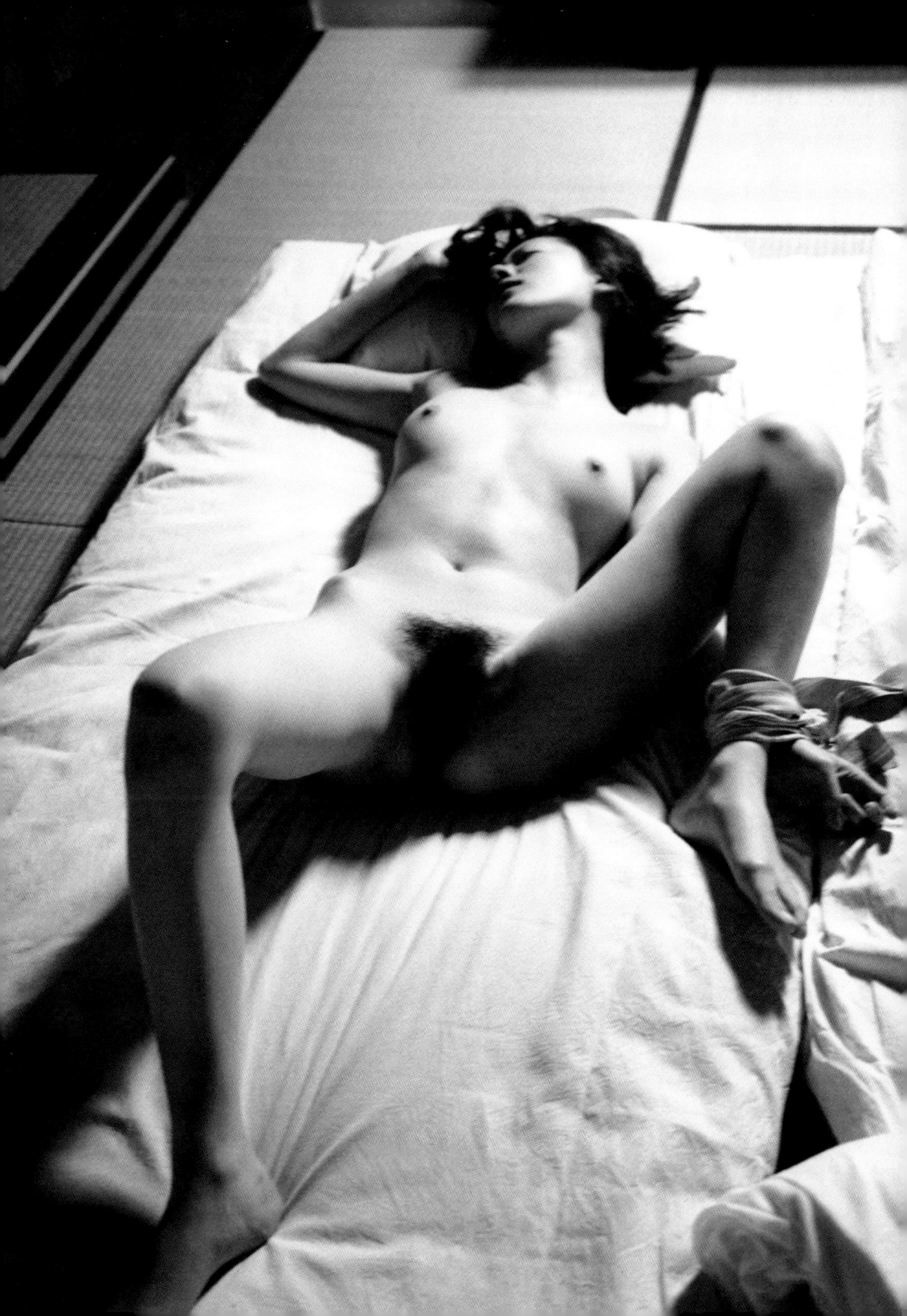

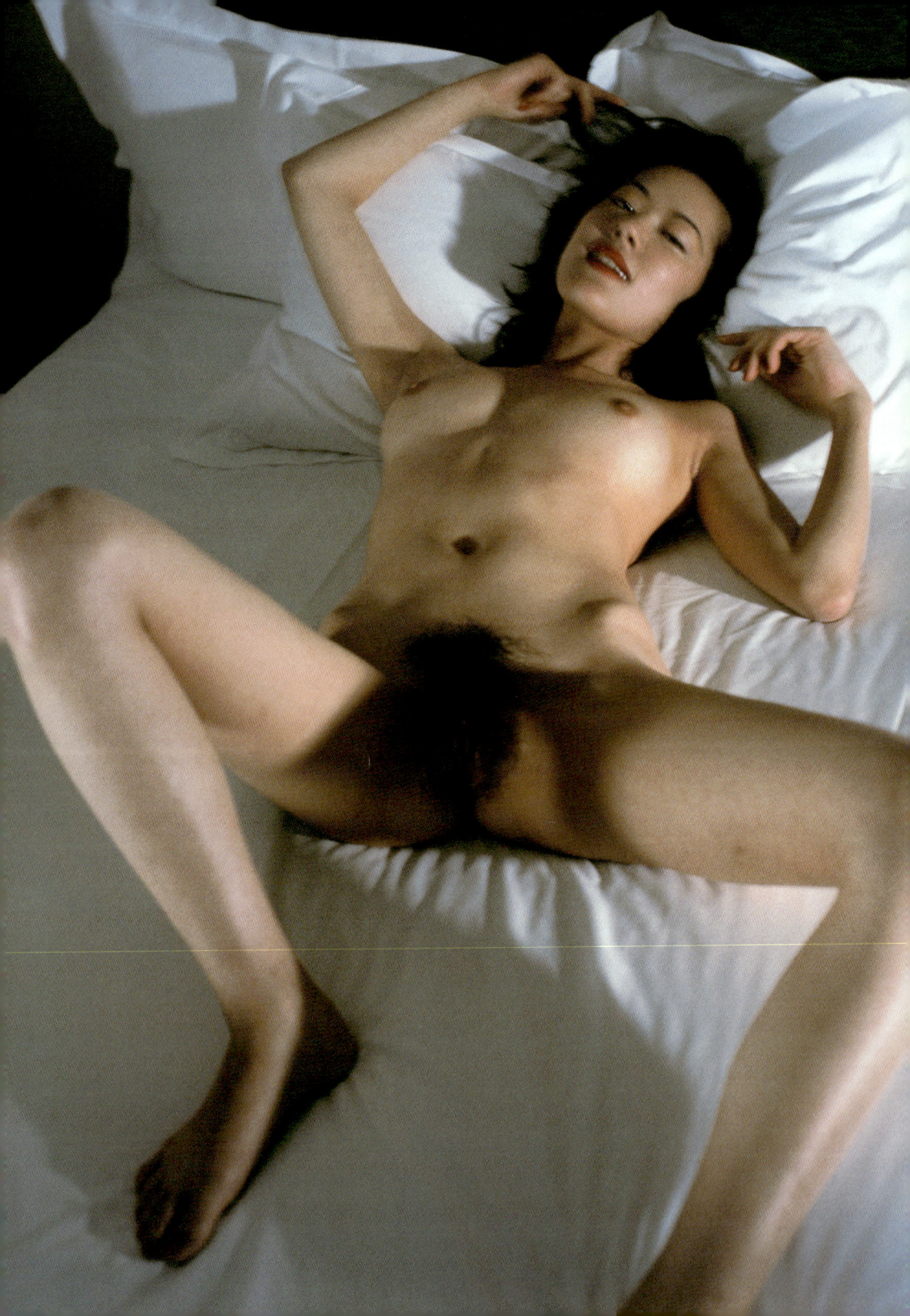

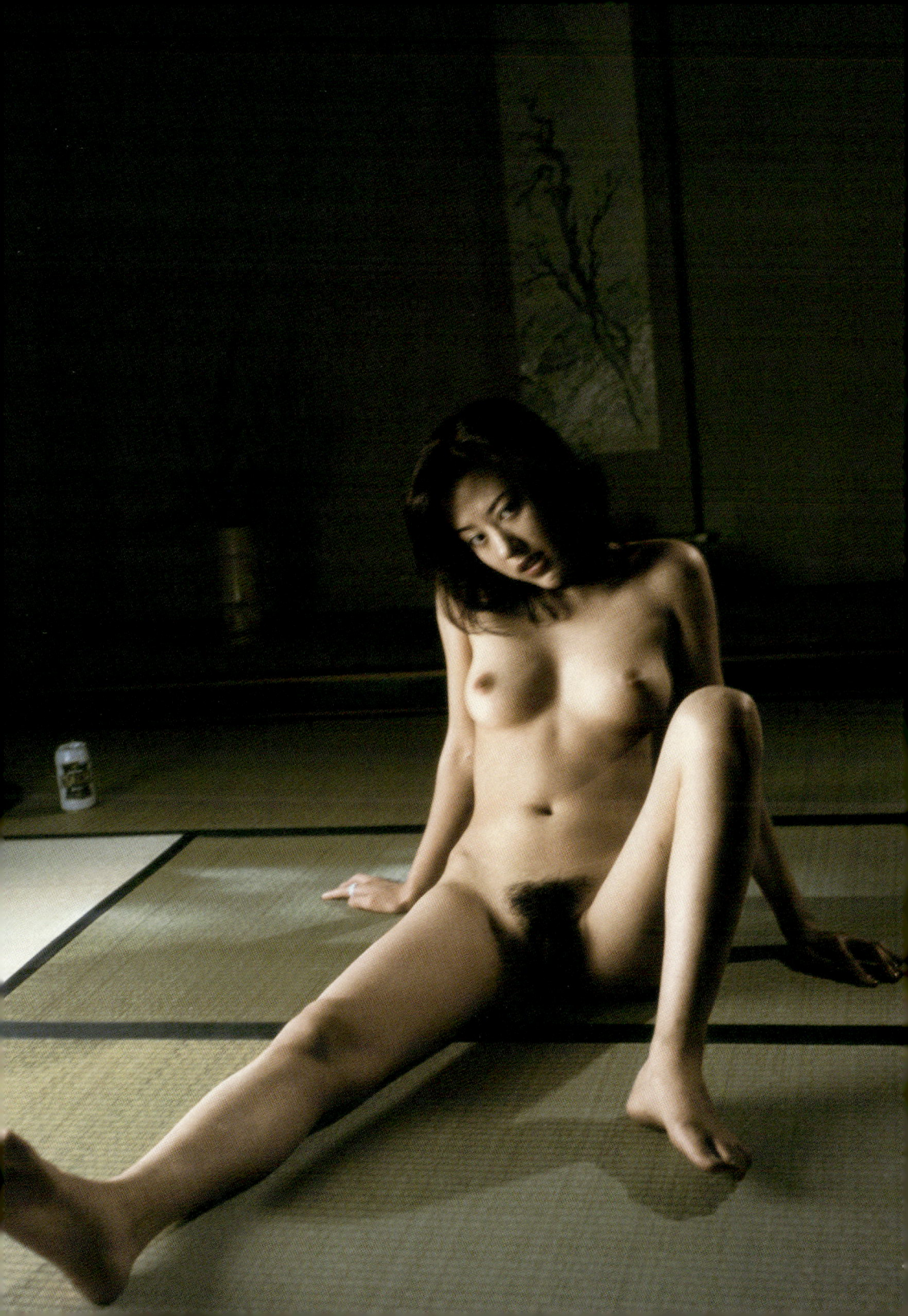

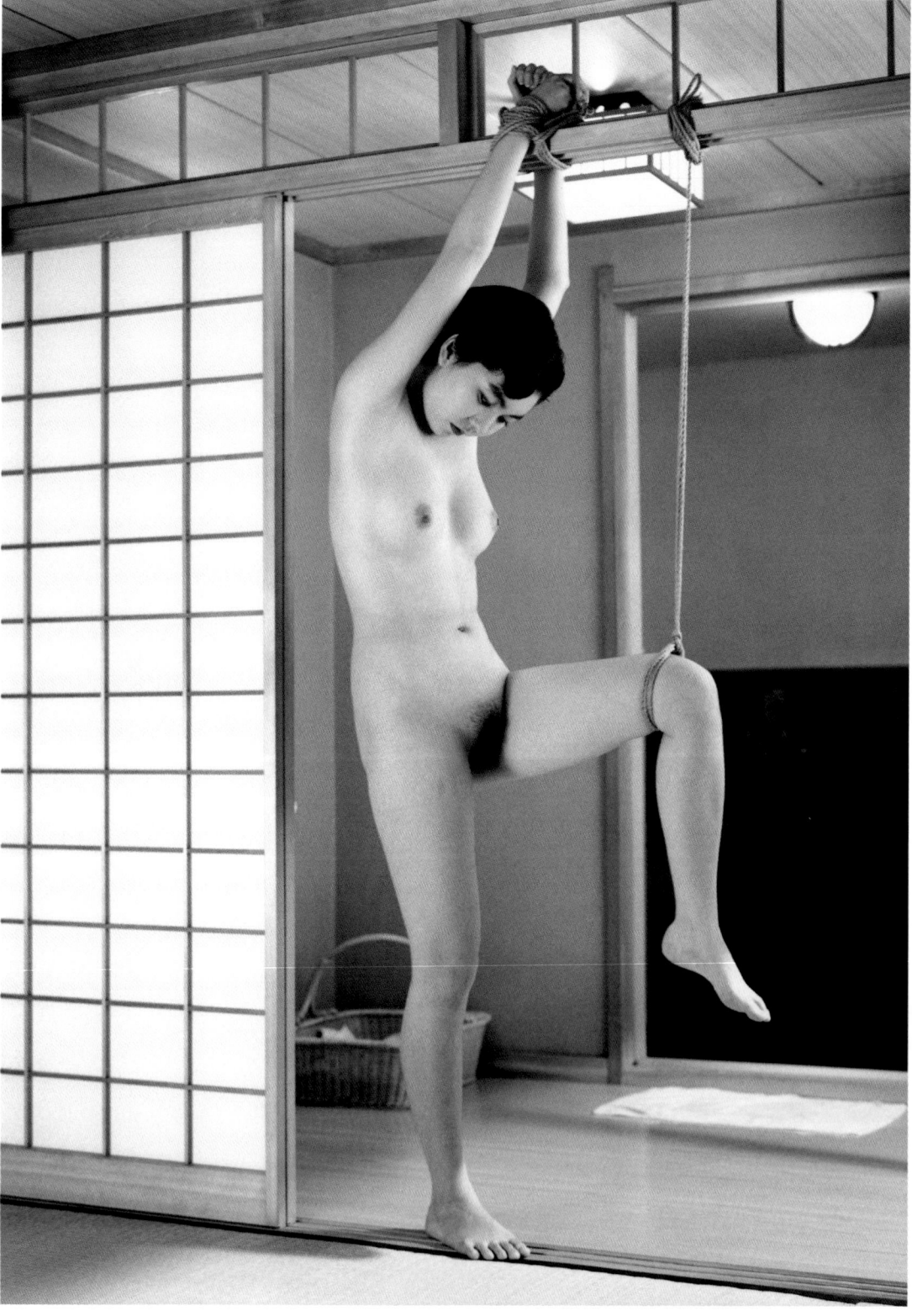

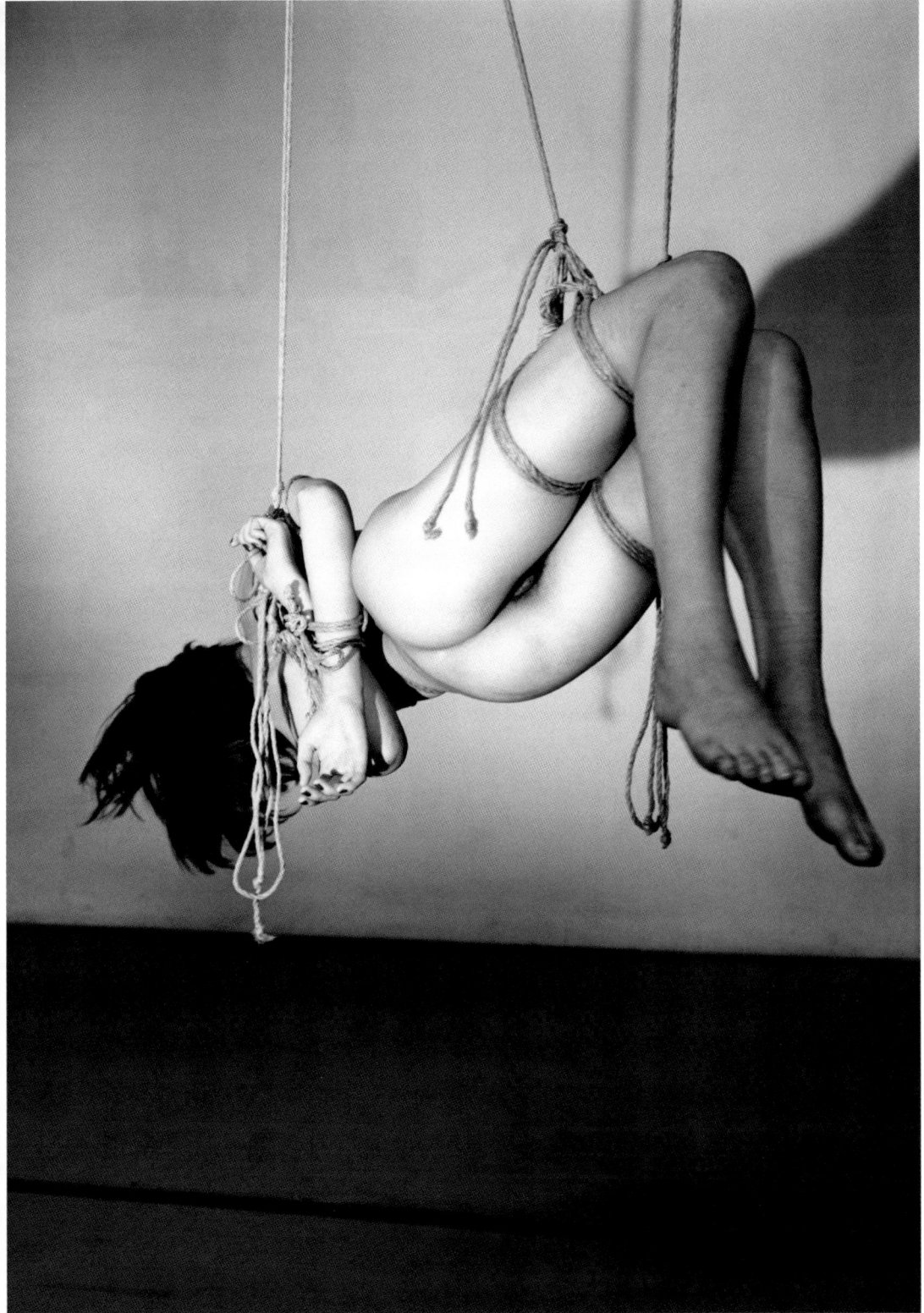

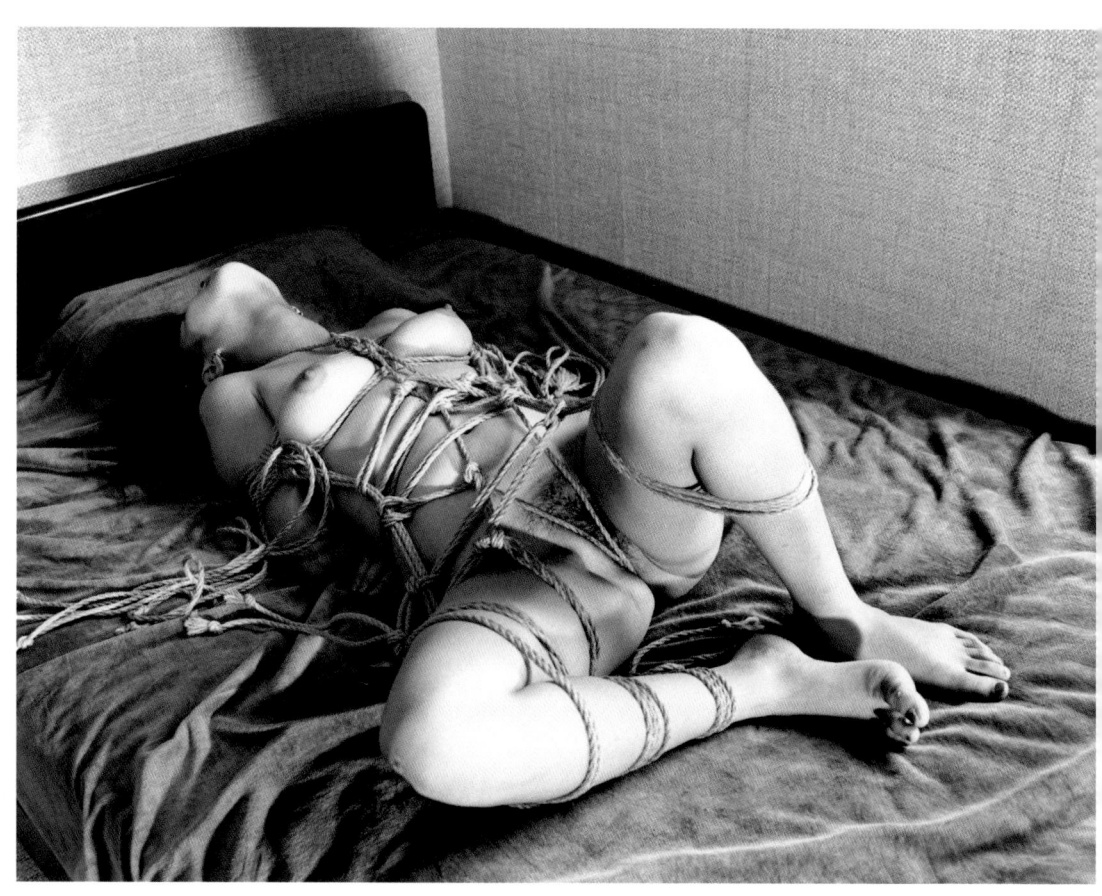

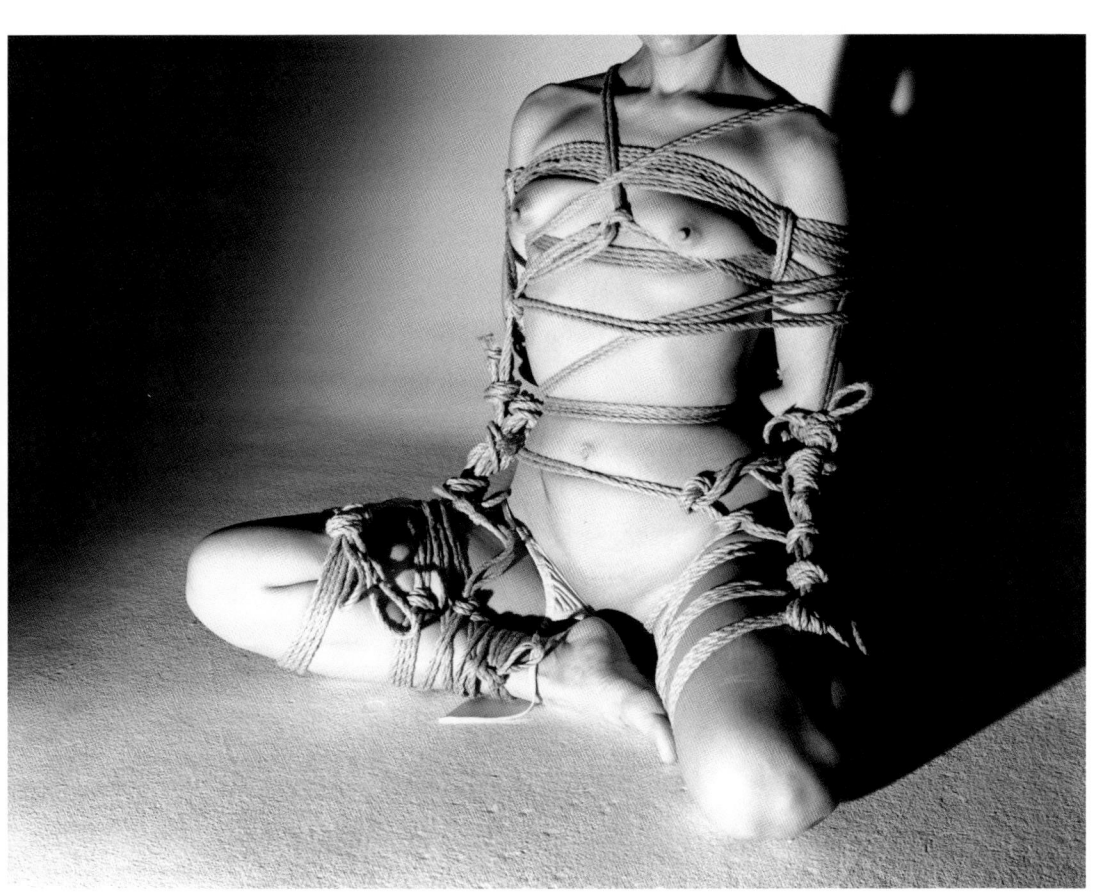

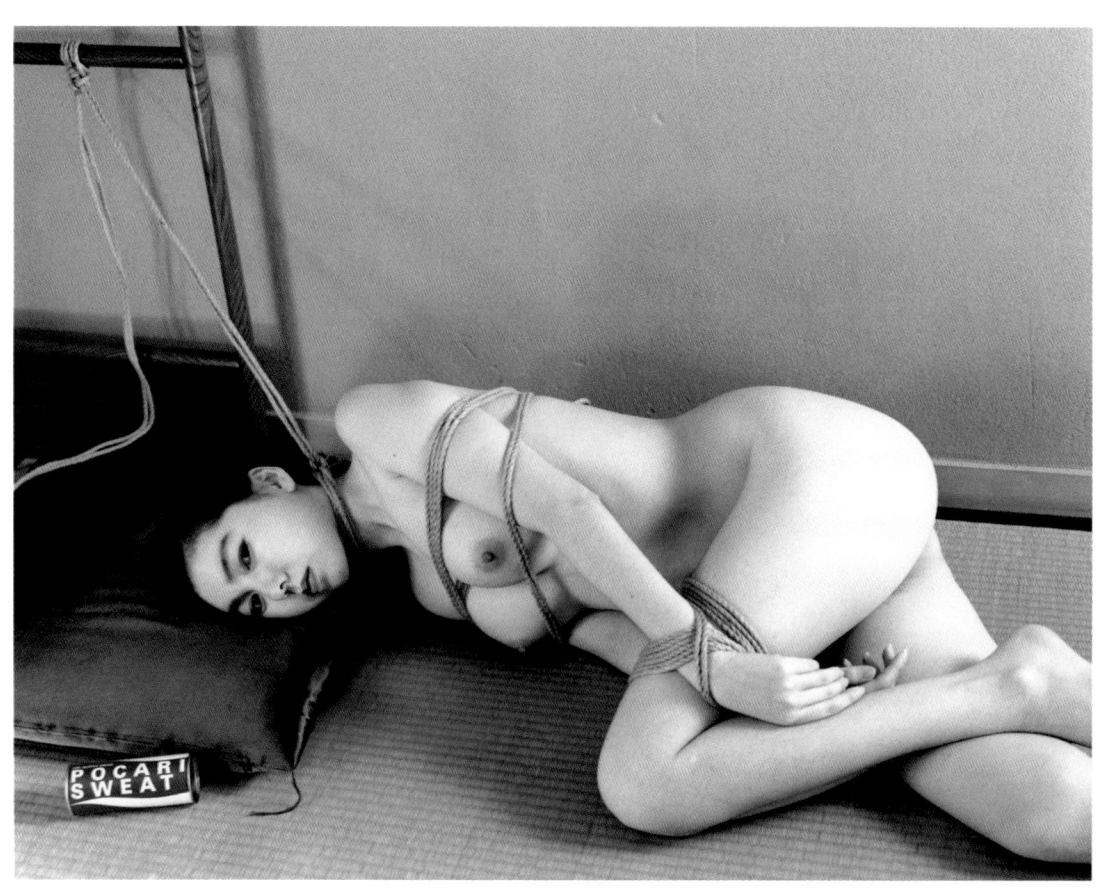

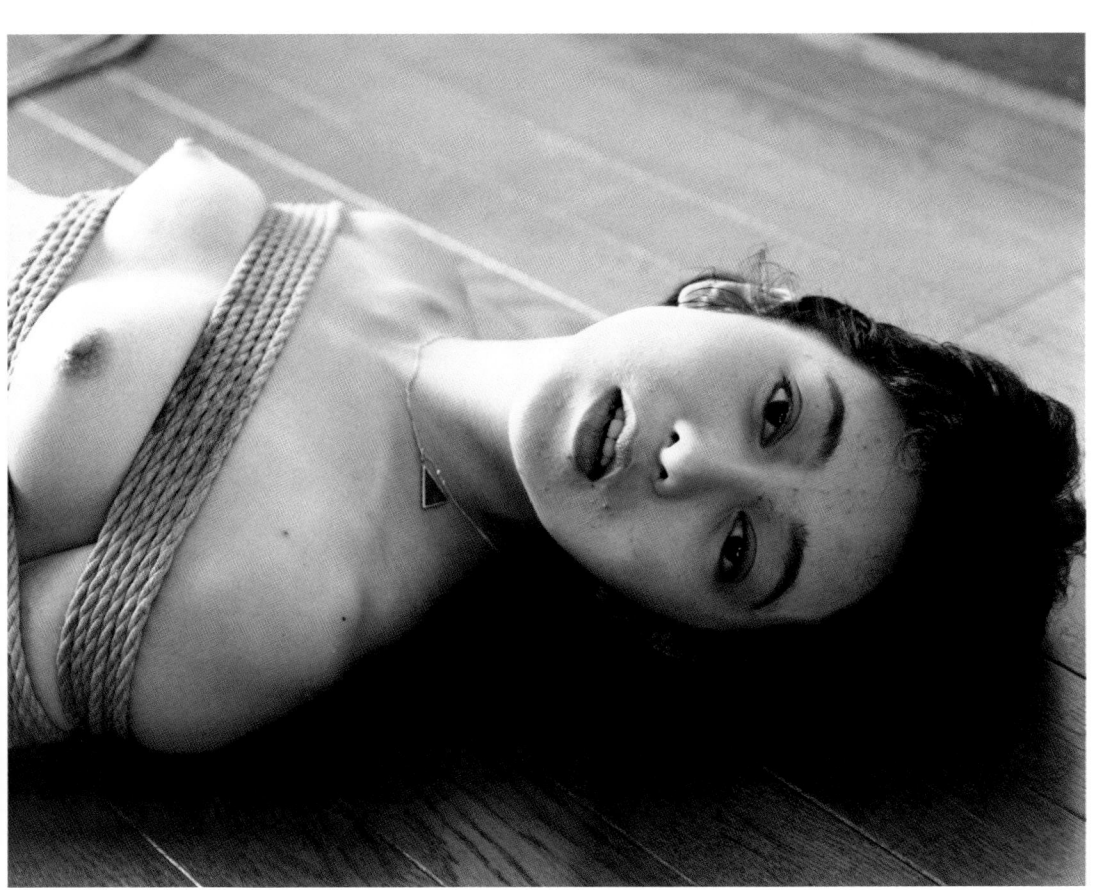

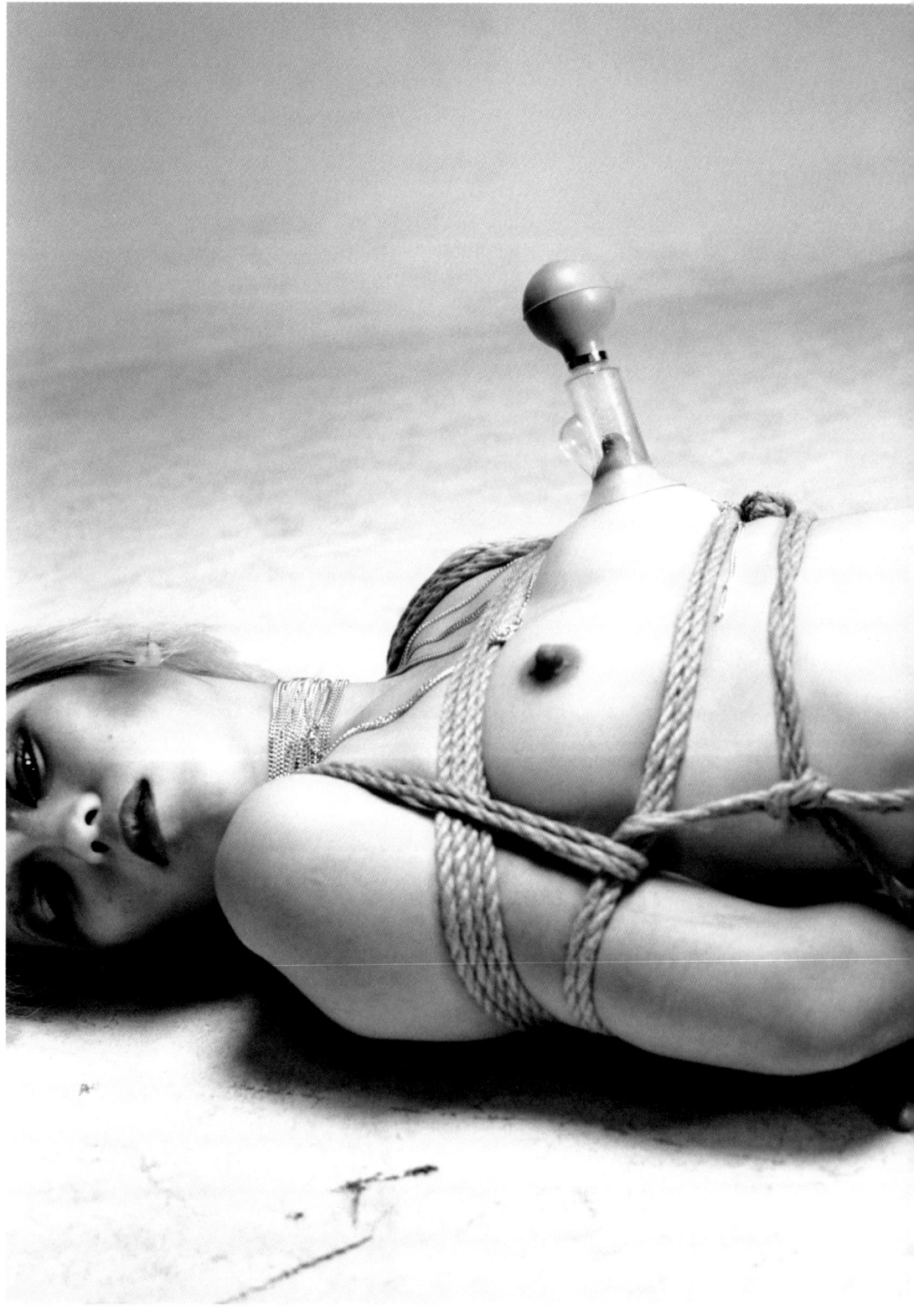

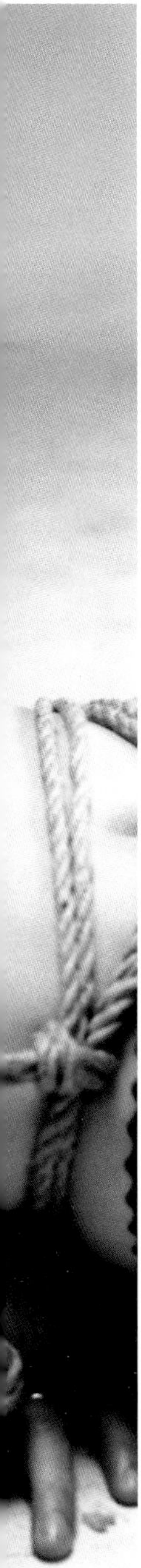
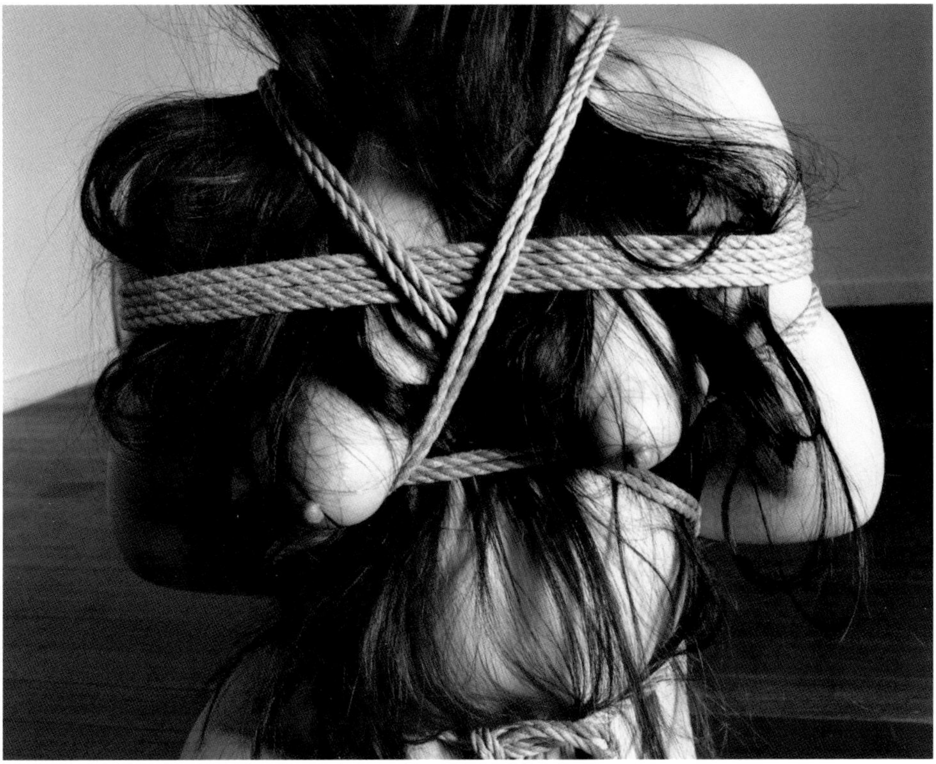
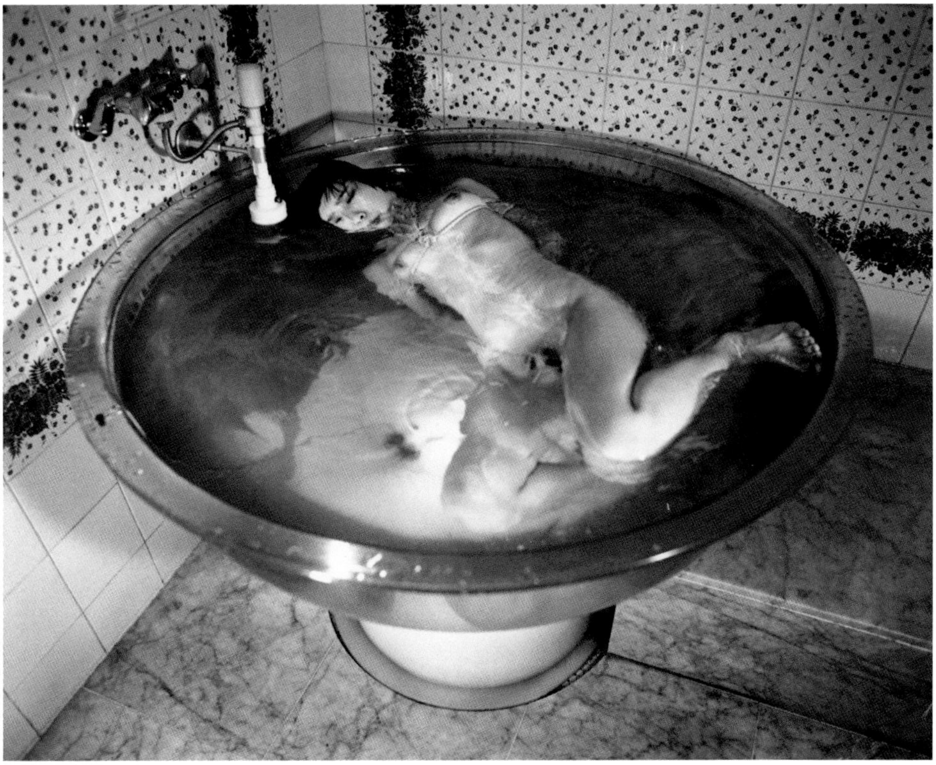

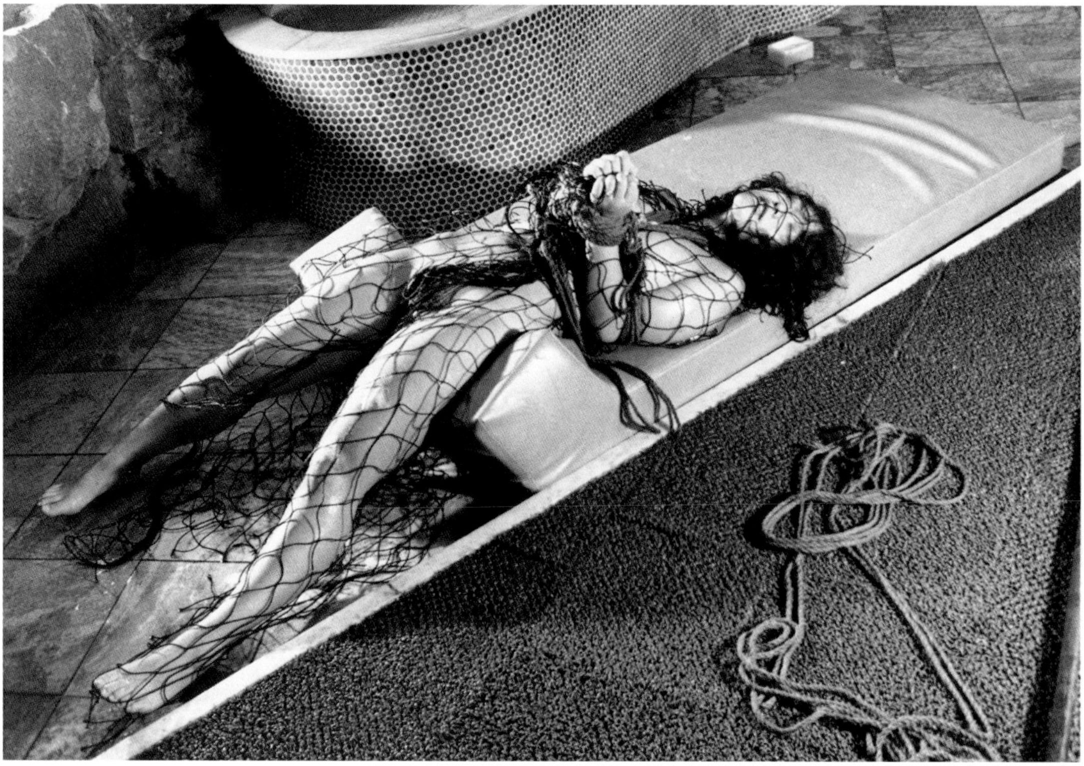

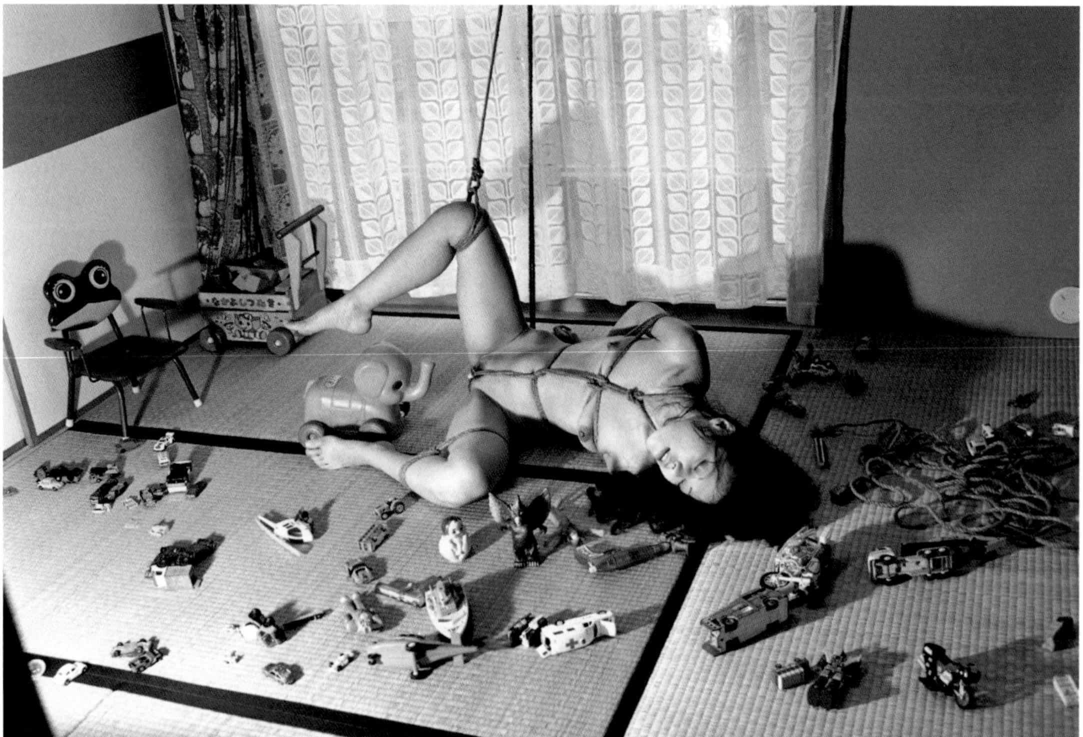

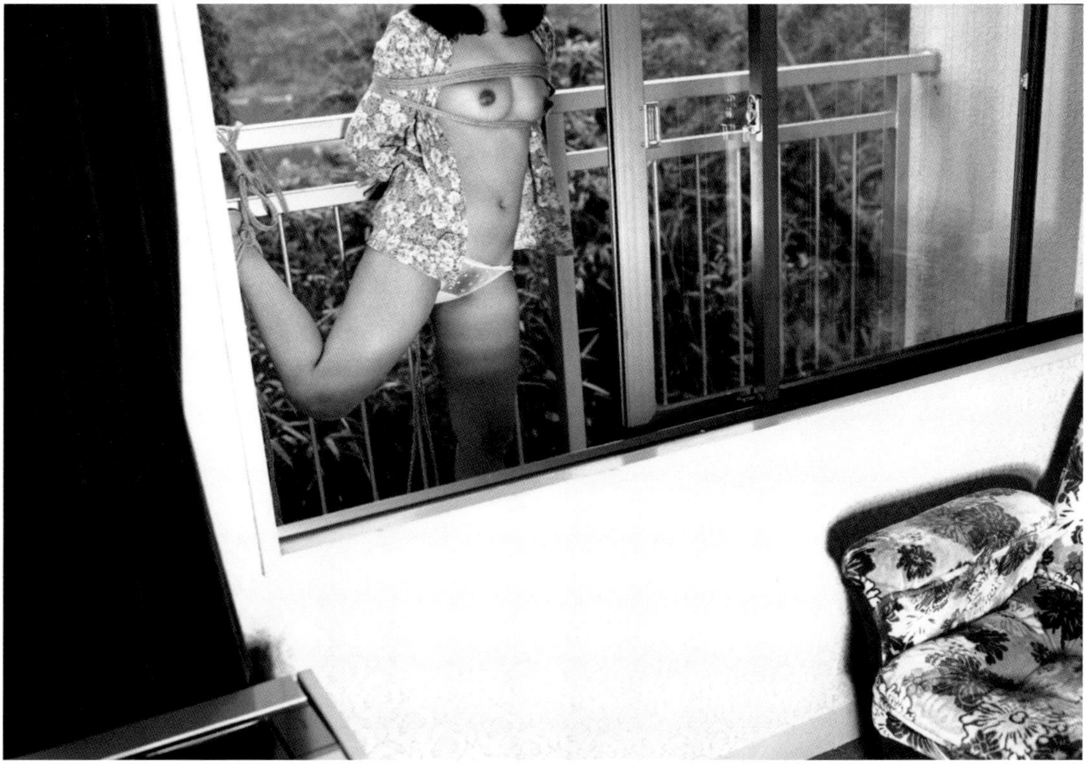

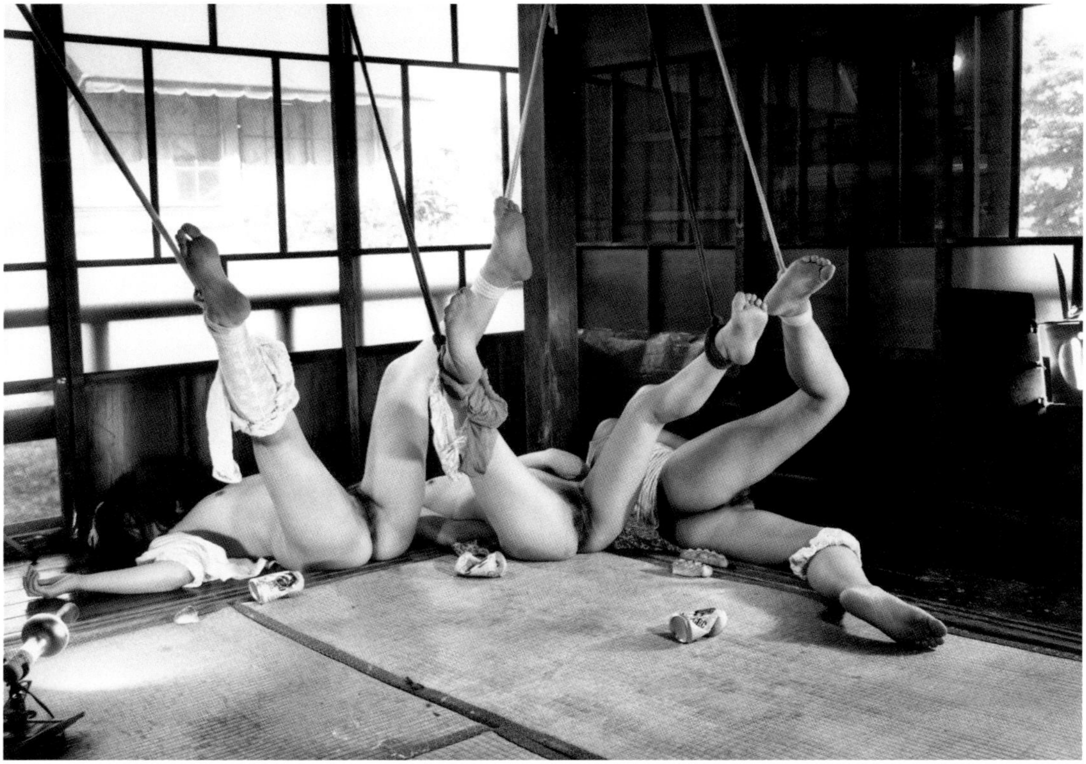

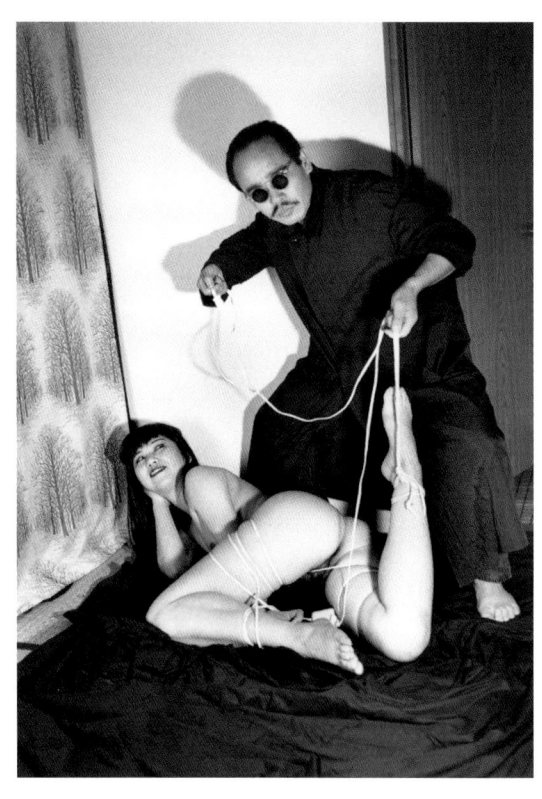
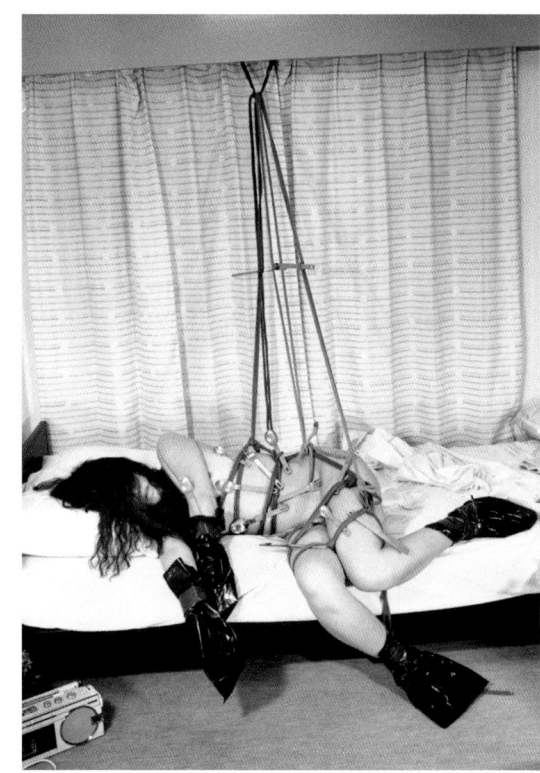
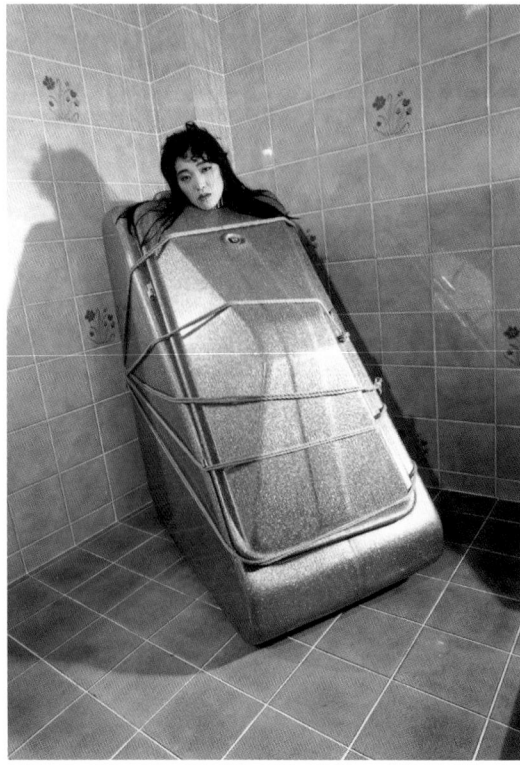
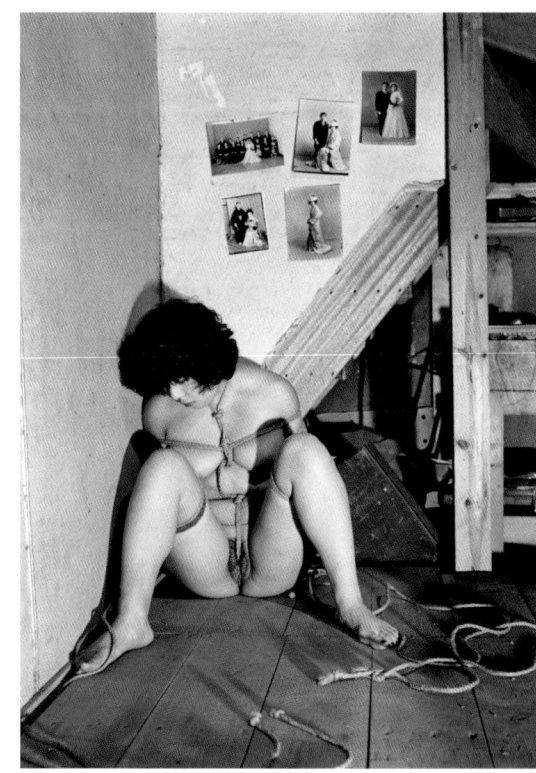

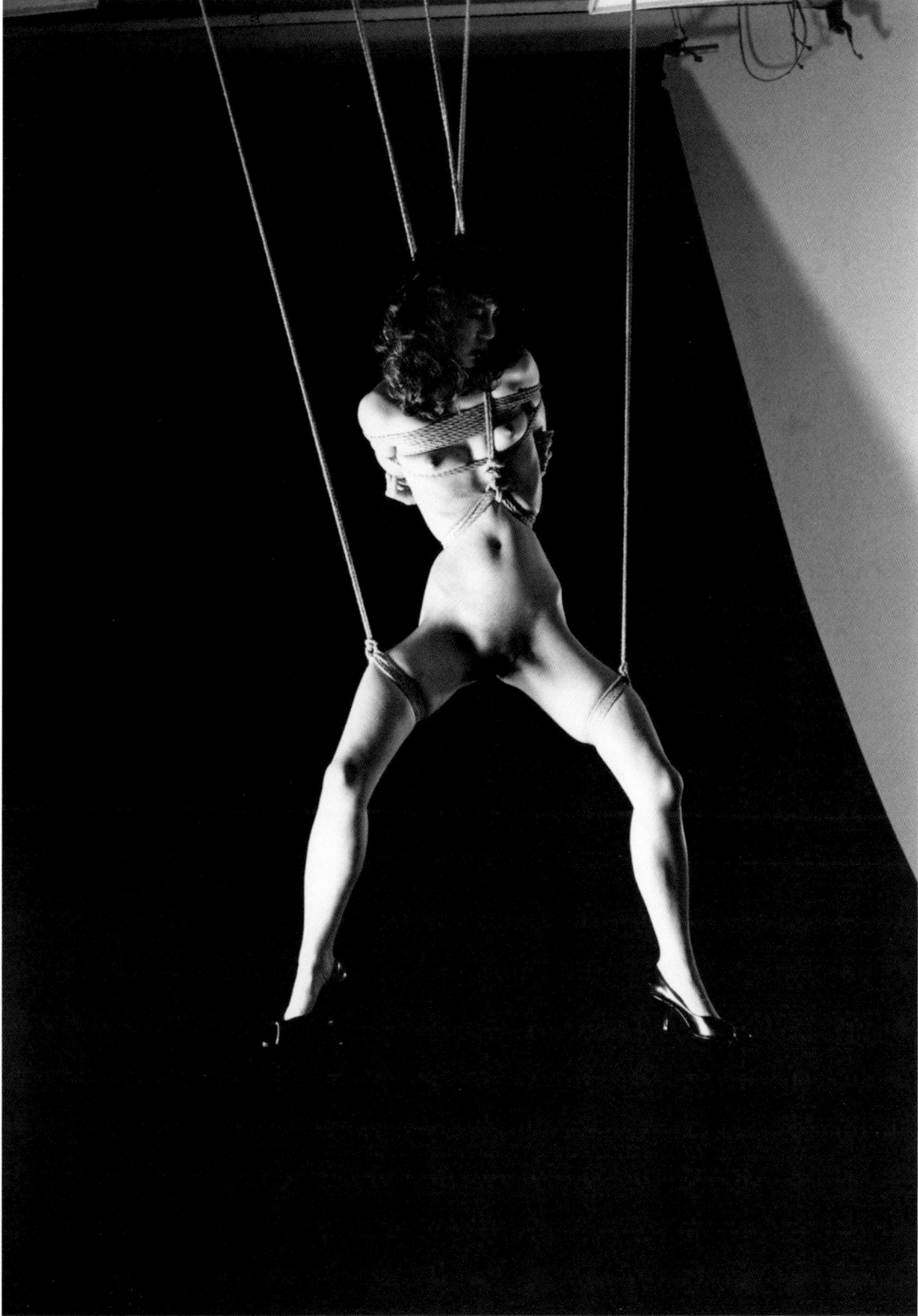

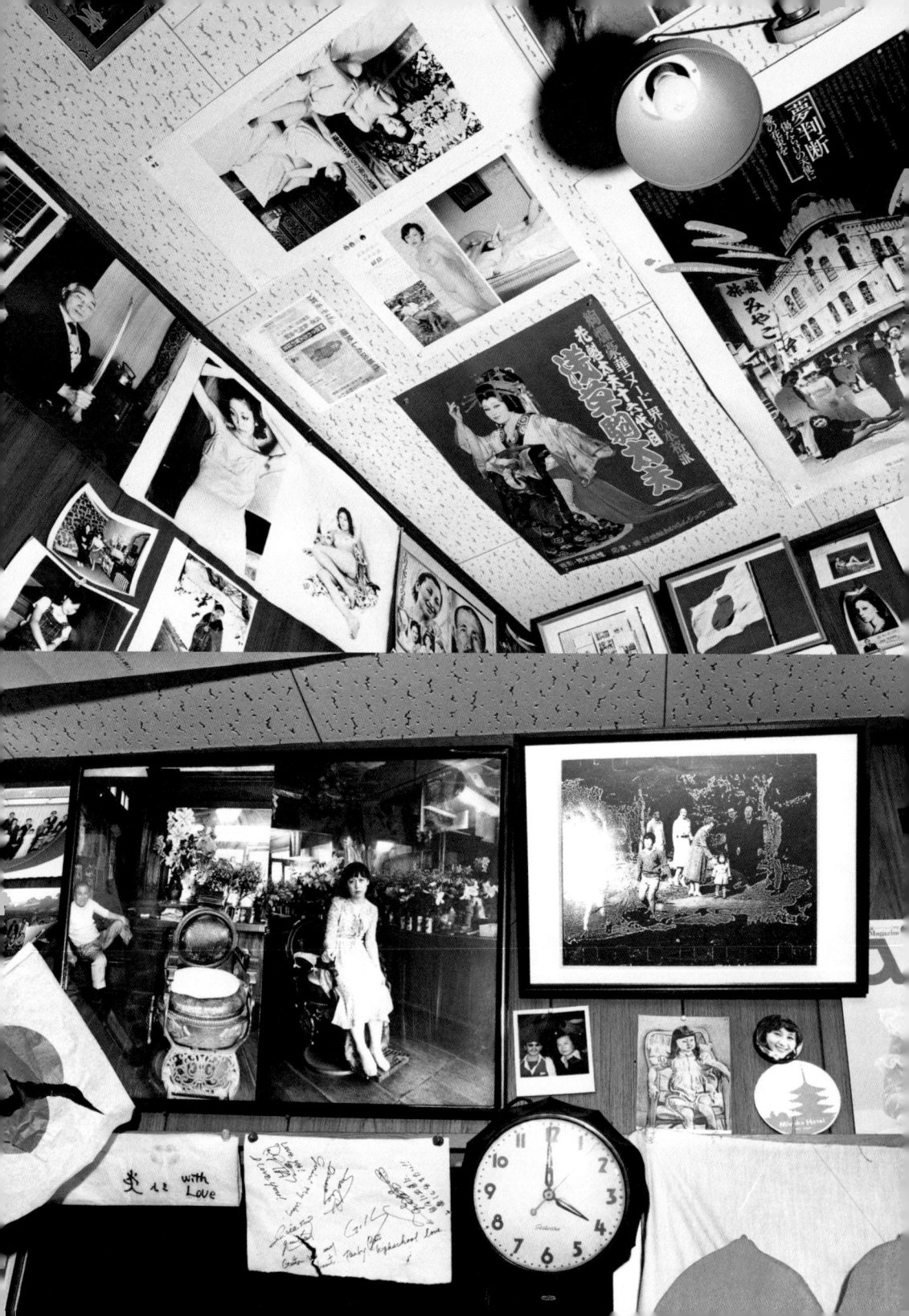

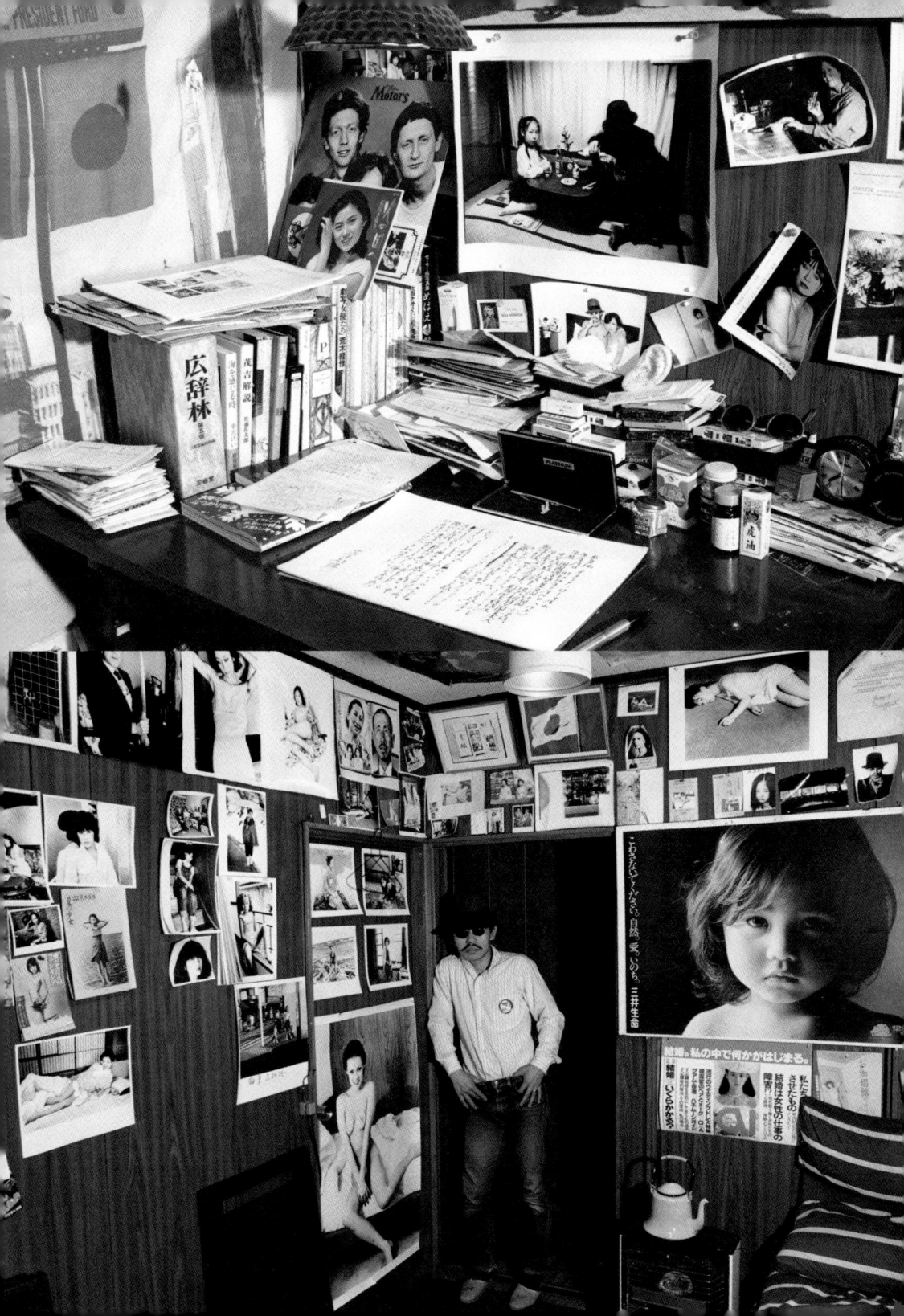

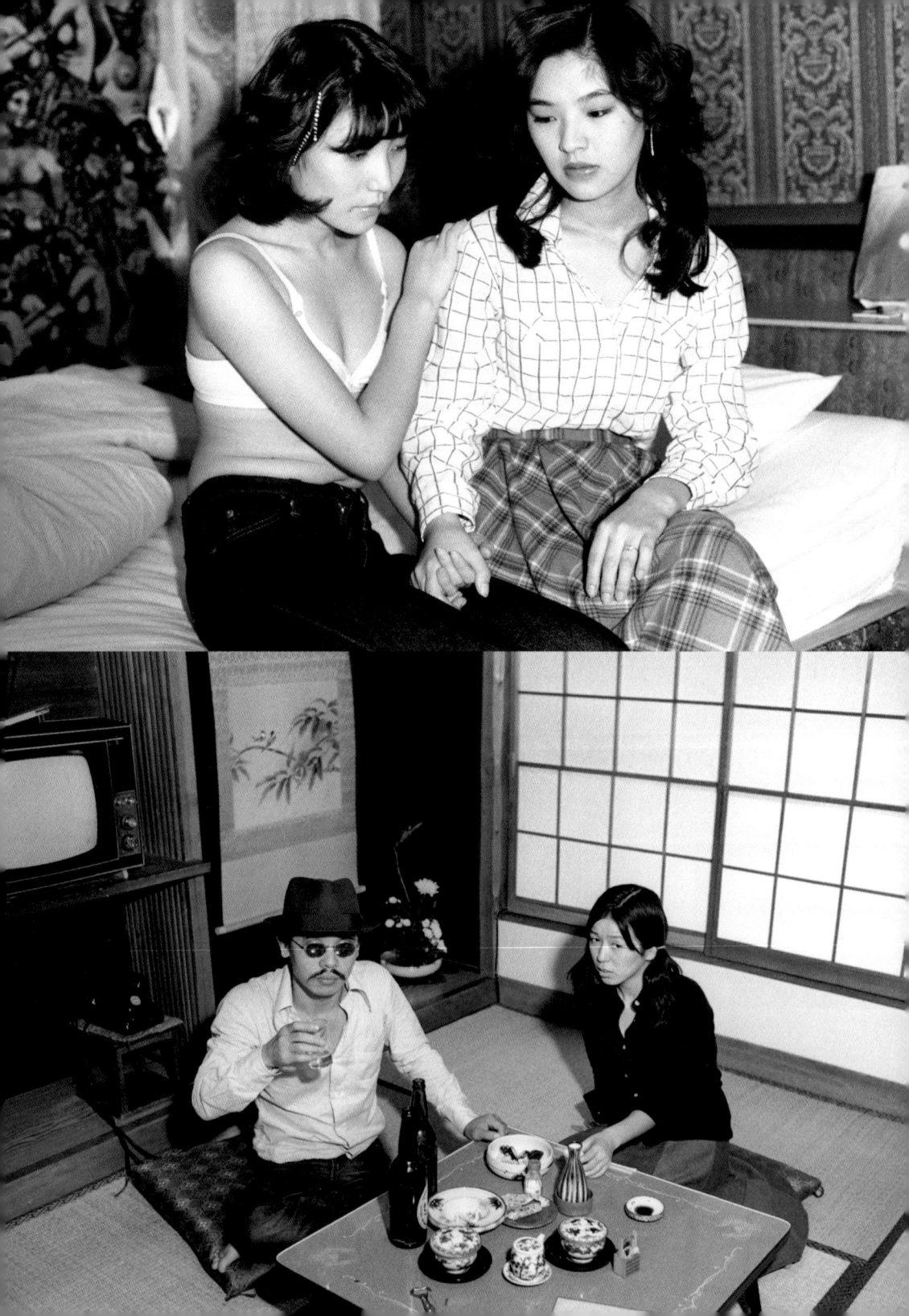

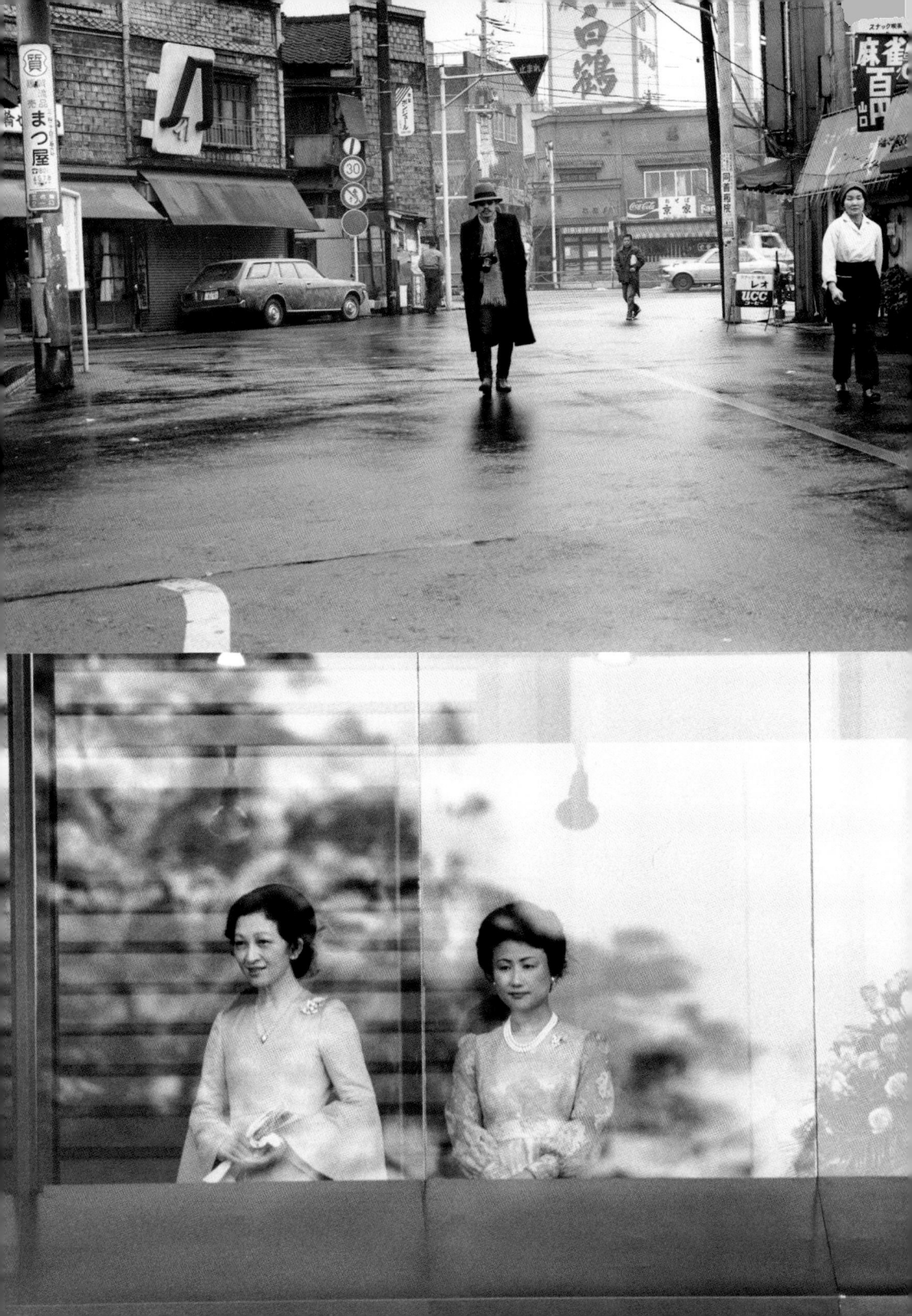

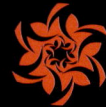

Flower Rondo

花曲

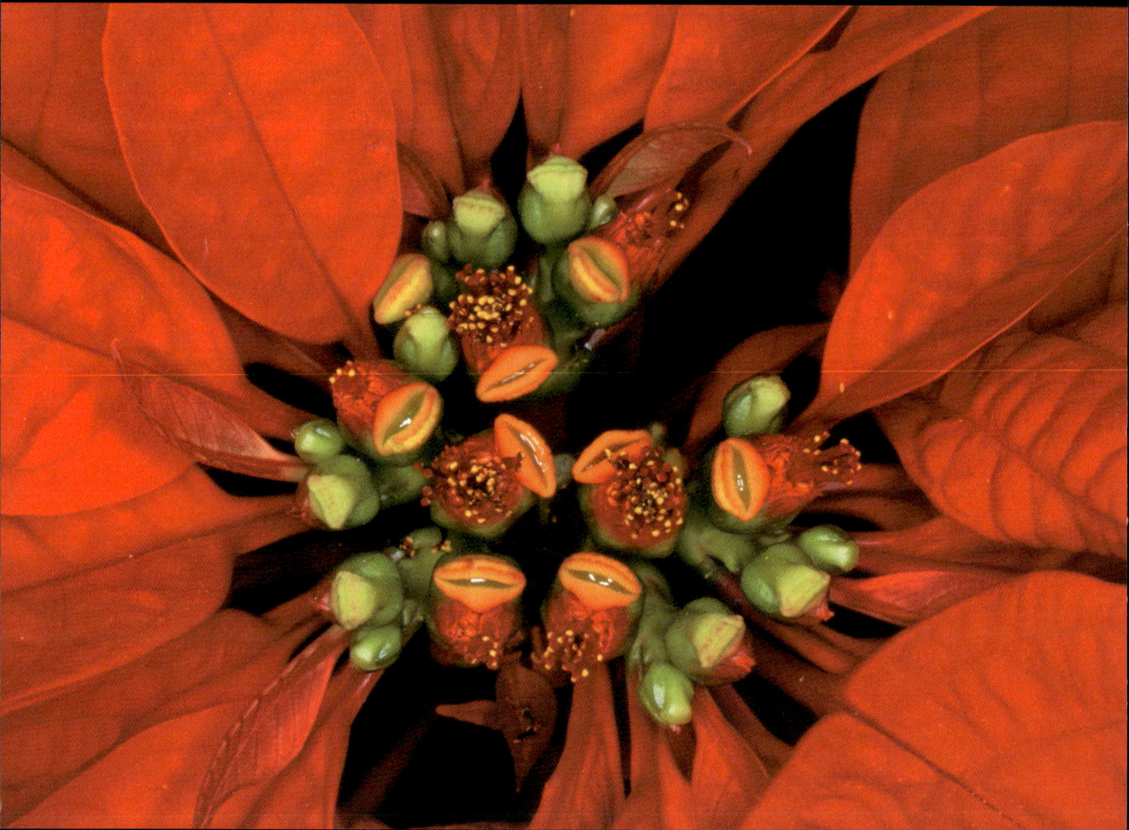

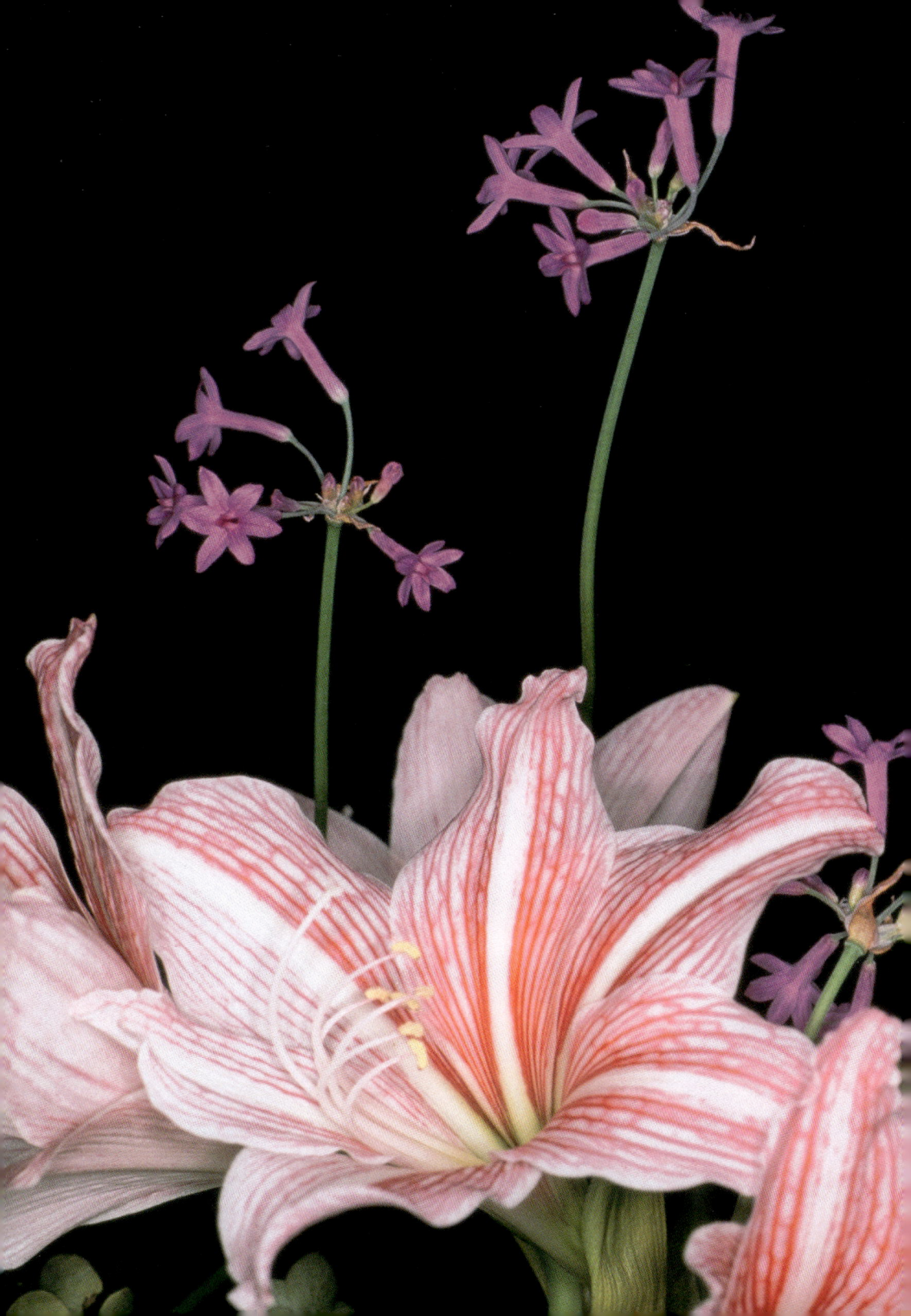

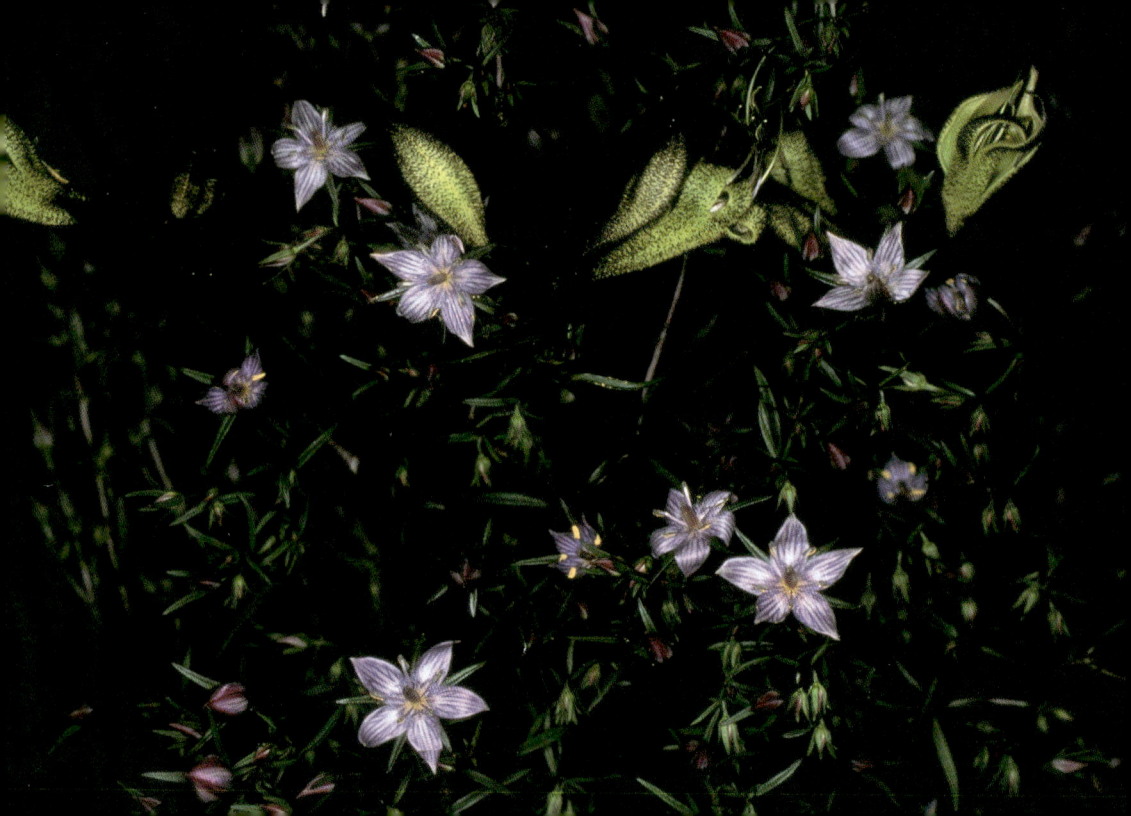

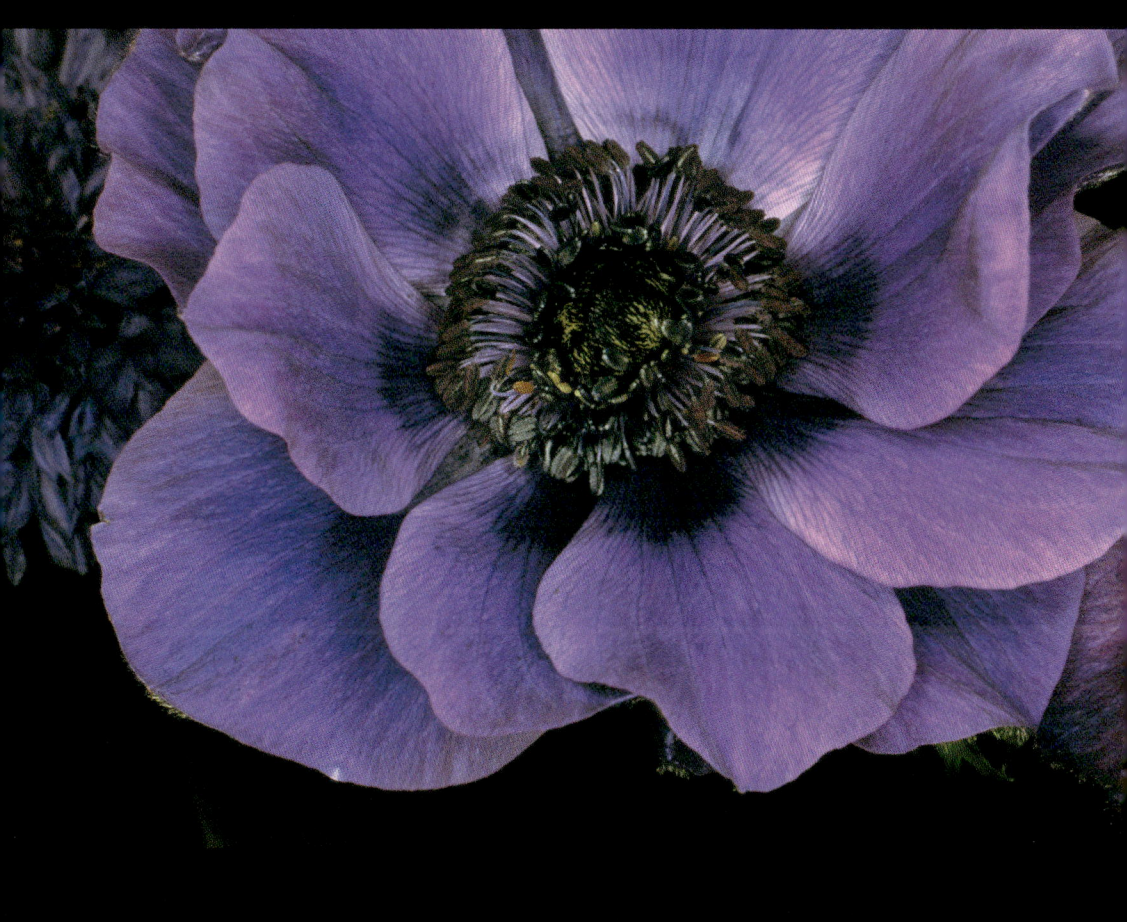

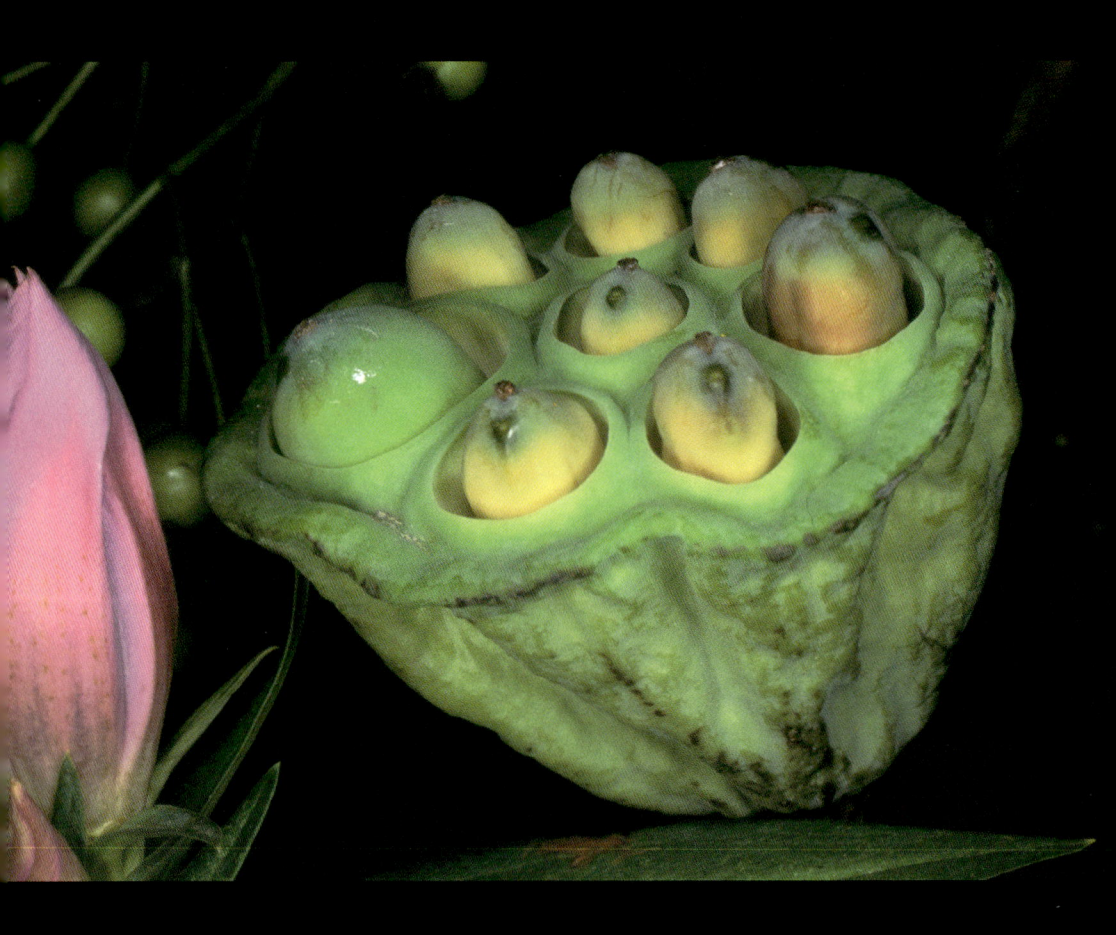

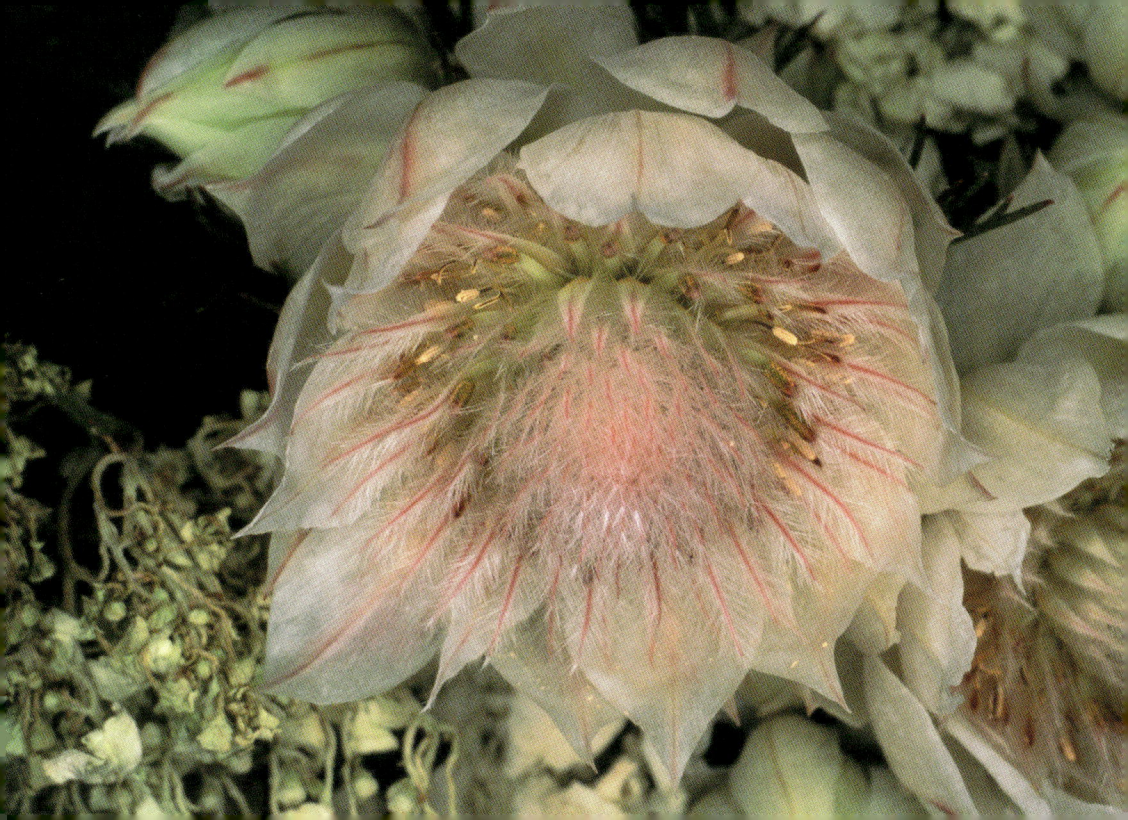

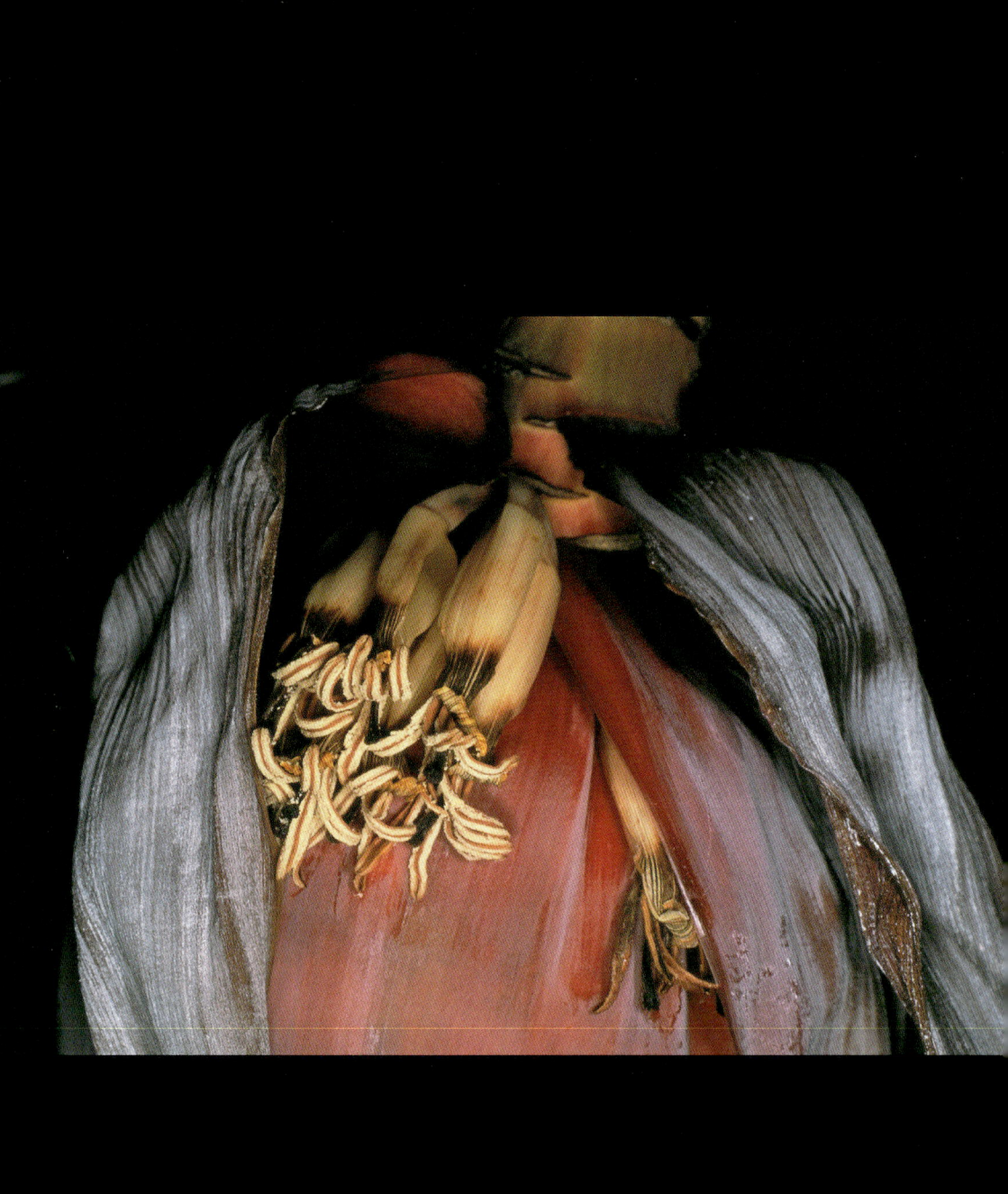

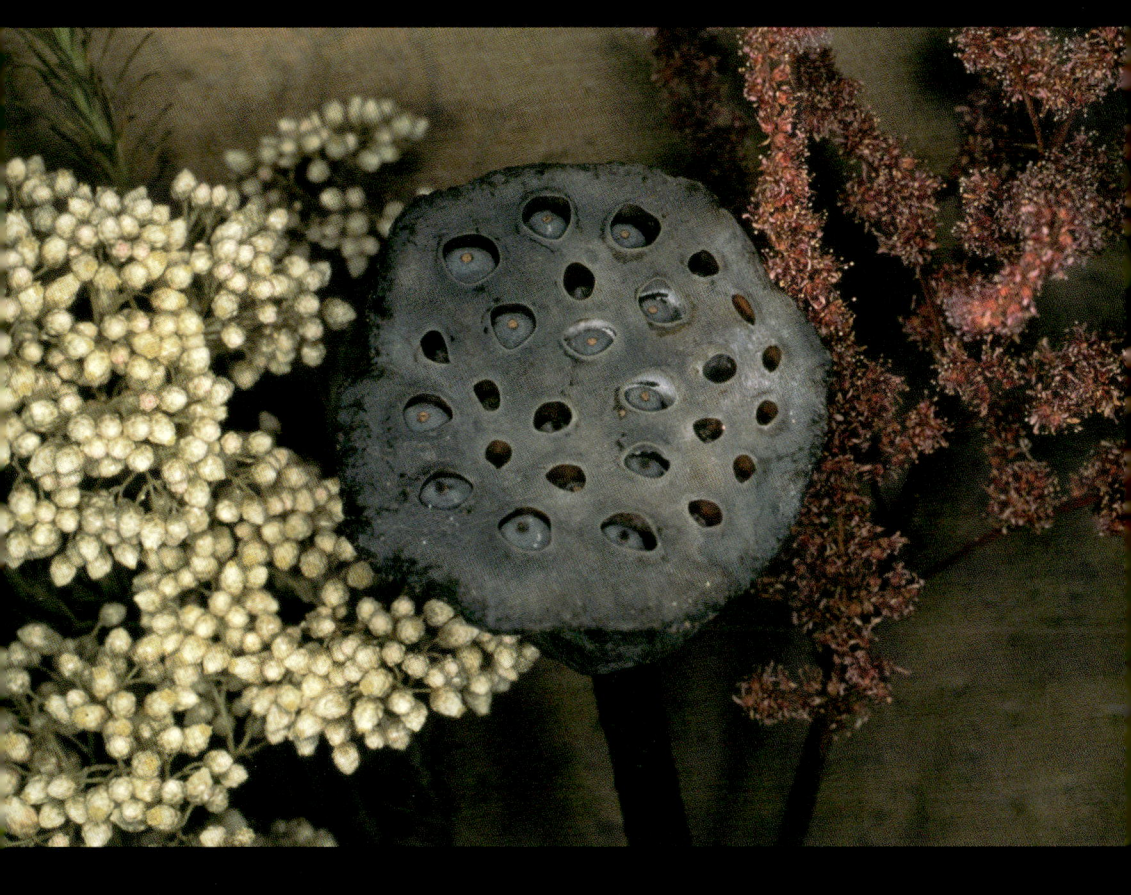

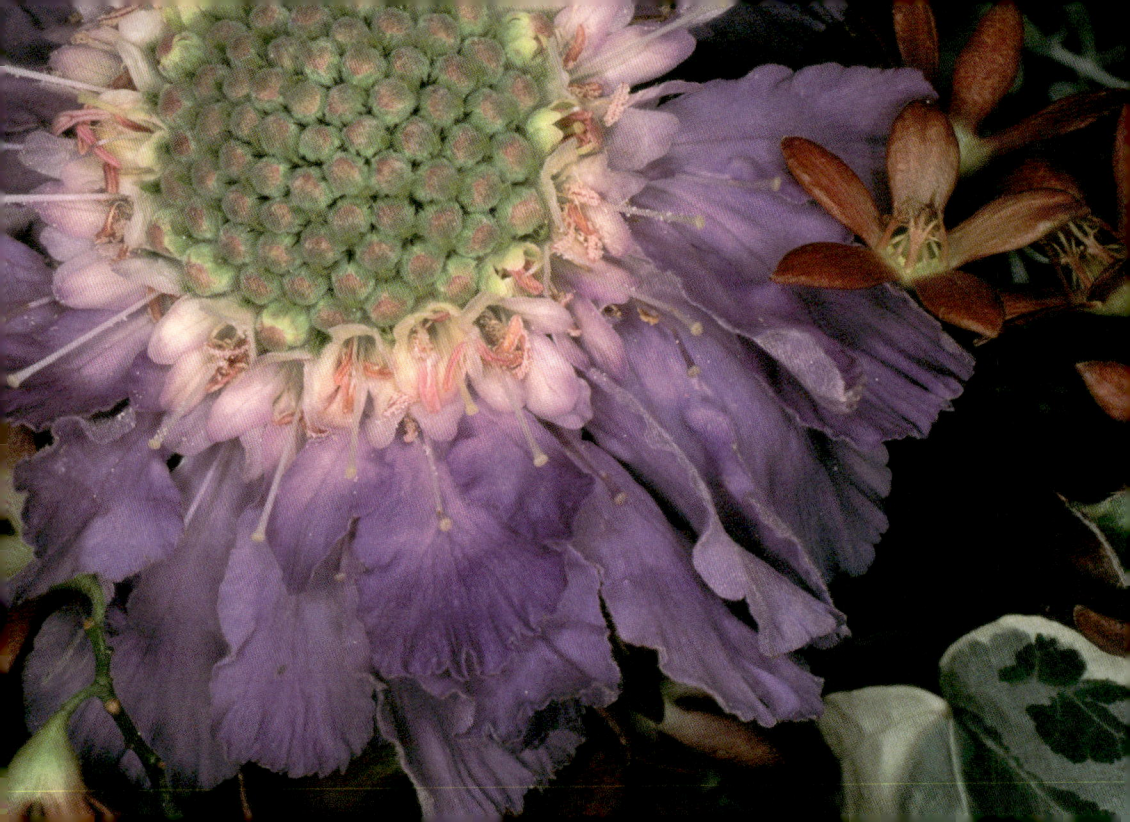

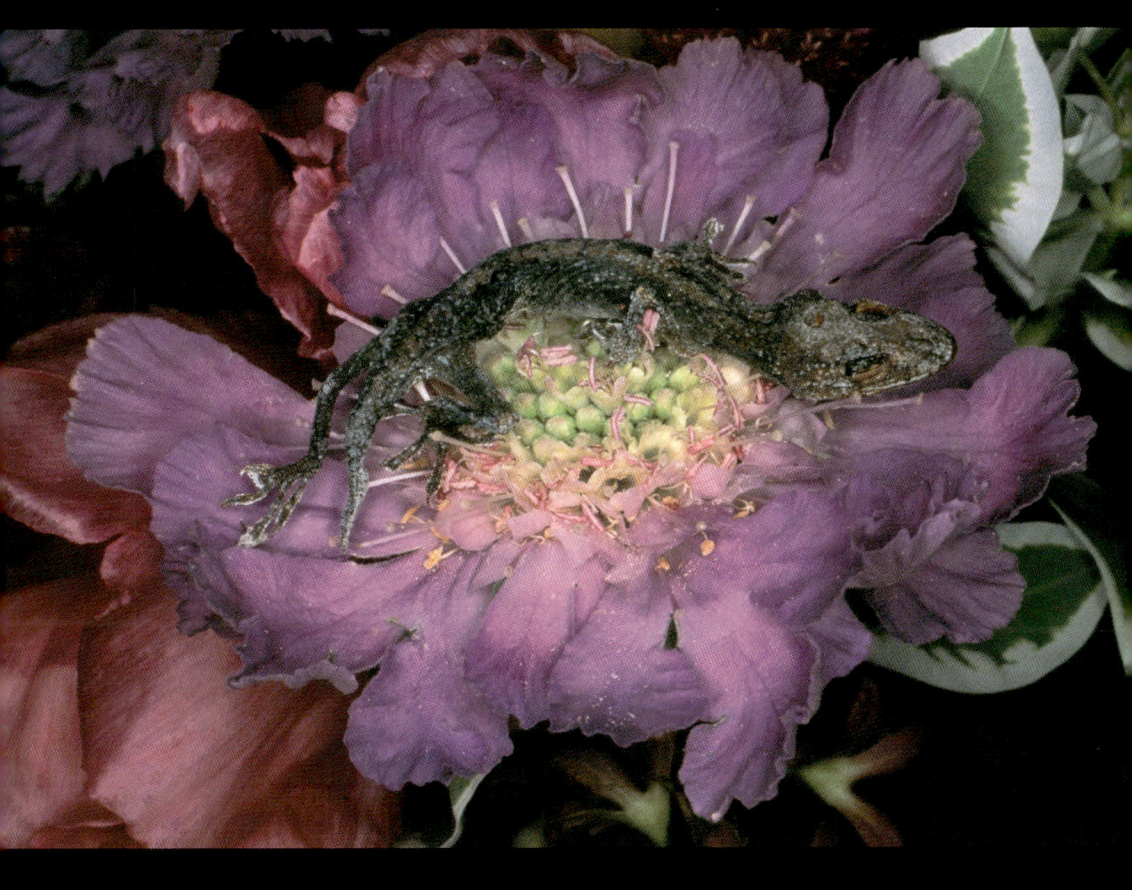

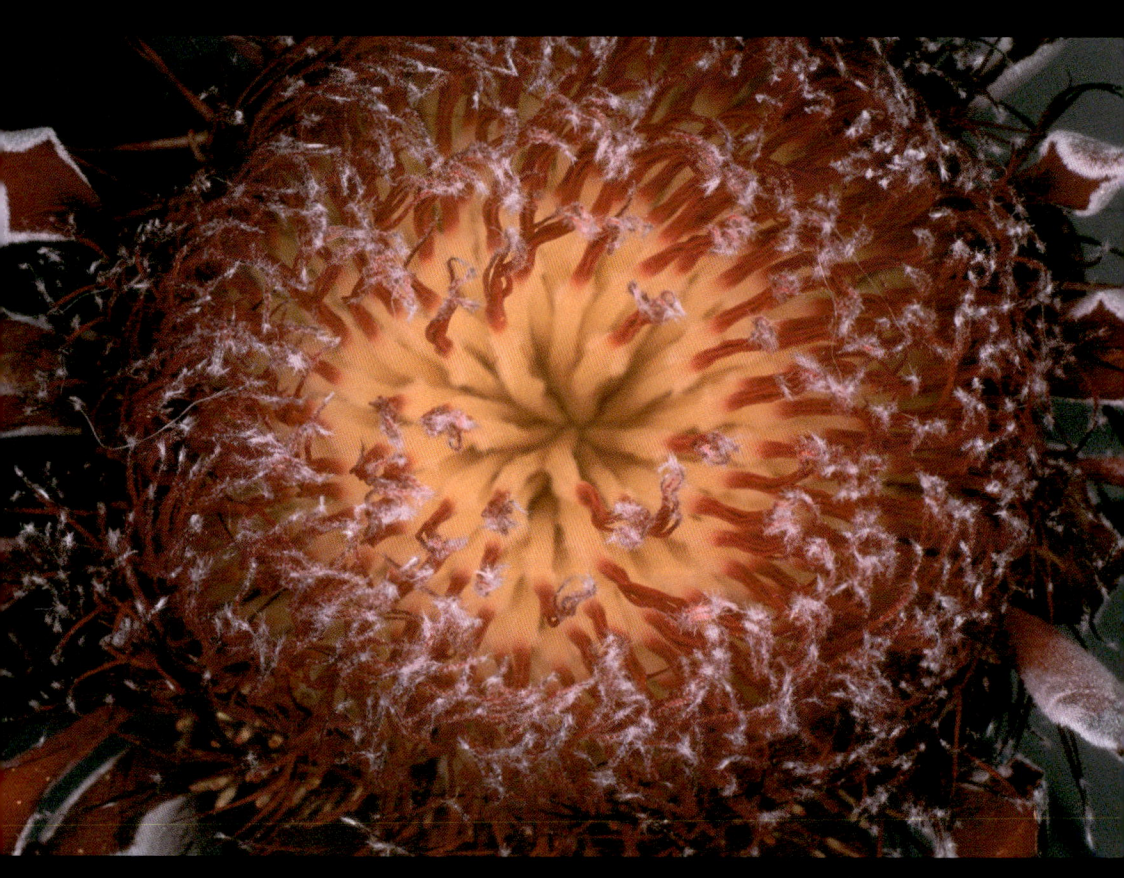

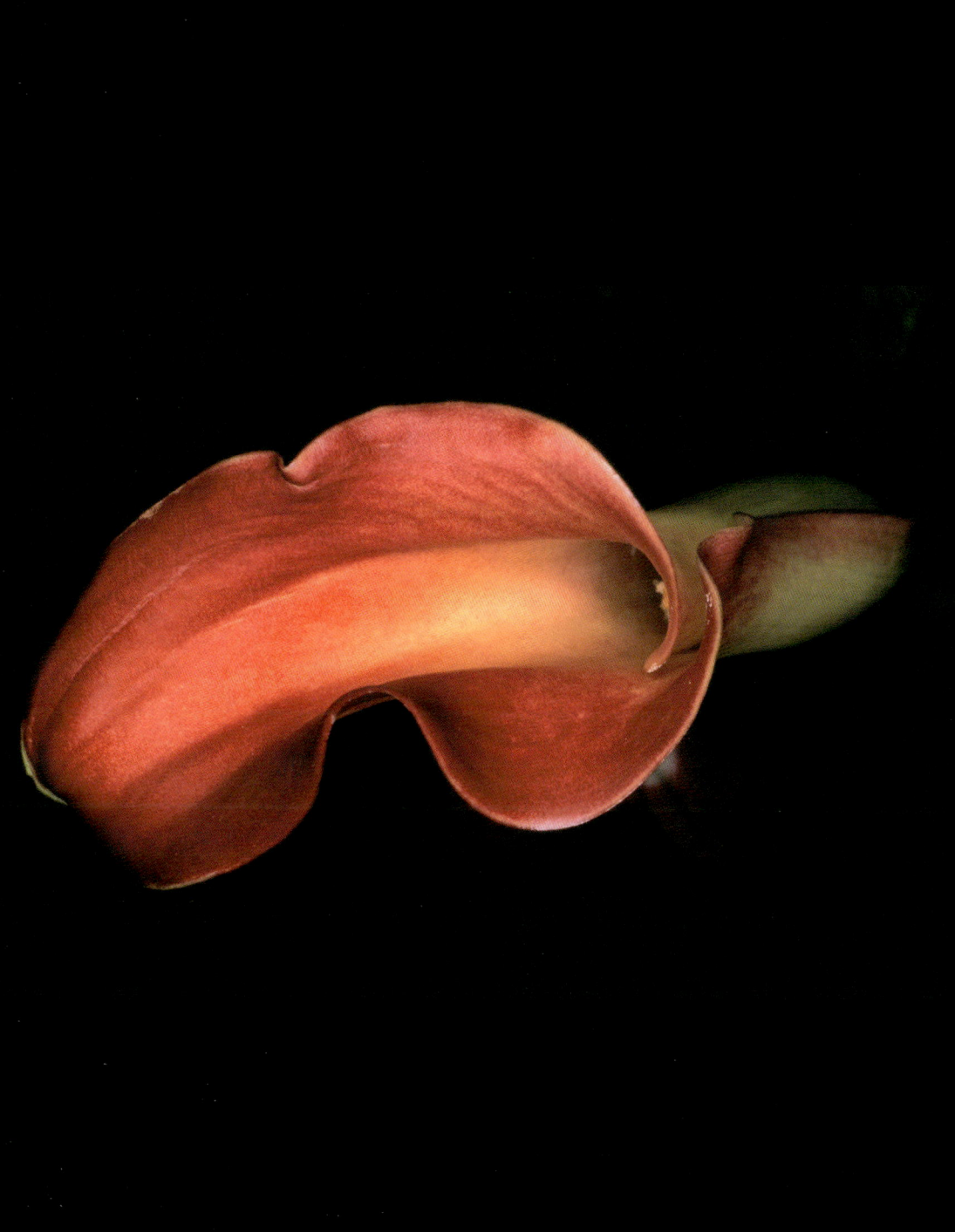

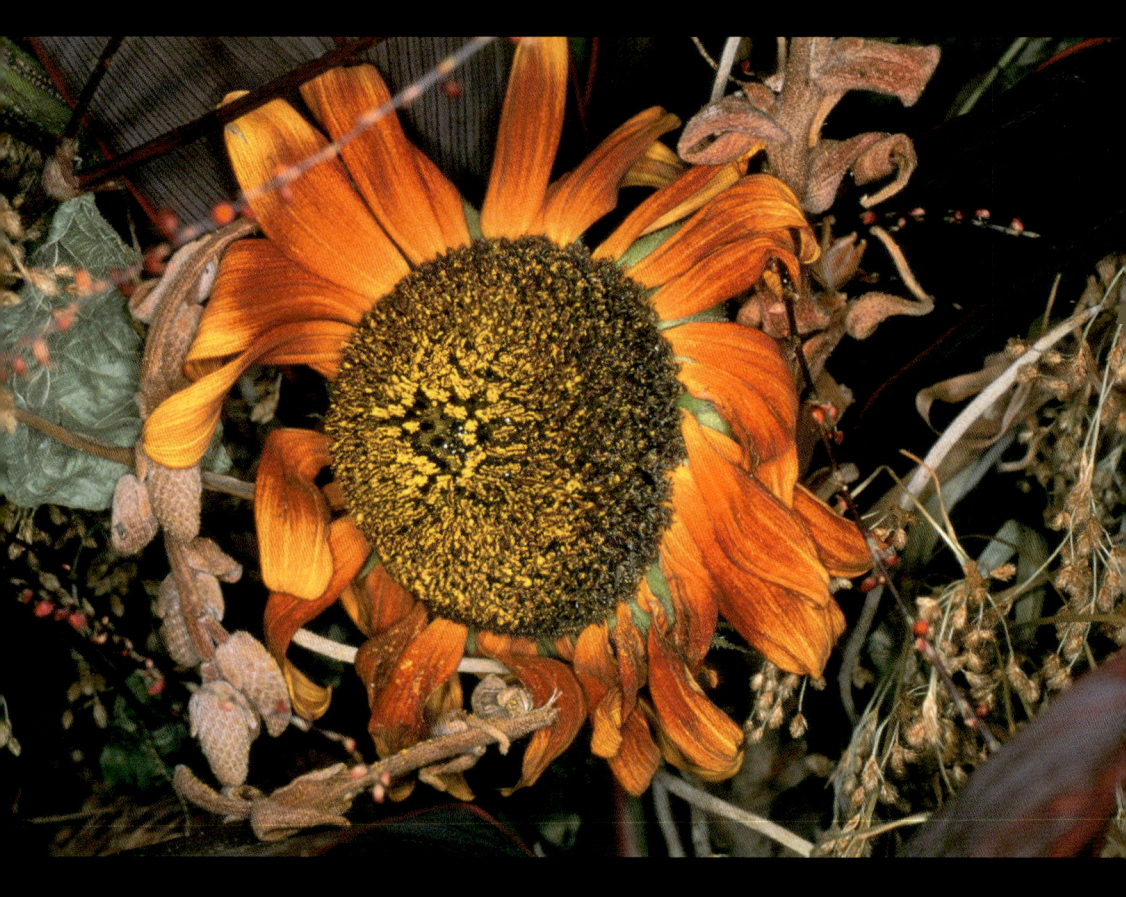

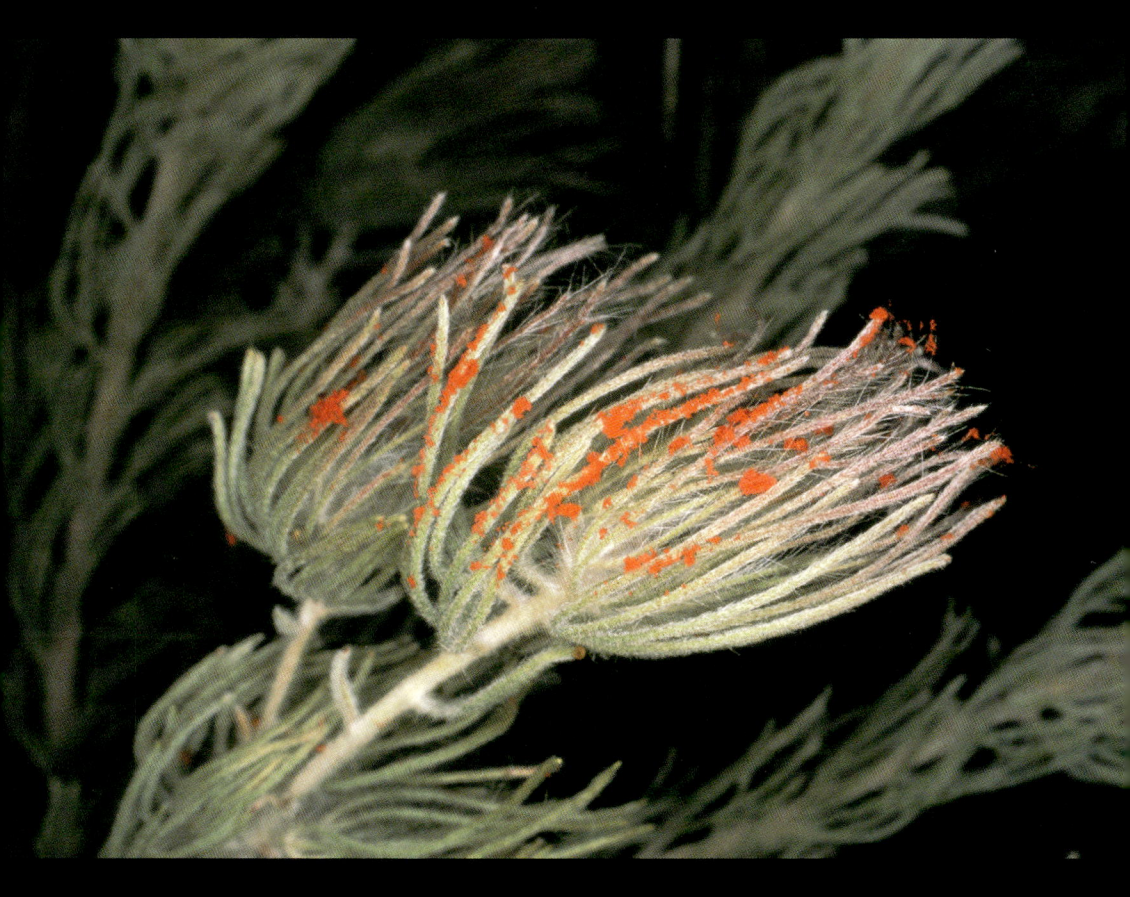

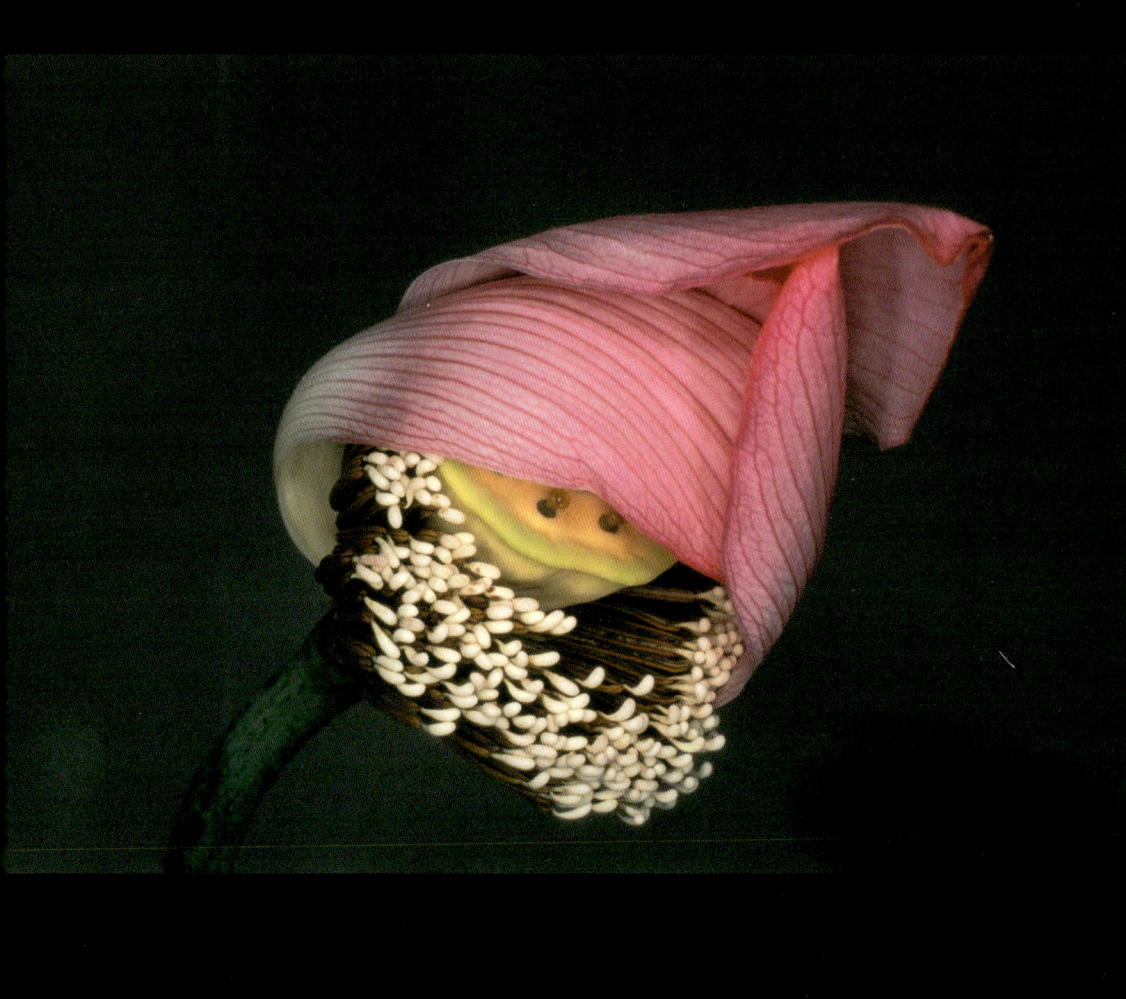

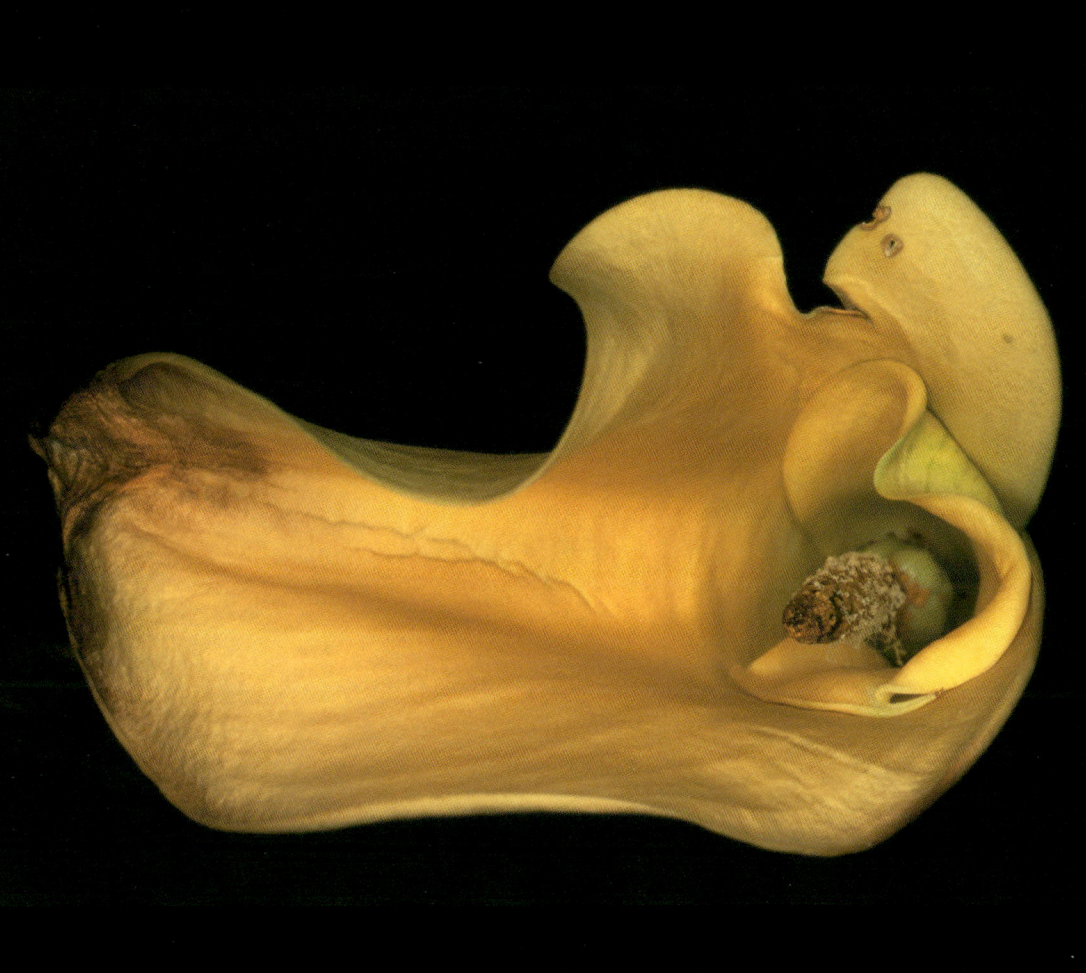

Private Photography

私写真

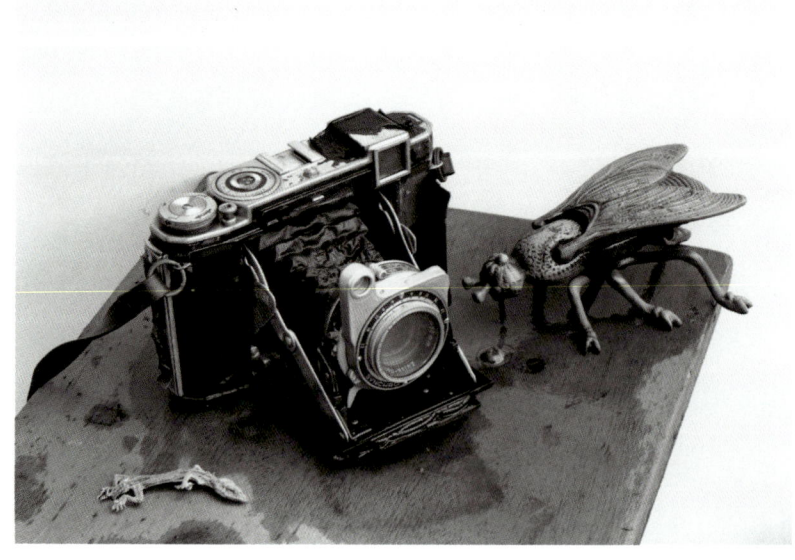

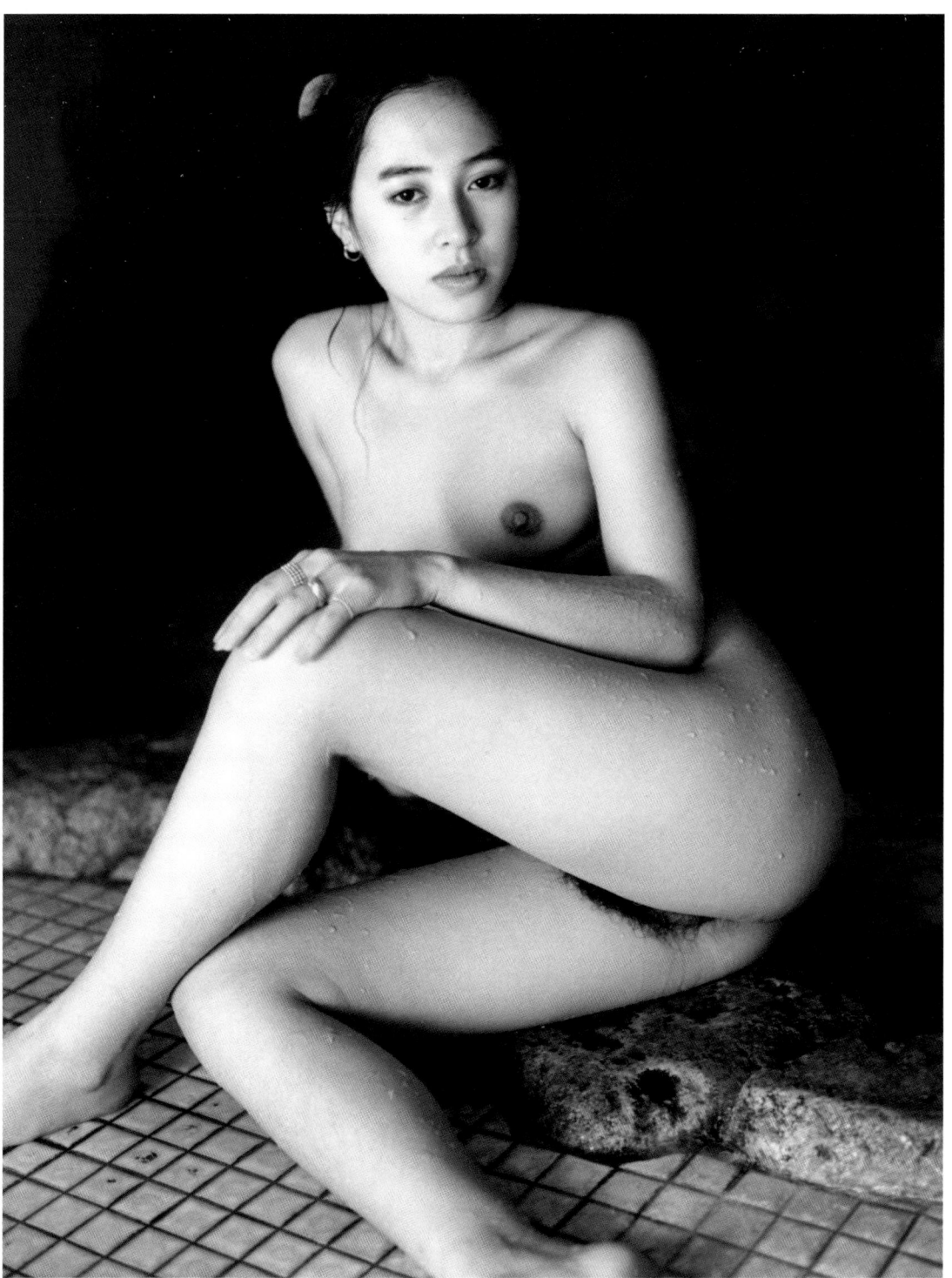

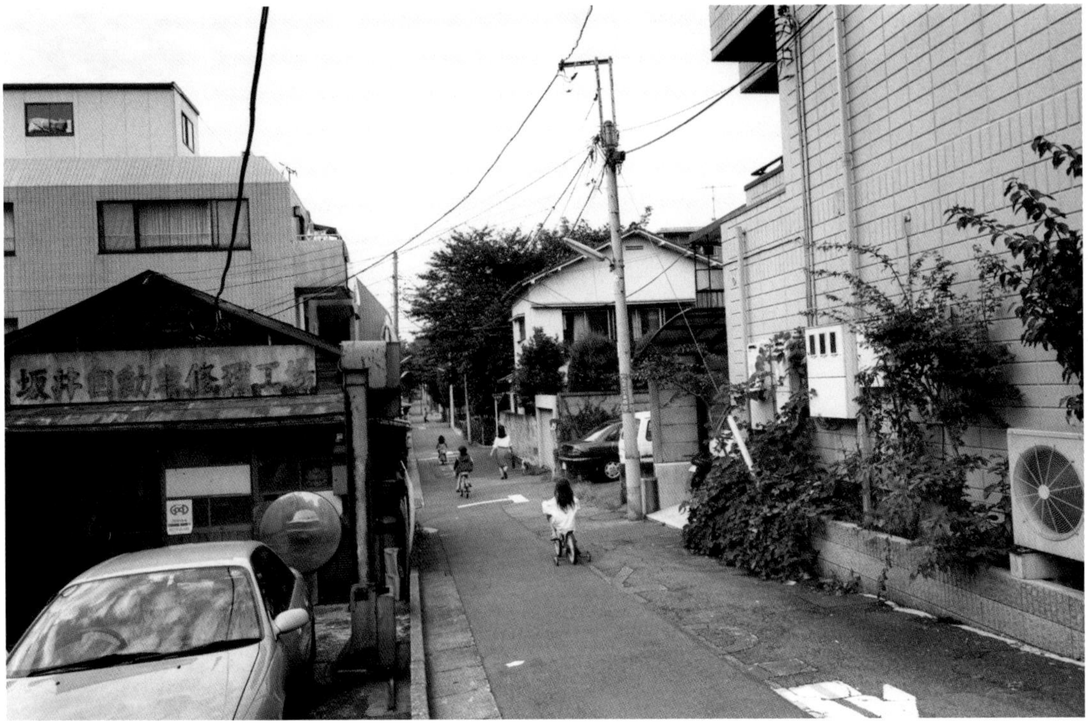
坂井自動車修理工

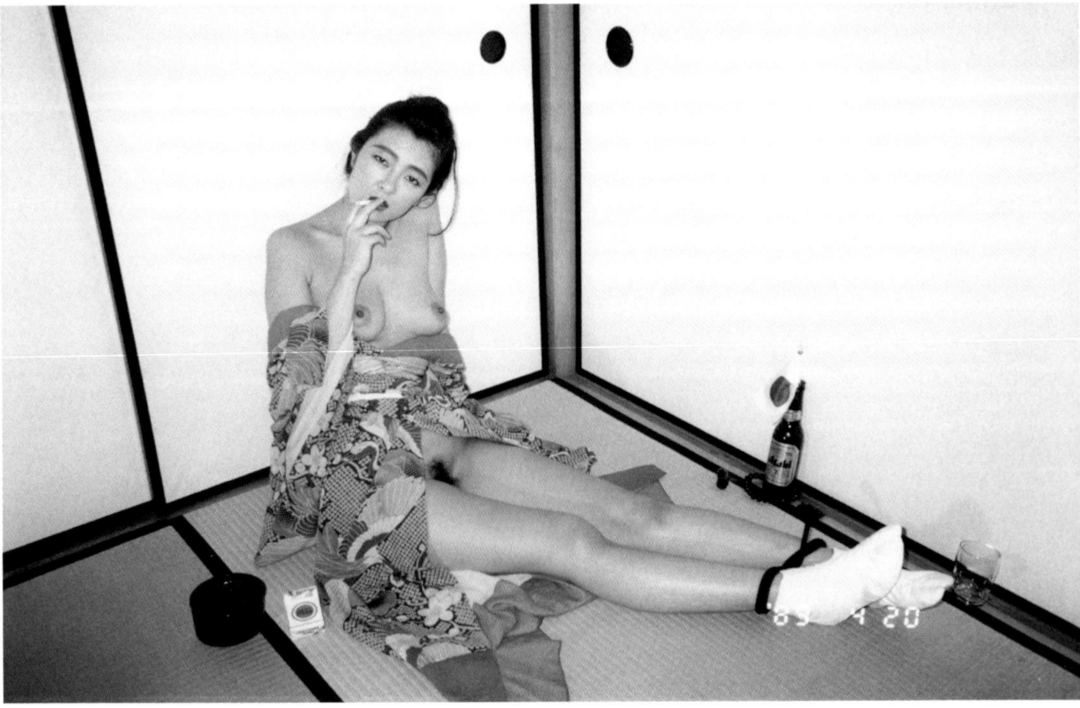

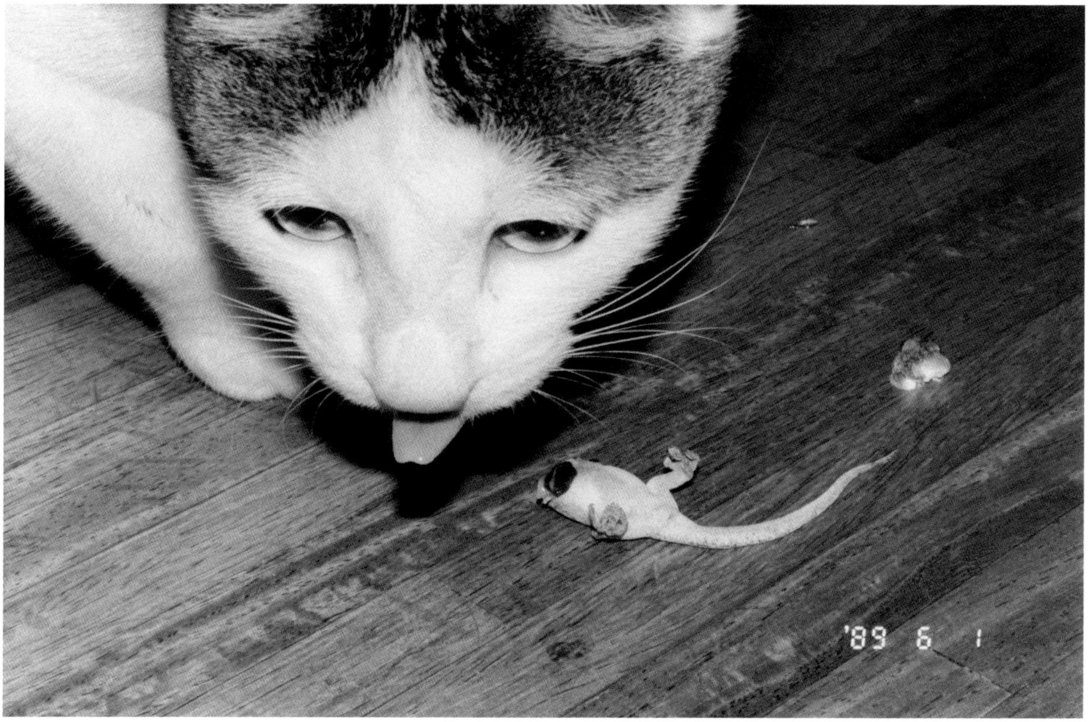
'89 6 1

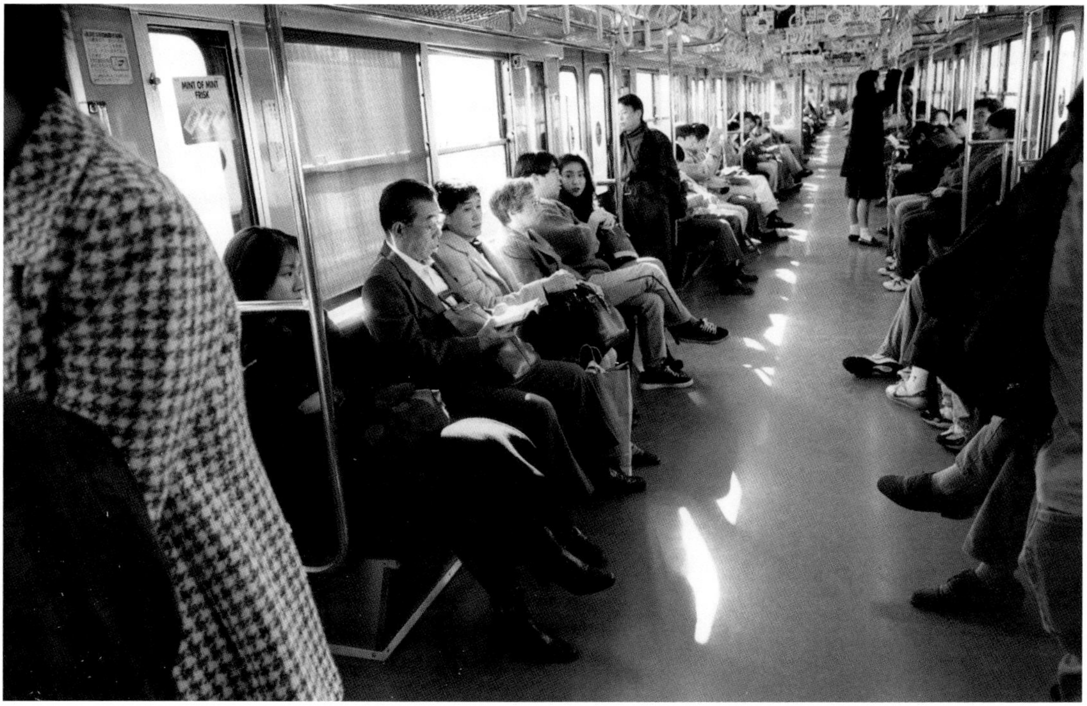
MINT OF MINT
FRISK

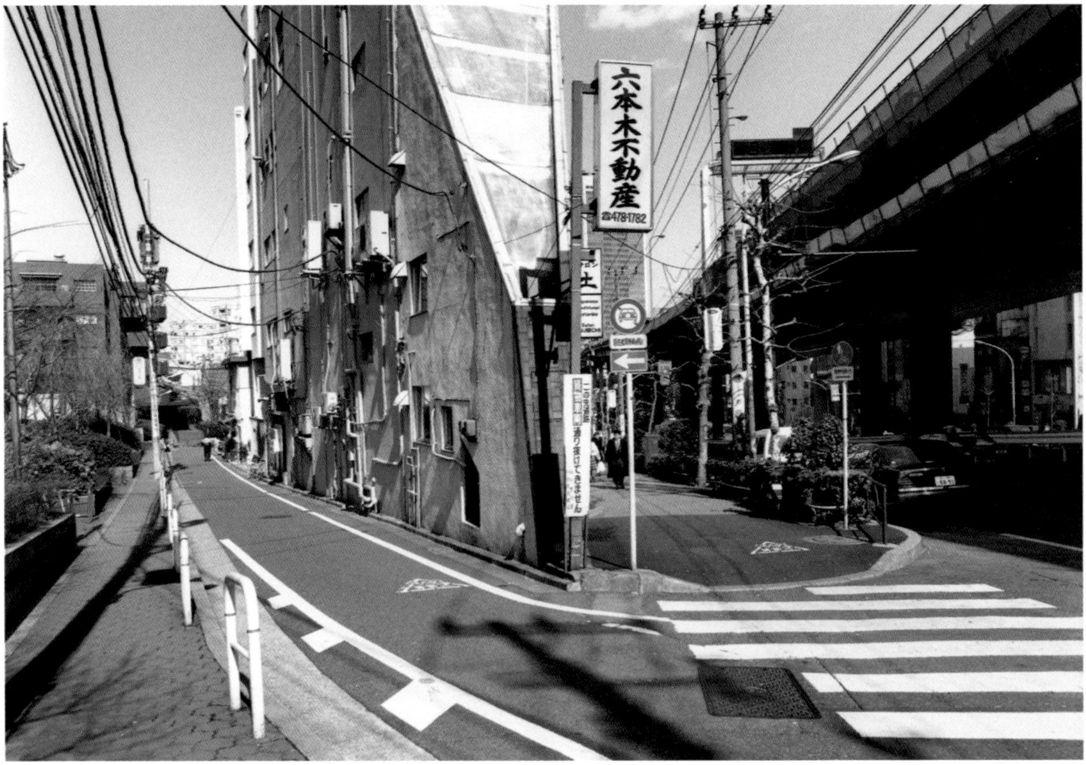
六本木不動産
478-1782

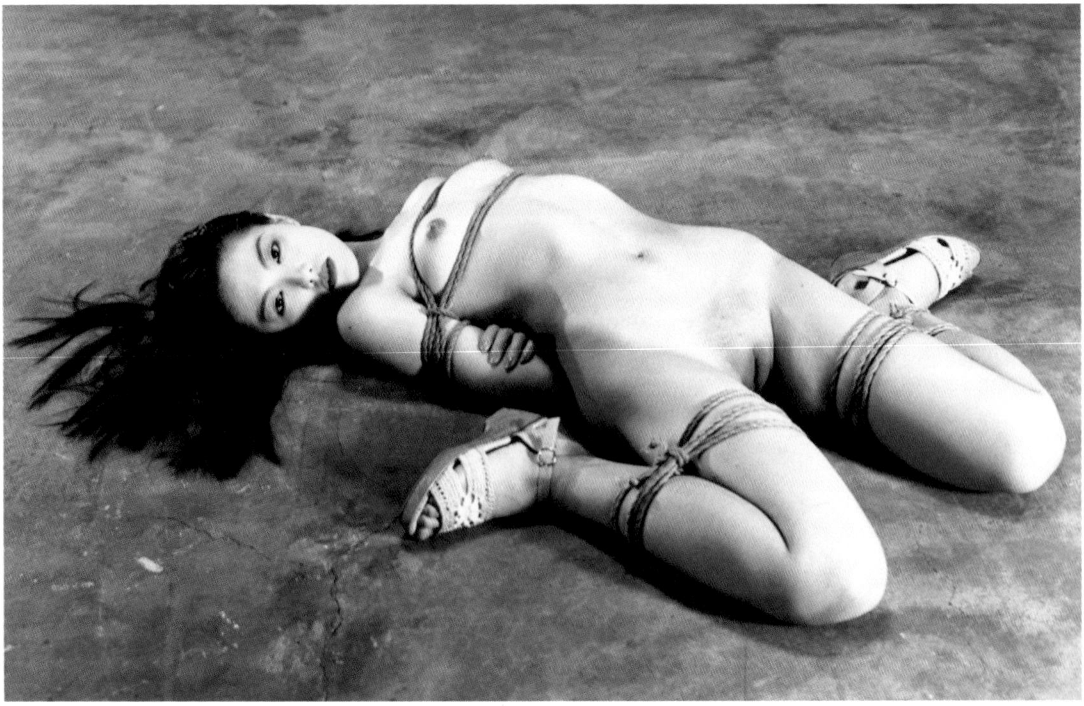

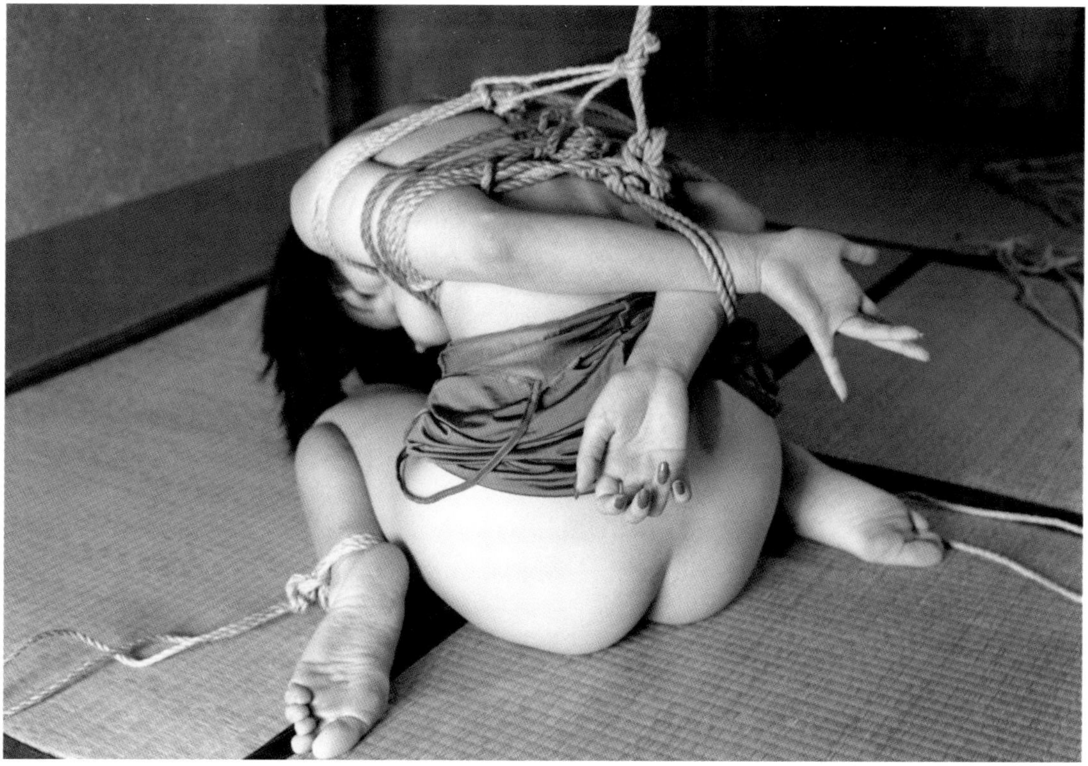

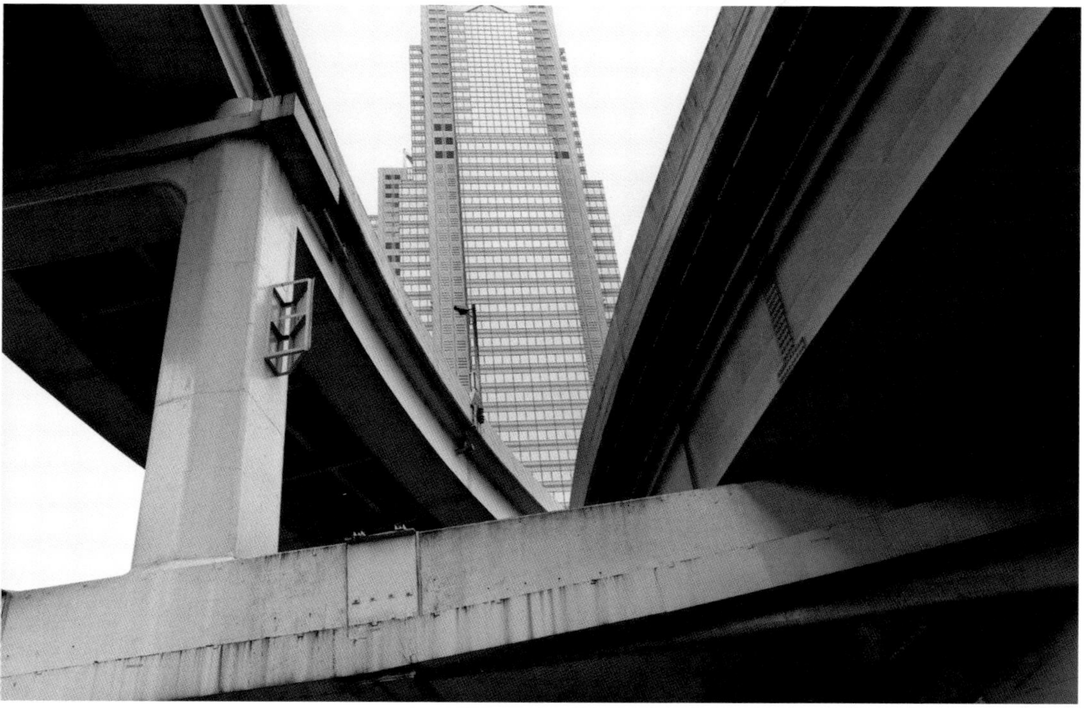

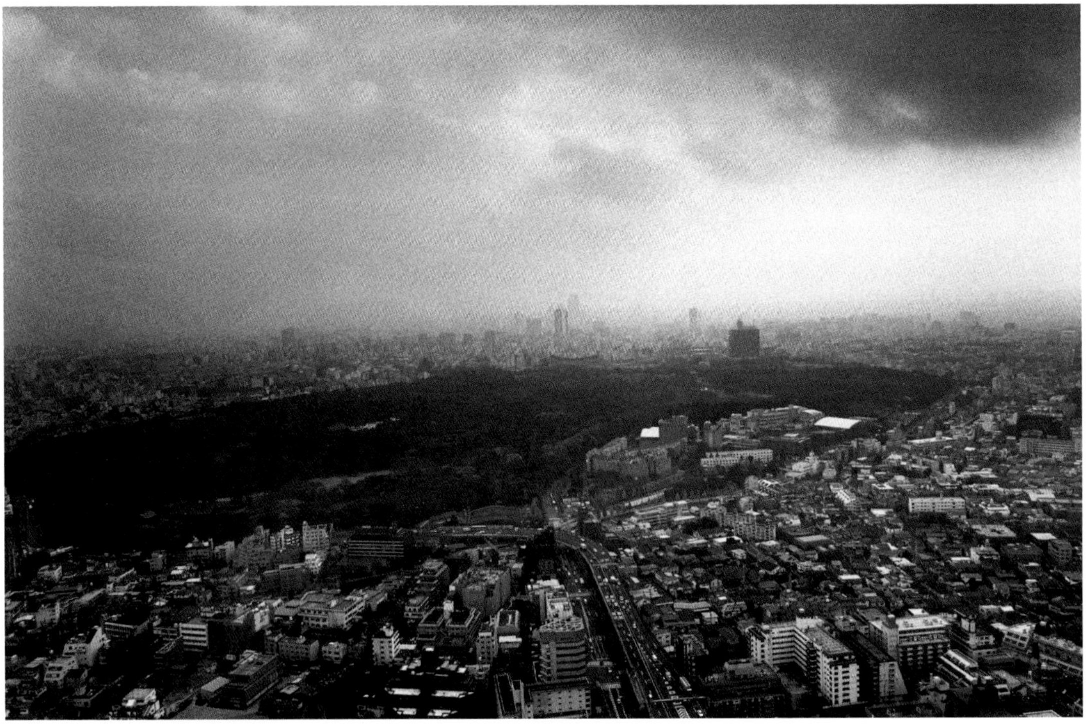

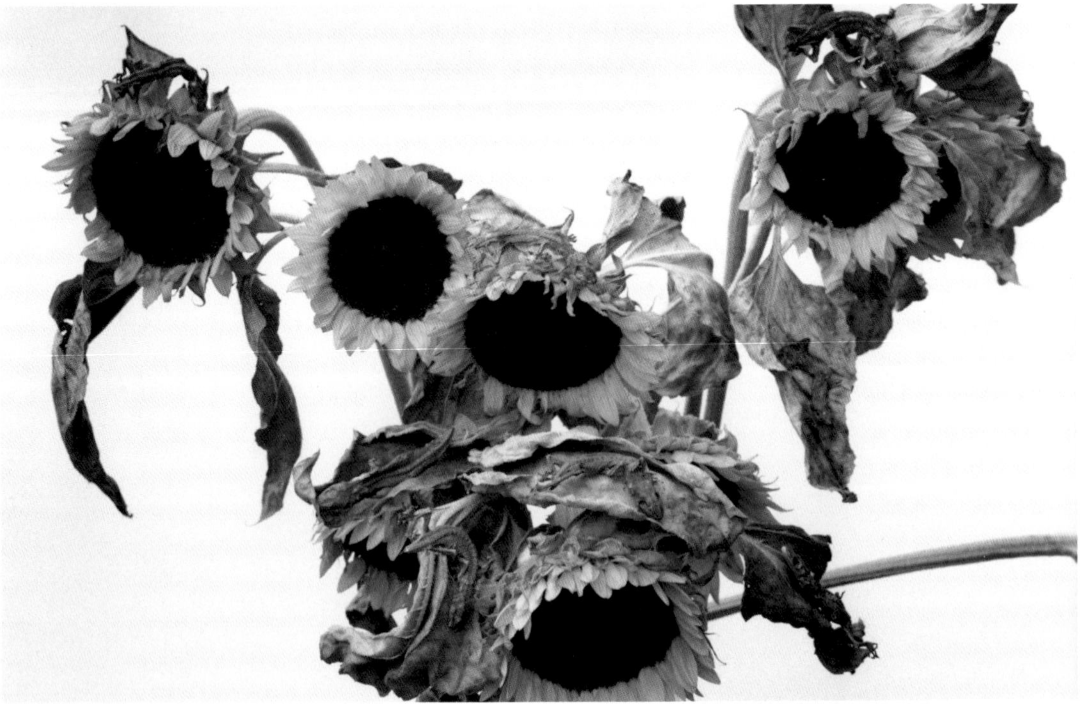

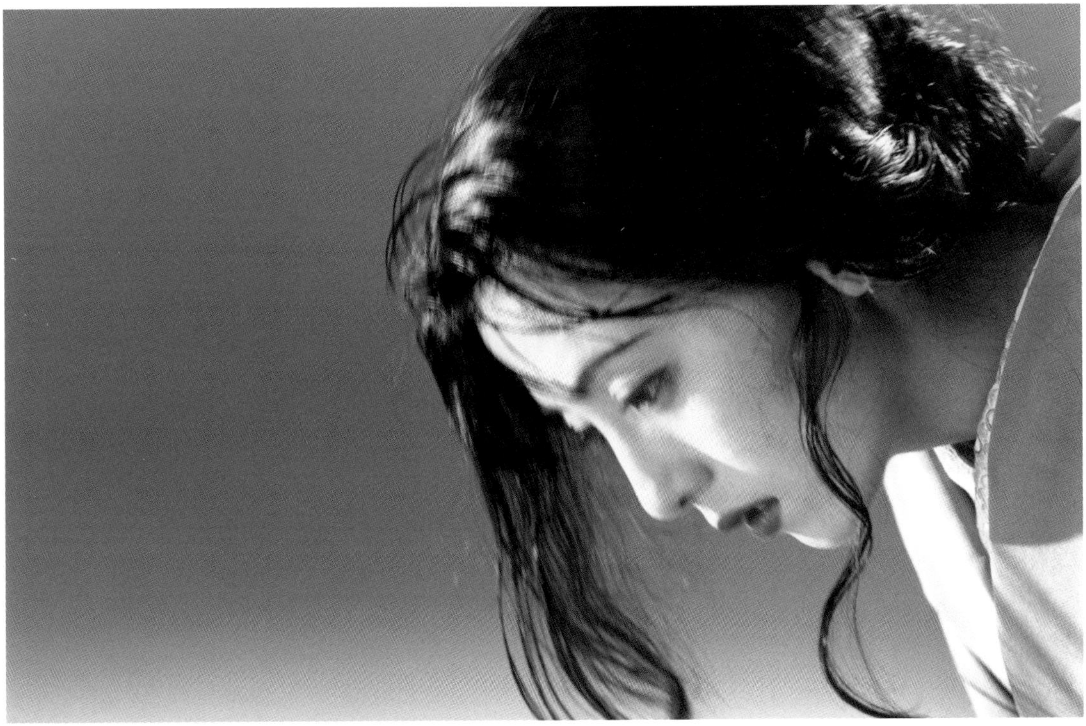

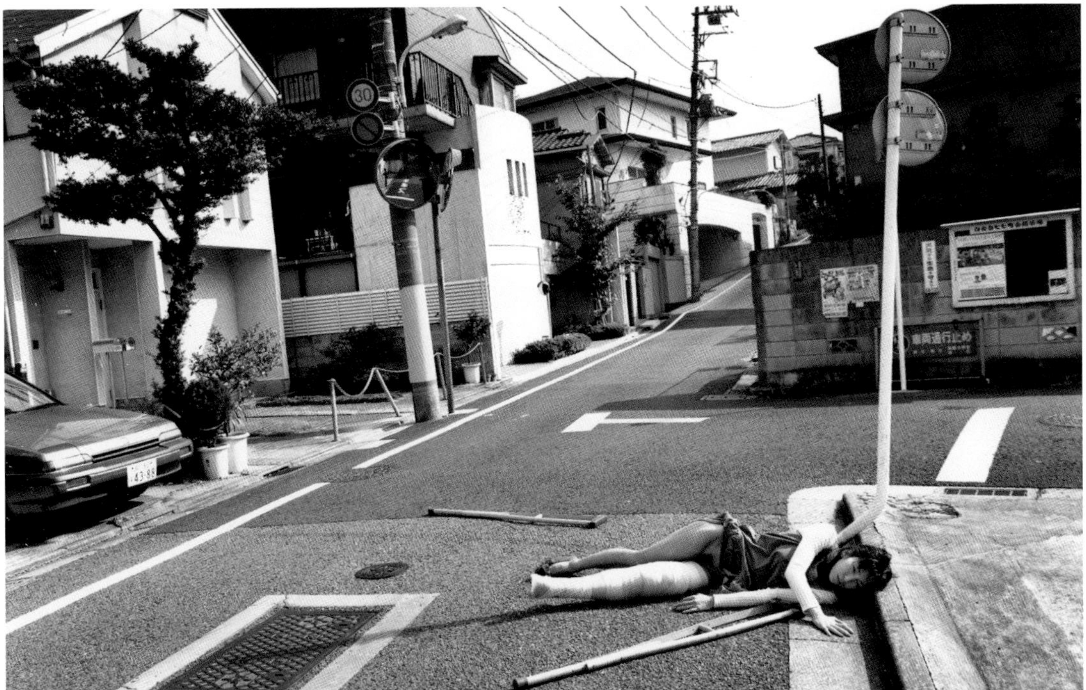
30
車両通行止め

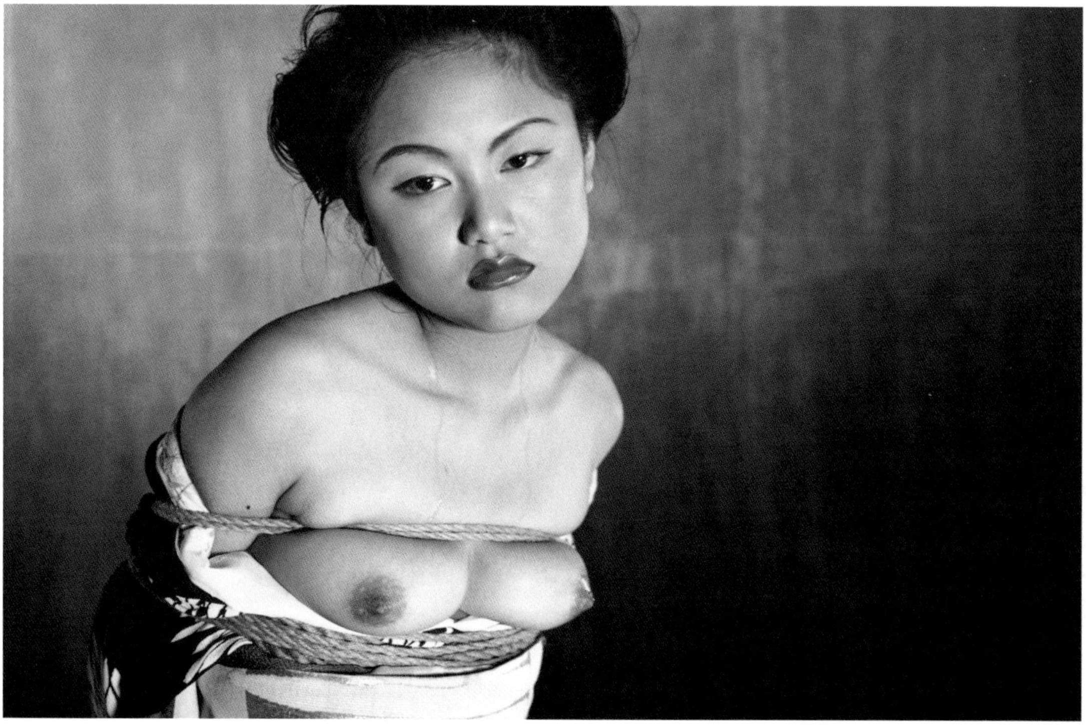

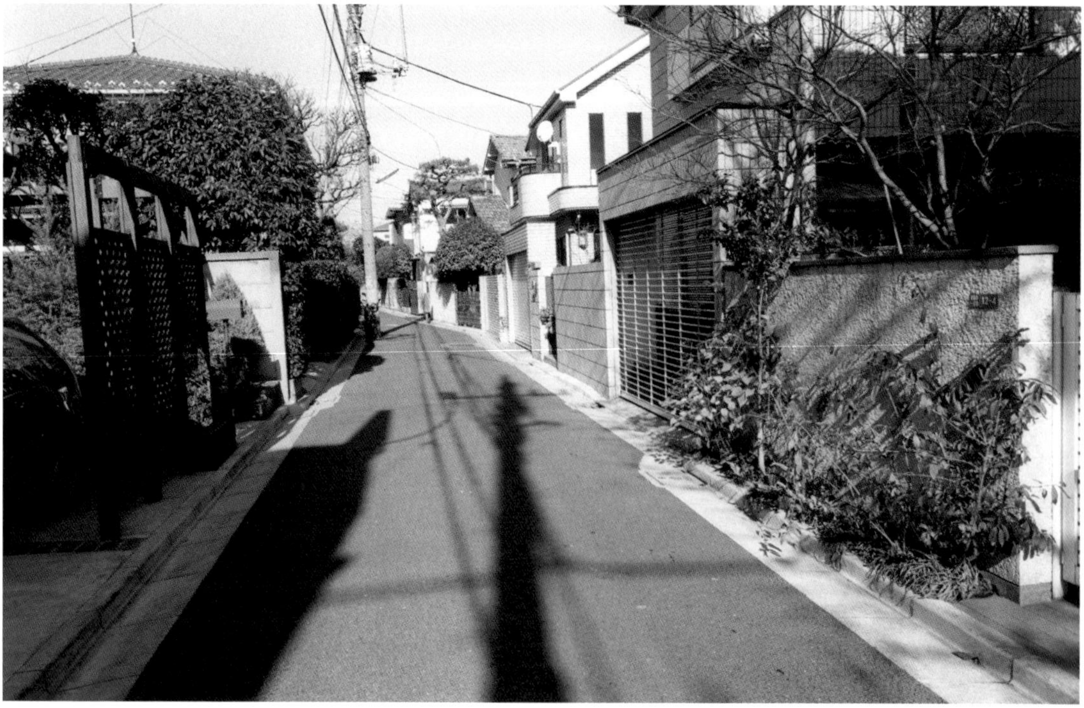

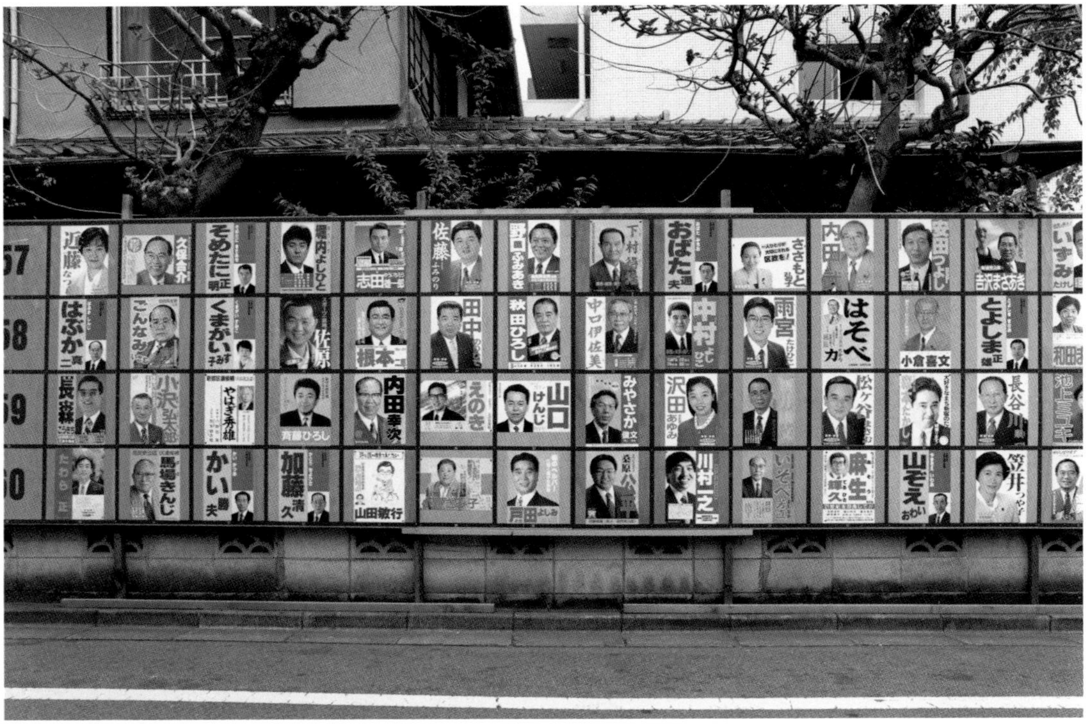
57
近藤
そめたに
志田
佐藤
野口ふみあき
おばた
ささもと
内田
いずみ
はぶか
くまがい
佐原
根本
田中
秋田ひろし
中口伊佐美
中村
雨宮
はそべ
小倉喜文
とよしま
和田
やはぎ秀雄
斉藤ひろし
内田幸次
えのき
山口
けんじ
みやさか
沢田
松ケ谷
長谷川
馬場きんじ
かい
加藤
清久
山田敏行
戸田よしみ
川村一之
いそべ
麻生
山ぞえ
おかい
笠井

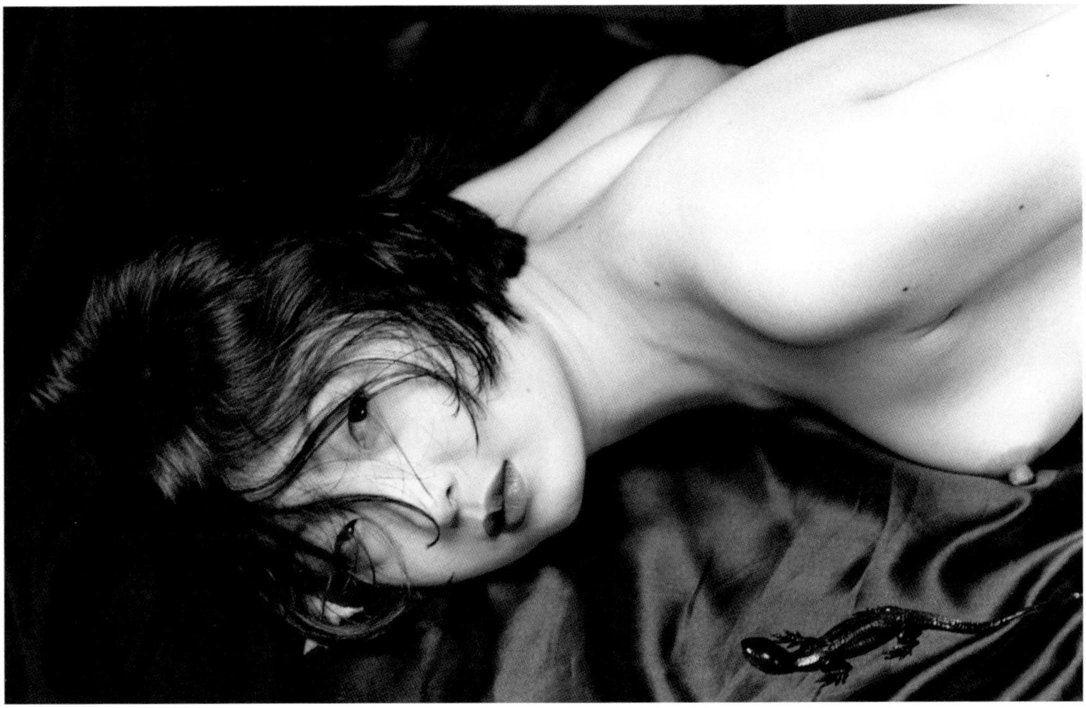

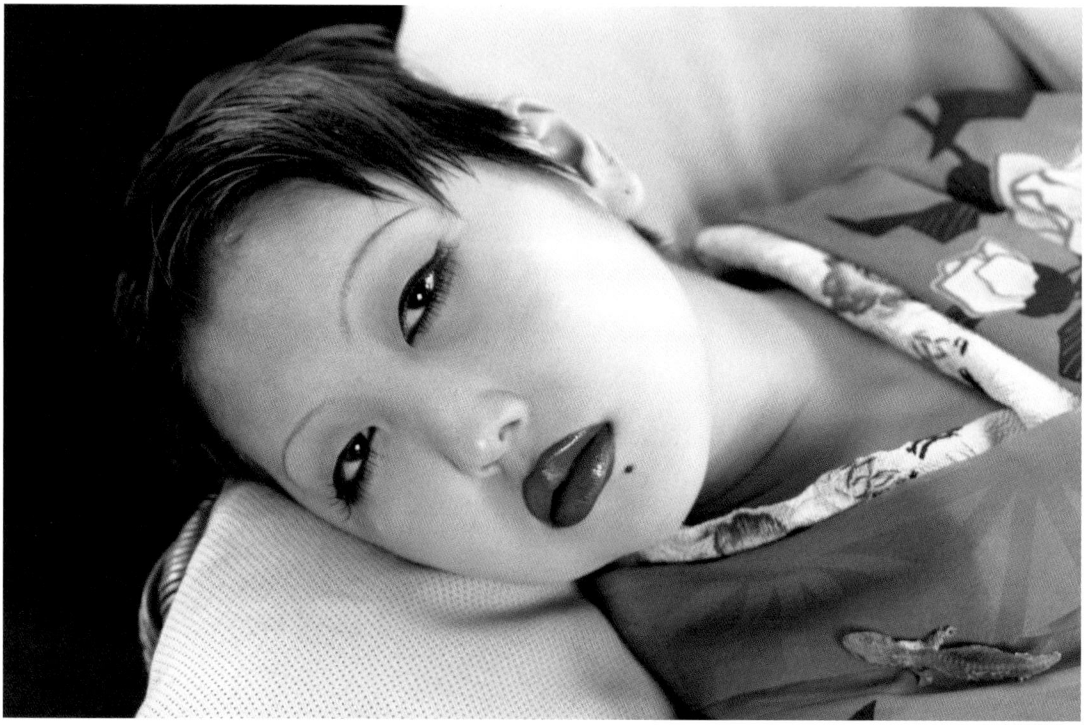

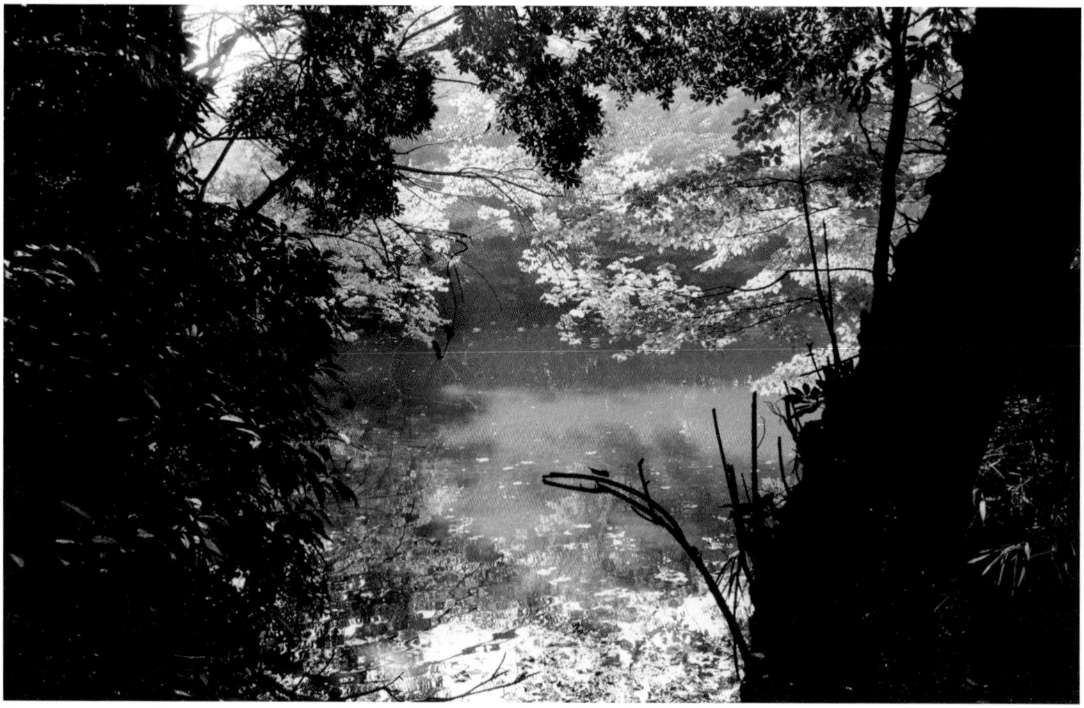

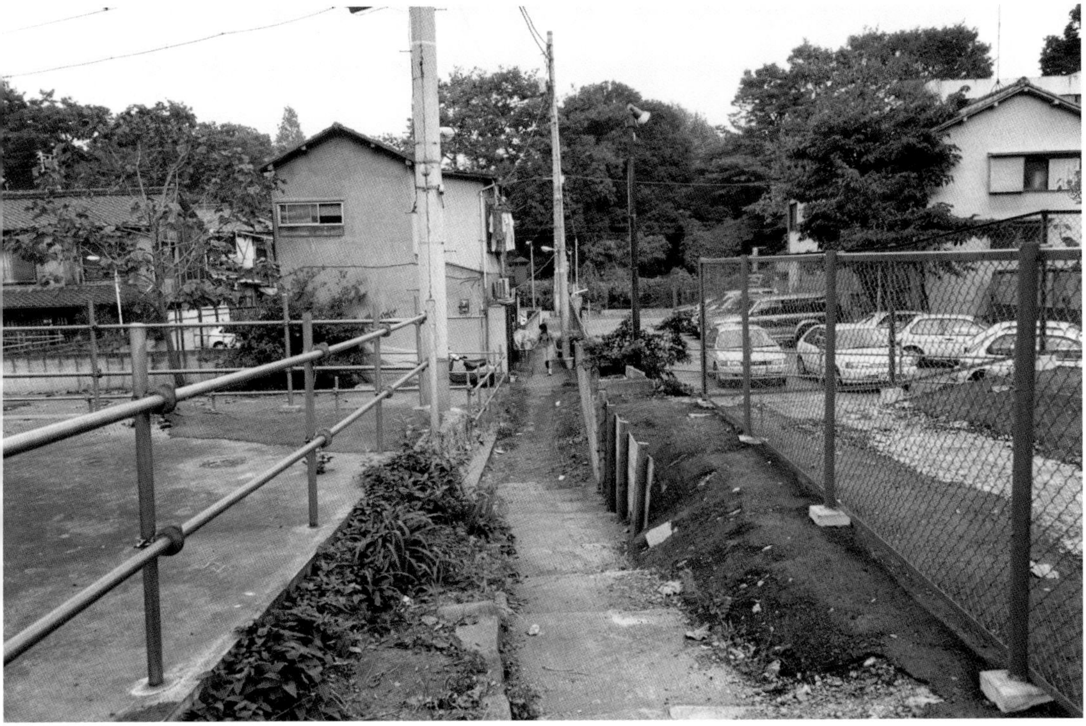

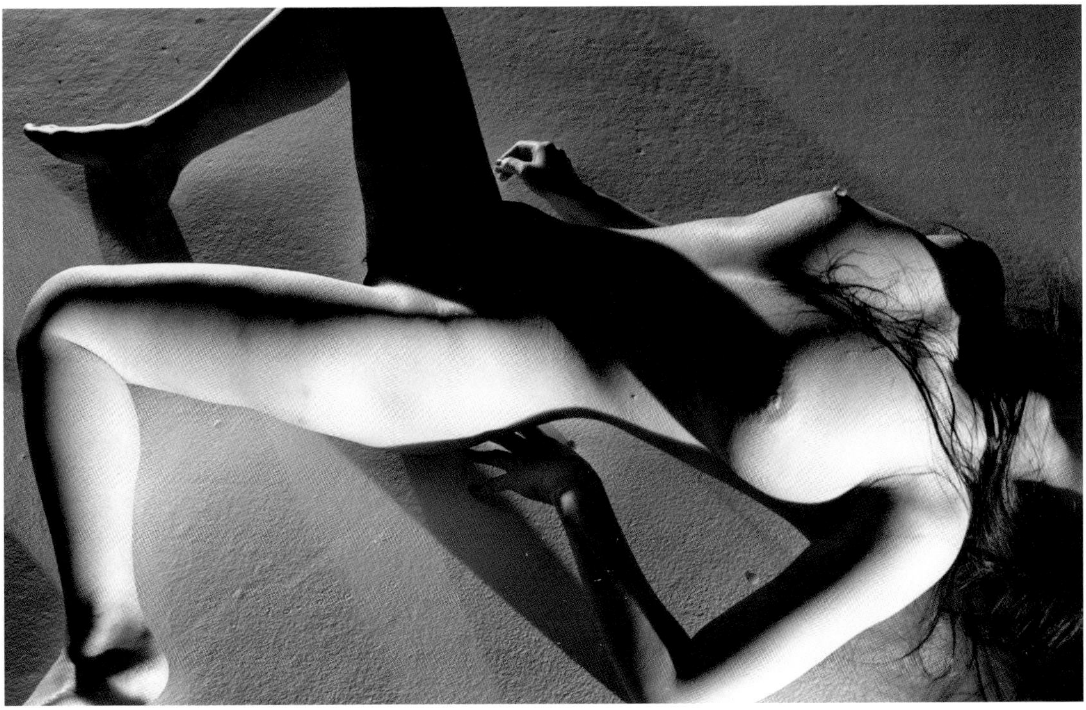

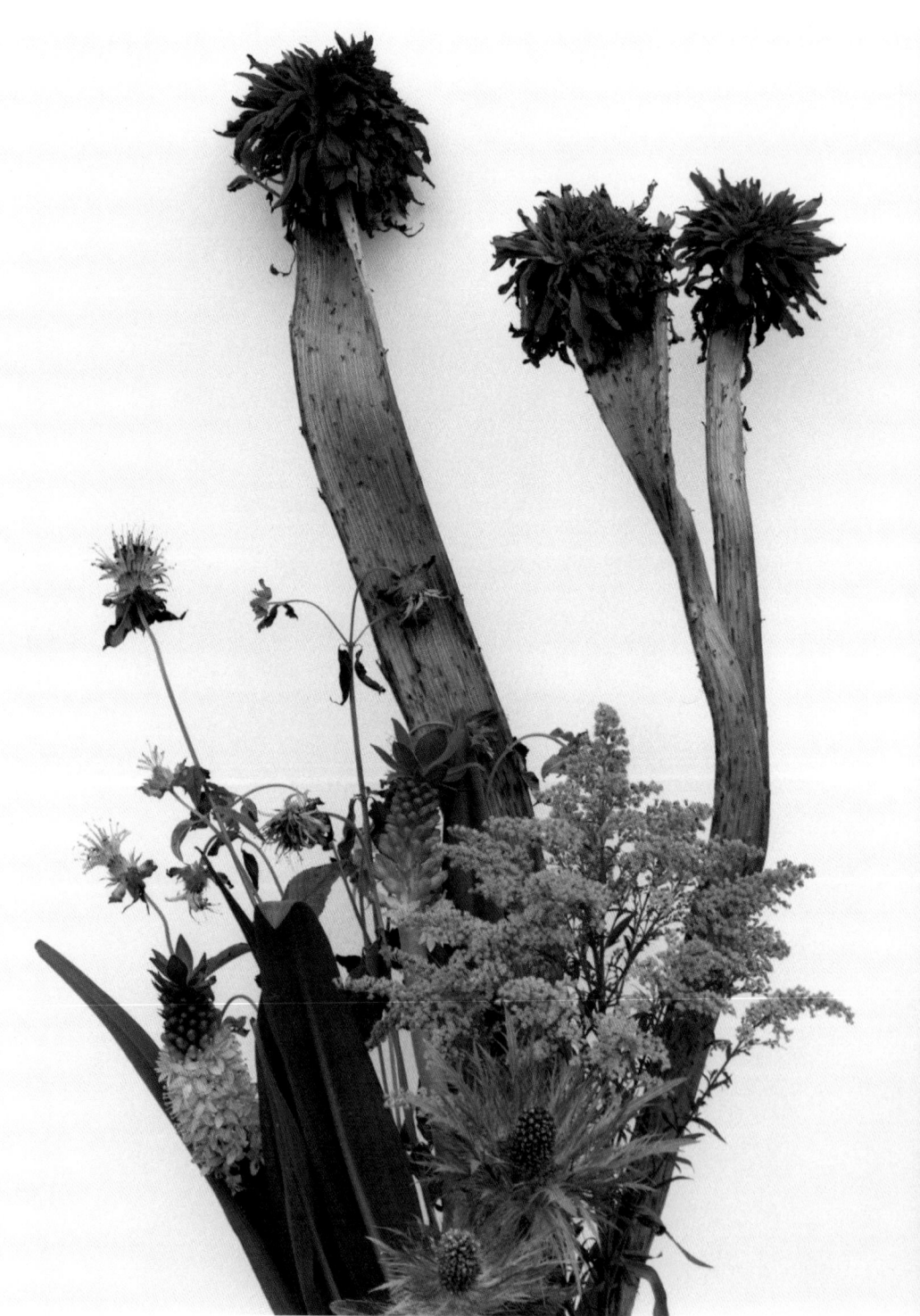

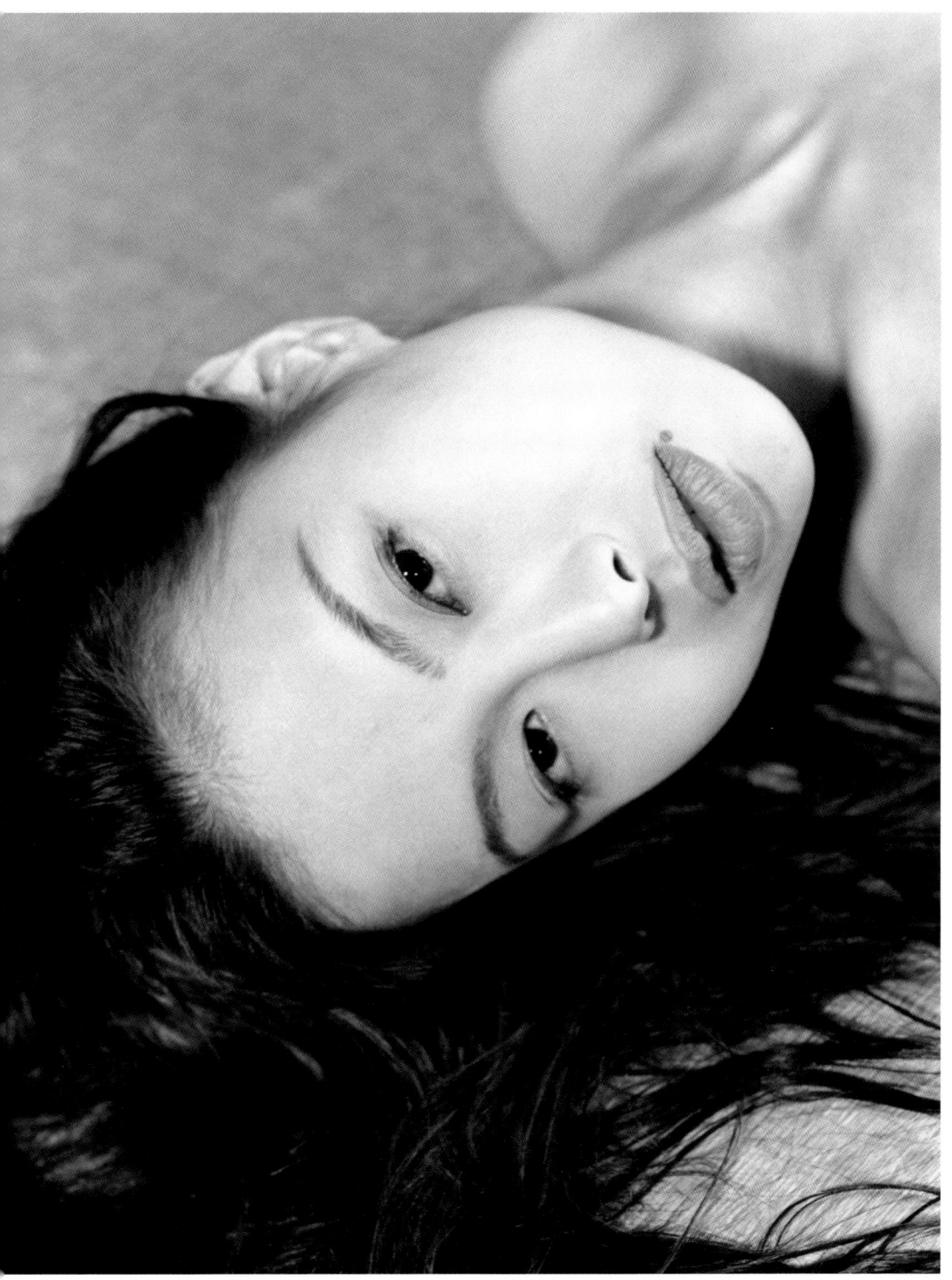

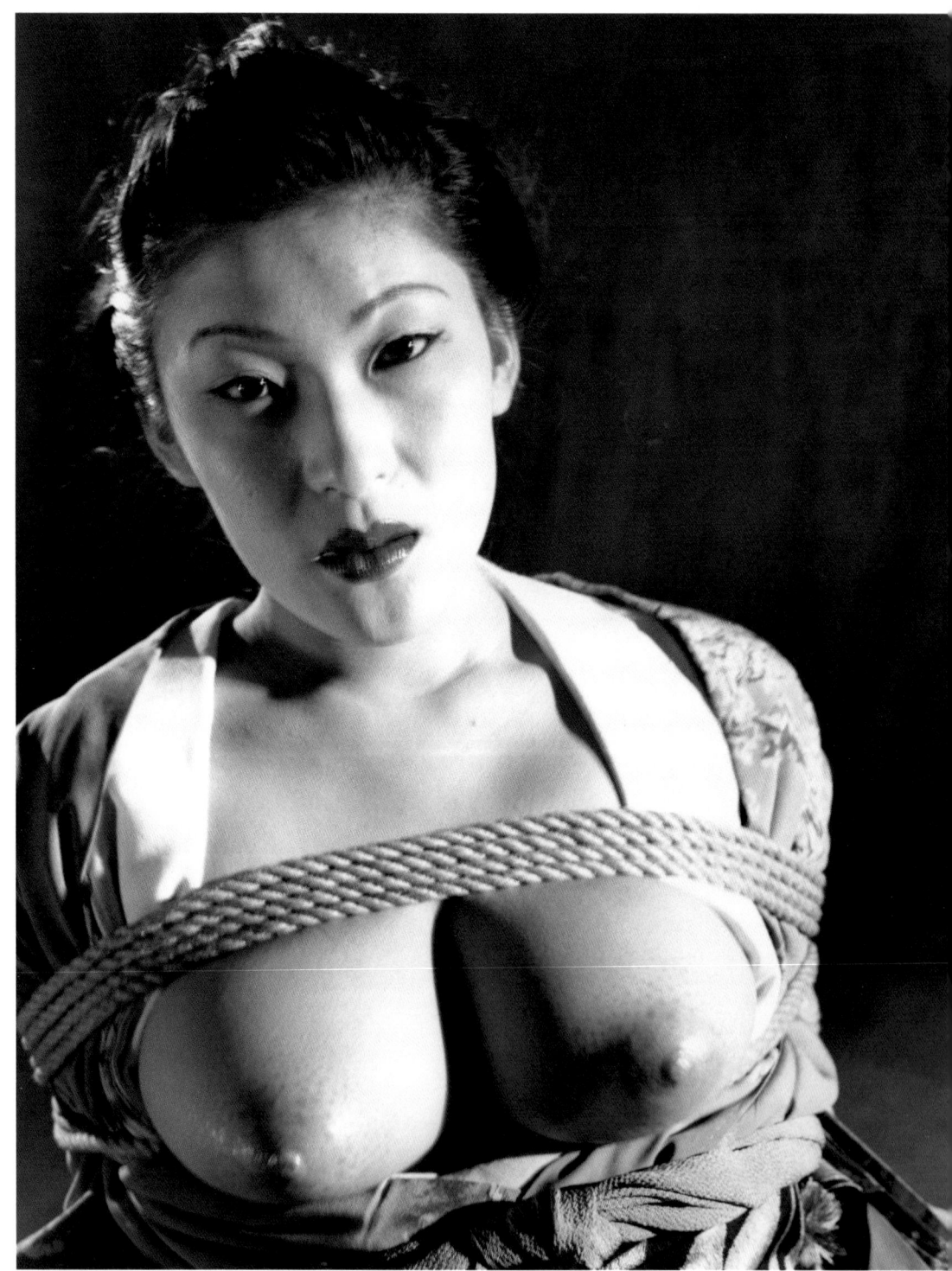

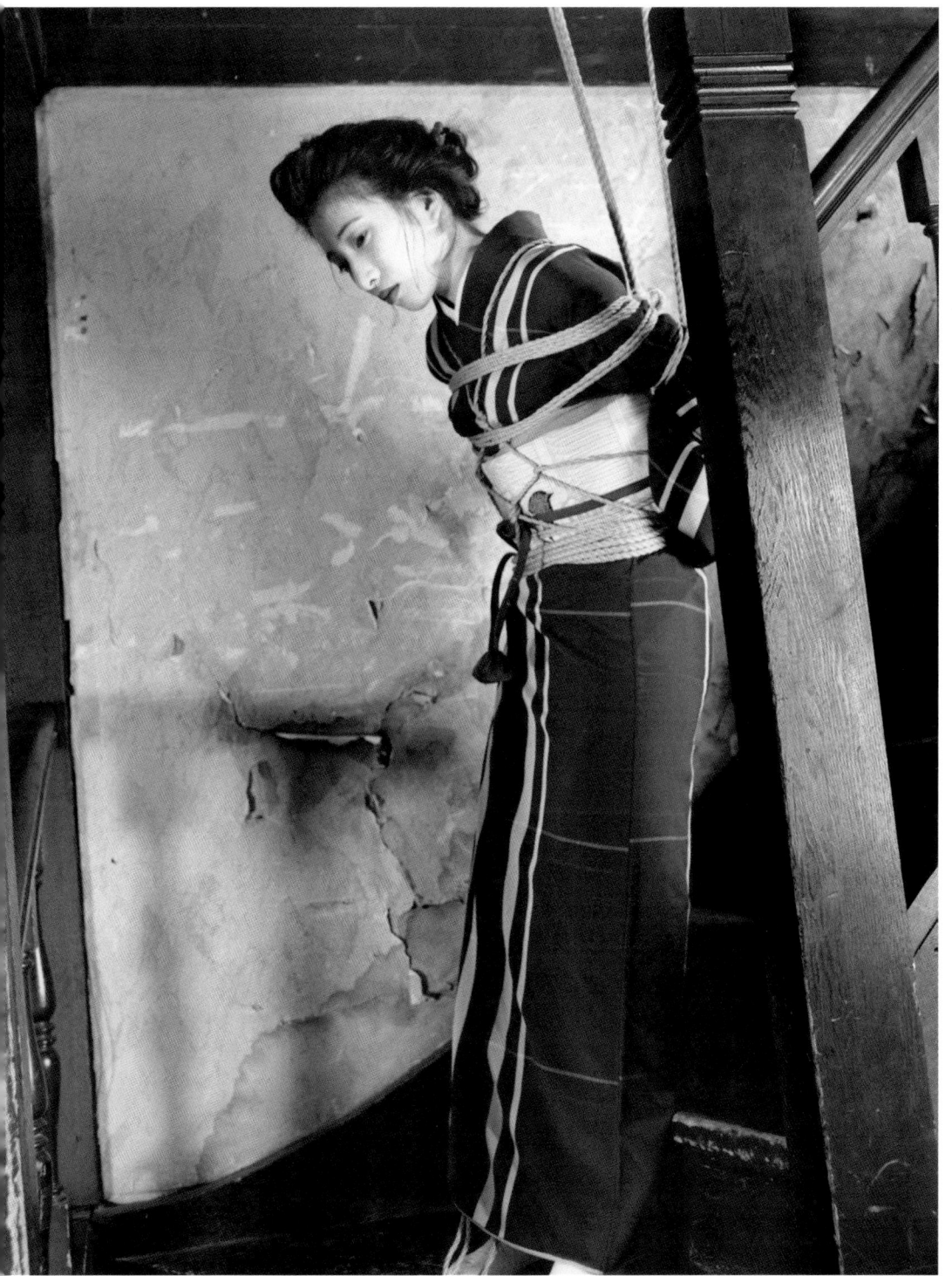

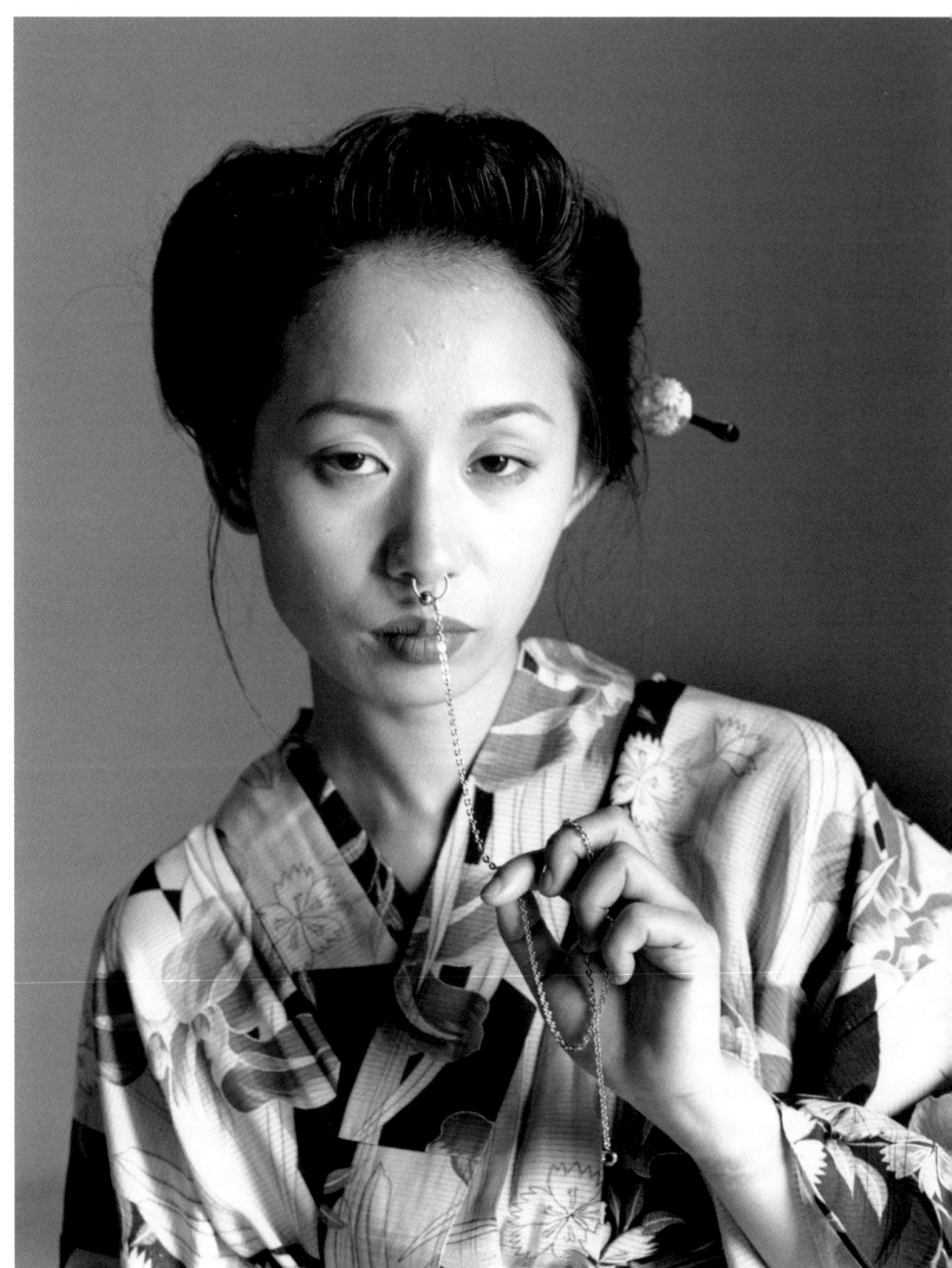

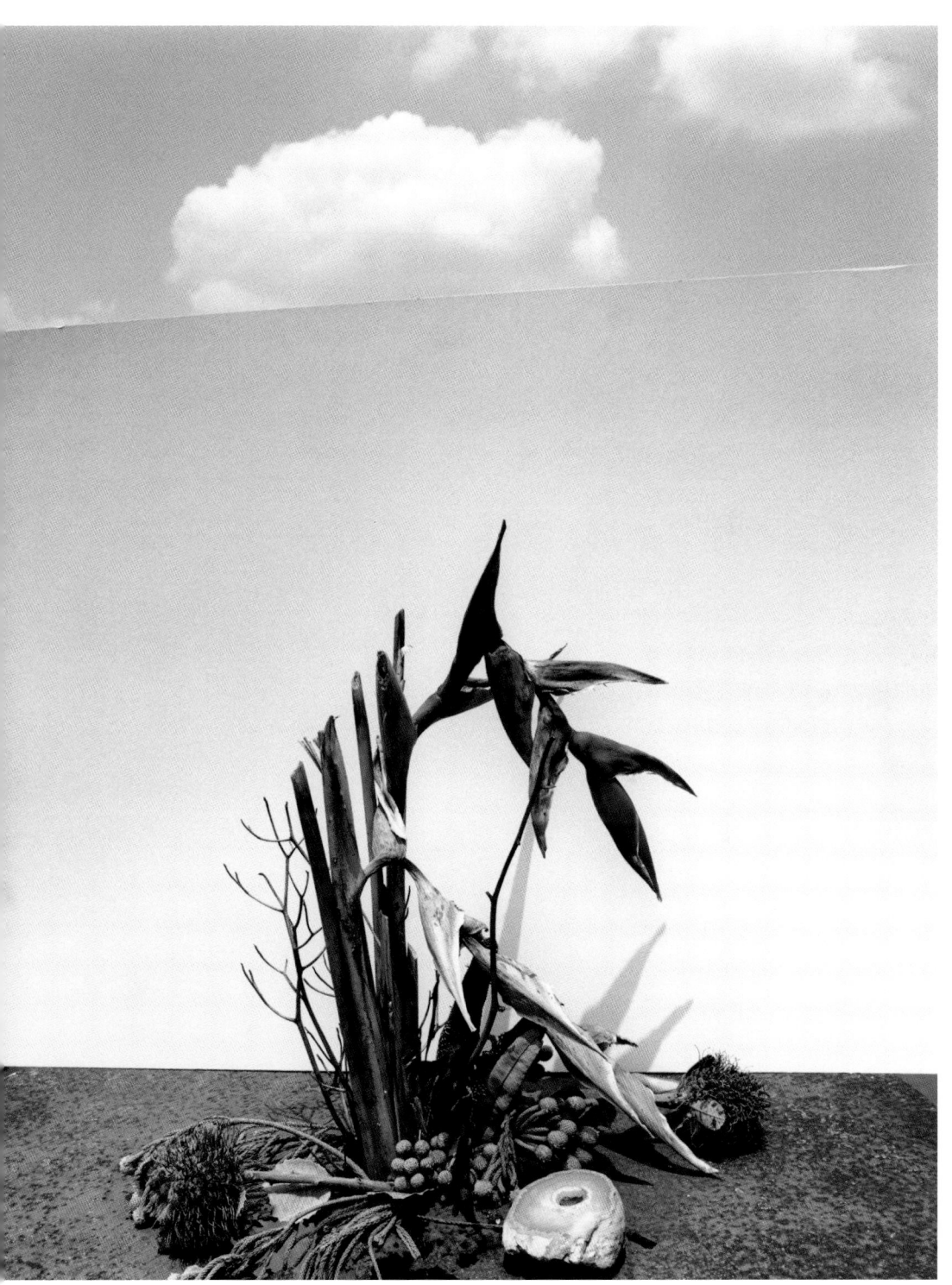

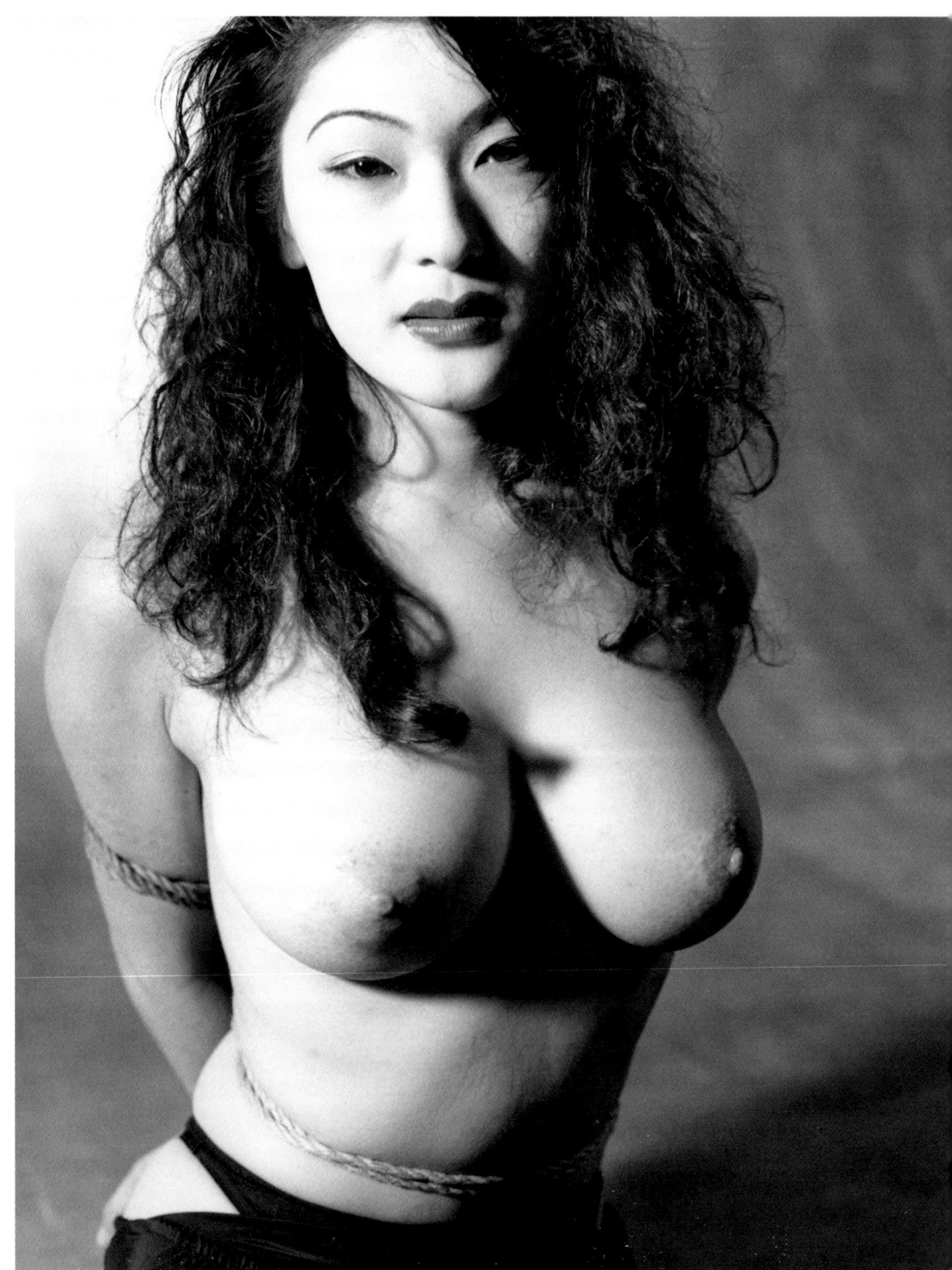

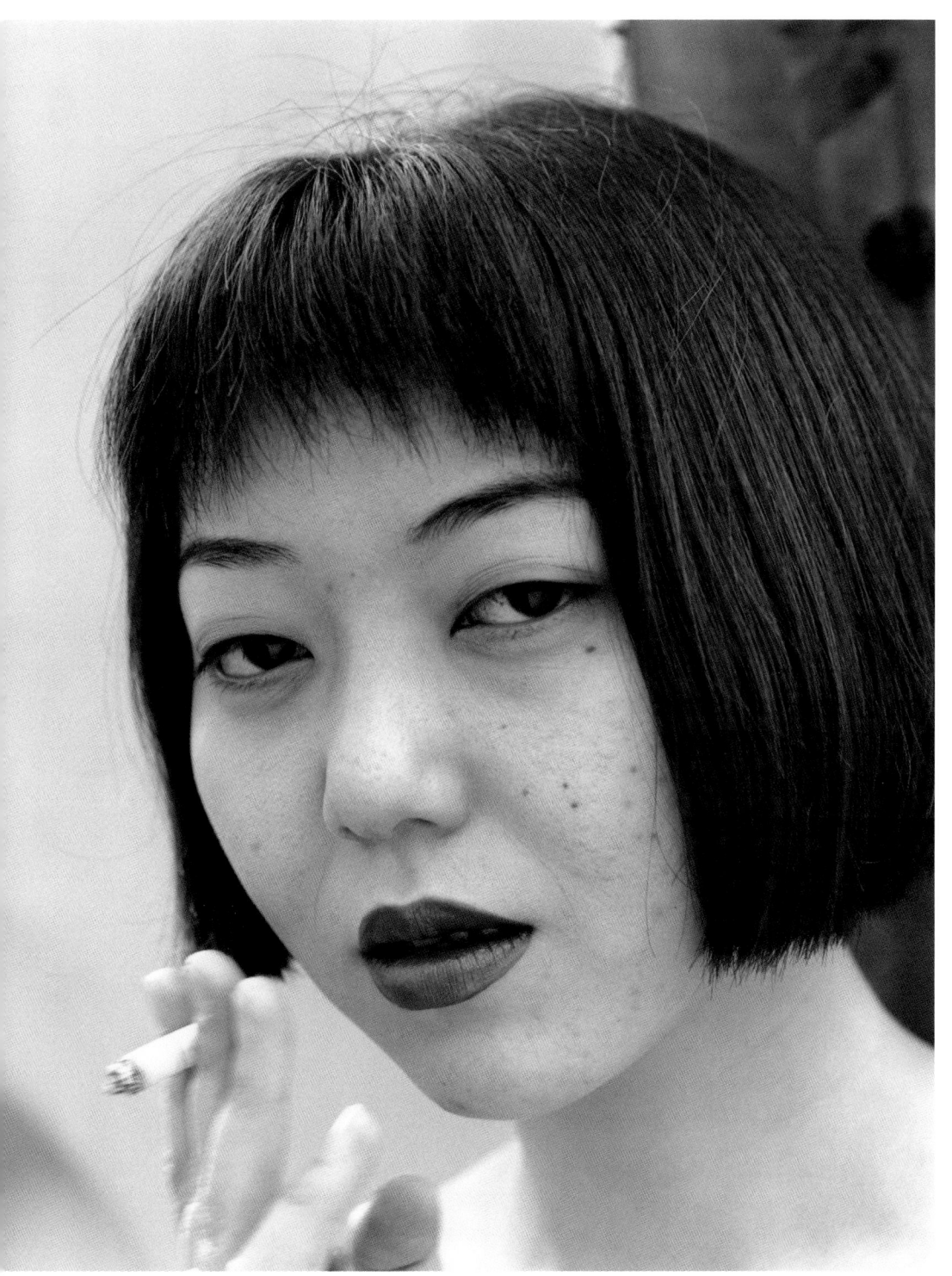

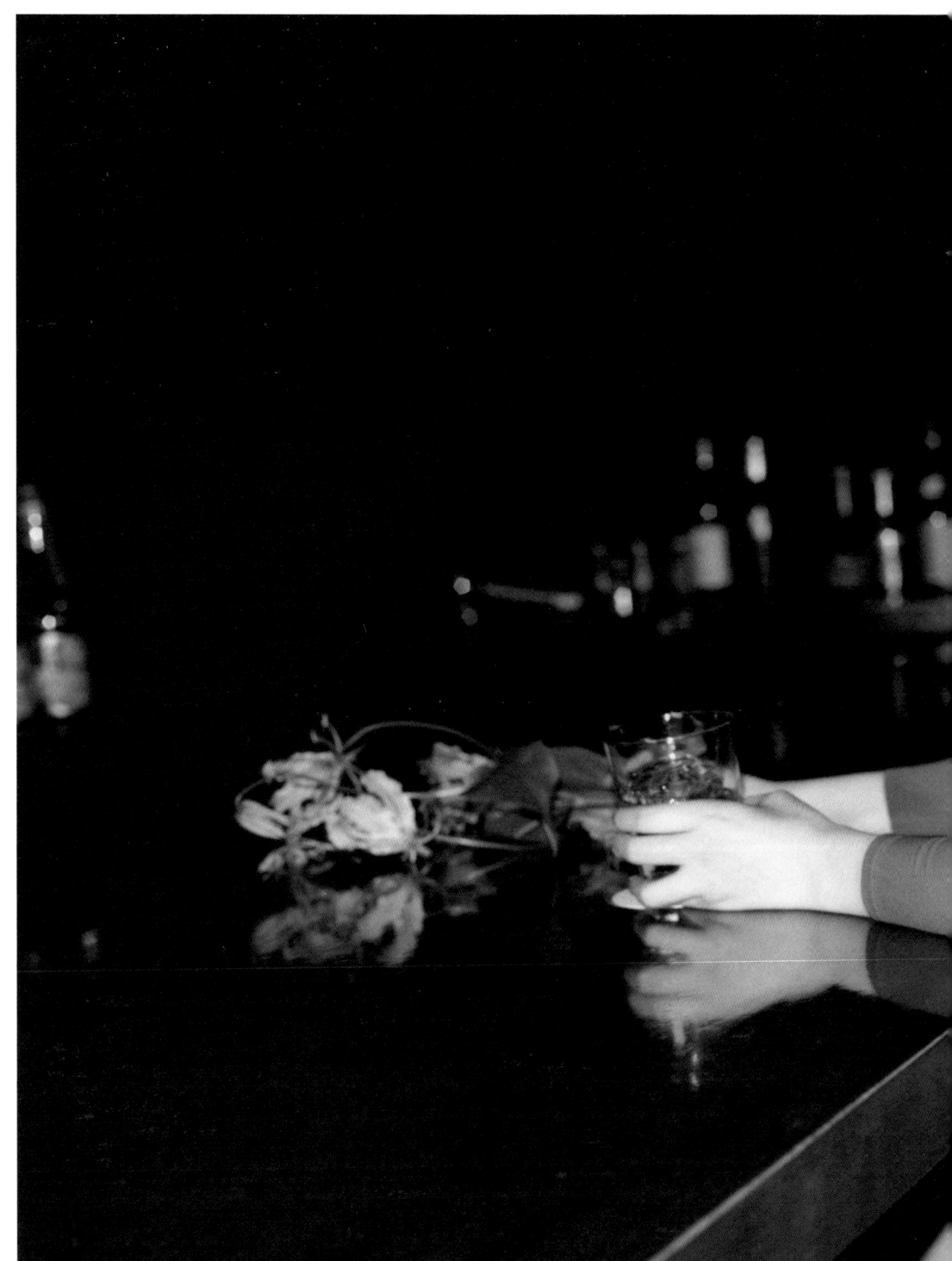

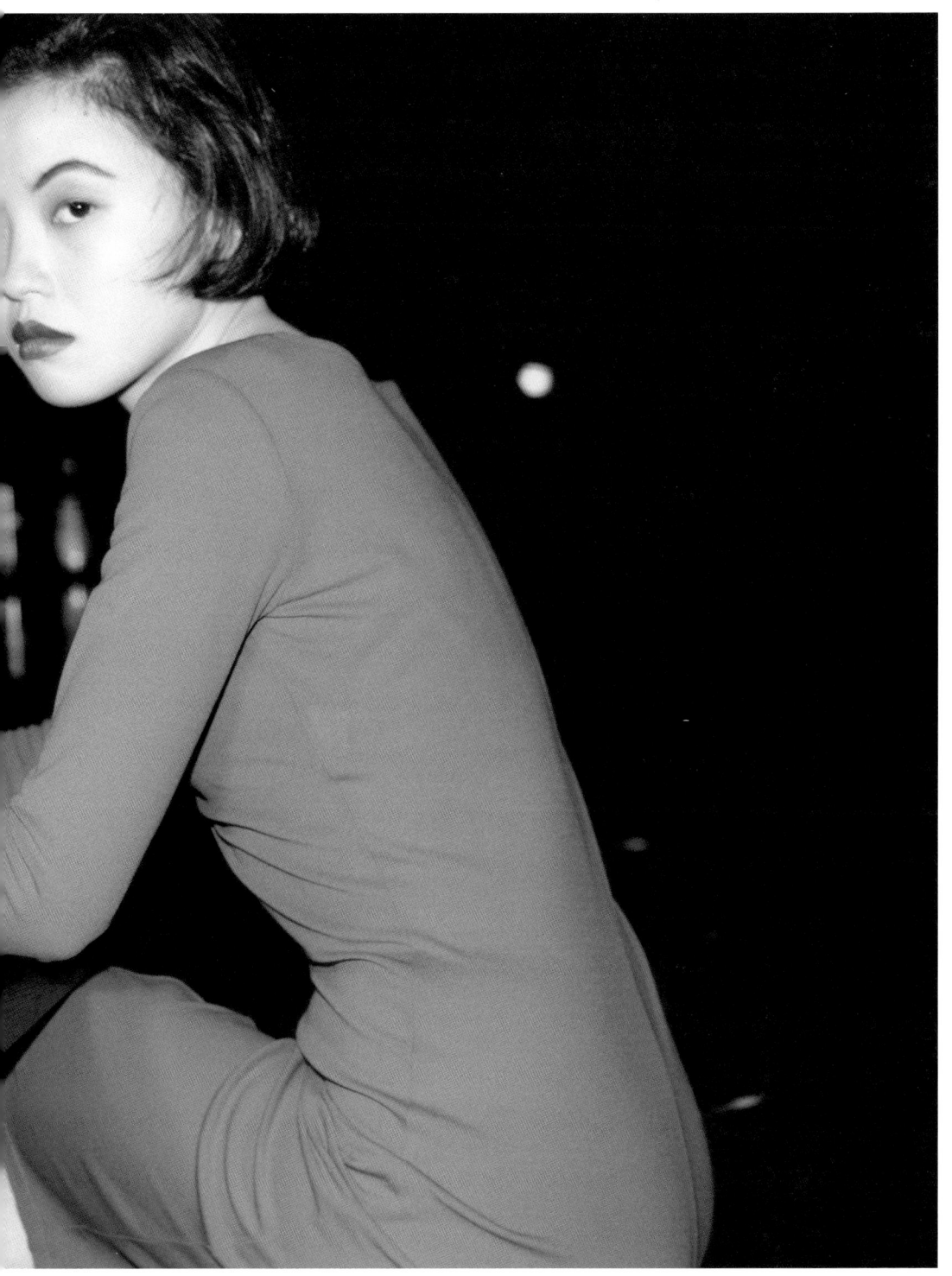

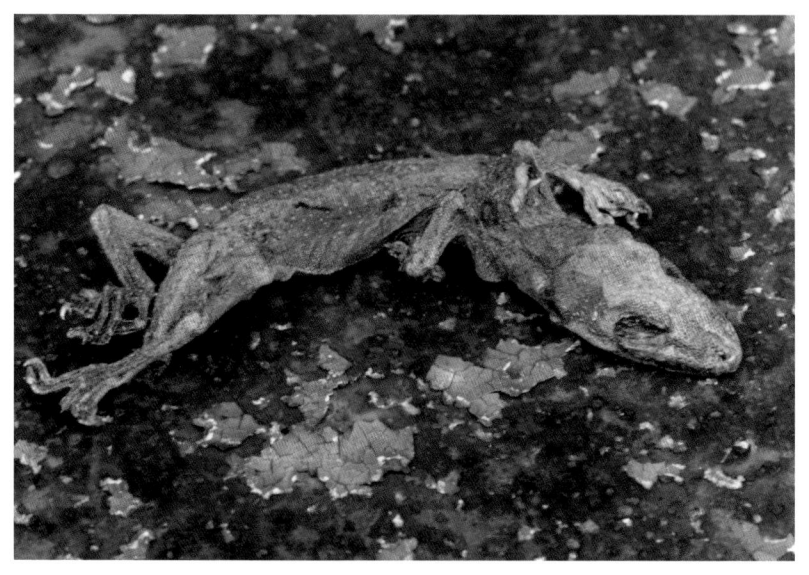

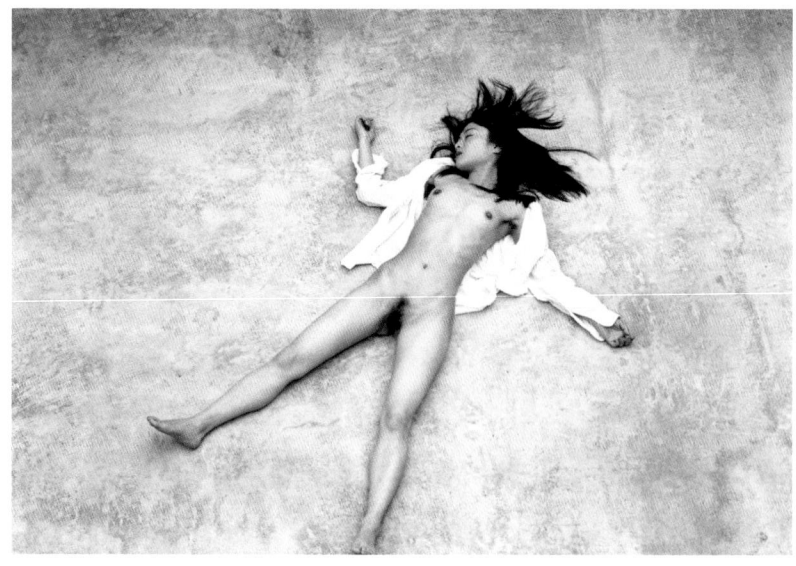

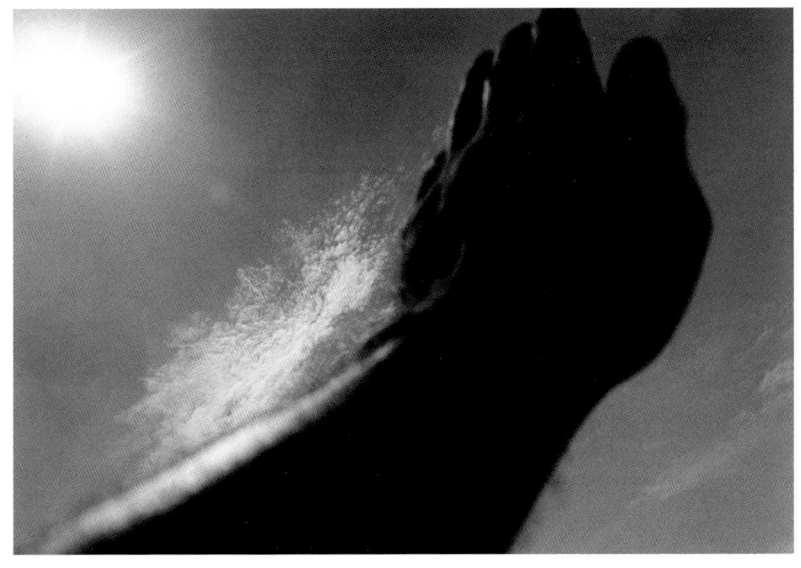

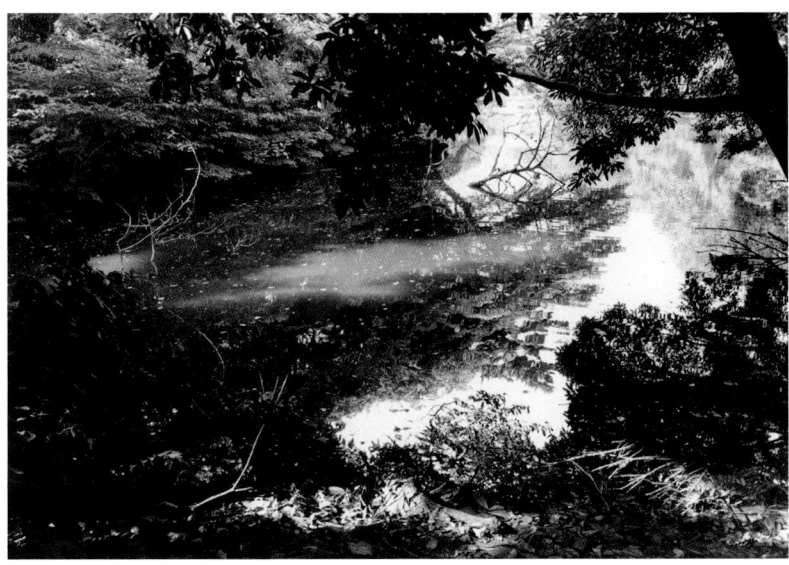

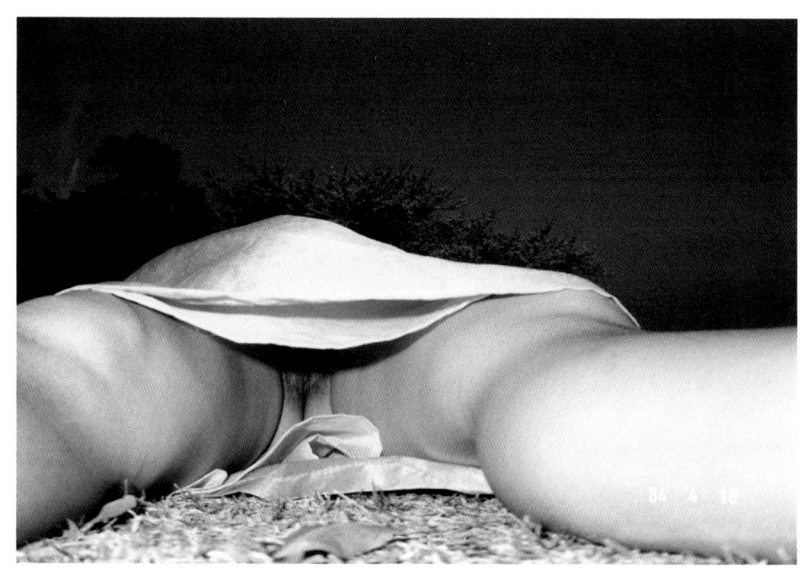

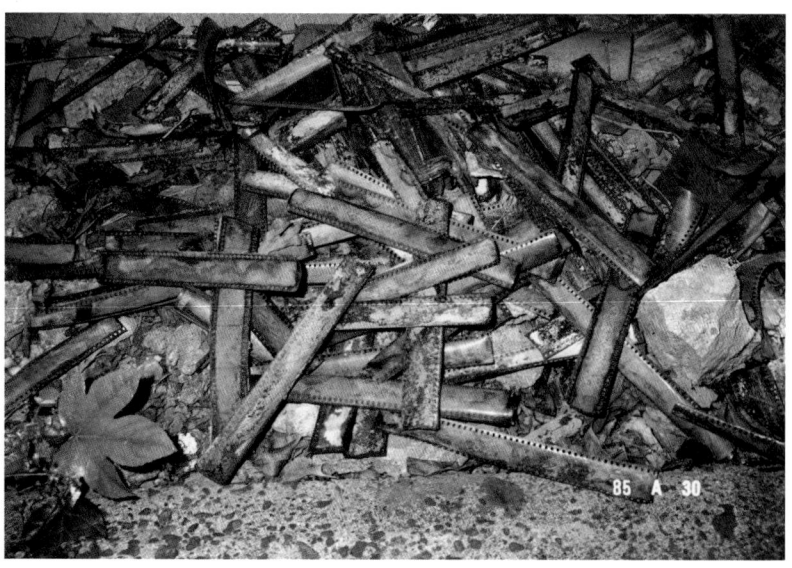

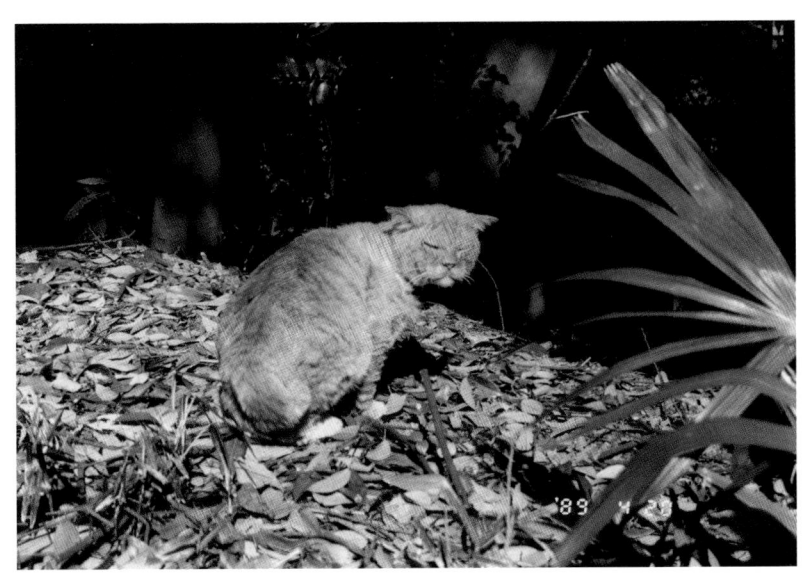

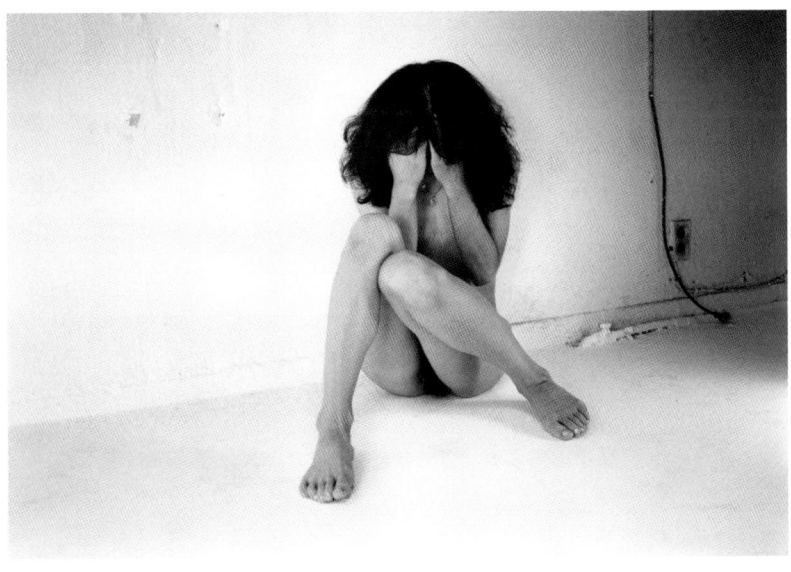

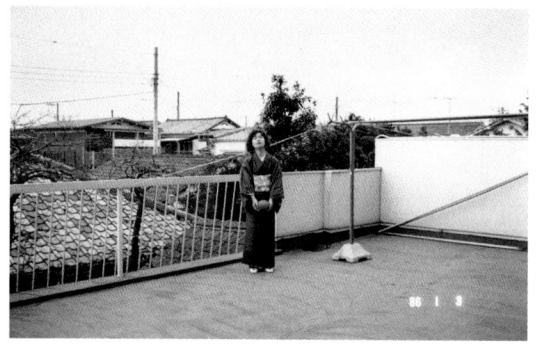 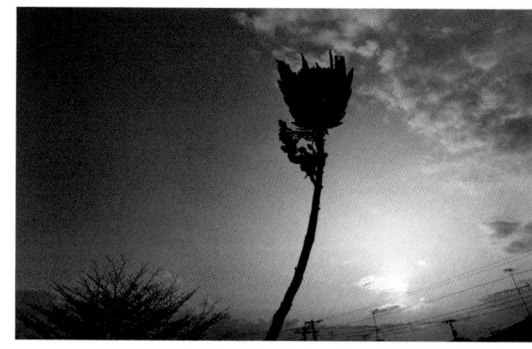

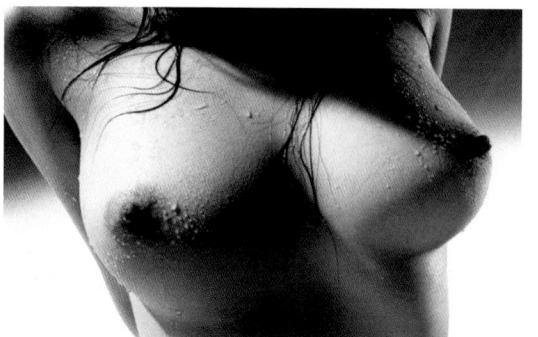 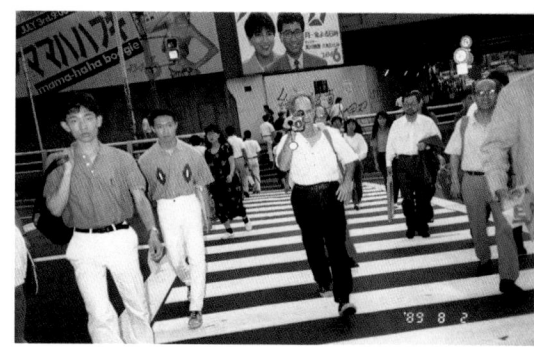

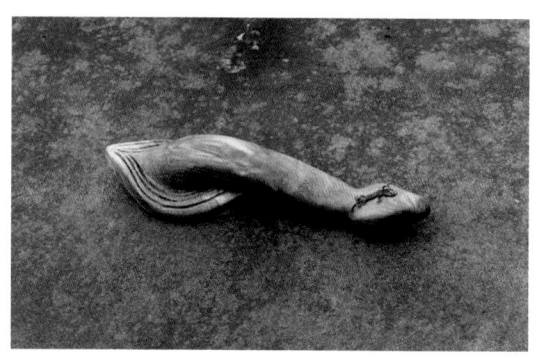 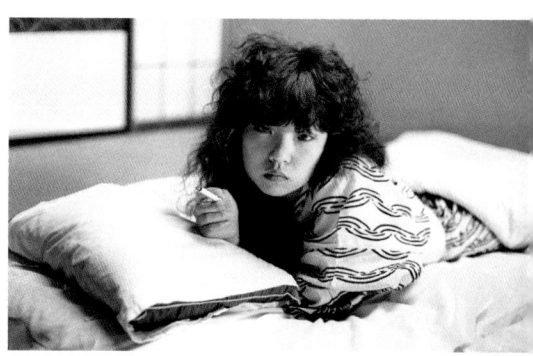

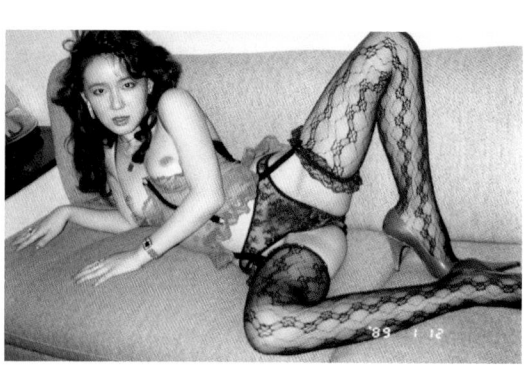 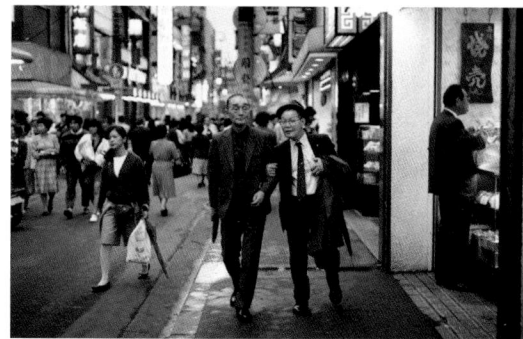

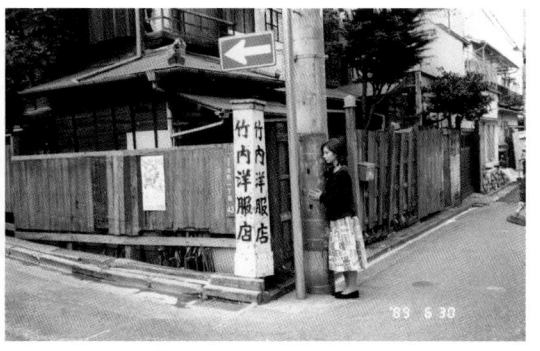
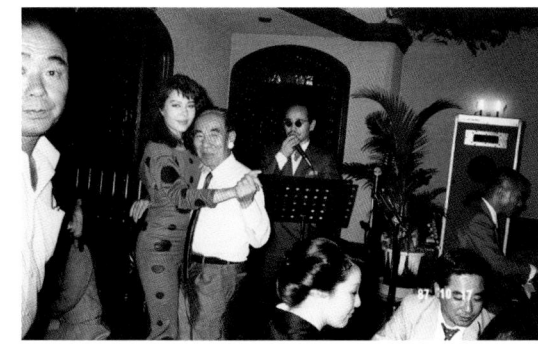
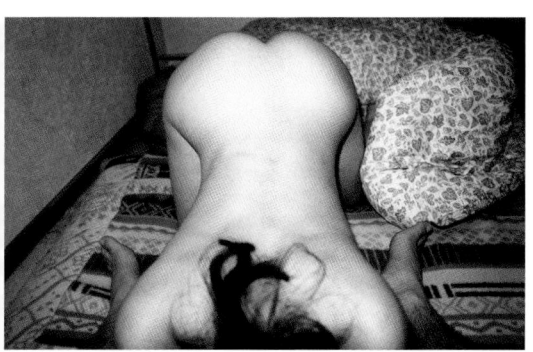
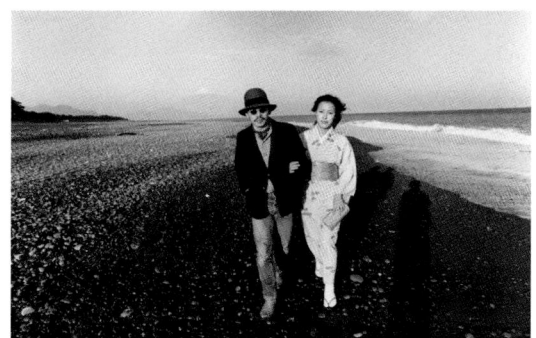
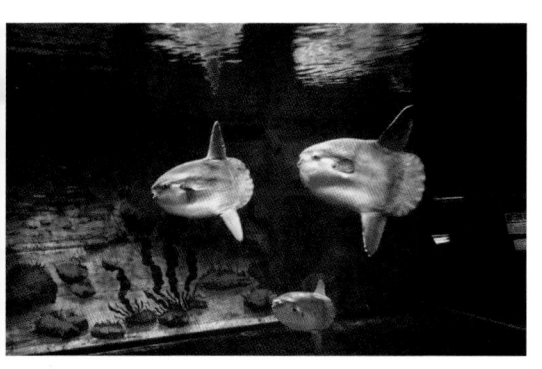
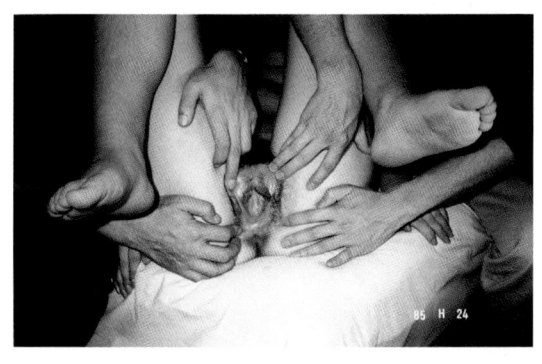
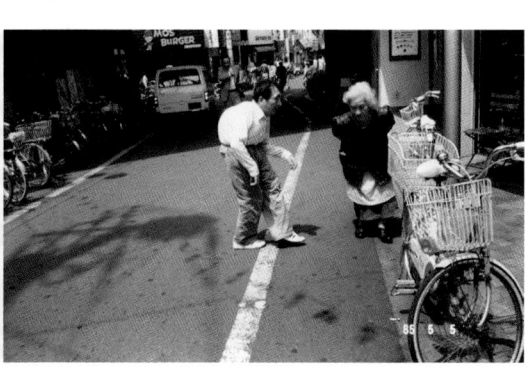
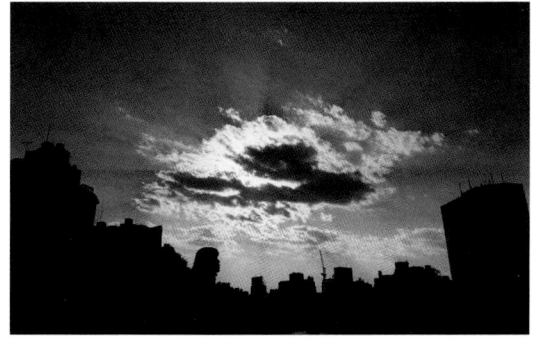

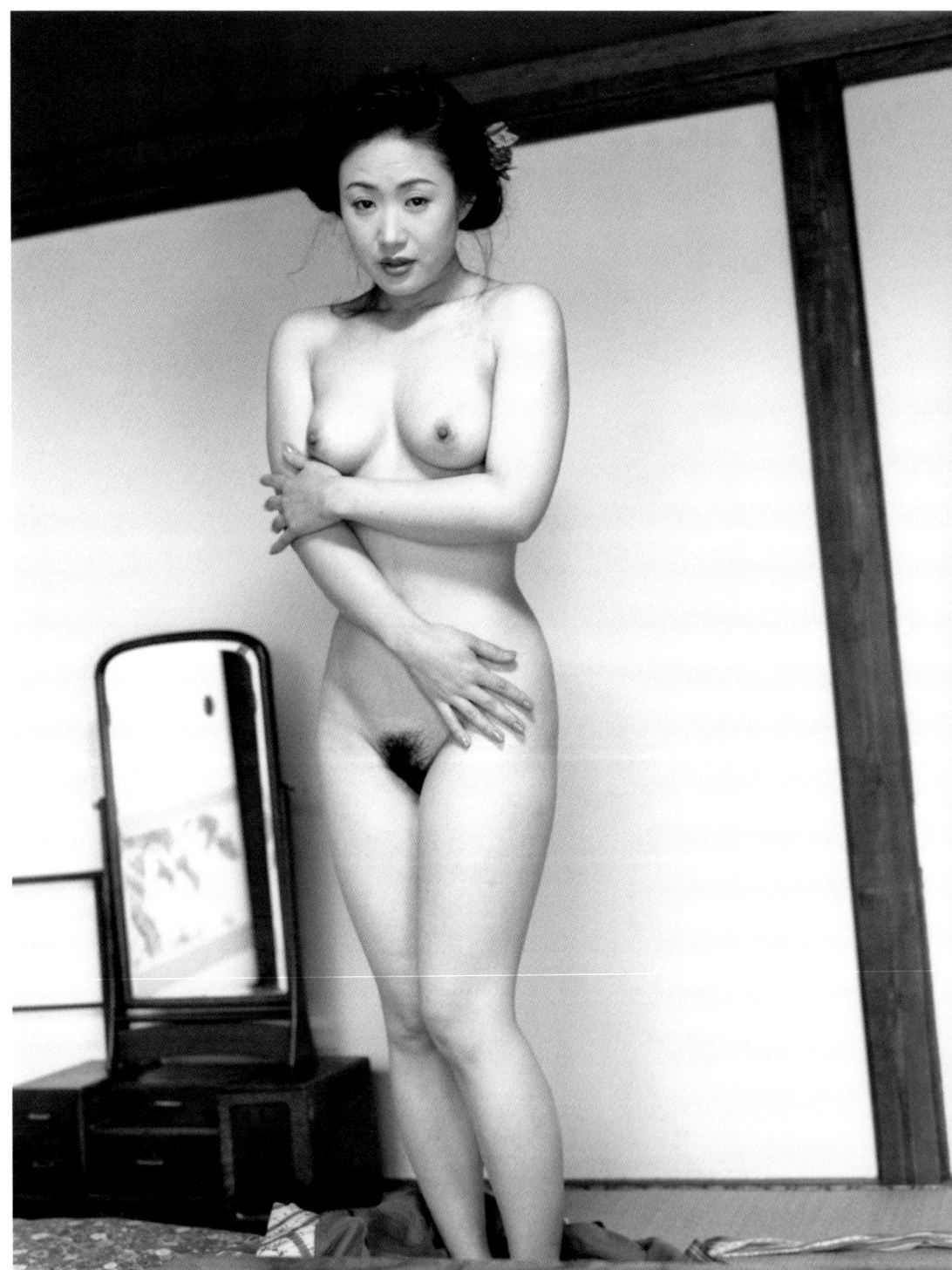

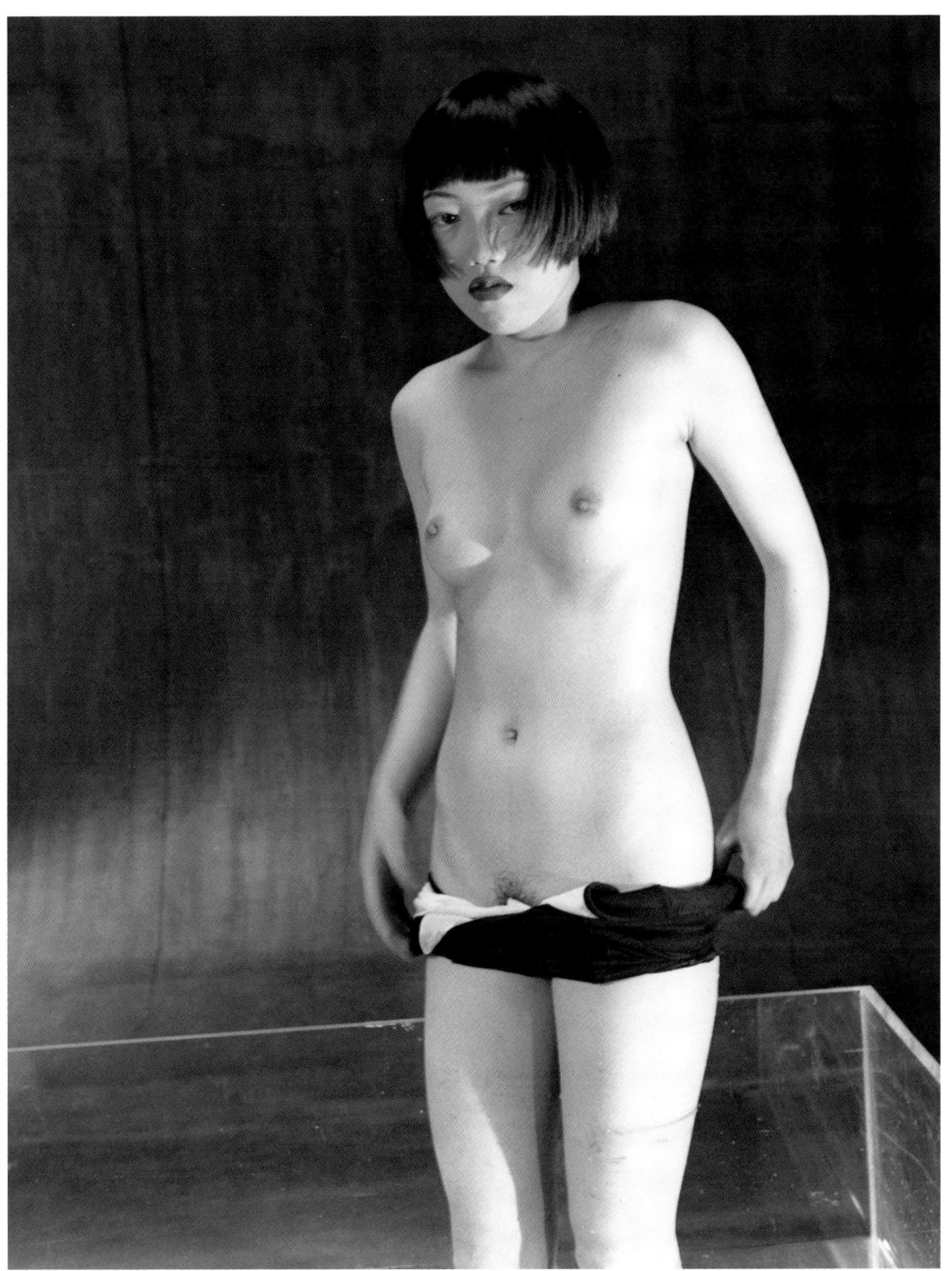

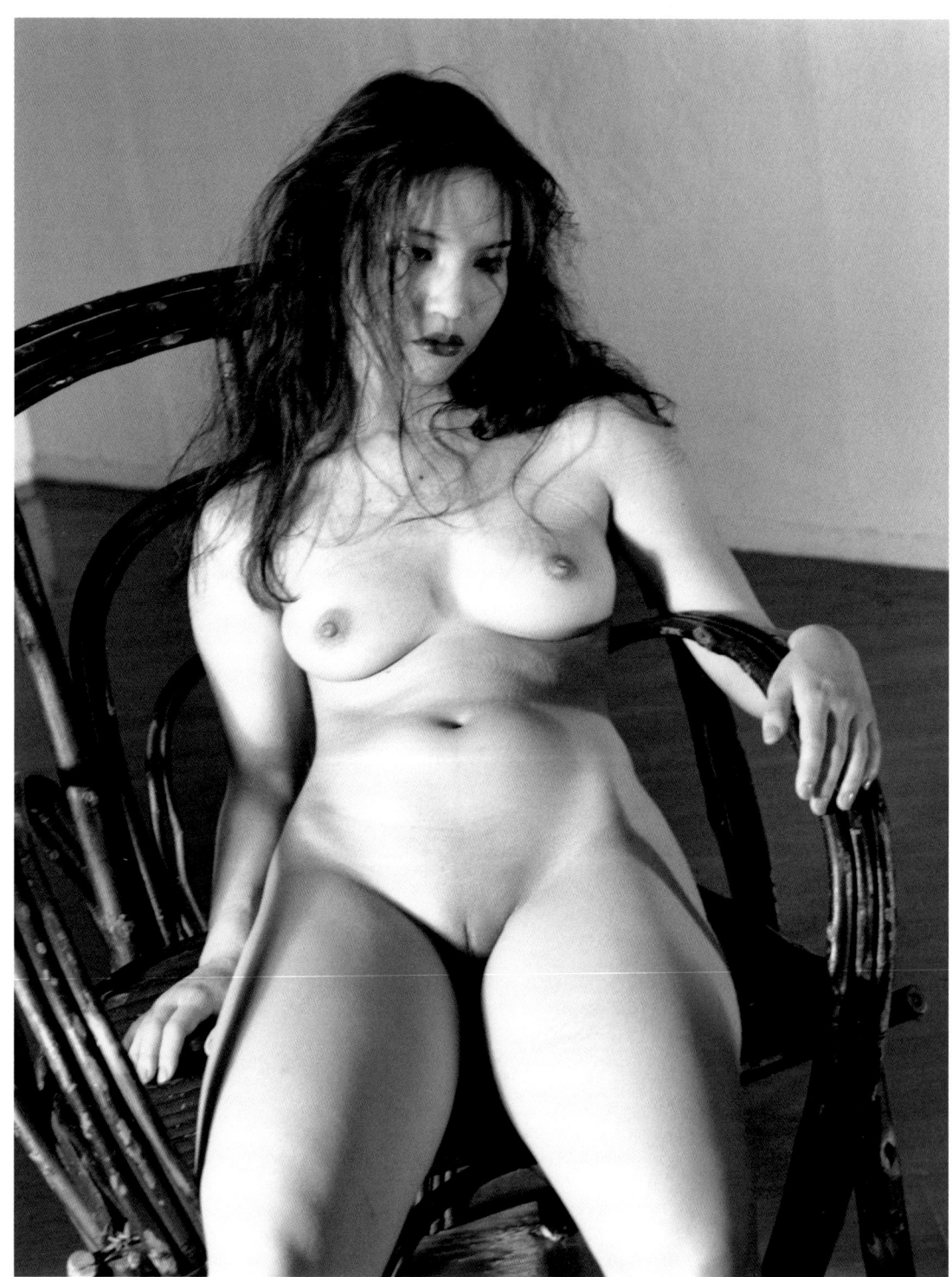

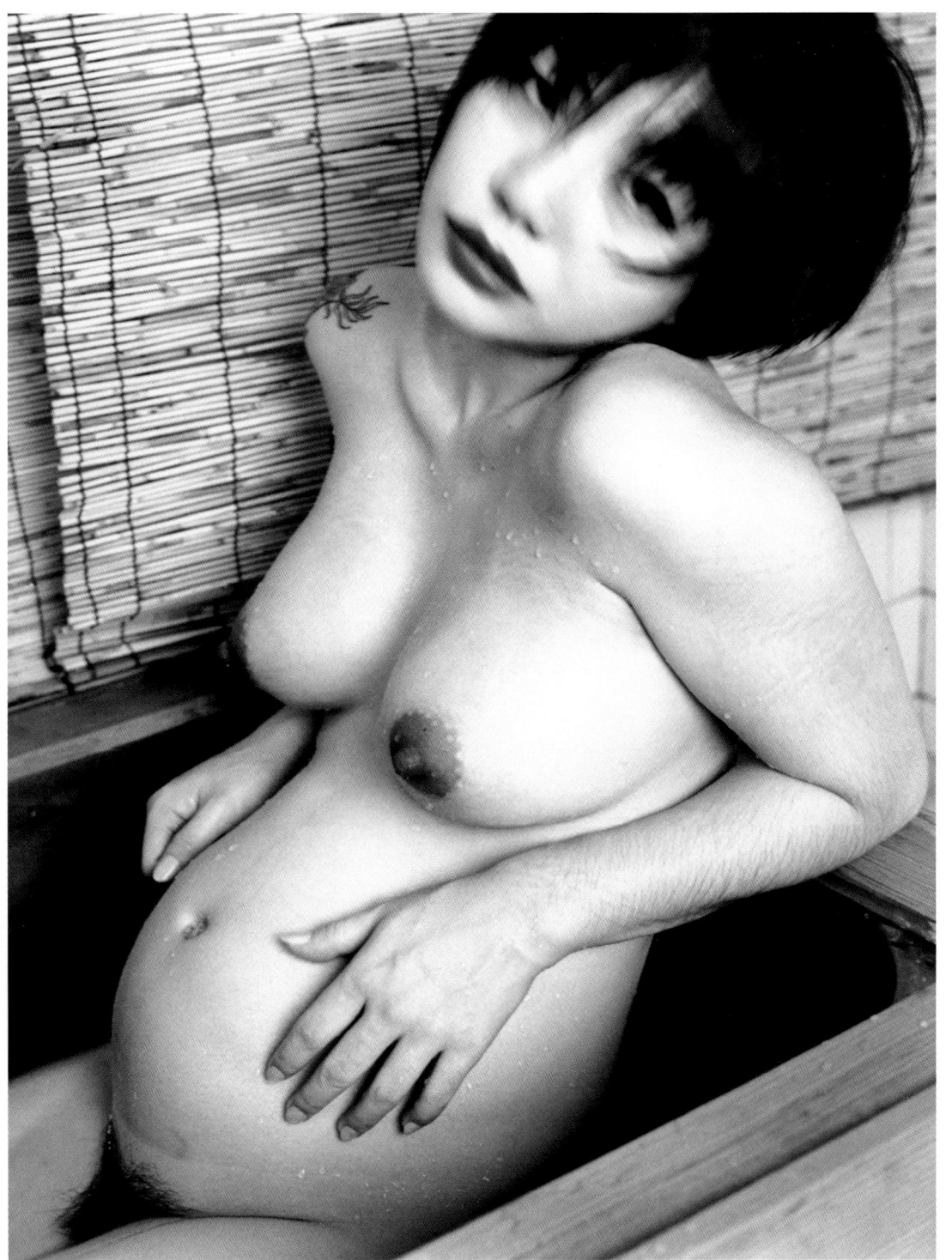

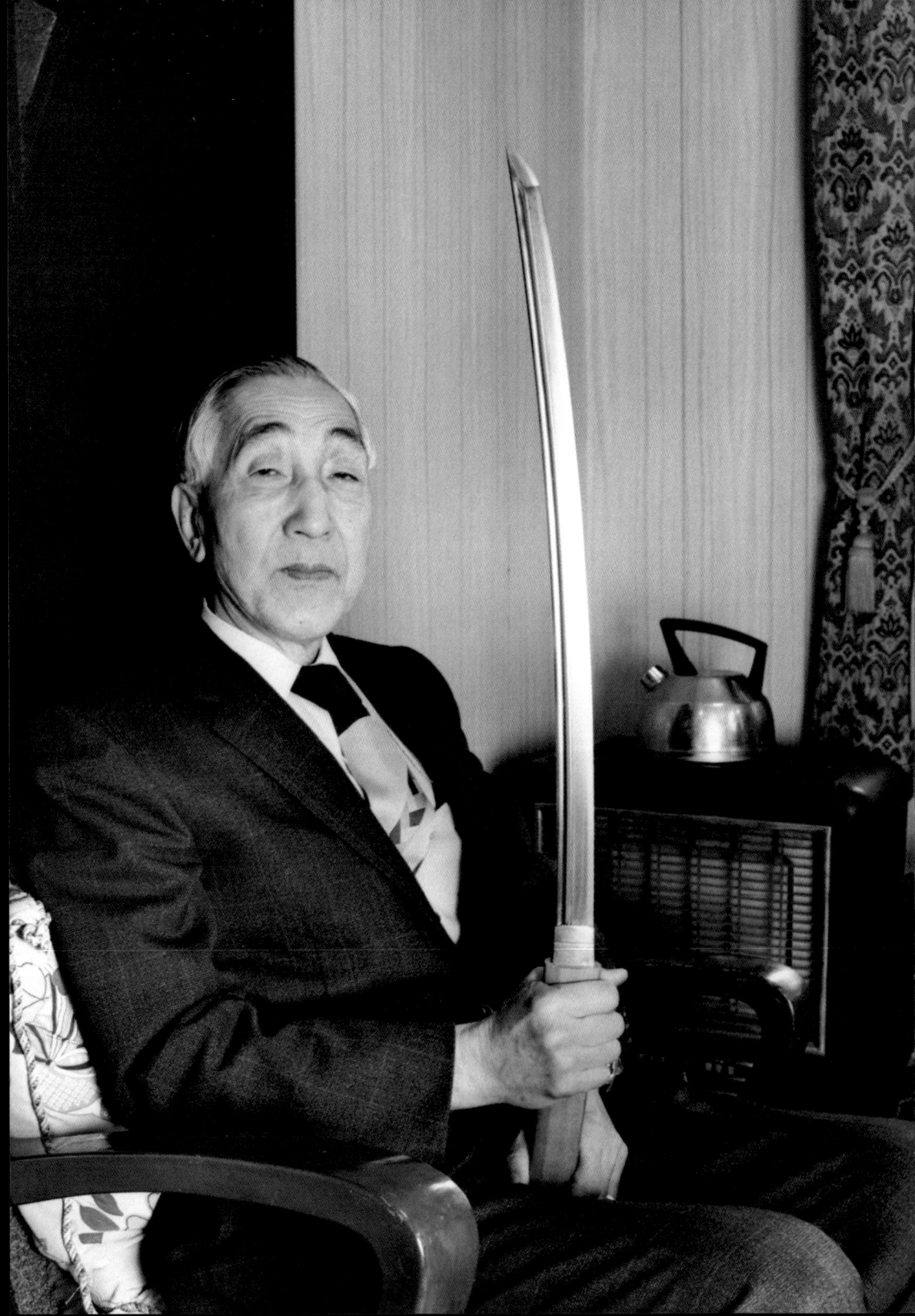

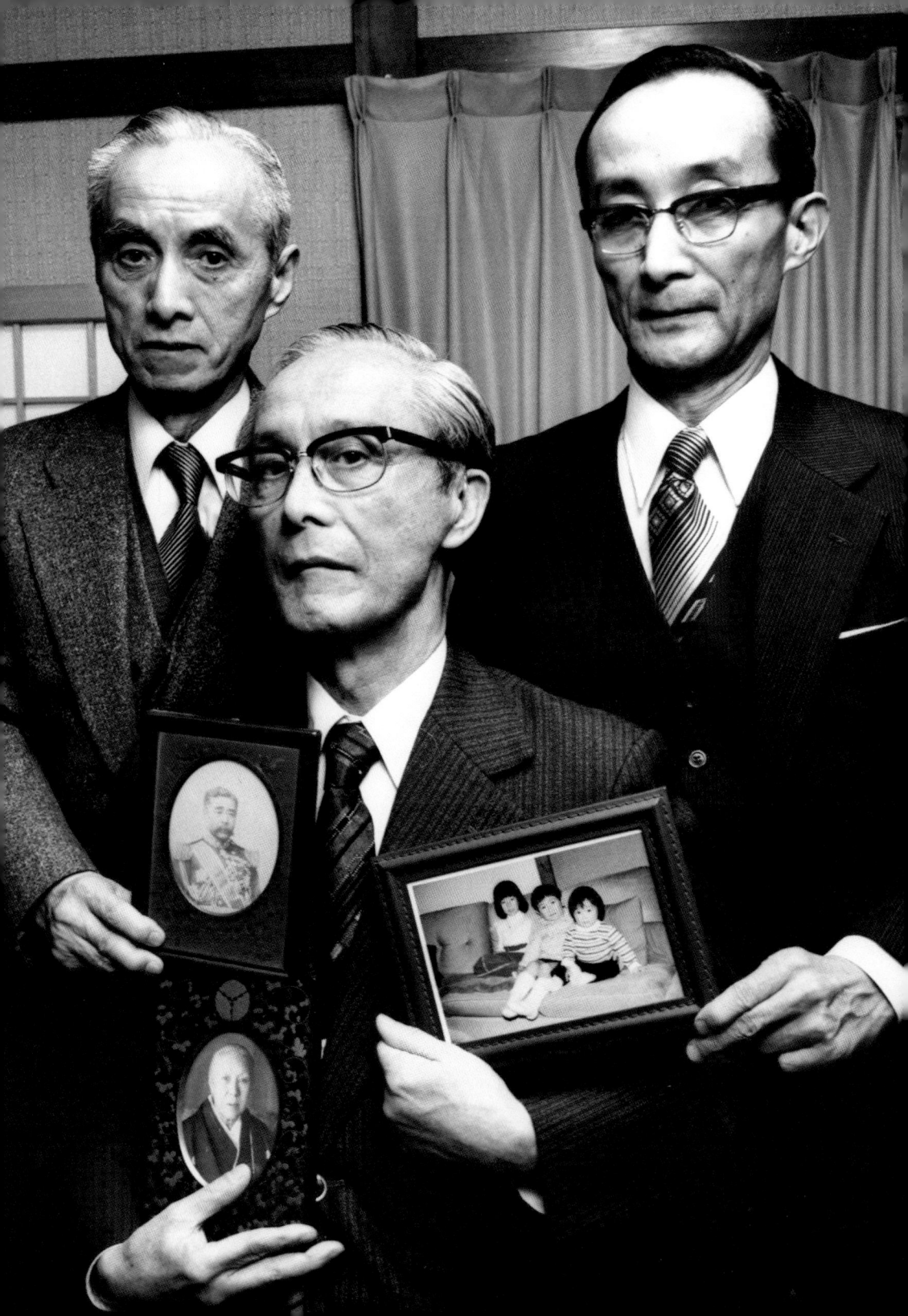

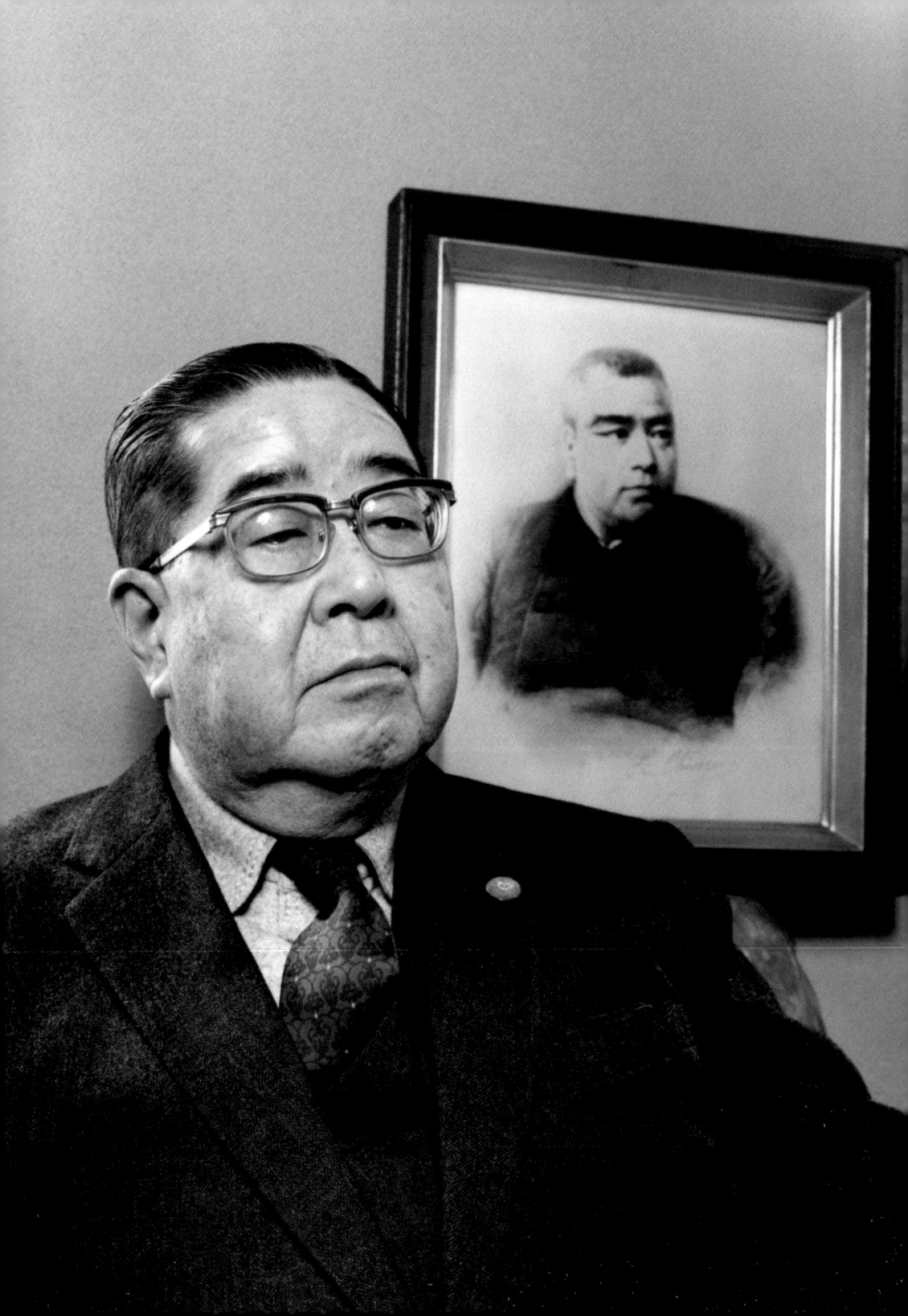

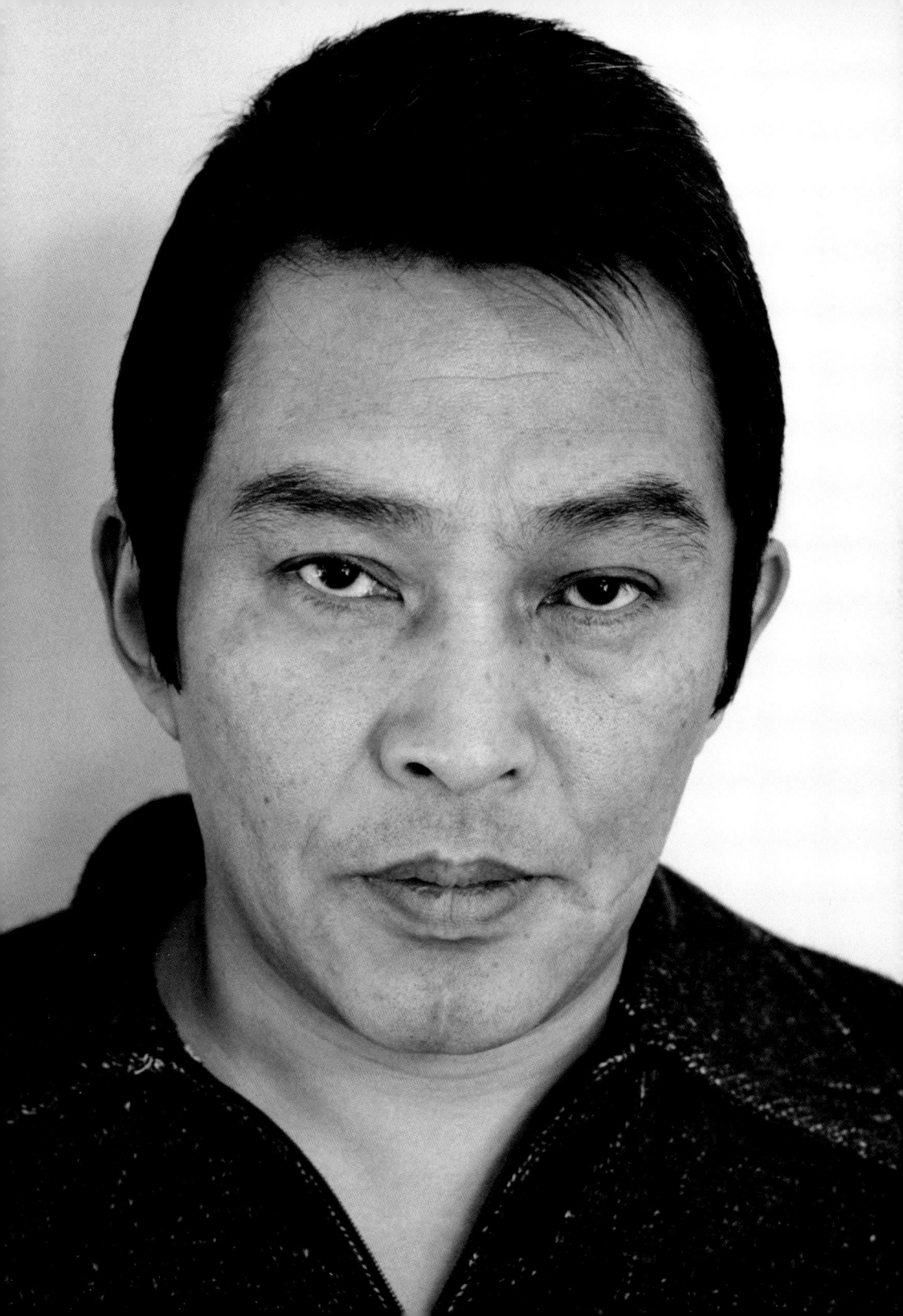

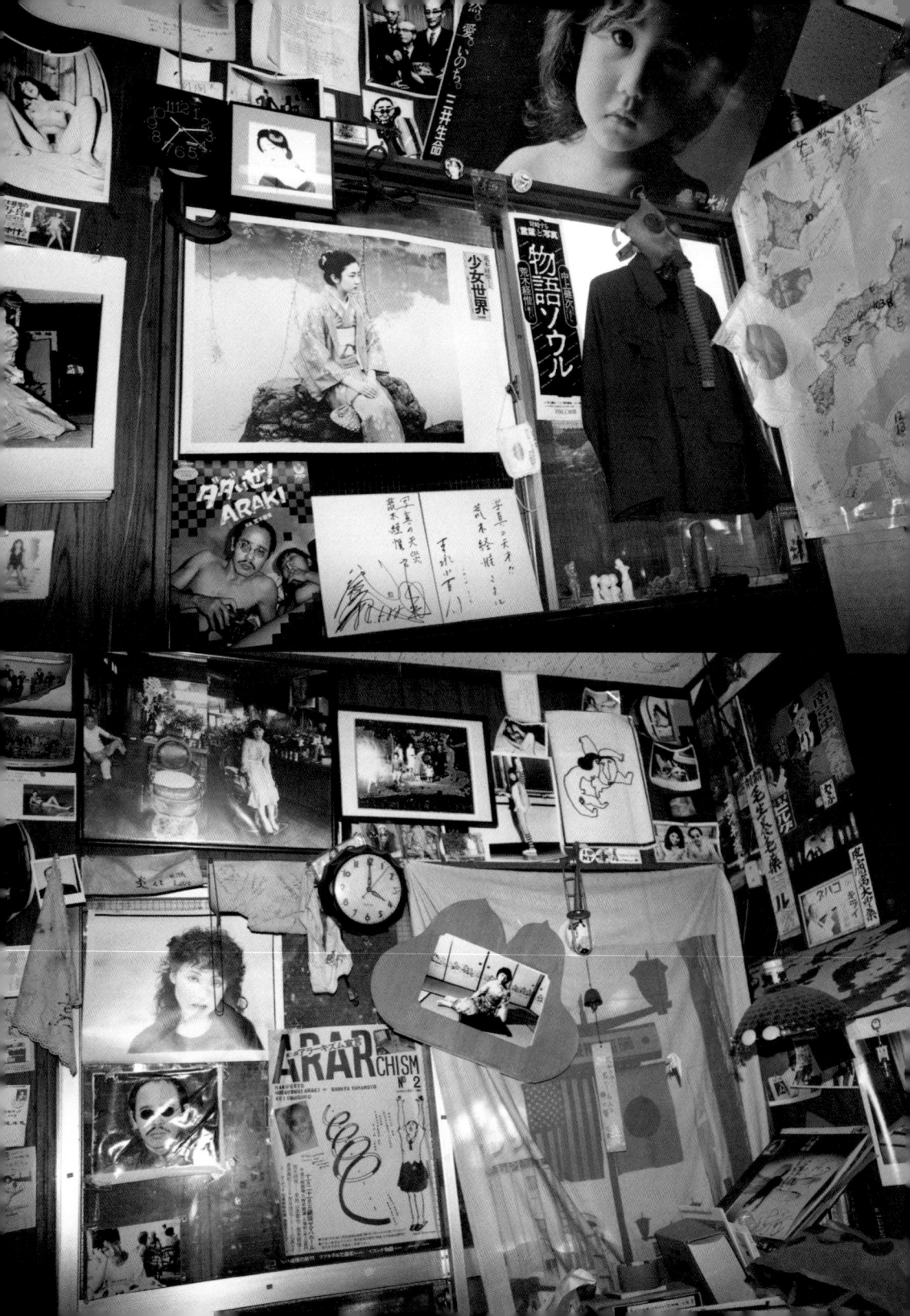

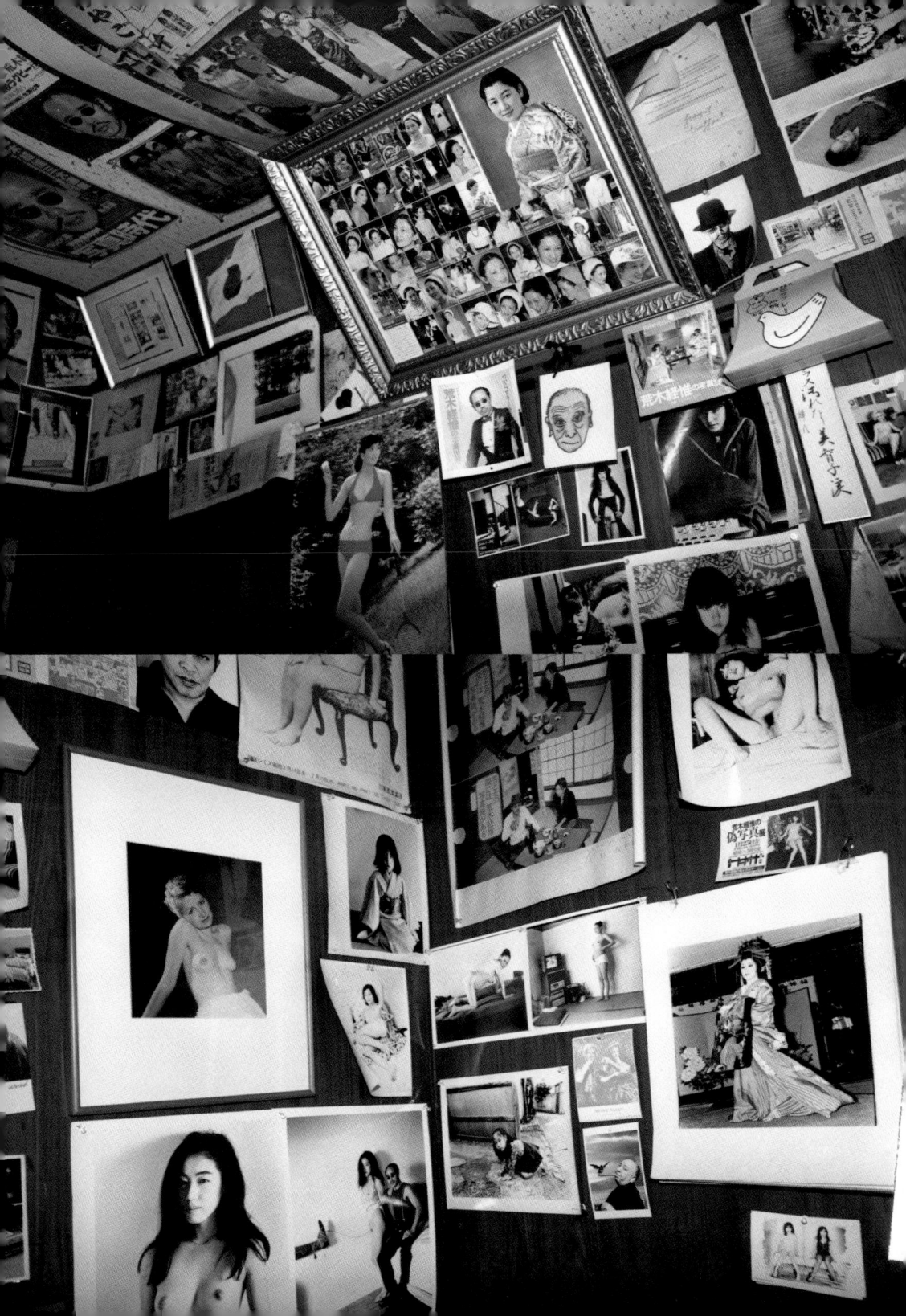

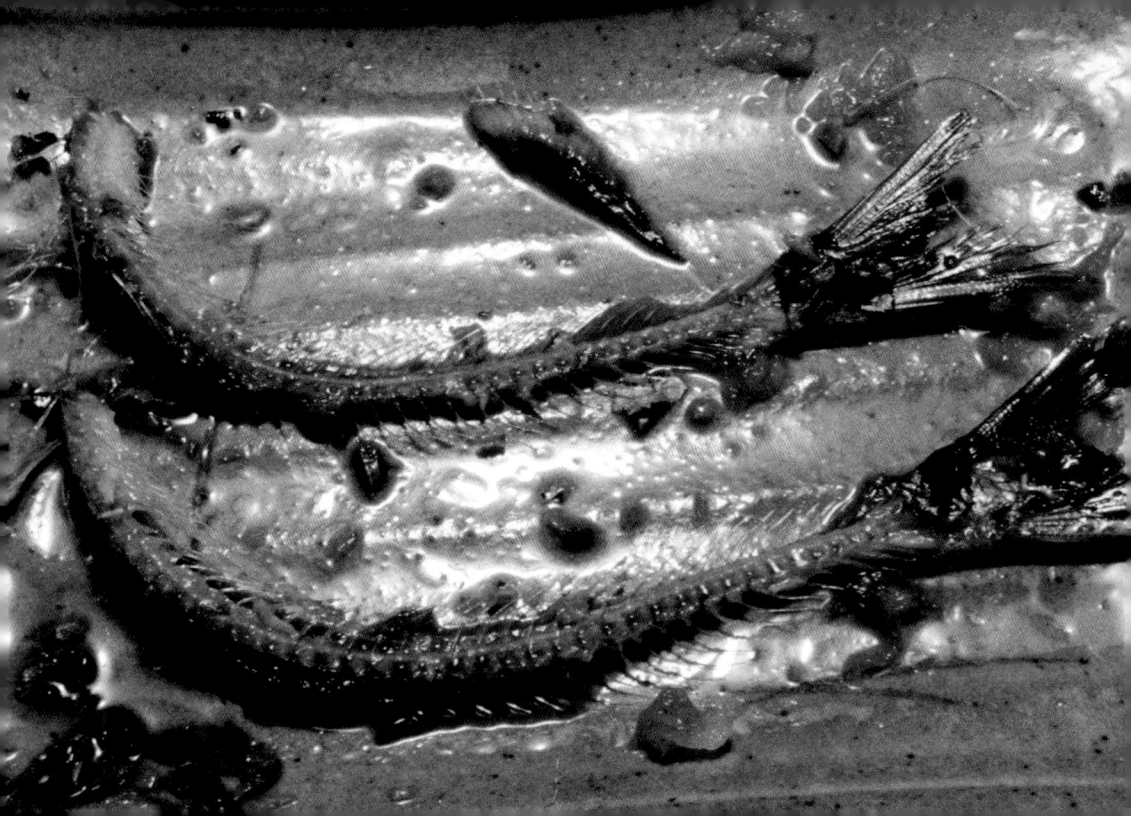

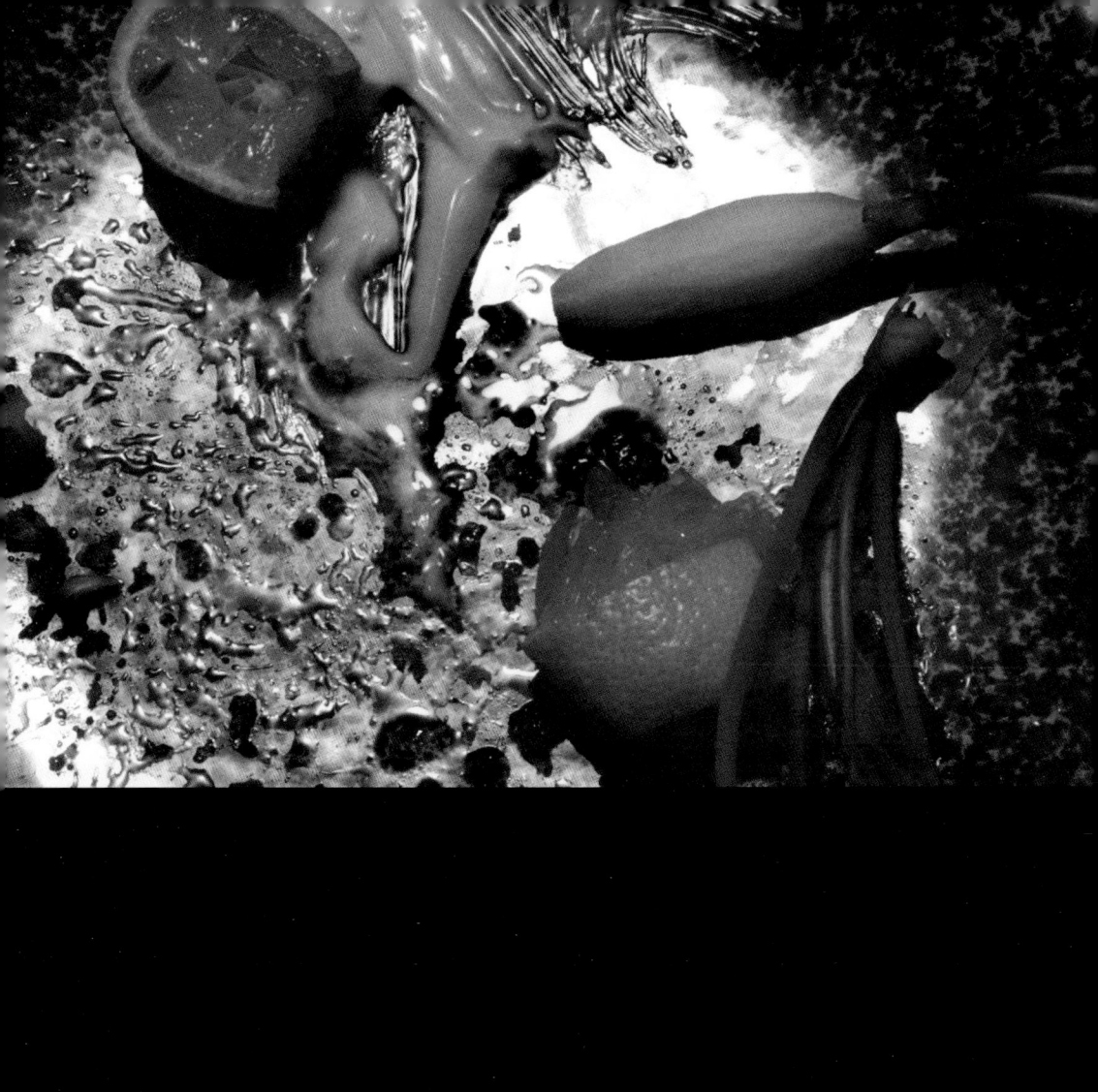

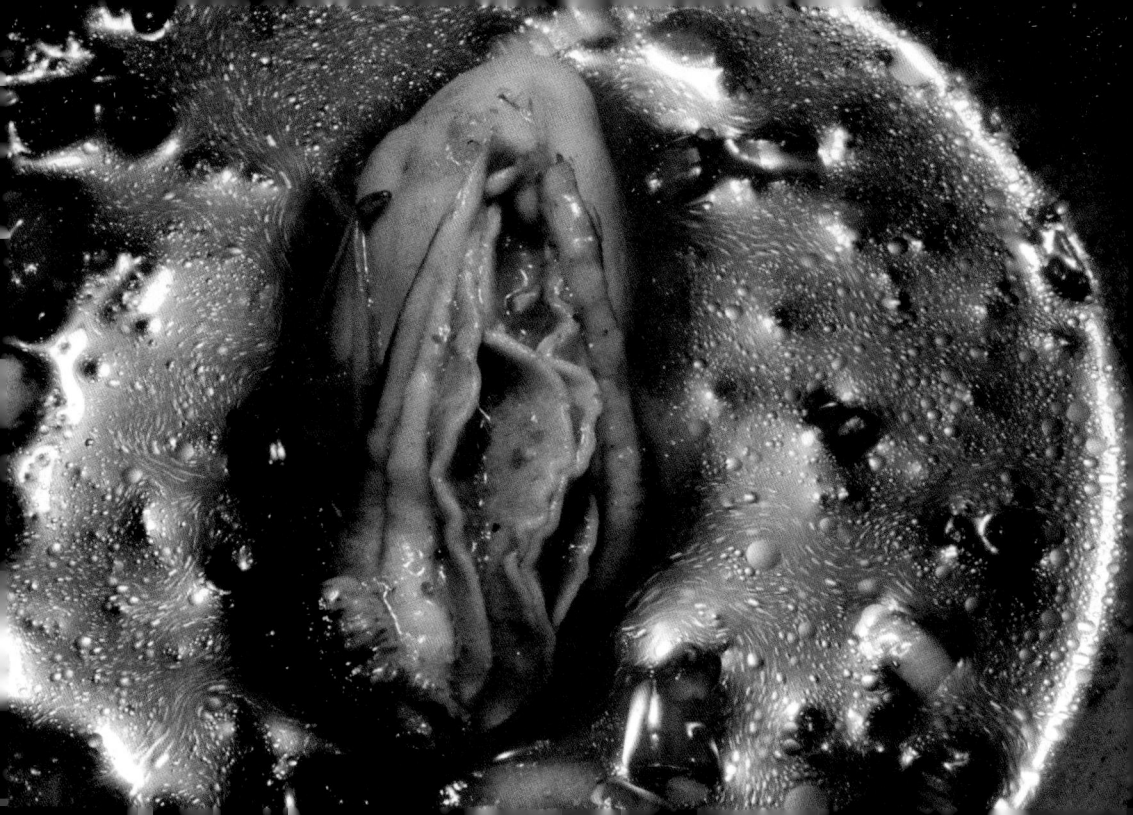

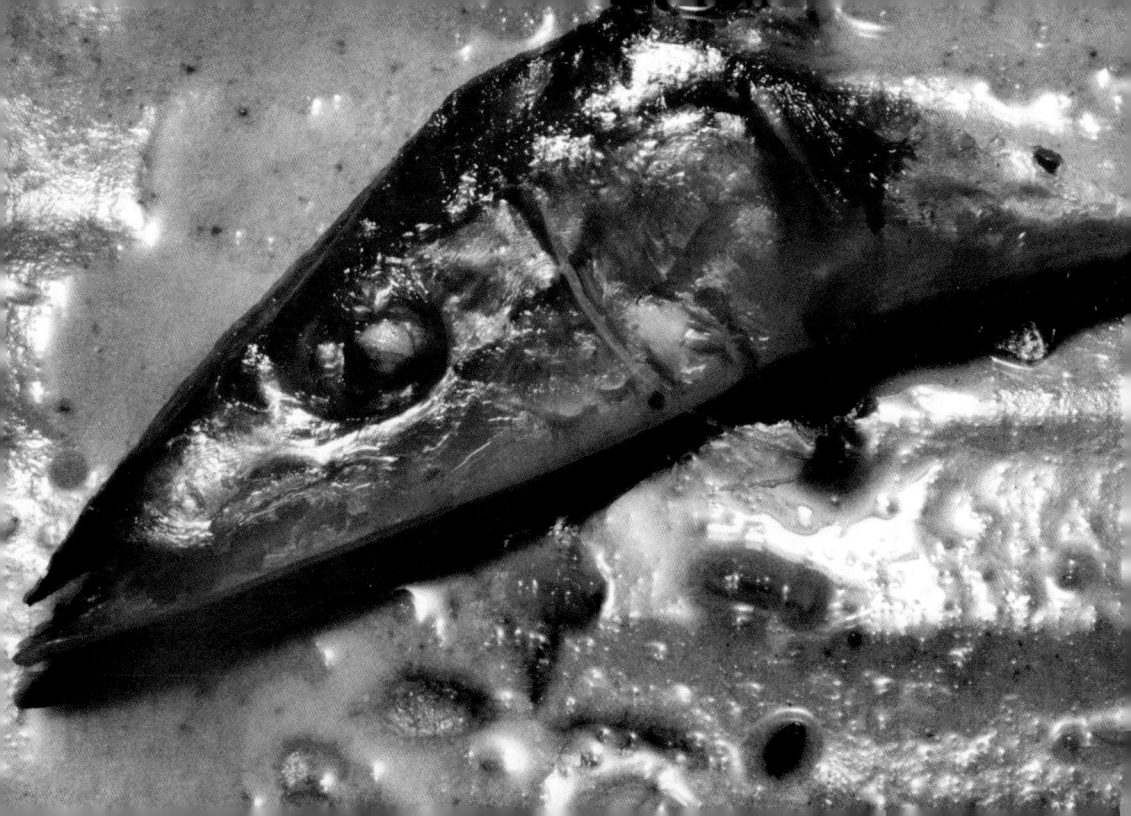

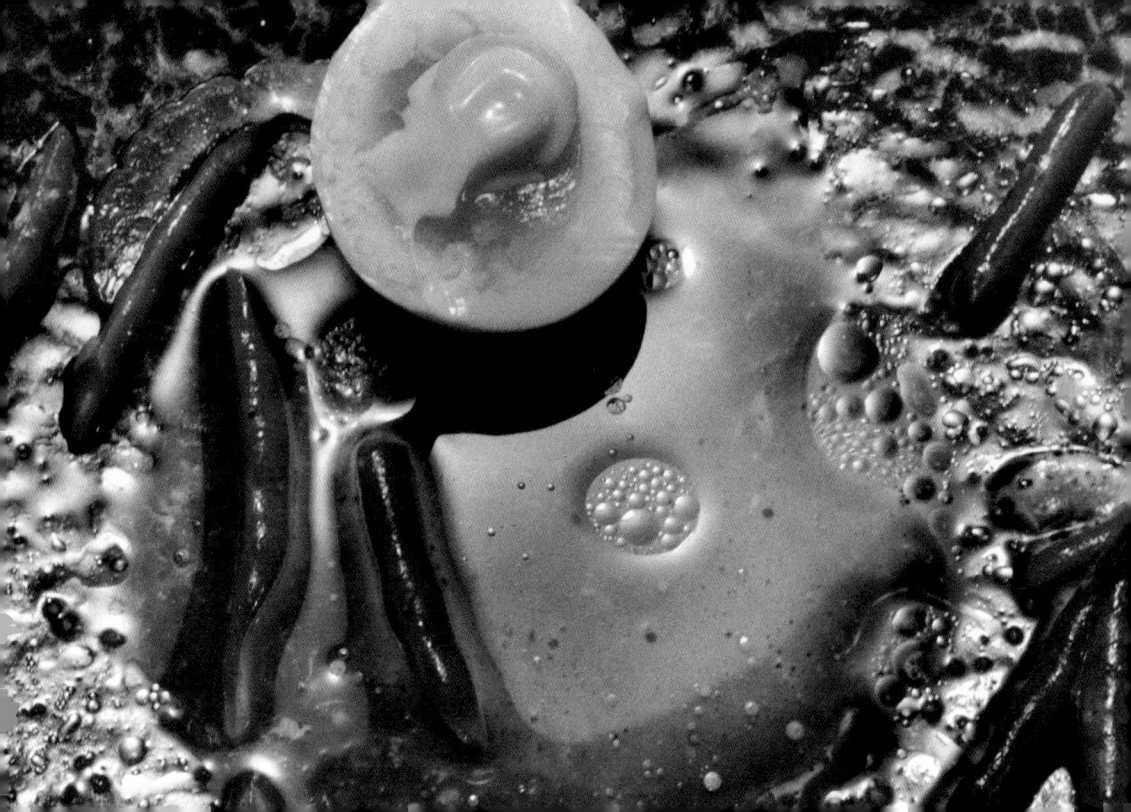

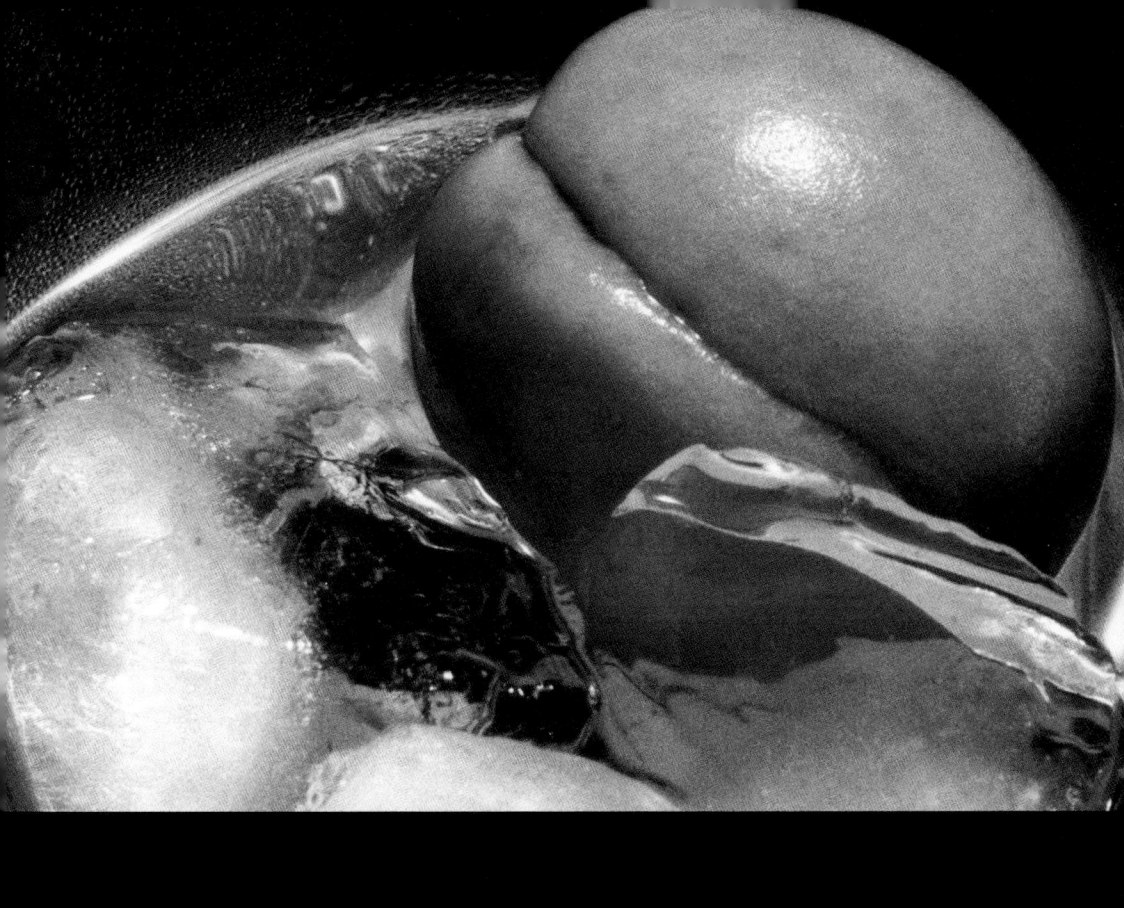

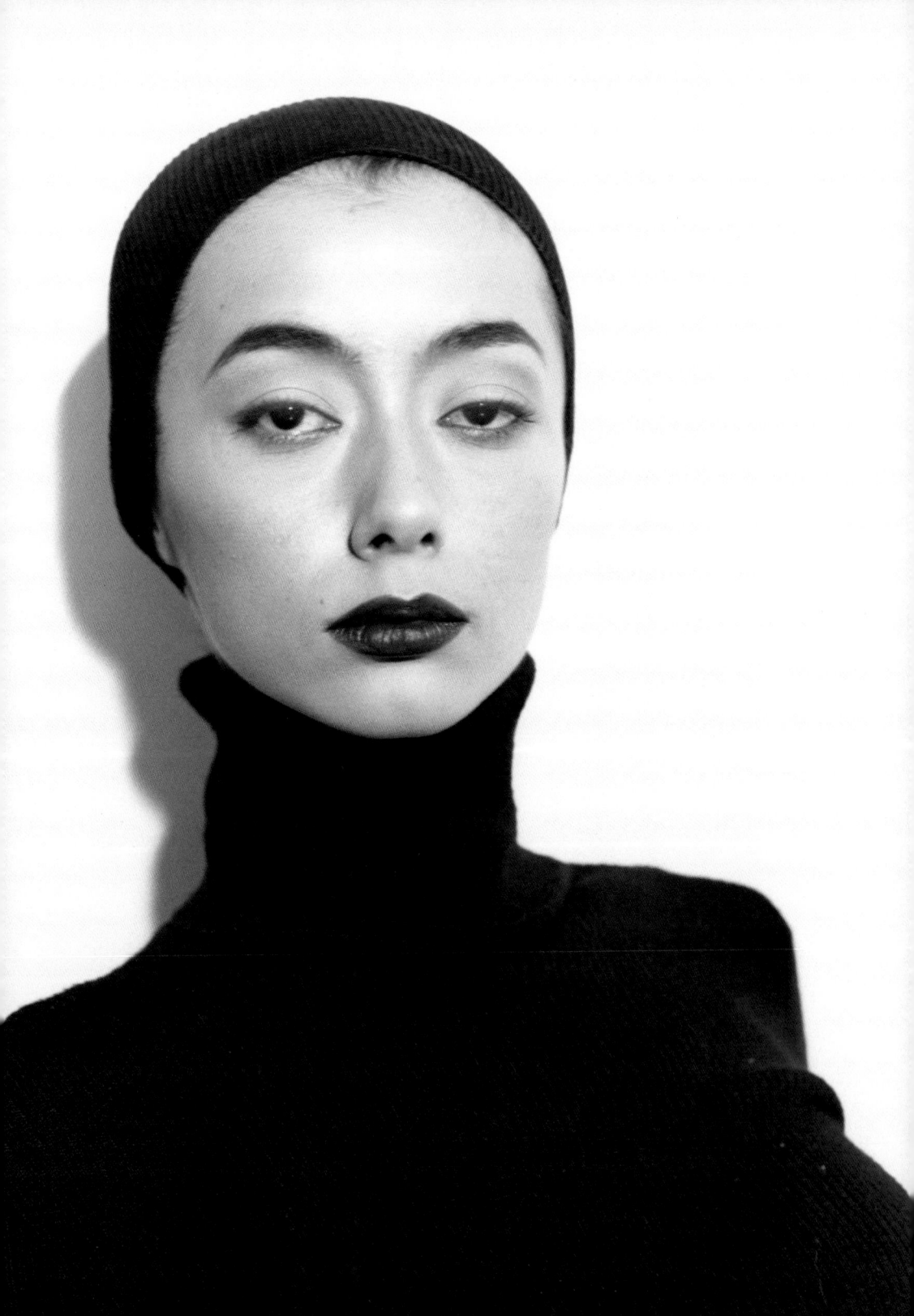

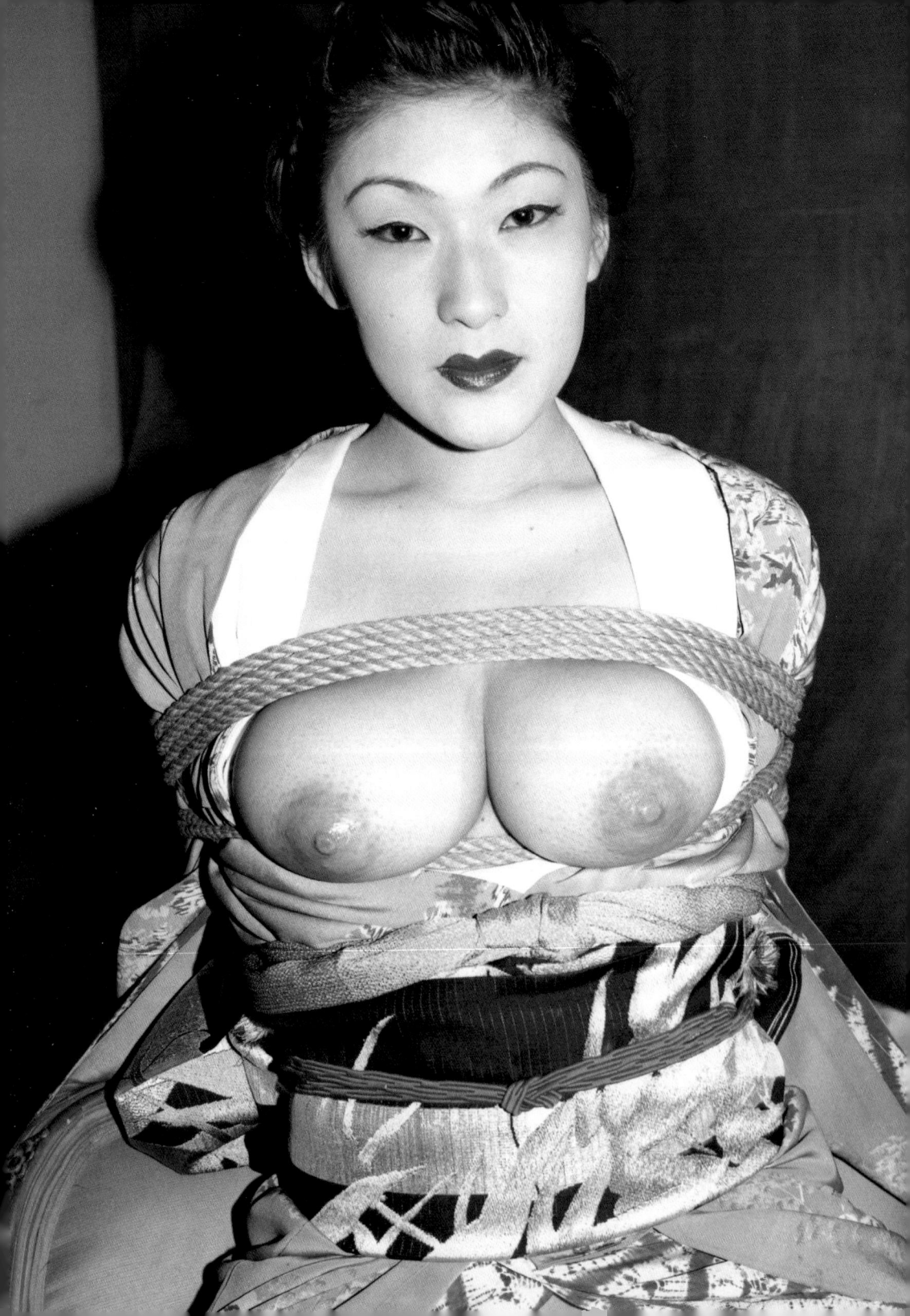

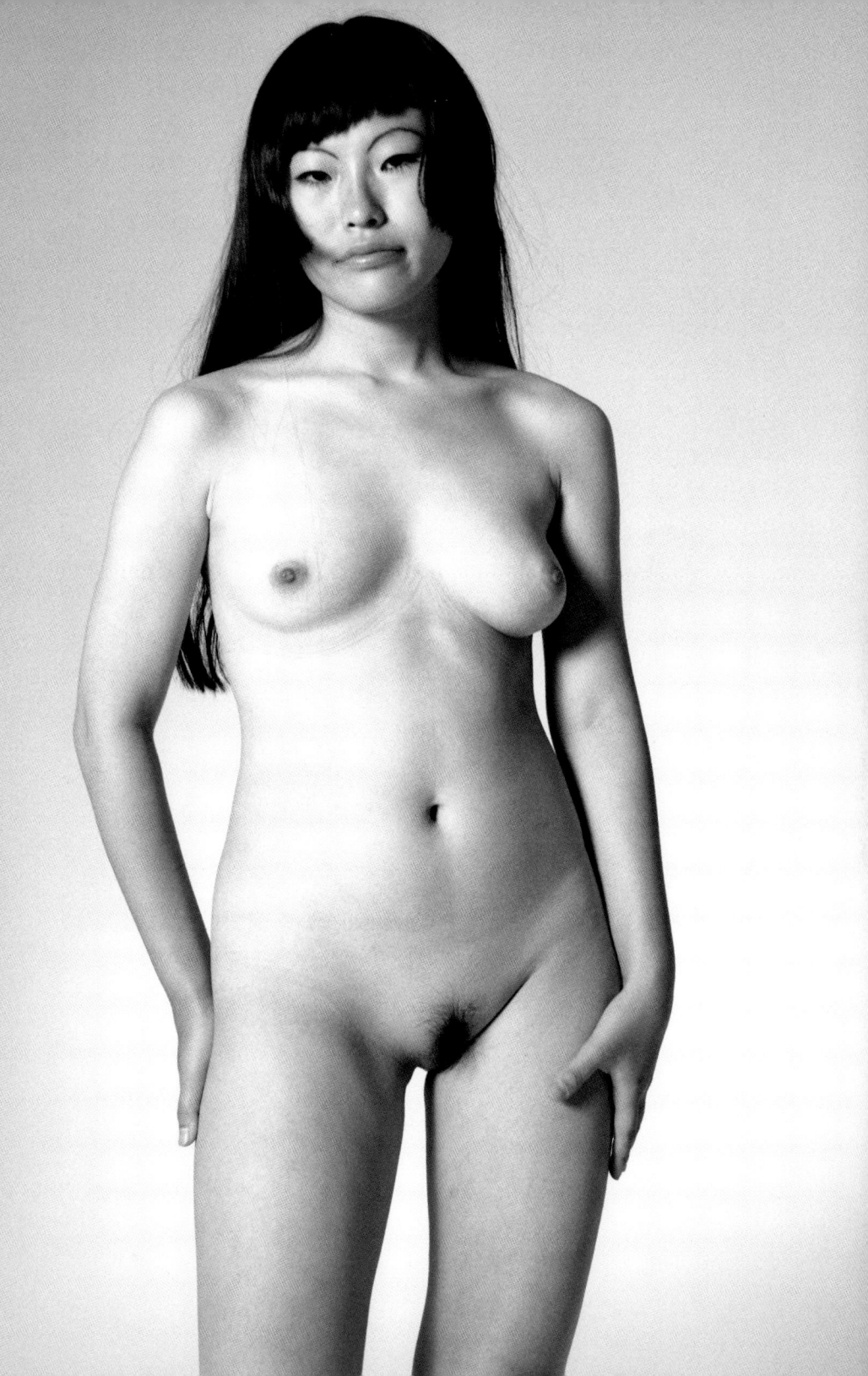

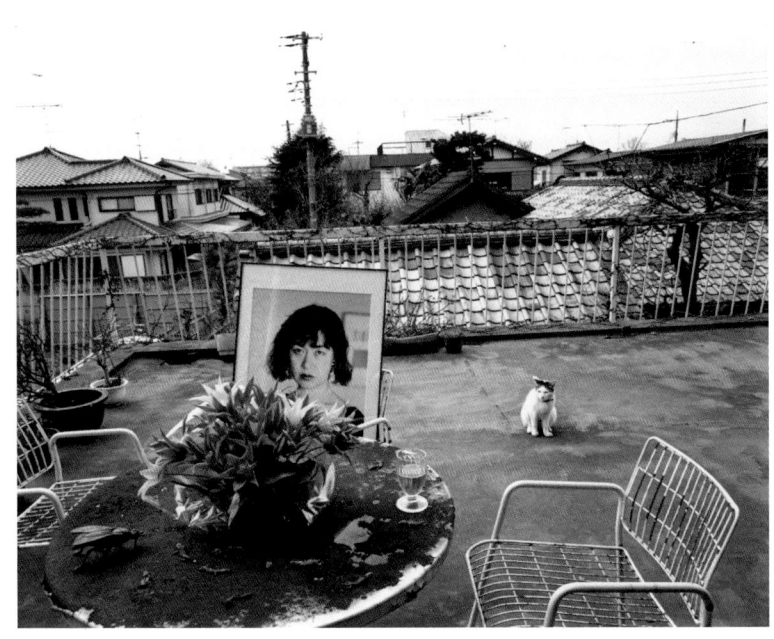

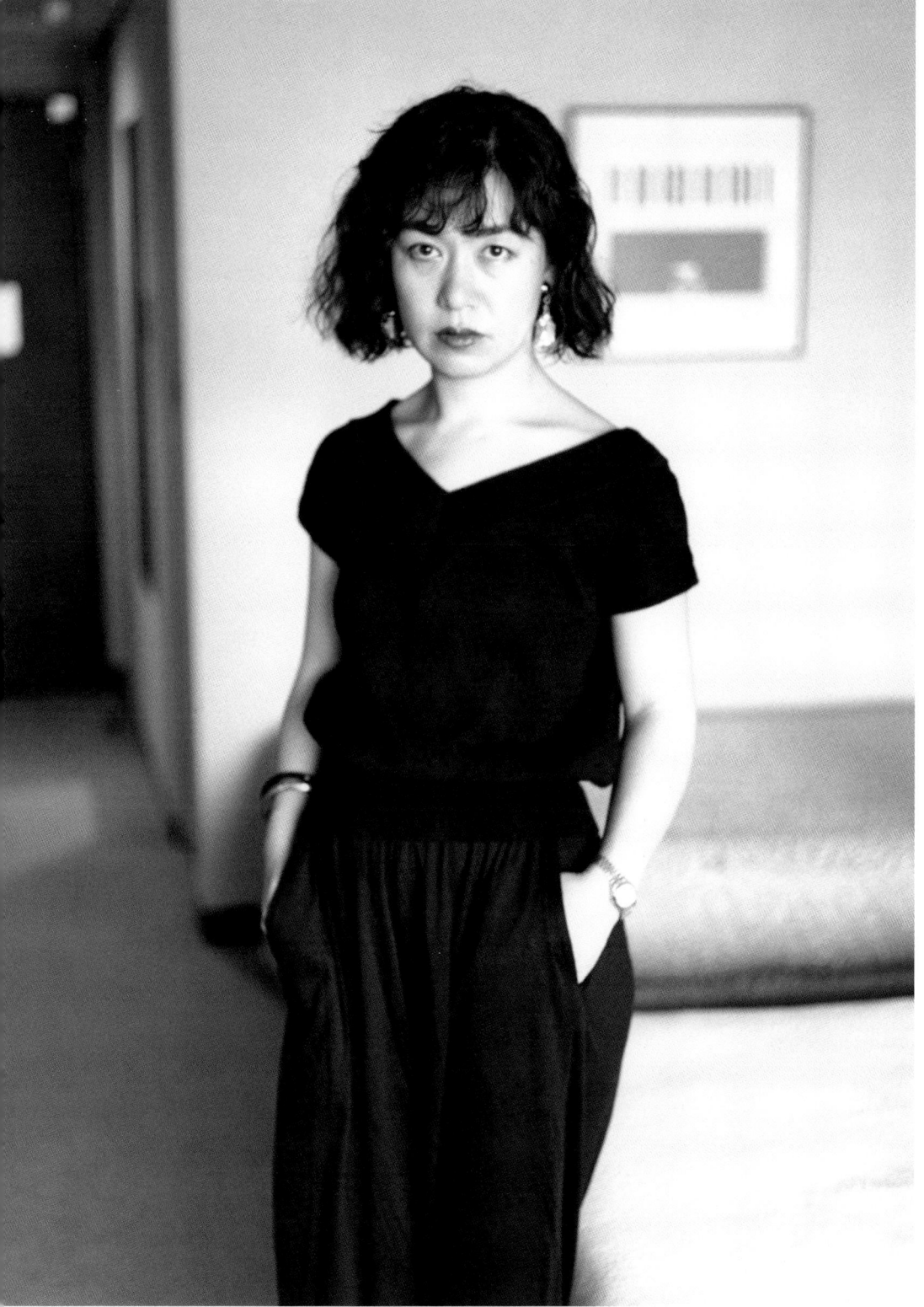

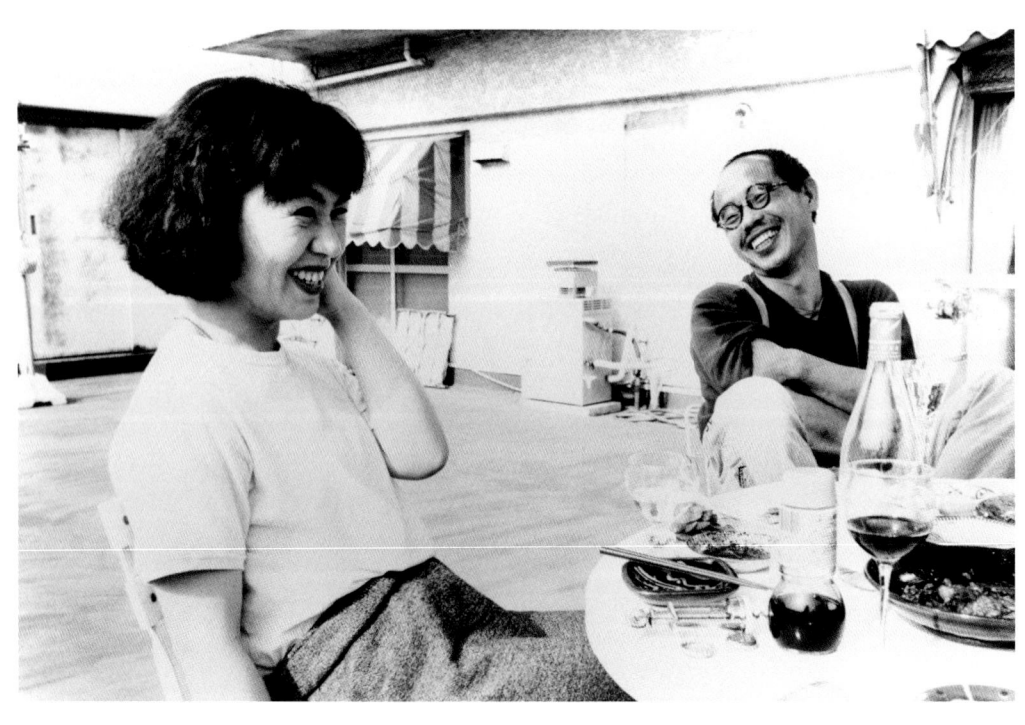

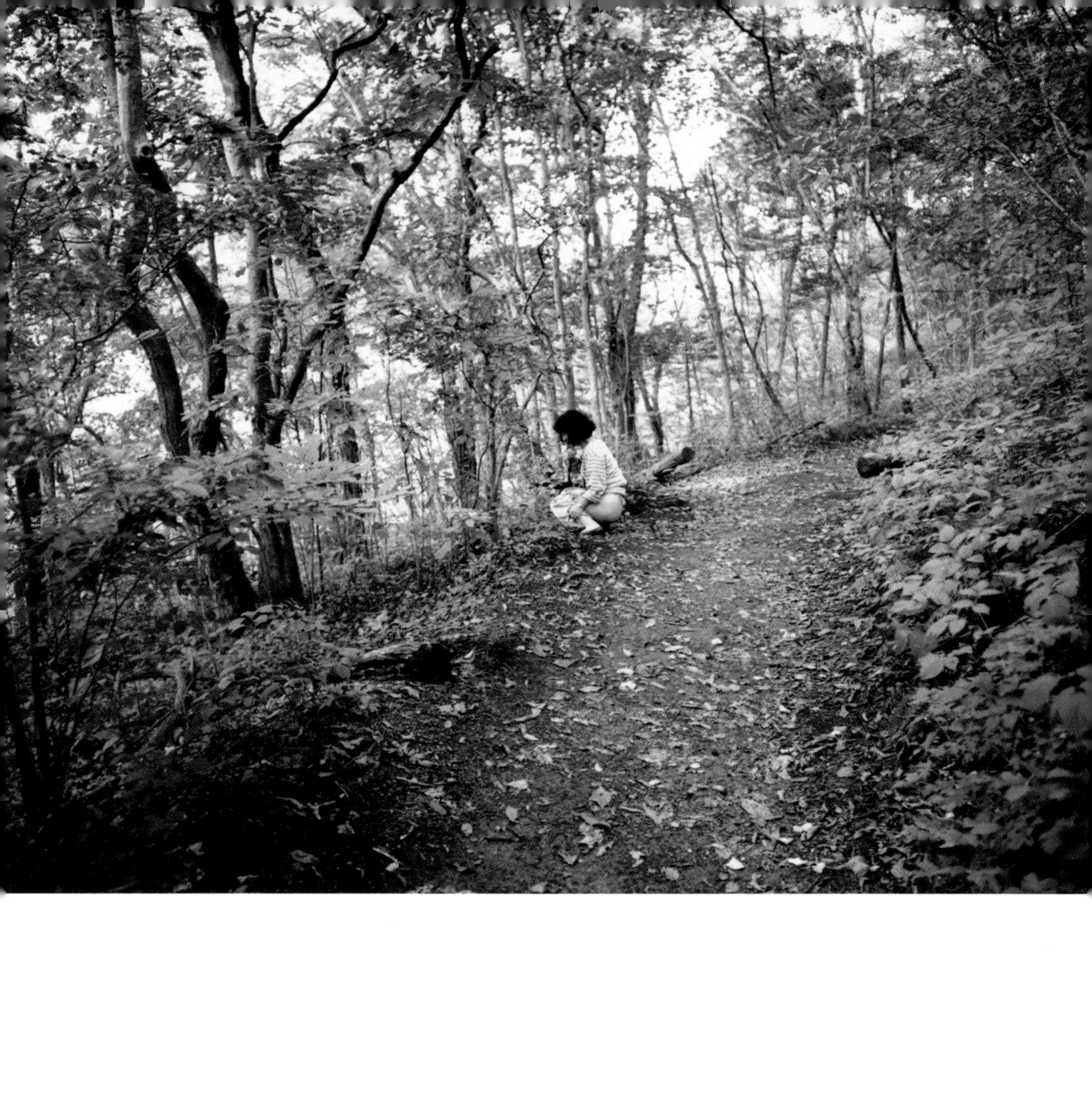

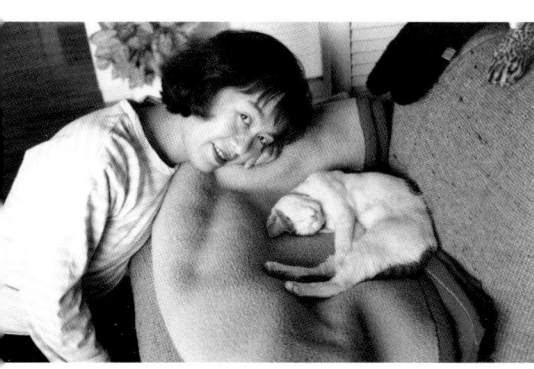
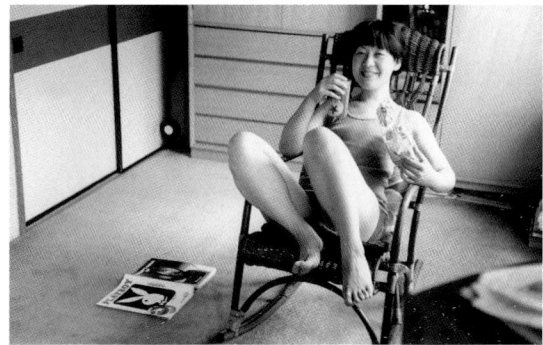

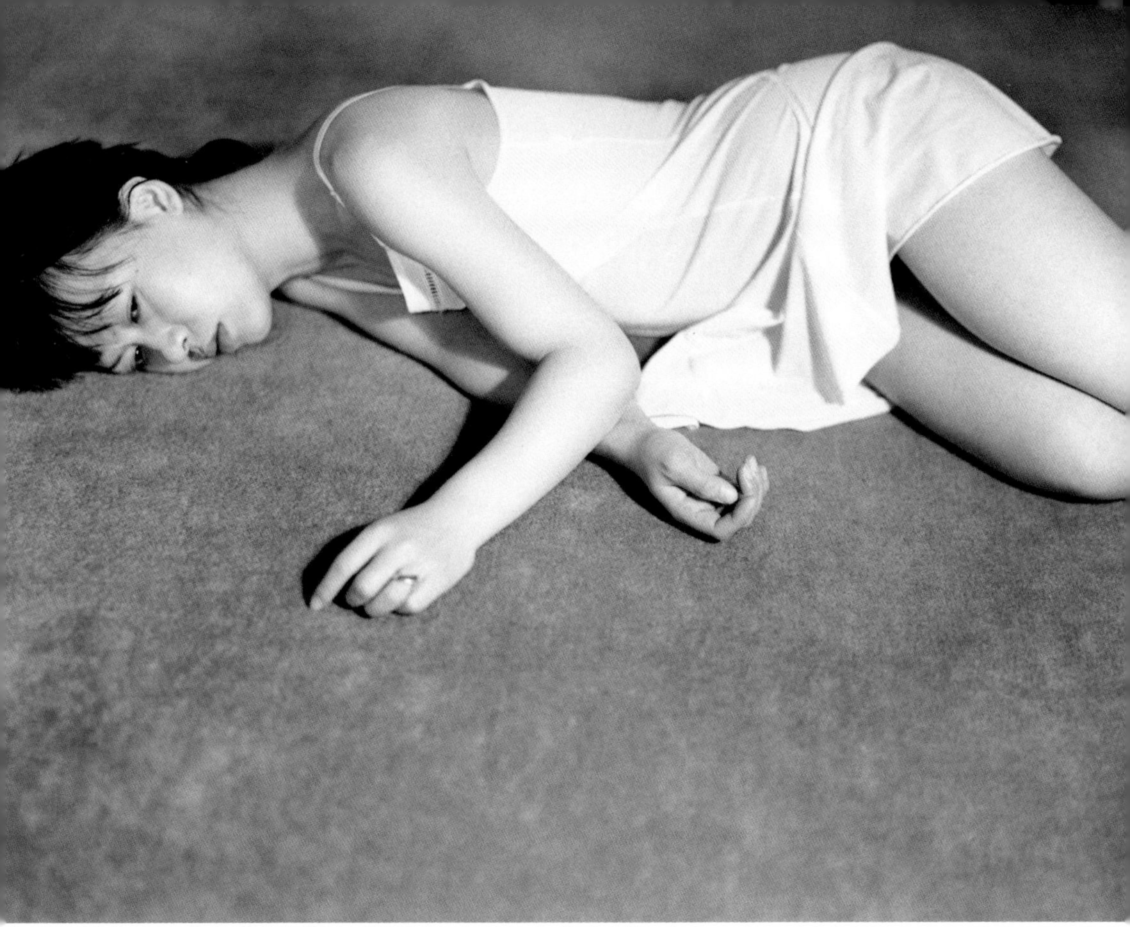

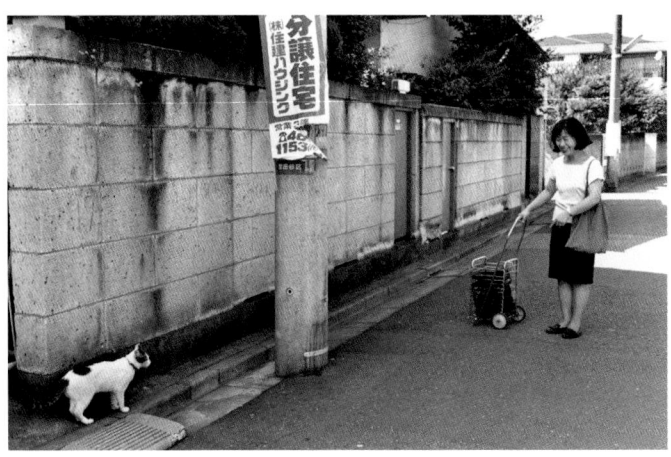

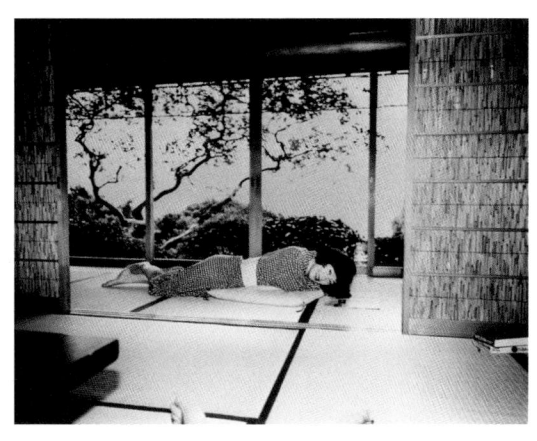

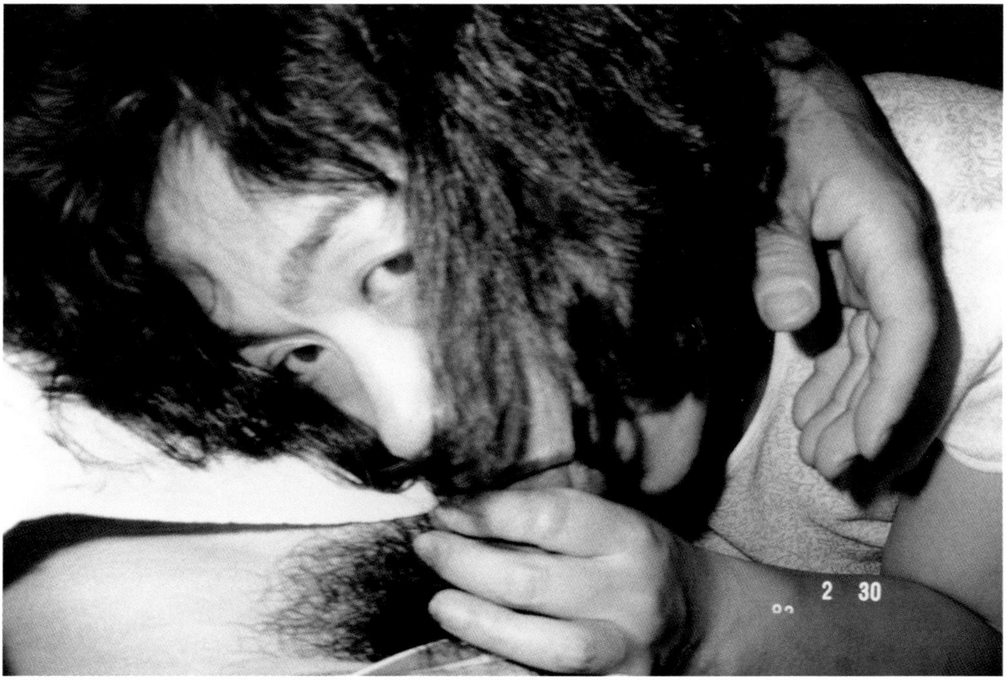

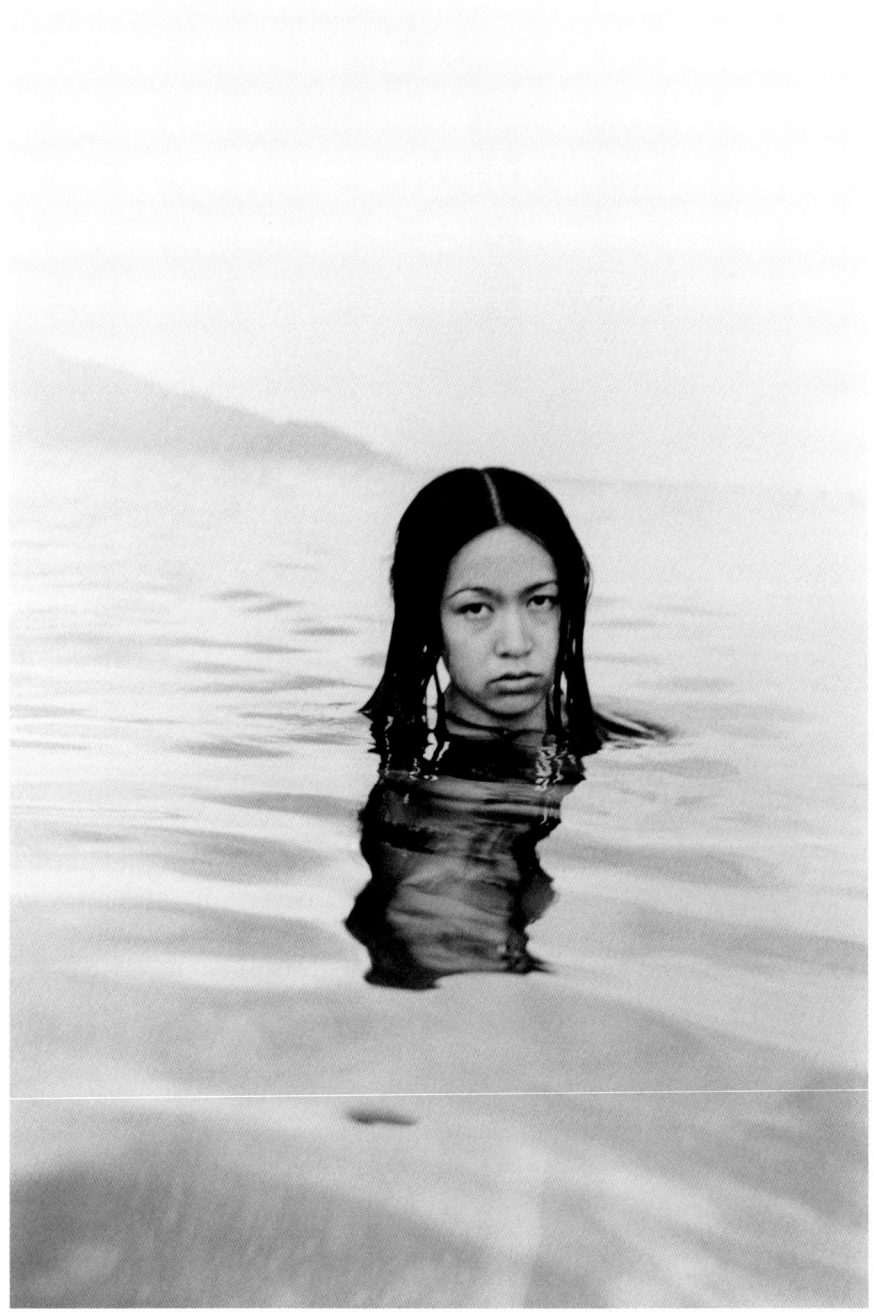

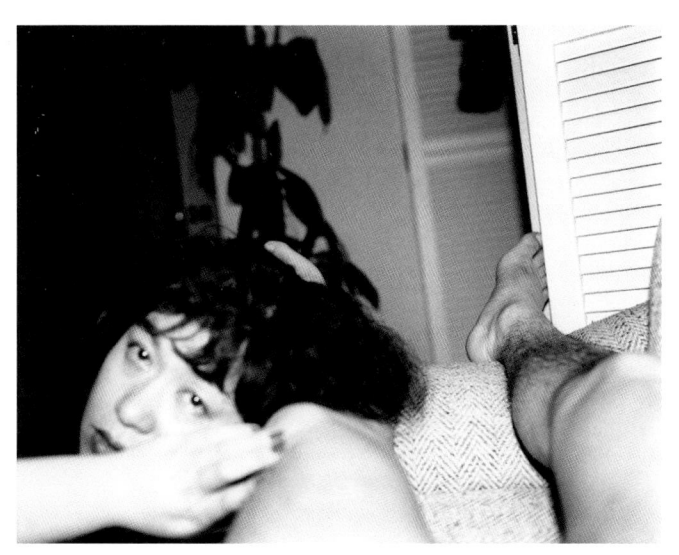

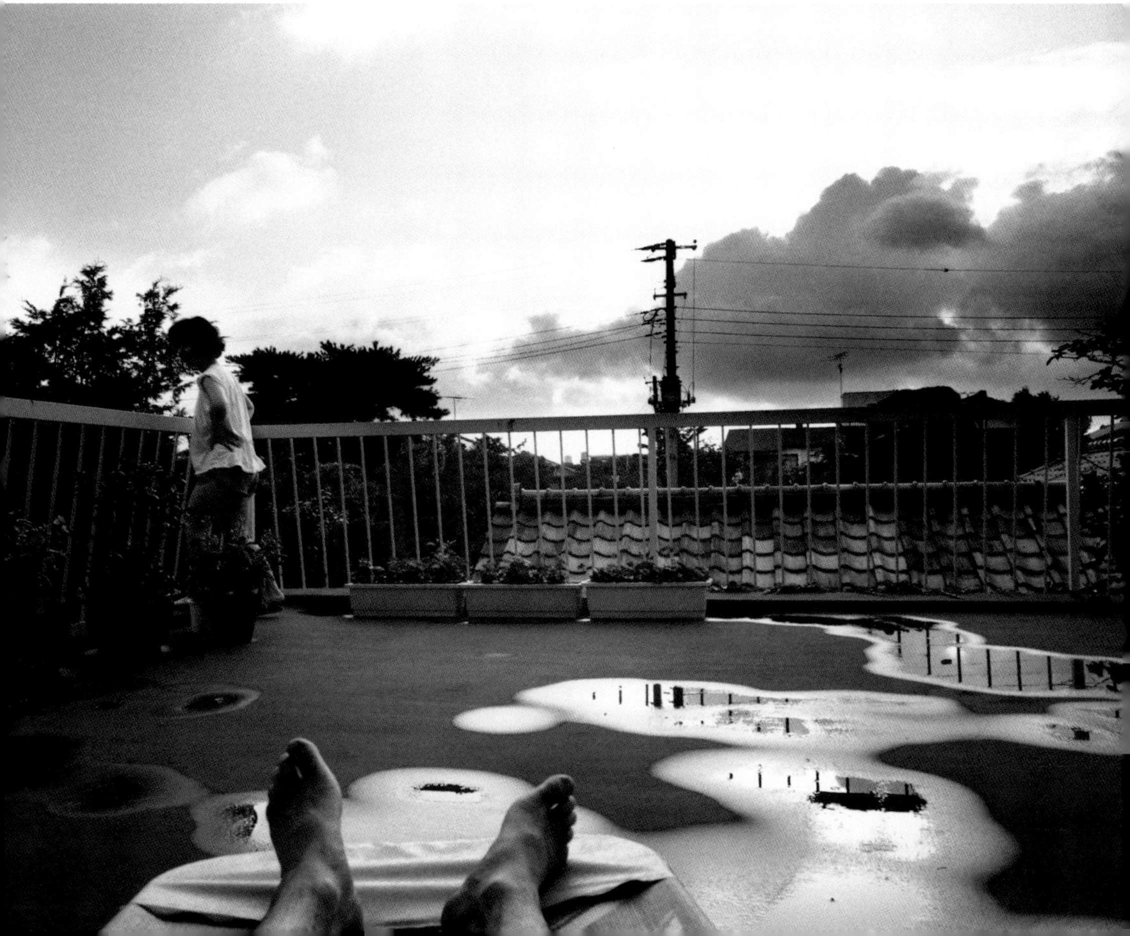

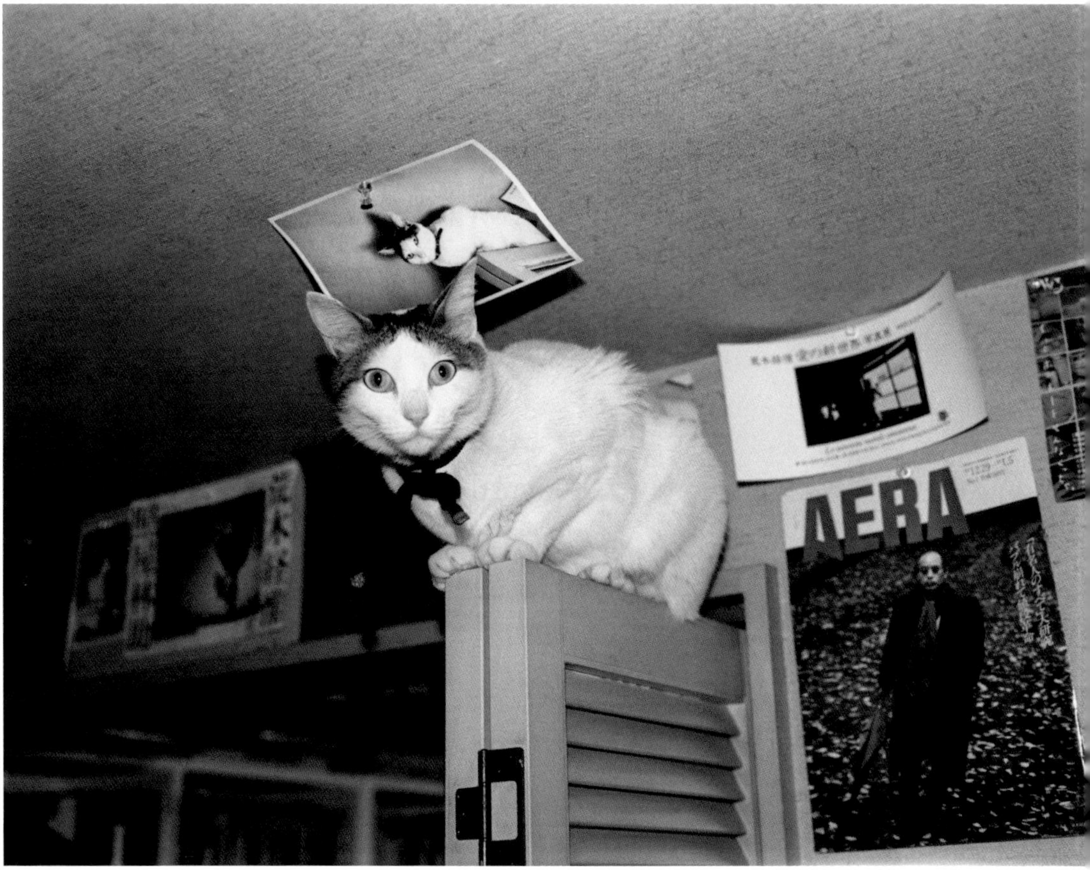

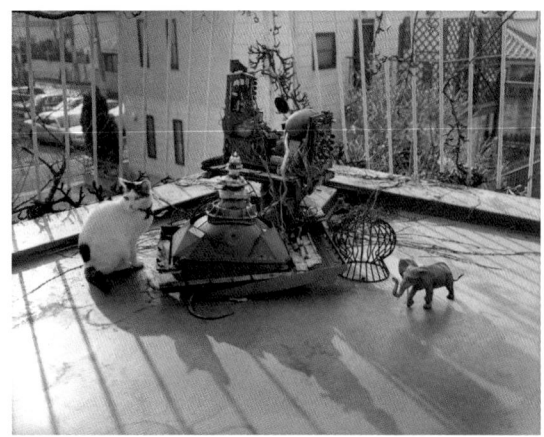

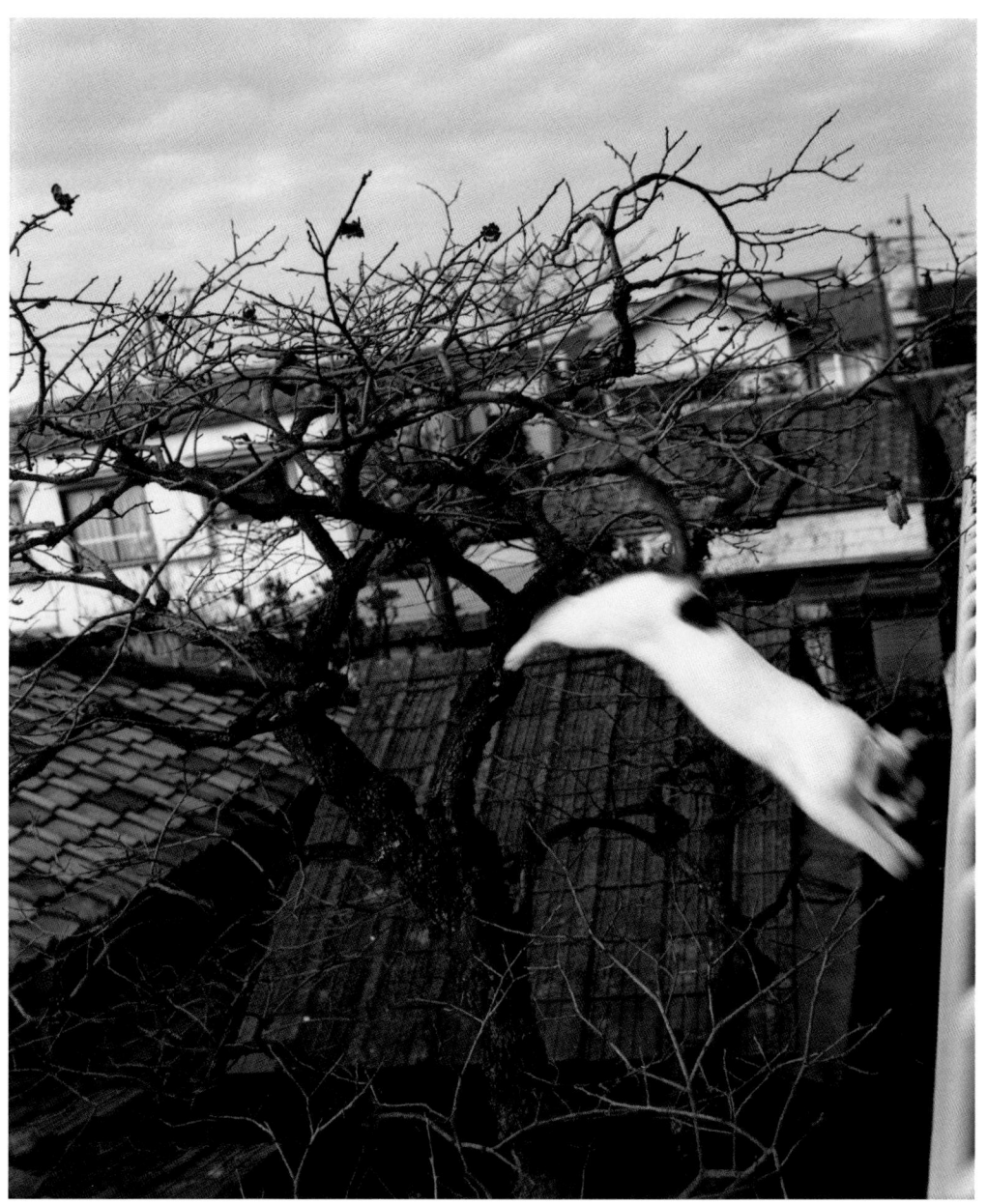

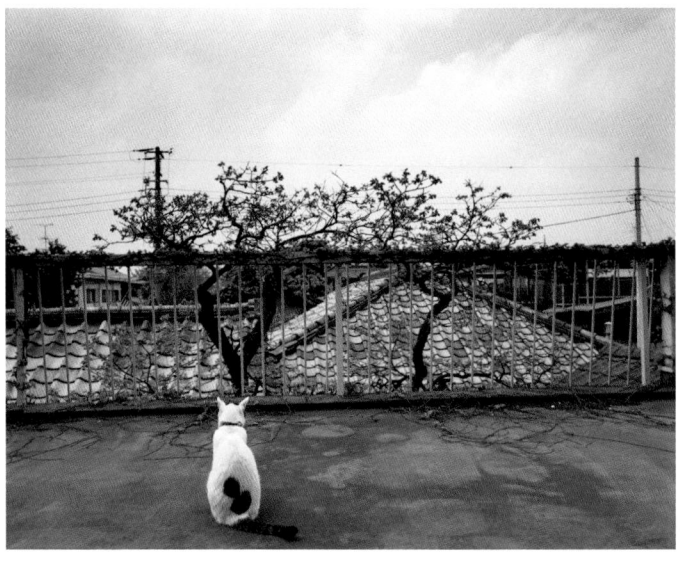

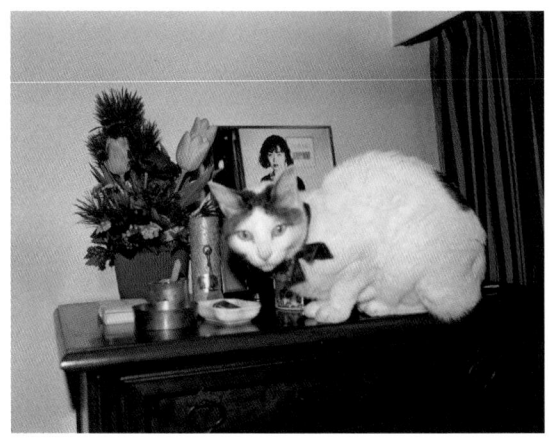
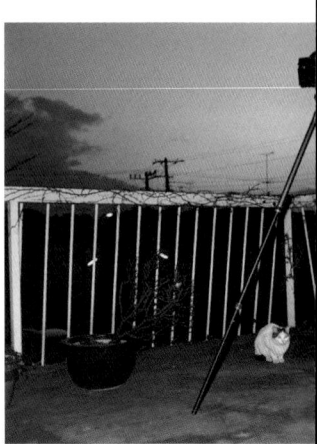

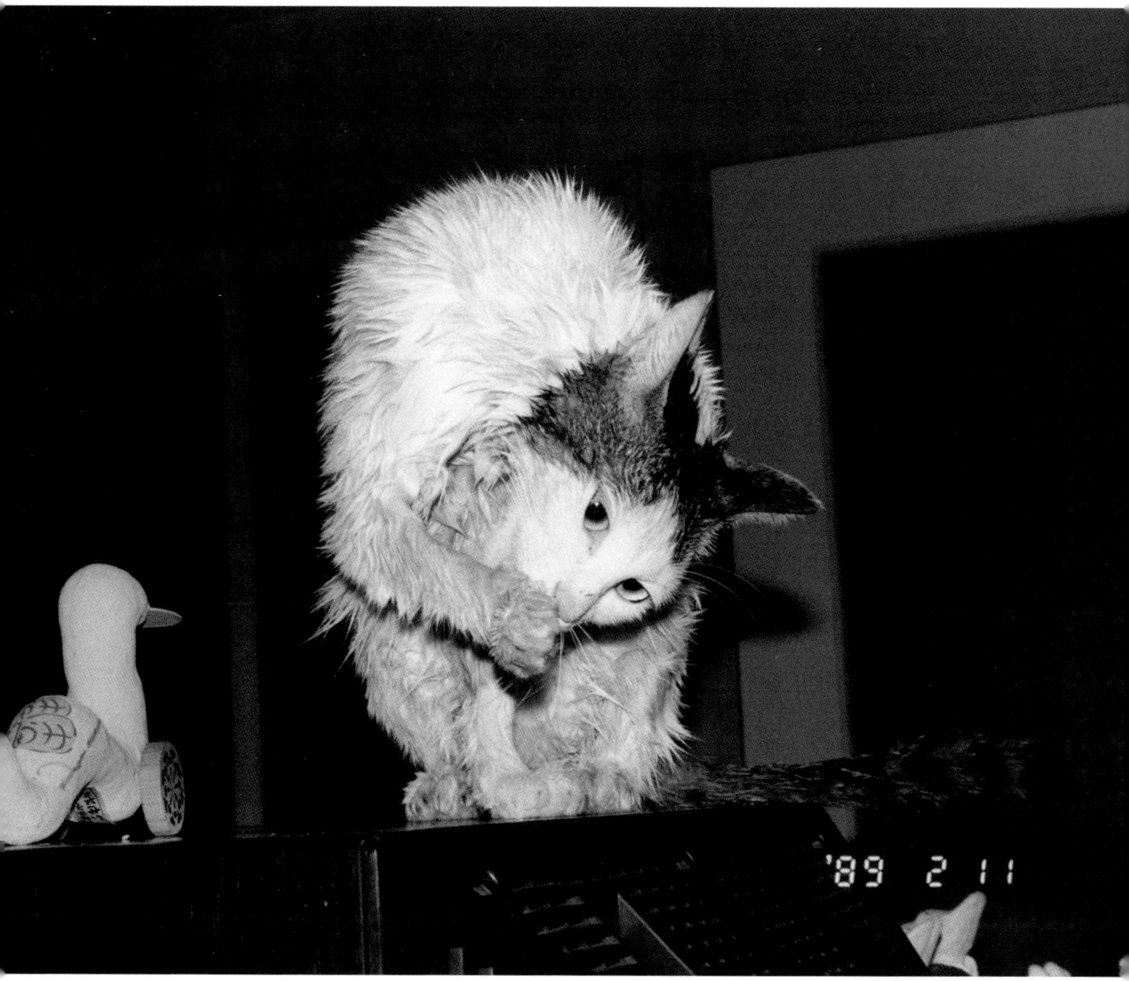

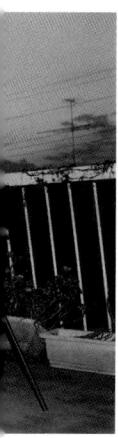

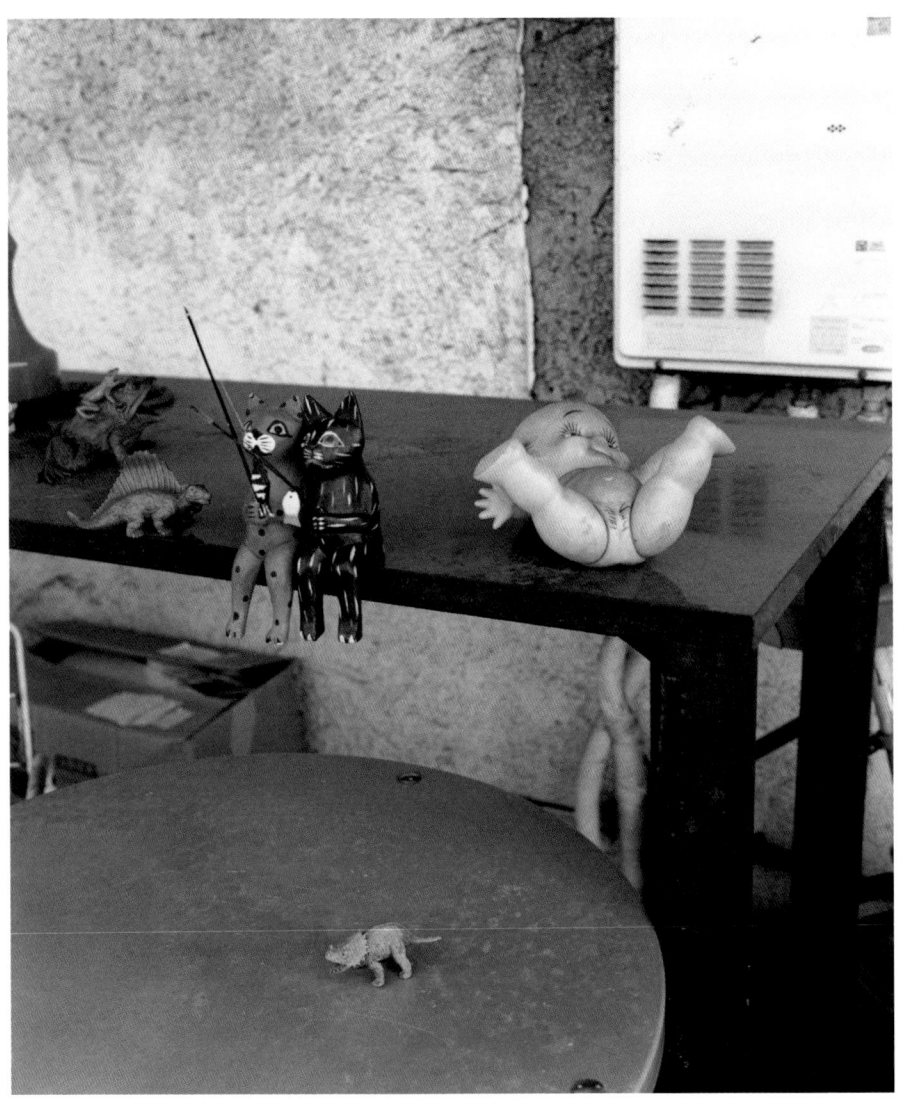

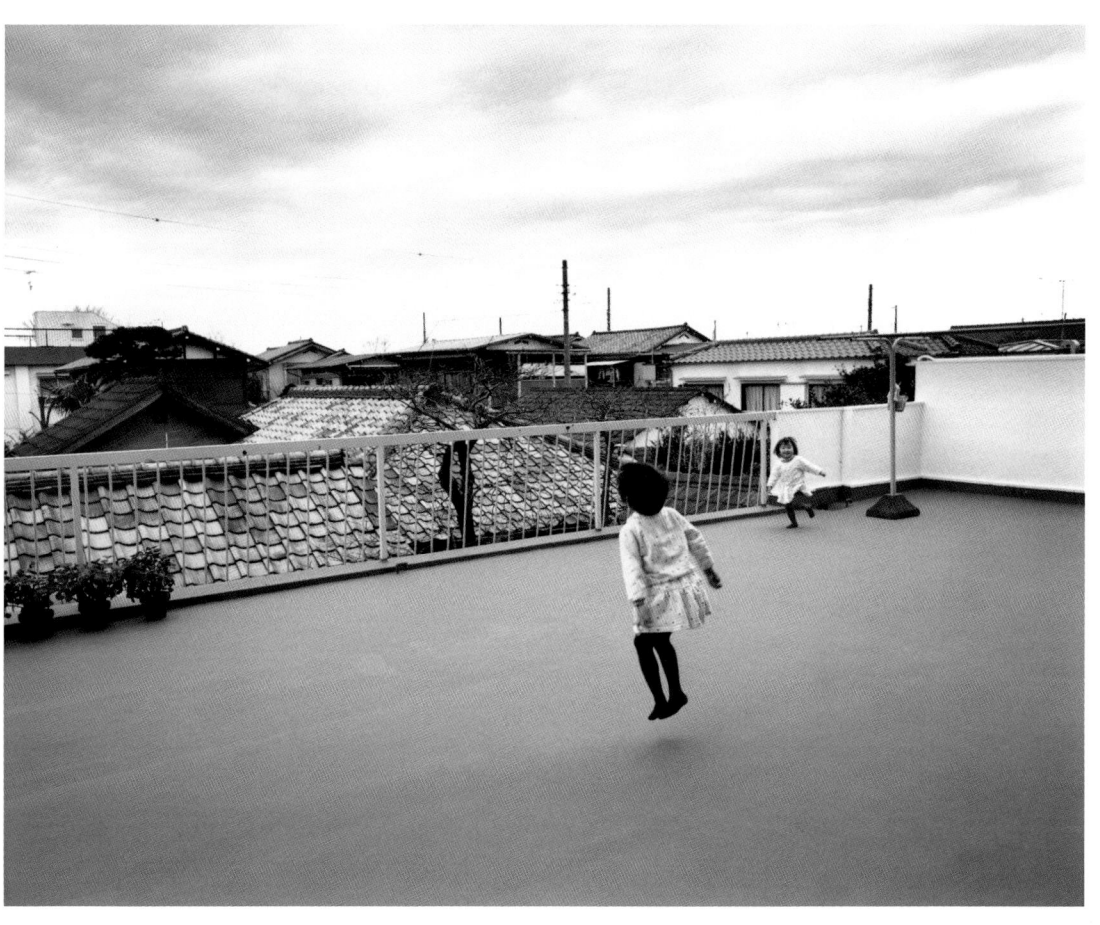

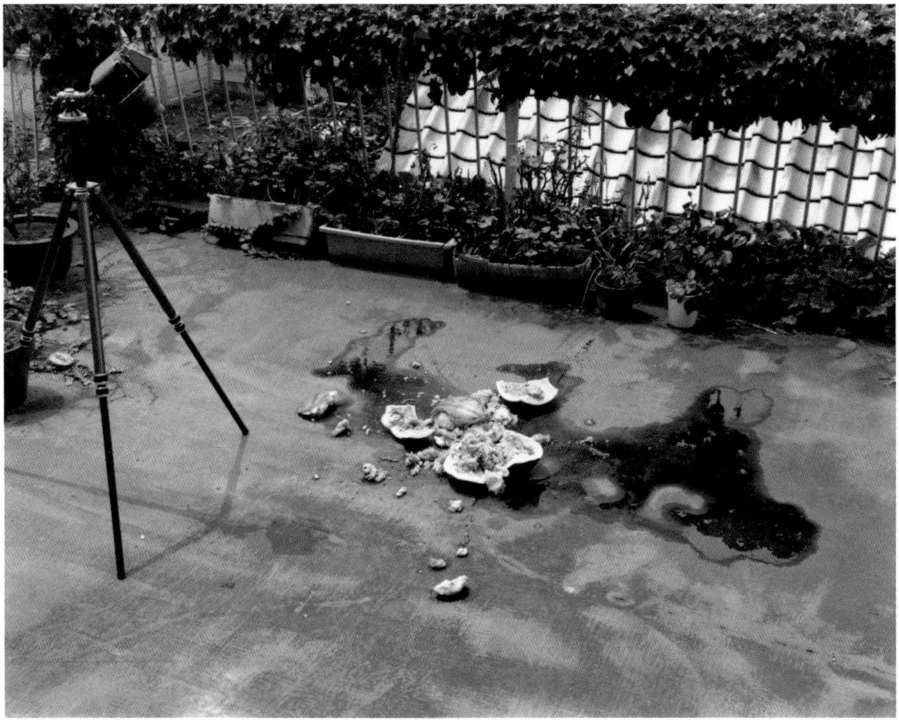

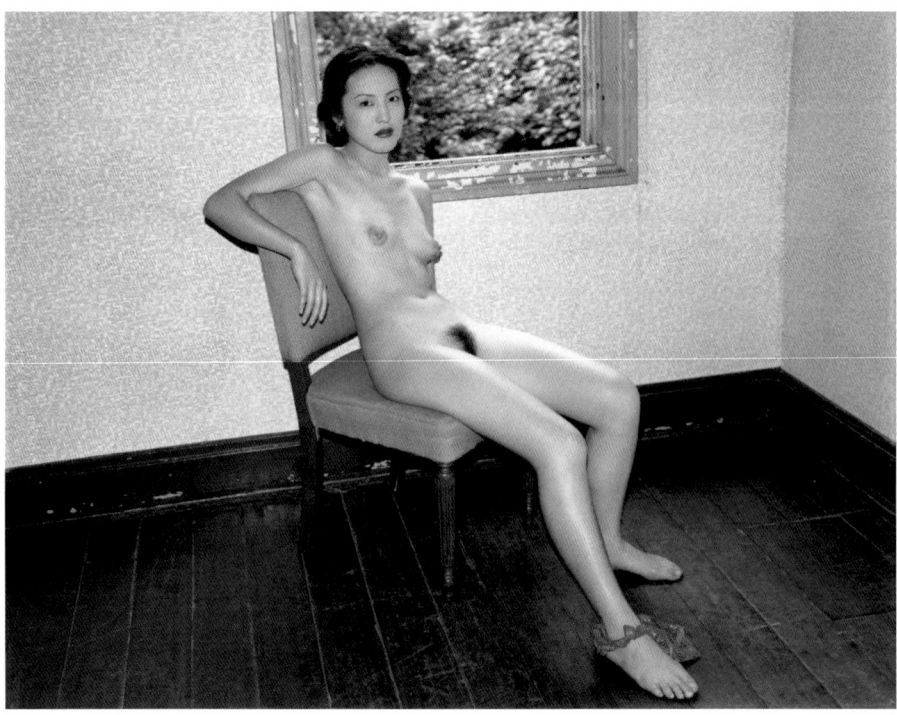

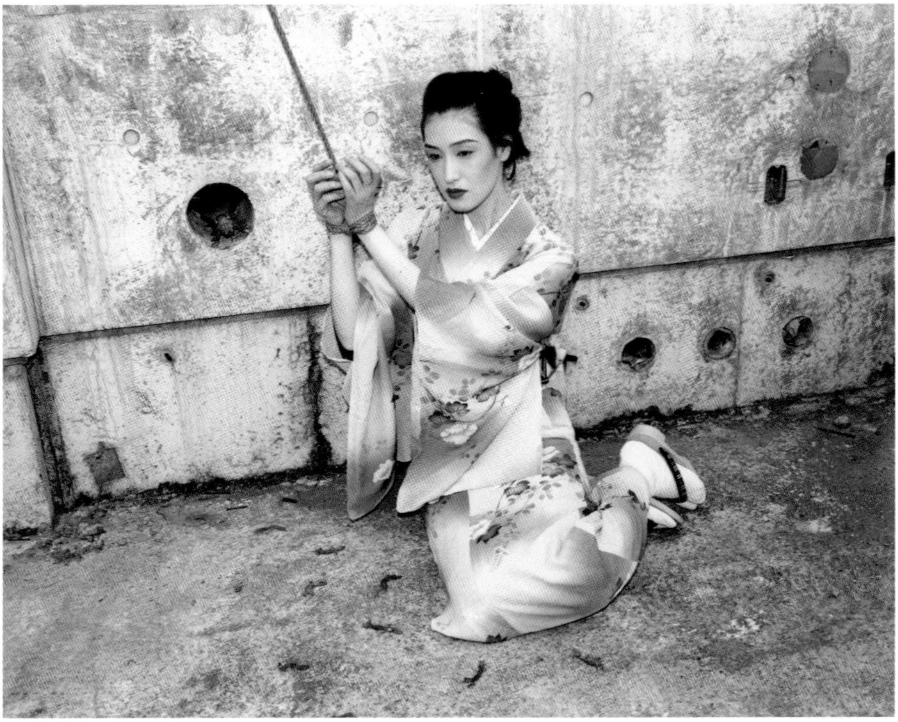

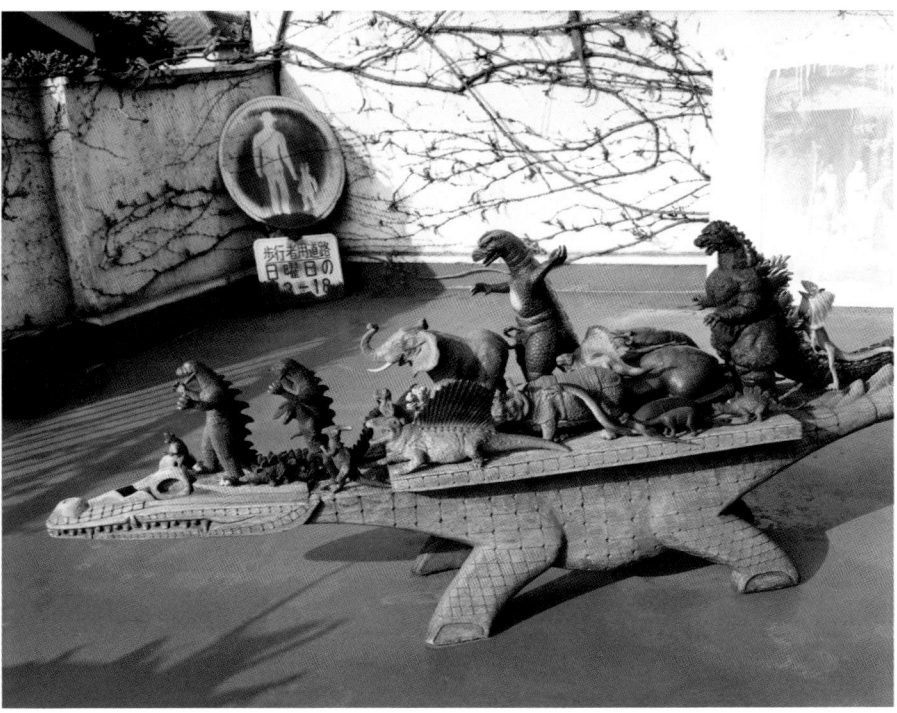

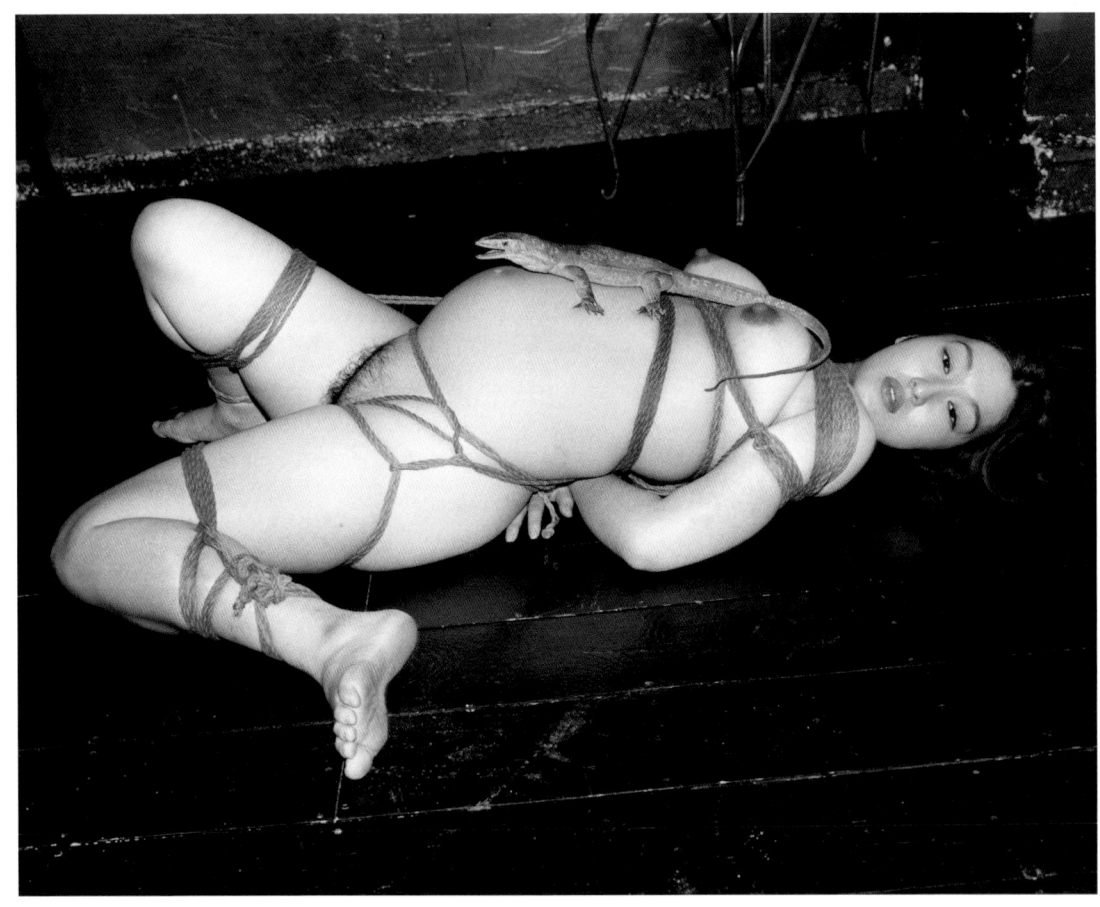

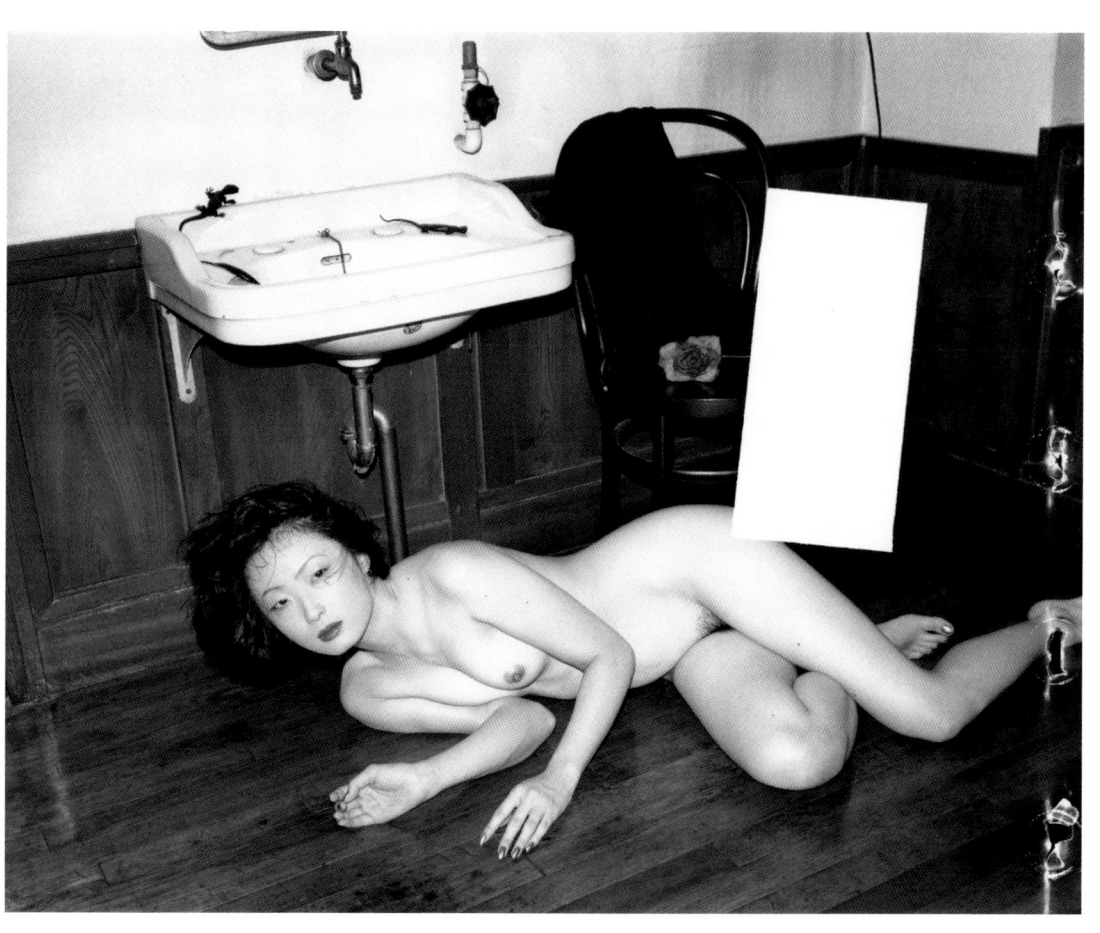

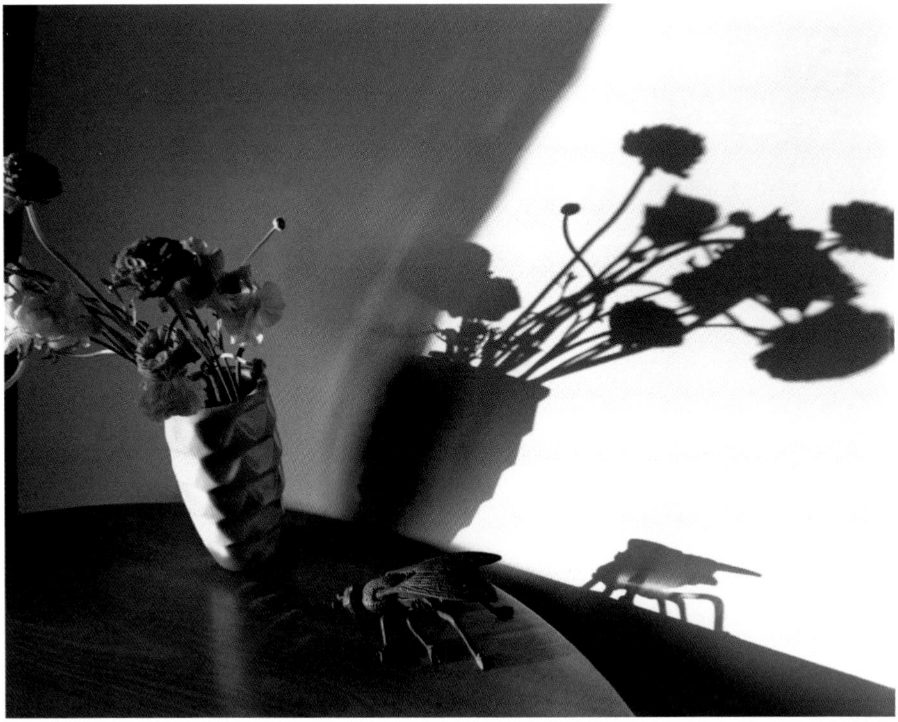

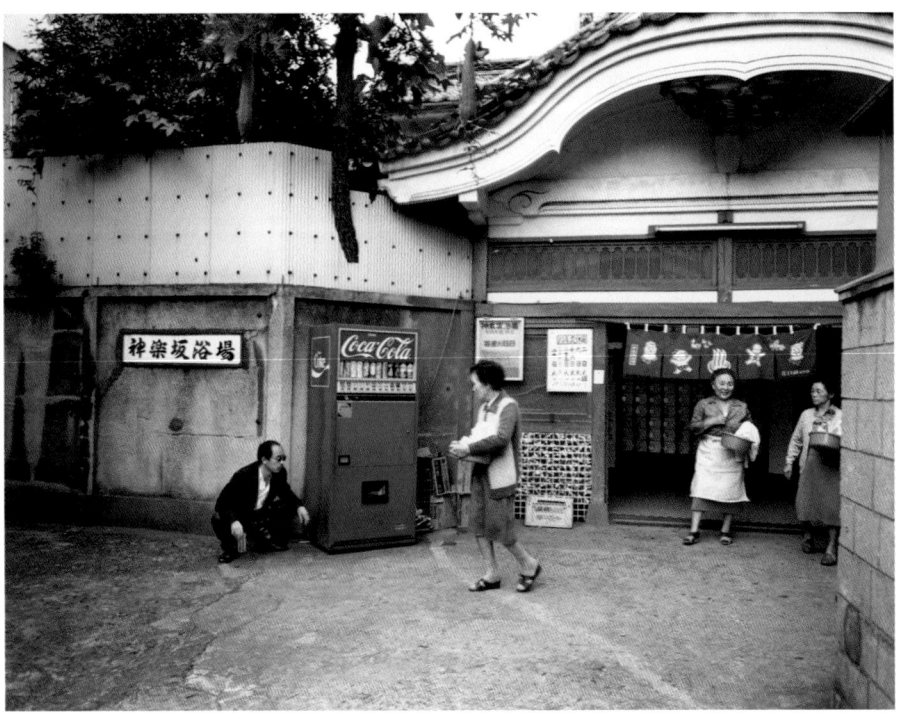

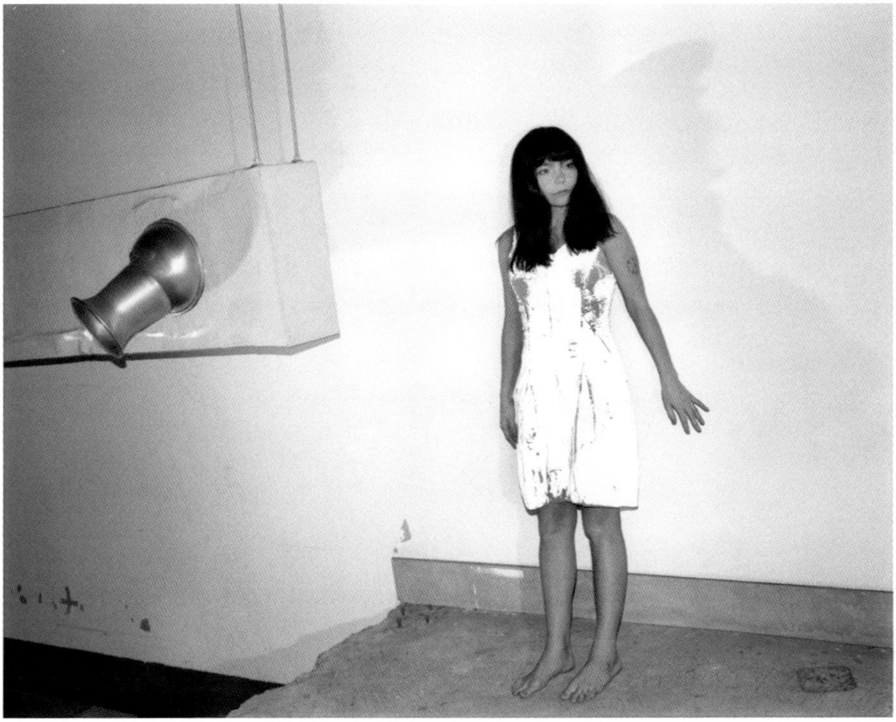

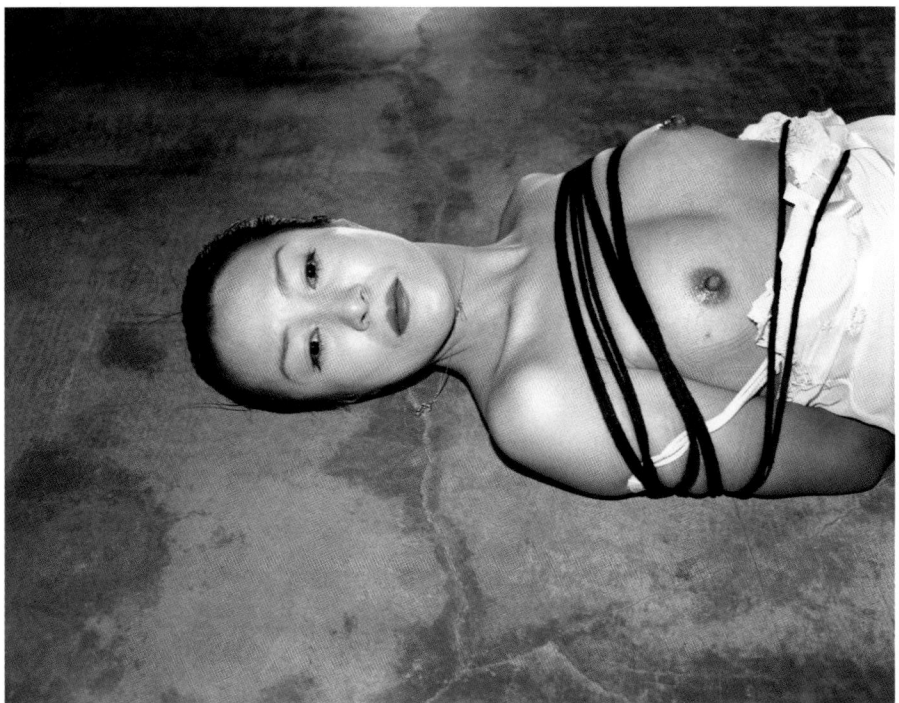

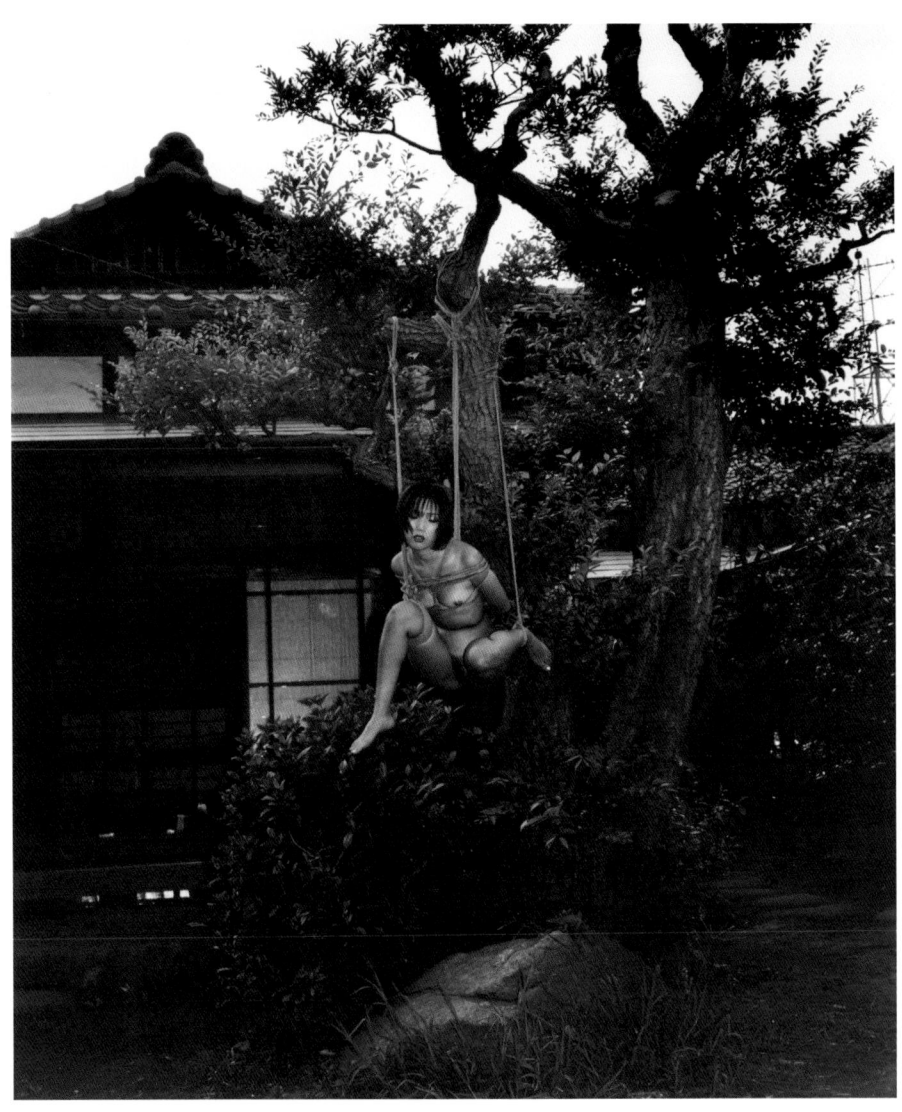

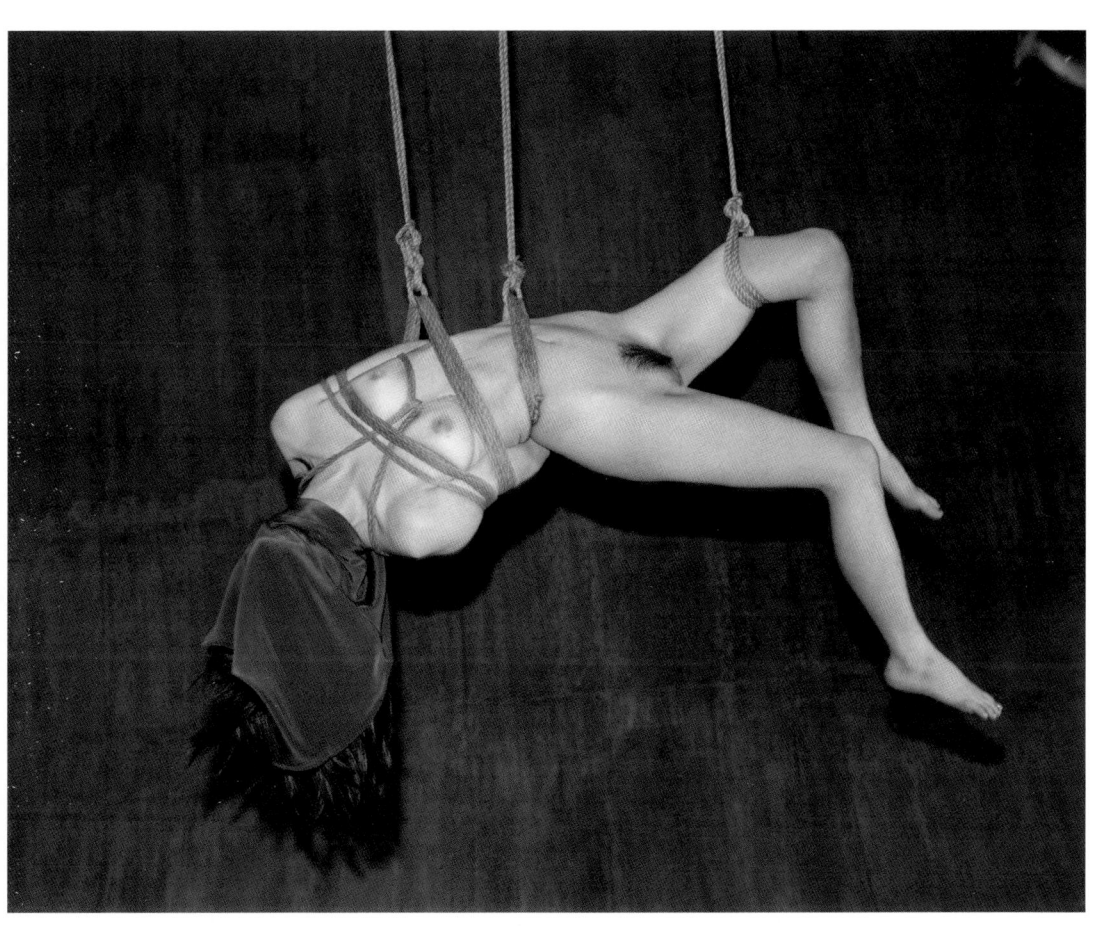

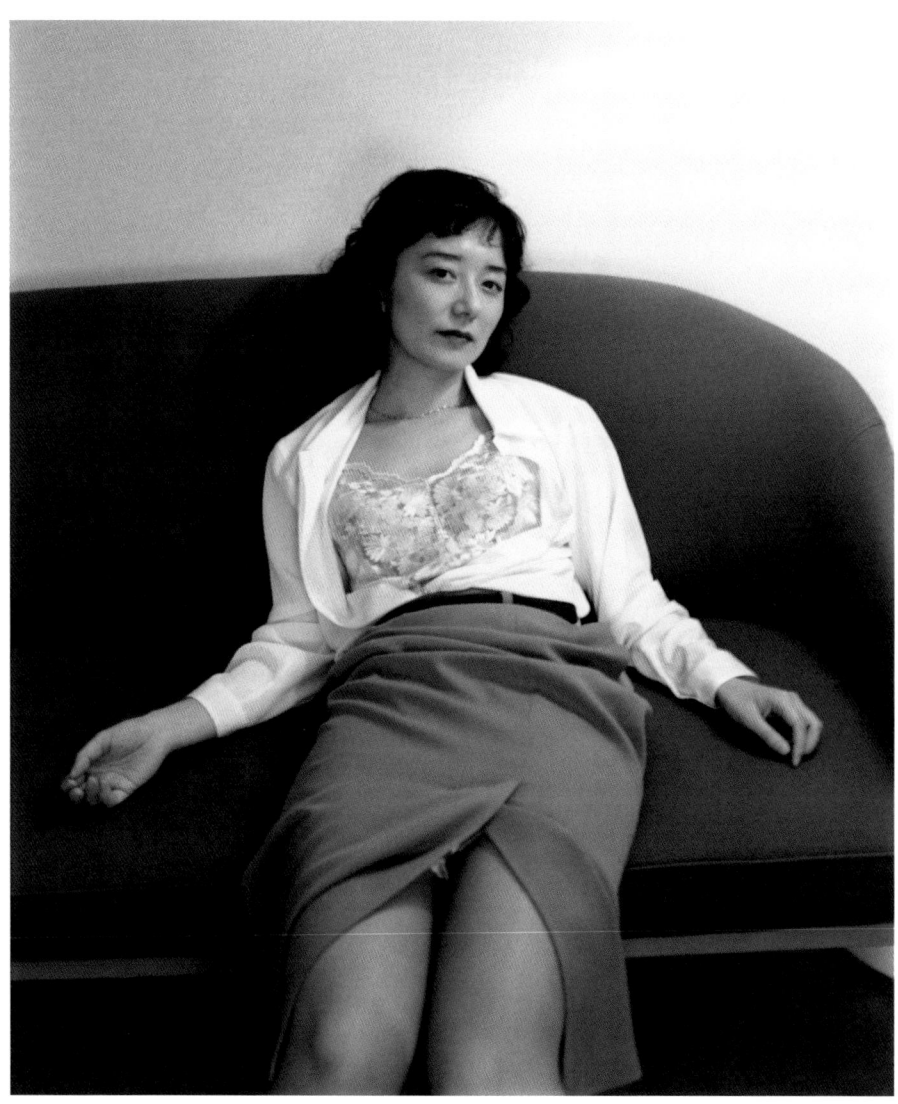

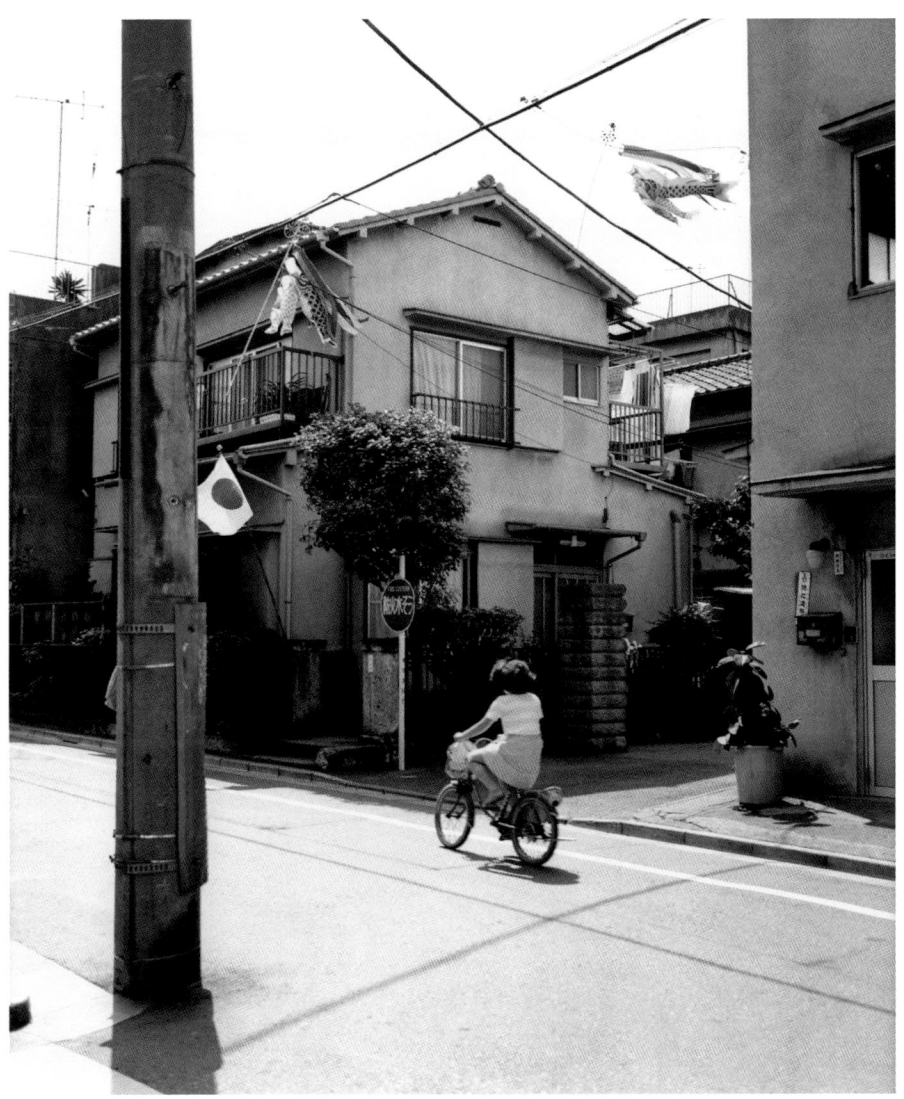

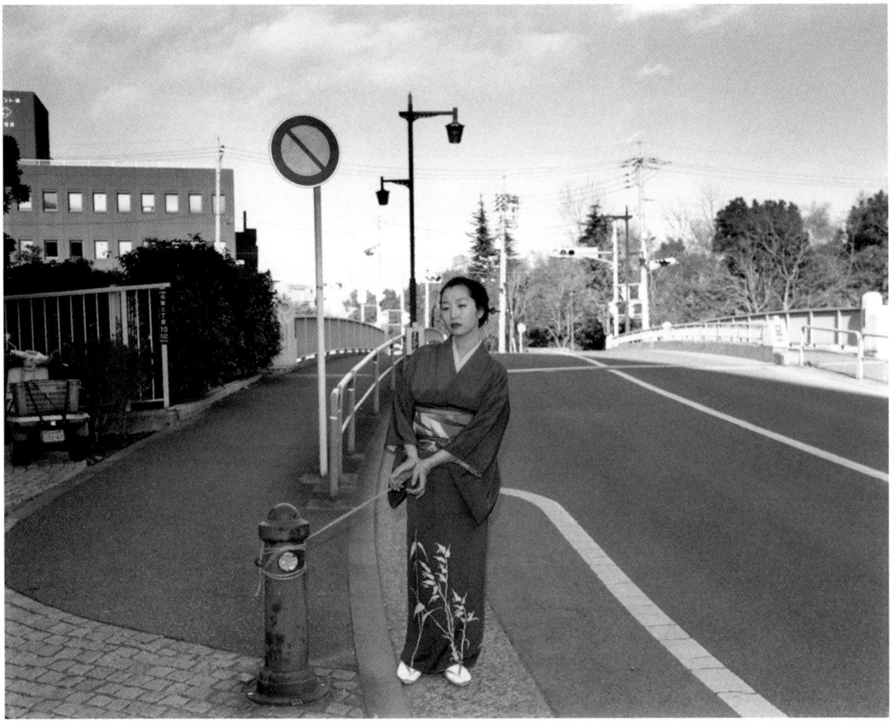

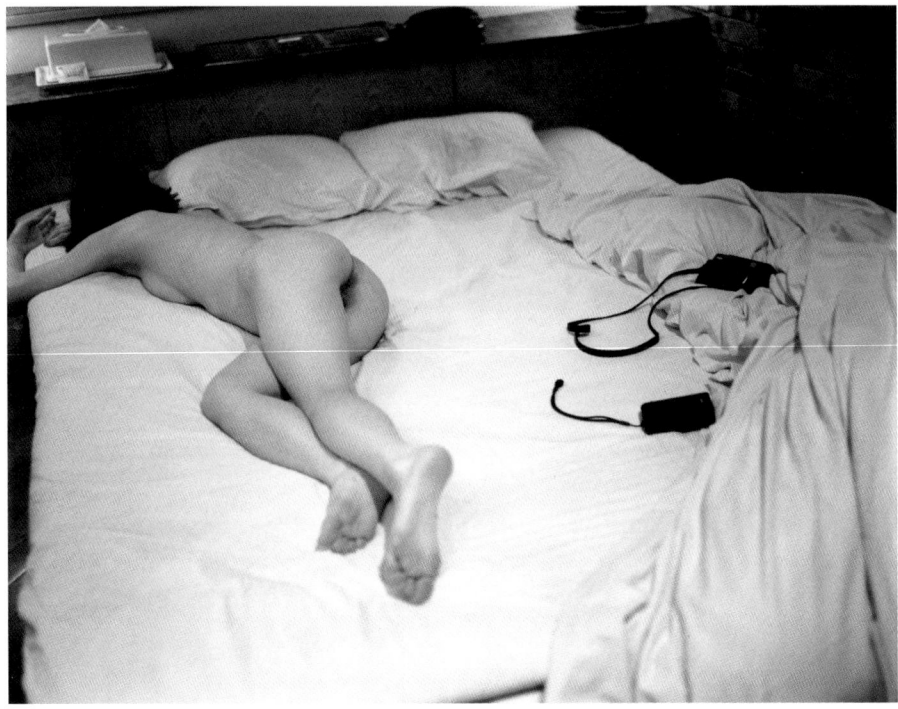

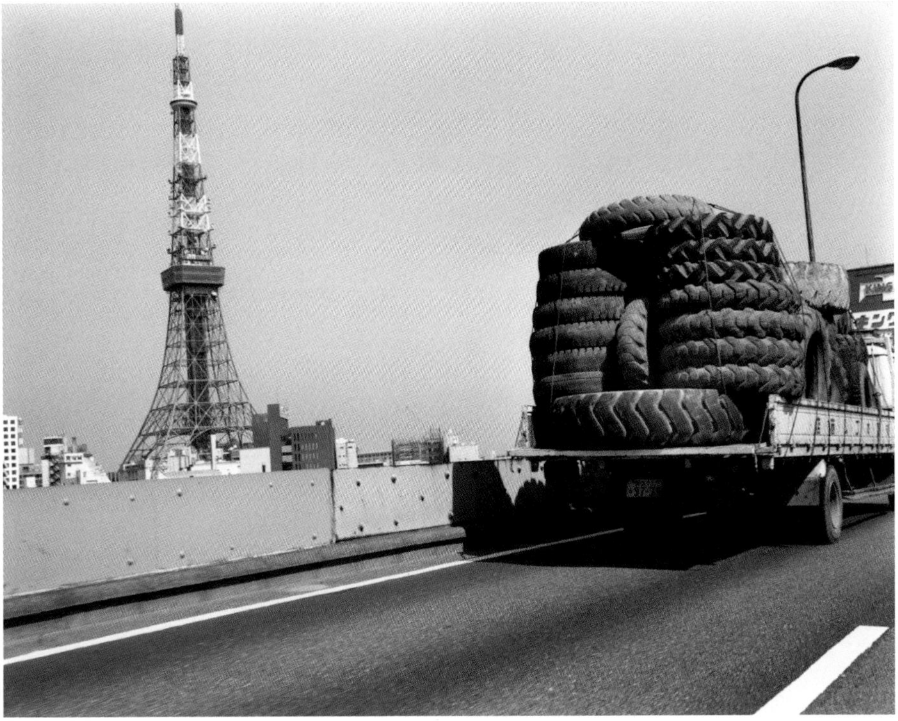

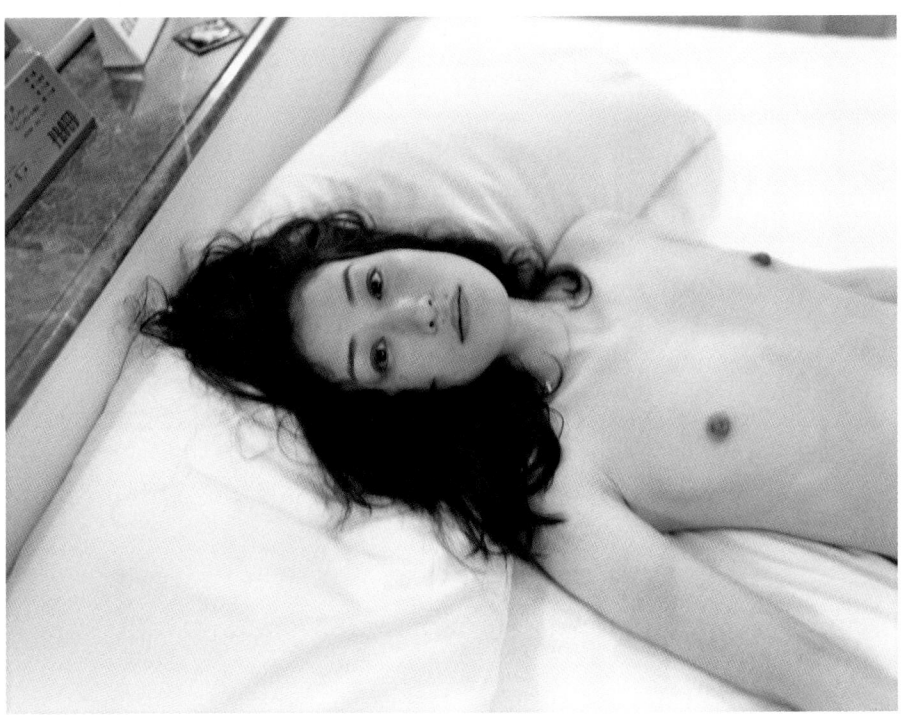

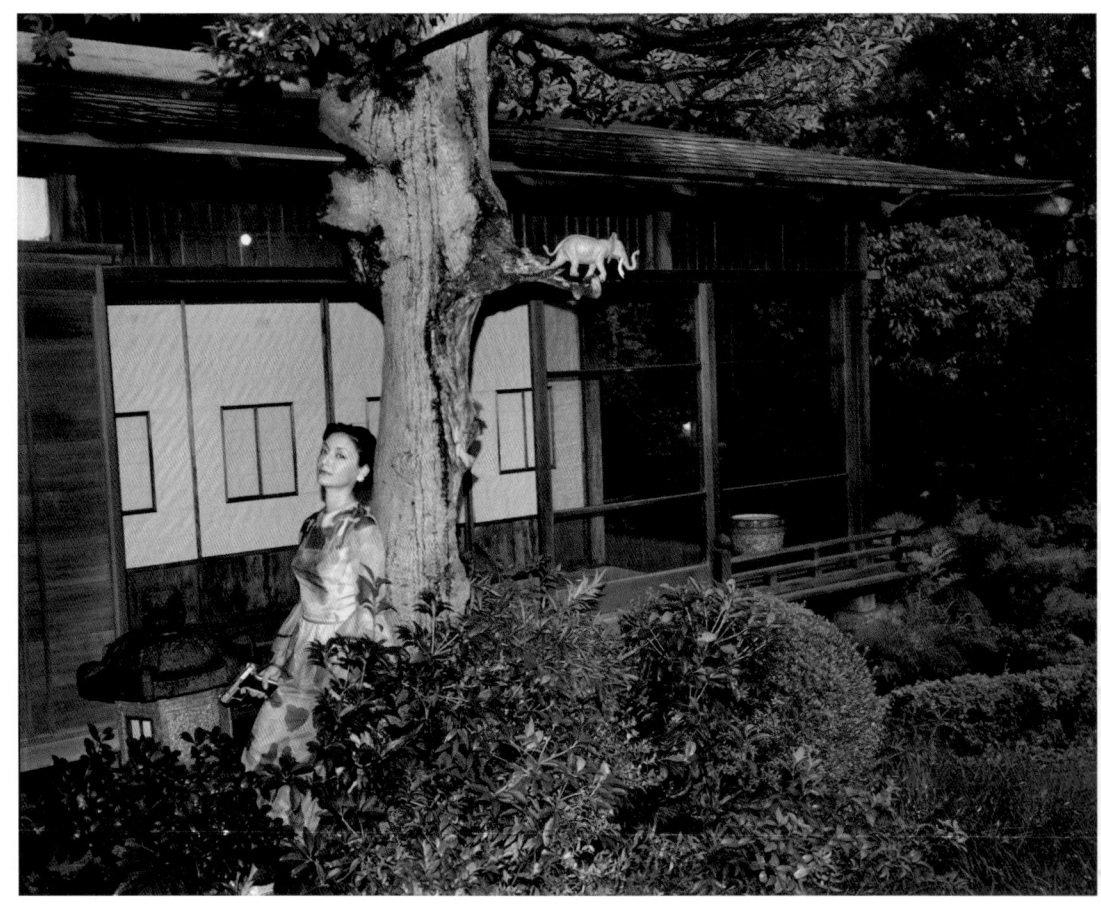

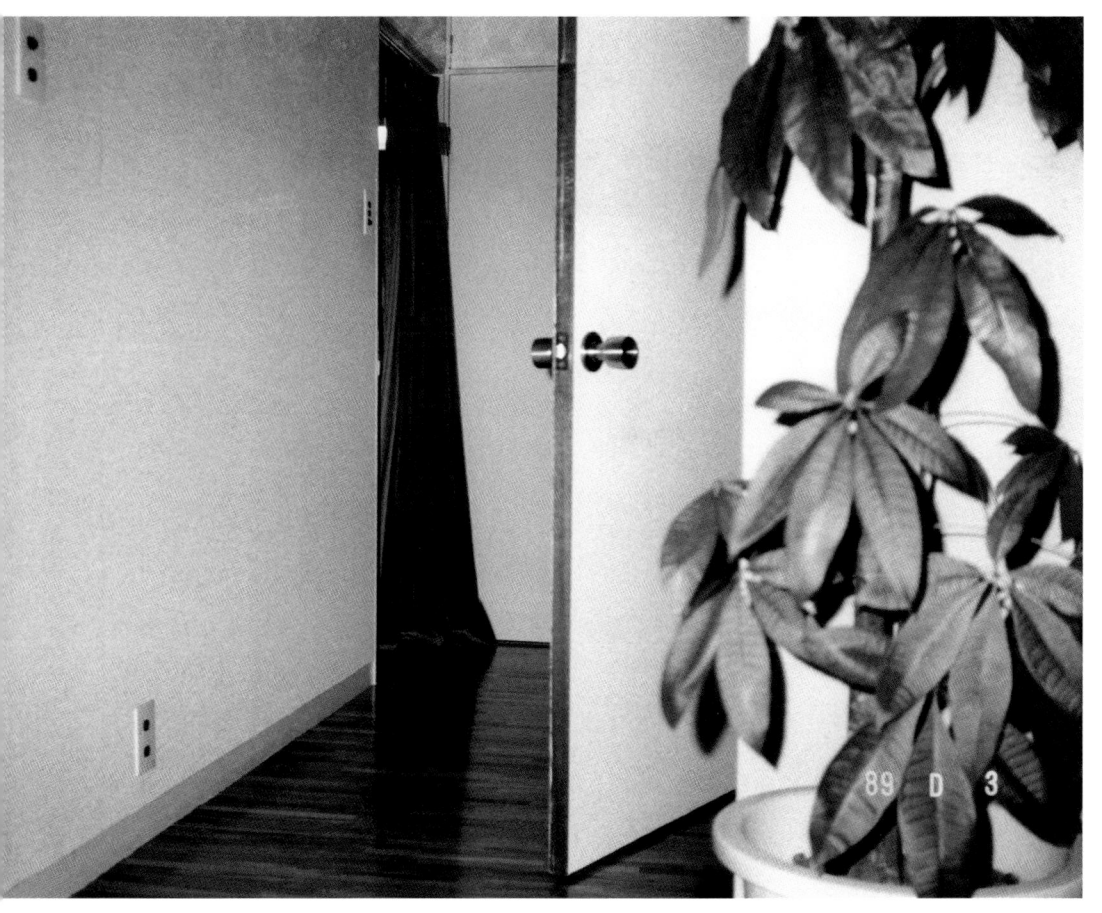

Kyoto White Sentiment

京都白情

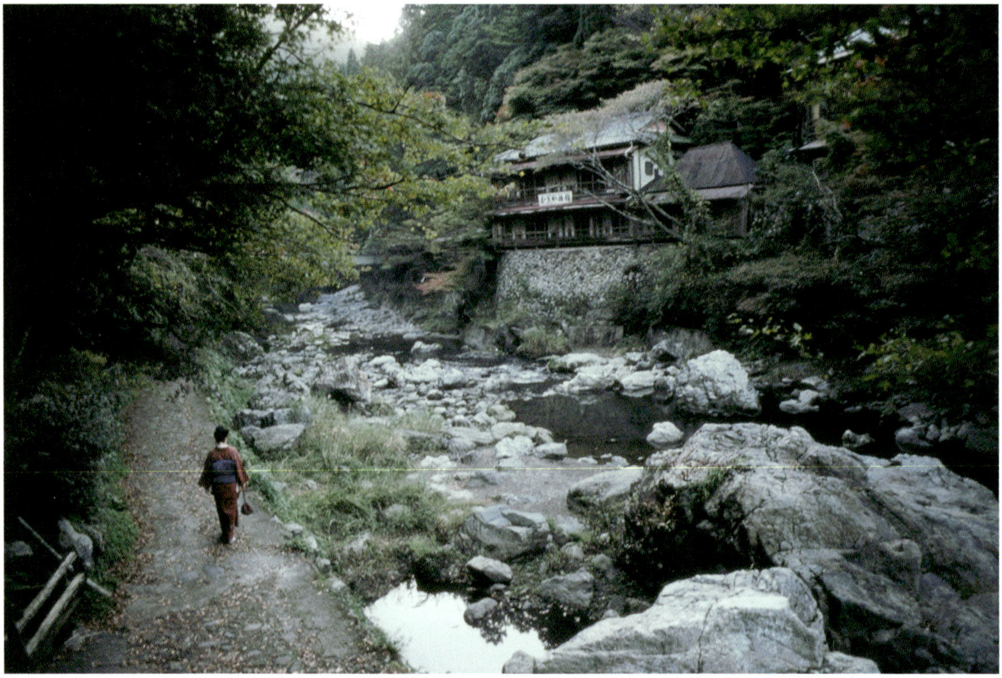

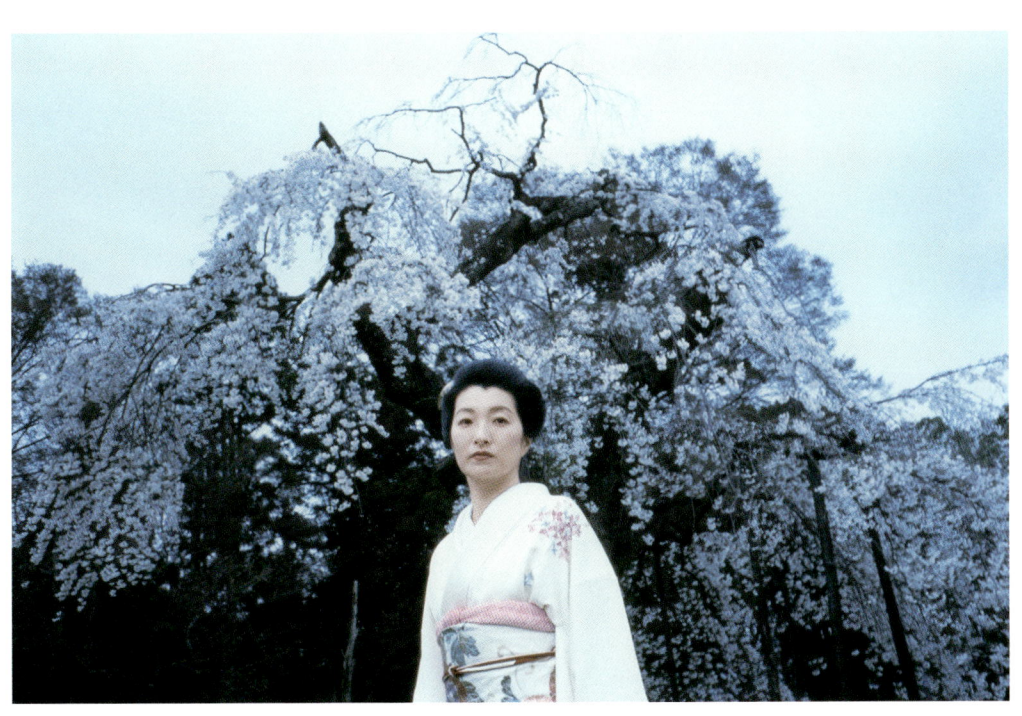

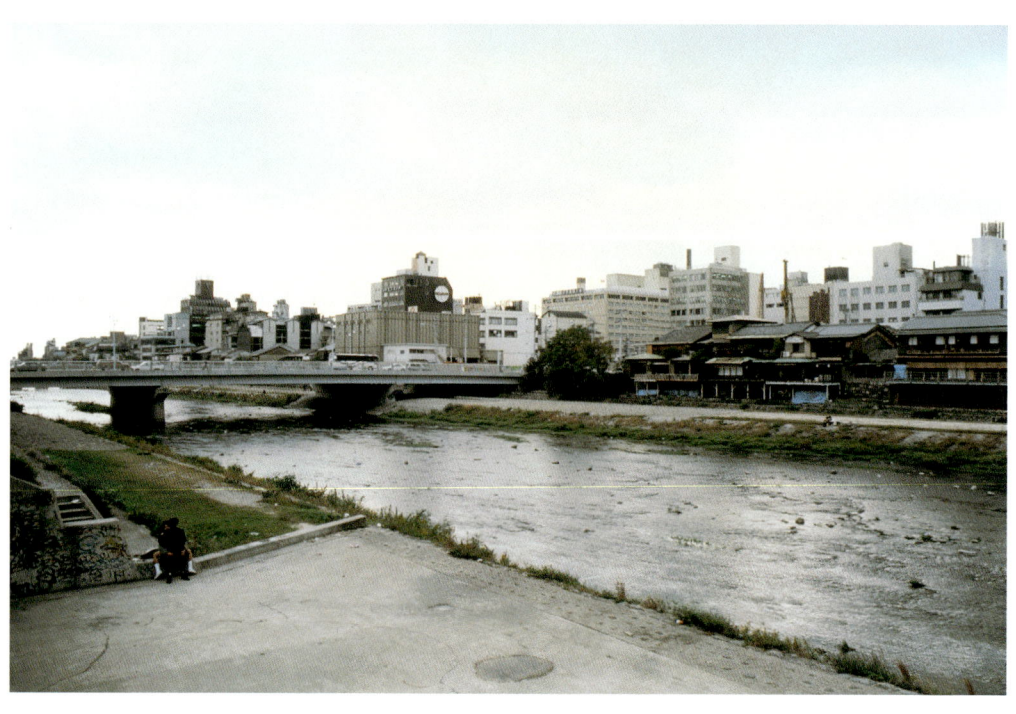

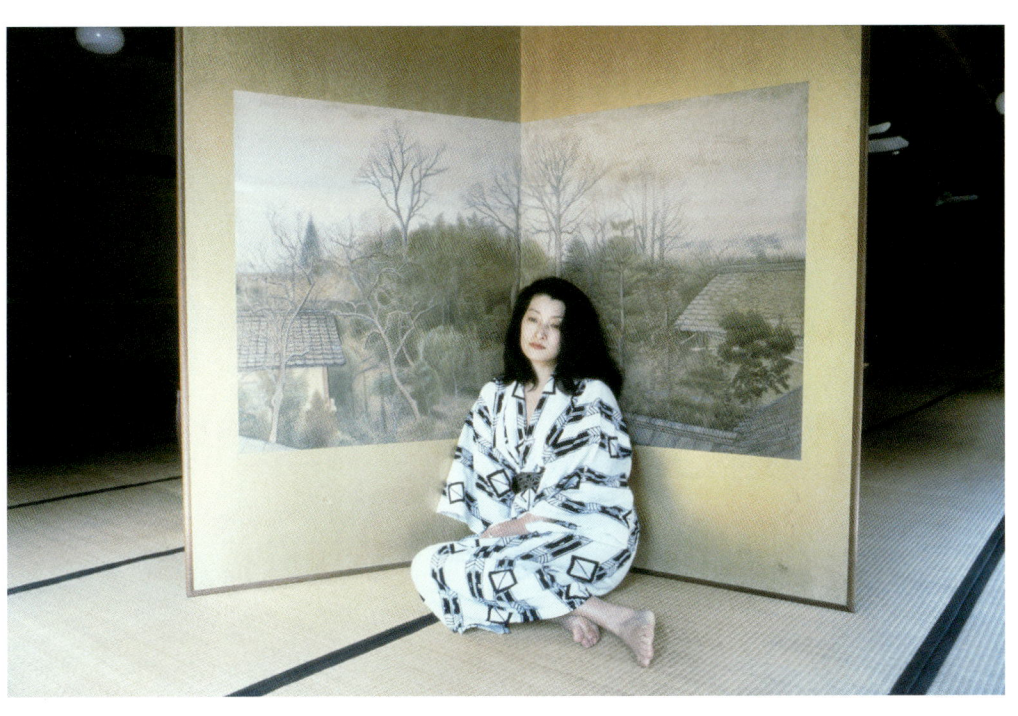

Chiro

チロ

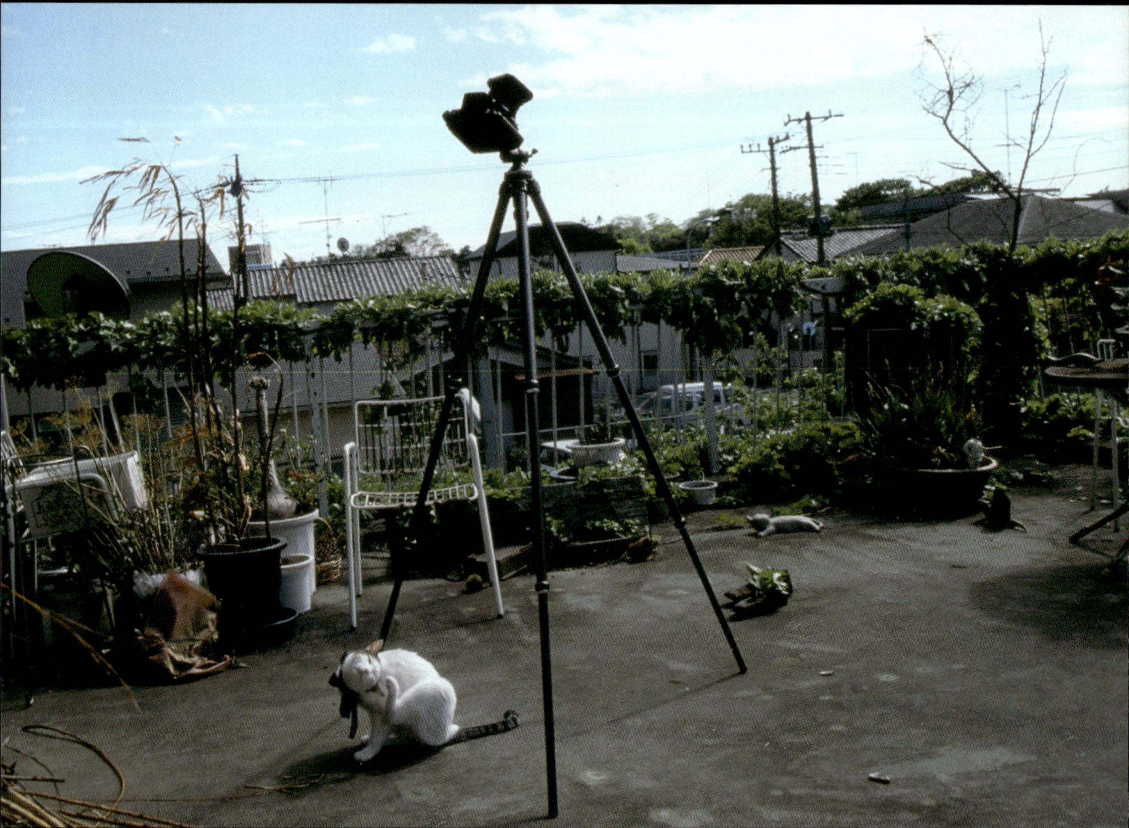

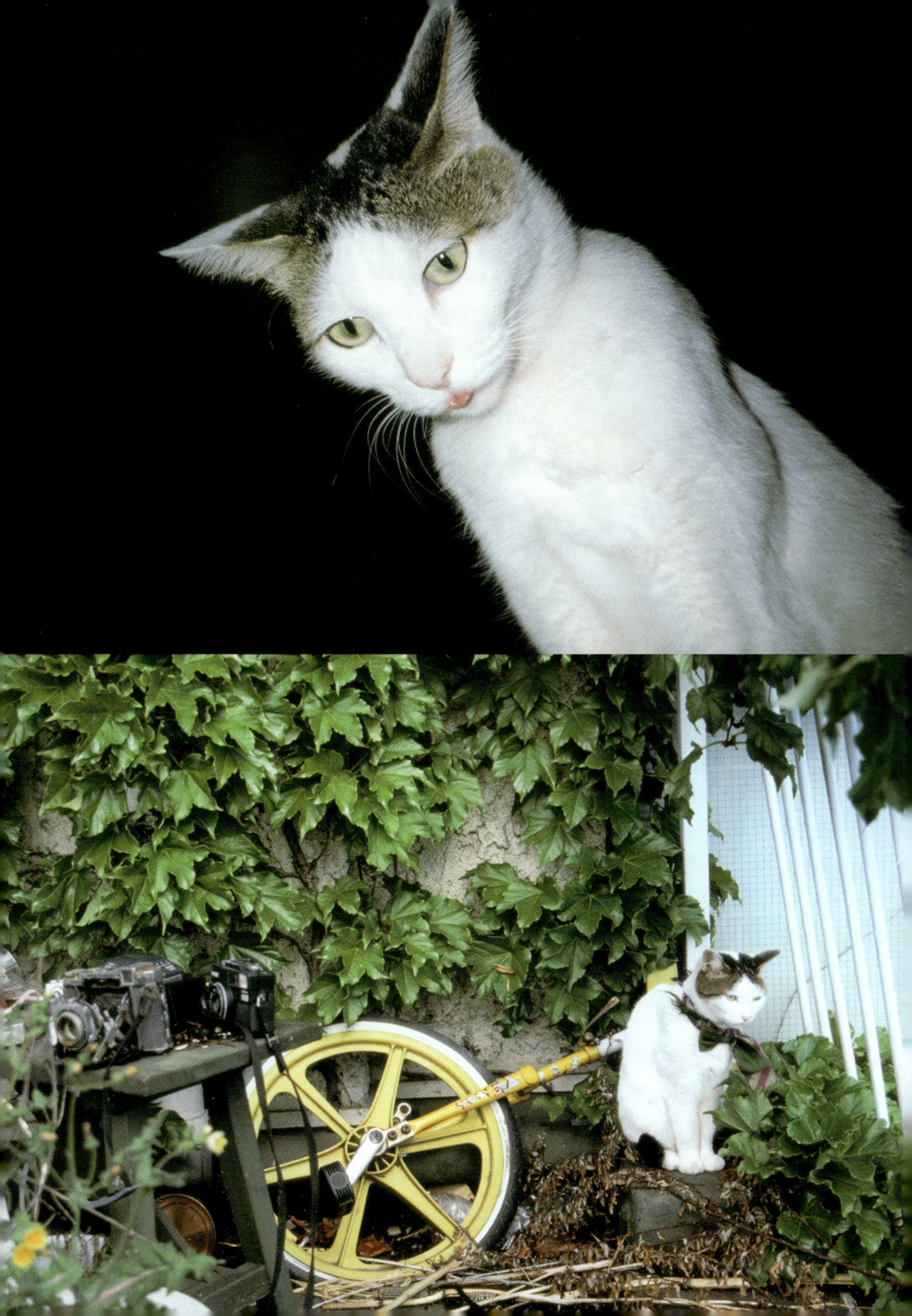

Novel
Photography

小説写真

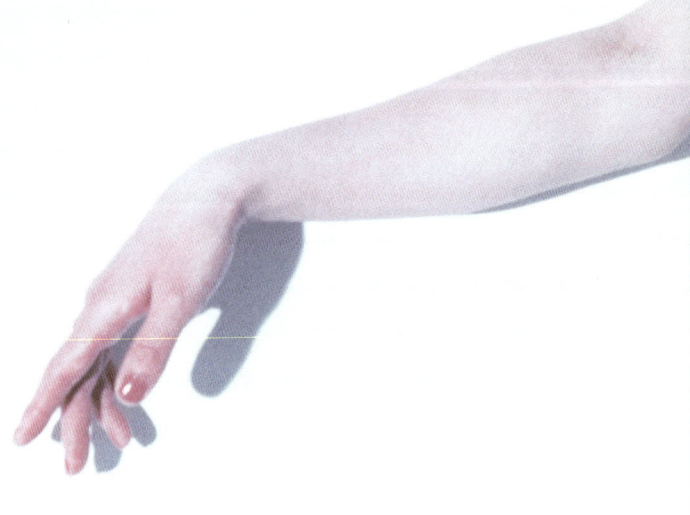

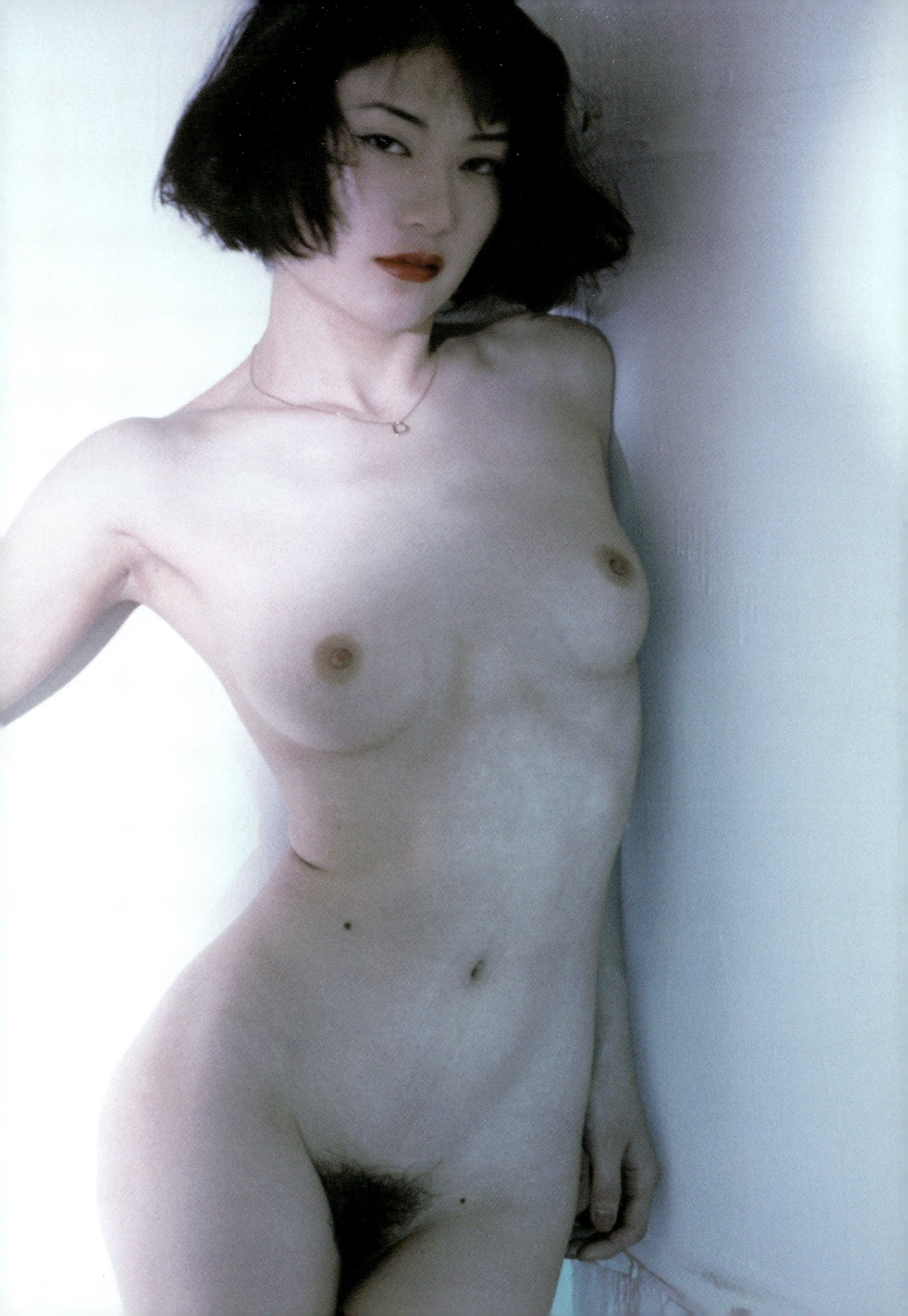

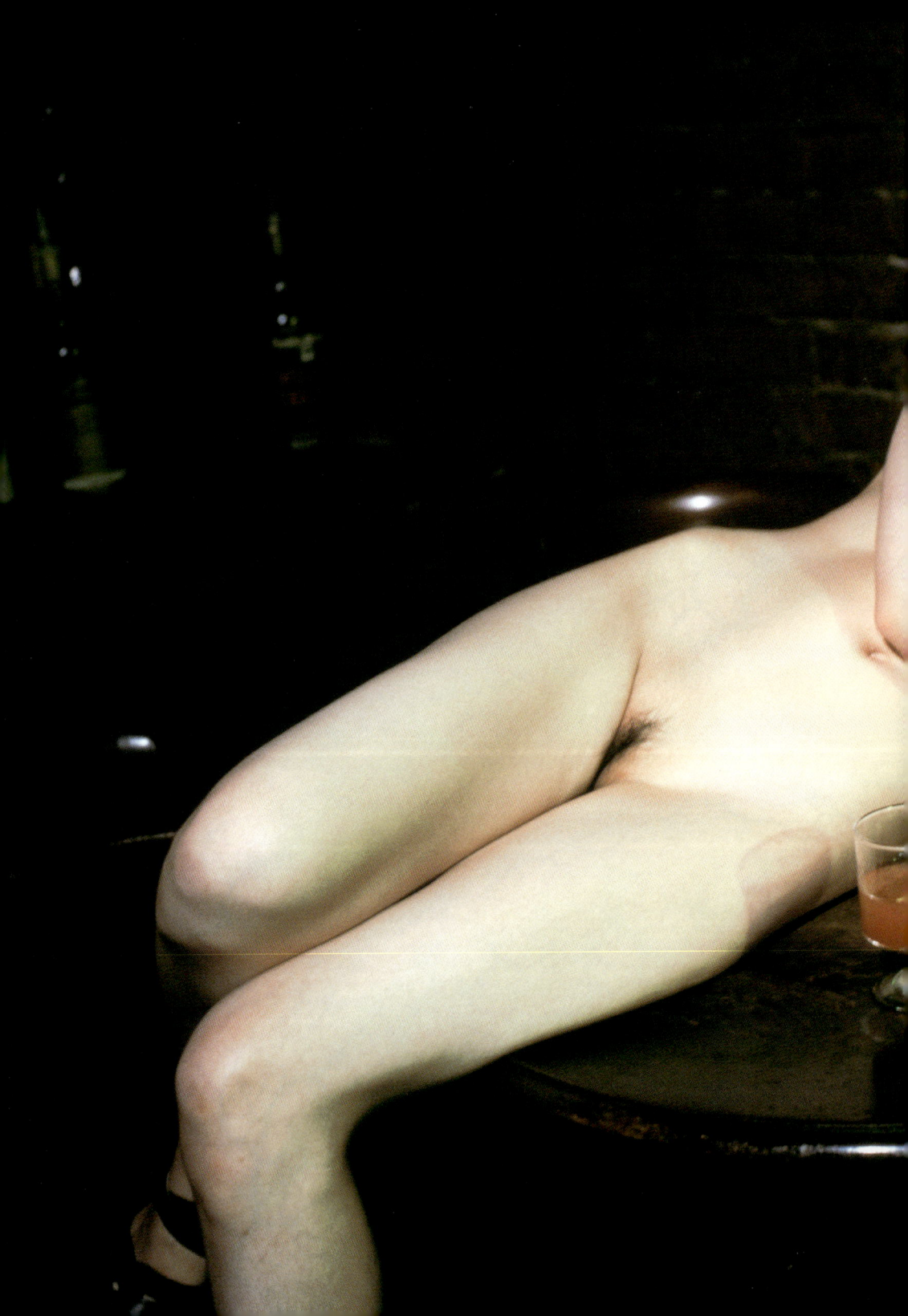

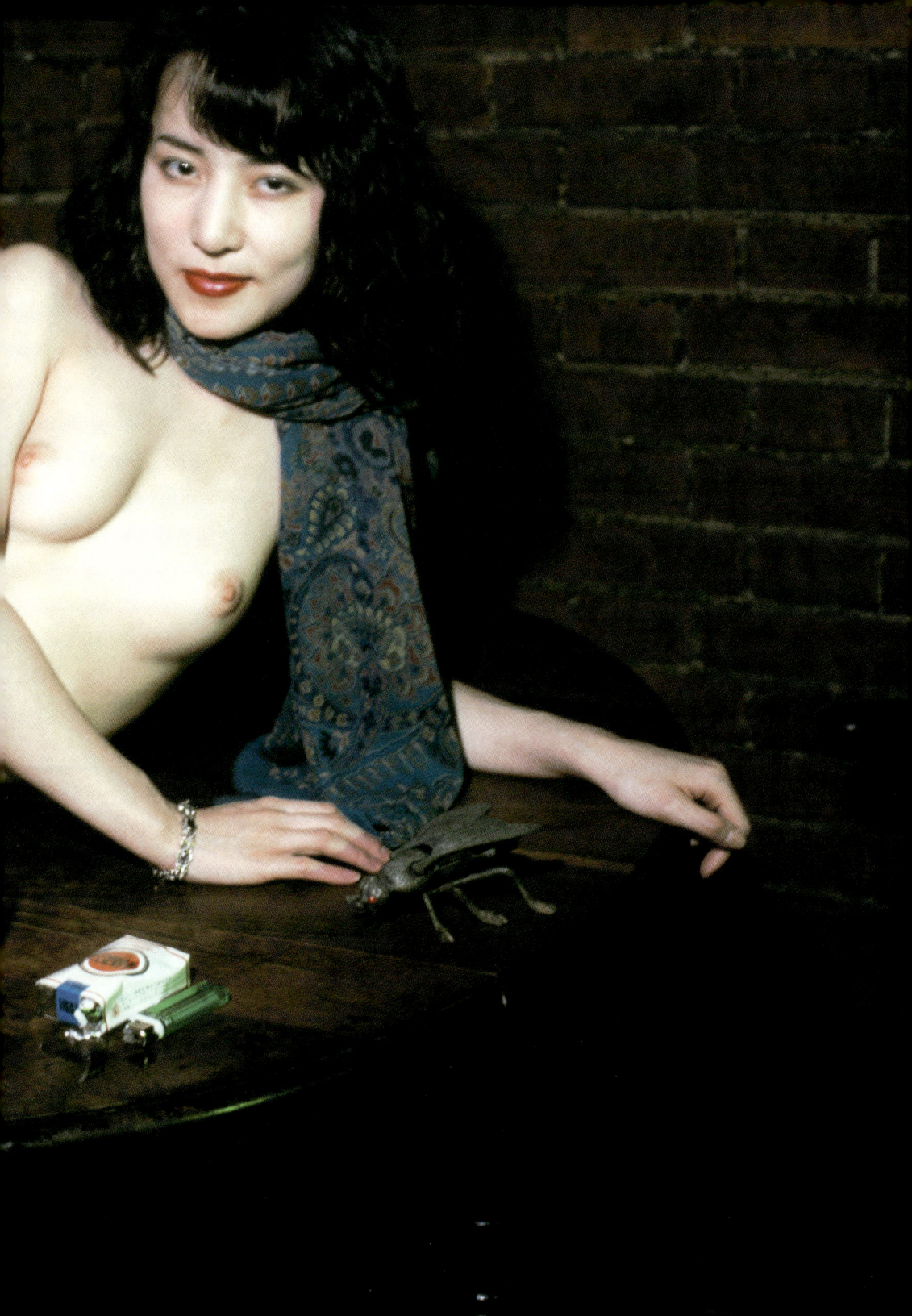

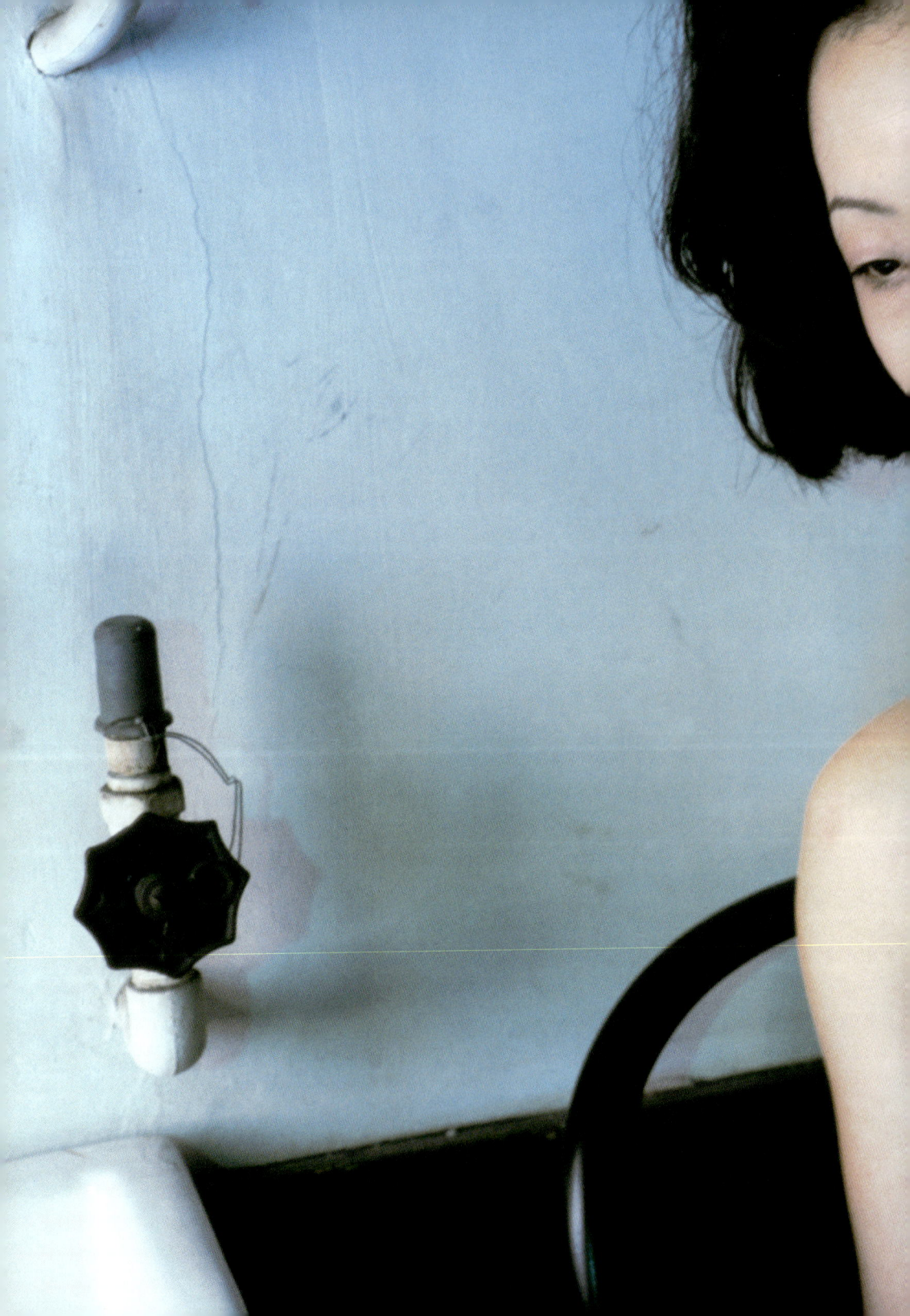

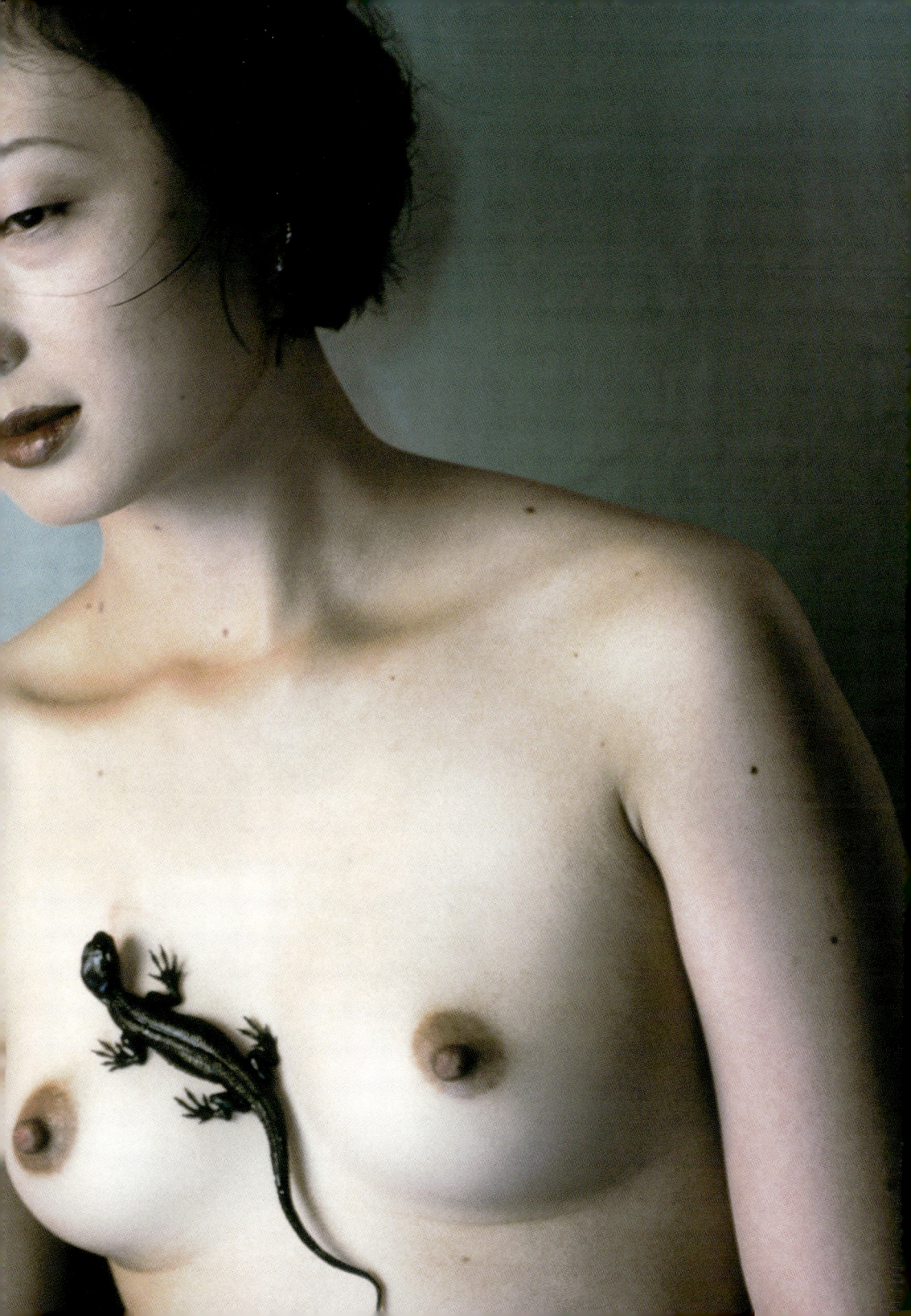

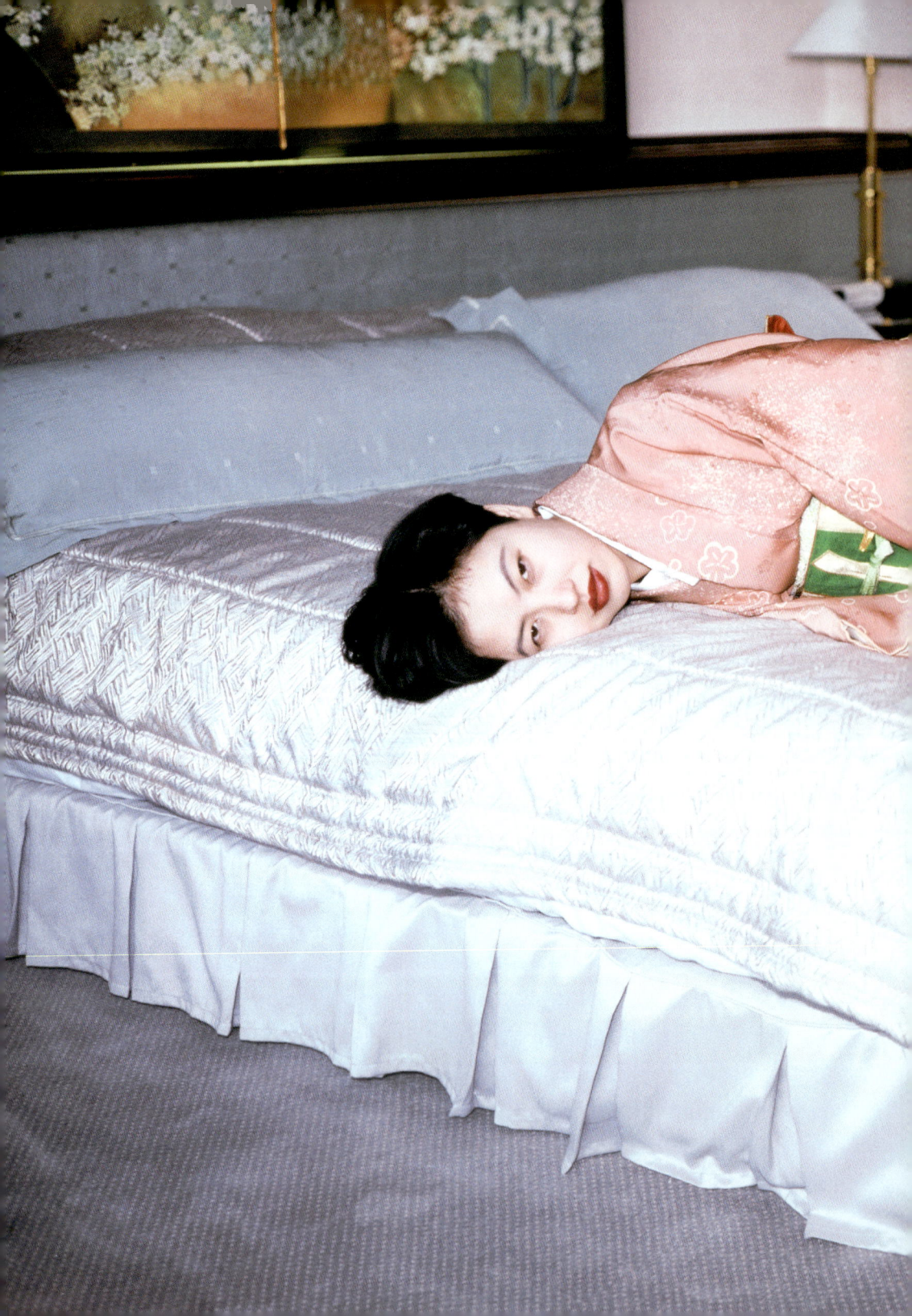

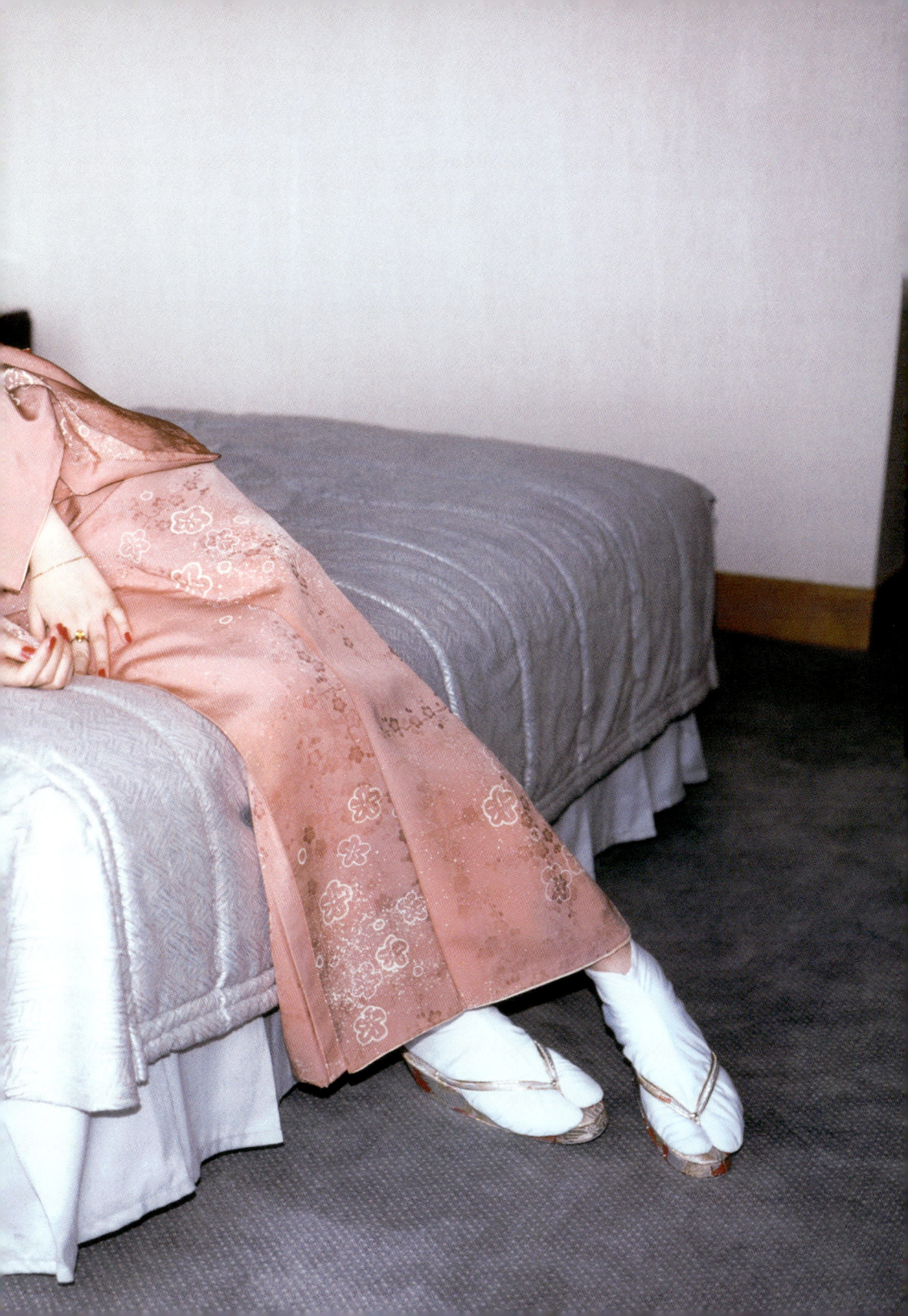

Tokyo Comedy

東京コメディー

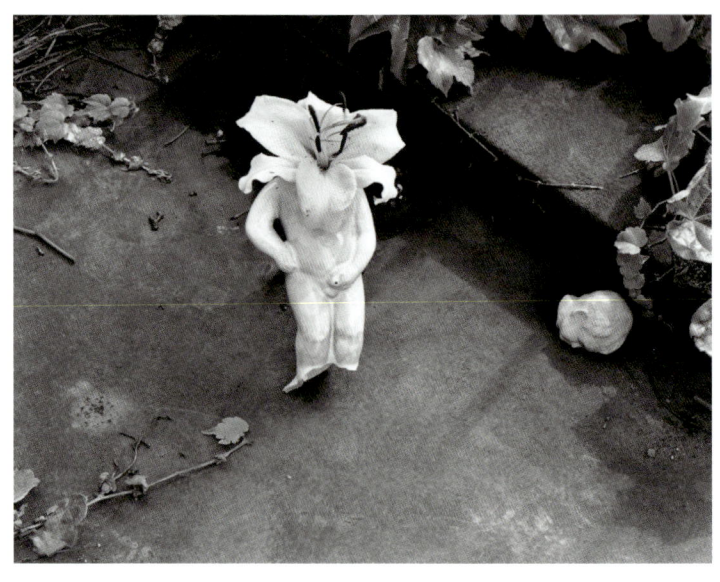

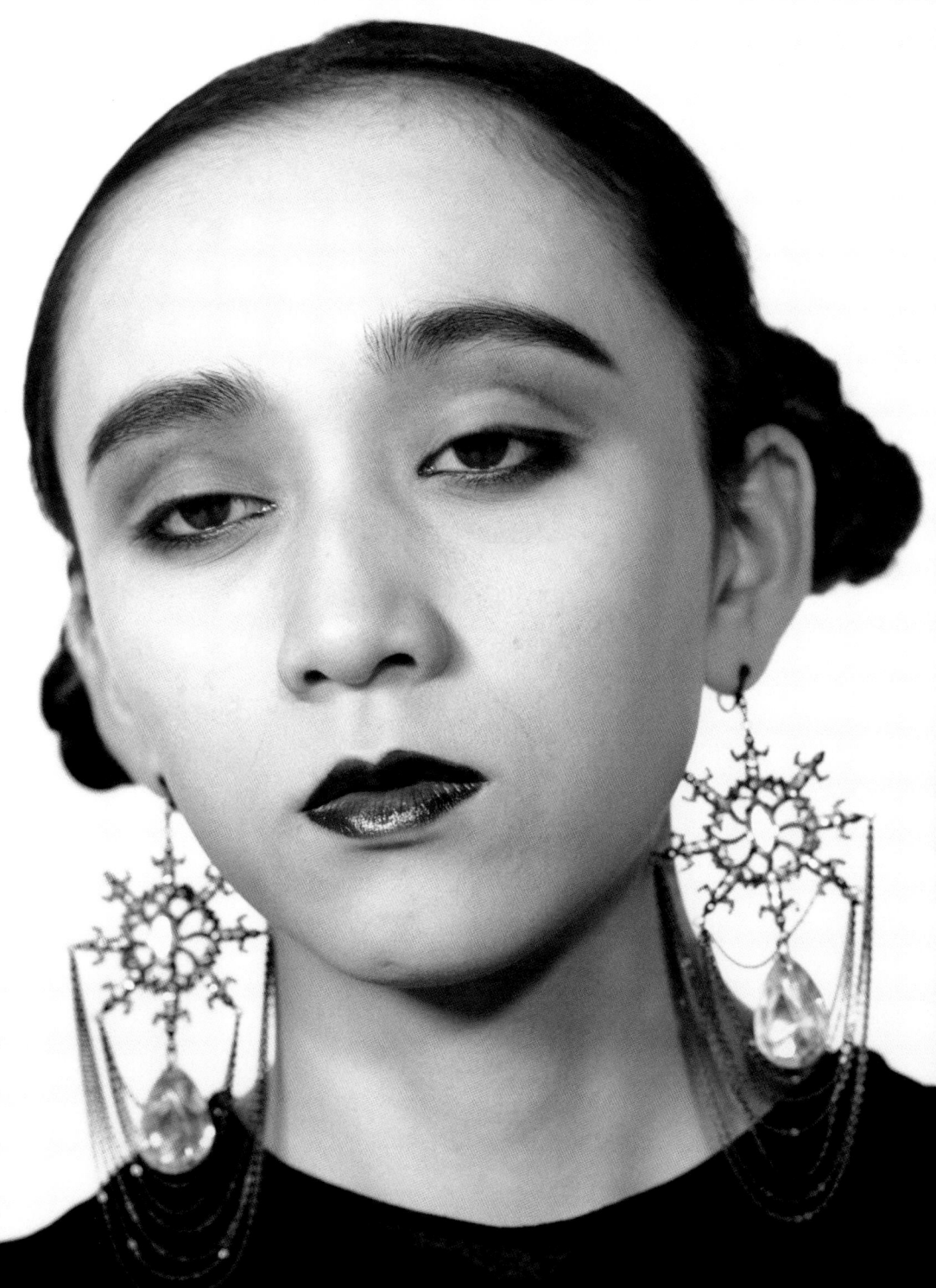

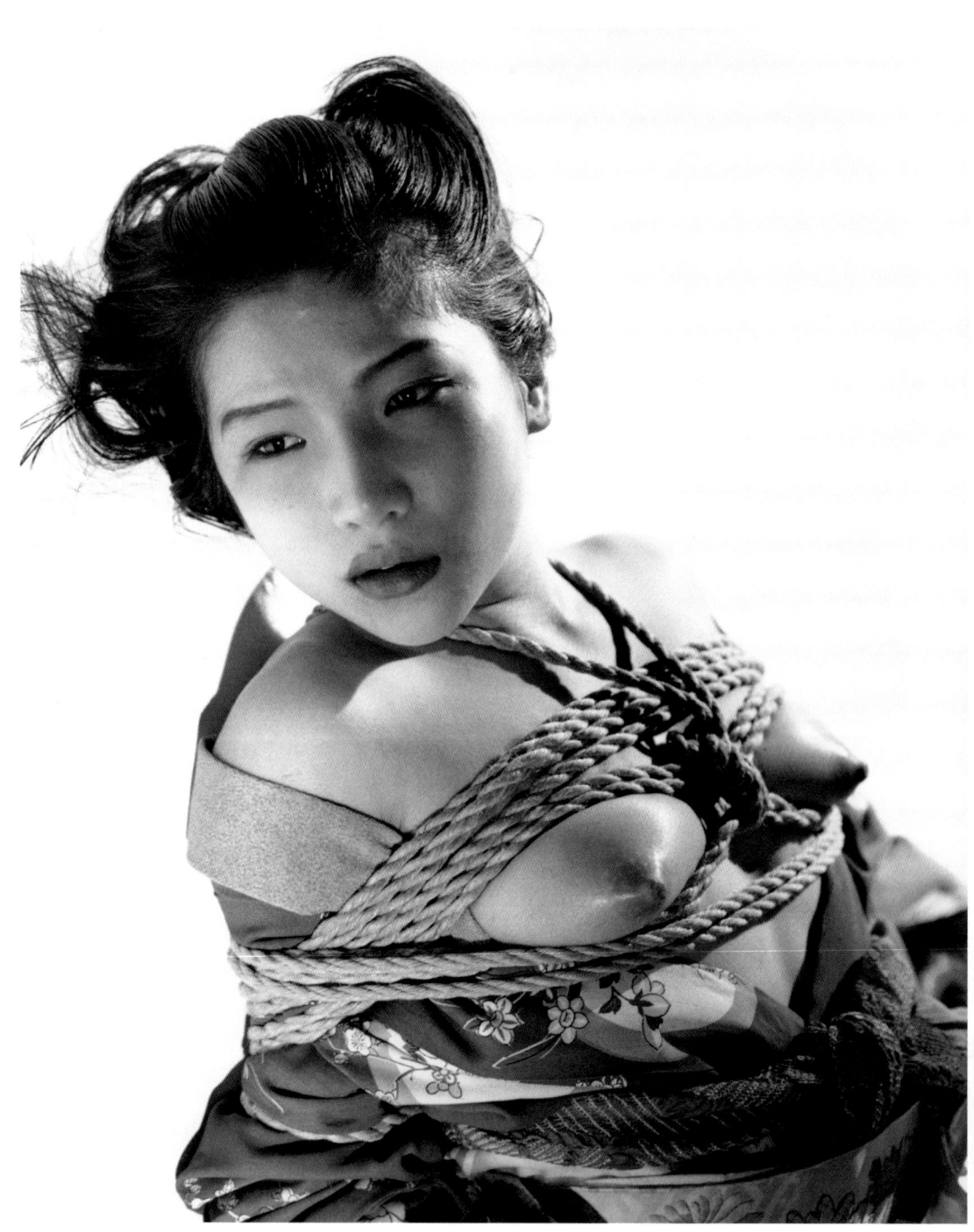

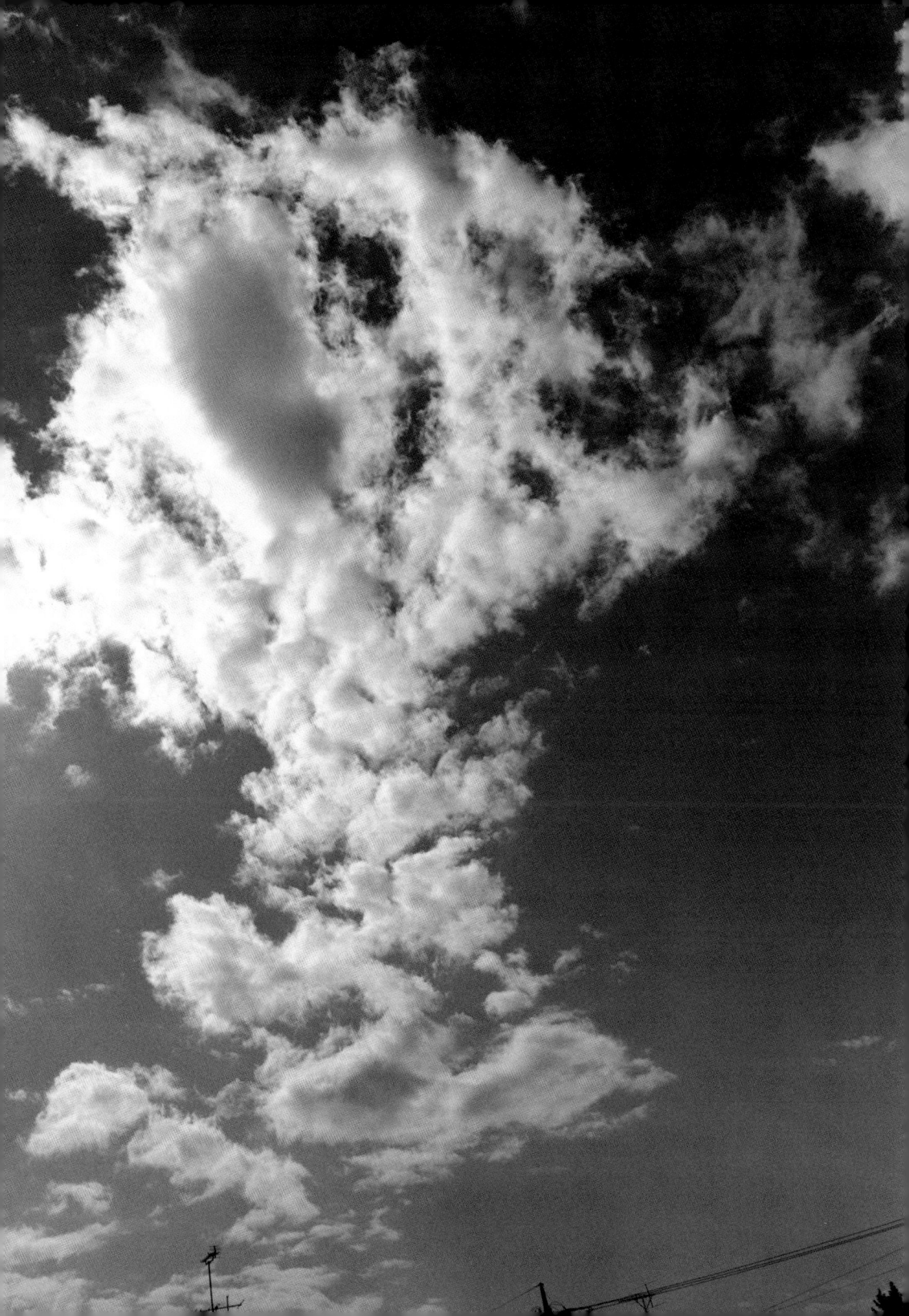

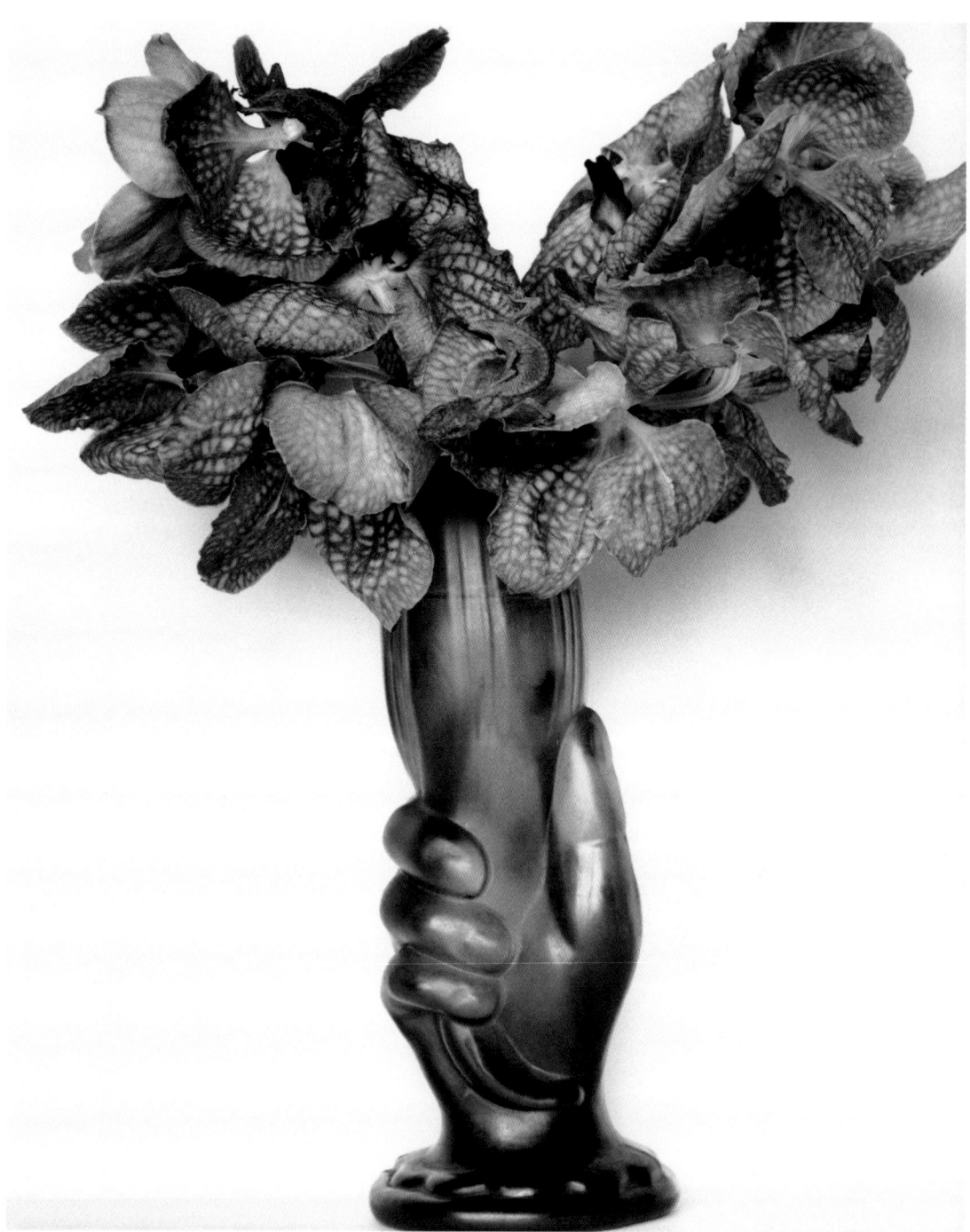

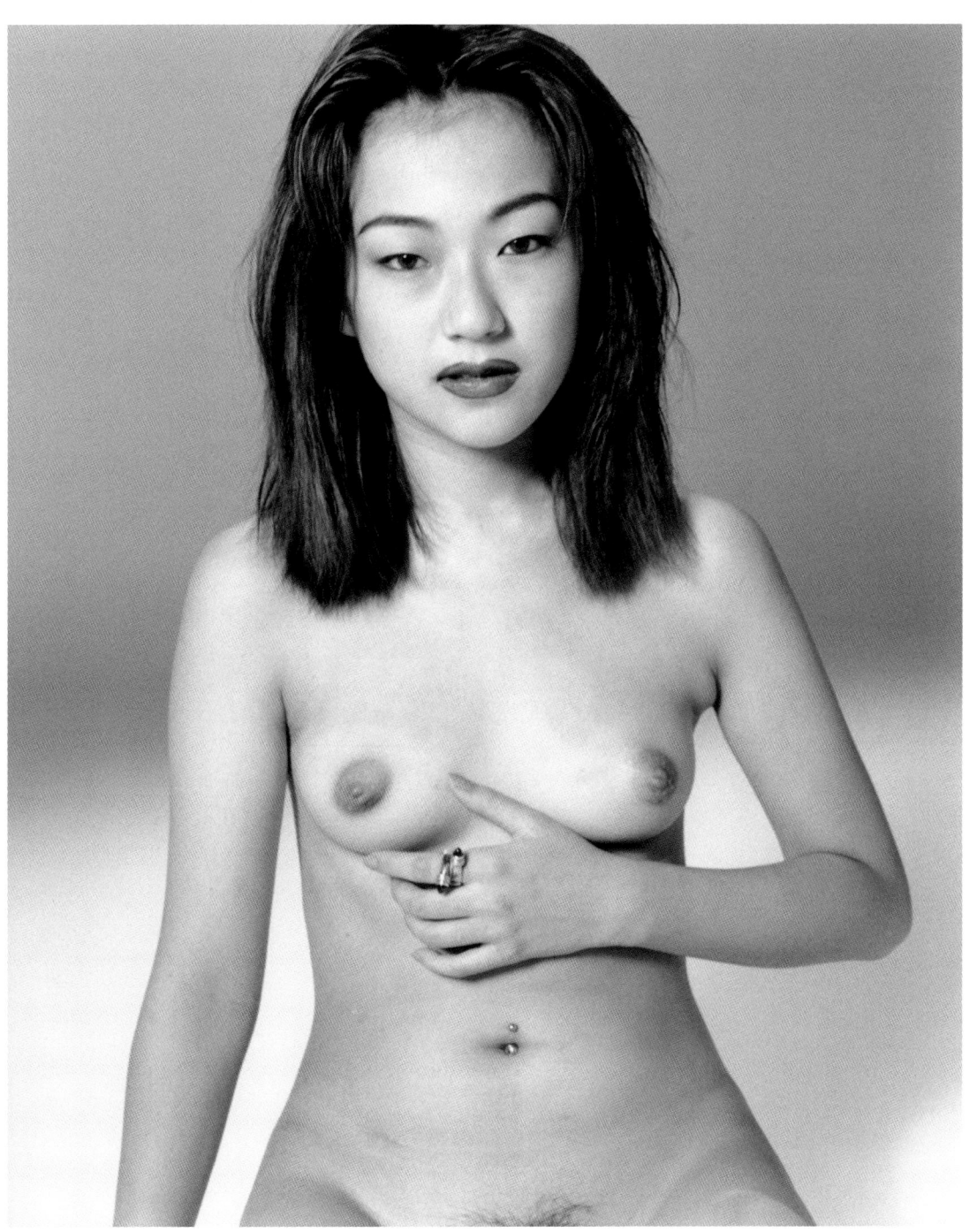

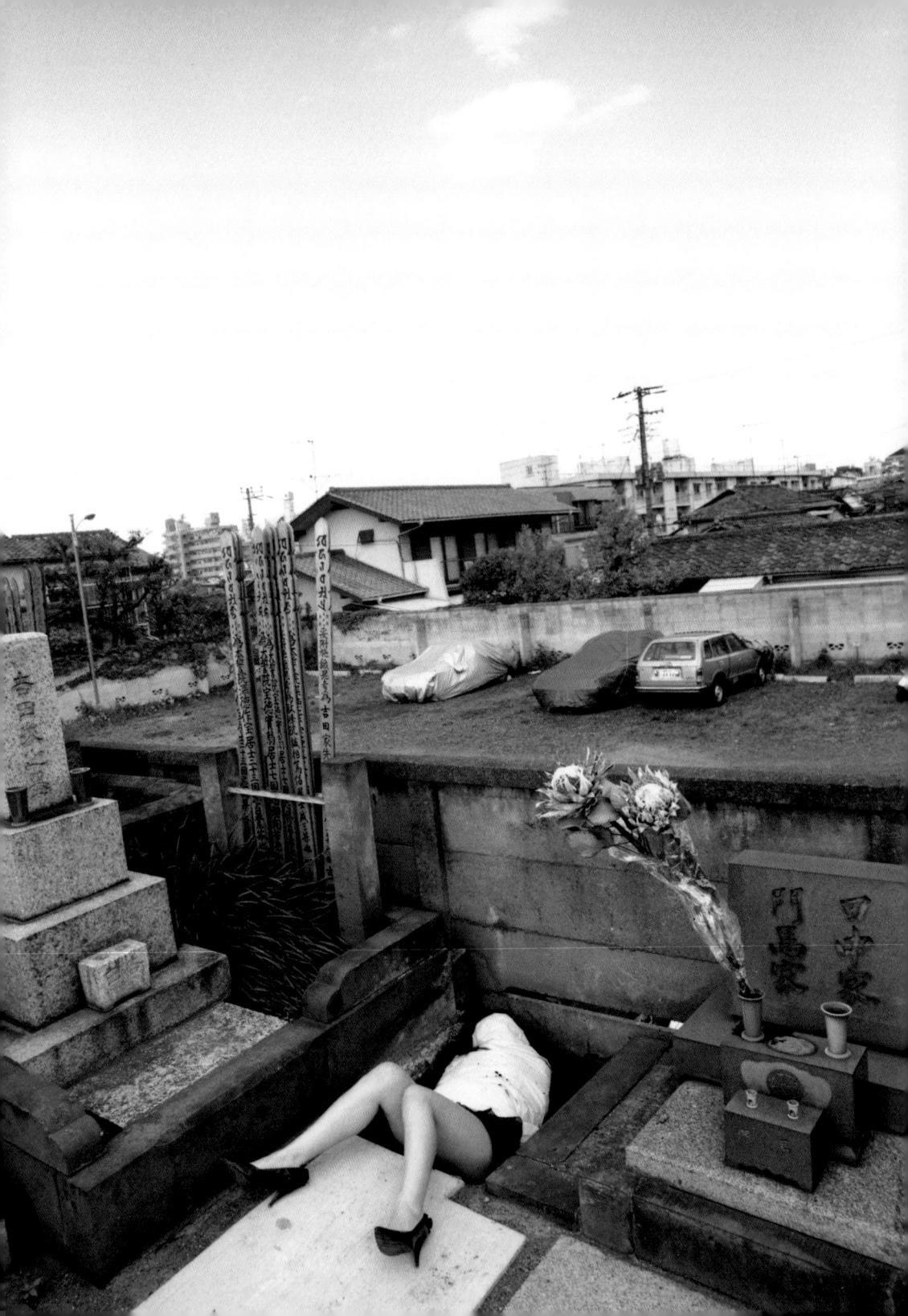

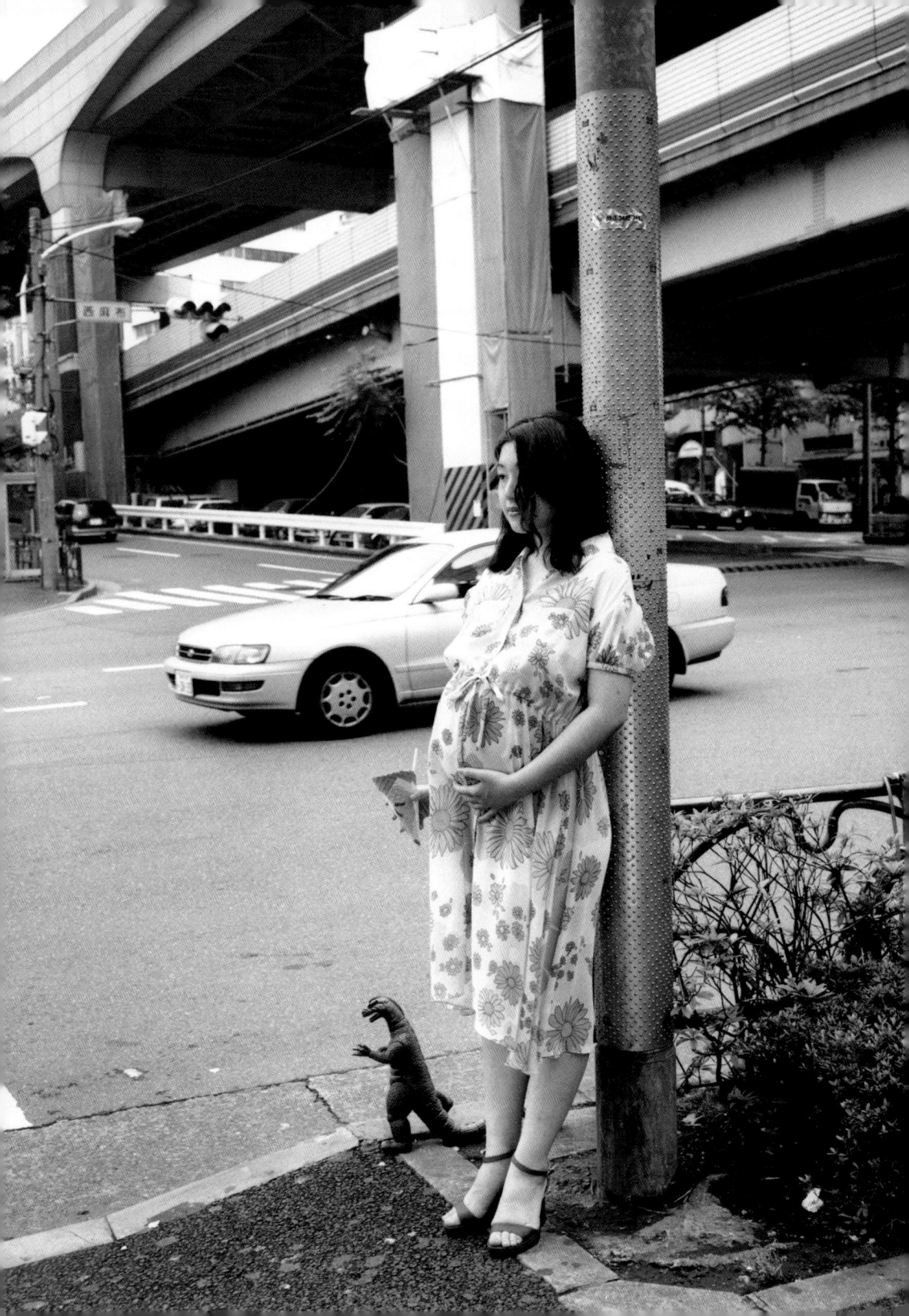

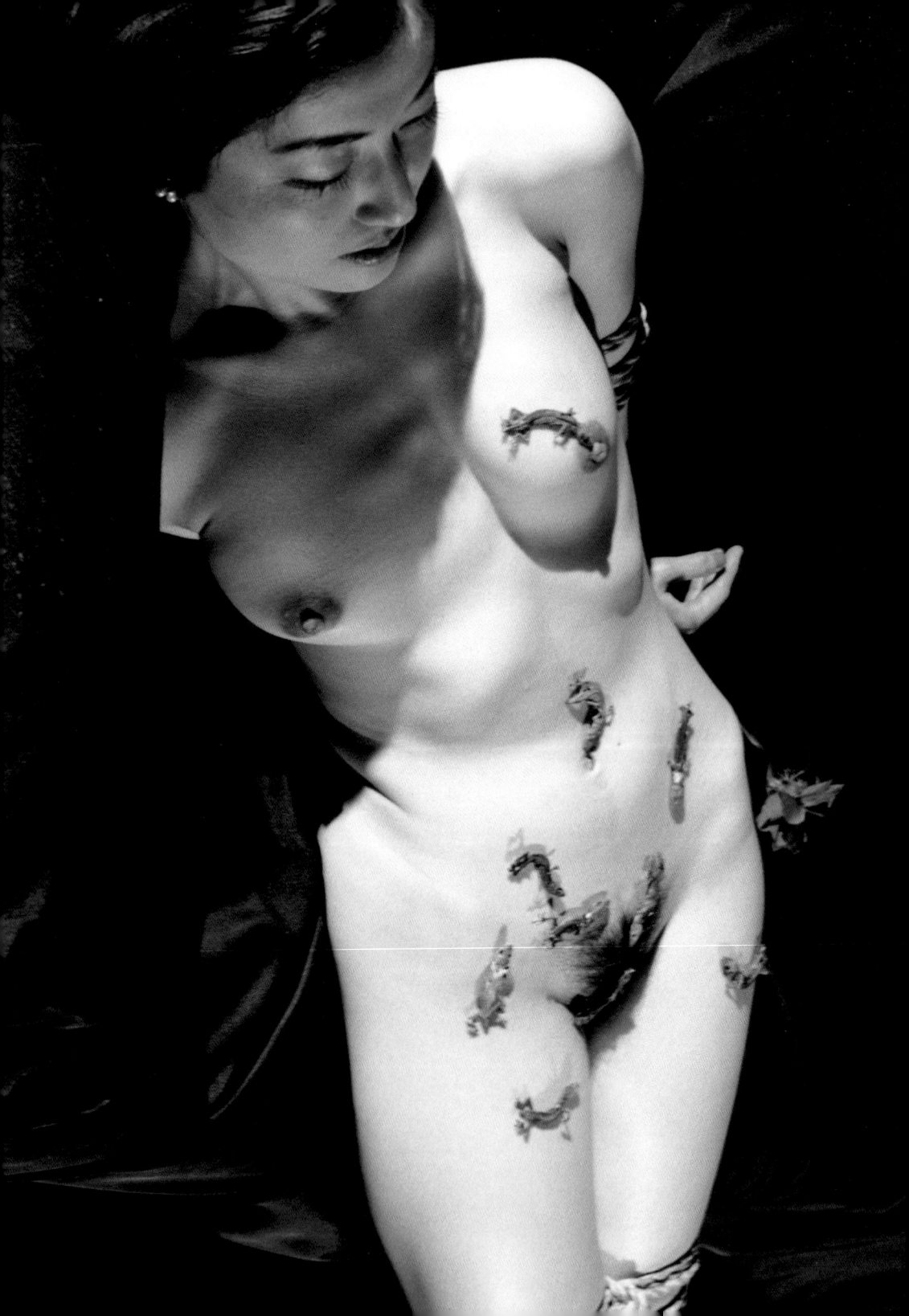

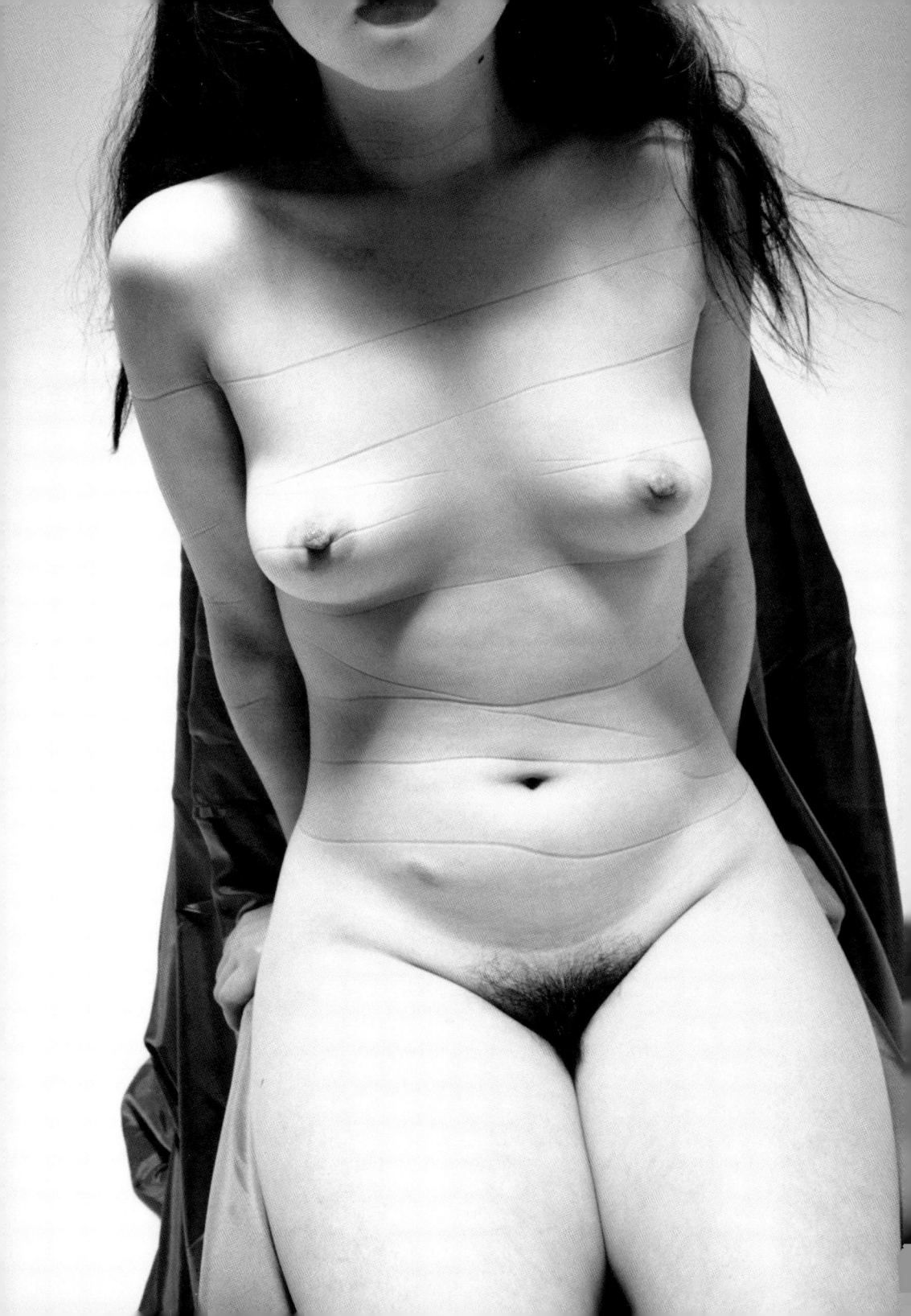

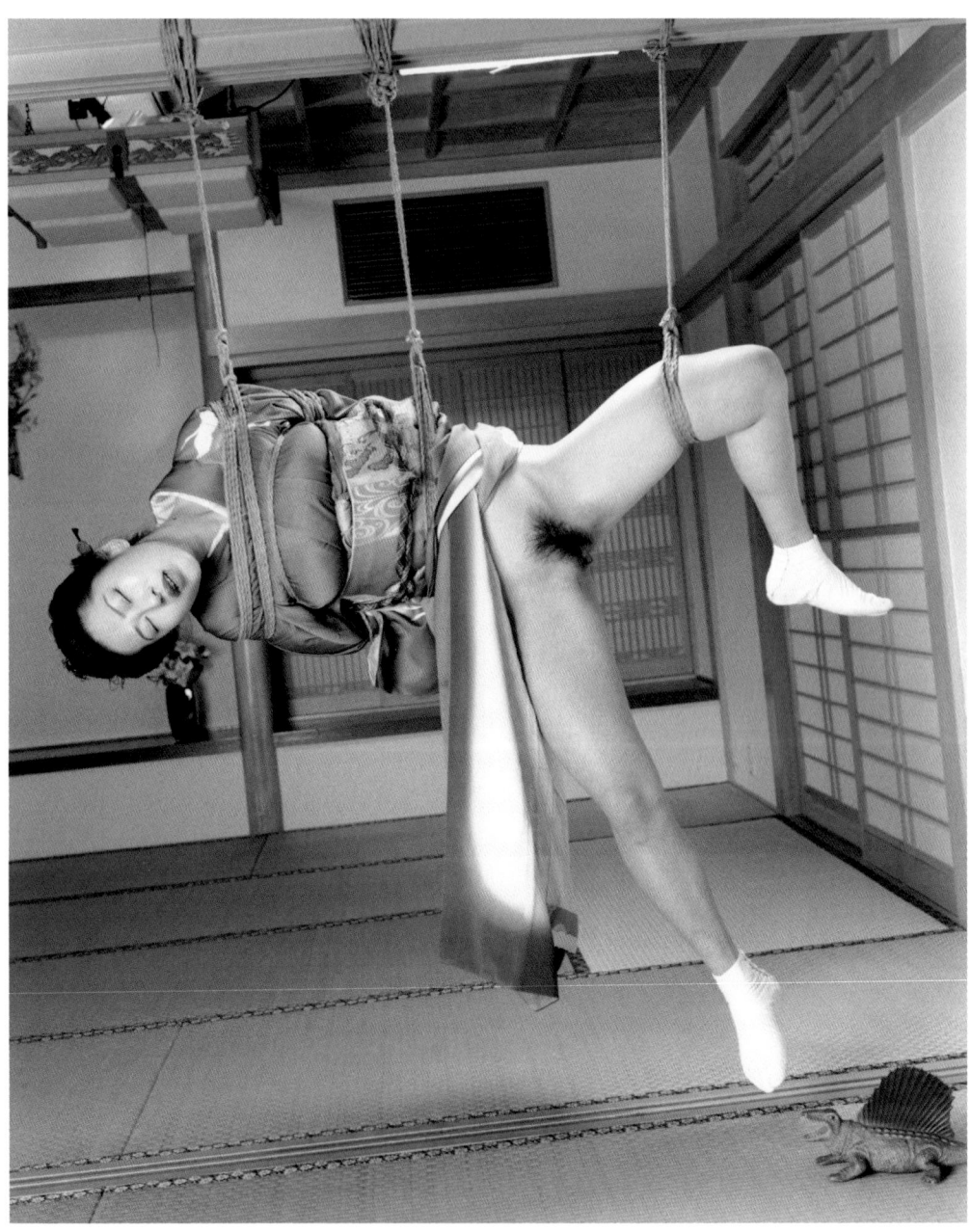

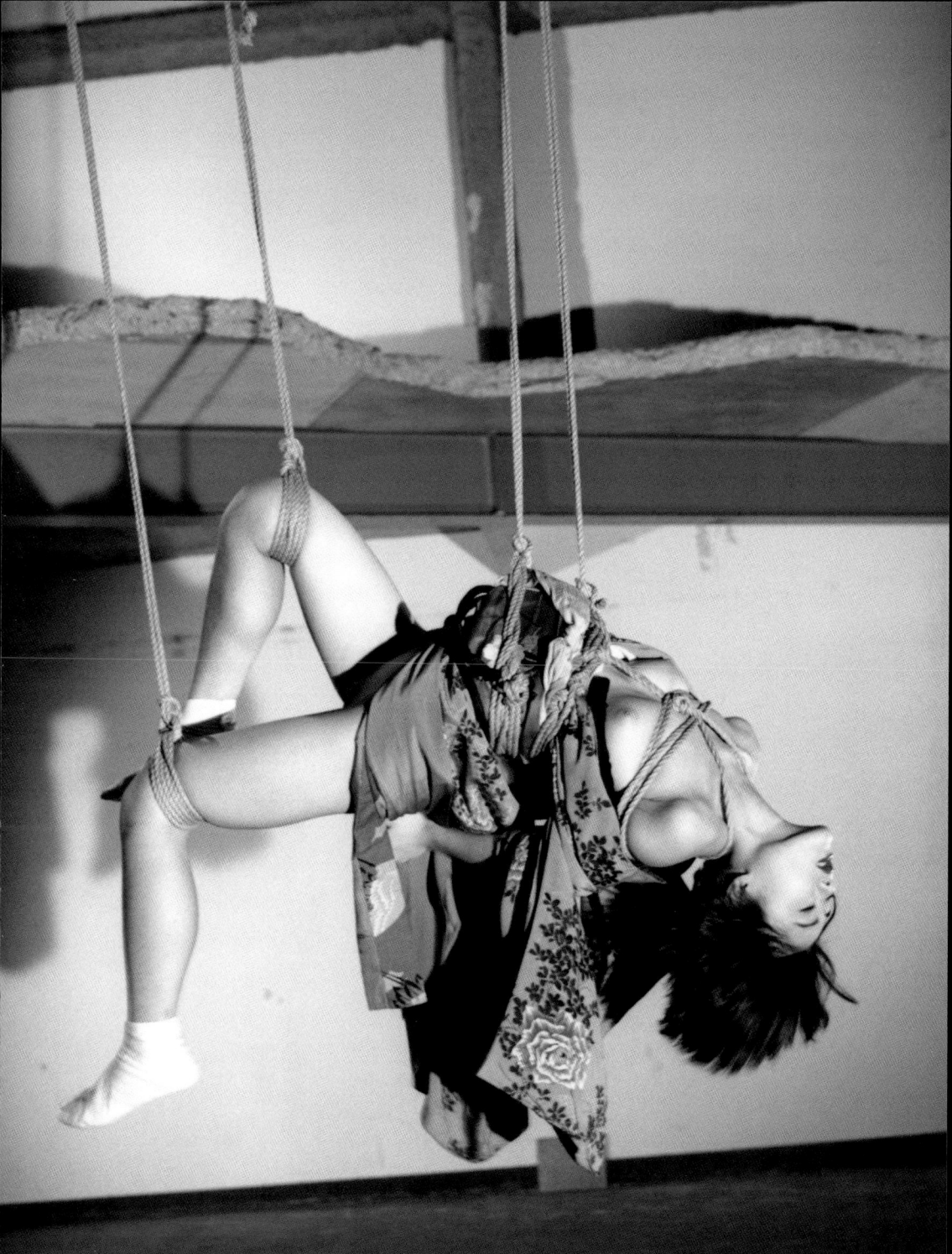

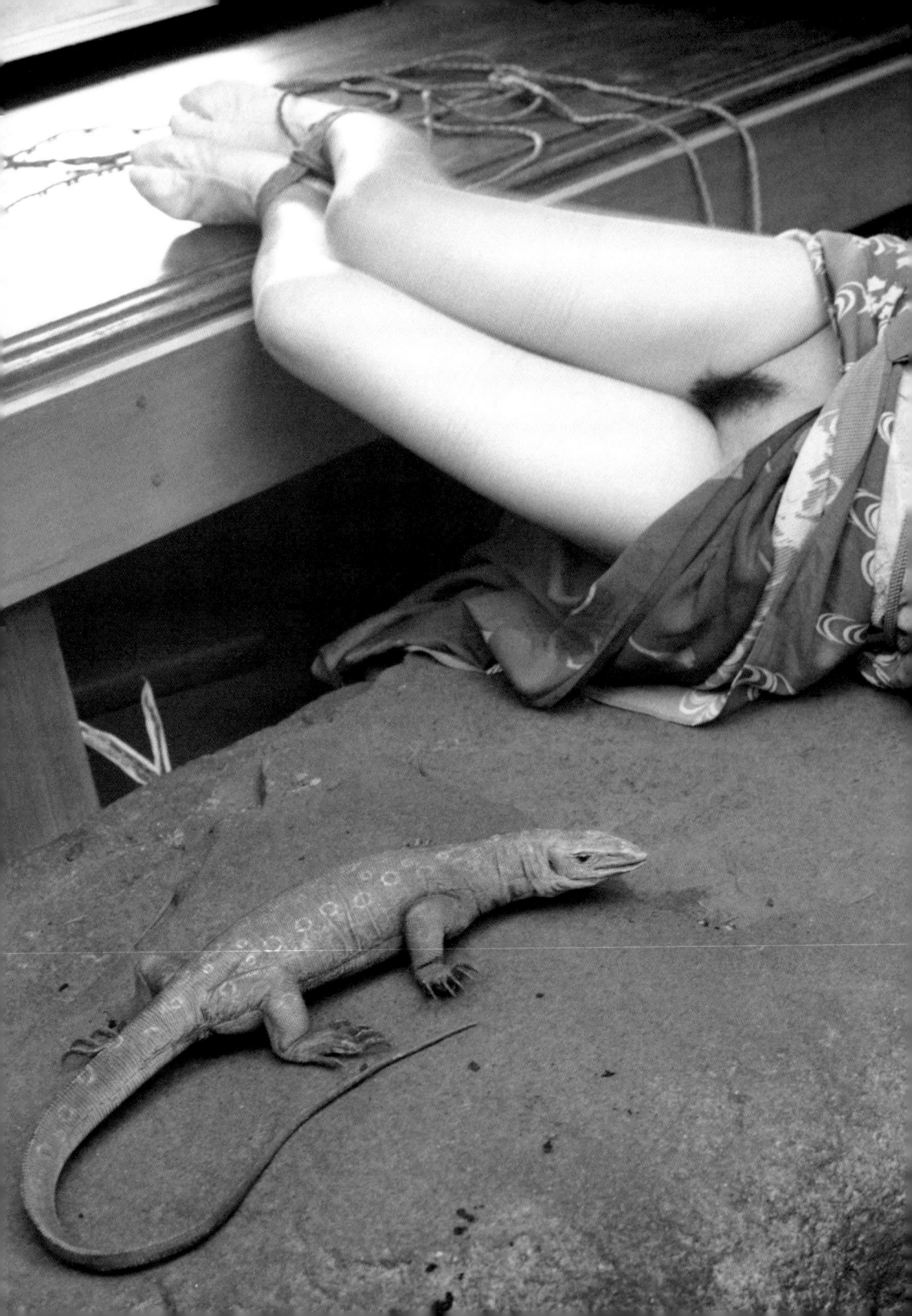

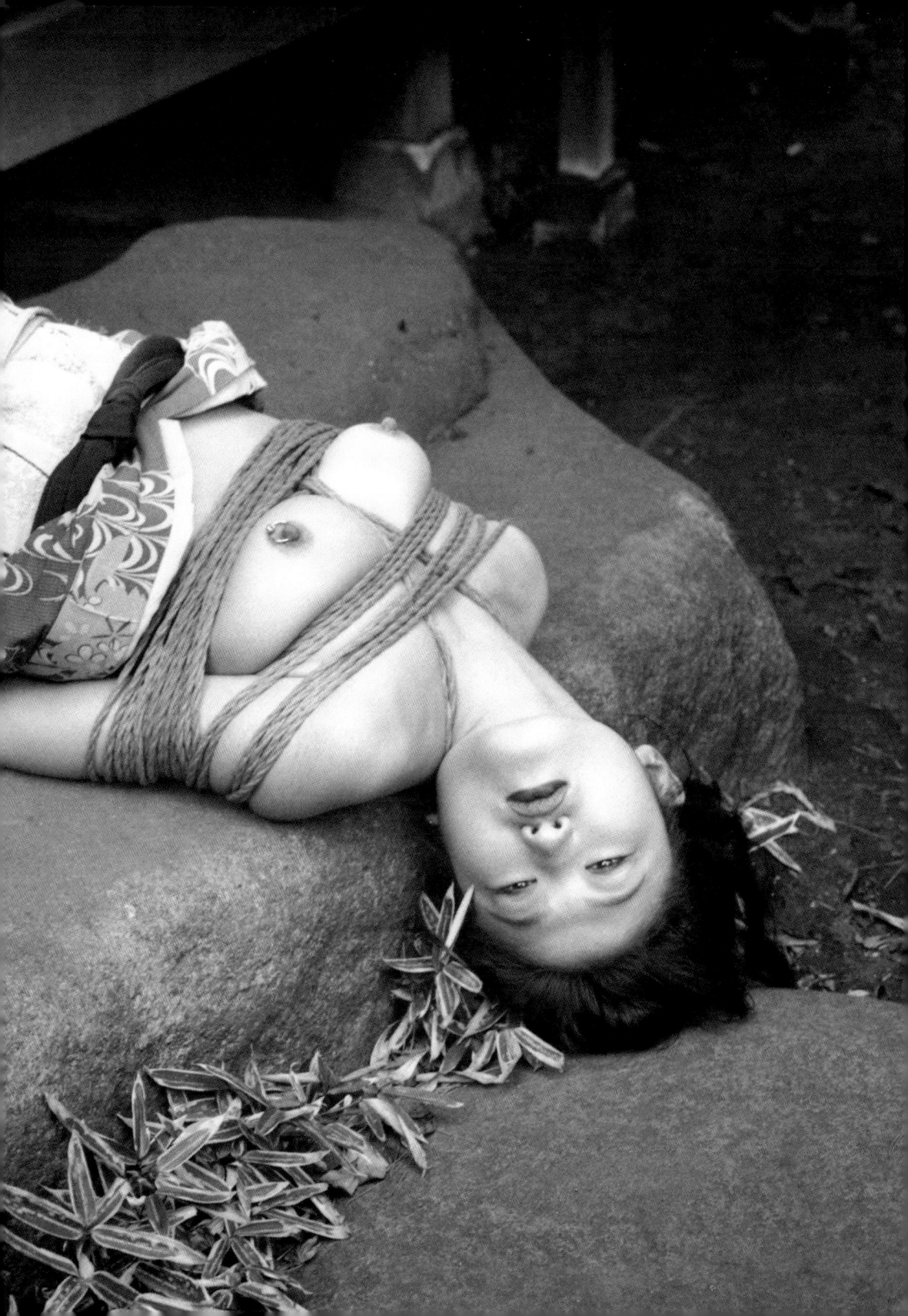

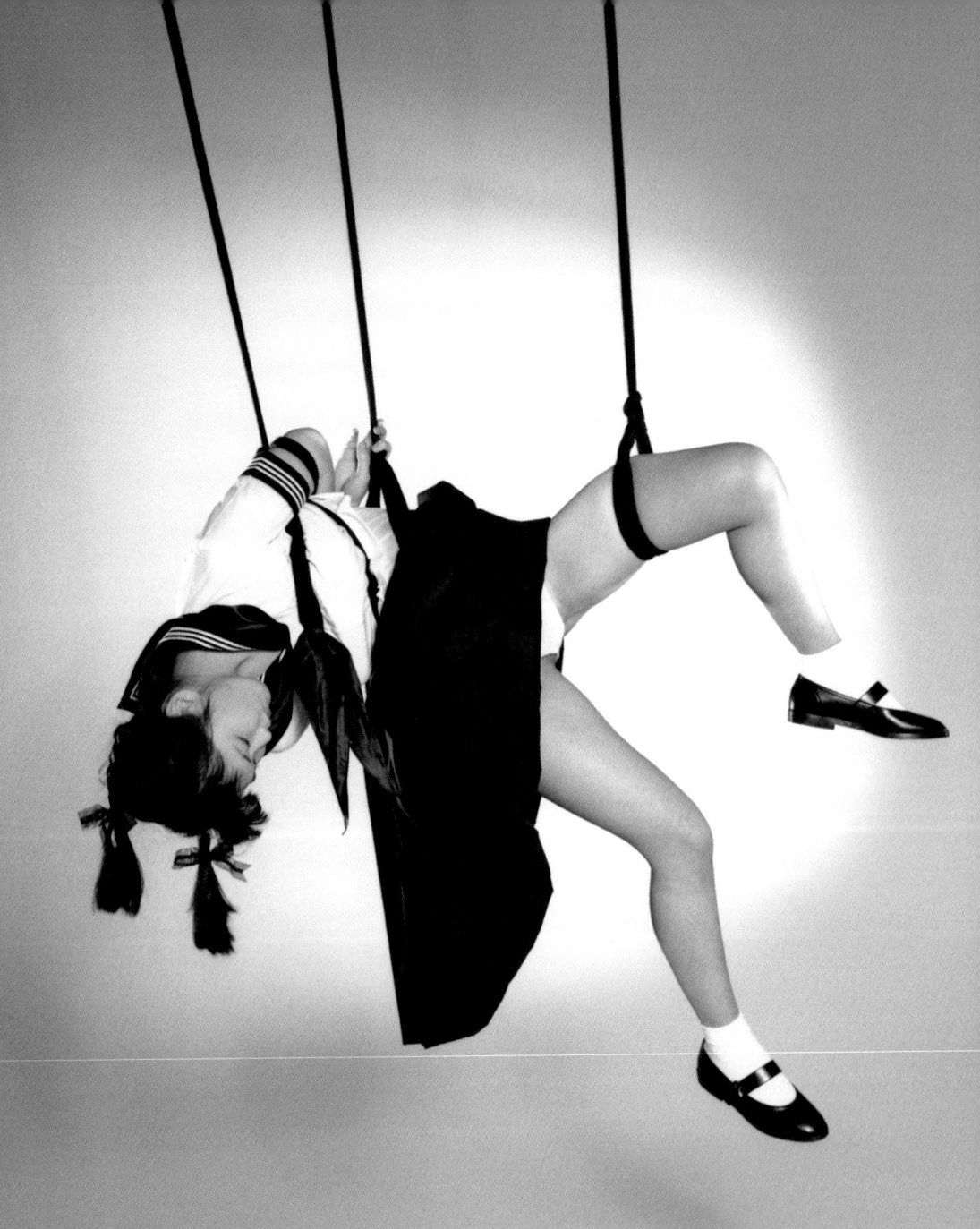

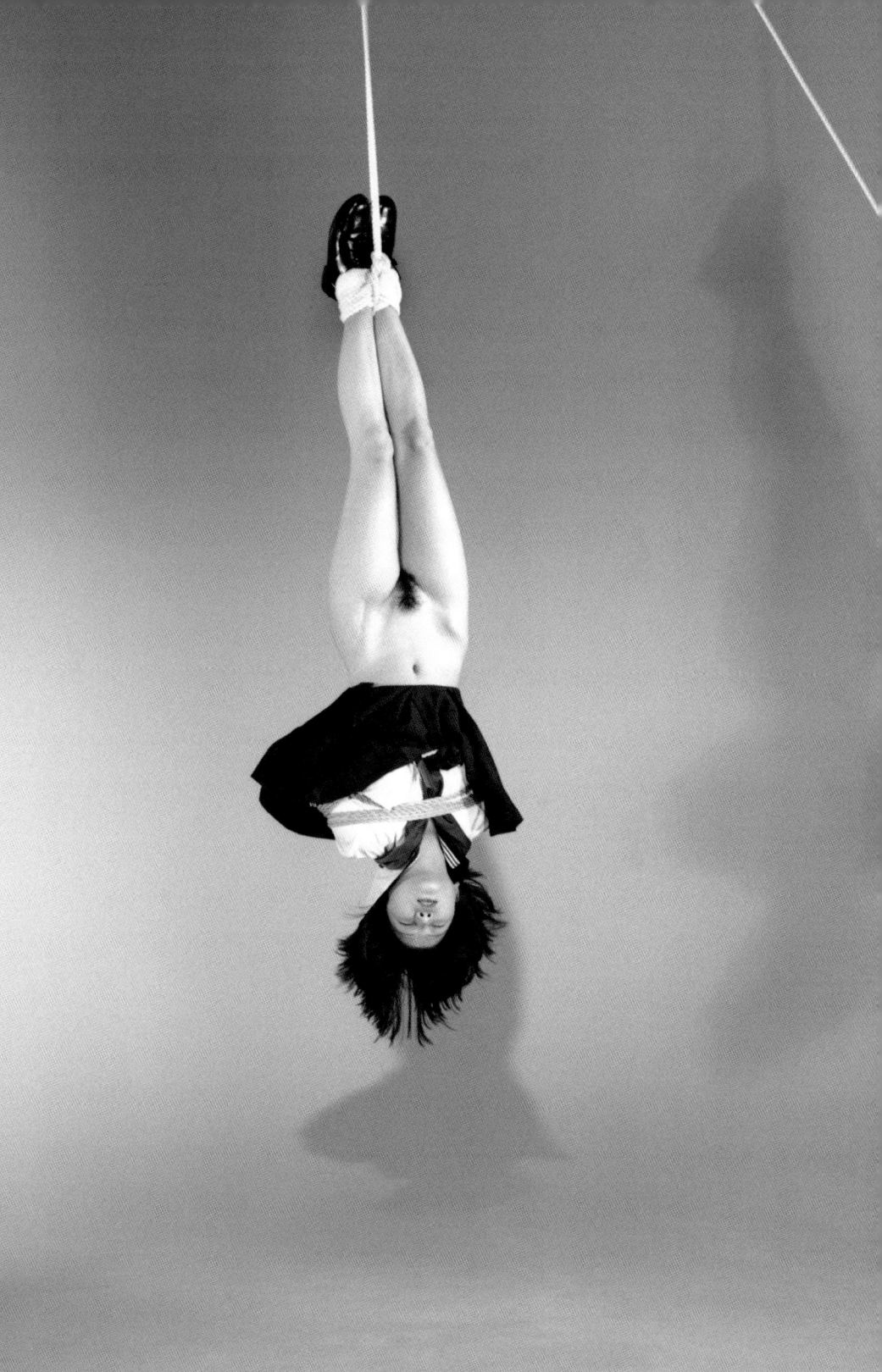

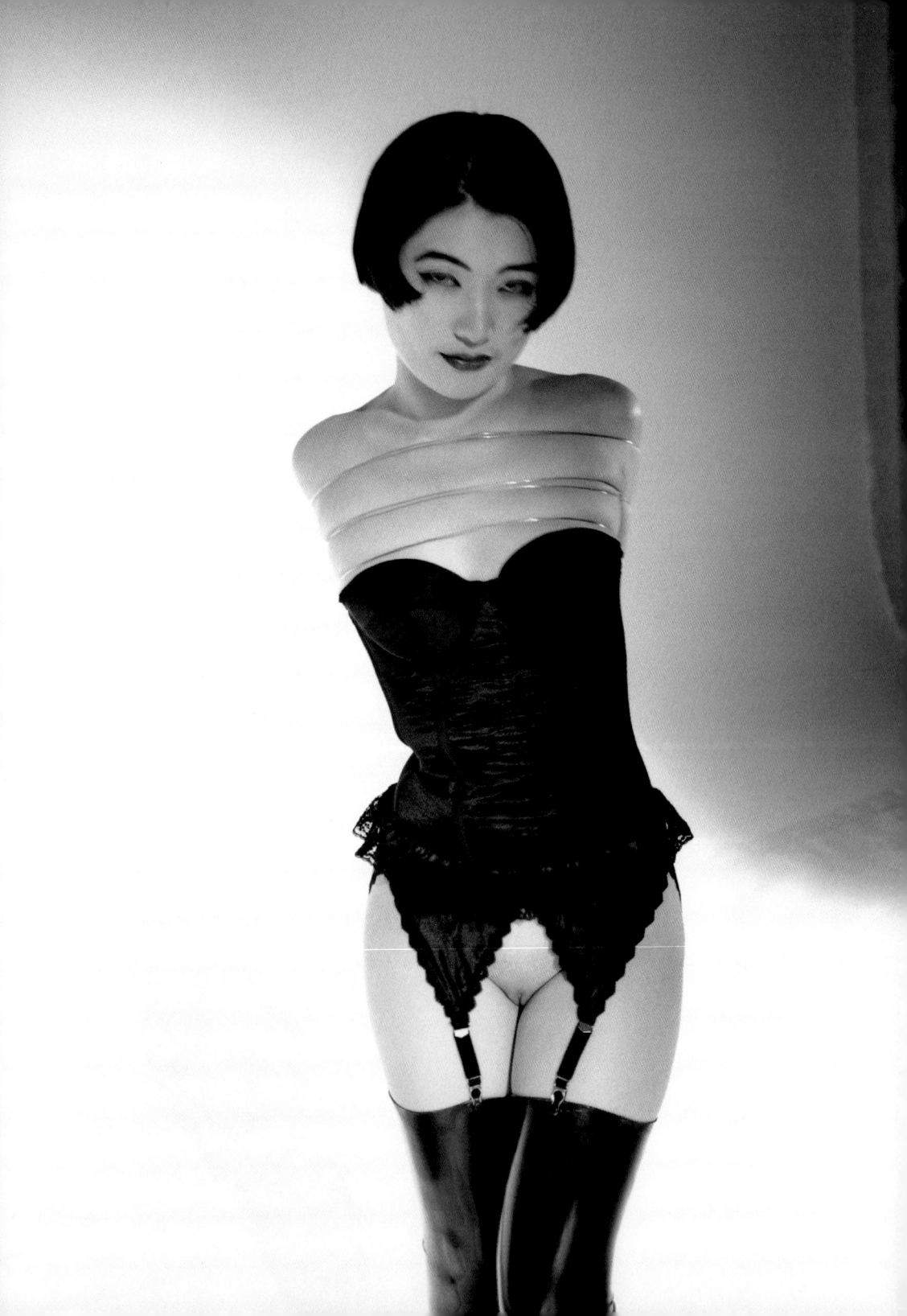

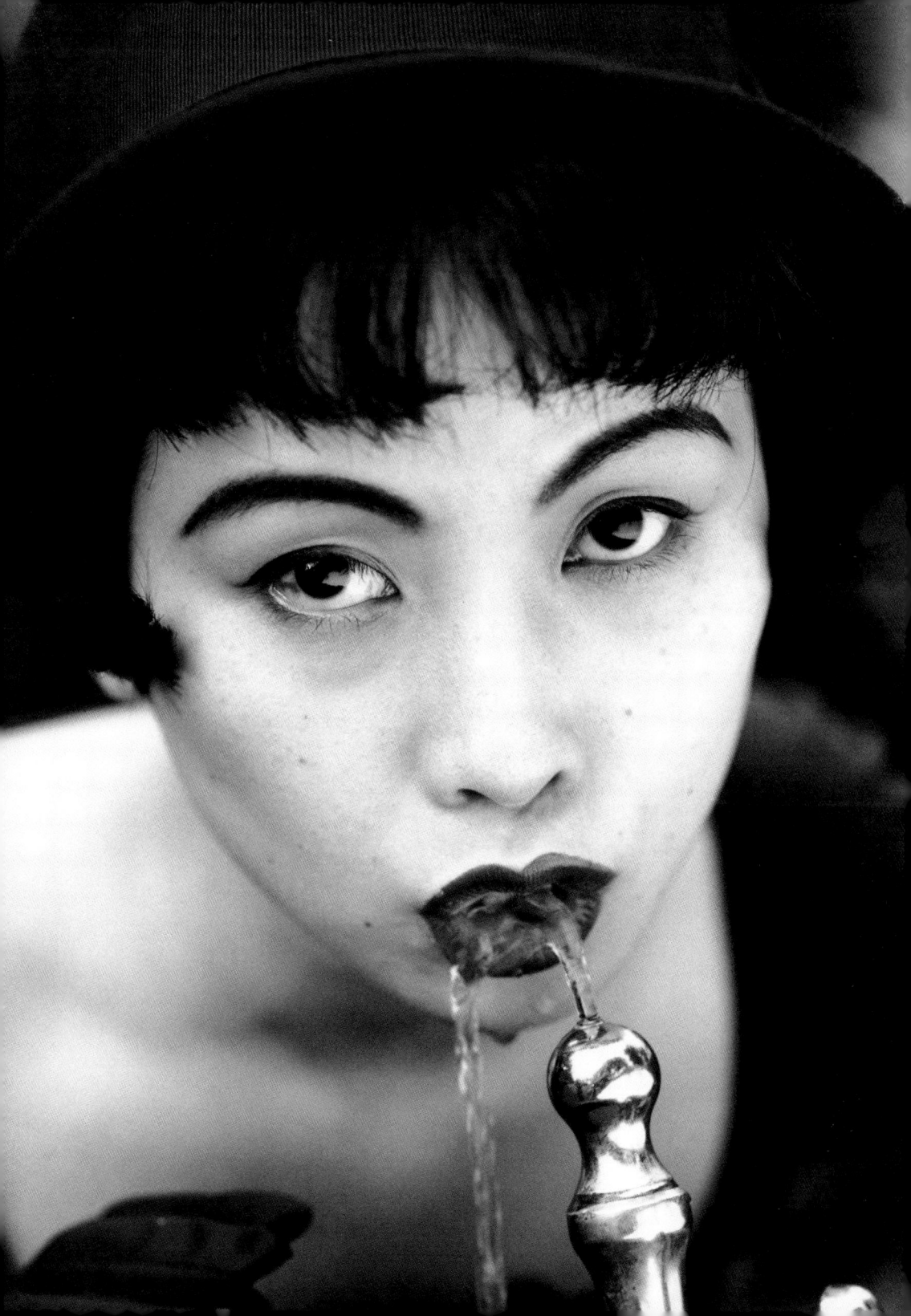

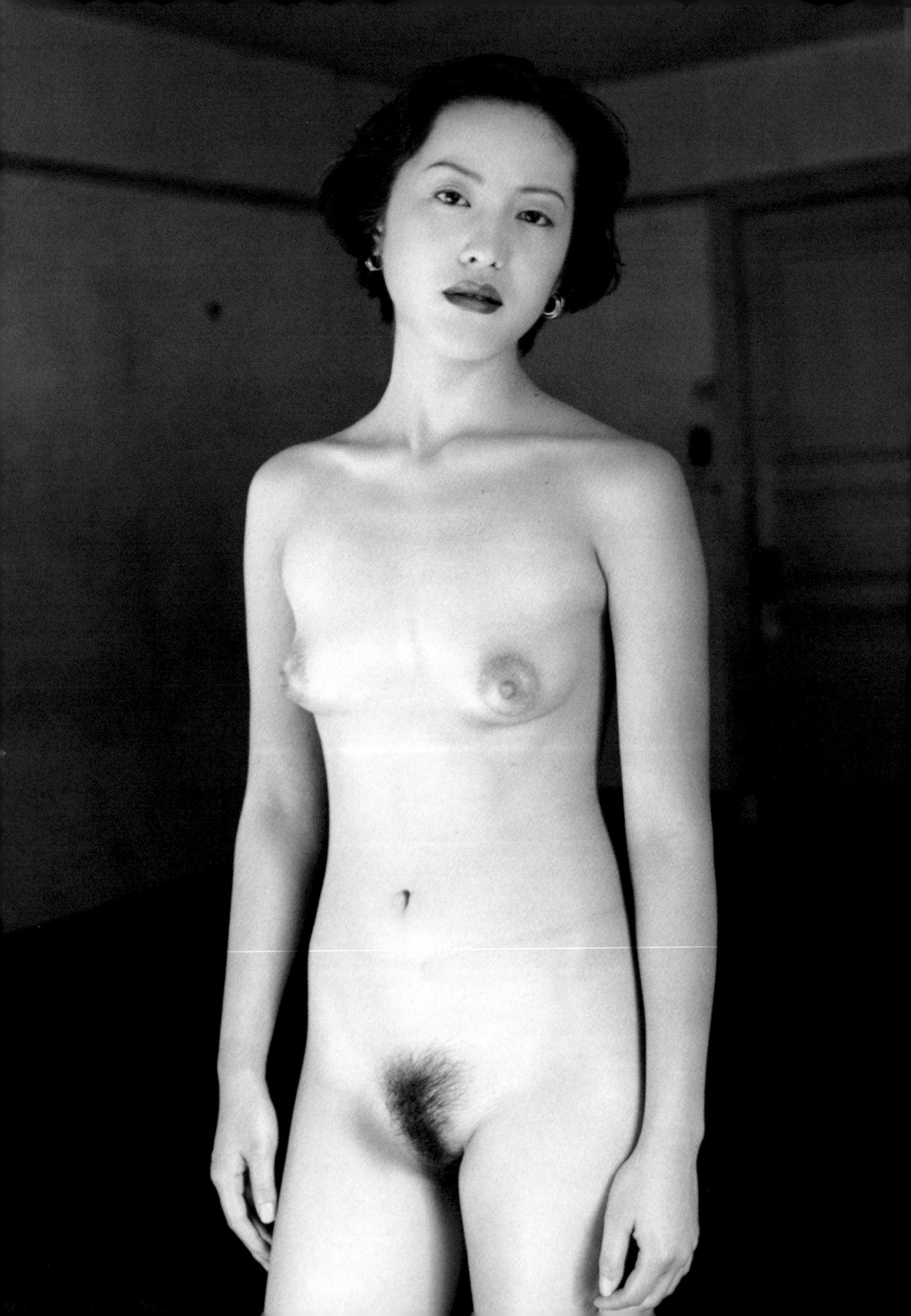

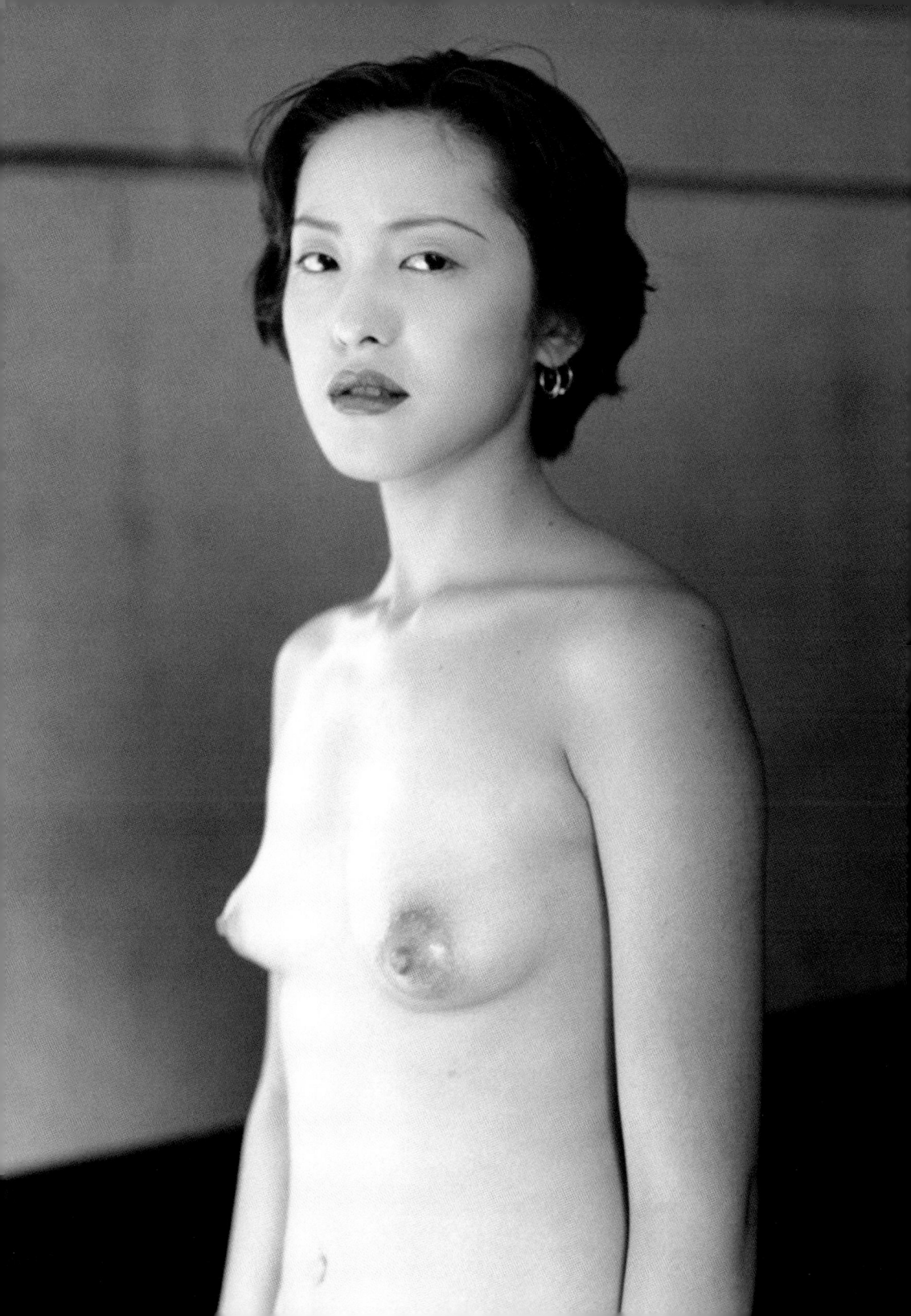

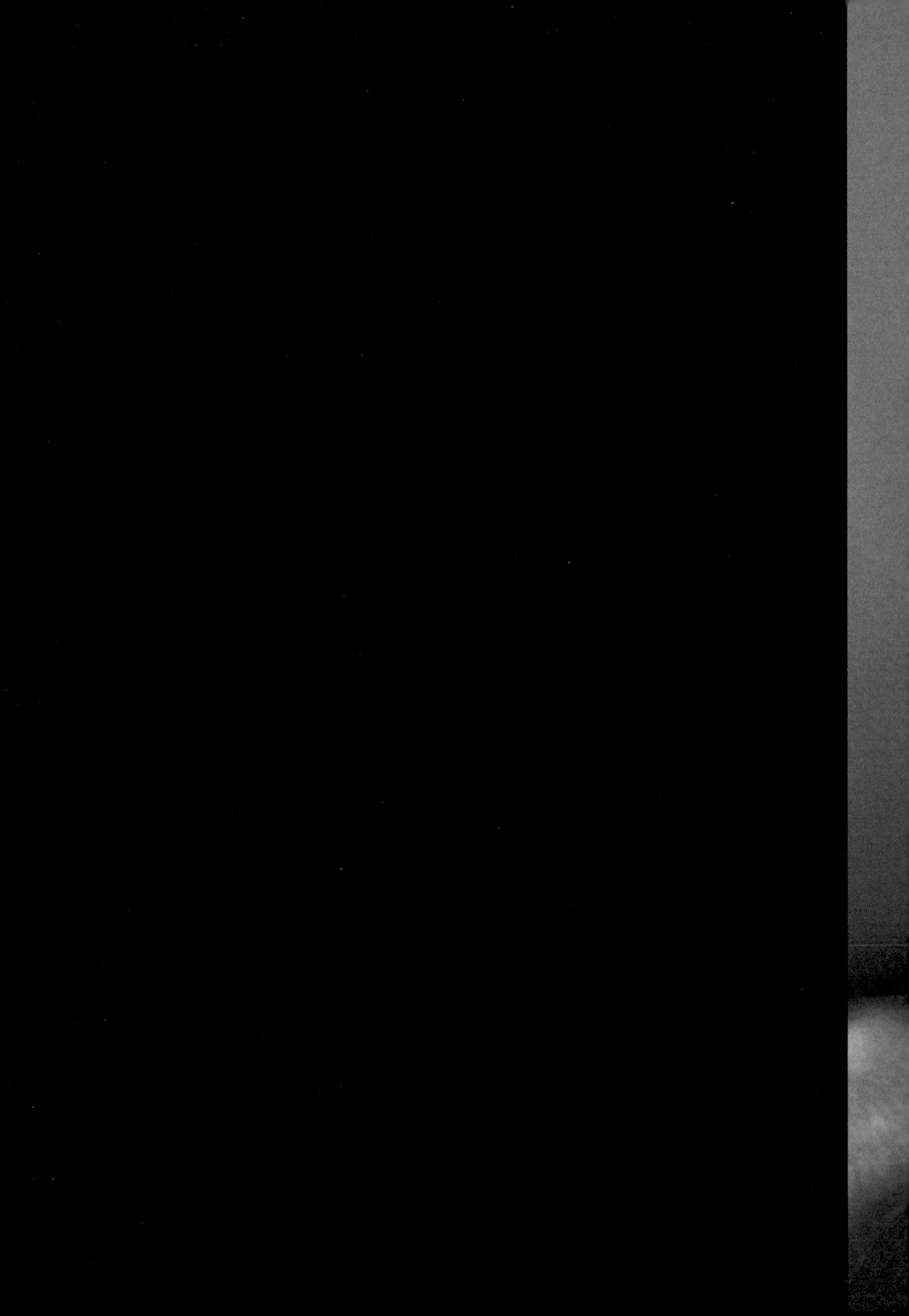

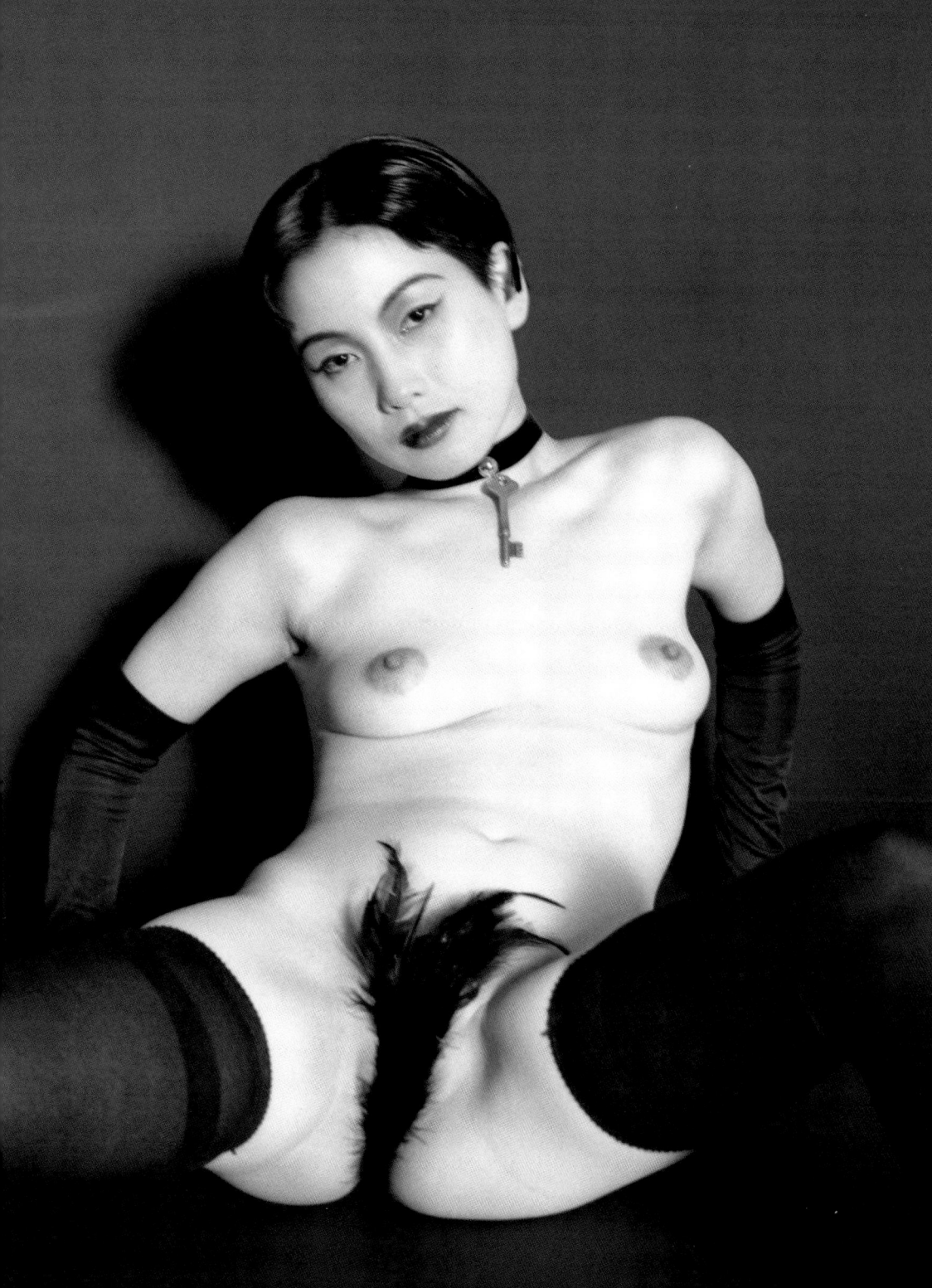

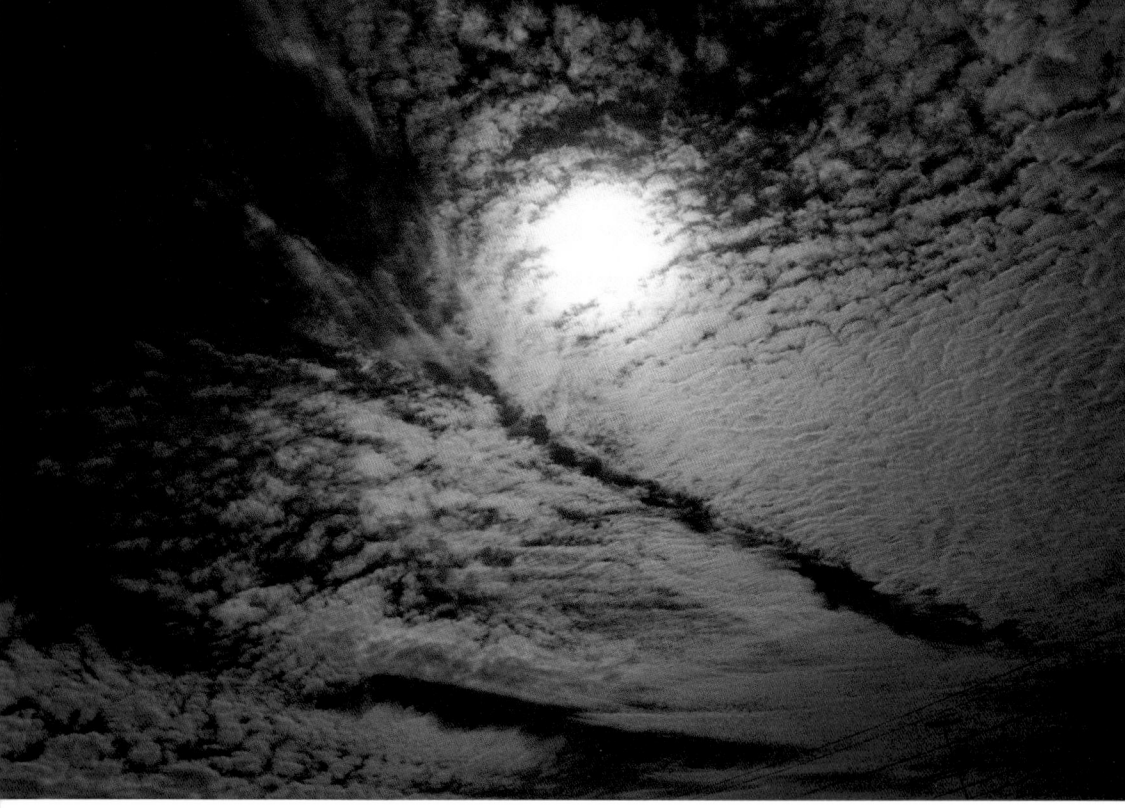

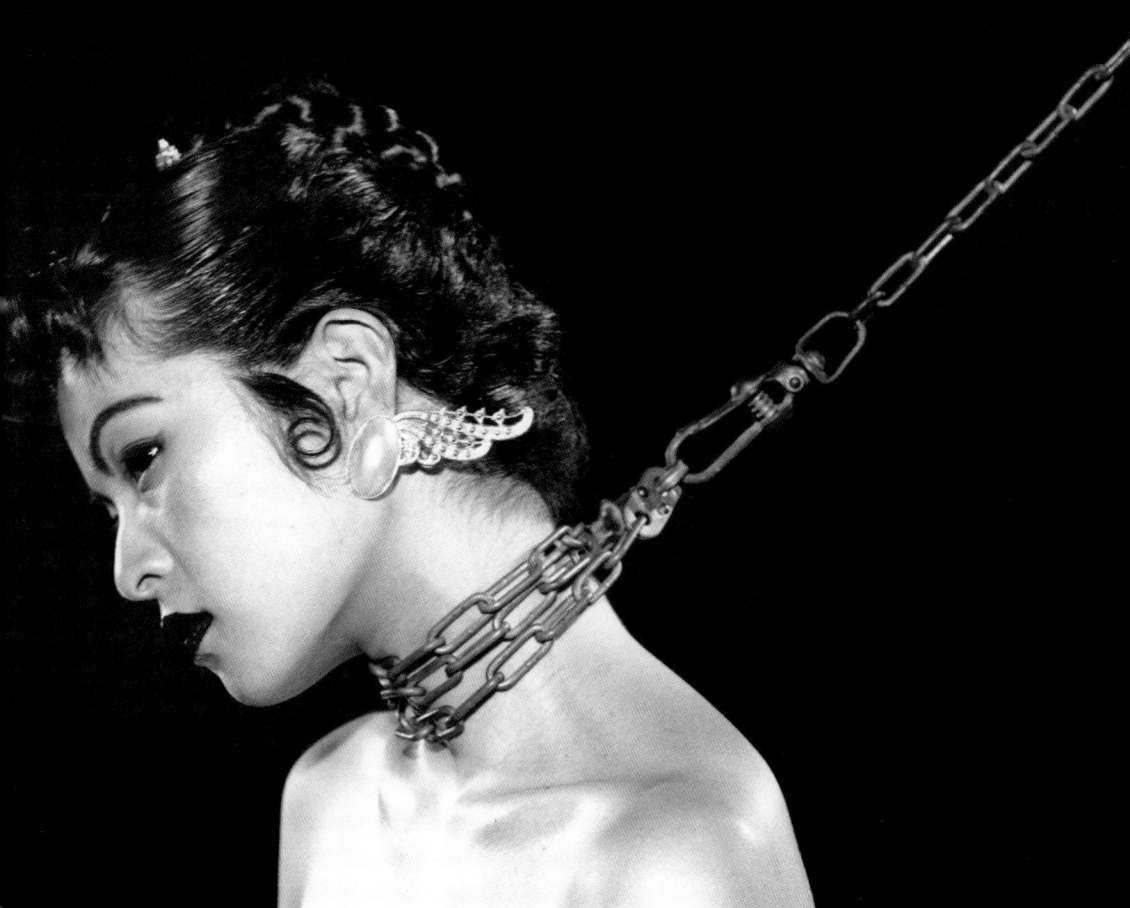

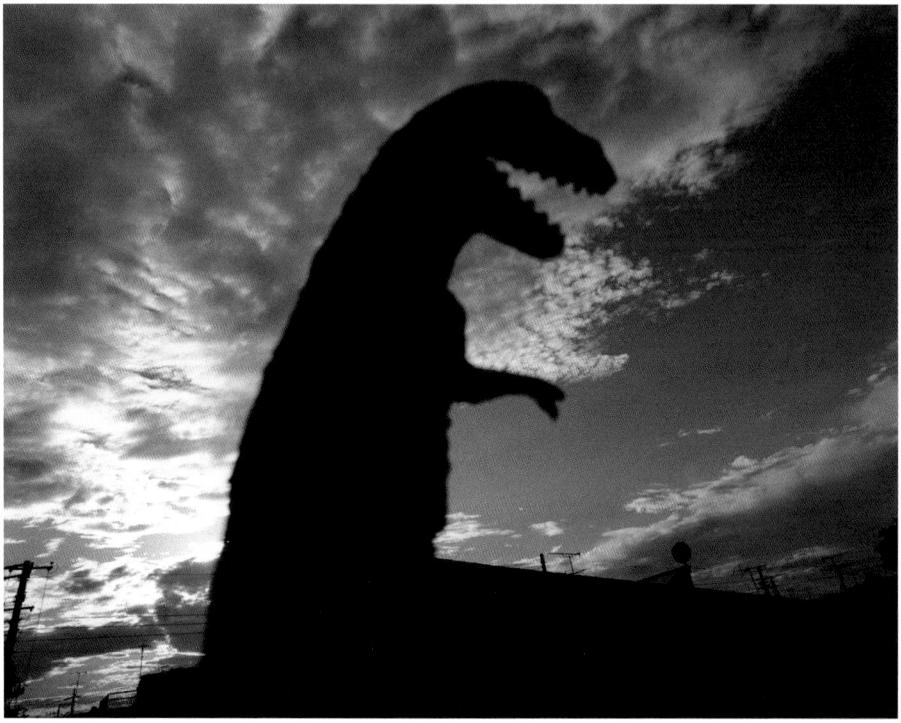

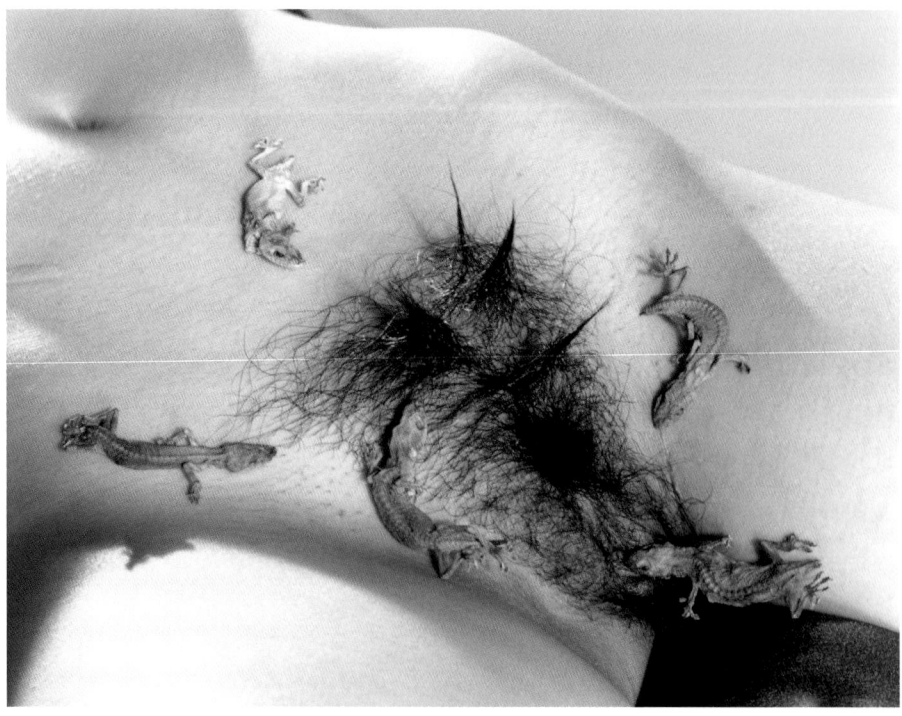

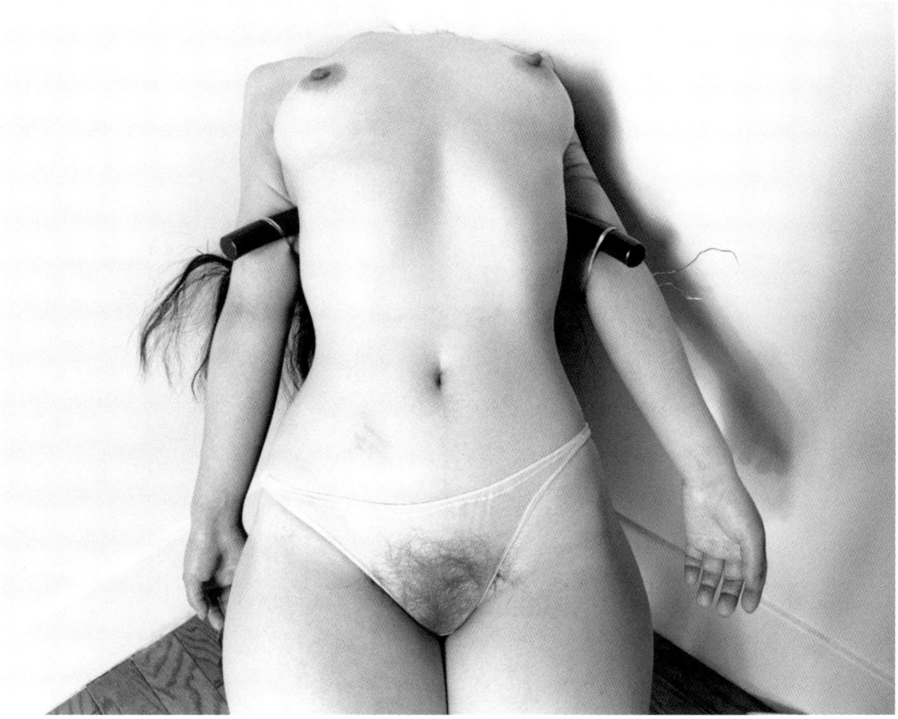

223

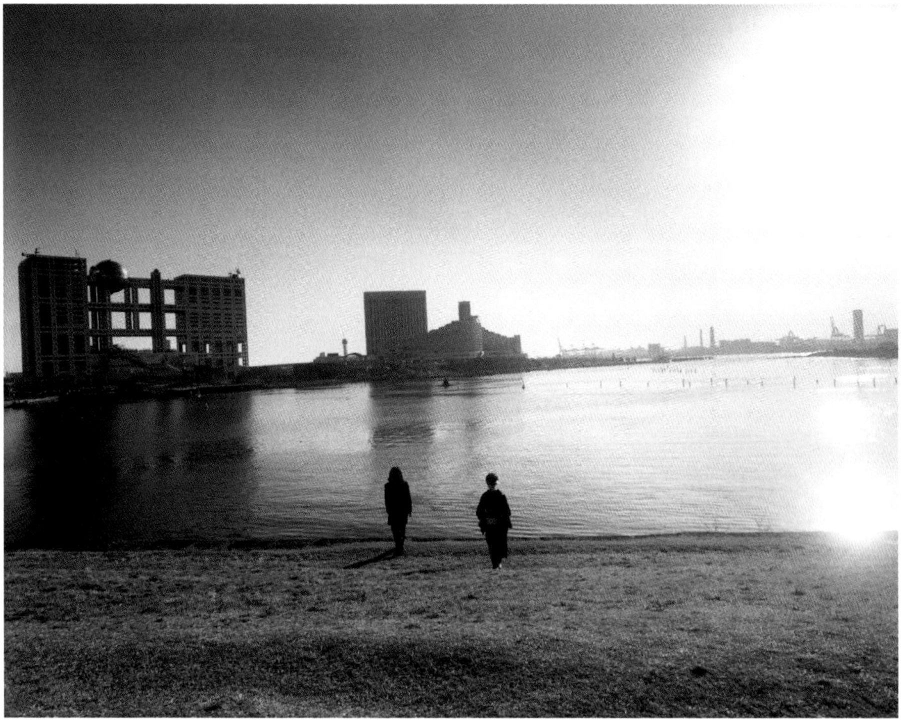

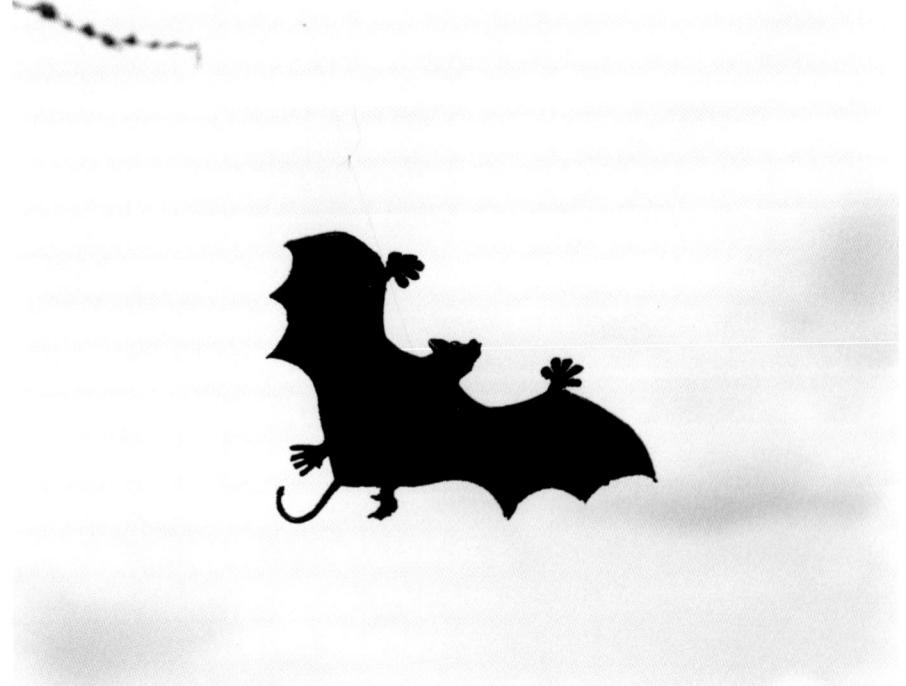

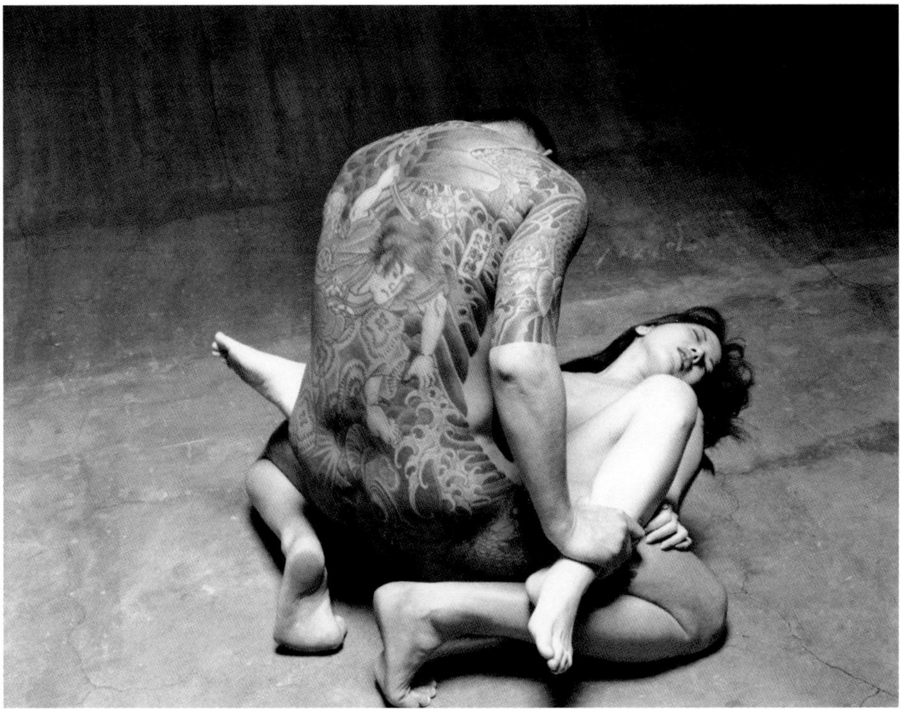

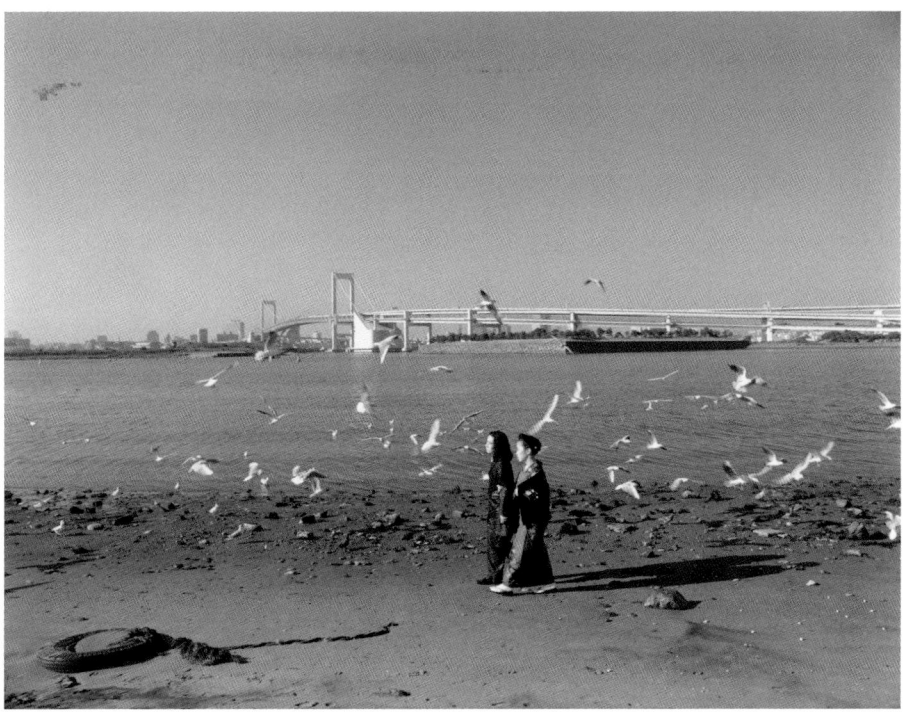

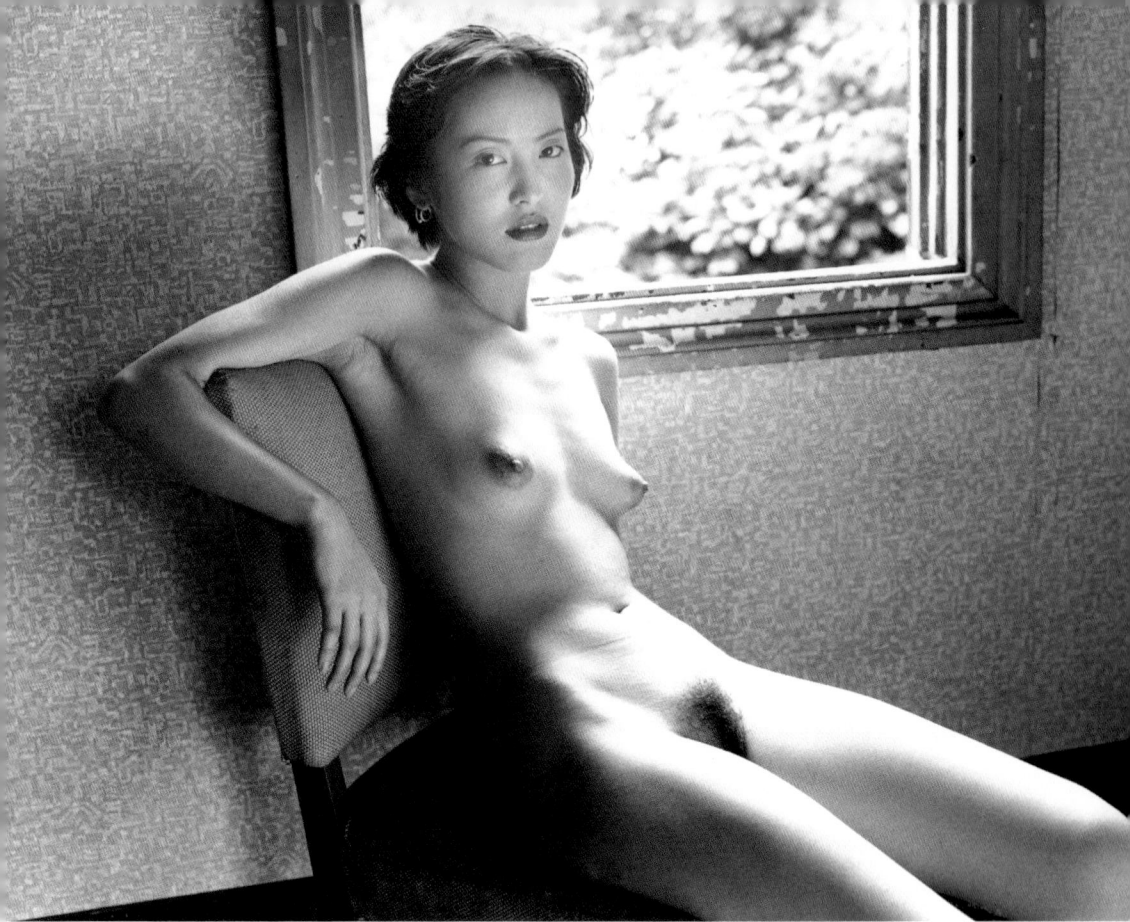

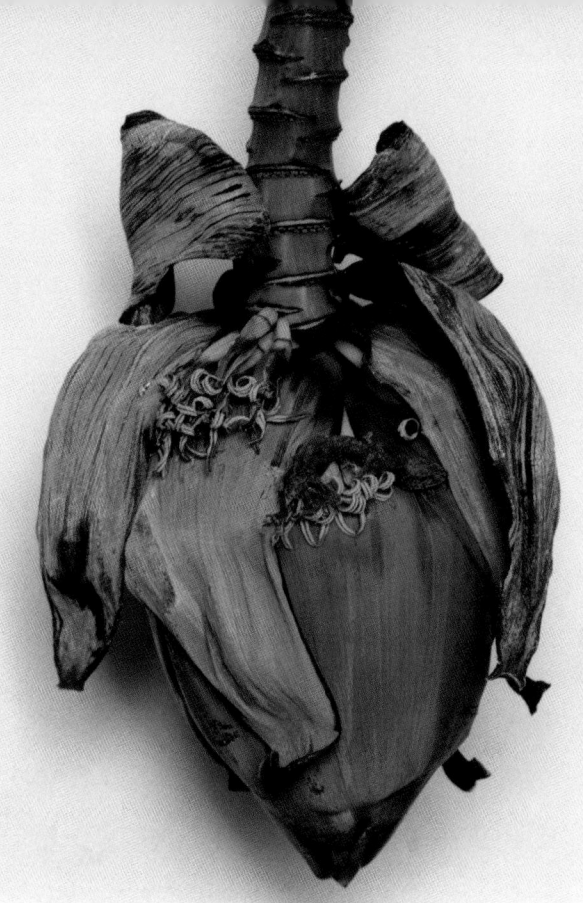

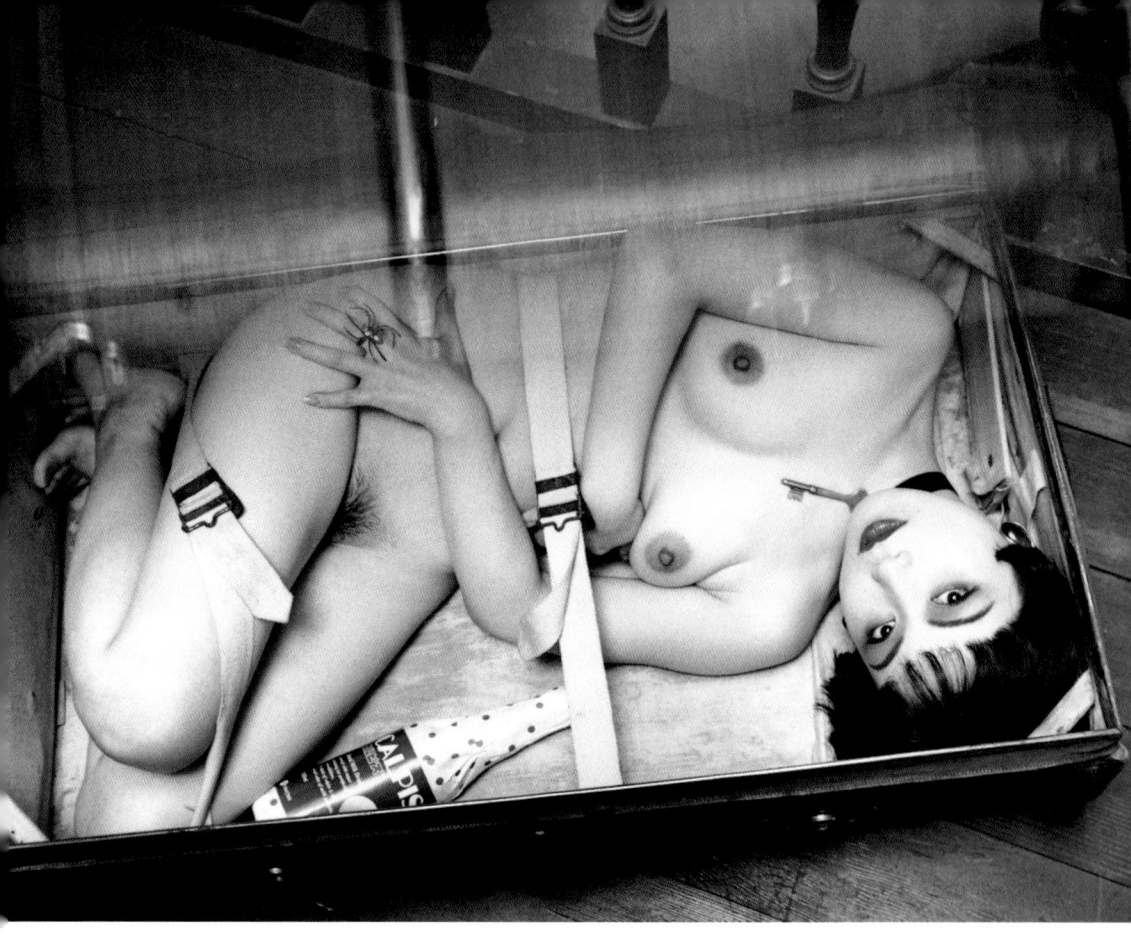

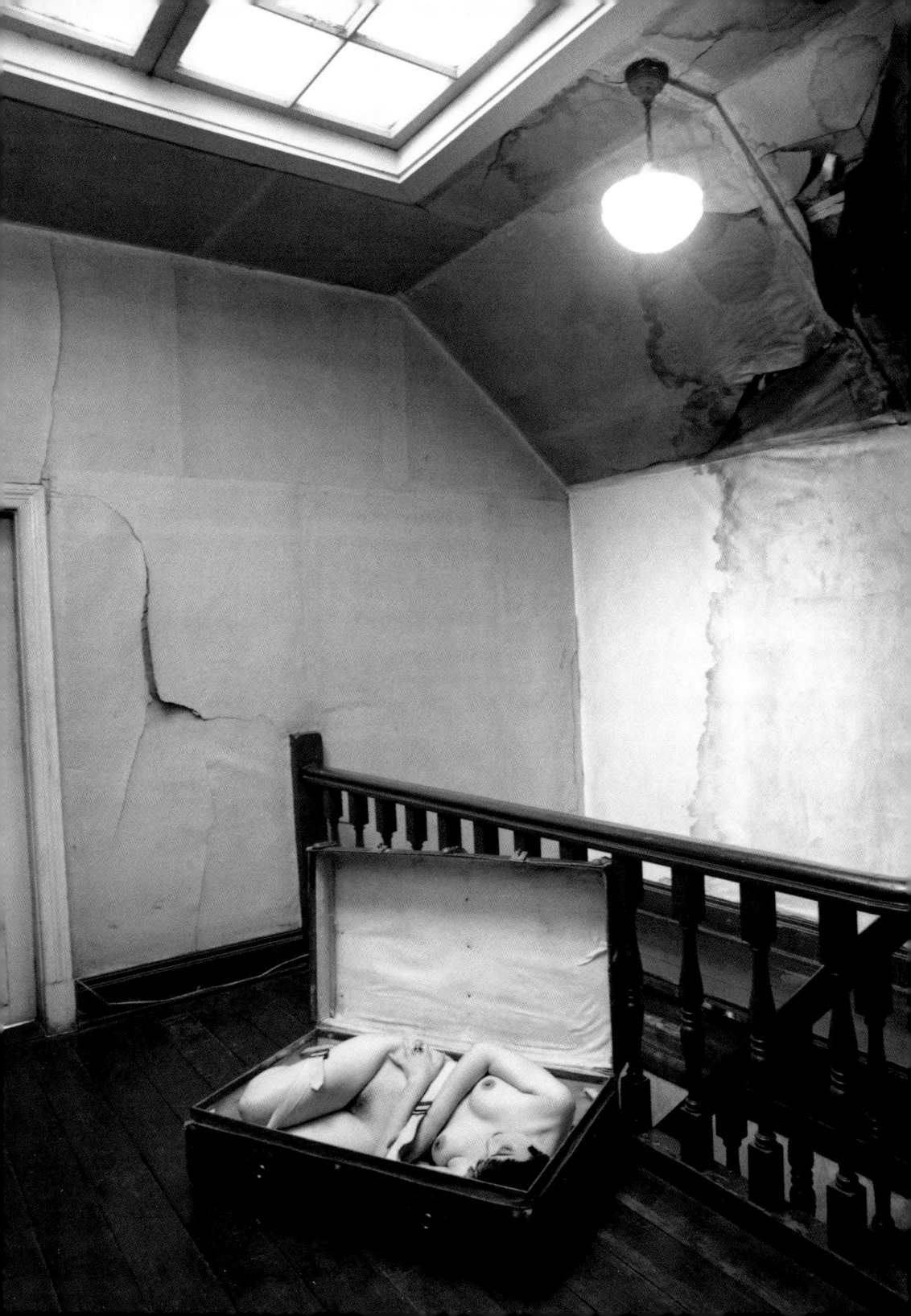

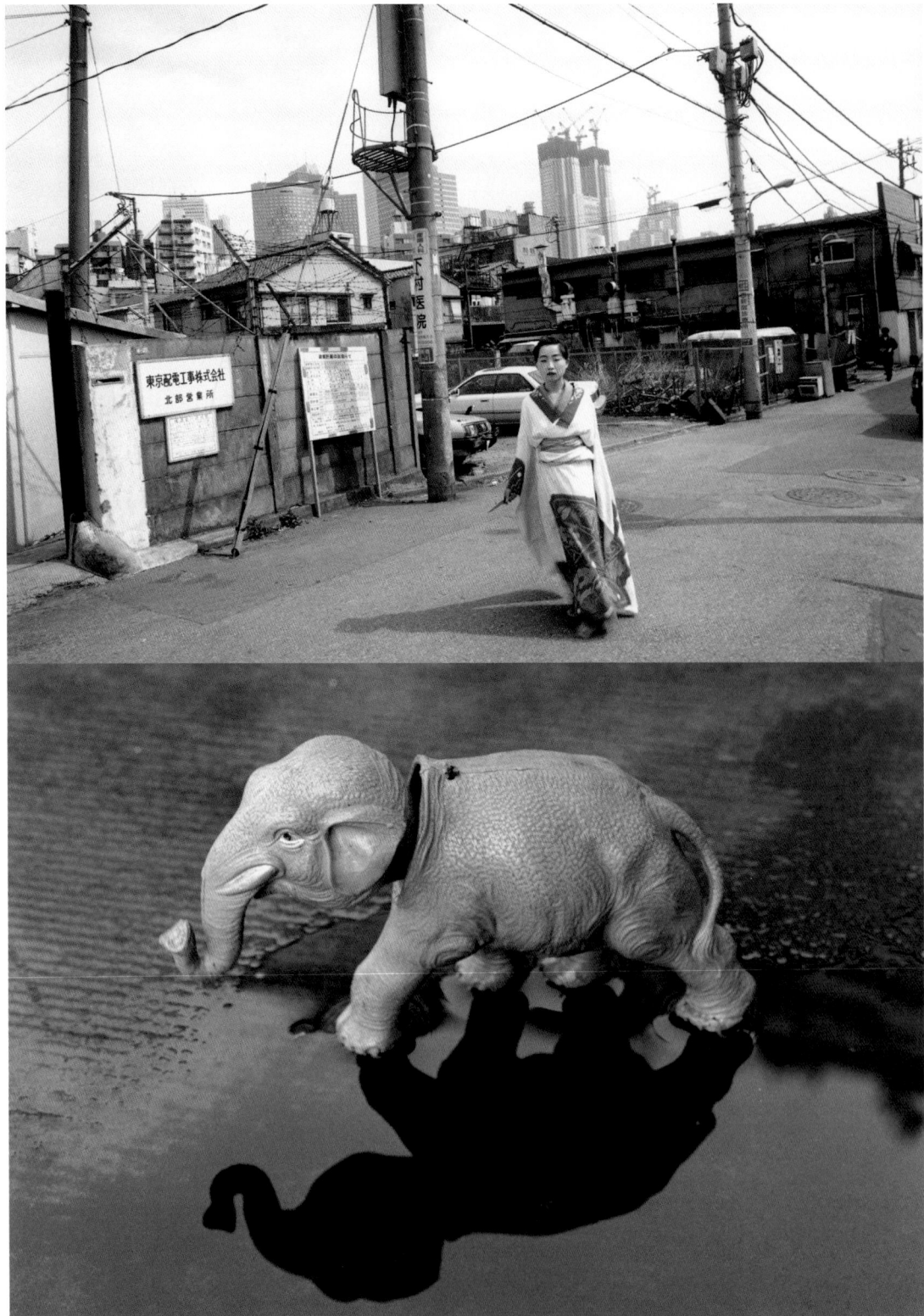

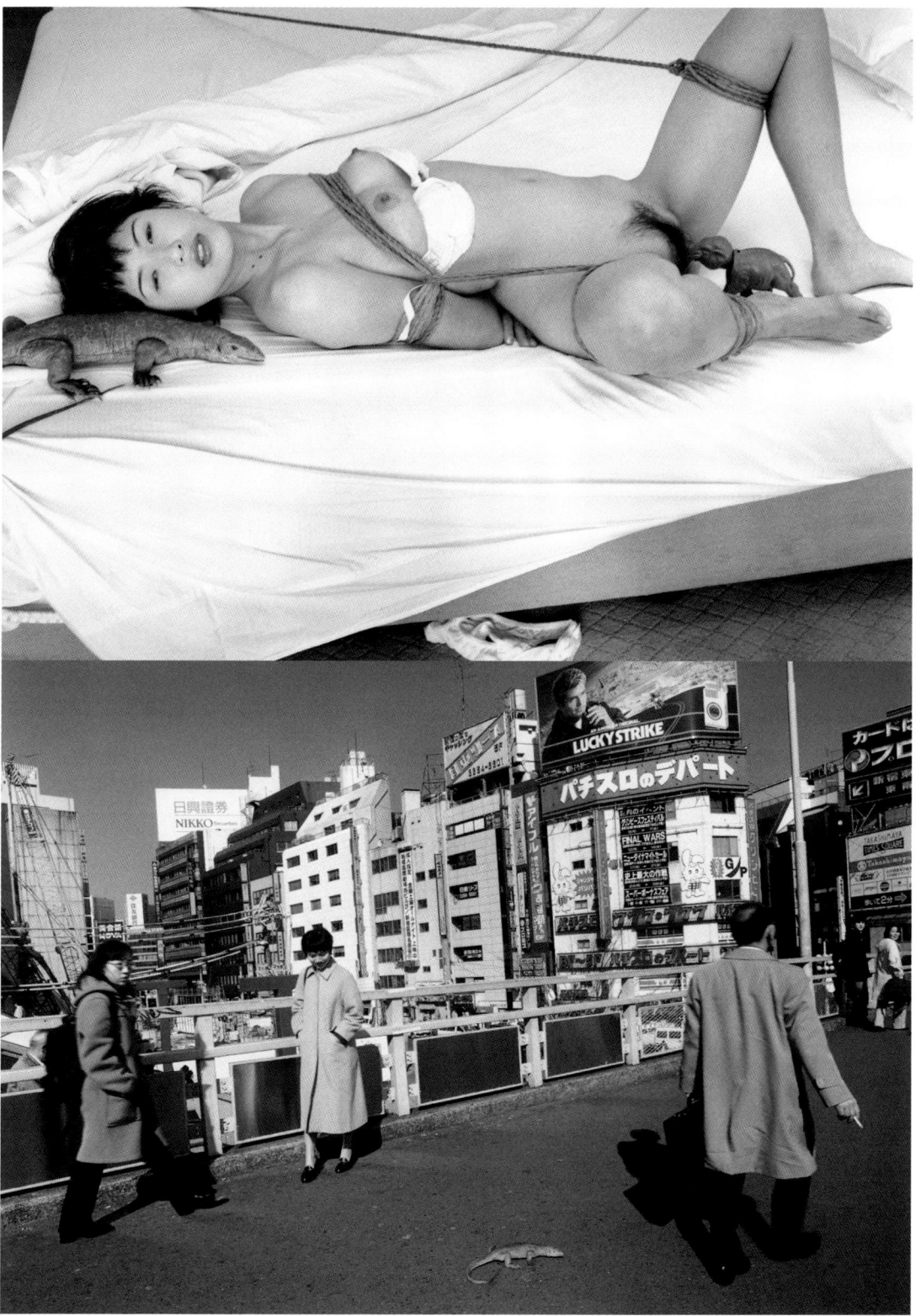

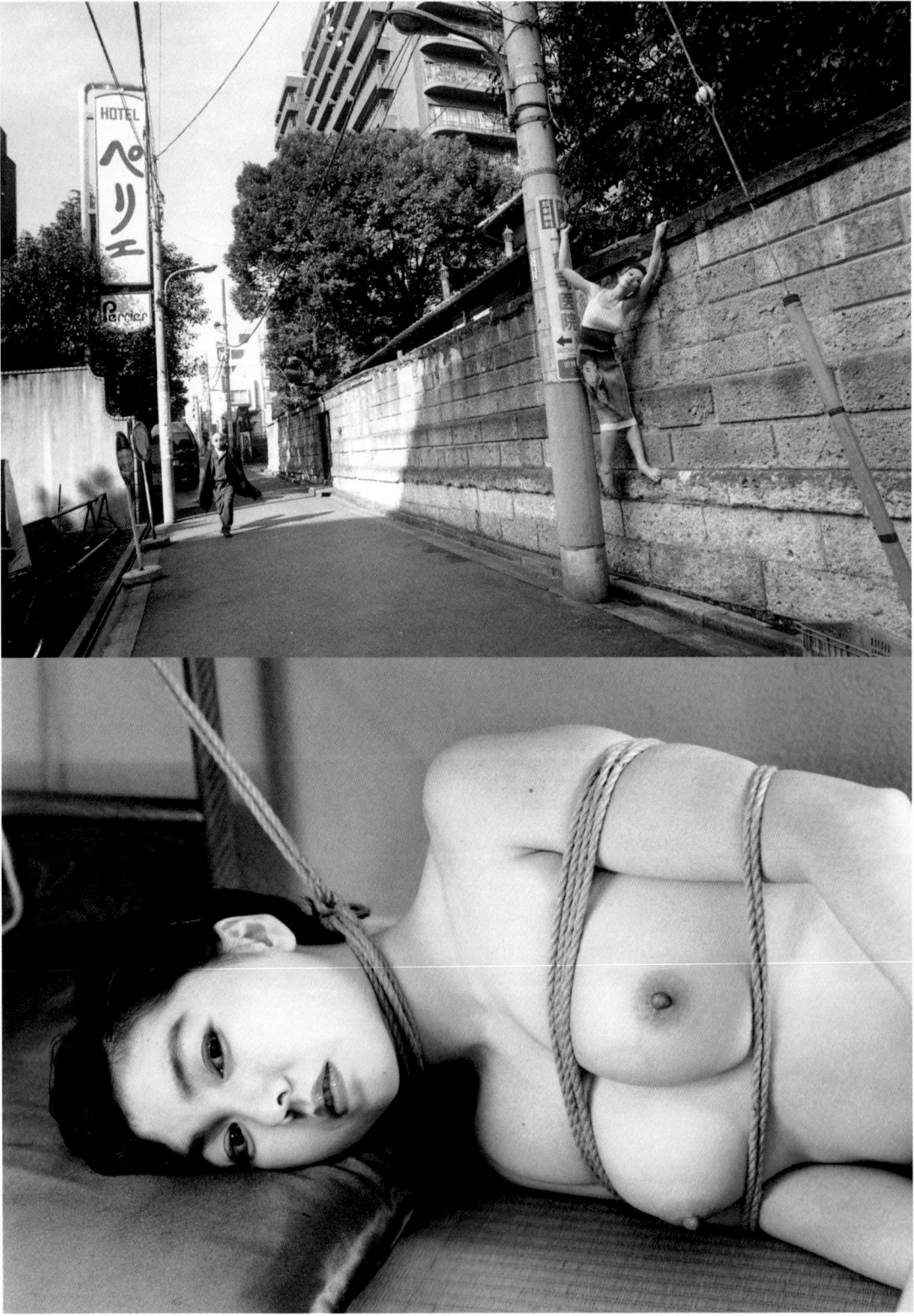

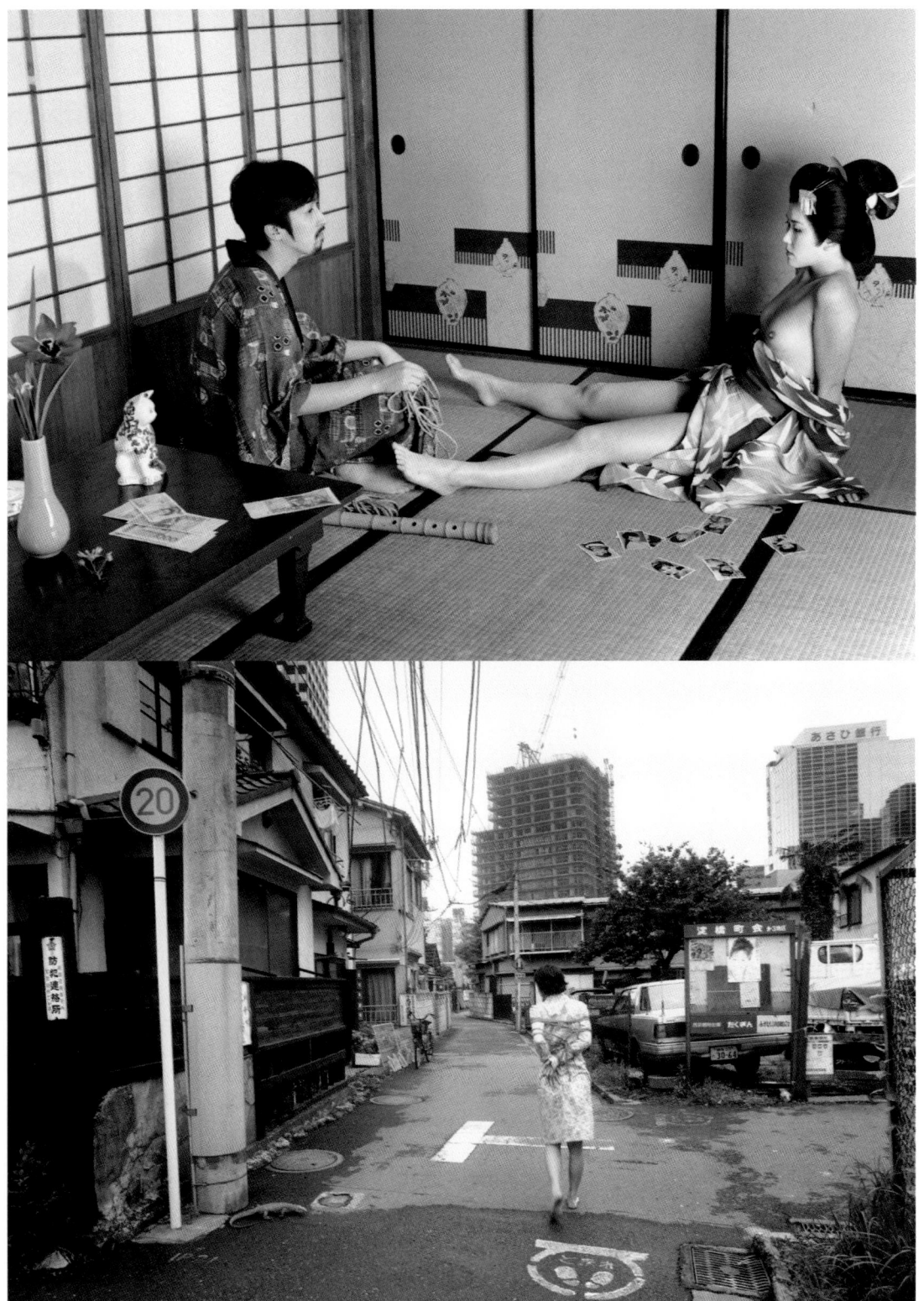

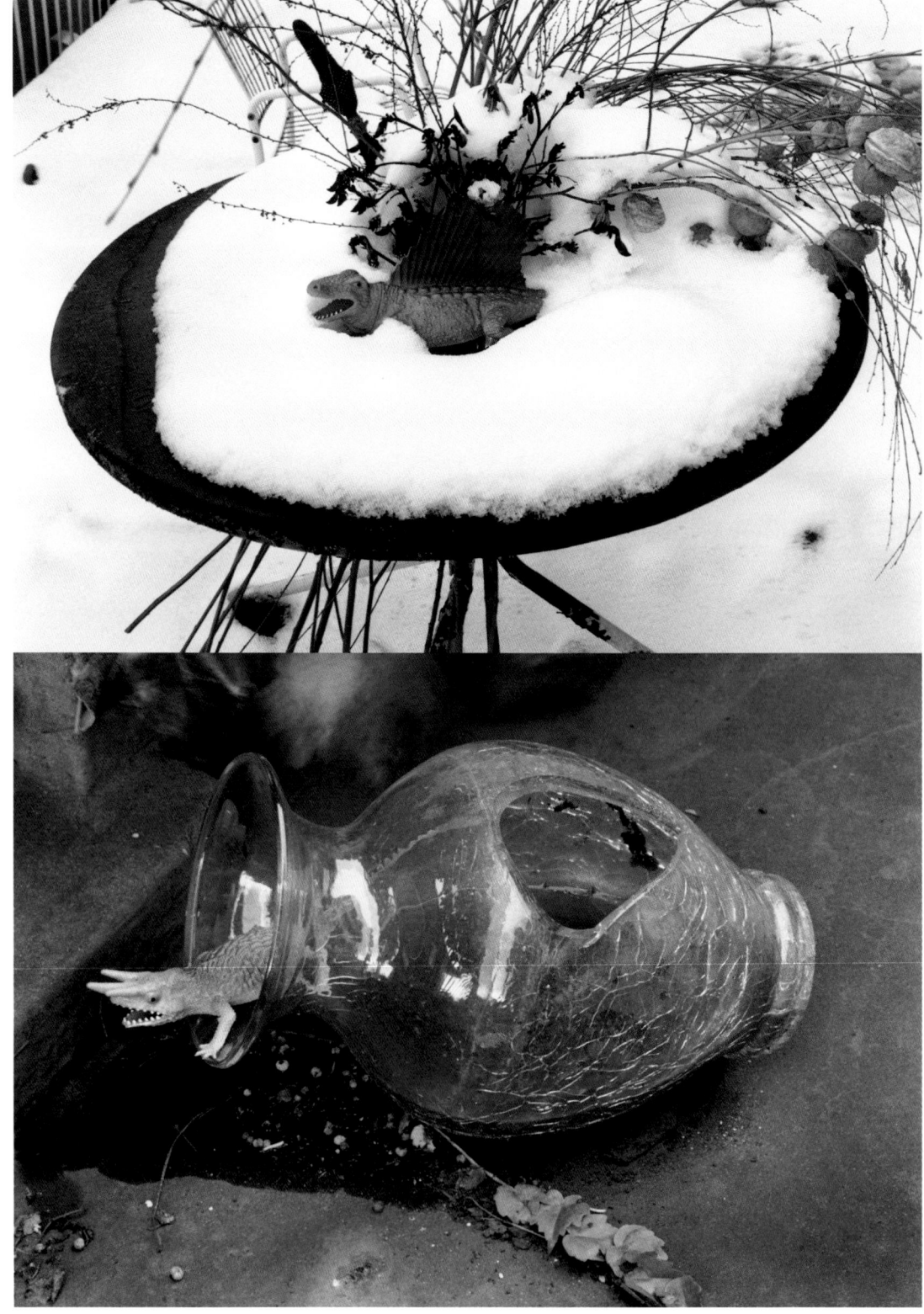

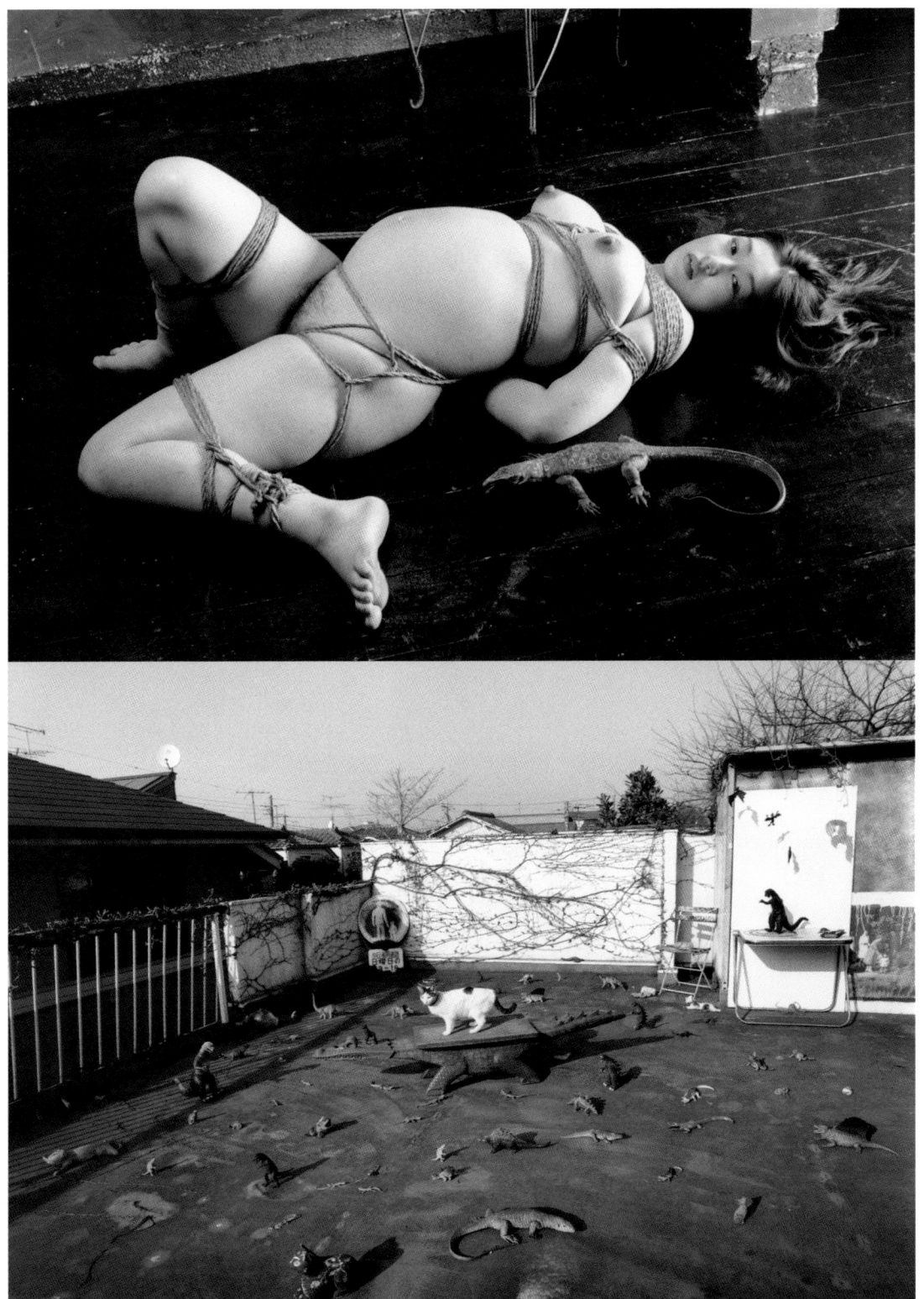

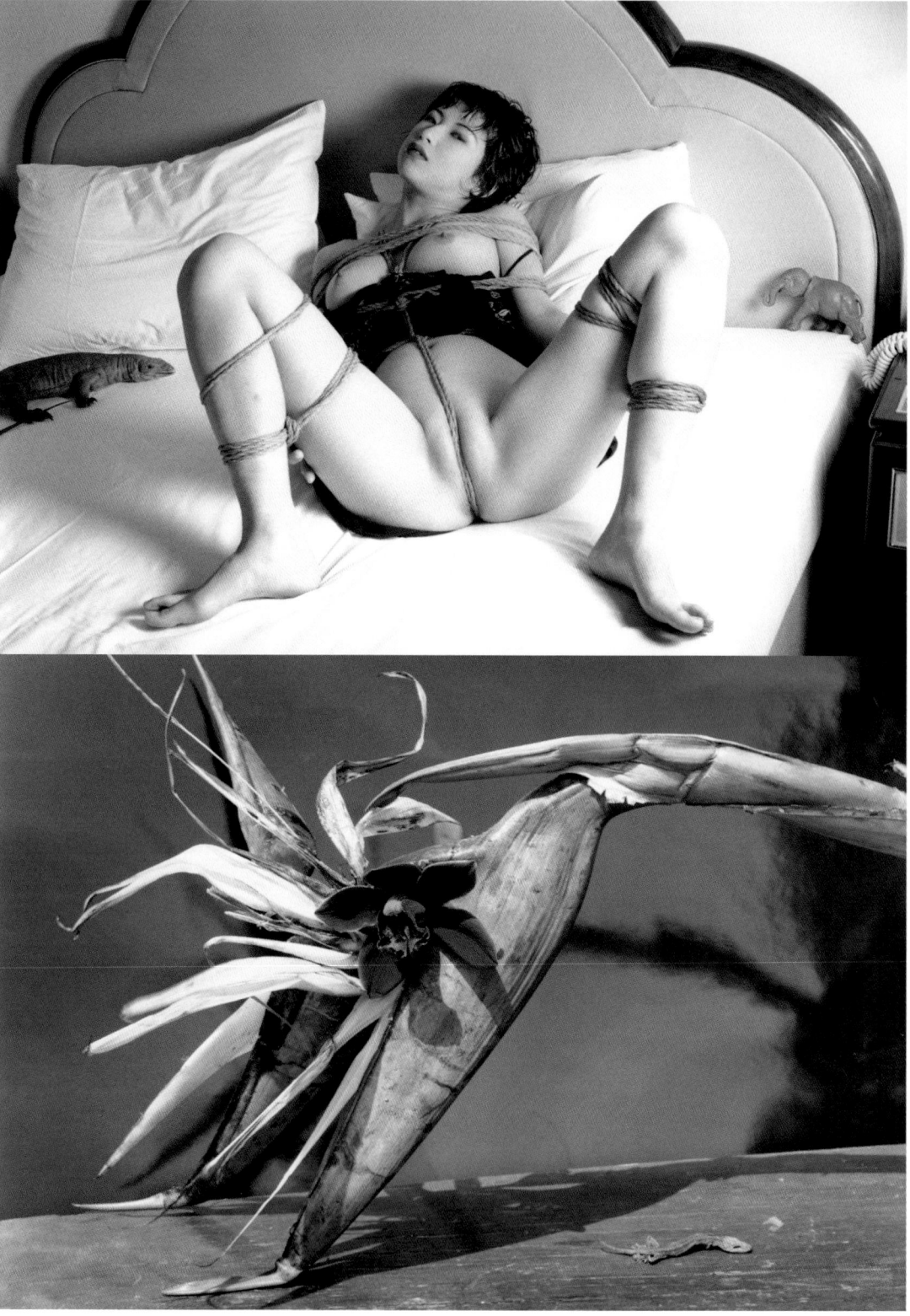

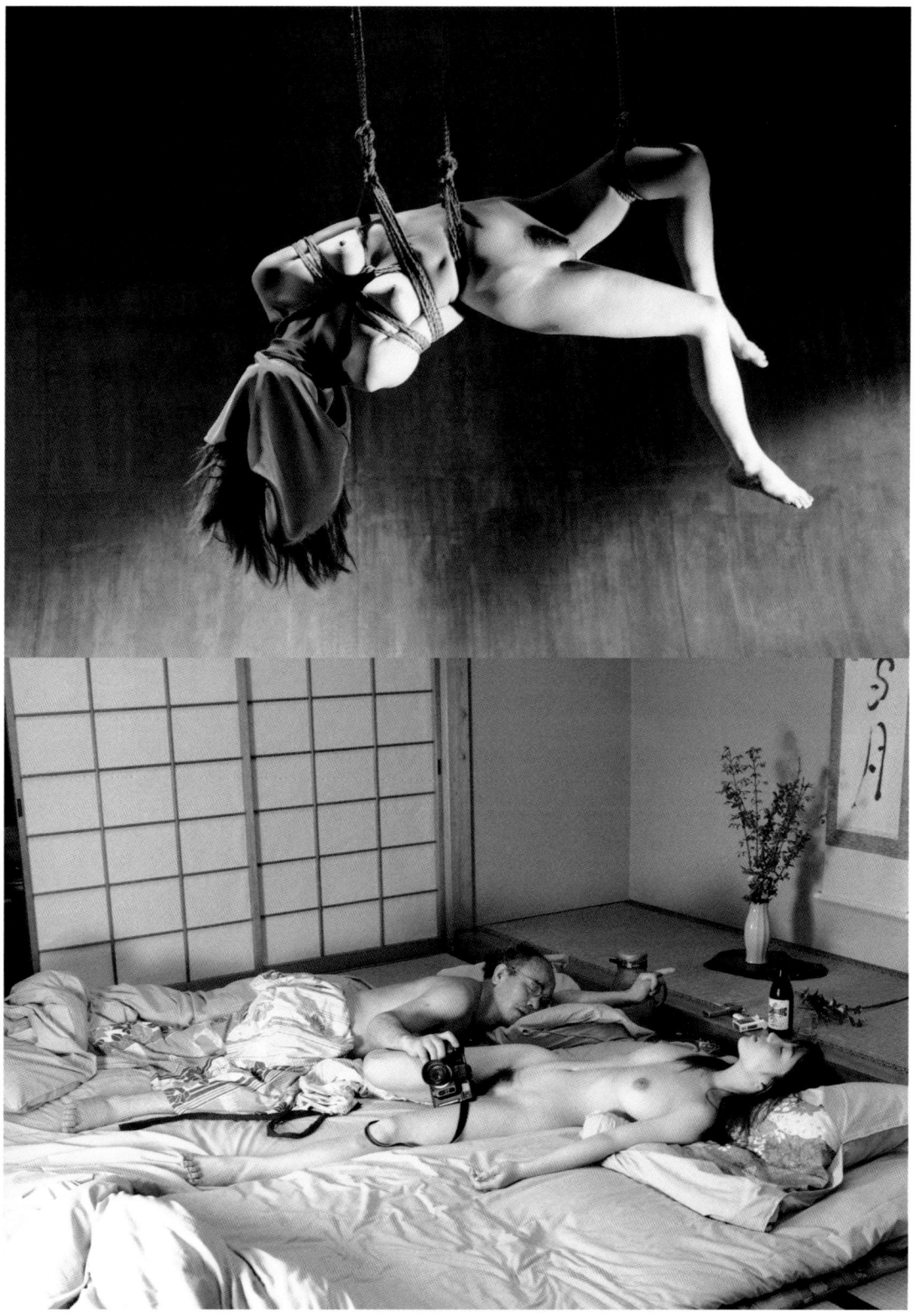

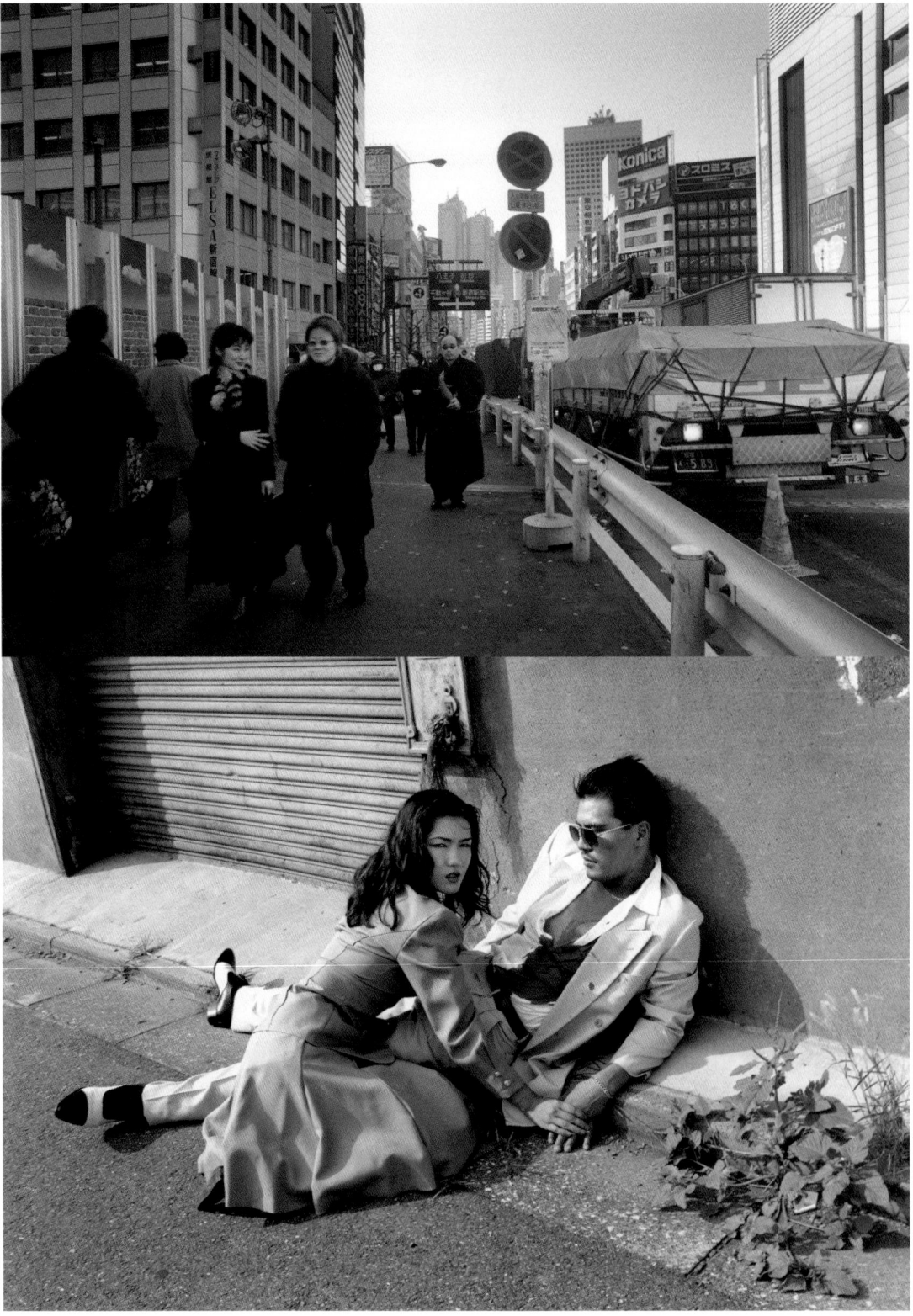

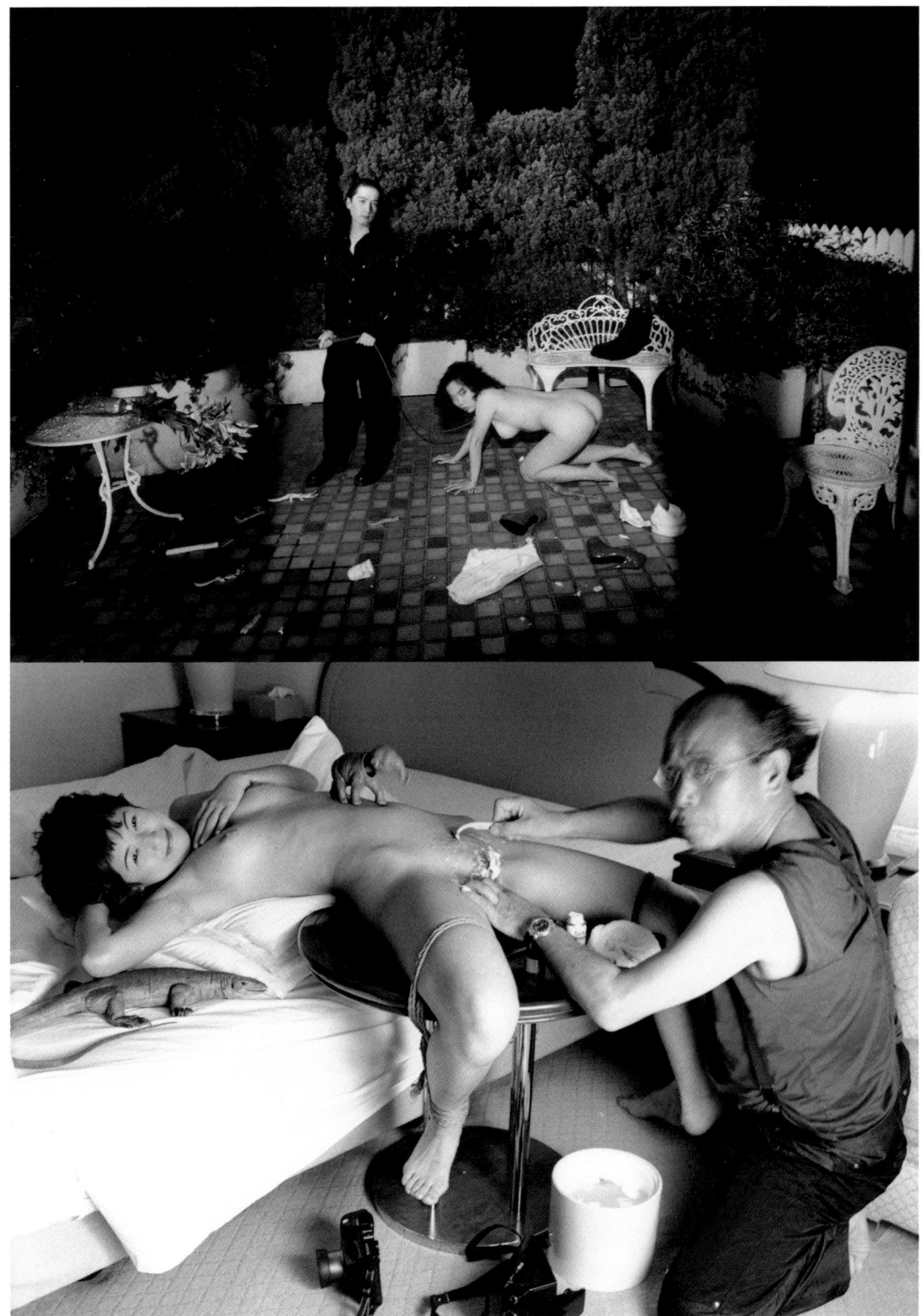

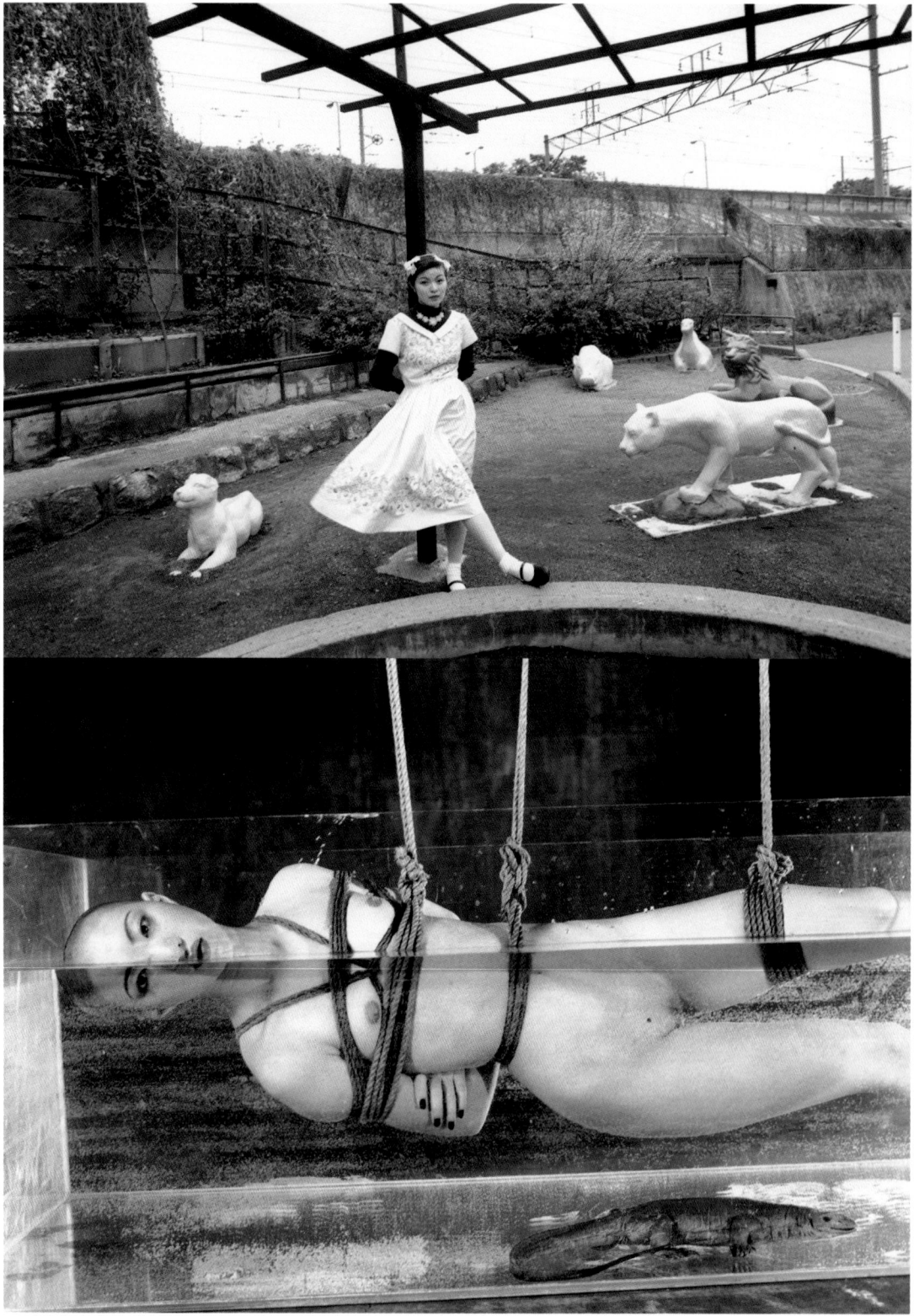

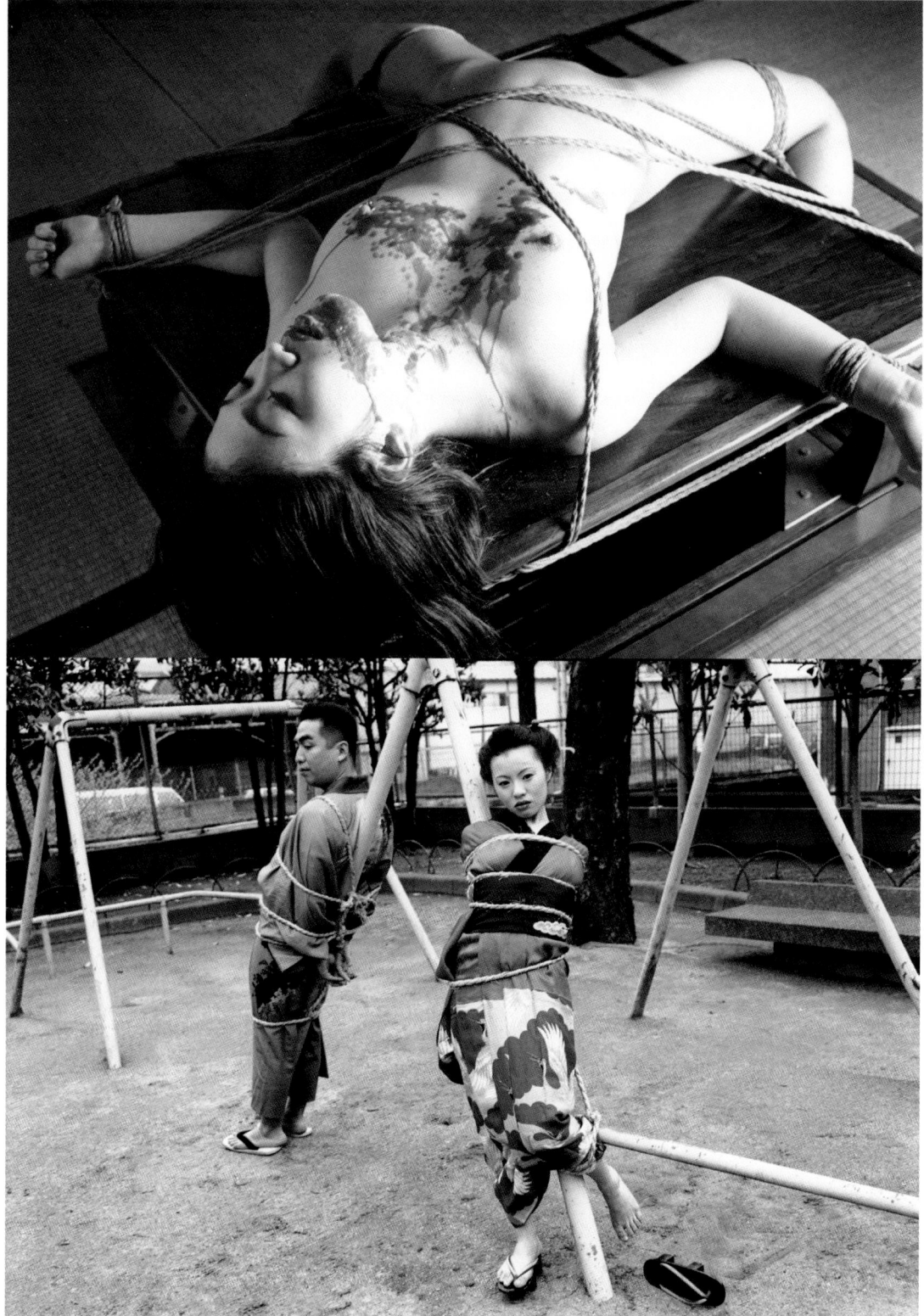

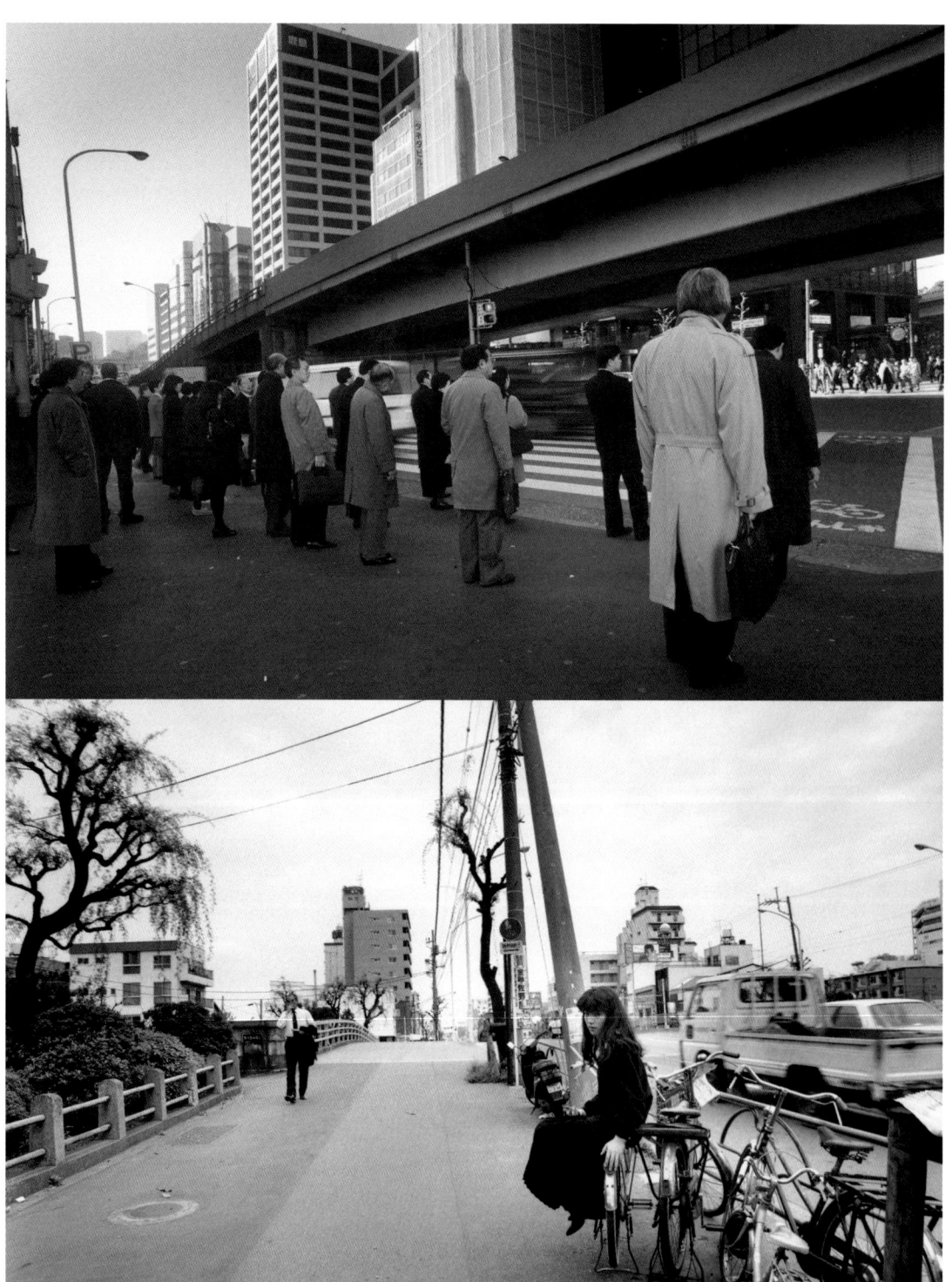

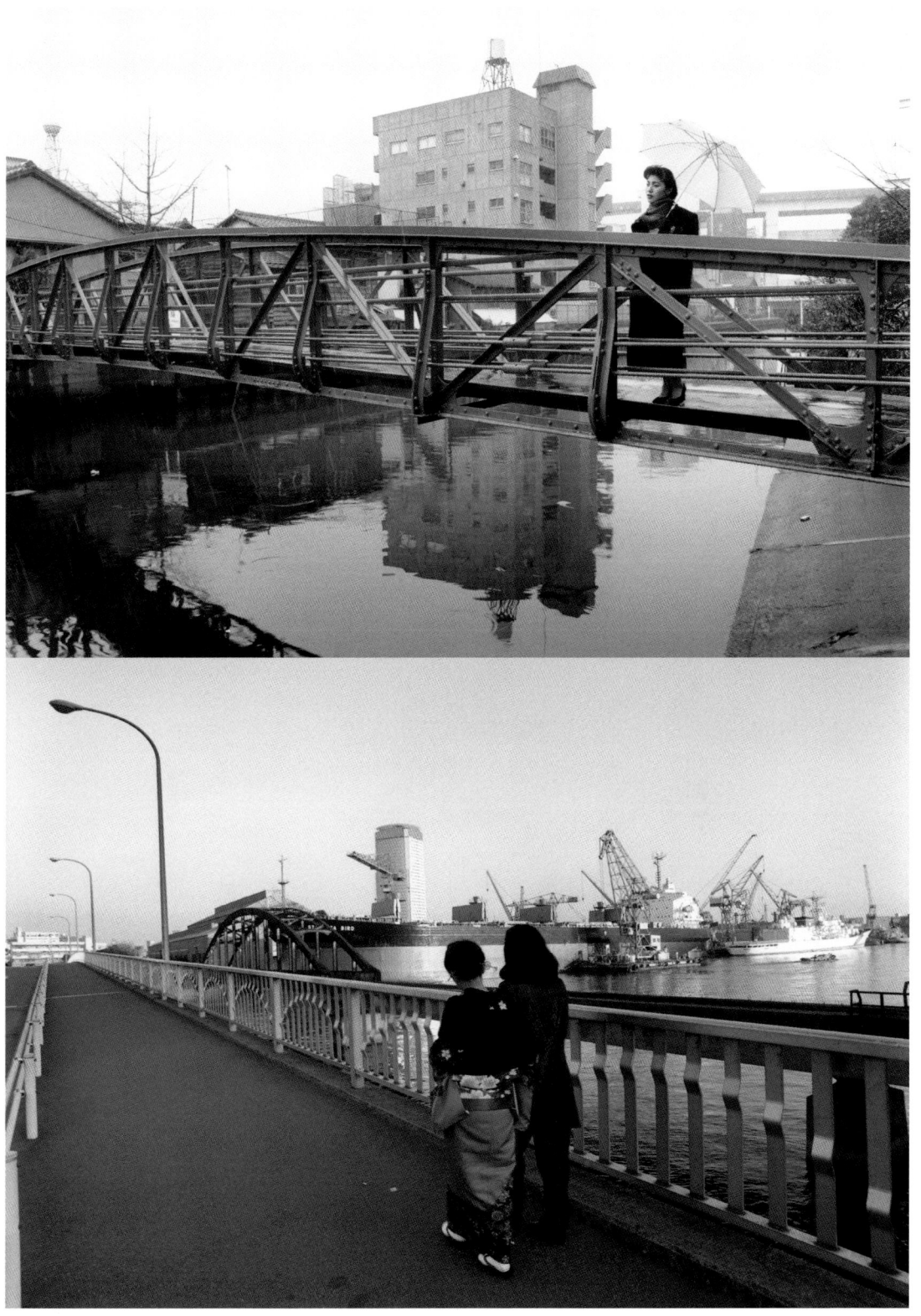

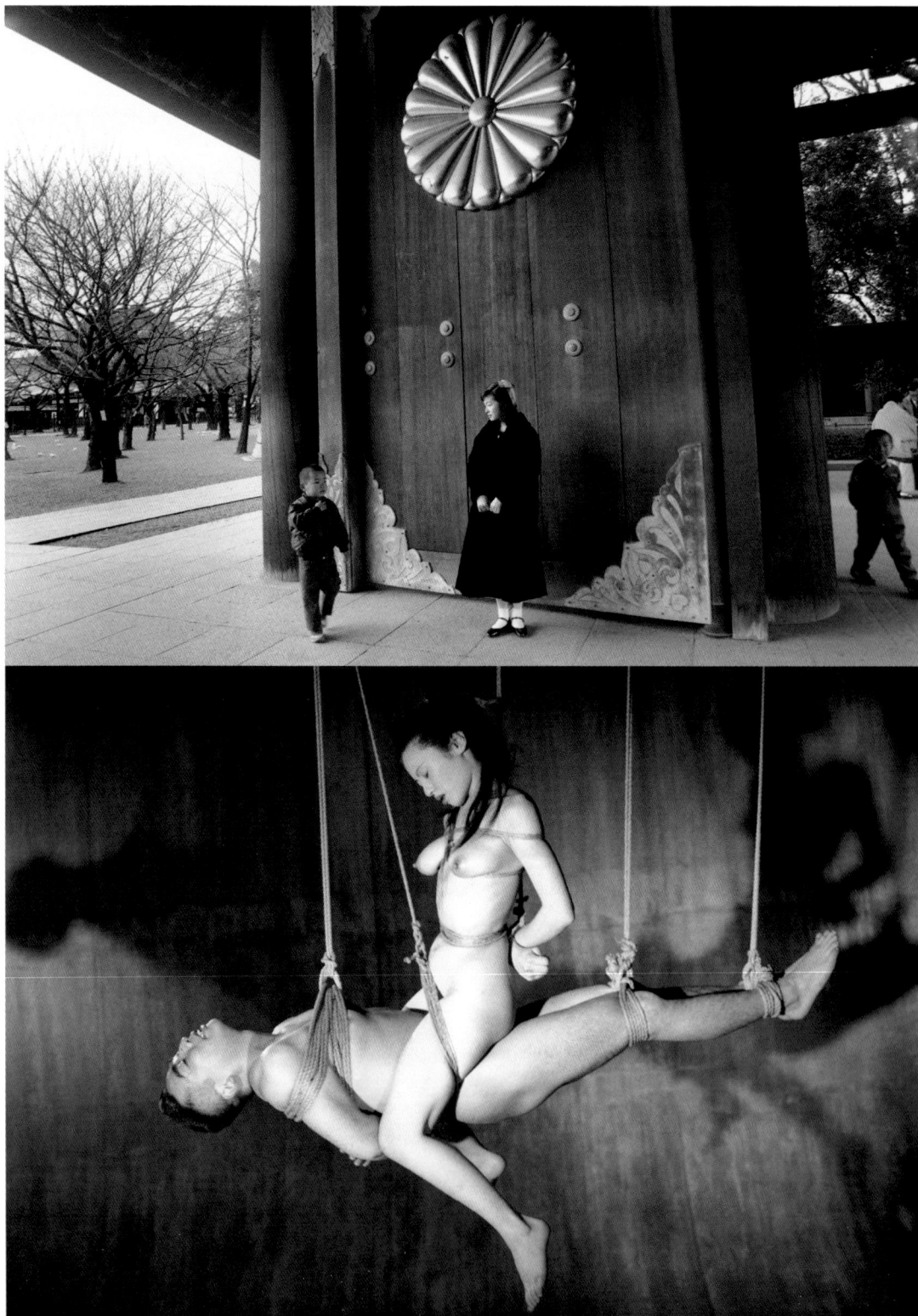

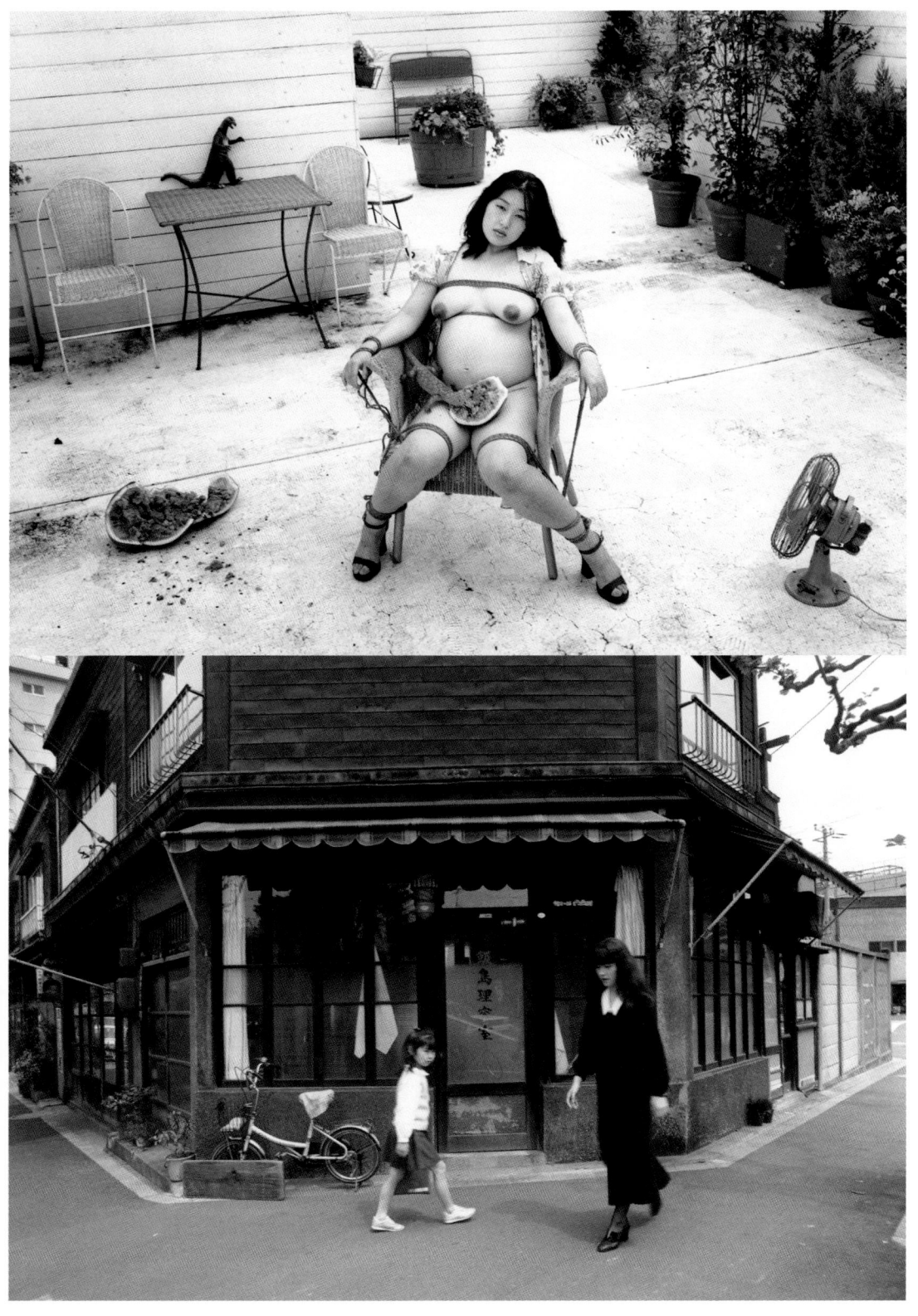

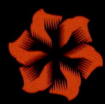

Angel's Festival

天使祭

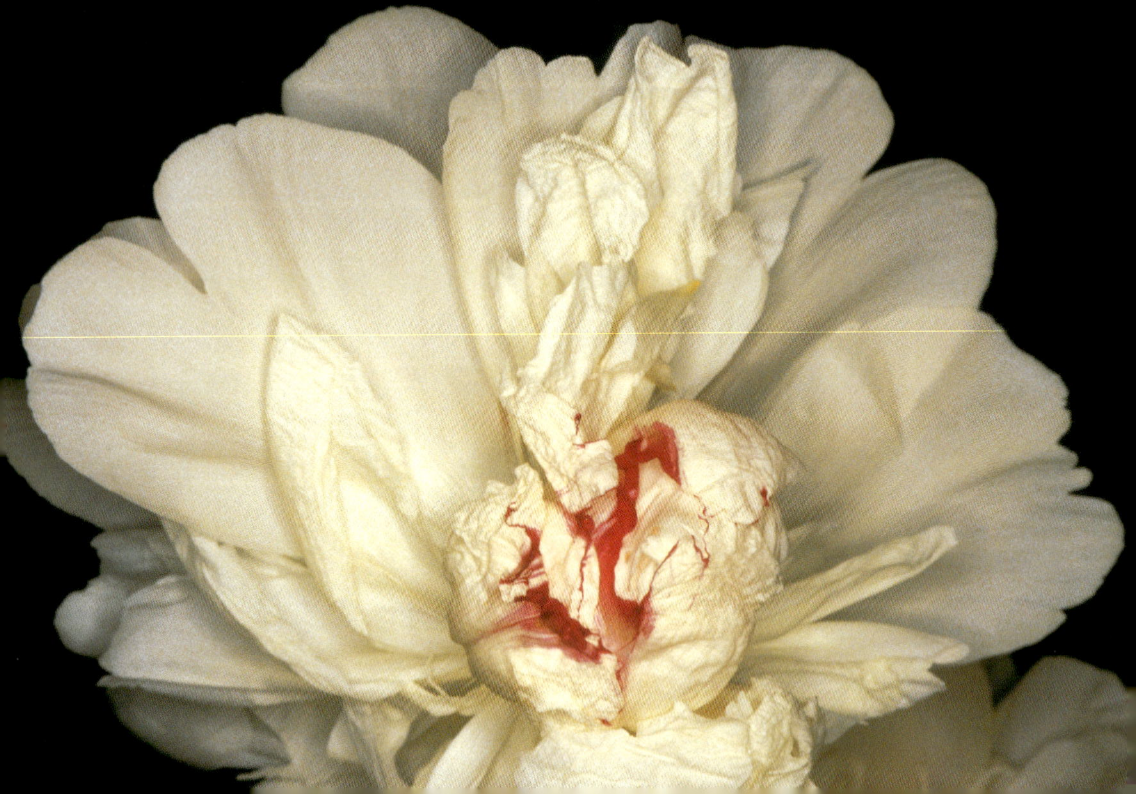

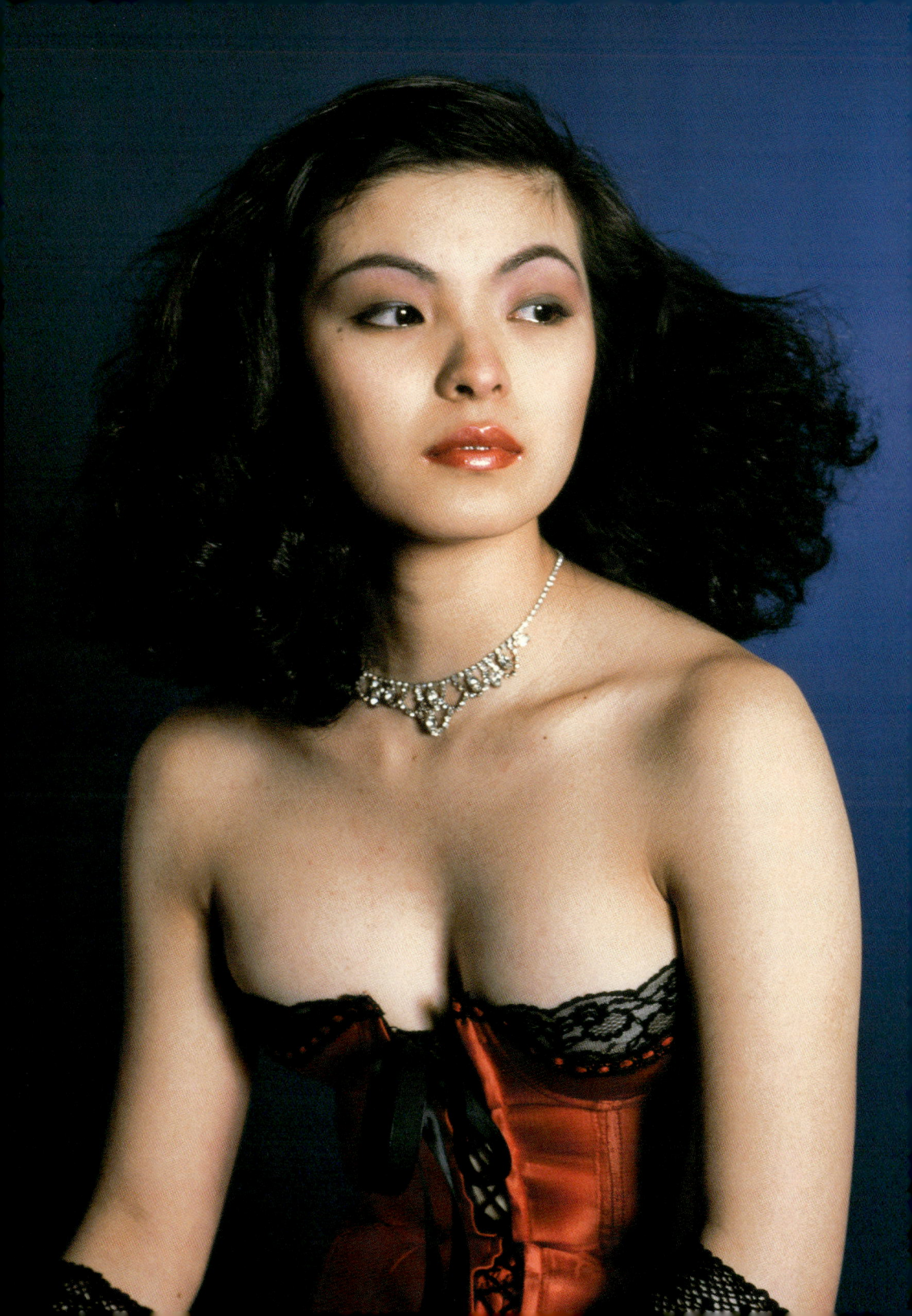

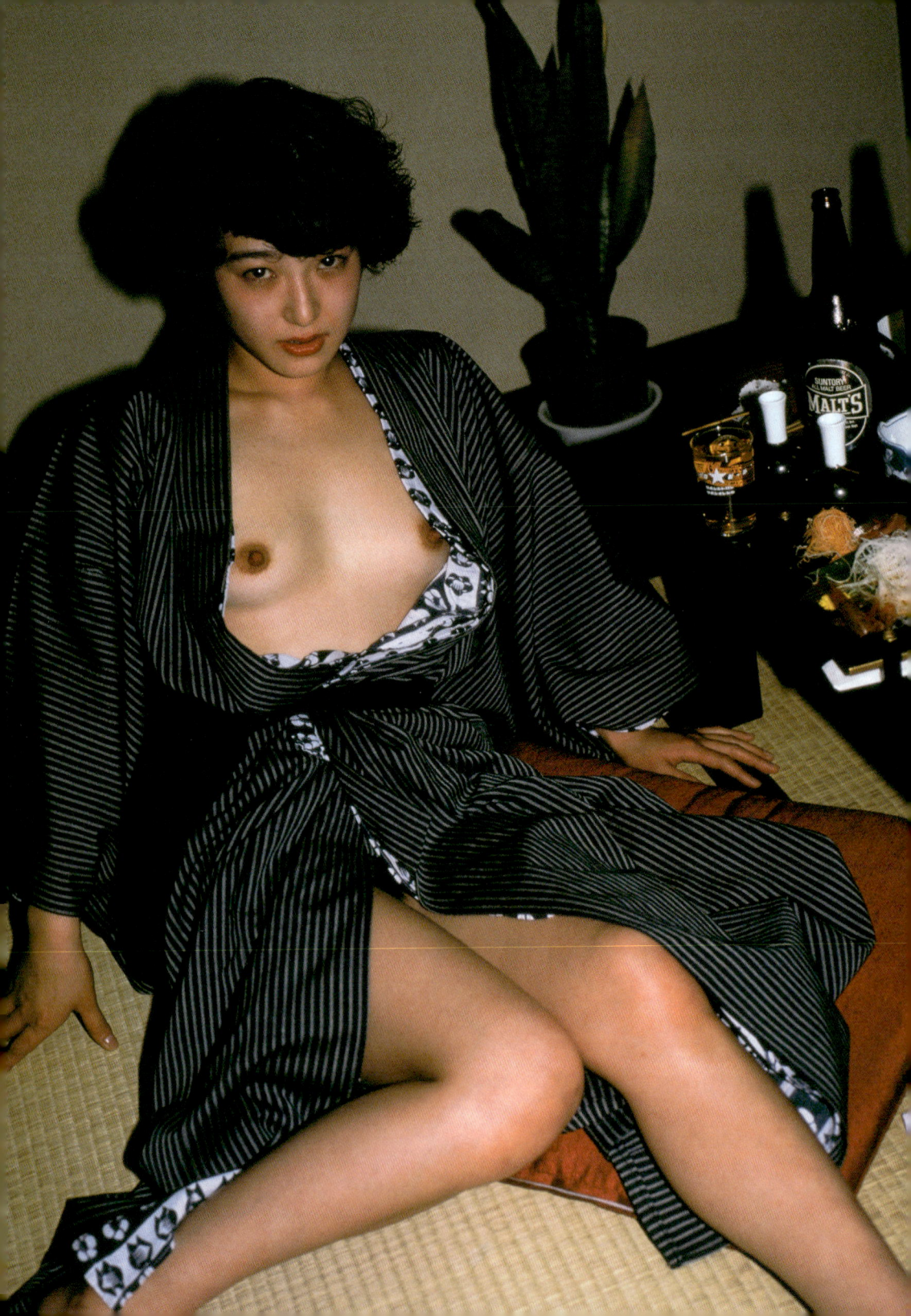

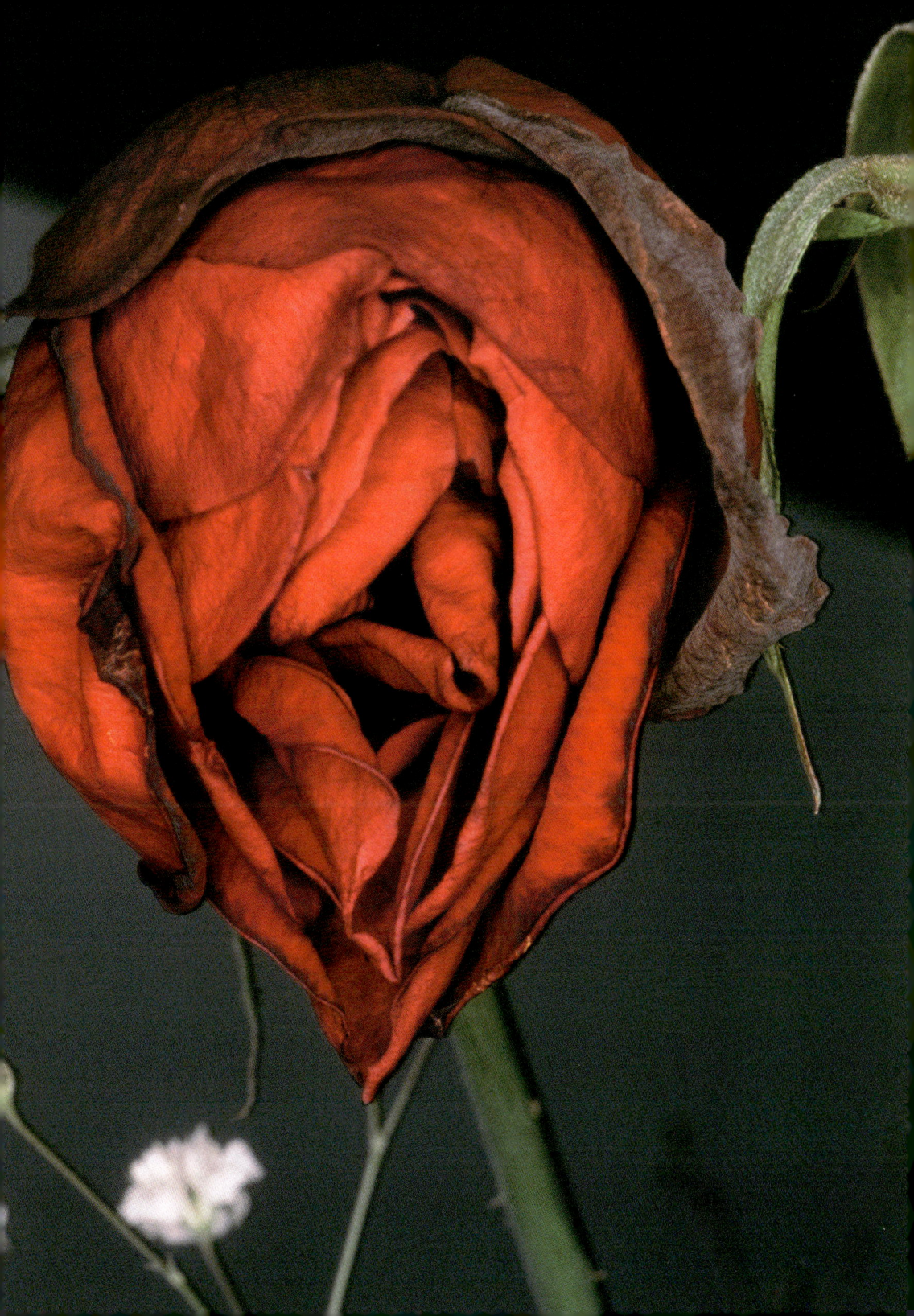

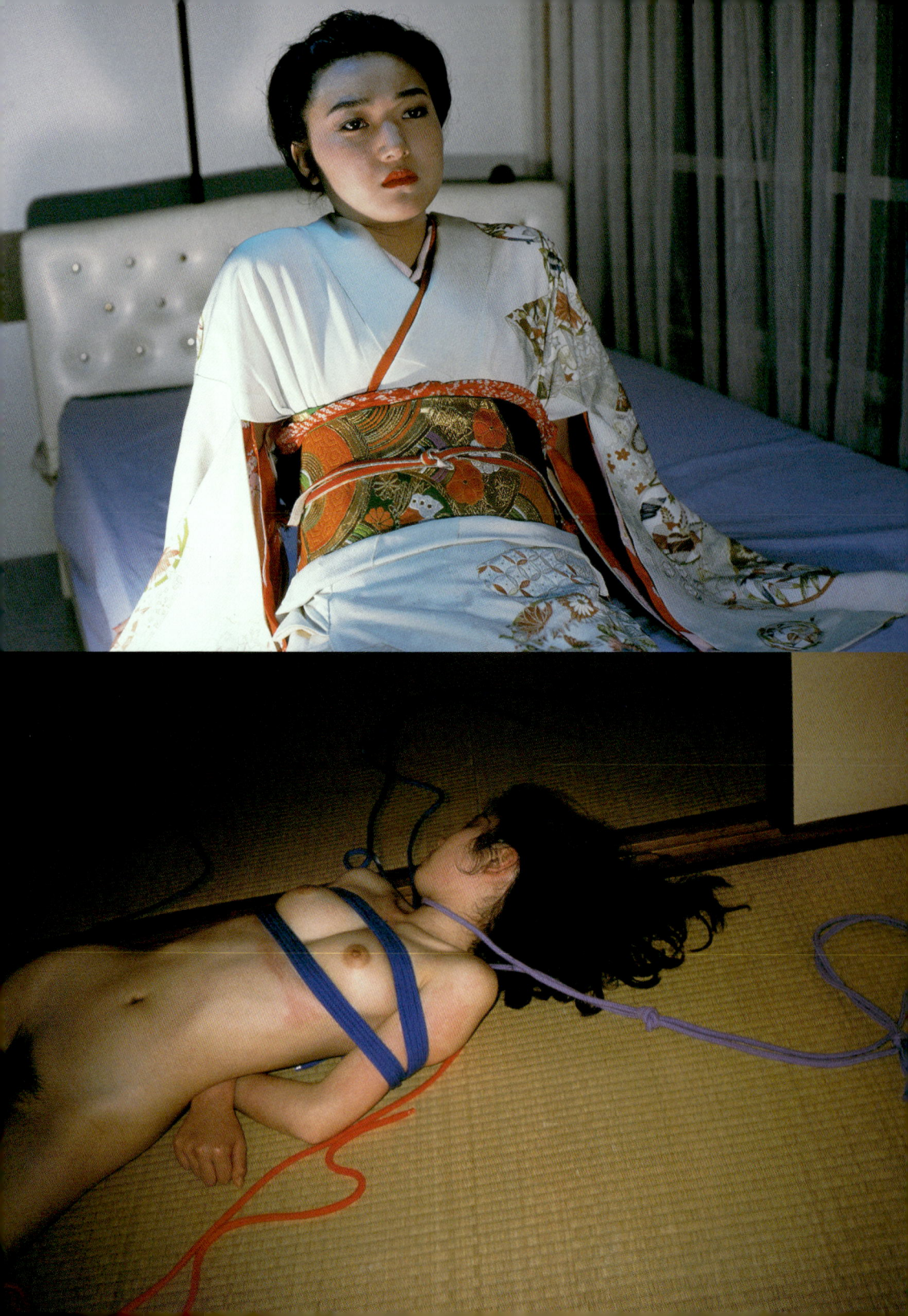

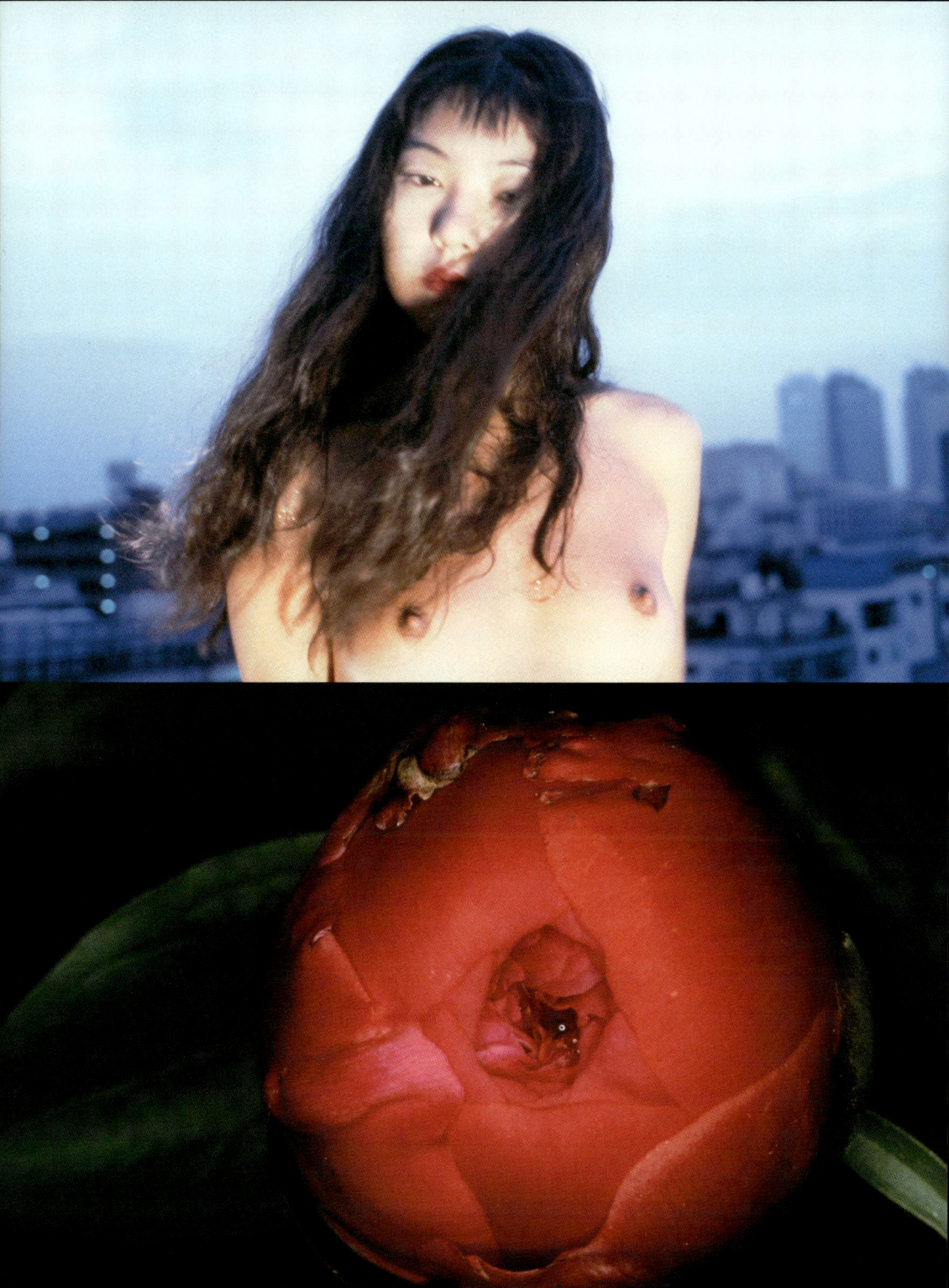

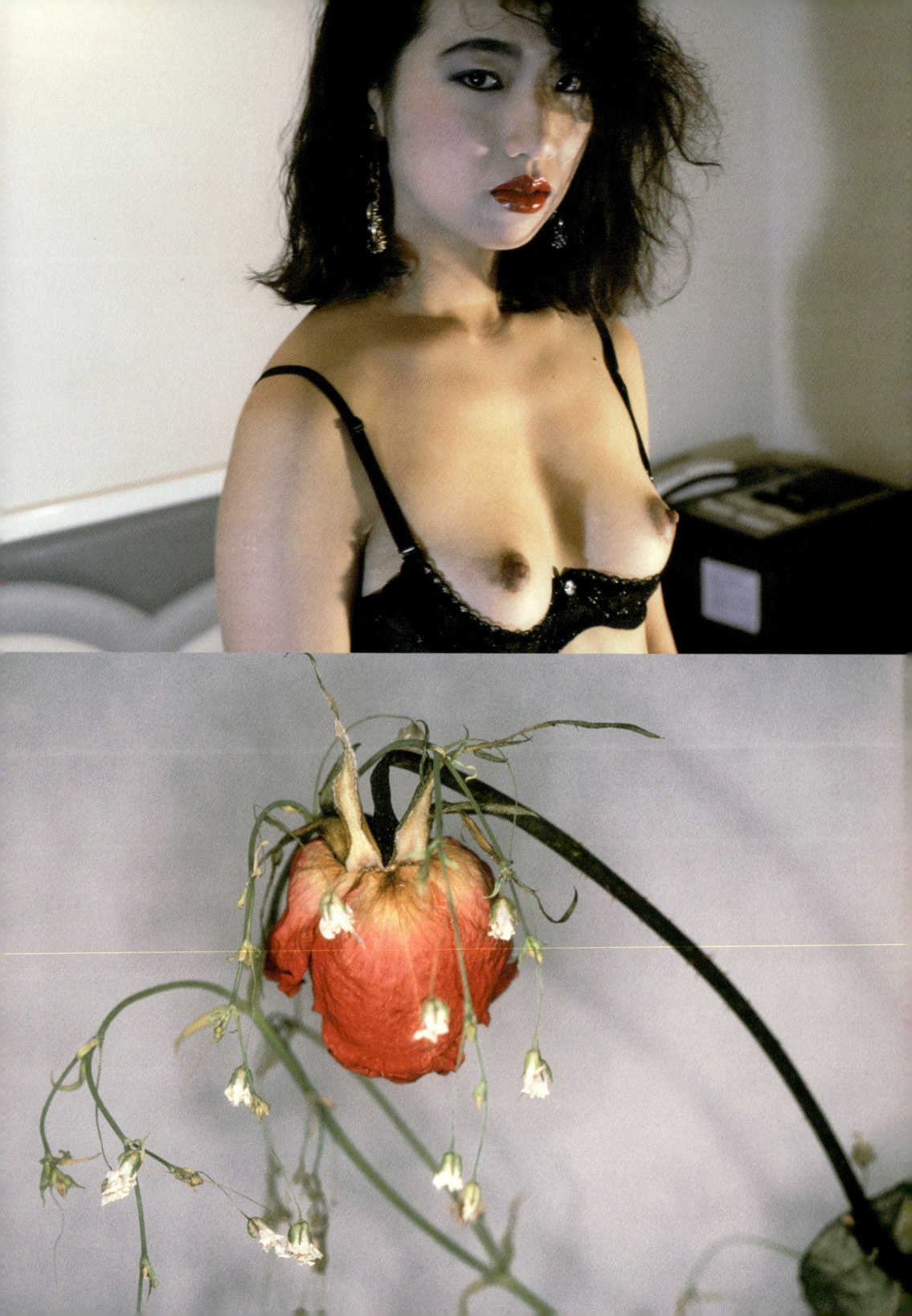

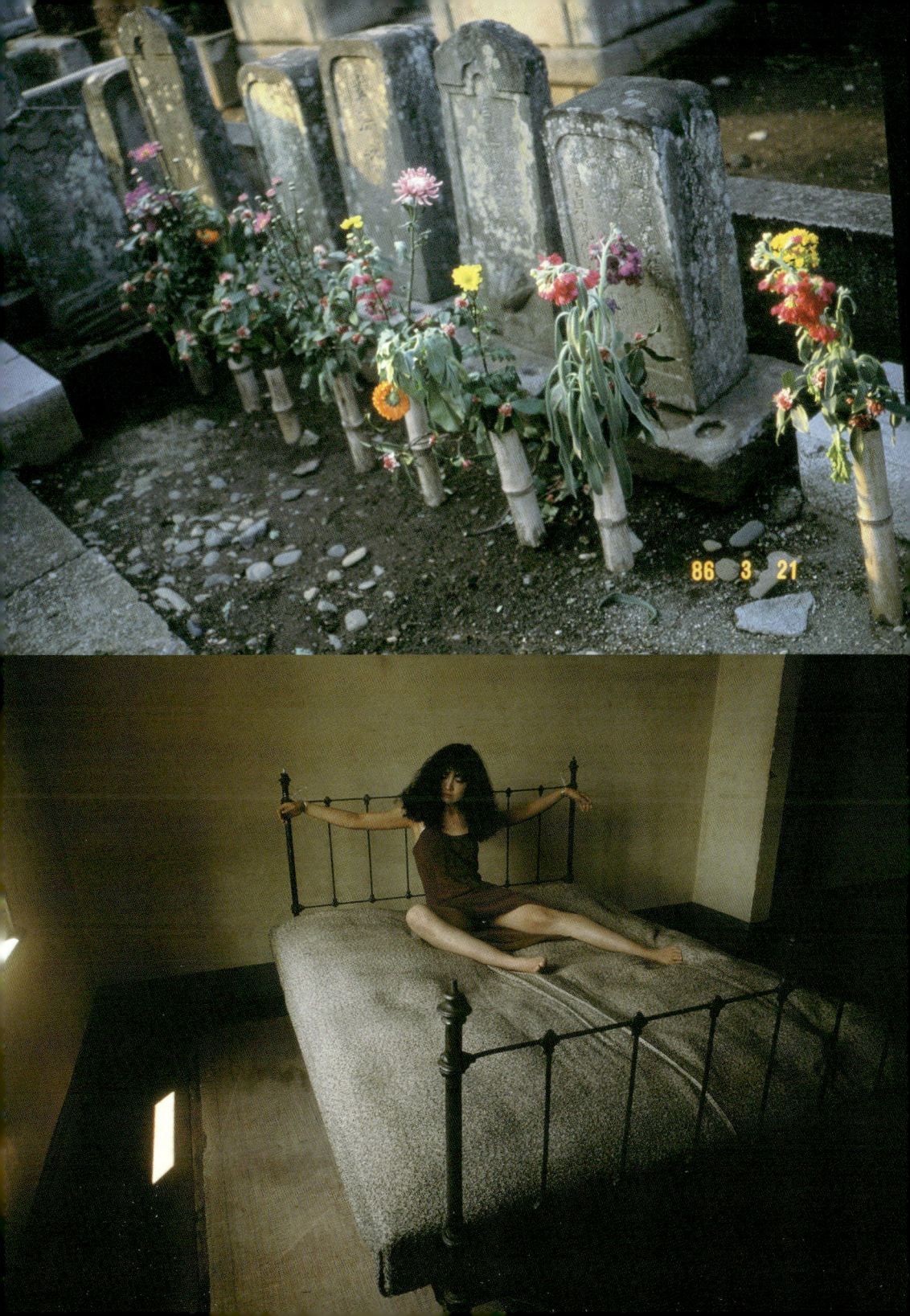

86 3 21

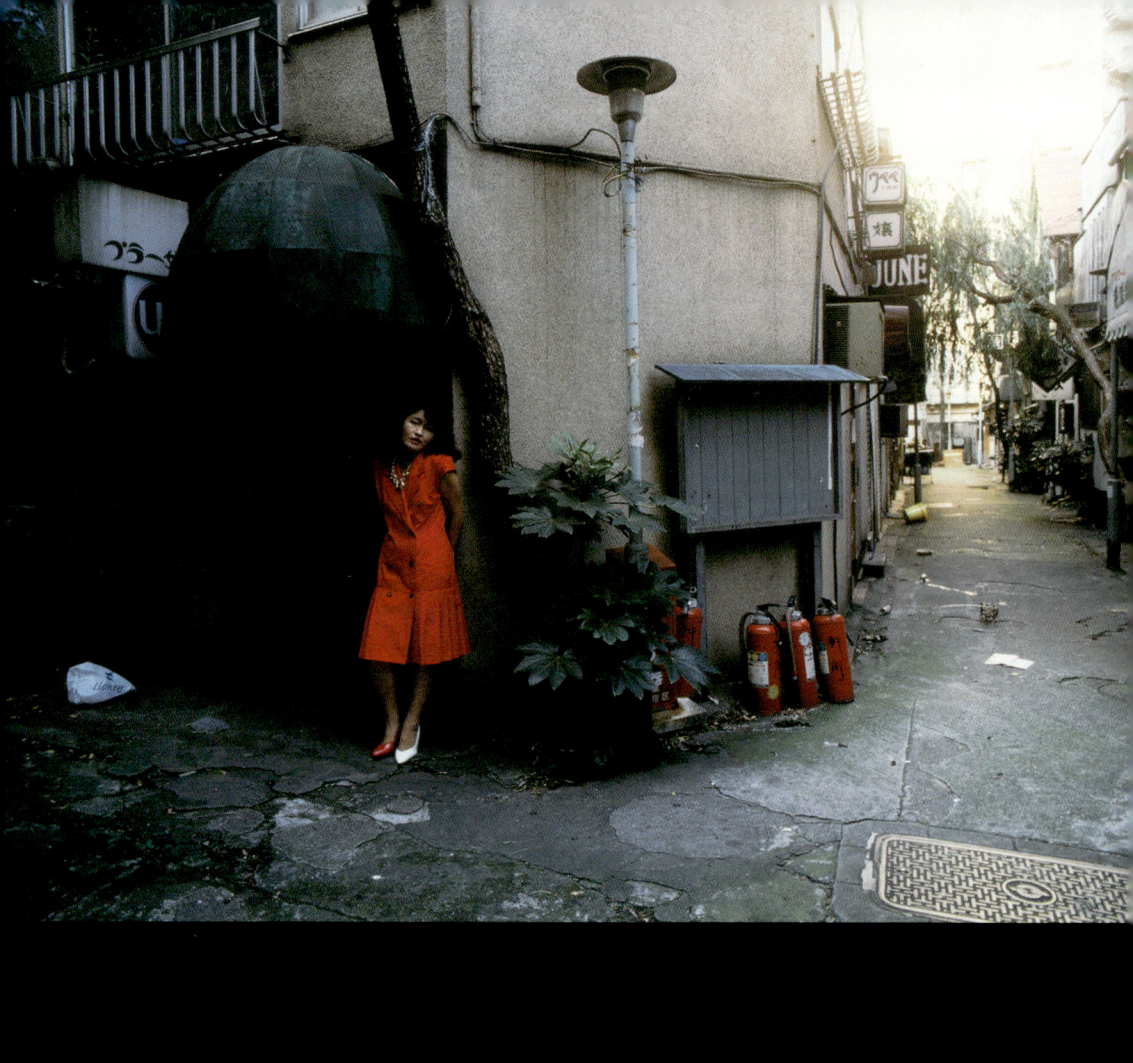

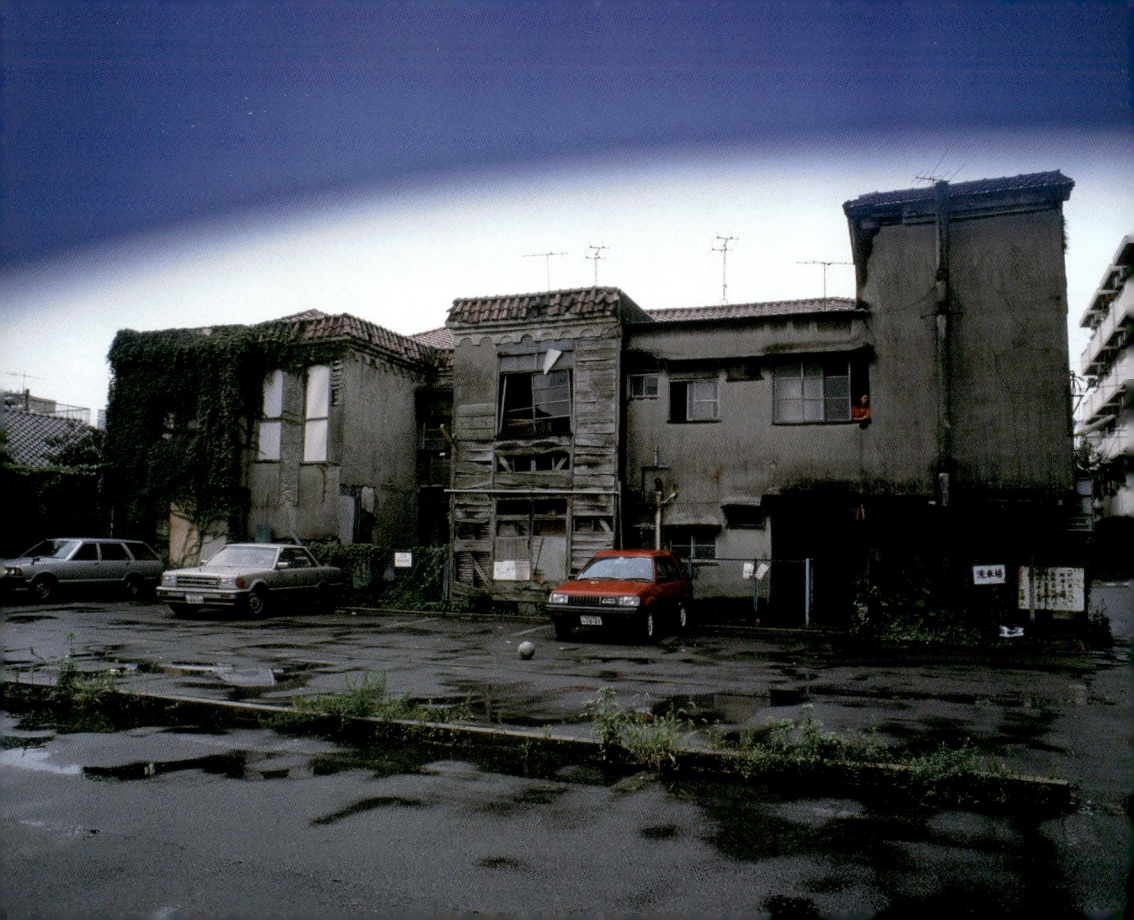

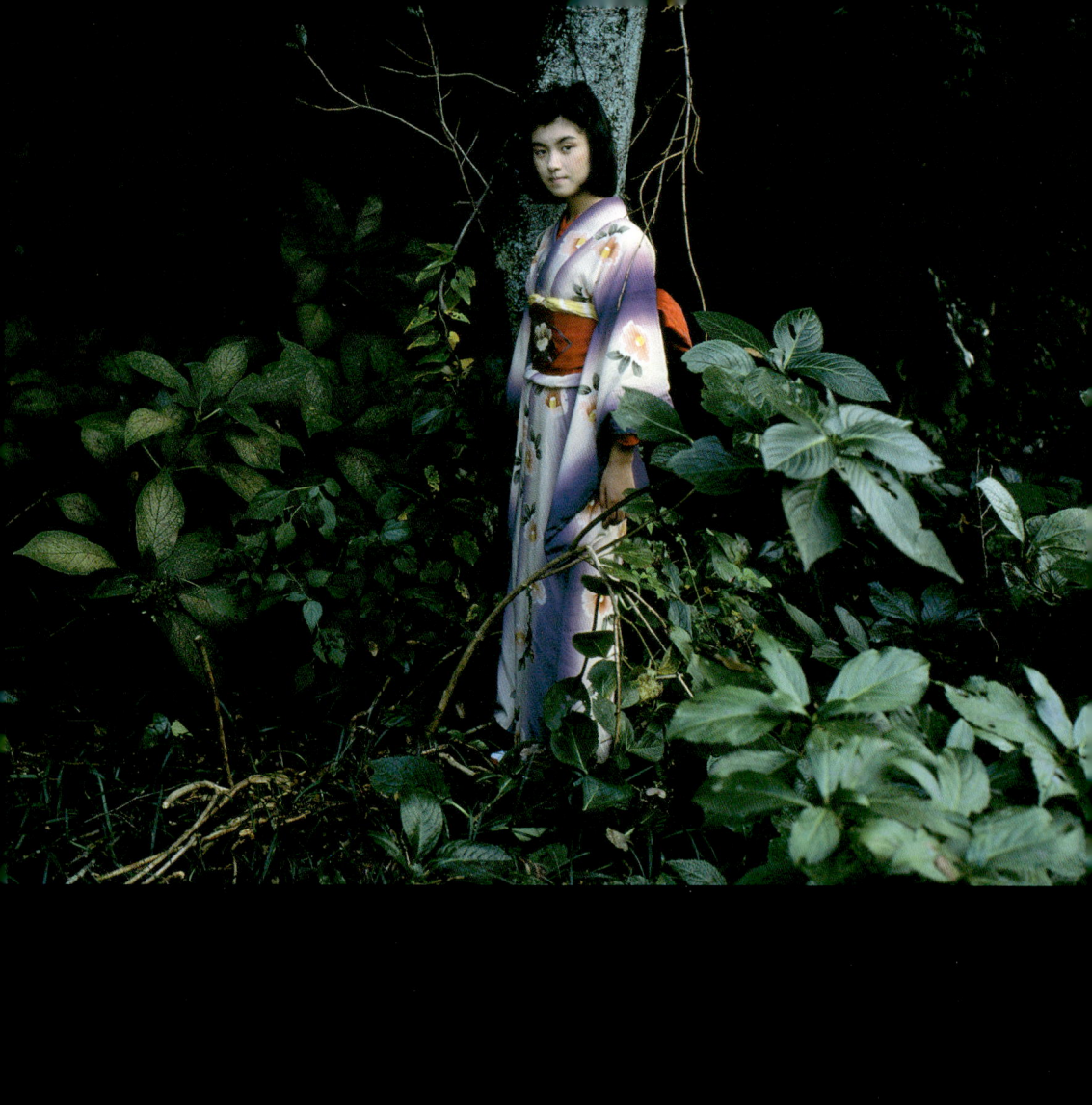

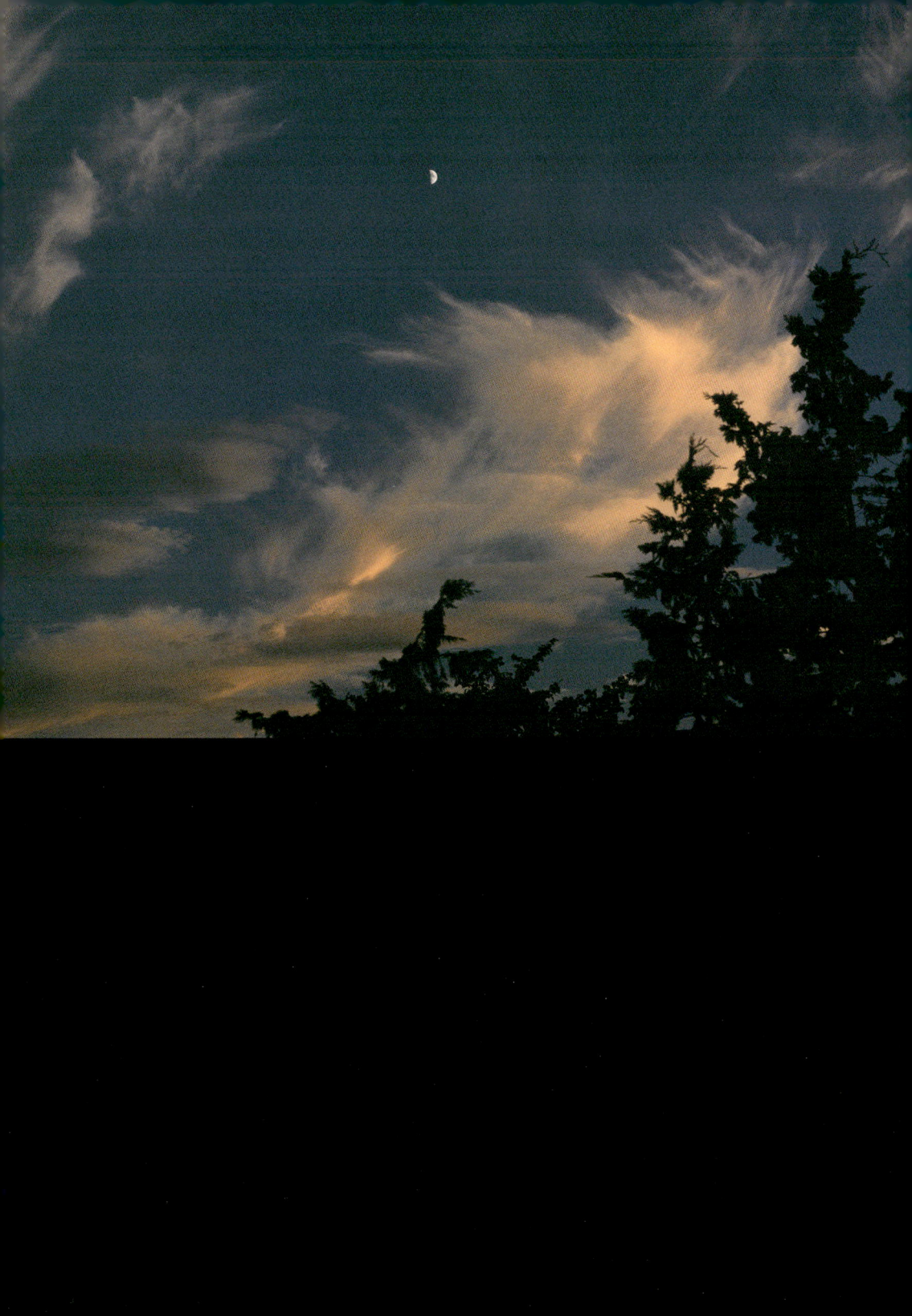

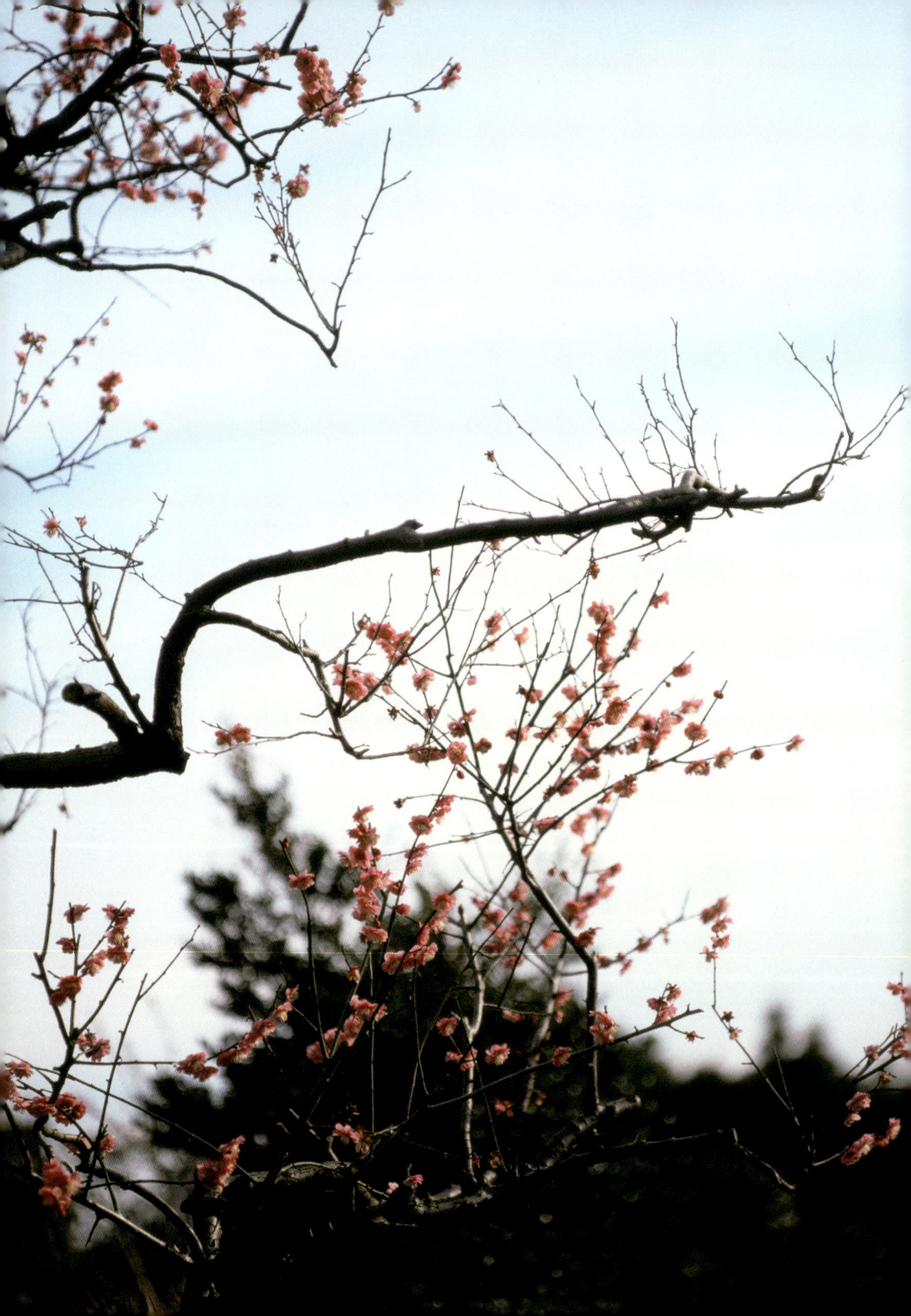

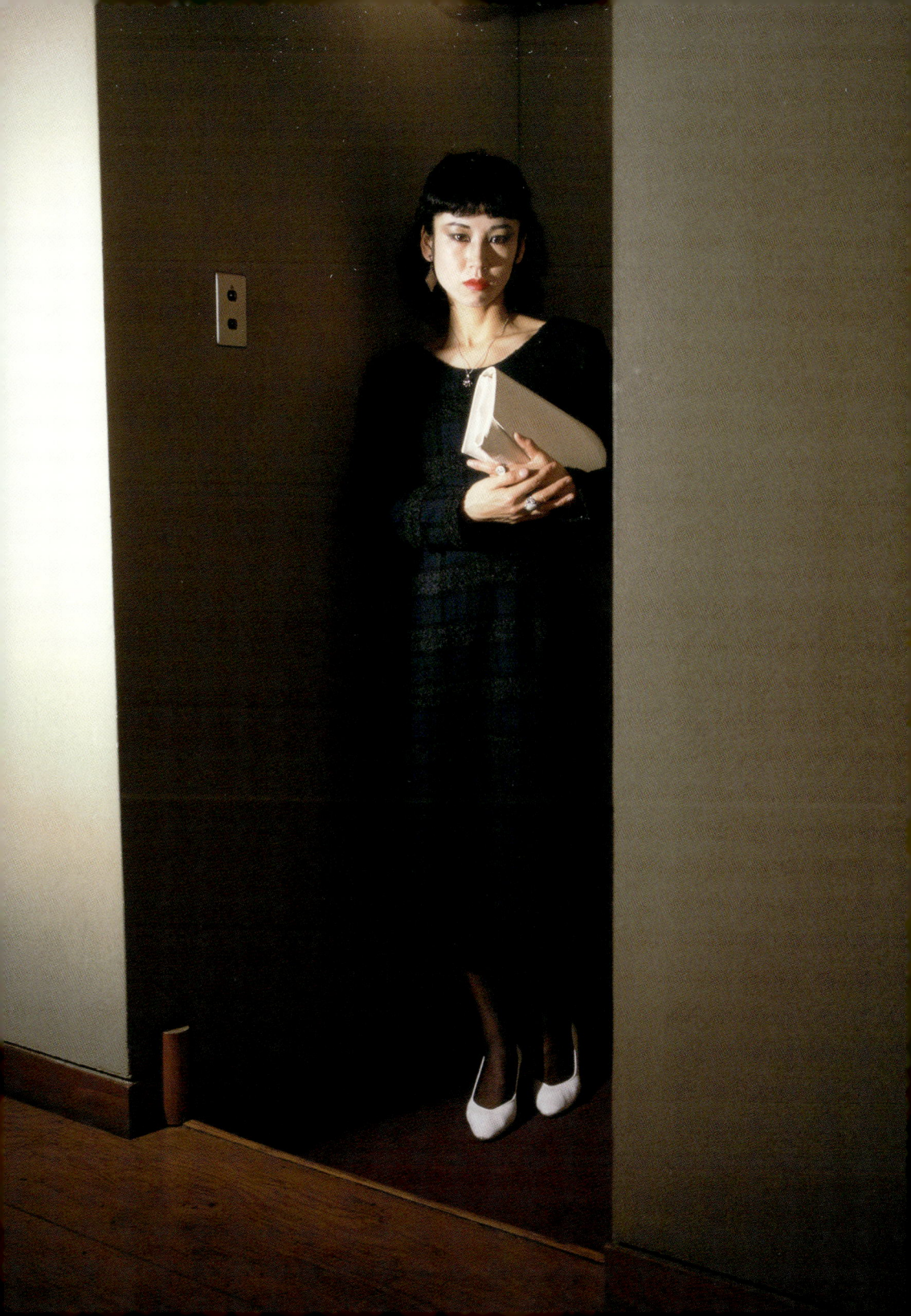

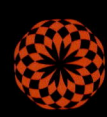

Tokyo Love

トーキョー・ラブ

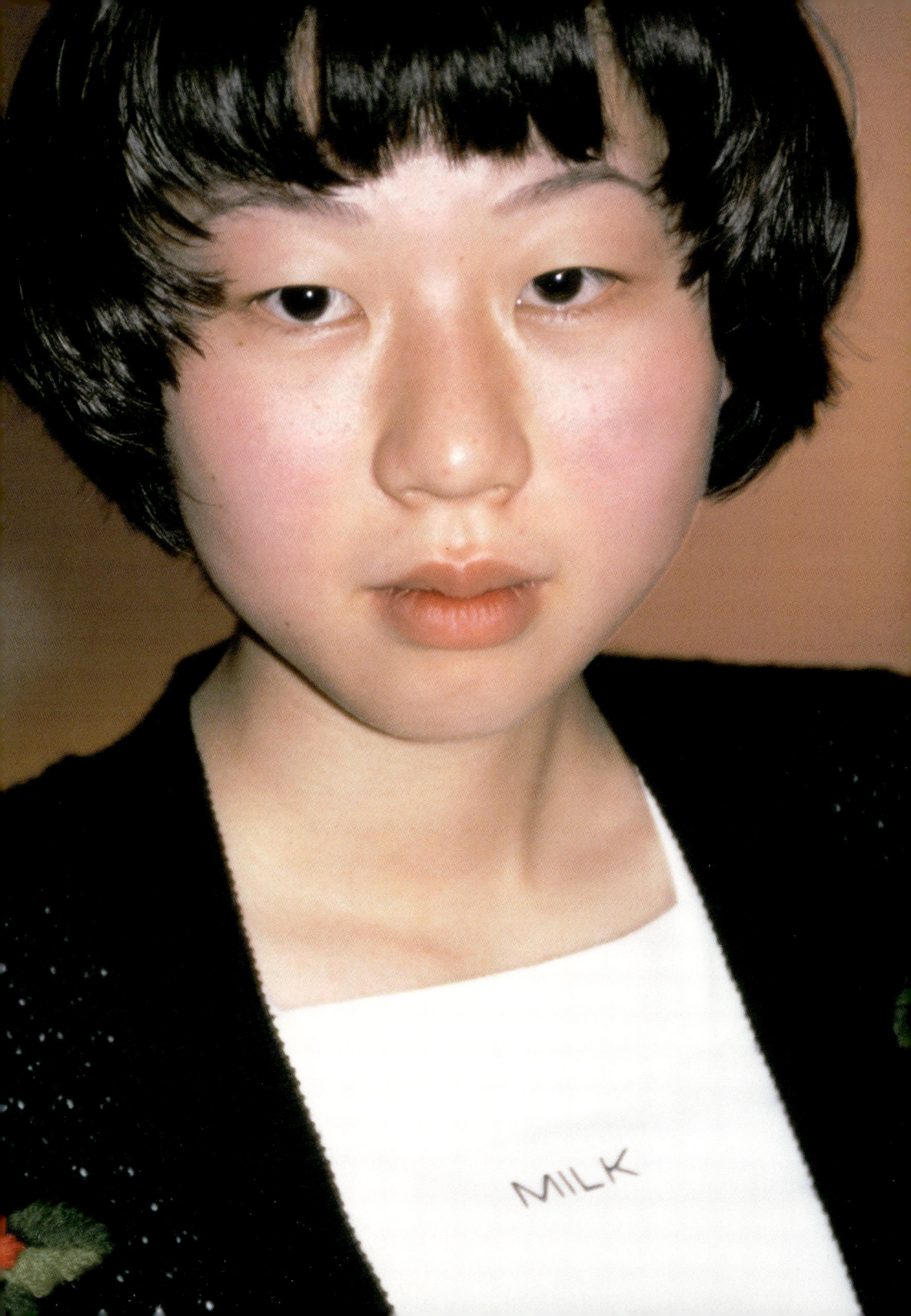

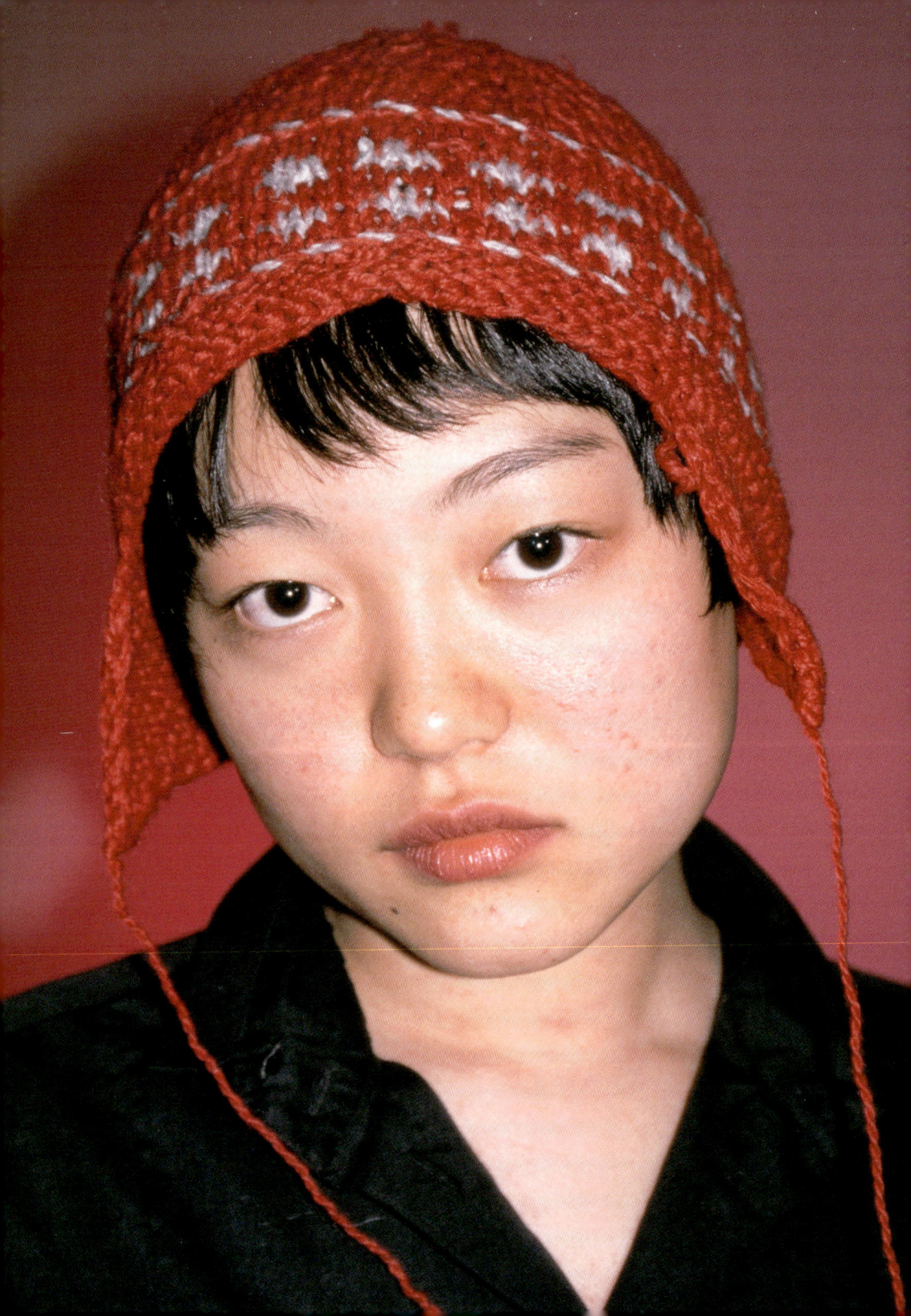

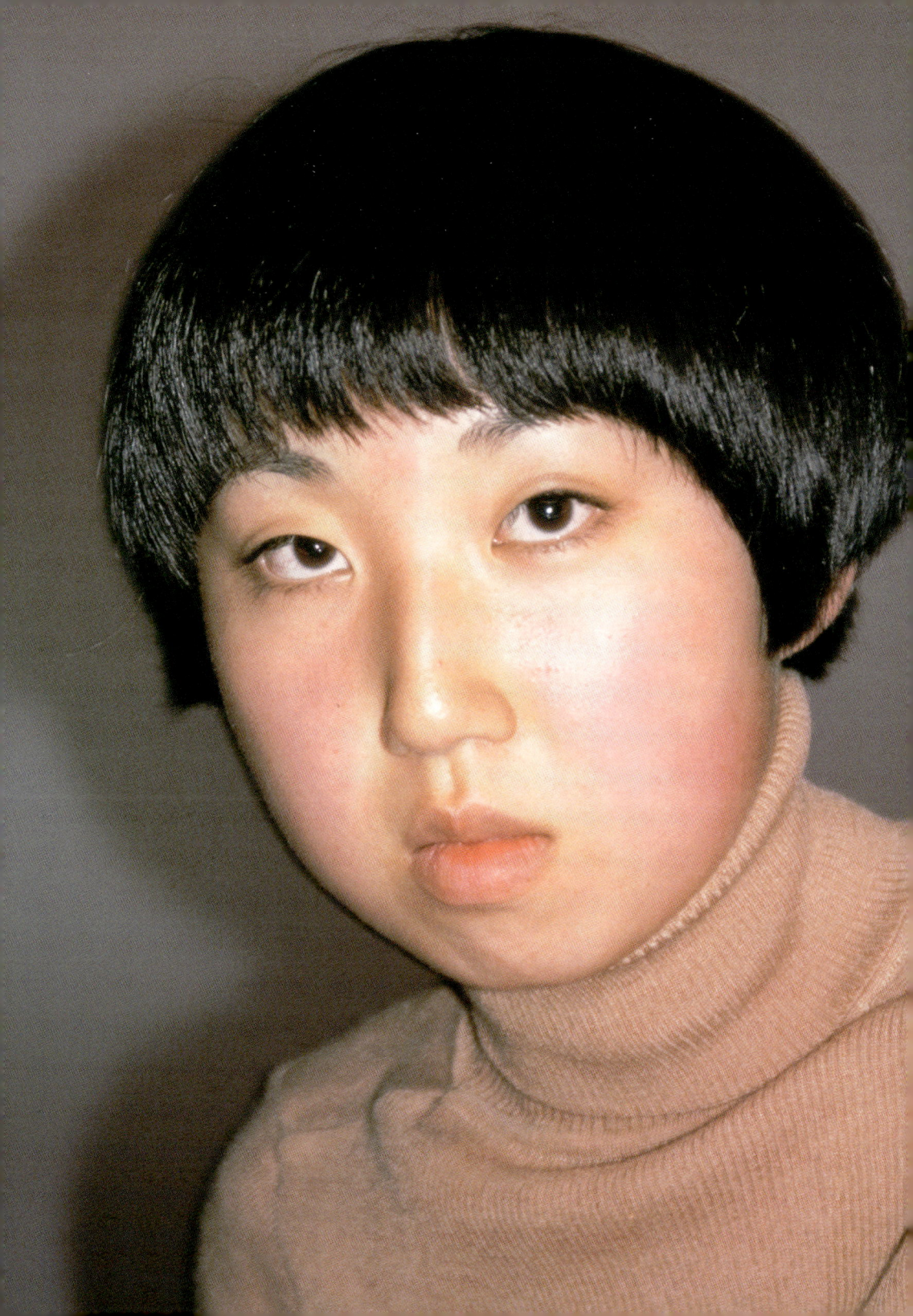

Naked Faces

顔写

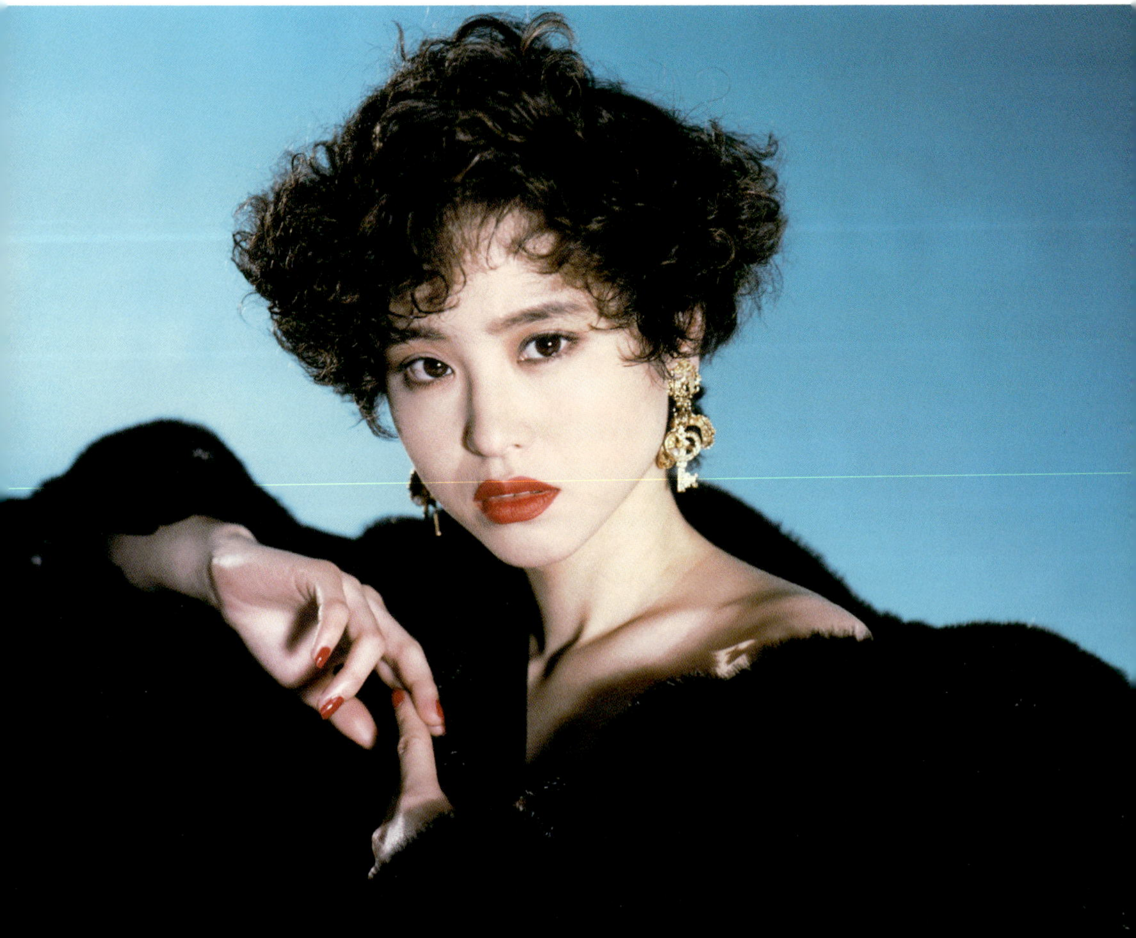

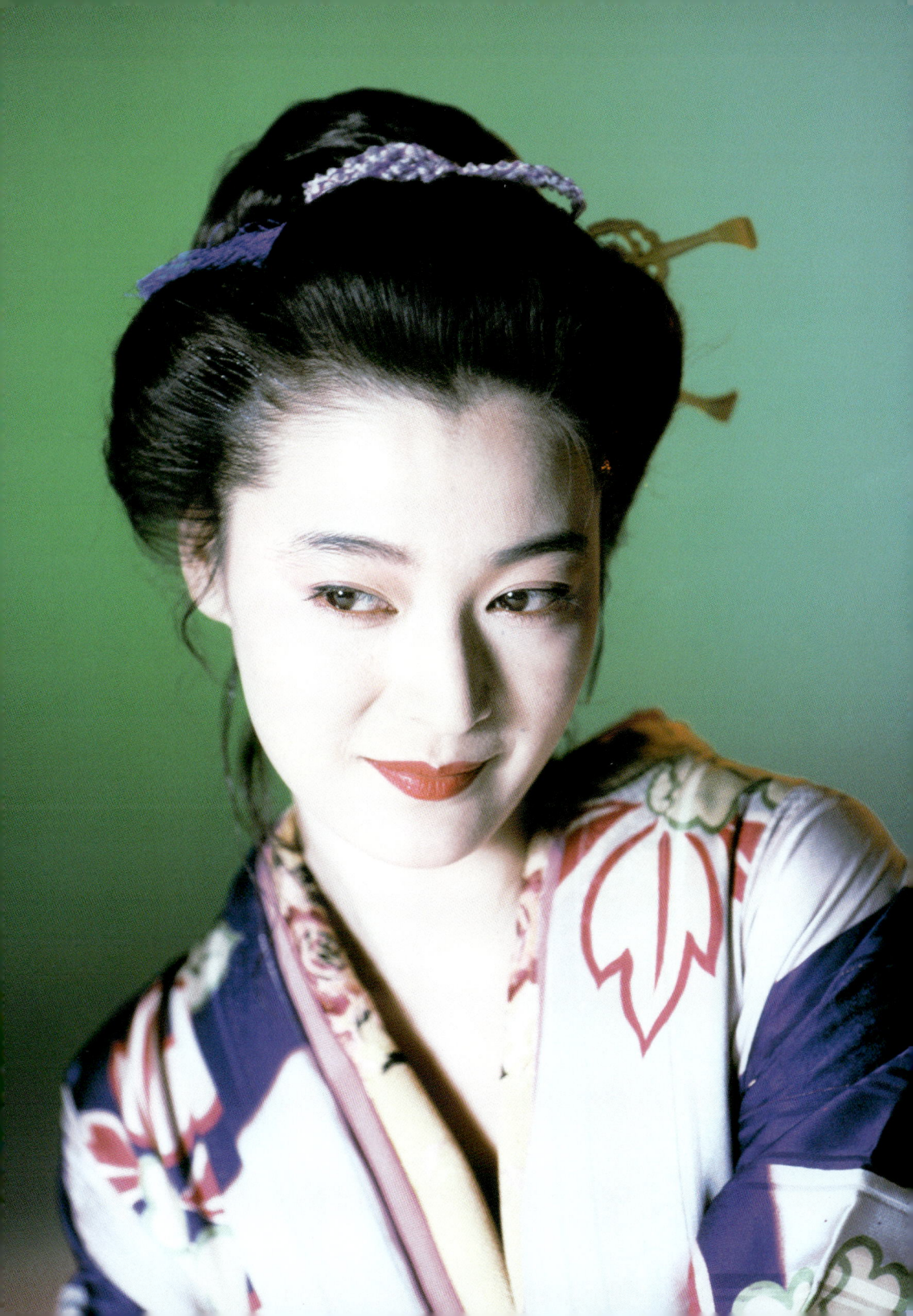

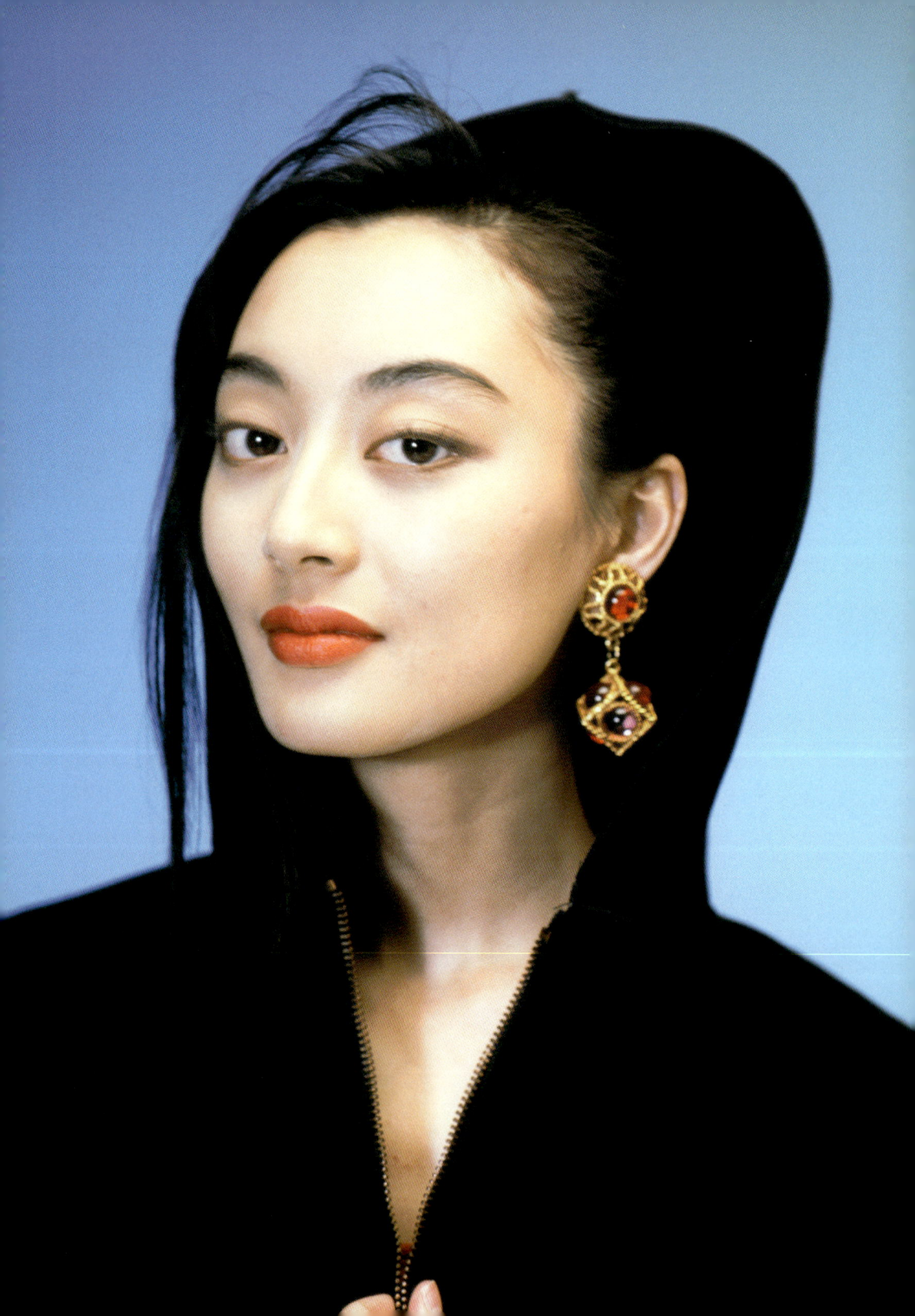

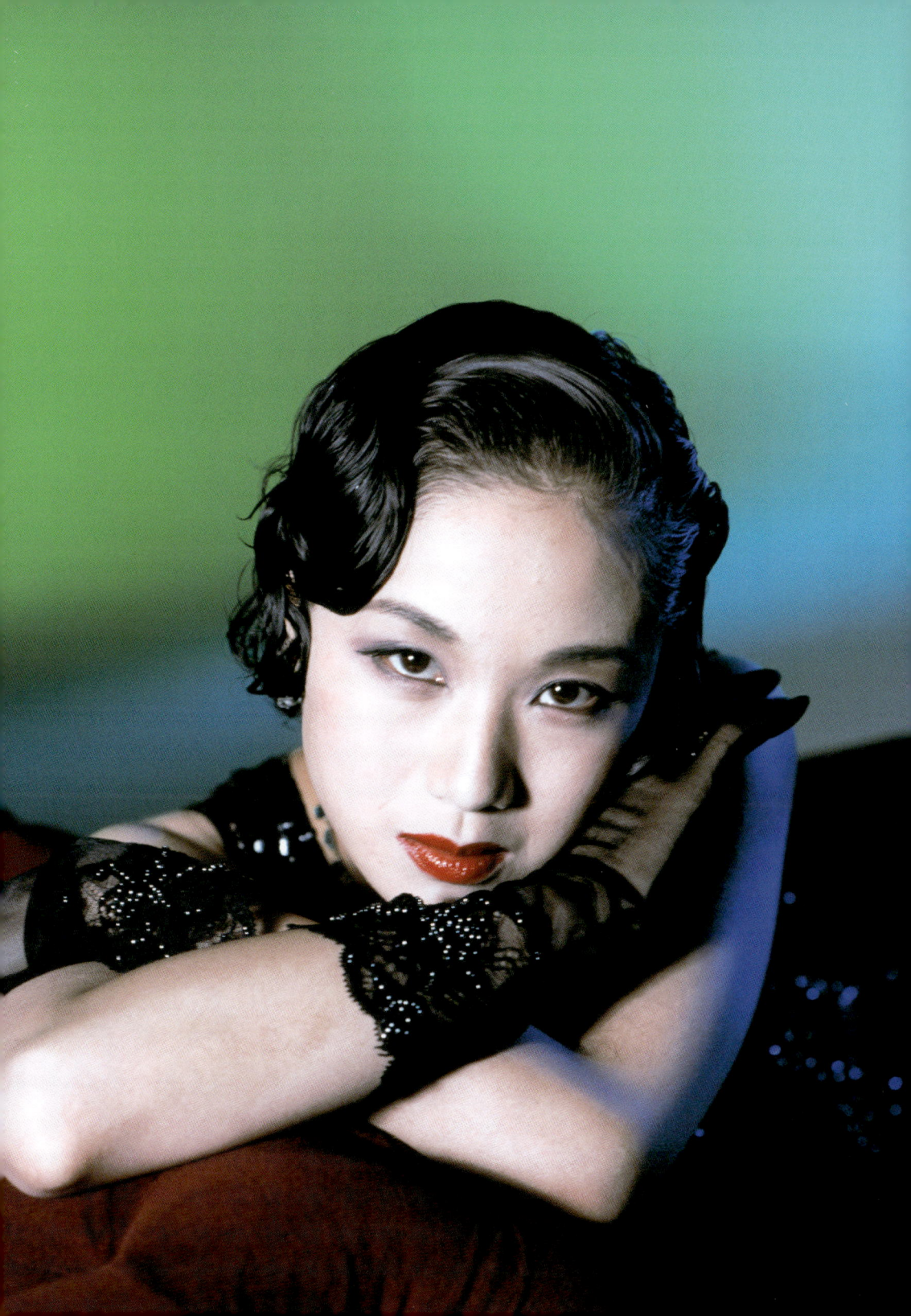

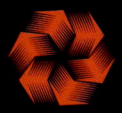

In Ruins

廃墟で

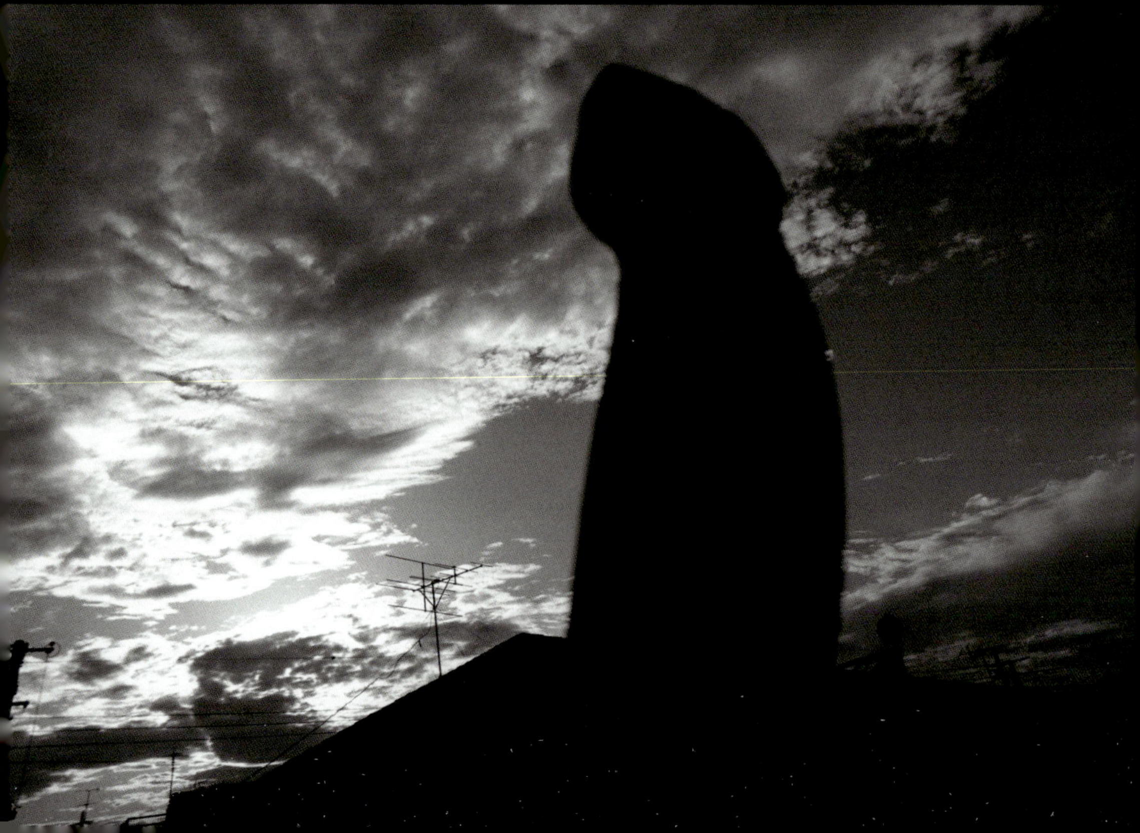

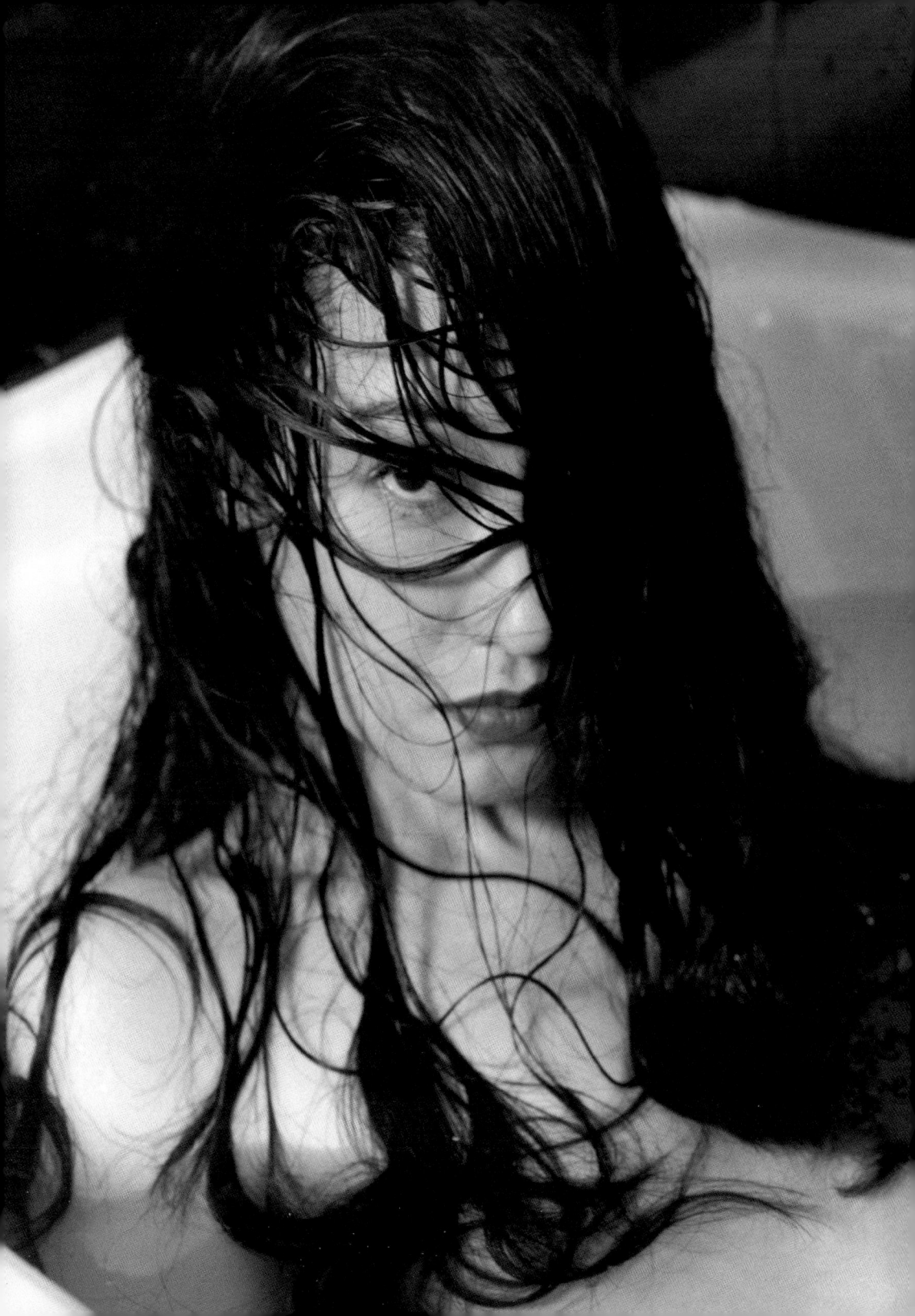

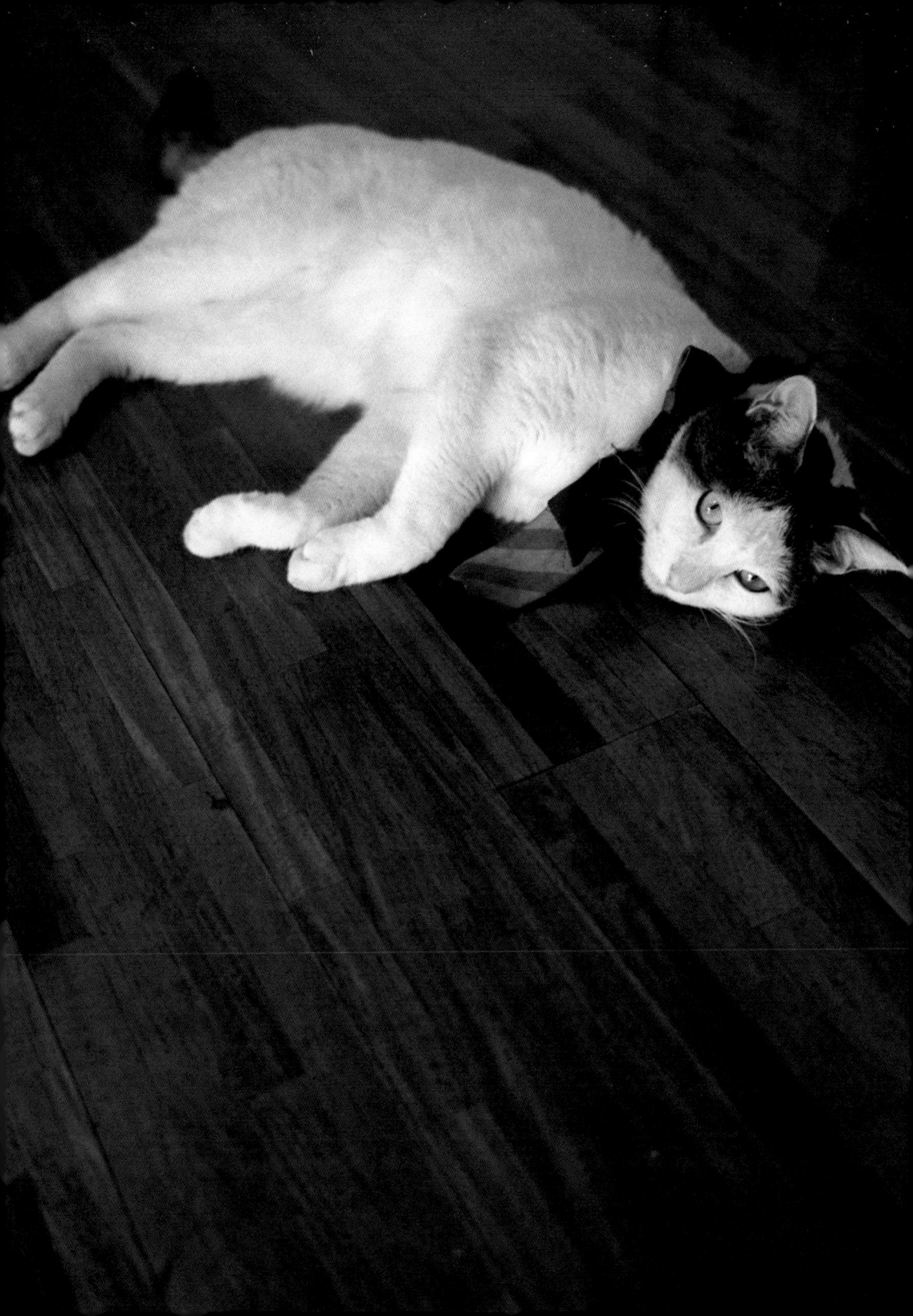

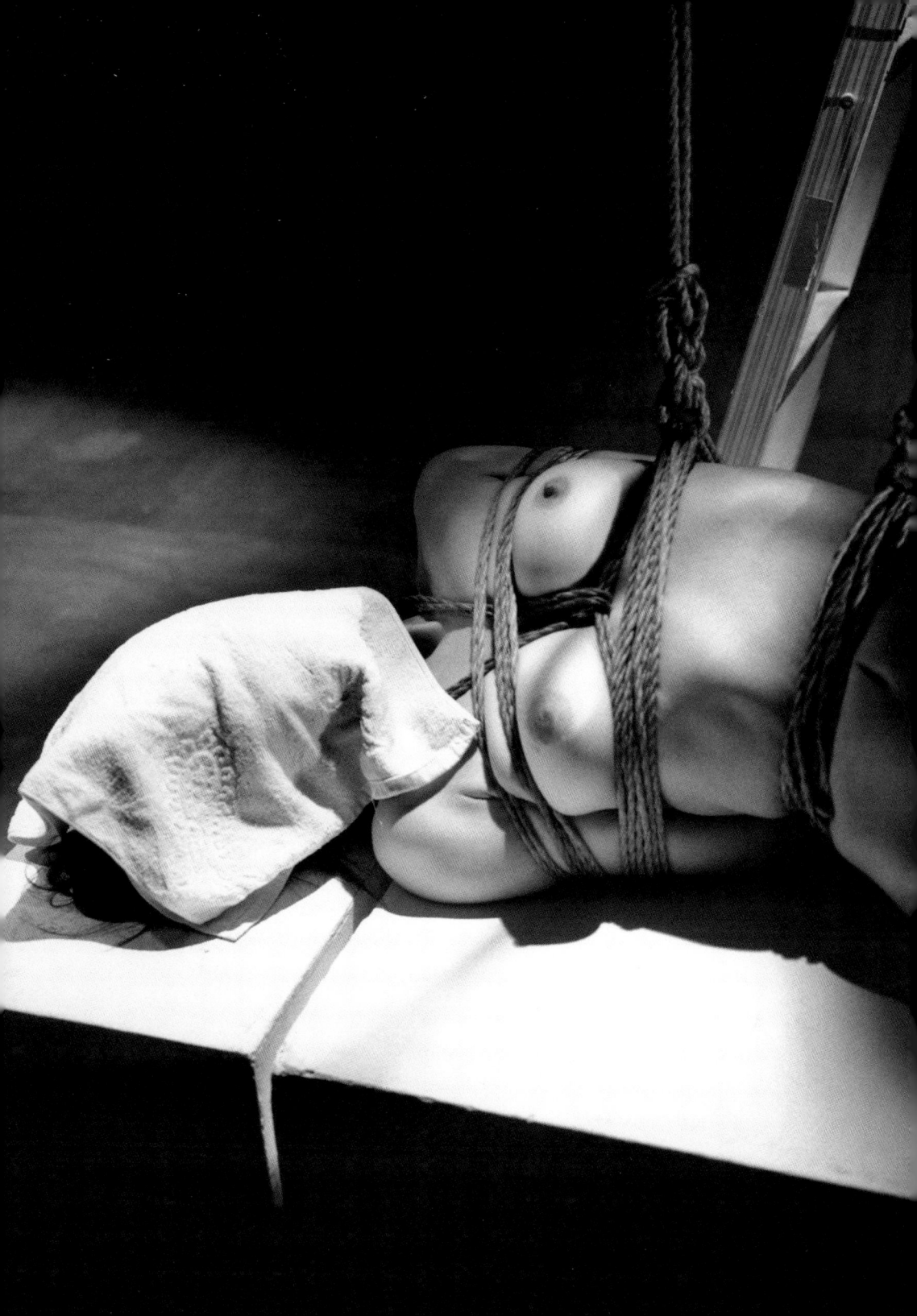

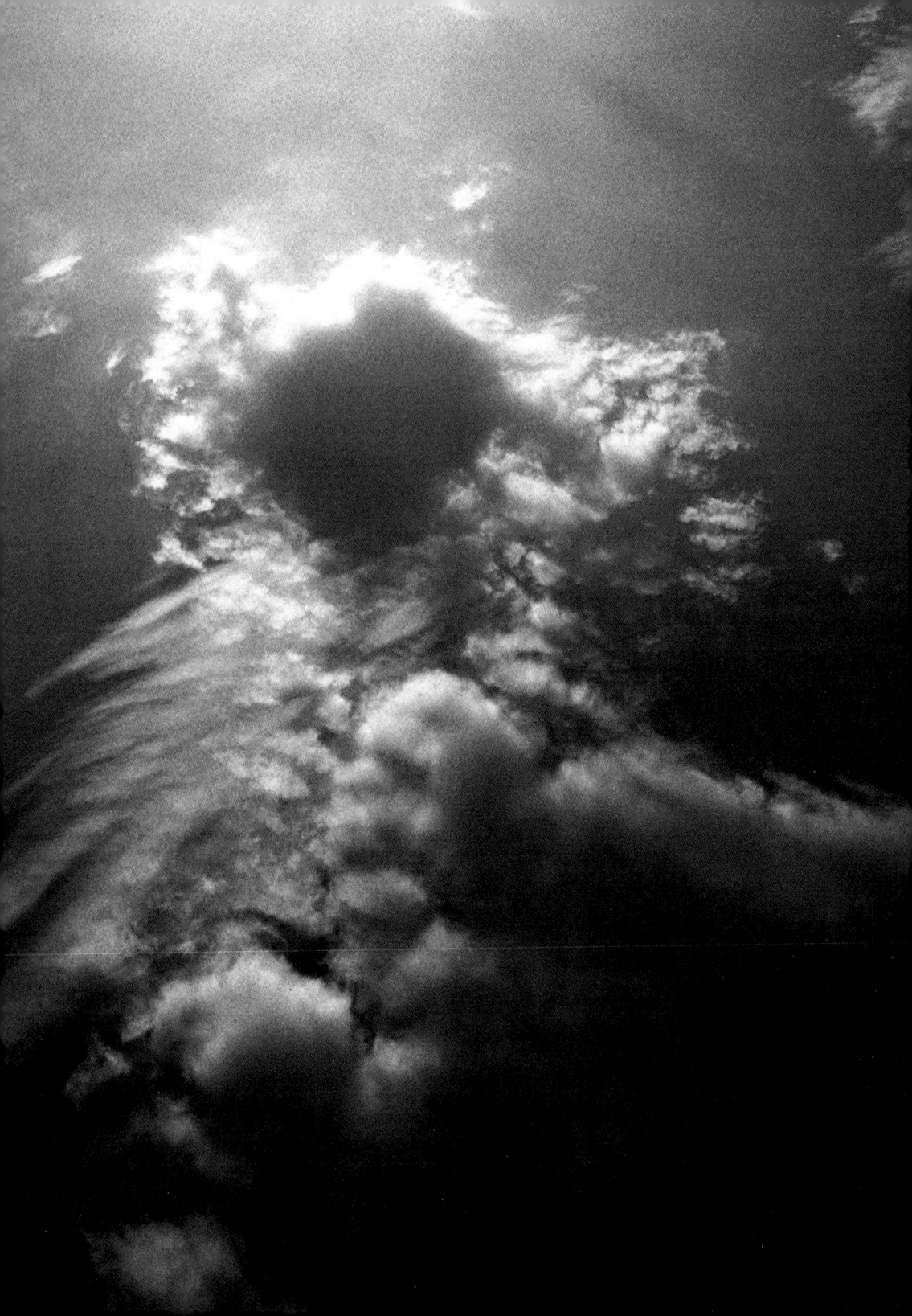

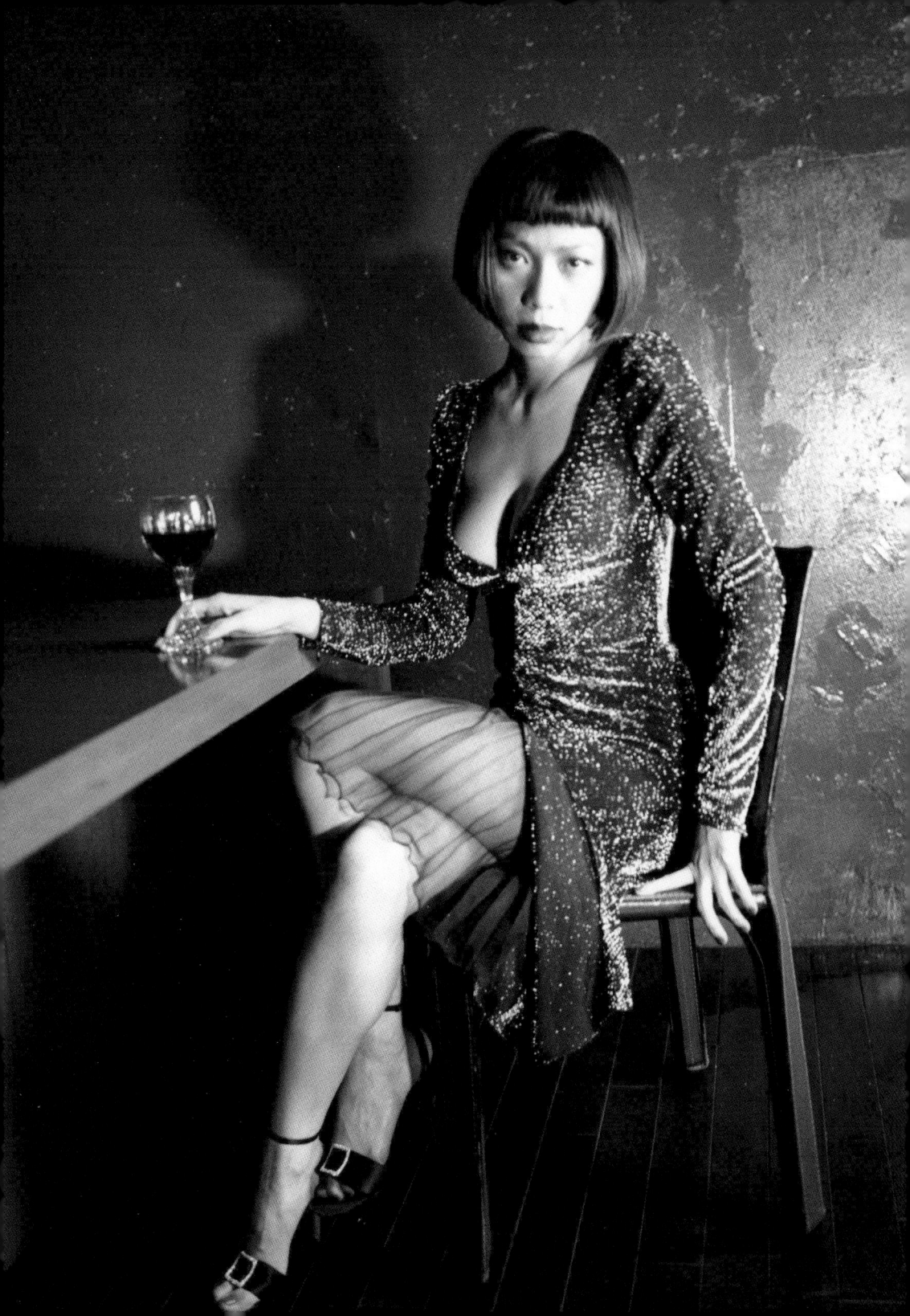

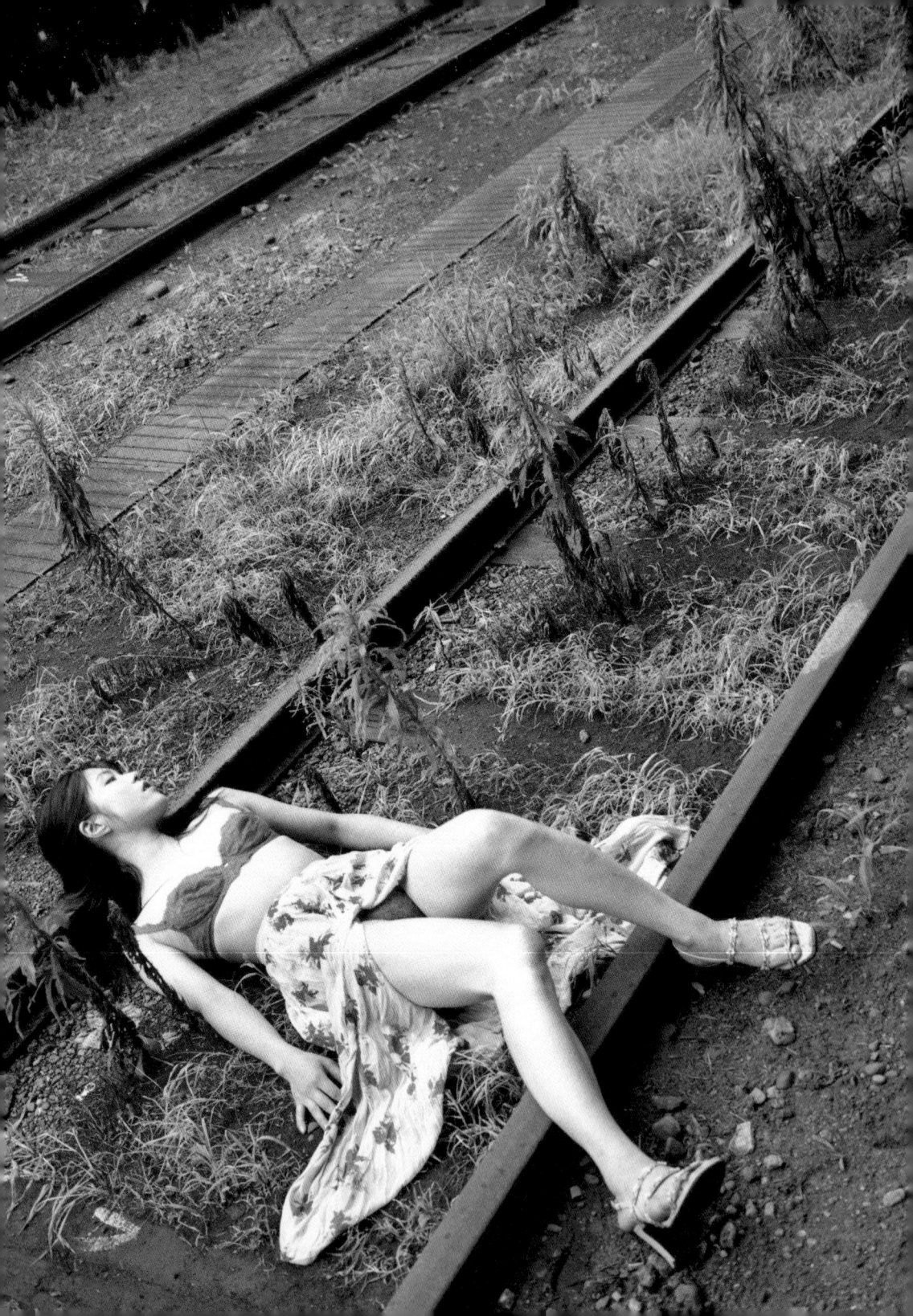

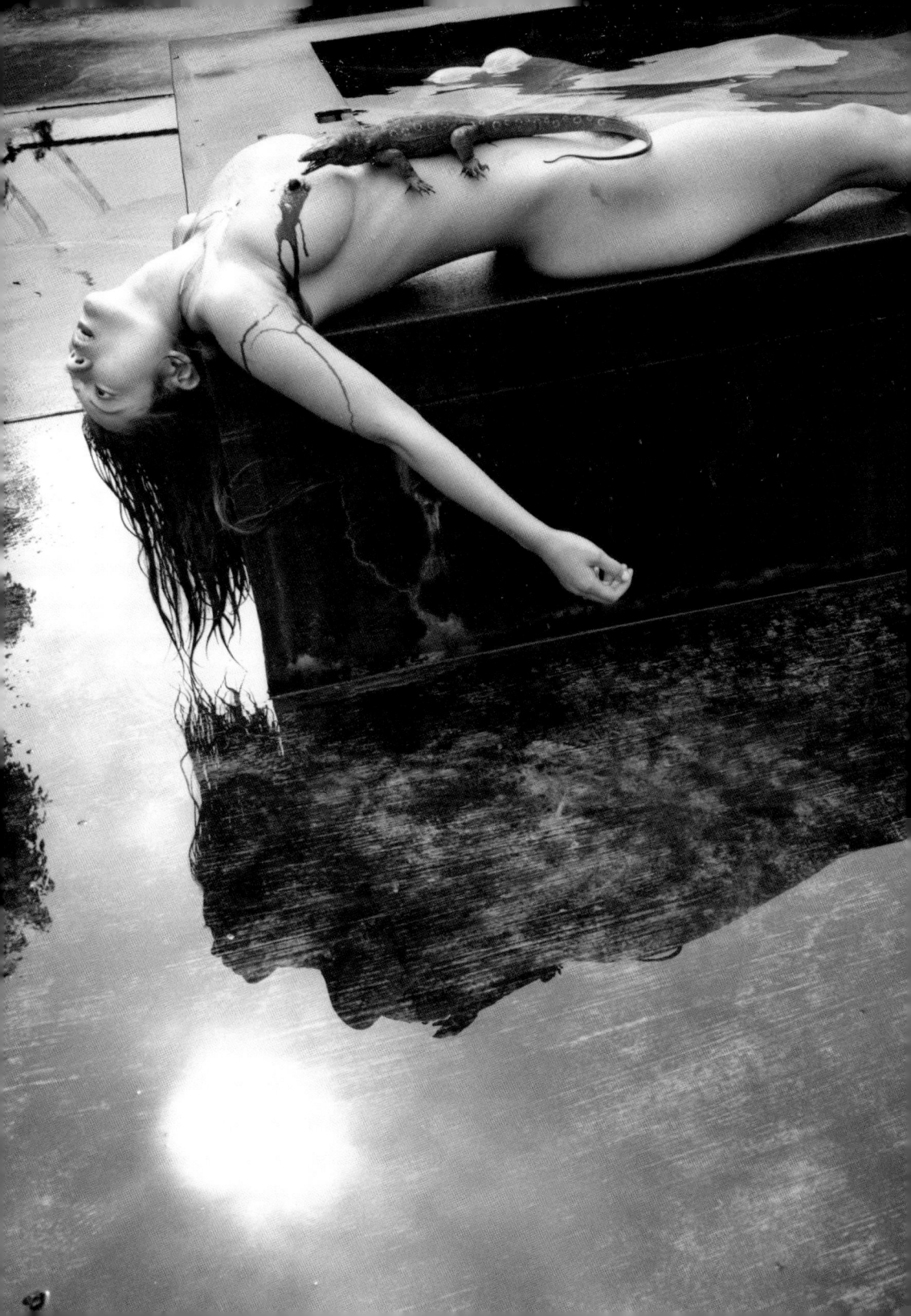

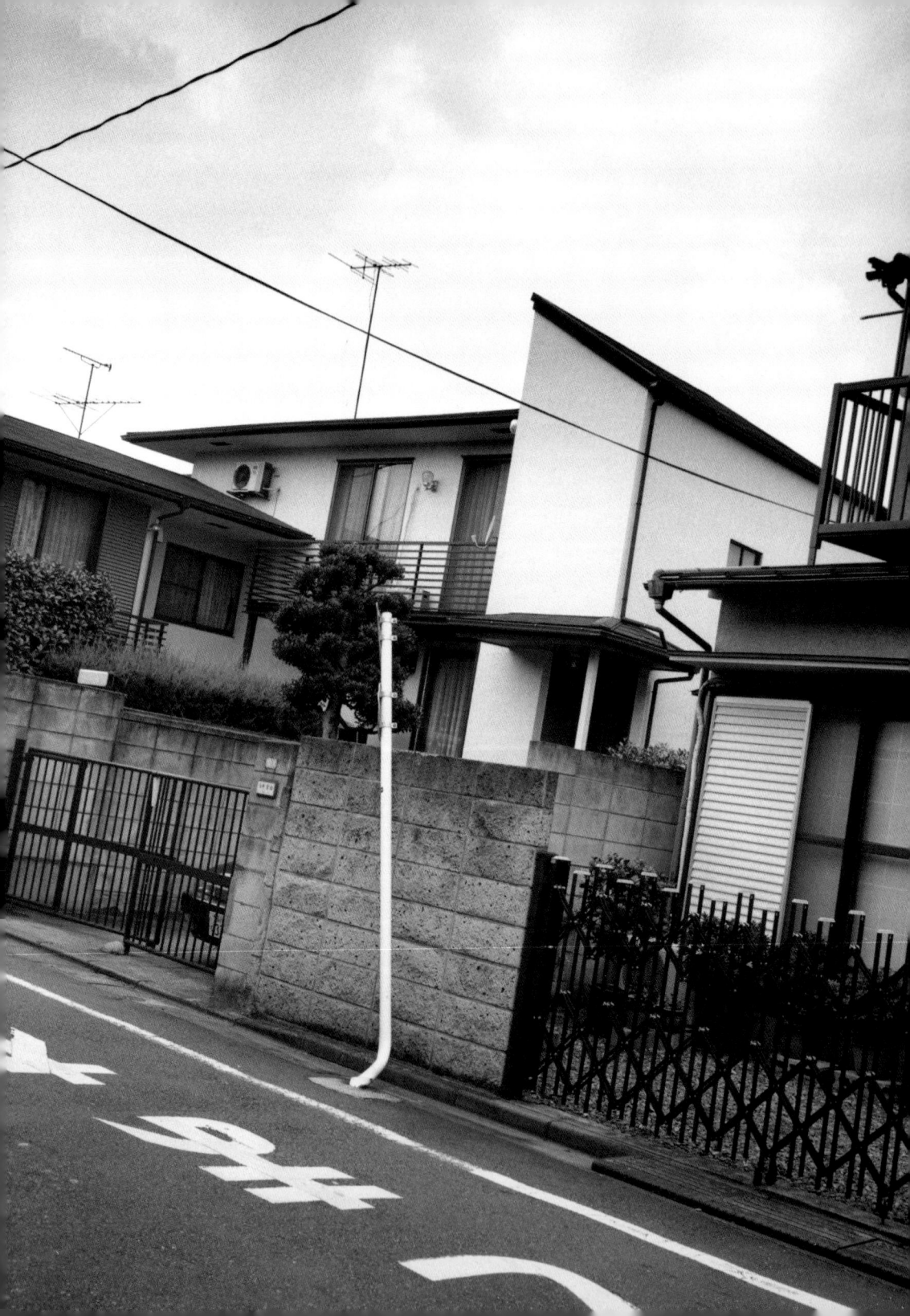

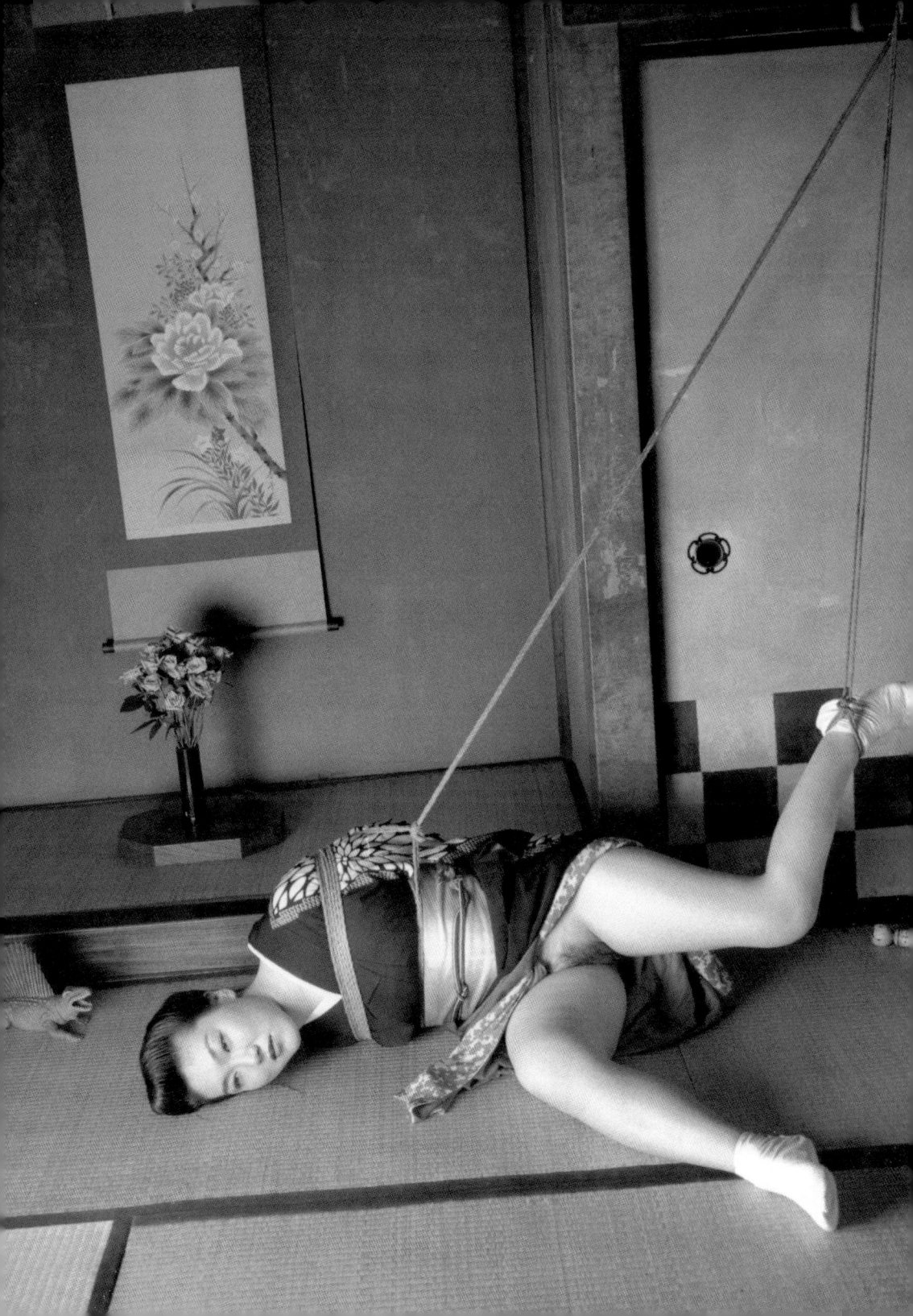

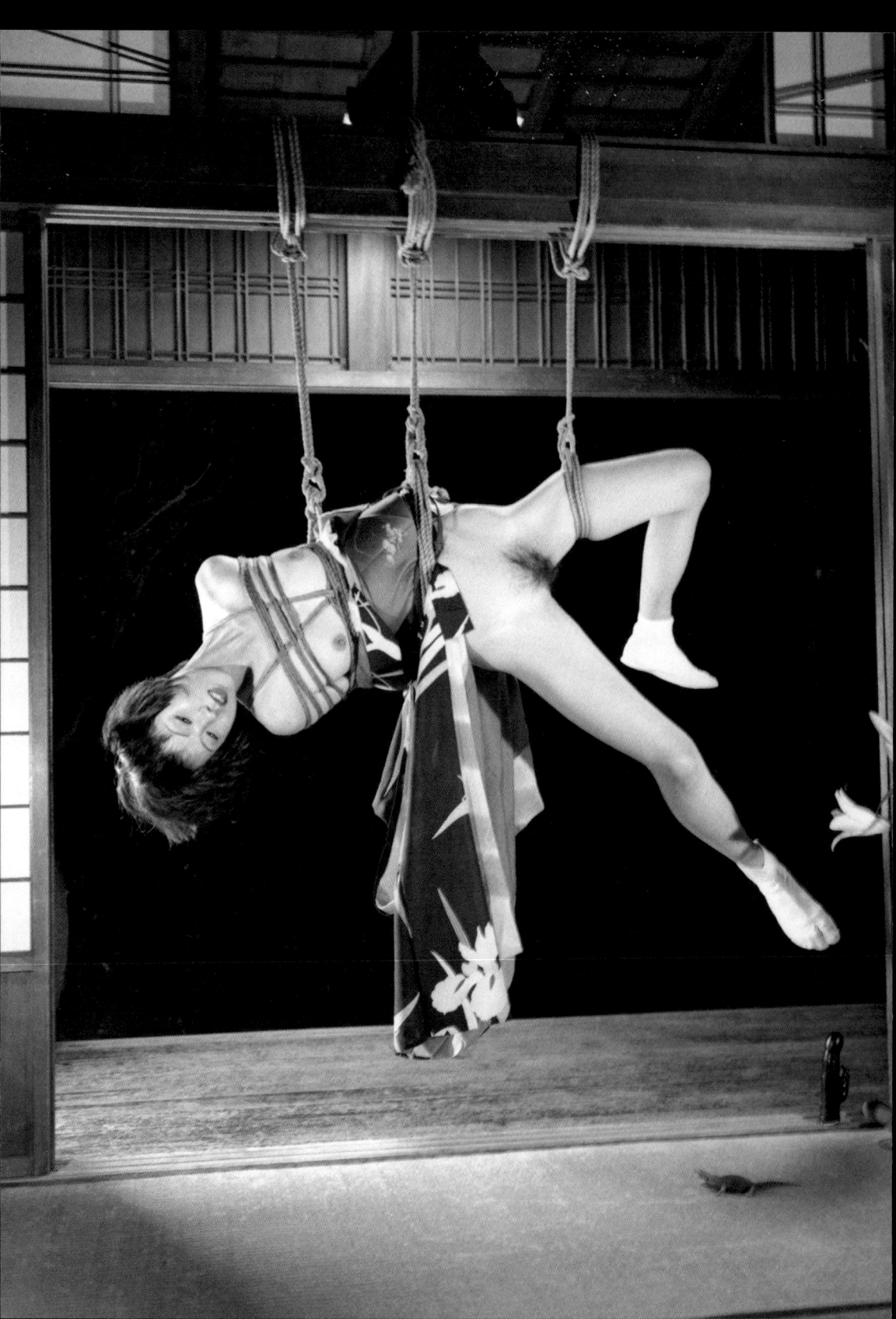

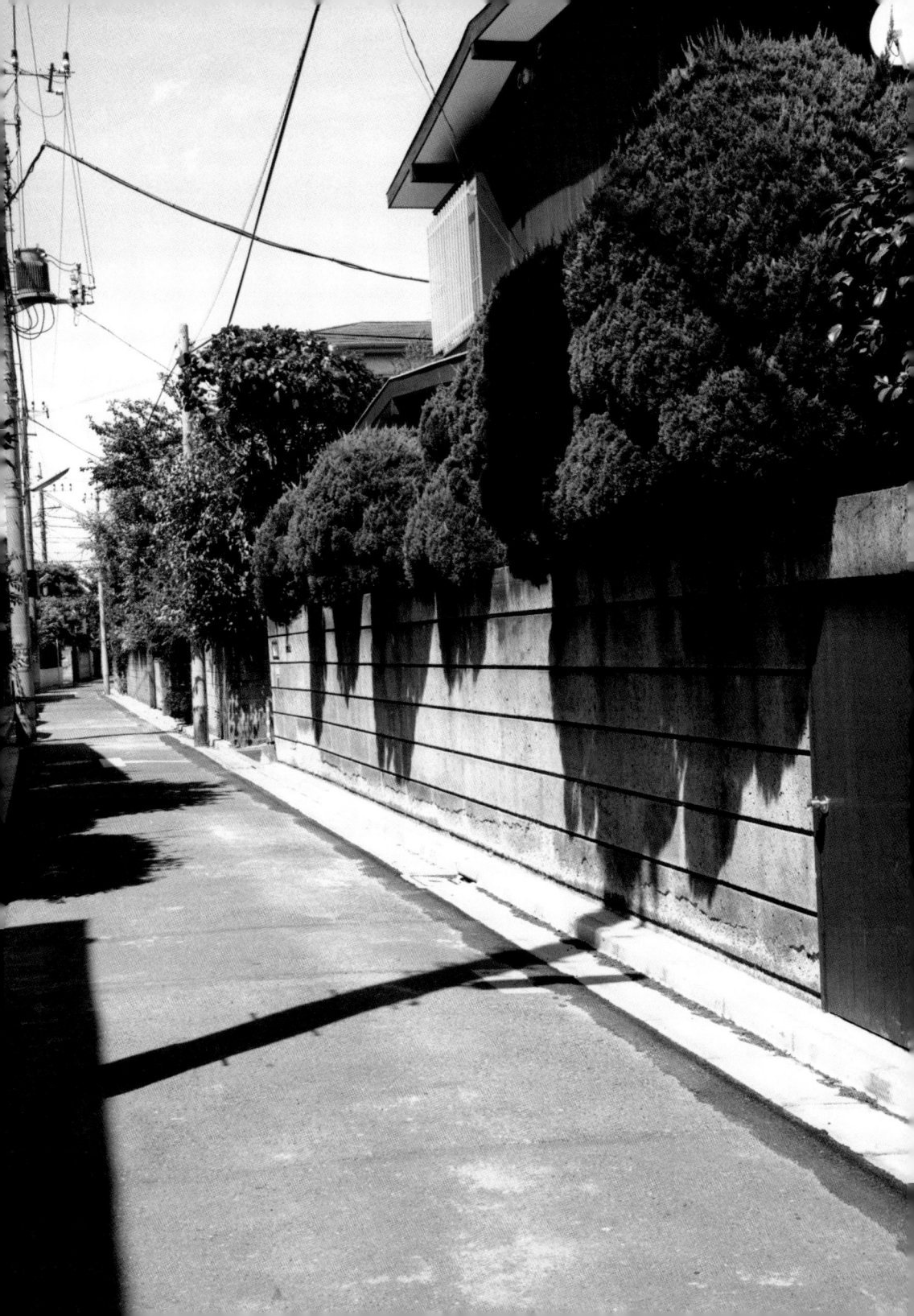

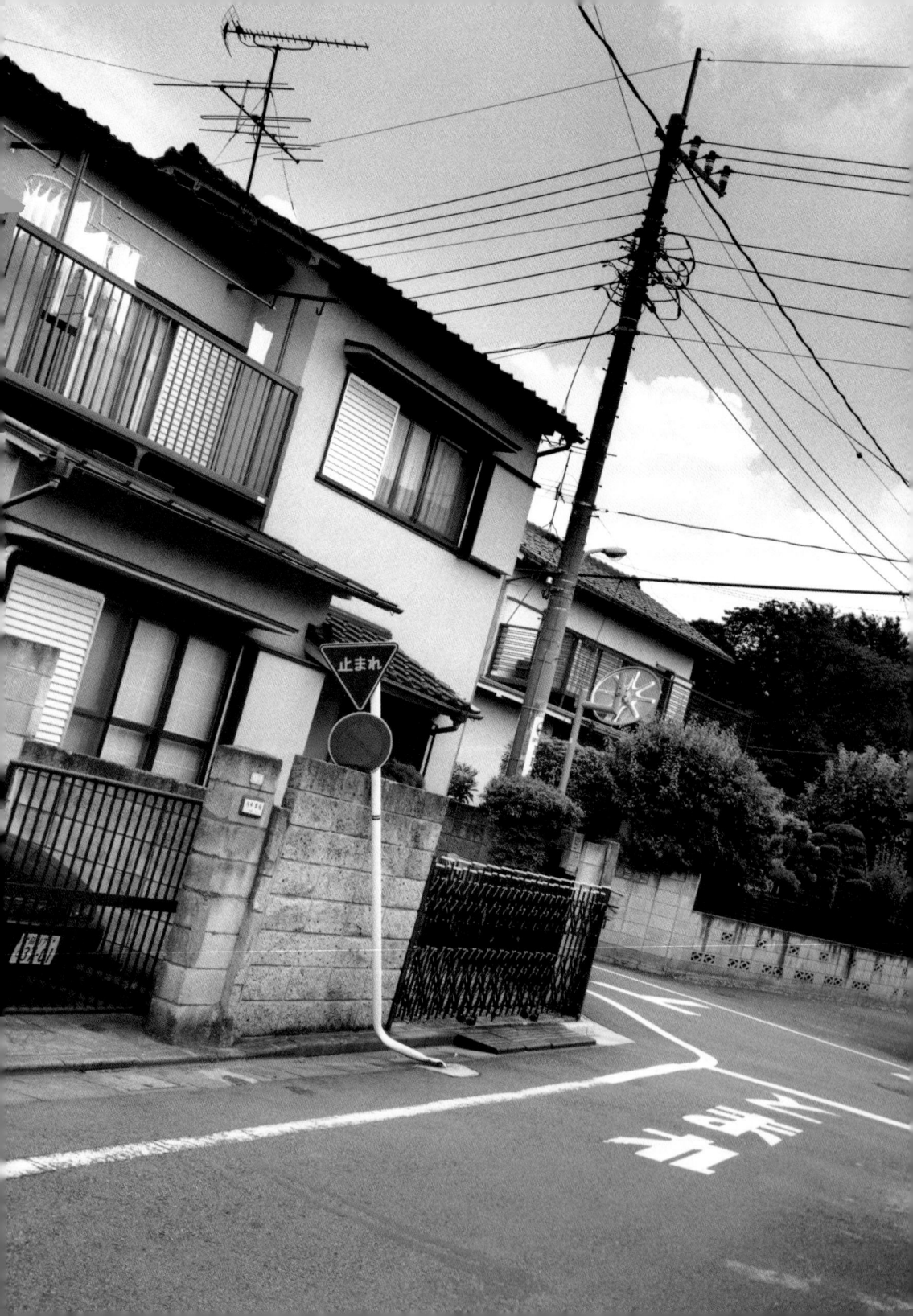

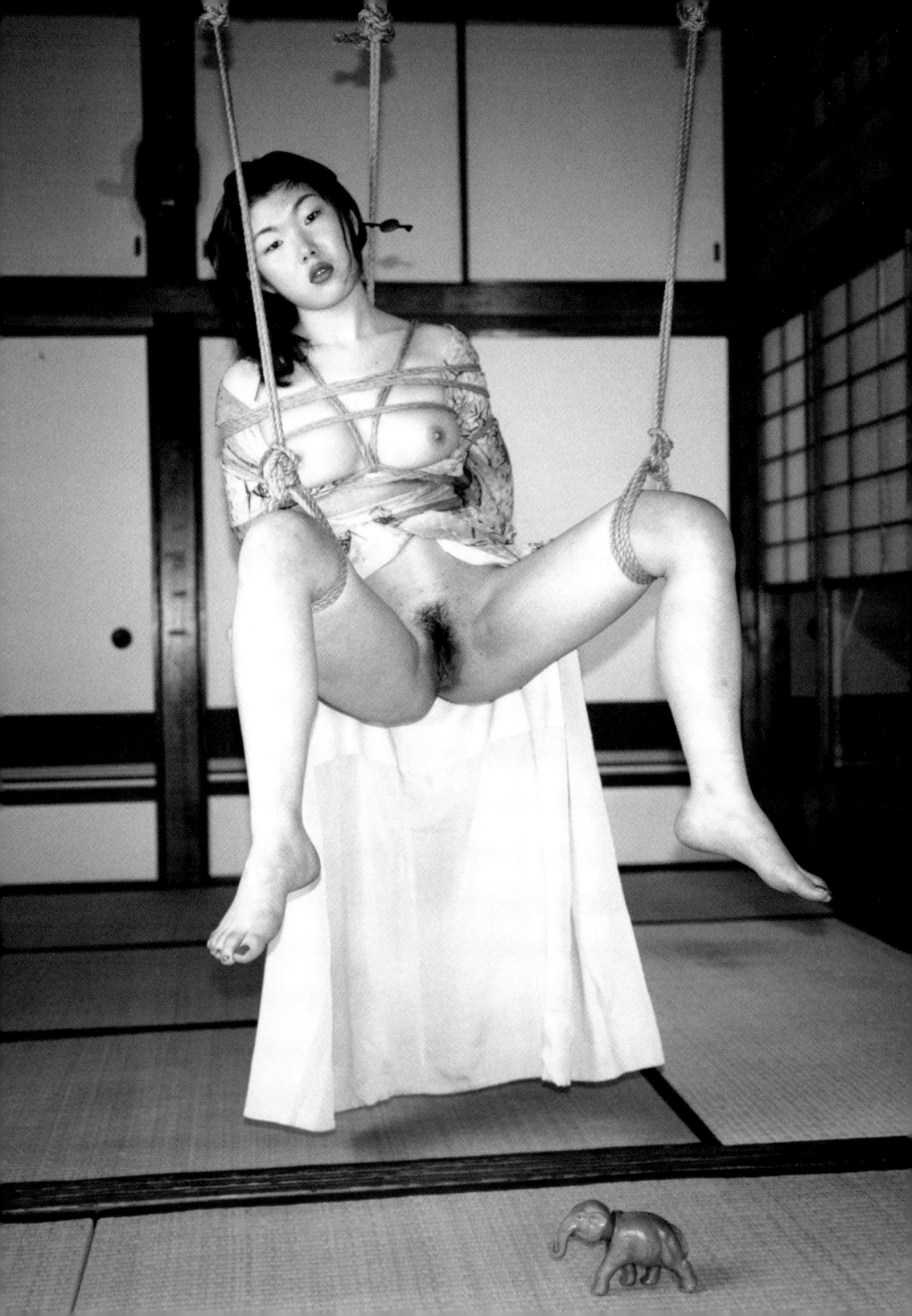

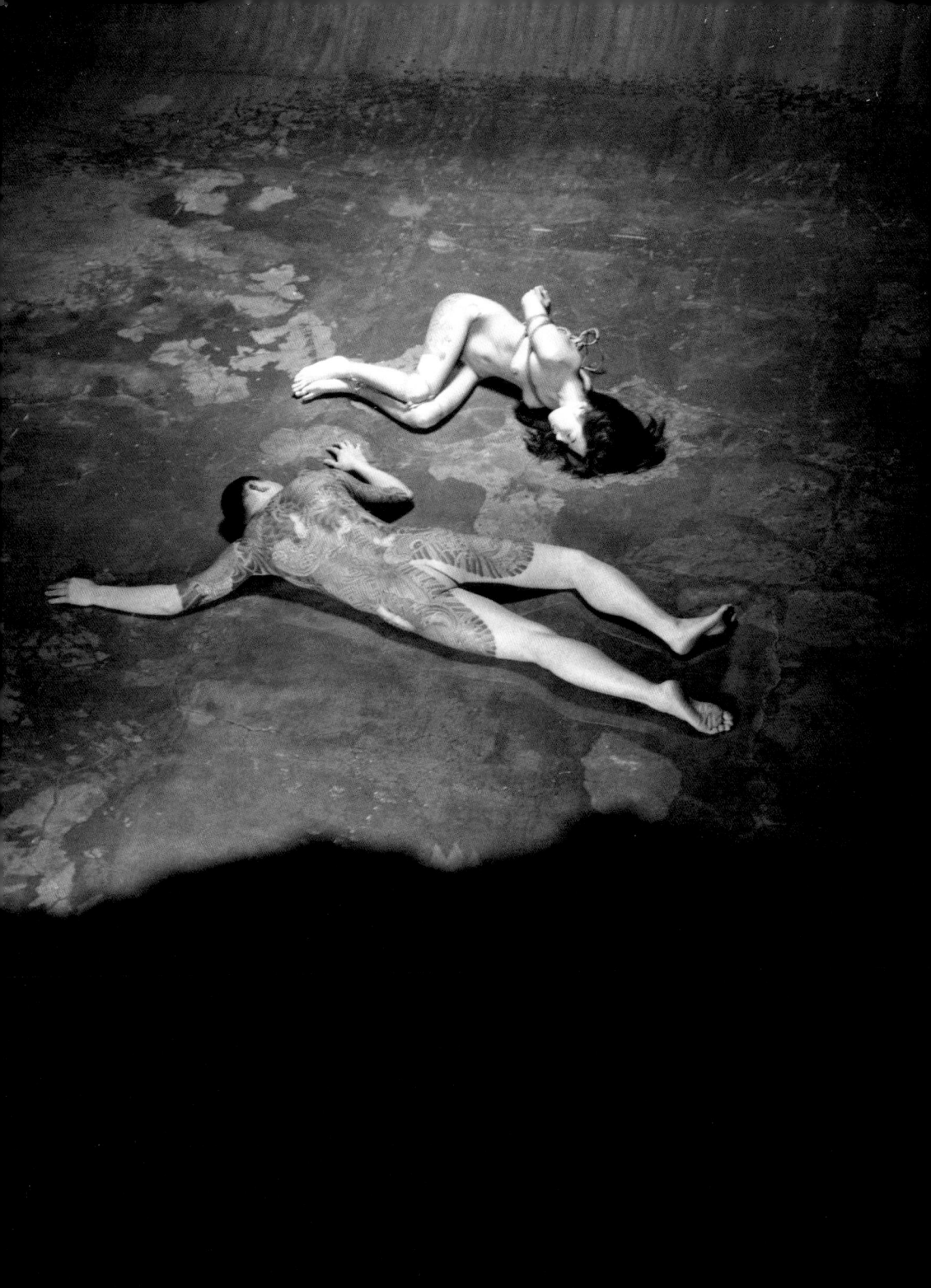

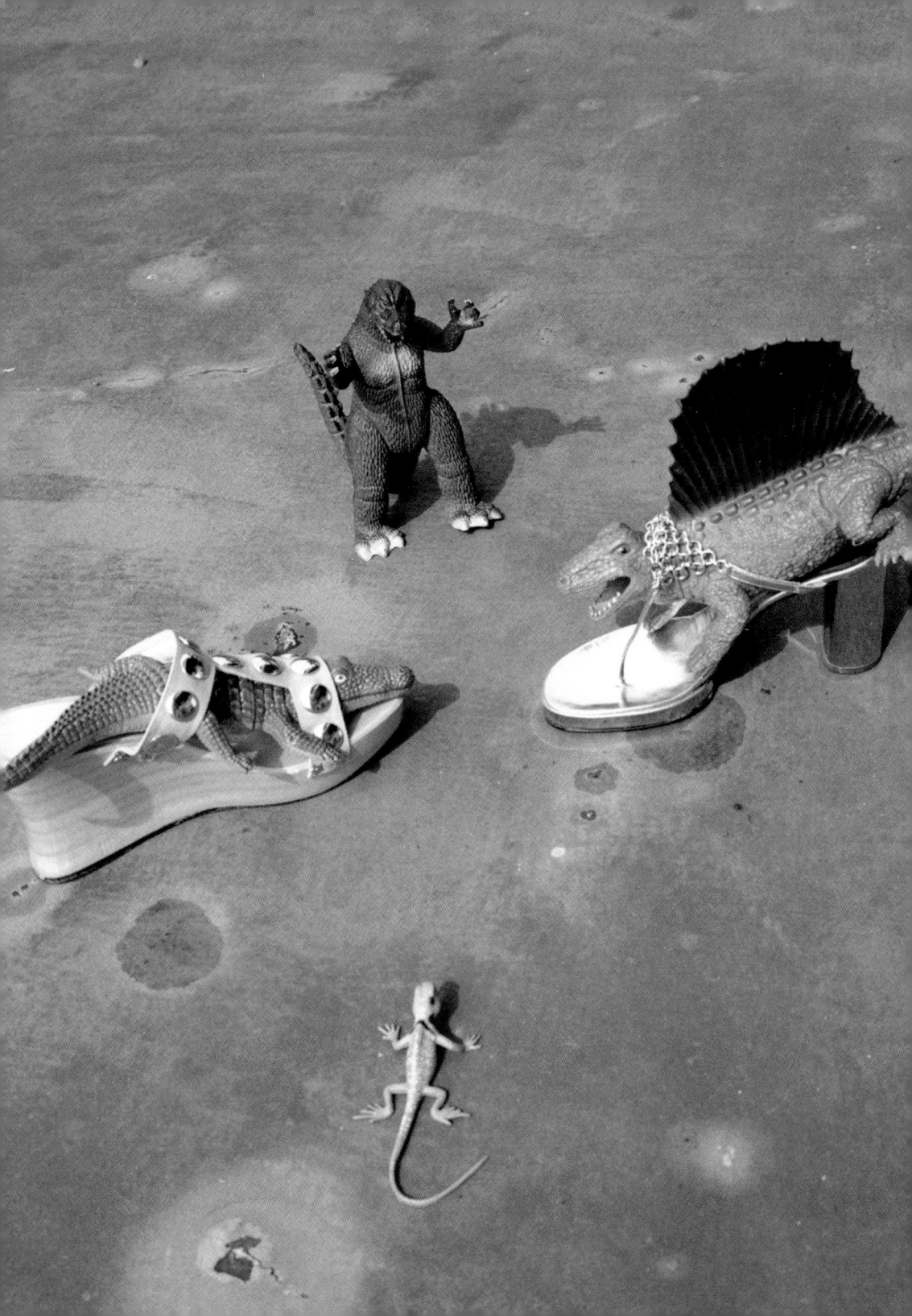

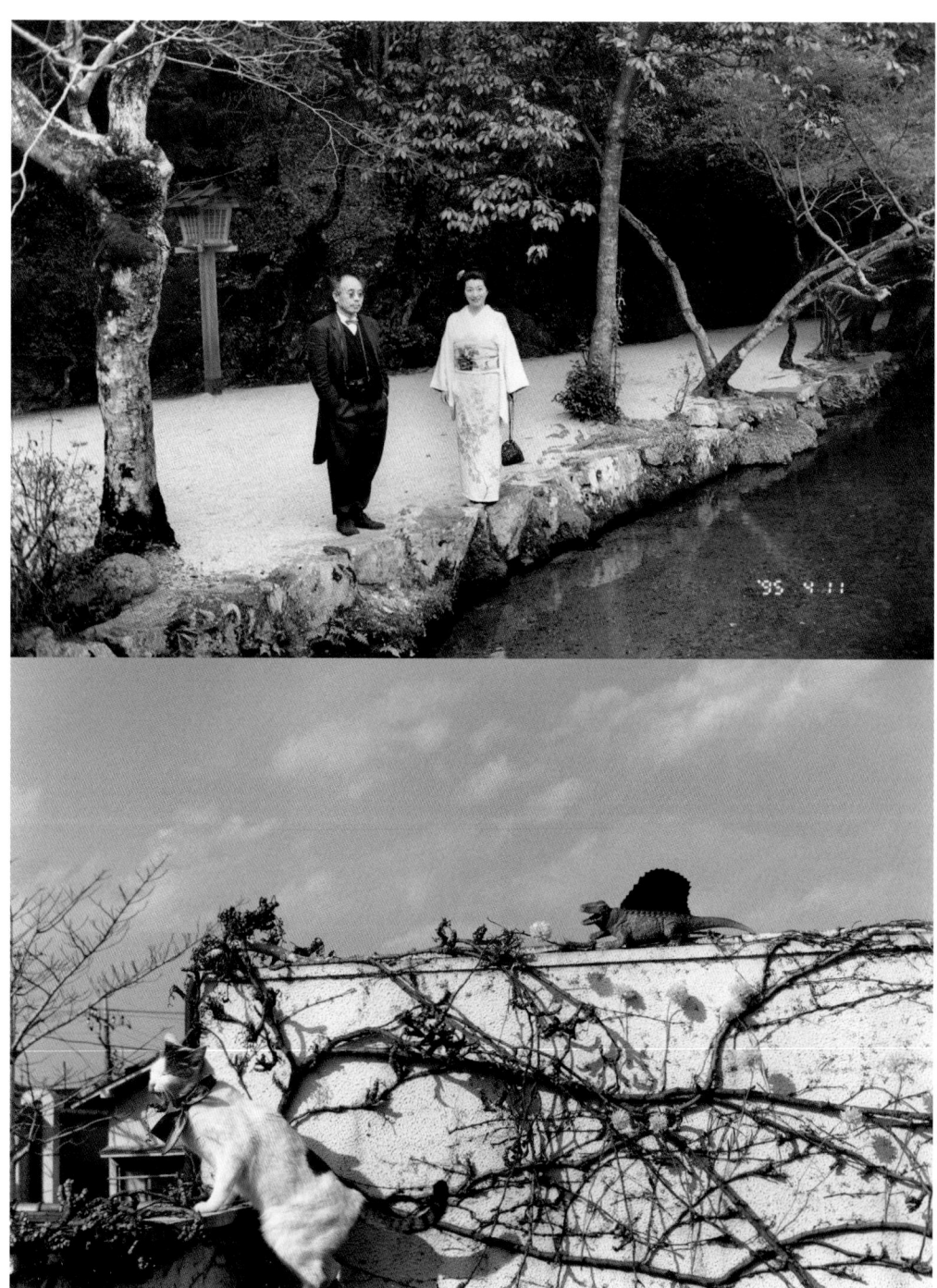

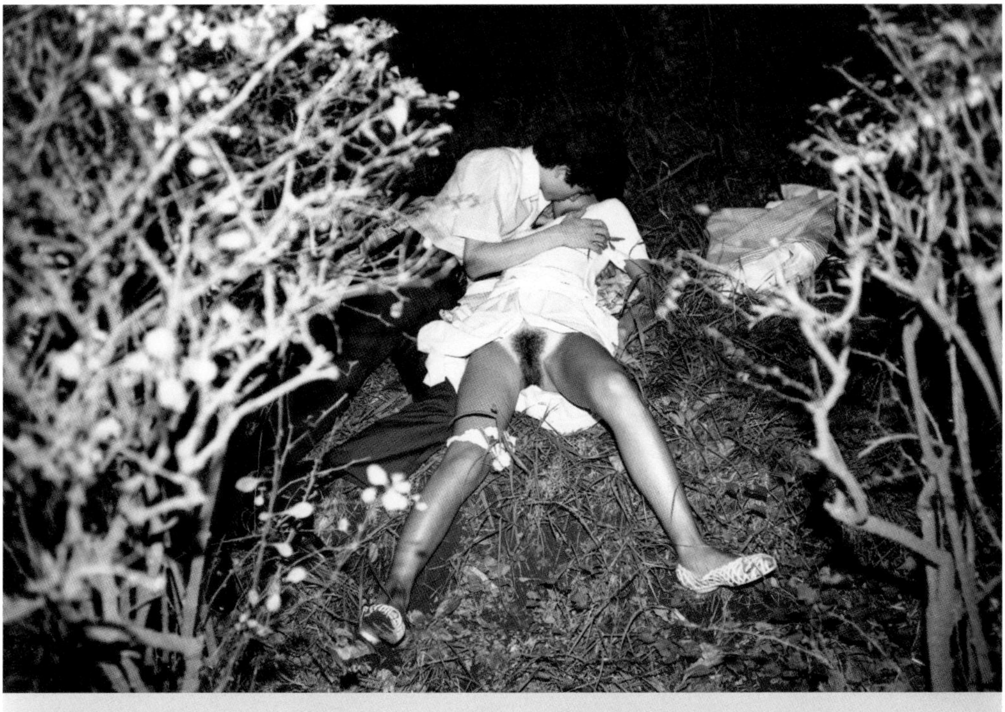

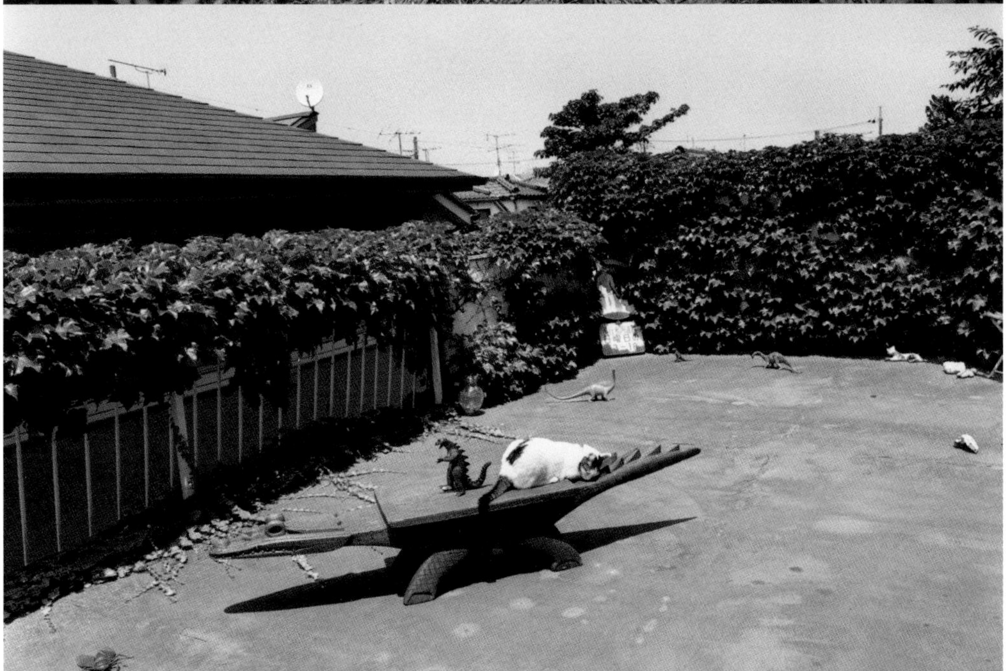

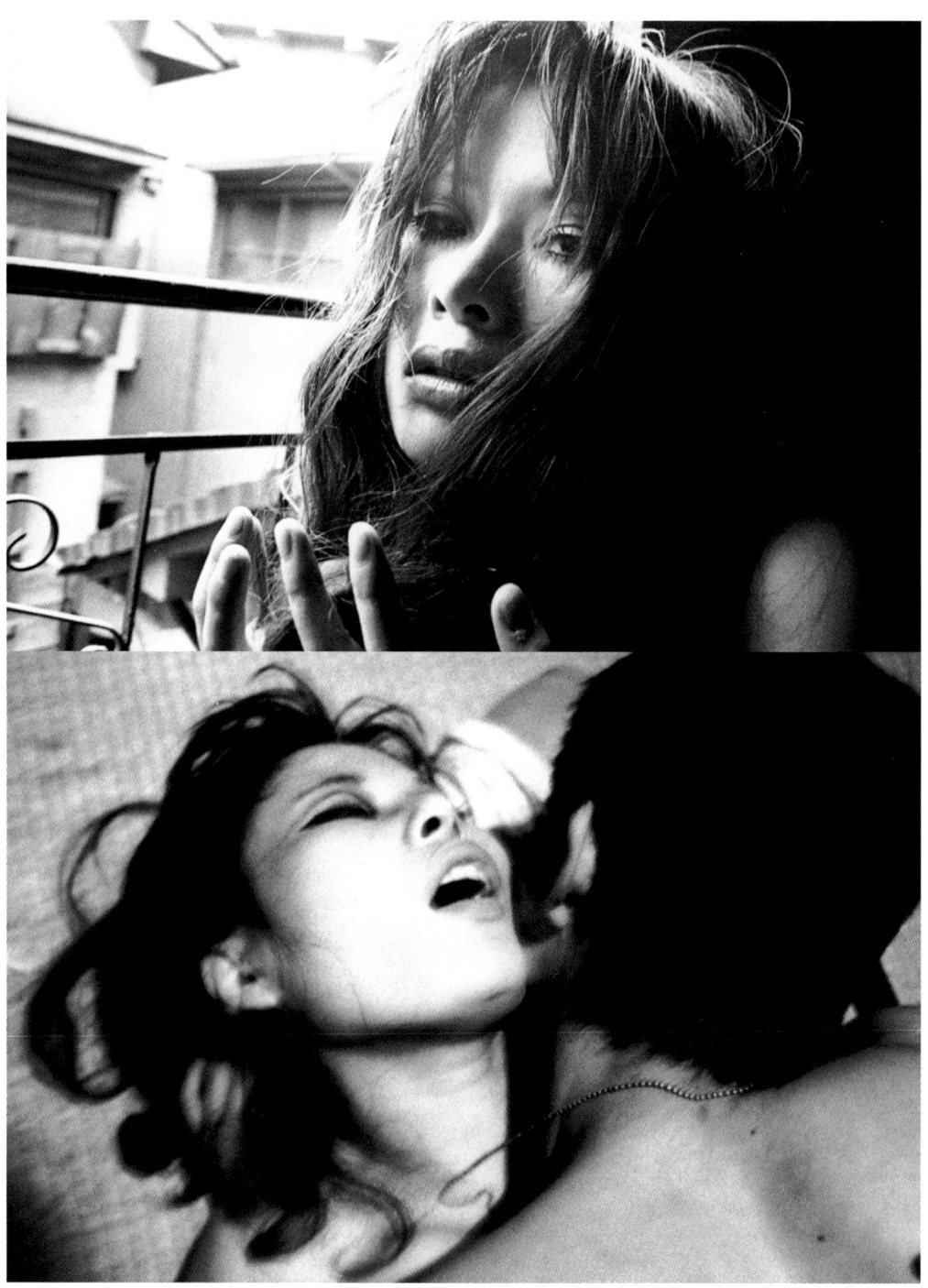

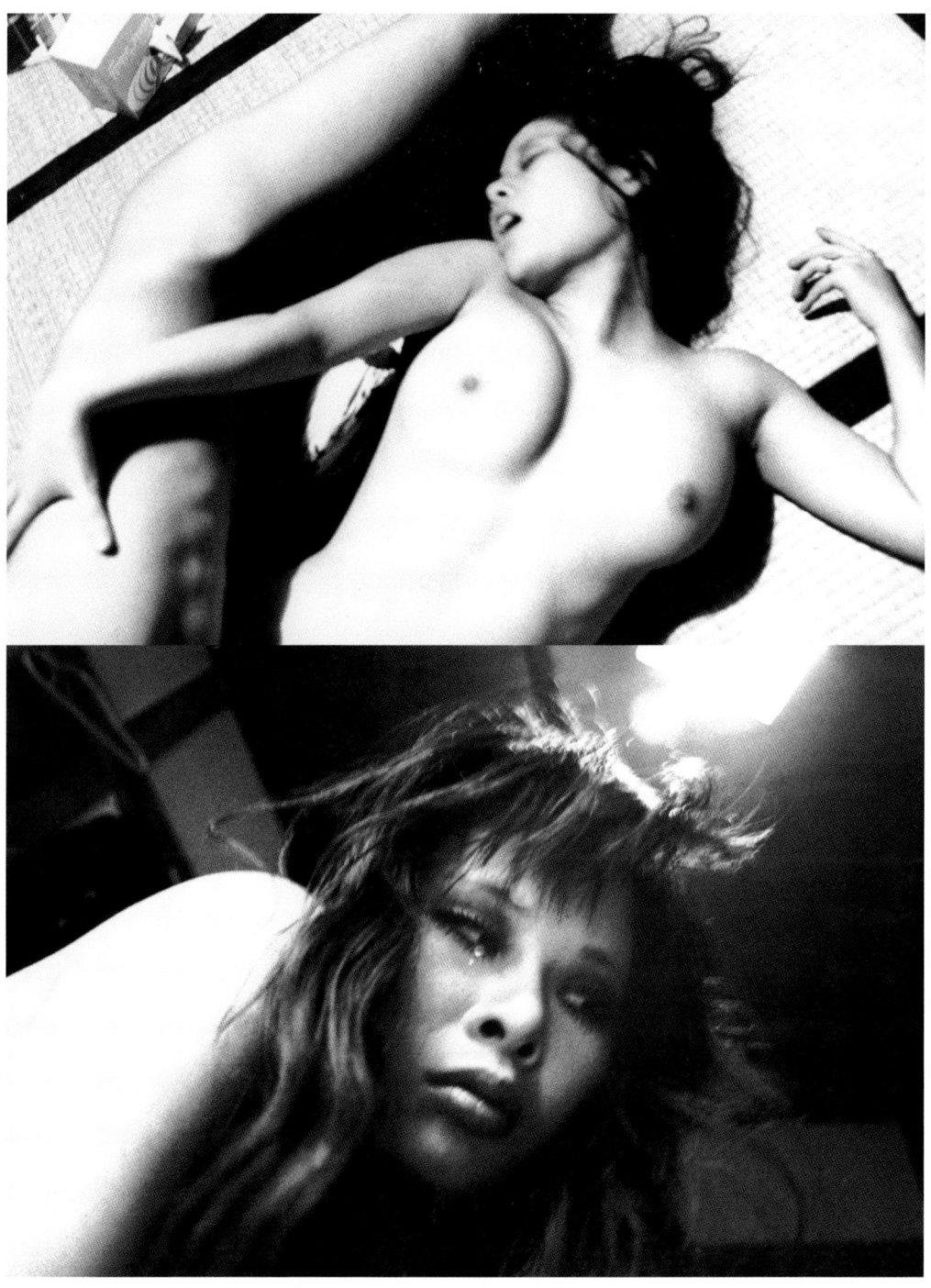

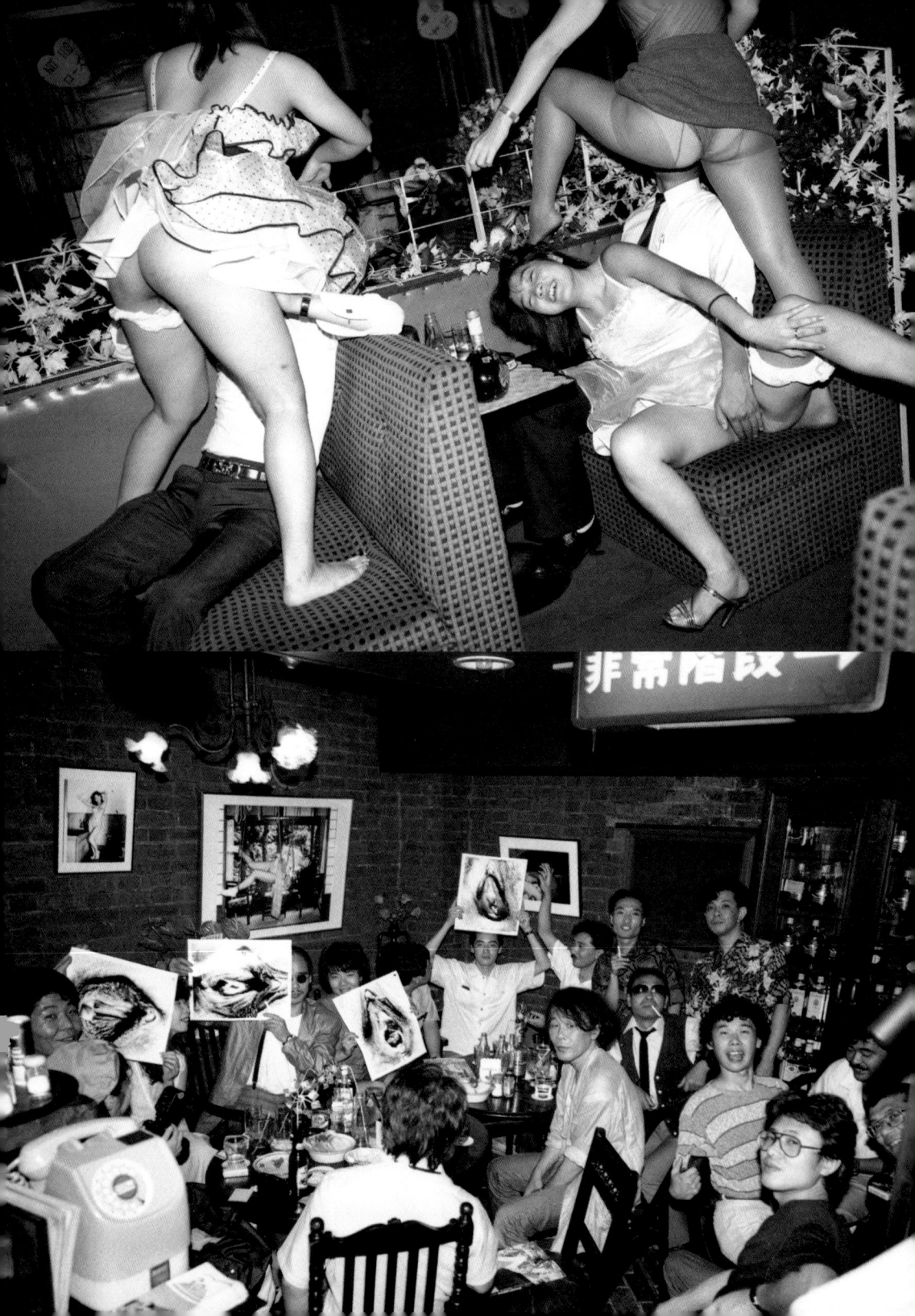

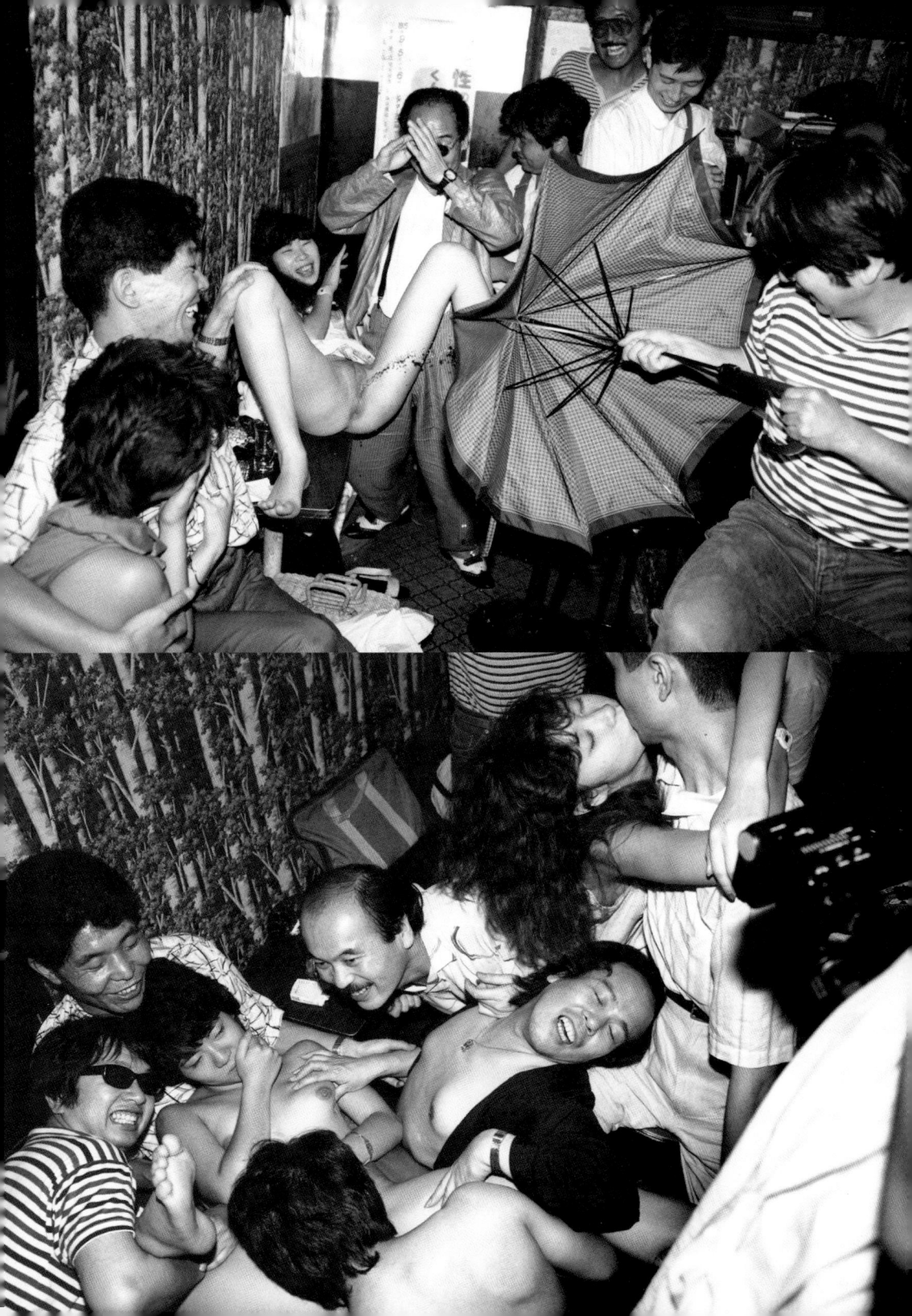

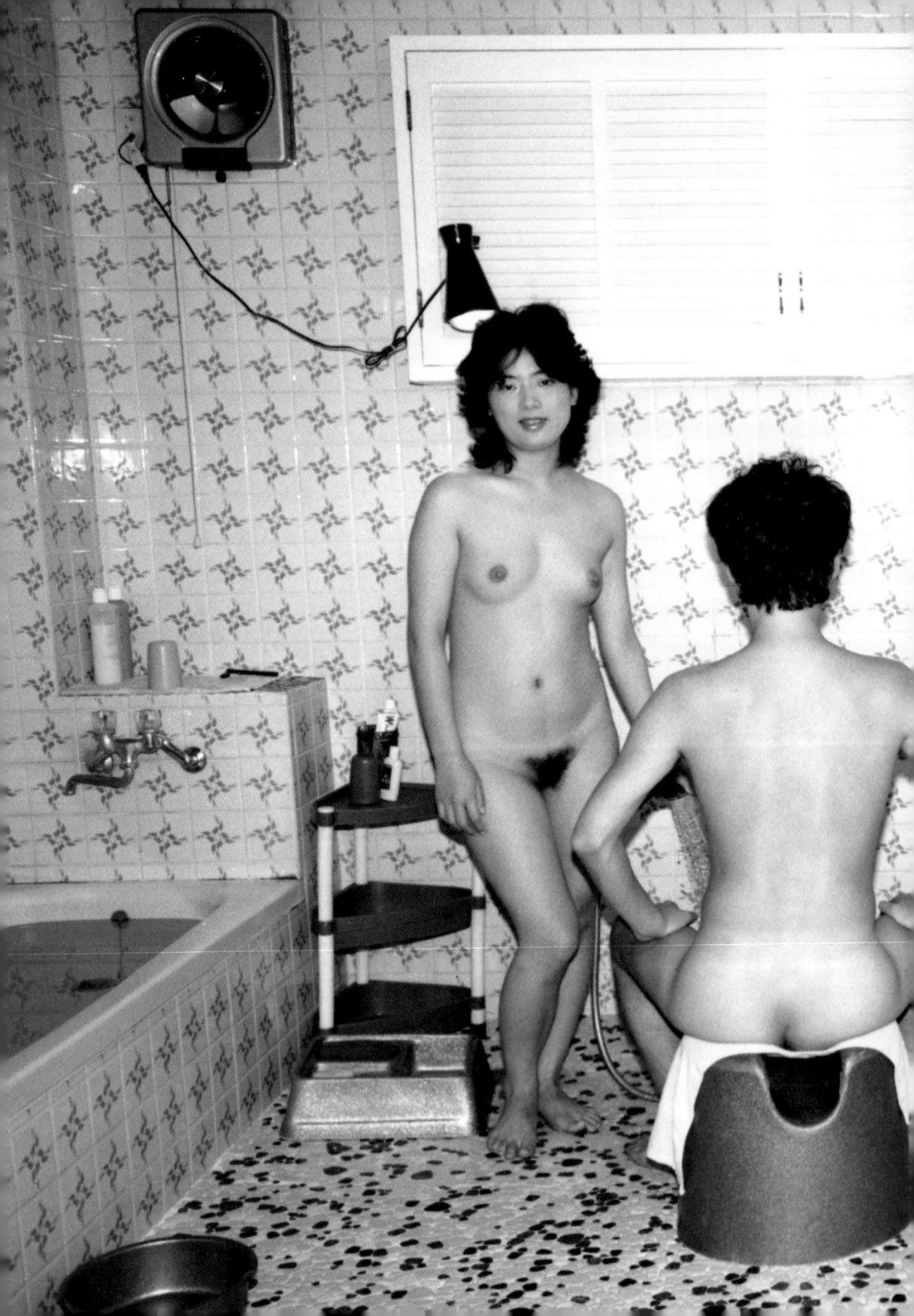

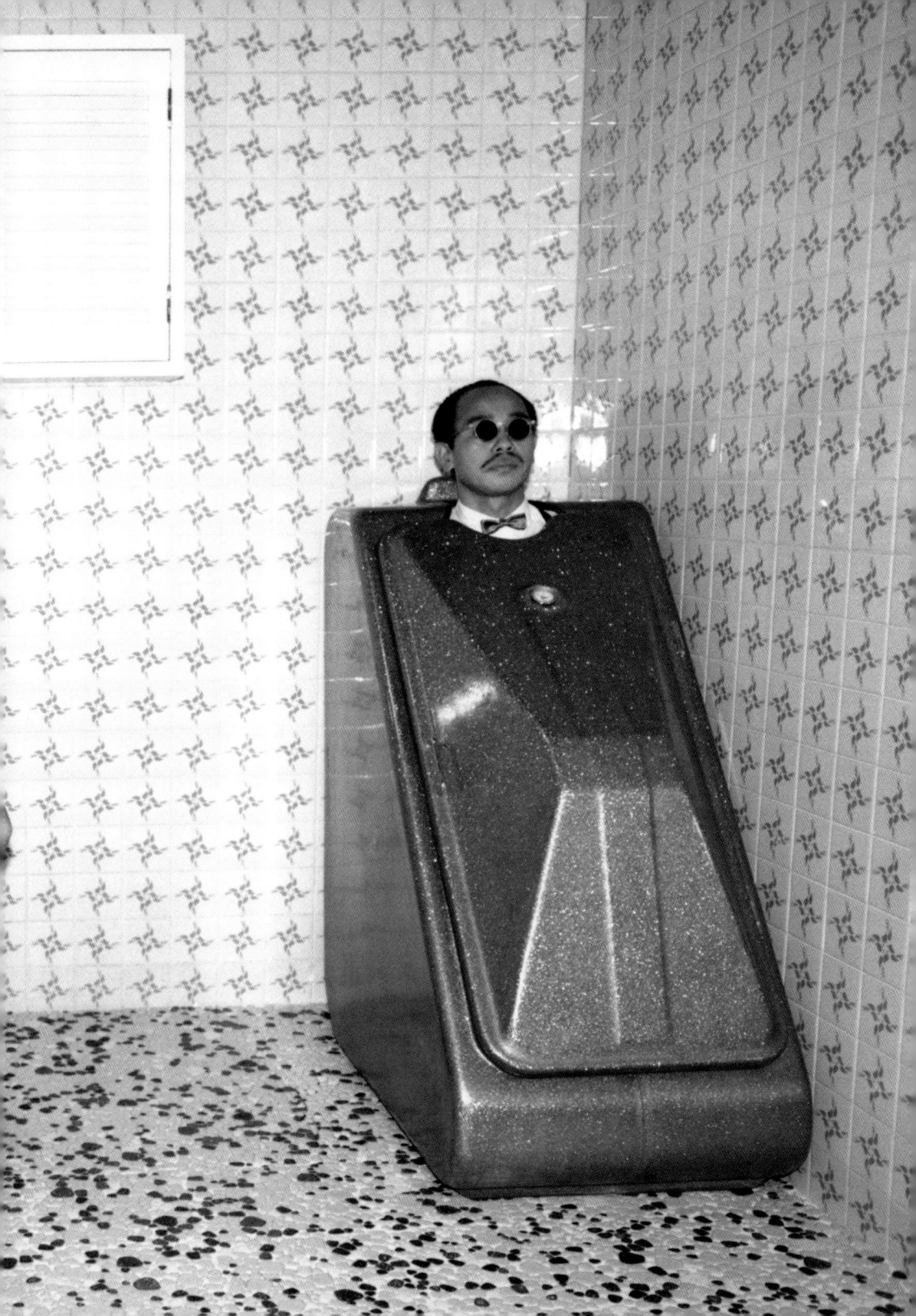

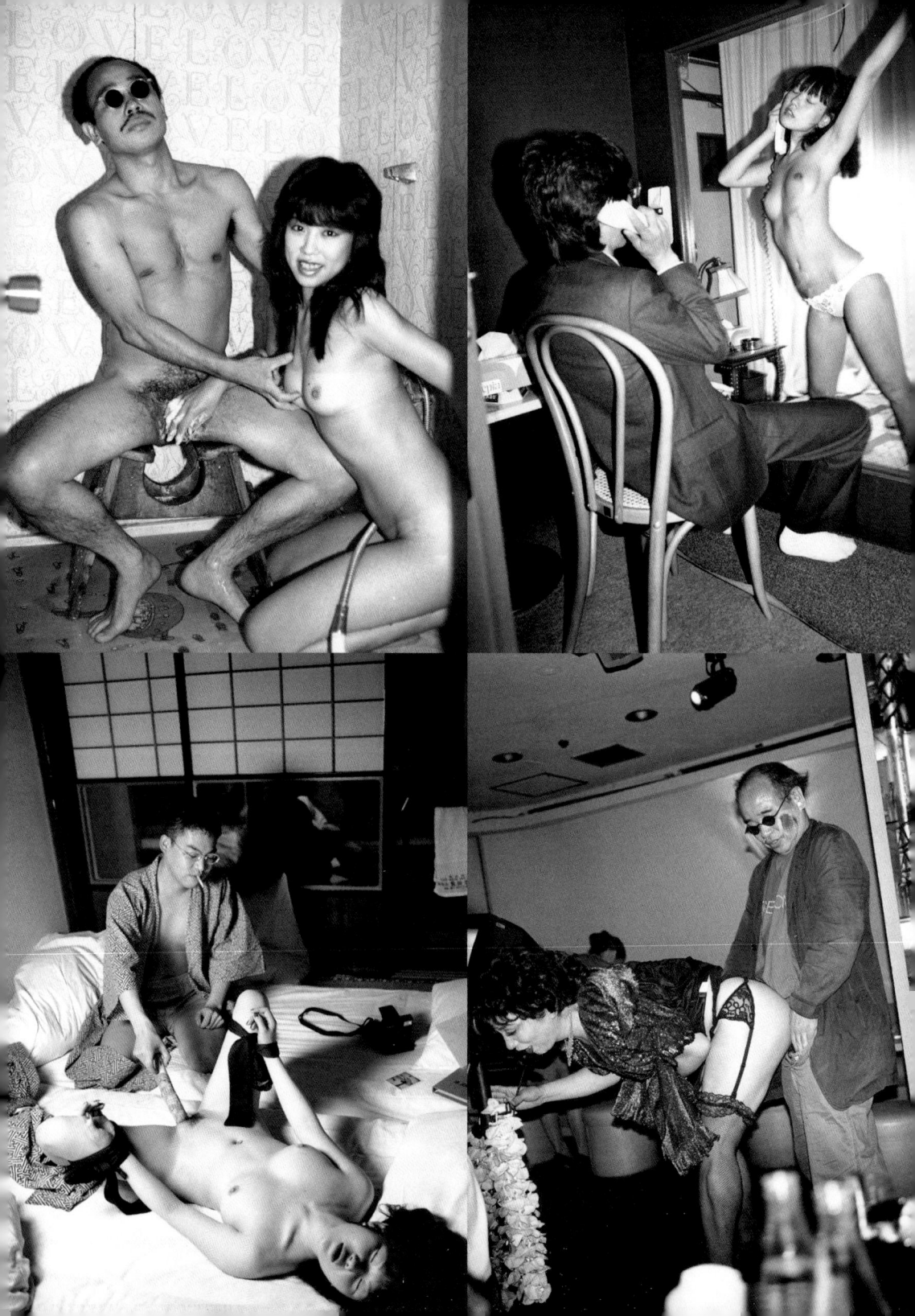

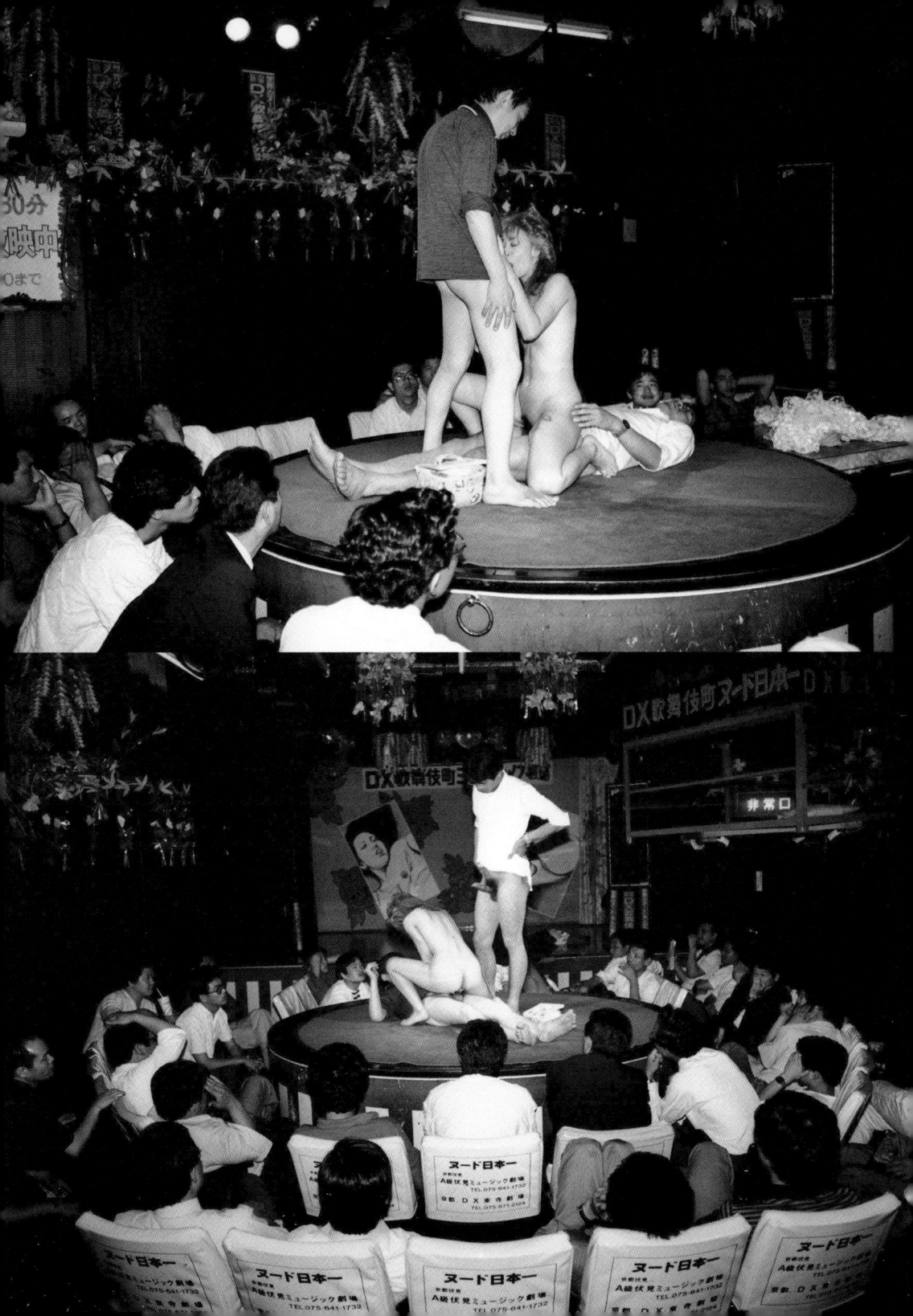

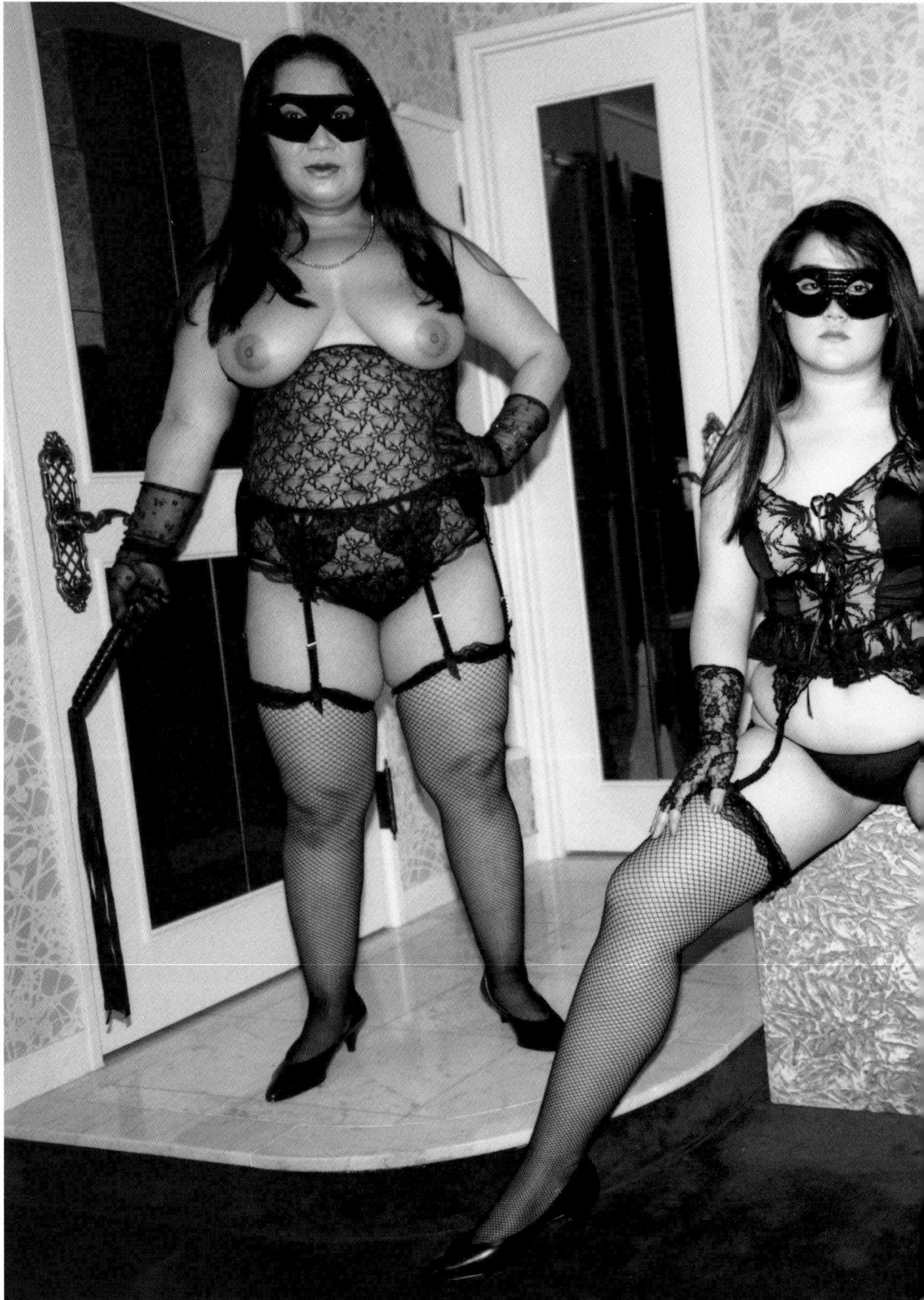

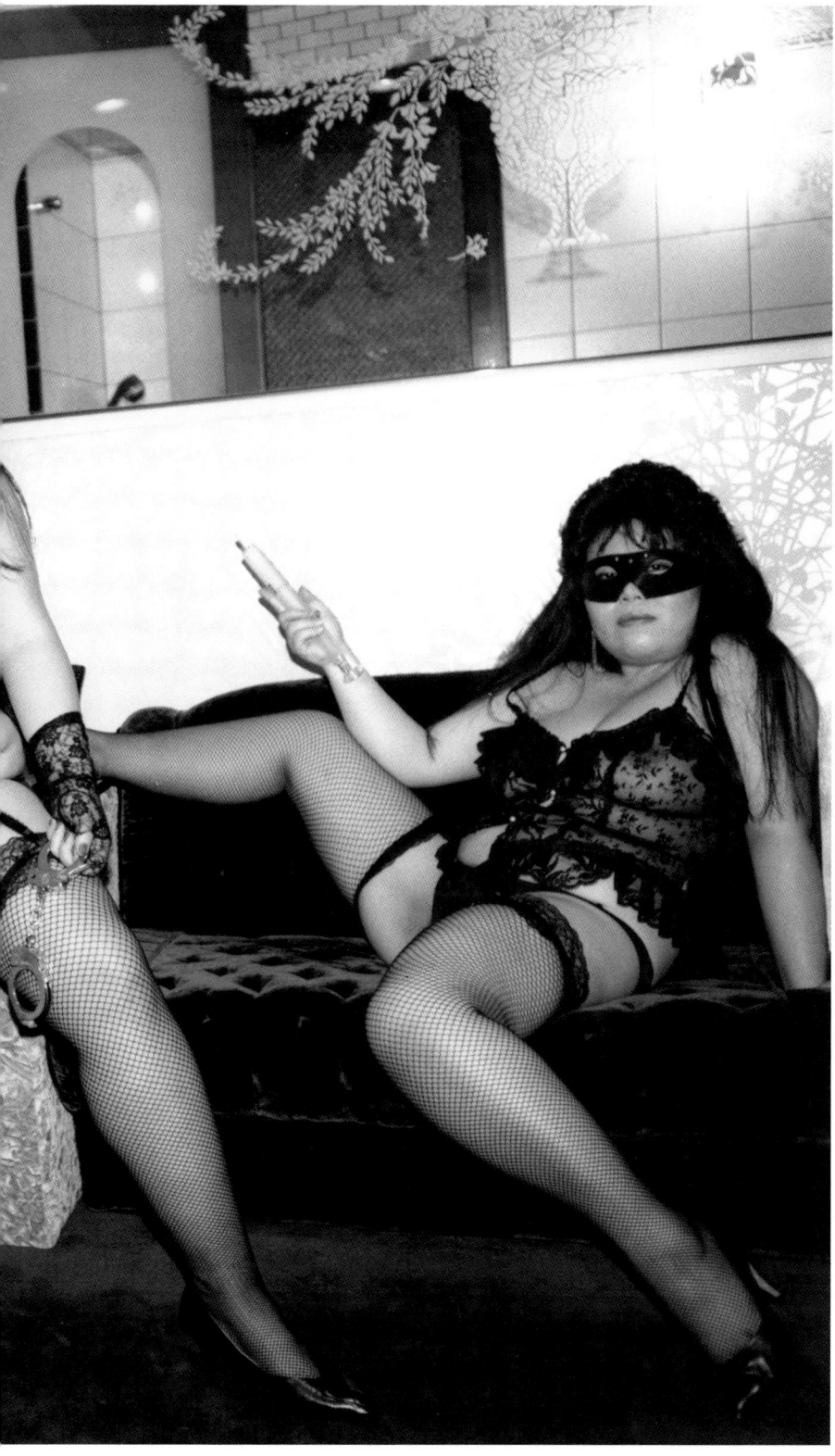

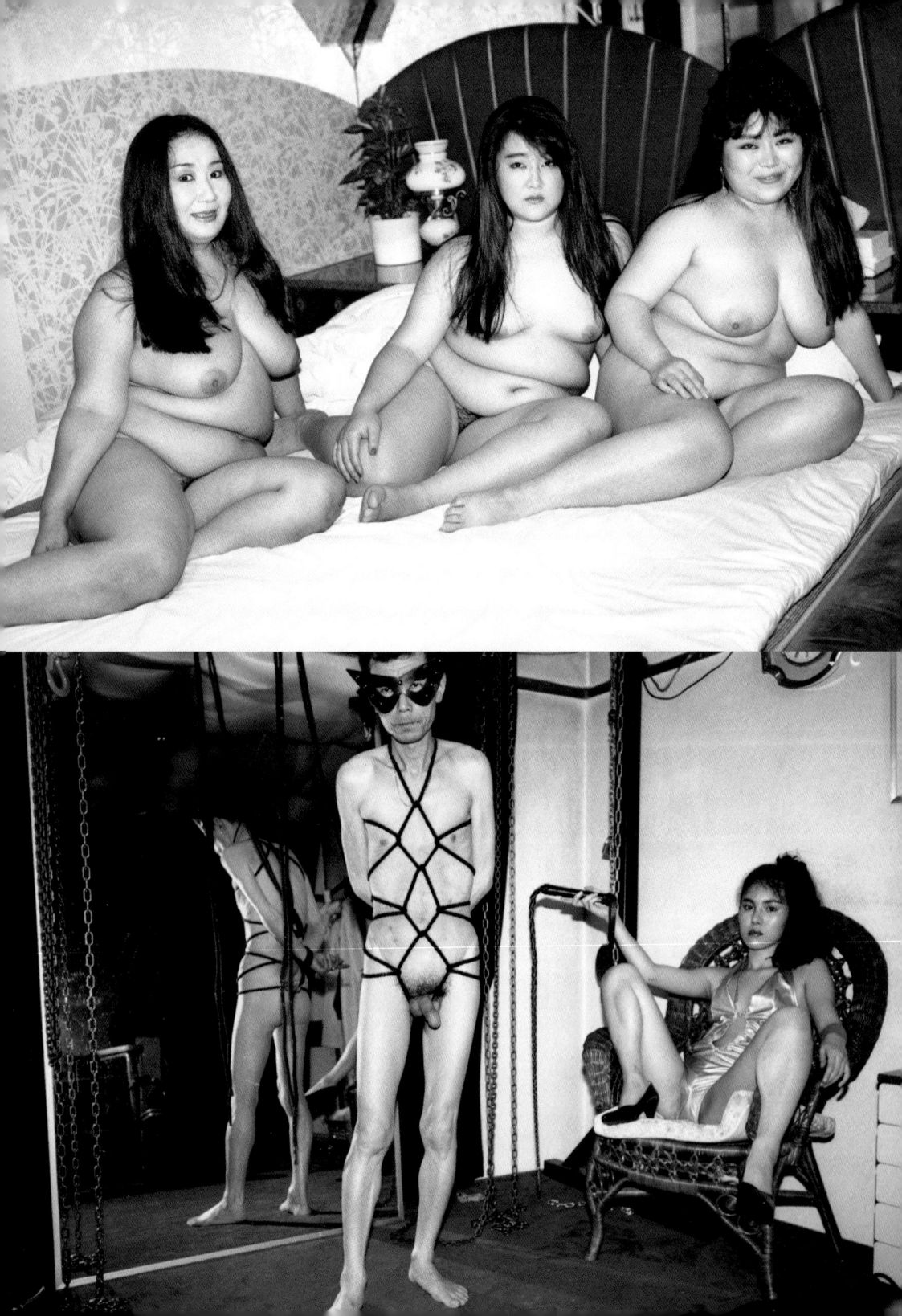

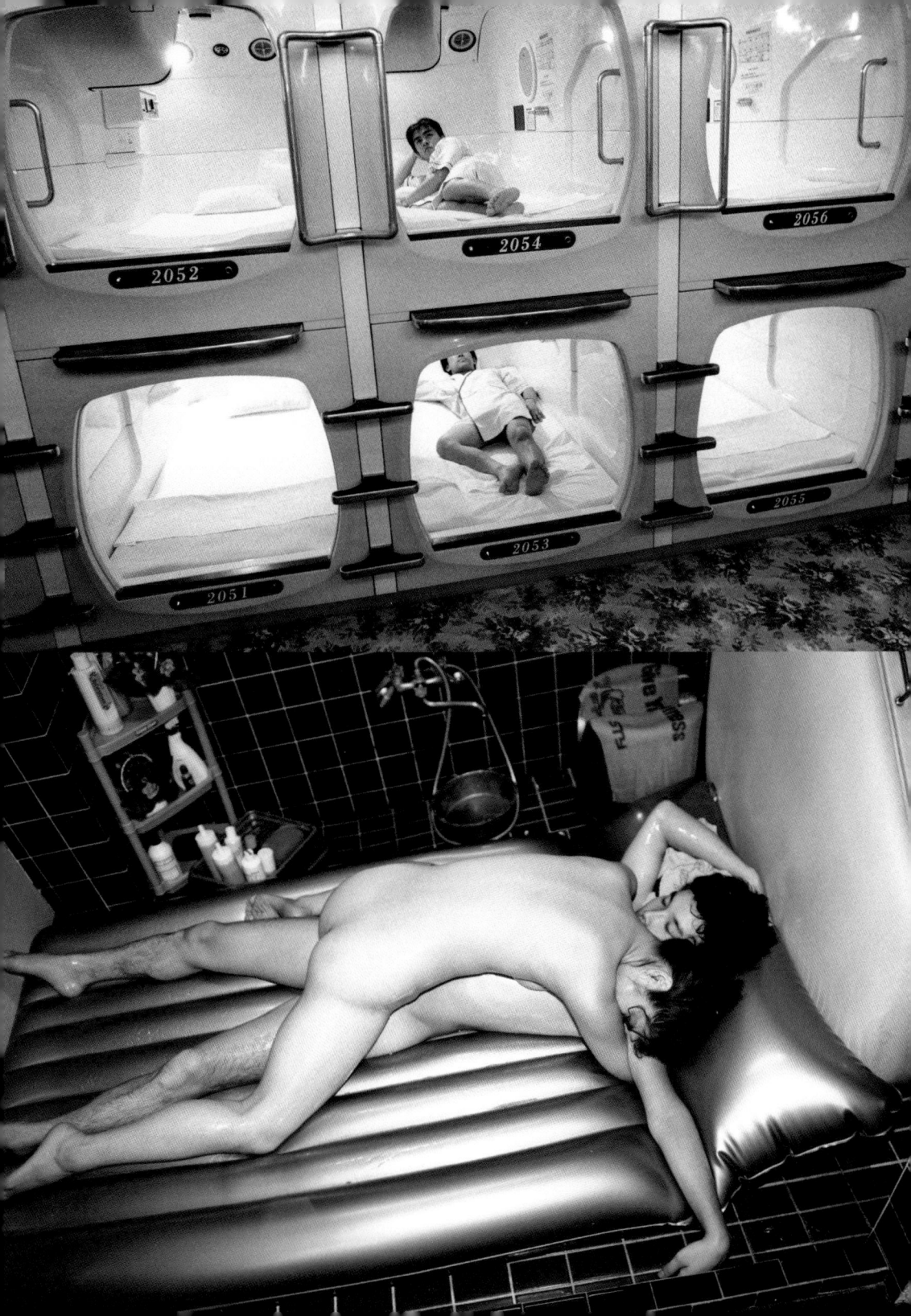

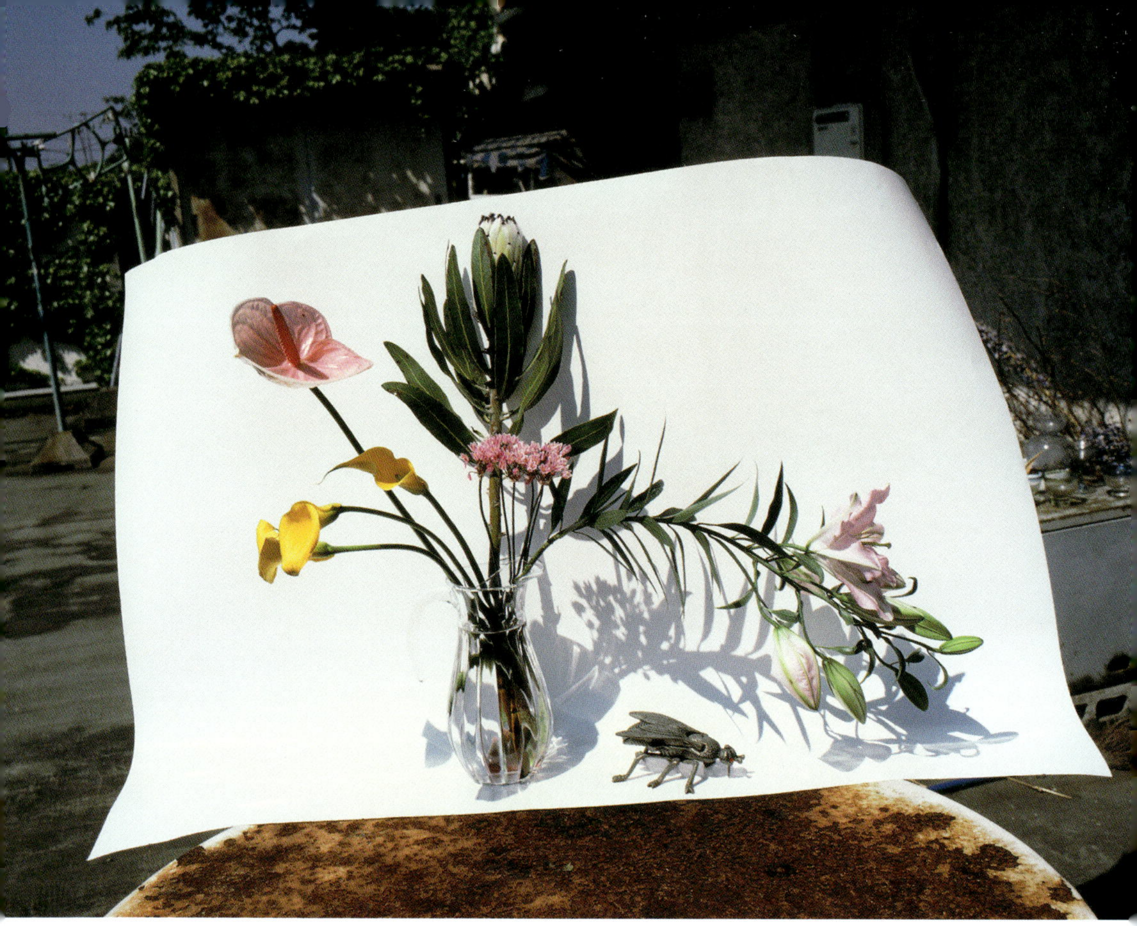

Sensual Flowers

花淫

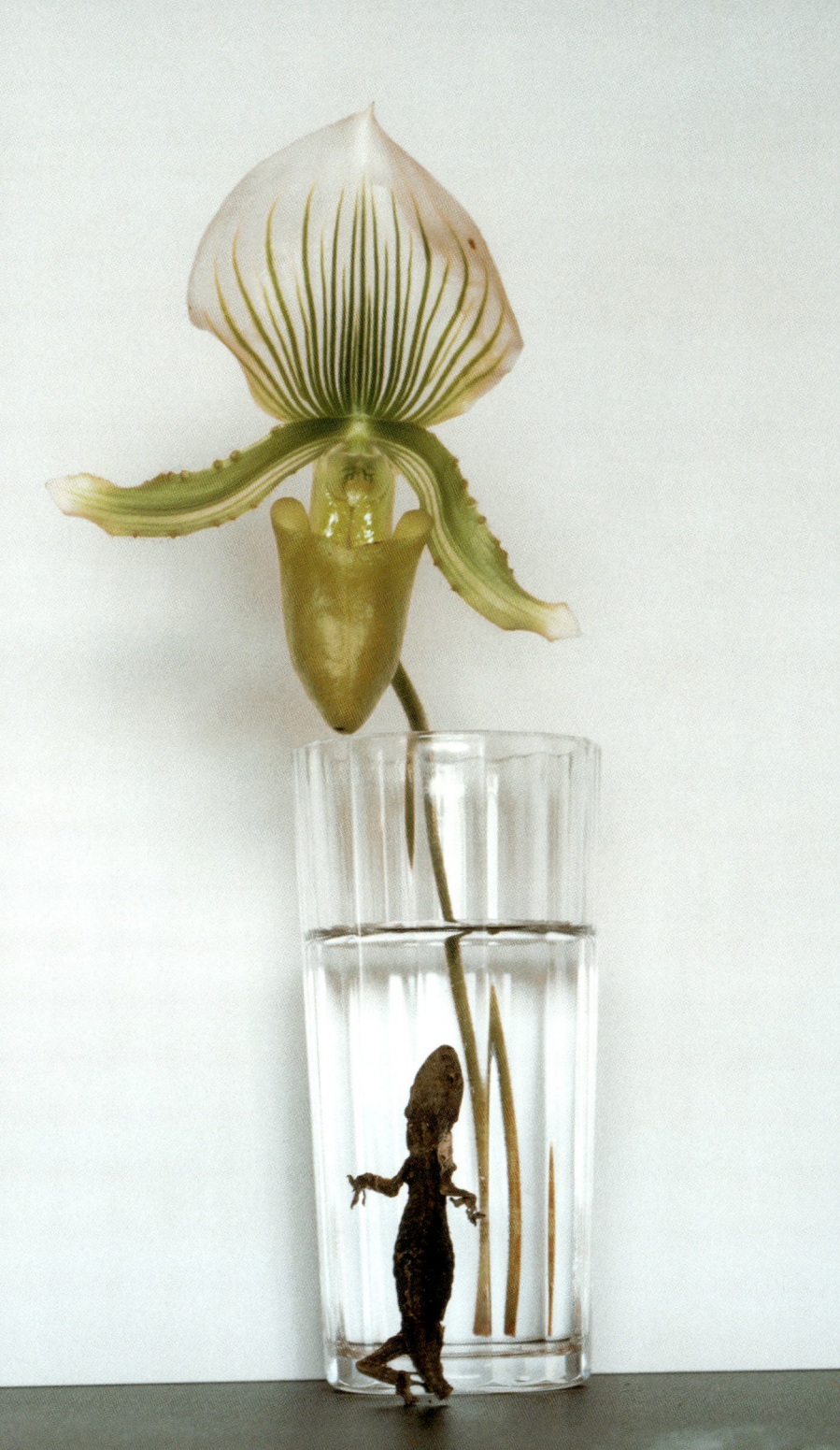

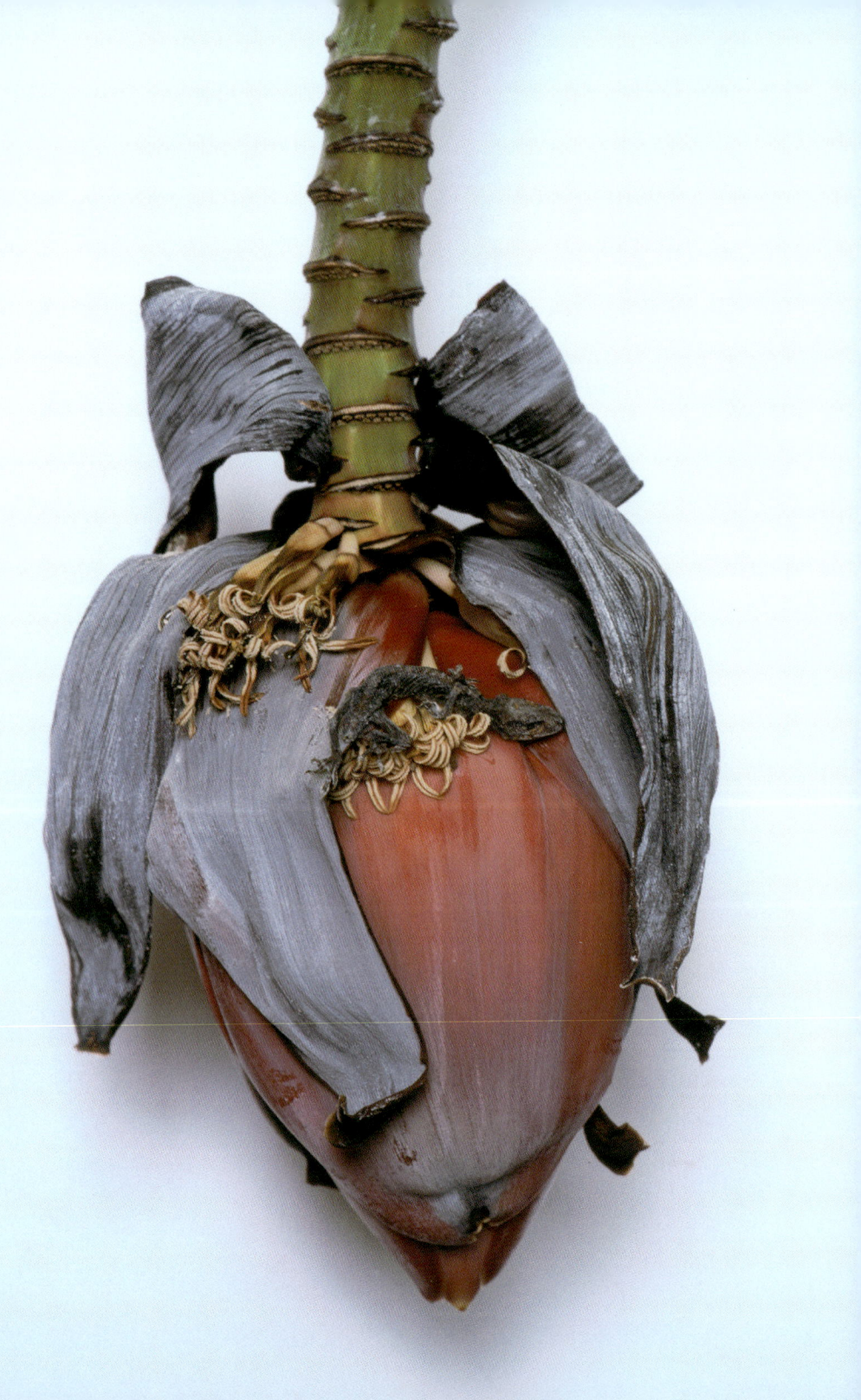

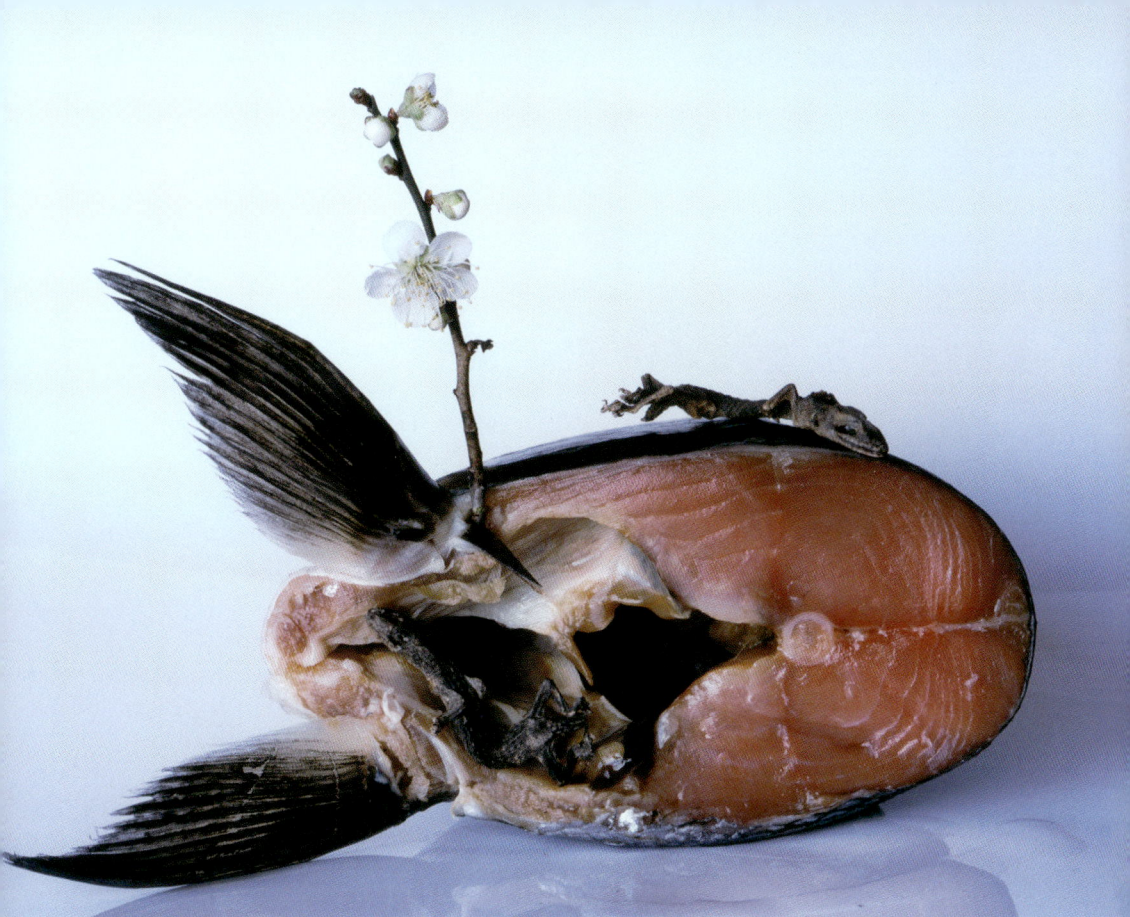

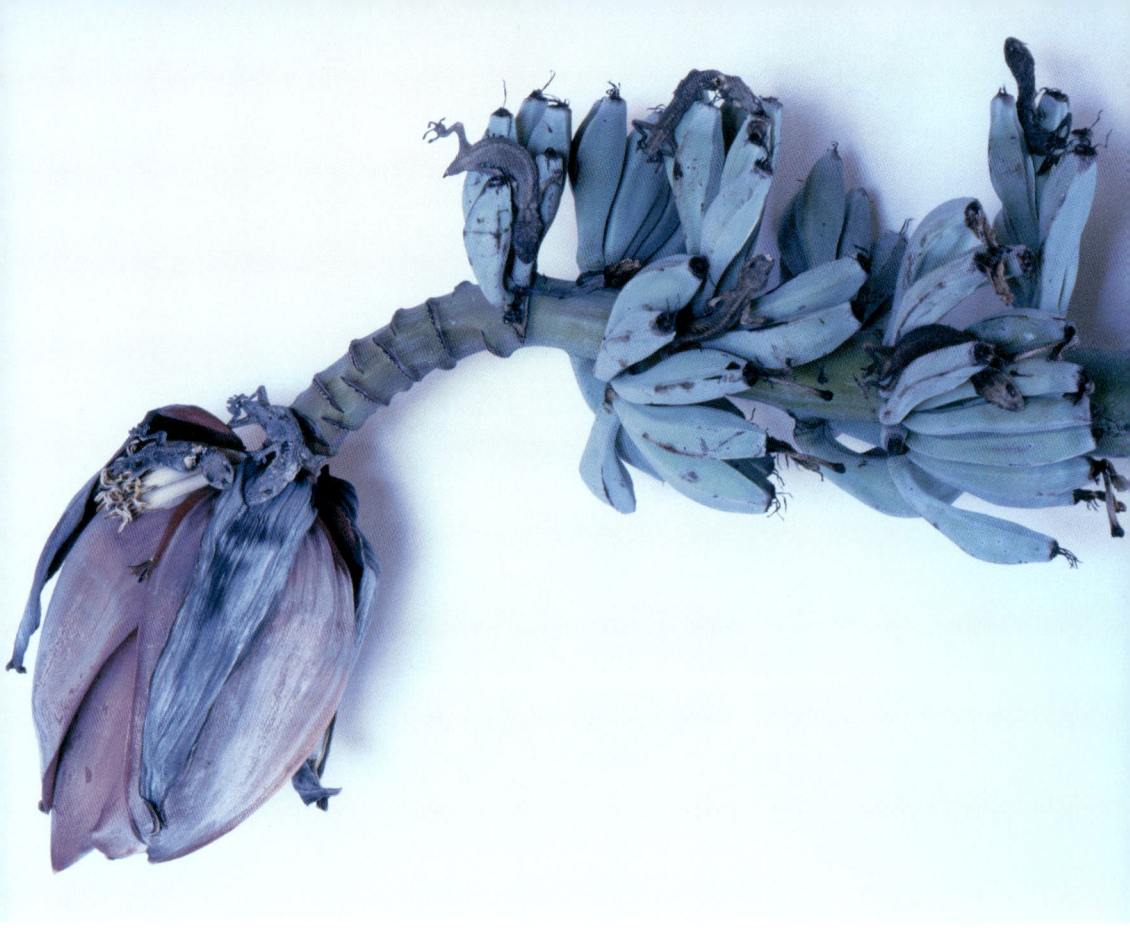

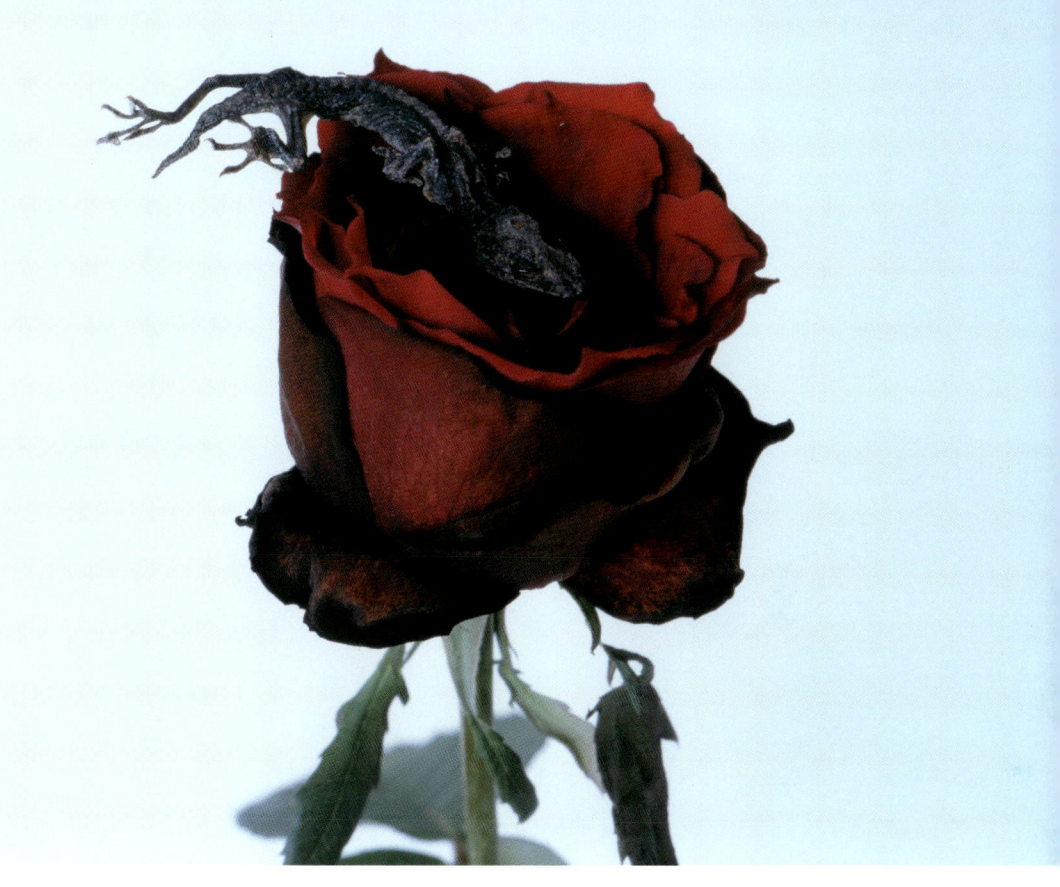

Erotos

エロトス

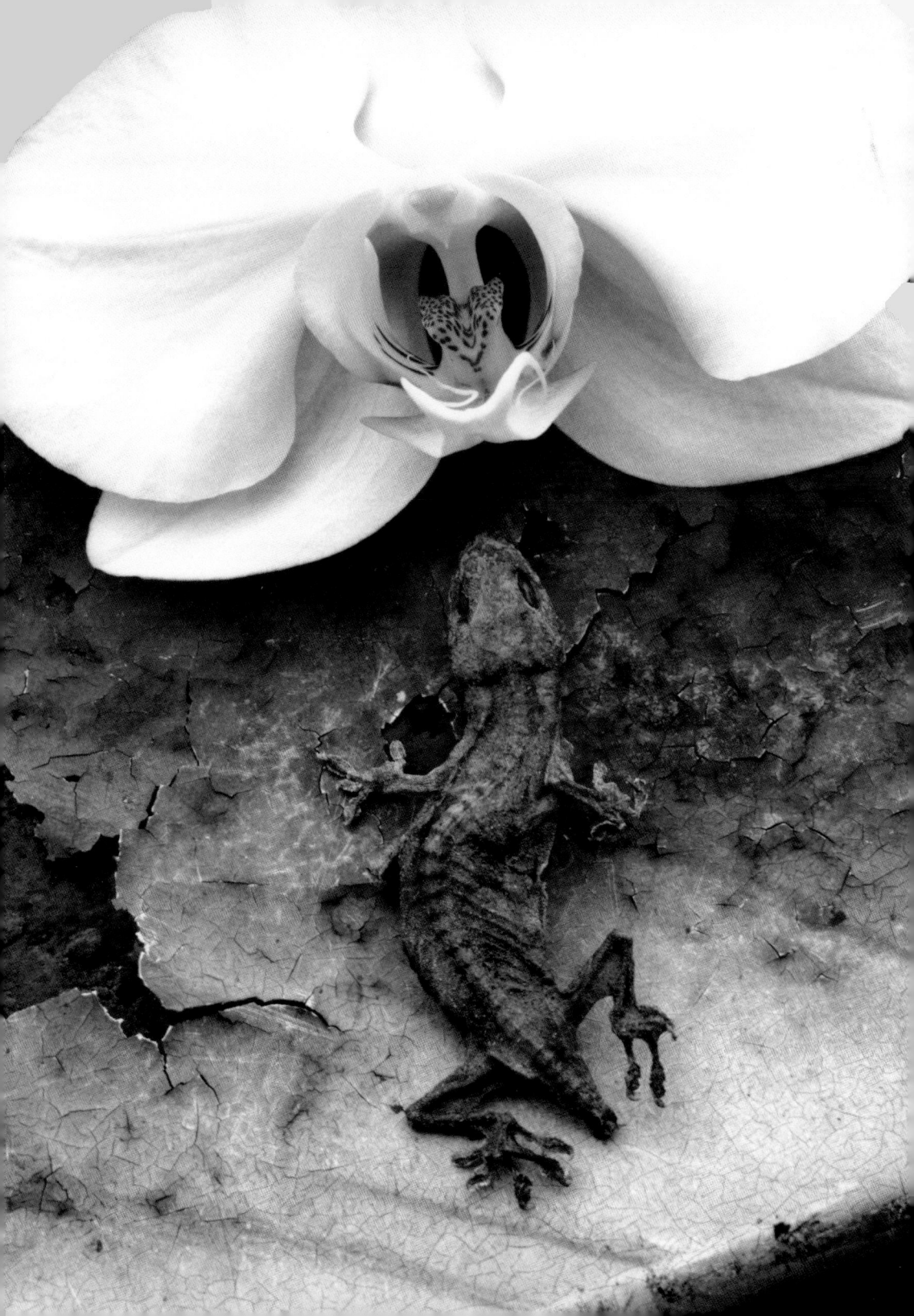

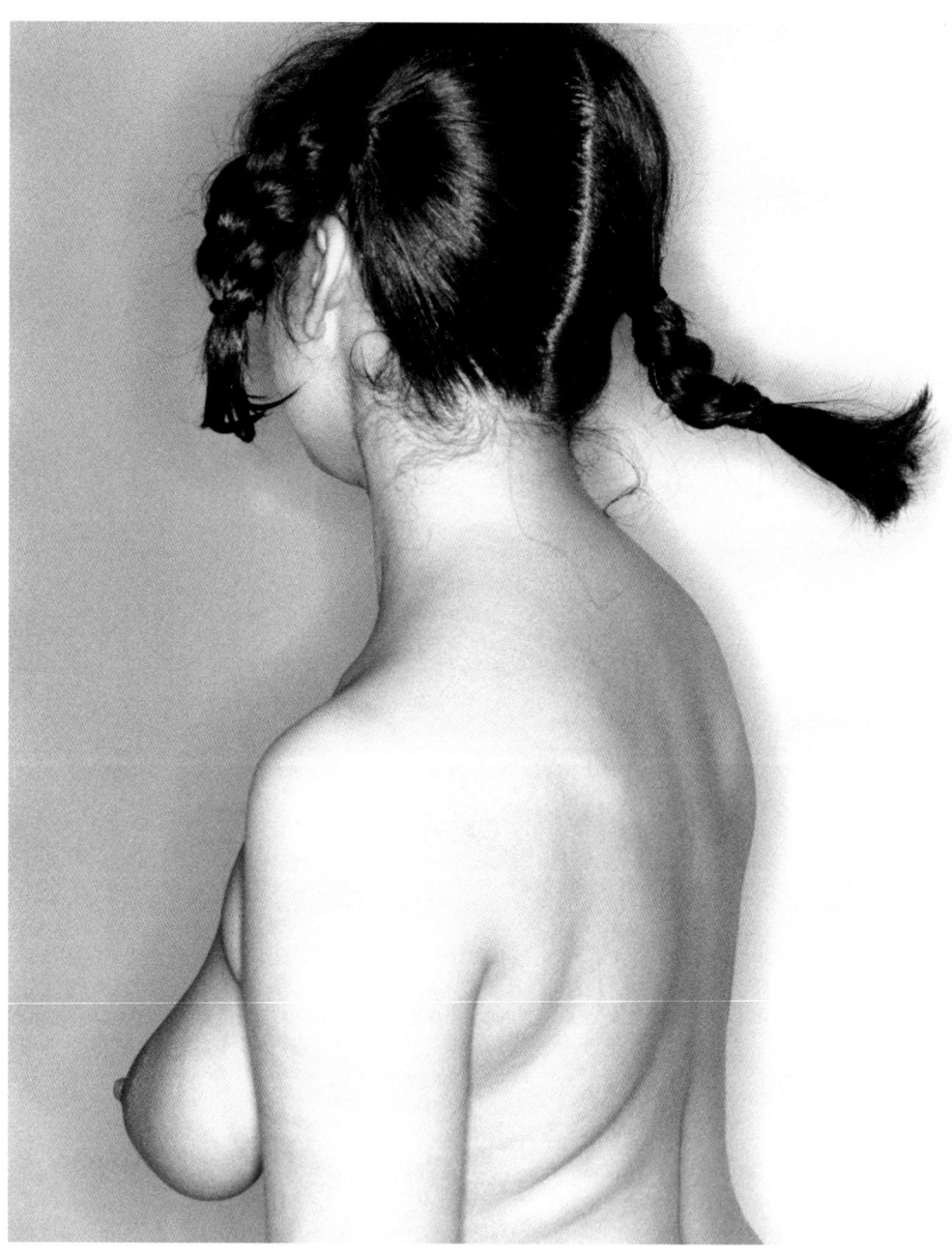

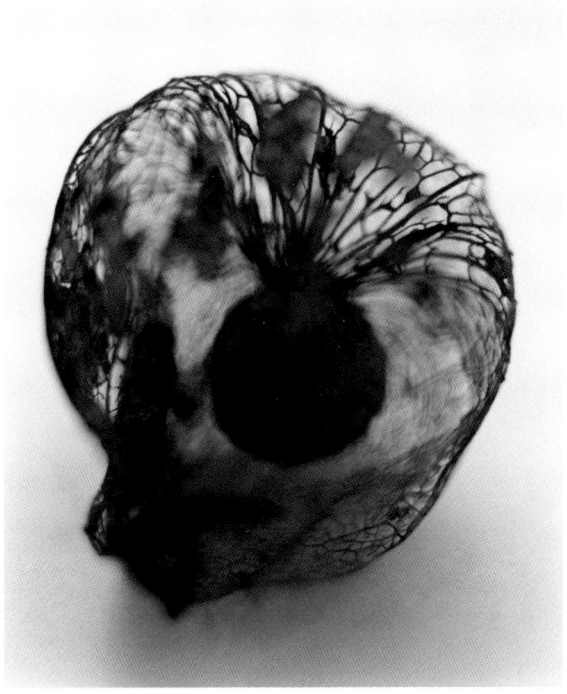

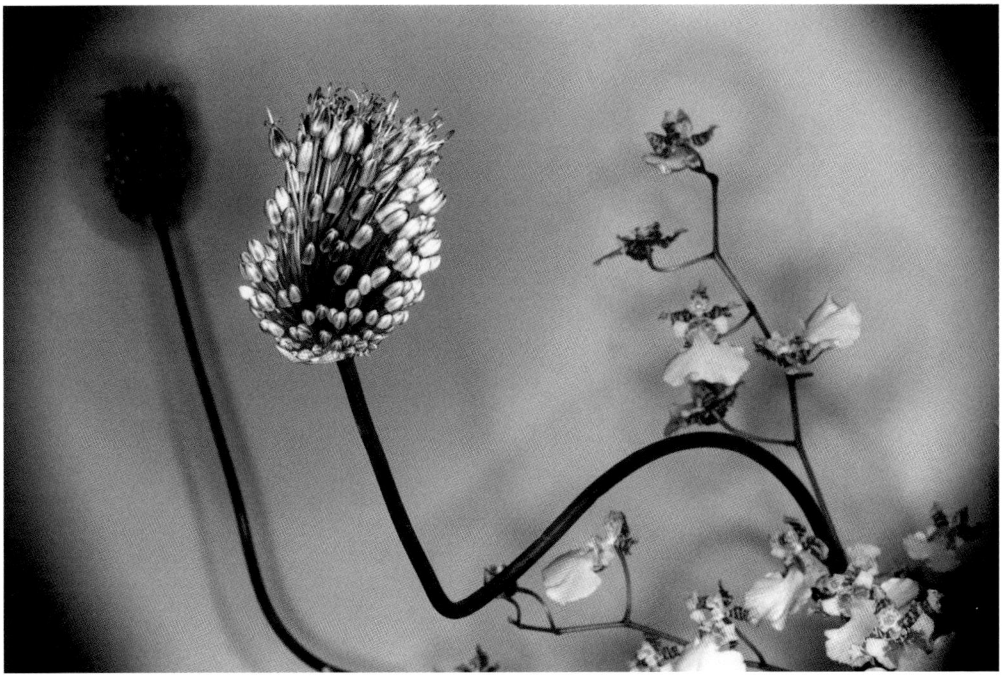

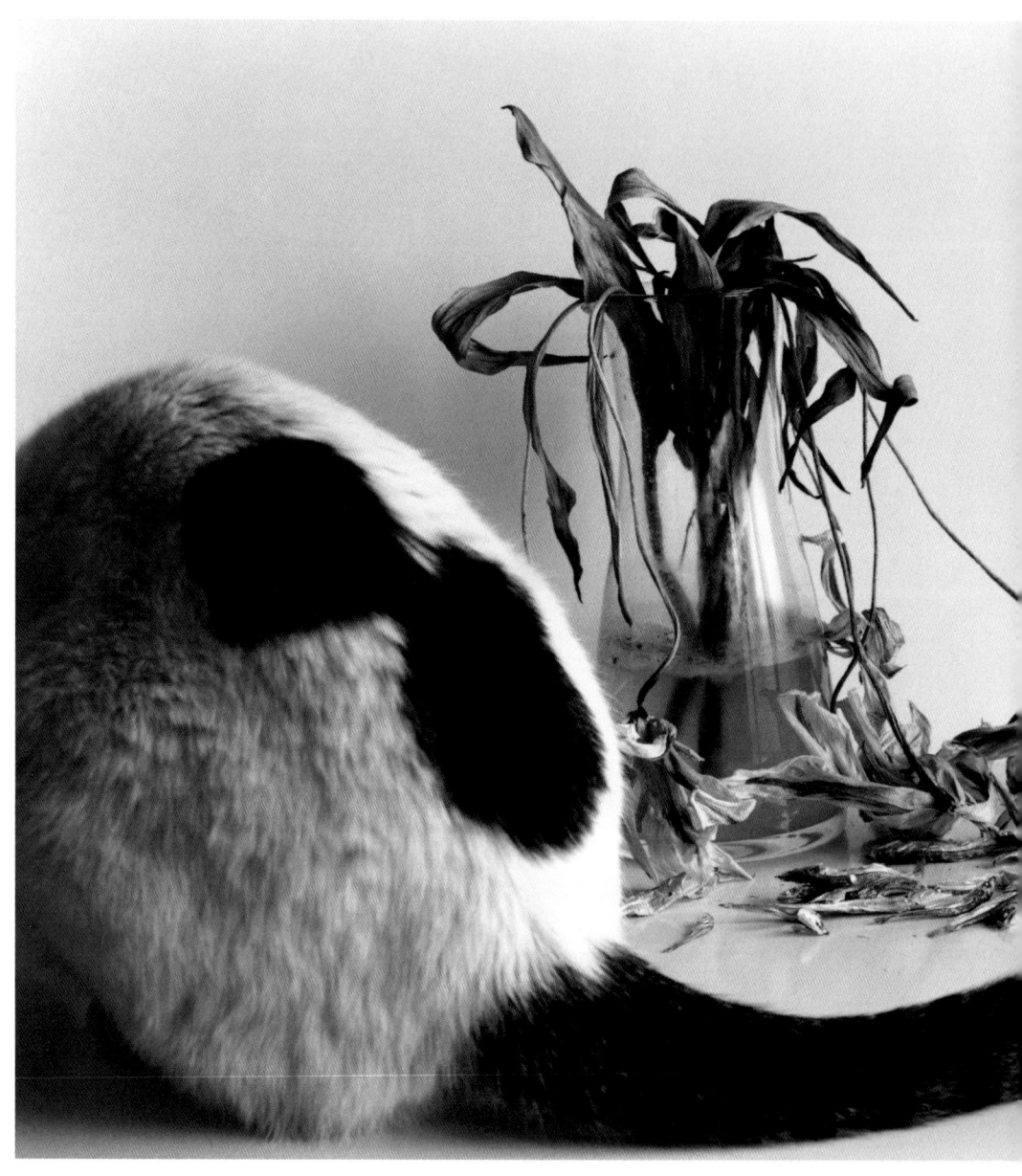

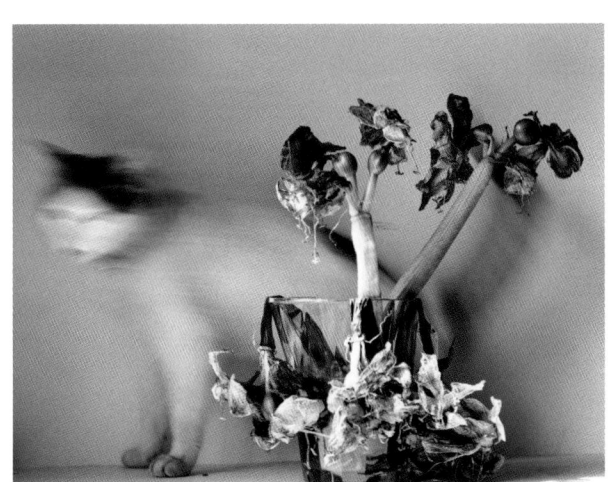

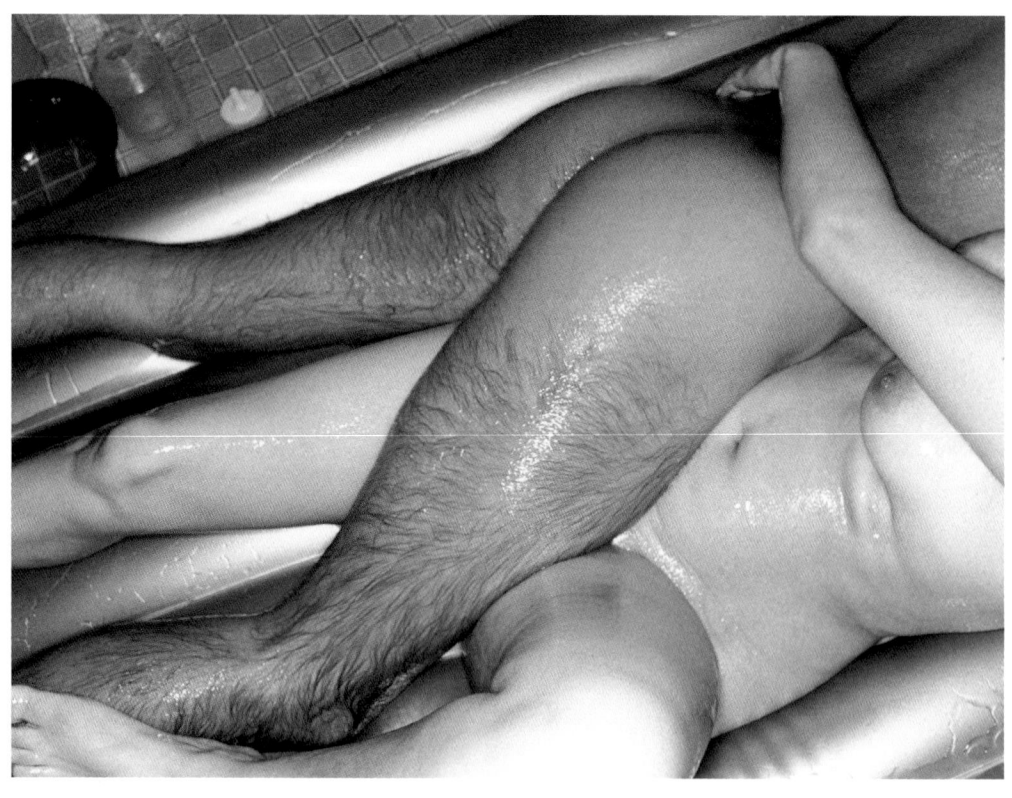

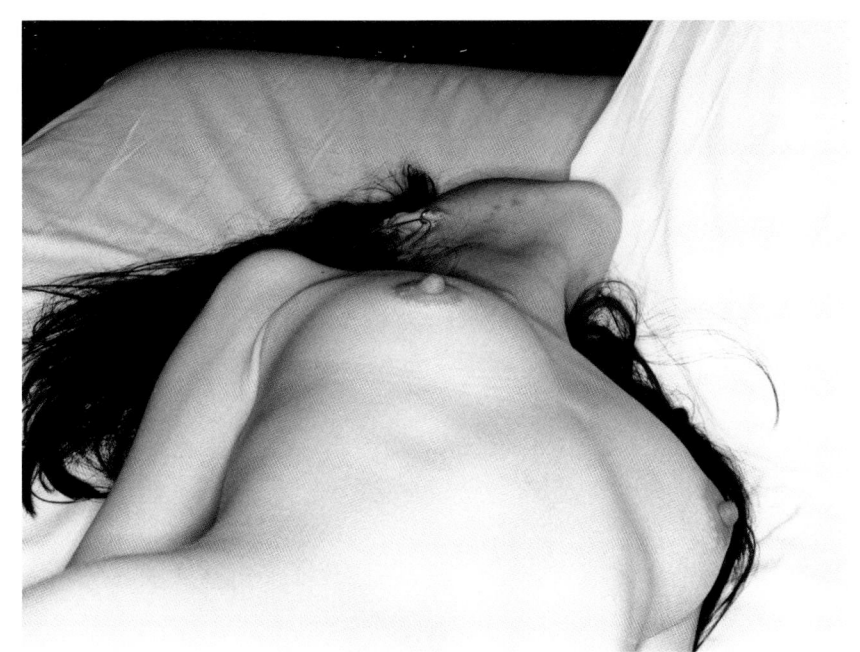

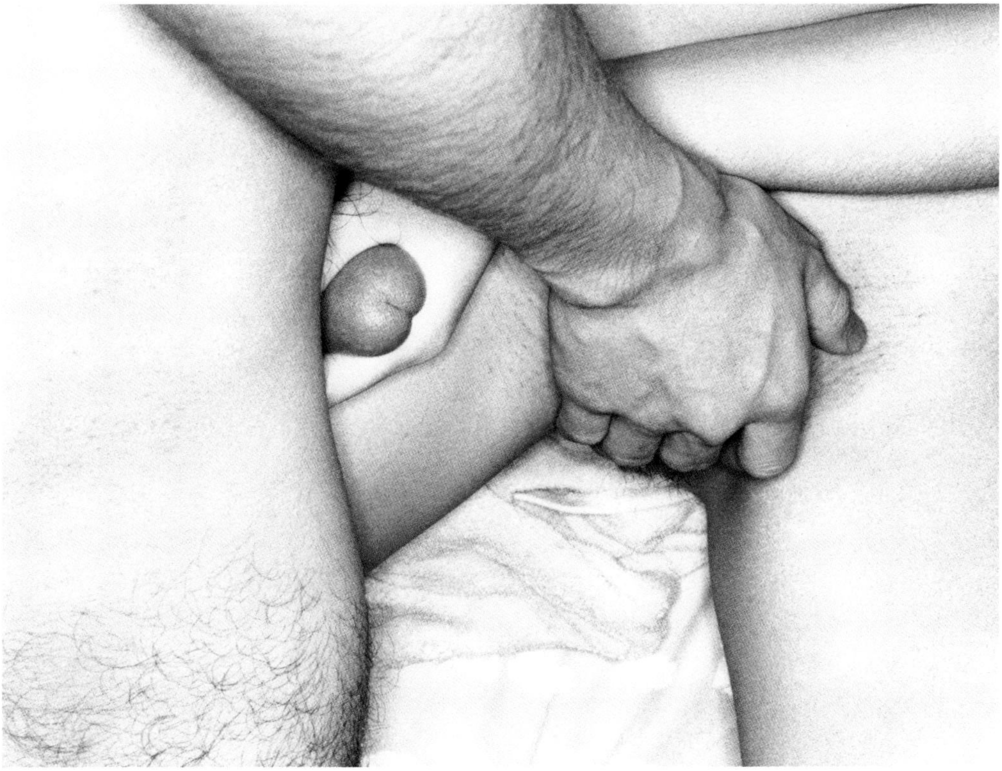

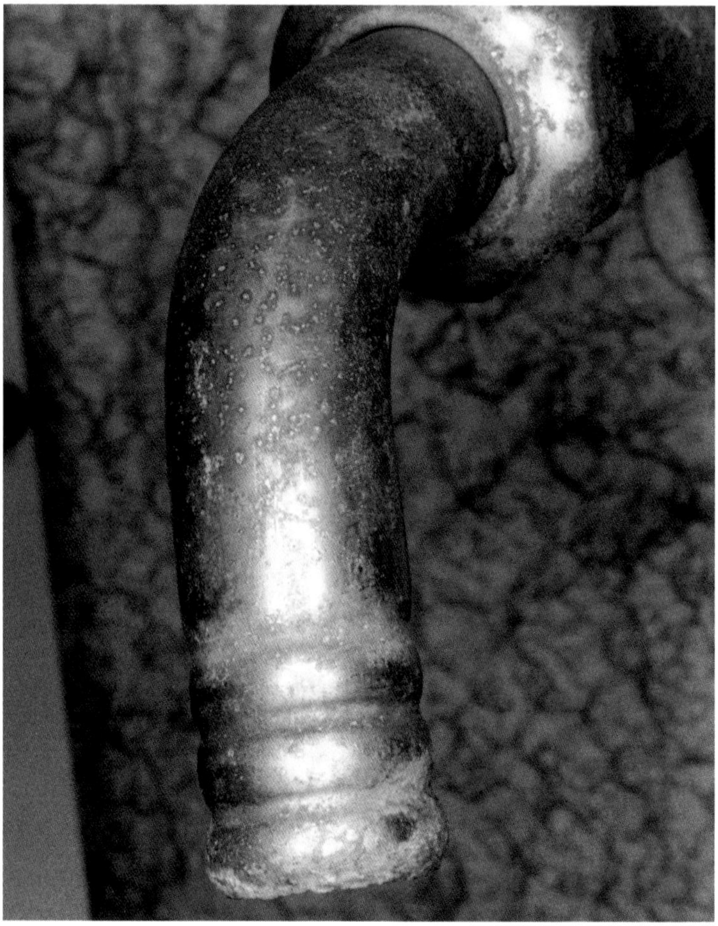

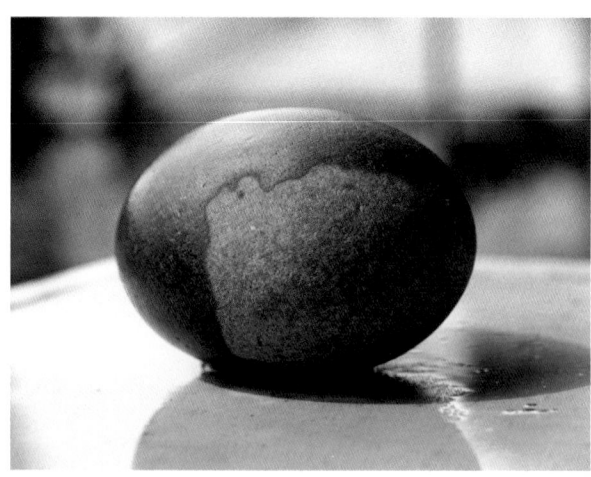

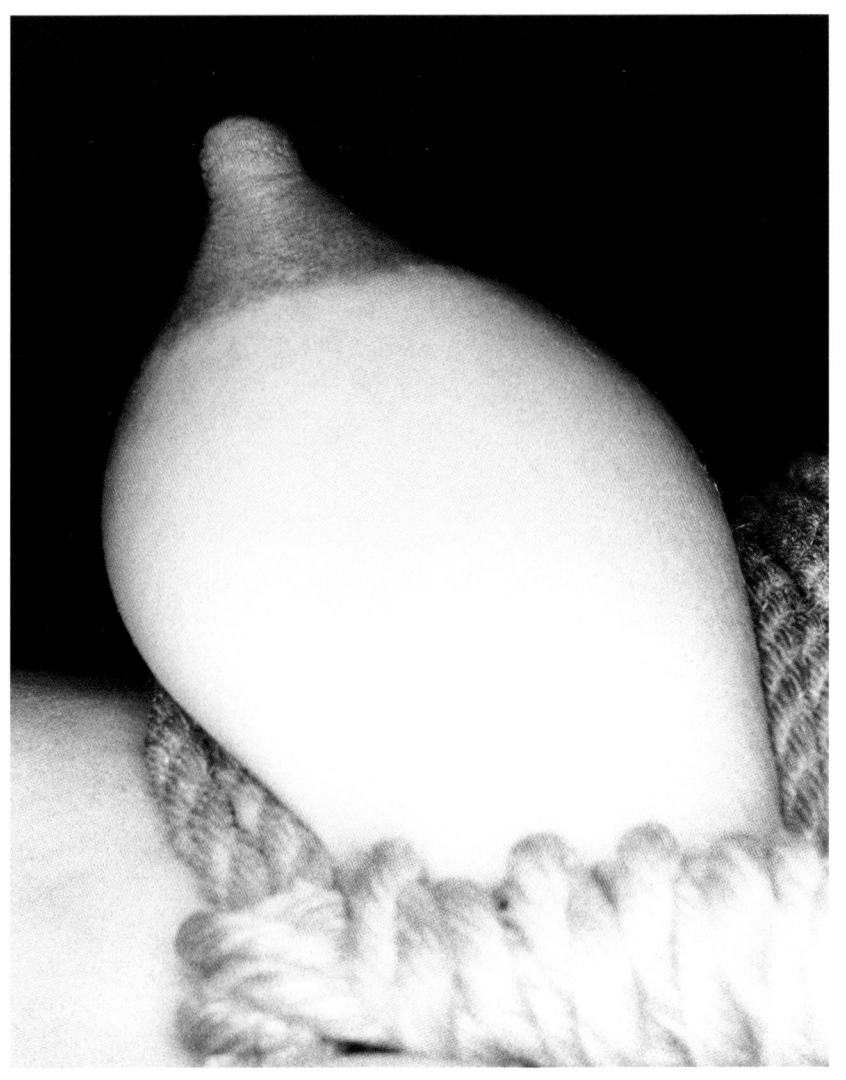

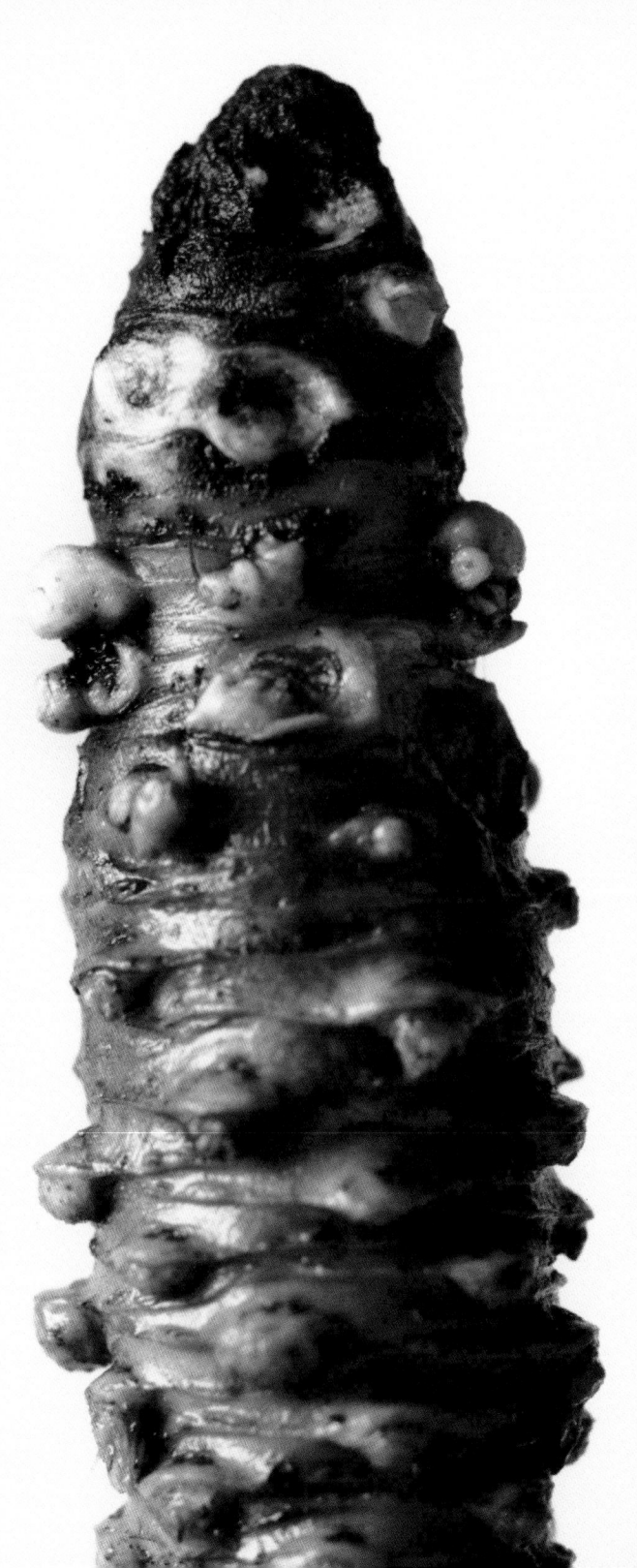

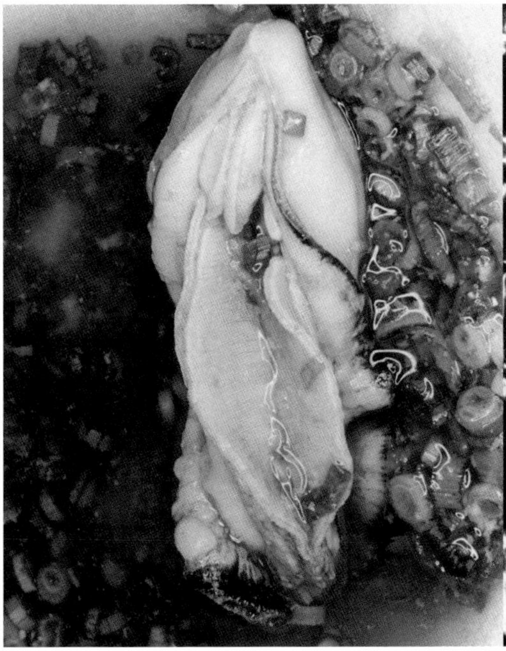

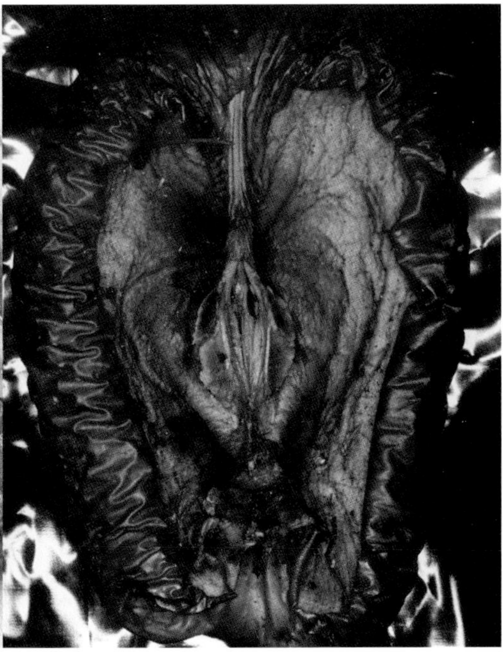

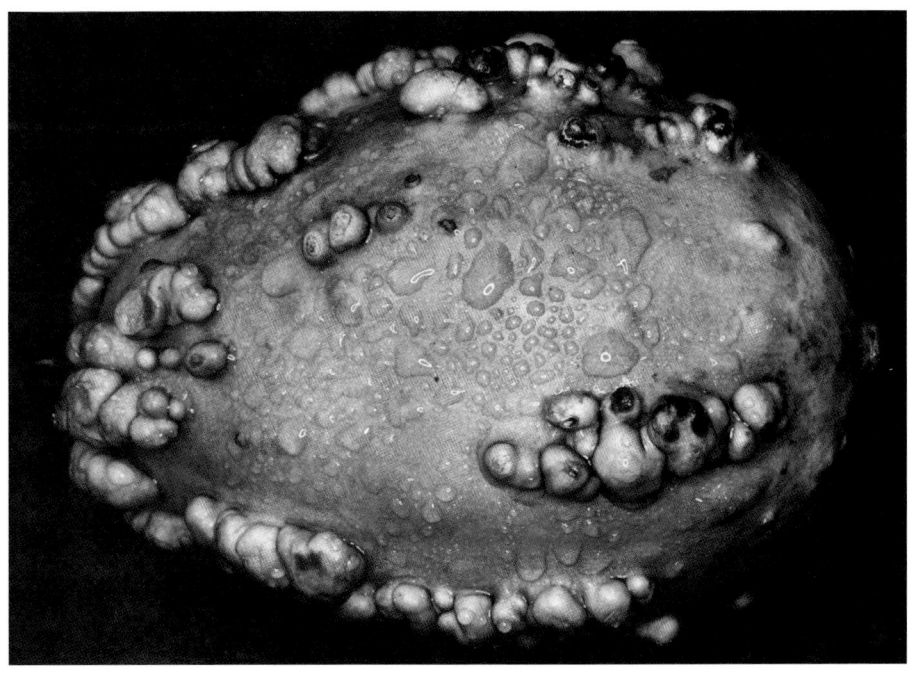

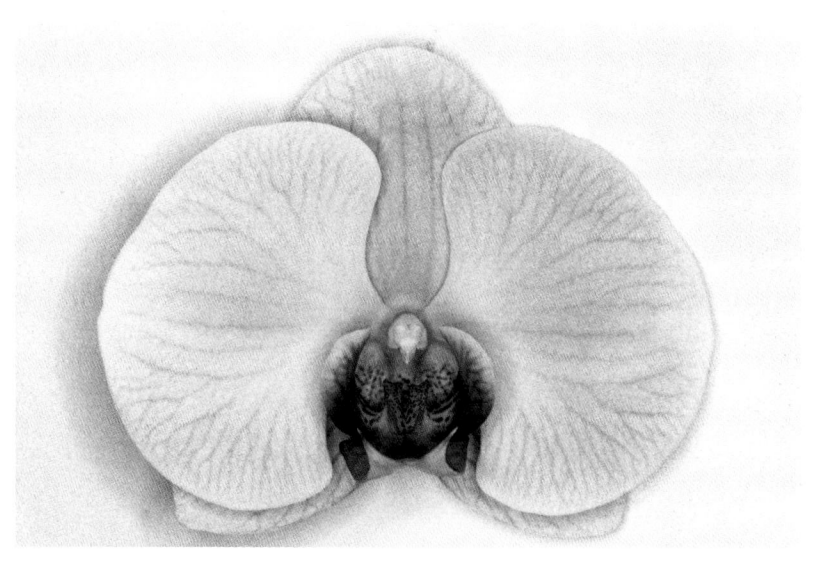

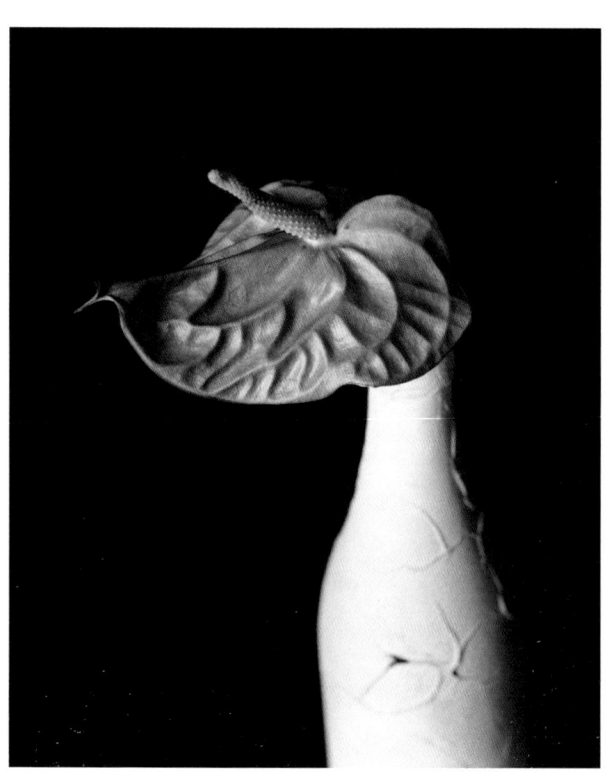

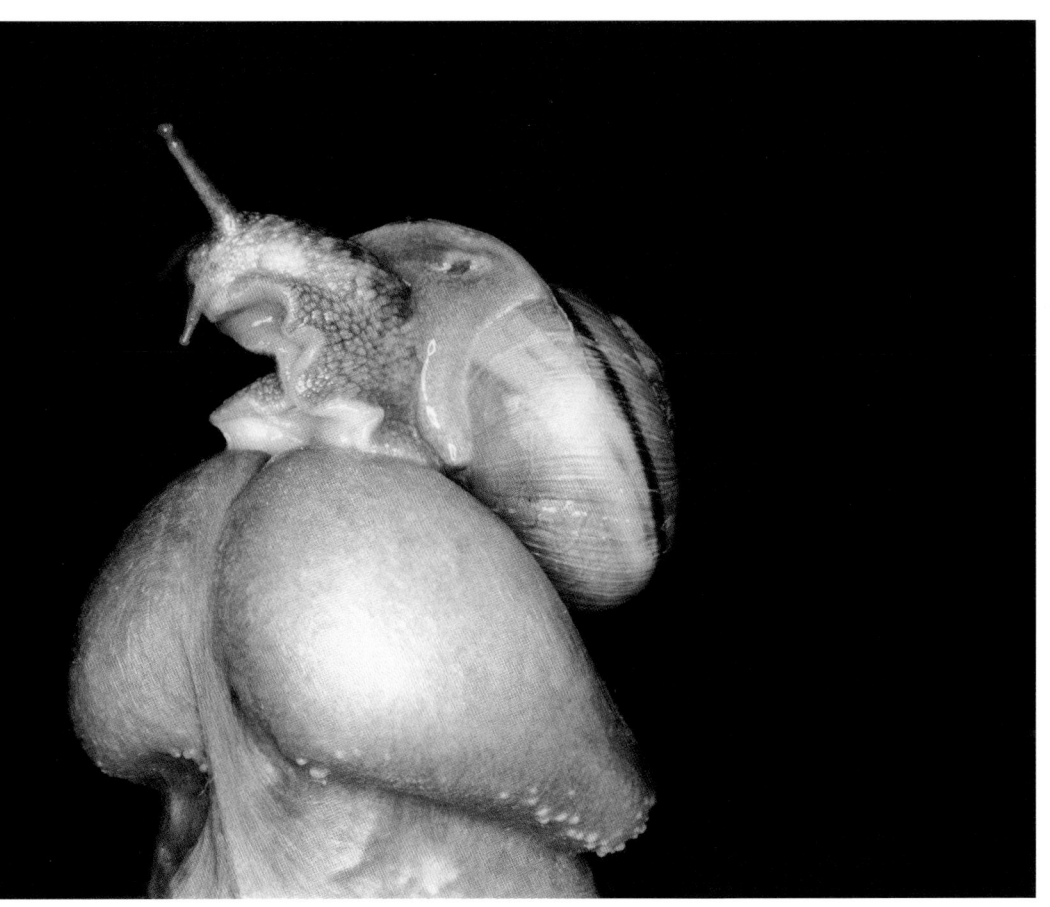

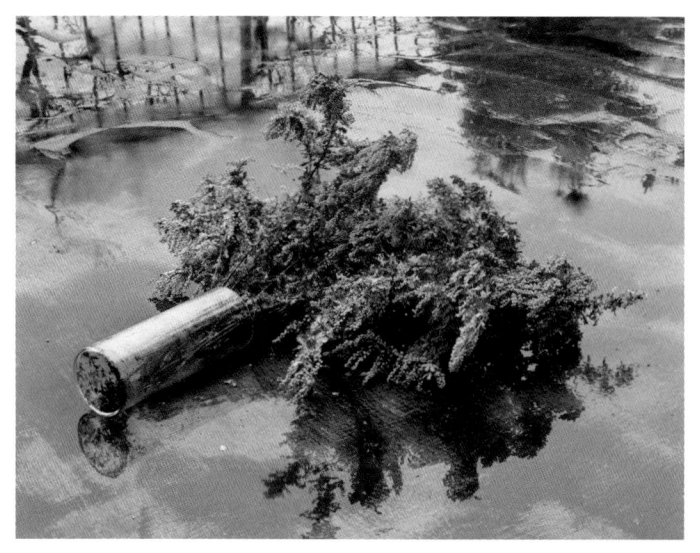

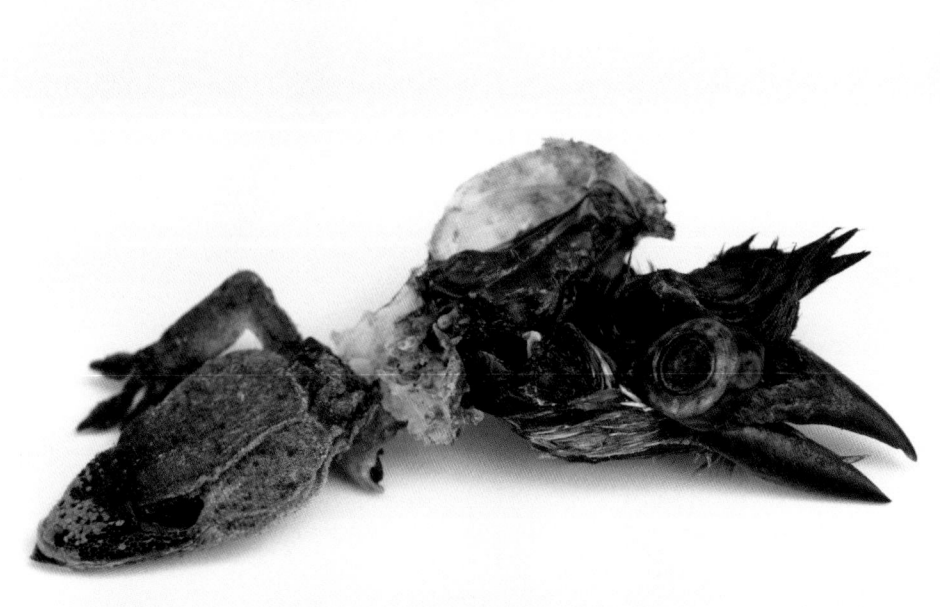

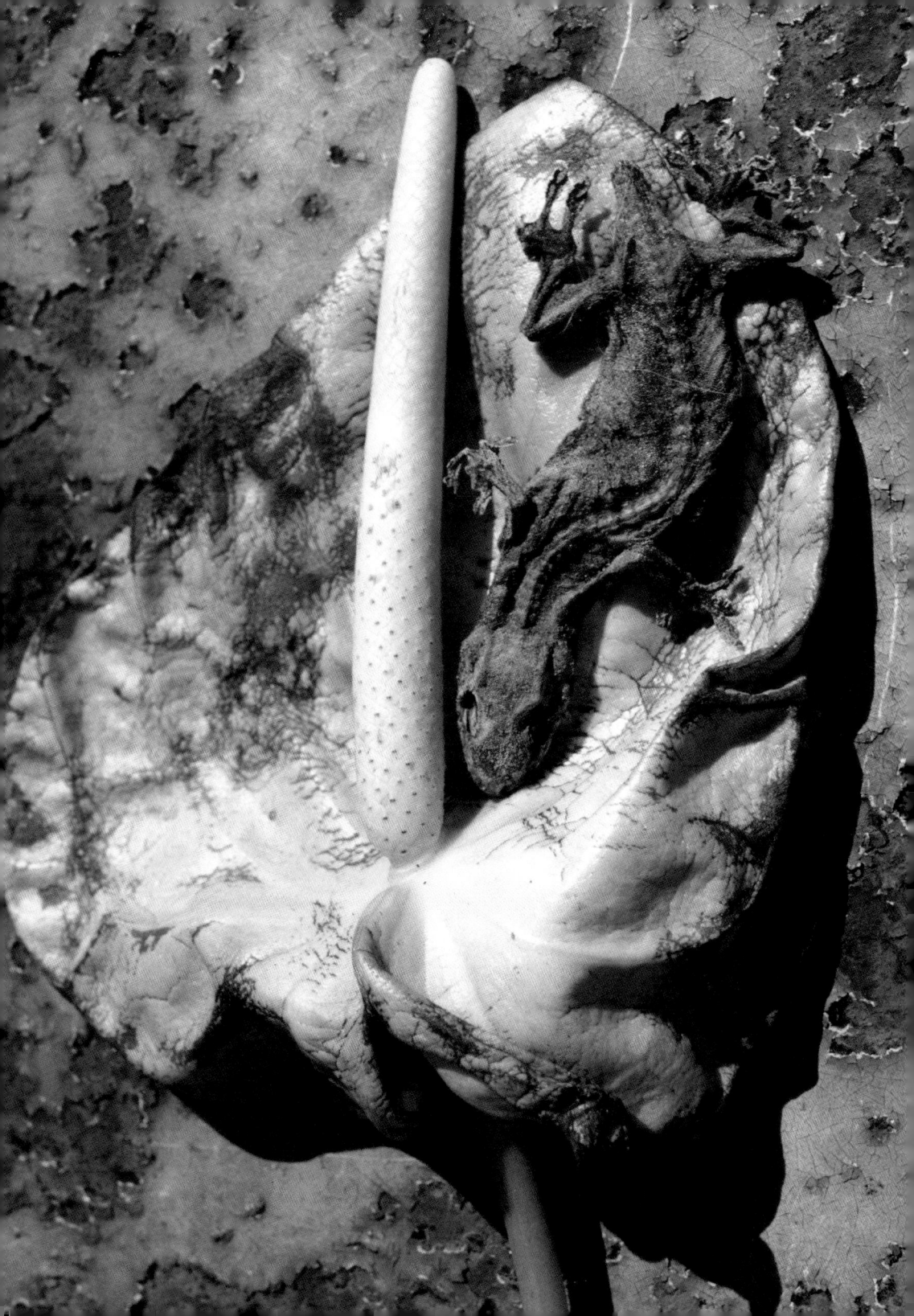

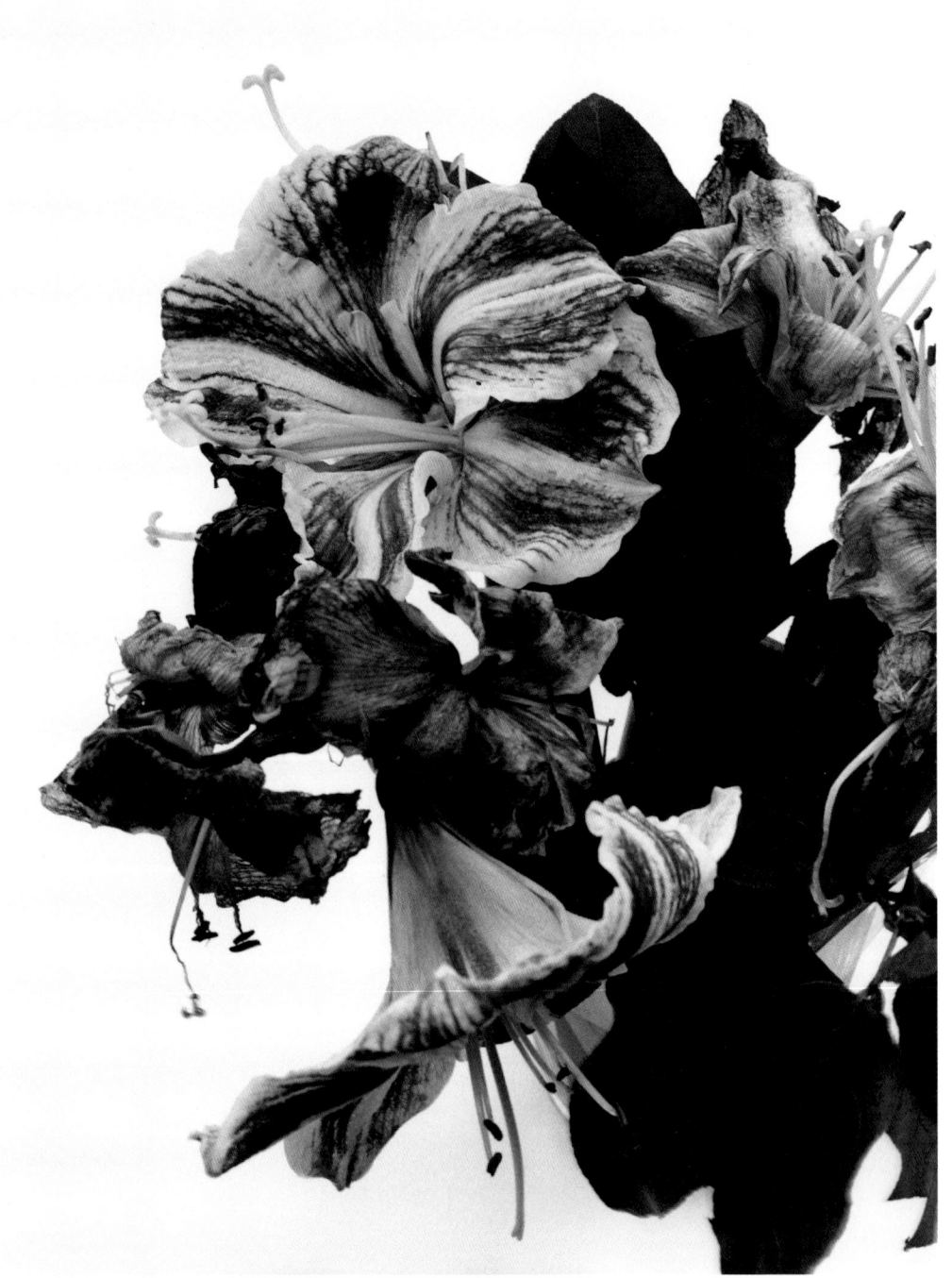

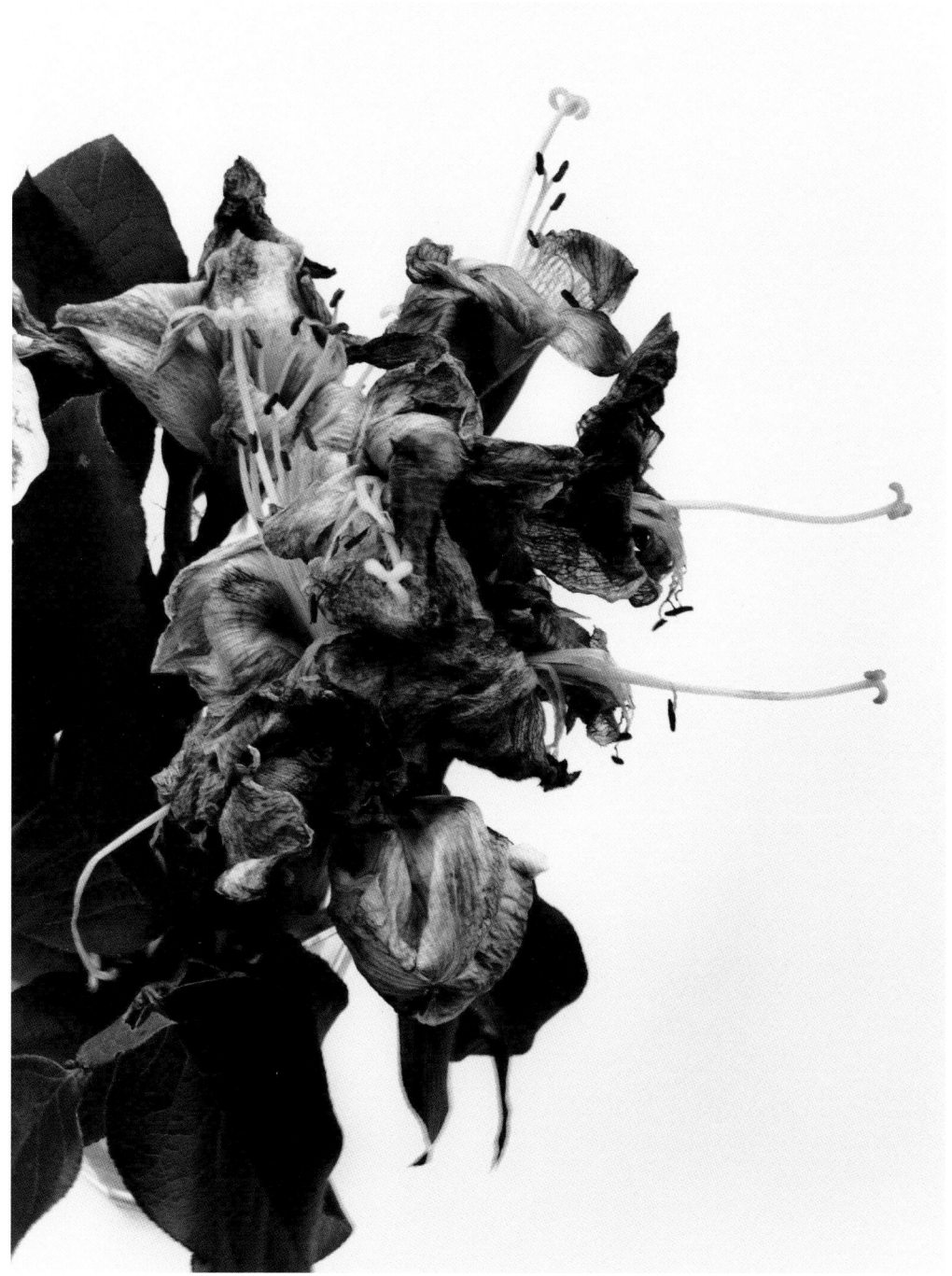

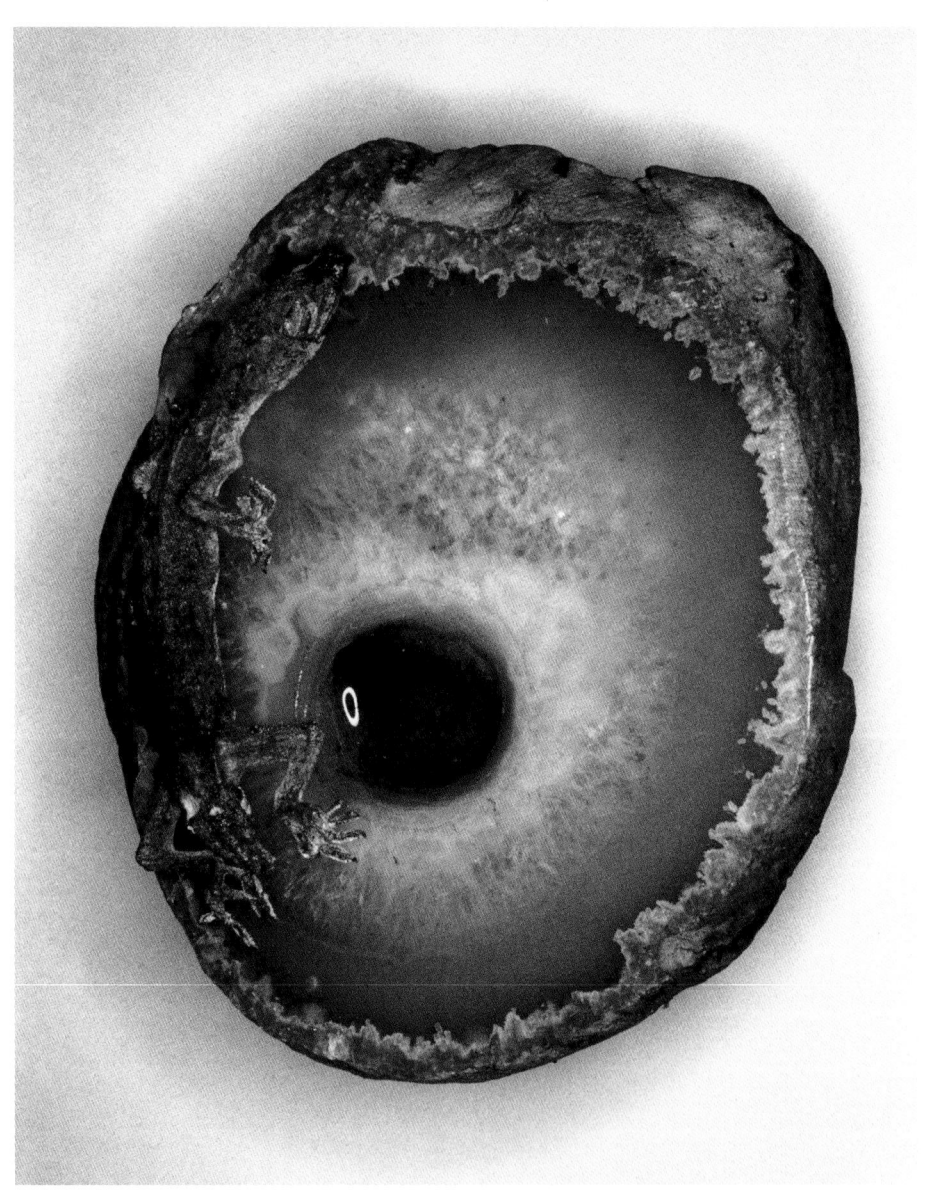

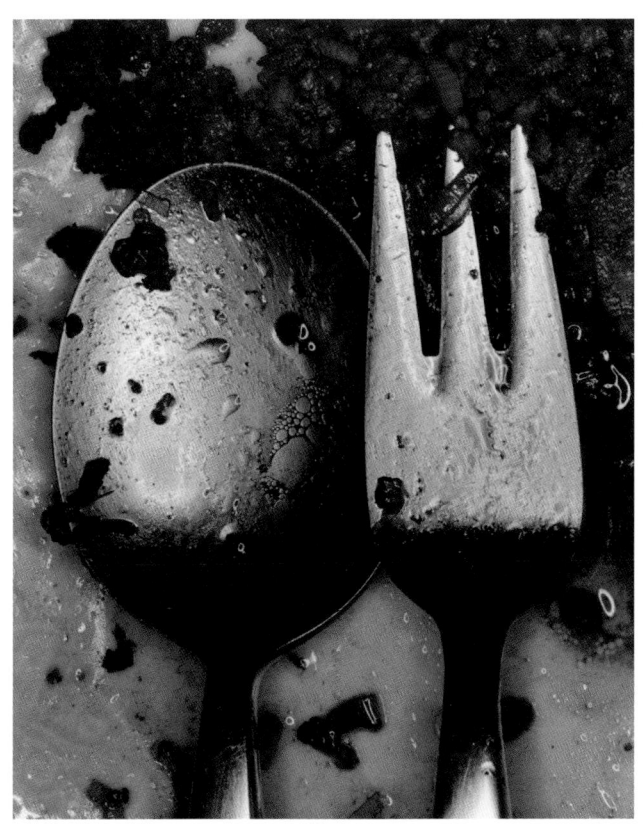

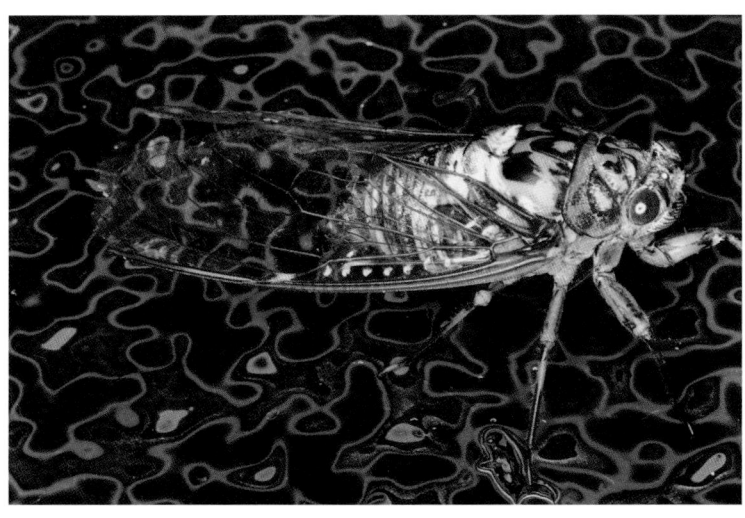

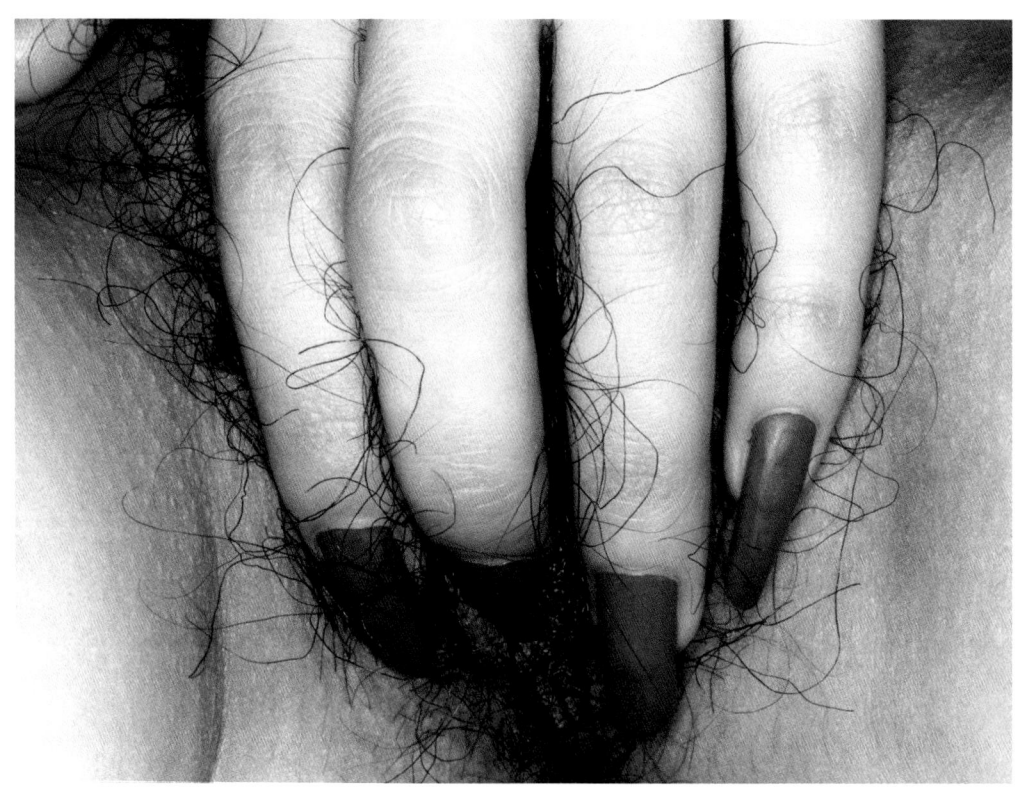

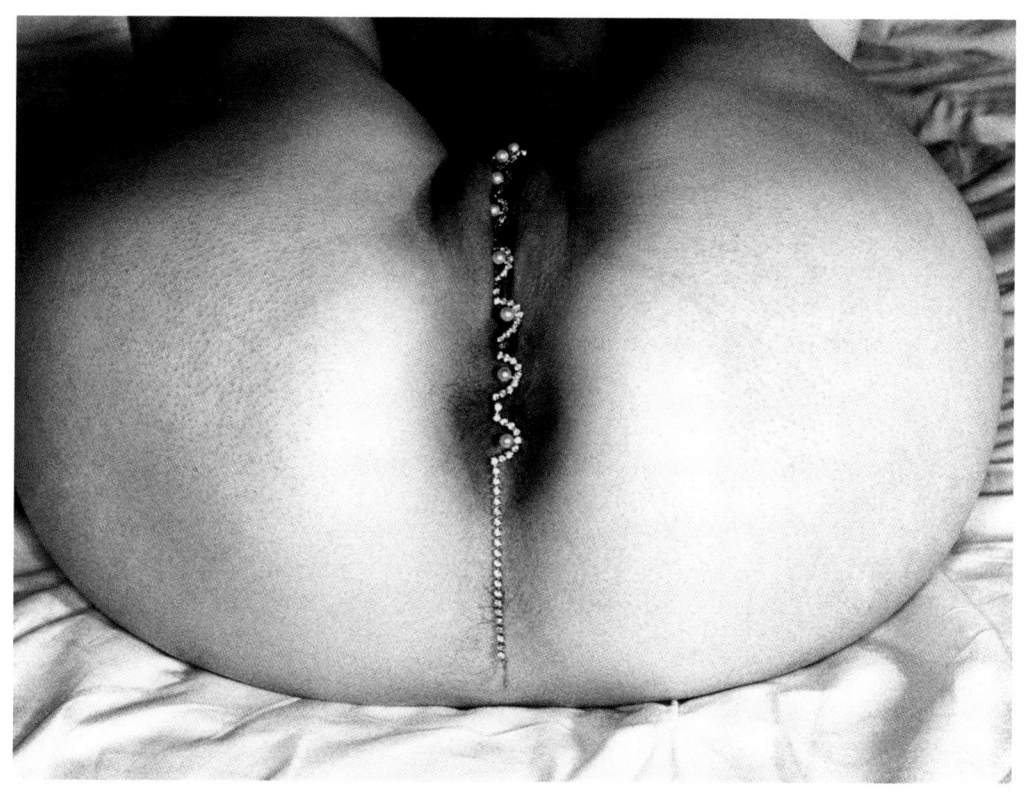

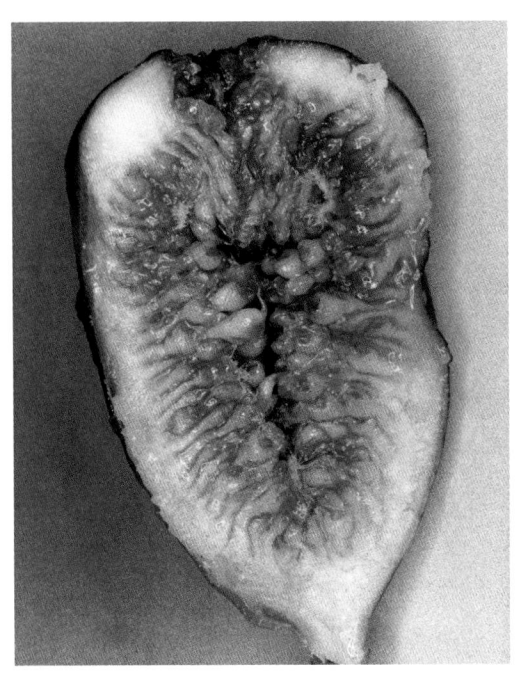

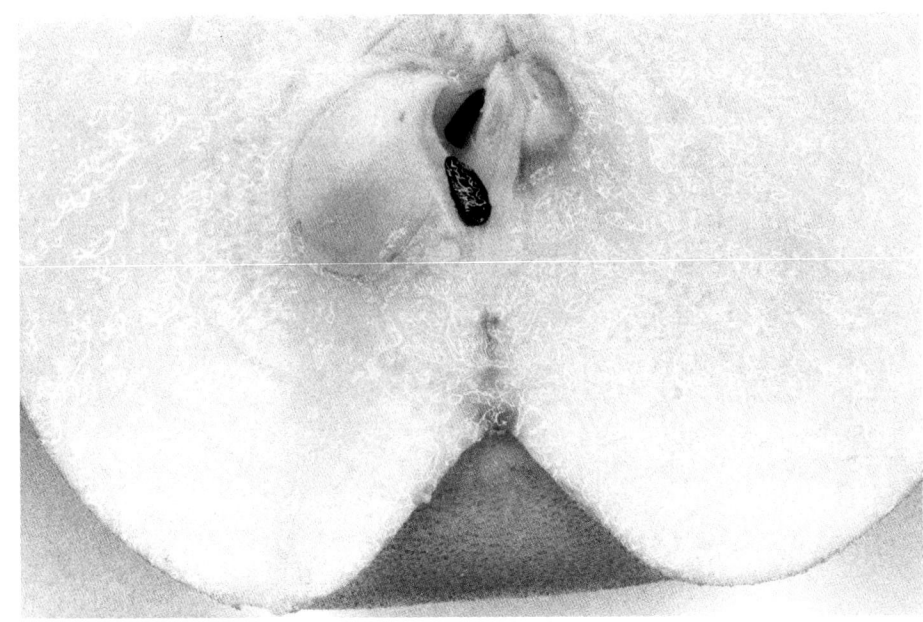

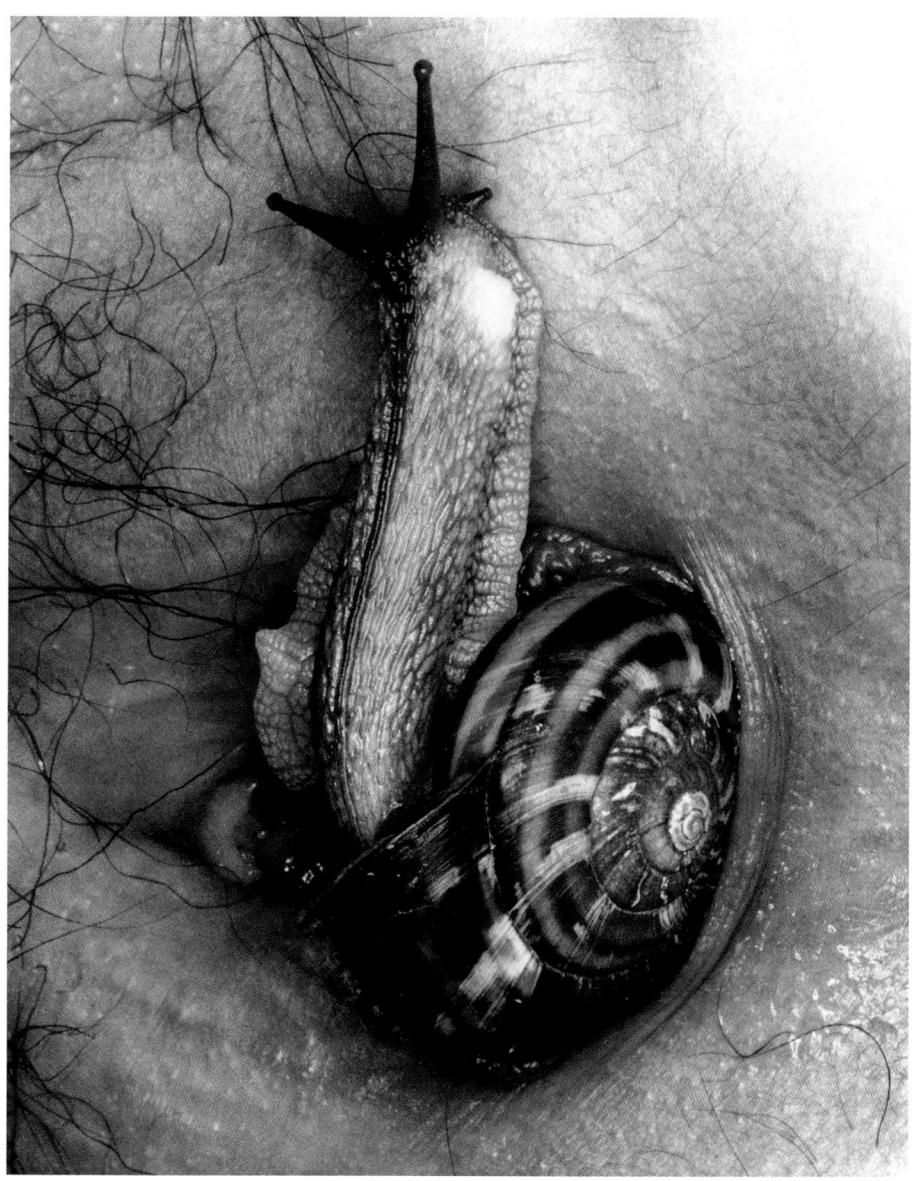

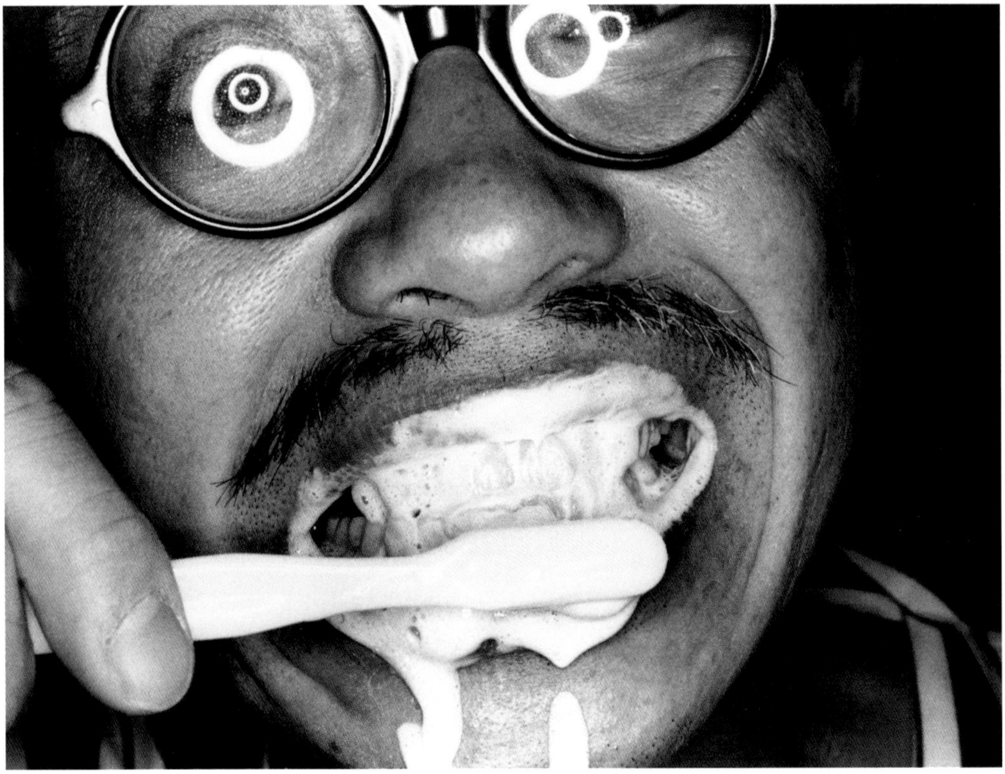

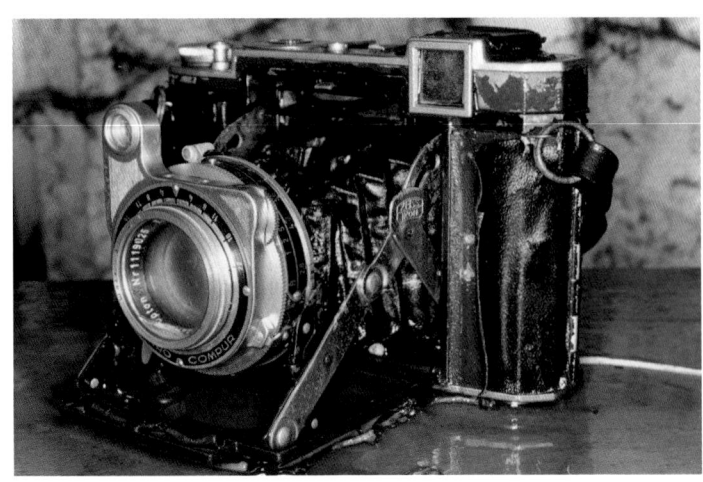

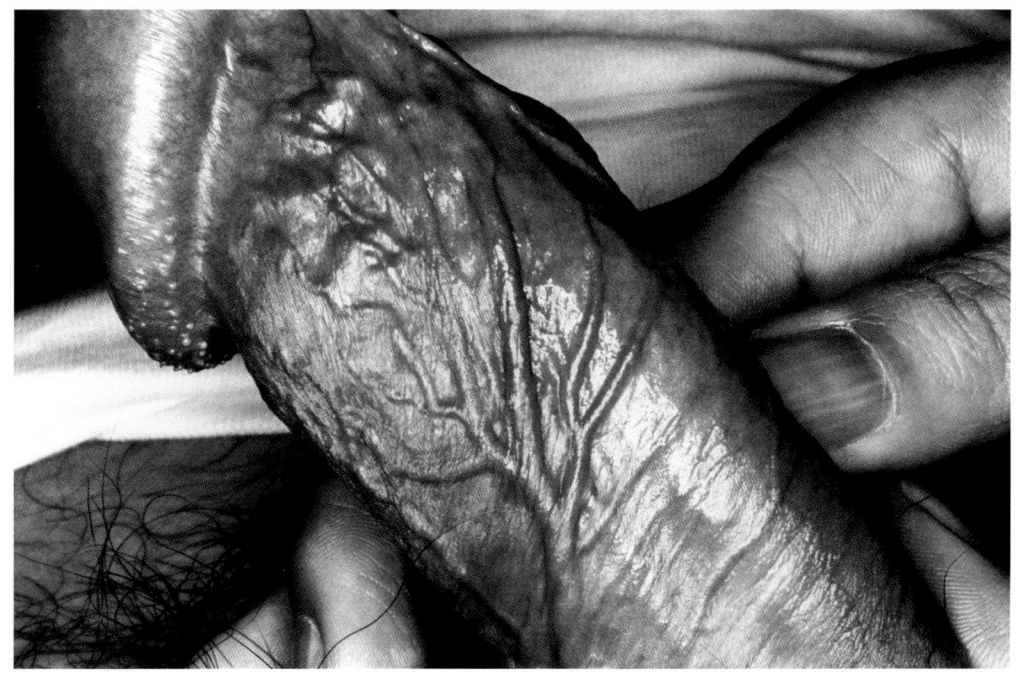

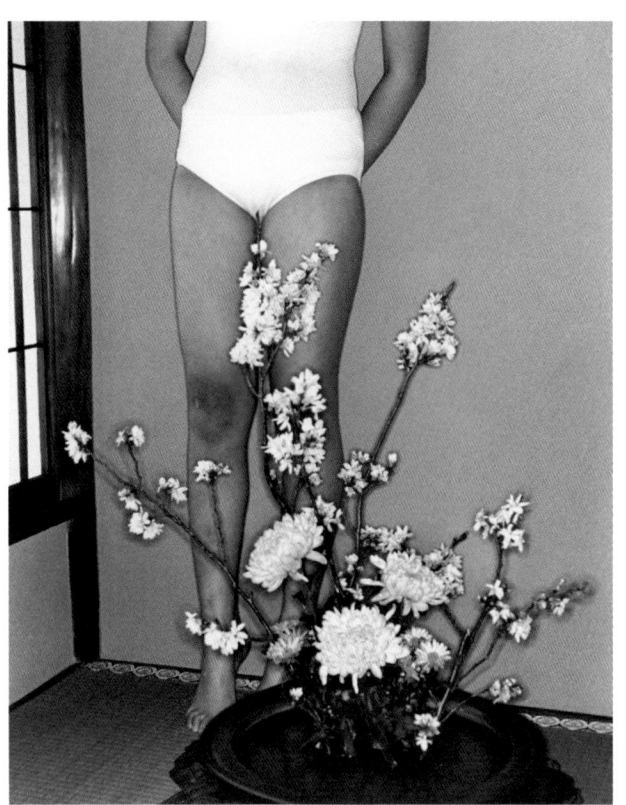

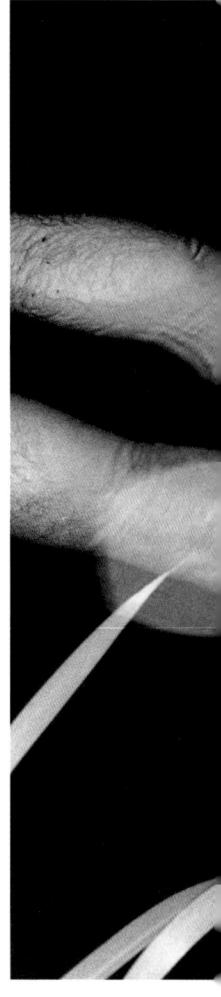

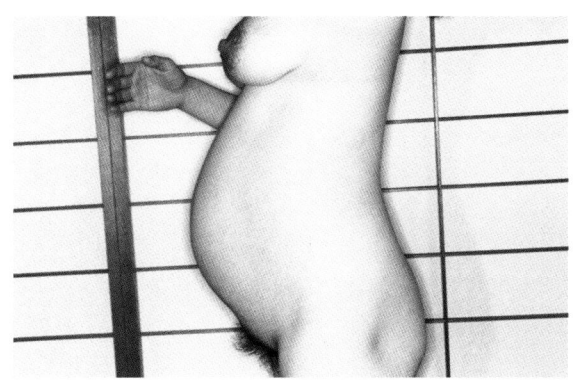

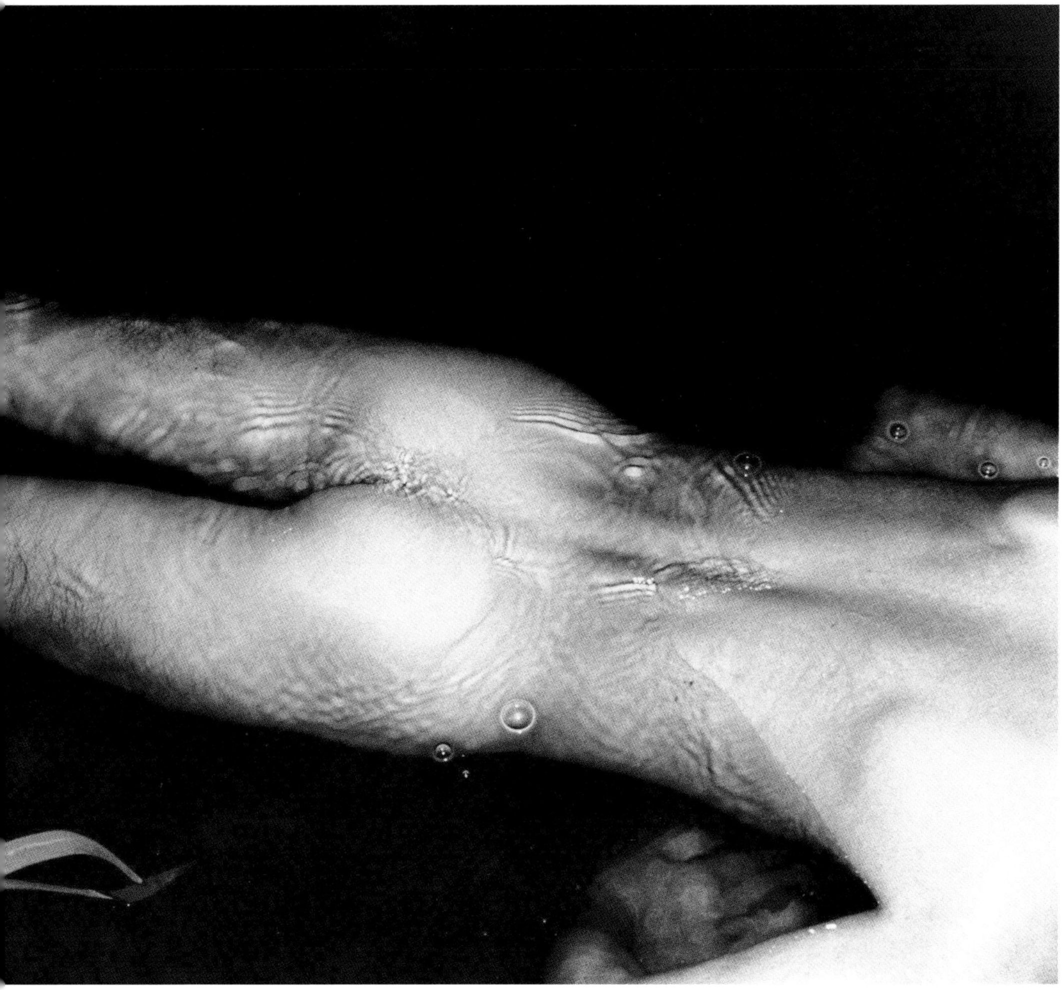

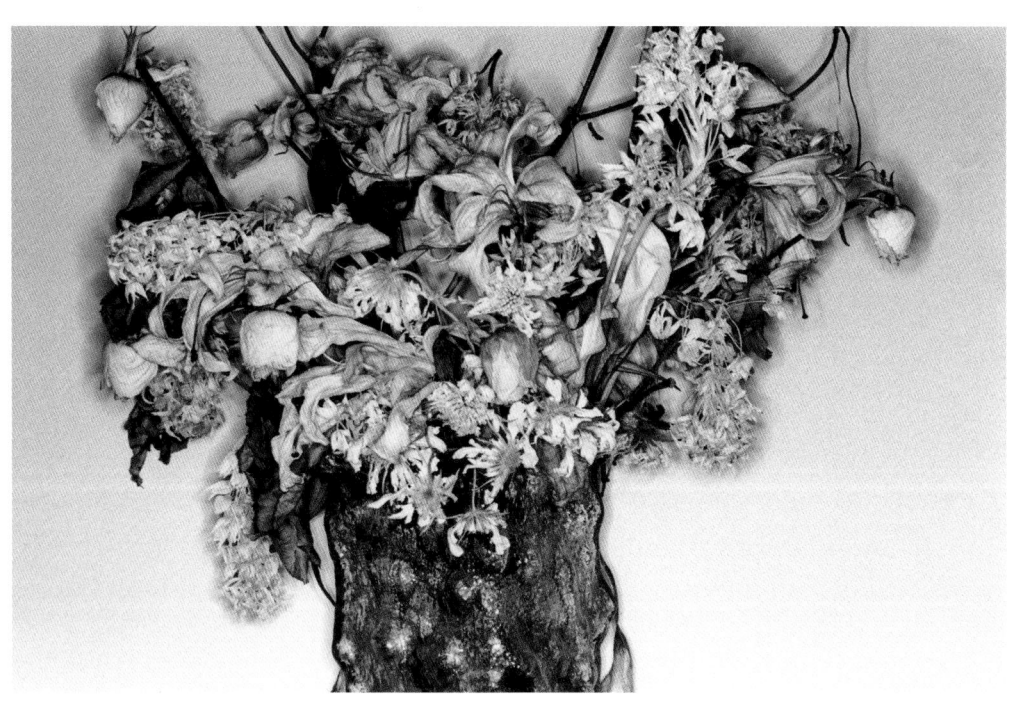

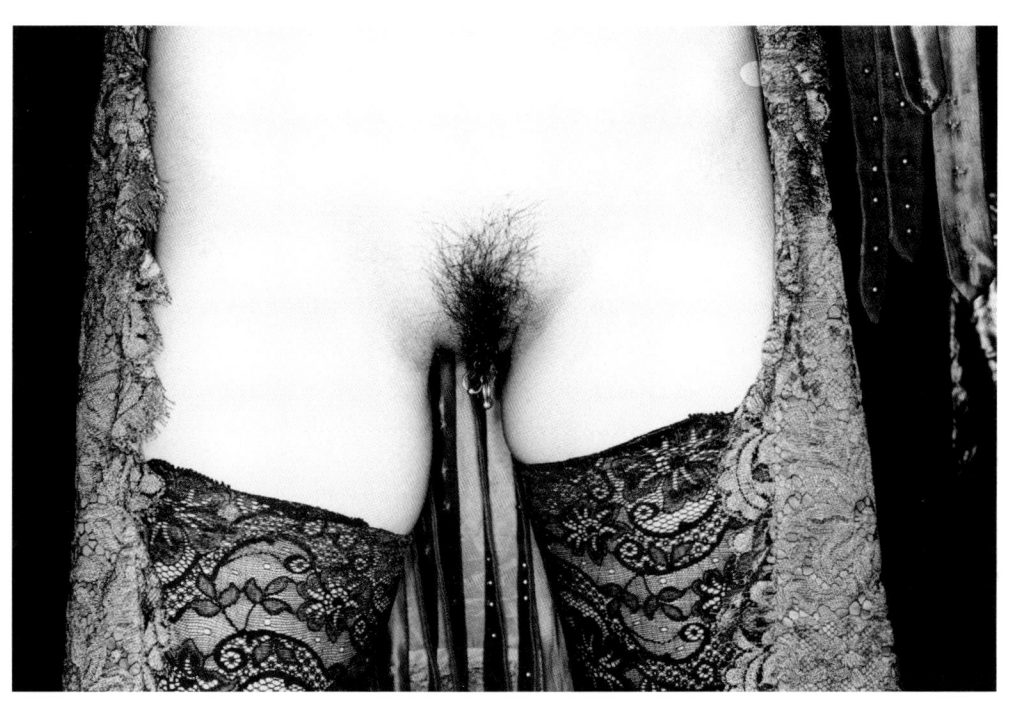

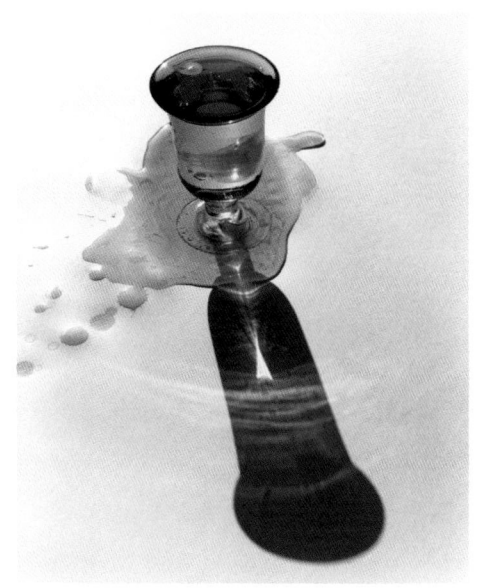

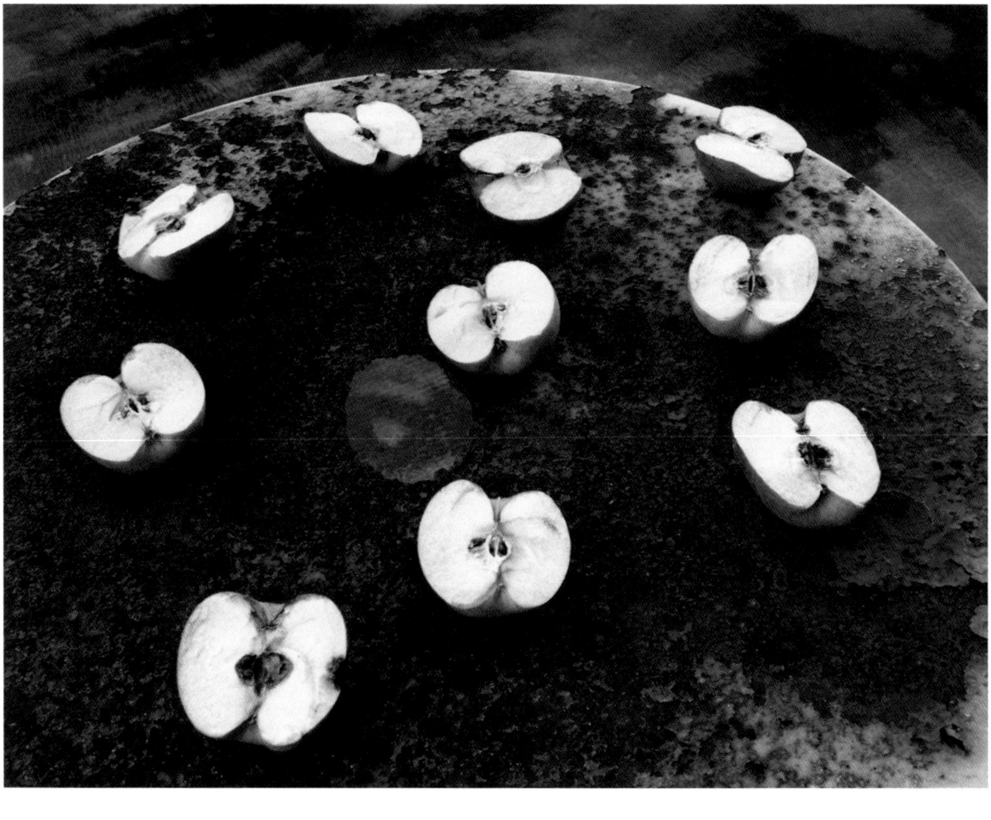

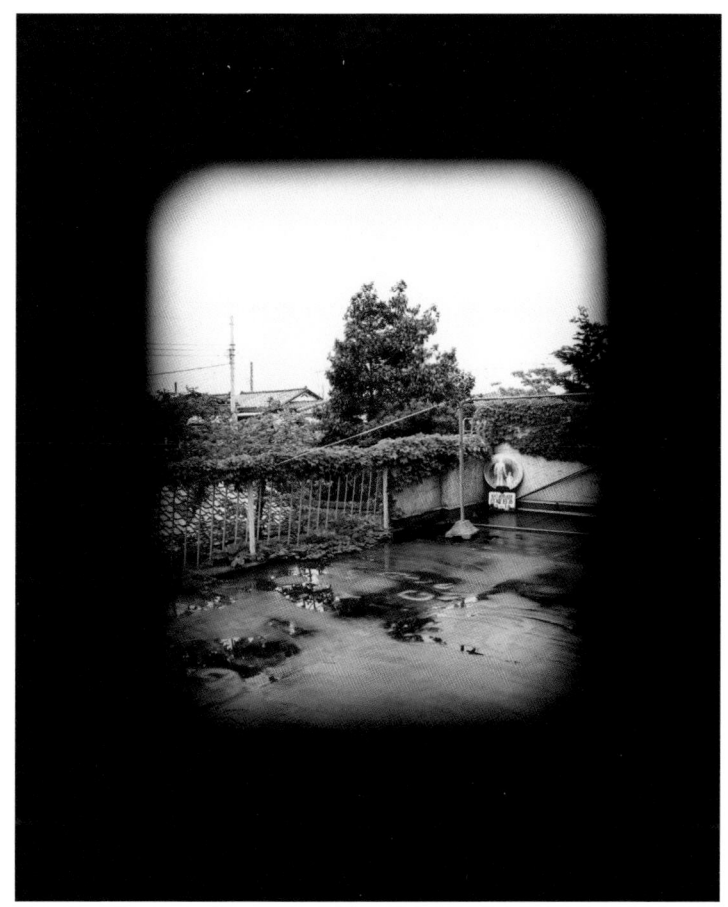

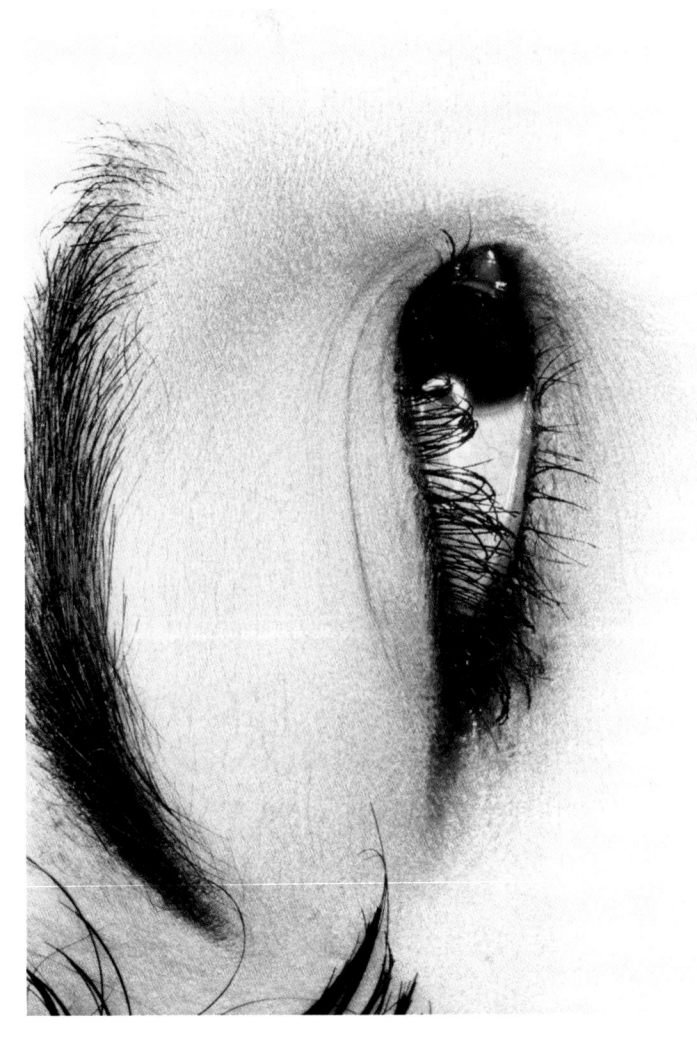

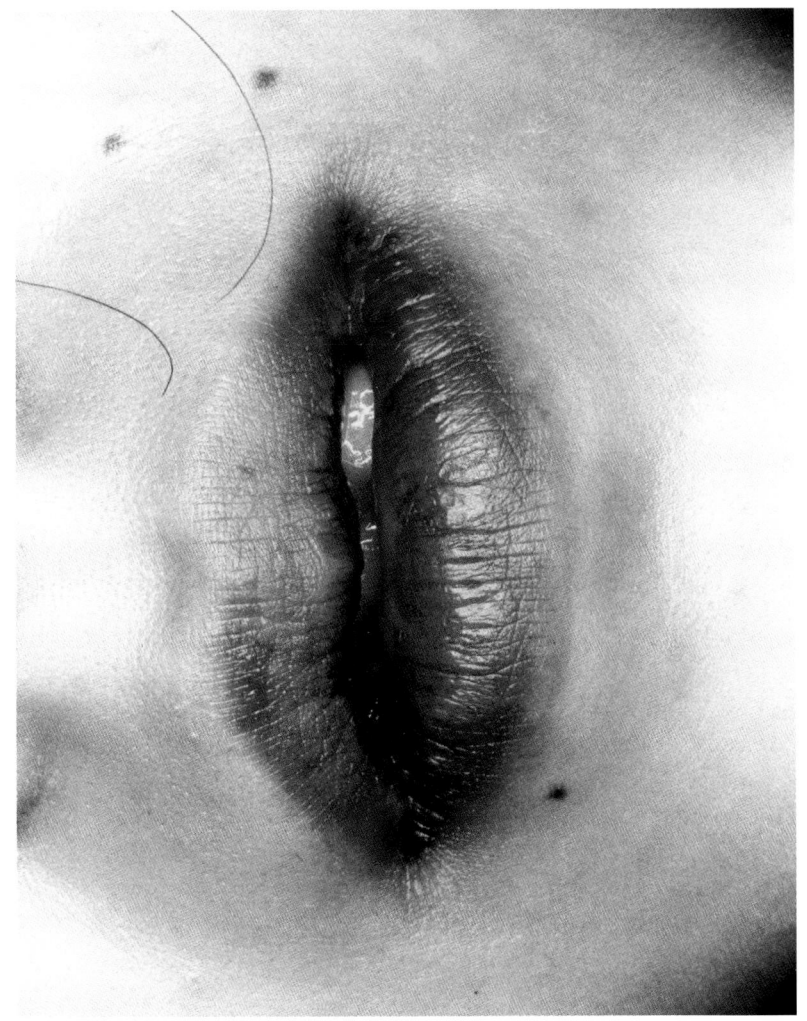

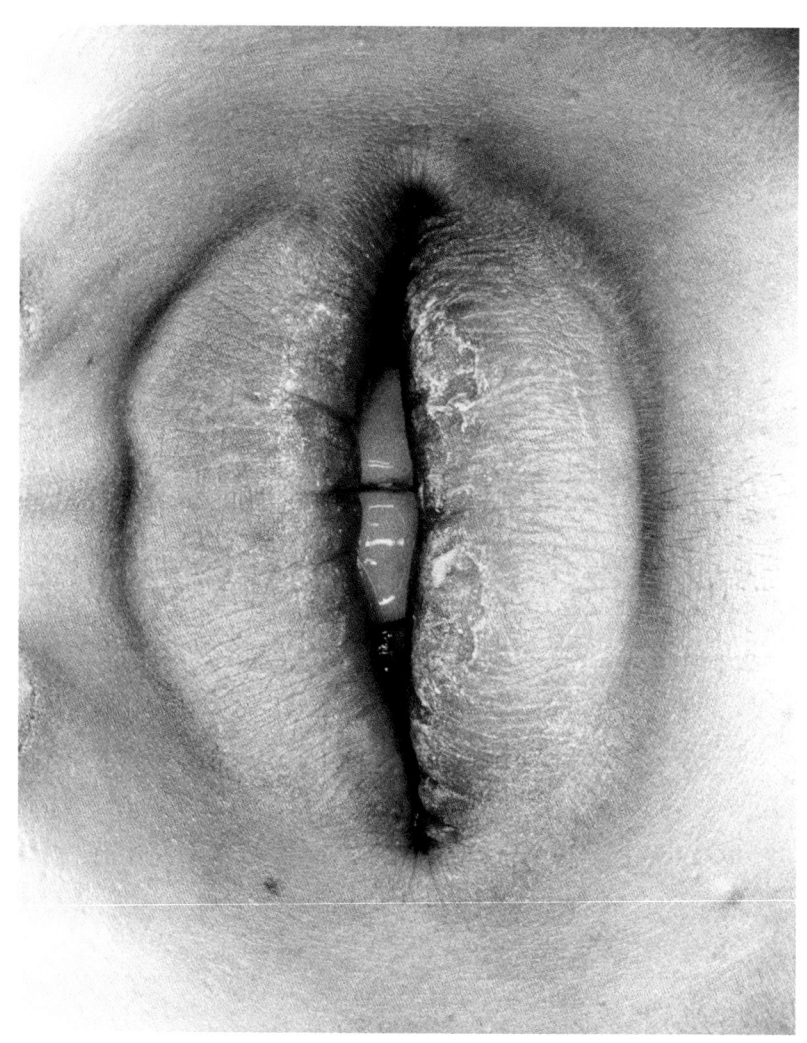

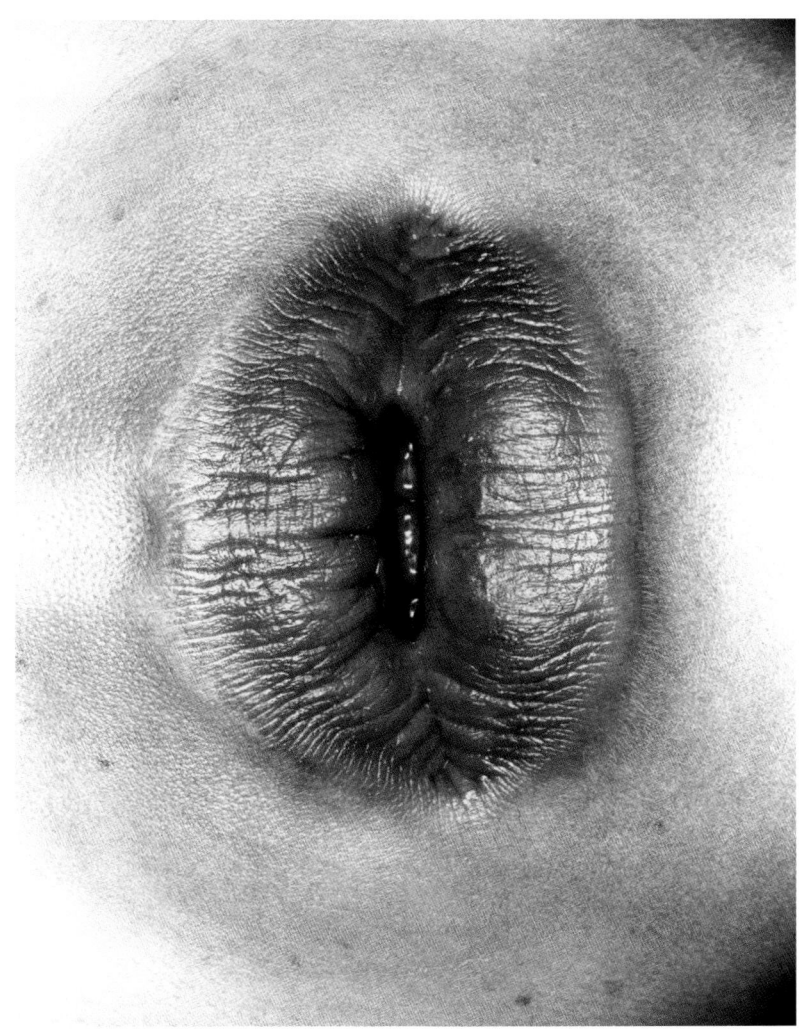

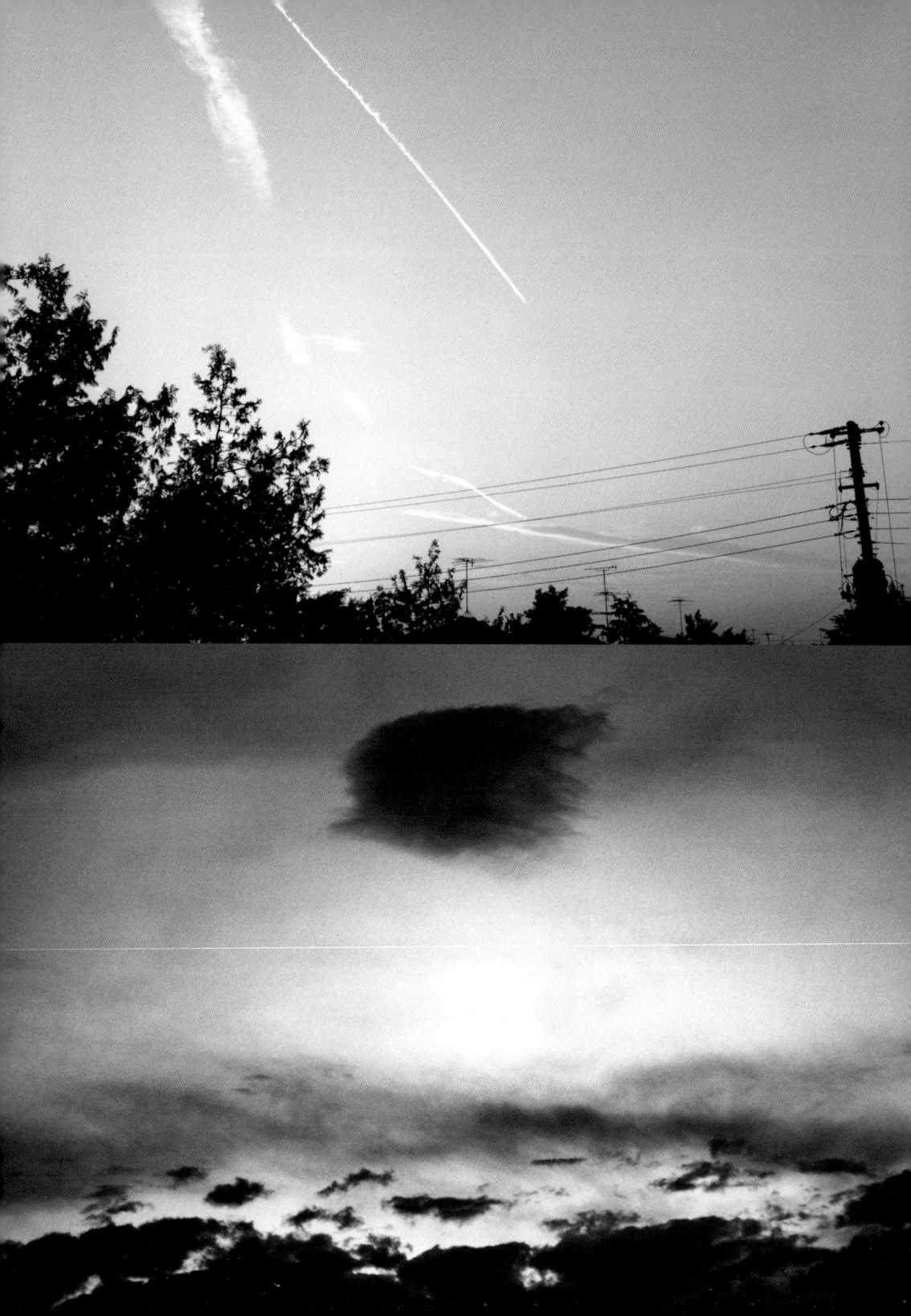

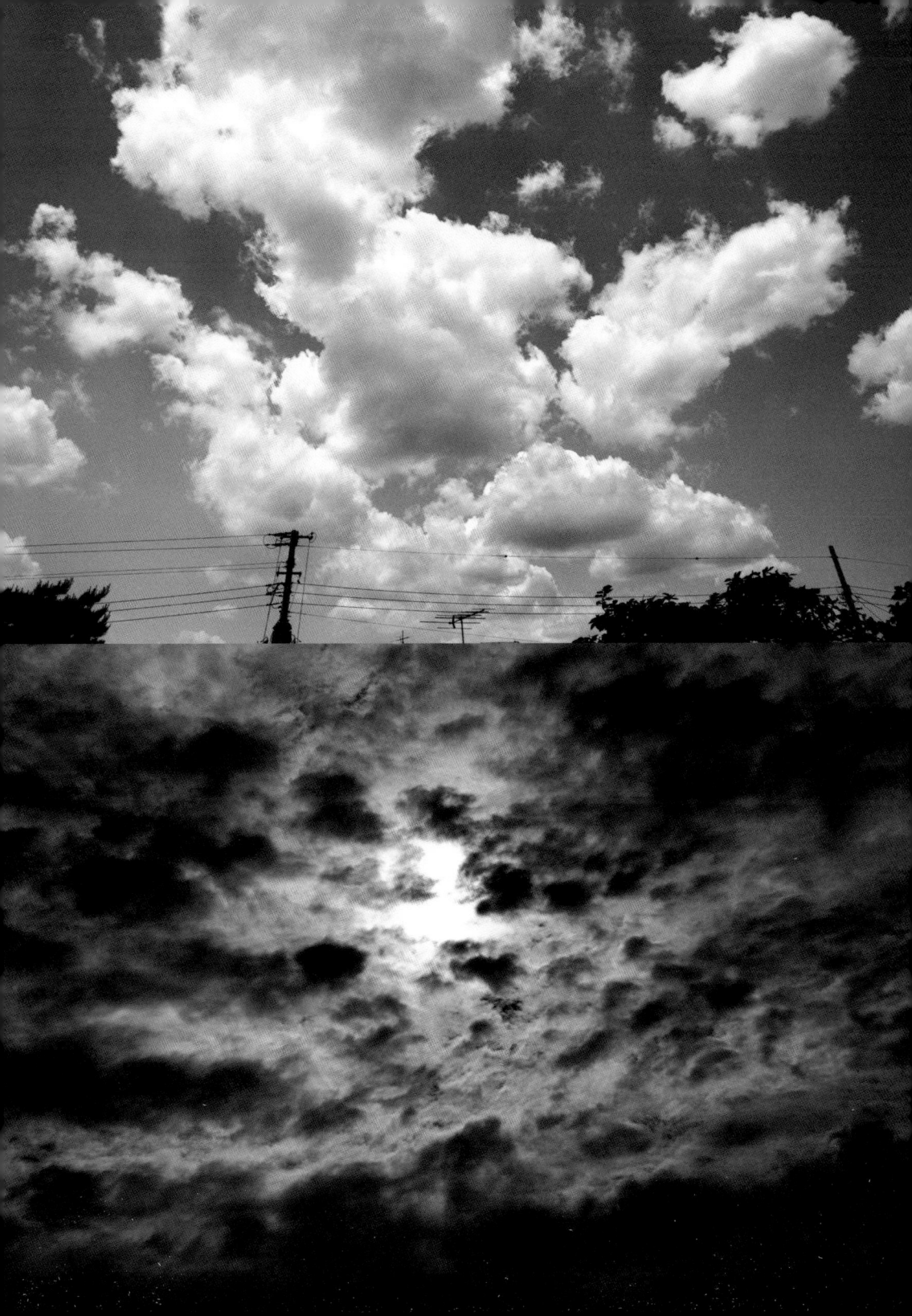

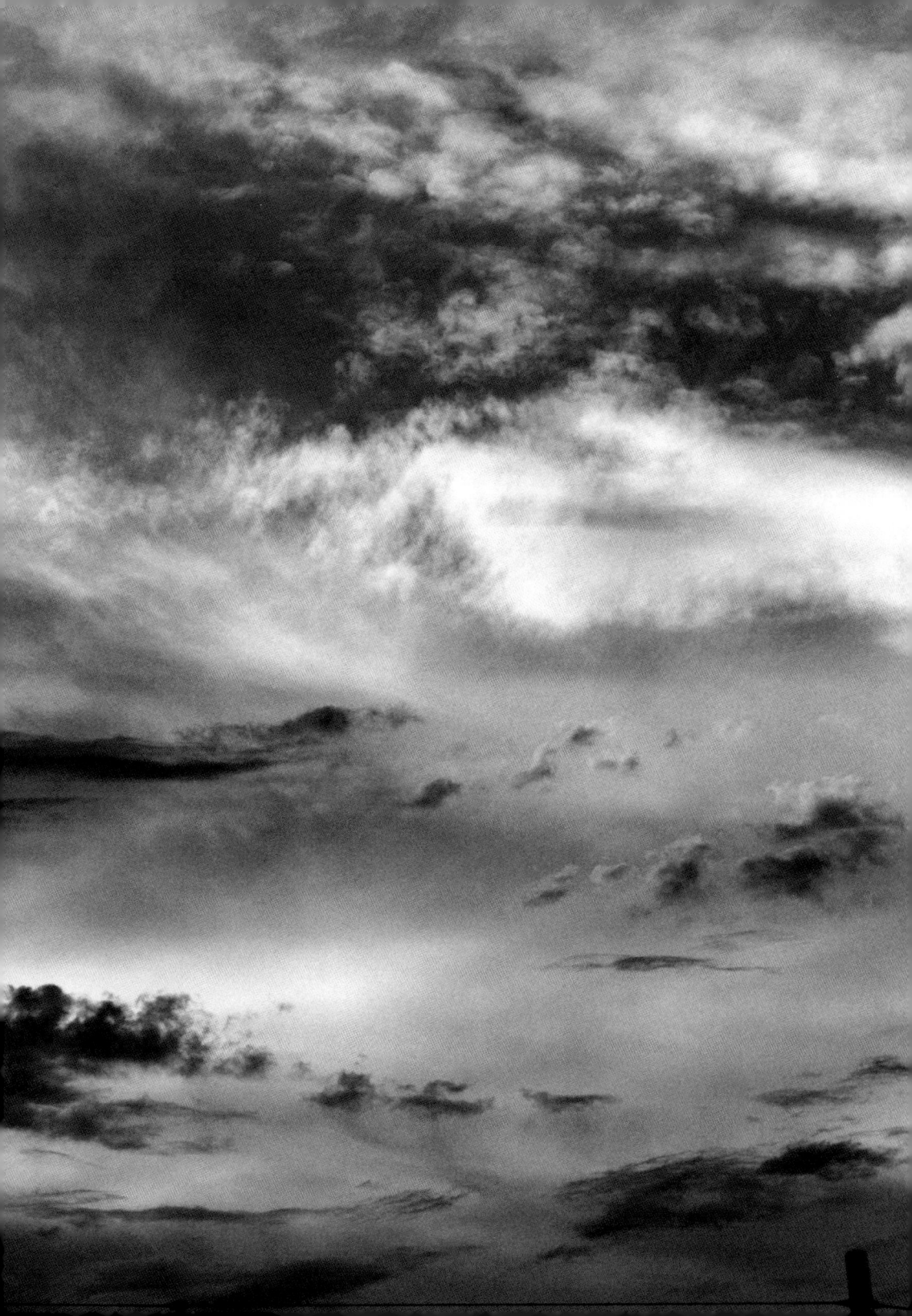

Sexual Desire

色情

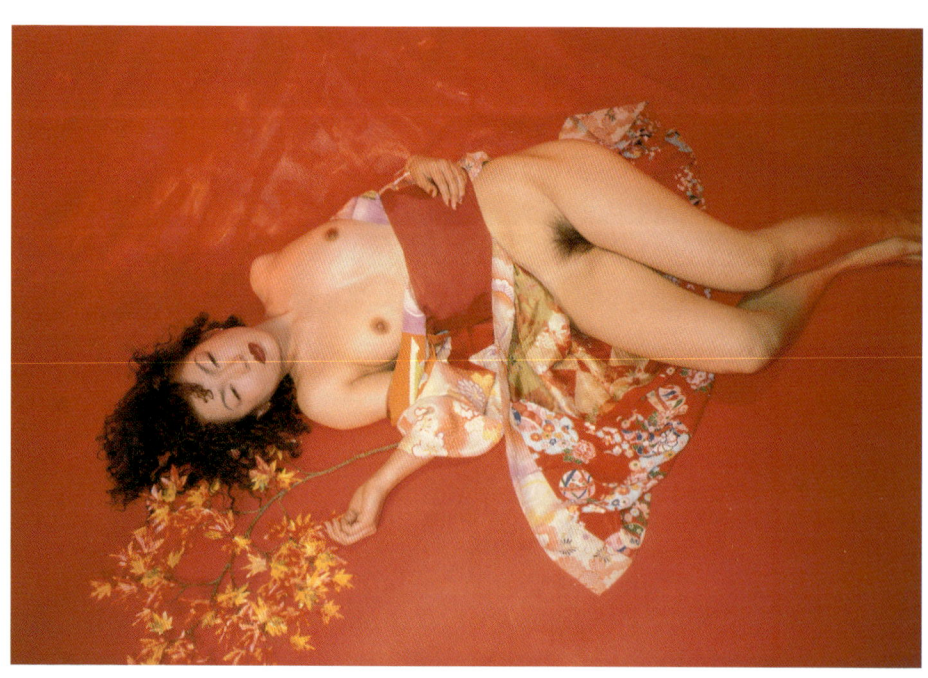

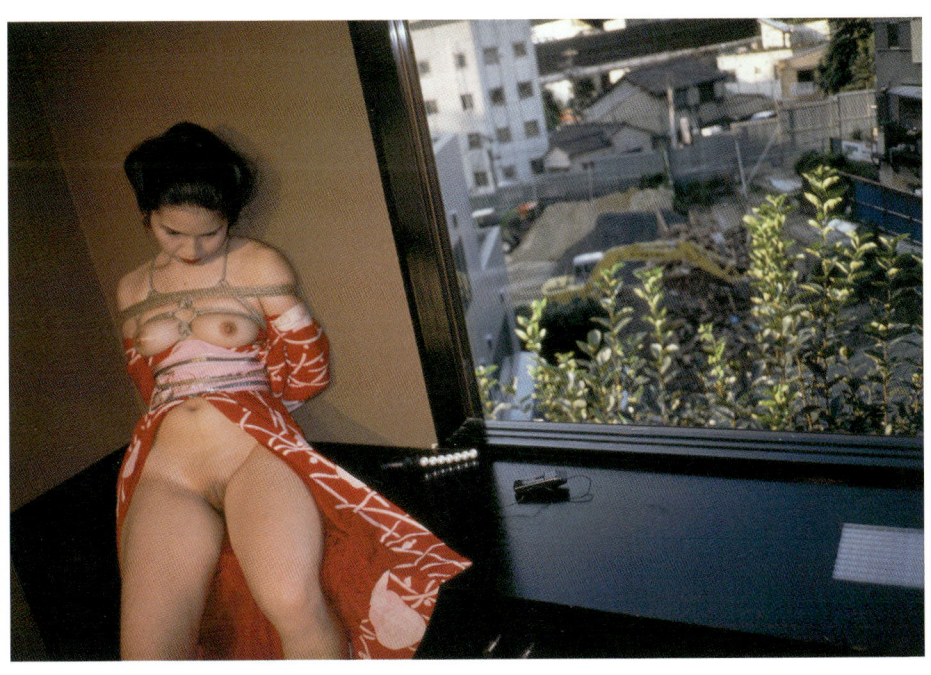

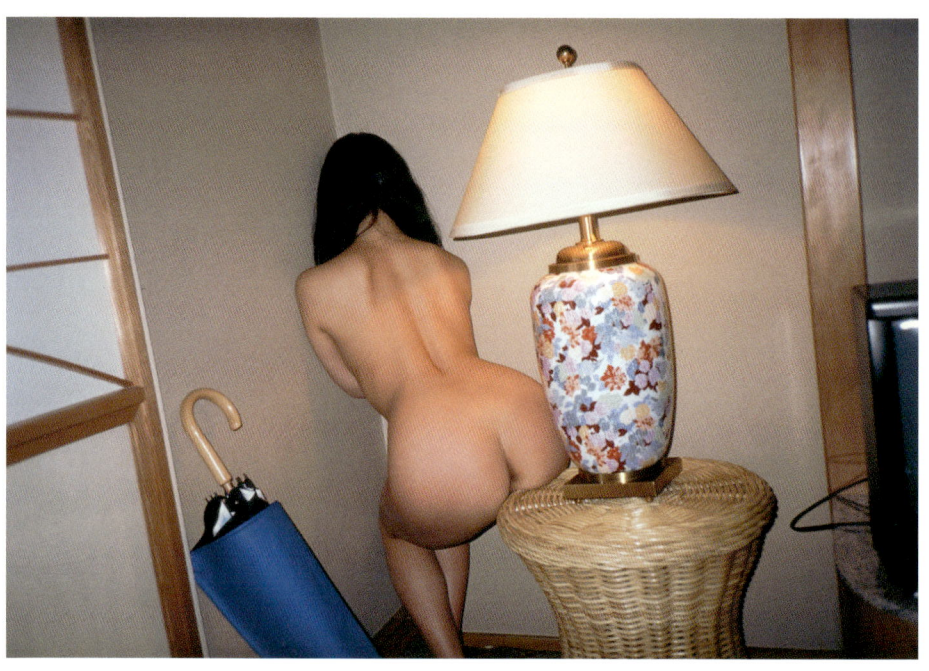

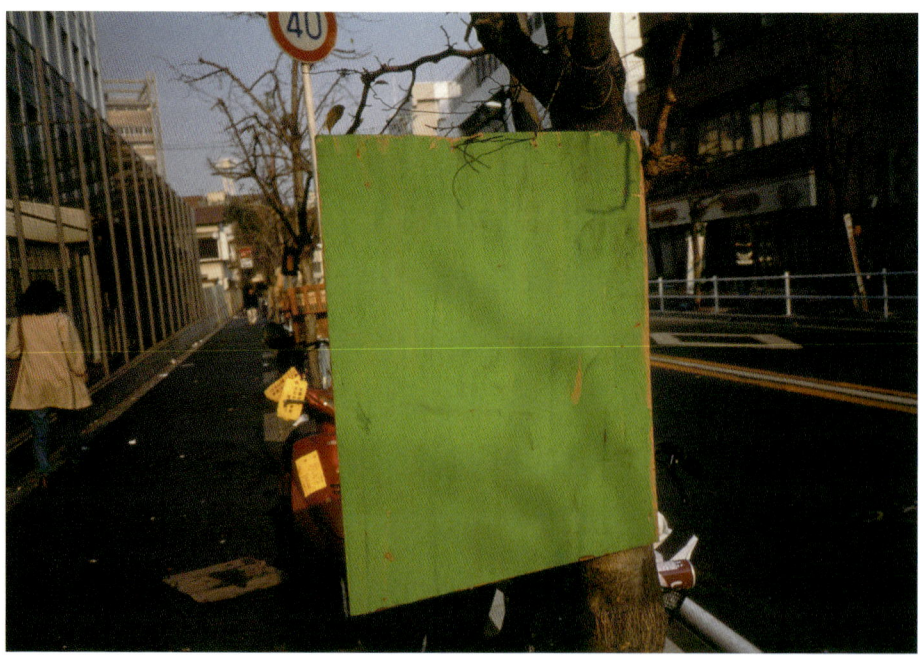

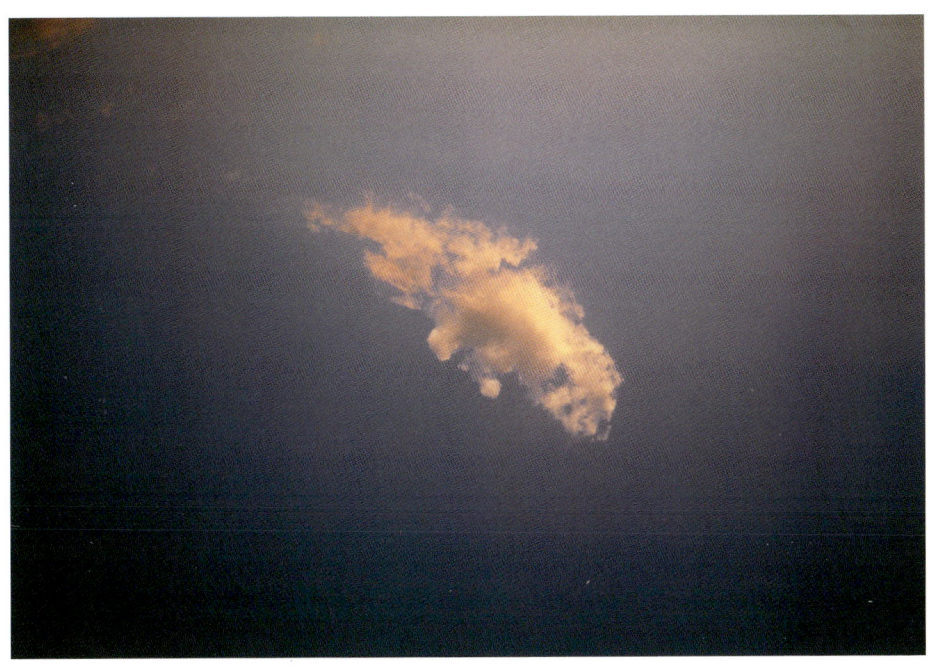

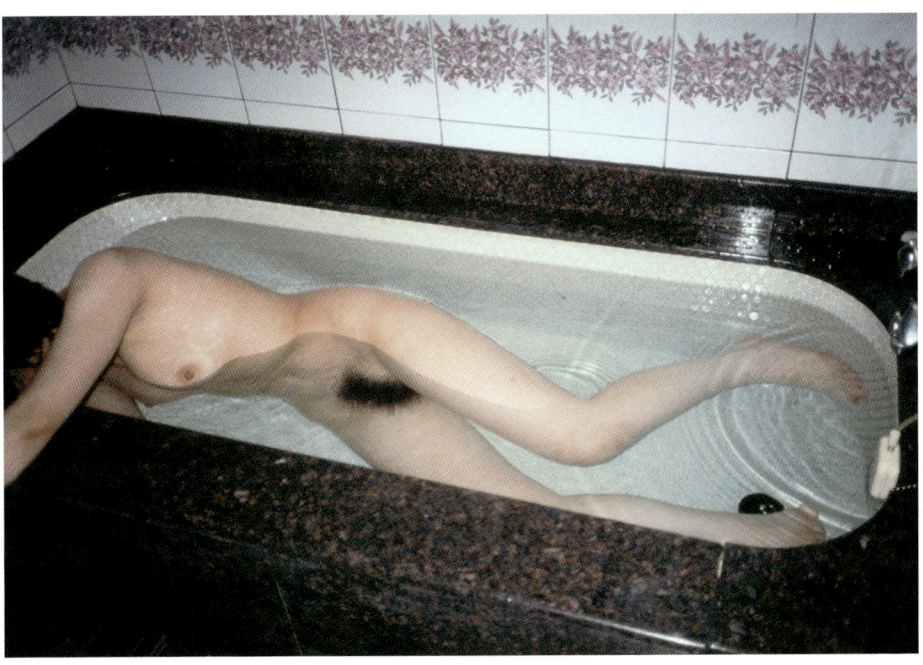

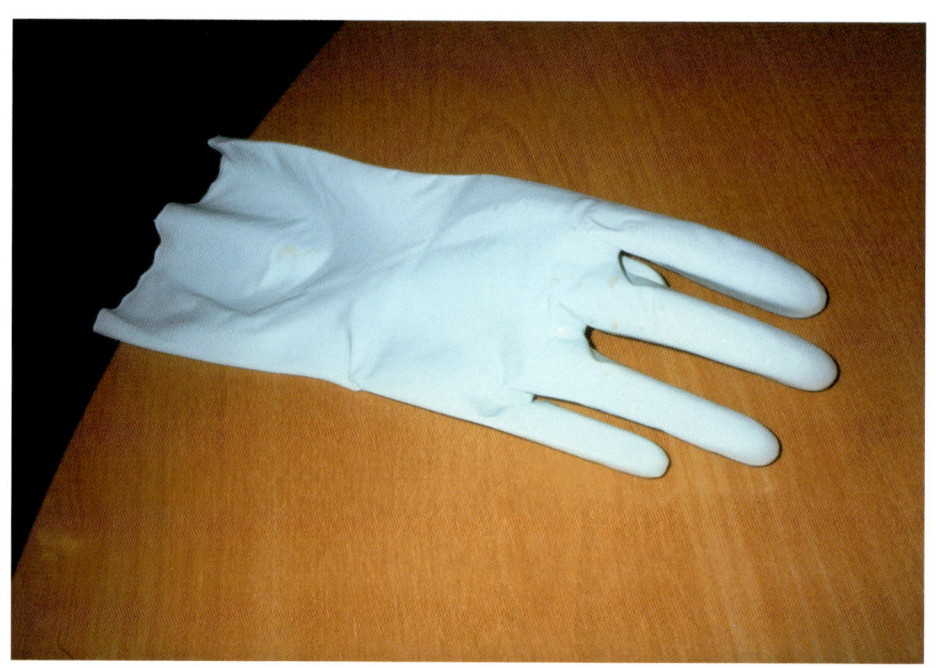

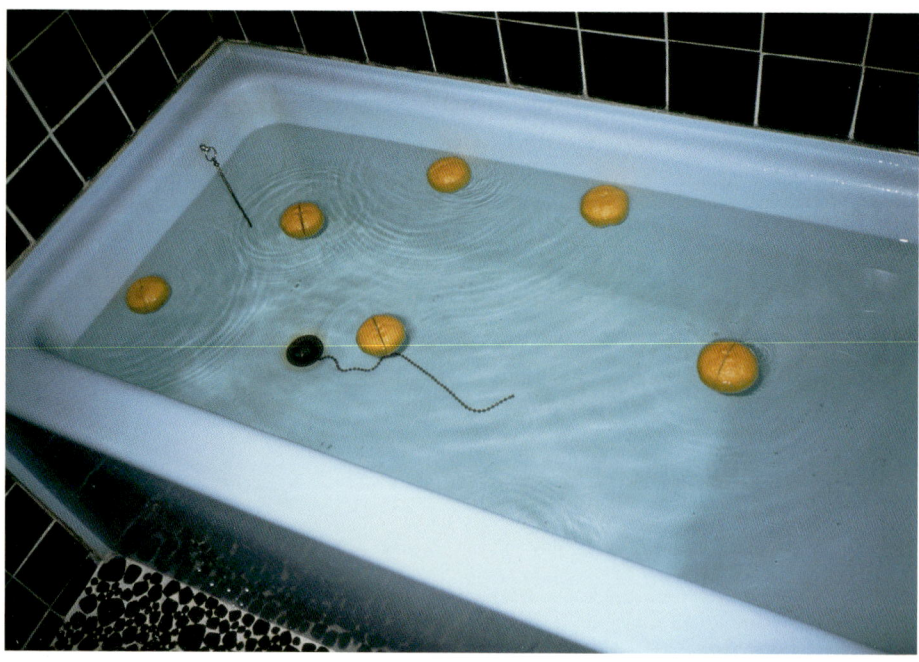

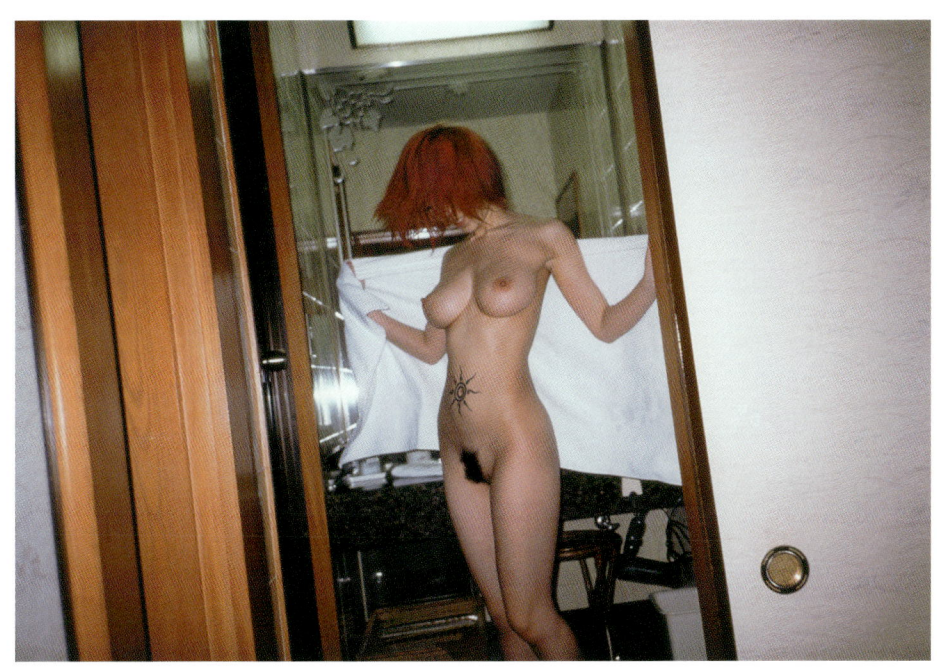

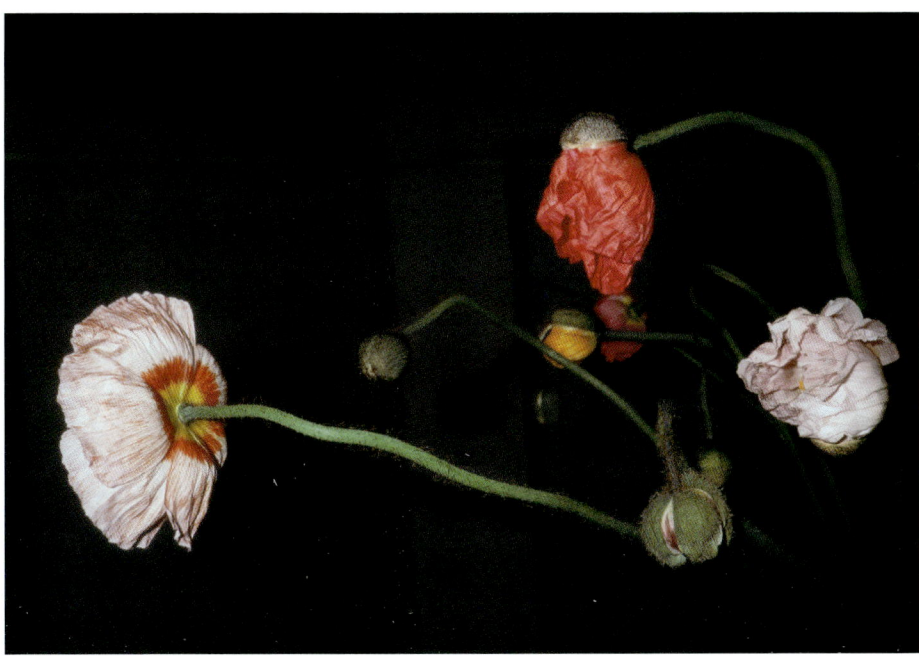

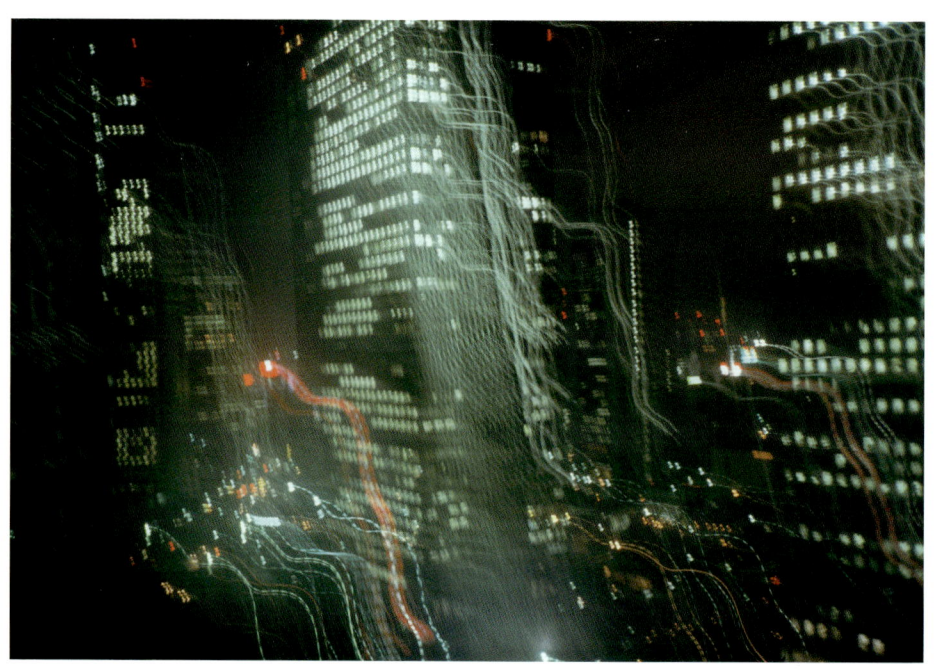

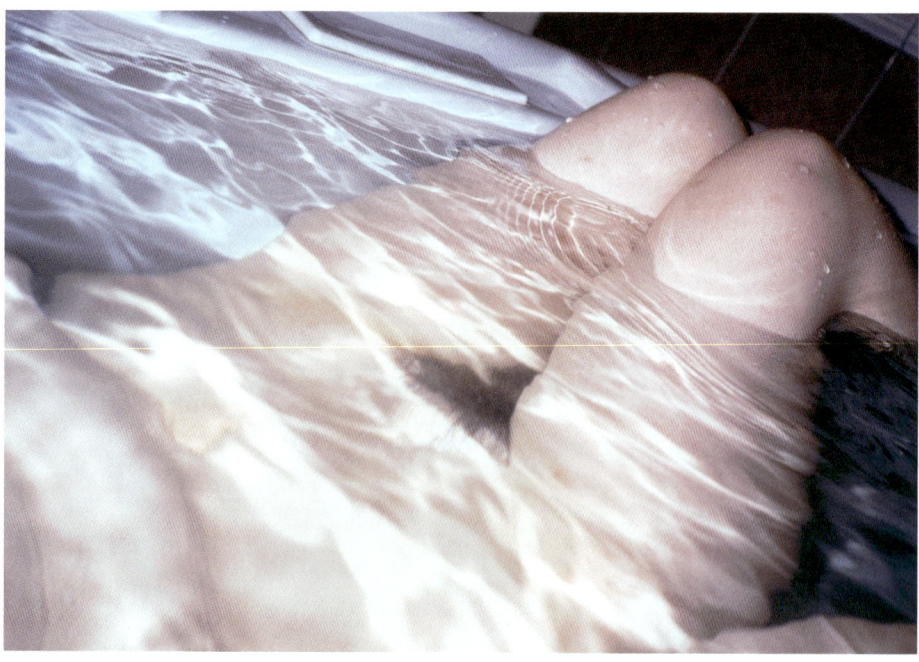

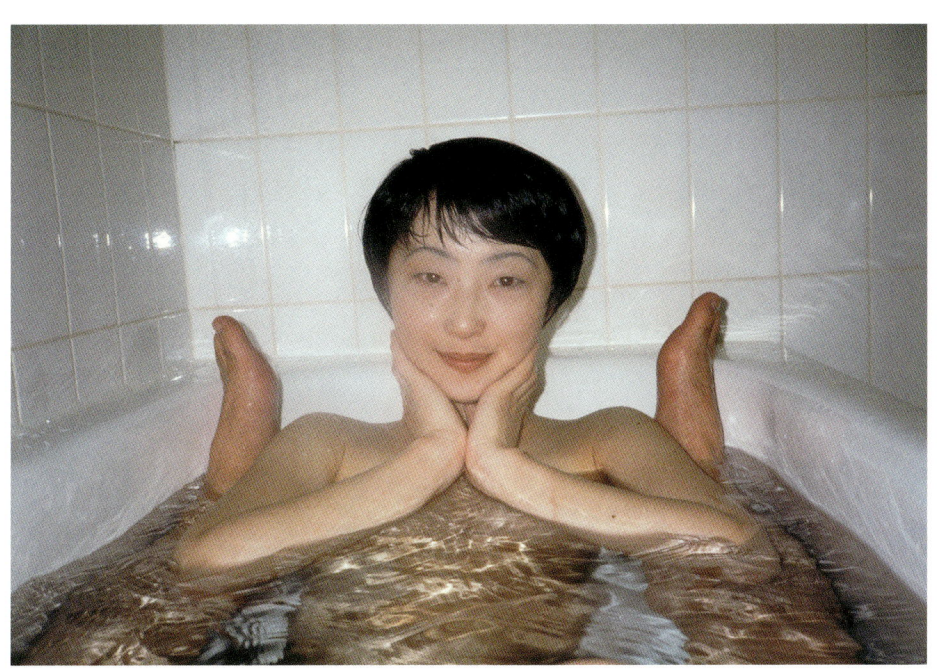

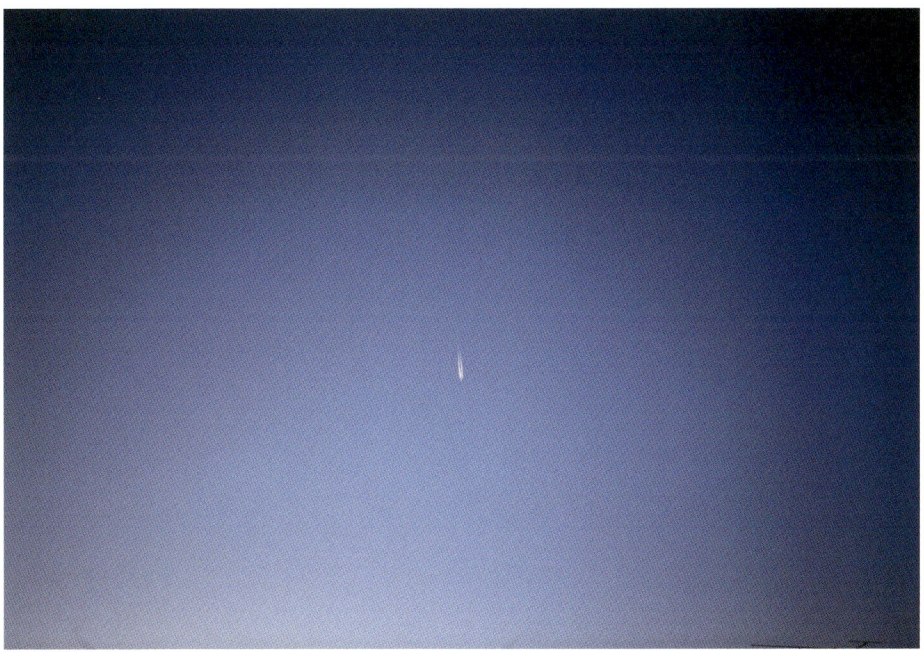

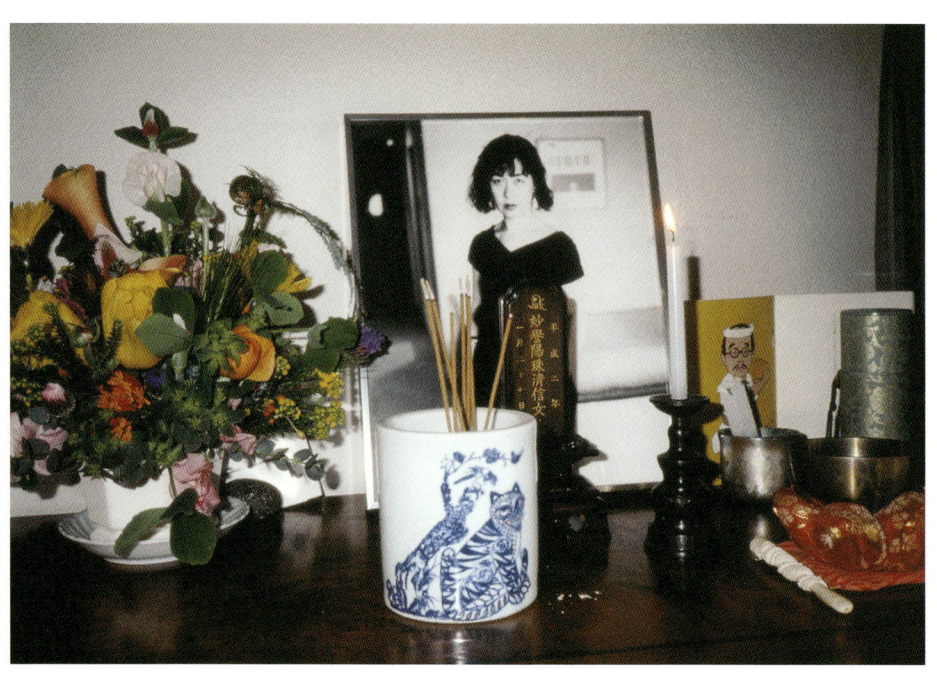

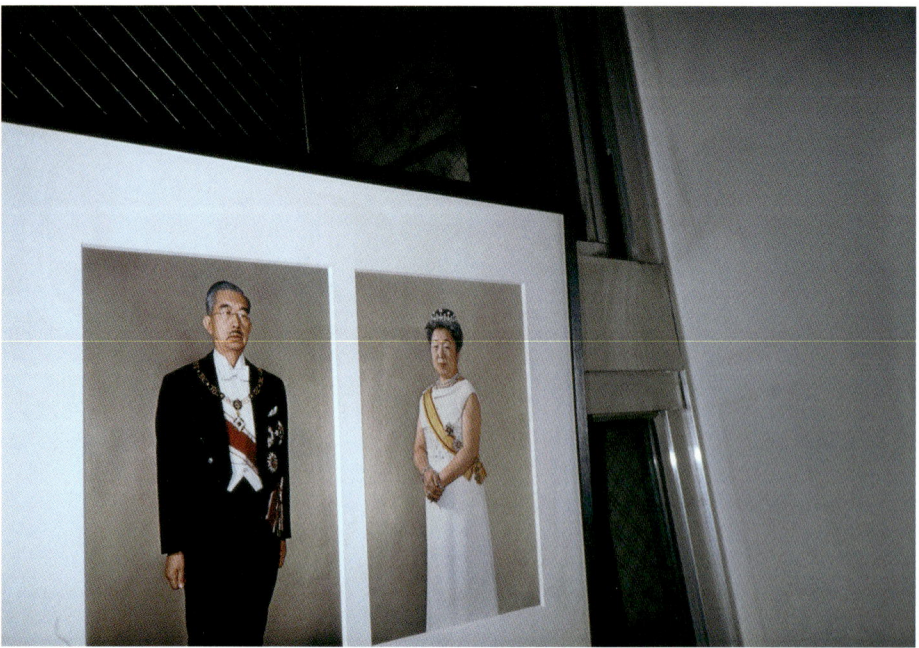

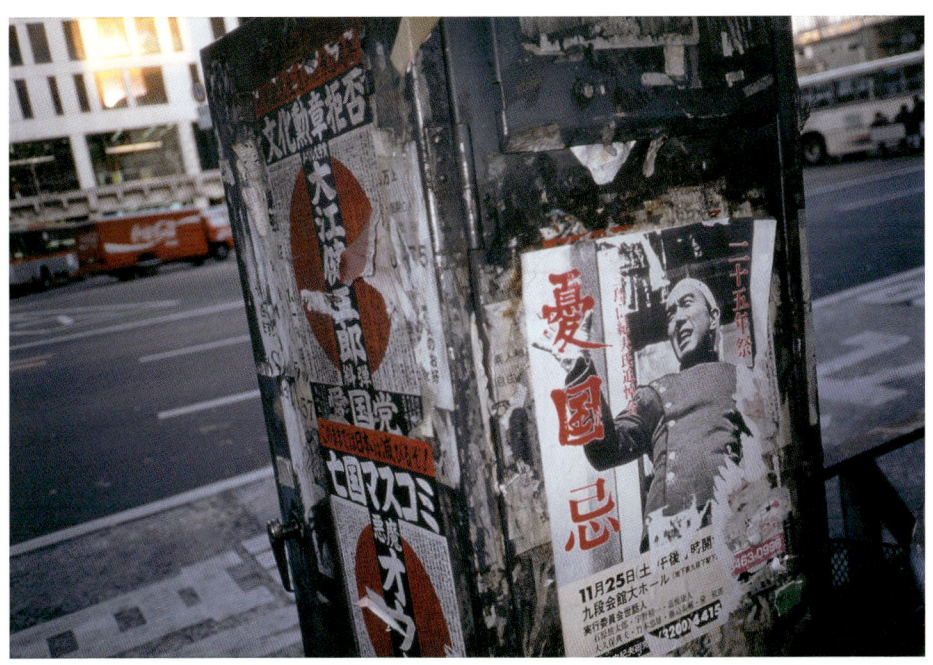

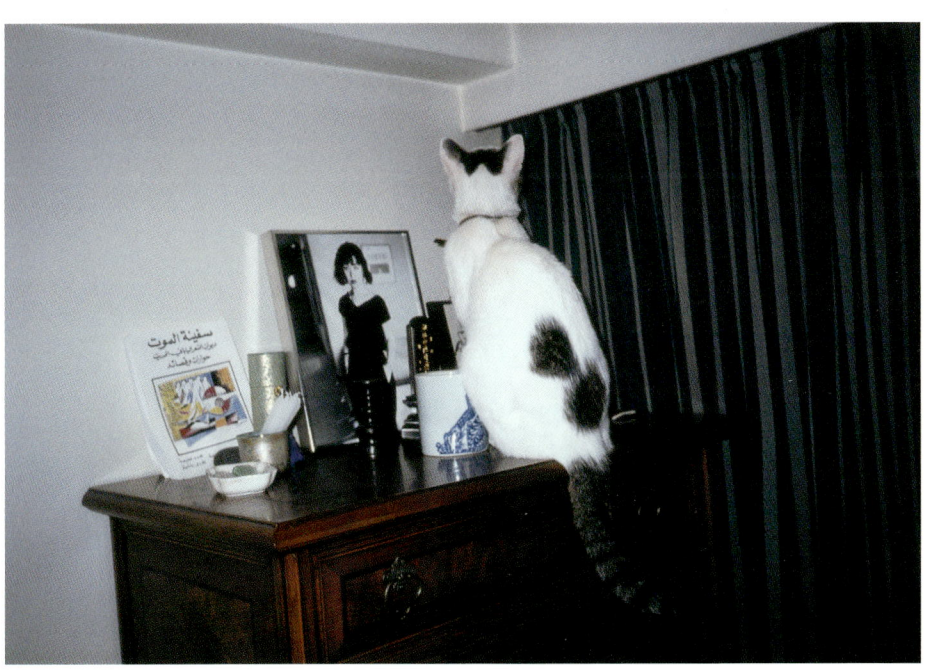

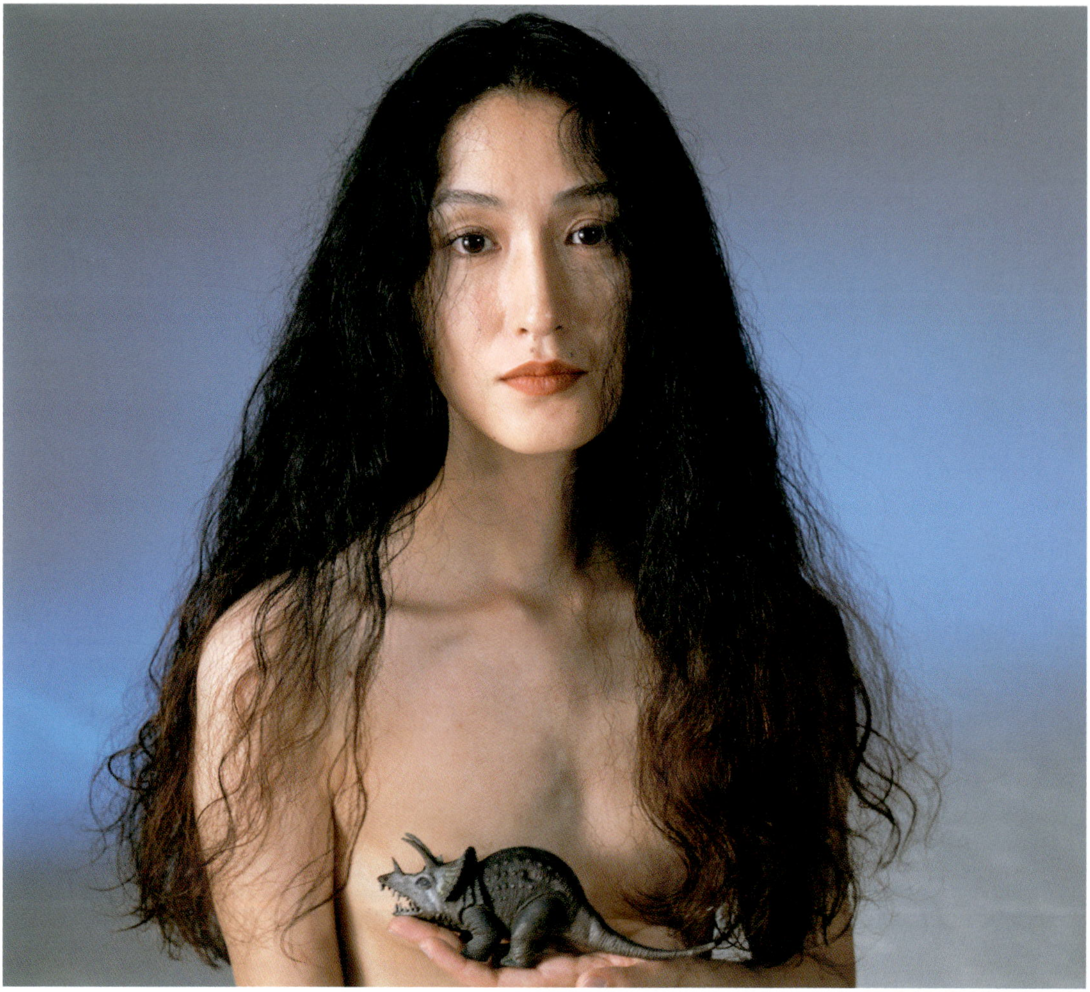

A's Paradise

Aの楽園

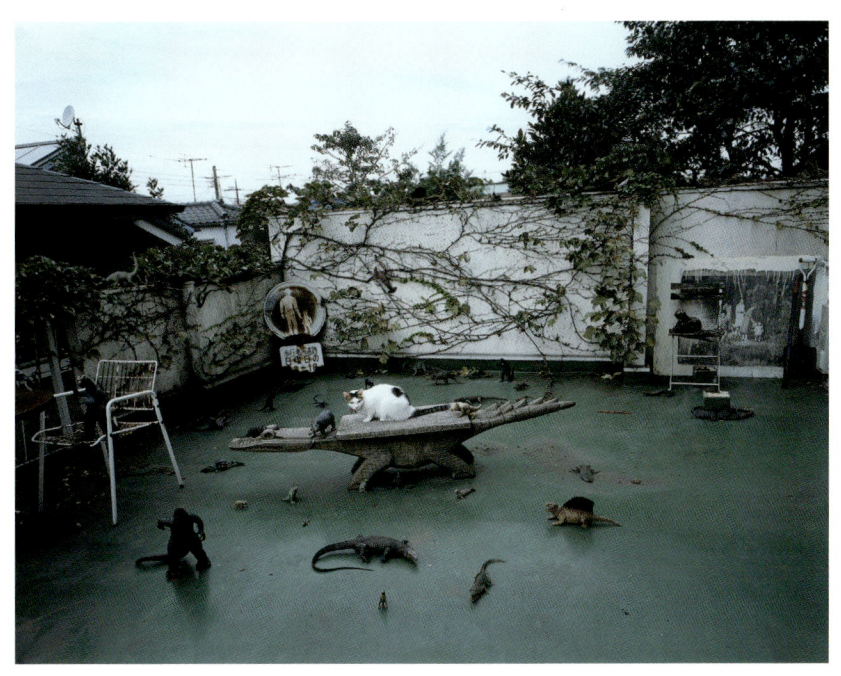

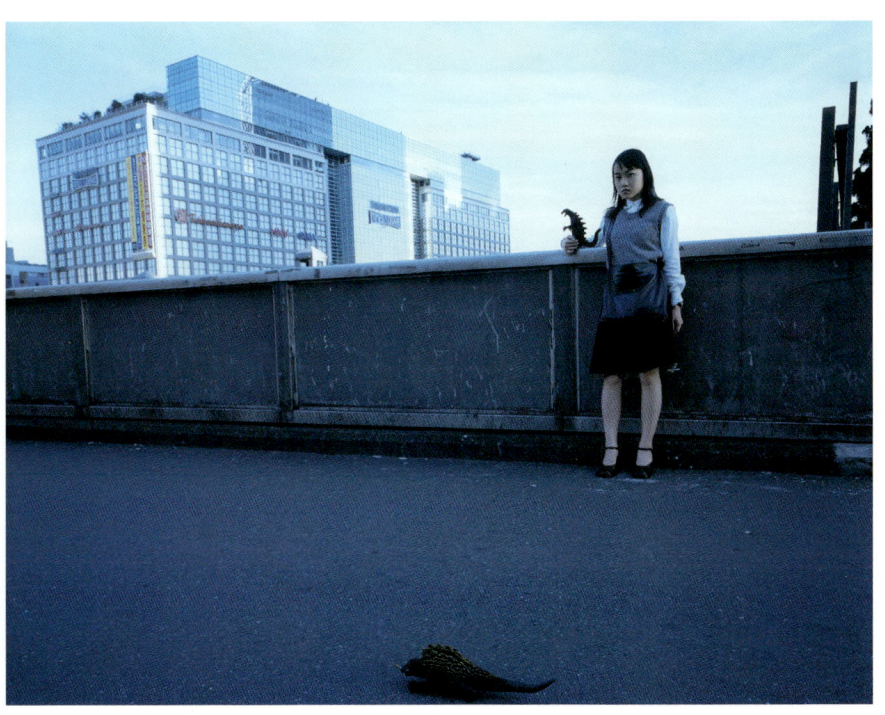

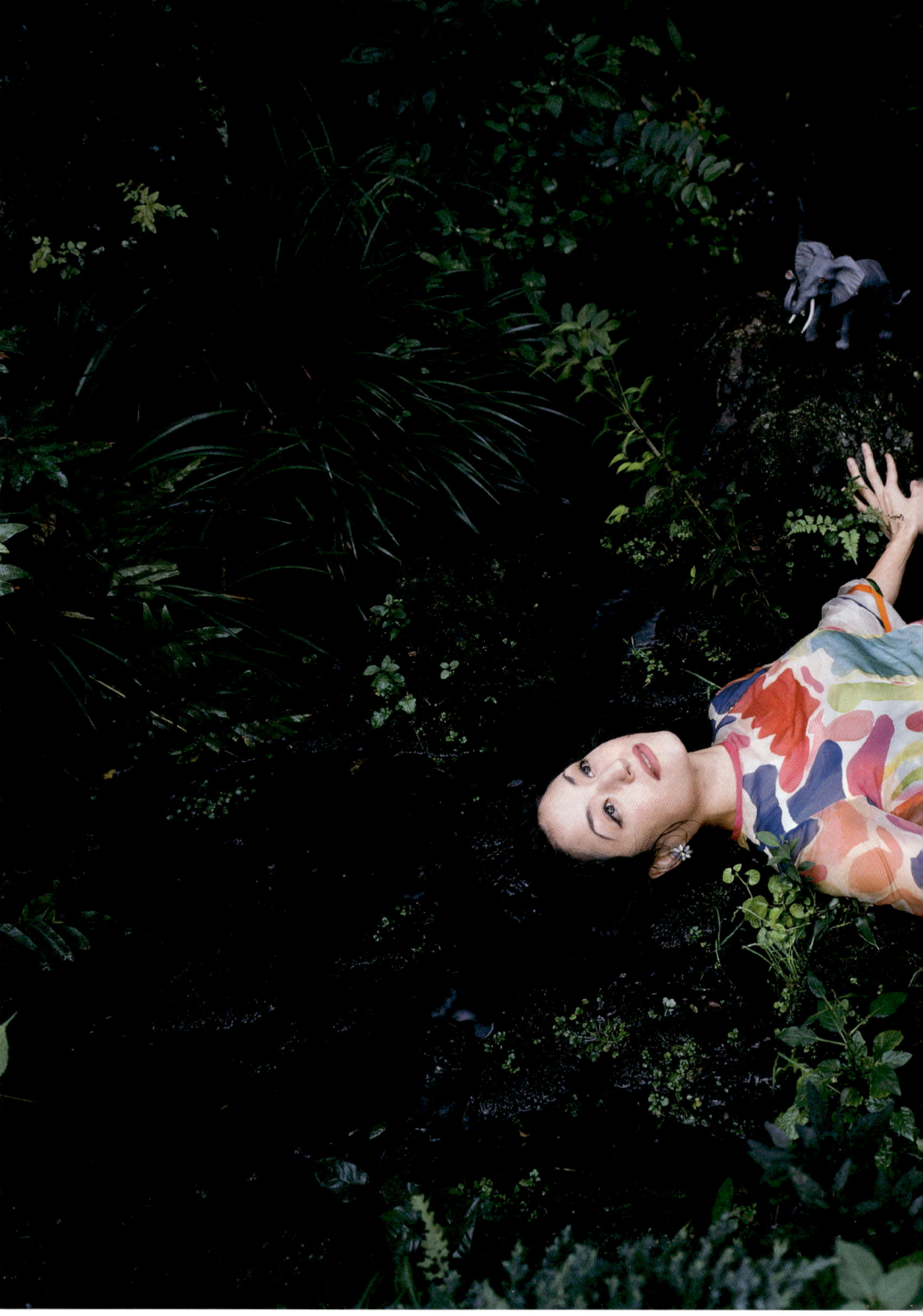

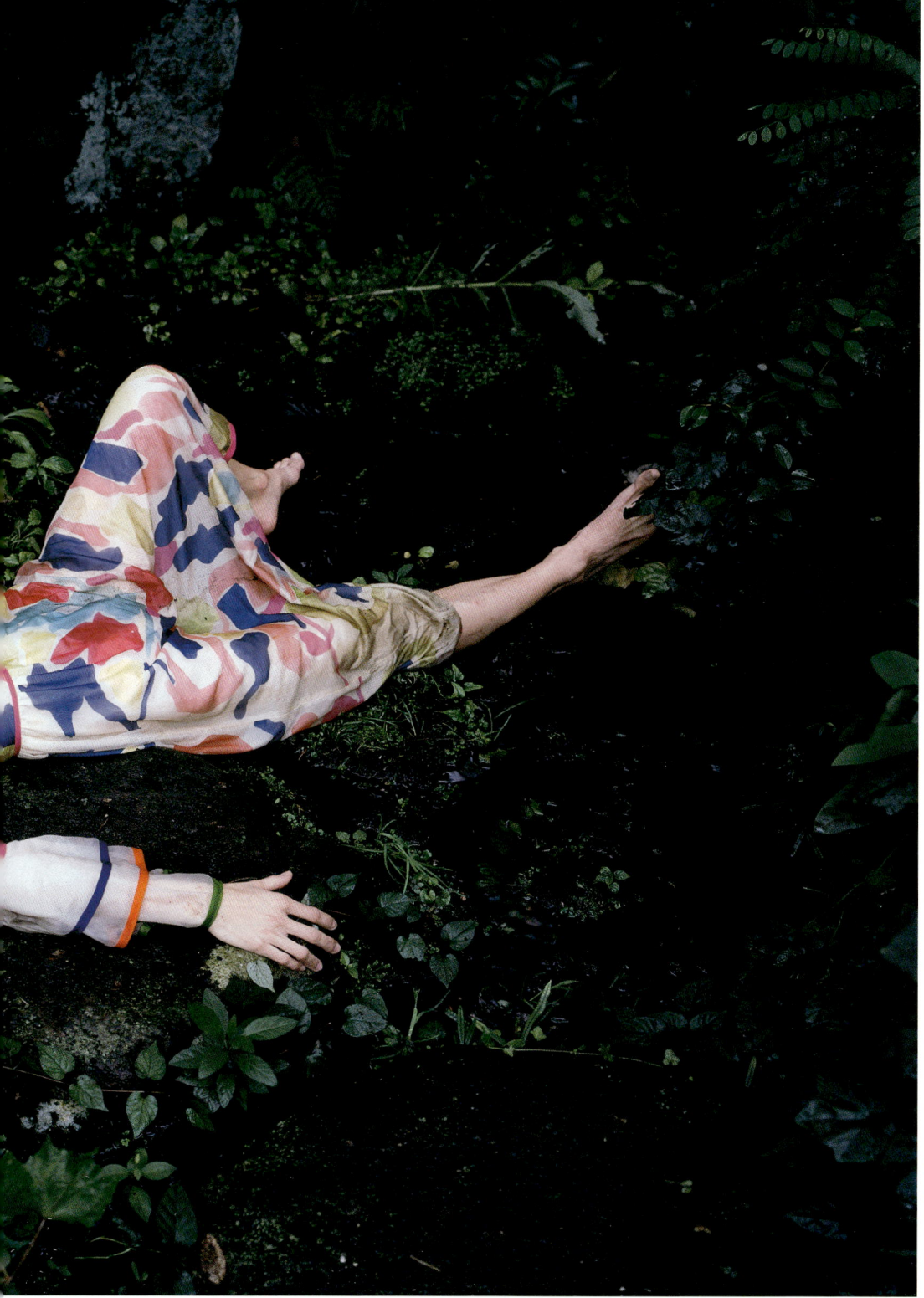

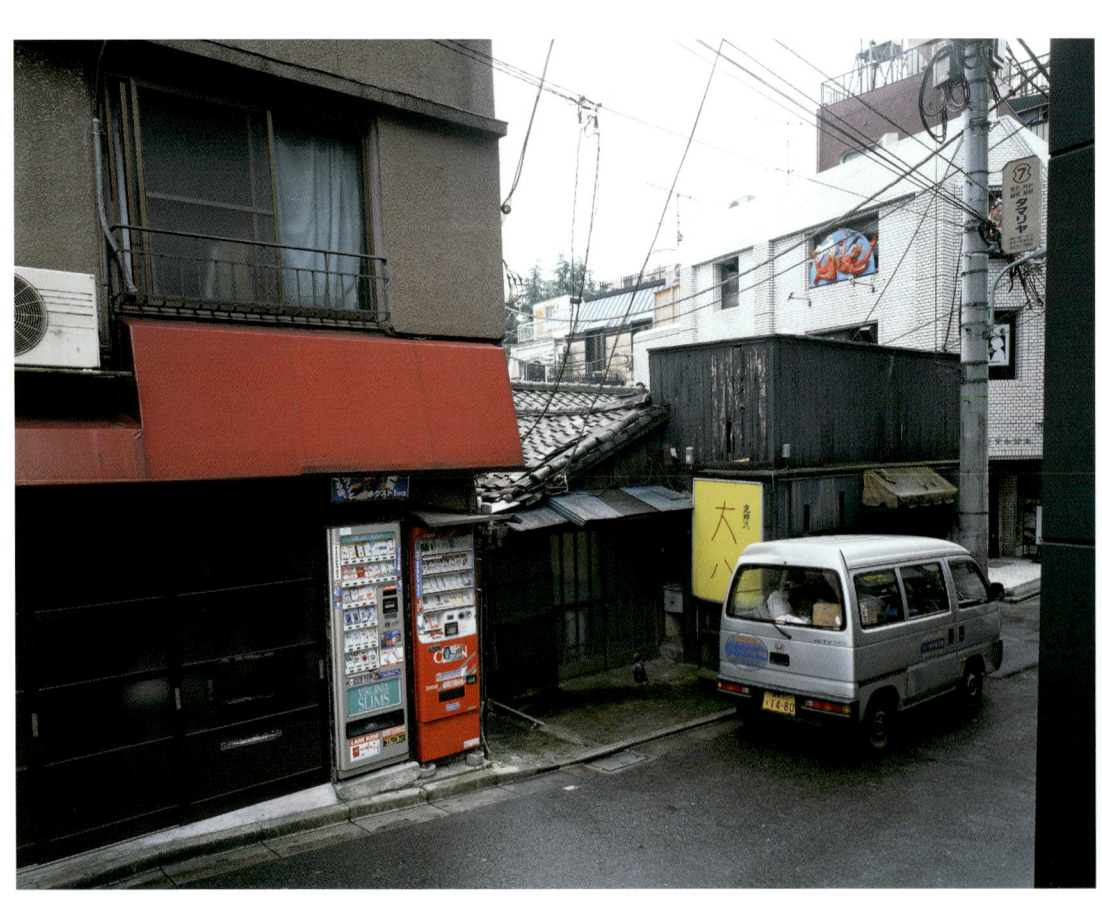

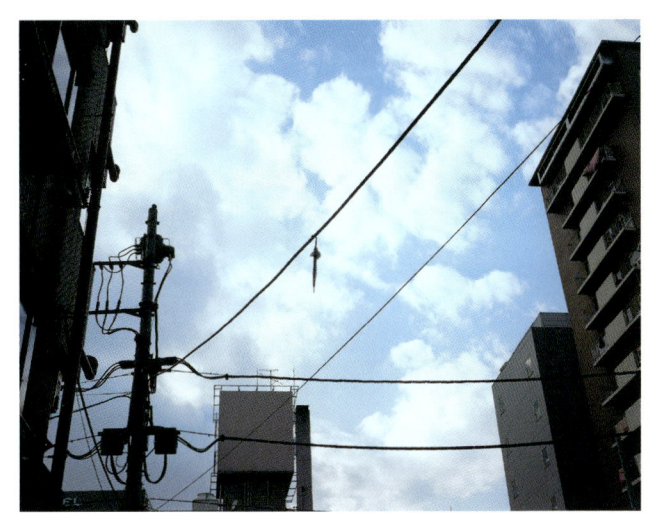

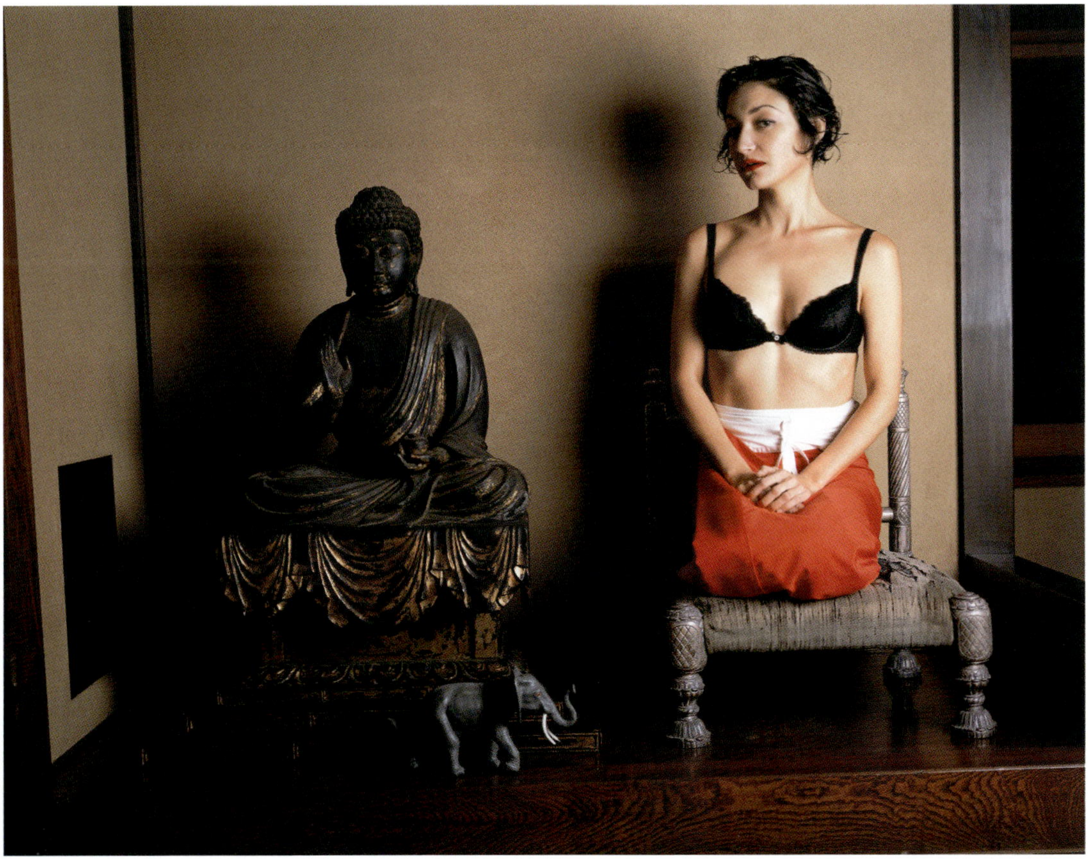

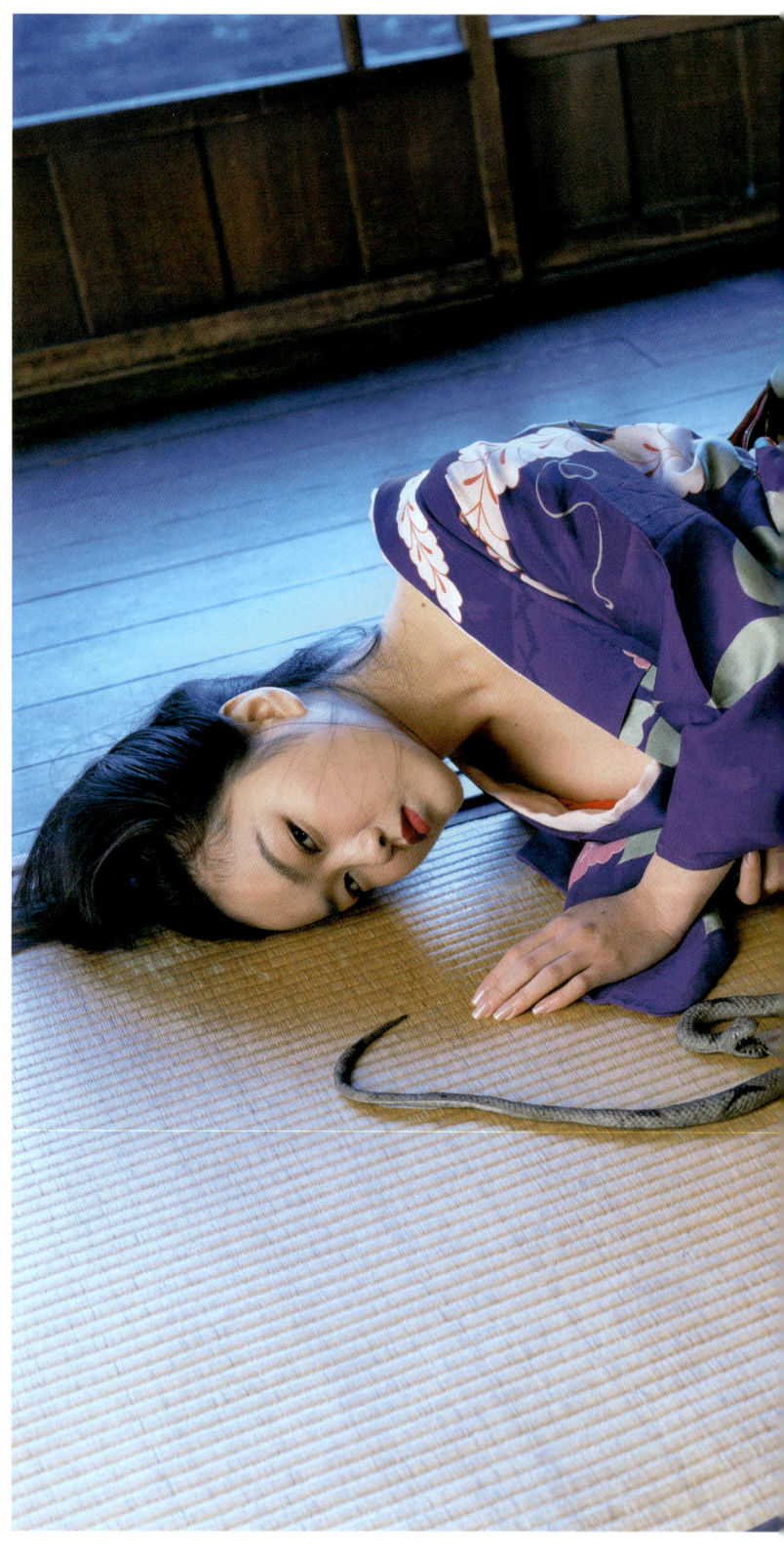

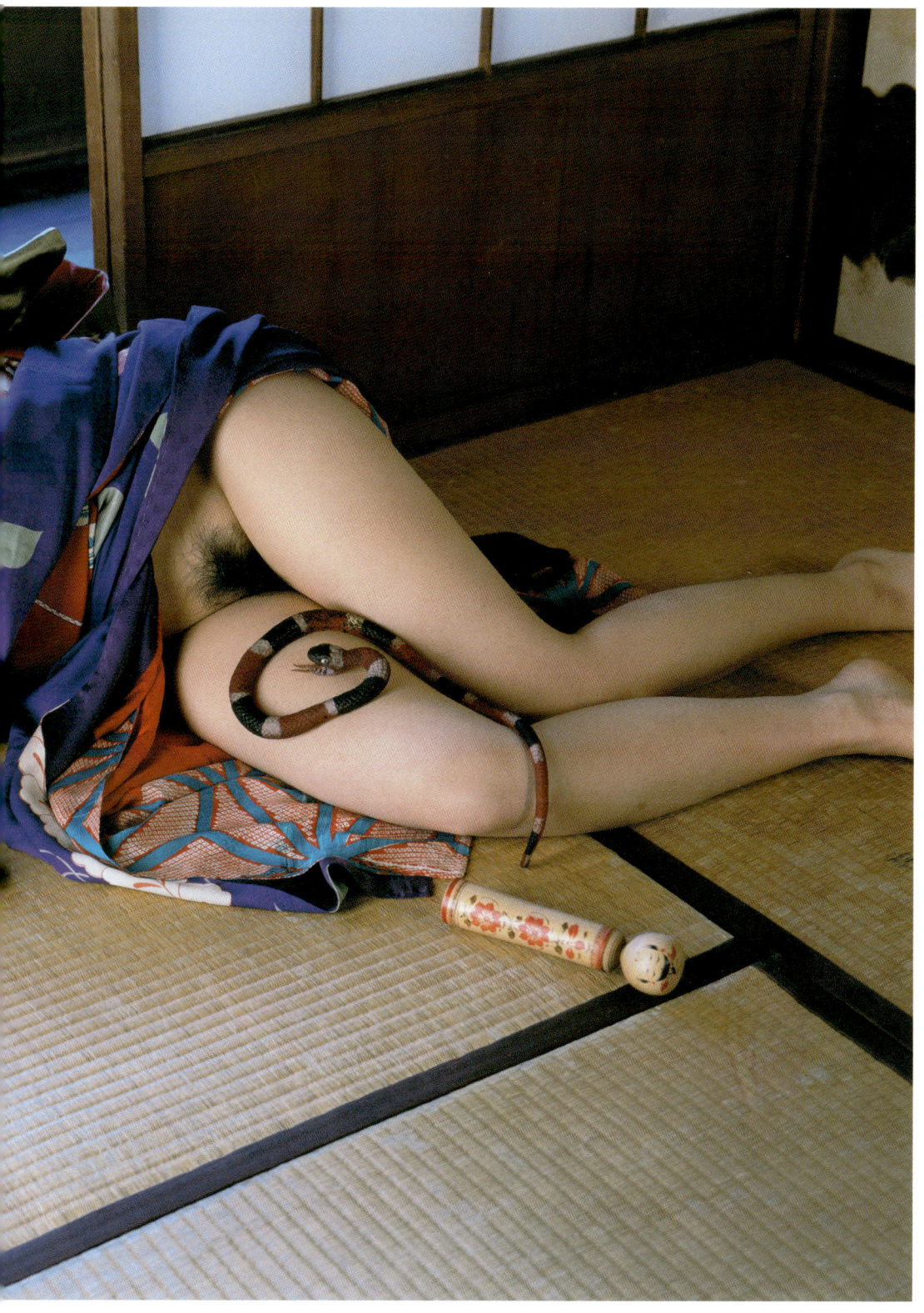

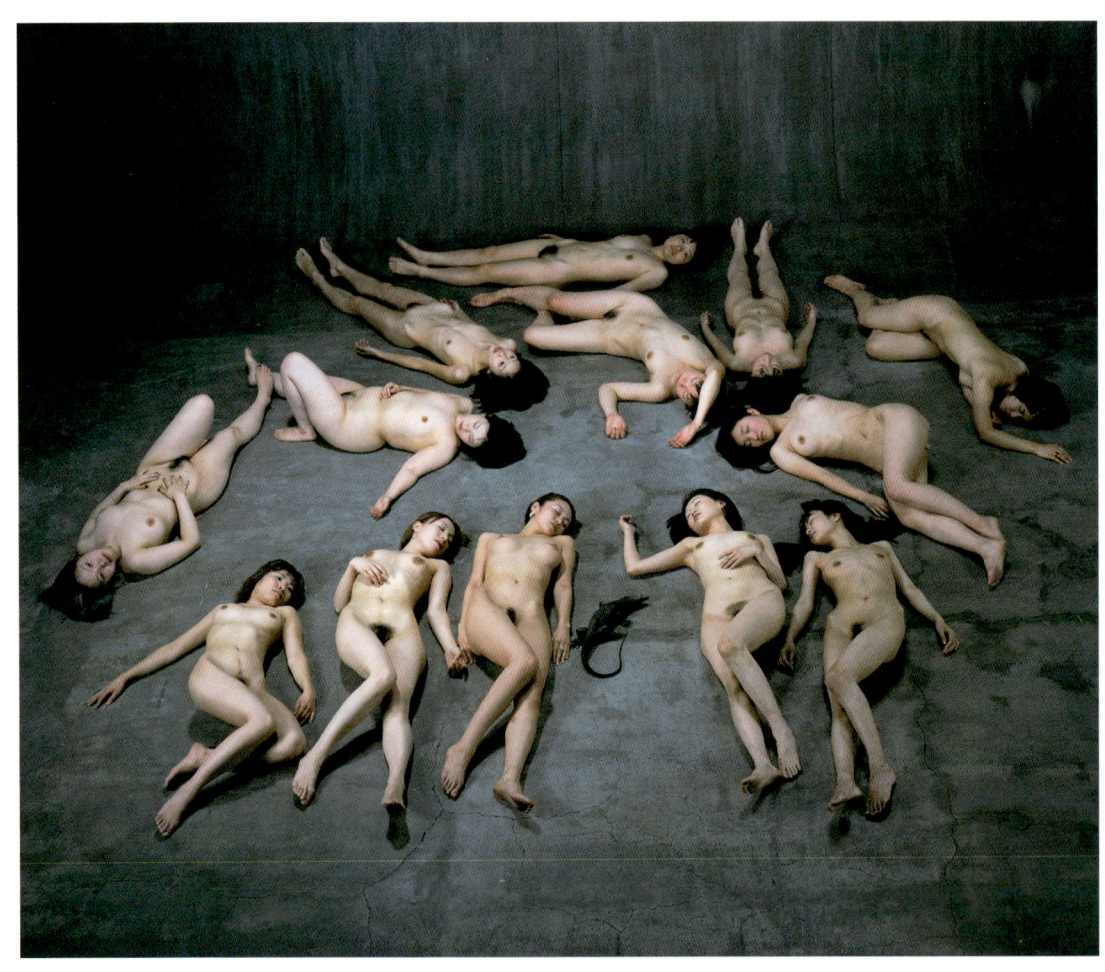

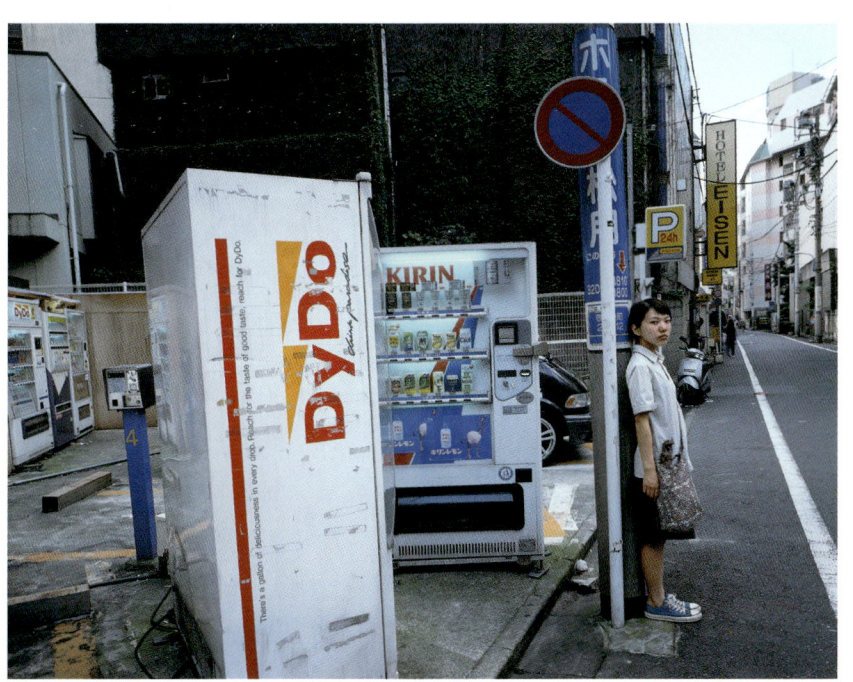

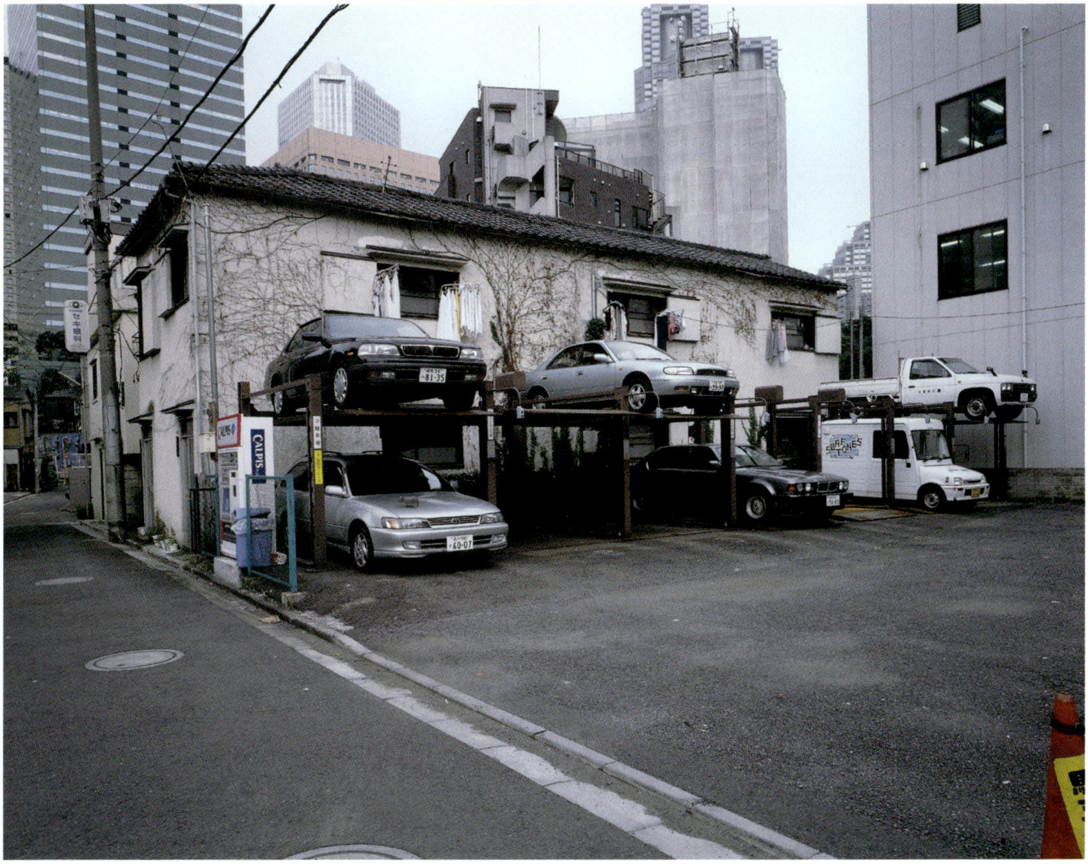

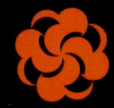

Tokyo Nostalgia

東京ノスタルジー

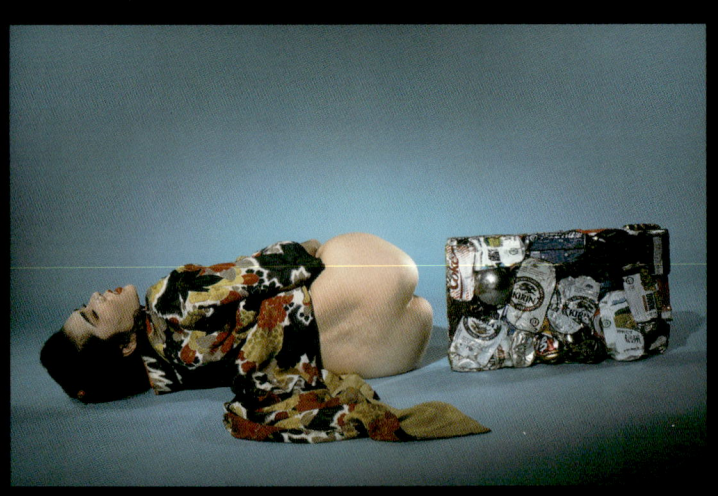

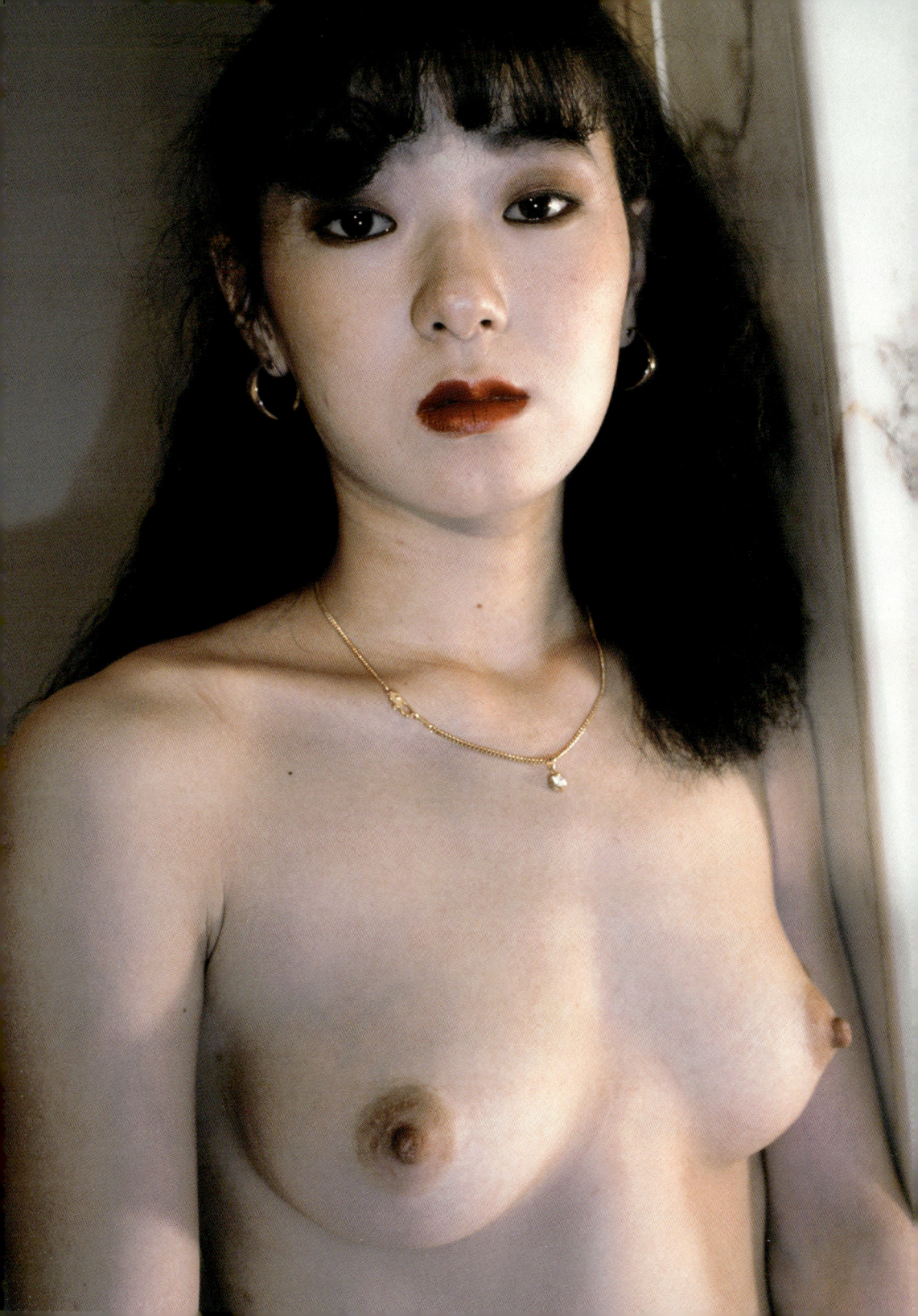

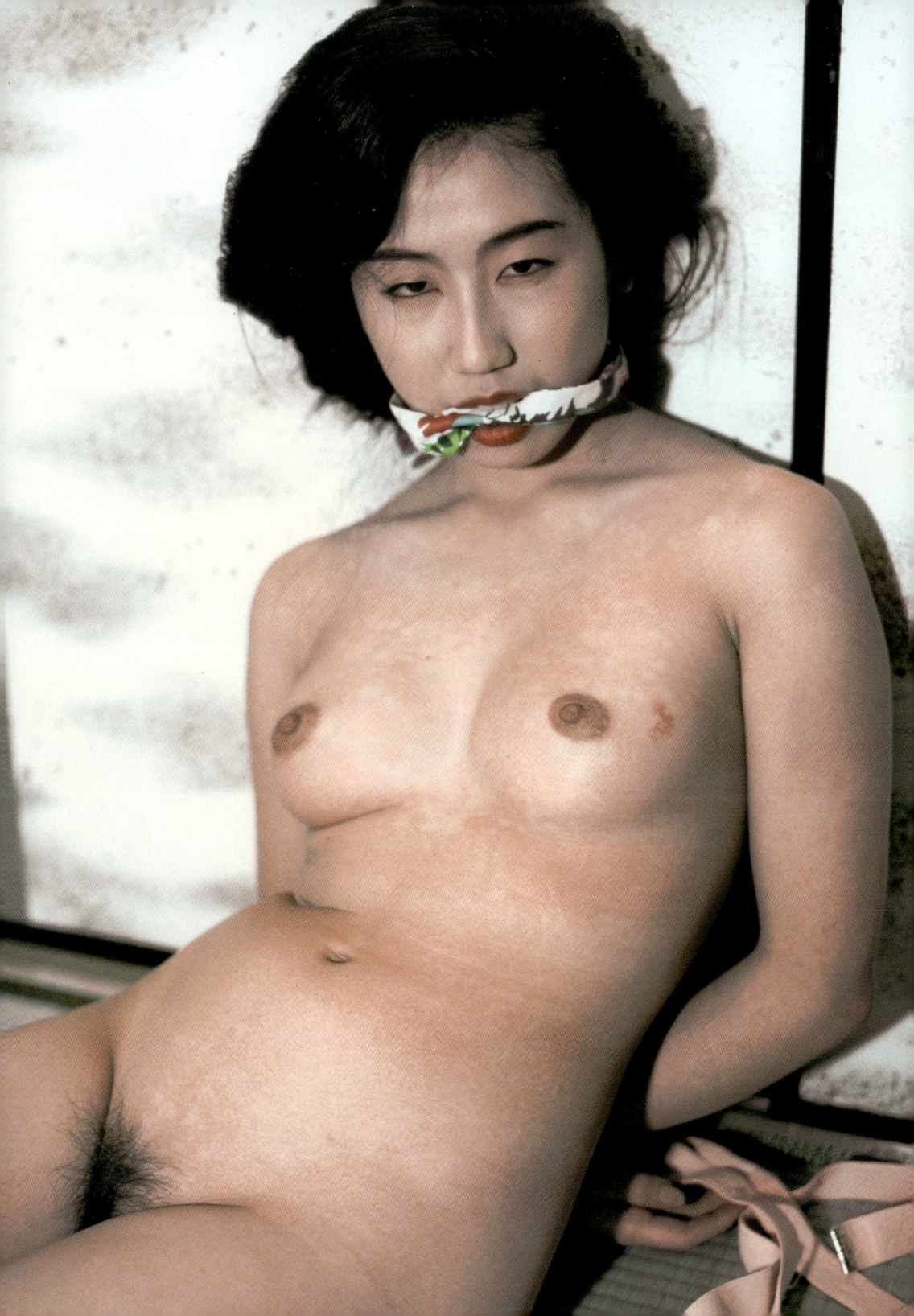

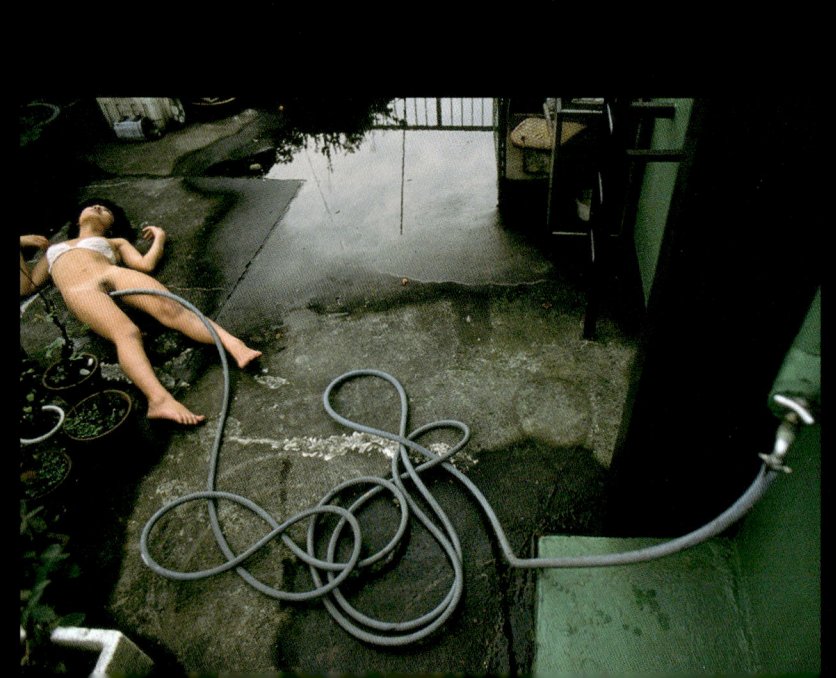

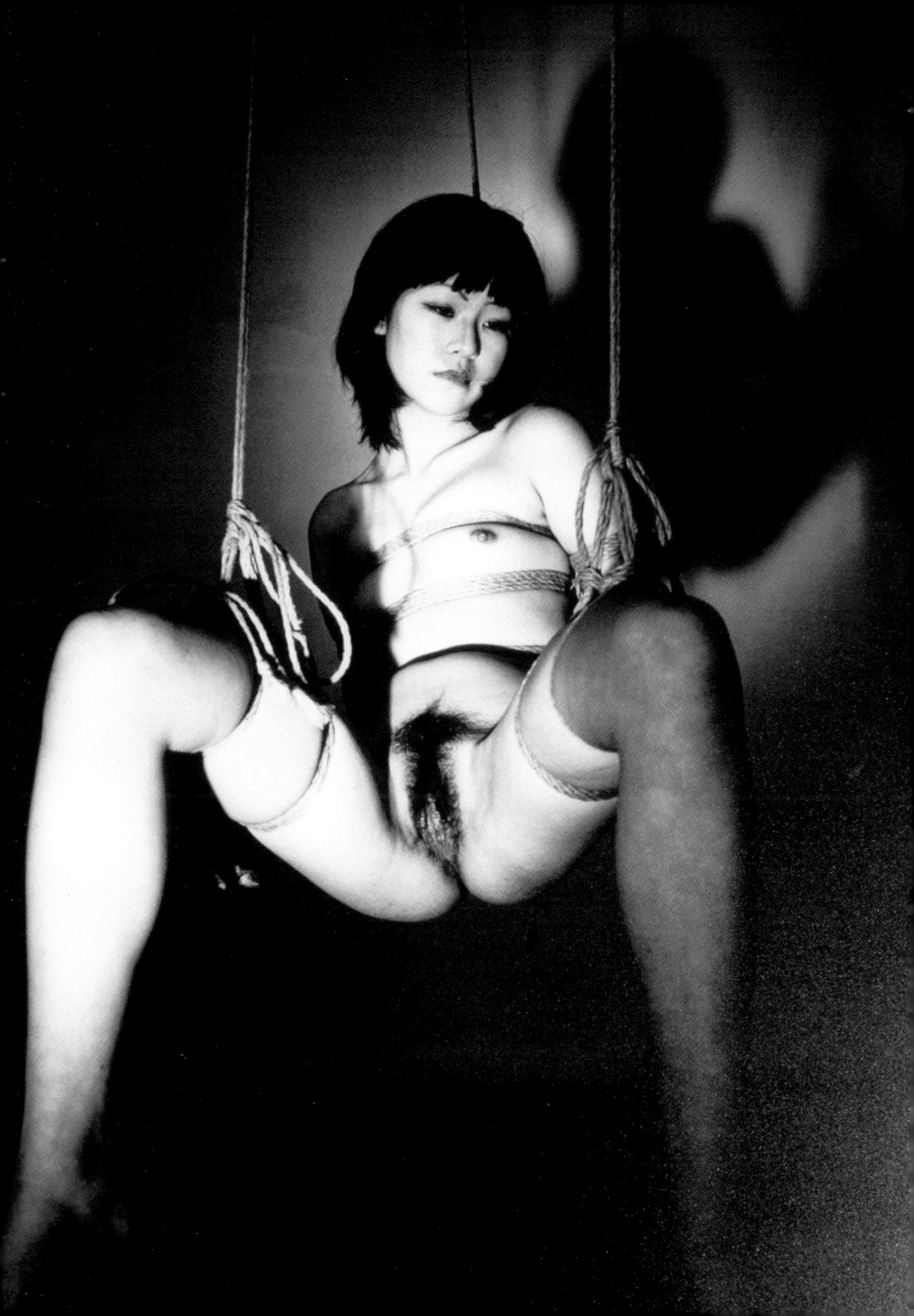

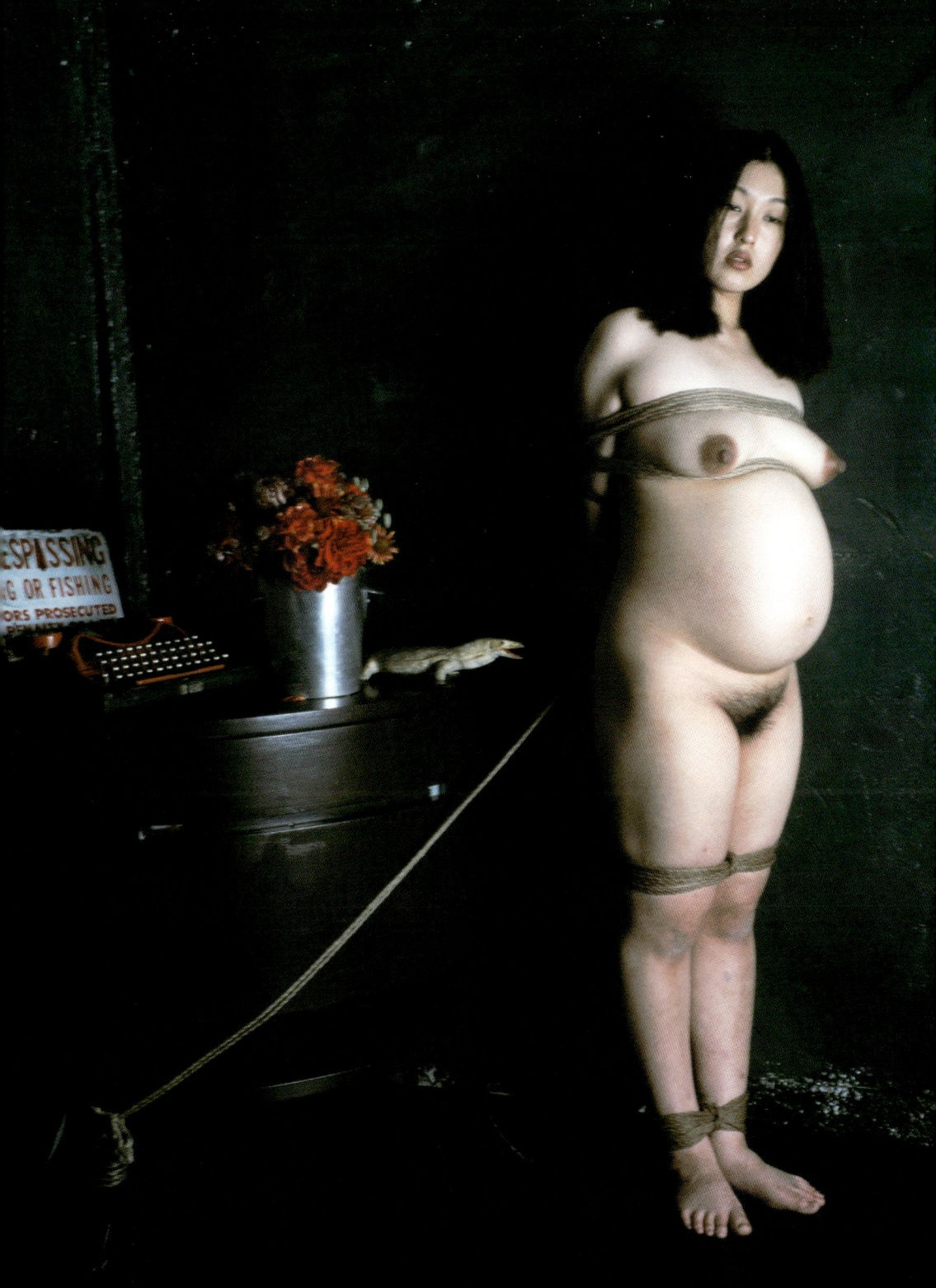

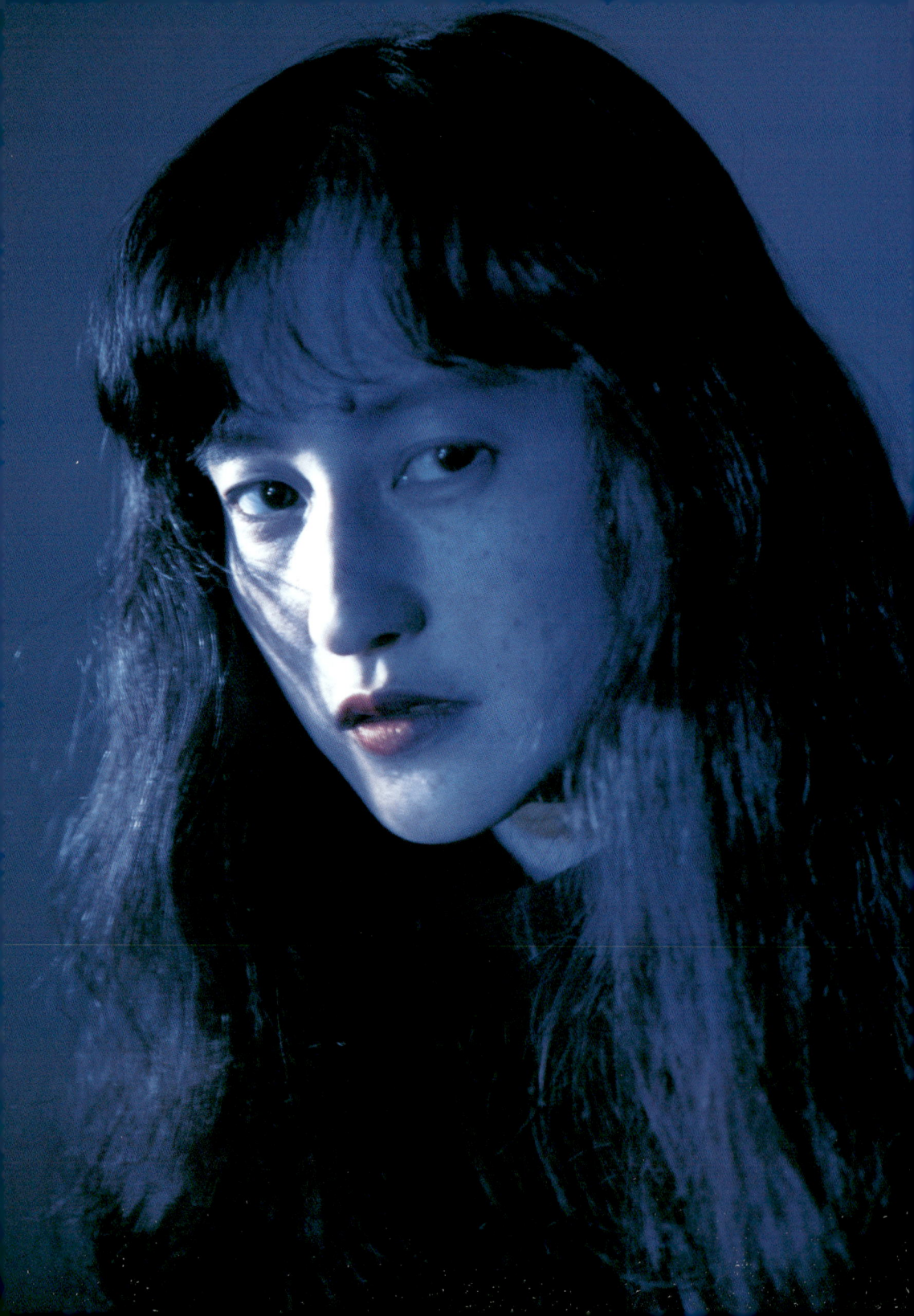

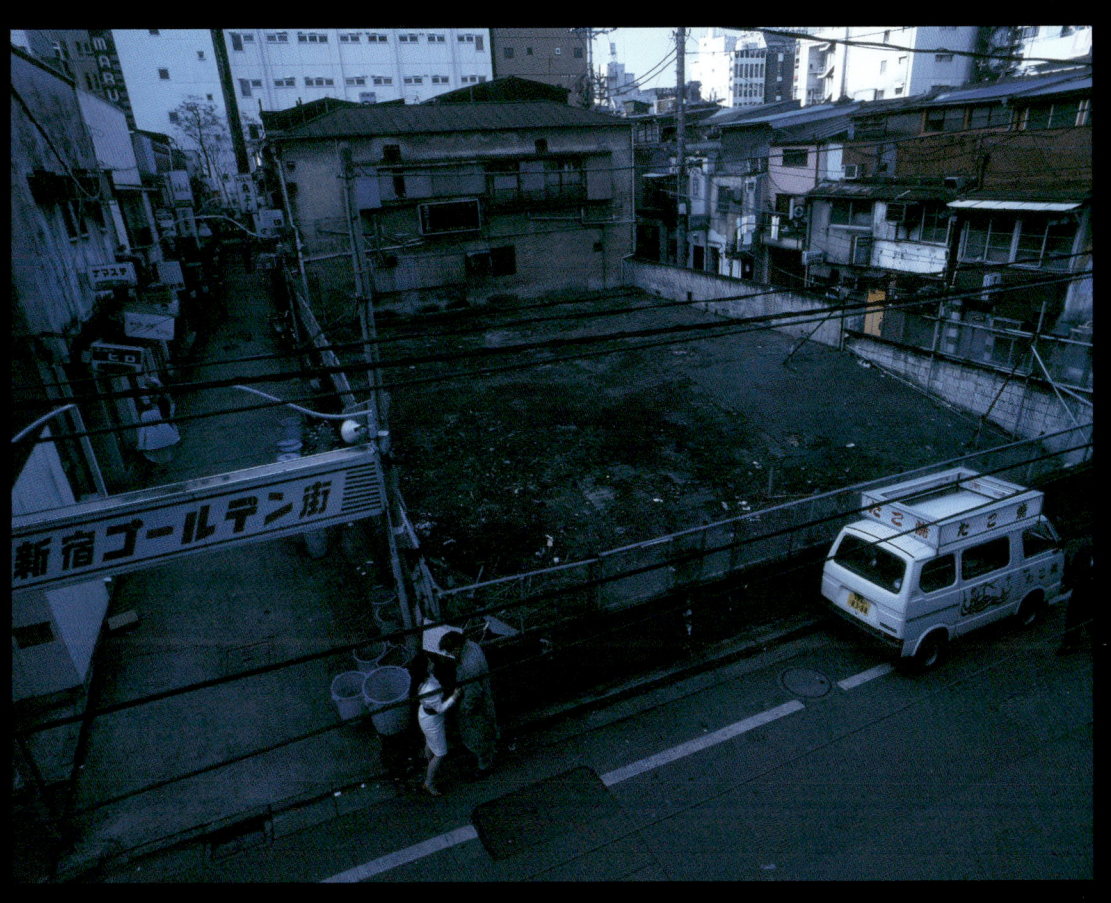

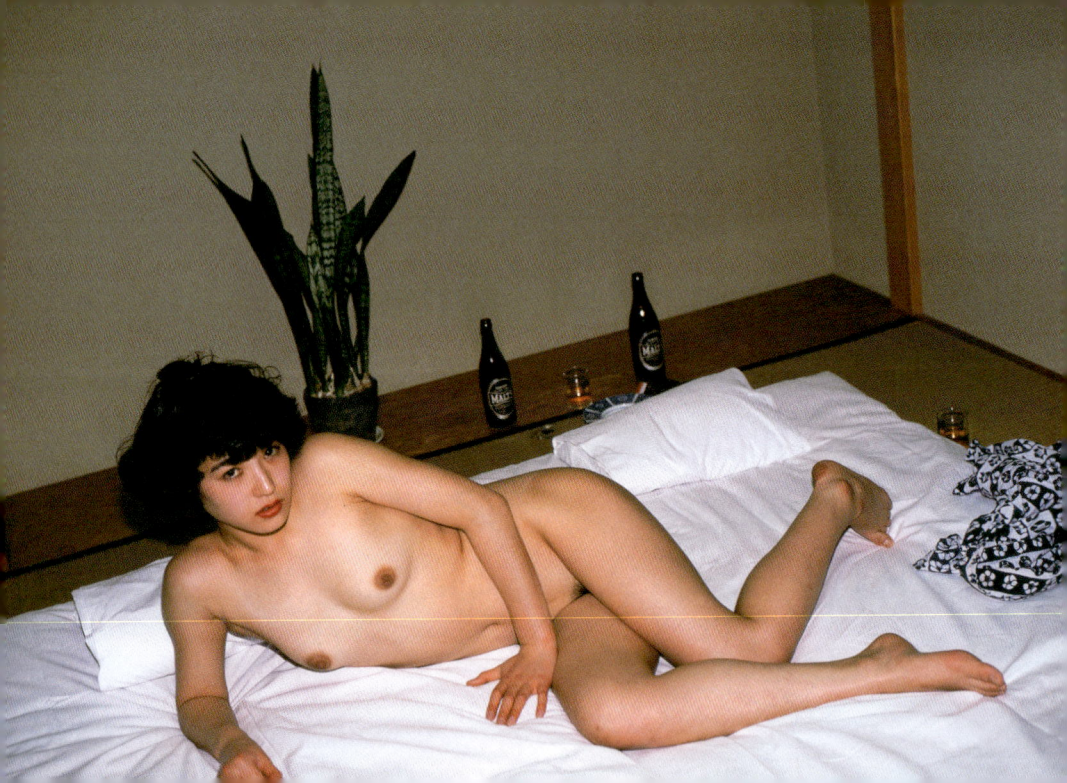

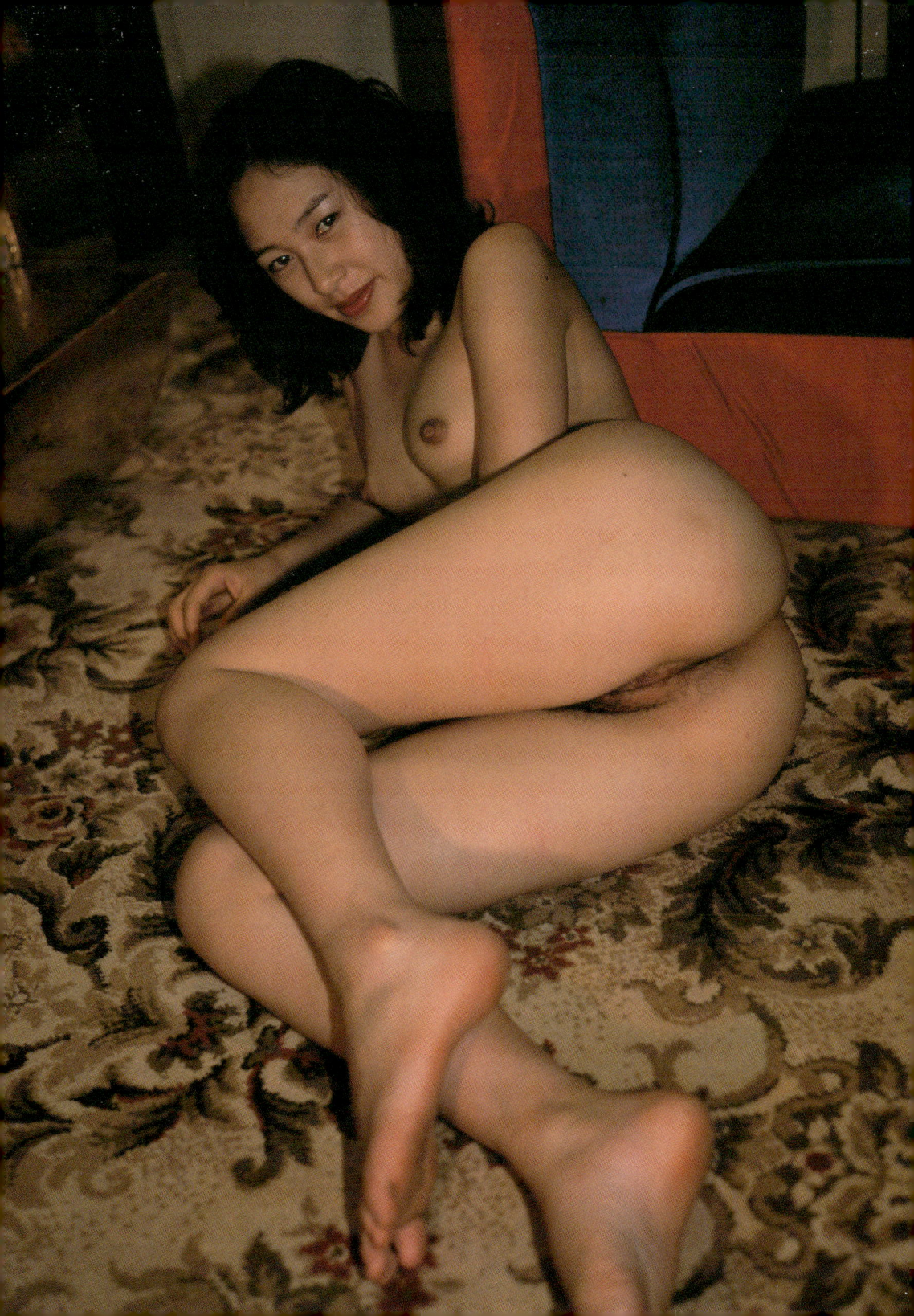

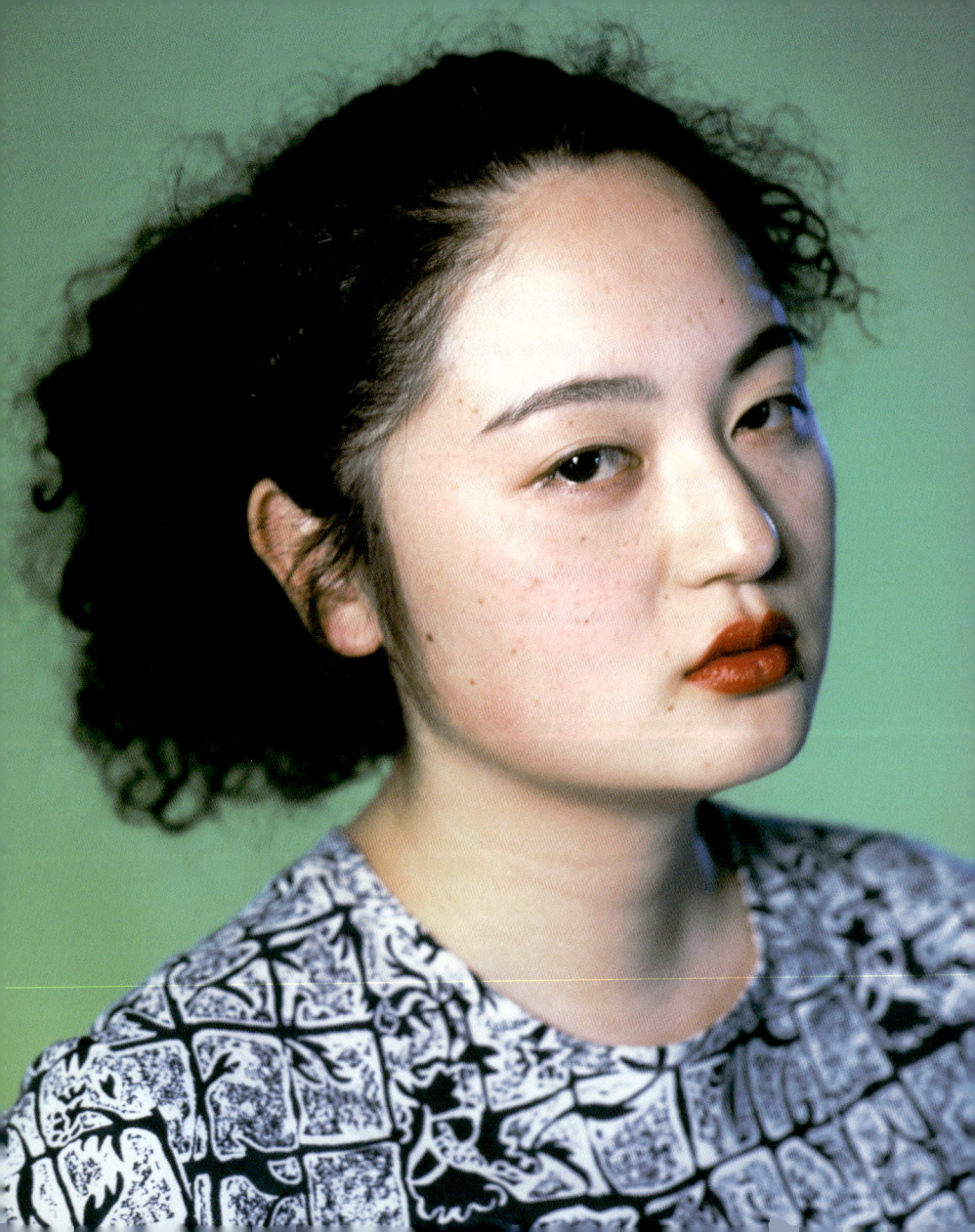

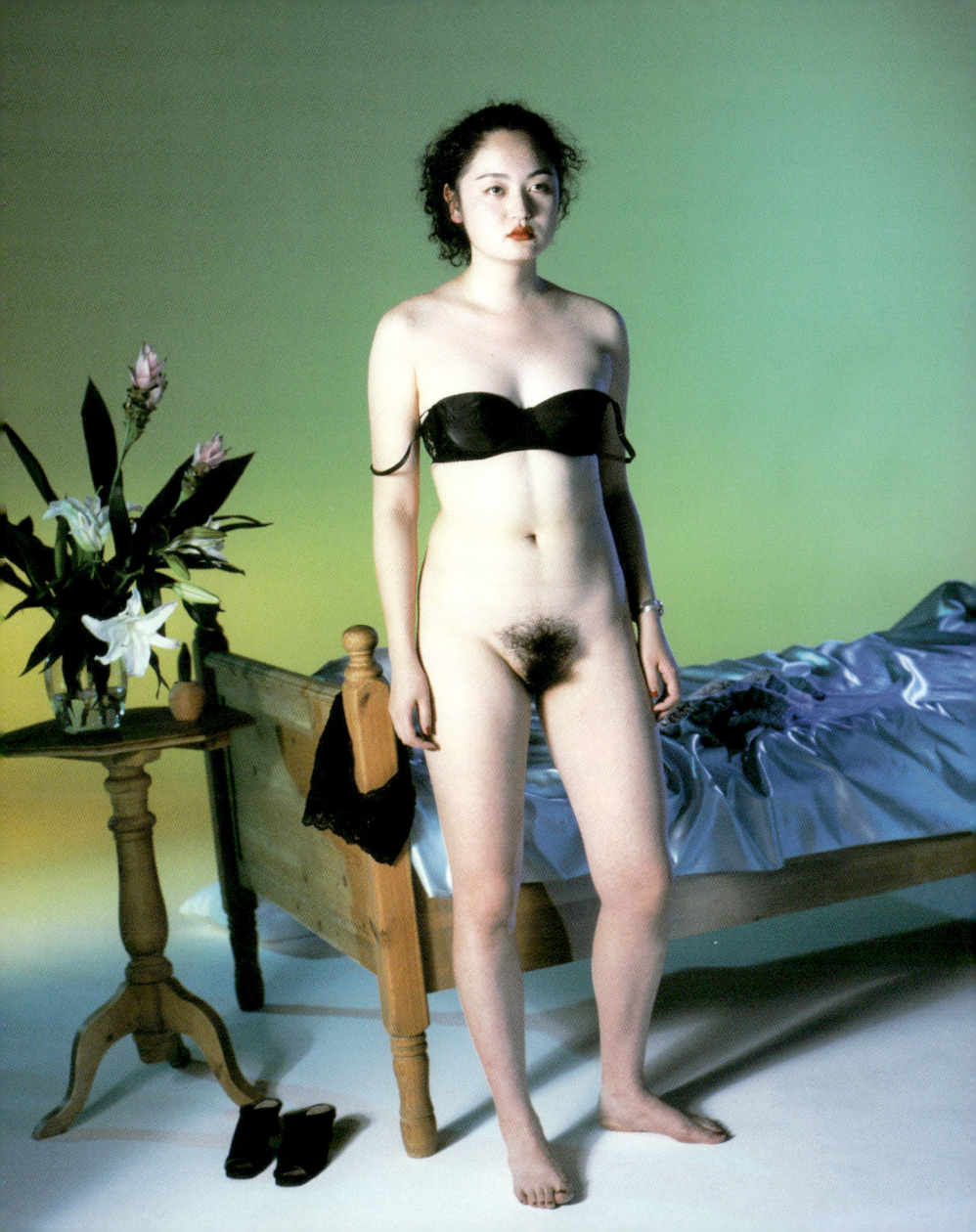

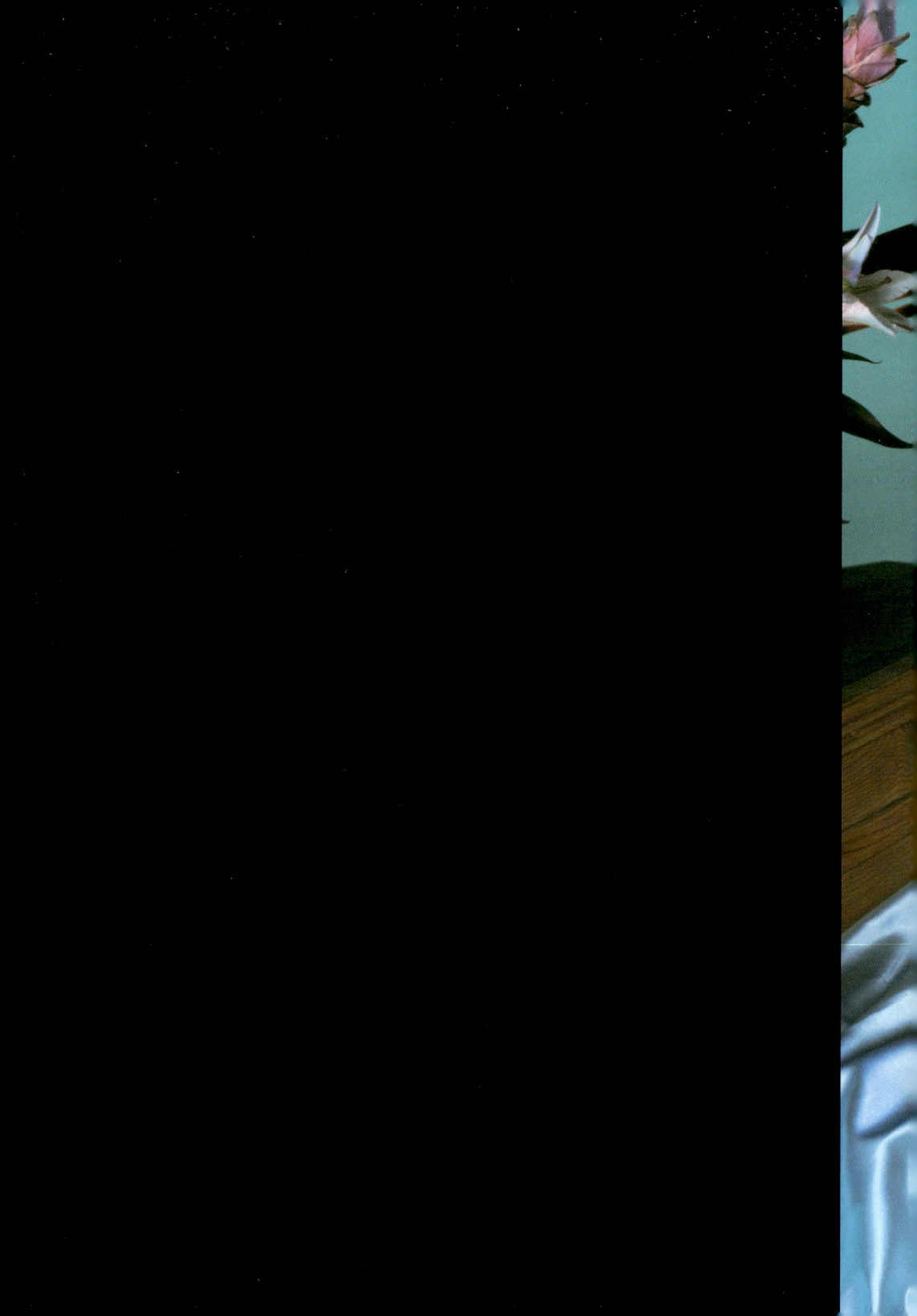

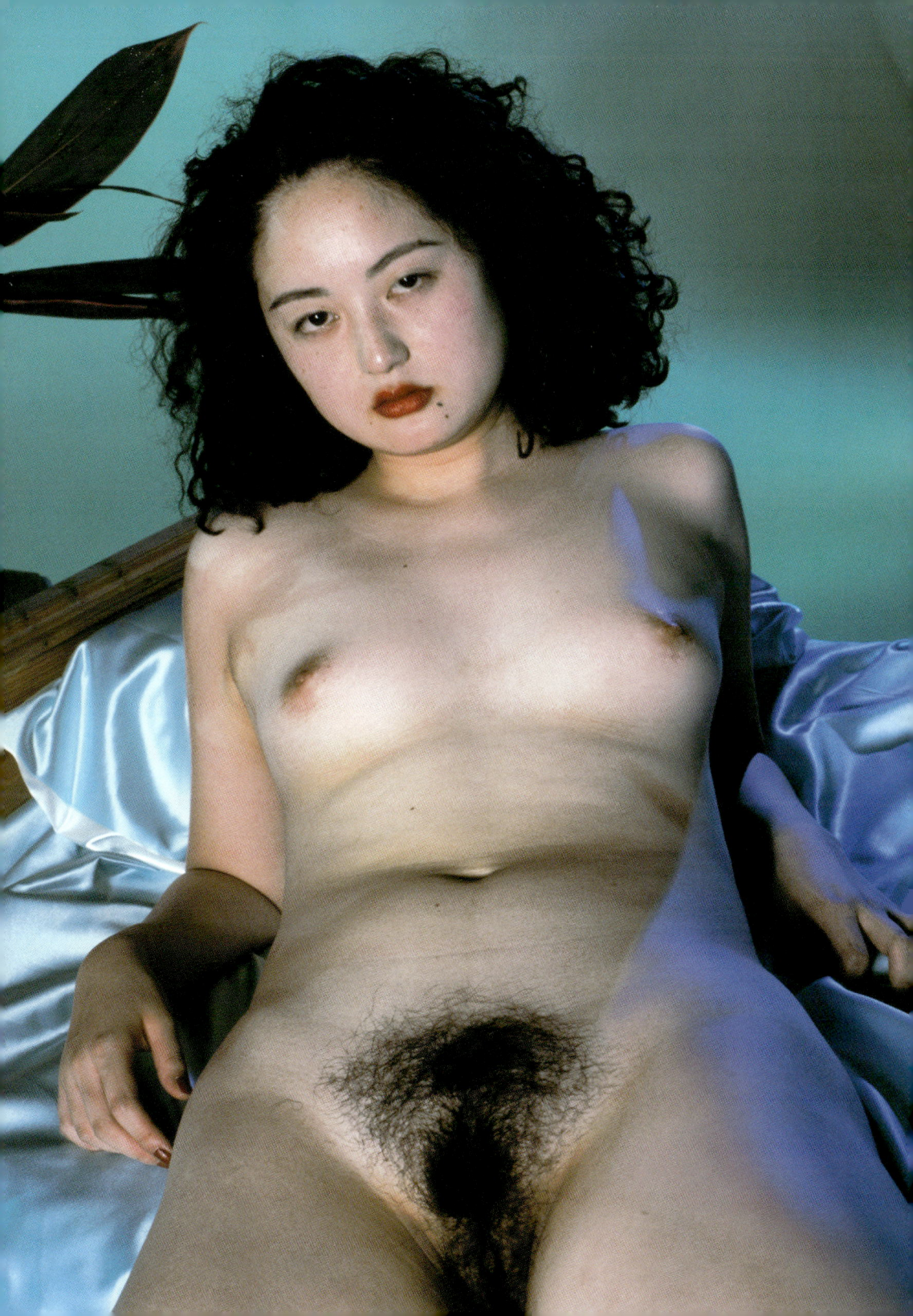

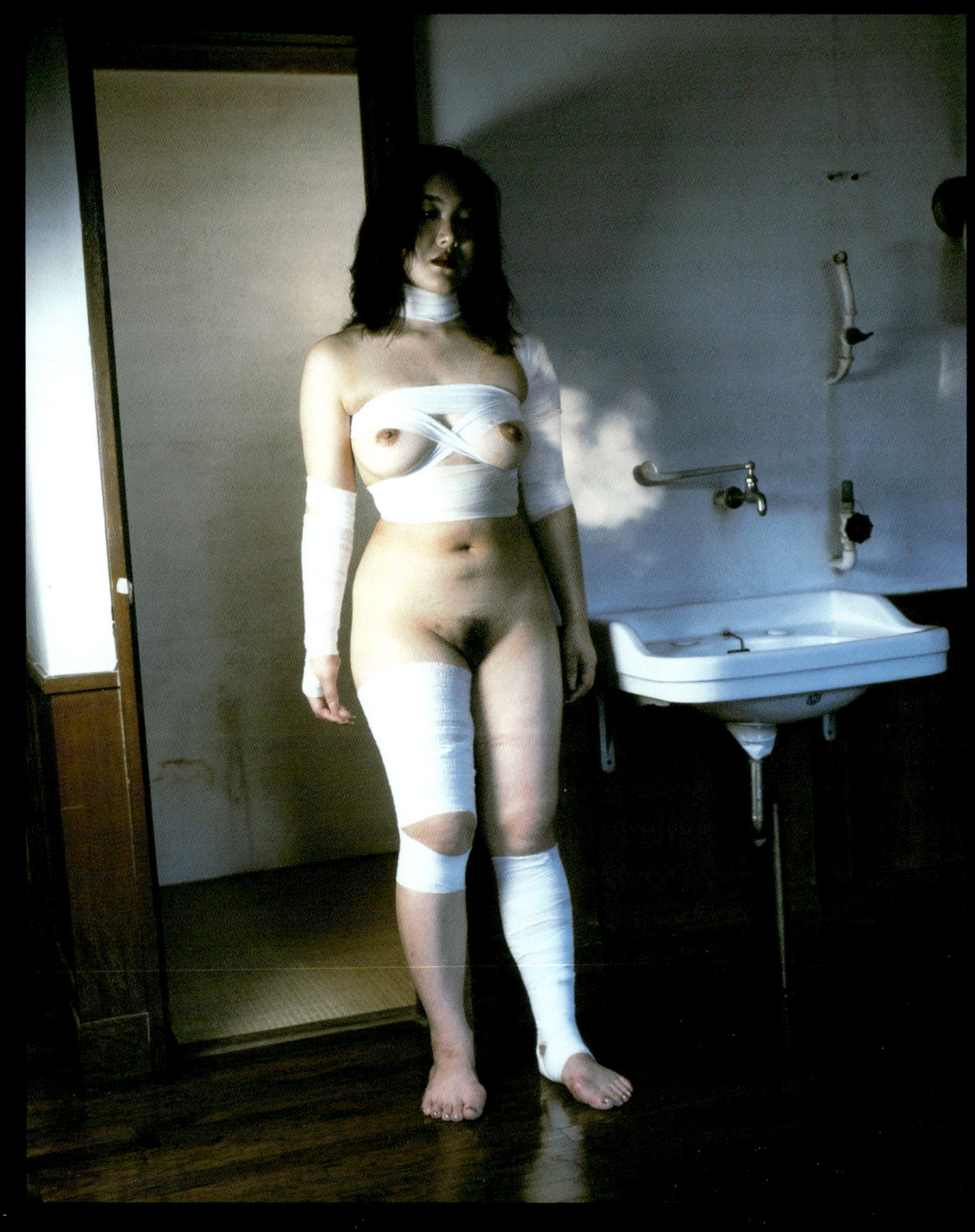

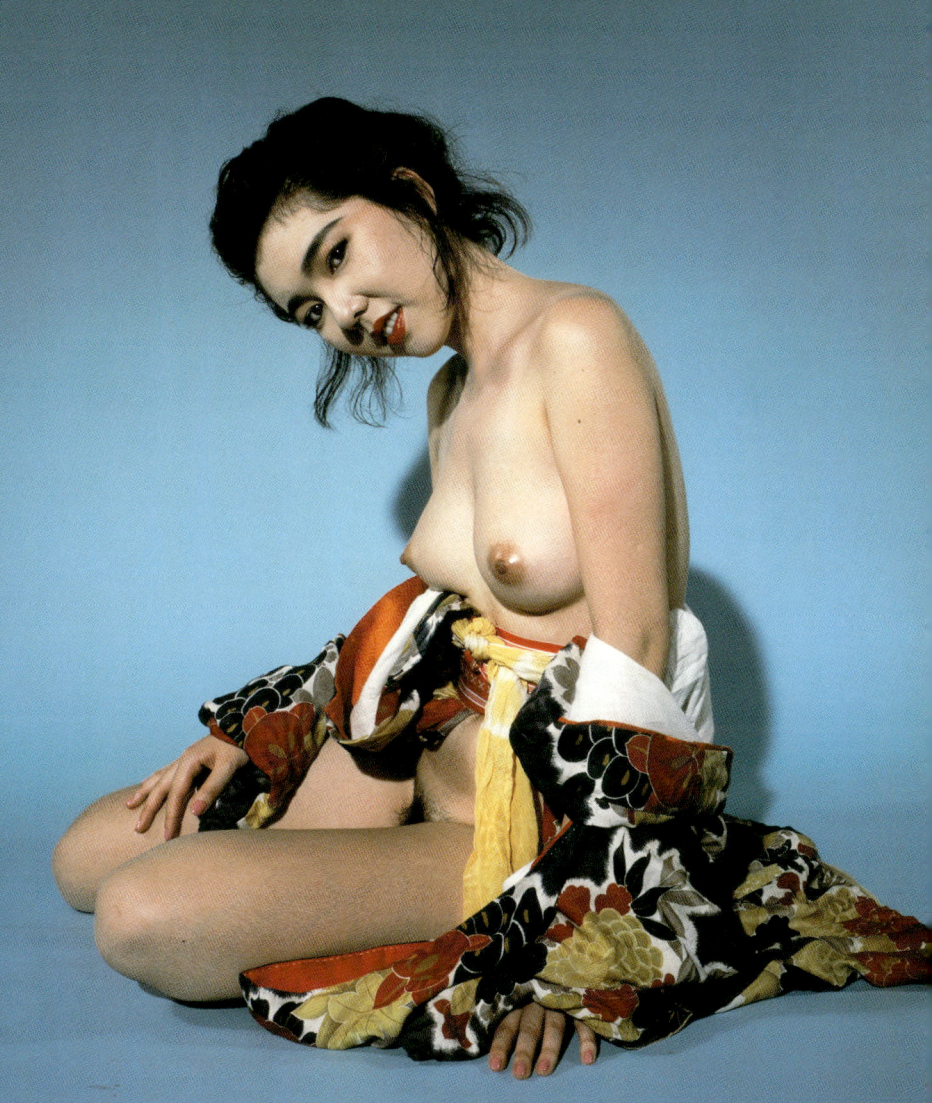

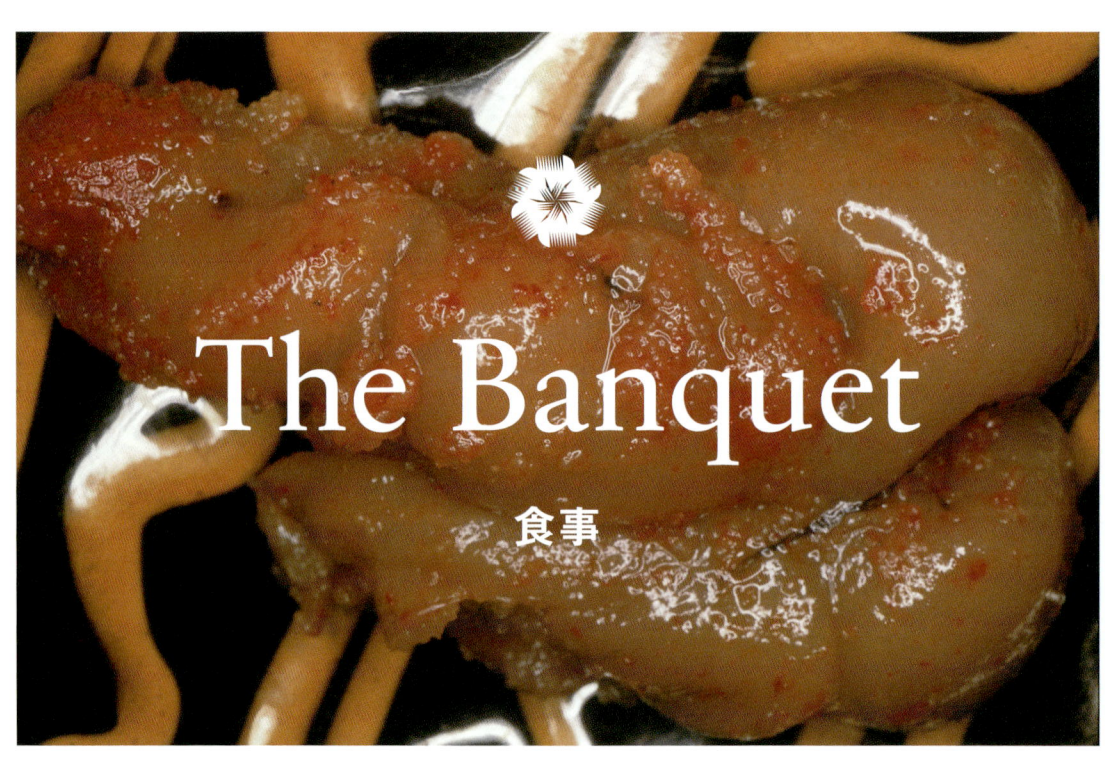

The Banquet

食事

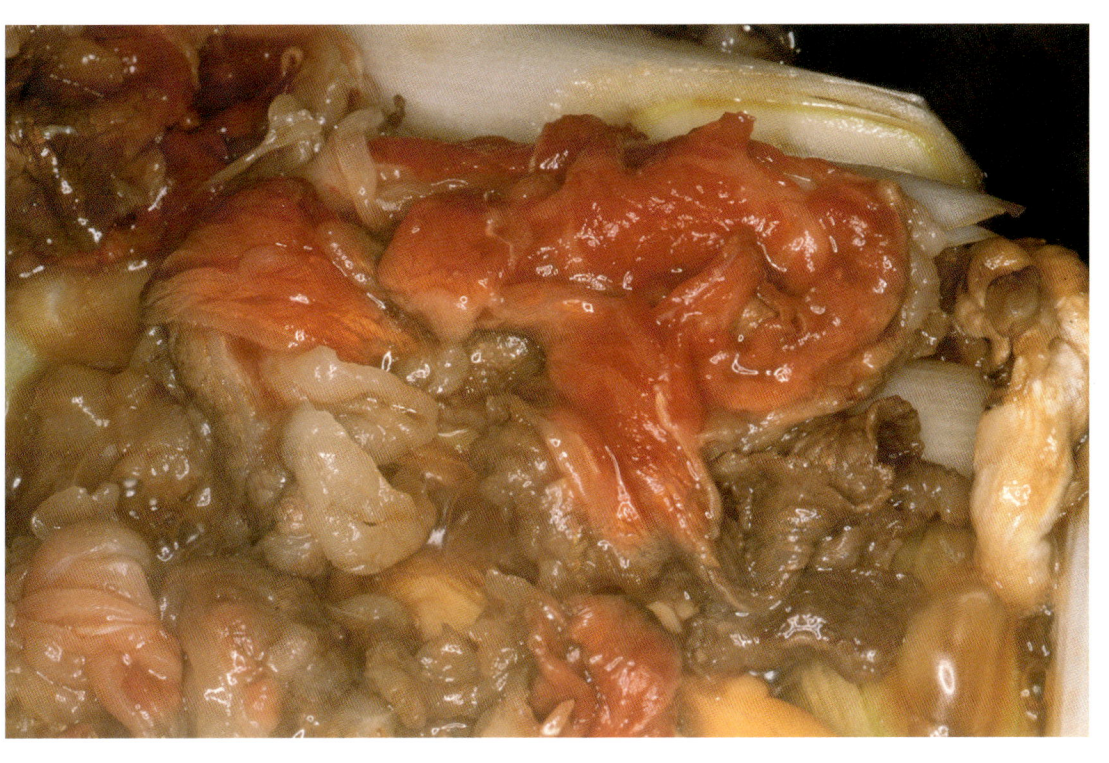

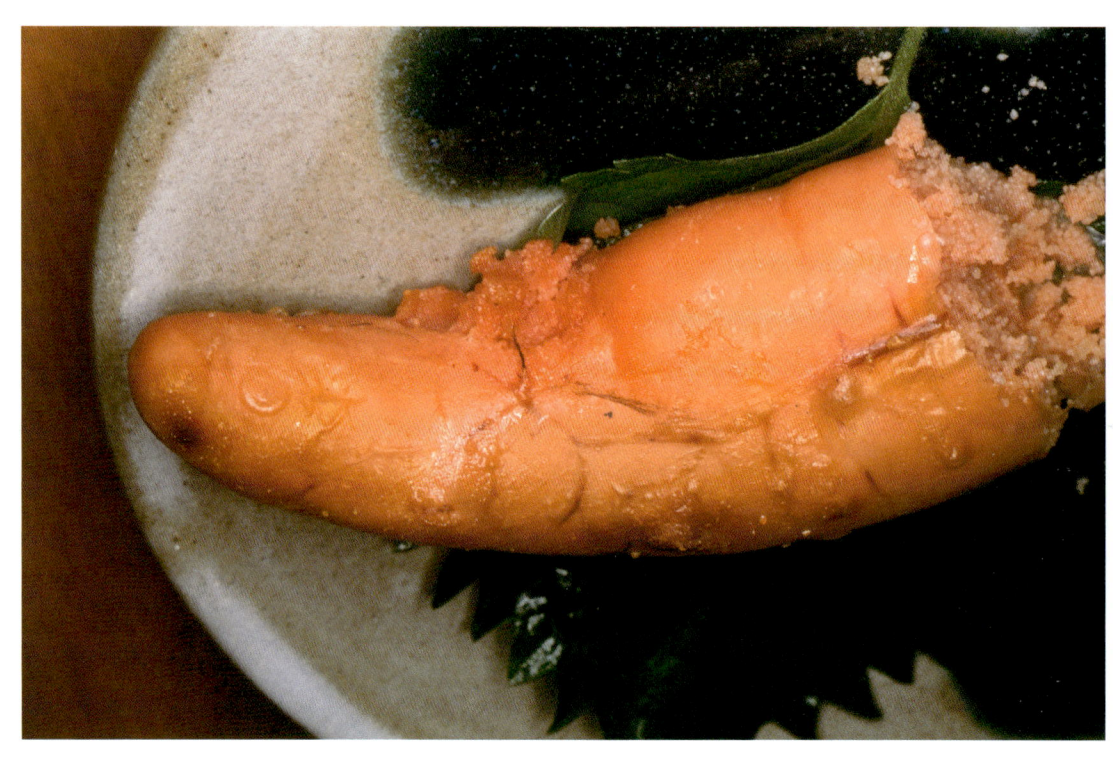

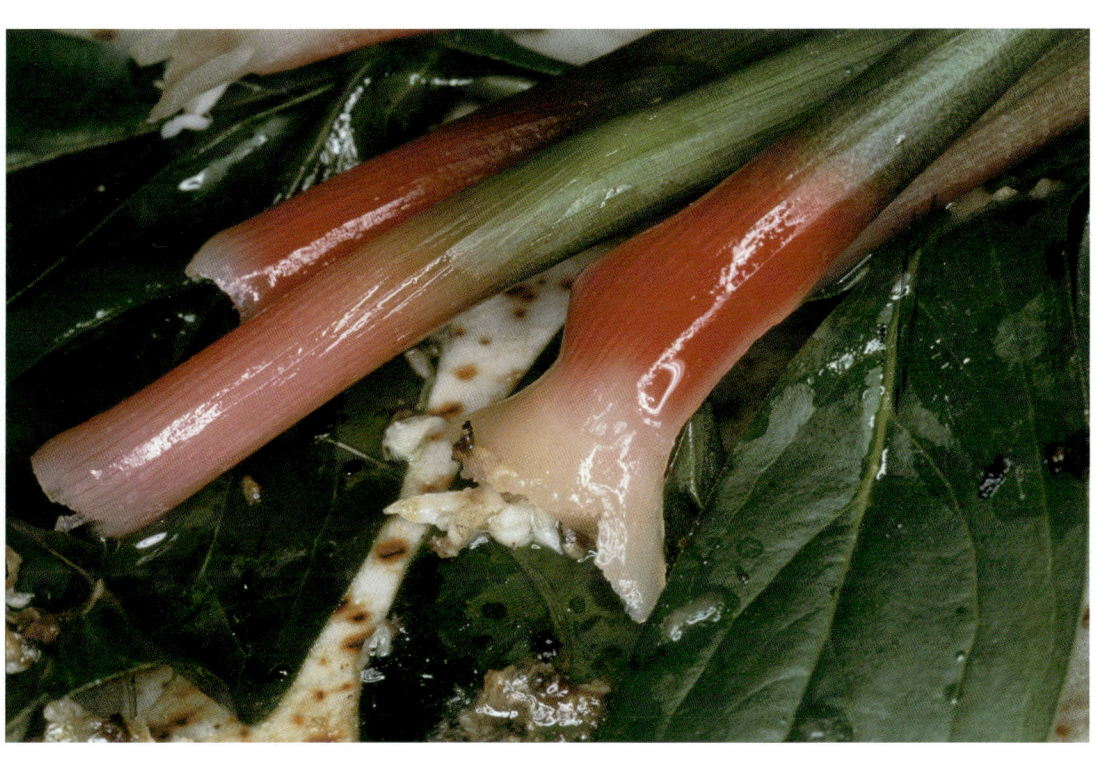

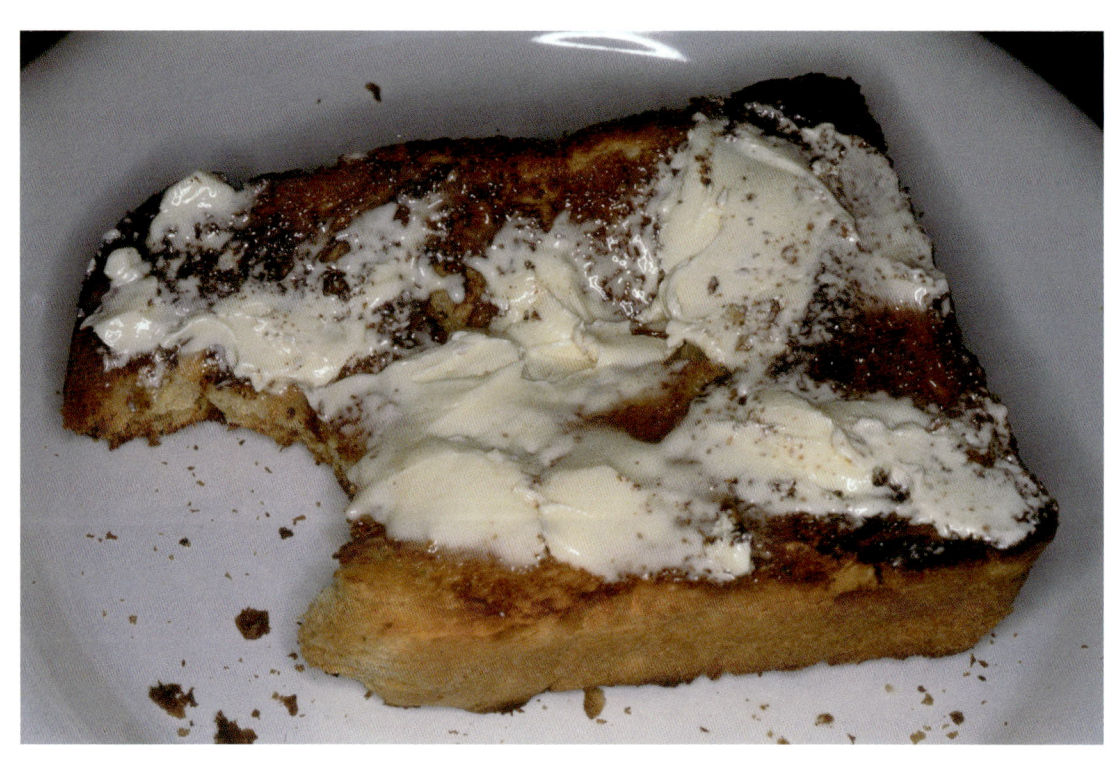

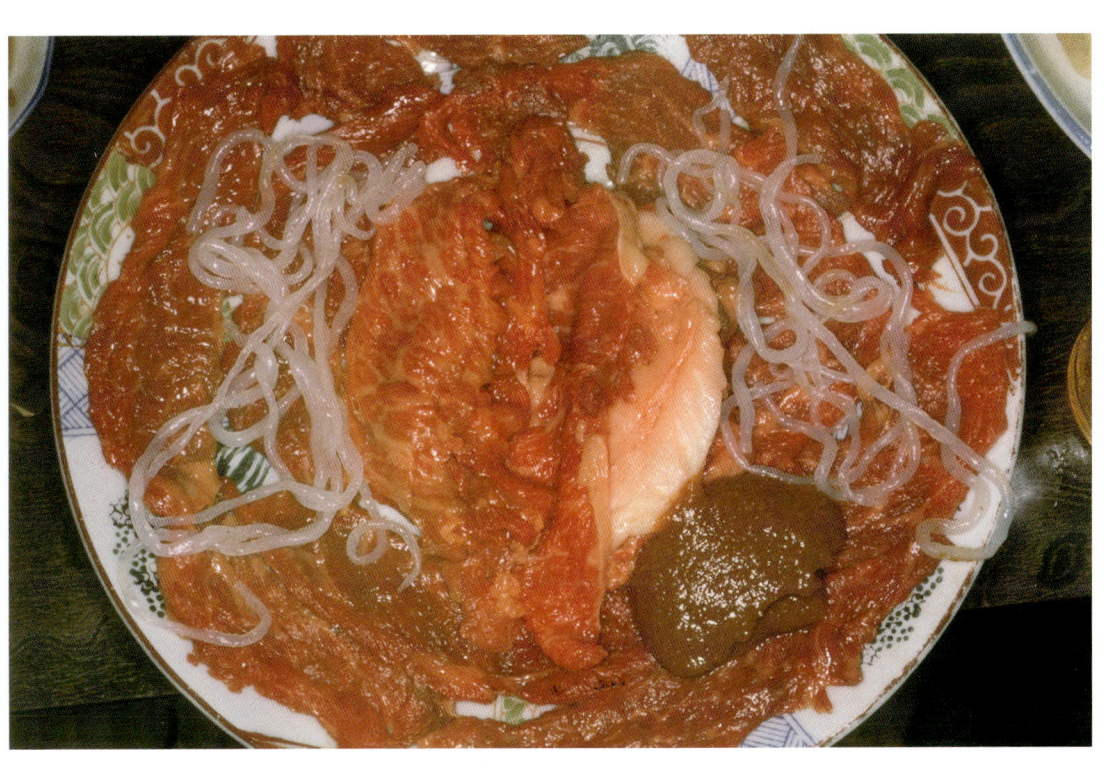

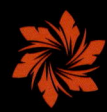

Shino

志乃

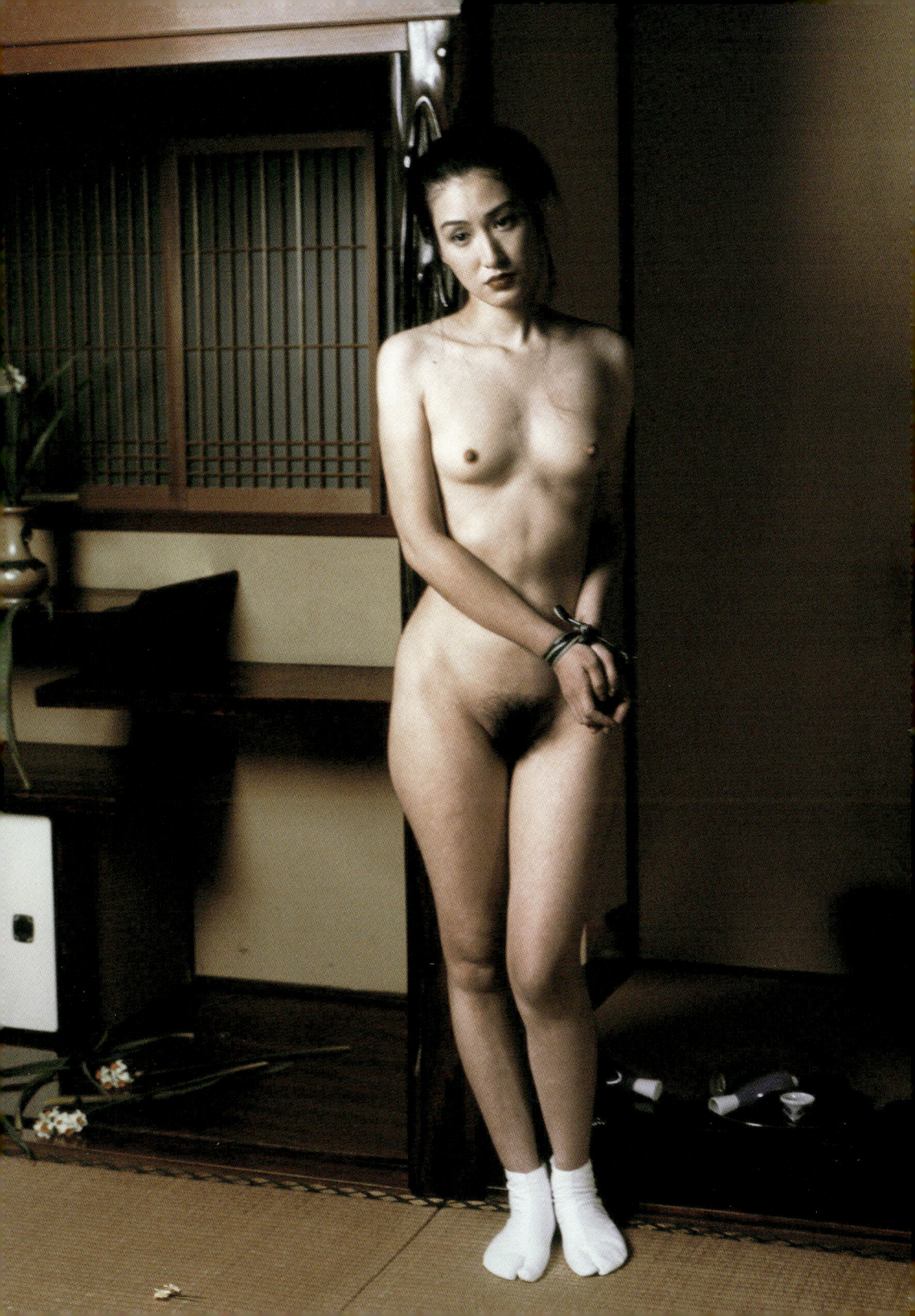

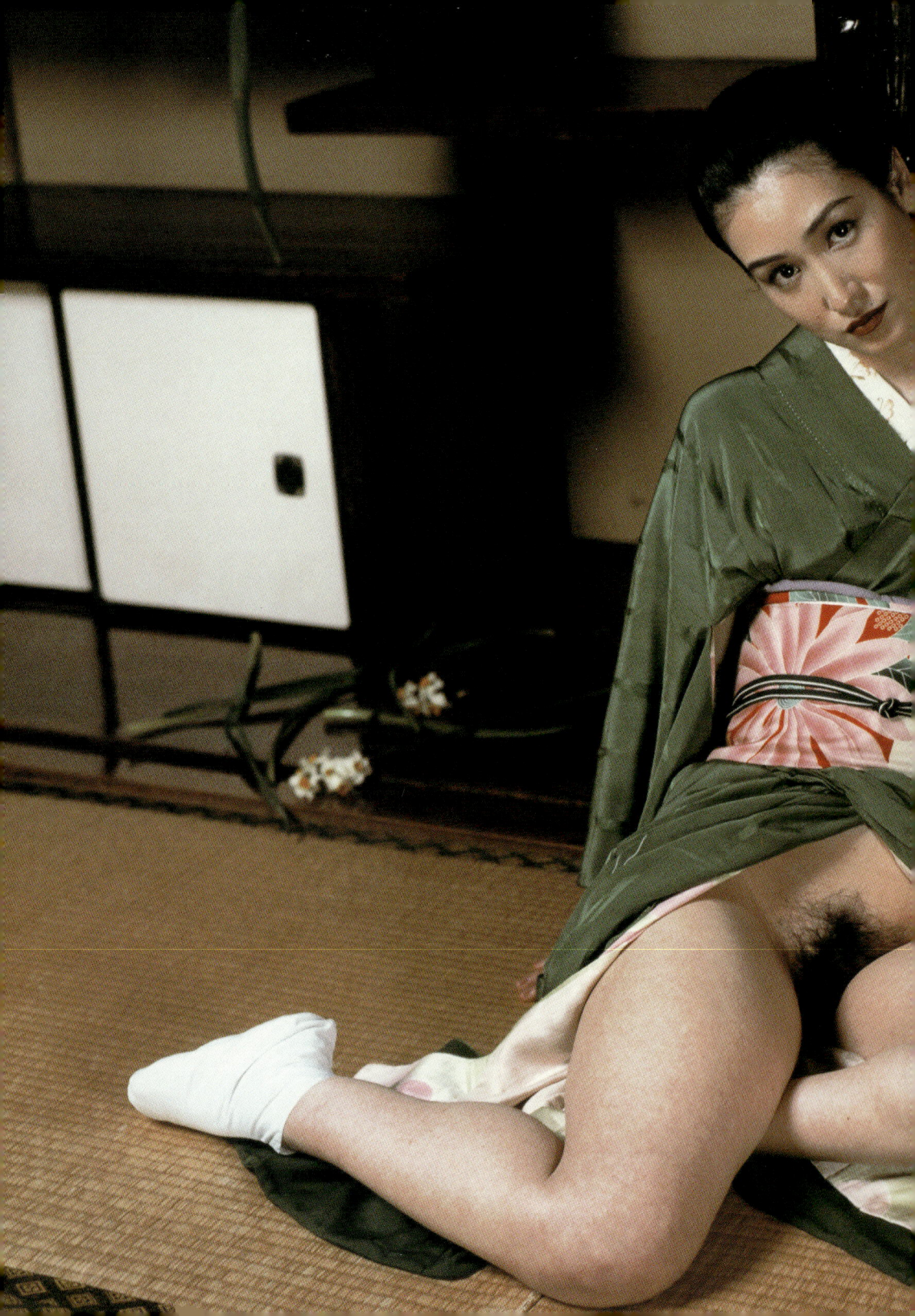

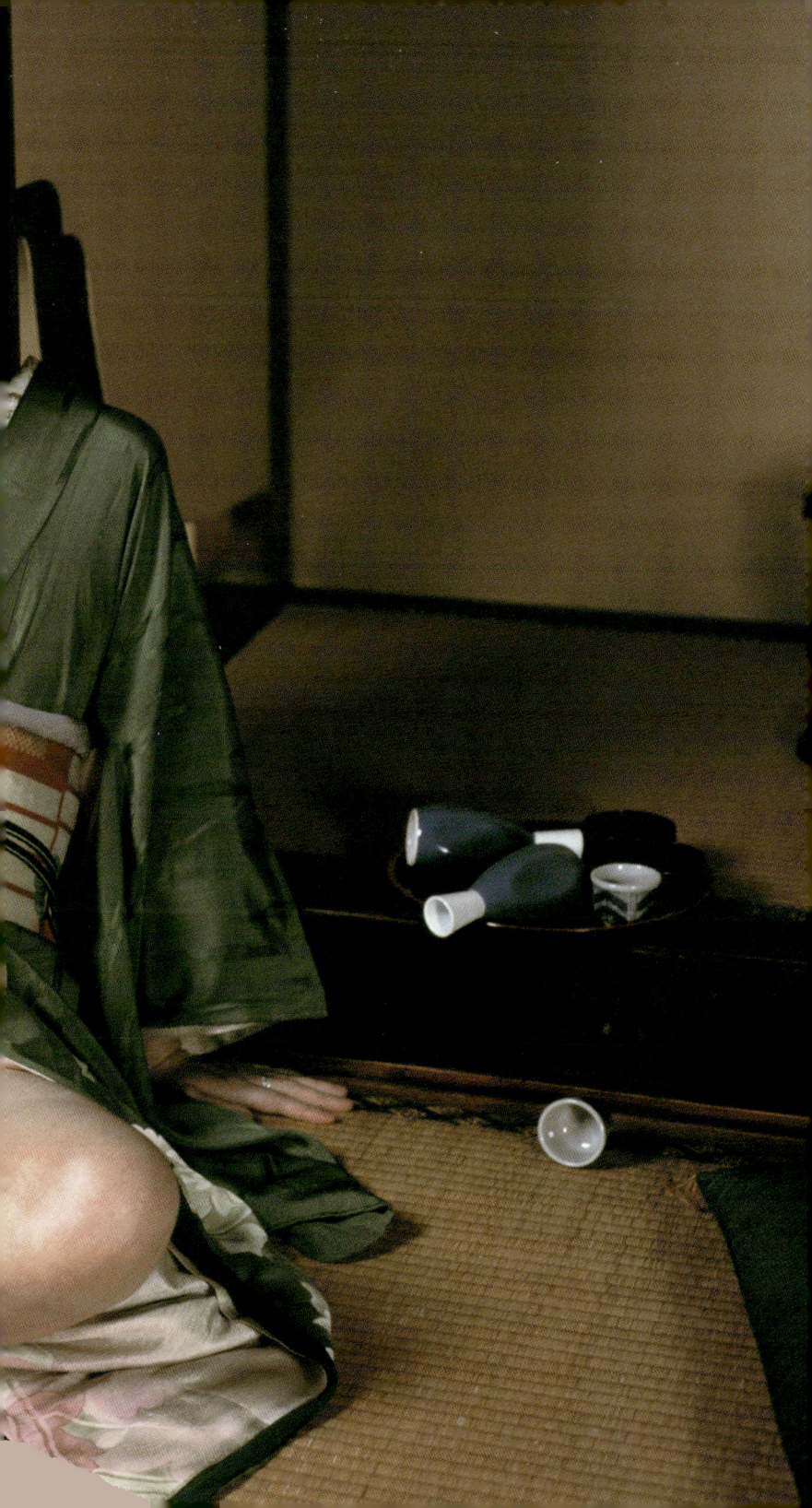

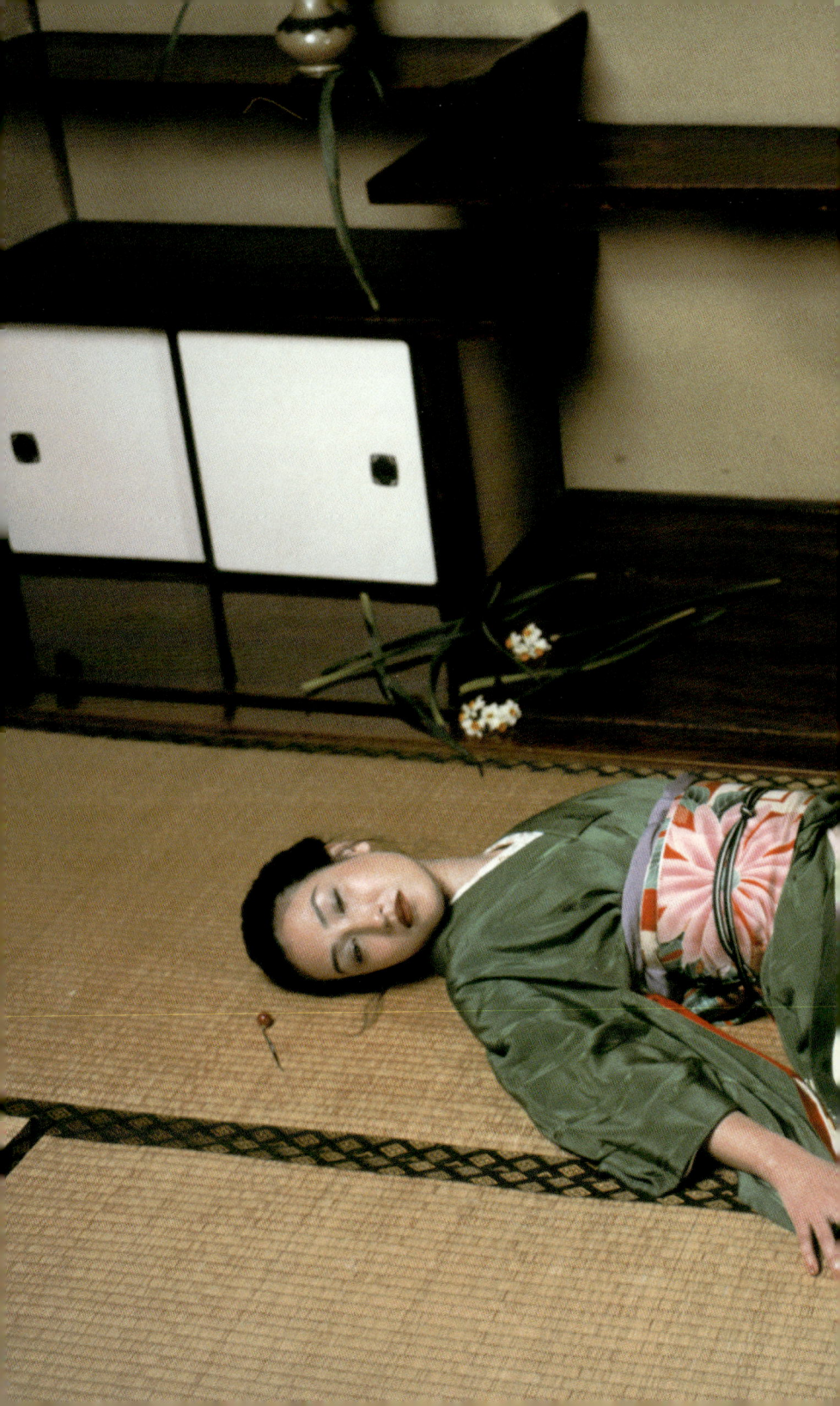

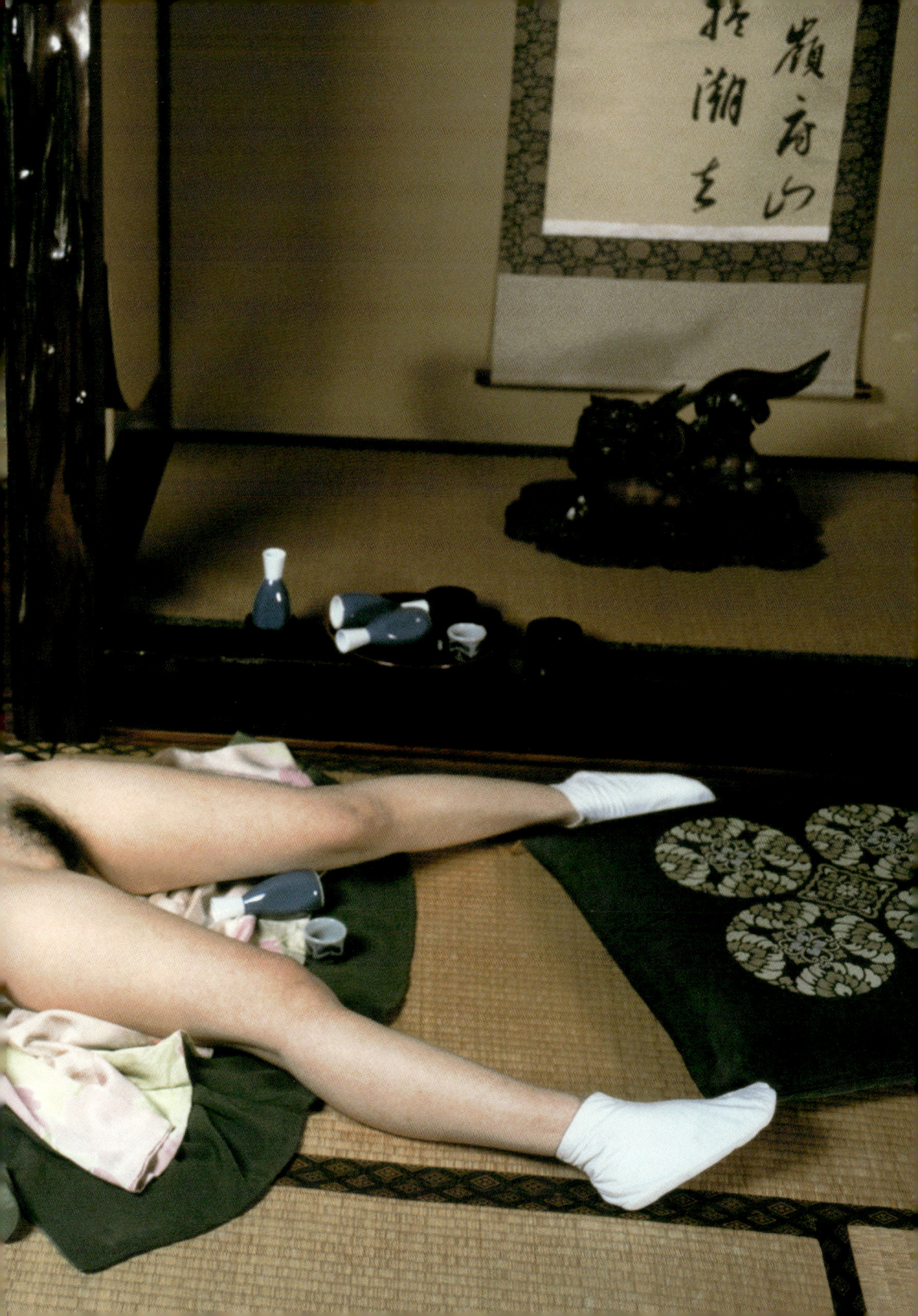

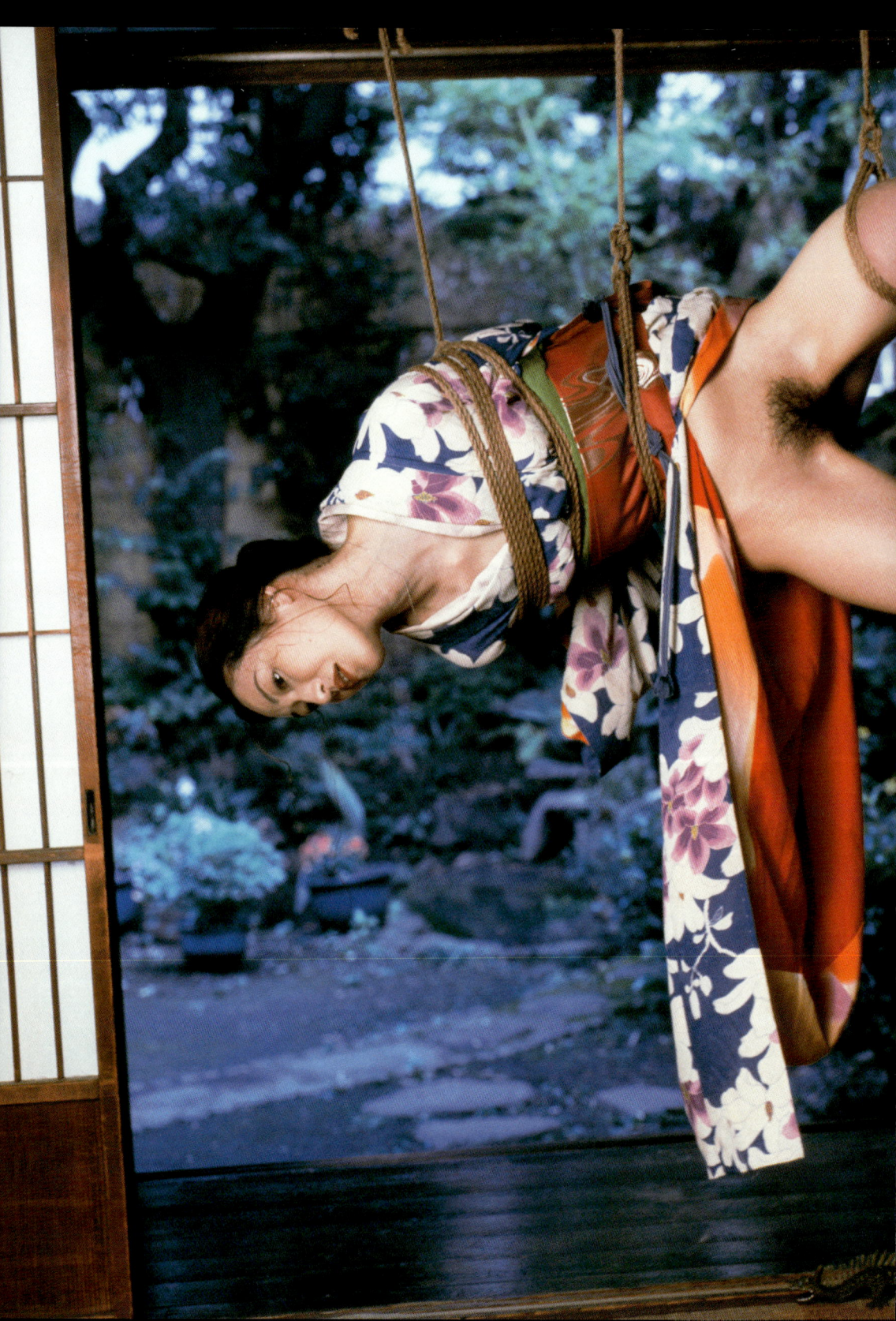

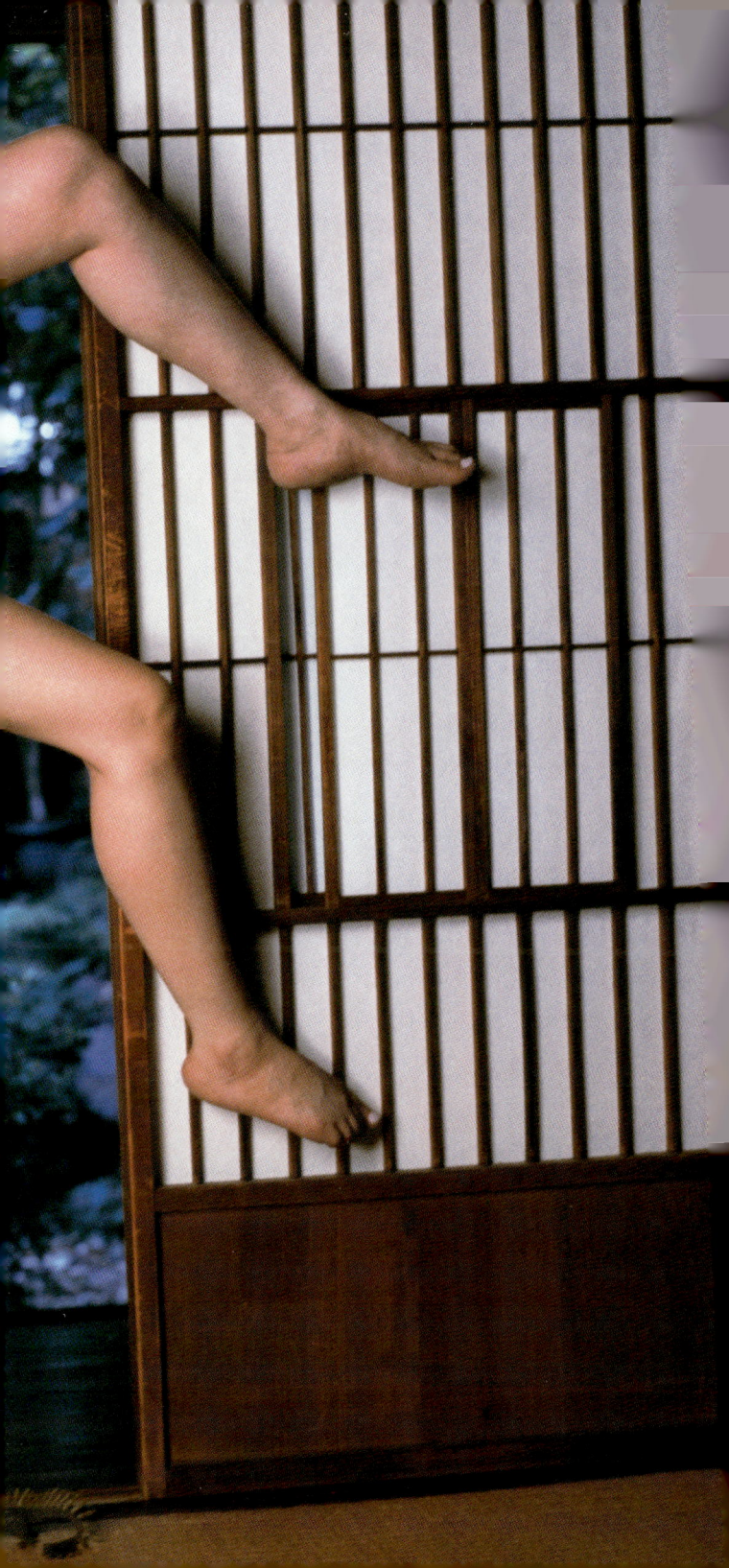

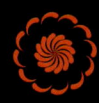

A's Lovers

Aの愛人

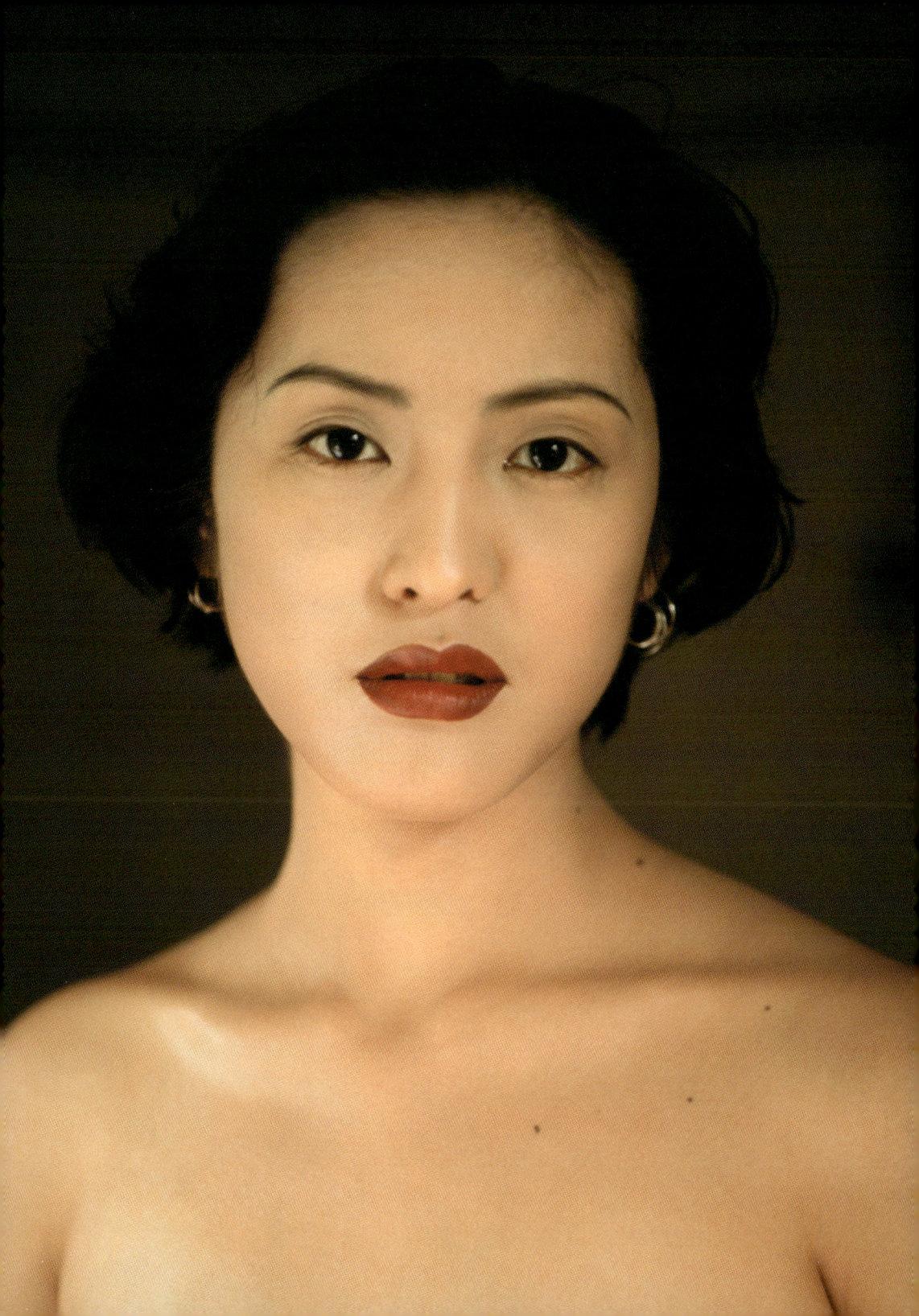

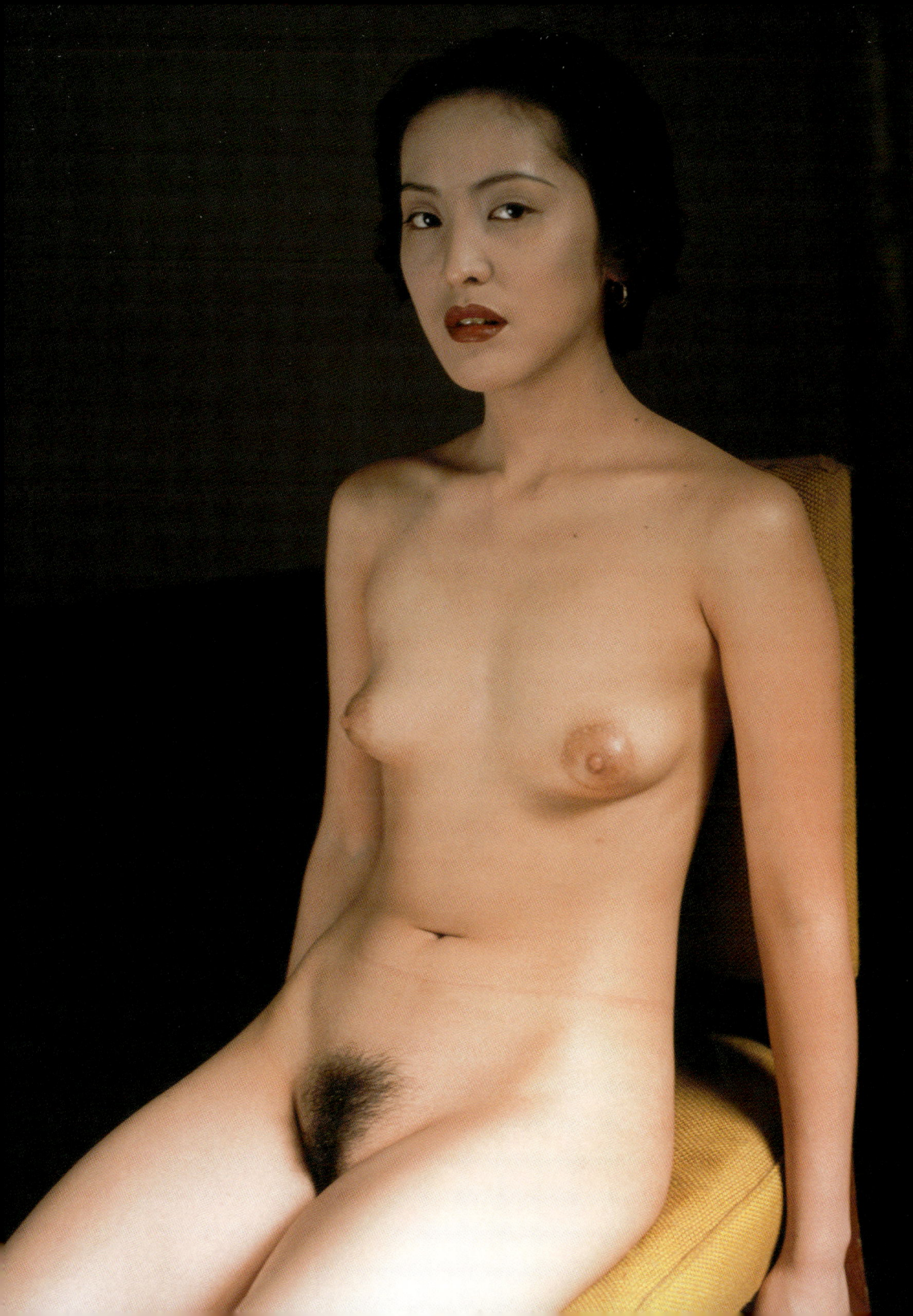

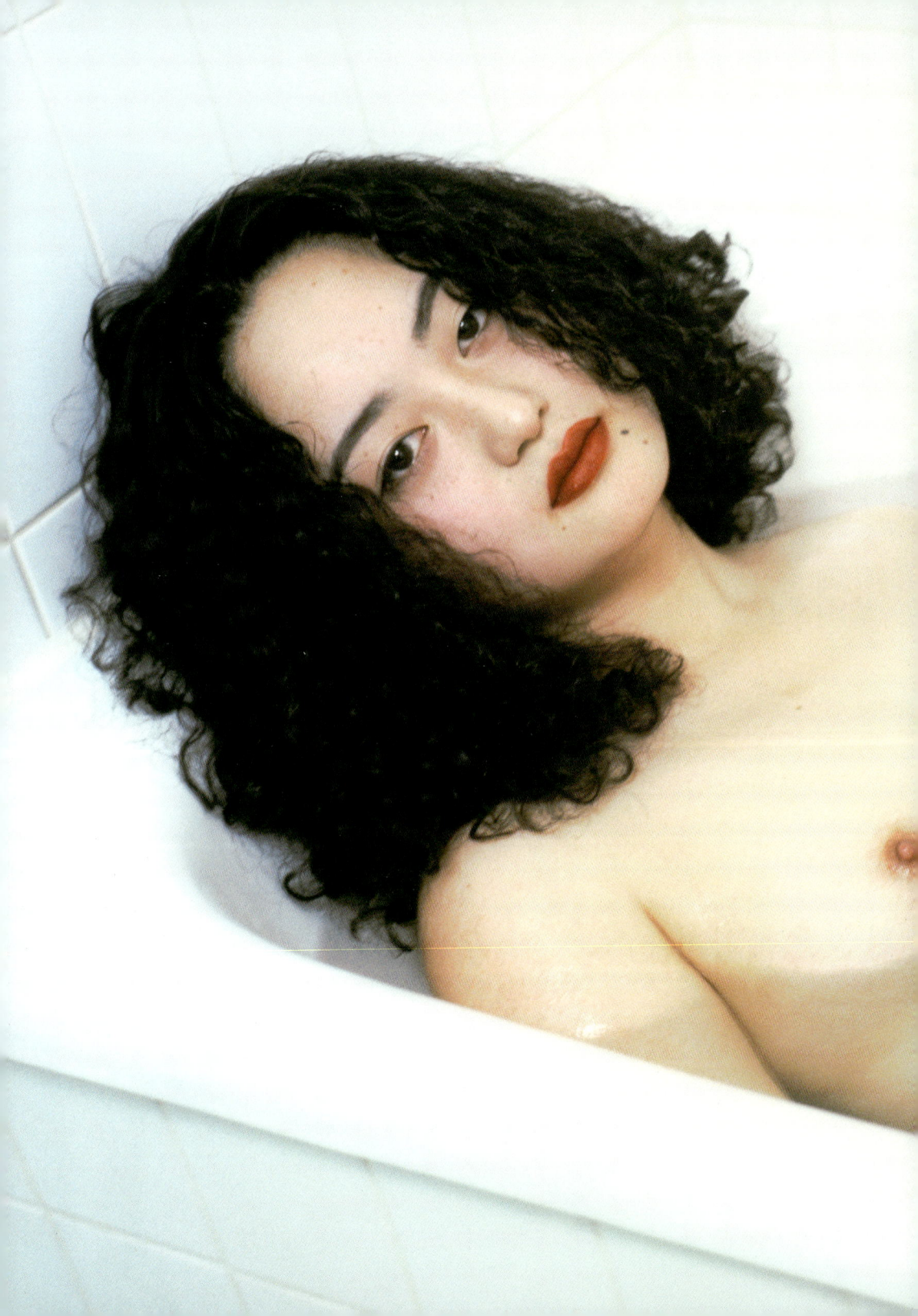

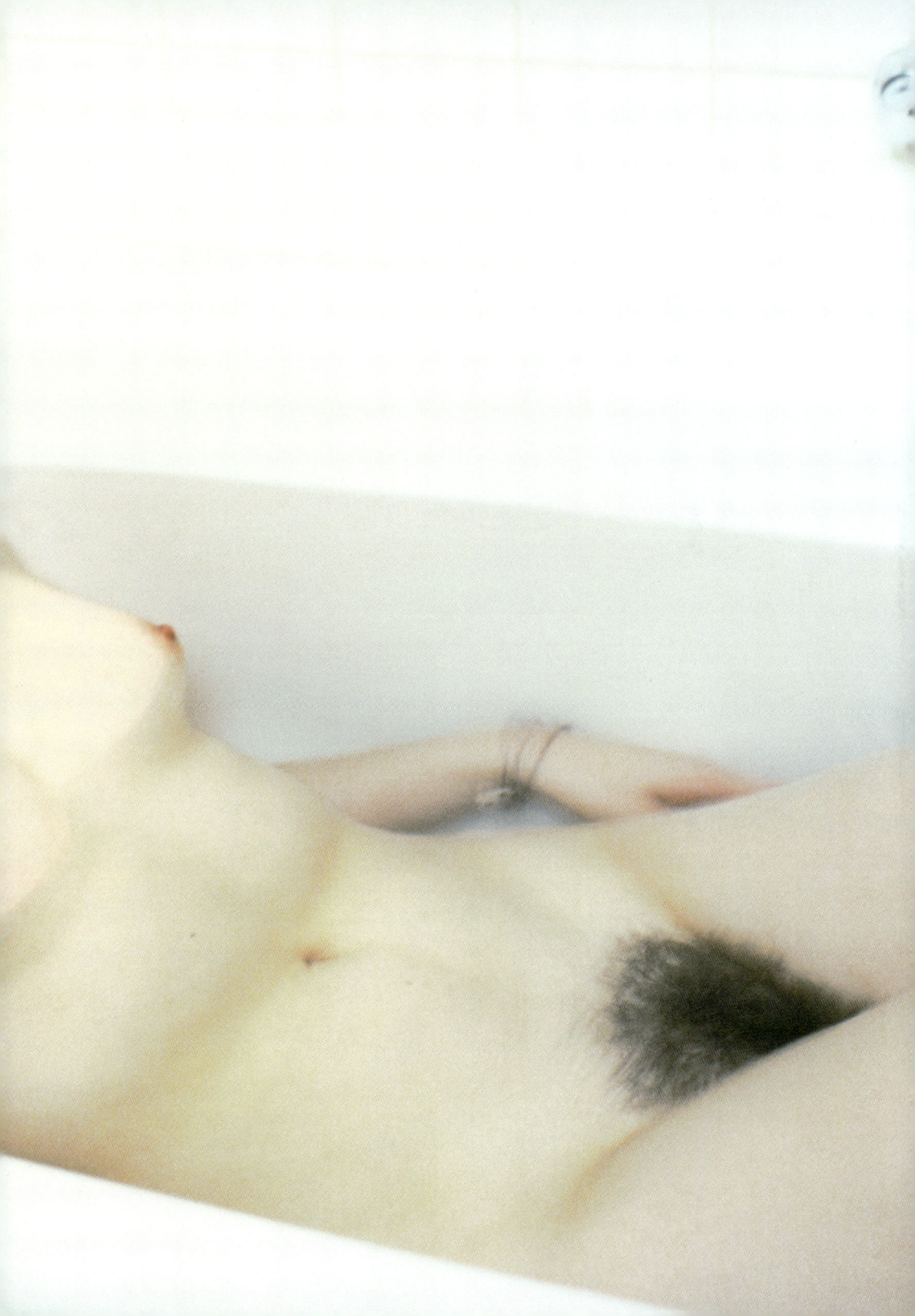

Photo-Maniac
Big Diary

写狂人大日記

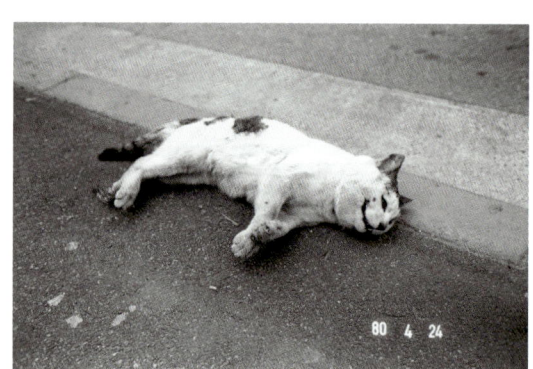

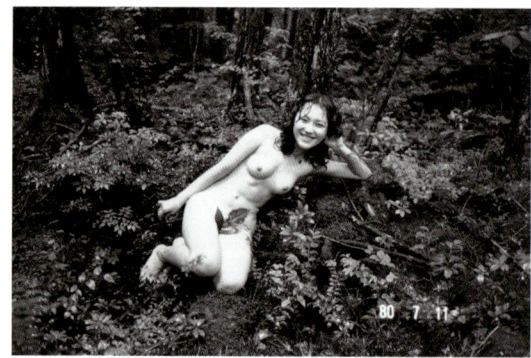

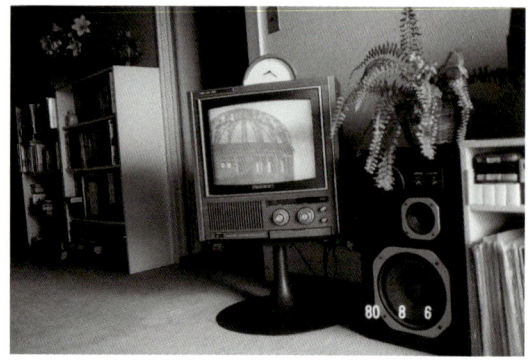

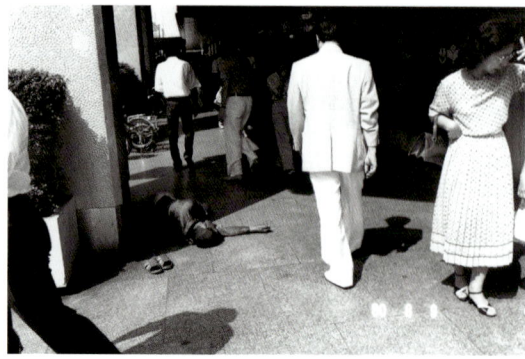

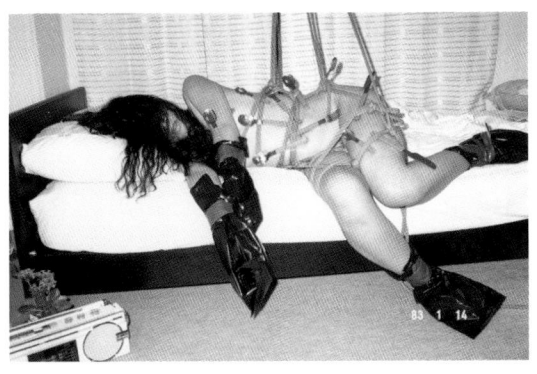
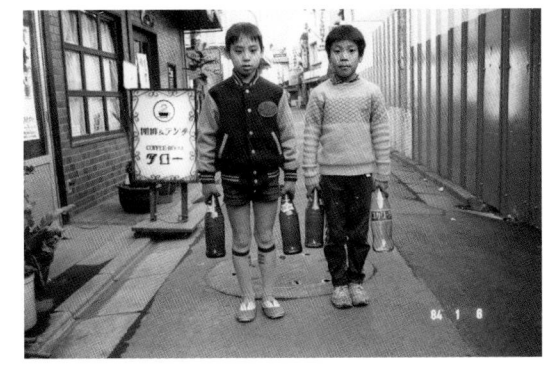
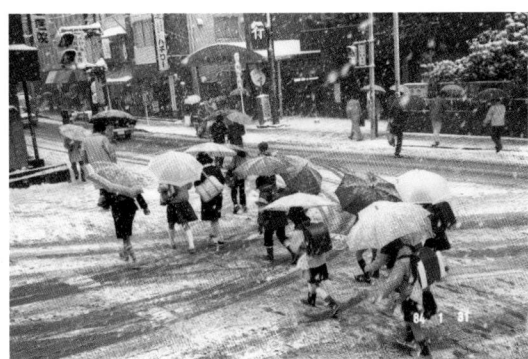
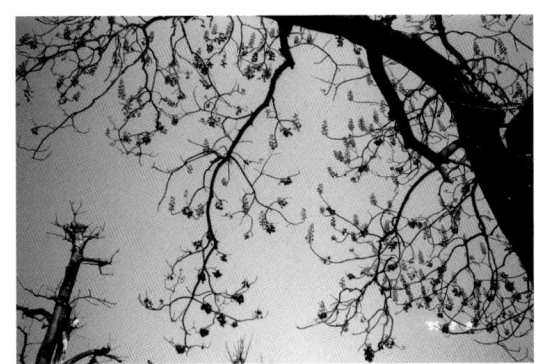
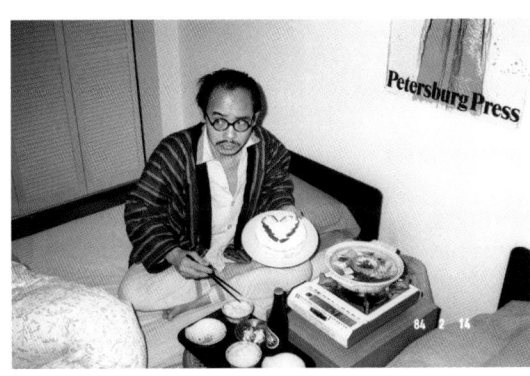
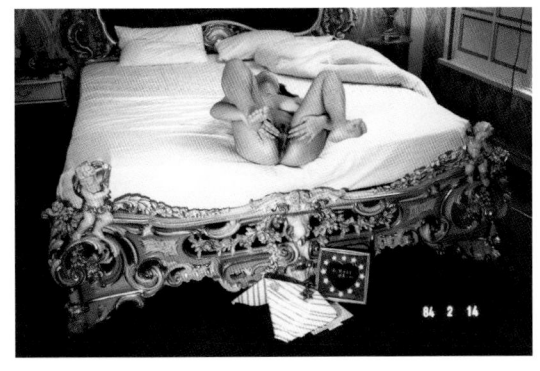
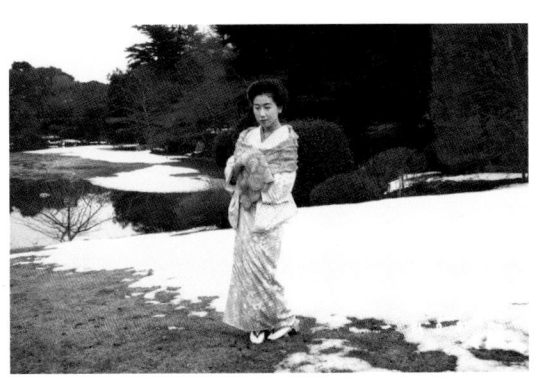
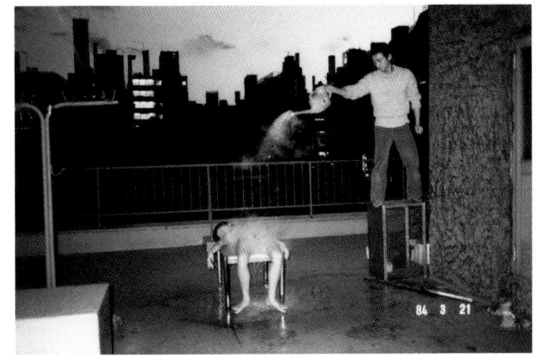

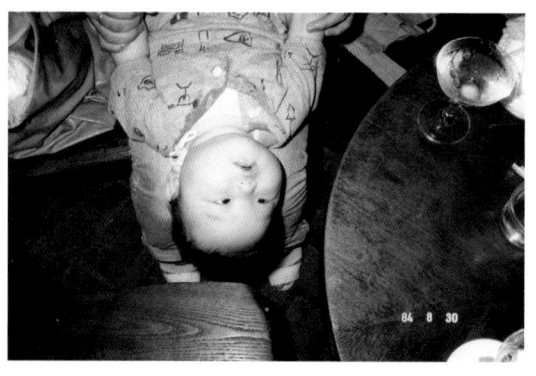

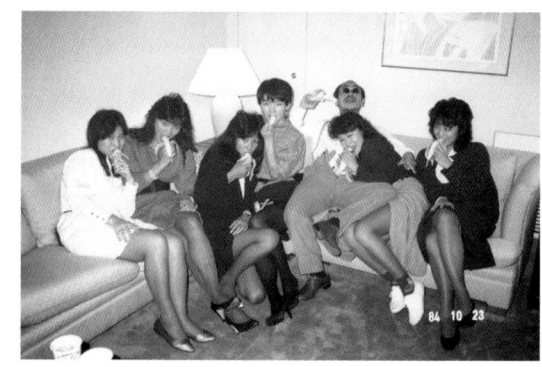

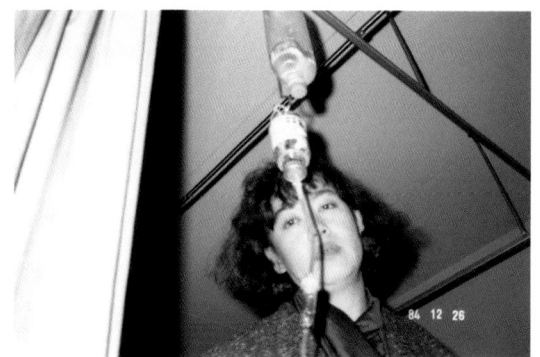

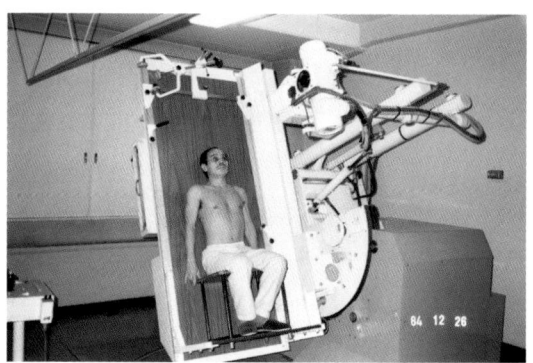

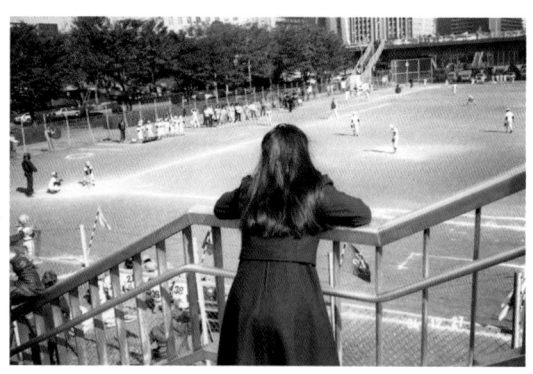

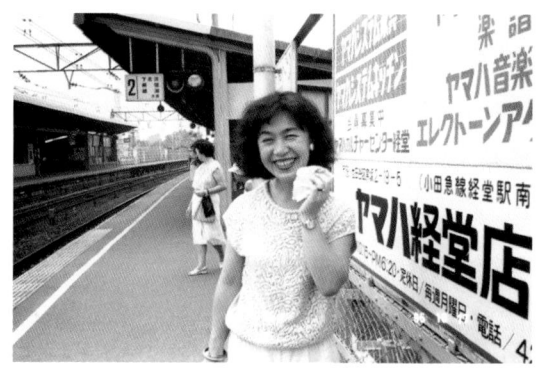

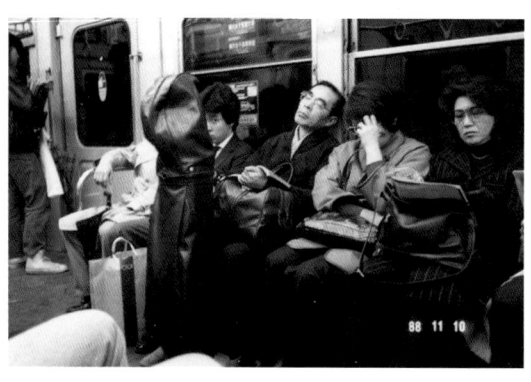

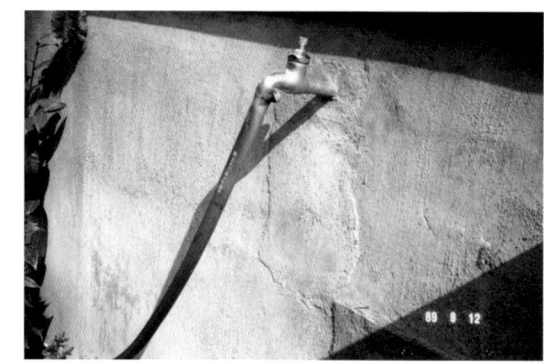

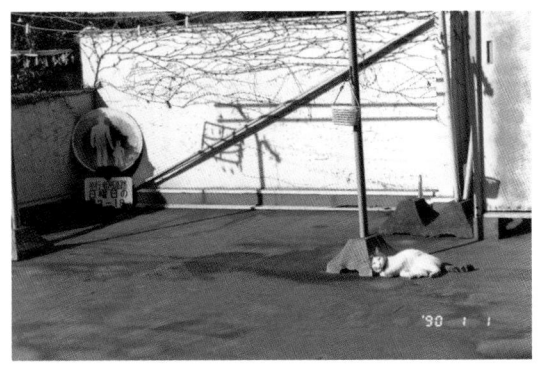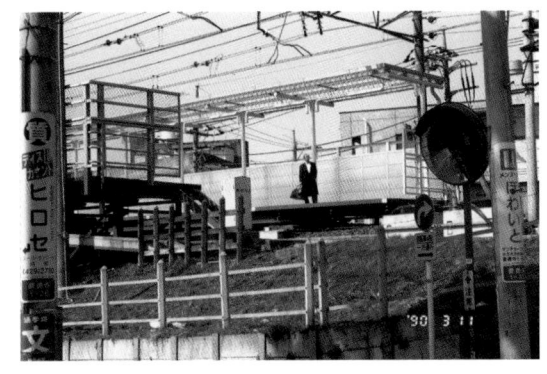
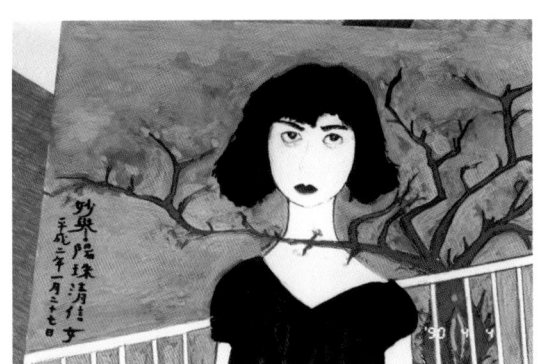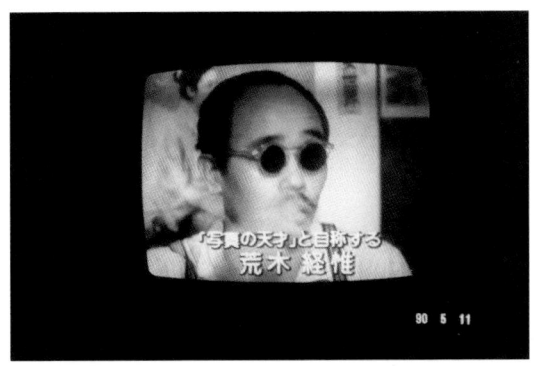
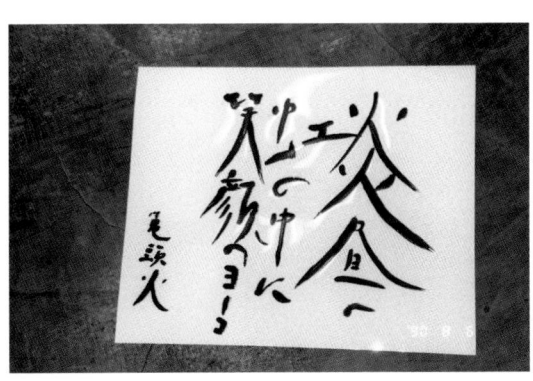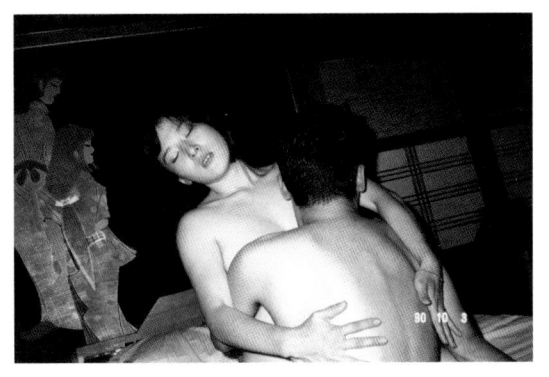
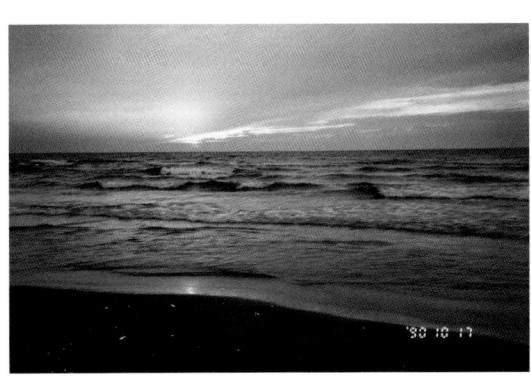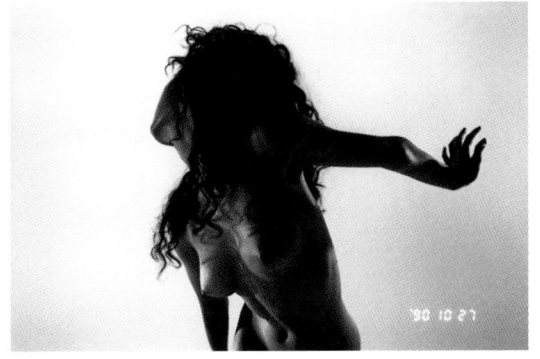

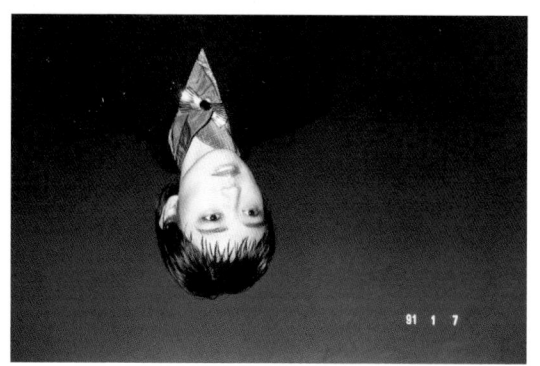
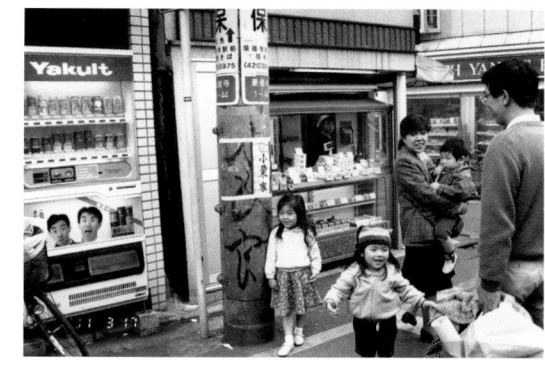
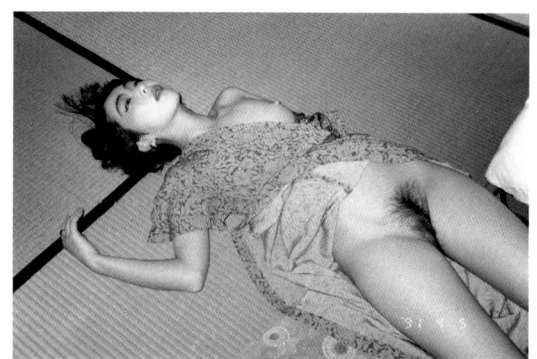
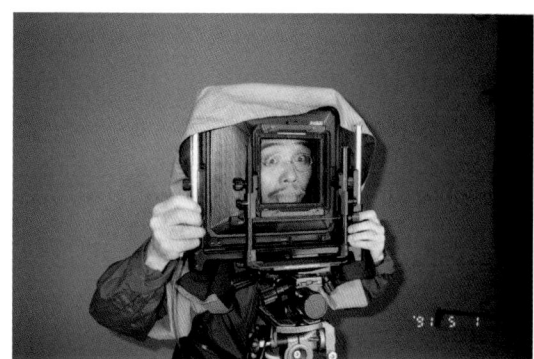
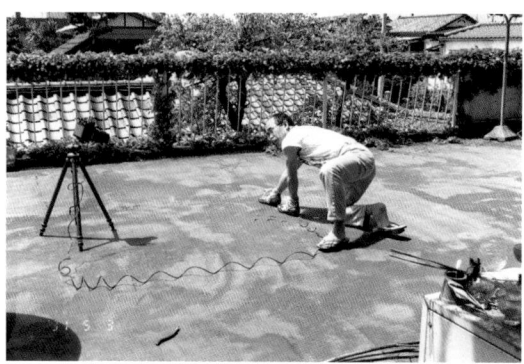
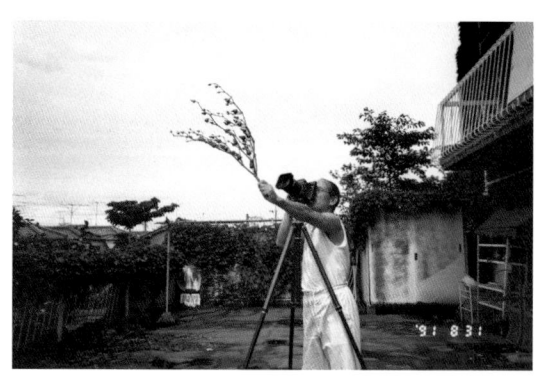

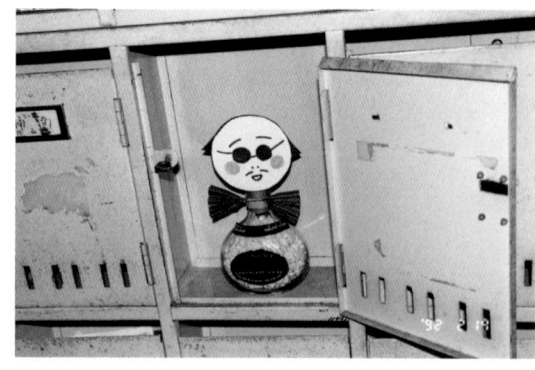

406

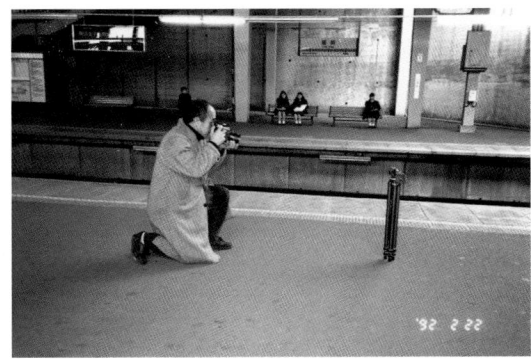
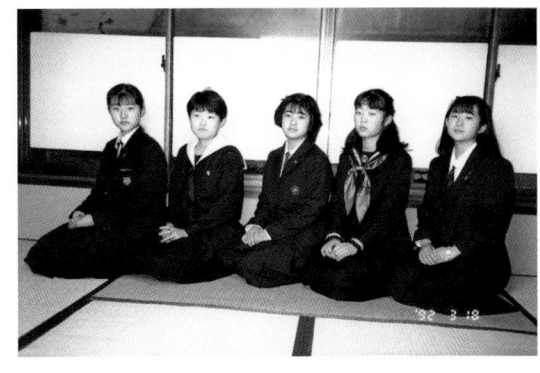
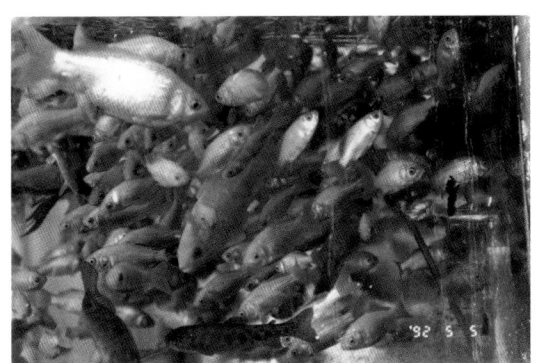
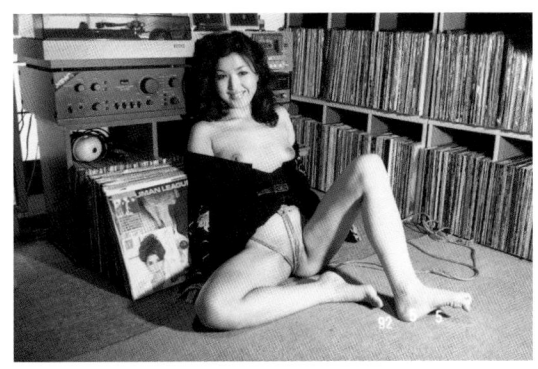
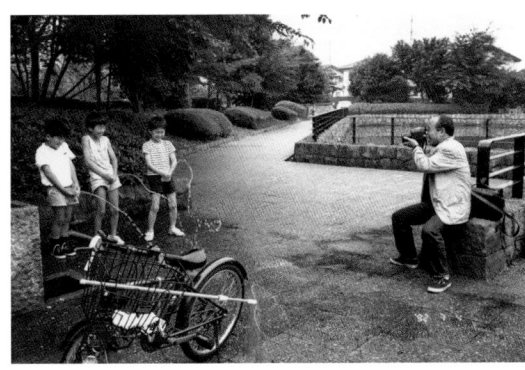
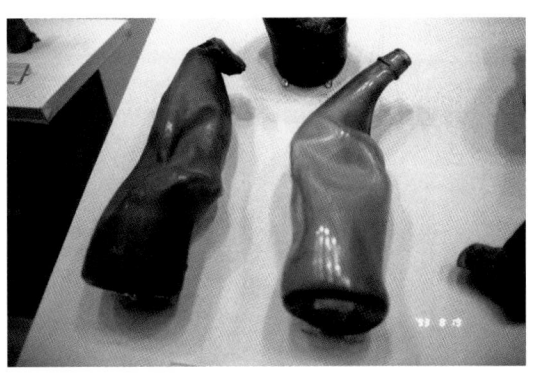
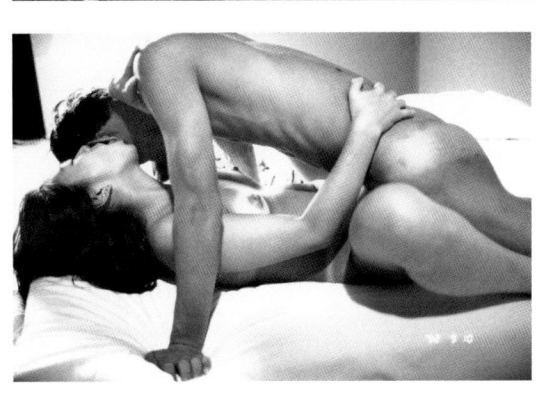
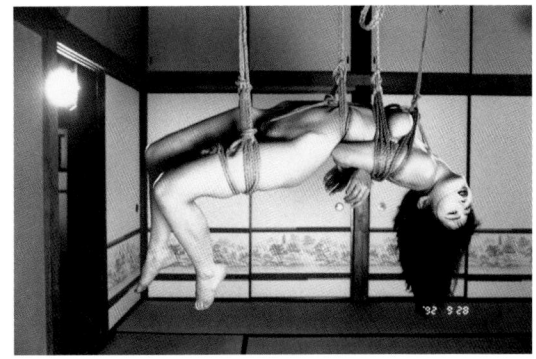

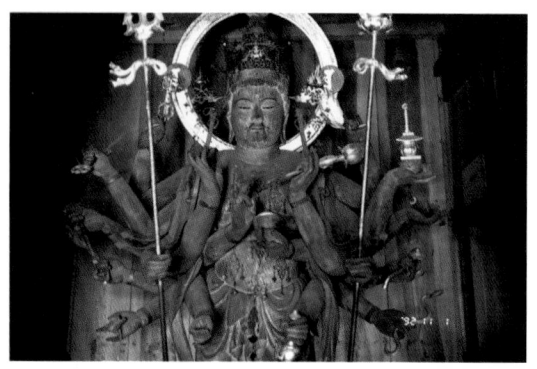
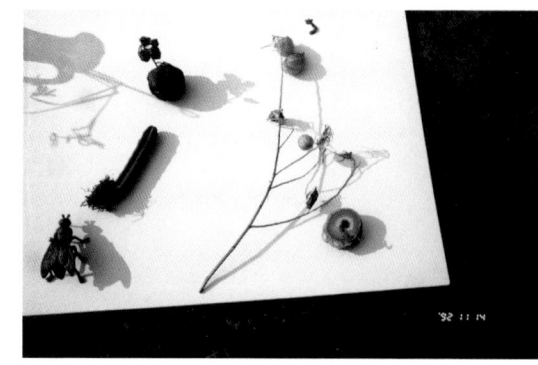
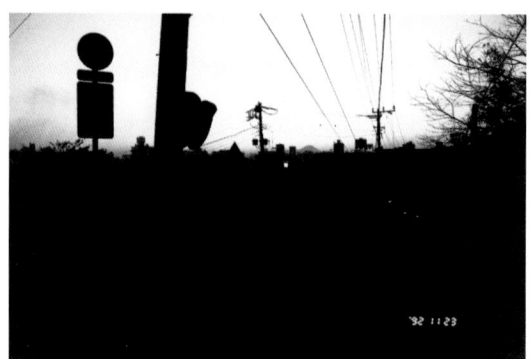
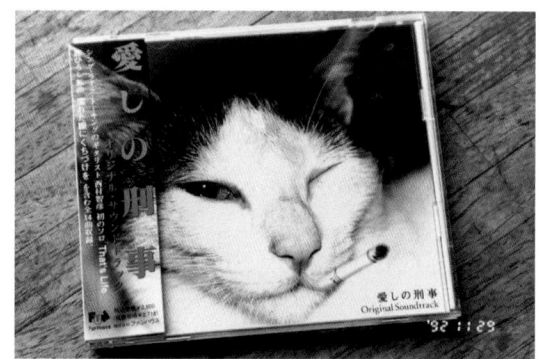
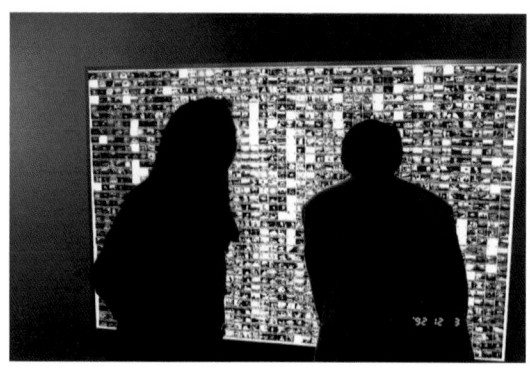
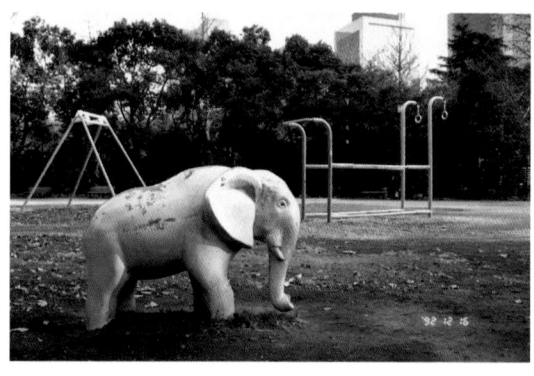
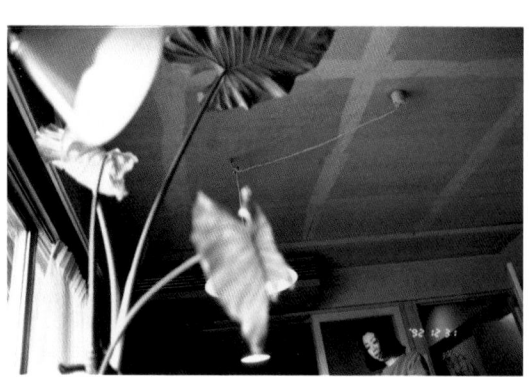
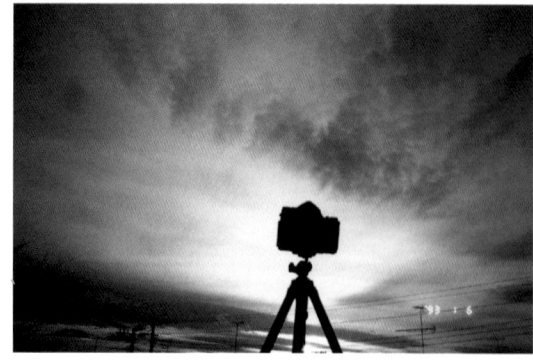

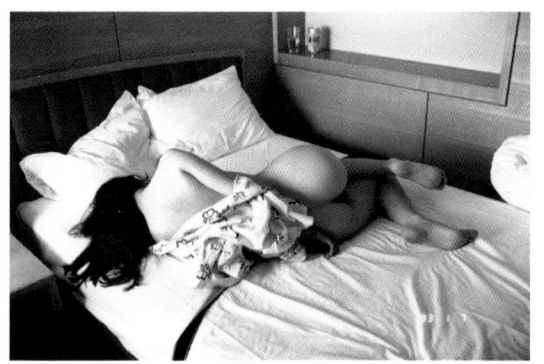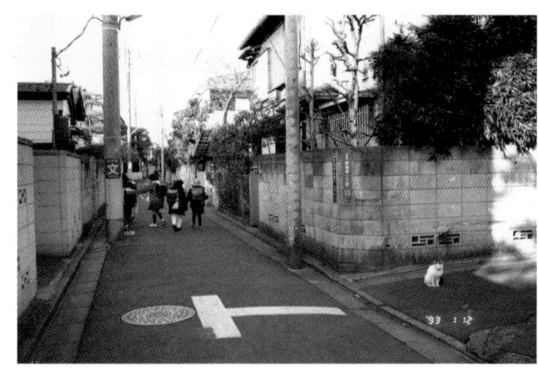
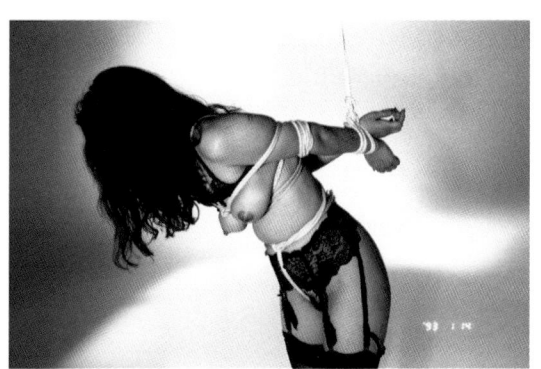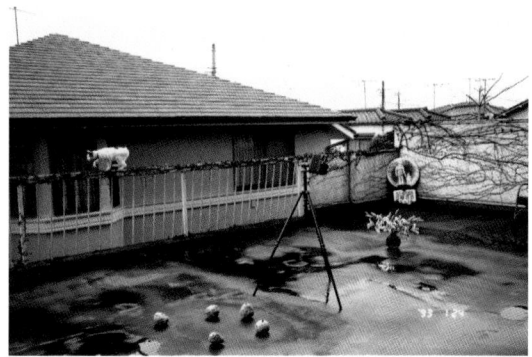
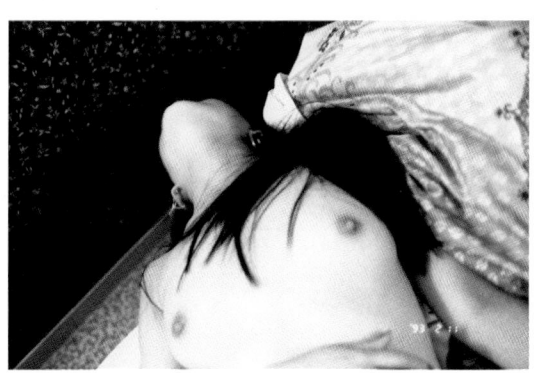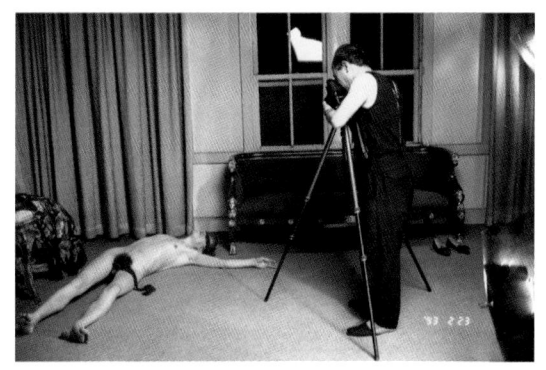
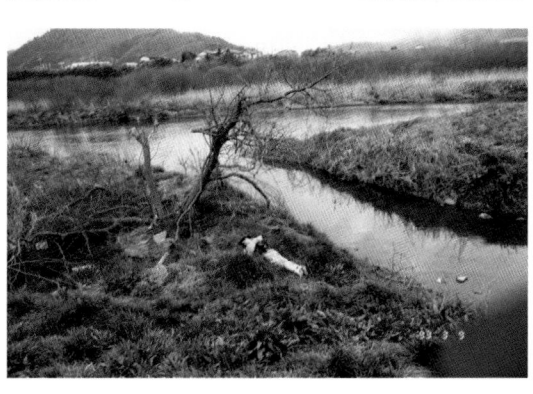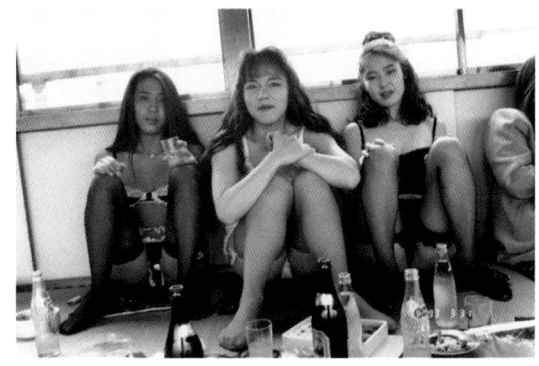

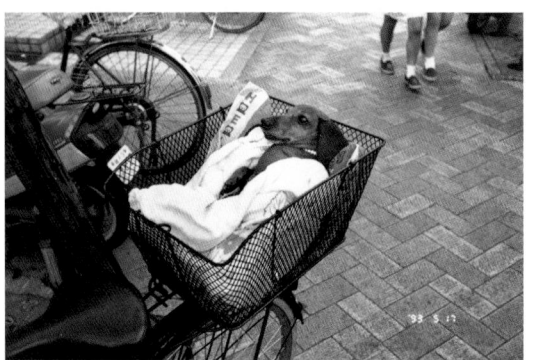 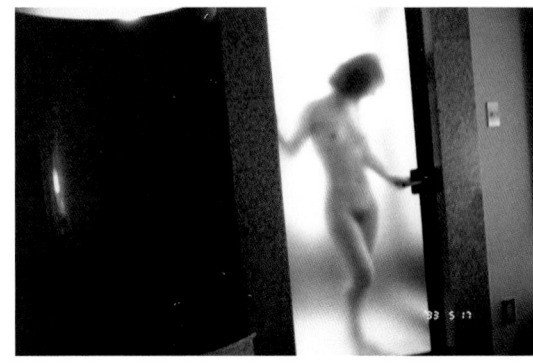

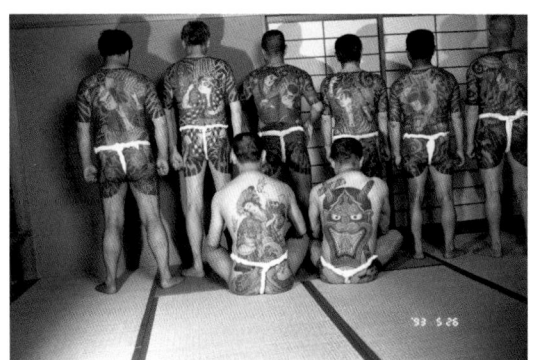 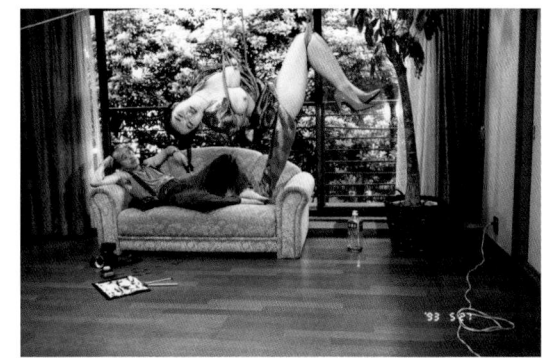

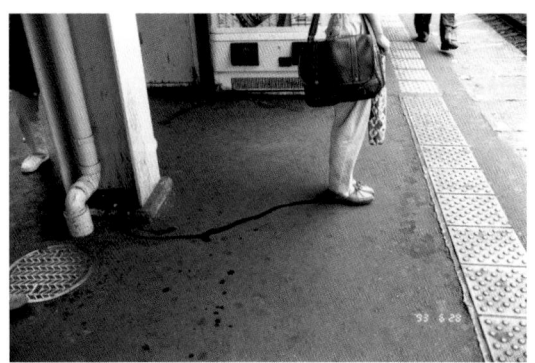 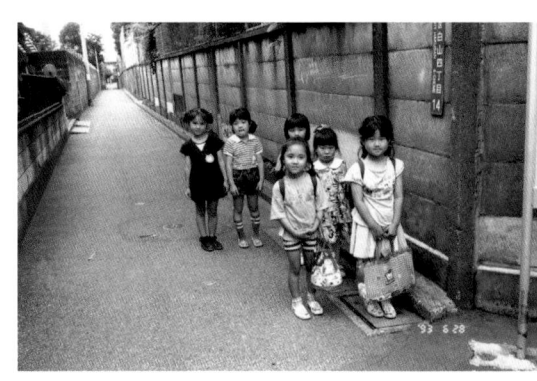

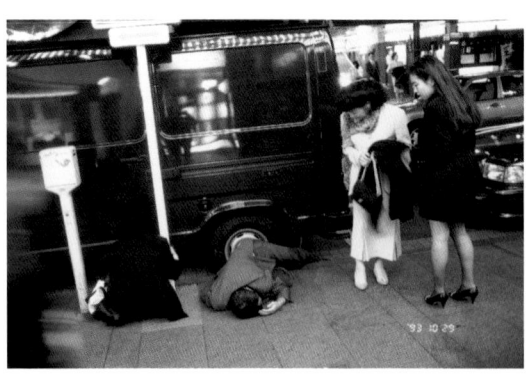 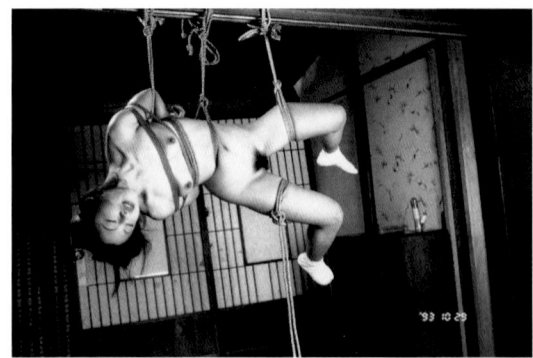

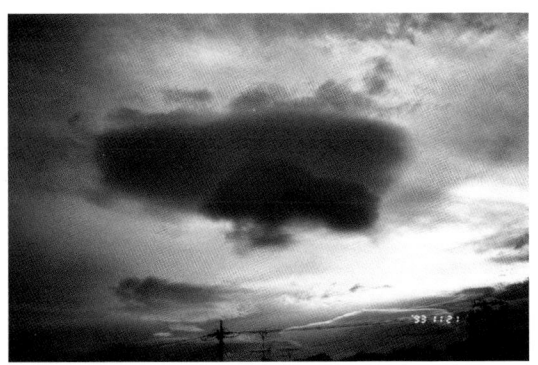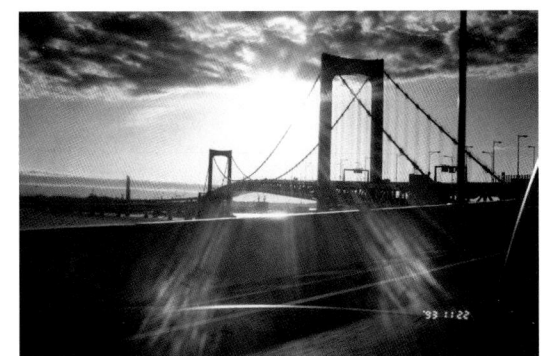
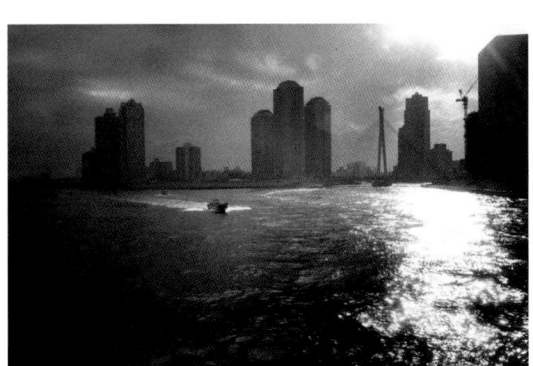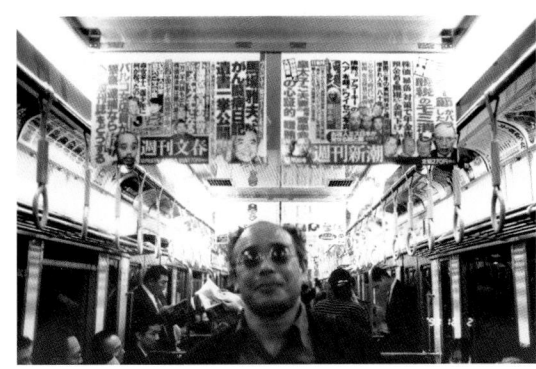
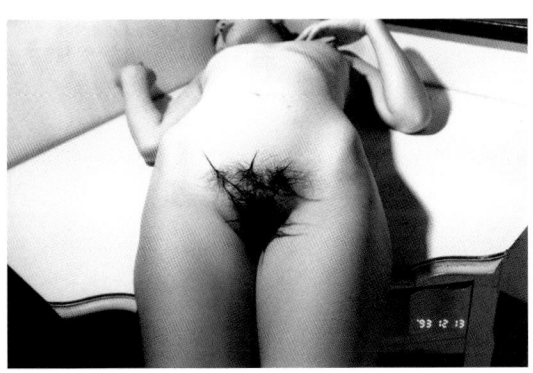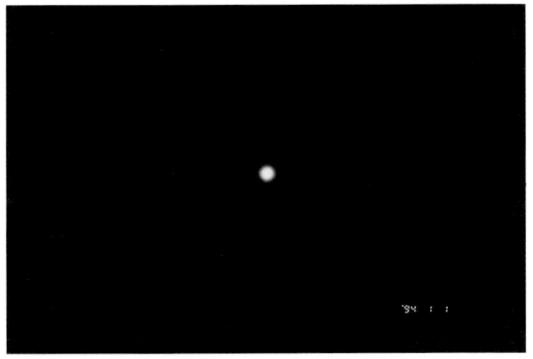
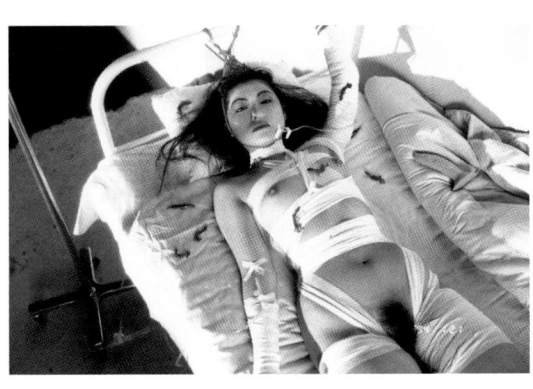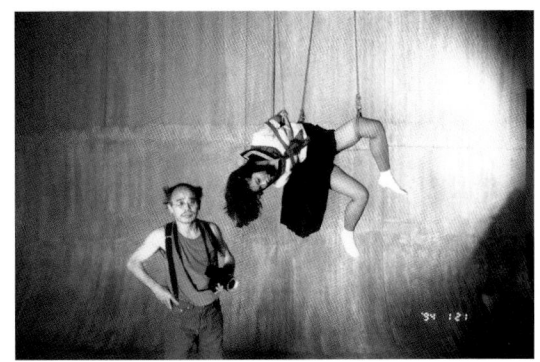

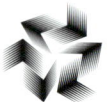

Color Rays

色光線

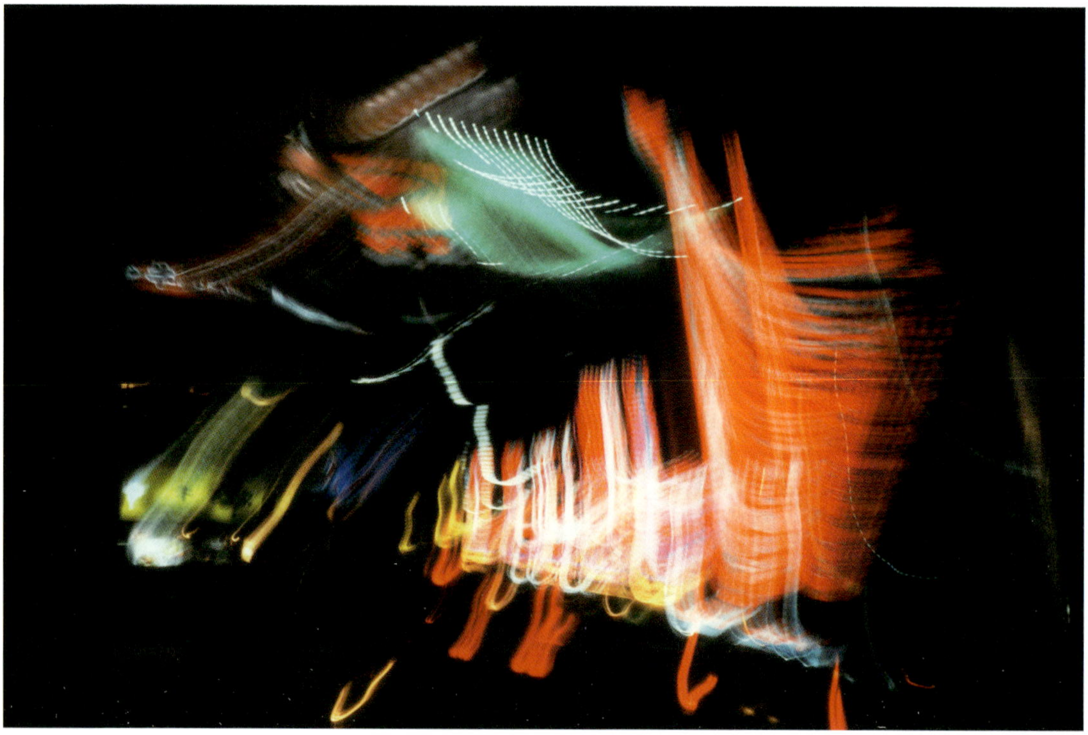

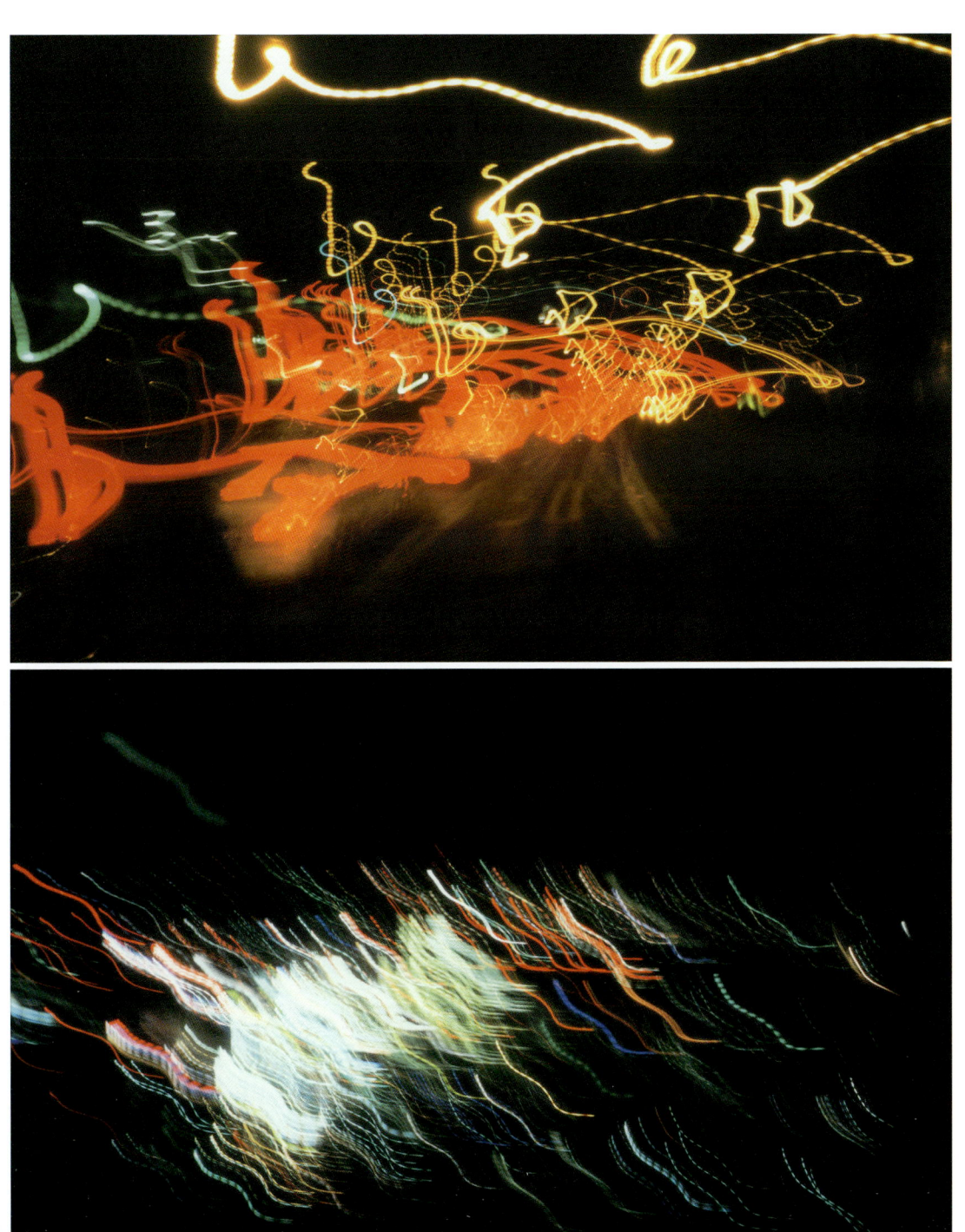

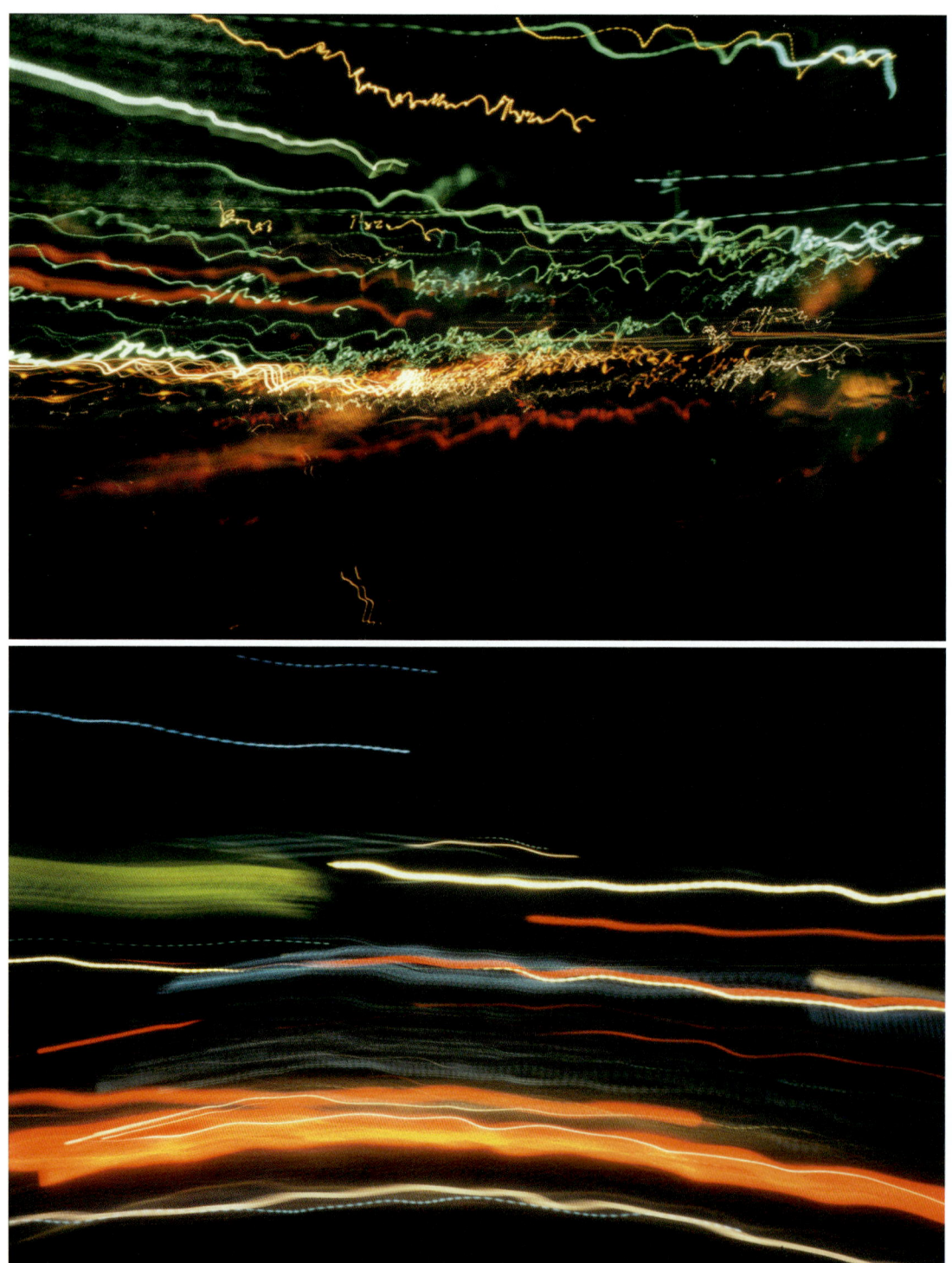

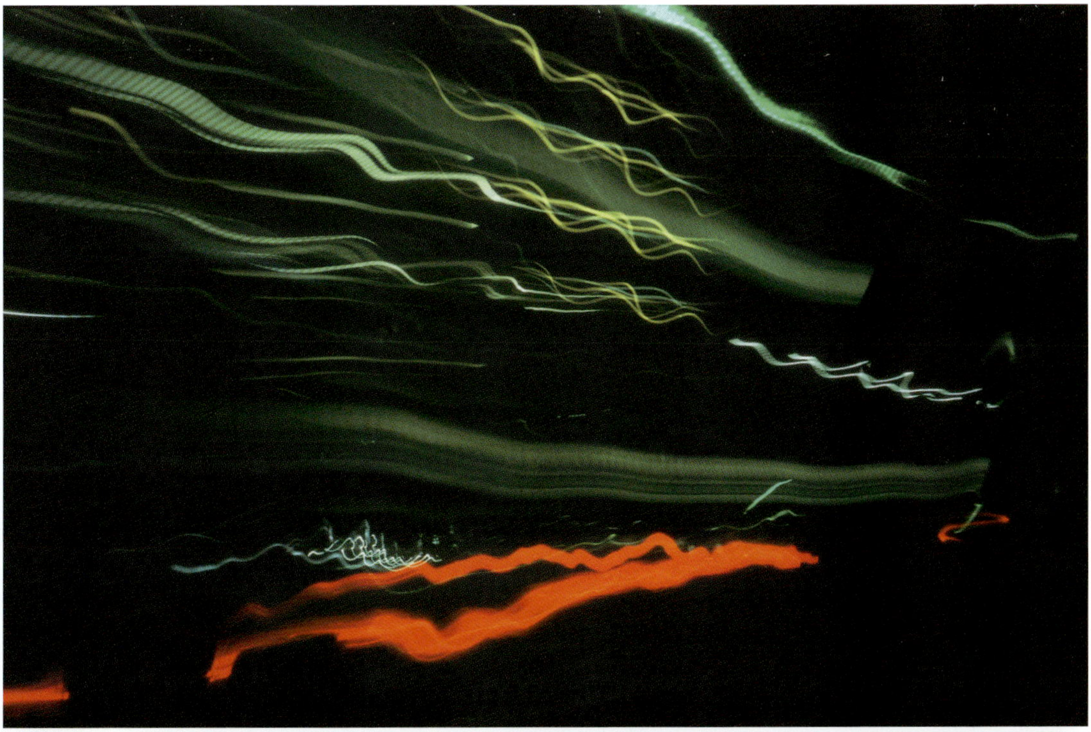

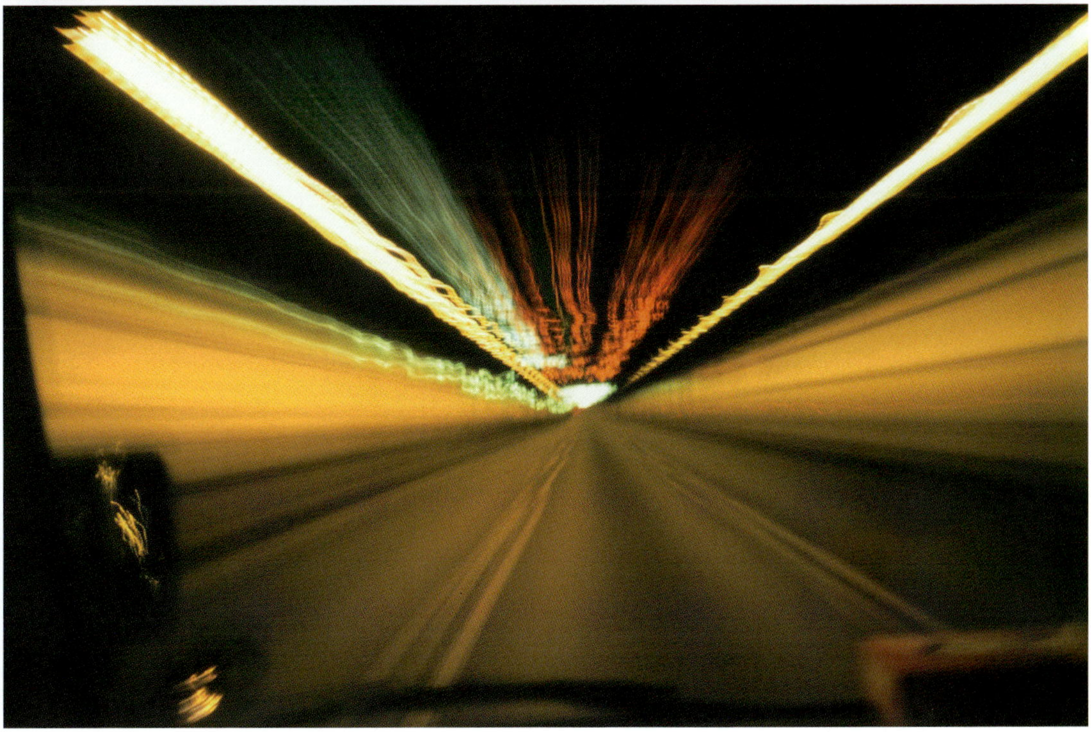

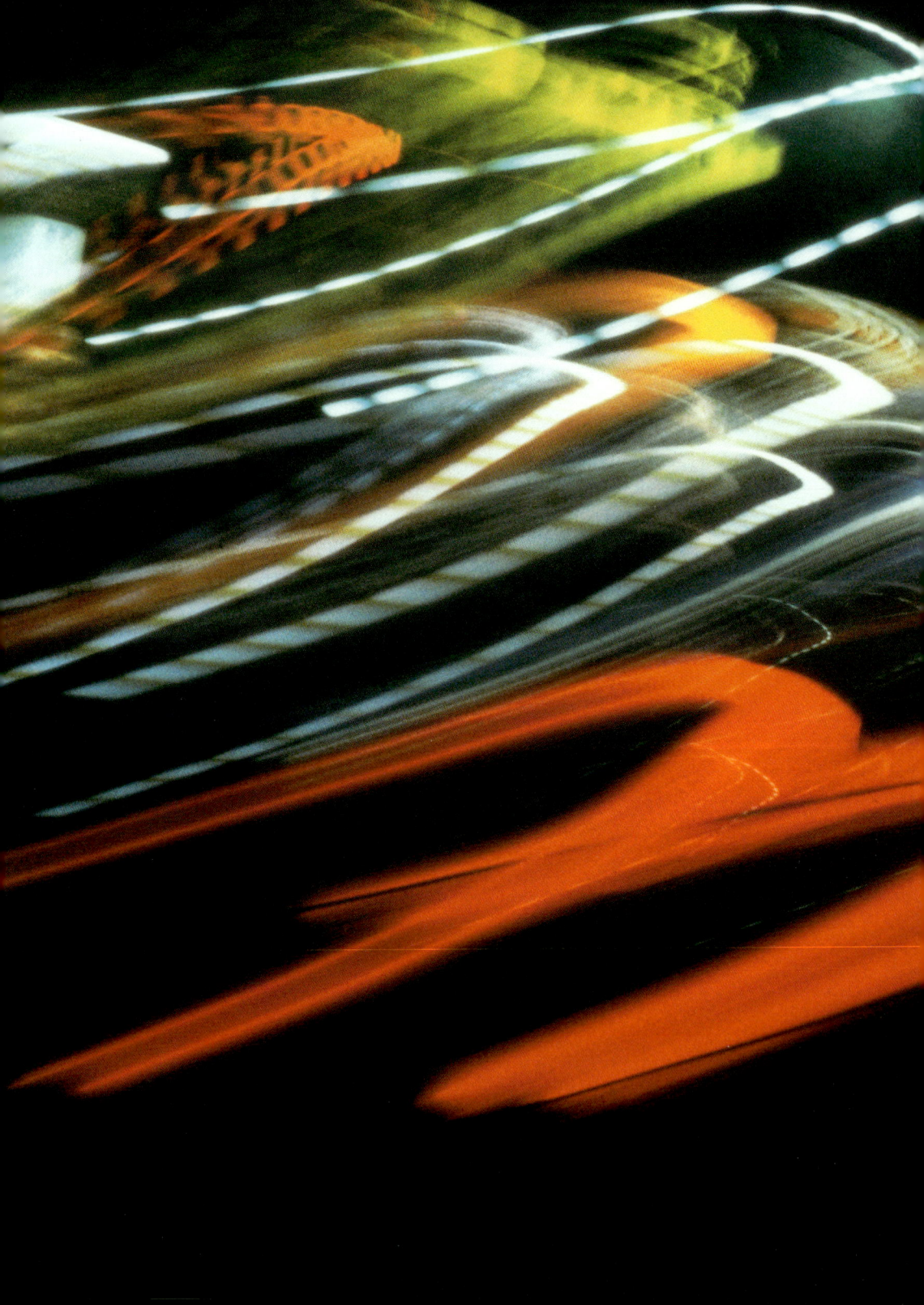

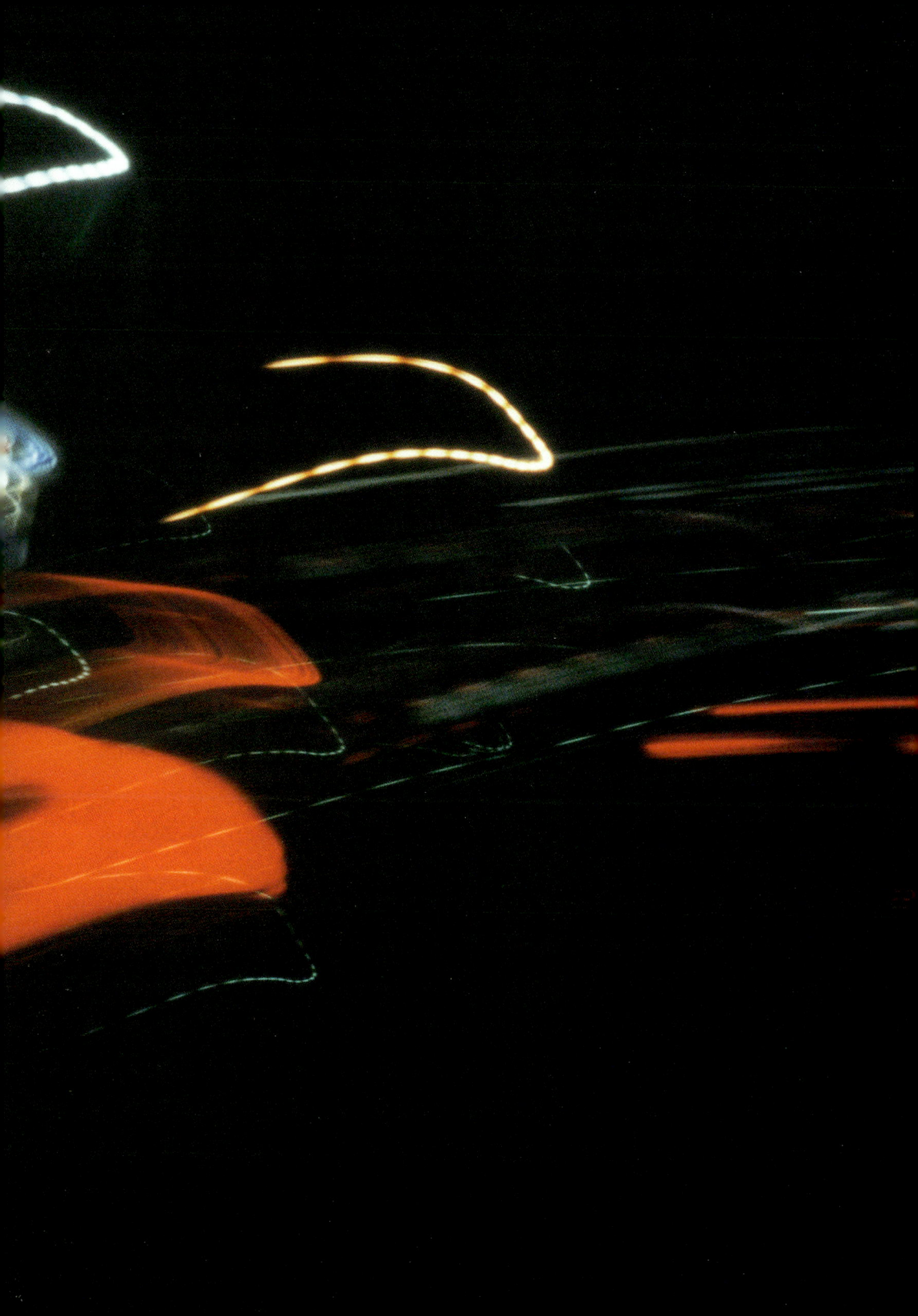

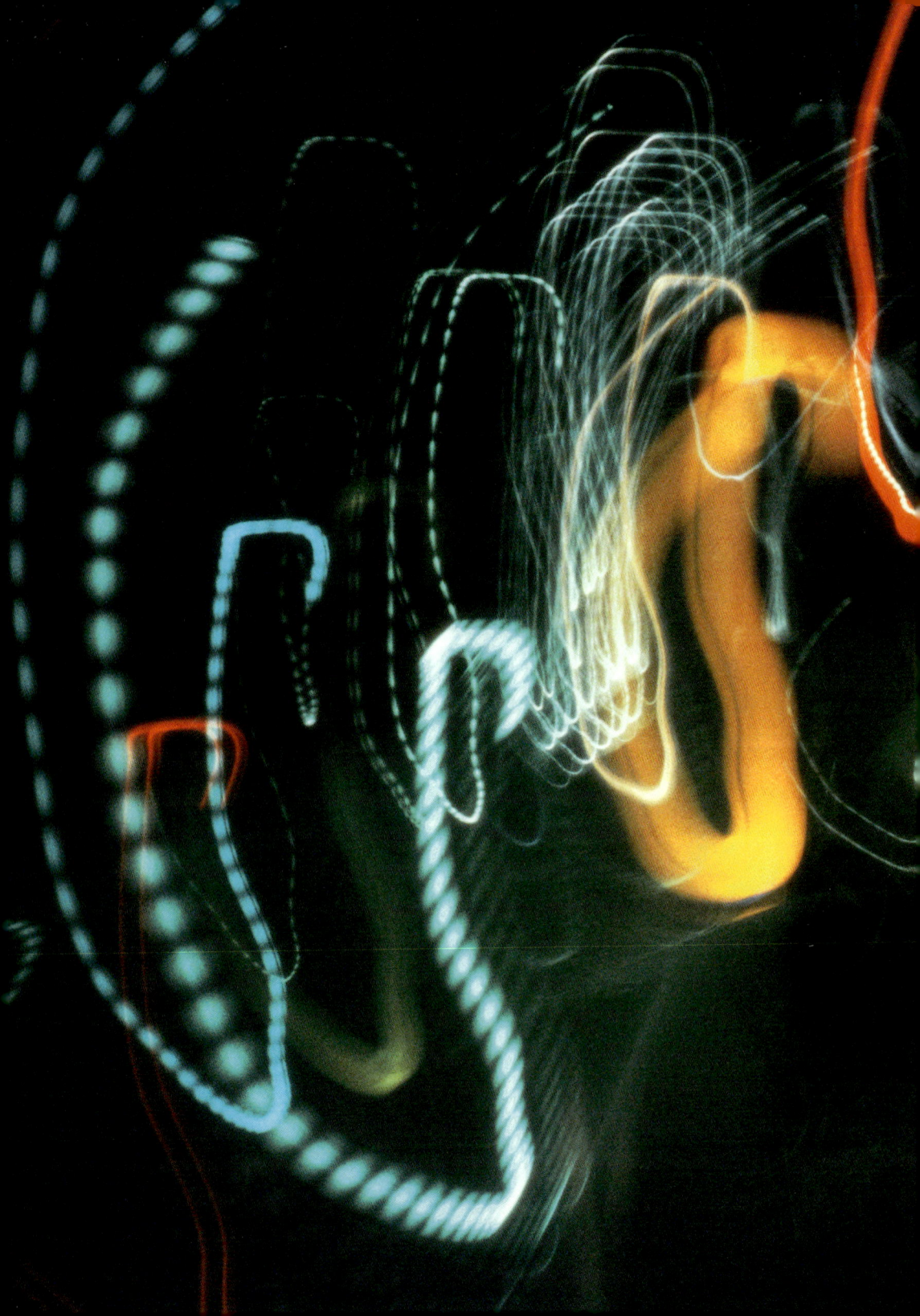

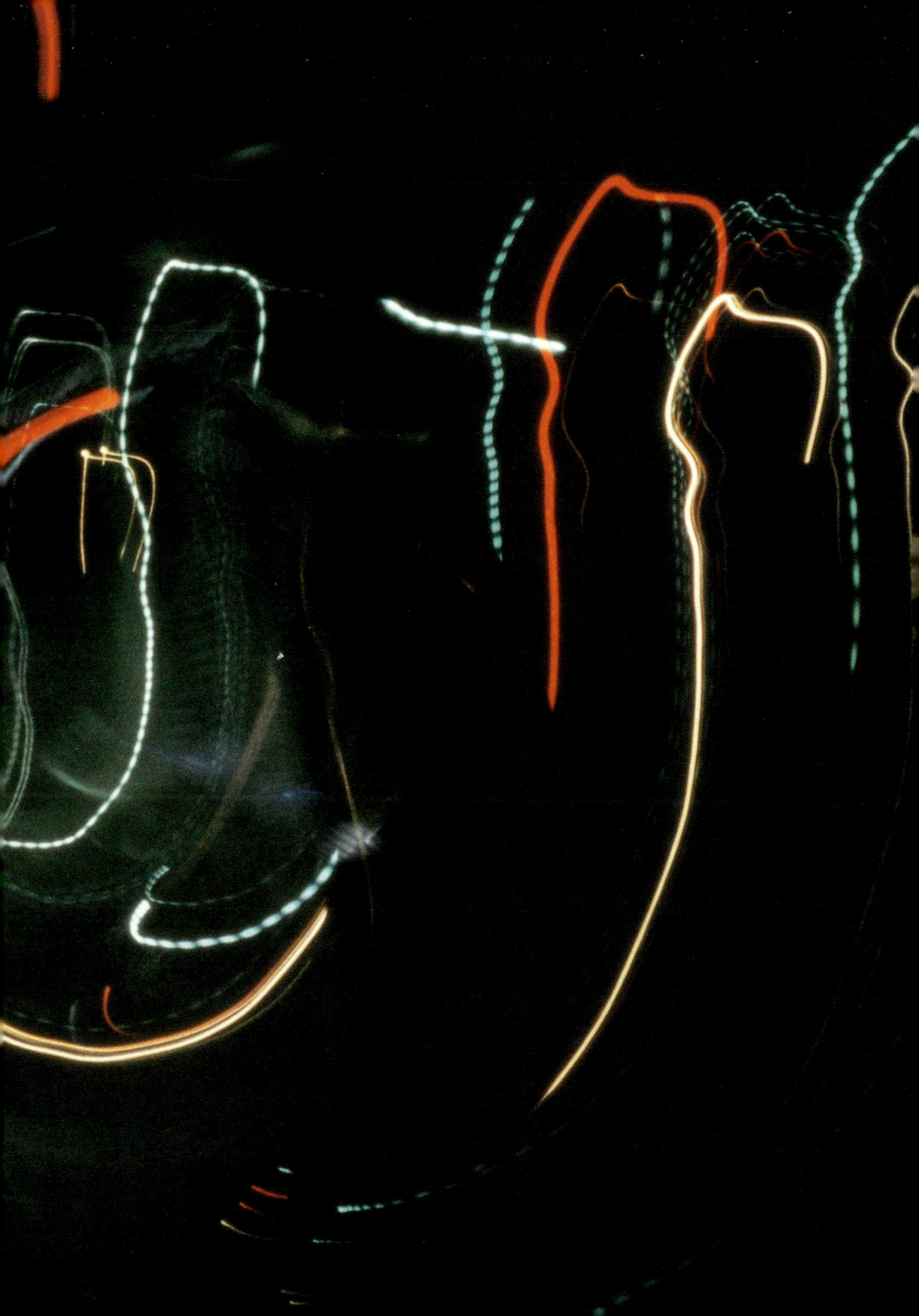

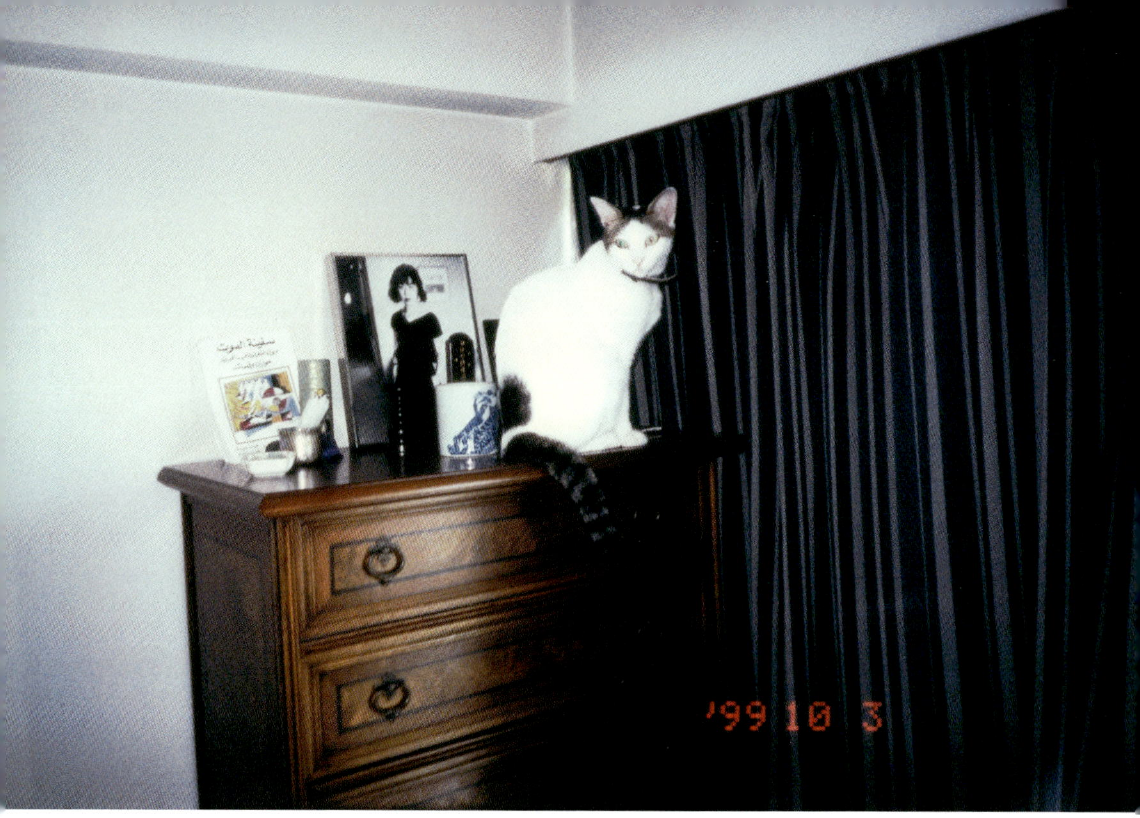

Private Diary

私日記

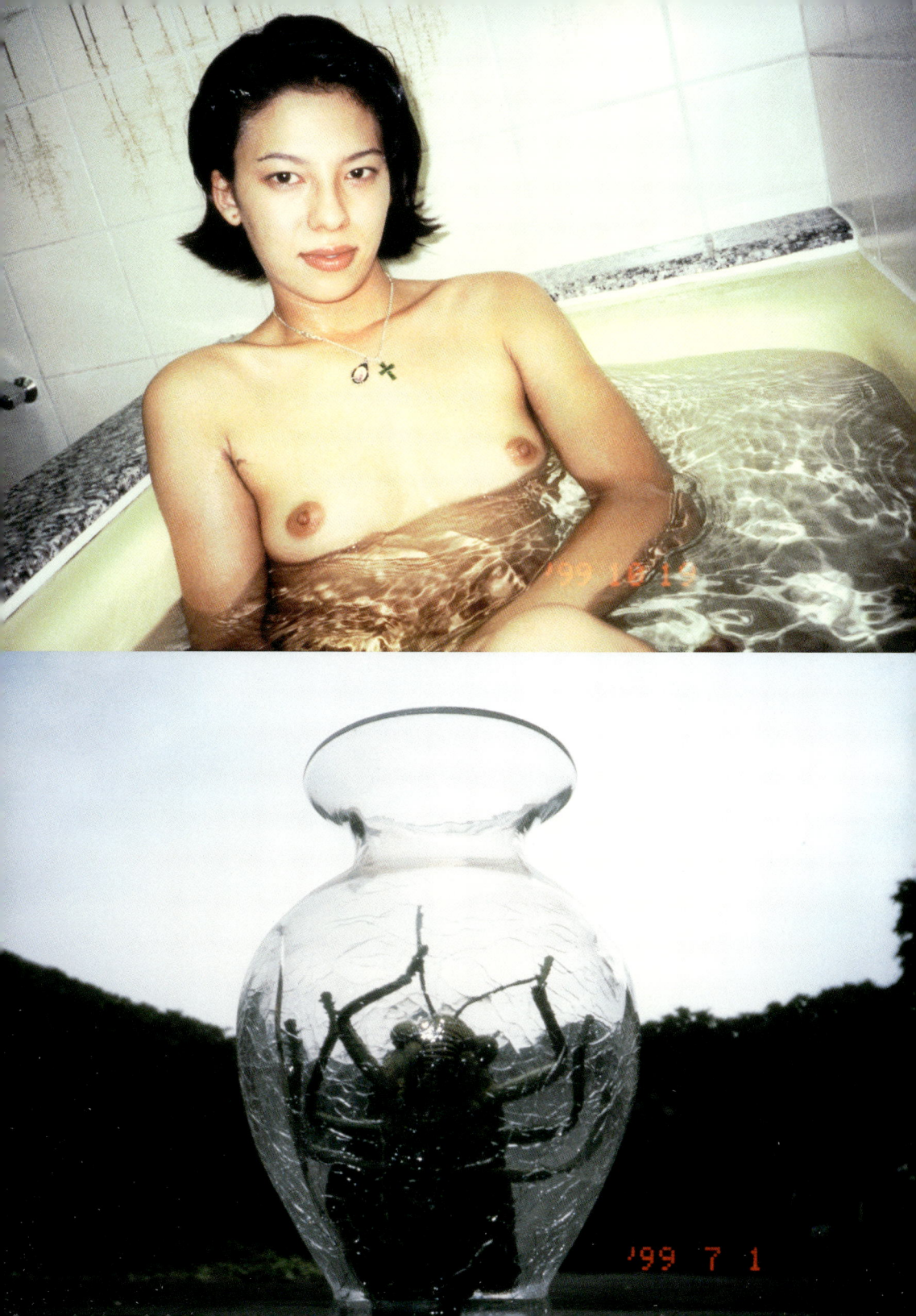

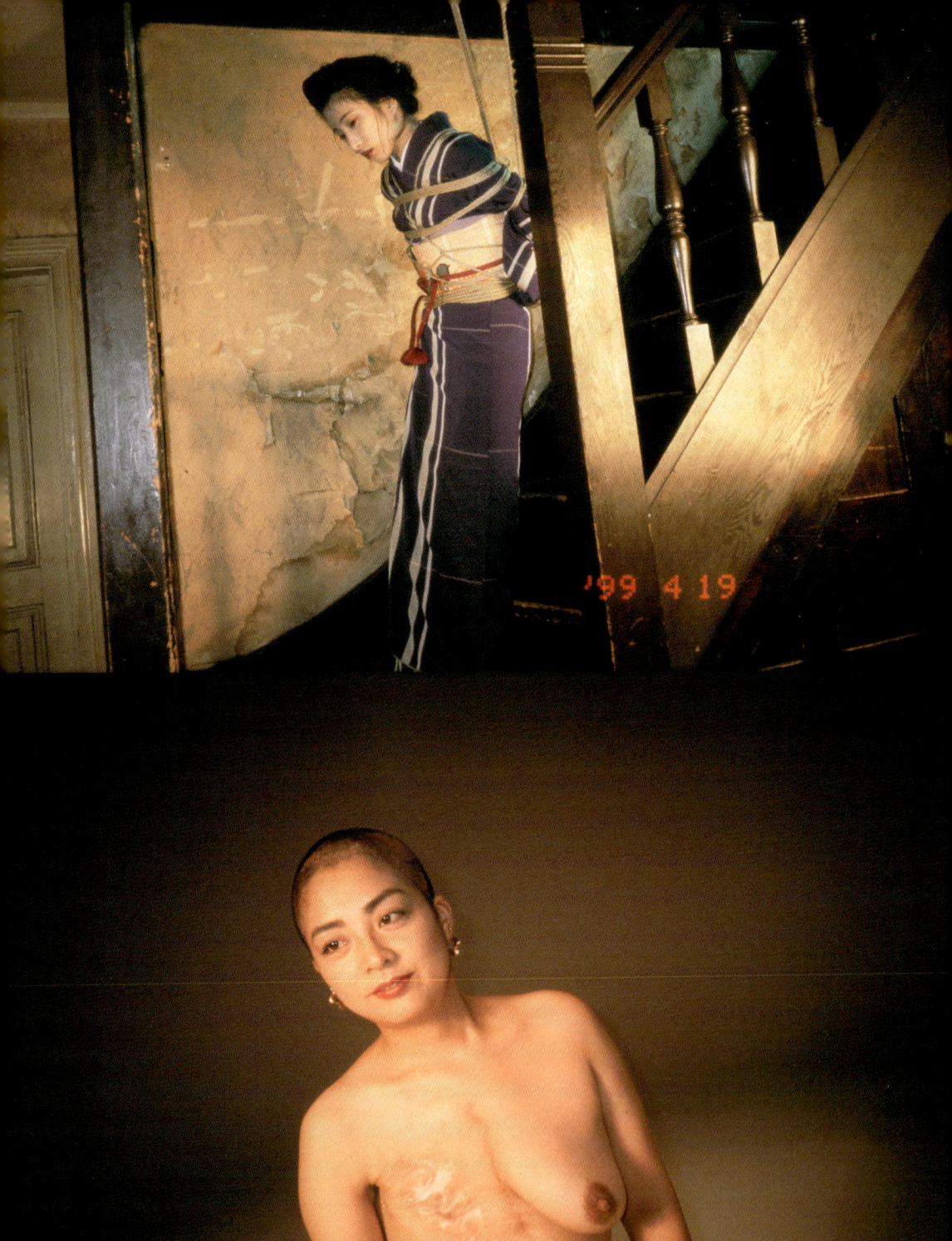

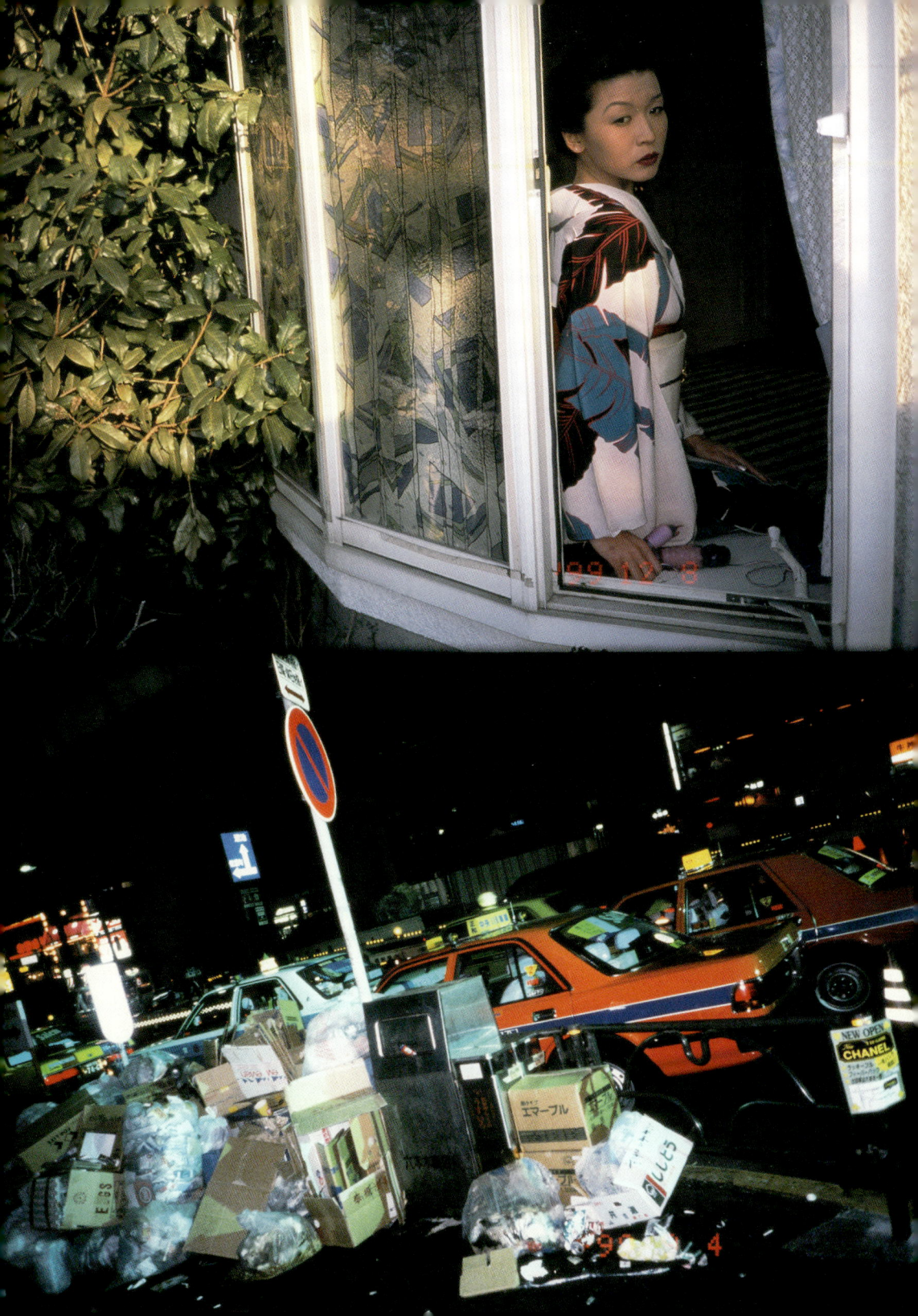

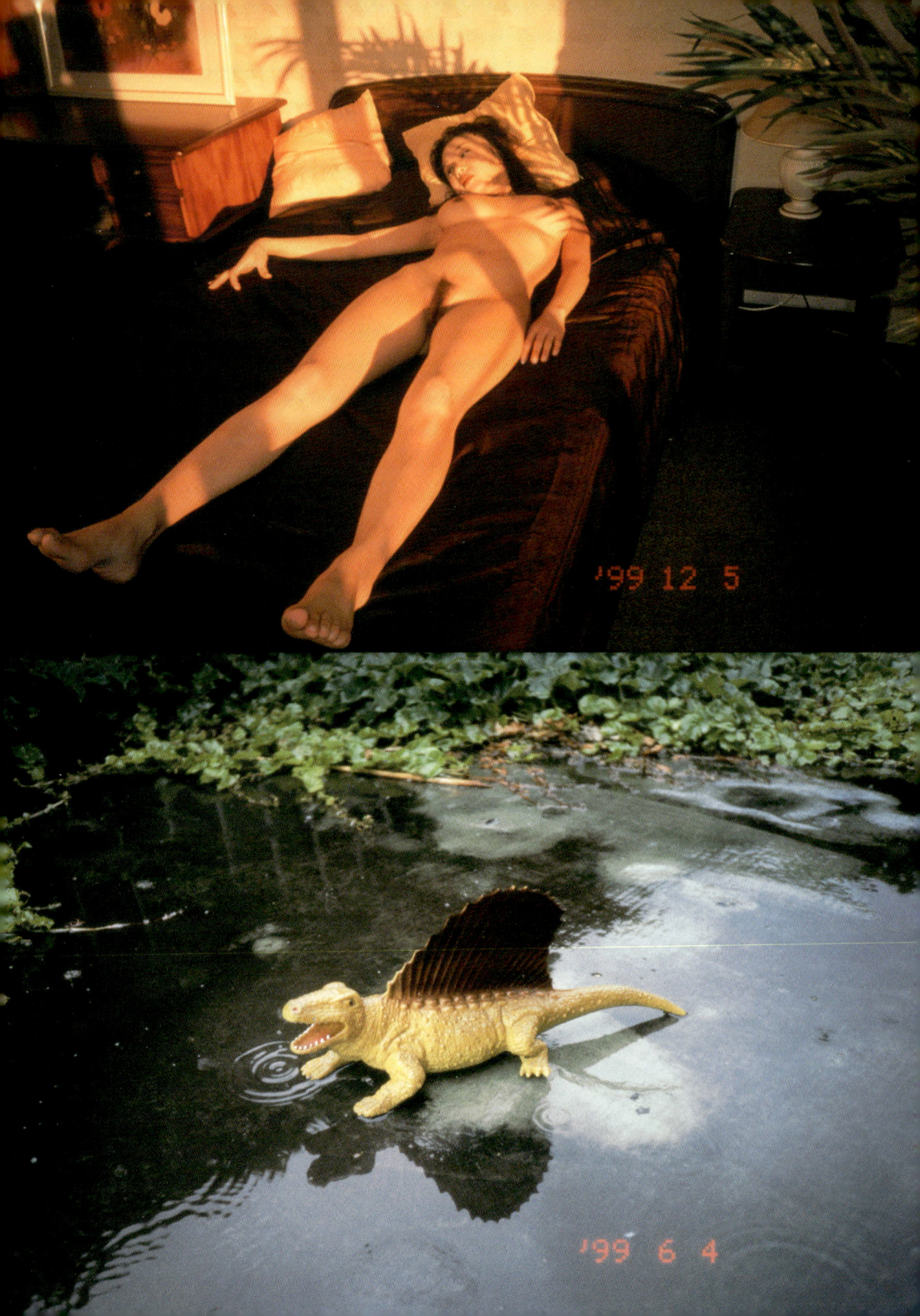

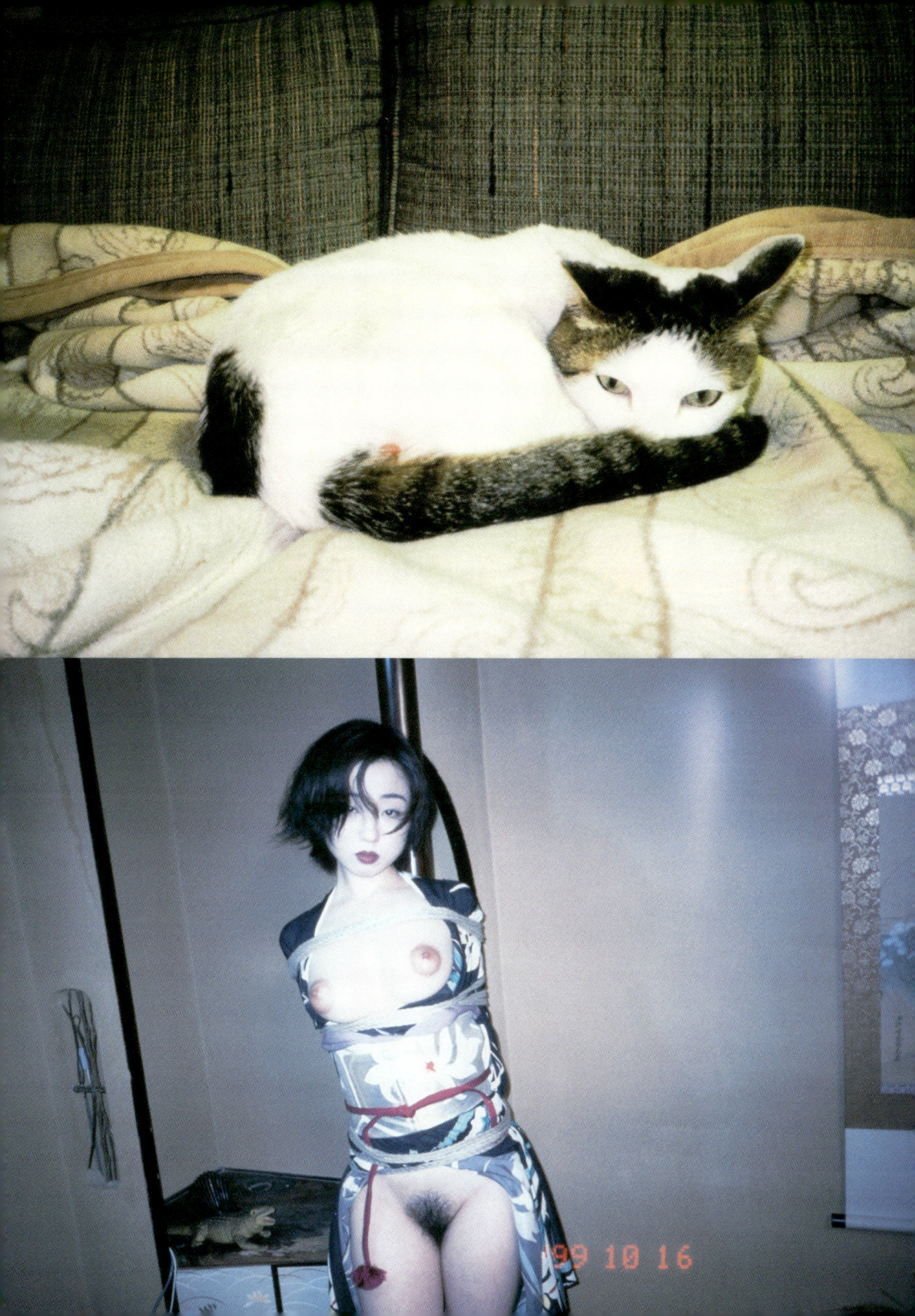

'99 10 16

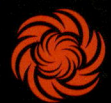

Tokyo Nude

東京ヌード

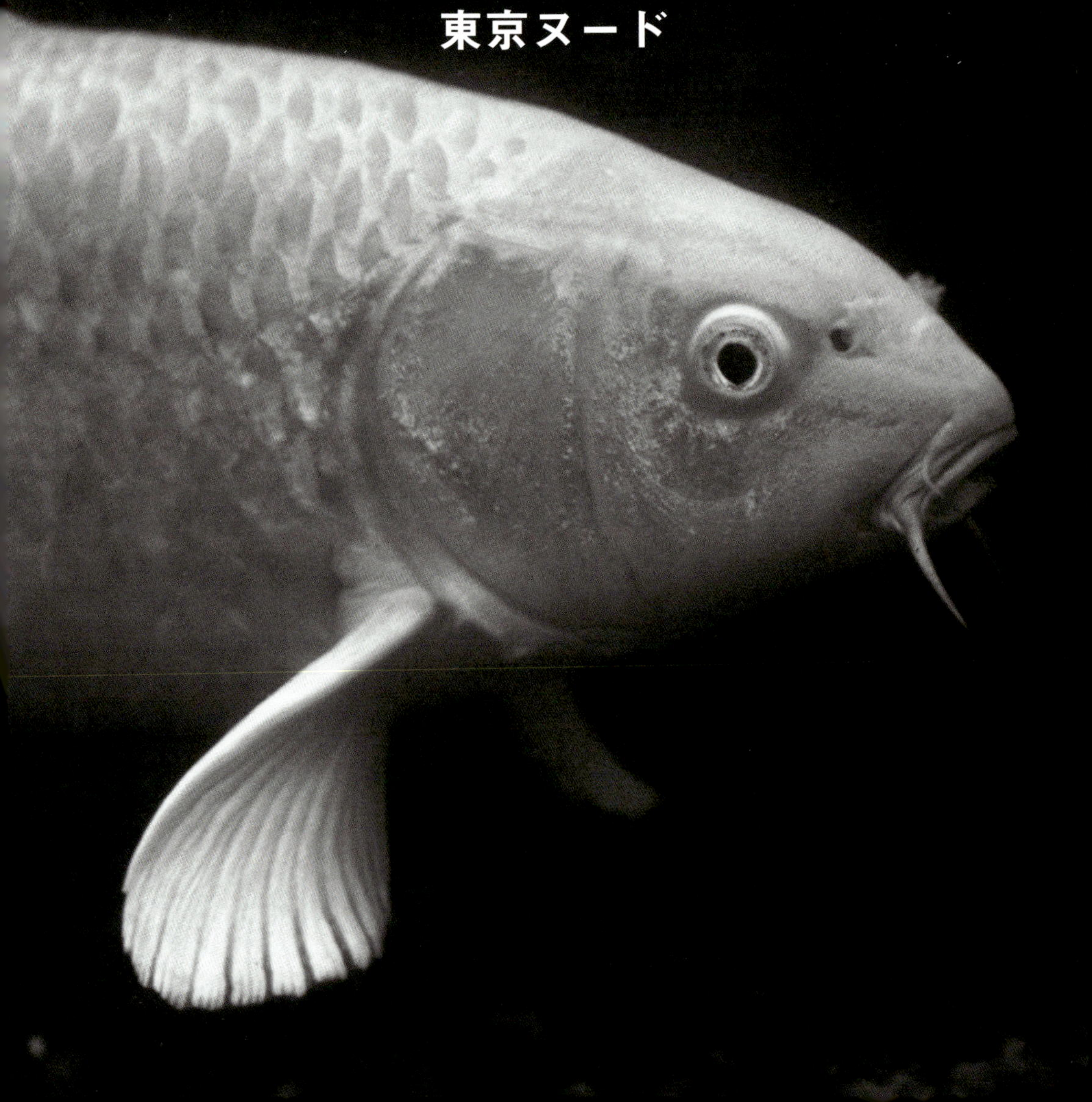

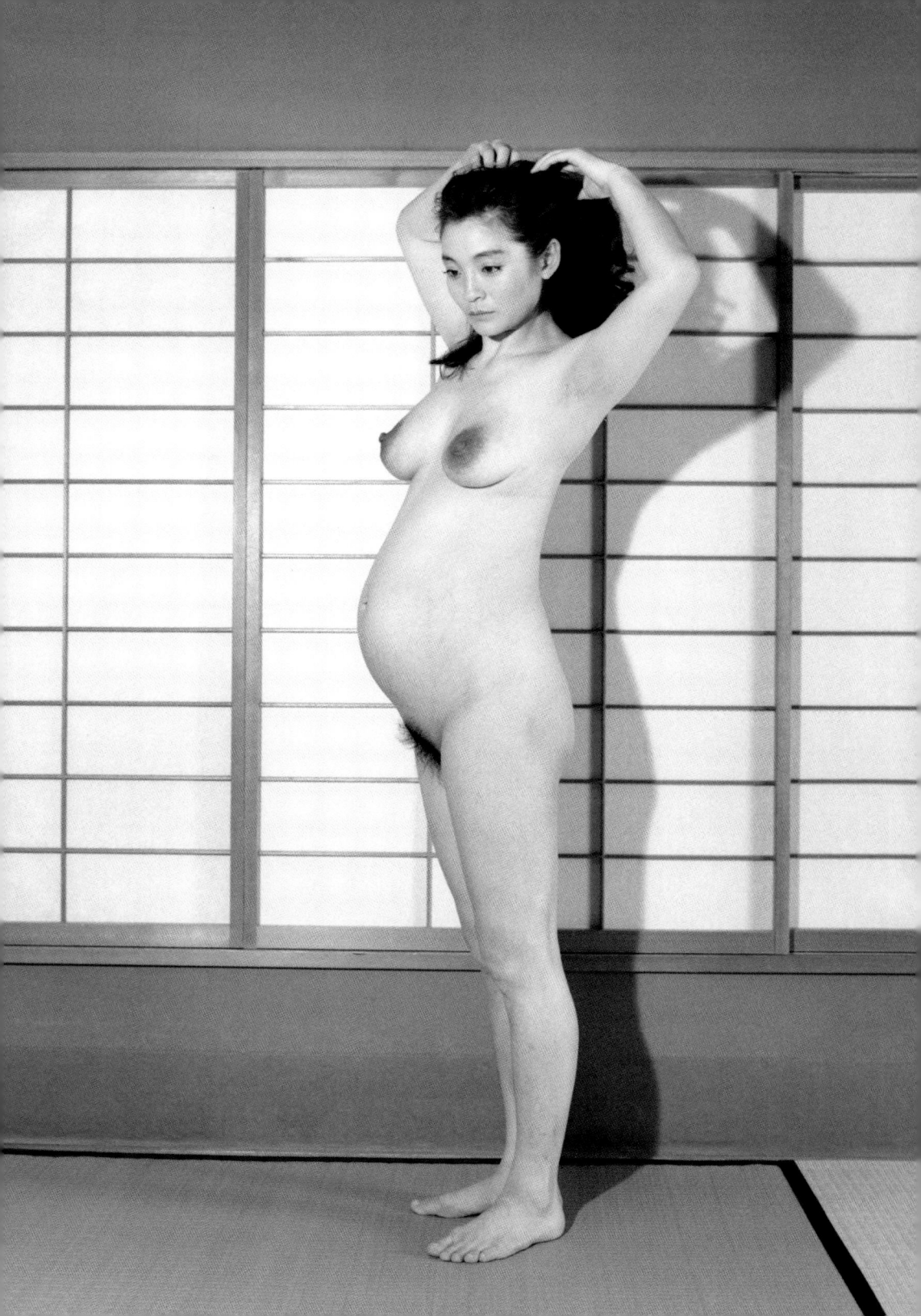

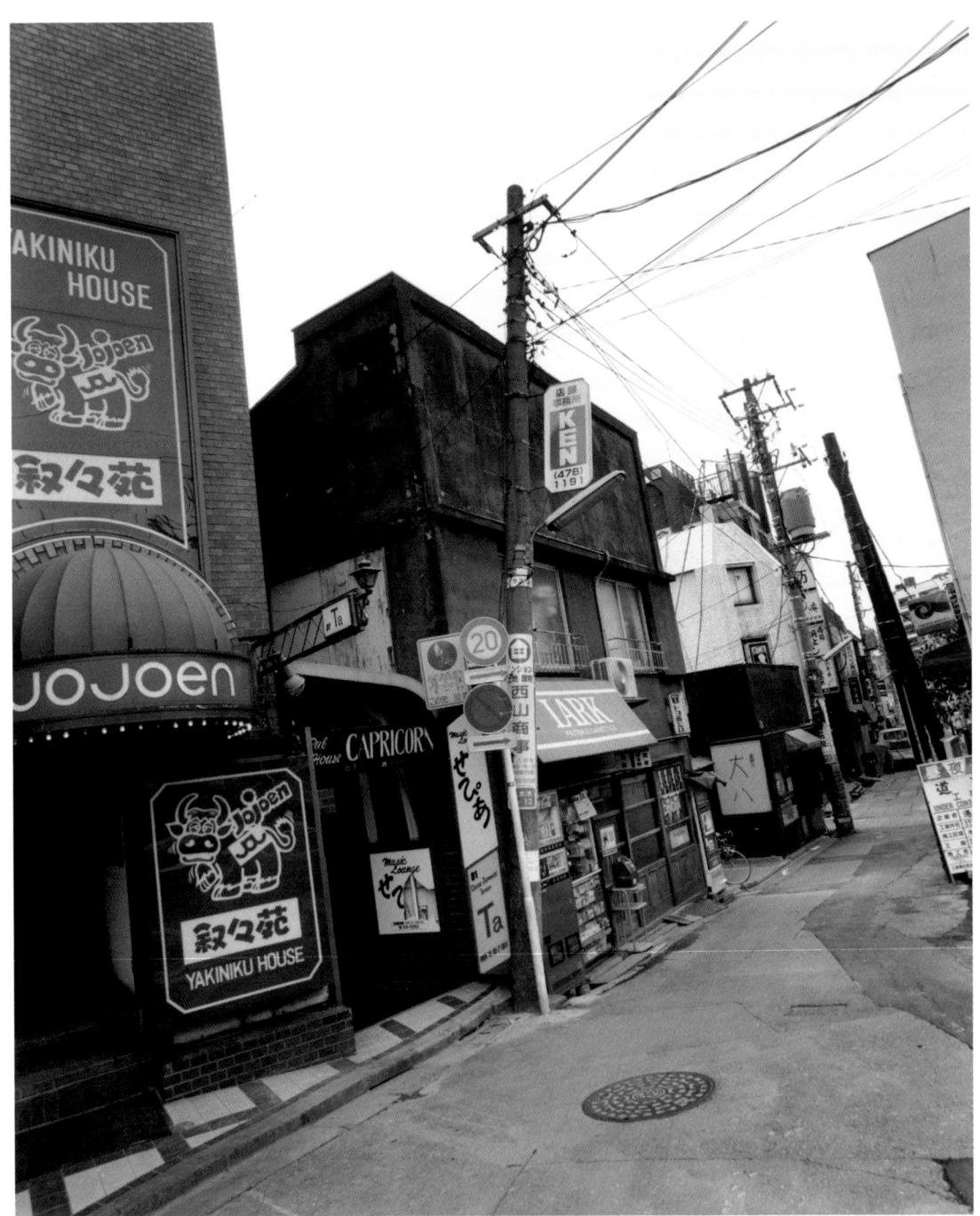

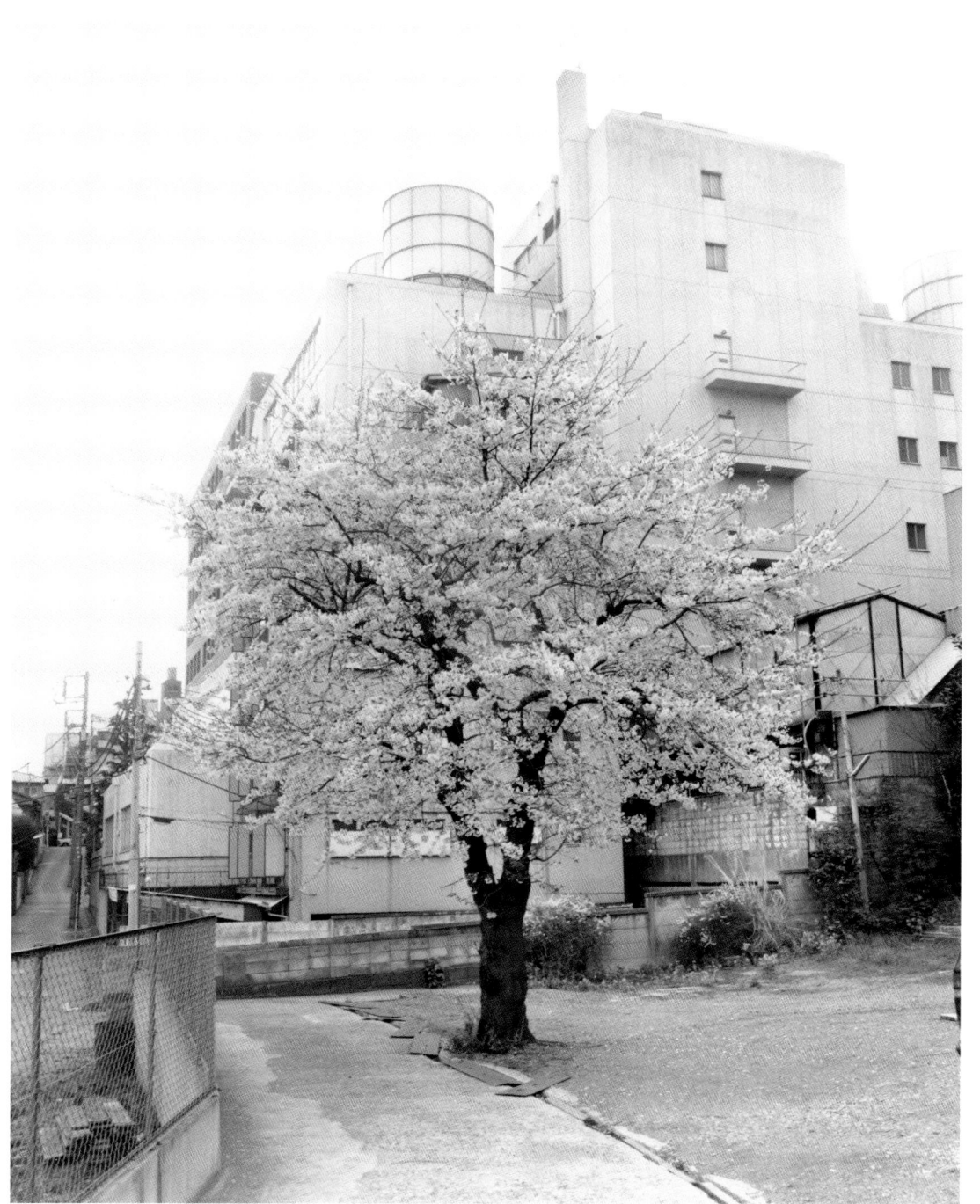

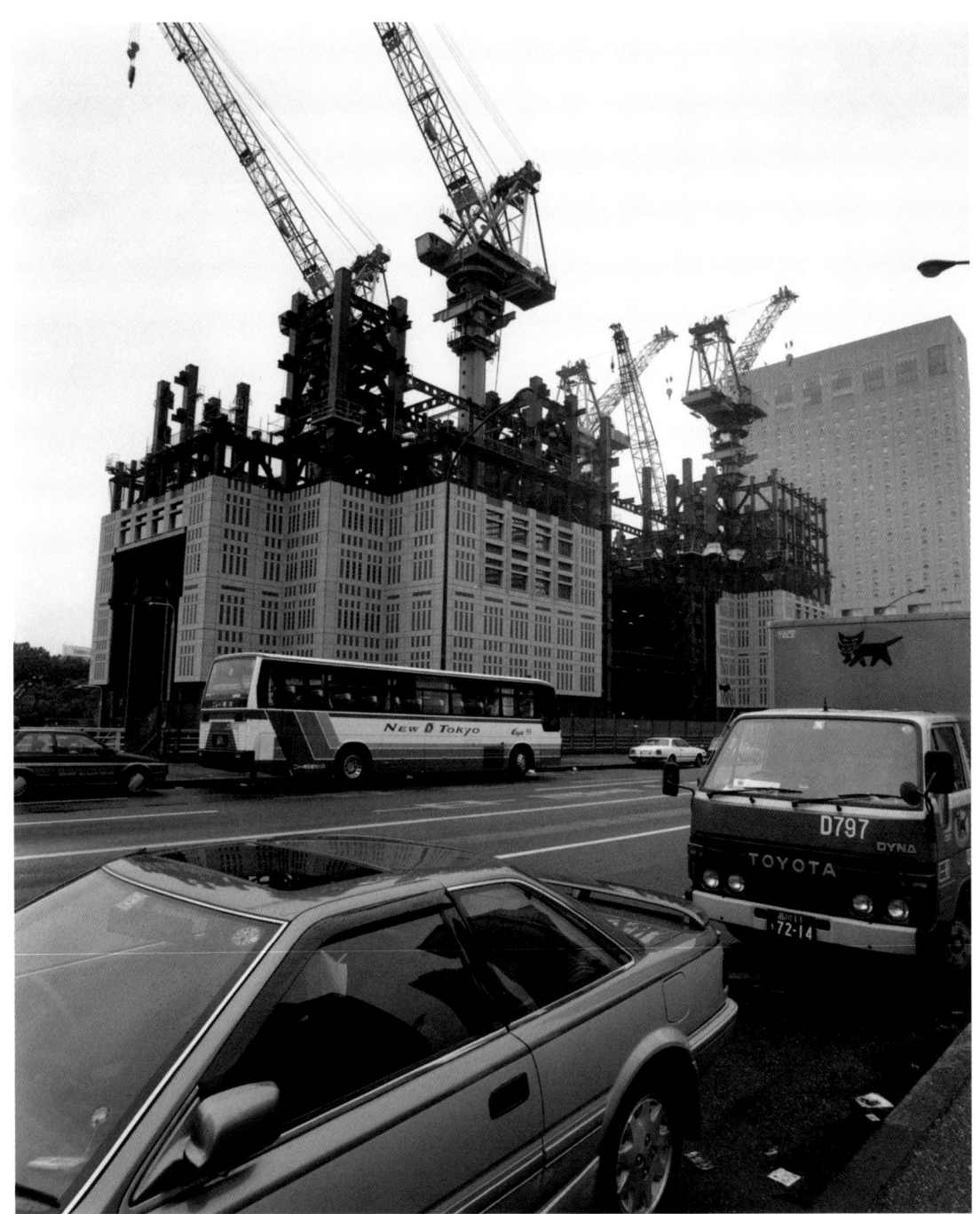

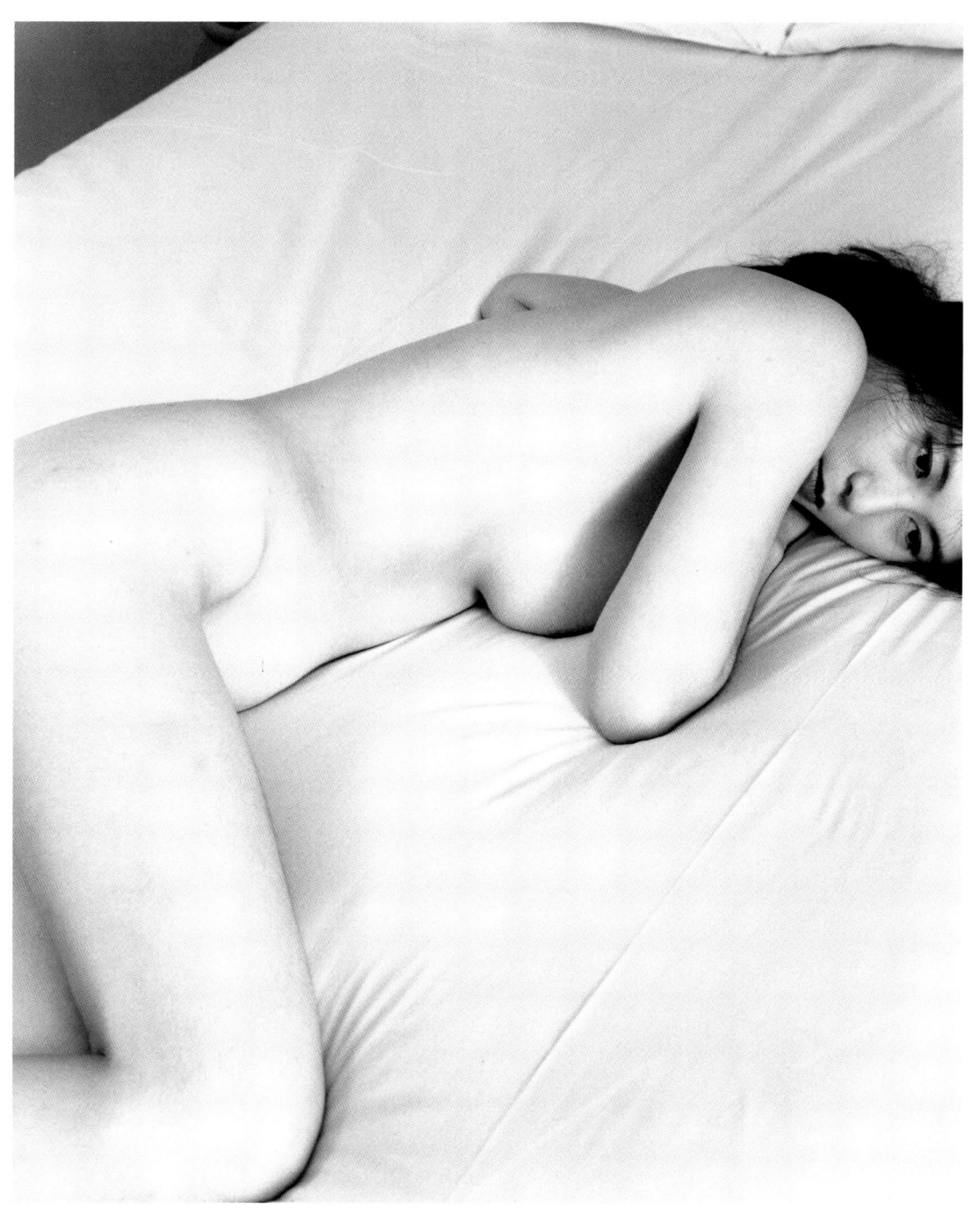

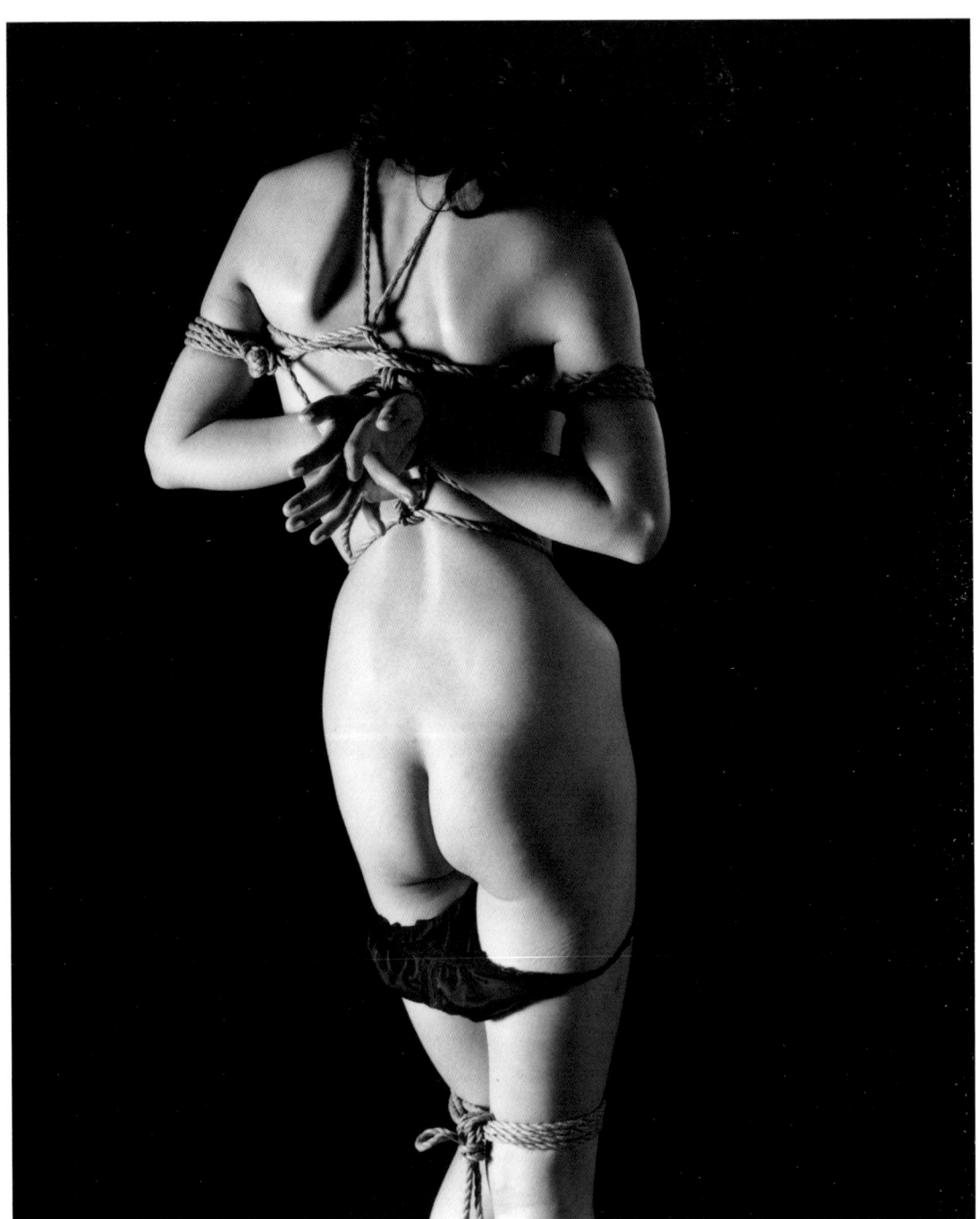

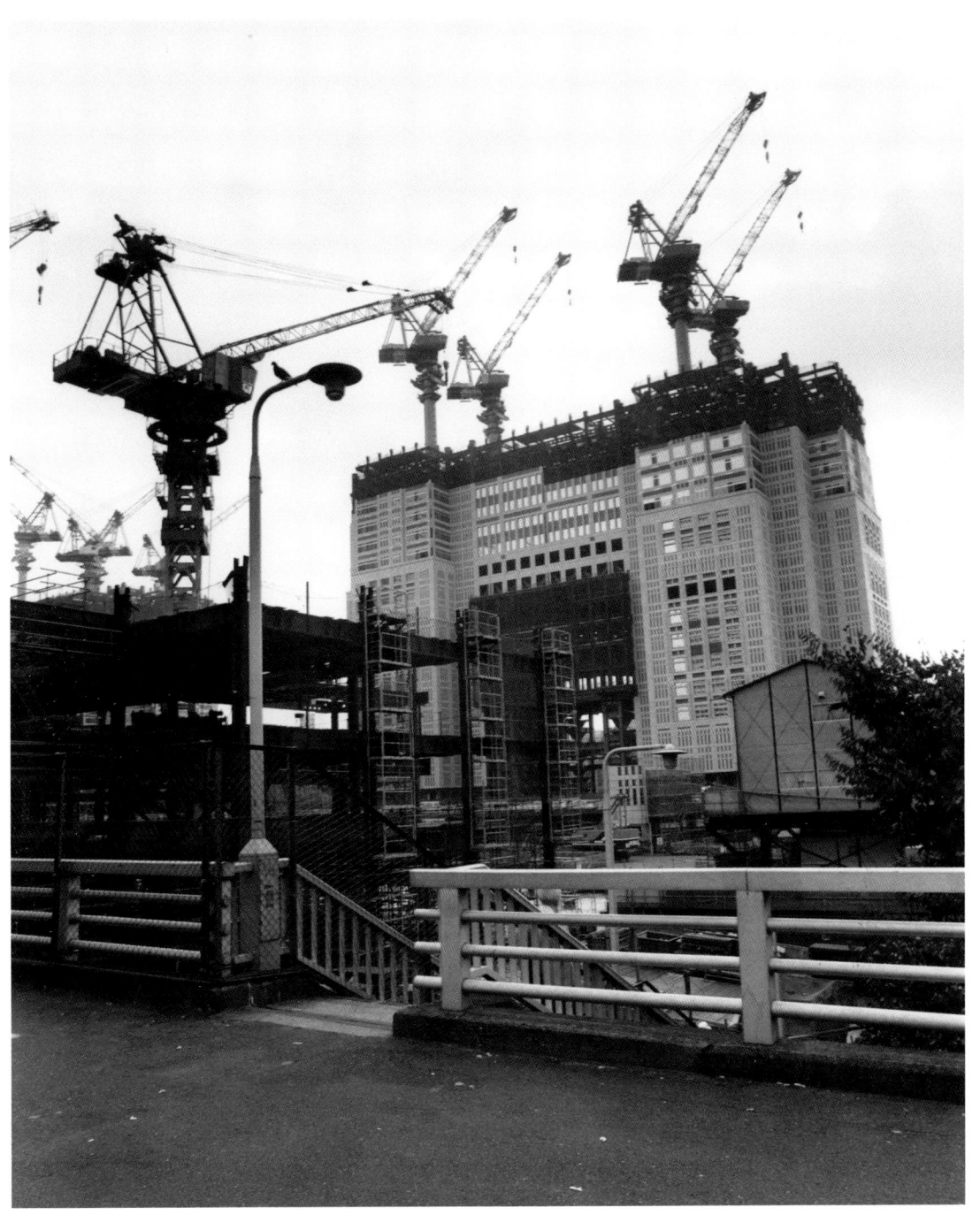

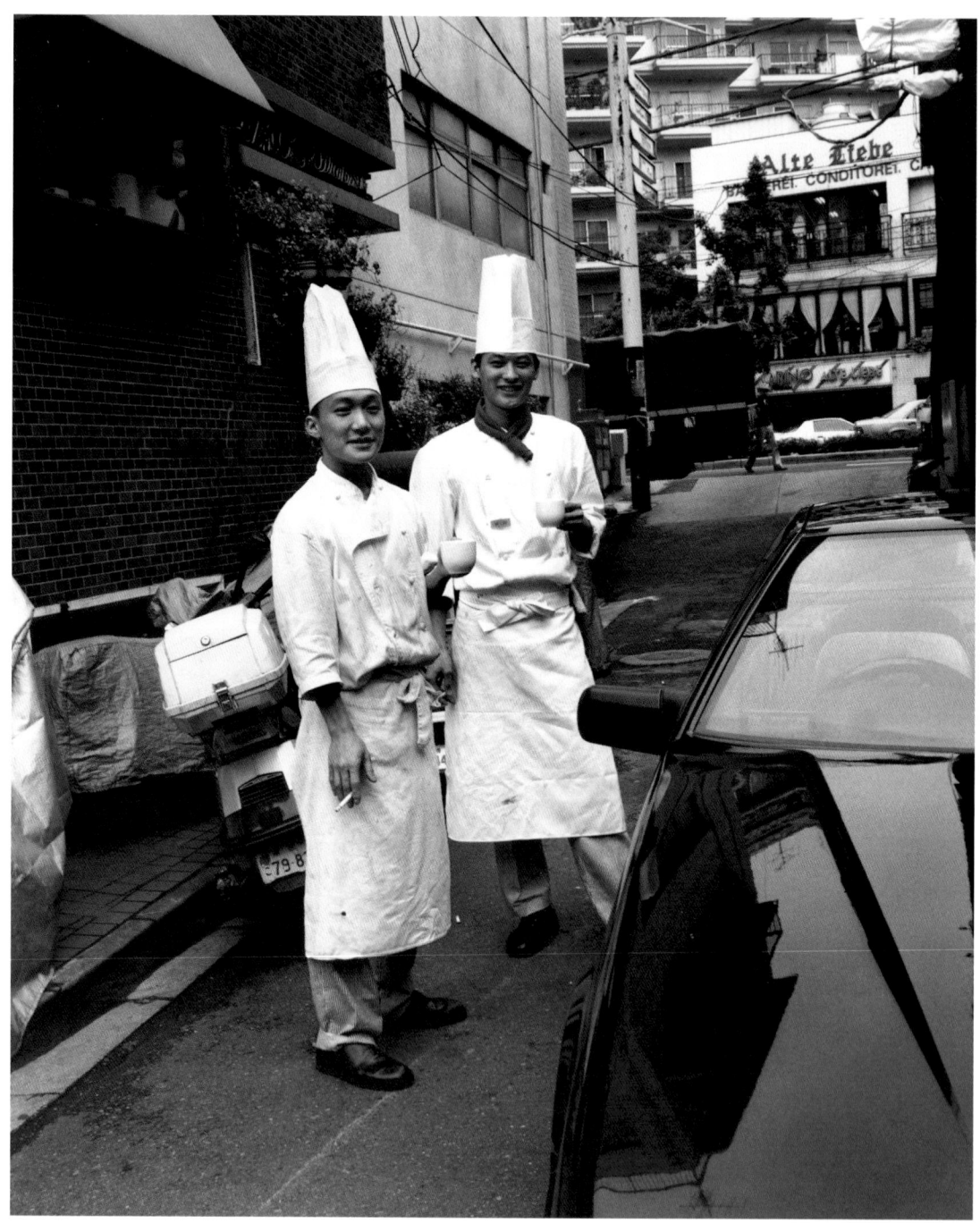

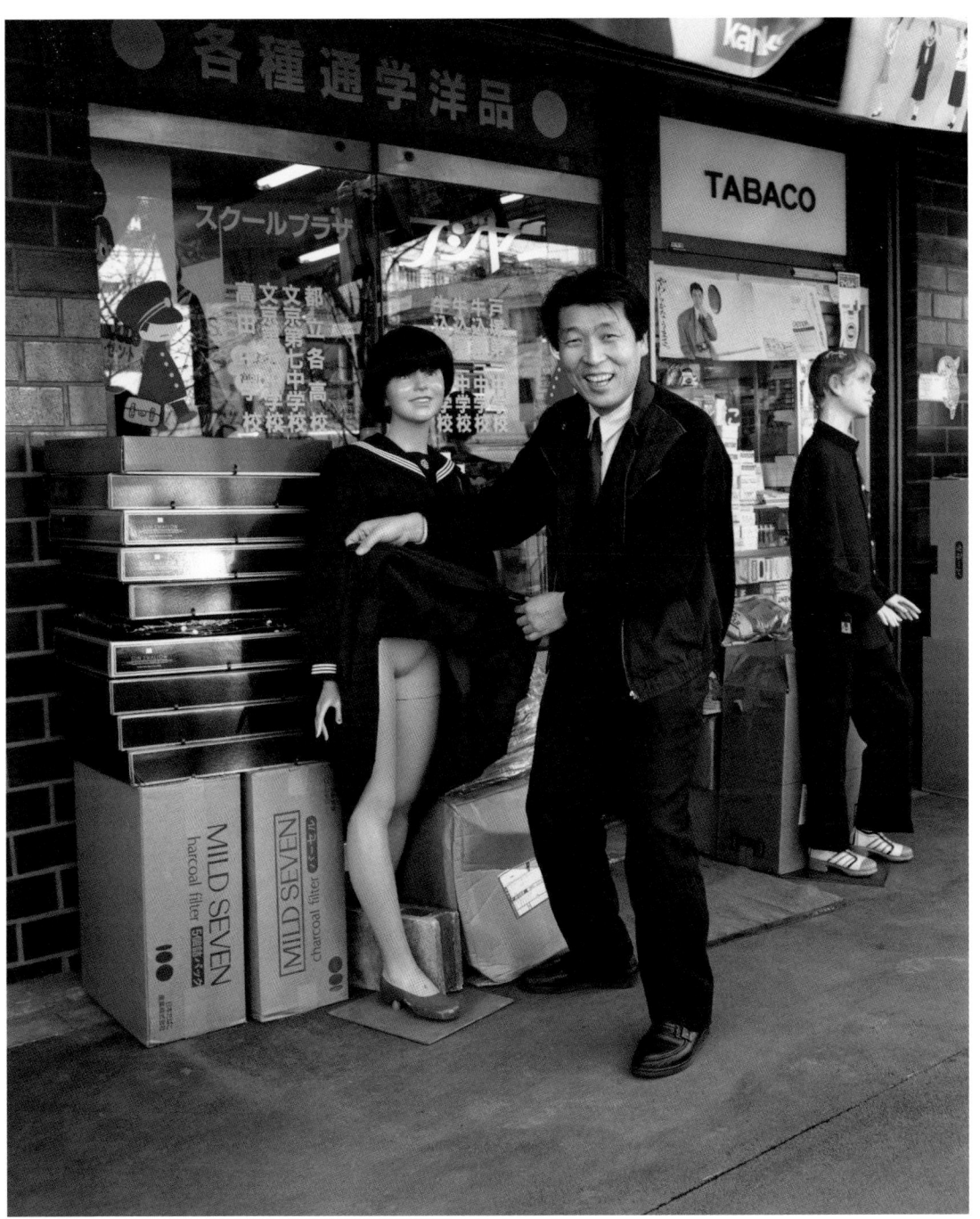

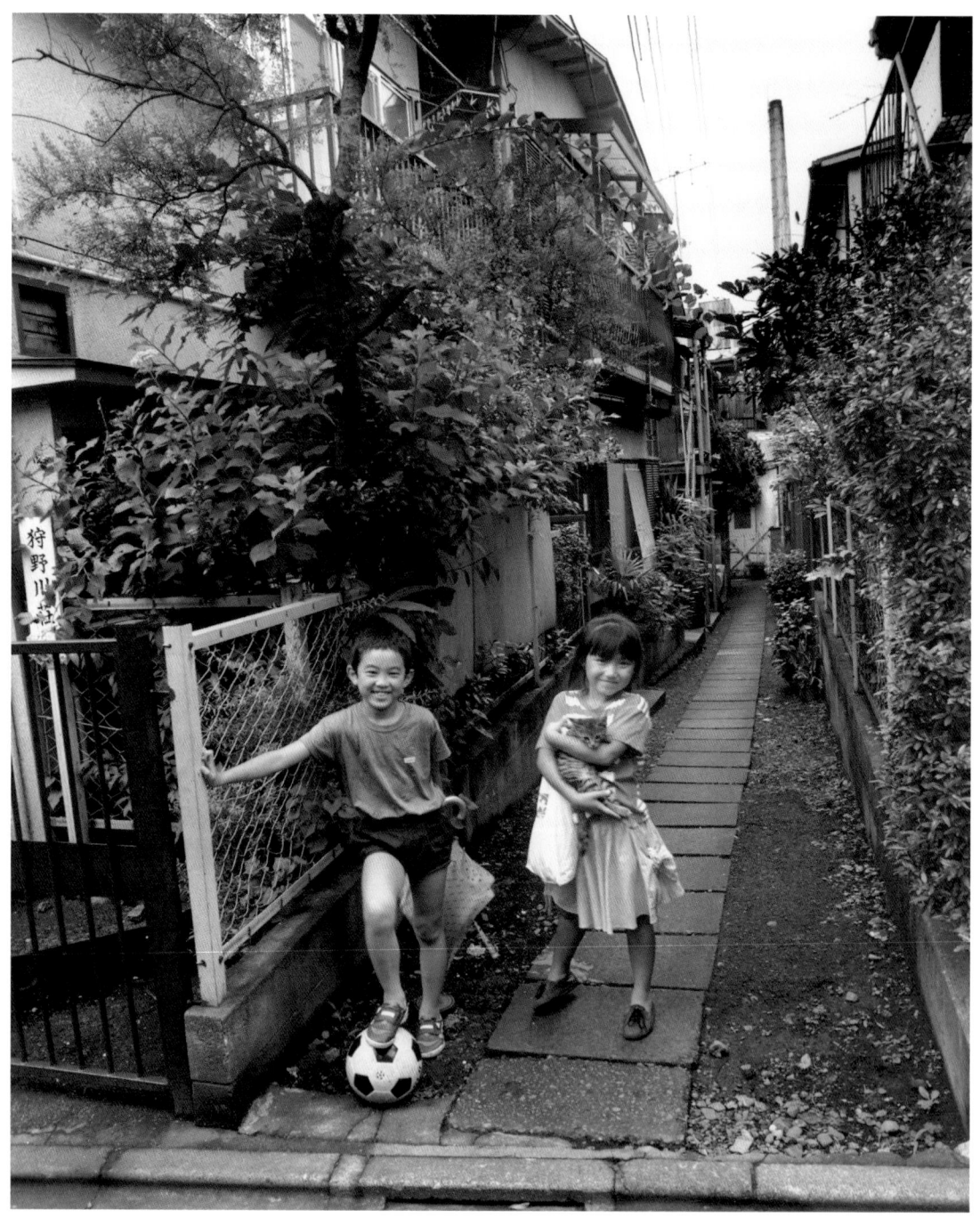

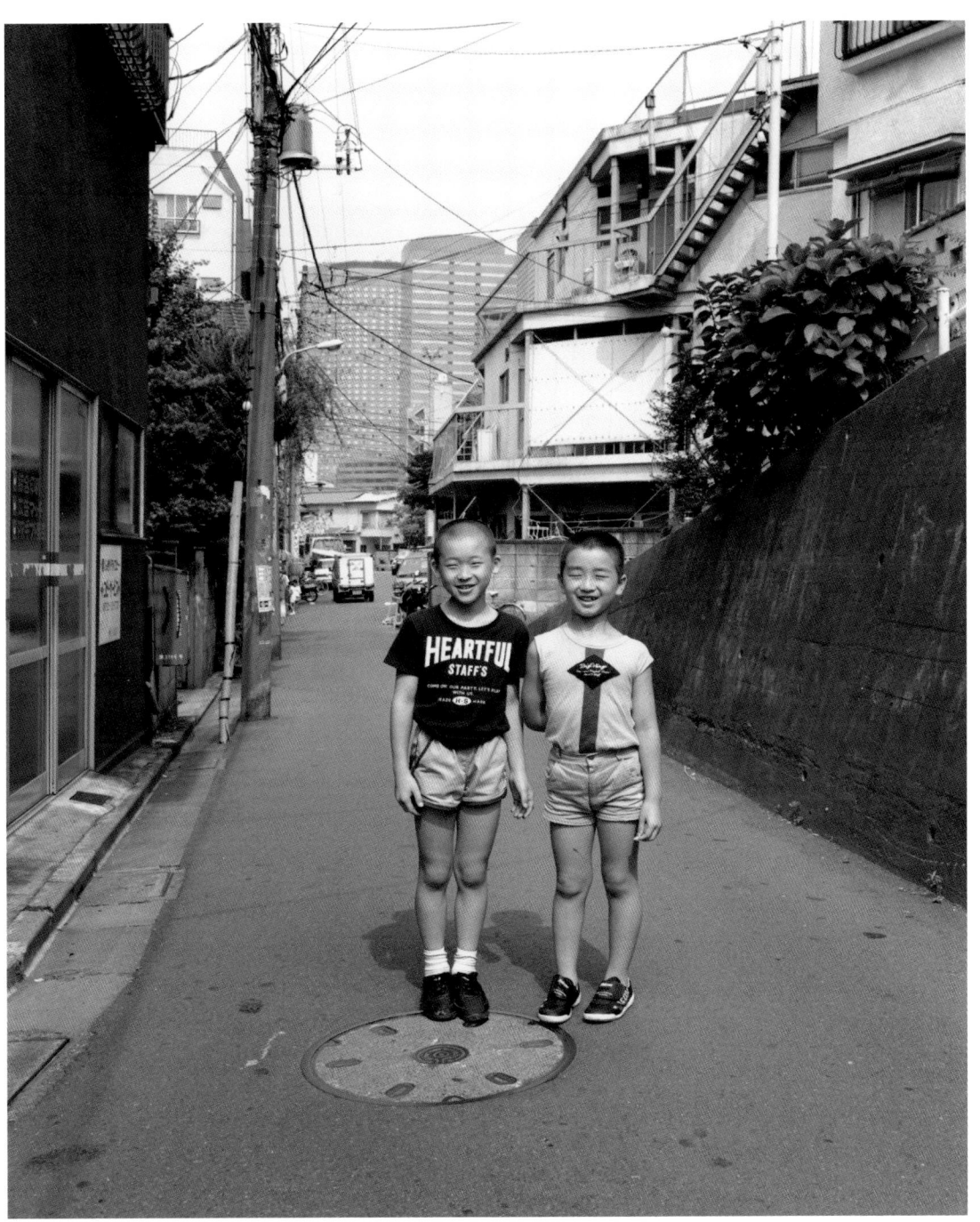

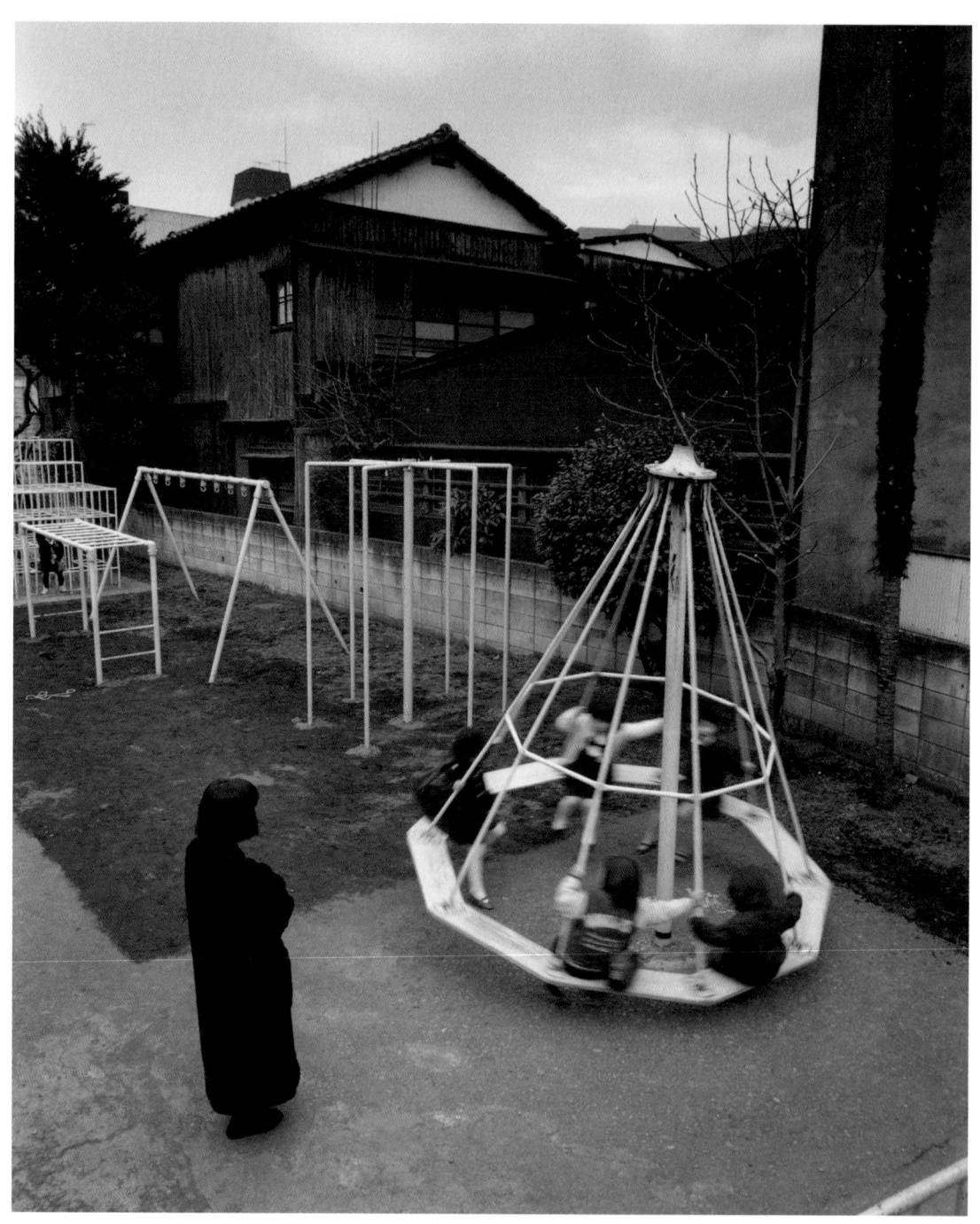

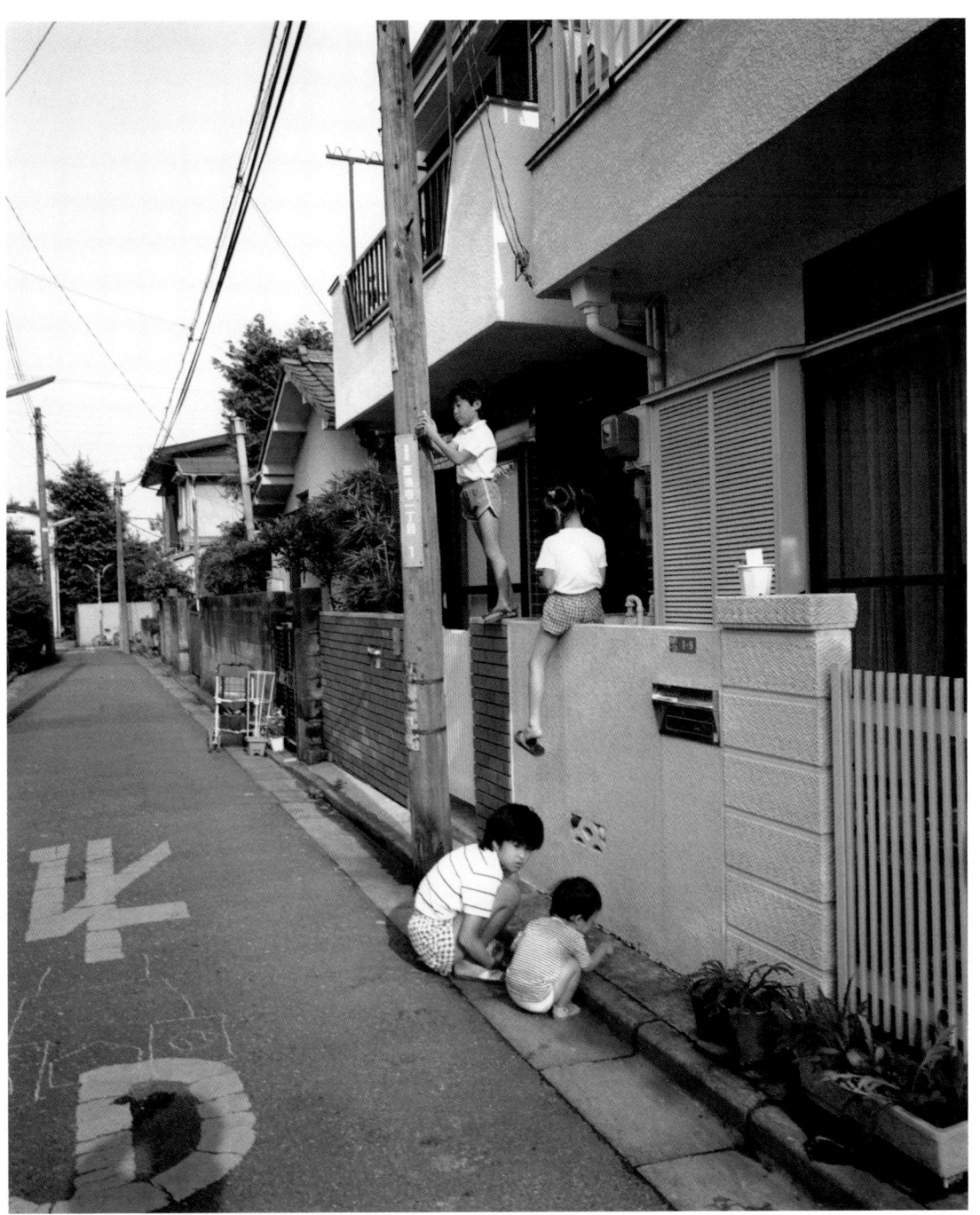

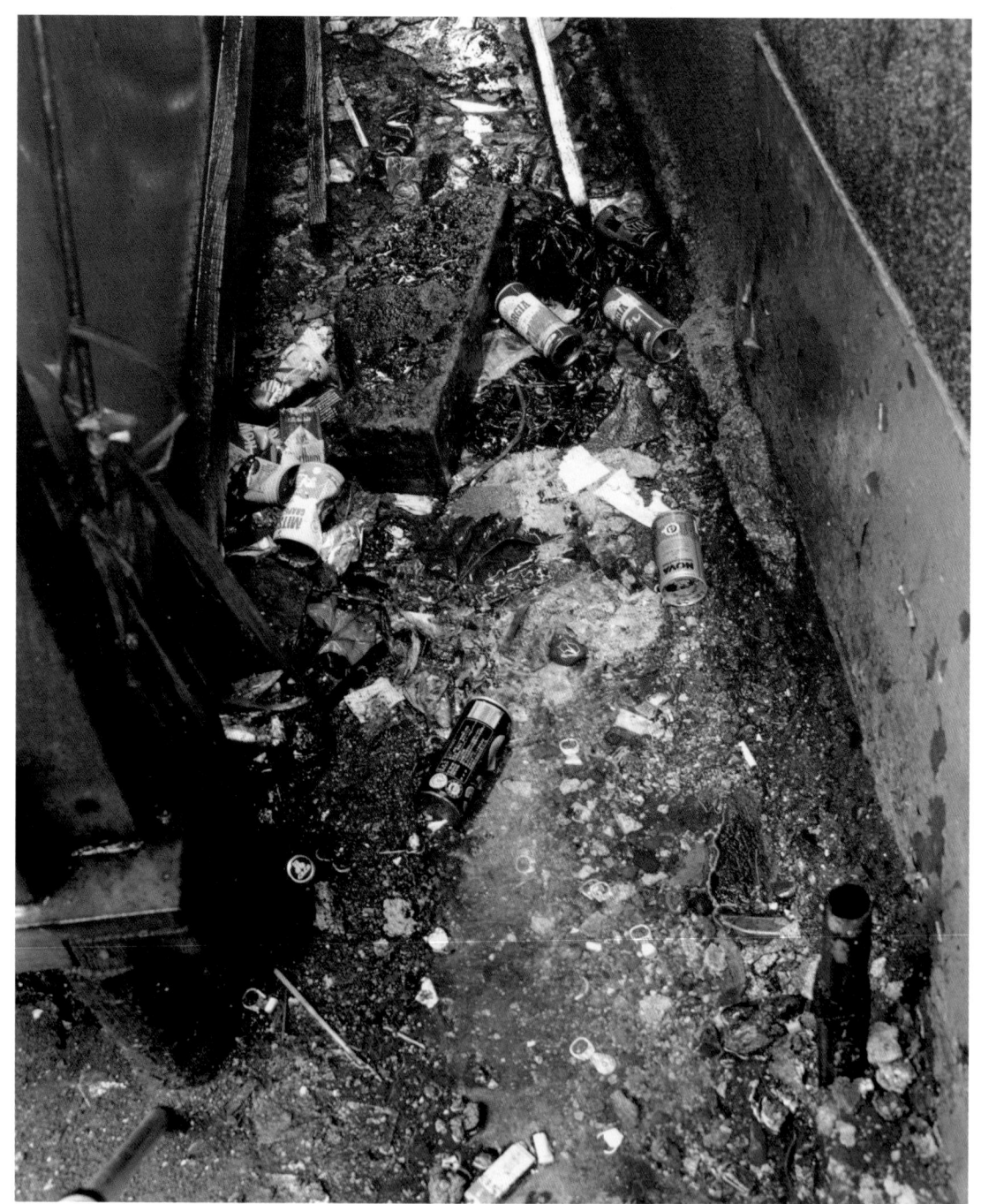

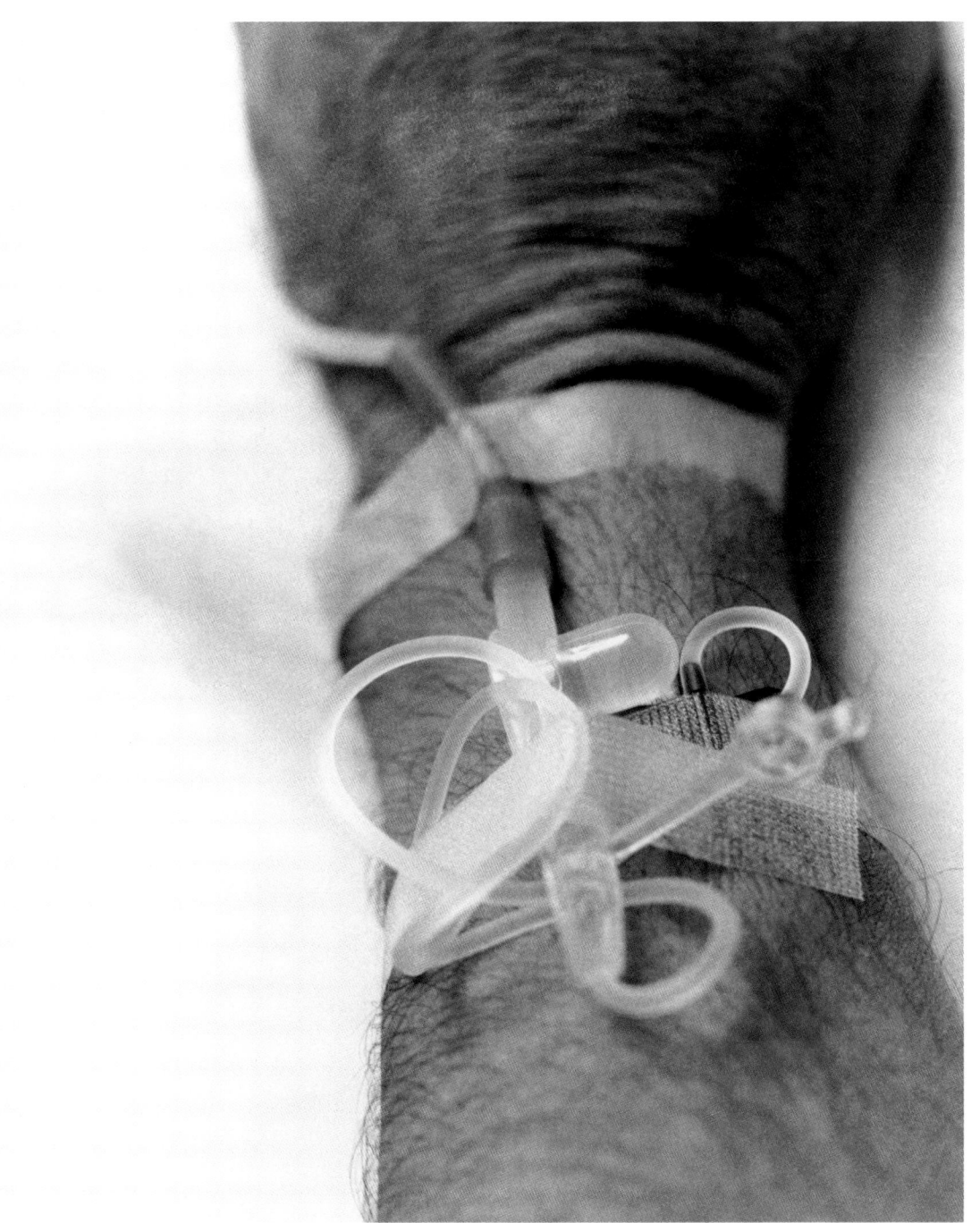

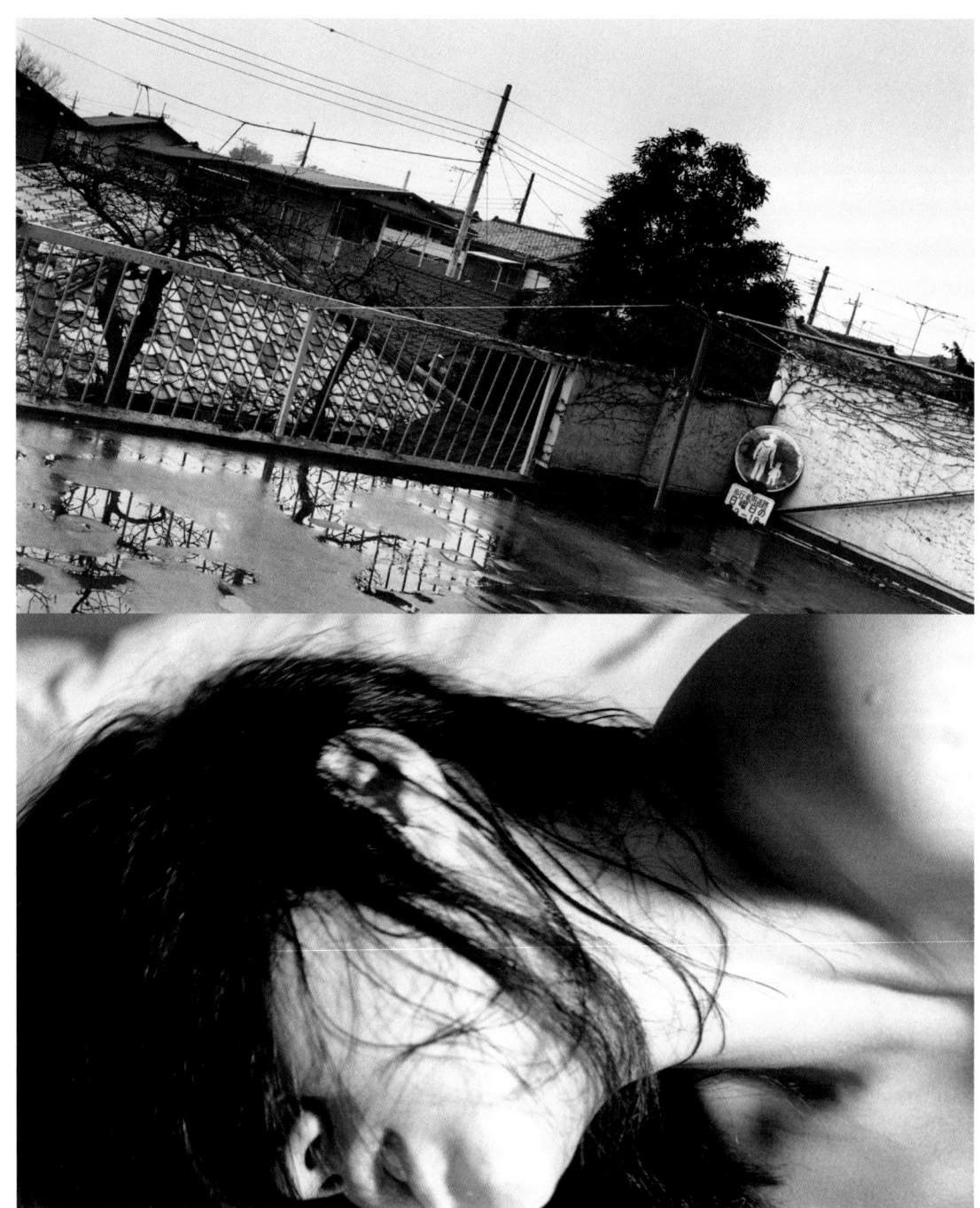

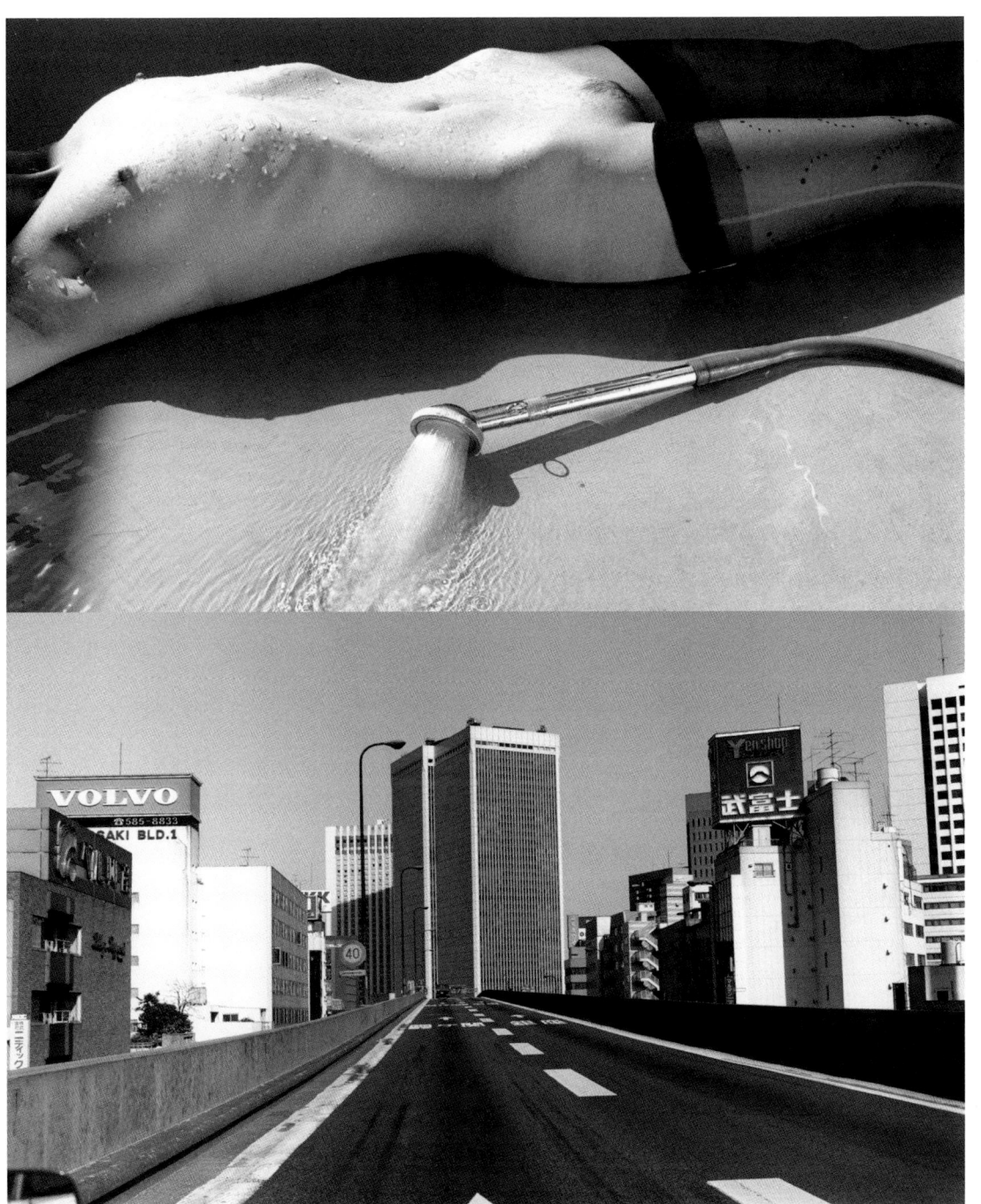

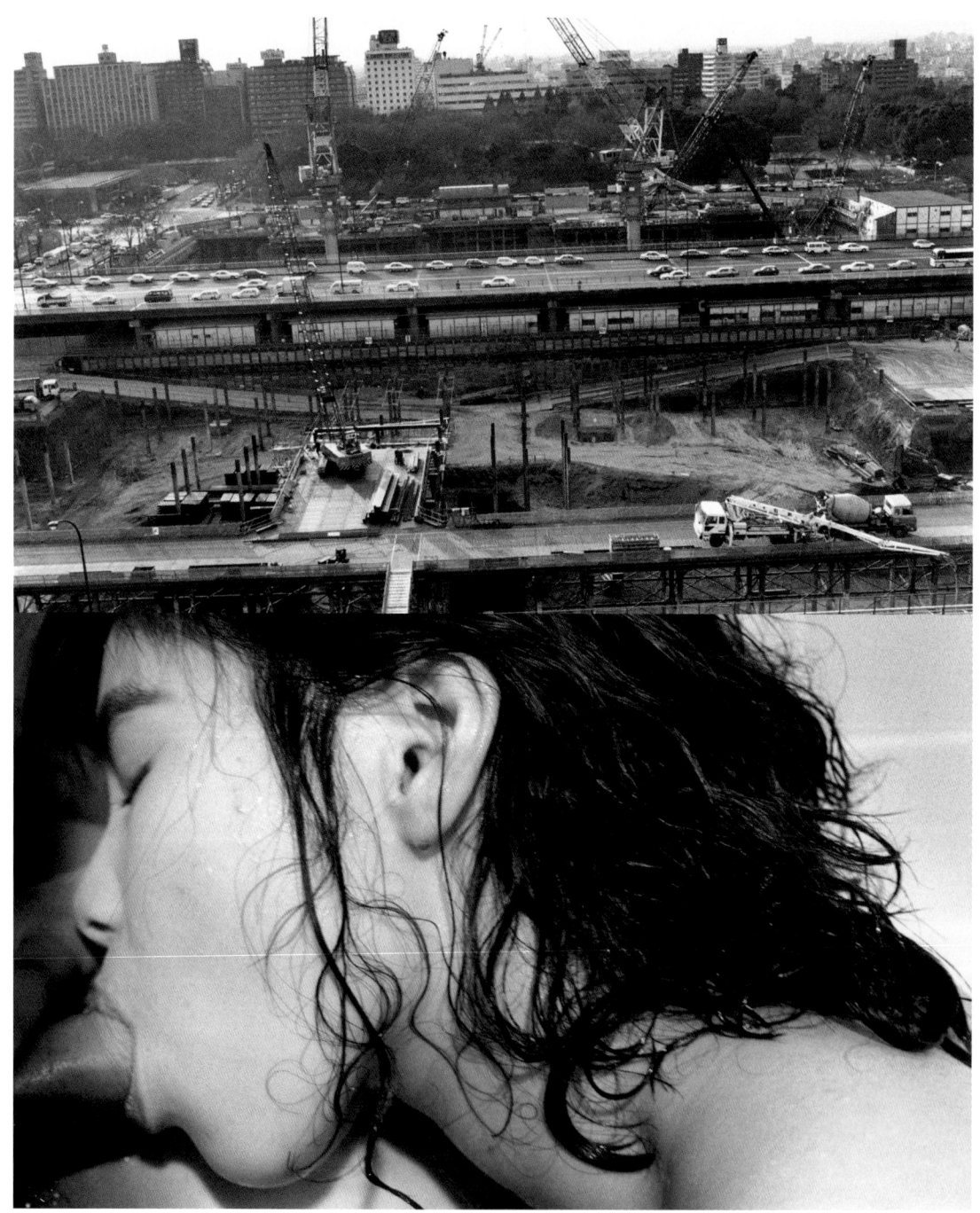

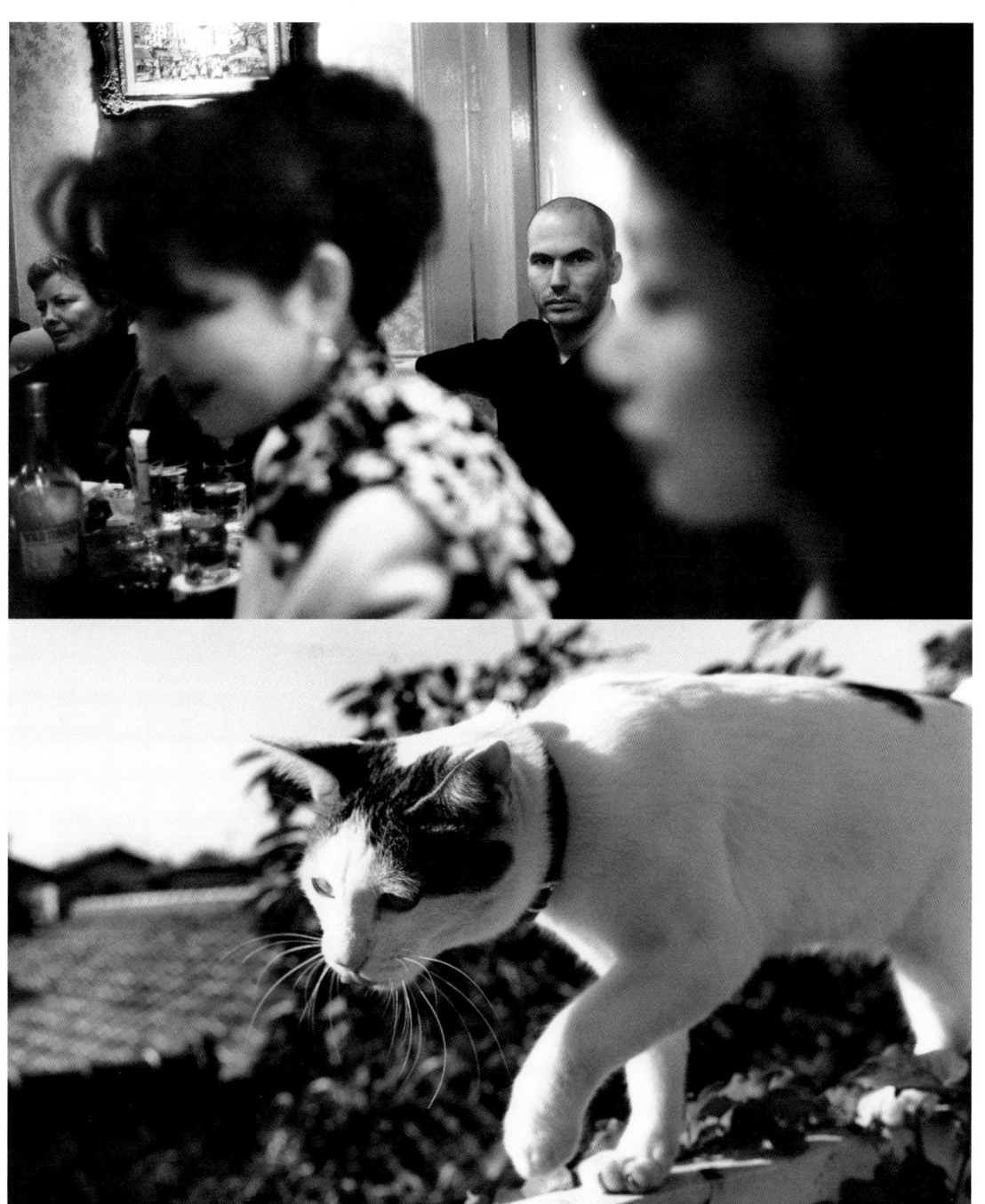

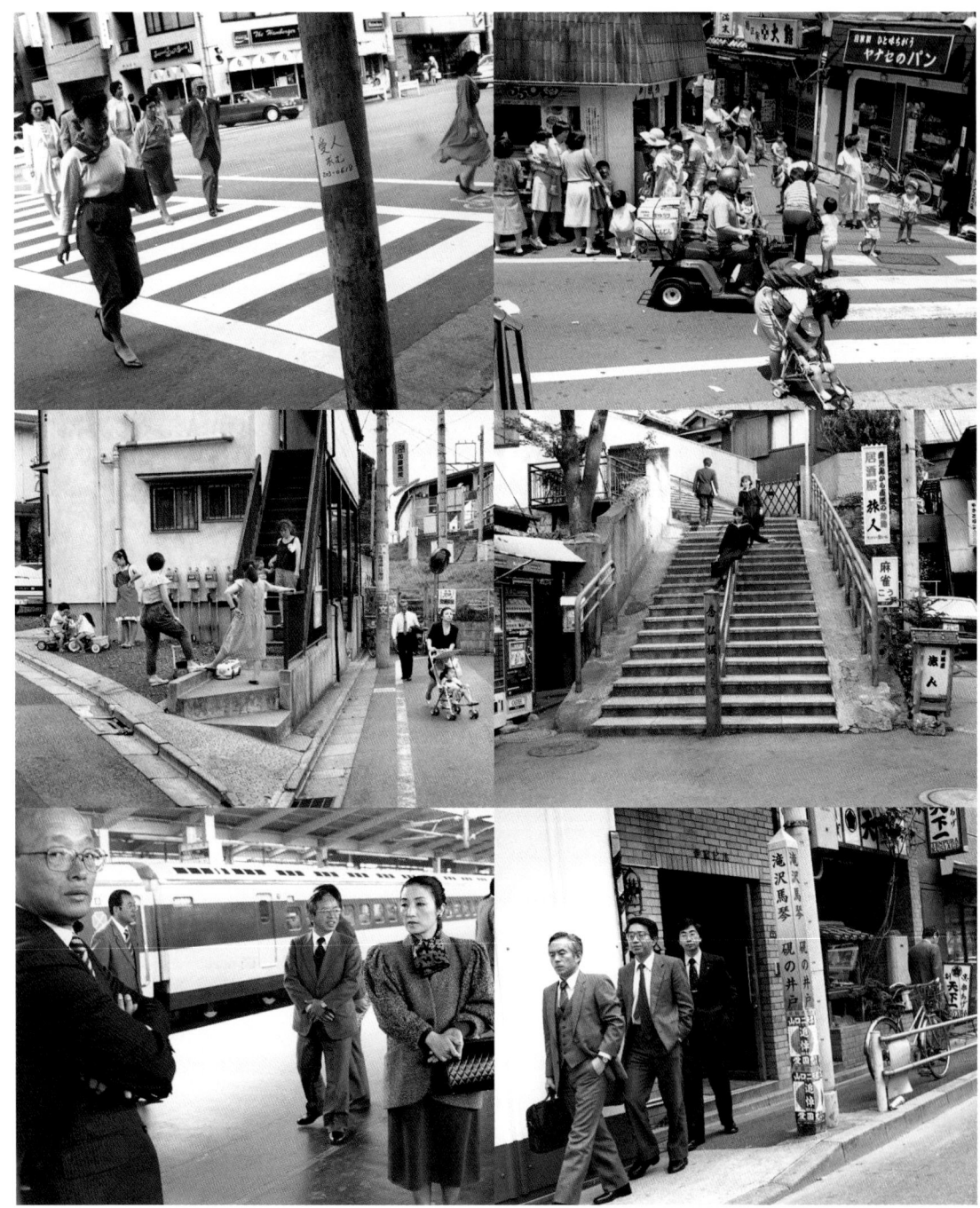

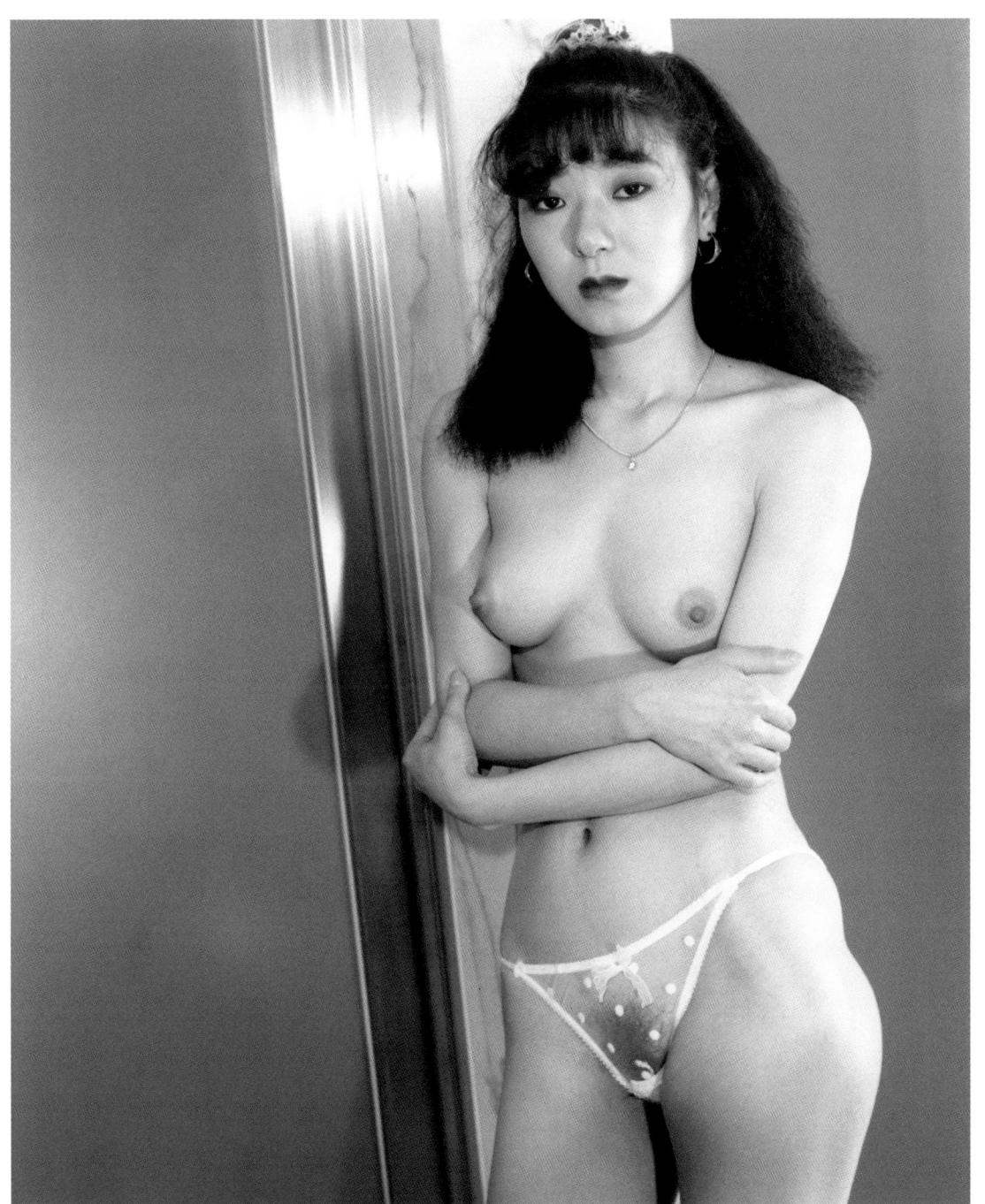

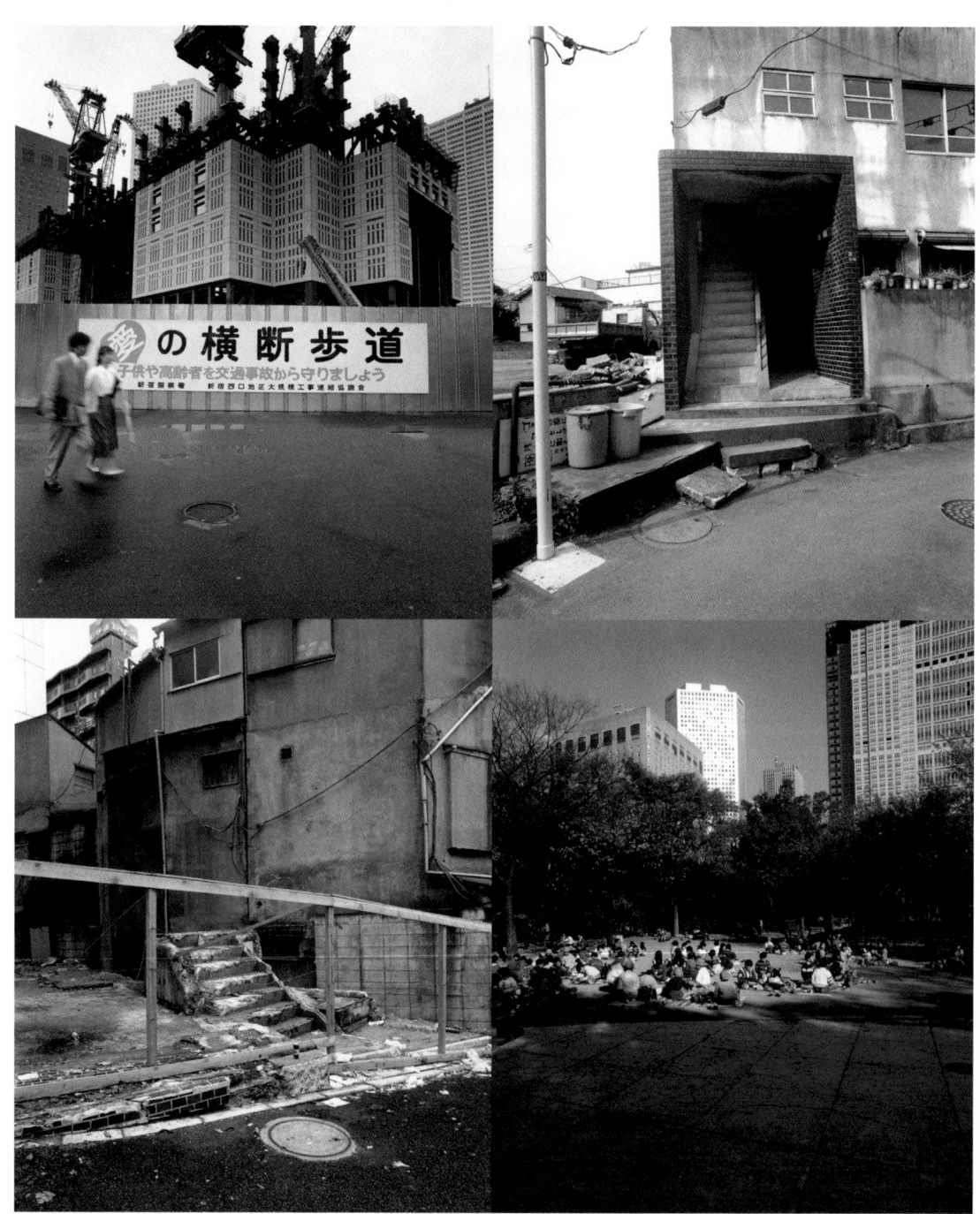

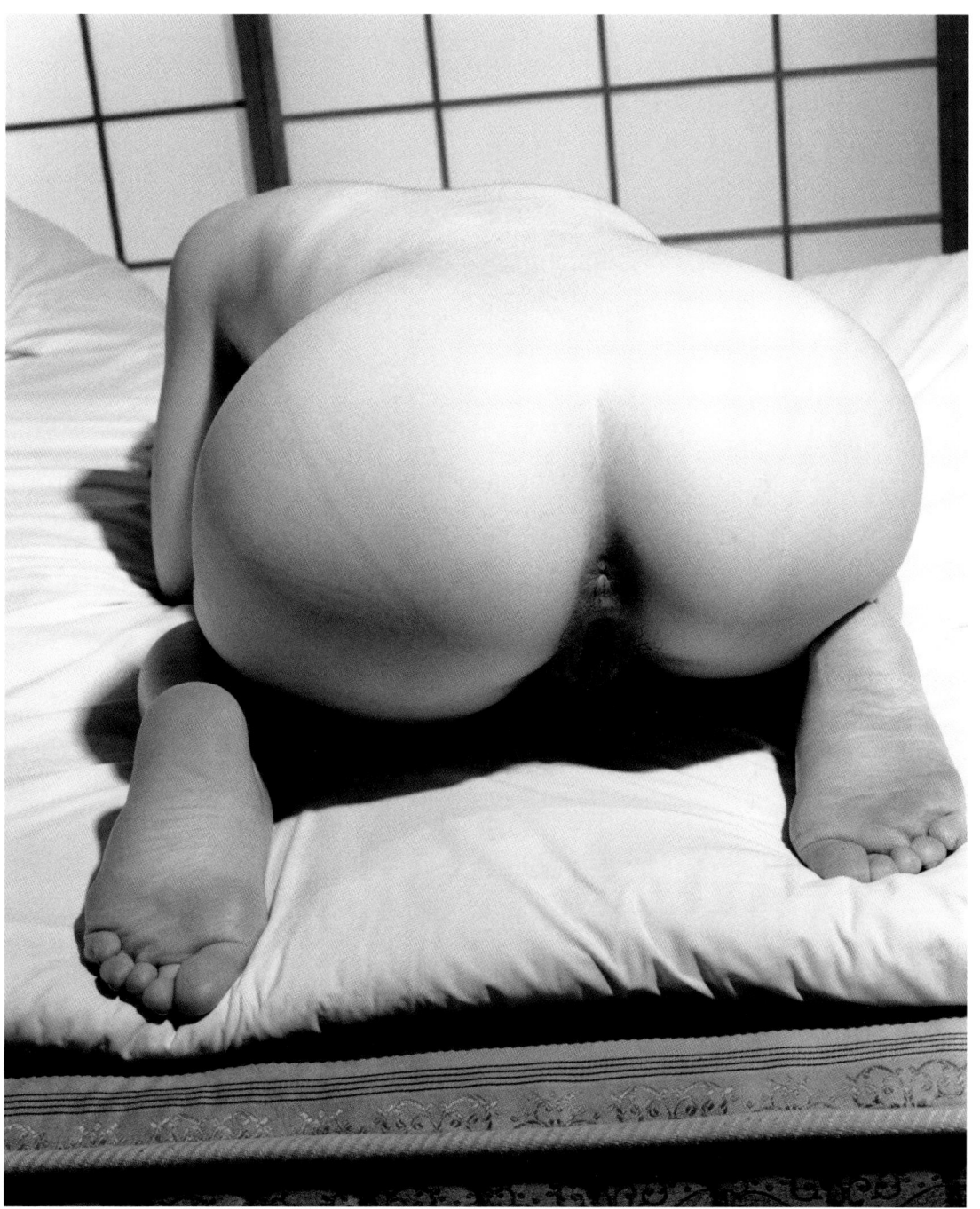

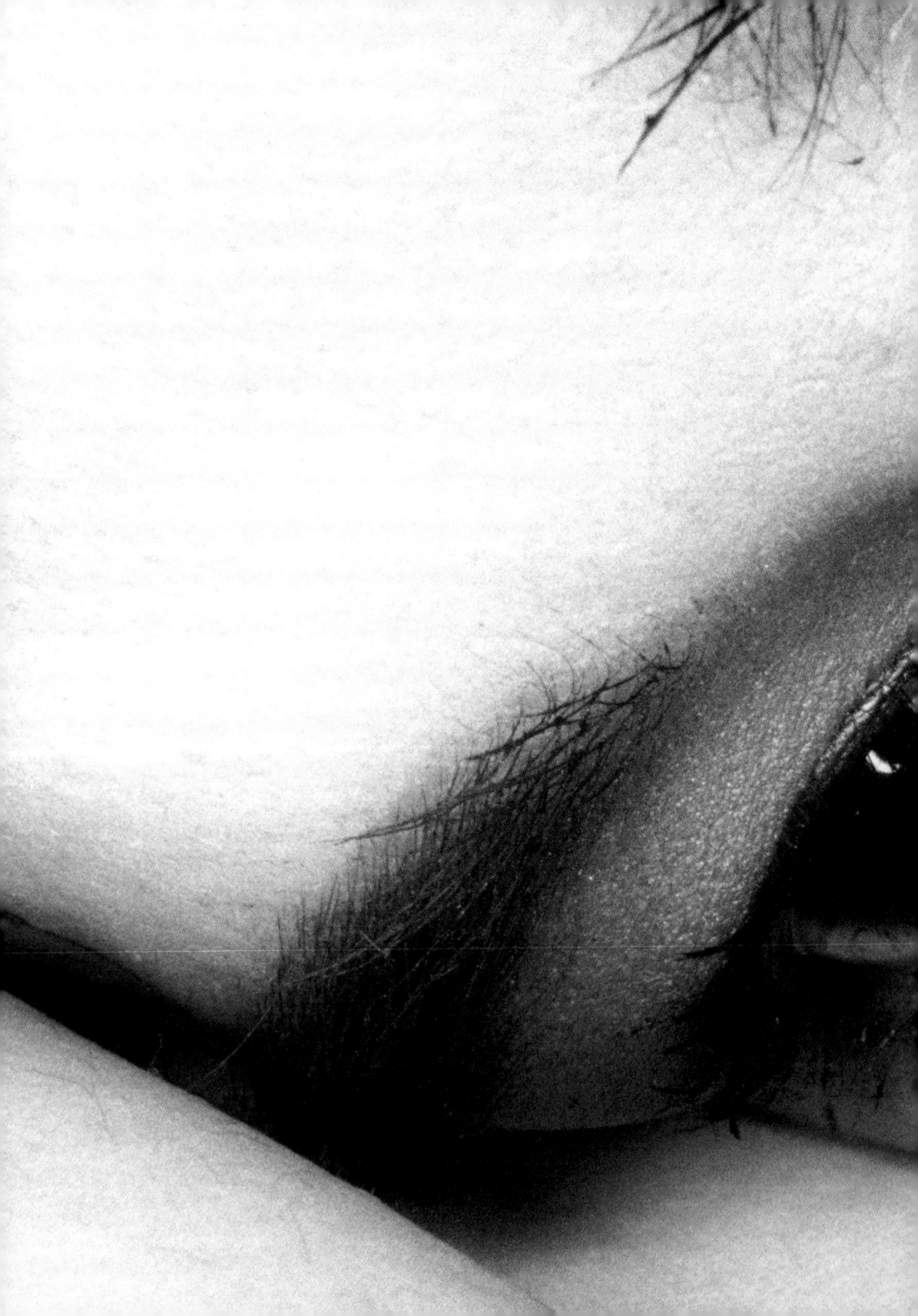

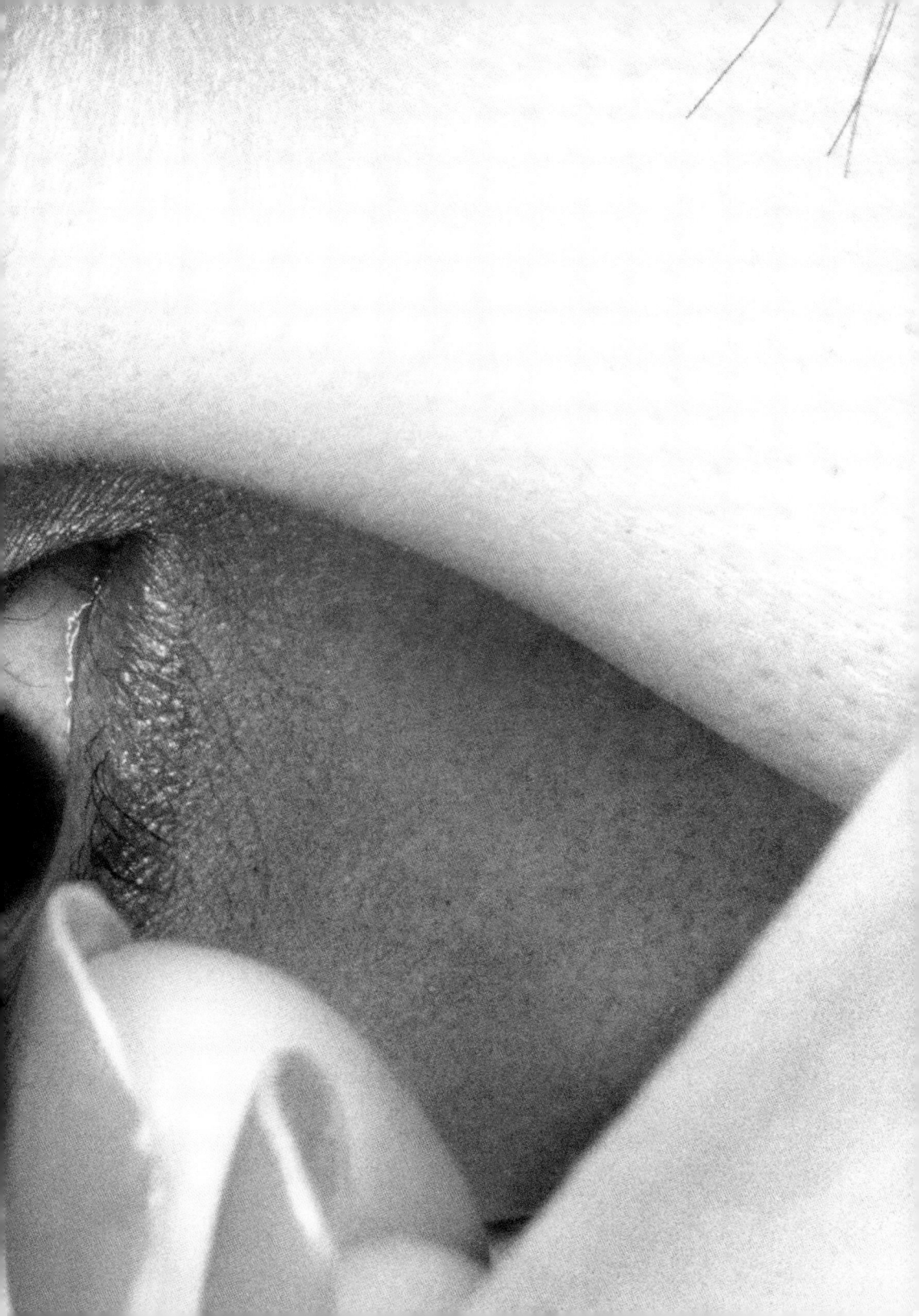

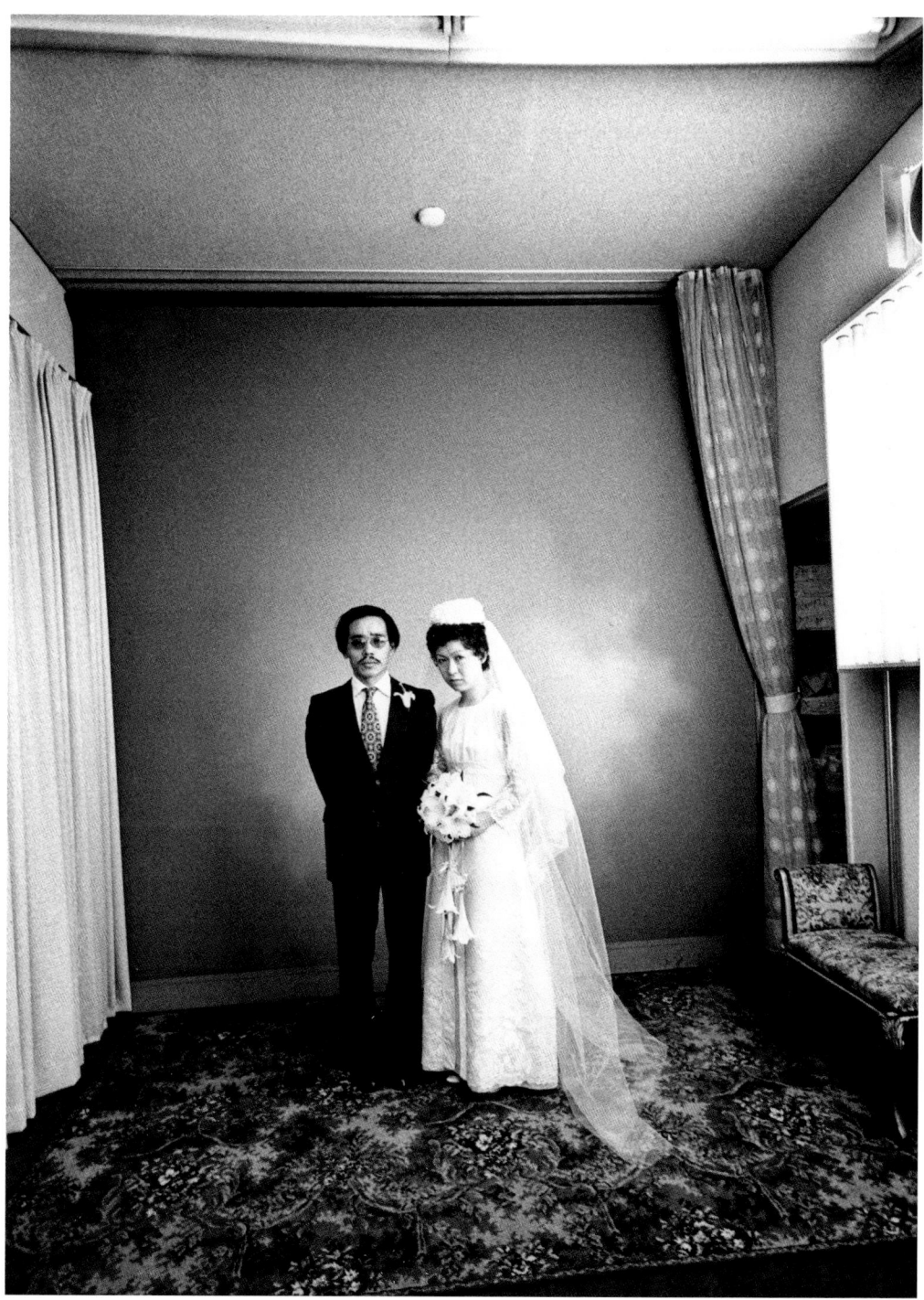

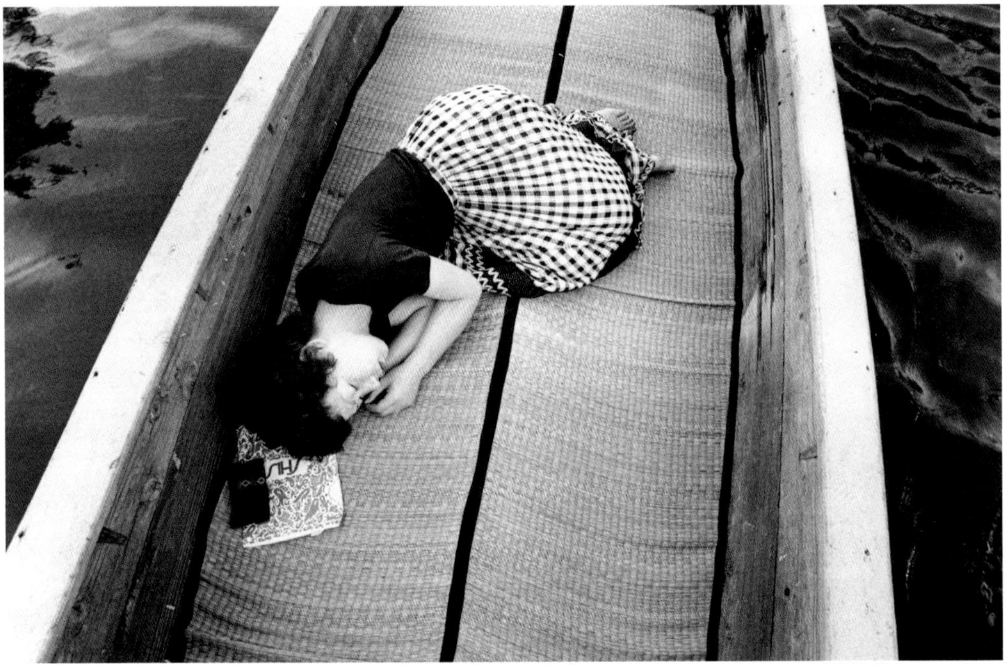

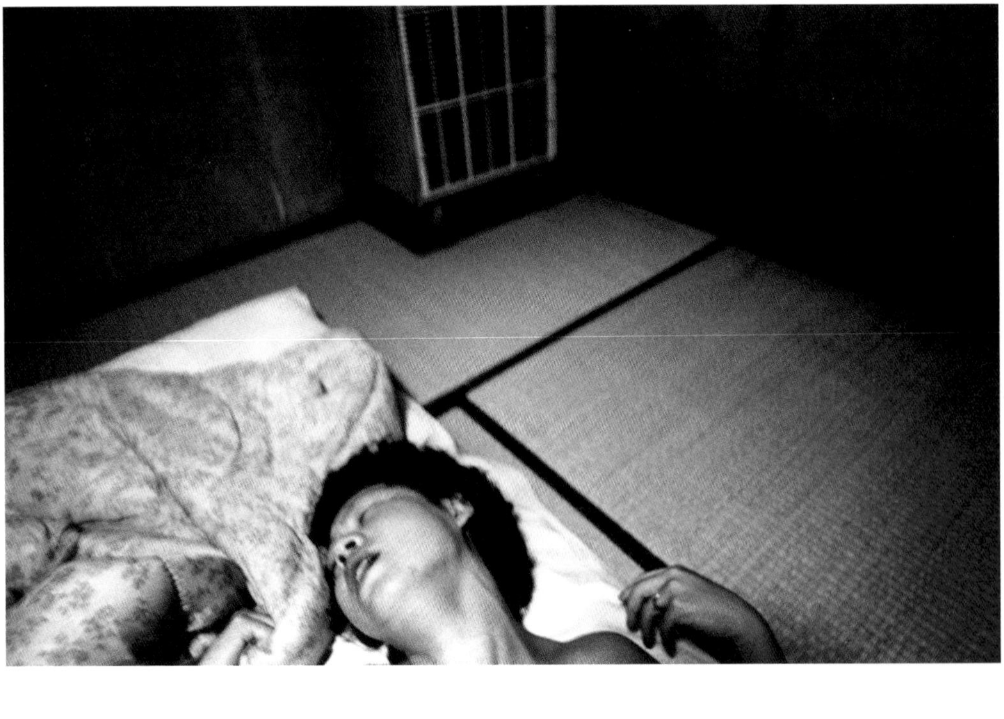

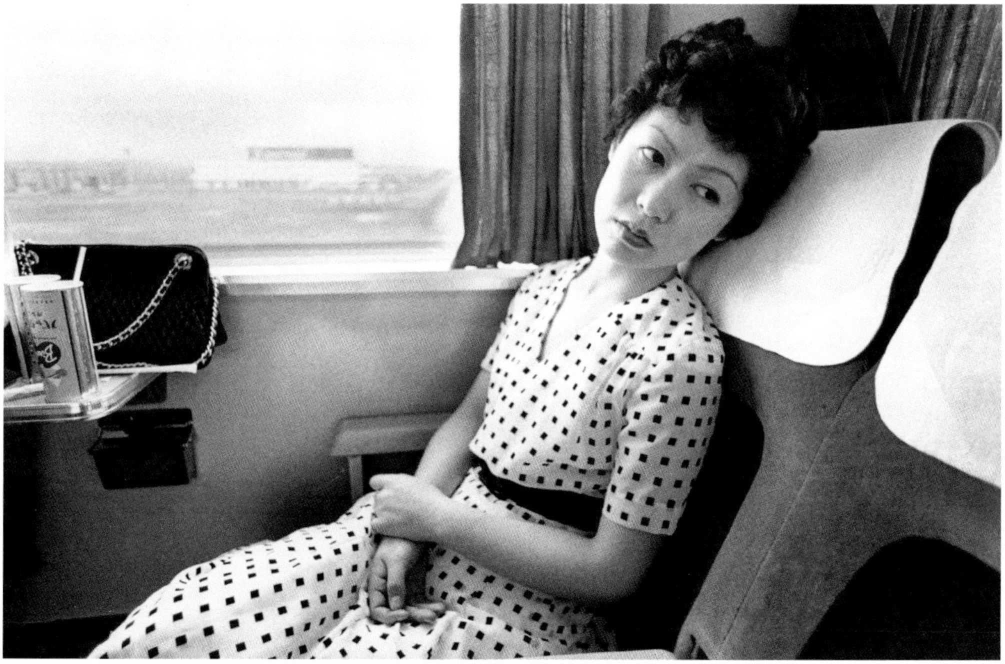

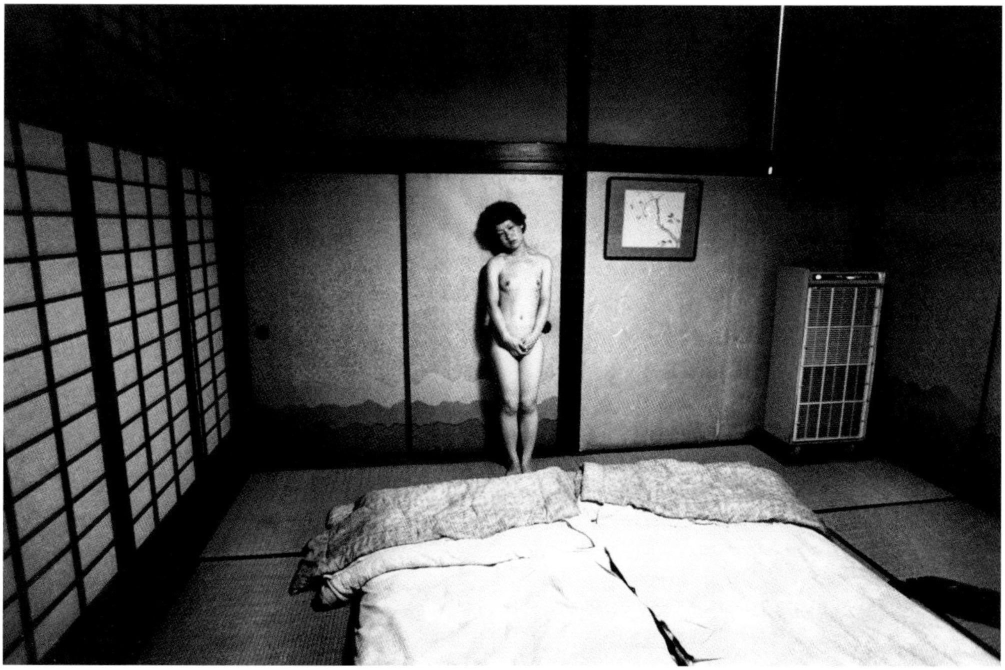

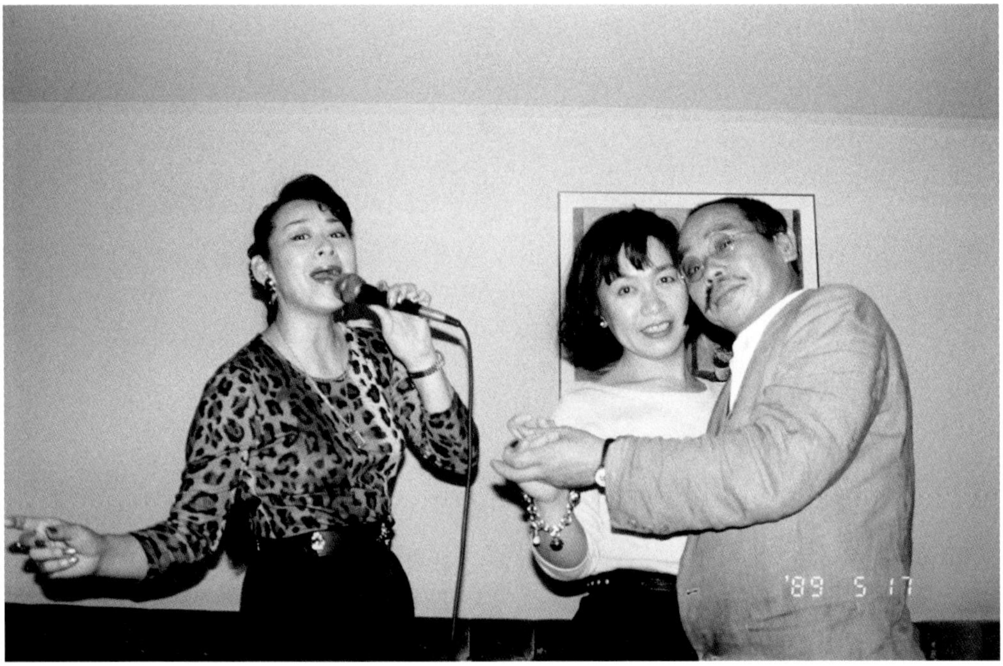
'89 5 17

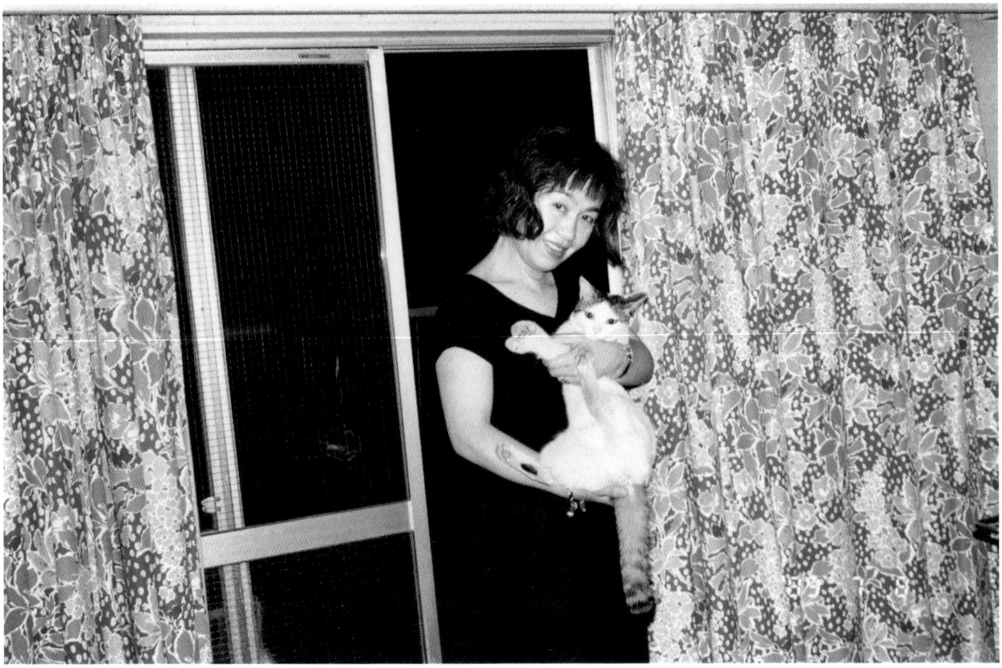

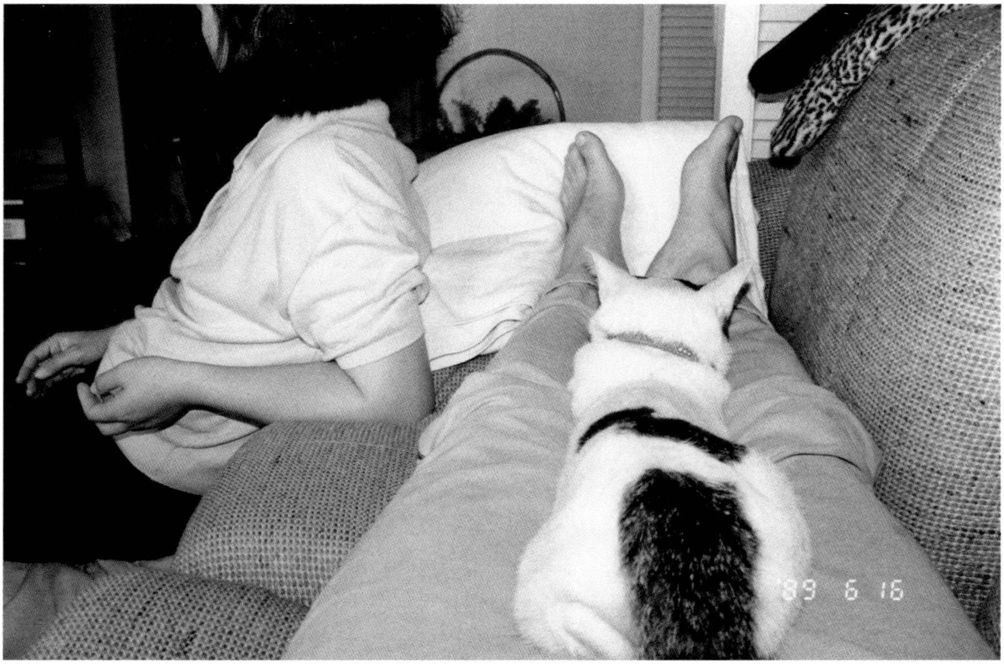

457

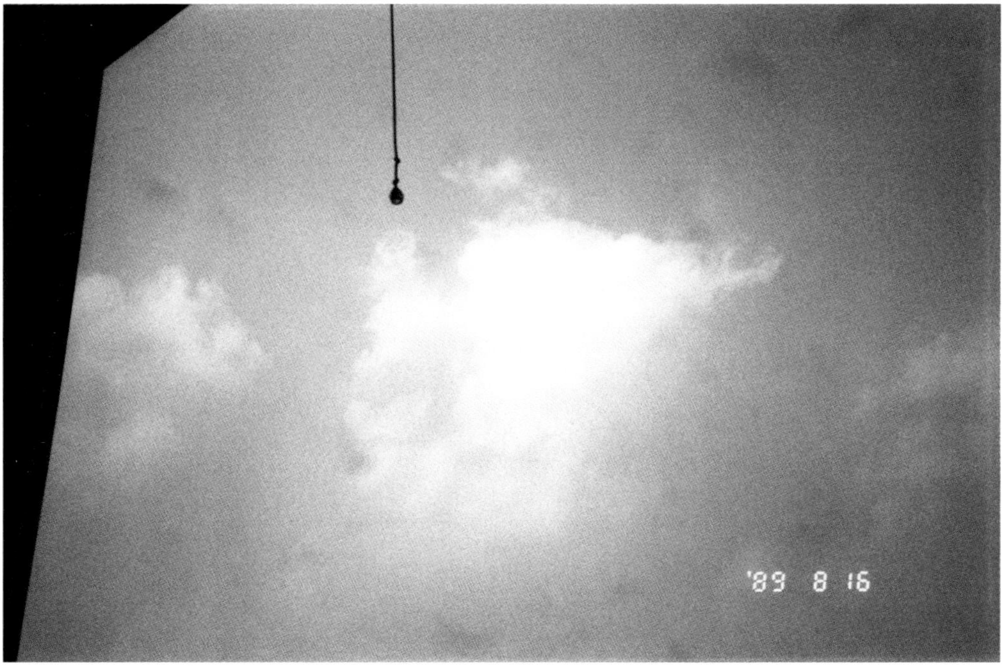

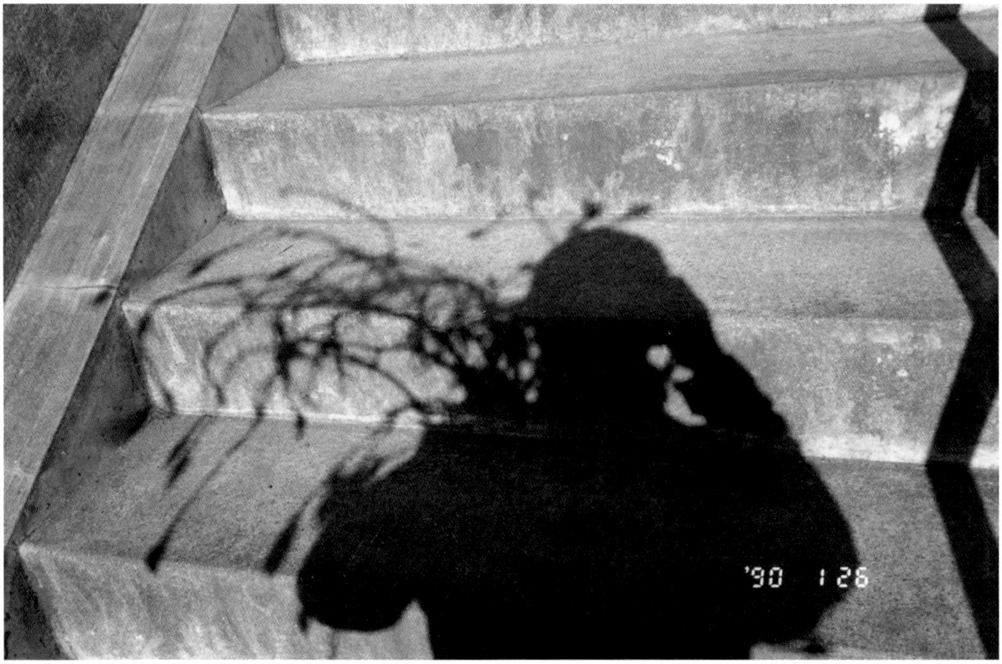

458

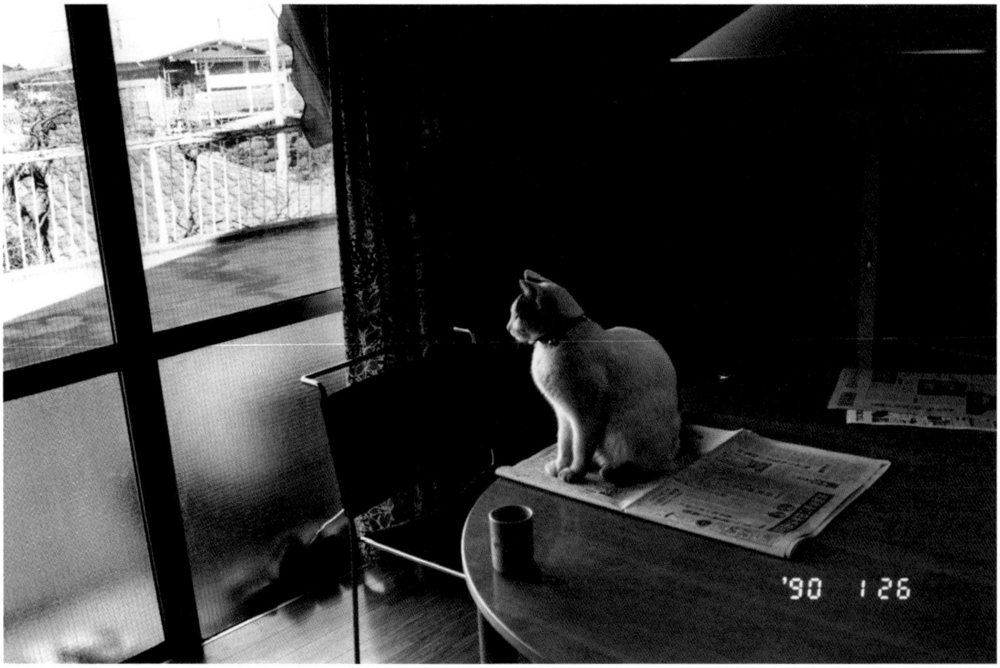

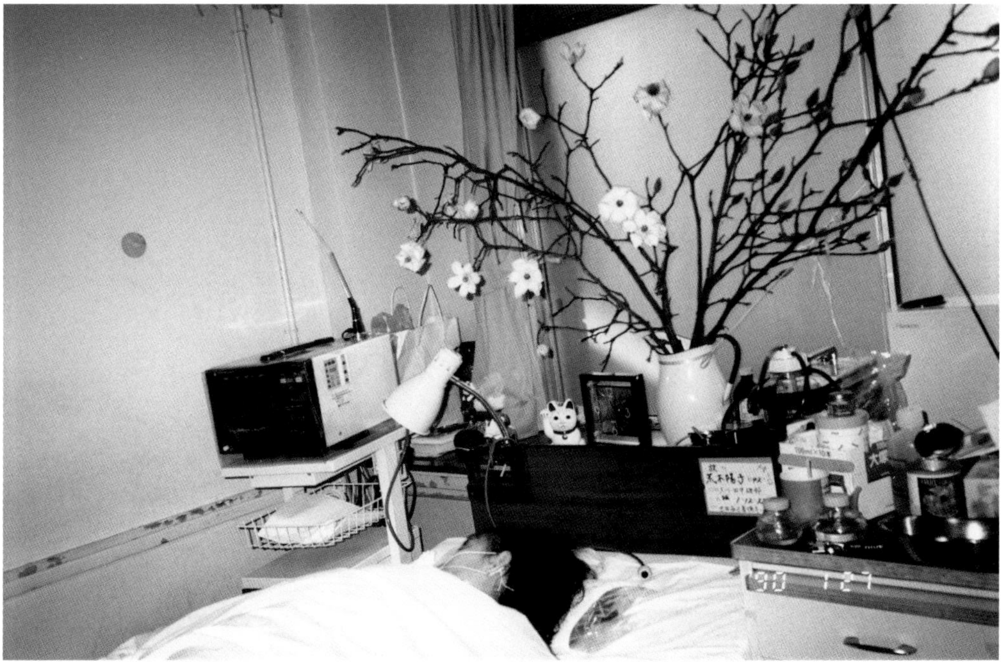
'90 1 27

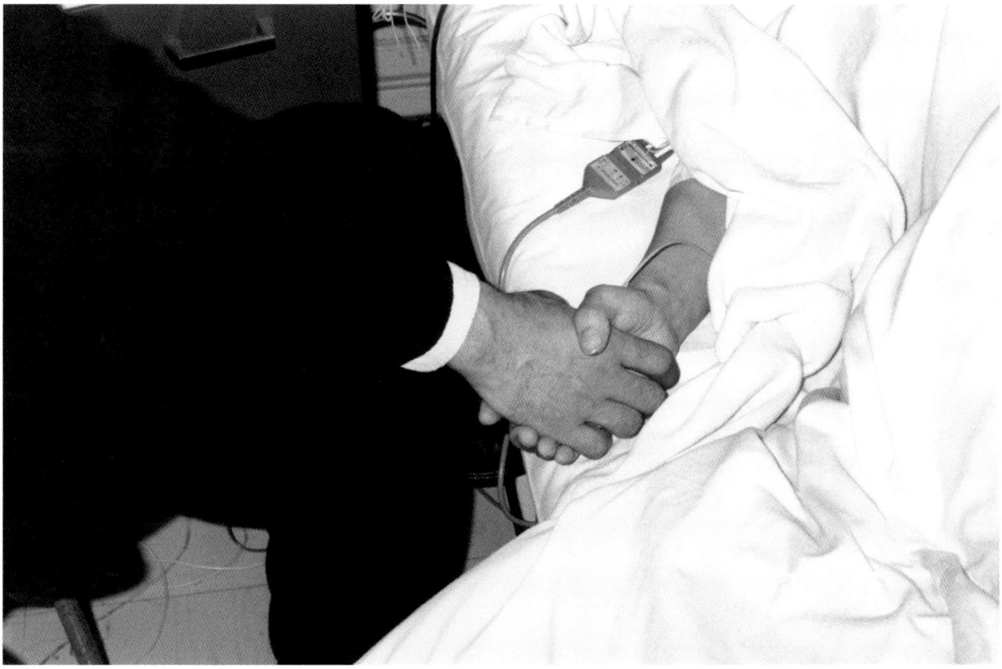

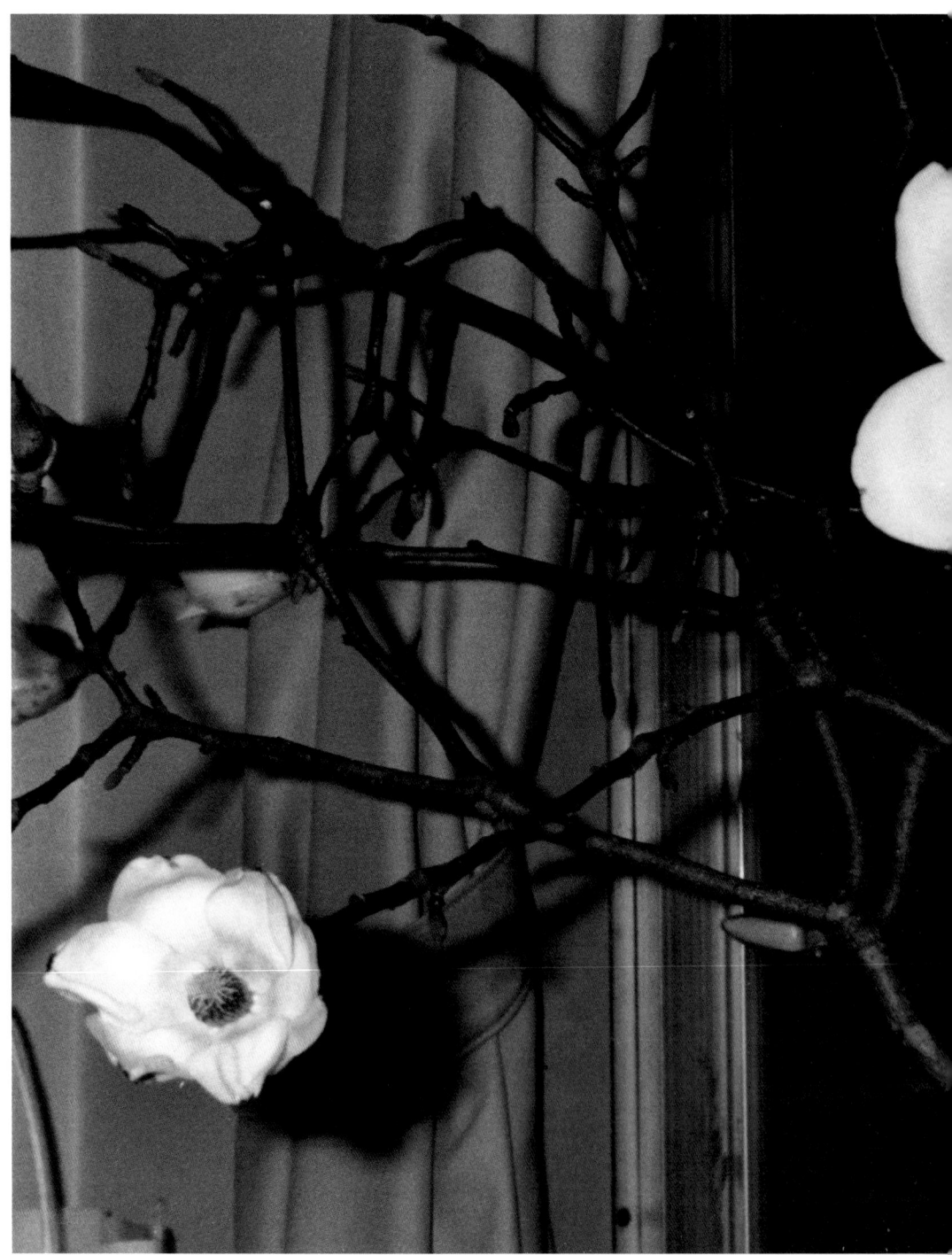

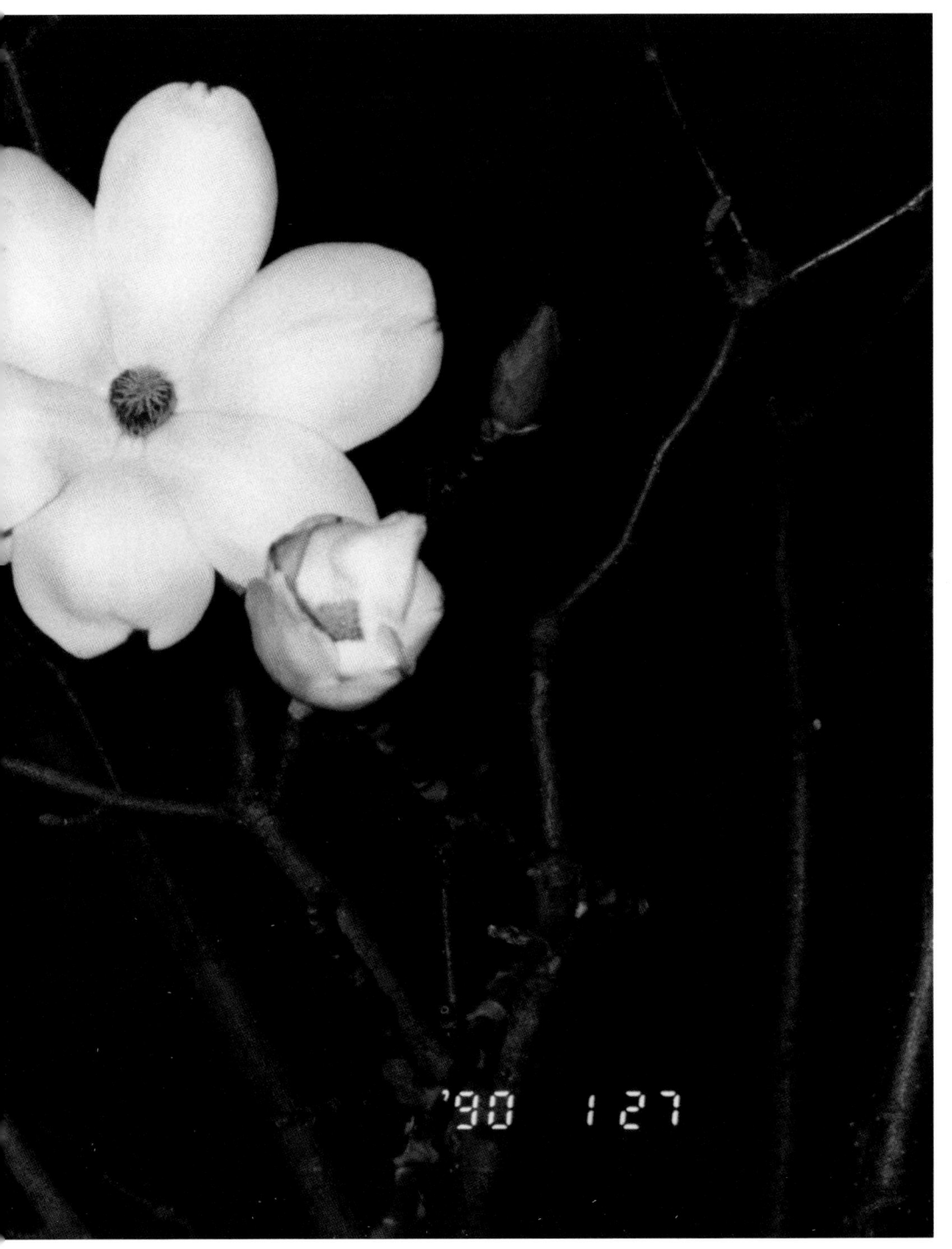

'90 1 27

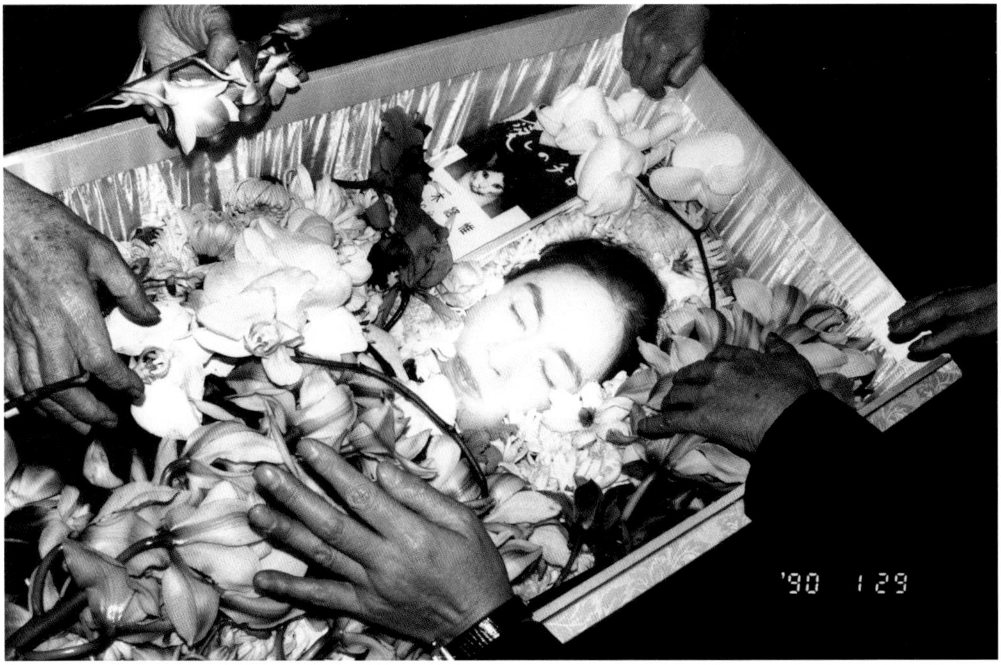

'90 1 29

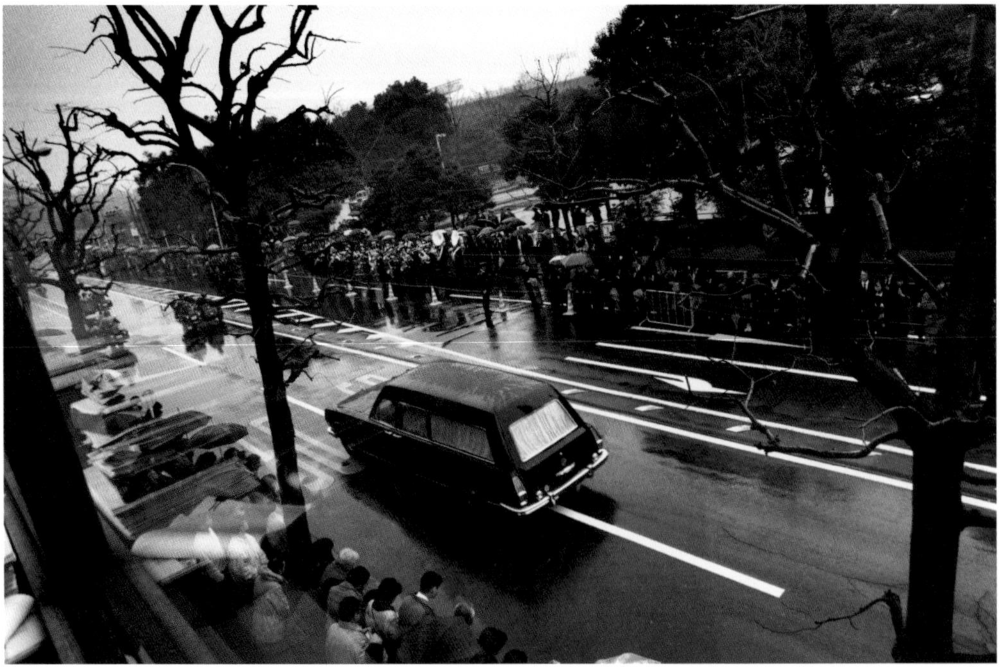

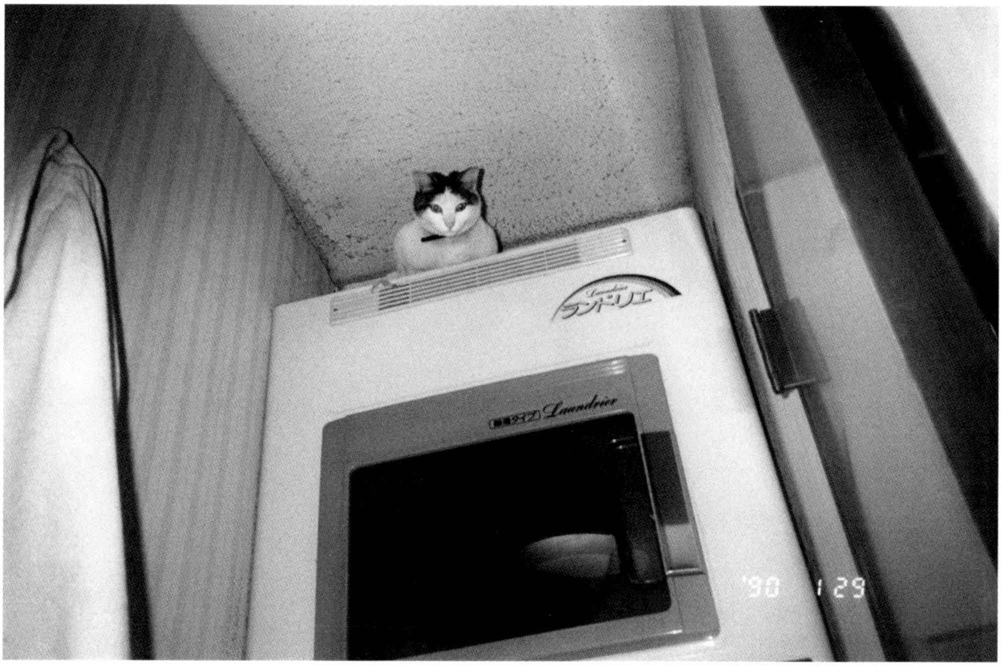
ランドリエ
Laundrier
'90 1 29

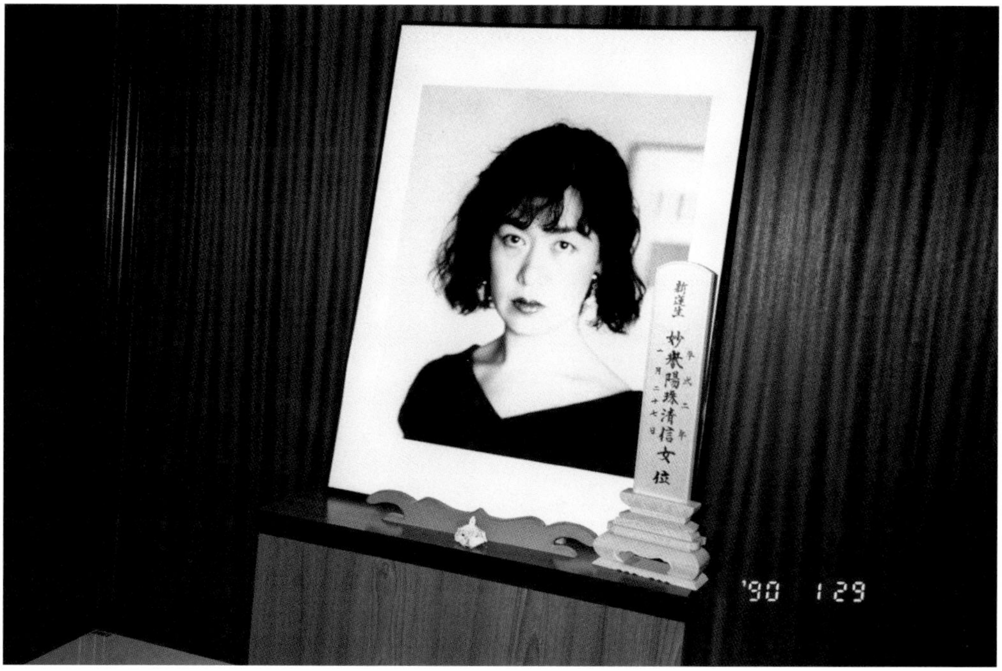
'90 1 29

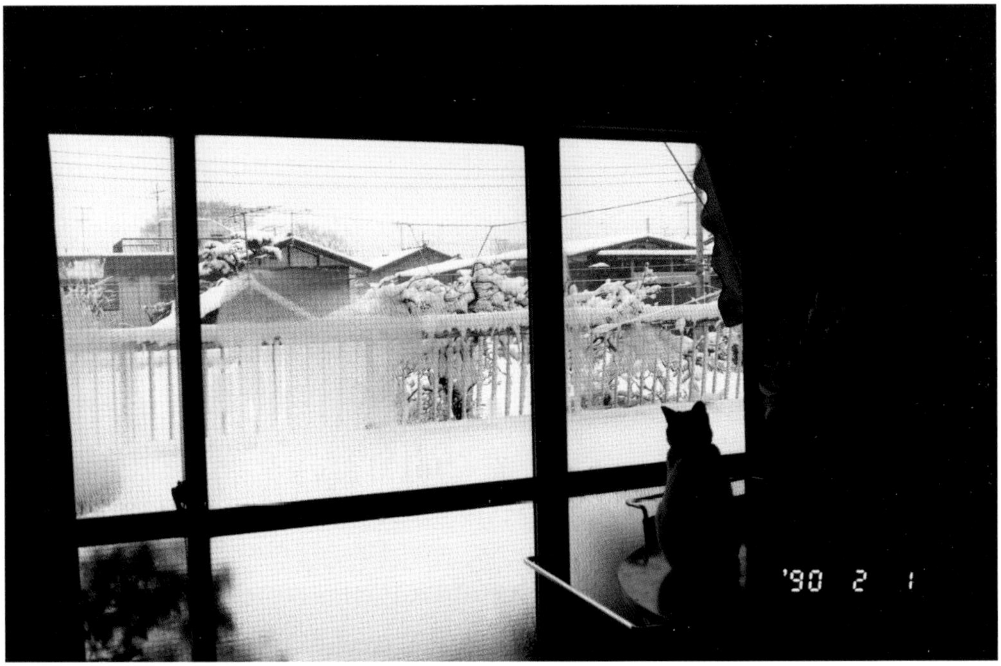
'90 2 1

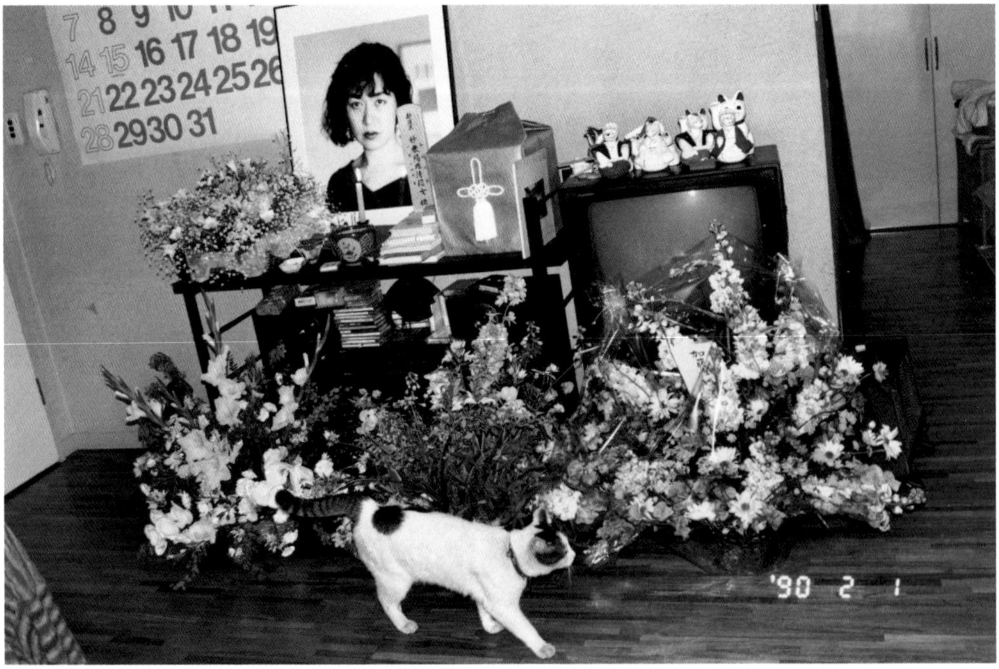
14 15 16 17 18 19
21 22 23 24 25 26
28 29 30 31
'90 2 1

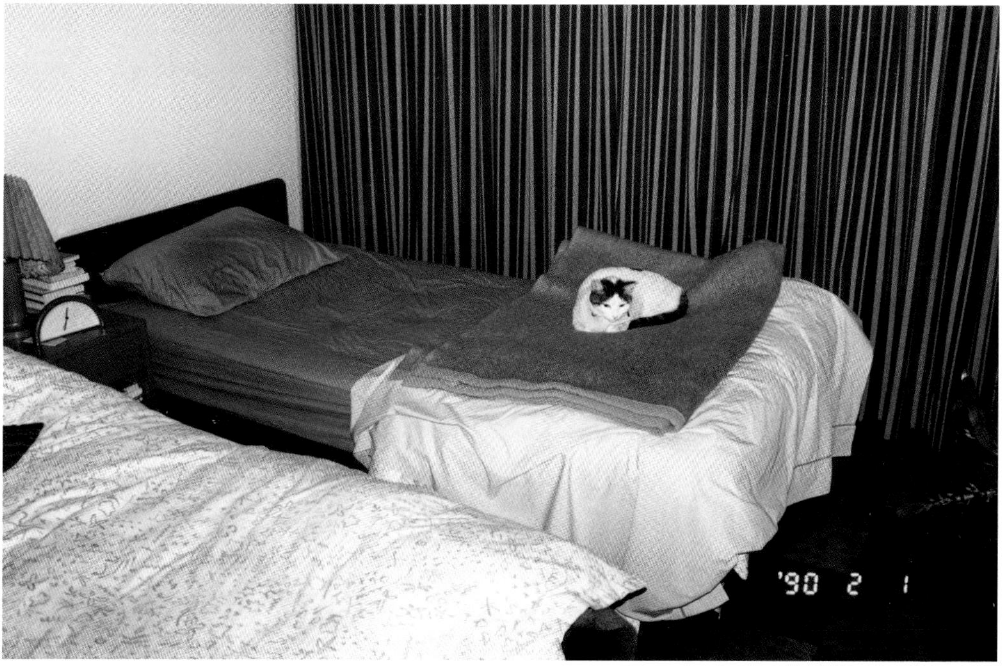

'90 2 1

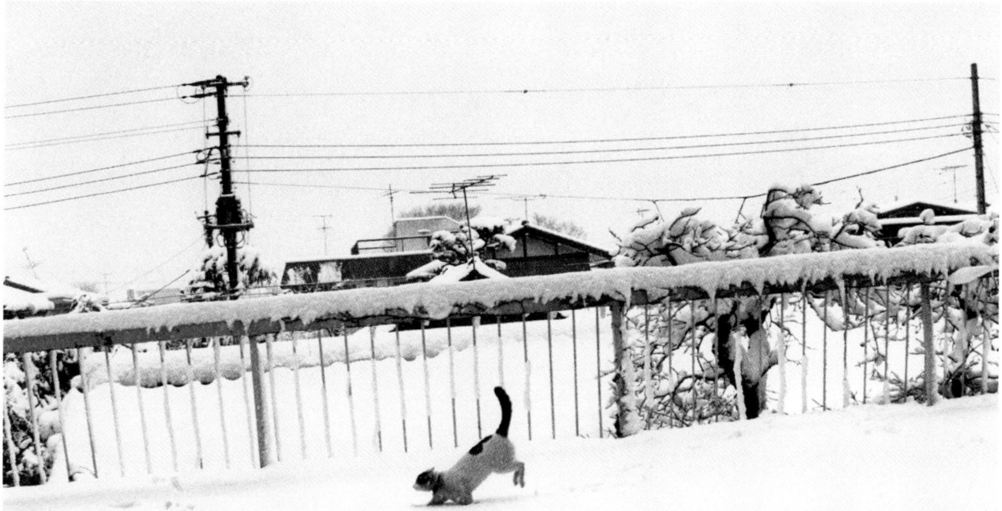

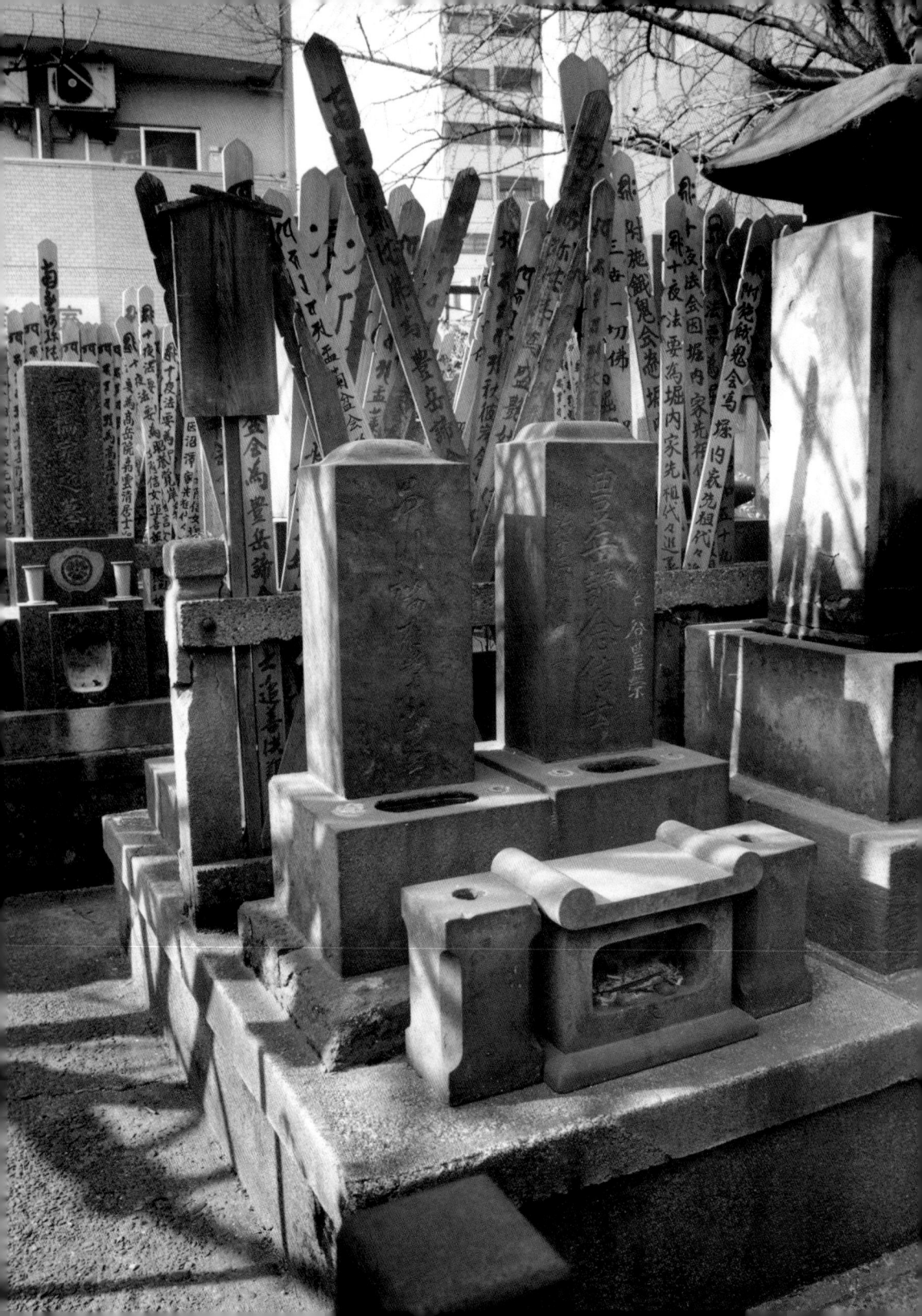

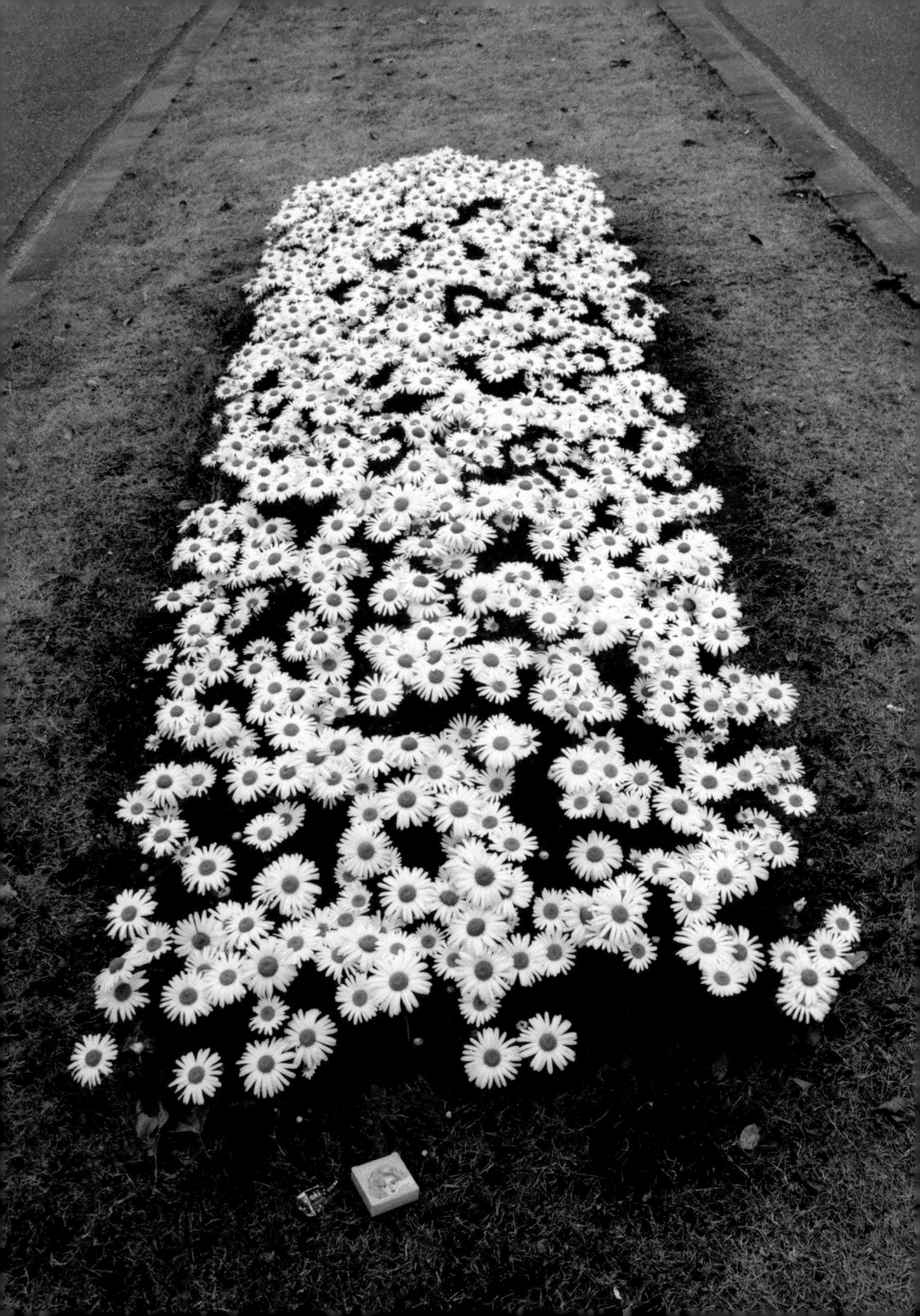

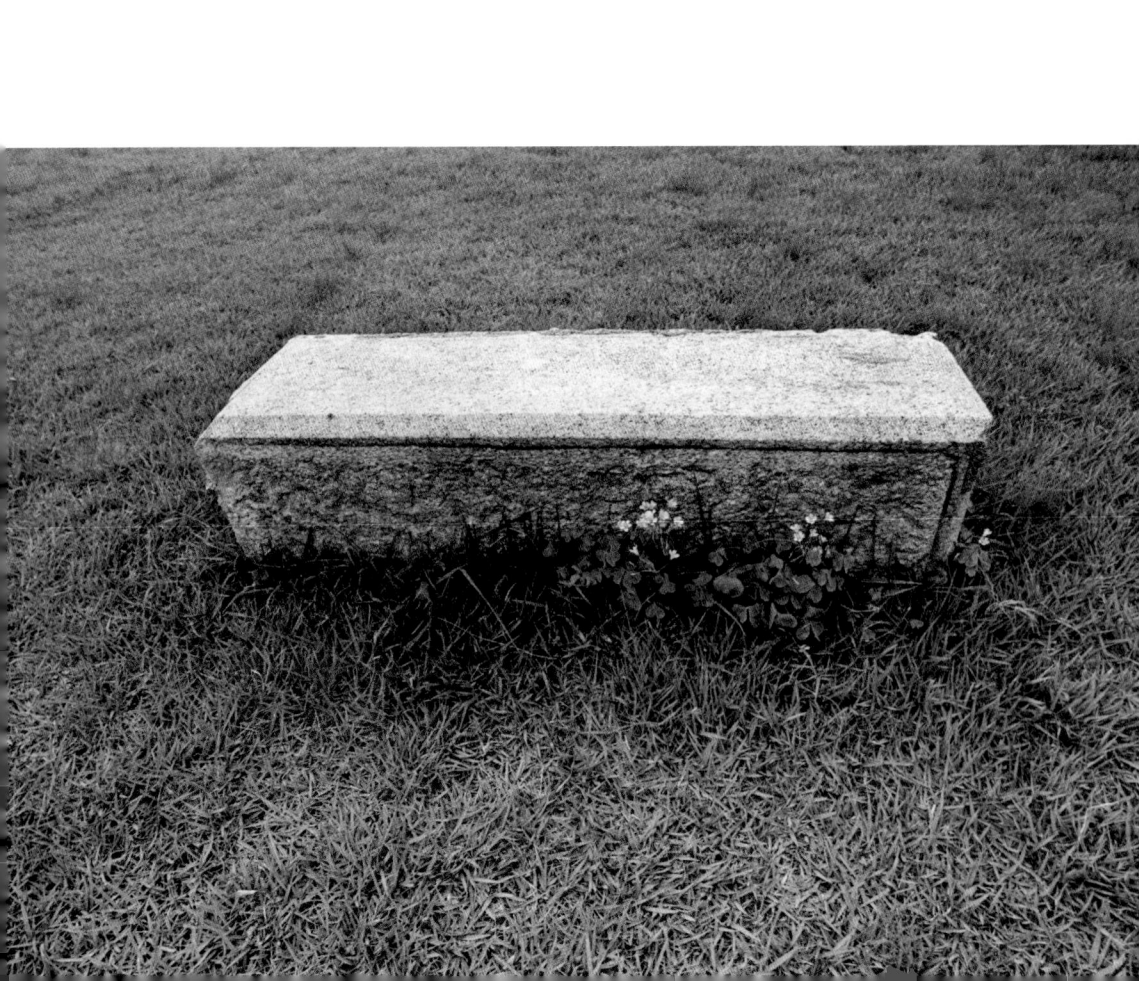

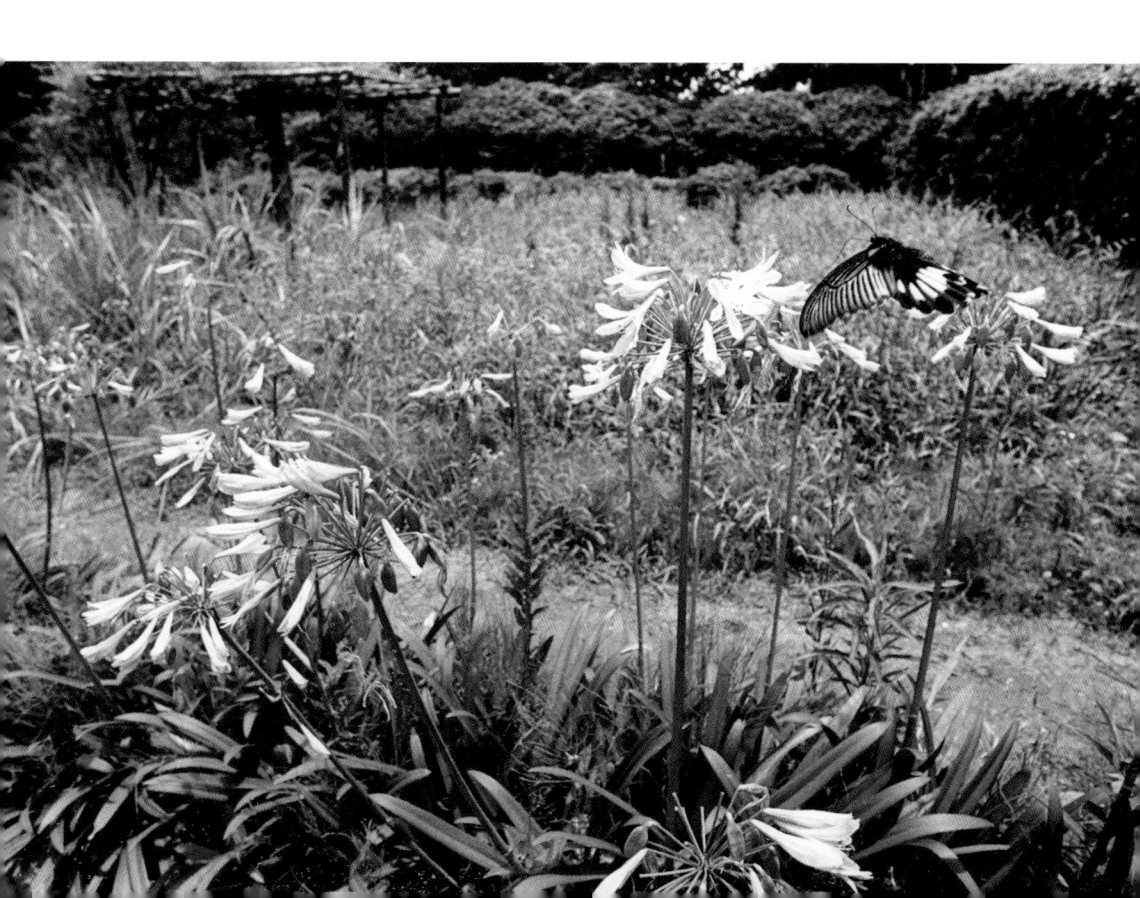

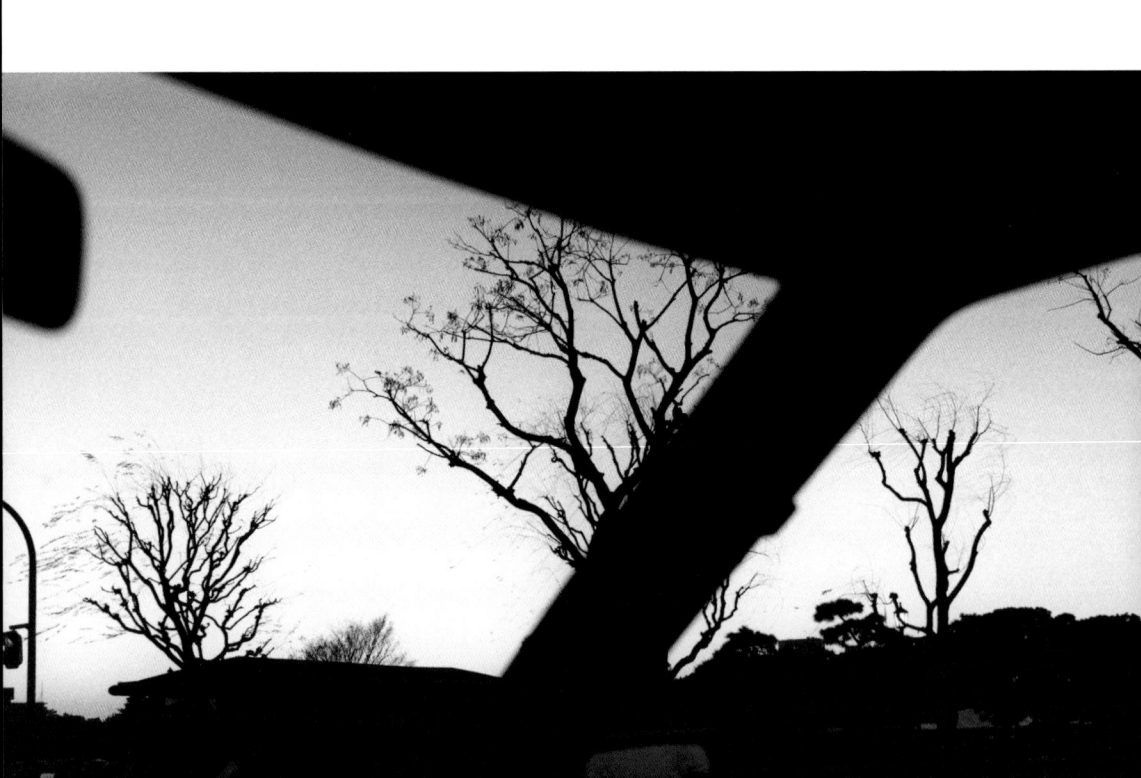

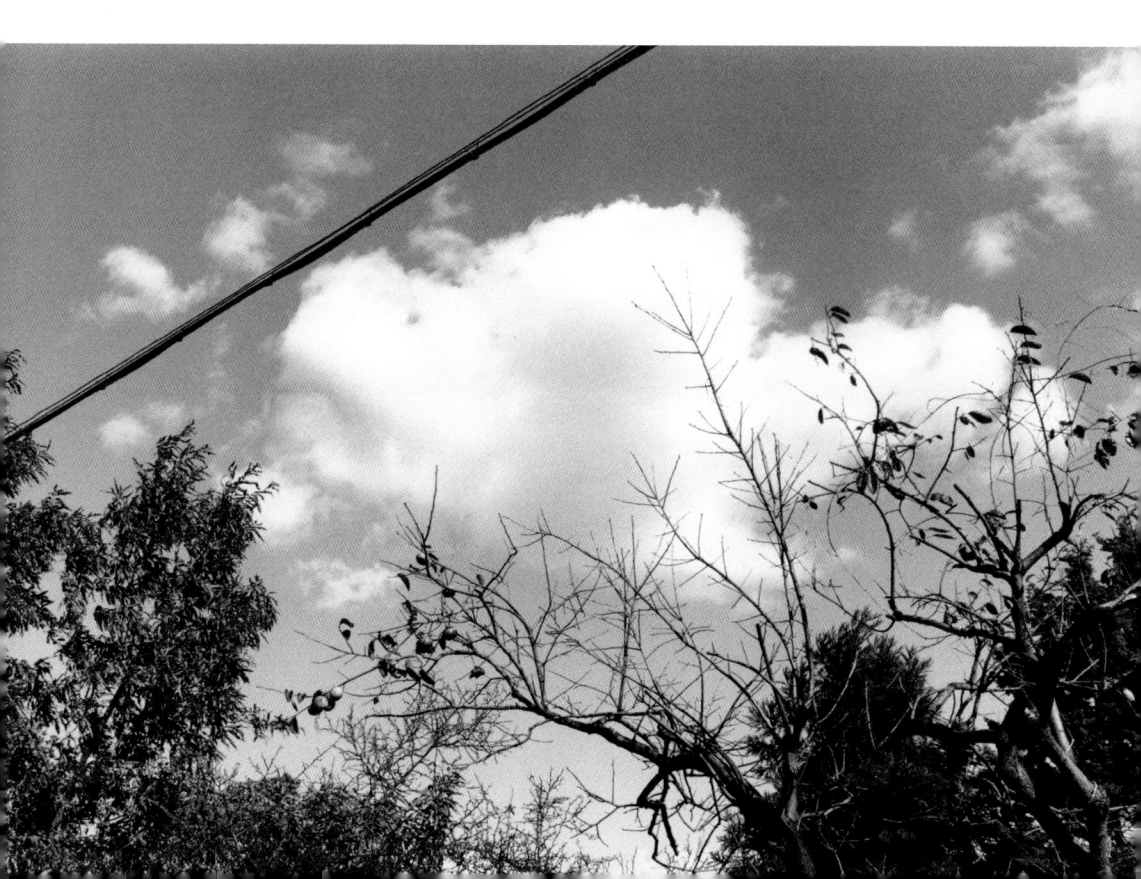

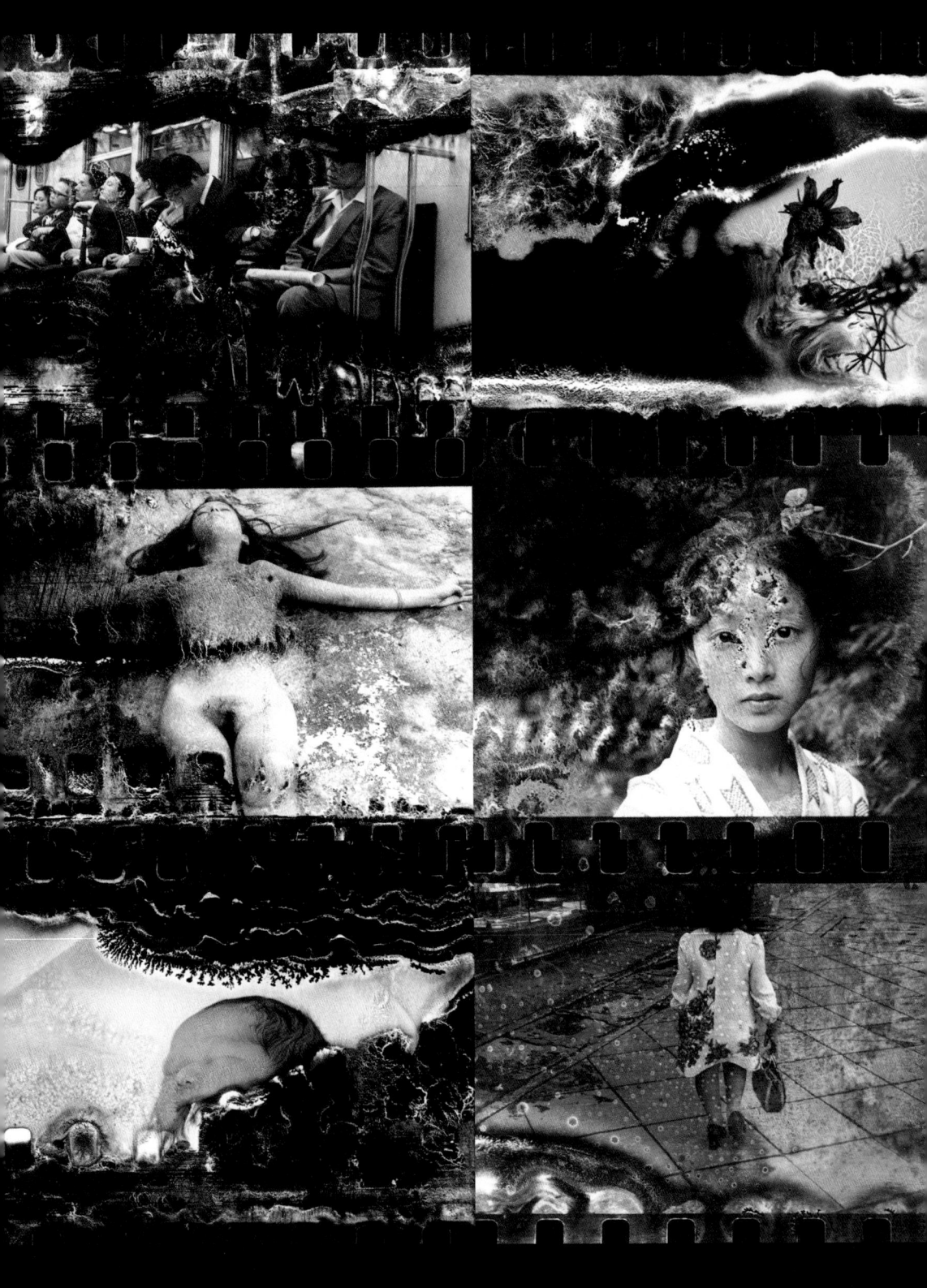

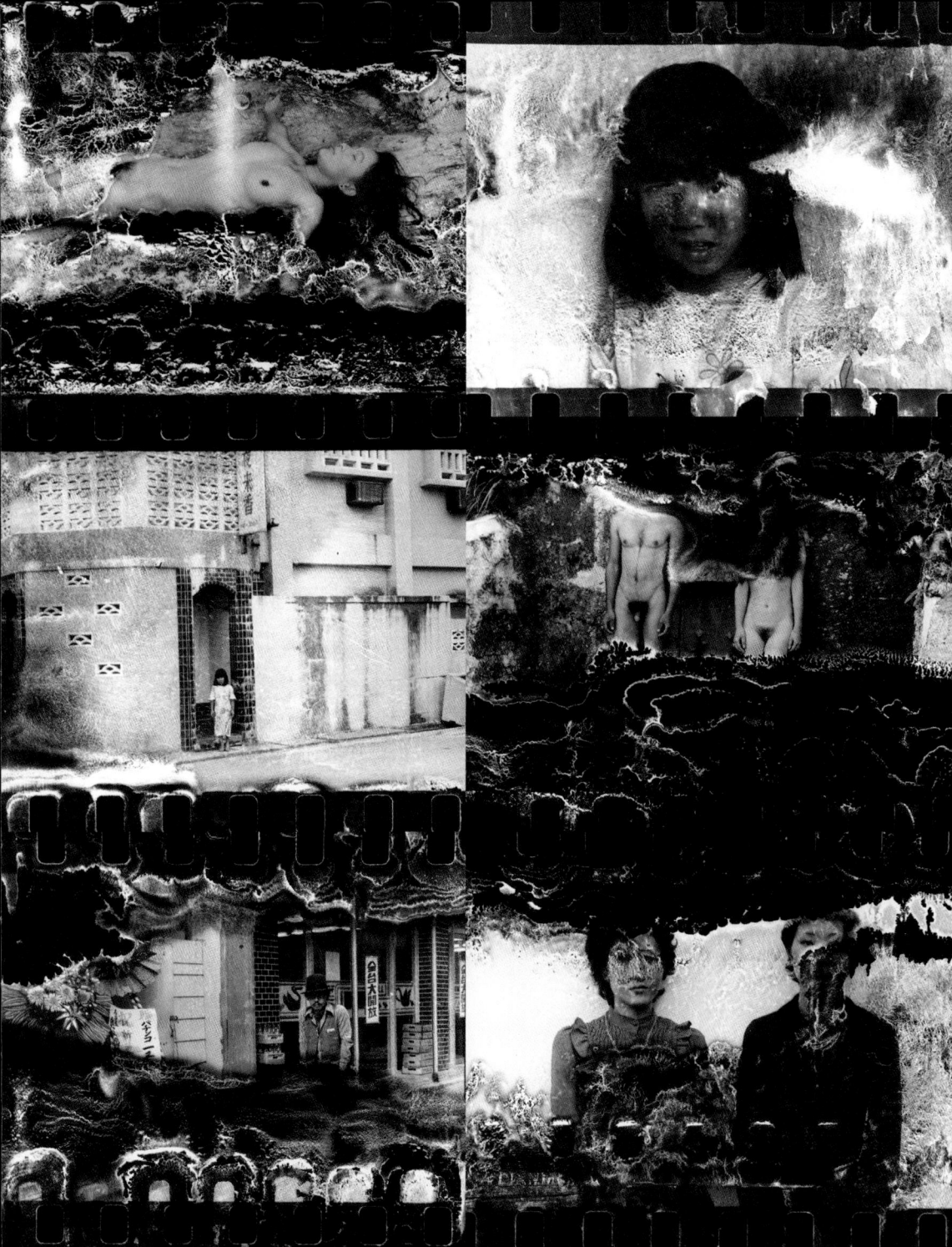

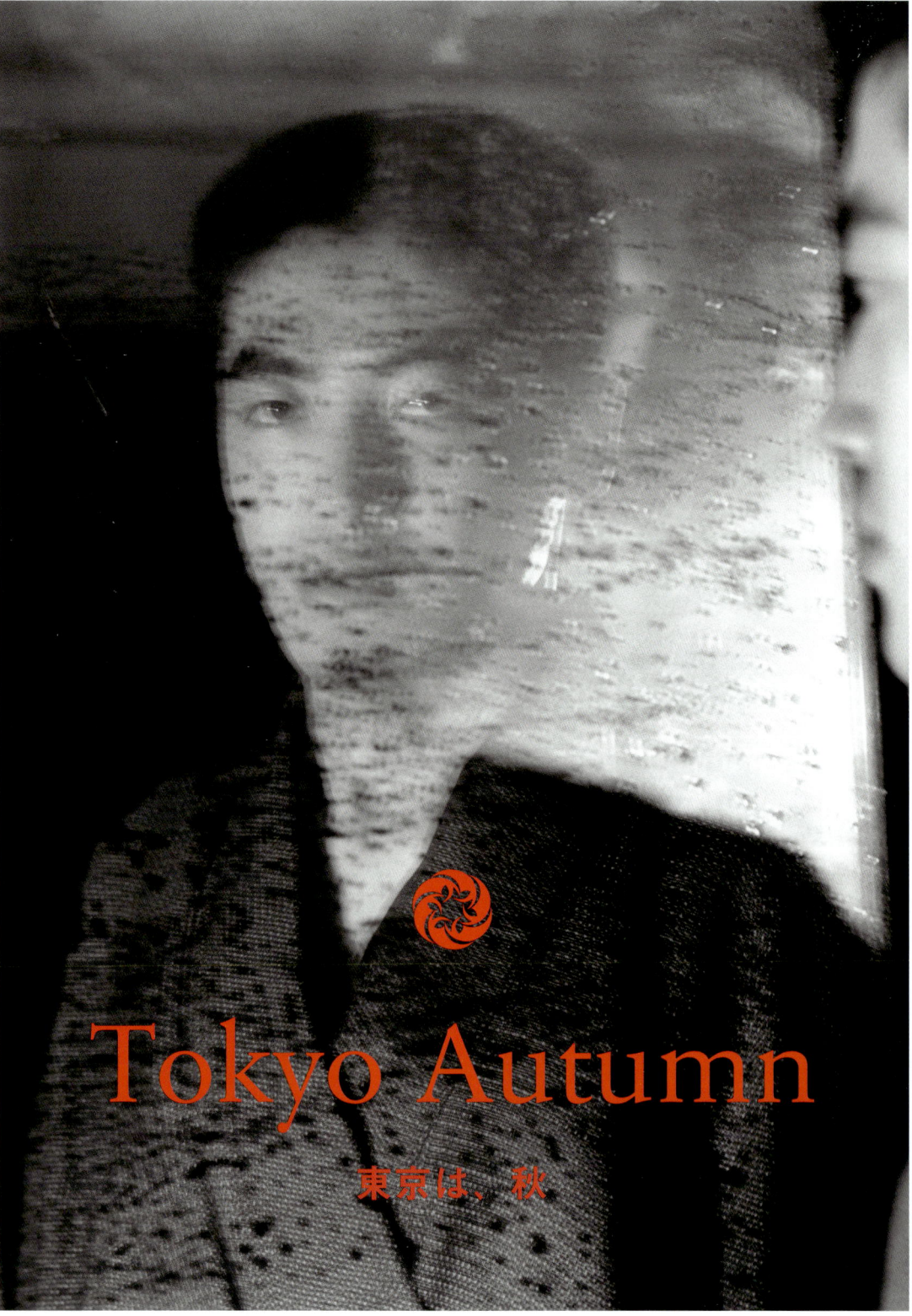

Tokyo Autumn

東京は、秋

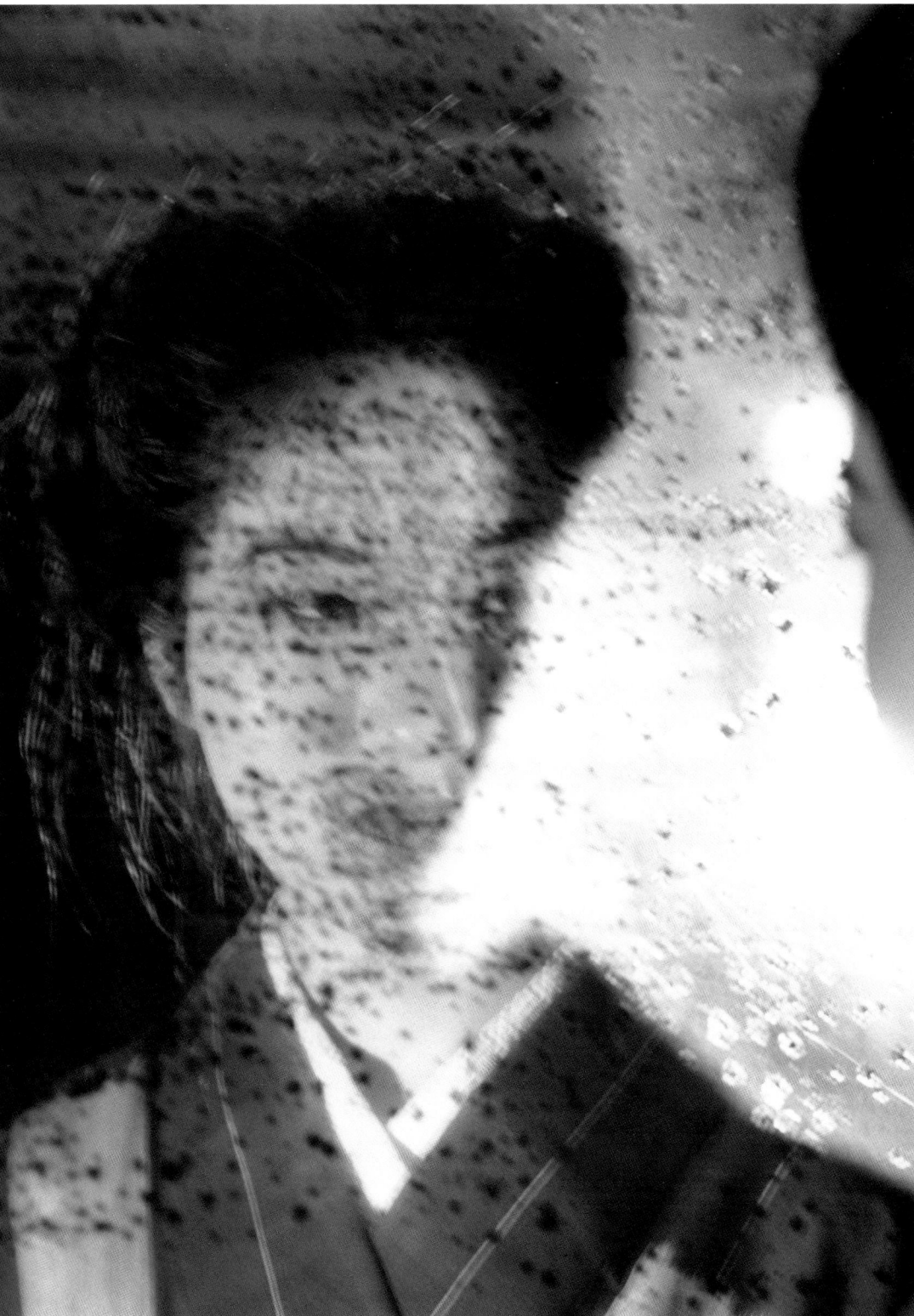

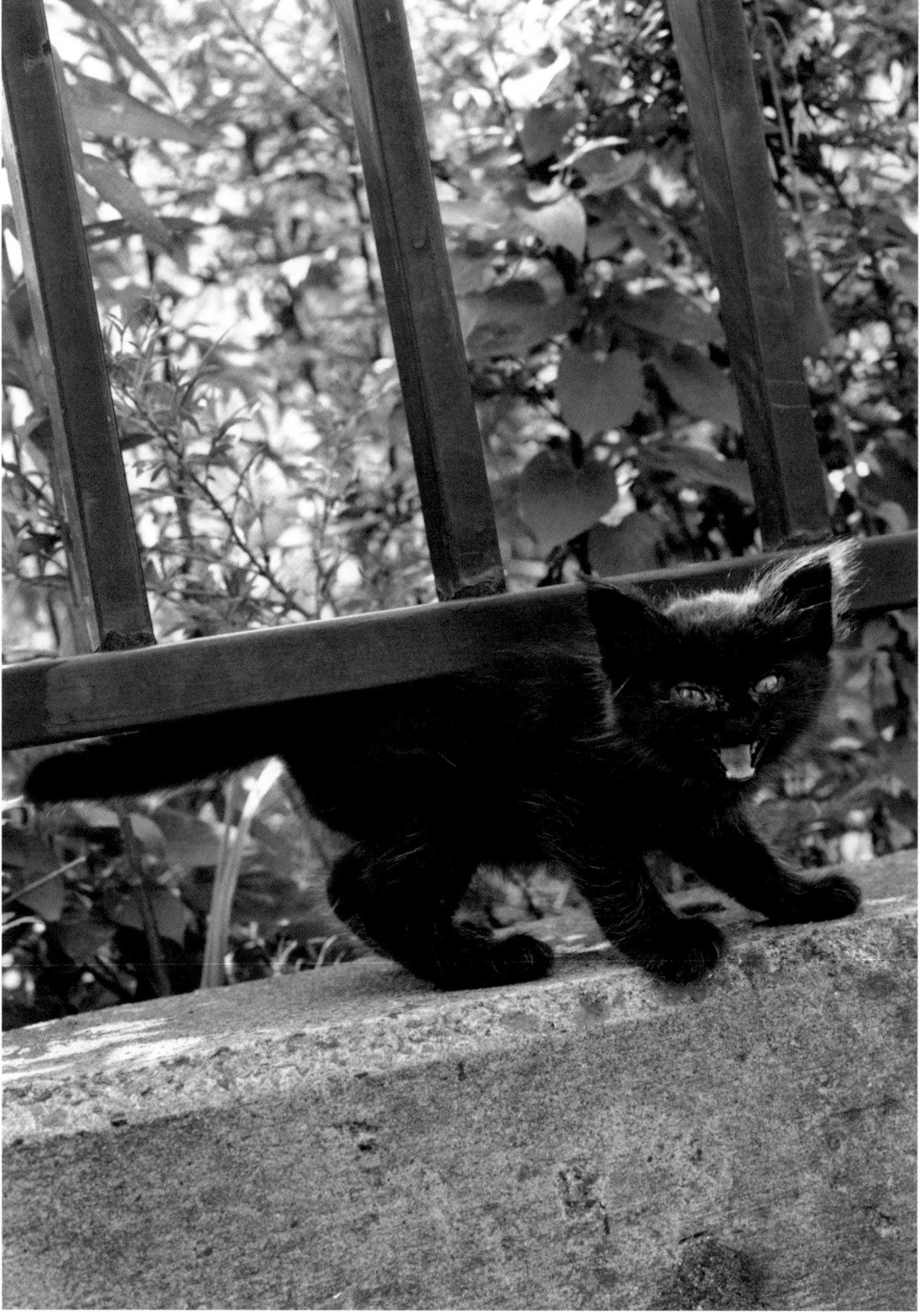

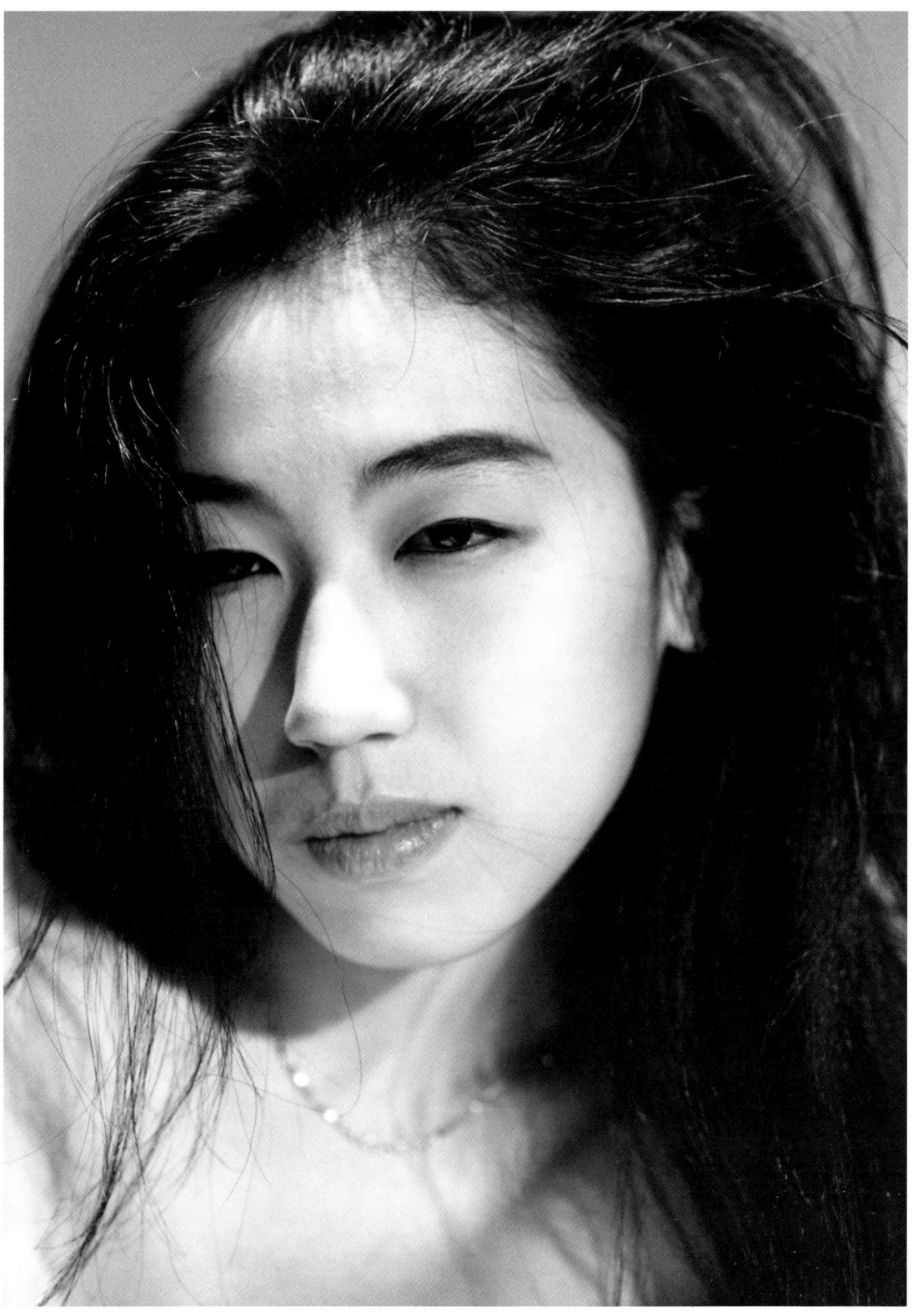

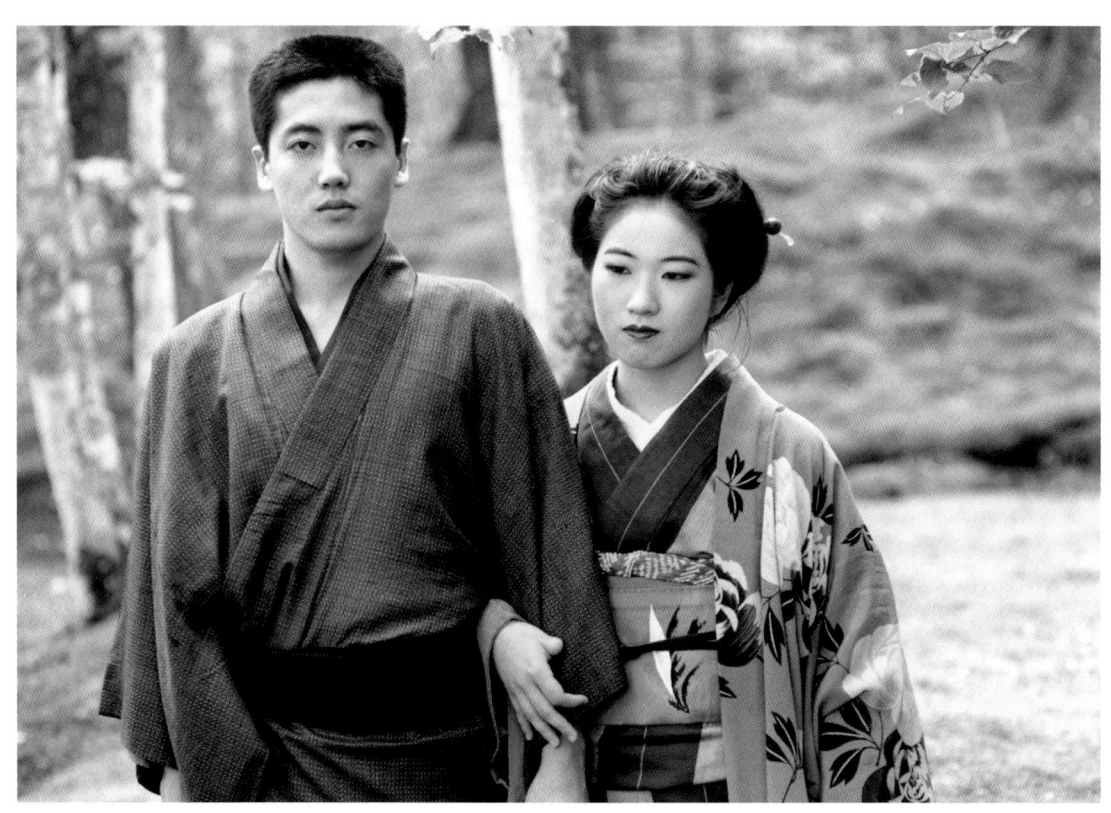

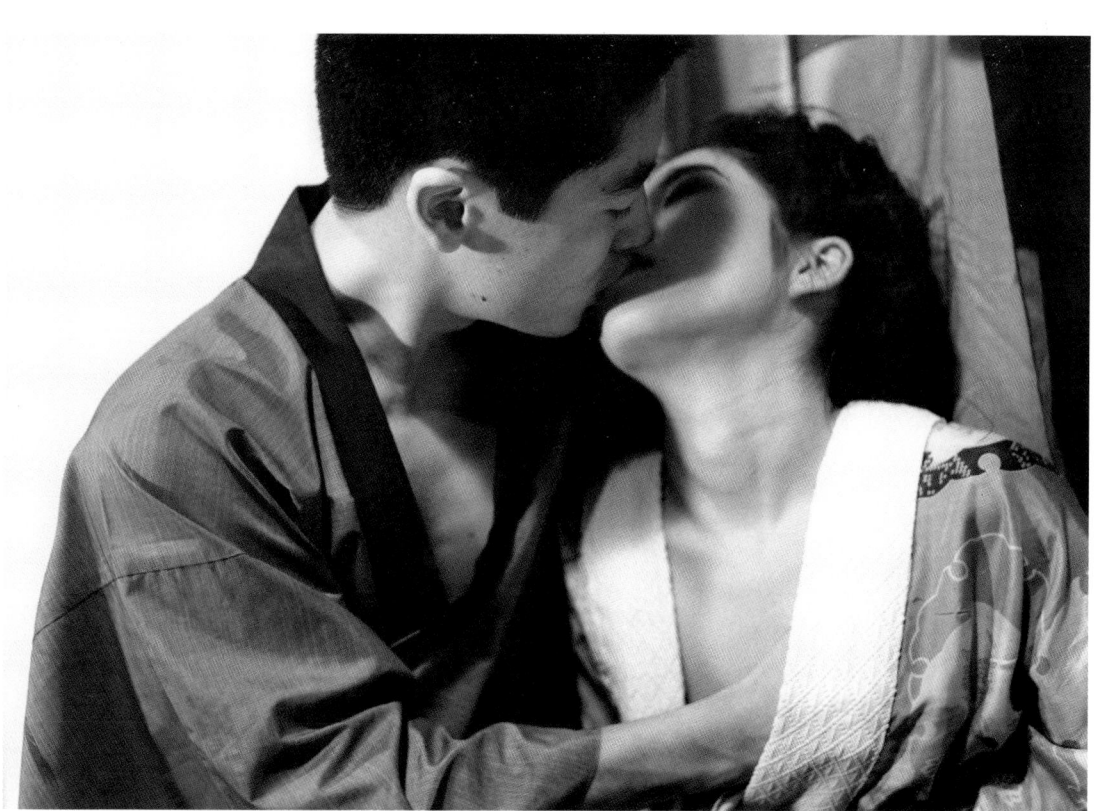

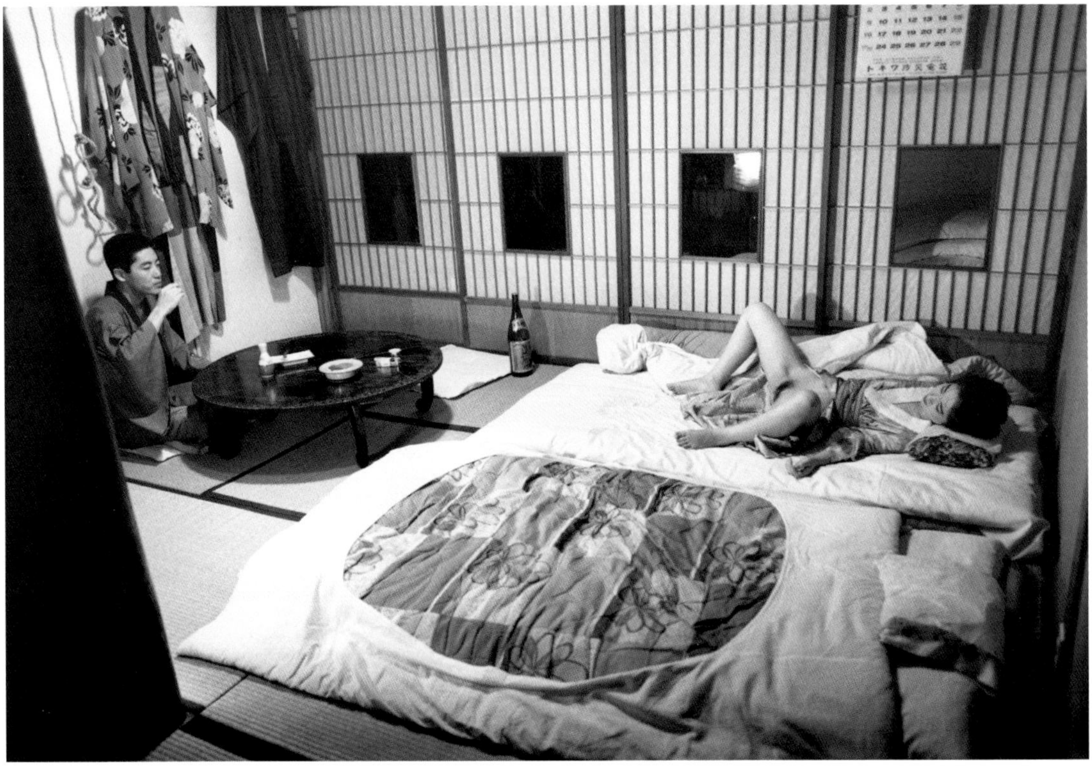

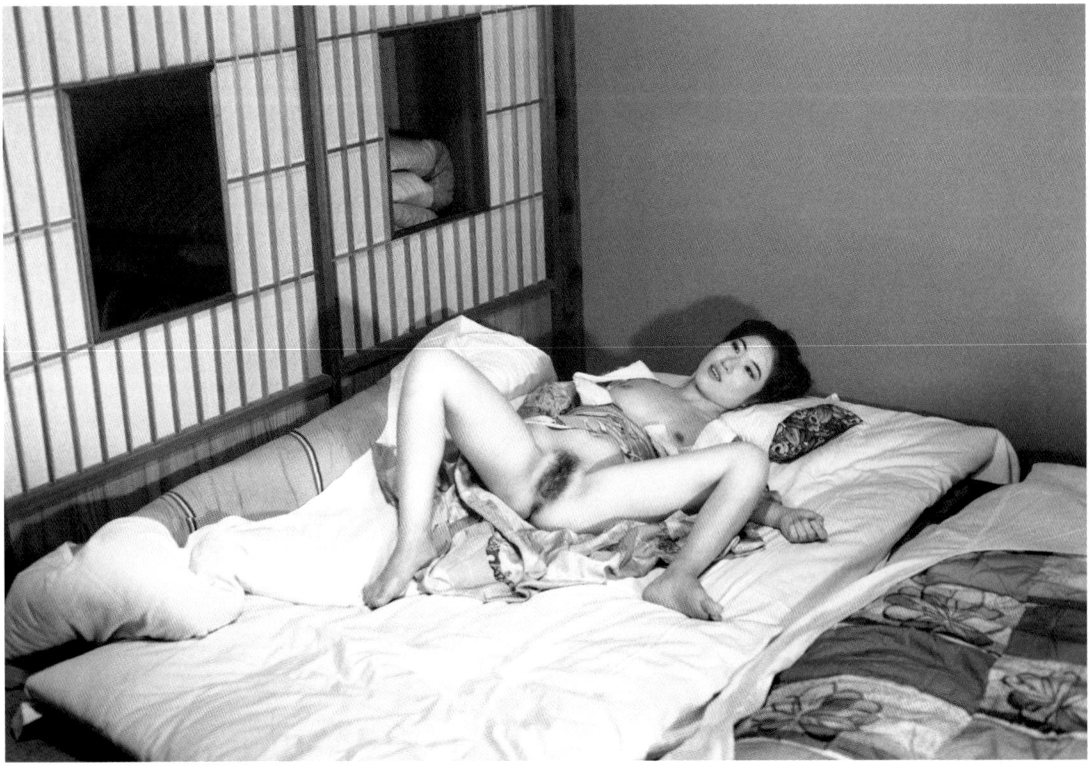

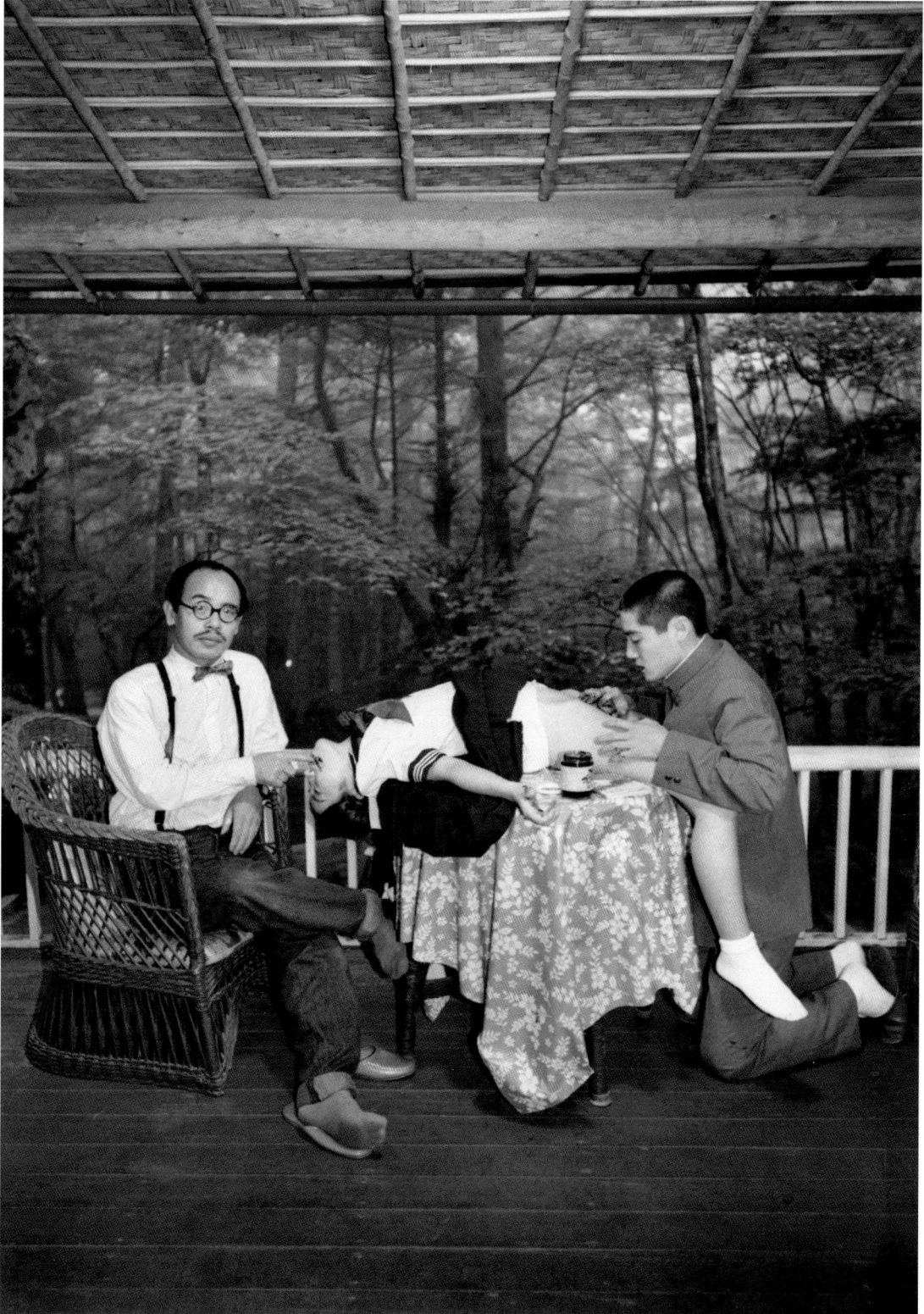

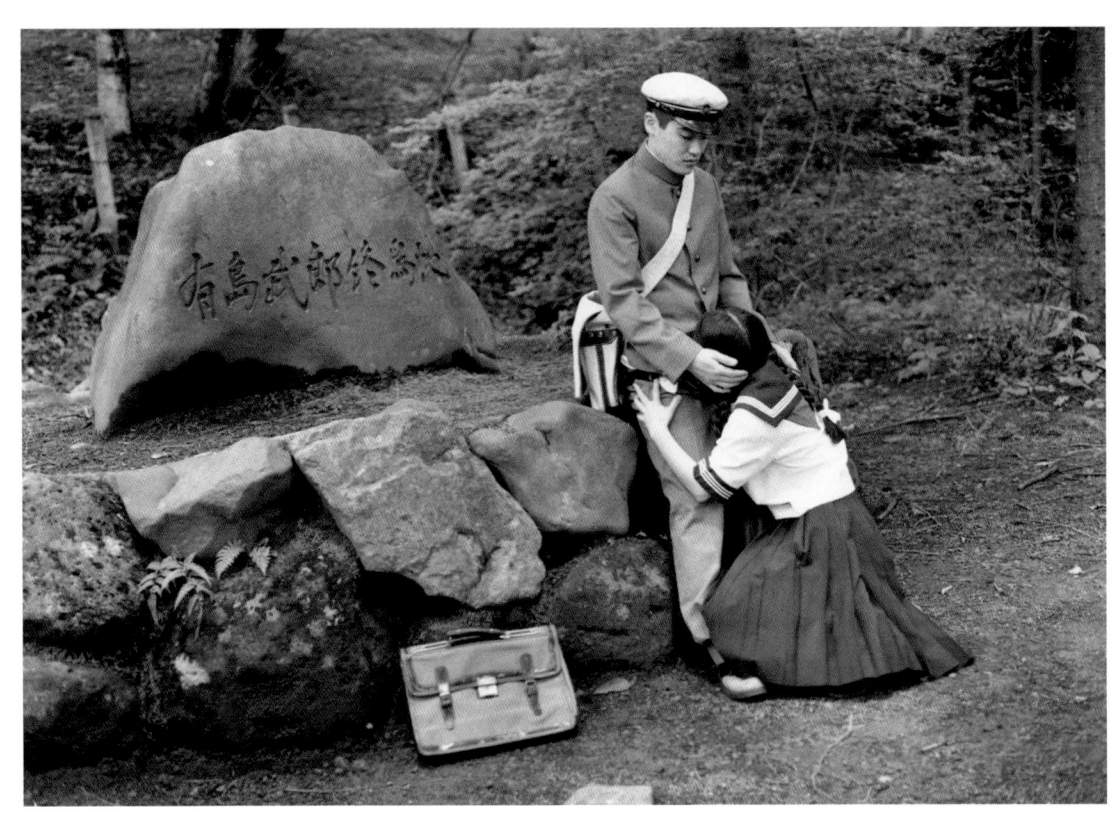

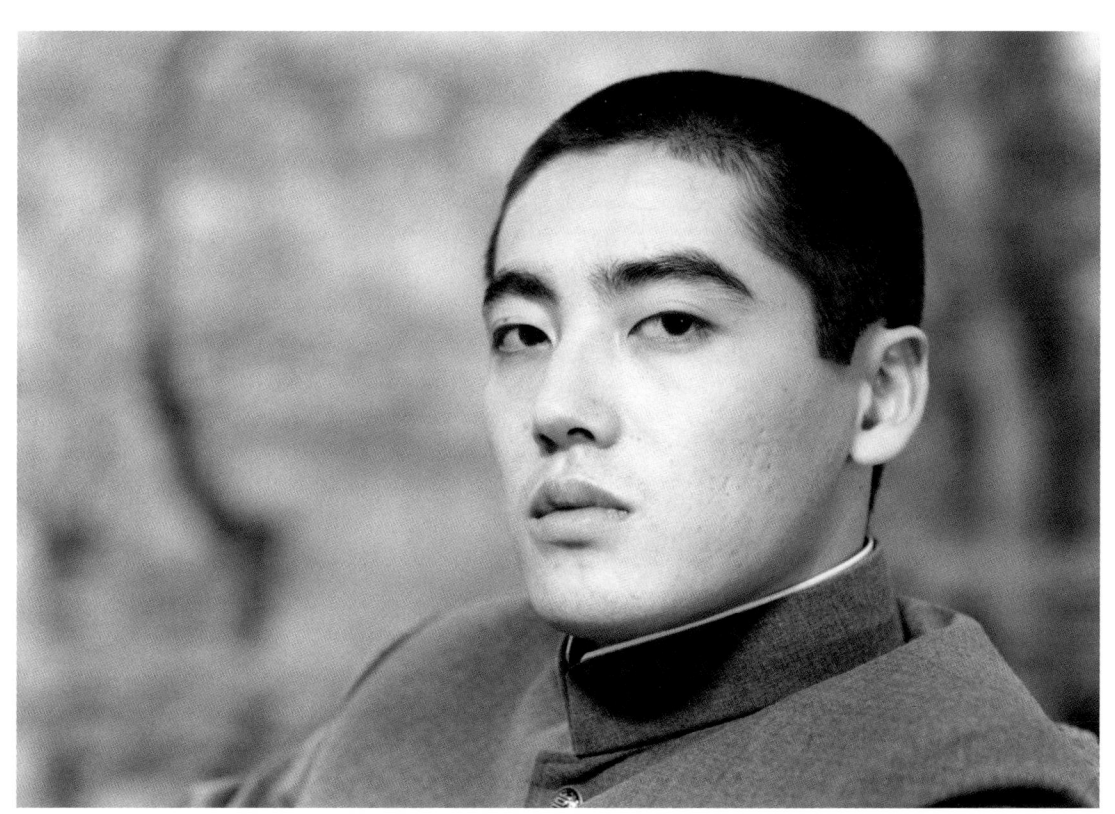

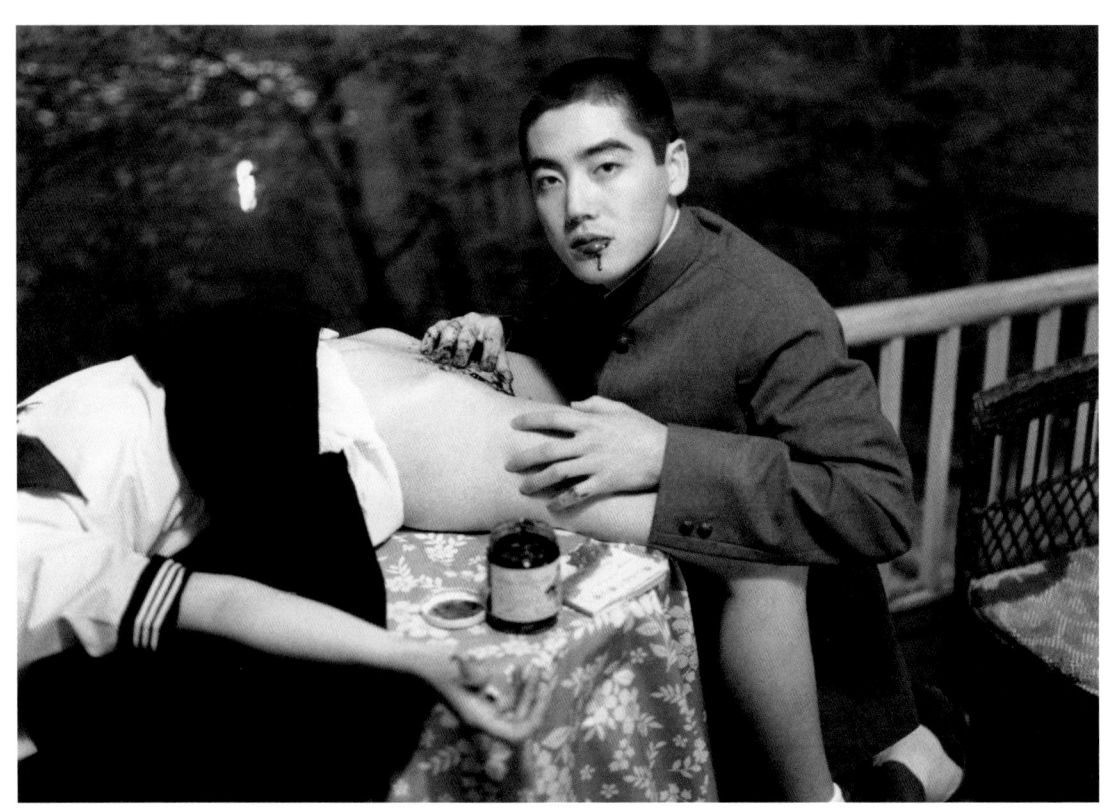

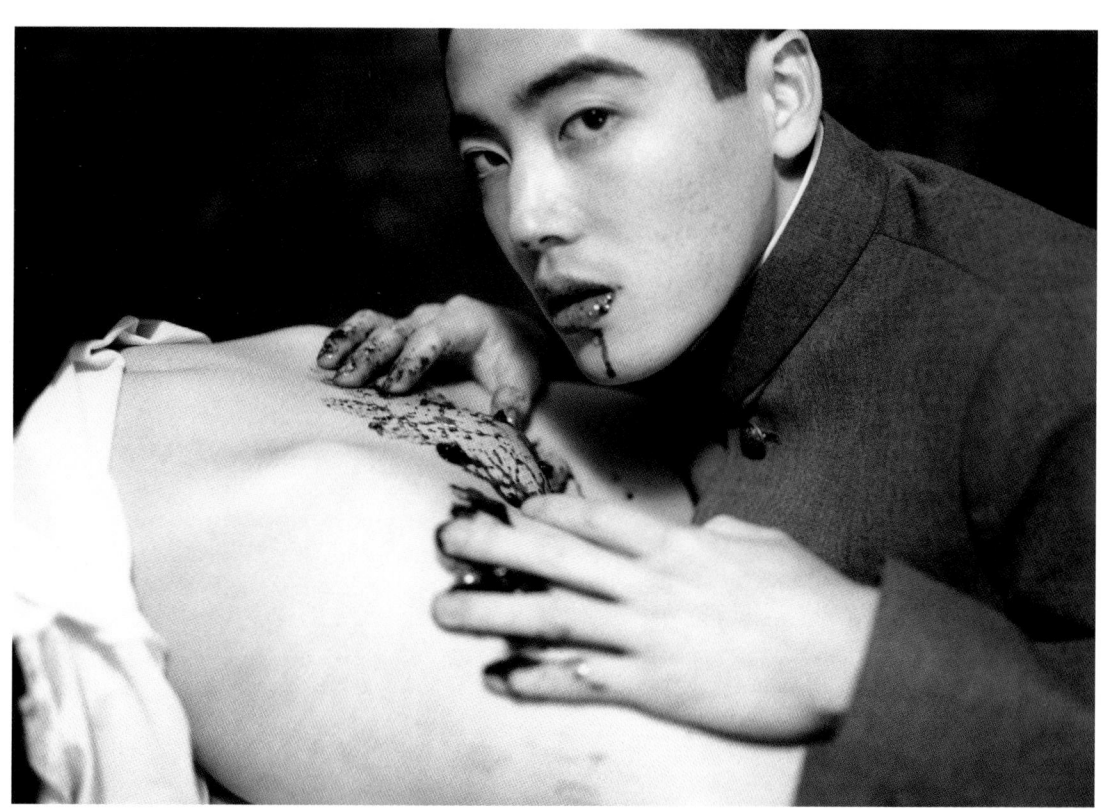

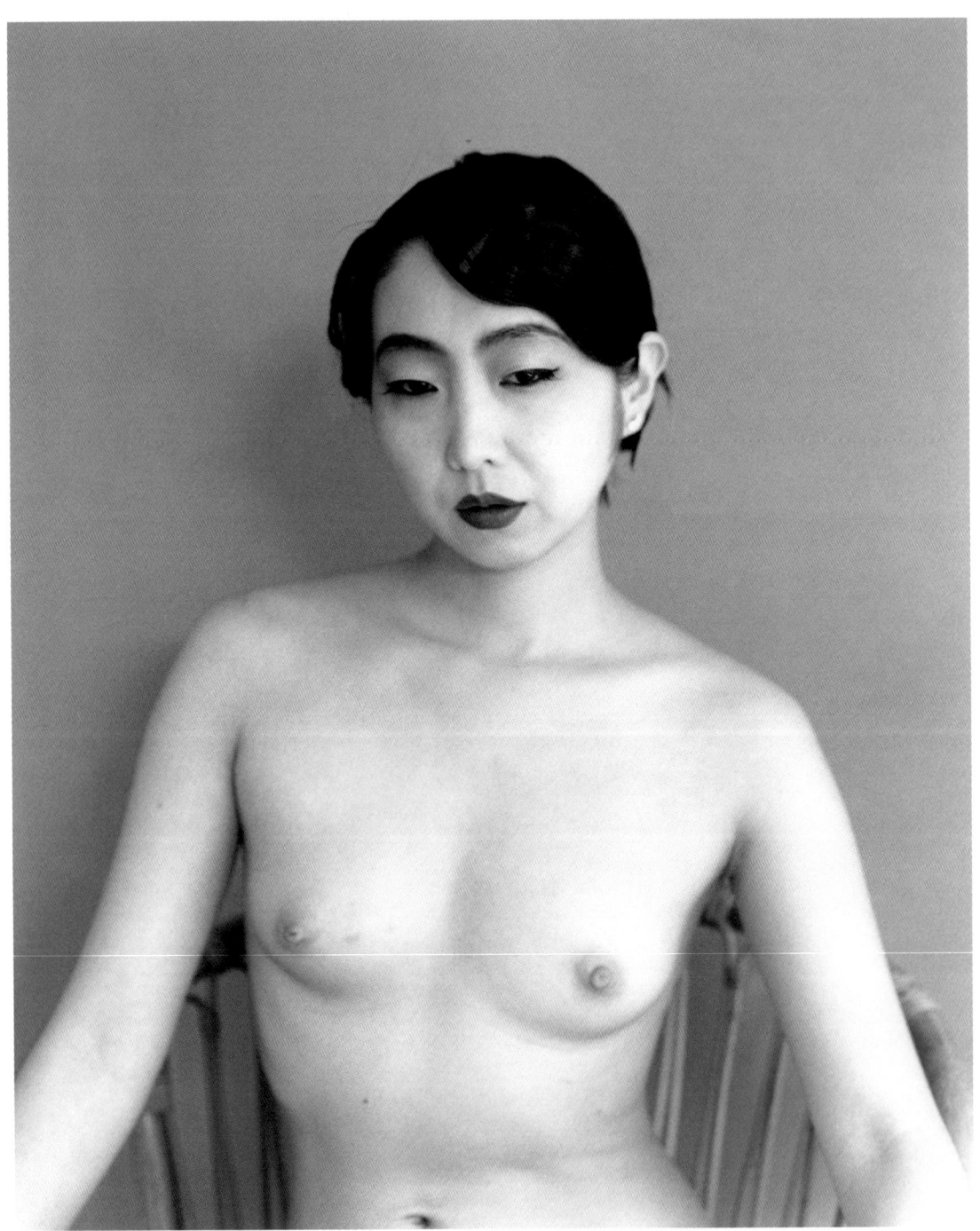

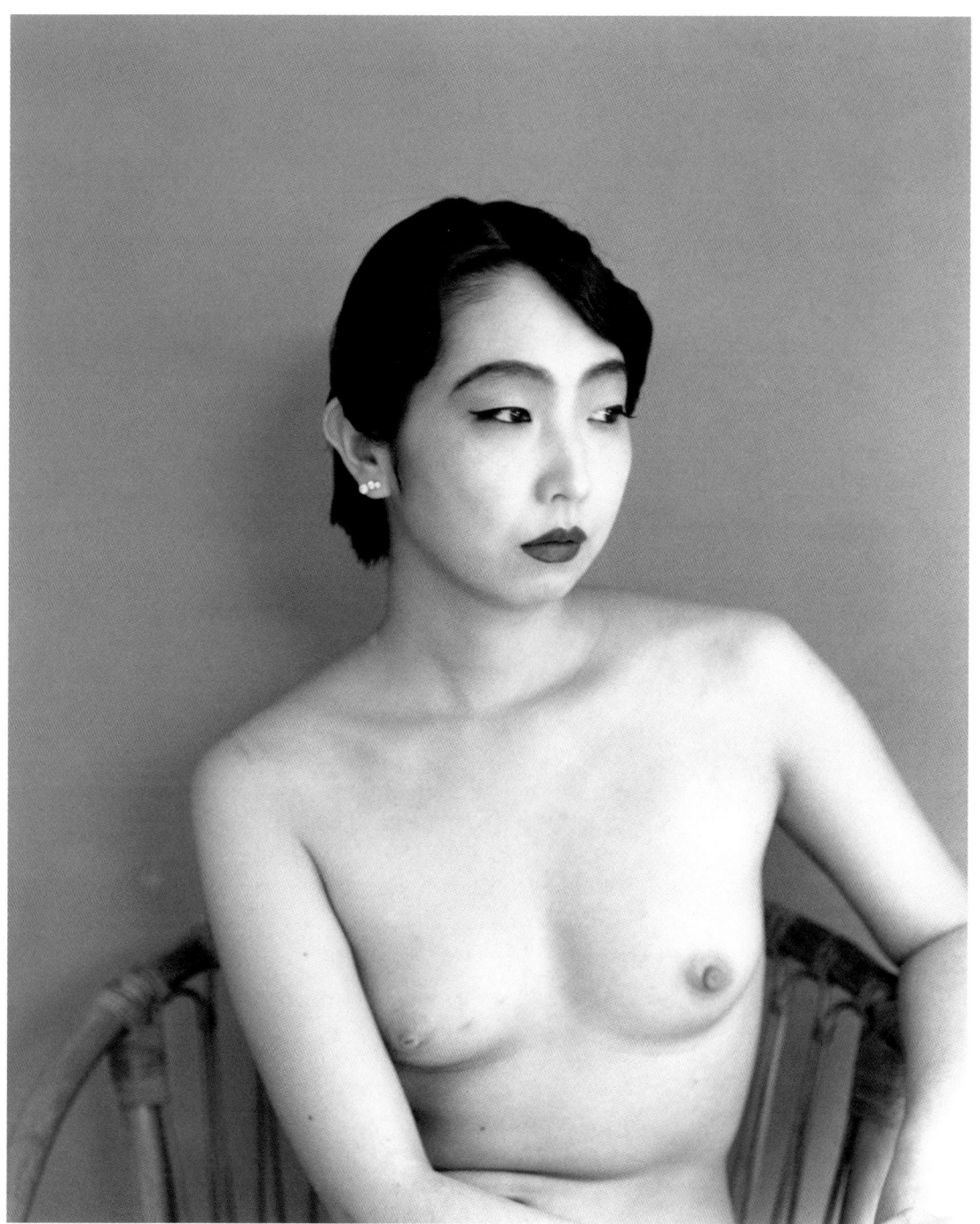

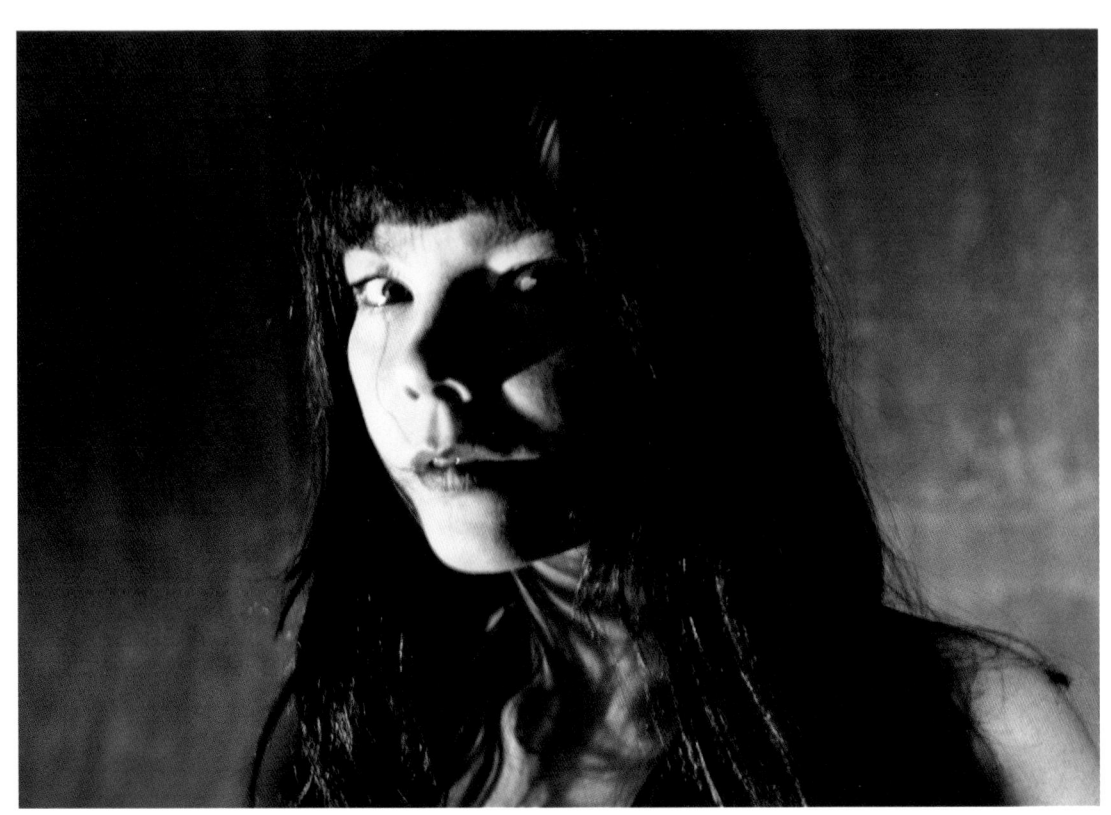

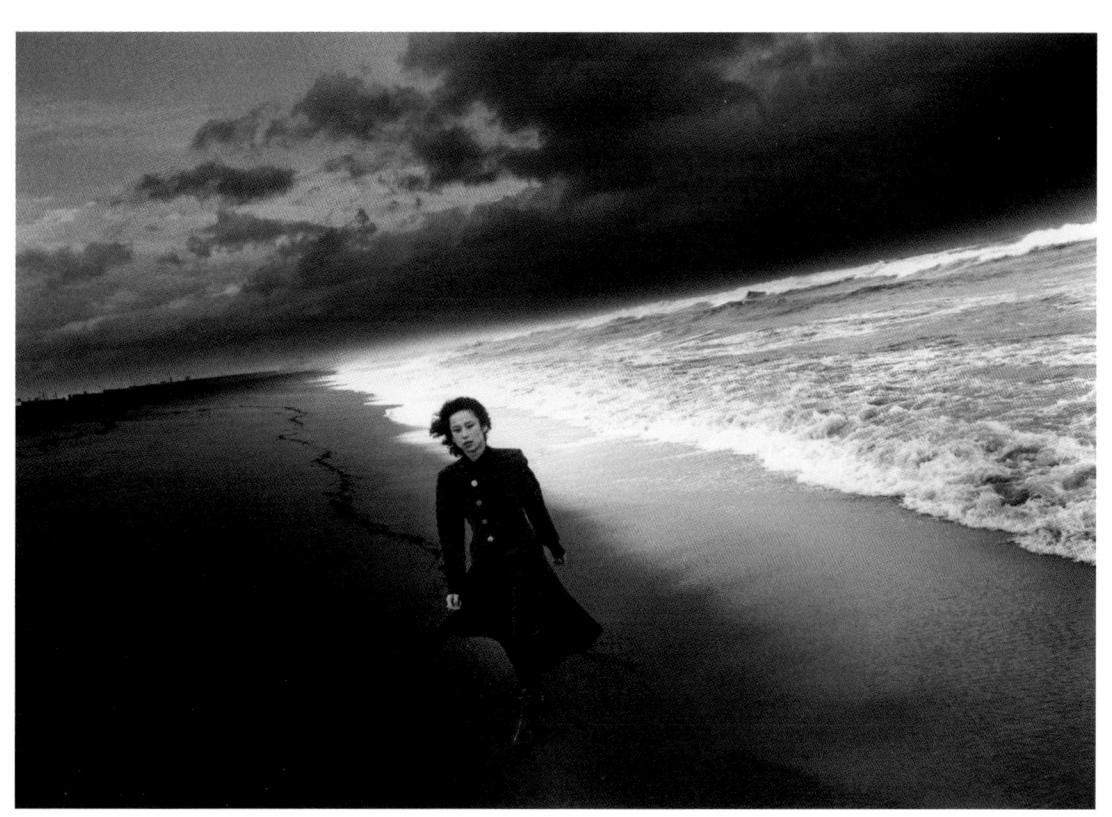

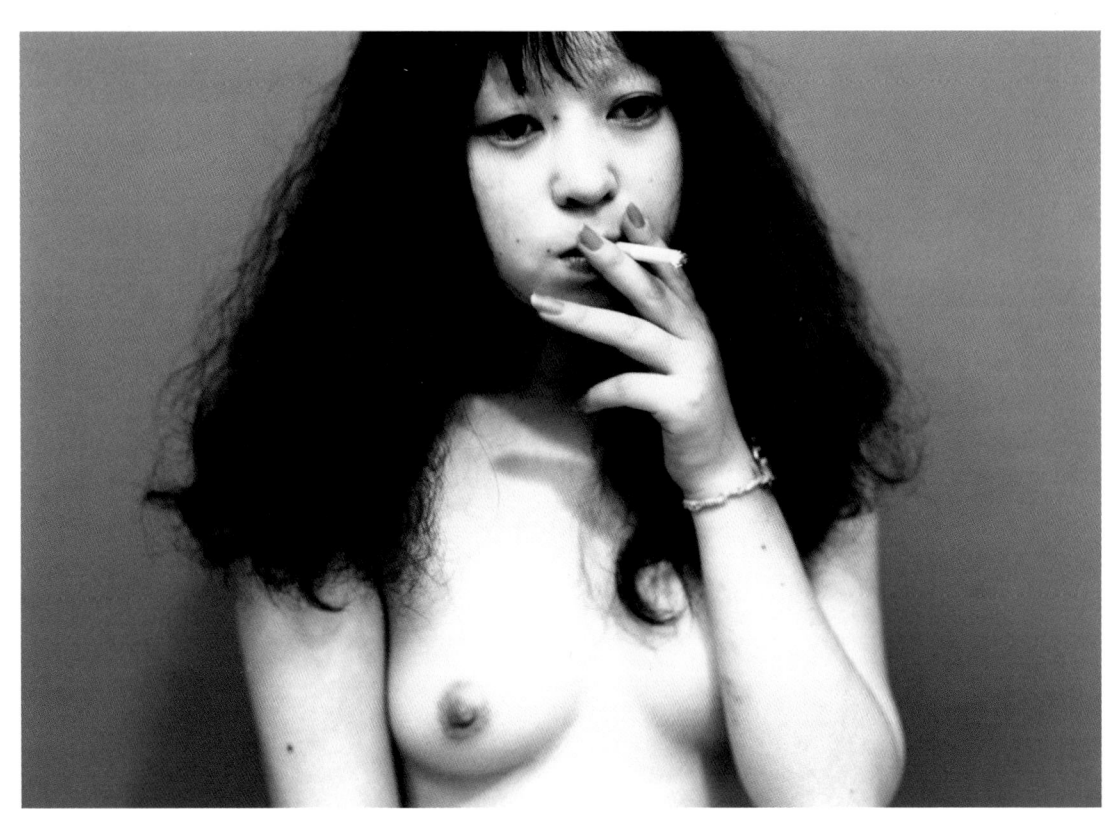

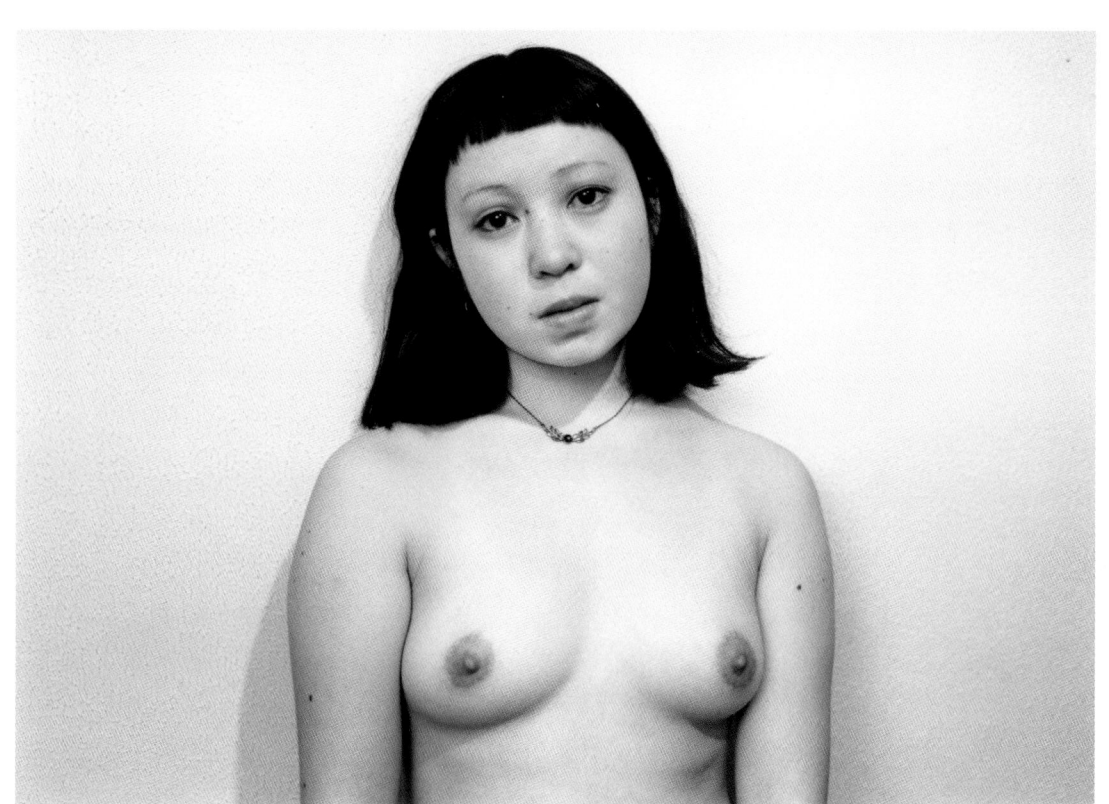

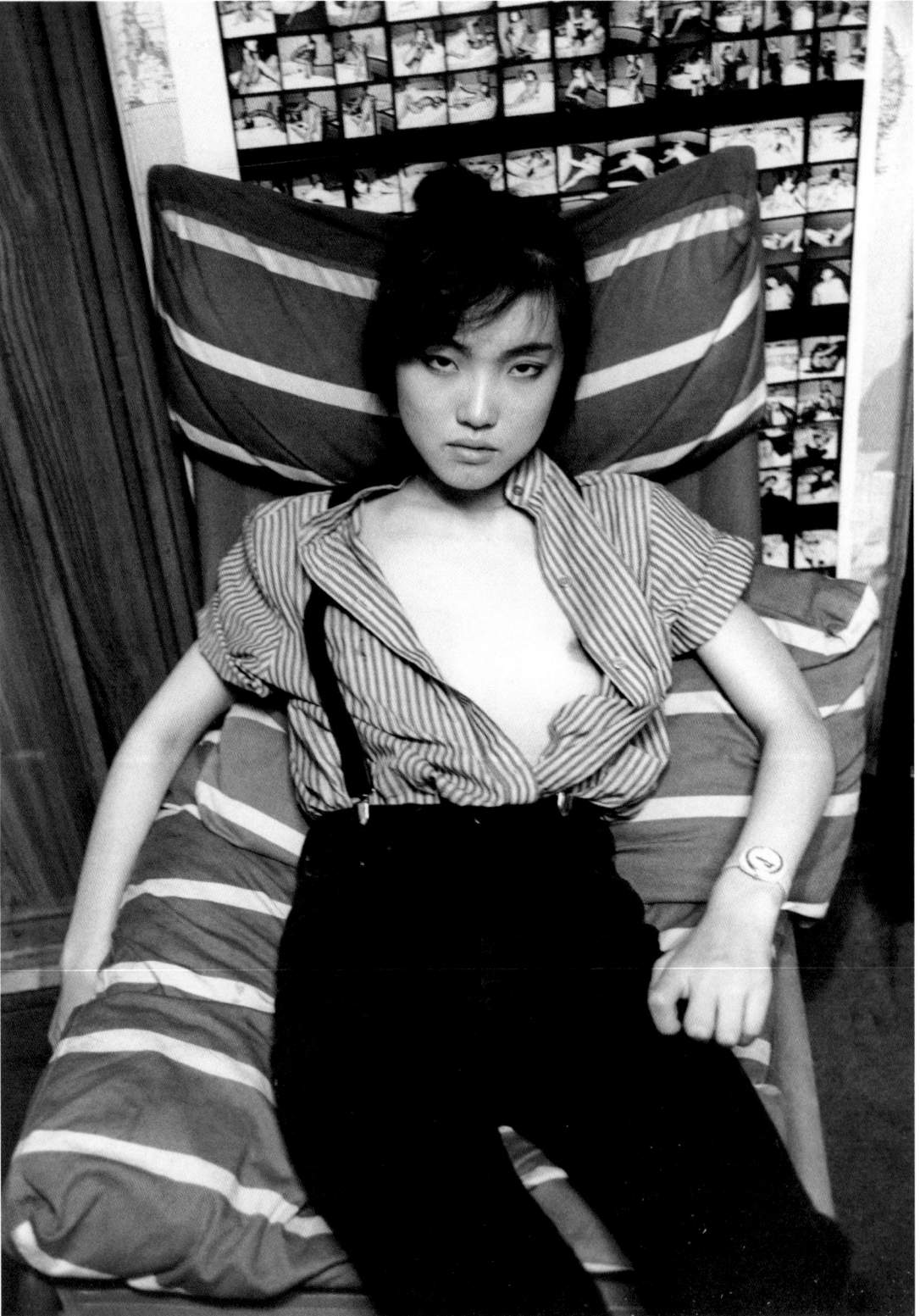

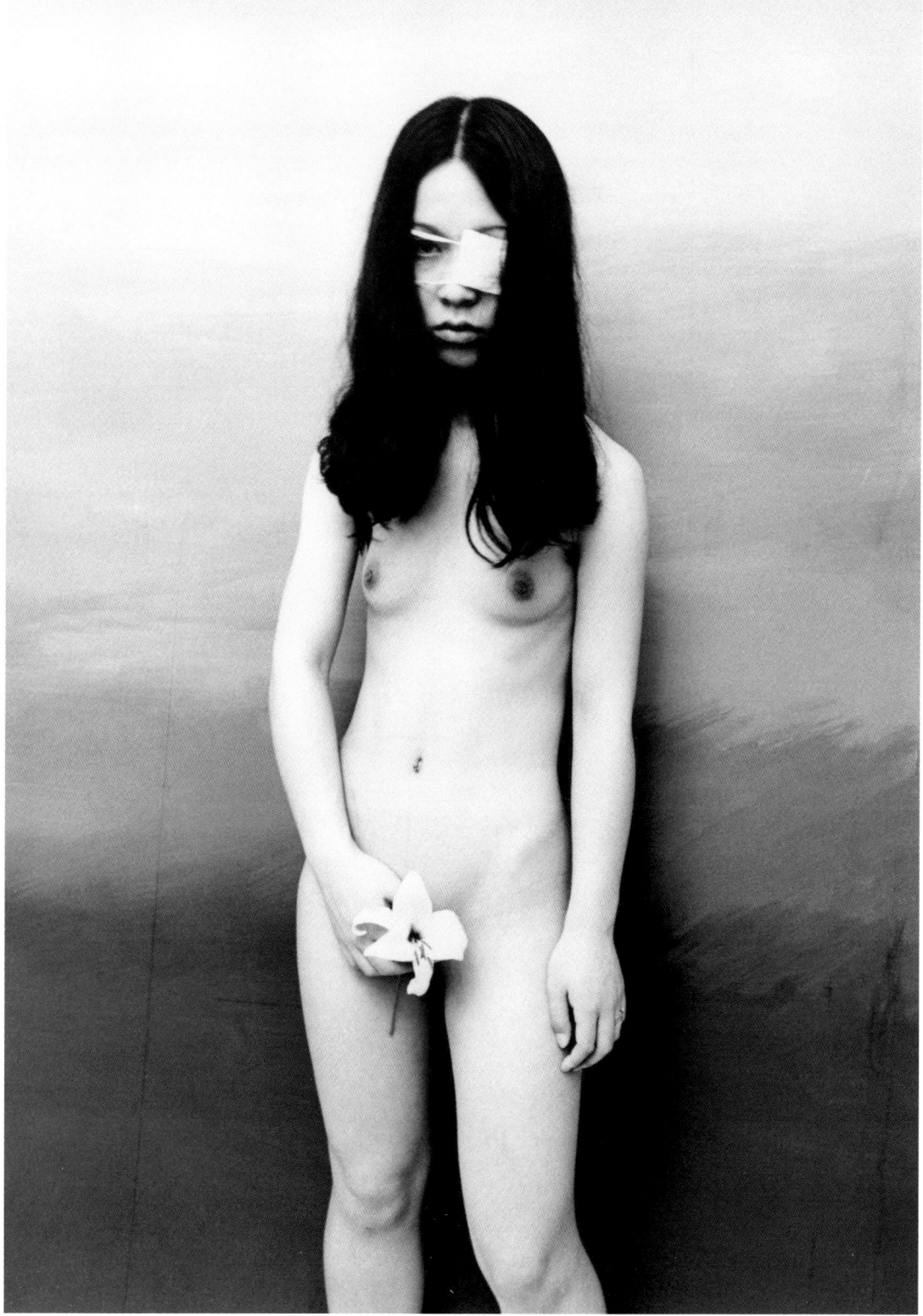

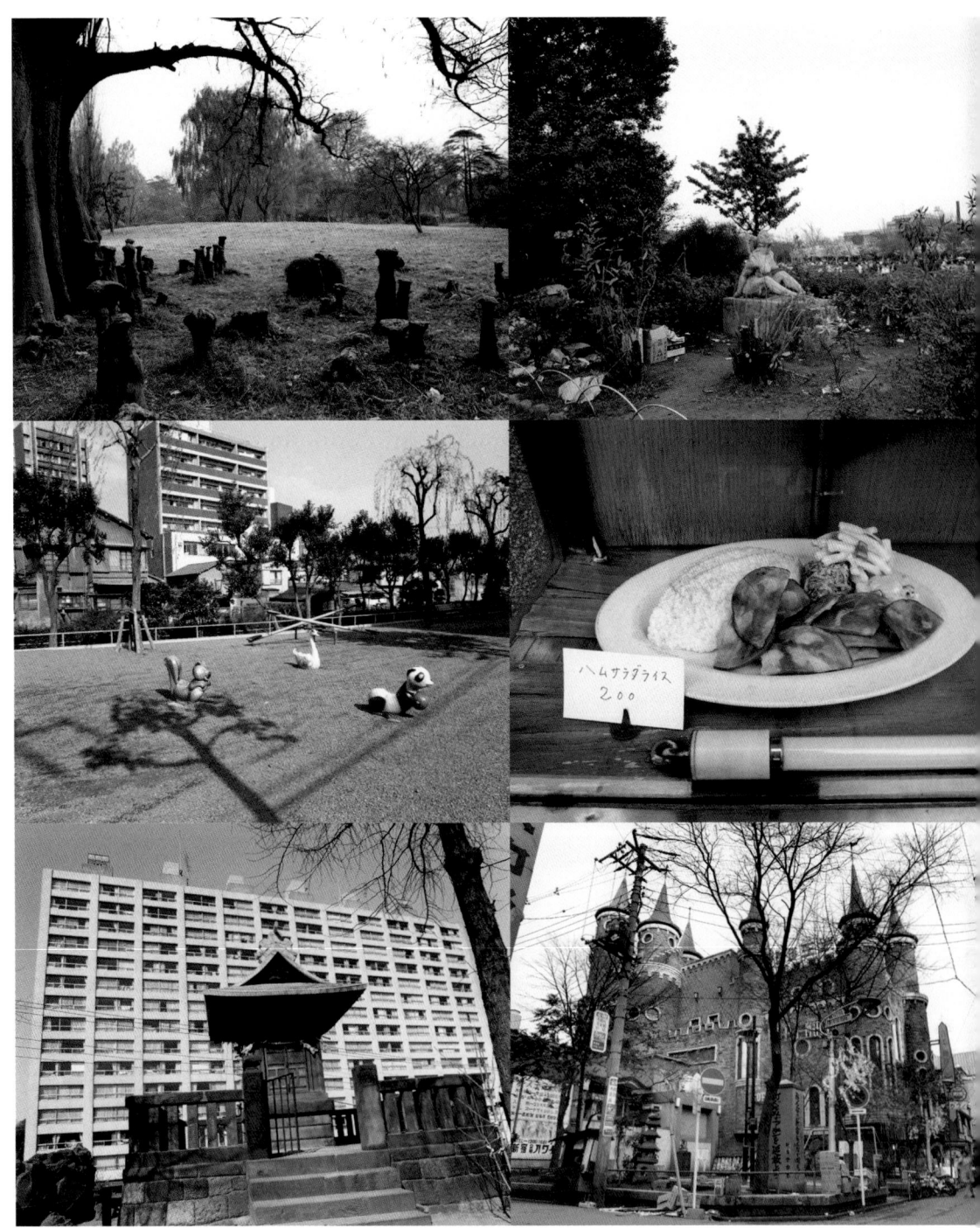

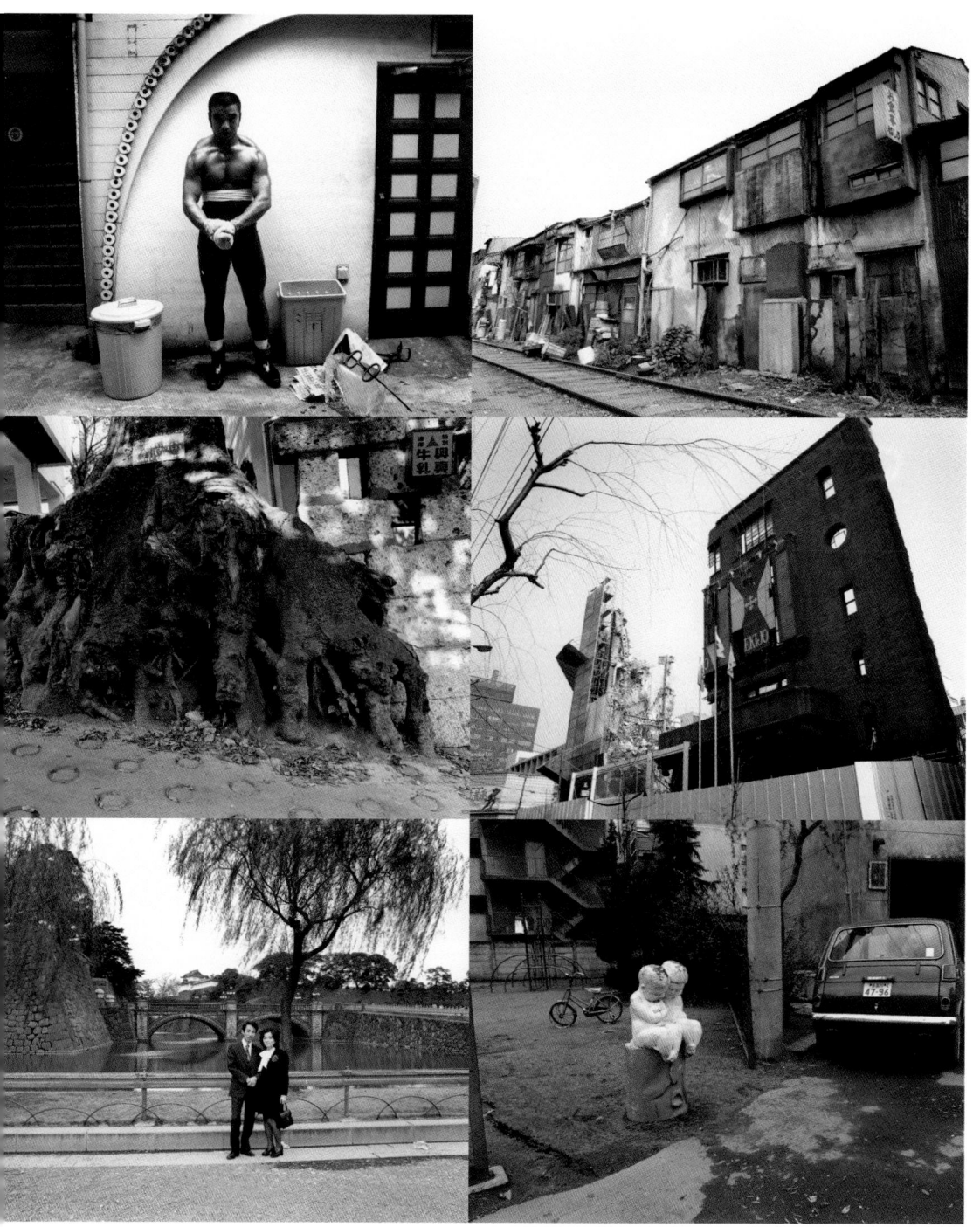

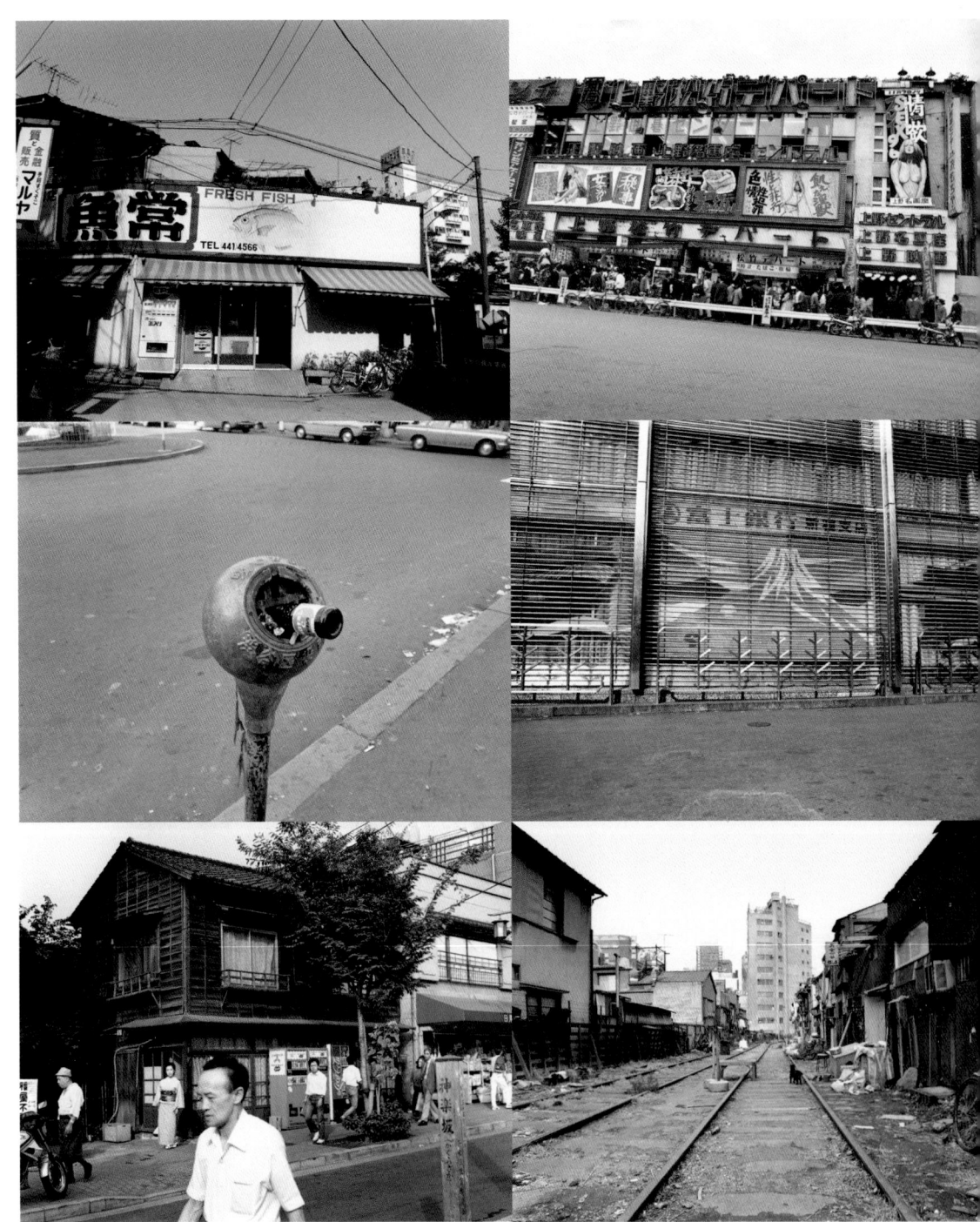

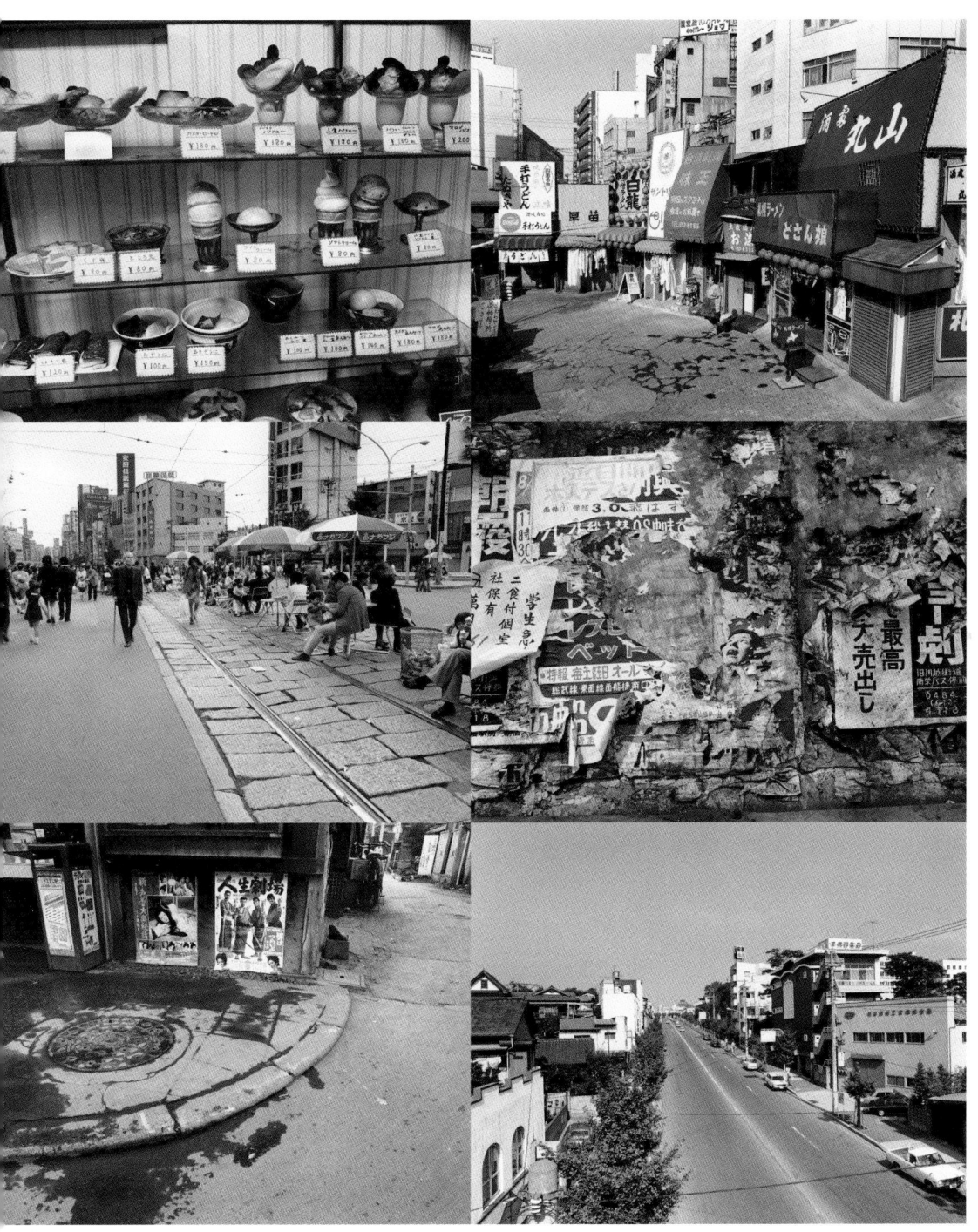

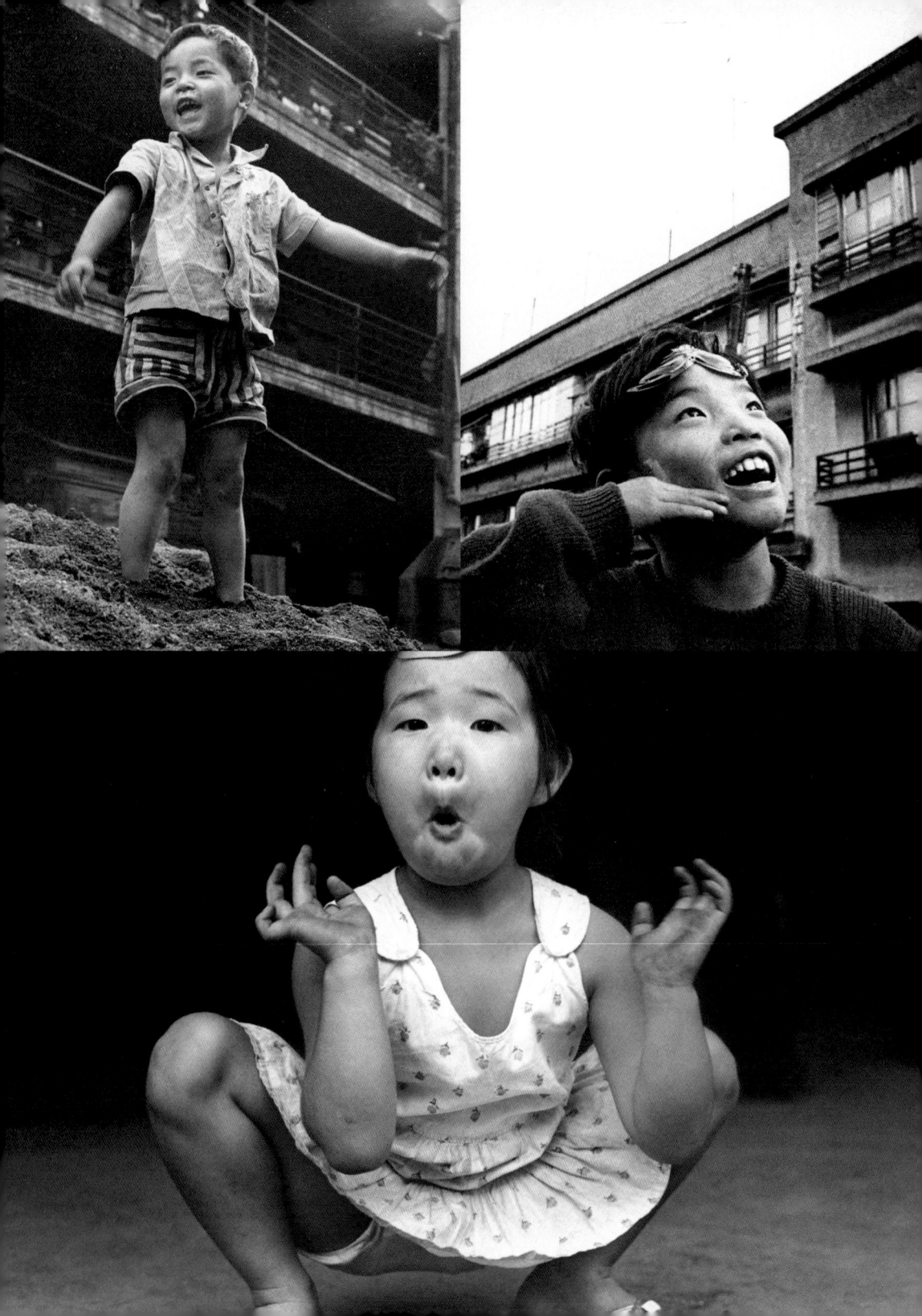

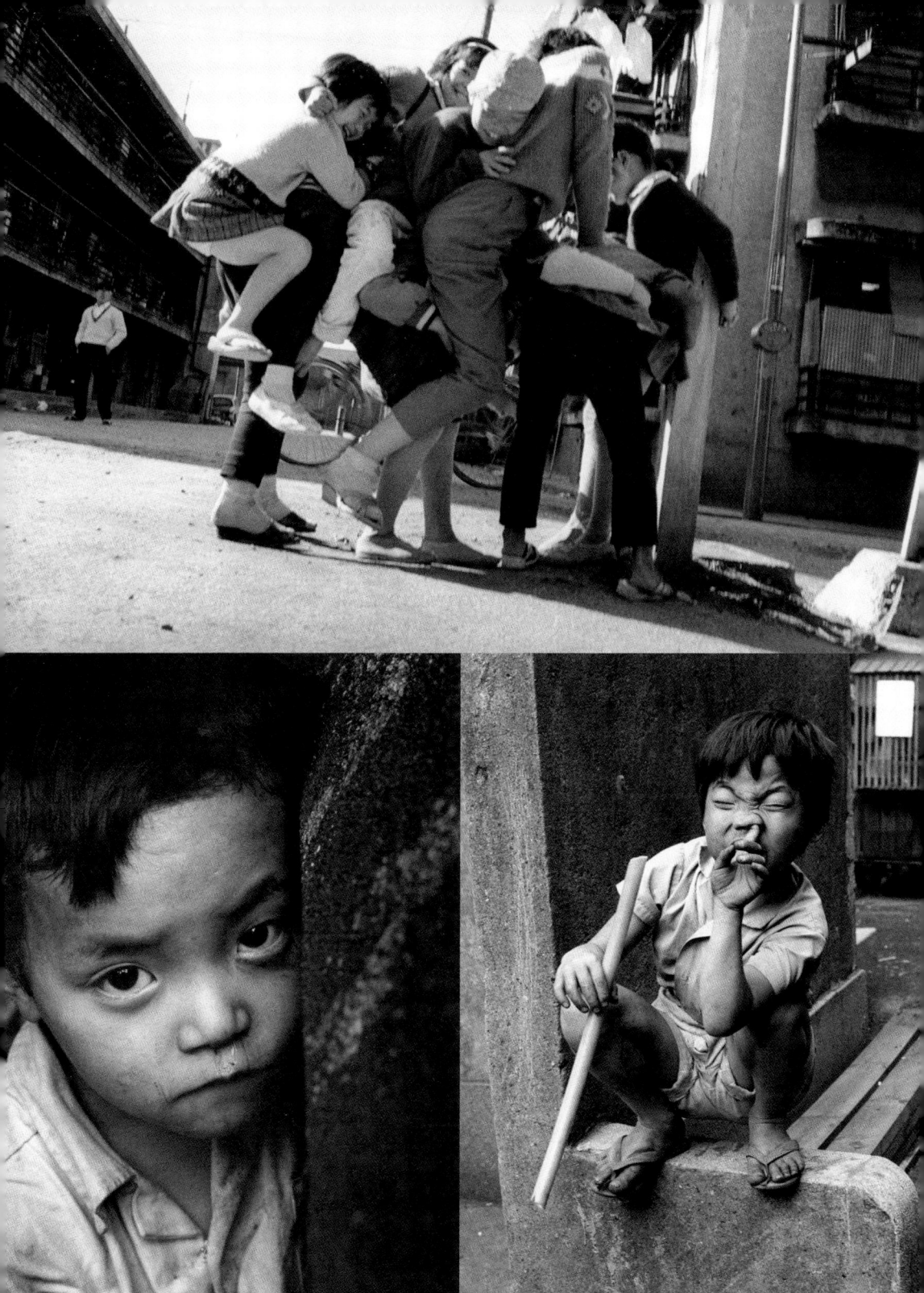

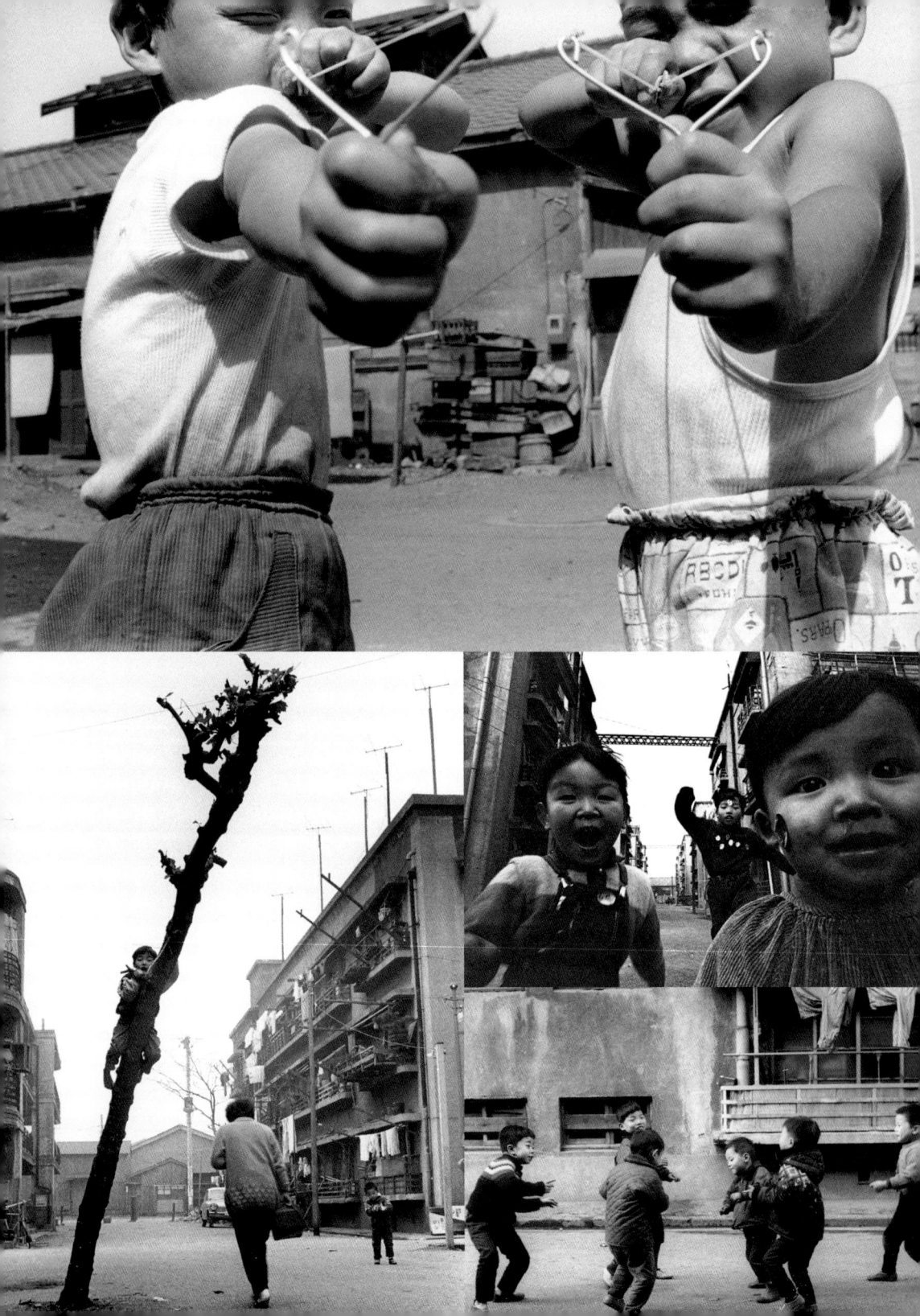

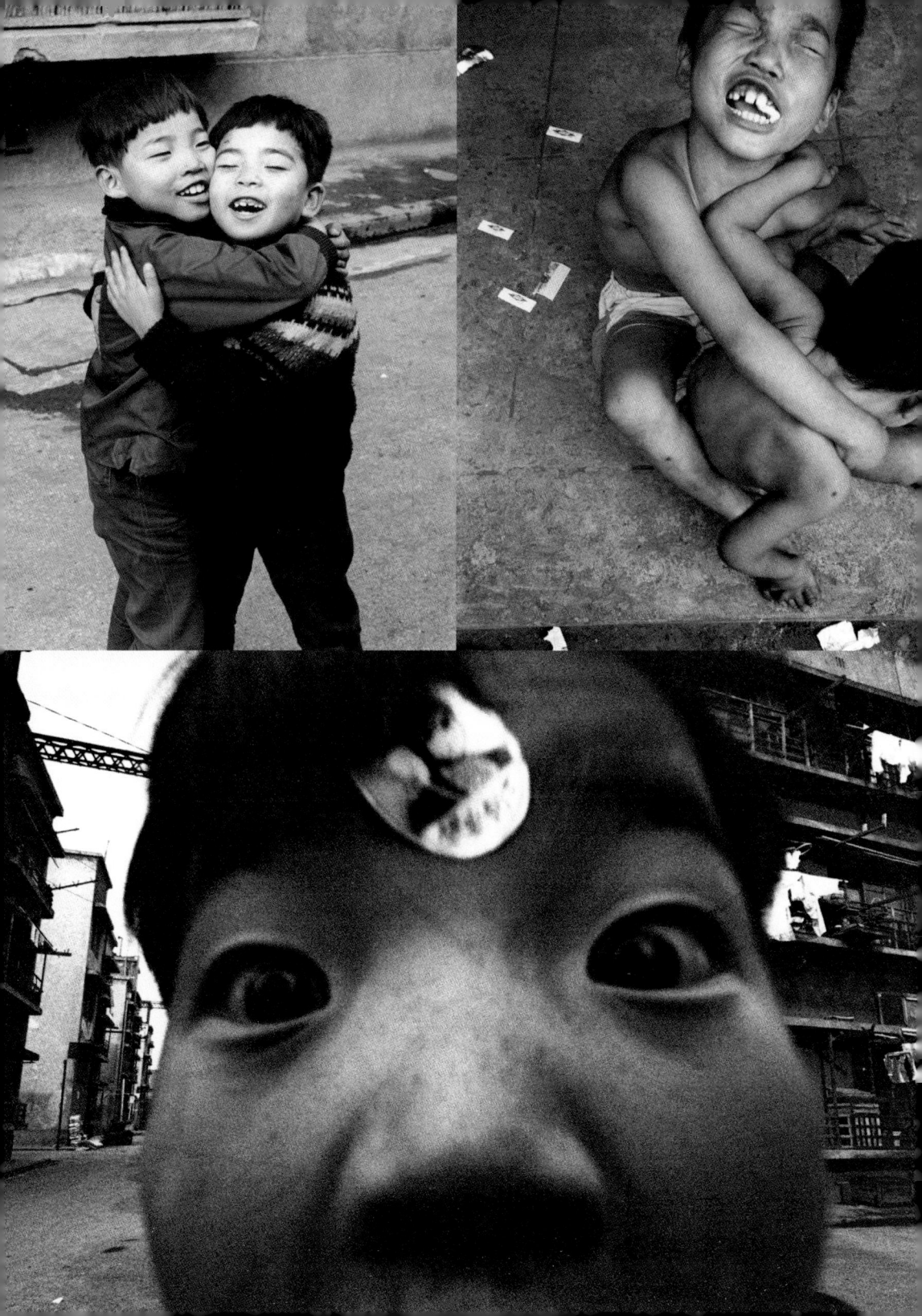

Biography

1940 Born May 25 in the Minowa area of Shitaya Ward (now Taito Ward), Tokyo. His father Chotaro and mother Kin run the Nimbenya *geta* (Japanese clog) shop. Nobuyoshi Araki (NA) is the fifth of seven children, with three brothers and three sisters.

1952 His father, an expert amateur photographer, presents him with a Baby Pearl camera. NA takes his first photos during a school excursion.

1959 Becomes a student at the engineering department of Chiba University, where he majors in photography and film.

1963 Graduates from Chiba University (his thesis is a black and white film called *Children Living in Apartments*), and starts work as a commercial photographer with ad agency Dentsu.

1964 Wins a photography contest organised by *The Sun* magazine with *Satchin*, photos of neighborhood elementary school boys.

1965 First one-man show, called 'Satchin and His Brother Mabo' (in Tokyo).

1967 NA's father dies.

1970 Creates *Xeroxed Photo Albums* (25 volumes, each in a limited edition of 70 copies) and sends them to friends, art critics, and people selected randomly from the telephone book. Puts on an exhibition called 'Sur-sentimentalist Manifesto No.2: The Truth about Carmen Marie.' which serves as his 'photographic manifesto.' The photos consist of enlargements of a woman's genitals.

1971 Marries Yoko Aoki (born 1947), a secretary at Dentsu, and publishes *Sentimental Journey* privately, a record of their honeymoon. He and four colleagues form a group known as Fukusha-shudan Geribara 5, which asserts that 'photos are copies.' Visits Okinawa (US territory at the time).

1972 Resigns from Dentsu.

1974 Photo Workshop School formed by NA, Shomei Tomatsu, Daido Moriyama, Eiko Hosoe, Masahisa Fukase, and Noriaki Yokosuka. NA's mother dies.

1976 Edits issue no. 7 of photo magazine *Workshop*, on the subject of 'Women' (Photo Workshop Editions). Photo Workshop School closes, and Araki's Private Photo School opens with about ten students (lasts until 1977).

1978 Leaves Minowa and moves to an apartment in Komae in the suburbs of Tokyo.

1979 Travels to New York for the opening of the group show 'Japan: A Self-Portrait' held at the International Center of Photography. First of a series of bondage shots for *SM Sniper* magazine.

1980 Does stills for the Seijun Suzuki film *Zigeunerweisen* (Gypsy Melodies).

1981 Sets up his own limited company (Araki Limited Company). Akira Suei launches *Shashin Jidai* (Photo Age) magazine, which contains three new series of works by NA. NA and Yoko celebrate their tenth wedding anniversary with a tour of Paris, Madrid and Buenos Aires. Works on *Pseudo-Diary of a High-School Girl*, his first film to be released.

1982 Opens a new office called Shashin-shinryojo (Photo Clinic). Visits South Korea with novelist Kenji Nakagami.

1986 Establishes his own style of slide-shows called 'Araki-nema,' using two slide projectors operated by his colleagues Shiro Tamiya and Nobuhiko Ansai.

1988 The police order *Shashin Jidai* to withdraw all copies of its April issue on grounds of obscenity. The magazine closes down, and NA is summoned to a police hearing. Chiro the cat comes to live with the Arakis. NA, Shiro Tamiya, and Nobuhiko Ansai set up the AaT Room imprint.

1990 January 27: Yoko Araki dies at the age of 42. NA wins the annual awards of both the Japanese Photographers' Society and the 2nd Photography Circle. Does stills for the Seijun Suzuki film *Yumeji*.

1991 Wins the Domestic Photographer's Award at the 7th Higashikawa International Photo Festival. Sakiko Nomura starts work as assistant to NA.

1992 Police accuse NA of exhibiting obscene photographs in his show 'Photo-Maniac Diary,' he is fined 300,000 yen. First one-man show in Europe, 'Akt-Tokyo: Nobuyoshi Araki 1971–1991,' opens at the Forum Stadtpark in Graz, Austria. The exhibition tours ten European cities (until 1995).

1993 The police declare the exhibition catalogue of 'Akt-Tokyo: Nobuyoshi Araki 1971–1991' obscene and arrest a curator of the Parco Gallery in Tokyo, where the catalogue is being sold at NA's show 'Erotos.' NA is also questioned, and his house and office are searched by police investigators. (In the end, the curator is not prosecuted.)

1994 First one-man show in the USA. Turns down an offer to exhibit at the Venice Biennale. Appears in a film version of *New World of Love* (published in 1993), directed by Banmei Takahashi. He plays himself, shooting still photographs. Directs the joint performance *From the Edge of Nirvana* by Marilia, Gozo Yoshimasu, and Kazuo Ohno, together with an Arakinema show.

1995 First one-man show in France, 'Journal intime,' is held at the Fondation Cartier pour l'art contemporain, Paris.

1996 First 13 volumes of the 20-volume *Works of Nobuyoshi Araki* published.

1997 NA's biggest one-man show, 'Tokyo Comedy' opens, celebrating the 100th anniversary of the Wiener Secession, Vienna. He attends the opening reception, and shows performance versions of Arakinema abroad for the first time.

Naoto Takenaka makes a film of *Tokyo Biyori* (Tokyo Fine Day), a photo-essay by NA and Yoko published in 1993. First retrospective exhibition in Japan, 'Araki Retrographs,' is held at Hara Museum of Contemporary Art, Tokyo.

1998 First seven volumes of the eight-volume *Literary Works of Nobuyoshi Araki* published. NA visits Shanghai, Taipei, and Bangkok to take photos and attend the opening of exhibitions.

1999 First one-man show at a Japanese public museum, 'Araki Nobuyoshi: Sentimental Photography, Sentimental Life,' opens at the Museum of Contemporary Art, Tokyo.

2000 'Viaggio Sentimentale,' a major exhibition of NA's work at an Italian public museum, opens at the Centro per l'Arte Contemporanea Luigi Pecci, Prato. He stays in Prato for 10 days, taking photographs (mainly portraits). The results are included in the exhibition.

2001 *Photographs from the End of the Century*, *Photographs from the New Century* and *Photography Again* are published under NA's own AaT Room imprint. The three books are planned and edited by NA himself.

2002 NA visits Venice for his two exhibitions, 'Suicide in Tokyo' at Padiglione Italia, Giardini di Castello, and 'Araki in Venice' at Fondazione Querini Stampalia.

2005 A large retrospective exhibition, 'Self, Life, Death,' is held at the Barbican Art Gallery, London.

2008 NA is awarded the Austrian Decoration of Honor for Science and Arts.

2010 The exhibition 'Araki Love and Death' opens at the Museo d'Arte in Lugano.

2012 The 'Photo Book Exhibition: Araki' at the Izu Photo Museum, Mishima, features more than 400 books by NA. He is awarded the Special Prize of the 54th Mainichi Art Prize.

2013 NA loses the vision in his right eye from a retinal artery obstruction. He uses the experience as an inspiration to exhibit 'Love on the Left Eye' at the Taka Ishii Gallery, Tokyo, the following year.

2017–19 Further solo exhibitions travel the world, like 'Araki. Tokyo' at the Pinakothek der Moderne in Munich, 'The Incomplete Araki' at New York's Sex Museum, and 'Impossible Love' at C/O Berlin.

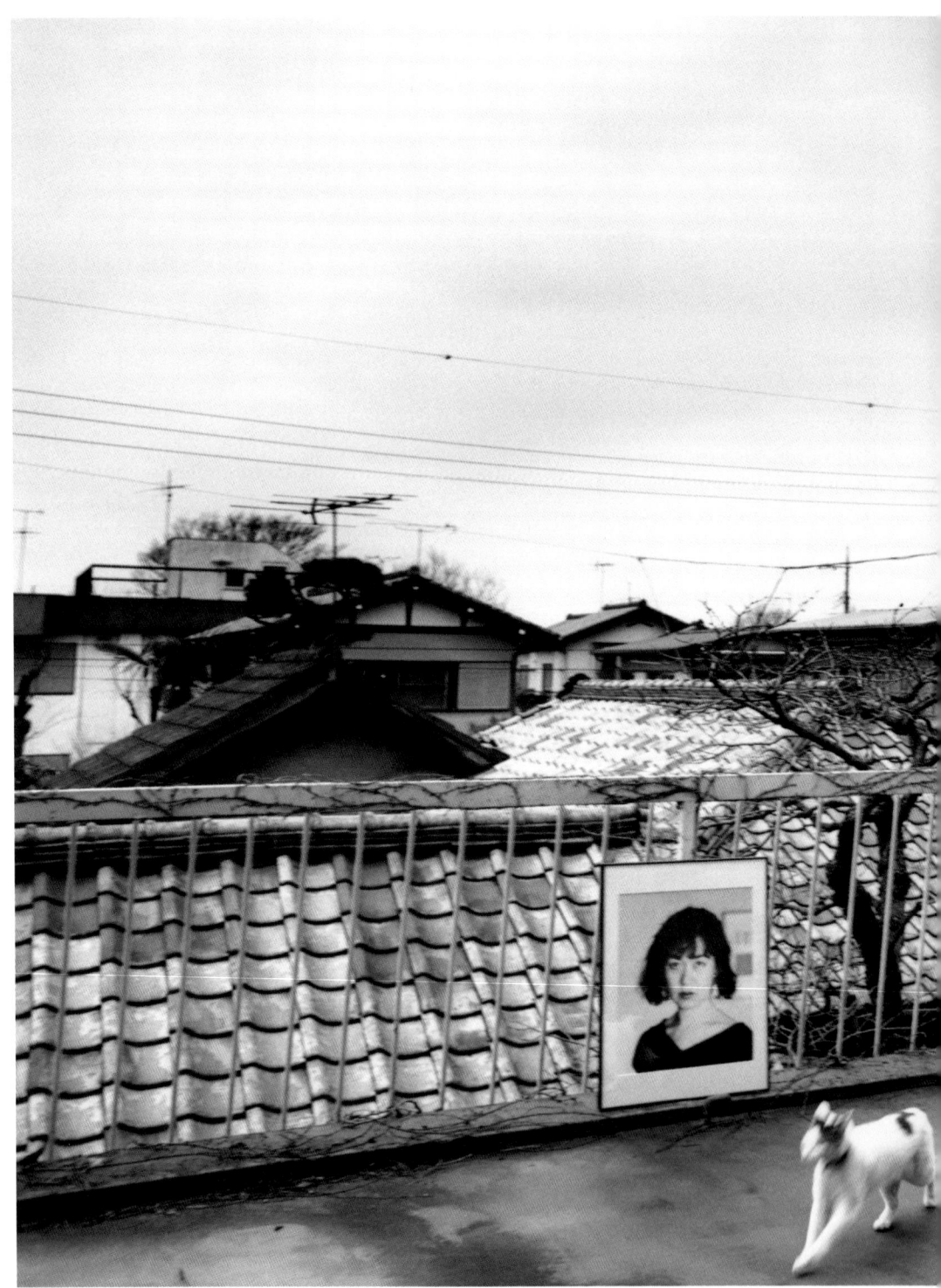

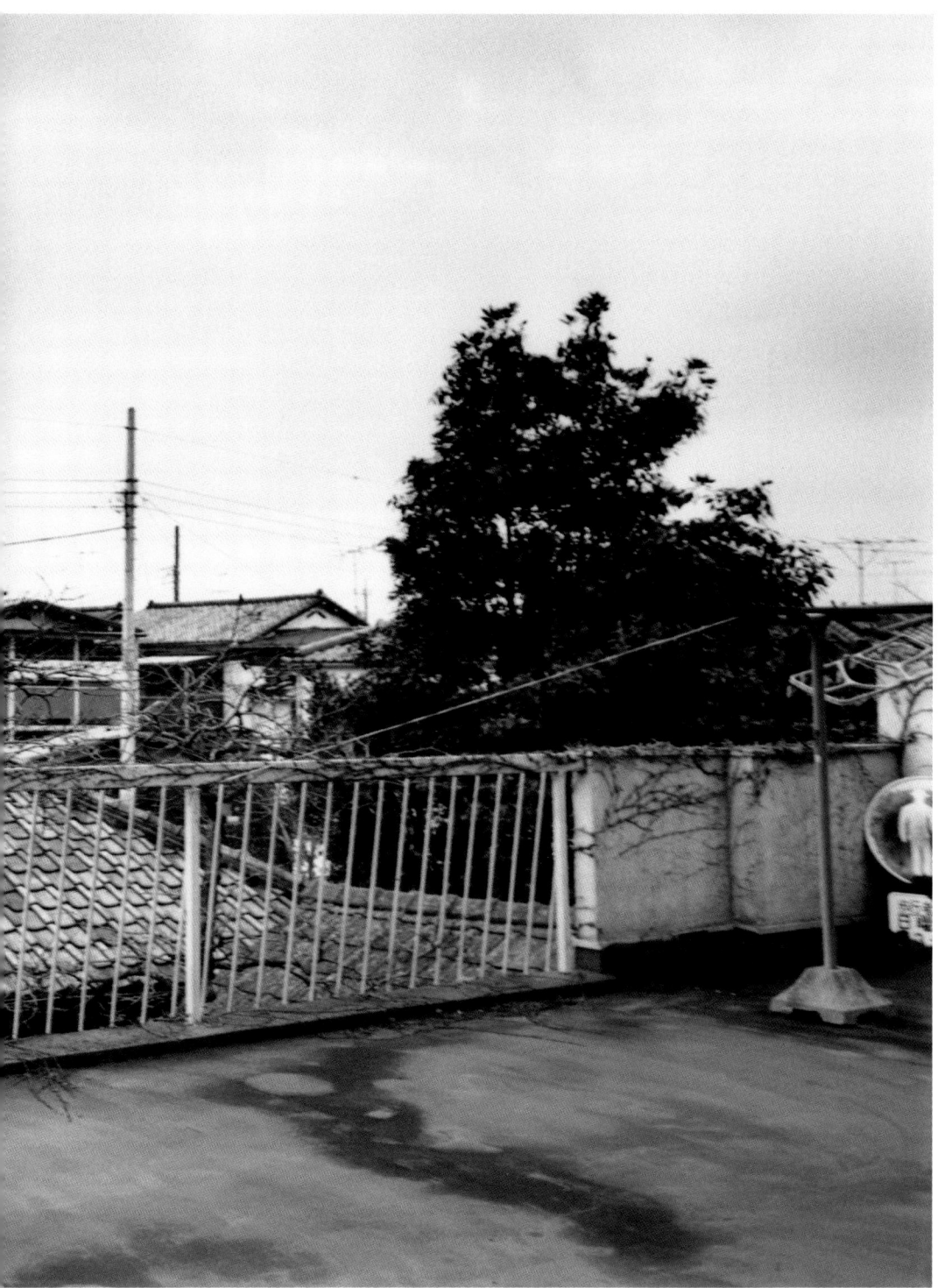

Selected Bibliography

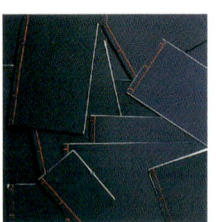

1970
Xeroxed Photo Albums
privately published
(25 vols., ltd. edns.
of 70 each)

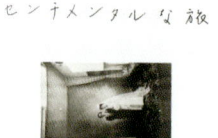

1971
Sentimental Journey
privately published
(ltd. edn. of 1,000)

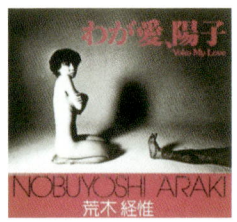

1978
Yoko My Love
Asahi Sonorama, Tokyo

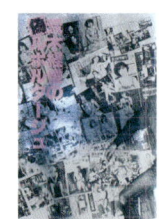

1980
*Nobuyoshi Araki's
Pseudo-Reportage*
Byakuya Shobo, Tokyo

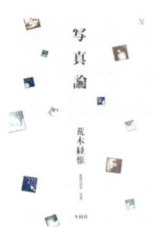

1981
Theory of Photography
Tojusha, Tokyo

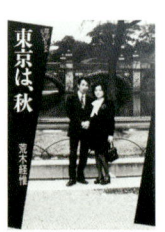

1984
Tokyo Autumn
Sanseido, Tokyo

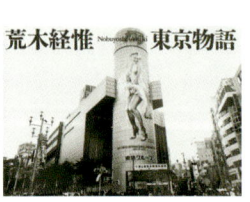

1989
Tokyo Story
Heibonsha, Tokyo

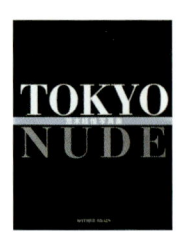

1989
Tokyo Nude
Mother Brain, Tokyo

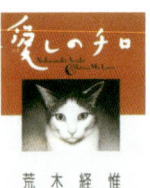

1990
Chiro, My Love
Heibonsha, Tokyo

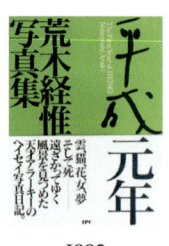

1990
The First Year of Heisei
IPC, Tokyo

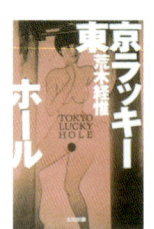

1990
Tokyo Lucky Hole
Ohta Shuppan, Tokyo

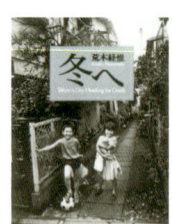

1990
*Towards Winter:
Tokyo, A City Heading
for Death*
Magazine House, Tokyo

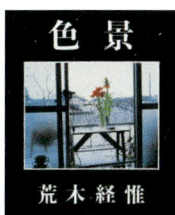

1991
Colorscapes
Magazine House, Tokyo

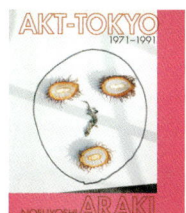

1992
Akt-Tokyo:
Nobuyoshi Araki 1971–1991
exhibition catalogue
Edition Camera Austria, Graz

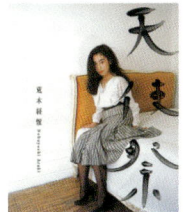

1992
Angel's Festival
Taiyo Shuppan, Tokyo

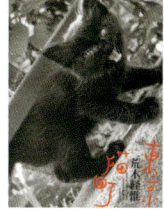

1993
Living Cats in Tokyo
Heibonsha, Tokyo

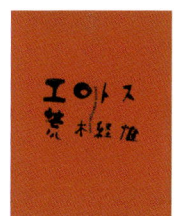

1993
Erotos
Libro Port, Tokyo

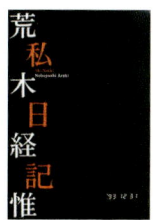

1994
Private Diary
AaT Room, Tokyo
(ltd. edn. of 1,000)

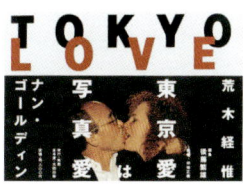

1994
Tokyo Love (with Nan Goldin)
Ohta Shuppan, Tokyo
(int. edn.: Scalo, Zurich, 1995)

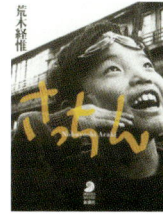

1994
Satchin
Shinchosha, Tokyo

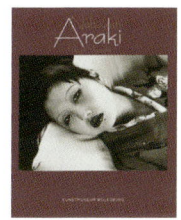

1995
Tokyo Novelle
exhibition catalogue,
Kunstmuseum Wolfsburg

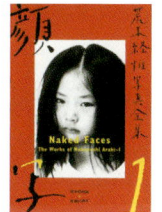

1996
The Works of
Nobuyoshi Araki—1,
Naked Faces
Heibonsha, Tokyo

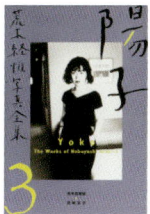

1996
The Works of
Nobuyoshi Araki—3, Yoko
Heibonsha, Tokyo

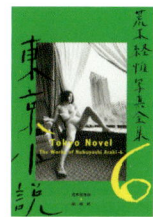

1996
The Works of
Nobuyoshi Araki—6,
Tokyo Novel
Heibonsha, Tokyo

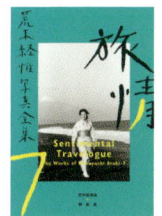

1996
The Works of Nobuyoshi
Araki—7,
Sentimental Travelogue
Heibonsha, Tokyo

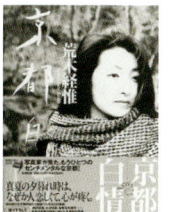

1996
Love Labyrinth:
Kyoto White
Sentiment
Shinchosha, Tokyo

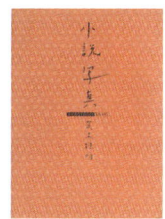

1996
Novel Photography
Recruit, Tokyo

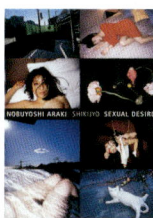

1996
Shikijyo: Sexual Desire
Edition Stemmle, Zurich
(Japanese edn.:
Tuttle Vista, 1997)

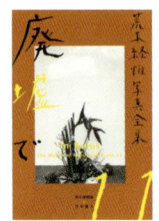

1996
*The Works of
Nobuyoshi Araki—11,
In Ruins*
Heibonsha, Tokyo

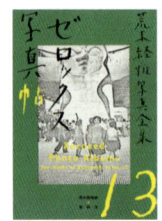

1996
*The Works of
Nobuyoshi Araki—13,
Xeroxed Photo Albums*
Heibonsha, Tokyo

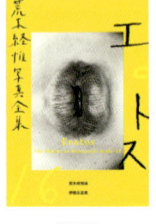

1997
*The Works of
Nobuyoshi Araki—16,
Erotos*
Heibonsha, Tokyo

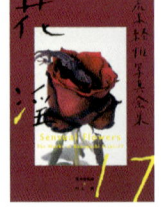

1997
*The Works of
Nobuyoshi Araki—17,
Sensual Flowers*
Heibonsha, Tokyo

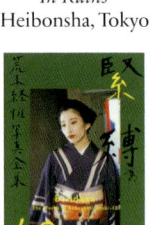

1997
*The Works of
Nobuyoshi Araki—18, Bondage*
Heibonsha, Tokyo

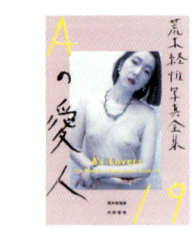

1997
*The Works of
Nobuyoshi Araki—19,
A's Lovers*
Heibonsha, Tokyo

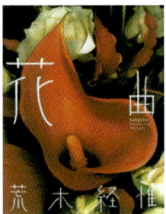

1997
Flower Rondo
Shinchosha, Tokyo

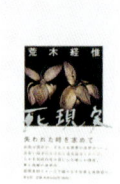

1997
Death Reality
Seidosha, Tokyo

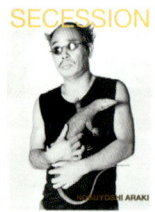

1997
Tokyo Comedy
exhibition catalogue,
Wiener Secession, Vienna

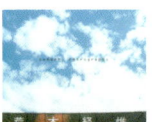

1998
Summer: Retrographs
Heibonsha, Tokyo

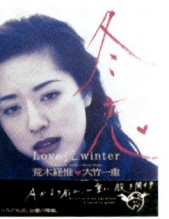

1998
Love in Winter
Bunkasha, Tokyo

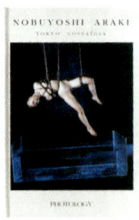

1998
Tokyo Nostalgia
Galleria Photology/
Photology, Milan

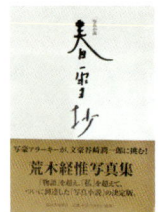

1999
*Photo-Novel:
Blind Love*
Photo-Planète, Tokyo

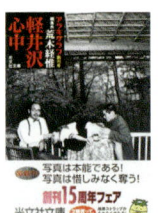

1999
*Double Suicide
in Karuizawa,
Araki Graph No. 1*
Kobunsha, Tokyo

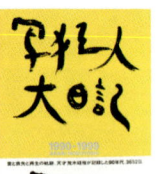

2000
*Photo-Maniac Big Diary
1990–1999*
Switch Publishing, Tokyo

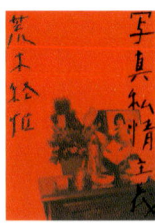

2000
*Photography:
Supreme
Sentimentalism*
Heibonsha, Tokyo

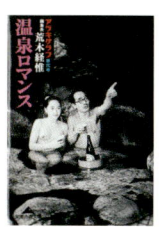

2000
Hot Spring Romance,
Araki Graph No. 2
Kobunsha, Tokyo

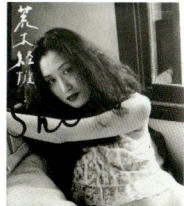

2000
Shino
Graphic Sha, Tokyo

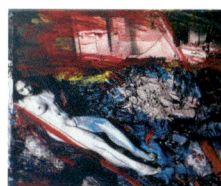

2001
Photographs from
the End of the Century
AaT Room, Tokyo
(ltd. edn. of 2,000)

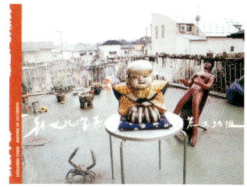

2001
Photographs from the
New Century
AaT Room, Tokyo
(ltd. edn. of 2,001)

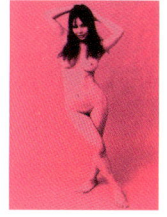

2002
Izumi, this bad girl
Bunyusha, Tokyo

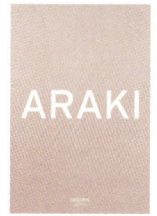

2002
Araki
TASCHEN, Cologne

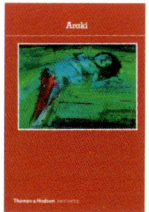

2007
Araki
Thames & Hudson,
London

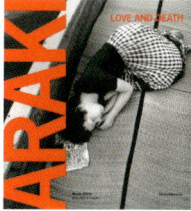

2010
Araki: Love and Death
Silvana Editoriale, Milan
(rev. edn.)

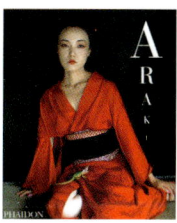

2011
Nobuyoshi Araki:
Self, Life, Death
Phaidon, London
(rev. edn.)

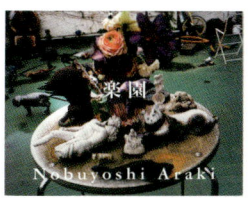

2011
Paradise
Rat Hole Gallery, Tokyo

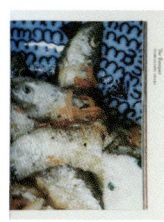

2012
The Banquet
Errata Editions, New York

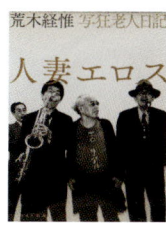

2013
Diary of a
Photomaniac Old Man
Wides Shuppan, Tokyo

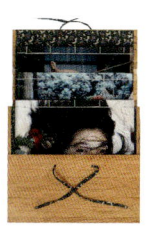

2012
Nobuyoshi Araki.
Bondage
TASCHEN, Cologne

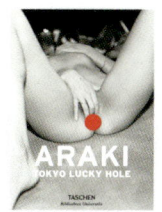

2015
Tokyo Lucky Hole
TASCHEN, Cologne
(rev. edn.)

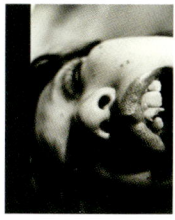

2018
Araki—impossible love
Steidl, Göttingen

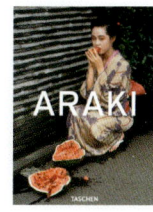

2020
Araki
TASCHEN, Cologne
(rev. edn.)

Credits

The chapters of this book were compiled from similarly named photo series or publications, plus additional photos taken from other books or series are follows:

Love in Winter:
Tokyo Novel, pp. 66, 89 (top)
Sensual Flowers, p. 68
Nobuyoshi Araki's Pseudo-Reportage,
pp. 86–88, 89 (bottom)
Akt-Tokyo: Nobuyoshi Araki 1971–1991, p. 74
Bondage, pp. 75–85

Private Photography:
Hot Spring Romance, Araki Graph No.2, p. 107
Kami in Pictures, pp. 108 (top), 109 (bottom),
129 (bottom)*Tokyo Novelle*, pp. 106, 110–113,
115, 116 (top), 118–125, 128, 129 (top),
132 (top right/below left), 134–136, 152
Tokyo Novel, p. 137
Sentimental Travelogue, pp. 132 (below right),
133 (below left)
Akt-Tokyo: Nobuyoshi Araki 1971–1991, pp. 108
(bottom), 109 (top), 130 (bottom), 132 (top left/
bottom left), 133 (top left/top right/below right)
Naked Faces, pp. 114 (top), 138–141
The First Year of Heisei, pp. 131 (top), 183
Nobuyoshi Araki's Pseudo-Reportage, pp. 142–143
The Banquet, pp. 144–149
Yoko, pp. 154–163
Chiro, My Love, pp. 165–167
Photography: Supreme Sentimentalism, pp.150, 152,
153, 164, 166, 168–182

In Ruins:
Tokyo Novelle, pp. 268
Photo-Novel: Blind Love, p. 273
Summer: Retrographs, pp. 272, 274/275
Tokyo Novel, pp. 276, 279, 280
Kyoto White Sentiment, p. 284 (top)
Chiro, My Love, pp. 270, 284 (bottom),
285 (bottom)
IZUMI, this bad girl, pp. 286, 287
Tokyo Lucky Hole, pp. 288–297

Erotos:
In Ruins, pp. 305, 319, 334–335, 340–343

Tokyo Nude:
Towards Winter:
Tokyo, A City Heading for Death,
pp. 430–439, 448, 466
Theory of Photography, p. 450/451
Sentimental Journey/Winter Journey,
pp. 453–465, 467–469
Death Reality, p. 472/473

Tokyo Autumn:
*Double Suicide in Karuizawa,
Araki Graph No.1*, pp. 474/475, 478–485
Living Cats in Tokyo, p. 476
A's Lovers, pp. 477, 486–492
Yoko, p. 493
Tokyo Novel, pp. 494–497
Satchin, pp. 498–501

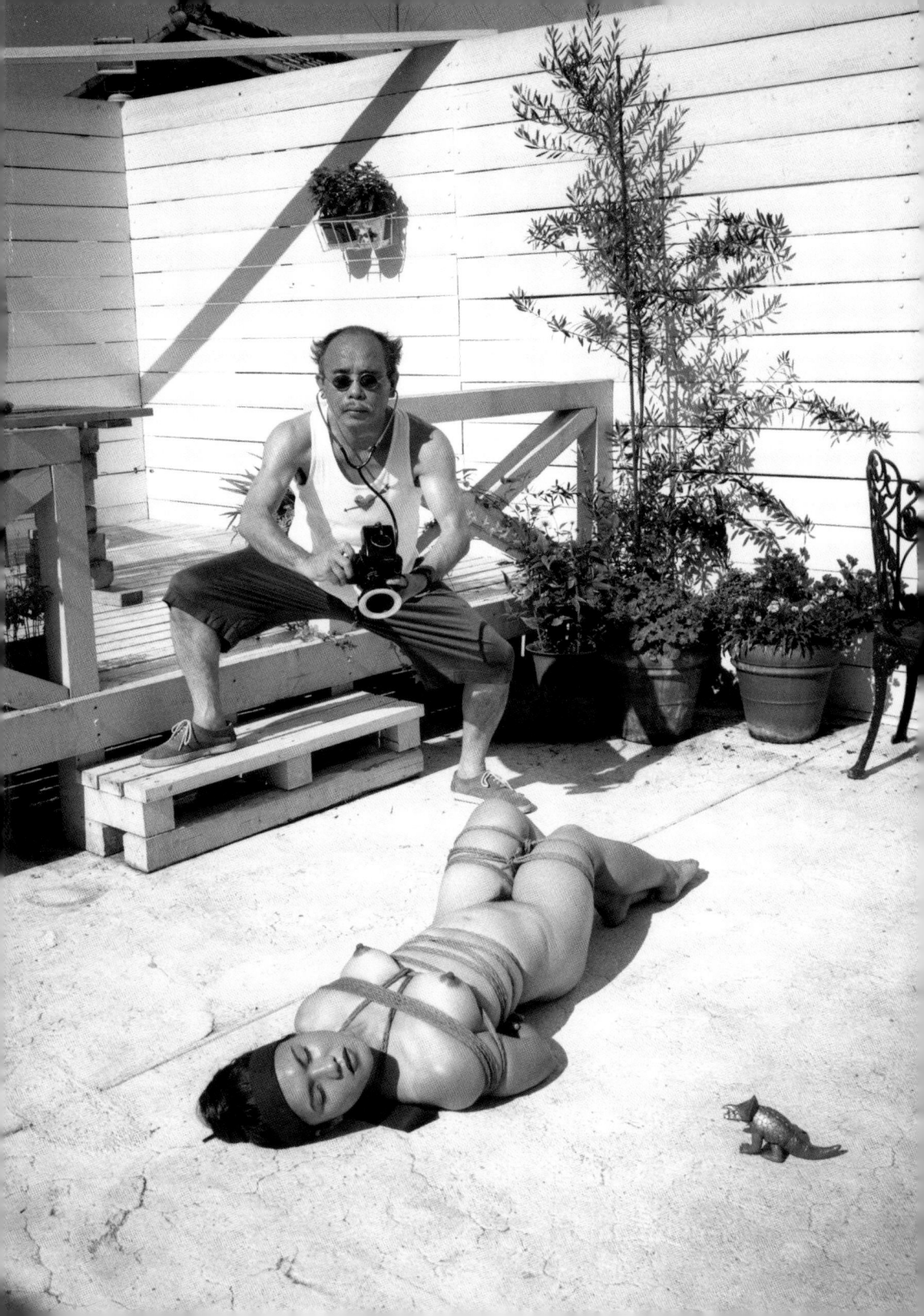

Imprint

**EACH AND EVERY TASCHEN BOOK
PLANTS A SEED!**
Each year, we offset our annual carbon emissions
with carbon credits at the Instituto Terra, a reforestation
program in Minas Gerais, Brazil, founded by Lélia and
Sebastião Salgado. To find out more about this ecological
partnership, please check:
www.taschen.com/institutoterra.
Inspiration: unlimited.
Carbon footprint: (almost) zero.

Want to see more? Visit taschen.com to view our current
publications, browse our latest magazine, and subscribe
to our newsletter.

© 2025 TASCHEN GmbH
Hohenzollernring 53, D–50672 Köln
www.taschen.com

Photos © Nobuyoshi Araki, Tokyo

Original edition: © 2002 TASCHEN GmbH

English translation: Mariko Oikawa
German translation: Stefan Barmann

Printed in Bosnia-Herzegovina
ISBN 978-3-8365-8252-0